CIVIL PROCEDURE

ASPEN PUBLISHERS

CIVIL PROCEDURE

Second Edition

RICHARD D. FREER

Robert Howell Hall Professor of Law
Emory University

Wolters Kluwer
Law & Business

AUSTIN   BOSTON   CHICAGO   NEW YORK   THE NETHERLANDS

Aspen Publishers
Attn: Permissions Department
76 Ninth Avenue, 7th Floor
New York, NY 10011-5201

To contact Customer Care, e-mail customer.care@aspenpublishers.com,
call 1-800-234-1660, fax 1-800-901-9075, or mail correspondence to:

Aspen Publishers
Attn: Order Department
PO Box 990
Frederick, MD 21705

Printed in the United States of America.

1 2 3 4 5 6 7 8 9 0

ISBN 978-07355-7830-2

Library of Congress Cataloging-in-Publication Data

Freer, Richard D., 1953 —
    Civil procedure / Richard D. Freer. – 2nd ed.
        p. cm.
    Rev. ed. of: Introduction to civil procedure. c2006.
    Includes index.
    ISBN 978-0-7355-7830-2
    1. Civil procedure — United States. 2. Civil procedure — United States — Cases. I. Freer,
        Richard D., 1953- Introduction to civil procedure. II. Title.

KF8839.F745 2009

347.73'5 — dc22

2009012941

About Wolters Kluwer Law & Business

Wolters Kluwer Law & Business is a leading provider of research information and workflow solutions in key specialty areas. The strengths of the individual brands of Aspen Publishers, CCH, Kluwer Law International and Loislaw are aligned within Wolters Kluwer Law & Business to provide comprehensive, in-depth solutions and expert-authored content for the legal, professional and education markets.

CCH was founded in 1913 and has served more than four generations of business professionals and their clients. The CCH products in the Wolters Kluwer Law & Business group are highly regarded electronic and print resources for legal, securities, antitrust and trade regulation, government contracting, banking, pension, payroll, employment and labor, and healthcare reimbursement and compliance professionals.

Aspen Publishers is a leading information provider for attorneys, business professionals and law students. Written by preeminent authorities, Aspen products offer analytical and practical information in a range of specialty practice areas from securities law and intellectual property to mergers and acquisitions and pension/benefits. Aspen's trusted legal education resources provide professors and students with high-quality, up-to-date and effective resources for successful instruction and study in all areas of the law.

Kluwer Law International supplies the global business community with comprehensive English-language international legal information. Legal practitioners, corporate counsel and business executives around the world rely on the Kluwer Law International journals, loose-leafs, books and electronic products for authoritative information in many areas of international legal practice.

Loislaw is a premier provider of digitized legal content to small law firm practitioners of various specializations. Loislaw provides attorneys with the ability to quickly and efficiently find the necessary legal information they need, when and where they need it, by facilitating access to primary law as well as state-specific law, records, forms and treatises.

Wolters Kluwer Law & Business, a unit of Wolters Kluwer, is headquartered in New York and Riverwoods, Illinois. Wolters Kluwer is a leading multinational publisher and information services company.

To Louise, Courtney, and Collin

Summary of Contents

Contents

Contents

Contents

Contents

Contents

Contents

Contents

Preface, Acknowledgments, and Conventions

Many students consider Civil Procedure the most difficult first-year law school course. The main reason is simple: Unlike your courses on Contracts, Torts, and Property, Civil Procedure is foreign to your experience. While everyone has had some exposure to principles addressed in the other core first-year courses, virtually no one spends any of her youth or young adulthood pondering the jurisdiction of the federal courts, the appealability of interlocutory orders, or the difference between local and transitory actions for venue purposes. Some students never break through the shroud of unfamiliarity to appreciate this course and why it is important. And it is indeed important—for a great many lawyers, Civil Procedure will address the most significant set of doctrines and principles in their practice. In my opinion, it is the most critical of first-year courses for the "real world."

The purpose of this book is simple: I wrote it to help students and lawyers demystify this foreign subject. I have attempted to do that in several ways. First, I try to explain concepts in real-world, common terms. When I was in law school, for instance, I could not figure out how a court could "attach" property. Nothing in my course made the idea any easier. I think we will find the idea fairly straightforward here. The book, like its author, is informal and (hopefully) occasionally funny.

Second, I have attempted to break complex doctrines into constituent parts. So, for example, instead of trying to approach the entire constitutional test for personal jurisdiction as one whole, we break it into smaller, easily understood components. And instead of asking you to memorize Rule 12 of the Federal Rules of Civil Procedure to determine when various defenses can be raised, we break it into three easily remembered principles that cover every possible permutation for an examination or a real-world case.

Third, we emphasize how various doctrines fit together. Sometimes, students master individual topics—such as subject matter jurisdiction and venue—but have no idea how they fit together. Throughout the book, you will see cross-references and footnotes that constantly force the reader to consider how various topics interrelate. For example, we emphasize that many of the most important elements of a Civil Procedure course—personal jurisdiction, service of process, subject matter jurisdiction, and venue—all relate to a single idea: that of choosing a place where litigation will take place. And we discuss in detail why that choice of "forum" is so important that litigants may spend a great deal of money and time arguing over where the litigation will proceed.

Fourth, throughout, there are hypotheticals to test your application of the principles discussed. And not imponderable hypotheticals, but hypos with answers provided and discussed. I have never forgotten that you need not only to know the doctrines, but to be able to apply them to a fact pattern on your examination.

Fifth, at various points, I have pulled together complex topics into analytical frameworks. So, for instance, after you study Chapter 2 on personal jurisdiction, we have an entire section pointing out how to use the tools acquired from the case law to address an examination question. This section takes you step by step through how you should analyze any exam question in that area, using each of the relevant factors identified by the Supreme Court.

Finally, though our focus is largely on legal doctrine, I have tried to convey an appreciation of the richness and depth of the subject, to put topics in context with each other and with the larger goal of the pursuit of justice. I believe this work will be helpful not only to students but to lawyers and judicial law clerks whose handle on (or memory of) Civil Procedure and federal jurisdiction may be less than they wish it to be.

There are 14 chapters in the book. They are arranged largely in chronological order, addressing the various issues that are confronted in bringing, defending, and litigating a case. You should realize, however, that there is no single "right" order in which to teach Civil Procedure. Professors and casebooks vary greatly in the order in which they address the subjects. So if the syllabus for your course looks different from our table of contents, do not worry. Each chapter in this book is intended to stand on its own—to be self-contained. At the same time, each, as noted above, will tell you how the material relates to other material throughout the course. So the order in which you approach the topics is irrelevant. This book will help you not only to master the individual areas of Civil Procedure, but to appreciate the whole of the course as well. That said, I do think it a good idea to read Chapter 1 before delving into any particular area. It gives you an overview of the course and discusses some background topics that will be relevant at various points along the journey.

So welcome to Civil Procedure. Don't let it scare you. Don't listen to the upper-division students who complain about how tough the course is. We will get a good handle on it, put the pieces together, and understand it. And we will have some fun doing it.

****

I have learned a great deal about Civil Procedure from my colleagues at Emory. I was fortunate to have a patient mentor and friend in Don Fyr on the Emory faculty; he is gone now, but is remembered fondly and has a continuing impact. Bill Ferguson, now also departed, taught me a good bit. Through the years my Emory colleagues Tom Arthur, Peter Hay, Robert Schapiro, George Shepherd, and Kimberly Robinson have been so generous with their time and talents that I can never hope to repay them; they are dear friends. I also am grateful for the honor to have known the late Judge Robert Howell Hall, whose contributions to the federal and state benches in Georgia are legendary; I am privileged and humbled to hold the chaired professorship that bears his name. I give a special note of thanks to H. Scott Fingerhut, Esq., of Miami, who took time from a very busy schedule to comment on manuscript. I am proud to call him not only a former student but a very dear friend.

I was privileged to visit at George Washington University Law School during the academic year 2006-2007, where I benefitted from the vibrant group of Civil Procedure scholars who welcomed me as one of the team—Jack Friedenthal, Todd Peterson, Peter Raven-Hansen, Jonathan Siegel, Joan Schaffner, Roger Trangsrud, and Amanda Tyler. And one of the treats of spending that year in Washington was getting to meet Sherman Cohn of Georgetown, with whom I had corresponded for years and learned a great deal.

My work has also been enriched by Civil Procedure colleagues at other schools. Debra Cohen, a former student and close friend, has been especially generous through the years. I am also indebted to Joe Bauer, Ed Brunet, Bob Casad, Howard Fink, Charlotte Goldberg, Cynthia Ho, Ben Madison, Colleen Murphy, Roy Sobelson, Joan Steinman, and Carl Tobias. I owe a special debt to my friend and coauthor of our casebook (now in its fifth edition), Wendy Perdue, with whom I have been privileged to work on that volume for over 15 years. And in the interesting world of e-mail, I am grateful to several professors I have never met, but who have made helpful suggestions for the casebook, which I have found useful here, including John Beckerman and Richard Seaman.

Research assistants at Emory have gone many extra miles on this work. I am grateful to Ethan Rosenzweig, Myra Mormile, Jennifer DiAngelo, Ashley Wilkes, and Katy Quarles for timely and meaningful contributions. I have undoubtedly stumbled despite the generous contributions of all these outstanding young people. This book has been long in the making, and I am ever indebted to my family for patience with me as I struggled with this task. The dedication of the book to them is only a small token of my appreciation.

****

Throughout the book, I cite the two standard multivolume works—Moore's Federal Practice and Wright & Miller's Federal Practice and Procedure—in abbreviated form, without noting the authors on specific volumes. Thus, they are cited as specific volumes of "Moore's Federal Practice" and "Wright & Miller," respectively. I am honored to be a contributor to both of these works. The citations to them are through the 2008 supplements. In addition, citations to Charles Alan Wright & Mary Kay Kane, The Law of Federal Courts (6th ed. 2002) are indicated "Wright & Kane, Federal Courts."

Richard D. Freer
Atlanta
April 2009

CIVIL PROCEDURE

Chapter **1**

The Study of Civil Procedure

§1.1   What This Course Is About: Civil Litigation and the Adversary System

Welcome to law school, and welcome to Civil Procedure. As you look through your list of courses, you encounter some familiar words, such as Property, Contracts, and Criminal Law. You also encounter at least one strange word — Torts. And then there is a class for which the words present no real problem, but as to which the words do not tell you much — that's our class, Civil Procedure. In this chapter, we discuss the course — what it addresses and why it is important — and some background topics that will set up our detailed study. Many students consider Civil Procedure the most difficult first-year class. If you are one of those students, take heart in the fact that you are not alone. More important, however, take steps to get a handle on the course. This book is intended to do just that.

Why does Civil Procedure give so many students trouble? There are two main reasons. First, Civil Procedure — unlike your other first-year courses — is foreign to your experience. Every person starting law school has had some exposure to Property, Contracts, Torts, and (perhaps) Criminal Law. For example, maybe you have entered a contract to rent an apartment or to buy a car. In fact, many of us have encountered issues relating to these core first-year classes in daily family life. When you were young, maybe you received an allowance for doing certain chores; that was a contract. Or maybe you left your shoes on the stairs and someone tripped over them and fell; that was a tort. Or maybe you and a sibling disagreed about the ownership or right to possess a CD or an article of clothing; that was a property dispute. These are everyday occurrences. But before coming to law school it is extremely unlikely that you encountered problems relating to *in personam* jurisdiction or the subject matter jurisdiction of the federal courts or the right to a jury trial. Put simply, Civil Procedure is full of topics most of us have never seen before law school.

Second, Civil Procedure presents a remarkable mix of different kinds of material. Some of the topics, including pleadings and discovery, are intensely mechanical, and demand memorization of some fairly wooden rules, including temporal limits on when parties must accomplish certain tasks. In contrast, most of the material is intellectually rich, and occasionally vexing. For example, personal jurisdiction is a particularly amorphous area in which you are expected to use a series of Supreme Court opinions to distill an analytical approach to contemporary problems. At the outset, it is worth noting that the different types of materials — from the relatively mechanical to the relatively amorphous — lend themselves to different approaches in your study. With the mechanical topics, there is often a clear right answer. But as to the amorphous topics (particularly personal jurisdiction and some aspects of the *Erie* doctrine), there is rarely a single right answer. In these areas, you should realize that reasonable people might disagree as to the ultimate outcome, so your goal is not so much to get the right answer as it is to come to a conclusion that is within the realm of reasonable answers. We talk about these different types of materials and approaches to them in each chapter.

Litigation

Civil Procedure is about *litigation*, which is the basic model by which disputes are resolved in our society. Suppose someone does something that harms you — maybe by negligently driving her car, or punching you in the nose, or breaching a contract, or stealing your property. How do you resolve your grievance with that person? One possibility is to engage in "self-help," by which you redress the wrong personally; you might want to punch the perpetrator in the nose, or enter her property to seize what she stole. This is usually a disastrous choice, because you simply compound the wrong by perpetrating one yourself. Another possibility is to contact the person who harmed you and demand some compensation or other remedy. This often works, as people quite frequently work out their differences informally. If such efforts fail, however, what do you do? The classic course for dispute resolution is *litigation* — the process by which you sue the wrongdoer, by which you "take her to court." The dispute is resolved by the judicial system through the litigation process. Litigation, then, is a socially acceptable method for resolving our disputes.

Indeed, litigation is *publicly funded* dispute resolution. The taxpayers provide the courtroom, the judge, and the bureaucratic instrumentalities by which the dispute (now usually called a *case* or *lawsuit*) is resolved. Obviously, not all disagreements in our society are determined by litigation. By far most disputes are resolved informally along the lines noted above — the parties work it out without filing a case. There is also a panoply of alternative dispute resolution (ADR) mechanisms by which parties can reach a resolution without going through the classic litigation process; we discuss the major ADR mechanisms (such as arbitration and mediation) in §1.3. But all these other methods for resolving disputes exist "in the shadow" of litigation. The fact that we call these other devices "alternatives" demonstrates that litigation is the norm. Again, that does not mean that *most* disputes are resolved by litigation. It simply means that litigation is the societally endorsed, publicly funded mechanism against which alternatives are measured.

Civil Litigation

Our course is about civil litigation. In this context, "civil" is juxtaposed to "criminal." For present purposes, it is helpful to think of litigation as falling into one or the other category. In a criminal case, a government (whether federal, state, or local) commences litigation against a defendant who has allegedly violated a law intended to keep the public peace. The goal of criminal litigation (called a *prosecution*) is to vindicate that public interest. If the criminal defendant is found guilty in the criminal litigation, the result can be some form of punishment — perhaps a fine, perhaps incarceration. Every day, in every newspaper, there are plenty of stories about criminal prosecutions. This course has nothing to do with them.

Instead, we deal with litigation aimed at vindicating *private* rights. Civil litigation is not brought by the government to punish someone for doing something against the public peace. Instead, it is brought by one who has been wronged by another.[1] That person is the *plaintiff* and the person who wronged her (whom she sues) is the *defendant.* In the civil suit the plaintiff seeks private remedies from the defendant for the harm done — often money[2] to compensate for damage done to the plaintiff's

---

[1] A government can be a party to civil litigation. For example, if the government concludes that one of its suppliers of goods has breached the contract between them, it can sue. The case would not be a criminal prosecution, but a civil case, by which the government seeks to vindicate its private rights.

[2] Money to compensate the plaintiff for harm done by the defendant is usually called *damages.* It is a common form of relief sought by plaintiffs, but is not the only one. In §1.2.3 we discuss damages and other commonly sought remedies.

automobile or to pay the medical bills incurred because of the defendant's actionable behavior. So in this course, we do not use the word *guilty*. That is a criminal law concept. Instead, we talk about a defendant's being *liable* to the plaintiff for some civil remedy, such as money to compensate for the wrong caused by the defendant's behavior.

Frequently, the same act or omission by the defendant will constitute both a crime and a civil wrong. The different goals of criminal and civil litigation can be demonstrated by looking at a simple example.

- ° While you are in class, suppose *D* breaks into your apartment and steals your television, DVD player, and stereo equipment; *D* then sells them to a third party. *D* has committed a burglary, and the government (probably the state) may prosecute *D* for that crime. If the state wins in that *criminal litigation*, *D* will be found guilty of burglary and will be punished, perhaps by a jail term.
- ° The criminal litigation vindicates the public's interest in dealing with one who violates basic rules by which we live in a decent society. But it does nothing *for you personally*. Putting *D* in jail does nothing to compensate you for the loss of your television, DVD player, and stereo equipment. To recover for those losses, you may file a *civil* case, seeking to recover money from *D* to permit you to replace the stolen items.[3] This is a civil case because it vindicates your personal rights against another. You would be the plaintiff and *D* would be the defendant. This course addresses *only* this latter type of litigation. Our society adopts the notion that this type of litigation is *adversarial*.

The Adversary System: Roles of the Parties, Lawyers, Jury, and the Judge

It is not enough for a government simply to provide a system for resolving disputes. The system must be perceived as legitimate. The government could decree that disputes between citizens will be resolved by a coin toss by a government official, with the result enforced by government officers. This would certainly resolve disputes (and more quickly than litigation), but it would not comport with any basic sense of justice. The civil justice system must strive to achieve the *fair* resolution of disputes.[4] To be legitimate, we insist that our system provide a fair method to determine the

---

[3] In many instances, your insurance company will have given you money representing the value of the stolen items (less whatever deductible you may have to pay under your insurance policy). Because of something called *subrogation*, the insurance company will then have the right to sue *D* to recover from *D* for the stolen items. Subrogation is discussed at §12.2. Don't worry about it now.

[4] Throughout the course, you will refer to the Federal Rules of Civil Procedure, which are included in a rules booklet that your professor undoubtedly asked you to purchase. These Rules apply in civil cases in federal (not state) courts, but most states have adopted rules modeled on them. Rule 1 provides that all the Rules "should be construed and

"truth" of what "really happened" and to apply the law to those facts. We can imagine different systems for determining the facts and the truth. For example, the government could investigate and determine when someone's rights have been breached by another and demand that the transgressor compensate the victim. Anglo-American civil justice has never embraced such a pervasive role for the government. Rather, we embrace the *adversary system* of litigation.

The adversary system is based upon self-interest. If an aggrieved person wishes to vindicate her civil claim by suing the person(s) who harmed her, she must take the initiative and sue. The government will not do it for her. And she must pursue the litigation vigorously. If she sues but then fails to keep the litigation going by appropriate action, the court may dismiss for "lack of prosecution." Once the parties are in the litigation process — which starts when the plaintiff sues the defendant — the adversary system requires each party to present her case and to attack the other's with partisan vigor. The adversary system is founded on the notion that the truth is best determined in the crucible of competition between adversaries. From this battle of self-interested combatants, an independent fact-finder (often a jury, but sometimes the judge) determines what likely happened. Thus, the system relies on partisan presentation by self-interested persons (not governmental investigation) to hone the evidence for presentation to a disinterested fact-finder. The purpose is to provide a fair, accurate, and efficient method of determining the likely facts and resolving disputes consistently, in accord with the law.

There are, of course, strict rules for this competition — including very important norms of professional responsibility for the lawyers. Thus, lying or destruction of evidence or other forms of cheating are not permitted. Lawyers who violate the norms can be sanctioned by the court and punished by the bar (including the ultimate sanction of disbarment). Parties who violate the norms can be sanctioned by the court. Within the rules, however, parties are expected to be self-interested, and their lawyers are required to represent them zealously. Within the rules, they may use every ploy, device, and creative effort to secure the best outcome for their client. They can be tough. They can be nasty. They can be sweet. They can be charming and engaging. They are to do what they think best to *win*. Litigation is competition. And it is usually a "zero-sum game" — which means that (usually) one side wins and one side loses.

In this adversary system, the judge's role — at least in theory — is rather limited. Classically, the judge is expected to be a passive umpire. She reacts to requests (called *motions*) by the parties for a variety of court orders (which we will study). At trial, she oversees the presentation of evidence

---

administered to secure the just, speedy, and inexpensive determination of every action and proceeding."

in accordance with the rules for admissibility (which you will study in an upper-division course on Evidence), but generally is not inquisitorial.[5] Again, our adversary system relies on the parties and their lawyers to determine what evidence to present and how to present it.

American judges are not completely passive. Judges — particularly in the federal courts (as opposed to state courts) — often ask questions of witnesses at trial, and raise various issues that the parties have failed to pursue. (When a judge raises an issue on her own — rather than in reaction to a motion by a party — she is said to act *sua sponte* — on her own motion.) If the adversary system were absolute, the judge would not take many (if any) *sua sponte* acts. But the adversarial ideal is not absolute. Let's face facts. Not all parties have equal skills or equal resources. Similarly, not all lawyers have equal skills or resources. Occasionally, a judge may inject herself into the questioning of a witness at trial to correct a mistake made by a lawyer. For example, if a lawyer failed to ask a witness about a particular issue that is relevant to the outcome, the judge might ask the question. After all, the goal is justice. The judge's limited intervention in such circumstances is probably a good thing. On the other hand, though, the judge is to remain impartial, and cannot allow herself to become so involved as to lose even the appearance of impartiality. Most judges are extremely good at drawing an appropriate line between avoiding undue involvement (on the one hand) and avoiding an unjust outcome based upon a technicality (on the other).

The role of judge as a largely neutral umpire has eroded significantly in the past generation, in response to increasingly complex litigation. As discussed in Chapters 12 and 13, civil litigation can become quite complex — with multiple claims and parties packaged into a single case. In some instances — especially in the class action (which we study in §13.3) — the court must become involved to ensure adequate representation of the interests of persons who, while not technically parties, may be affected by the outcome of the litigation. Lessons learned in complex litigation have permeated procedural rules generally, and it is now becoming routine to think of "managerial judges" — judicial officers whose job description has become increasingly bureaucratic. As we see in §§8.5 and 8.6, judges (especially in the federal courts) are required to take an active role in ensuring that the case keeps moving; to some judges, the job has become less judicial and more bureaucratic. In part, the emergence of managerial judges reflects the wide perception of a "litigation explosion" over the past few decades. There is much debate about the level of frivolous litigation filed in this country, and concern with abusive litigation has spurred some procedural innovations requiring greater oversight by judges. We see such provisions throughout the course.

---

[5] Judges in most continental European countries, in contrast, are inquisitorial, and take an active role in formulating the presentation of evidence at trial.

Litigation Is a (Potentially Lengthy) Process

Based on television shows and movies, most of us think of litigation as the trial itself — the nerve-wracking, dramatic moments in the courtroom, with the judge presiding, the jury listening and watching attentively, and a witness testifying on the stand in response to questions by razor-sharp lawyers. Of course, there are such moments in the real world. But most litigation moments — even in trial — are not riveting. More important, you should understand that the trial is just the tip of the iceberg. Litigation is a *process* that *may* lead to trial. In fact, the overwhelming majority of civil cases *never* go to trial. An empirical study of federal civil cases in 2002 found that only 1.8 percent of cases go to trial.[6] Why? Because in the vast majority of cases, the parties reach a settlement sometime during the process. In others, the court may terminate the case without trial, through motions to dismiss, for summary judgment, or other pretrial mechanisms for resolution.

It is important to understand that litigation is usually a lengthy process. Depending on the court system, litigation of a case that does go through trial will usually be measured in years, not in months. Why? Because there are many more parts to the process than the trial. Indeed, the plaintiff and her lawyer have a great deal to do even before filing the case. For one, they must decide *where* to file the case. As we will see, parties often spend a great deal of time and money litigating over *forum selection* — that is, whether the case is in a proper court. The decision implicates a variety of important doctrines, including personal jurisdiction, subject matter jurisdiction, and venue. In addition, there are questions of tactics and strategy: What location would be most convenient for the plaintiff and perhaps not ideal for the defendant? What court system (federal or state) might be most advantageous to the plaintiff (perhaps in terms of her lawyer's familiarity with the judges or the geographic area from which a jury will be drawn)? In what court is the litigation most likely to proceed more rapidly? In what court is the lawyer most comfortable? The question of forum selection is enormously important — and the course spends a good deal of time on it.

Further, before filing suit, the plaintiff and her lawyer must determine what to put in the complaint. More specifically, what *claims* (or *causes of action*) will the plaintiff assert, and what remedies will she seek? These are important questions, the answers to which are informed by the *substantive law*. Some substantive law is created by the legislative branch of government, for example, when Congress permits plaintiffs to sue to recover for deprivations of federal civil rights under 42 U.S.C. §1983. But

---

[6]*See* Marc Galanter, *The Vanishing Trial: An Examination of Trials and Related Matters in Federal and State Courts*, 1 J. Empirical Legal Stud. 459 (2004) (the percentage given in text for 2002 is contrasted with data from 1962, when 11.5 percent of cases went to trial).

many claims are created by *common law* — that is, by court decision. Most of the claims treated in Contracts, Torts, and Property are common law claims.

Civil Procedure does not prescribe the elements of these various claims. Those elements — what one must allege and prove to win a case — are prescribed by the substantive law, covered in other courses (notably Contracts, Torts, and Property). Civil Procedure provides the mechanism — the process (litigation) — by which disputes over such substantive claims are resolved. Civil procedure is "trans-substantive" — it provides a theoretically content-neutral mechanism for resolving disagreements. In other words, Civil Procedure establishes the method by which someone would vindicate a right given her by the law you learn in courses such as Contracts, Torts, and Property.

Once the plaintiff files the case — once it is in what we can call the "litigation stream" — the law of Civil Procedure prescribes the rules by which the plaintiff and the defendant proceed. Though movies and television focus on the trial, the case must progress through various stages of litigation — including pleadings, motions, discovery, possible pretrial adjudication, conferences, and meetings — before getting anywhere near trial. That takes time. Again, outside small claims matters and some family law disputes, for which there are usually streamlined simplified procedures, the litigation stream in most cases takes years. In some especially congested courts, it is possible that the parties will not get to trial (if the case goes to trial) for five years after filing. During that time, the parties are engaged in pretrial litigation (and waiting in line for trial). Section 1.4 presents an overview of the litigation process, focusing on how the various subjects of Civil Procedure fit together.

Litigation Is an Expensive Process

We said above that litigation is publicly funded dispute resolution. That means that the public pays for the courthouse, the judge, and the bureaucracy necessary to support the system. But the public does not pay the costs and attorneys' fees incurred in the litigation. Each party bears her own costs and attorneys' fees, at least initially.

It is important to distinguish between these two categories of expense. Costs are the general expenses of litigation *other than* attorneys' fees. These include fees charged to file a case, fees incurred in notifying the defendant of the litigation, expenses of discovery, witness fees, and the like. Attorneys' fees, obviously, are the fees charged by the lawyer to represent the party. Generally, attorneys bill for their services by the hour. They keep detailed records of the hours spent on each matter, and often bill monthly or quarterly. Instead of billing by the hour, the plaintiff's lawyer may take the case on a contingent fee, which means the lawyer recovers a fee only if the plaintiff recovers from the defendant. A contingent fee is set as a percentage of the recovery, and is agreed to in advance. It is important to consider how the requirement that each party bear her own costs and attorneys' fees affects the bottom line in litigation.

- *P* sues *D* for breach of contract. Let's assume that under the relevant substantive law of contracts, *P* is entitled to recover $300,000 from *D*. In other words, *D*'s breach of the contract with *P* caused *P* $300,000 worth of harm. *P* sues *D*. The case proceeds through the various stages of litigation and, after three years, goes to trial. After hearing all the evidence, the jury agrees with *P*'s version of the facts and returns a verdict of $300,000 for *P*. The court enters judgment in *P*'s favor for $300,000.
  - From all appearances, *P* has prevailed completely, and should be ecstatic. But is she? She has to pay her lawyer, who, let's say, took the case on a one-third contingent fee. So the lawyer gets $100,000 (one-third of *P*'s recovery). In addition, *P* has had to pay various costs — including filing fees and expert witness fees — of, say, $10,000.
  - The law provided that *P* was entitled to recover $300,000 — in other words, that $300,000 would compensate her for the harm caused by *D*. It is often said that the recovery was to "make her whole." But did it? Though the jury agreed that *P* should get $300,000, in fact she will pocket (in our hypothetical) $190,000. She had to pay $100,000 in attorneys' fees and $10,000 in costs.[7]
- Now let's see it from *D*'s viewpoint. Suppose *D* is convinced that she did not do any of the things *P* alleges. She litigates the case through trial and the jury returns a verdict in *D*'s favor. The court enters judgment for *D*. The judgment provides that *D* does not owe anything to *P*.
  - From all appearances, *D* has prevailed completely, and should be ecstatic. True, she does not have to write a check to *P*. But she has been writing checks to her lawyer all along. She may have paid $150,000 in attorneys' fees and $10,000 in costs.
  - According to the law, *D* did nothing wrong. Yet she has been sued and is out of pocket $160,000.

In both situations — whether *P* won or *D* won — we have a nagging sense that the result is not fair. When *P* won, she was supposed to get $300,000 but really only got $190,000. When *D* won, she was faultless, but ended up $160,000 in the hole. Some commentators have argued that the

---

[7] Not only that, but it took a long time to vindicate the claim. The harm of $300,000 was caused, say, three years before *P* wins her case. If she had had that $300,000 over the three years, she would have been making interest on the money. So one might expect the law to require *D* to pay interest on the claim. Generally, however, interest begins to accrue only when the judgment is entered. So *P* has lost three years' worth of interest on that money.

law should permit "shifting" of costs and attorneys' fees. Put bluntly, the argument goes, the loser should be required to pay the winner's costs and attorneys' fees. This "loser pays" system is followed in many other countries, including Great Britain. The American system has adopted something of a middle course — known, not surprisingly, as the "American Rule."

In litigation in the United States, each party pays her own costs and attorneys' fees as the case progresses. Once the case is resolved, however, the American Rule provides for some shifting of the ultimate liability — generally the prevailing party may recover her costs — *but not her attorneys' fees* — from the losing party. In the federal system, this rule is reflected in Federal Rule 54(d)(1), which creates a presumption that the winner is entitled to recover her costs from the loser.[8] Detailed coverage of this point is beyond our scope, but it is worth noting that not every litigation expense qualifies as a cost under Rule 54(d)(1).[9] Instead, that Rule permits shifting of only certain litigation expenses set forth in 28 U.S.C. §1920. In addition, statutory caps limit the amount that can be recovered for certain costs. Quite frequently, the limited amount recovered does not come close to the expense actually incurred. Thus, though it is generally said that the prevailing party recovers her costs from the loser, in fact the recovery will not reimburse that party for her out-of-pocket expenses.

More significantly, the American Rule creates a presumption that each side bears her own attorneys' fees — by far the most significant expense incurred in litigation. Persons are free to contract around the American Rule — and frequently do. It is commonplace for parties entering a contract to provide that — in the event of litigation — the prevailing party will recover attorneys' fees from the loser. (In fact, you are probably a party to such a contract — check your contracts with credit card and insurance companies.)

Occasionally, courts recognize a common law exception to the American Rule, and order a party to pay the other party's attorneys' fees. For example, in *Chambers v. NASCO, Inc.*,[10] the Supreme Court upheld a general power to make such an order against a party who engages in bad faith, vexatious litigation. For the most part, though, courts are reluctant to create exceptions to the general rule. This attitude reflects a general sense

---

[8] This presumption is subject to some exceptions. For our purposes, the important exception will be discussed in §4.5.3, which addresses 28 U.S.C. §1332(b). That statute permits the court to force a prevailing plaintiff to pay her own costs and the defendant's costs if the plaintiff recovered less than a certain amount. Don't worry about it now.

[9] Costs recoverable under Rule 54(d)(1) are usually called *taxable* costs. The word has nothing to do with whether one pays income tax. Taxable simply refers to the types of costs recoverable. We discuss this topic in more detail in §9.3. *See generally* 10 Moore's Federal Practice §54.101.

[10] 501 U.S. 32, 43-51 (1991).

that fee-shifting provisions should come from the legislative branch.[11] Congress has passed many statutes addressing the award of attorneys' fees, some of which permit the prevailing party to recover her fees from the losing party. The broadest fee-shifting provisions permit recovery by successful parties claiming discrimination in violation of various federal laws.[12]

Outside such piecemeal efforts, however, federal and state legislatures have continued to embrace the American Rule. While there is a facial appeal to the "loser pays" system, as seen above, proponents of the status quo fear that broad shifting of attorneys' fees would make plaintiffs too timid to attempt to vindicate their rights. A plaintiff — particularly one of limited means — might eschew the right to sue if losing meant that she would have to pay the defendant's attorneys' fees. Indeed, there may be something particularly American about the American Rule — it seems consistent with our sense of individual justice and paying one's own way. There are strong arguments (and feelings) on both sides of the debate. Suffice to say that every effort to abandon the American Rule has failed. The result is simply that litigation — even for the winner — is an expensive proposition.

§1.2 Background and Recurring Themes

§1.2.1 Federalism

Throughout your career as a law student and lawyer, you will encounter issues relating to the relationship between the federal and state governments. In your first-year studies, you address such issues in Constitutional Law as well as in Civil Procedure. In this section, we discuss basic background materials that play a role in Civil Procedure.

Each person in the United States is subject to the authority of at least two governments — the federal government and that of a state.[13] The federal government (or national government) is one of limited powers. The

---

[11] *See, e.g.,* Alyeska Pipeline Serv. Co. v. Wilderness Society, 421 U.S. 240, 263 (1975) (rejecting the notion that the judiciary can "jettison the traditional rule against nonstatutory allowances to the prevailing party . . .").

[12] *See, e.g.,* 42 U.S.C. §1973l(e) (Voting Rights Act); 42 U.S.C. §3613(c)(2) (Fair Housing Act).

[13] Some people in the United States don't live in states, but in federal enclaves such as the District of Columbia or territories such as Guam or the Commonwealth of Puerto Rico. For such persons, the federal government plays two roles — that of the national sovereign and also that of the local sovereign. For instance, Congress (in its role as legislature for the federal government) passes laws of national application and also passes local laws to govern the District of Columbia.

Constitution of the United States (which is included in your Federal Rules booklet and which you should read at your leisure early in your studies) does several things. For starters, the Constitution *creates* the federal government. Without it, there would be no national government. There would be instead 50 separate sovereigns, un-united. After the War of Independence there were 13 colonies. The leaders of that generation understood that certain functions were best performed centrally. For example, it made no sense to have each colony coin separate money, or to impose barriers to travel or trade among the colonies, or for each colony to raise its own army. The Founders concluded that things like coinage and commerce and defense should be handled centrally.

The first experiment at centralization — the Articles of Confederation — did not work well. Finally, the Framers met in Philadelphia to work out a Constitution, forging a national government to perform certain tasks, and leaving the independent state governments in charge of the rest. Thus, in the Constitution, the independent states forming the United States actually *cede* power to form the new national government. This process emphasizes that the federal government is one of limited powers. As the Tenth Amendment makes clear, powers not ceded to the federal government in the Constitution remain vested in the states or in the people. So the federal government is not an oppressive omnipresence — it exists solely because the states and the people decided to centralize certain functions in a national power.

The Constitution spells out the powers of each of the three branches of the federal government. Article I concerns the legislative branch, and establishes that all federal legislative power is vested in the Senate and House of Representatives. It also establishes rules for when those bodies shall meet, how membership is allocated, and age and residency requirements. It expressly lists the powers to be exercised by the national legislature and restricts the states from various acts, including imposing duties and entering treaties. Article II addresses the executive branch, and provides that the national executive power is vested in the President of the United States. It details the requirements for office and the powers of the presidency, including the authority to appoint (with the advice and consent of the Senate) various federal officers, including federal judges. You will study Articles I and II in considerable detail in your course on Constitutional Law.

In Civil Procedure, we focus on Article III of the Constitution, which establishes the judicial branch of the federal government. It requires the existence of only one federal court — the Supreme Court of the United States — but permits Congress to establish lower federal courts, as discussed in §4.3. Consistent with the limited nature of federal power, it establishes that the federal judicial power extends only to certain types of cases (listed in Article III, §2, paragraph 1). This is an extremely important point in Civil Procedure — federal courts *can only hear certain kinds of disputes*. If a case does not fall within this federal "subject matter jurisdiction," it can only be heard in a *state* court.

Thus, from the outset, keep in mind that there are two completely separate sets of courts — federal courts and state courts. State courts, essentially, can decide *any* type of dispute. But federal courts can only hear a limited range of disputes. We discuss these points in detail in Chapter 4. For now, it is enough to note two of the types of cases that can be heard in federal courts — those between citizens of different states (called *diversity of citizenship* cases) and those arising under federal law (called *federal question* cases).

- *P*, a citizen of New York, enters a contract with *D*, a citizen of California. *D* breaches the contract by failing to perform as required by the agreement. *P* may sue *D* in a federal court, because the dispute is between citizens of different states.[14] The Founders thought it important to permit the federal courts to entertain such interstate disputes, as we see in §4.5.2.[15]
- *P* claims that *D* terminated her employment in violation of federal law prohibiting discrimination on the basis of national origin. *P* may sue *D* in federal court, because her claim arises under federal law. The Founders thought it important to permit the federal courts to entertain disputes involving federal law, as we see in §4.6.1.[16]

Let's not get distracted by detail. For now, focus on the big picture — the federal judicial system has limited subject matter jurisdiction. Courts in that system can only decide cases falling within the judicial power of Article III, §2, paragraph 1 of the Constitution; the two main examples are cases between citizens of different states and cases arising under federal law.

In addition, Article III, §1, provides extraordinary protection to federal judges. They are appointed by the President, with approval required by the Senate. Federal judges appointed under Article III never face an election, cannot be removed by the voters, and have lifetime tenure, during which their pay cannot be reduced. They can only be removed by impeachment (which has happened only a handful of times in our nation's history). In §4.4, we discuss this remarkable job security accorded federal judges.

---

[14] By statute, the amount in controversy in a diversity of citizenship case must exceed $75,000. We discuss this in §4.5.3.

[15] Interestingly, *P* is not *required* to file this case in federal court. If she prefers, she can litigate in state court.

[16] Here, too, *P* generally is not *required* to file the case in federal court. If she prefers, she can litigate the federal claim in state court. There are some (very few) federal question claims that must go only to federal court — over which federal courts have "exclusive federal question" jurisdiction. There are very few of these, though. See §4.6.1.

The point is simple: The Founders thought it important to give federal judges freedom to make decisions without fear of reprisal. A federal judge can rule against local interests without fear of being voted out of office. Likewise, she can rule against Congress without fear that that body will reduce her salary. State court judges, in contrast, do not have these protections; generally, they face an electorate at some point to get or to keep their jobs.

In addition to forming the national government and vesting its three branches with power, the Constitution also guarantees individual rights and liberties. Thus, for instance, neither the federal nor state government may abridge an individual's freedom of speech,[17] or impose cruel and unusual punishment on anyone, or deprive someone of life, liberty, or property without due process of law. It is helpful to think of such rights this way: By joining the Union, the states surrendered absolute power. By becoming a member of the United States, each state essentially agreed that it would not abridge free speech, would not impose cruel and unusual punishment, and would not deprive persons of life, liberty, or property without due process. (There are, of course, other individual liberties; we mention these three for simplicity.) One of the major topics in Civil Procedure — personal jurisdiction — concerns one of these federal constitutional limitations on state power. Specifically, due process requires that a state cannot enter a binding judicial order against someone unless that person has sufficient contacts with the state. We study this in detail in Chapter 2.

So for our purposes, it is important at this stage to focus on three things. First, the relationship between the federal and state governments is complex and evolving, and will be studied in Constitutional Law and Civil Procedure (and other courses in the upper division of law school). Second, federal courts have authority to adjudicate only certain types of cases, while state courts can entertain virtually any type of dispute. Third, the Constitution imposes limits on the power of states (including the state courts). One of these is that a state court cannot enter a valid judicial order without affording the defendant due process. We now turn to the structure of judicial systems. One of the important issues we consider is the interaction of the federal and state court systems.

---

[17] The First Amendment to the Constitution provides that the federal legislature may not abridge freedom of speech. As you will study in Constitutional Law, the Fourteenth Amendment is interpreted as incorporating several of the protections of the Bill of Rights — including free speech — and providing that they are also not subject to encroachment by *state* governments.

§1.2.2 Roles of Trial and Appellate Courts (and the Interaction Between the State and Federal Courts)

The federal government and each state has a judicial *system* — a group of courts that serve different functions in the resolution of disputes. These systems can differ markedly from state to state, but some characteristics are common to all. An important common characteristic is the bifurcation between *trial* courts and *appellate* courts. Each system must have a trial court. Indeed, most of our course on Civil Procedure addresses activities in the trial court. The basic litigation stream discussed in §1.1 — involving pleadings, discovery, motions, and adjudication, including trial — takes place in the trial court. The process may take years or it may be over very quickly (as when the defendant defaults or the court dismisses the case early in the proceedings).

In the trial court, a single judge presides over the case at a time. In most systems (including the federal system), the same judge oversees the case at every stage of the trial court litigation. In some states, such as California, different judges may rule on different aspects of the case; for example, one judge might rule on motions and another may oversee the trial. But even in such a system, only one judge is involved in making determinations at a time. (If the case goes to trial, a jury might be empaneled to decide the facts, but the judge presides over the trial.) The trial court is called a court of *original* jurisdiction, which signifies that the case is instituted there and the outcome of the dispute is determined there. The trial court provides the mechanisms for processing the case, including discovery, and for determining the facts, applying the law to the facts, and thus determining who wins and who loses. Unless the parties settle the case, the trial court eventually enters a judgment, declaring who wins and what, if any remedy, is to be awarded. Movies and television shows about lawyers focus on events in the trial court. Here — at least at trial — we have the courtroom drama — the witnesses breaking down on the stand, the jury swayed by the articulate lawyer.

In appellate courts, there is no jury, there are no witnesses, there is no presentation of evidence. Instead, lawyers for each party present oral argument (often 30 minutes per side) to a panel, usually of three judges. The appellate court does not determine what happened and apply the law to those facts — that is the role of the trial court. The role of an appellate court is to determine whether the trial court did its job properly. If so, the appellate court can affirm the judgment of the trial court. If not, the appellate court can reverse or vacate the judgment and remand to the trial court for further proceedings. The party instituting the appeal is the *appellant*. The other party is the *appellee*. Interestingly, there is no federal constitutional right to appeal the result in a civil case. Thus, in federal courts the right to appeal from the federal district court to the United States Court of Appeals is created only by statute; it is a matter of legislative grace. The same is true in many, but not all, state courts. In general, one may appeal only from a final judgment — that is, the trial court's ultimate decision on the merits of the entire dispute. The numerous interlocutory (or non-final) decisions of the trial court generally cannot be appealed as they are made, but must await entry of the final judgment.

On appeal, the appellate court does not second-guess everything the trial judge did. Generally, it reviews only those things to which a party made a timely objection at the trial court and which that party then raised on appeal. Because the appellate court does not entertain the presentation of evidence — does not, for instance, see witnesses testify — it is not in a position to second-guess the trial court's determination of the facts. Instead, it defers to the trial court on such issues, and will reverse only if the trial court's findings are "clearly erroneous." The appellate court makes this determination by reviewing the trial court record — reading the transcript of the trial, reviewing the documents and other evidence adduced at trial, etc. On questions of law, however, the appellate court does not defer to the trial court. Rather, it determines the law *de novo* — afresh, on its own. So if the trial court made an error of law — for example, by putting the burden of proof on the wrong party, or misstating the law, or allowing the introduction of improper evidence — the appellate court may reverse the judgment and remand for further proceedings, including, if necessary, a new trial. We discuss standards of appellate review in detail in §14.7.

Not every trial court error will result in reversal, however. The error must be "prejudicial," as opposed to "harmless." That is, sometimes a trial judge will make a mistake, but the mistake did not likely affect the outcome of the case. Such an error is harmless, and will not result in a reversal. But some errors do affect or at least taint the outcome. Such errors are prejudicial, and will result in reversal.

From this brief discussion, it is clear that our system of justice values *finality*. There is one trial court and, generally, one chance to litigate issues. If a party does not like the outcome, she can appeal, but the appellate court will reverse only if there was a clearly erroneous factual finding or a prejudicial error of law. *But, unless the judgment is set aside or a new trial ordered, or unless it is reversed on appeal, the disgruntled party does not get another chance to litigate the issues.* So if one does not like the result of her case at trial court, there is no opportunity to "do over" or to take a Mulligan.[18] Indeed, in Chapter 11, we study doctrines that limit the party's ability to relitigate issues *even in a different case.*

In most judicial systems, including the federal system, there are actually two levels of appellate courts. The first, known in many states (and

[18]*Mulligan* is a golf term. When you hit a lousy tee shot, taking a Mulligan means you hit a new tee shot and do not count the lousy one. Mulligans are wonderful if you play like I do.

the federal system[19]) as the Court of Appeals,[20] performs the function we just discussed. It is there to ensure that the trial court reached plausible factual findings, and applied the right law and applied it correctly. It is an "intermediate" court, because it is perched above the trial court but below the jurisdiction's supreme court. That supreme court is also an appellate court.

Before discussing the role played by supreme courts, however, we should note that not all judicial systems have an intermediate court. In Nevada, for instance, there is no court between the trial court and the supreme court. In Virginia, there is a Court of Appeals, but it has very limited jurisdiction, and does not hear appeals in general civil cases. Where the intermediate court does exist — as in the federal system and in most states — appeal to that court is usually "of right." That means that a party who loses at the trial court has a right to have the appellate court review the case (assuming, of course, that the party taking the appeal satisfies the procedural requirements for doing so). Again, in the federal system, this right is not secured by the Constitution, but is granted by statute.

Generally, there is no right to appeal, however, to the jurisdiction's supreme court.[21] In most civil cases, review by the supreme court is discretionary. Thus, the court is not required to hear any particular civil case,[22] and does so only if convinced by the party seeking review that the case is sufficiently important to warrant its attention. So though the supreme court is an appellate court, and serves the appellate function described above, it does so in a very selective way. Because it hears such a small number of cases, it looks for those in which a pronouncement by the ultimate court is needed to bring clarity and certainty to the law. For example, the Supreme Court of the United States may agree to hear a case that raises an issue on which the various Courts of Appeals have reached different conclusions. Thus, supreme courts generally act only when a case raises an important issue on which there is some uncertainty or other need for definitive guidance. Supreme courts rarely agree to review a case

---

[19] In the federal system, the Court of Appeals is divided geographically into circuits, most of which have a numerical name. For instance, the United States Court of Appeals for the Eleventh Circuit (which lawyers simply call "the Eleventh Circuit") hears appeals from federal trial courts in Florida, Georgia, and Alabama. Congress sets the geographic boundaries by statute. In addition, Congress sets the geographic boundaries of the federal trial courts — the United States District Courts.

[20] Not all states follow suit. In California, this court is known as the Court of Appeal (singular). In New York, it is called the Appellate Division.

[21] Again, there are some exceptions. In Nevada, there is a right to appeal trial results to the Nevada Supreme Court. Such appeal of right of a civil case to the supreme court is extremely rare.

[22] Remember, we deal in this course with civil cases. In many states, the supreme court is required to review criminal convictions in which the death sentence is imposed.

simply to correct some mistake on an established matter — that is something the intermediate court of appeals ought to do.

The chart below shows the typical tripartite court system, with the trial court at the bottom, the intermediate appellate court in the middle, and the supreme court at the apex. On the left side are the names of those courts in the federal system. The trial court is the United States District Court, which is always followed with a geographic description. For example, in California there are four federal trial districts: The Southern District sits in San Diego, the Central District in Los Angeles, the Northern District in San Francisco, and the Eastern District in Sacramento. In some states, there is only one district, such as the United States District Court for New Jersey. As noted above, the intermediate court in the federal system is the United States Court of Appeals (for whatever circuit is involved). The federal supreme court is the Supreme Court of the United States, which, as you know, consists of nine Justices and sits in Washington, D.C.

On the right side of the chart is the model for most state judicial systems. Trial courts have various names in the different states[23] (and sometimes even within a state). Remember that in some states there is no intermediate court of appeals. The high court in most states is known simply as the supreme court.[24] That court is often called the *court of last resort* because it is the highest court in that judicial system. Courts below it are sometimes called *inferior courts*. This is not a pejorative statement; it does not mean that such courts are not as competent as others. It simply means they are below another court in the judicial system. Thus, a trial court is inferior to an intermediate appellate court. The trial court and intermediate appellate court are both inferior to the supreme court.

Federal System		*State System*
U.S. Supreme Court	HIGH COURT	State Supreme Court
U.S. Court of Appeals	INTERMEDIATE	Court of Appeals (typically)
U.S. District Court	TRIAL COURT	Various names, e.g., District, Circuit, Superior

It is important to understand that the supreme court of each state is the final arbiter on the meaning of state law. No federal court — not even the Supreme Court of the United States — has any authority to tell the Iowa Supreme Court what Iowa law is or should be. Most of us have a sense

---

[23] In New York, the trial court is called the supreme court.

[24] Here, too, there is some state variation. In New York, the high court is the Court of Appeals. In Massachusetts, it is the Supreme Judicial Court.

that somehow almost any issue can be decided by the Supreme Court of the United States. On television news, we often hear people say, "I'm going to fight this to the highest court in the land — all the way to the Supreme Court." Well, fine. Just realize that the highest court in the land on matters of state law is not the Supreme Court in Washington, D.C. The highest court in the land on issues of Arizona law is in Phoenix. The highest court in the land on issues of New York law is in Albany.

It is also important to understand that a case filed on one side or the other — either in the federal trial court or a state trial court — is appealed *through that system.* In other words, a case filed in the state trial court in California is appealed to the California Court of Appeal and ultimately to the California Supreme Court (if that court agrees to hear the case). A case cannot be appealed from a state trial court to a federal appellate court; neither can a case filed in a federal trial court be appealed to a state appellate court.

For our purposes, there is one very important exception to the model we just laid out: The Supreme Court of the United States may exercise appellate review over state court decisions, *but only if two things are true.* First, the case must have been appealed all the way through the state system. That means that review at the United States Supreme Court is precluded until a party has sought review by the highest court of the state system that could hear the case (usually, that is the state supreme court).

- ◦ *P* sues *D.* The case is fully litigated and the trial court enters judgment for *P. D* appeals to the intermediate court of appeals, which affirms the judgment. *D* cannot seek review by the United States Supreme Court because the intermediate court of appeals is not the state's highest court. *D* must seek review at the state supreme court. If that court agrees to hear the case, the party who loses there can seek review by the United States Supreme Court.
  - ◦ What if the state supreme court refuses to hear the case? After all, the state supreme court's review is usually discretionary. Then the party who lost at the intermediate court of appeals can seek review by the United States Supreme Court, because review was sought at the highest state court. The requirement, then, is not that the state's highest court actually render a decision. Rather, a party must have "exhausted" all options in the state system before seeking review at the United States Supreme Court.[25]

Second, the United States Supreme Court can review *only* matters of federal law.[26]

---

[25] *See* Costarelli v. Massachusetts, 421 U.S. 193 (1975).
[26] This is the upshot of 28 U.S.C. §1257.

- ° The Iowa Supreme Court holds that the state law on abortion prohibits abortions in the third trimester of pregnancy. The United States Supreme Court has no authority to review this holding, because it concerns state law, on which the state supreme court is the authoritative body.
- ° The Iowa Supreme Court holds that the state law on abortion does (or does not) violate federal constitutional principles concerning personal privacy. The United States Supreme Court may review this issue, because it is one of federal law — the meaning of the federal Constitution.

Thus, the Supreme Court of the United States exercises its appellate jurisdiction in two types of cases. First, it has discretion to review decisions of the United States Courts of Appeals.[27] These are cases that have been litigated through the federal system — from the United States District Court to the United States Court of Appeals and, now, to the court of last resort in the federal system. Second, it has discretion to review rulings from state courts if (1) a litigant has sought review at the highest state court that could entertain the matter and (2) the issue presented is one of federal law.

As seen above, Supreme Court review in either instance — over judgments by the United States Court of Appeals or over judgments from the highest state court on matters of federal law — is discretionary. A party seeking review by the Supreme Court files a petition for writ of *certiorari*. The writ is granted, and the case reviewed by the Supreme Court, only if at least four of the nine Justices agree that the case should be heard. Such action is extremely rare. In an average year, litigants will seek *certiorari* in more than 7,000 cases; it will be granted in about 100. So the odds of Supreme Court review of any case are exceptionally long. If the Court agrees to hear the case, the party who sought review is called the *petitioner* and the other party is called the *respondent*.[28]

Again, note that lower federal courts — the United States District Court and the United States Court of Appeals — do not have appellate jurisdiction over cases decided in the state courts. Many students seem to have the idea that federal courts are somehow superior to state courts — that a federal court somehow can review what state courts do. As we have just seen, though, federal appellate review of state judgments is quite rare — it can be done only by the Supreme Court, only over matters of federal law, and only in the extraordinary situation in which the Supreme Court grants a writ of *certiorari*.[29]

---

[27] This is established in 28 U.S.C. §1254(1).

[28] So in a Supreme Court opinion, the party whose name is listed first was not necessarily the plaintiff (who filed the case in trial court). Rather, it is the party who lost in the court immediately below, and who (successfully) sought Supreme Court review.

[29] The United States Supreme Court has *original* (as opposed to appellate) jurisdiction in certain limited situations. Original jurisdiction, as we saw above, means that it sits as a trial court. Under Article III, §2, paragraph 2 of the Constitution, the Supreme Court has

Finally, we need to understand the doctrine of *precedent*, or *stare decisis*. The Latin phrase means "to stand by things decided." When an appellate court makes a holding on a question of law, that holding is *precedential*. That means that it binds all lower courts within that judicial system on that question of law; no inferior court in that judicial system can take a different approach on that question of law. Of course, precedent can be overturned — either by the appellate court that set the precedent or by a higher court.

- Suppose the Georgia Court of Appeals (an intermediate appellate court in that state's judicial system) holds that state law recognizes a particular claim — that it allows someone who has suffered a particular harm to sue the perpetrator of the harm. Lower courts in that judicial system — that is, trial courts in Georgia — must follow that rule on that question of law. The holding of the Court of Appeals establishes precedent for the lower courts in Georgia.
- Suppose the Georgia Supreme Court decides to review the question and concludes that state law does *not* recognize that claim. The state supreme court's holding on this question overturns the Georgia Court of Appeals' holding.[30] All courts in the Georgia judicial system (trial courts and the intermediate appellate court) must follow the precedent set by the state supreme court.

Obviously, decisions by the United States Supreme Court bind all courts in the United States, federal and state, *on matters of federal law*. Thus, the Supreme Court is the ultimate arbiter on the meaning of federal statutes and the Constitution. As suggested above, *stare decisis* is not immutable. A court may determine that relevant changes in law and society lead to the conclusion that precedent be overturned. In 1896, the Supreme Court held that separate but equal facilities for different races did not violate constitutional norms.[31] In 1954, in the landmark decision of *Brown v. Board of Education*,[32] the Court overturned the 1896 holding. In 1842, the Supreme Court held that federal courts could fashion their own common

---

trial jurisdiction in cases affecting ambassadors and other public ministers and consuls, and in cases in which a state is a party. Such cases are rare, and usually not discussed in Civil Procedure.

[30] If the supreme court were reviewing the same case in which the court of appeals had made its pronouncement, we would say that the supreme court reversed the lower court's judgment. The term *reverse* connotes that a higher court disagreed with a lower court in the context of the same case. The term *overrule*, in contrast, refers to a subsequent ruling *in a different case* that rejects the holding of an earlier case. Examples of such "overturning" of precedent are given in the next paragraph of the text, with *Brown* and *Erie*.

[31] Plessy v. Ferguson, 163 U.S. 537 (1896).

[32] 349 U.S. 294 (1954).

law for the resolution of disputes between citizens of different states.[33] In 1938, in the famous decision of *Erie Railroad Co. v. Tompkins*,[34] addressed in Chapter 10, the Court overturned the 1842 holding as having usurped state power in violation of the Tenth Amendment to the Constitution. The circumstances that justify a departure from the doctrine of precedent are subject to debate and can be the source of considerable controversy. Your professor may discuss them in Civil Procedure or, more likely, in Constitutional Law or a course on Legal Methods.

§1.2.3   The English Influence and the Bifurcation of Law and Equity

The United States evolved, of course, from British colonies. Not surprisingly, then, much of our procedure and much of our law finds root in England. One pivotal event in English history was the Norman Conquest, which was ensured when William the Conqueror defeated the Britons in the Battle of Hastings in 1066. William revolutionized many things in Britain, including the administration of justice. Before William, the justice system consisted of local courts, run by feudal lords and barons. The local control of these courts reflected the scattered, feudal nature of life in England at the time. William did much to pull the feudal fiefdoms into a more unified whole that mirrored a single country.

William established three sets of royal courts, which did not replace the feudal courts, but existed alongside them. The courts were the King's Bench, the Court of the Exchequer, and the Court of Common Pleas. Each court entertained only certain types of disputes, each of which was denominated by a particular *writ*. For instance, to sue for an intentional tort, the plaintiff would seek a "writ of trespass *vi et armis*," while to sue for negligence the plaintiff would seek a writ of "trespass *on the case*."[35] Over time, the royal courts gradually expanded the types of cases they could hear — by expanding the number of writs they would grant. The local barons were not happy about this, because the expansion of the royal courts' jurisdiction resulted in a contraction of the jurisdiction of the local feudal courts. Ultimately, though, there was little they could do about it, and over time the feudal courts waned in importance.

---

[33] Swift v. Tyson, 41 U.S. 1 (1848).

[34] 304 U.S. 64 (1938).

[35] It's important to keep in mind that in law school you encounter familiar words in unfamiliar contexts. The word *trespass* is widely used in common parlance to mean the unlawful entry onto another's land. As used here, the word has a broader meaning — a wrong committed against another's property or her person. The English common law courts recognized a dizzying array of writs for various forms of trespass. For example, if someone stole your personal property, you would sue in trespass *de bonis asportatis*.

While expanding their jurisdiction, the royal courts, over the centuries, did two other things, both of which made them less desirable as tribunals of justice. First, they became increasingly rigid; the courts emphasized form over substance. Many plaintiffs with legitimate claims and solid proof lost because of some arcane procedural slip-up.[36] Second, the royal courts were not creative when it came to awarding relief to those plaintiffs who did win. Basically, they recognized one remedy: *damages*, which is a monetary payment. Damages are to this day an important remedy, but there are many cases in which damages cannot make the plaintiff whole.

- *D* trespasses across *P*'s real property[37] every day. *P* sues and wins. The royal courts would permit *P* to recover money to compensate her for the damage by *D*'s trespass. Note how this remedy is aimed only at past behavior — it makes *D* pay for the trespassing she has already done. But it does nothing to prevent future trespassing. If *D* wants to keep trespassing, she may do so, and the only sanction will be payment of damages. In all likelihood, the damages will not be prohibitive, and *D* may find it worth her while simply to pay to trespass daily. Because of the limited remedy of damages, *D* can essentially force *P* to grant her a license to travel across *P*'s land.
  - What *P* wants is a court order telling *D* that she cannot trespass, punishable by holding *D* in contempt of court (which may result in a fine or imprisonment of *D*). Stated in terms lawyers use, *P* wants an *injunction* — an order prohibiting *D* from taking some act in the future. But the royal courts simply did not grant injunctions.
- *D* steals a diamond ring from *P*. *P* sues and wins. The royal courts would require *D* to pay *P* money sufficient to purchase a new diamond ring. But *P* doesn't want a new ring — she wants the one that was stolen, because it had great sentimental value. She wants what lawyers call *specific relief* — a remedy that relates to this particular piece of property. The royal courts, however, would not grant such relief. It was basically damages or nothing.

These two factors — the elevation of form over substance and the limited remedy available — led plaintiffs to seek relief outside the royal courts. Specifically, they started going to the King's Council, which was a

---

[36] As we see in §7.2, the common law rules of pleading a case were quite unforgiving. If the plaintiff chose the wrong writ (which she had to choose at the outset of the case, when she might not have been clear on the facts), she would lose, even if at trial she showed that she had a right to recover on a different writ.

[37] Real property, or "realty," is land. Many students equate the word "real" with "tangible," and thus conclude that a car is real property, because they can touch it, so it is in some sense real. Don't make that mistake. Real property is land. Period. If you own something that is not land, it is personal property, sometimes called *chattels*. Personal property can be tangible (like a car) or intangible (like an ownership interest in a corporation, usually represented by a stock certificate).

group of officers serving the King. These suitors would ask the King's Council to intervene and to "do justice" in their case. Gradually, the Chancellor, who was a member of the King's Council, began to issue orders in individual cases. These orders were issued on behalf of the King's Council and were aimed at achieving "equity." By about the middle of the fourteenth century, this practice had developed into a separate court, called Chancery (named, obviously, after the Chancellor).

Thus, nearly seven centuries ago in England, there were two completely separate sets of courts: the law courts (which consisted of the royal courts) and the equity (or Chancery) courts. Today, in the twenty-first century, on this side of the Atlantic, this bifurcation of law and equity is still important (as you will see throughout your legal career). But let's complete the story in old England. Over the centuries, equity practice expanded, and the equity court developed a series of useful remedies that were unavailable in the law courts. Equity upheld the assignment of claims (which law courts would not do) and enforced trusts (which law courts also would not do). The equity court even became so brazen that it would issue an order forbidding the enforcement of a judgment from a royal court if the judgment were obtained through fraud. Such an order seemed so invasive of royal court jurisdiction that King James I commissioned a group, headed by Francis Bacon, to resolve the debate. The commission concluded that the equity court indeed had the power to issue an injunction to stop a party from enforcing a fraudulent judgment from a law court. Importantly, because the injunction was issued against the party, and not against the court or judge, it was not an impermissible encroachment of the royal courts' power.

Afterward, the law and equity courts continued to develop independently. They adopted different procedures and terminology. Law courts employed a jury to determine the facts of a case, while equity courts did not. Trials in law courts featured live testimony by witnesses, while equity favored presentation of evidence through sworn written statements, or *affidavits*. At law, a case was known as a "legal action," while equity adjudicated a "suit at equity." At law, the court's adjudication resulted in a "judgment," while at equity the court entered a "decree." At law, the judicial officer was the "judge," while at equity the judicial officer was the "chancellor." Law courts enforced their judgments *in rem*, which (as we discuss in Chapter 2) means "against the property." Equity courts, in contrast, enforced decrees *in personam*, or "against the person."

- ○ A law court enters a judgment against *D* for $50,000. If *D* does not pay the money to *P*, the court will enforce the judgment by issuing an order to the sheriff to seize *D*'s property (her house, her car, her bank account, whatever the sheriff can get) and have it sold at a public auction. The first $50,000 raised at the auction would go to *P* (with the rest going to *D*). If the auction failed to fetch $50,000, *P* is just out of luck. The judgment at law is enforced against the property — and if the property is insufficient to cover the judgment, tough.

  ◦ An equity court enters a decree requiring D to return a stolen diamond ring to P. D refuses to do so. The sheriff can arrest D and put her in jail until she agrees to return the ring. The equity decree is enforced against the person, so the court can coerce D to do as she was ordered. As my dear late friend Donald Fyr used to say, "equity is into behavior modification."[38]

Most important, law and equity courts differed in the remedies available. Again, law courts were largely limited to awarding damages. There are different types of damages, as you will see, particularly in your courses on Contracts and Torts. Compensatory damages, as the name makes clear, compensate the plaintiff for the harm occasioned by the defendant's act. Punitive damages, as the name also implies, are aimed at punishing a defendant for particularly egregious behavior. It is important to understand, though, that not all awards of money constitute damages. For instance, restitution of unjust enrichment is not damages, and historically was pursued in equity.

  ◦ D performs services for P, for which the bill is \$120. P gives D a \$100 bill and a \$50 bill, mistakenly thinking that the latter was a \$20 bill. D has been unjustly enriched by \$30. P's claim is not for damages, but for restitution, to disgorge the amount overpaid.

Equity courts, as noted, developed a broad range of remedies. These include the injunction (which is an order commanding that the defendant either do or refrain from doing something), specific performance (which commands a party to perform in accordance with its agreement in a contract), rescission (which "undoes" a document, such as a contract, thus allowing both sides to be free of obligations under the document), and reformation (under which the court essentially redrafts a document to accord with the parties' true intentions). Equity also developed the "cleanup" doctrine, which allowed it to award damages, so long as they were incidental to the principal equitable relief sought. To this degree, then, equity could award a remedy usually available only at law (damages). The converse was not true, however; thus, the law courts did not grant equitable relief.

  ◦ P, the owner of real property, sues in equity for a decree ordering D to move out of the premises after D's lease had expired. The equity court can grant the injunction ordering D to move and, as incidental to the

---

[38] Don Fyr was my mentor in law teaching, and was my daughter's Godfather. He died in 1994. He was a wonderful guy, who cared greatly about teaching.

decree, order *D* to pay damages to cover the lost rent for the period during which she overstayed.

One abiding tenet of equity jurisprudence has been that one cannot obtain an equitable remedy if the legal remedy (of damages) is adequate to make her whole. If the harm done to the plaintiff can be vindicated by an award of damages, she must sue at law, and cannot invoke equity jurisdiction. Thus, the first order of business for a plaintiff in equity is to allege that her legal remedy of damages is inadequate. We saw examples above: the plaintiff for whom the diamond ring had sentimental value and the plaintiff who did not want the defendant trespassing across her property.

This dual set of courts — law and equity — with their different procedures, terminology, methods of enforcement, and remedies, were imported to the American colonies. Throughout most of its history as an independent nation, the United States followed the practice of maintaining separate courts of law and equity. In 1938, though, Congress abolished separate law and equity dockets in the federal courts. It provided instead for a single type of civil case, known as a "civil action." Under the Federal Rules of Civil Procedure, adopted in that year, there is uniform procedure in all cases in the federal courts, regardless of whether they would have been law or equity in bygone days. Most states did the same, and abolished separate law and equity courts. But not all have done so. Every state is free to do as it pleases. In Delaware, for example, there are still separate law and equity courts. In Virginia, until 2006, the main trial court (the Circuit Court) was divided into law and equity sides, in which the historical terminological and remedial differences persisted. In that year, Virginia finally abolished the distinctions and now uses a unified procedure in all cases.

The fact that the federal system and those of most states have merged law and equity into a single trial court, though, does not mean that the distinction between law and equity is not important. It is. To this day, all jurisdictions differentiate between legal and equitable remedies, and a plaintiff cannot obtain an equitable remedy without demonstrating that her legal remedy (of damages) is inadequate. Moreover, in federal court the Seventh Amendment preserves a right to jury trial in civil cases "at law" but not at equity. As discussed in §9.2.2, determining whether a litigant has a right to jury trial can be difficult, and involves the historic lines of demarcation between law and equity.

§1.3   Alternatives to Litigation

We know that litigation is the basic model for dispute resolution in our society. We also know that it is usually an expensive and time-consuming process. Some critics note not only the expense and delay, but also question the underlying premise of the adversary system; some feel that the polarizing effects of that system may obscure rather than reveal the truth. Further, some commentators criticize the fact that most litigation is a zero-sum game: One side wins and the other side loses. Many disputes, they argue, are sufficiently subtle that there should be some "give" on both sides of the case. Moreover, litigation forces the parties to focus on the past, rather than on building a harmonious future relationship.[39] For these and other reasons, recent decades have seen increasing interest in alternatives to litigation. Most Civil Procedure casebooks have at least some materials on alternative dispute resolution (ADR). And most law schools offer upper-level courses on ADR and on specific forms of litigation alternatives.

It is worth noting that American society has long embraced ADR in specific settings. For instance, in the workplace, it has long been commonplace that the litigation model has been supplanted by statutes concerning workers' compensation. These statutes provide that a worker injured on the job cannot sue her employer. Instead, the employer is required to pay a certain benefit — set by statute or regulation — for specific types of injuries. Under workers' compensation programs, then, workers waive their right to sue their employers in return for an absolute right to recover a specific dollar sum immediately. The award is made without need of showing that the employer was at fault. Workers' compensation programs are a common alternative to tort litigation.

The commonest form of ADR, of course, is settlement. People with disputes work them out all the time, often obviating the need even to file a case. But, as we saw above, a settlement is usually struck with litigation in the background — that is, if the parties do not settle the dispute, one of them will sue. Settlement is really a form of *negotiation* — the parties may structure the outcome in a way that makes most sense for them. They can avoid the "winner takes all" mentality of litigation and structure an outcome in which each side gives and each side receives. In a dispute between businesses that foresee an ongoing relationship, perhaps the settlement will involve future conduct toward each other. In the upper division of law school, you may take a course on negotiations; such classes are frequently taught by adjunct professors, who are "real-world" lawyers with a wealth of valuable experience to be shared.

Often, serious settlement negotiations do not commence until after a case has been filed and the parties have engaged in some stages of litigation. In the discovery phase of the case, for instance, each side may get a

---

[39] Of course, many disputes are between people who would prefer never to deal with each other again, such as in the typical automobile crash case. But many disputes are between people who envision an ongoing relationship, such as businesses or family members. In such situations, the parties may wish to resolve the dispute as quickly as possible, to allow an agreeable future.

"reality check" about what the evidence actually shows. Maybe an event that seemed clear-cut at the time has more nuance when witnesses give testimony. Also, as each side spends increasing amounts in lawyers' fees, the incentive to negotiate a settlement often increases. Many disputes will not settle early — the parties have their heels dug in. But with the passage of time and expenditure of money, the parties may become more willing to approach the bargaining table.

When most people invoke the phrase "ADR" they are referring to two dispute-resolution mechanisms: arbitration and mediation. It is important to understand the differences between them. It is also important to understand that while each traditionally has been voluntary, an increasing number of judicial systems are requiring disputants to try one or the other; in other words, after filing litigation, some parties find themselves engaged in mediation or arbitration because the judge ordered them to do so. This "mandatory ADR" is a relatively new phenomenon. Traditionally, ADR has been voluntary; parties to litigation may choose to submit to mediation or arbitration, or parties to a contract may have waived the right to sue in favor of some form of ADR. Indeed, you may be surprised to learn (when you look at the fine print of some contracts you have signed) how often you have done just that.

Arbitration is quite similar to litigation; the parties submit their dispute to a decision by a third party. The third party, however, is not a judge paid by the taxpayers. She is a civilian, chosen and paid by the parties; in some cases, there is a panel of multiple (usually three) arbitrators. And the hearing does not take place in a courthouse built with taxpayer funds. It takes place in somebody's office. The American Arbitration Association (AAA), a private entity, has offices throughout the country, and provides training for arbitrators as well as a venue for arbitration hearings. Many contracts provide that disputes between the parties must be arbitrated under the auspices of the AAA. The collective bargaining agreement between Major League Baseball and the players' union provides for arbitration of some salary disputes.

An arbitration hearing looks like a trial, at which each side presents evidence. But the hearing is far less formal than a trial. The rules governing admissibility of evidence at trial do not apply, and the arbitrator(s) often allow the introduction of hearsay. Evidence is frequently proffered in written form instead of oral testimony. In arbitration, there is no formal discovery, but the arbitrator often facilitates the parties' exchange of relevant information. Like litigation, arbitration usually results in a winner and a loser. The advantages over litigation are usually simple: Arbitration is cheaper and less time-consuming than formal litigation.

Parties to arbitration often waive significant rights. There is no right to a jury trial in arbitration, and there is usually little, if any, appellate review.

The victorious party may ask a court to confirm and enforce the arbitration award. The losing party can petition a court to vacate the arbitration award, but on very limited grounds. Usually, the arbitrator's misapplication of the law is not a basis for setting aside an arbitration award. Critics assert that arbitration thus can become essentially a "lawless" dispute resolution.

Mediation is quite different from litigation. Here, the parties ask a third party to help them reach a settlement. The mediator is less interested in who is right than in getting the parties to find common ground. The mediator is often creative in suggesting ways for the parties to get the dispute behind them and get on with their lives. Often, mediators realize that parties need a chance to tell their story, and structure hearings to allow each side to do so. In addition to being cheaper and less time-consuming than formal litigation, mediation usually avoids the zero-sum game: The object is to reach accord, rather than to declare a winner and a loser.

In recent years, feminist scholars have debated whether the mediation model, with its emphasis on cooperation and communication, is more hospitable to women than the adversary system of litigation.[40] In addition, some commentators criticize ADR as forcing compromise upon persons who have a right to vindication and remedy. At a broader level, the use of ADR forces us to consider a very basic question: What is the purpose of litigation? It might be seen as essentially private — litigation is intended to resolve disputes peacefully, and thus to prevent disputants from resorting to self-help. It might also be seen, however, as serving a public function — as private citizens using governmental power to force other citizens to abide by the norms we have set for appropriate behavior.[41] Under such a view, the adversary system of litigation is not seen as excessively combative, but as necessary to vindicate the rules of civil society. As one leading commentator concluded: "We train our students in the tougher arts [of litigation] so that they may help secure all that the law promises, not because we want them to become gladiators or because we take special pleasure in combat."[42]

At this point you may not — indeed, perhaps you *should* not — have an overarching view of the role of litigation in our society. As you study Civil Procedure, you will occasionally become inundated with detail, enmeshed in specifics. This is as it should be. The details are important. But from

---

[40] *See, e.g.,* Trina Grillo, *The Mediation Alternative: Process Dangers for Women,* 100 Yale L.J. 1545, 1607 (1991) ("To the extent that women are more likely than men to believe in communication as a mode of conflict resolution and to appreciate the importance of an adversary's interests, [the adversary system of litigation] does not always suit their needs."). Professor Grillo concludes, however, that mediation often does not serve women well.

[41] Owen Fiss, *Against Settlement,* 93 Yale L.J. 1073, 1089 (1984) (describing litigation as "an institutional arrangement for using state power to bring a recalcitrant reality closer to our chosen ideals").

[42] *Id.* at 1090.

time to time you will also find yourself taking a view from higher altitude — pondering the big questions of the role of litigation and the administration of justice. As we said in §1.1, Civil Procedure presents students with a stunning array of material — from the nuts and bolts to the big picture. In the next section, we put the various topics together to survey the entire course.

§1.4 The Big Picture in Civil Procedure

Many students struggle for a sense of how the various topics in Civil Procedure relate to one another. Some get a good grasp of the various pieces of the course — they understand individual topics in isolation — but do not see how those pieces fit together. In fact, the topics covered in our course do fit into a cohesive whole. This section describes that whole and provides a framework of the course. It does so in a largely chronological way, by reflecting how litigation unfolds in the usual case. It is imperative to understand, however, that there is no single right order in which to cover the topics in this course. Your professor may cover them in a different order from the way they are addressed in this book. There is nothing wrong with that. No matter what order, however, it will facilitate understanding to see how the pieces fit together.

Most Civil Procedure professors spend a great deal of time on topics concerning the selection of the forum in which litigation will proceed. For reasons we discuss in the various chapters, litigants and lawyers care a great deal about where litigation takes place. For now, suffice to say that we will see cases in which parties paid millions of dollars in attorneys' fees and expenses to vindicate their choice of forum. It is a very important issue.

Four topics in the course relate directly to forum selection. First (here, but not necessarily in your course) is *personal jurisdiction*, which governs the geographic question of whether the plaintiff may sue the defendant in a particular *state*. As we see in Chapter 2, this is a far more complex question than may meet the eye, and is affected both by state statutes and the Due Process Clauses of the Constitution. The statutory and constitutional analyses are aimed at determining whether a particular state has sufficient "power" over the defendant to enable it to enter a judgment that will bind the defendant. Second, and closely related, is the topic of *notice*. It is not enough simply to show that a state has personal jurisdiction over the defendant. In addition, due process requires that the defendant be given notice of the proceedings against her and an opportunity to defend. We address these topics in Chapter 3.

Thus, together, personal jurisdiction and notice ensure that the plaintiff can sue the defendant *in a particular state*. The next question is what court *in that state* hears the case. This question raises the topic of *subject matter jurisdiction*, treated in Chapter 4.[43] Specifically, the choice is between litigating in the state court system or the federal court system. As noted in §1.2.1, the federal courts have limited subject matter jurisdiction, which means that they can entertain only specific types of disputes. The topic raises constitutional and statutory considerations as to the allocation of judicial business between the federal and state governments. Keen awareness of the requirements for invoking federal subject matter jurisdiction — and an understanding of the policy reasons for the various forms of federal subject matter jurisdiction — is part of the arsenal of any litigation lawyer.

The last topic addressing forum selection is *venue*, addressed in Chapter 5. Venue is concerned with the geographic question of *where* the litigation will proceed *within the chosen judicial system*. Subject matter jurisdiction informs us that a particular case can go to a federal district court, but it does not tell us *which* federal district court. The nation is divided into federal districts, and federal statutes prescribe proper venues for various types of cases in the federal system. So if the plaintiff wants to sue in federal court in California, the venue question would determine where the case goes — to the Southern District of California (in San Diego), the Central District of California (in Los Angeles), the Northern District of California (in San Francisco), or the Eastern District of California (in Sacramento).

In Chapter 6, we study the avenues available to the defendant for challenging the plaintiff's choice of forum. The timing and method for raising an objection may vary depending on whether the objection is to personal jurisdiction, notice, subject matter jurisdiction, or to venue. The rules here are fairly mechanical and can be harsh. Failure to abide by them may result in waiver of an otherwise valid defense. So, in sum, Chapters 2 through 6 all deal broadly with the topic of forum selection.

From there, we assume that the case is in a proper forum, and walk through the litigation in a typical case. Chapter 7 addresses *pleadings*, which are the documents in which parties set forth their claims and defenses, such as the complaint and the answer. This is a fairly mechanical topic, in which historical perspective is helpful. In this area, we will see that a case may be ended without trial. Specifically, for instance, the

---

[43] Many professors start with subject matter jurisdiction before addressing personal jurisdiction. Again, there is no single right way to approach these topics. In my view, personal jurisdiction should go first because it is the broader question. It asks whether the plaintiff can sue the defendant in Texas (or any other particular state). If the answer is yes, the next task (it seems to me) is to determine the proper court in Texas (or whatever state). But there is nothing wrong with starting with subject matter jurisdiction.

defendant may successfully move to dismiss for any of a variety of grounds, or the plaintiff may win a judgment based on the defendant's failure to respond to the complaint properly. The pleadings, at best, basically put the parties on notice of the general claims by the plaintiff and defenses raised by the defendant. They are based upon the parties' best understanding of the facts. Modern procedure recognizes, however, that that understanding of the facts is largely uninformed. In the *discovery* phase of litigation, discussed in Chapter 8, we see that each party has very broad (perhaps surprisingly broad) rights to gain access to evidence held by the other party, and to force that party to clarify its position on relevant matters.

Thus, together, pleadings and discovery constitute an education process in which each party finds out about the other side's position and evidence. In a fundamental way, the judicial system's desire for free exchange of information and evidence seems at odds with the adversary system discussed in §1.1. After all, if the point is to win, why should a party have to cough up information that hurts her case? Yes, the goal of each party is to win. But the goal of the process is to do justice — to achieve the just and fair resolution of the dispute. So litigation is not unfettered warfare. The search for the truth is fostered by disclosure within the rules. Sometimes the discovery process demonstrates that there is no claim there, and leads to dismissal. Sometimes it convinces the defendant that she really did do something wrong and caused harm to the plaintiff, which may lead to settlement. In all events, the American system is based in part on a very broad duty to cooperate in ascertaining the truth by allowing the adversary to have access to information.

In Chapter 9, we address actual adjudication of the dispute. Many cases disappear before getting to this point — perhaps because the court dismissed the case, perhaps because the defendant defaulted, perhaps because the parties settled. Cases that do survive to this stage will not necessarily be tried. It may be that there is no dispute on a material issue of fact, in which case the dispute is simply over the interpretation of a legal issue. In such a case, the court can rule through a procedure known as summary judgment. If, on the other hand, the parties dispute material issues of fact, the case will be tried. Here, we consider the important and sometimes vexing issue of whether the parties are entitled to a jury trial. And in cases involving a jury, it is important to allocate authority between the jury and the judge. One way or another, whether by summary judgment or trial, the dispute is adjudicated and the case ended with the court's entry of judgment.

At this point, the losing party may seek appellate review, which we address in Chapter 14. Before going there, however, the intervening chapters address other topics. One is the *Erie* doctrine, which many people consider the most difficult topic in Civil Procedure. *Erie* is a subject of surpassing importance, because it goes to the heart of the relationship between the state and federal governments. It is important to note, though, that *Erie* raises its troubling specter in rather limited circumstances. It is only an issue when the case is in federal (not state) court. And, even there, it generally arises only when the federal court is exercising diversity of citizenship jurisdiction — that is, the case is in federal court because of the citizenship of the parties. The question addressed by *Erie* is whether the federal judge in such a case must apply state law (or, on the other hand, is free to ignore state law and fashion her own approach). *Erie* is something of a freestanding issue. It can be raised almost anytime in the course.

Remember that Chapter 9 ended with the court's entering a judgment in the case. In Chapter 11, we assess whether that judgment precludes anyone from litigating anything in a different case. The preclusion doctrines of claim and issue preclusion (also known as res judicata and collateral estoppel) emphasize the importance of finality. In general, our system is committed to the notion that a litigant has one opportunity to litigate a matter. She does not get to litigate the same claim or the same issues serially in different cases. So the preclusion doctrines demonstrate how broadly a judgment operates. They may prohibit a plaintiff from asserting the same claim again. They may prohibit someone from litigating a particular issue again.

In Chapters 12 and 13 we complicate the litigation. Through Chapter 9, with its entry of judgment, we presumed a fairly simple case — the typical case of one plaintiff suing one defendant. In real life, there are many such cases. But many cases, on the other hand, involve multiple claims and multiple parties. The rules of joinder, addressed in Chapter 12, define the scope of a single civil case. Specifically, they define how many claims and how many parties may be packed into a single case. In this area, we dip back to topics covered in Chapter 4, about the subject matter jurisdiction of the federal courts. Why? Because each claim asserted in federal court — not just the original claim by the plaintiff against the defendant — must be supported by a basis of federal subject matter jurisdiction. Thus, this area is a rich one for professors. They can test the mechanical joinder provisions of the Federal Rules of Civil Procedure and topics of federal subject matter jurisdiction in a single fact pattern.

Chapter 13 continues themes established in Chapter 12, by addressing special multiparty litigation. Specifically, we discuss interpleader and the class action. Interpleader is a very specific type of litigation in which claimants are vying for ownership of money or some tangible property. In the class action, a representative sues on behalf of a group. Because the result of the litigation binds the class members, we encounter important issues of due process. Beyond this, the class action is controversial because it creates potentially devastating liability for a defendant by aggregating potentially thousands of claims in a single case. The device has always been at the center of a tug-of-war between the plaintiff's bar and business interests.

In 2005, however, large business interests succeeded in urging Congress to pass the Class Action Fairness Act, which funnels many class actions from state to federal court. This funneling is, at least in theory, substance-neutral, which means that it does not affect the substantive law to be applied in the case. On the other hand, there is a general sense that federal courts are less hospitable to class actions than state courts. Thus, critics charge, the Class Action Fairness Act is actually a version of tort reform sold to the public as a mere procedural provision. That is, the Act forces tort class actions from state to federal court, where they are likely to be thwarted not on the basis of the substantive law, but on procedural grounds. This recent issue, then, raises in microcosm profound topics of federalism and the efficacy of our procedural system for the administration of justice.

So again, welcome to law school and welcome to Civil Procedure. Throughout the course, you will see a wide range of subjects — some easy, some hard, some mechanical, some amorphous. Most of them are foreign to your experience; unlike issues presented in your other first-year courses, you probably have not seen them before. This book is intended to make you comfortable with those issues.

Chapter 2

Personal Jurisdiction

§2.1 Defining the Issue

Many students consider personal jurisdiction the most difficult topic in Civil Procedure. The main reason is clear: The concept of personal jurisdiction is foreign to your life before law school. In §1.1, we said that Civil Procedure itself is more foreign to your experience than any other course in the first year of law school. Even in this course, however, personal jurisdiction takes the cake for many students as the most arcane topic.

The difficulty in grasping the basic idea of personal jurisdiction is compounded by the fact that most professors study the topic historically. It can be frustrating to take so long to get to an understanding of what the law of personal jurisdiction is *today*. But the historical approach is a good thing. Indeed, in my opinion, it is the only way to "get it." Most professors start with a difficult but wonderful case decided in 1878, the very name of which still resonates with lawyers years after graduating from law school: *Pennoyer v. Neff*. From there most courses launch into a series of cases tracing the development of personal jurisdiction doctrine through over more than a century and a quarter.

It is important to study the historical development with one thing in mind: The goal is to develop an analytical framework for addressing personal jurisdiction problems that might arise *today*. That framework will pull together various threads we see in the historical tour. Moreover, the historical tour will drive home an important point: The law in this area (as in others) is constantly evolving. The principles distilled at the end of the tour might be thrown into question by a Supreme Court decision the next day. By going through the historical development and seeing how things build and fit together, however, you will be equipped to adjust to future changes.[1] So please be patient as you study personal jurisdiction. It takes a while to get to the point at which we see what the law is today.

Now, with that advice in mind, what is personal jurisdiction all about? As we said in Chapter 1, this course concerns *litigation*, which is the process by which parties submit their disputes to a court — the judicial branch of the government (state or federal) — for resolution. The court (state or federal) is an arm of the government (state or federal). During any case, the court makes orders commanding the parties to do various things. For starters, it issues a *summons*, which commands the defendant to appear and to defend against the plaintiff's accusations.[2] If the defendant fails to do so within the prescribed time, the court may enter a default judgment against her.[3] If the defendant does respond and the parties litigate the dispute, at some point the court enters an order, called a judgment, declaring the relative rights and liabilities of the parties. In other words, it decides who wins (and what, if anything, the winner recovers). In so doing, it decides the "merits" of the case.

The government (state or federal) cannot command anyone to do anything (and cannot decide the merits of the dispute) unless it has some basis of authority over that person. For lack of a better term at this stage, let's refer to this authority as *power*.[4] The government (state or federal) must have some *power* over the litigants to enter valid orders affecting them and their rights. If the government does not have this power over the litigants, the orders made by its courts, including the final judgment, are void. So personal jurisdiction is the power the court must have *over the parties*

---

[1] This chapter is designed to walk through the historical development of personal jurisdiction doctrine and, in §2.6, to suggest an analytical framework for addressing personal jurisdiction problems on your exam.

[2] The summons is discussed in detail at §3.3.1. Don't worry about it now.

[3] Default judgments are discussed in detail at §7.5.3. Don't worry about them now.

[4] Some professors do not like using the word *power* in this context. Some feel that using it gives too much weight to early cases, particularly *Pennoyer*, in which the Court spoke in terms of power. I am not one of those professors, and I think the term is a helpful shorthand for describing the authority a court must have over the parties to the litigation. Just be sensitive to the fact that your professor might not use this shorthand.

to the case to enter orders that bind those parties. There are two related and very important points in this notion: (1) personal jurisdiction is exercised by the (state or federal) government (through its courts) over the *parties* to the litigation;[5] and (2) if the government does not have personal jurisdiction over the litigants, the orders entered by its court are void.

Why would such orders be void? Because (as we see throughout this chapter), the Due Process Clauses of the Constitution require that a defendant be sued in an appropriate forum. They provide the defendant with protection from litigation in a forum with which she has no relevant contact. Stated another way, constitutional principles of due process limit the ability of a government (through its courts) to impose binding orders on a litigant. A government may do so only if it has appropriate power over the litigant. Interestingly, this constitutional protection, like most legal protections, can be relinquished, either by choice or by failing to raise an appropriate objection. Thus, the defendant can waive a personal jurisdiction objection. We discuss this possibility in detail in §6.2. For now, we assume that the defendant does not waive her due process protection against being sued in an inappropriate forum.

One very good question that may occur to you is whether the standards for asserting personal jurisdiction are (or should be) different in federal court than in state court. (Remember the introduction to the difference between federal and state courts in §1.2.1.) We address the question in some detail in §2.5. There, we see that the general rule — subject to very few exceptions — is that the standards are the same in federal as in state court. Those exceptions need not concern us now. So for our purposes now, let's take it as a given that whether a *federal* court would have personal jurisdiction involves the same analysis as whether a *state* court would have personal jurisdiction.

Any court will *always* have personal jurisdiction over the plaintiff. Why? Because she *chose to sue in this court* and thereby agreed that the court could enter binding orders as to her. By suing, the plaintiff voluntarily submitted herself to the jurisdiction of the court. The big question — one on which your course may spend weeks — is whether the court has sufficient power — has personal jurisdiction — *over the defendant*. The forum court[6] can have power, in the sense of personal jurisdiction, over either of two things: the defendant's *person* or her *property*. Stated another way, the court might have one of two "jurisdictional predicates" — it may exercise power either (1) over the defendant herself or (2) over her property.

---

[5] This kind of power is contrasted with subject matter jurisdiction, which, as we see in Chapter 4, is exercised not over the parties but over the case — over the dispute itself. More on that later.

[6] Throughout your legal career, the word *forum* will be popular. For now, the forum simply means the state in which *P* sues *D*. Remember, it does not matter whether *P* sues in a federal court or a state court for these purposes.

To illustrate these principles, let's address a hypothetical with several permutations. These fact patterns show the types of problems encountered in personal jurisdiction — the kinds of problems you may well have to address on your final exam. Let's not worry at this point about what the right answer is. After all, you have not yet learned the tools for analyzing these problems. For now, let's just get a sense of what the issues are and why the question of forum selection — choosing which court will resolve the dispute on the merits — is important.

- *D* is a citizen of West Virginia. She was born and raised there and has traveled to various states on the East Coast. At age 20, she and a friend go on vacation to Hawaii. It is the first time *D* has been west of West Virginia. While in Hawaii, *D* gets into a dispute with *P*, who is vacationing in Hawaii from Utah. After *D* returns home, *P* sues *D*, claiming that *D* punched *P* in the nose in a hotel in Hawaii. The underlying facts and law — about whether *D* actually punched *P* in the nose, whether such an act was excused (as, for example, self-defense), and what damages, if any, were suffered — are the "merits" of the dispute.[7] We do not care about those yet. At this stage, we consider *only* what court will decide the merits of the dispute. (Indeed, throughout Civil Procedure, we are not concerned with the substantive rules of law that govern the dispute (you learn those in other classes), but with the processes by which the merits are decided in court.)
- Can *P* sue *D* in Utah? Think about why *P* would like to do so. First, she would not have to travel; she would get to litigate at home and could employ a lawyer she might already know. Second, she might think that the jury and judge would view her more sympathetically than they view the "out-of-stater" *D*. The jurors are drawn from the local community and the judge may well be running for re-election in the local community sometime soon,[8] so it is not unreasonable to think they might favor the local litigant.
- The serious question is whether Utah has power *over D*. *D* has never been to Utah. She did not send anything to Utah. She became involved — in Hawaii — in a dispute with a Utah citizen. Does that give Utah power over *D*? After reviewing the cases, we will answer this question by saying no. Even now, there is something that suggests that it would not be fair to *D* to force her to litigate in Utah.
- Suppose, however, before *P* sues *D* anywhere, that *D* goes on a skiing trip to Utah. While *D* is in Utah, *P* files suit against *D* in Utah and has the proper officer serve the appropriate papers for the suit

[7] The merits of the dispute are determined by applying substantive rules of law, such as those you learn in the other first-year courses of Contracts, Torts, and Property.

[8] As noted in §1.2.1, state court judges are often elected. Federal judges, as we see in §4.4, are not; they are appointed for life and never face an electorate. This difference leads some to conclude that state judges may be more politically motivated to rule in favor of the local litigant against an out-of-state litigant. After all, the job security of a Utah state judge is in the hands of Utah voters, not West Virginians.

on *D* in Utah. Now, does Utah have power over *D*? Does it matter that *D*'s presence in Utah had nothing to do with the altercation in Hawaii? After review of the cases, we will probably decide that Utah does have personal jurisdiction over *D* in this scenario.

- Can *P* sue *D* in West Virginia? *P* certainly will not *want* to do this, because it means she will be litigating on *D*'s home turf. And *P* will have to hire a lawyer in a state in which she probably knows no one. On the other hand, there is no doubt that West Virginia courts would have power over *D*. After all, *D* is a citizen of West Virginia. Does it matter that the dispute occurred in Hawaii? Ultimately, we will decide that West Virginia has personal jurisdiction over *D* even for a suit involving an altercation in Hawaii.

- Can *P* sue *D* in Hawaii? Again, this is not ideal for *P*, because it means litigating in unfamiliar surroundings and hiring a lawyer in a state in which she probably knows no one. So for *D*, this may be better than going to Utah. On the other hand, Hawaii is not *D*'s home turf, and litigating there will impose significant burdens on *D* too.

  - But notice another aspect of this situation: Though neither party has much of a contact with Hawaii (each has vacationed there), the underlying dispute arose in Hawaii. Litigation is publicly funded dispute resolution. Doesn't Hawaii have an interest in determining who was at fault — *P* or *D* — for a breach of the public peace? Is this interest relevant to whether Hawaii has power over *D*? Ultimately, we will probably conclude that this factor has some bearing on personal jurisdiction, and that Hawaii would have personal jurisdiction over *D* for this case.

- Can *P* sue *D* in California? Neither *P* nor *D* has any connection with California. Moreover, unlike Hawaii, California itself has no interest in the matter. The dispute involves the public peace of Hawaii, not California. Why should the California taxpayers pay their judges and court personnel, and burden their jurors, with a dispute that does not have any connection with the state?

  - But suppose, before *P* sues *D* anywhere, that *D* goes on vacation to California to learn to surf. Knowing this, *P* sues *D* in California and has the proper officer serve the proper papers on *D* in California. What is different about this hypothetical and the preceding one? Here, *D* has some connection with California (having gone there to learn to surf), though her contact is unrelated to the dispute with *P*. Does this connection give California power over *D*? Ultimately, we may conclude that California does have personal jurisdiction over *D*.

- Finally, suppose *P* finds out that *D* has money on deposit with a bank in Illinois. Can *P* sue *D* in Illinois? Here, the power would not be over *D* herself, but over *D*'s *property*. As discussed in §2.2, Illinois' power over this property might give Illinois a specialized type of personal jurisdiction, called *quasi-in-rem*.

Now let's start acquiring the tools to address problems like these. Begin with these background principles in mind:

- The forum (the court resolving the merits of the case) must have power over D or her property to enter binding orders to D.
- If it does not have such power over D or her property, any order entered by the court is void.
- The analysis of whether the forum has power in this sense is the same whether the forum is a federal court or a state court.
- A court always has personal jurisdiction over the plaintiff, because the plaintiff has invoked its jurisdiction, and thus has waived any objection as to whether the court lacked power over her.
- A defendant may waive an objection to a court's lack of power over her, and permit a court otherwise lacking personal jurisdiction to enter valid orders to her.[9]

One last prefatory point. You may read (or your professor may say) that due process imposes two distinct requirements: personal jurisdiction and notice. This is true. Each is such a large topic, however, that they are treated in separate chapters. This very long chapter addresses only personal jurisdiction. Chapter 3 addresses the due process requirement that the defendant be given notice of the claims against her and an opportunity to respond.

§2.2   The Types of Personal Jurisdiction (*In Personam, In Rem*, and *Quasi-in-Rem*) and the Concept of Full Faith and Credit

In §2.1, we noted that a court might gain personal jurisdiction by exercising power over either the defendant herself or her property. In other words, the jurisdictional predicate might be the person or her property. There are three kinds of personal jurisdiction, the names of which invoke Latin phrases that reflect the jurisdictional predicate used: *in personam, in rem*, and *quasi-in-rem*.

In Personam *Jurisdiction (and the Effect of an* In Personam *Judgment)*

In personam jurisdiction is exercised over the defendant herself, because she has some appropriate connection with the forum. This fact is reflected by the word *personam*, which (even to those of us who did not take Latin) clearly refers to the person. We cover the kind of connection

---

[9] In Chapter 6, we discuss in detail how a defendant may assert the objection that the forum lacks personal jurisdiction. Some professors cover this material along with the personal jurisdiction cases, so you may need to address some of that material (particularly in §6.2) while studying the personal jurisdiction cases.

required for the exercise of *in personam* jurisdiction in great detail. By way of examples, perhaps the defendant is domiciled in the forum, or perhaps she has committed an act there, or has done something that caused an impact there (like sending a defective widget into the forum, which exploded and injured someone). Historically, this form of jurisdiction involved literal physical power over the person. At common law, the sheriff for the local court actually arrested the defendant — even in a civil case — to ensure her attendance in the case. The sheriff did this with a writ of *capias ad respondendum*. It was a stark reminder that the jurisdiction was being exercised *in personam*, because it actually resulted in taking the defendant into the custody of the government.

Today, we no longer arrest the defendant in civil cases. But there must be some symbolic "seizure" of the defendant to show that the government is exercising power over her. Today, that symbolic seizure is performed by the service of "process" on the defendant. We discuss service of process in detail in §3.3. For now, we note only that process (the documents that are delivered to the defendant to inform her that she has been sued) consists of a copy of the plaintiff's complaint and a document called a *summons*. The court issues the summons; thus, that document emanates from the government and is the *symbol* of the government's power over the defendant. When the appropriate person serves process on the defendant, the justice system is acting out the government's exercise of power over the defendant.

A valid judgment *in personam* against a defendant creates a personal obligation — a debt — that the plaintiff is entitled to recover from the defendant. Suppose, for example, that the court determines on the merits that the plaintiff is entitled to recover $100,000 from the defendant. It will enter a final judgment reflecting this determination. That judgment creates a legal debt for the defendant to pay the plaintiff $100,000. The defendant might discharge this debt by writing a check to the plaintiff for the judgment amount.

If the defendant does not (or cannot) pay the judgment amount to the plaintiff, the plaintiff will want to enforce the judgment. The plaintiff can "execute" on that judgment by asking the court to seize the defendant's property in that locality and to sell it at a public auction to raise the $100,000. We discuss this auction process in addressing the case of *Pennoyer v. Neff* in §2.4.1. For now, it is enough to understand that this legal procedure is available for the enforcement of an *in personam* judgment. Through it, the defendant's property can be seized and sold to satisfy the debt created by the *in personam* judgment.[10]

---

[10] The valid *in personam* judgment creates a "lien" on the defendant's land in the locality. That lien is a right held by the plaintiff against that property, to have her debt repaid by the sale of the property at public auction.

Full Faith and Credit

A valid *in personam* judgment against the defendant not only creates a personal obligation for her, but is also entitled to full faith and credit. This concept is discussed in detail in §11.5. In short, the Constitution — at Article IV, §1 — provides that the valid judgments of the courts of one state are entitled to enforcement in the courts of the other states. Full faith and credit is an important statement of the interdependence of the American states — a valid judgment entered by a court in Kansas is entitled to recognition by the courts of Florida.

This fact is particularly important for the plaintiff trying to collect her judgment. Let's say the plaintiff's valid judgment against the defendant (for $100,000) was entered by a state court in Kansas. Suppose the defendant refuses to pay the plaintiff. The plaintiff then executes on the judgment by having the court seize the defendant's property in Kansas and sell it at auction. But let's say the auction only fetches $60,000. (That is, the sale of the defendant's Kansas property only raised $60,000 at auction.) The judgment has been satisfied to that extent, but there is still a *personal obligation* of the defendant to pay the plaintiff the remaining $40,000.

Now let's say the plaintiff discovers that the defendant has a vacation house (or a bank account or a race car or any other property) in Florida. Because of full faith and credit, the plaintiff can institute an action in Florida and ask a Florida court to enforce the Kansas judgment. Once the Florida court is satisfied that the judgment is entitled to full faith and credit (because the Kansas court had valid *in personam* jurisdiction over the defendant), it will recognize the Kansas judgment. That means that the plaintiff can then have the Florida court "domesticate" the Kansas judgment and enforce it (for the remaining $40,000) by seizing the defendant's property in Florida and selling it at public auction to raise the remaining amount due. If the sale fetches only $25,000, the plaintiff can go to another state in which the defendant has property (if there is one) and repeat the process until the entire $100,000 judgment is satisfied.

In Rem *and* Quasi-in-Rem *Jurisdiction (and the Effect of Such Judgments)*

In rem and *quasi-in-rem* jurisdiction are different from *in personam* jurisdiction in a fundamental way: In each, the jurisdictional predicate is not the defendant herself, but her property. The difference is clear from the presence of the word *rem* in their titles. The Latin word *res* means "thing." Rem, then, refers to the fact that a thing — property — is the jurisdictional predicate. As you will learn in other courses, property comes in many forms. There is tangible property, such as a book or a yacht or a building — something you can touch. There is also intangible property. For instance, if you borrowed money to pay your tuition, you owe the lender the money in return (plus interest, no doubt). The lender thus owns intangible property — sometimes called a *chose in action*[11] — which is the right to collect the money from you. And of course there is real property, which is land.[12]

Usually, the plaintiff will prefer to proceed *in personam*. Why? Because, as we just saw, a valid *in personam* judgment against the defendant creates a *personal obligation*, which can be enforced by having the defendant's property seized and sold at public auction. But sometimes the plaintiff simply cannot proceed *in personam*.[13] In such cases, occasionally, the defendant might nonetheless have some property in the forum. With *in rem* and *quasi-in-rem* jurisdiction, the defendant's property in the forum might give a court there jurisdiction to adjudicate matters that affect the defendant.

Suppose the plaintiff wanted to sue the defendant in Kansas but that, for whatever reason, Kansas would not have *in personam* jurisdiction over the defendant. But suppose the defendant had property in Kansas. Say, for instance, that the defendant's parents lived in Kansas and they created a college fund for the defendant, which they put in a Kansas bank. The plaintiff, unable to get *in personam* jurisdiction, may be able to have the court establish *in rem* or *quasi-in-rem* jurisdiction over the defendant by seizing the defendant's bank account to use as the jurisdictional predicate.

Do not confuse this type of seizure of property (as a jurisdictional predicate) with the seizure we talked about five paragraphs above (to enforce an *in personam* judgment). In the latter (to enforce an *in personam* judgment), the court had *in personam* jurisdiction and entered a valid judgment. The seizure of the property in that instance was simply a means to get the defendant to pay what she owed to the plaintiff. That seizure of property routinely takes place after entry of judgment and after the defendant has refused or simply failed to pay the judgment amount to the plaintiff.

Here, we are talking about something fundamentally different. Here, there is no *in personam* jurisdiction, so there is no *in personam* judgment to enforce. The plaintiff is trying the next best thing — *in rem* or *quasi-in-rem* jurisdiction. To do that, the court must have power over the defendant's property. And, as seen in our discussion of *Pennoyer v. Neff* in §2.4.1, the Supreme Court has long held that such seizure must take

---

[11] This is a "law French" term, essentially referring to a type of intangible property such as the right to sue someone. You will probably encounter it in your Property class.

[12] We saw this at §1.2.3, footnote 37, and it bears repeating. Do not make the mistake of thinking that real property refers to tangible property. Real property (or realty) is land. It is also tangible, because you can touch it. So all real property is tangible, but not all tangible property is real.

[13] For example, perhaps the state's statutory grants of *in personam* jurisdiction do not apply, even in a case in which such jurisdiction would be constitutional. See §§2.3, 2.5.

place at the outset of the litigation. Why? To ensure that there is something over which the court actually has power, and that it will not be transferred or destroyed during the litigation. Just as in common law times the court arrested the defendant to ensure that he would be before the court, so the court in *in rem* and *quasi-in-rem* cases must seize the defendant's property at the outset of the litigation (or, as your professor might say, *ab initio*, which means "at the beginning").

So we know that *in rem* and *quasi-in-rem* jurisdiction are similar in that each employs the defendant's property as the jurisdictional predicate. So how do they differ? True *in rem* cases are quite rare. They involve a dispute over *ownership* of the property that is the jurisdictional predicate, and (believe it or not) purport to determine the ownership interest in that thing *as to every person in the world*. There are only a few such cases, and they are deeply rooted in history. The best example may be in admiralty, to determine the ownership of a ship. The court in this *in rem* proceeding seizes the ship[14] and determines who owns it. In theory, this judgment binds everyone in the world. That is an odd and obviously fictive concept. But it is probably best to emphasize that true *in rem* cases are rare and involve ownership of the property that was used as the jurisdictional predicate.

What about *quasi-in-rem*? There are two types of this form of jurisdiction, known by number: *quasi-in-rem* of the first type (which we will abbreviate QIR-1) and *quasi-in-rem* of the second type (which we will call QIR-2). QIR-1 cases adjudicate the *ownership* of the property that is used as the jurisdictional predicate, and purport to determine that ownership as between and among the parties to the case. Thus, QIR-1 is quite similar to true *in rem* — it is litigation about who *owns* the property. The only difference from true *in rem* is that a QIR-1 judgment does not purport to bind the whole world. This is not a big deal. As noted, there are very few true *in rem* cases. The key is to emphasize the similarity between true *in rem* and QIR-1: They are about ownership of the very property being used as the jurisdictional predicate.

    ○ *P* claims that she owns certain real property (remember, that is *land*, see footnote 12 above) in Montana because she has established a right to it by adverse possession. (You will learn about adverse possession in your

---

[14] That sounds strange, I know. We can imagine a court's seizing a fund of money or a diamond ring, simply by ordering the sheriff (or like officer) to go out, get it, and bring it into the courthouse, where it can be kept by the clerk pending litigation (or *pendente lite*, as the Latin scholars say). But how does a court seize a ship or, for that matter, land? Basically the court orders the sheriff to post signs on the property announcing that it is subject to the authority of the court. In addition, in the case of real property, the court will ensure that notice is filed in the registry of deeds, to indicate to anyone checking the title records that the property is in the "possession" of the court, so no one can transfer it in the meantime.

course on Property. Under that doctrine, one who has occupied real property openly for a period set by law may cut off the ownership rights of the person who held the deed to the property.) *D* holds the deed to the property and believes that *P* has not satisfied the requirements for adverse possession. We have no idea who should win this case — the merits of the suit will be determined much later. Right now, we're just trying to figure out what court will address the merits.

    ° *P* resides in Montana, which is where the disputed real property is located. *D* resides in Maine and, aside from claiming to own the real property, has no other contact with Montana.

        ° *P* sues *D* in Montana, and asks the court to declare the respective rights to the land. Assuming *P* cannot proceed *in personam* against *D*, she can proceed by QIR-1. To do so, she should have the court attach the property at the outset of the case to establish its power over the property. The court would have the authority, under QIR-1, to determine who — between *P* and *D* — owns the property. If the attachment was proper and other requirements met, the QIR-1 judgment would be valid as to the question of ownership.

        ° Why? Because a judgment is valid to the extent the court had jurisdiction. That is why we said that an *in personam* judgment creates a personal obligation on the defendant — the court had jurisdiction (power) over the defendant herself and thus could create that personal obligation. In a QIR-1 case, however, the court had jurisdiction only over the property, and thus its judgment is valid only to affect that property itself, and not to impose a personal obligation on *D*.

That brings us to QIR-2. Such a case is similar to *in rem* and QIR-1 in that the court's jurisdiction is over property, and not over the person of the defendant. But here — unlike with *in rem* and QIR-1 — there is no dispute over who owns the property. The dispute between the parties has nothing to with who owns the property — it is clear that the defendant owns it. Rather, the dispute is one that *would be* in personam *if we could get* in personam. The property is relevant as a jurisdictional predicate only because the plaintiff cannot obtain *in personam* jurisdiction over the defendant. So the dispute is unrelated to ownership of the property, and might be about anything at all.

    ° *P* is a lawyer, who performed legal services for *D*. *D* failed to pay *P* for the legal services. *D* resides in another state, however, and would not be subject to *in personam* jurisdiction. *D* does, however, own land in the forum state. *P* may proceed against *D* through QIR-2, by using *D*'s land as the jurisdictional predicate. (This is the underlying fact pattern in the famous case of *Pennoyer v. Neff*, discussed in §2.4.1.)

        ° *P* would prefer to proceed *in personam*, because such a judgment would create a personal obligation that *P* could enforce by seizing other property of *D*'s and having it sold at auction. In a QIR-2 case, the court cannot create such a personal obligation, because it does not have power over the person of *D*. The QIR-2 judgment, however, will be valid to the extent the court has power — which is, of course, to the extent of the value of the property.

○ Suppose *P* proceeds QIR-2 and *D* defaults. The court enters a default judgment against *D*, holding that *D* owes *P* $15,000. Because *D* defaulted (and thus will probably not give *P* the $15,000 voluntarily), *P* asks the court to have *D*'s property — the property used as the jurisdictional predicate — sold at auction. Suppose the sale at the auction fetches $10,000. The QIR-2 judgment is valid, but only to that extent — only to the tune of $10,000. *P* cannot take the judgment to a court in another state under full faith and credit to seek enforcement for the other $5,000.

○ Remember, *P* could do that if the judgment had been *in personam*. Because it was QIR-2, however, the court only had power to the extent of the value of the property, which is set by the auction, and therefore is $10,000.[15] *P* has a $5,000 unsatisfied claim against *D*, and can sue *D* to get it. But *P* cannot use this QIR-2 judgment any further — the court's power was over the property, and that has been exhausted.

Recap

In sum, then, *in personam* jurisdiction operates on the person of the defendant. The plaintiff seeking money undoubtedly prefers *in personam* because a valid *in personam* judgment against the defendant creates a personal obligation (a debt) for that person to pay the plaintiff. The plaintiff can enforce that judgment by having the defendant's property seized and sold to raise money for the judgment. The judgment is entitled to enforcement in other states under the principles of full faith and credit. *In rem* and both versions of *quasi-in-rem* exercise jurisdiction not over the defendant, but over the defendant's property. *In rem* and QIR-1 are similar in that the dispute between *P* and *D* is over who owns that very property. With QIR-2, in contrast, the dispute is something unrelated to the ownership of the property. In *in rem* and both versions of *quasi-in-rem*, the court's judgment may be valid, but not to create a personal obligation; rather, it is valid only to the extent of the property that served as the jurisdictional predicate.

Jurisdiction by Necessity

We end this subsection with a brief reference to "jurisdiction by necessity." This is a theory, espoused by different commentators over time, that a court may exercise personal jurisdiction when there is no other forum

---

[15] The fair market value of the property is irrelevant. The property is worth only what someone is willing to pay for it at auction. That is the amount of money that goes into the registry of the court and is available for satisfying the claim.

in the world in which justice may be had. The Supreme Court has mentioned the theoretical possibility of such a basis of jurisdiction but has never embraced it.[16] In one case, plaintiffs sued non-U.S. defendants in Texas. After the Court rejected personal jurisdiction under traditional analyses, the Court also rejected the plaintiffs' invitation to adopt the concept of jurisdiction by necessity. It characterized the theory as "a potentially far-reaching modification of existing law" and refused to address it in the absence of a well-developed factual record.[17] Specifically, it noted that the plaintiffs failed to show that they could not pursue their claims against the defendants "in a single proceeding in Colombia or Peru."[18]

It is not clear that the Court was seriously suggesting that the absence of a *single* foreign forum in which to sue *all* defendants in a single case would justify jurisdiction in the United States, notwithstanding the defendants' lack of relevant contacts with this country. Such a suggestion would indeed be radical, since it would still be probable that the plaintiffs could proceed against the foreign defendants in individual litigation in foreign countries. Surely Colombian defendants can be sued in Colombia and Peruvian defendants in Peru. The existence of fora in which the defendants could be sued — even separately — would seem to obviate any need for an American court to take the case on the basis of jurisdiction by necessity. Moreover, it seems unlikely that courts in the United States want to be put in the position of declaring that a foreign tribunal — if available — would be so inadequate as to justify personal jurisdiction in the United States. Thus, jurisdiction by necessity remains only a theoretical possibility.[19]

---

[16] In *Shaffer v. Heitner*, 433 U.S. 186, 211 n.37 (1977), the Court mentioned the possibility of jurisdiction when "no other forum is available to the plaintiff." On the facts of this case, however, the plaintiff could pursue litigation in various U.S. courts, so the Court did not have to take a position on jurisdiction by necessity.

[17] Helicópteros Nacionales de Colombia, S.A. v. Hall, 466 U.S. 408, 419 n.13 (1985).

[18] *Id.*

[19] Some commentators have considered *Mullane v. Central Hanover Bank & Trust Co.*, 339 U.S. 306 (1950), as a case involving jurisdiction by necessity. *See, e.g.*, George B. Fraser, *Jurisdiction by Necessity — An Analysis of the* Mullane *Case*, 100 U. Pa. L. Rev. 305 (1951). *Mullane*, discussed at §3.2, establishes the constitutional requirement for notice to be given to one whose rights may be affected by litigation. It involved claims relating to a pooled trust fund having thousands of beneficiaries — some known and some not, some residing in the forum state and some not. Having a single court oversee the administration of the trust, as upheld in *Mullane*, is a commonsense pragmatic reaction to the reality that people from many states may invest in another state. Though the courts of many states could be involved, it would be a nightmare. So if *Mullane* involves jurisdiction by necessity, it is of a different type than the one discussed in text, in which the motivation is not convenience and common sense, but the lack of another forum.

§2.3 The Statutory and Constitutional Dimensions of Personal Jurisdiction

The major focus of your studies on personal jurisdiction will be whether the exercise of jurisdiction comports with the requirements of due process. This is a *constitutional* inquiry. It is not, however, the only relevant inquiry in determining whether a court has personal jurisdiction. There is also a *statutory* inquiry. In this section, we introduce why there are two such levels of assessment then address each in detail in §§2.4 and 2.5.

There are two "due process" provisions in the Constitution (or, technically, in amendments to the Constitution). The Fifth Amendment provides (among other things) that the federal government may not deprive anyone of "life, liberty, or property, without due process of law." This provision is part of the Bill of Rights, ratified in 1791. The Fourteenth Amendment (among other things) makes a similar provision about *state* governments — no state may deprive one of "life, liberty, or property without due process of law." This provision was adopted after the Civil War, as part of Reconstruction, and became effective in 1868. These clauses set the outer boundary for the exercise of personal jurisdiction.[20] In other words, due process defines the absolute limit to which a court can exercise power over a person or her property. It is helpful to think of the due process limit as a large circle. Judgments entered in cases that fall within the circle are valid, and thus are entitled to full faith and credit (as discussed in §2.2). Judgments entered in cases falling outside the circle, however, are void, and thus are *not* entitled to full faith and credit. As we will see, defining the constitutional limit on personal jurisdiction is occasionally difficult, and the line can be blurry. But the line is there, and courts need to be aware of it to avoid overreaching their power.

The mere fact that a case falls within the "due process circle," however, does not mean that a court has personal jurisdiction. Why not? Because the power to exercise jurisdiction under the Constitution is not self-executing. Courts do not automatically have the power to exercise personal jurisdiction. That power must be given to them by statute (which, of course, is an act of the legislative branch of the government). In other words, the constitutional power (to the full extent of the due process circle) is available to a court, but only if the legislative branch of the government gives it to the court. The state legislature is not required to grant its courts the full extent of the constitutional power to exercise personal jurisdiction. They may, in other words, declare that the courts of their state exercise only a portion of the authority permitted by due process. (We

---

[20] In §2.5, we discuss whether the due process limits are different under the Fifth Amendment and the Fourteenth Amendment. For now, we refer simply to due process limits on the power of a court to exercise personal jurisdiction, and assume (for now) that they are the same for federal and state courts.

discuss why a legislature might do this in §2.5.) A state court, then, cannot exercise personal jurisdiction — even over a case that clearly, without question, falls within the due process circle — unless the state legislature has enacted a statute permitting the court to do so.

Each state has a series of statutes granting personal jurisdiction to its courts. Some such statutes are ubiquitous. For example, every state grants its courts *in personam* jurisdiction over defendants who are served with process while present in the state, and over persons who reside in the state, and over businesses incorporated in the state. In addition, each state has a statute (or series of statutes) permitting its courts to exercise *in personam* jurisdiction over nonresidents in various circumstances. Such statutes — generically called *long-arm* statutes — can vary considerably from state to state. And each state also has attachment statutes permitting the attachment of property for the exercise of *in rem* and *quasi-in-rem* jurisdiction.

Analytically, then, the statutory question always comes first. Unless there is a statute granting personal jurisdiction in the case, the fact that the case falls within the due process circle is irrelevant. So on an exam (and in the real world), you first assess whether the facts of the case fall within a statutory grant of personal jurisdiction. If they do (or arguably do), you must make the constitutional analysis to assess whether the exercise of jurisdiction on the facts comports with due process.

For our purposes, though, we address these two levels of analysis in reverse order. We discuss the constitutional analysis first (in §2.4) and then look at the statutory issues (in §2.5). We do this for two reasons. First, most courses spend substantially more time on the constitutional analysis, so it is clearly more important for your purposes. Second, once we have discussed the constitutional issues, the statutory analysis is simply easier. After these discussions of both the constitutional and statutory analyses, §2.6 presents an analytical framework for any personal jurisdiction question you may face on your exam (or in the real world), tying together both levels of analysis.

§2.4 Constitutional Analysis

§2.4.1 The Traditional Approach: *Pennoyer v. Neff*

The most famous personal jurisdiction case is *Pennoyer v. Neff*.[21] It is the starting point for understanding personal jurisdiction law, but cannot be appreciated without an understanding of the (fairly complicated) facts.

---

[21] 95 U.S. 714 (1878).

The opinion presented in your casebook is a decision by the United States Supreme Court, rendered in 1878. That decision, however, is the culmination of two cases. Many professors spend a good bit of time and care with the facts of *Pennoyer*. Here is the fascinating story behind the cases.

The Facts

John Mitchell was a lawyer in Multnomah County (Portland), Oregon. He claimed to have performed legal work (of about $300[22]) for Marcus Neff, for which Neff allegedly did not pay. Mitchell sued Neff in a Multnomah County state court to recover that sum. Neff, however, was living in California at the time Mitchell sued him. Because Neff could not be found in Oregon, Mitchell could not proceed *in personam*. (At the time, *in personam* jurisdiction could only be exercised by having the defendant served with process within the forum state.) So Mitchell tried to proceed *quasi-in-rem* of the second type (QIR-2). (If these terms are unfamiliar, review §2.2.) That case was *Mitchell v. Neff*. It never resulted in a published opinion in the Oregon court system, but the validity of the judgment entered in *Mitchell v. Neff* is at the basis of *Pennoyer*.

QIR-2 requires that the court have power over some *property* that belongs to the defendant, but the dispute is not about ownership of that property. (Again, see §2.2.) Neff owned a large parcel of land in Multnomah County, which Mitchell wanted to use as the jurisdictional predicate for his case against Neff. Mitchell filed suit and had notice published in a newspaper, as required by Oregon law. The problem (it will turn out) was that neither Mitchell nor the Oregon court saw any need for the court to seize Neff's land at the outset of the case. There is no question that Neff owned the land. He got it from the federal government under the Oregon Donation Law, by which the federal government urged people to settle in the then-new state.[23]

Because he was in California and had no access to the publication notice in the Oregon newspaper, Neff knew nothing about Mitchell's case against him, and failed to respond to the suit within the time required by law. Accordingly, the Oregon court entered default judgment in *Mitchell v. Neff*, in favor of Mitchell. That gave Mitchell a piece of paper — a judgment — from the court in Oregon, which said, in effect, that Neff owed Mitchell $300 (approximately). Obviously, Neff did not write Mitchell a check for the money. What happens when a defendant fails for whatever reason to

---

[22] Actually, it was $253.14. With the addition of costs and any interest on the claim accruing after entry of the judgment, let's call it $300.

[23] This method of getting land from the federal government is sometimes referred to (as it is in the *Pennoyer* opinion) as having received a "patent" for the land. Do not confuse this with getting a patent on an invention. A land patent is just a grant of land from the government.

pay the judgment that has been entered against him? To this day, as we saw in §2.2, the answer is the same: A court will seize some property of the defendant's and have it sold at public auction to pay off (satisfy) the judgment. That is what happened here. The Multnomah County court had Neff's land in Multnomah County seized and sold at public auction. Who showed up to bid for it at the auction? Mitchell, and nobody else. Mitchell bid the amount of the judgment and was the winner of the auction. Thus, the land was delivered to Mitchell via a sheriff's deed, pursuant to the order that the land be sold to satisfy the judgment.

Before going further with the story, you should understand how the public auction works. The topic was introduced in §2.2. In theory, anyone could have shown up at the auction and bid on the land. Because the auction is intended to raise money to satisfy the judgment, it is hoped that the auction price will at least equal the amount of the judgment. If it does not, the proceeds are used to satisfy the judgment partially. If it does, the proceeds satisfy the judgment fully. If there is excess, the government keeps the excess funds in an account for the defendant.

- P obtains a judgment against D for $50,000. (The judgment might have been entered after P and D went all the way through a trial or by default or any other way in which judgments are entered.) P wants her $50,000. D refuses to pay (for whatever reason). P seeks an order (writ) from the court to seize some property of D's for sale at auction to raise the $50,000. The court issues a "writ of execution" to the sheriff, commanding her to seize the property. It might be land, or an automobile, or a bank account, or any other kind of property. Then the sheriff oversees the sale of the property at public auction.
  - Suppose at the auction, X is the high bidder, at $70,000. X pays $70,000 to the court and gets ownership of the property. If the property was land, the sheriff would transfer it to X by executing a sheriff's deed, which is then recorded in the register of deeds as a public record that X owns the land. What happens to the money? The court pays $50,000 to P (to satisfy her judgment) and the remaining $20,000 is kept in an account for D. She can get it whenever she wants. If she is absent, it will sit in the account, earning interest at a rate set by law.
  - Suppose at the auction, X is the highest bidder, at $40,000. X pays $40,000 to the court and gets ownership of the property. The court pays P the $40,000, and the judgment against D is satisfied to that amount. That means, of course, that P still has a claim of $10,000 against D. If the judgment were valid and *in personam*, the judgment would be unsatisfied to the tune of $10,000, and P might be able to enforce it against other property of D in the forum or even in another state under full faith and credit (this was discussed at §2.2).

Now back to our story. See how Mitchell played two roles at the auction: P (the plaintiff) and X (the buyer at the auction). There is nothing wrong with that. We just need to keep the two roles separate. As bidder, he offered the judgment amount (about $300). He paid that to the court and got a sheriff's deed to the land. As plaintiff, Mitchell was entitled to the $300. So the court paid him that money. So, by playing both the role of the bidder and the plaintiff, Mitchell came out of the deal with a deed to Neff's land and without being out of pocket any money. Again, there is nothing wrong with playing both roles; it probably happens frequently. (Though, as we will see, Mitchell was a crook and was probably up to no good here.)

Just days after receiving the sheriff's deed, Mitchell sold the land (at a huge profit; the land was apparently worth about $15,000) to a new player in the controversy, Sylvester Pennoyer. In return for the payment, Mitchell gave Pennoyer a deed to the land. Pennoyer moved onto the land and everything was fine until Neff came back from California. Needless to say, Neff was shocked to find Pennoyer living on his land. Neff sued Pennoyer in federal court to recover the land.[24] Neff claimed that he got the land originally from the federal grant under the Oregon Donation Law, and that the sheriff's deed purporting to transfer it to Mitchell was void. (If the deed to Mitchell was void, Mitchell's deed to Pennoyer was also void.) The entire case thus depended on whether the sheriff's deed to Mitchell was valid; if so, it cut off Neff's ownership of the land. That issue, in turn, depended on whether the underlying judgment in the case by Mitchell against Neff was valid.

The federal trial court[25] ruled in favor of Neff. According to that court, the judgment in *Mitchell v. Neff* was void. Thus, the sheriff's deed (based on that judgment) that purported to transfer title from Neff to Mitchell was also void. That meant, of course, that Mitchell had no valid title to convey to Pennoyer, so Neff got his land back. That court based its decision, however, on very narrow grounds: It determined that the publication notice given in the newspaper violated Oregon law because Mitchell's sworn statement (affidavit), which he was required to give as a prerequisite to giving publication notice, was inadequate. On "writ of error," the U.S. Supreme Court affirmed the judgment[26] — in other words, agreed that

---

[24] In §1.2.1, we noted that federal courts can only entertain certain types of cases. Among these are cases between citizens of different states. The case by Neff against Pennoyer qualified, because Neff was a citizen of California and Pennoyer was a citizen of Oregon. This form of subject matter jurisdiction is discussed in detail in §4.5.

[25] At that time, federal trial courts were known as circuit courts for the particular district in which they sat. The court deciding Neff's case against Pennoyer was the circuit court for the district of Oregon. Today, the federal trial court is known as the district court, and intermediate court of appeals in the federal system is known informally as the circuit court.

[26] When *Pennoyer* was decided, there was no intermediate court of appeals between the federal trial court and the U.S. Supreme Court. Today, a decision by the federal trial court in Oregon would be appealed to the U.S. Court of Appeals for the Ninth Circuit, which hears appeals from federal trial courts in several western states, including Oregon. In the days of

Neff should win — but did so on different, and far broader, grounds. It is that opinion by the Supreme Court that you read in your casebook.

The Holding

In *Pennoyer*, the Court held that the judgment in *Mitchell v. Neff* was void because the Oregon state court that rendered the judgment did not have jurisdiction over Neff's property. More specifically, the Oregon court lacked what we today would call valid QIR-2 jurisdiction. Why? Because Neff's property had not been attached *at the outset of the case*. Instead, Mitchell did not have it attached until after the court had entered its default judgment against Neff. At that point, Mitchell had the property attached in an effort to satisfy his judgment against Neff.

The Court's actual holding, then, concerns only QIR-2 jurisdiction, and requires that the jurisdictional predicate in such a case (which is, of course, property belonging to the defendant) be seized by the court *at the outset* of the litigation. Without such seizure, there is simply no property over which the court can exercise power. As the Court explained:

> [T]he jurisdiction of the court to inquire into and determine [the defendant's] obligations at all is only incidental to its jurisdiction over the property. Its jurisdiction in that respect cannot be made to depend upon facts to be ascertained after it has tried the cause and rendered the judgment. If the judgment be previously void, it will not become valid by the subsequent discovery of property of the defendant, or by his subsequent acquisition of it. The judgment, if void when rendered, will always remain void: it cannot occupy the doubtful position of being valid if property be found, and void if there be none. . . . [T]he validity of every judgment depends upon the jurisdiction of the court before it is rendered, not upon what may occur subsequently.[27]

It is important to understand the basis of the Supreme Court's holding. Though the trial court based its decision on a perceived problem with Mitchell's affidavit under Oregon law, the Supreme Court did not address that issue. Rather, it held that the failure of the Oregon state court to seize the jurisdictional predicate (Neff's property) at the outset of the case violated federal constitutional and statutory provisions concerning full faith and credit. As we discussed in §2.2, full faith and credit provides that a valid judgment is entitled to enforcement in other states. Consequently, the Court explained in *Pennoyer*, a void judgment (such as that in *Mitchell v. Neff*) is not entitled to enforcement in other states — or even in the state in which it was rendered. Because the Oregon state-court judgment

---

Pennoyer, as today, the Supreme Court was not required to hear an appeal taken to it. Rather, it has discretion as to which cases to decide, as discussed in §§1.2.1 and 1.2.2.

[27] 95 U.S. at 728.

in *Mitchell v. Neff* was void, it was not entitled to respect in the subsequent case in federal court in *Neff v. Pennoyer*.[28]

The Court then discussed the adoption of the Fourteenth Amendment to the Constitution. As noted in §2.3, that amendment, among other things, prohibits *states* from denying citizens of property without "due process of law." Before the adoption of the Fourteenth Amendment, the Fifth Amendment prohibited the *federal* government from denying citizens of due process, but the body of the Constitution was silent regarding such actions by *state* governments. The Fourteenth Amendment was ratified in 1868, which was after entry of the judgment in *Mitchell v. Neff*. Thus, the Fourteenth Amendment technically did not apply in *Pennoyer* because it was not adopted in time to affect the judgment in *Mitchell v. Neff*. Nonetheless, the Court left no doubt that a judgment rendered without a proper jurisdictional predicate (such as the judgment in *Mitchell v. Neff*) would constitute a denial of due process (and thus a violation of the Fourteenth Amendment). As the Court said, "proceedings in a court of justice to determine the personal rights and obligations of parties over whom that court has no jurisdiction do not constitute due process of law."[29]

After *Pennoyer*, there is no doubt that the constitutional propriety of personal jurisdiction is judged by principles of due process. Moreover, the due process assessment determines whether the judgment is entitled to full faith and credit. In other words, if a court lacks personal jurisdiction, its judgment would deny the litigants of due process. Because the judgment would be void under due process, it would not be entitled to full faith and credit. Thus, though technically *Pennoyer* could be based only on full faith and credit (because the Fourteenth Amendment had not been ratified in time to apply to the judgment in *Mitchell v. Neff*), today the assessment is made under due process.

Though the precise holding in *Pennoyer* concerned QIR-2 (because the attempted jurisdictional basis in *Mitchell v. Neff* was Neff's property in Oregon), the opinion discusses other bases of personal jurisdiction. It provides a primer on jurisdictional thought that continues to shape our thinking. In a famous (and very long) paragraph of the opinion, Justice Stephen Field[30] invoked two "principles of public law," which emanated from international law. First,

> every State possesses exclusive jurisdiction and sovereignty over persons and property within its territory. As a consequence, every State has the power

---

[28] "Whilst [federal courts] are not foreign tribunals in their relations to the State courts, they are tribunals of a different sovereignty, exercising a distinct and independent jurisdiction, and are bound to give to the judgments of the State courts only the same faith and credit which the courts of another State are bound to give them." 95 U.S. at 732-733.

[29] 95 U.S. at 733.

[30] Justice Field was a younger brother of David Dudley Field, who was an important law reformer in the United States in the nineteenth century. See §7.2.

to determine for itself the civil status and capacities of its inhabitants; to prescribe the subjects upon which they may contract, the forms and solemnities with which their contracts shall be executed, the rights and obligations arising from them, and the mode in which their validity shall be determined and their obligations enforced; and also to regulate the manner and conditions upon which property situated within such territory, both personal and real, may be acquired, enjoyed, and transferred.[31]

The second principle, which is really a corollary to the first, is

that no State can exercise direct jurisdiction and authority over persons or property without [which means "outside"] its territory. The several States are of equal dignity and authority, and the independence of one implies the exclusion of power from all others. And so it is laid down by jurists, as an elementary principle, that the laws of one State have no operation outside of its territory, except so far as is allowed by comity; and that no tribunal established by it can extend its process beyond that territory so as to subject either persons or property to its decisions.[32]

Clearly, *Pennoyer* is based upon the notion of physical "power" — a state has power over people and things inside its boundaries. Such power is demonstrated by the fact that the courts of the state can seize people and property found within the state. Thus, California has power over people and things inside California, and Oregon cannot exercise authority over such people or things. More precisely, Oregon cannot exercise *direct* authority over people or things in California. The Court in *Pennoyer* did recognize, however, that a valid judgment by an Oregon court might have an *indirect* effect in California.

○ *X* owns land in California. There is a dispute about whether *X* agreed to transfer that land to *A*. An Oregon court with *in personam* jurisdiction over *X* litigates the dispute and determines that *X* did agree to convey the property to *A*. The Oregon court can enter an *in personam* judgment ordering *X* to execute a deed transferring the property to *A*. Though this Oregon judgment has an effect in California (because it results in transfer of property in California from *X* to *A*), the effect is *indirect* and therefore permissible. That is, the effect in California is ancillary to Oregon's exercise of *in personam* jurisdiction over *X*. Because Oregon had *in personam* jurisdiction over *X*, it had the power to command *X* to do something (even something that has an effect in California).
○ Neff owns land in Oregon, but lives in California. Mitchell contends that Neff owes him money for legal services rendered. Mitchell sues Neff using

---

[31] 95 U.S. at 722.
[32] *Id.*

QIR-2 in Oregon, and uses Neff's Oregon land as the jurisdictional predicate. Neff defaults, so Mitchell wins. If done properly, the default judgment in this case would dispose of Neff's land in Oregon at a judicial sale to the highest bidder. Though this Oregon judgment has an effect in California (by affecting the Oregon holdings of a California resident), the effect is *indirect* and therefore permissible. If Oregon had QIR-2 jurisdiction over Neff's land, it would have the power to dispose of the property, notwithstanding the incidental effect on a Californian.

If all this is true — if states have all this power — why didn't Oregon have authority to make the order it made in *Mitchell v. Neff*? The two *Pennoyer* principles quoted above have to be tempered slightly, because a state in the United States does not have absolute power to do anything it wants to people and property within its boundaries. Why? Because of the Constitution of the United States. That wonderful document does several things. For present purposes, though, it creates the federal government by vesting in that government powers otherwise belonging to the states. Put bluntly, states give up some of their powers to join the Union. Thus, Justice Field said in *Pennoyer*, "[t]he several States of the Union are not, it is true, in every respect independent, many of the rights and powers which originally belonged to them being now vested in the government created by the Constitution."[33] He continued to note that states of the United States possess authority of independent (international) states "except as restrained and limited" by the Constitution.

And, as we discussed above, concepts of due process and full faith and credit limit a state's power to exercise personal jurisdiction. So states of the United States do not have *unfettered* power over persons and things inside their boundaries. The Constitution limits their power. One such limitation — emanating from the constitutional principles of due process and full faith and credit — is that a state may not enter a judgment unless it has a proper jurisdictional predicate. According to *Pennoyer*, a state can exercise QIR-2 jurisdiction only if it seizes the property serving as the jurisdictional predicate at the *outset* of the case. Because this was not done, the judgment in *Mitchell v. Neff* was unconstitutional and thus void. Thus, the sheriff's deed to Mitchell was void, which means that his deed to Pennoyer was void. Neff won.[34]

---

[33] 95 U.S. at 722.

[34] Notice what this means in the human drama. Mitchell bought the property for about $300. He sold it to Pennoyer for many times that amount (about $15,000). Because of the holding by the Supreme Court, however, Pennoyer lost the land for which he spent so much money. So who's to blame? Not Neff, an illiterate homesteader who, by all accounts, was an honorable man. Not Pennoyer, who was a beloved figure in Oregon history, and went on to serve as governor of the state. Mitchell is the bad guy. He was a Pennsylvania lawyer who abandoned his wife and left the East Coast with a good deal of his clients' money (and with his mistress) and went to Oregon. There, he married his mistress without divorcing

What the Opinion Said About In Personam *Jurisdiction*

The opinion in *Pennoyer* is famous and influential for more than its narrow holding about the constitutional need to seize property at the outset in QIR-2 cases. In it, the Court also discussed other bases of personal jurisdiction, and clarified the understanding of those bases. Concerning *in personam* cases — "where the entire object of the action is to determine the personal rights and obligations of the defendants"[35] — *Pennoyer* sets forth what are still considered the "traditional bases" of jurisdiction. Early in the opinion, when discussing the relevant Oregon statute, the Court mentioned three such bases.

First, a defendant can be subject to *in personam* jurisdiction if she "appear[s] in the court."[36] This basis is generally known as *consent*. As we noted in §2.1, a defendant may waive the constitutional protection from being sued in a forum that does not have personal jurisdiction. Accordingly, she can consent to jurisdiction in any state. As we see in §6.2, sometimes such consent is voluntary, and sometimes it is the result of failing to object appropriately to an attempted exercise of jurisdiction. There is no question to this day that a defendant can consent to personal jurisdiction in any state, either willingly or by making a mistake.

Second, *Pennoyer* recognized that a state may exercise *in personam* jurisdiction over "a resident thereof."[37] This exercise of jurisdiction makes sense. After all, if someone resides in the forum that person is within the boundaries of the state and thus subject to the power of the state's courts. Again, there is no doubt to this day that states have *in personam* jurisdiction over those who have this sort of ongoing association with the forum. It is likely that Justice Field intended to connote not simple residence but the concept of "domicile." In a later case (*Milliken v. Meyer*, discussed in §2.4.2), the Court spoke of jurisdiction based on domicile rather than "residence." We define and discuss domicile in detail in §4.5.3, regarding a different issue. In short, a person has only one domicile, and can never have more than one. It is established by presence there plus forming the subjective intent to make that her permanent home. It remains the person's domicile until she establishes a new one elsewhere. Residence may be a

---

his first wife. He became a successful land lawyer in Oregon but also a scandalous member of the community. A local paper published the love letters he wrote to his second wife's younger sister. Interestingly, his personal life did not keep him from serving as a United States Senator from Oregon. He was convicted of land fraud (unrelated to the *Pennoyer* case) and sentenced to jail; he died while the case was on appeal. For a fascinating and entertaining account of the characters involved in this great case, *see* Wendy Collins Perdue, *Sin, Scandal, and Substantive Due Process: Personal Jurisdiction and* Pennoyer *Reconsidered*, 62 Wash. L. Rev. 479 (1987).

[35] 95 U.S. at 727. See also §2.2.
[36] 95 U.S. at 720.
[37] *Id.*

more fleeting concept, and a person can have more than one residence. For instance, suppose you attend law school in a state with which you previously had no contact. Suppose also that after law school you intend to return to what you consider your home state. Though you may now reside in the state where you go to school, you are domiciled in your home state. In all likelihood, in *Pennoyer*, the Court meant that one is subject to jurisdiction where she is domiciled.

Third, a state has *in personam* jurisdiction over a defendant "found within the State."[38] Generally, this is referred to as "presence" as the basis of jurisdiction. There is nothing wrong with using that shorthand expression if we understand that it does not envision jurisdiction based simply on the fact that the defendant was present in the forum once upon a time. Rather, she must be *served with process while present* in the forum. This is the archetypal form of *in personam* jurisdiction.

In addition, later in the opinion, the Court noted another basis for *in personam* jurisdiction. The Court confirmed that a state may "require a nonresident entering into a partnership or association within its limits, or making contracts enforceable there, to appoint an agent or representative in the State to receive service of process" for cases involving that business.[39] This may actually be seen as an amalgam of two bases already seen: consent and presence. A state may require anyone doing business or entering a contract within the state to appoint someone to receive service of process. A defendant who does so may be consenting to jurisdiction or the case may involve the "constructive" presence of the defendant in the state. By and large, a person can have an agent perform various functions for her. Thus, appointing an agent for service of process in another state may be seen as the defendant's being present in that state through an agent. These notions are developed further in §2.4.2.

The Need for a Jurisdictional Predicate and for Notice to the Defendant

In *Pennoyer*, the Court made clear that the Constitution (due process and full faith and credit) requires not only a jurisdictional predicate, but also that the defendant be given notice and an opportunity to defend herself in the forum. This notice consists of *process*, which, as we saw in §2.1, consists of a copy of the complaint and a summons, which is the document symbolizing the court's exercise of power over the defendant. (Service of process is discussed in detail in §3.3.) The *Pennoyer* Court drew a sharp distinction between two general types of service: personal service and "constructive" service. The former is exactly what it sounds like: The defendant is given (personally) the requisite papers. Constructive service

[38] 95 U.S. at 720.
[39] 95 U.S. at 735.

refers to something short of personal service. One form is publication, in which notice is published in a newspaper of general circulation in the forum. Mitchell arranged for such notice in *Mitchell v. Neff*.

According to *Pennoyer*, personal service is absolutely required for *in personam* cases. Moreover, because the Court stressed that a court cannot have a direct effect outside the state boundary, "[p]rocess from the tribunals of one State cannot run into another State, and summon parties there domiciled to leave its territory and respond to proceedings against them."[40] Under *Pennoyer*, then, the only proper form of *notice* for an *in personam* case is personal service of process on the defendant (or her agent) in the forum state.

Oddly, when we think about it, this form of notice subsumes the various jurisdictional predicates for *in personam* jurisdiction. Remember that the Court recognized consent and residence as predicates for jurisdiction, in addition to service of process on the defendant (or her agent) in the forum. If, however, the only notice that can be used is service of process in the forum, the predicates of consent and residence seem superfluous. Suppose *P* wants to sue *D* in Oregon, and that *D* is domiciled in Oregon. We know that her domicile in Oregon gives Oregon a jurisdictional predicate for *in personam* jurisdiction over *D*. But the only way to give notice, at least according to *Pennoyer*, is to serve process on *D* in Oregon. Thus, why not just use that basis (presence when served) as the jurisdictional predicate?

We will see in succeeding sections that the Supreme Court will relent on the requirement that service of process be effected in the forum state. The day will come when process from one state can reach into another.

As we saw above, the jurisdictional predicate for QIR-2 (and, by implication, for QIR-1 and true *in rem* cases) is the attachment of the property by the court in the forum at the outset of the proceedings. The notice requirement may then be satisfied by constructive notice, such as publication in a newspaper. Even here, there is some overlap of functions. The Court indicated that the seizure of the property itself will also give notice. As Justice Field said, "The law assumes that property is always in the possession of its owner, in person or by agent; and it proceeds upon the theory that its seizure will inform him . . . that he must look to . . . proceedings authorized by law. . . ."[41] Such "notice" is pretty fictive. So it must, according to the Court, be augmented by publication notice. *Pennoyer* made it clear, however, that publication notice would not suffice in an *in personam* case.

---

[40] 95 U.S. at 727.
[41] *Id.*

Cases Involving Status

Relatively late in the opinion, the Court in *Pennoyer* affirms that a state may "authorize proceedings to determine the status of one of its citizens toward a nonresident, which would be binding within the State, though made without service of process or personal notice to the nonresident."[42] It then discusses the best example of such a status case — divorce proceedings. A suit for divorce is not a proceeding *in personam*. Rather, it is litigation to determine the interests of persons (the spouses) in the "thing" of marriage. Thus, it is in the nature of an *in rem* or QIR-1 case. The fact that one spouse resides in the forum permits that person to maintain the divorce proceeding without having to serve process on the other party in the state. Publication notice will suffice — again, because this is not an *in personam* proceeding.

This result is dictated by practical reality. If divorce were an *in personam* proceeding, one spouse could prevent the other from getting a divorce simply by moving to another state. It is in everyone's interest to allow the resident spouse to maintain the case in the forum. Note, however, that only the status issue can be determined in this way. If one spouse sought recovery of money from the other (e.g., alimony or child support), the court would have to be able to exercise *in personam* jurisdiction.[43]

Some Hypotheticals

Let's apply the law according to *Pennoyer* to some fact patterns.

- *P* sues *D* in Oregon. *D* is served with process in Oregon, but refuses to participate in the litigation. The Oregon court enters a default judgment in favor of *P* for $10,000. Is the judgment valid?[44]
- *P* sues *D* in Oregon. *D* is served with process while in California, just over the boundary from Oregon. *D* refuses to participate in the litigation. The Oregon court enters a default judgment in favor of *P* for $10,000. Is the judgment valid?[45]
- *P* sues *D* in Oregon. *P* has an officer go to serve process on *D* in Oregon. As the officer approaches *D*, however, *D* steps over the boundary from Oregon into California. The officer goes to the California side of the boundary and punches *D* in the nose, rendering *D* unconscious. The

---

[42] 95 U.S. at 734.

[43] Or QIR-2 over some property in the forum owned by the nonresident spouse.

[44] Yes. The Oregon court had the jurisdictional predicate of presence in the forum when service was effected. Notice consisted of service of process in the forum.

[45] No. Service was not effected in the forum. *Pennoyer* requires that the defendant be served with process in an *in personam* case inside the forum state. The Oregon court has no power in California.

officer then drags *D* across the border into Oregon. When *D* regains consciousness, the officer serves process on *D*. Does Oregon have *in personam* jurisdiction over *D*?

- ∘ We are tempted to say no, because we are outraged by the officer's behavior. But does *Pennoyer* say anything at all about *how* a defendant becomes present in the forum? No. Does it say anything at all about whether the exercise of jurisdiction is "fair"? No. It talks about power over people and things within the state. *D* was present in the forum when served with process. Obviously, *D* can sue the officer for committing a tort.[46] Moreover, the officer committed a crime by punching *D*, so the state could prosecute the officer for the crime.[47] Is there anything in *Pennoyer*, however, that indicates that these facts should matter when it comes to the question of whether Oregon has jurisdiction over *D*?

- ∘ It is probable, under the *Pennoyer* power principle, that Oregon *would* have *in personam* jurisdiction over *D*. After all, *D* was served within the forum, and that's all the Supreme Court required. On the other hand, there is nothing that *requires* Oregon courts to exercise such jurisdiction.

In cases such as these, courts routinely invoked what came to be called the *force and fraud exception* to jurisdiction. This exception recognized that the state could constitutionally exercise personal jurisdiction, but that, under the circumstances, it would be unseemly to do so. Thus, the court refuses to countenance the bad behavior by the officer. Think about the enormous theoretical difference between saying (1) there is no jurisdiction and (2) there is jurisdiction but the court refuses to exercise it. Because nothing in *Pennoyer* says anything about fairness, it seems the second option is the more accurate reflection of the law of that case.

- ∘ *H* and *W* are married, living in Pennsylvania. *H* abandons *W*, and moves to Oregon. *W* sues *H* for divorce in Pennsylvania. *H* cannot be served with process personally in Pennsylvania. Notice is given only by publication. The Pennsylvania court enters a judgment declaring the couple divorced. Is the judgment valid?

  - ∘ Yes. This is not an *in personam* case. Rather, it is one to determine the status of persons in a thing — the marriage. The opinion in *Pennoyer* makes it plain that states must have the authority to render such binding judgments based on the residence of one of the parties to the marriage in the state.

---

[46] By the way, where would *D* sue the officer, California or Oregon?

[47] By the way, which state would prosecute? Did the officer commit a crime in California? In Oregon? In both?

- Same case, and in addition to a decree of divorce, *W* seeks an order that *H* pay her $500 per month in alimony and child support. Can the Pennsylvania court validly enter such an order based on publication notice?[48]
- *P* sues *D* for damages of $10,000 in Oregon. *D* is not present in Oregon. *P* has the court attach property belonging to *D*, and present in Oregon. The attachment is made at the outset of the suit. Notice is given by publication. *D* defaults. The court enters judgment in favor of *P* for $10,000. Is the judgment valid?
  - Yes, but only to the extent of the value of the property attached. This is a QIR-2 case. The jurisdictional predicate of attaching the property at the outset of the case is satisfied, as is the requirement of publication notice. The value of the property will be established at the public auction.

§2.4.2   Stretching *Pennoyer*: *Harris v. Balk*, *Hess v. Pawloski*, and Others

The Supreme Court decided *Pennoyer* in 1878, during the horse-and-buggy era. In the ensuing decades, Americans became far more mobile. The horse and the wagon and the train gave way to the automobile and the airplane. It became easier to go into a state, have an impact there (maybe by committing a tort or breaching a contract), and to get out before being served with process there. Yet, under *Pennoyer*, one could only get *in personam* jurisdiction in limited ways: residence, consent, presence in the forum when served with process, or presence of an agent in the forum for service of process. Thus, if one wanted to sue a nonresident of the forum — and if the nonresident did not have an agent in the forum and would not consent to jurisdiction — one had to be able to serve process on the nonresident in the forum. The wily defendant could easily avoid jurisdiction by staying out (or getting out) of the forum.

Something had to give. Somehow, the Supreme Court had to expand the availability of personal jurisdiction to adapt to modern realities. Eventually, as seen in §2.4.3, in the mid-twentieth century, the Court recast the basic due process inquiry. Before that, however, in the early part of that century, the Court expanded the availability of personal jurisdiction by stretching the principles established in *Pennoyer*. There are three principal areas in which the Court stretched *Pennoyer*: QIR-2, *in personam* involving businesses, and *in personam* involving individuals.

---

[48] No. The requested relief — requiring *H* to pay money — goes beyond a determination of status. *W* cannot sue *H* *in personam* for such relief in Pennsylvania without serving process on *H* in Pennsylvania, which is impossible on these facts.

QIR-2 Expansion: Harris v. Balk

In cases in which *in personam* jurisdiction was impossible because the defendant could not be served with process in the forum, *Pennoyer* permitted QIR-2. As long as the defendant had property in the forum, it was attached at the outset of the case, and the defendant was given publication notice, a QIR-2 judgment would be valid. The only example we have seen (*Mitchell v. Neff*) involved attachment of the defendant's land in the forum.[49] Nothing in *Pennoyer*, however, limited QIR-2 to jurisdiction over *tangible* property.[50]

The Supreme Court expanded the availability of QIR-2 jurisdiction dramatically in 1905 in *Harris v. Balk*.[51] In that case, Balk owed money to Epstein. Epstein wanted to sue Balk to recover the money, but he wanted to sue in Baltimore (Epstein's home), rather than going to North Carolina, where Balk lived. Epstein could only proceed *in personam* against Balk in Maryland, though, if he could serve process on Balk there. Balk did not go anywhere near Maryland, so *in personam* was out of the question. What about QIR-2? Balk seemed safe from suit in Maryland on that score as well, because he did not own any property in that state. But here's where Balk was in for a surprise. A man named Harris happened to owe money to Balk. When someone owes money to you, you have a property right (the debt). You can try to enforce that property right by suing on the debt. That right to sue to enforce the debt is "property" of yours, but it is intangible property. You cannot touch it or see it, but it is there.

Harris went to Maryland. Epstein somehow heard about this, and brought suit against Balk (QIR-2) to recover the money Balk owed him. But he needed to attach some property of Balk's. Epstein had Harris served with process in Baltimore, and asked the Maryland court to make Harris place the money he owed Balk in the registry of the court. Harris did so, and deposited the money he owed Balk. Epstein had it attached at the outset of the case and proceeded QIR-2 against Balk. The Supreme Court upheld QIR-2 jurisdiction.

The upshot of *Harris v. Balk* is that QIR-2 jurisdiction can be exercised even over *intangible* property. In essence, when Harris went to Maryland, the debt he owed to Balk went to Maryland. Thus, property of Balk's was in Maryland. Epstein attached it by suing Balk under QIR-2 and having Harris served with process for the sole purpose of making Harris

---

[49] Remember, however, that the attachment was defective because it was not undertaken at the outset of the case. This was the reason the judgment in *Mitchell v. Neff* was struck down in *Pennoyer v. Neff*. See §2.4.1.

[50] We drew distinctions between tangible and intangible property and defined real property in footnote 12. Remember that all real property is tangible but not all tangible property is real. If that doesn't make sense, revisit that footnote.

[51] 198 U.S. 215 (1905).

surrender the money he owed to Balk.[52] Once Harris did that, that money (which belonged to Balk) was attached as the jurisdictional predicate for the QIR-2 proceeding against Balk. It's brilliant, and it's completely consistent with *Pennoyer*.

Notice how the holding in *Harris* makes it more difficult for someone to avoid being sued in another state. Before *Harris*, someone in Balk's position could avoid jurisdiction in another state simply by (1) refusing to go to the state and (2) making sure she did not own property in that state. After *Harris*, however, one can be sued under QIR-2 wherever her debtor happens to go.

The Supreme Court did not address QIR-2 jurisdiction again for over 70 years, when it decided *Shaffer v. Heitner*.[53] In that case, discussed in §4.2.4, the Court overruled *Harris v. Balk*. But let's not get ahead of ourselves. The point now is to note how the Court in the early twentieth century expanded personal jurisdiction by stretching concepts from *Pennoyer*.

In Personam *Expansion Regarding Businesses*

In the nineteenth century, it was clear that a corporation could be sued in the state in which it was incorporated.[54] Thus, if a corporation were formed ("chartered") in Pennsylvania, there is no question that it was subject to *in personam* jurisdiction in Pennsylvania. There was some doubt, however, about whether the corporation could be sued in another state. For a long time, this limitation did not impose great hardship, because corporations usually were engaged only in local, intrastate business. In the late nineteenth century, however, this began to change. Increased industrialization and concentration of wealth in corporate hands, along with increased opportunities to travel, vastly increased the interstate transaction of business by corporations and other forms of business. As it became more likely that a Pennsylvania corporation might do business in Virginia, the desire to sue the Pennsylvania business in Virginia also increased.

---

[52] The court holds what is often called a proceeding *in garnishment* to seize Balk's property, which happens to be in the hands of Harris. Harris could have contended that he owed Balk nothing and litigated that issue. As it turns out, he admitted his debt to Balk and deposited the money in the court in Maryland. Because the Maryland court's QIR-2 judgment against Balk was valid, Balk was precluded from suing Harris to recover the debt. Harris had already paid the debt by surrendering it to the court in Maryland.

[53] 433 U.S. 186 (1977).

[54] A corporation is a business form that is seen as an entity — separate from the people who own it and those who run it. The entity comes into existence only upon the satisfaction of the formation requirements, which each state is free to prescribe. A corporation is usually formed in a single state, and then seeks permission to do business in other states. Not all business is transacted by corporations. There are other business structures, including the partnership. Historically, the partnership was not seen as an entity unto itself, but as an amalgam of its partners.

In *Pennoyer*, the Court suggested that states could essentially coerce *in personam* jurisdiction from businesses formed in another state by requiring them to appoint agents for service of process. The appointment of a local agent was a *quid pro quo* — that is, it was made in exchange for being allowed to do business in the state. Then, at least in cases arising from the transaction of that business, a plaintiff could have process served upon the agent and force the out-of-state business to defend in the forum. The result is consistent with *Pennoyer*: The jurisdictional predicate is consent and notice is given by serving process on the defendant's agent within the forum state.

But what gives a state the authority to coerce the appointment of an agent for service of process? In the case of the corporation, the answer has long been clear: One state can deny a corporation formed in another state to enter. Thus, Virginia could simply exclude a Pennsylvania corporation from entering Virginia. Why? Because the Privileges and Immunities Clause of the Constitution (Article IV, §2) does not apply to corporations.[55] That clause, which provides that the citizens of one state "shall be entitled to all privileges and immunities of citizens in the several states," means (roughly)[56] that Virginia must accord to Pennsylvanians the privileges and immunities it accords its own citizens. But, again, the clause just does not apply to corporations. Thus, Virginia could bar a Pennsylvania corporation from entering the state. And if it can exclude the corporation altogether, it certainly has the lesser power of permitting the corporation to enter, *conditioned upon* its appointment of an agent for service of process and its consenting to *in personam* jurisdiction.[57]

But states encountered a problem in this regard in the early twentieth century. Then, though the Privileges and Immunities Clause clearly does not apply to corporations, the Supreme Court concluded that a different part of the Constitution — the Commerce Clause — prohibited a state from excluding a corporation that was engaged in interstate commerce within its boundaries.[58] In other words, if a Pennsylvania corporation's activities in Virginia were part of interstate commerce (and not simply local activity), Virginia could not exclude the corporation. If Virginia could not exclude the Pennsylvania corporation, how could Virginia condition its activities on the appointment of an agent for service of process and on its consenting to *in personam* jurisdiction?

[55] Paul v. Virginia, 75 U.S. 168, 177 (1869).

[56] This aspect of privileges and immunities is studied in detail in the course on Constitutional Law.

[57] *See* Lafayette Ins. Co. v. French, 59 U.S. 404, 407 (1855) ("A corporation created by Indiana can transact business in Ohio only with the consent, express or implied, of the latter state. This consent may be accompanied by such conditions as Ohio may think fit to impose. . . .").

[58] International Textbook Co. v. Prigg, 217 U.S. 91 (1910).

The answer came by an ingenious shifting of emphasis from consent to another basis of *in personam* jurisdiction under *Pennoyer*. In *International Harvester Co. v. Kentucky*,[59] the defendant corporation (formed outside Kentucky) set up business in Kentucky very deliberately, in an attempt to qualify as the transaction of interstate business. The corporation contended that Kentucky thus had no authority to exclude it and, accordingly, no authority to coerce its consent to jurisdiction. The Supreme Court upheld jurisdiction over the corporation in Kentucky. True, jurisdiction could not be based on consent. But, the Court held, the corporation was *present* in Kentucky, and jurisdiction could be upheld on that *Pennoyer* basis. Thus, when consent was cut off as a basis for jurisdiction, presence stepped in to fill the void.

The Supreme Court then embarked on a series of decisions in which it discussed how much activity was required to find an out-of-state corporation to be "present" in the forum.[60] Over time, courts got sloppy and started talking about whether an out-of-state corporation was "doing business" in the forum. If it was, they concluded, the corporation was subject to *in personam* jurisdiction. Why is this sloppy? Because *Pennoyer* did not say that doing business was a basis for *in personam* jurisdiction. Rather, as we saw in §2.4.1, it gave four traditional bases for such jurisdiction: presence, consent, residence, or presence of an agent. But the phrase (which is quite inexact anyway) took hold, and in thousands of opinions courts wrestled with what constitutes "doing business." We see this point again in our discussion of the *International Shoe* case in §2.4.3.

In Personam *Expansion Regarding Individuals:* Hess v. Pawloski

We have just seen that a state may, at least in certain instances, coerce consent to jurisdiction from a corporation. This authority flows from the fact that the state could often exclude the corporation from entering its borders, because corporations are not protected by the Privileges and Immunities Clause of the Constitution. There is no question, however, that the Privileges and Immunities Clause applies to individuals, so a state does not have the blanket authority to exclude a human from entering. But this fact did not stop states from attempting to base *in personam* jurisdiction on similar notions of implied consent. The Supreme Court upheld such an effort in 1927 in the famous case of *Hess v. Pawloski*.[61]

In that case, Hess, a citizen of Pennsylvania, drove his car in Massachusetts, where he was involved in an auto wreck with Pawloski, a citizen of Massachusetts. Pawloski sued Hess in an *in personam* action in Massachusetts, seeking damages for the wreck. He did not sue, however, until

---

[59] 234 U.S. 579 (1914).
[60] *See, e.g.*, People's Tobacco Co. v. American Tobacco Co., 246 U.S. 79, 87 (1918).
[61] 274 U.S. 352 (1927).

after Hess had returned to Pennsylvania. Thus, Hess could not be served with process in Massachusetts. But Massachusetts had a statute allowing its courts to exercise *in personam* jurisdiction over nonresidents involved in a motor vehicle collision in Massachusetts. The statute provided that by operating a motor vehicle in Massachusetts, the nonresident had consented to jurisdiction and to the appointment of a Massachusetts state official (the registrar of motor vehicles) as her agent for service of process. It also provided that the plaintiff must serve process on the state official and that a copy of the process be sent to the nonresident at his residence. Pawloski followed the statute diligently, served process on the state officer, and ensured that a copy of process was mailed to Hess in Pennsylvania.

Such nonresident motorist statutes are ubiquitous today. Before discussing the constitutional propriety of *in personam* jurisdiction over Hess in Massachusetts, we should note that such statutes provide for what we will call *specific jurisdiction*. That means that jurisdiction is created only for a claim that arises from activity within the forum; particularly, it created *in personam* jurisdiction over Hess, but *only* for the motor vehicle crash. This specific jurisdiction is to be contrasted with *general in personam* jurisdiction, under which a defendant can be sued in the forum for a claim that arose anywhere in the world. We revisit this theme in §2.4.5. *Hess* simply provides our first example of specific jurisdiction. *Pennoyer* did not make any such distinction between specific and general jurisdiction.

In *Hess*, the Court upheld *in personam* jurisdiction in Massachusetts (and, in so doing, paved the way (so to speak) for all states to pass such nonresident motorist statutes). It noted, citing *Pennoyer*, that "process of a court in one State cannot run into another."[62] But notice how nicely crafted the Massachusetts statute was — it did not permit service of process in Pennsylvania. Rather, the service was effected in Massachusetts, on Hess's *agent*, which is, of course, allowed by *Pennoyer*. Moreover, the jurisdictional predicate was Hess's consent, which also is recognized by *Pennoyer*.

But how did Hess consent to jurisdiction in Massachusetts? By operating his motor vehicle there. And how does a state have the right to coerce such consent? Interestingly, the Court held, though the Privileges and Immunities Clause means that a state cannot exclude an individual from entering a state, *it can exclude her from entering in a motor vehicle*. In *Kane v. New Jersey*,[63] Justice Oliver Wendell Holmes, writing for the Court, concluded that the state interest in highway safety justified a state's excluding a motorist who refused to appoint a local officer as agent for service of process for actions arising from the operation of the motor

---

[62] 274 U.S. at 355.
[63] 242 U.S. 160, 167 (1916).

vehicle. Accordingly, the Court in *Hess* concluded, a state also has the power to permit a motorist to enter based on her *implied* consent. In other words, a state can stop a motorist at the border and require that she appoint an agent for service of process for a case arising from the operation of the vehicle in the state. Since that is true, the Court concluded, the state may simply allow the motorist to enter, on condition that she thereby impliedly consents to *in personam* jurisdiction and to the appointment of a local agent for service of process.

Hess is brilliant. Notice how it is consistent with *Pennoyer*: The jurisdictional predicate is consent and the notice consists of service of process *within the forum* on the defendant's agent. In *Hess* and similar cases, the Court adapted *Pennoyer* to the new, more mobile world. It pushed the idea of consent to include implied consent. And it seized upon the idea of service of process upon the defendant's agent in the forum to include an agent appointed by operation of law.[64]

Though we are about to embark on a tour of the modern era of personal jurisdiction, you should understand that nonresident motorist acts such as that upheld in *Hess* operate in every state every day. You probably did not realize it, but every time you have driven across a state line, you have — by operation of law — consented to being sued in that state concerning a motor vehicle crash and you have appointed a state officer as your agent for service of process in such a case.

In 1940, the Court decided a case that does not seem to get recognized much in Civil Procedure courses, but which is nonetheless significant as a bridge from *Pennoyer* to the modern era. In *Milliken v. Meyer*,[65] the Court upheld *in personam* jurisdiction based on the defendant's domicile in the forum. As was suggested in discussing *Pennoyer* above and we will see in detail in §4.5.3, a person has only one domicile at a time; it is the state in which she has been present and that she intends to make her permanent home. A person retains her domicile until she acquires another one. Domicile in this sense is probably what the *Pennoyer* Court had in mind when it spoke of a state having *in personam* jurisdiction over its "residents." As the Court made clear in *Milliken*, there is a *quid pro quo* — when one takes up domicile in a state, she gets certain privileges and benefits from the state. It is only fair, in return, that the domiciliary be amenable to jurisdiction in the state's courts.[66]

---

[64] Among other things, the Court in *Hess* justified the result by noting that its holding tended to put nonresident motorists on the same footing with residents. By this it meant that a Massachusetts resident, involved in a motor vehicle wreck in Massachusetts, could be sued in that state based on her residence there. Remember, residence is a basis of *in personam* jurisdiction under *Pennoyer*.

[65] 311 U.S. 457 (1940).

[66] On the other hand, it is certainly conceivable that one could establish a sufficient tie with a state of residence (even if not her domicile) to justify the exercise of *in personam*

Significantly, *Milliken* upheld *in personam* jurisdiction over a domiciliary *even though the defendant was not personally served with process in the forum.* The case involved a domiciliary of the forum who was absent from the state.[67] The Court required only a "reasonable method" for apprising the defendant of the action. Thus, we see an important weakening of the seemingly inflexible requirement in *Pennoyer* that notice of an *in personam* case consists only of service of process in the forum state. *Milliken* opens the door for *in personam* jurisdiction based on other forms of notice and, more significantly, for the possibility (soon to be realized) that process can cross state lines. We turn to that modern era now.

§2.4.3 The Modern Era: *International Shoe*

In 1945, the Supreme Court decided *International Shoe Co. v. Washington,*[68] which ushered in the modern era in personal jurisdiction jurisprudence. Judges, lawyers, professors, and students have spent the ensuing decades trying to figure out (1) what *International Shoe* means and (2) how, if at all, it is to coexist with *Pennoyer.* Even professors who do not spend a great deal of time on historical treatment of personal jurisdiction invest a good bit of time on *International Shoe.*

The International Shoe Company (Shoe) manufactured shoes in St. Louis. The question in the case was whether it was amenable to *in personam* jurisdiction in Washington for a proceeding brought by the state to force the company to pay unemployment tax there.[69] Lawyers for Shoe had structured the company's activities in Washington very carefully, in an effort to avoid *in personam* jurisdiction there. For instance, Shoe employed salesmen who resided in the state and who were paid on commission. Shoe did not own any land in the state, but did occasionally rent rooms in which to display shoe samples. It permitted salesmen to show only one shoe of a pair; the argument was that by failing to ship an entire pair, Shoe was not really doing business in Washington. In addition, the salesmen had no authority to accept offers. Rather, they forwarded the

---

jurisdiction. For instance, a student or member of the military might reside for several years in a state that she does not consider her domicile.

[67] This can happen easily. Remember, a person has only one domicile at a time. So if a domiciliary of Illinois moves to California for four years to attend college, but has no desire to make California her permanent home, she is still a domiciliary of Illinois — even though she is absent from Illinois.

[68] 326 U.S. 310 (1945).

[69] Each state has an unemployment compensation system, which is funded by a tax on businesses in the state. Shoe contended that it did not have to pay the tax because it was not doing business in Washington. The state sued Shoe to collect the tax. The question of whether Washington had personal jurisdiction over Shoe is the same for this action as it would have been for any *in personam* case against Shoe.

offers to buy shoes to St. Louis, where all decisions were made; again, the idea was to set things up so Shoe would not be subject to jurisdiction in Washington. Notice also that the shoes were shipped "f.o.b." from St. Louis. This means "free on board," which requires the purchaser to pay the freight charges to get the shoes from St. Louis. Thus, Shoe argued, it did not ship anything into Washington and should not be held amenable to jurisdiction there.

At the end of §2.4.2, we saw that courts had strayed a bit from the *Pennoyer* bases of jurisdiction when addressing *in personam* jurisdiction over businesses. Instead of adhering to the bases provided by *Pennoyer*, they had come to base jurisdiction on whether the corporation was "doing business" in the forum. Through the years, the courts had found that a corporation that had engaged in soliciting business in the forum "plus some additional activities" there would be deemed to be doing business and thus would be amenable to *in personam* jurisdiction there. In *International Shoe*, the Supreme Court of Washington held that Shoe had engaged in "solicitation plus other activities" and thus could be sued there under this theory. The Supreme Court of the United States, in the opinion in your casebook, upheld jurisdiction in Washington, but recast the jurisdictional inquiry in very famous terms that continue to vex us today.

The Court cited *Pennoyer* in noting that "historically," *in personam* jurisdiction was "grounded on [a court's] de facto power over the defendant's person. Hence his presence within the territorial jurisdiction of a court was prerequisite to its rendition of a judgment personally binding him."[70] Now, however, that we no longer need to arrest the civil defendant,

> due process requires only that . . . to subject a defendant to a judgment *in personam*, if he be not present within the territory of the forum, he have certain minimum contacts with it such that the maintenance of the suit does not offend traditional notions of fair play and substantial justice.[71]

You will come to know that phrase in your sleep. It is the famous *International Shoe* (or, as many people call it, *minimum contacts*) test for whether the exercise of personal jurisdiction is constitutional. You will read various cases in which the Court attempts to explain what this phrase means. As we attempt to determine that meaning, however, it is helpful to keep several points in mind:

---

[70] 326 U.S. at 316.

[71] *Id.* (internal quotation omitted). The Court quoted *Milliken v. Meyer*, discussed in §2.4.2, for the language "traditional notions of fair play and substantial justice." *Milliken* upheld *in personam* jurisdiction over a domiciliary of the forum even without personal service in the forum.

(1) Nowhere in this passage or elsewhere did the Court in *International Shoe* purport to overrule *Pennoyer*. Thus, the question arises: Is the *International Shoe* formulation merely an alternative to *Pennoyer*, or does it replace *Pennoyer*?

(2) Notice that the Court sets out the "minimum contacts" language only *after* referring to the case in which the defendant "be not present within the territory of the forum." This seems to imply that "presence within the territory of the forum" remains a viable basis for the exercise of *in personam* jurisdiction. Indeed, it seems likely that the minimum contacts test is intended as an *alternative* to the defendant's presence in the forum as a basis for jurisdiction. As we see in §2.4.4, the Supreme Court finally addressed this issue in 1990 (and failed to resolve it definitively).

(3) The phrase seems to have two parts: one about "contacts" and the other about "fair play." We will see that the Court soon did come to consider the formulation as embodying two prongs of analysis: one about contact and the other about fairness.

(4) There is not a single term in the famous phrase that anyone can define. What are *minimum contacts*? What are *traditional notions*? What is *fair play and substantial justice*? The majority opinion itself admits that the inquiry "cannot be simply mechanical or quantitative," but must be more nuanced.

Let's be honest: The quoted words are classic weasel phrases; they can mean almost anything to anyone. Justice Black's wonderful concurring opinion in *International Shoe* drives this point home. He concurred with the result in the case because he thought Washington clearly had *in personam* jurisdiction over Shoe. He decried the Court's use of "vague Constitutional criteria" and "uncertain elements" as confusing a simple case. On this score, Justice Black was absolutely right: *International Shoe* introduces open-ended, imprecise language for determining whether the exercise of *in personam* jurisdiction is constitutional. This uncertainty is shown in subsequent cases in §2.4.4. The Court's embrace of amorphous words created great uncertainty and unpredictability.

But at another level, Justice Black was wrong. He was concerned that the weasel words would be used to *limit* the ability of a state to exercise *in personam* jurisdiction. This is why he discussed the Tenth Amendment (which retains for the states powers not given to the federal government). He was concerned that the states' power to determine their jurisdiction was being usurped by the federal bench. In fact, however, the minimum contacts test has been read quite broadly by state and federal courts, and Justice Black's concern of unduly limiting state power proved wrong. His broader fear that open-ended words create unnecessary uncertainty, however, has been borne out emphatically.

After laying out the now-famous minimum contacts test,[72] the Court then discussed jurisdiction over a corporation by addressing when a corporation is "present" in the forum state. It put the word in quotations because a corporation is present anywhere only because of the activities of people working on its behalf. It then indicated that an "estimate of the inconveniences" imposed upon the defendant by jurisdiction in the forum was a relevant consideration, and constructed a four-part model for when jurisdiction is appropriate. The model assessed two variables: (1) the level of activity of the defendant in the forum and (2) whether the claim asserted against the defendant is related to the defendant's activities in the forum. The *Pennoyer* regime did not deal with such nuances: Either there was jurisdiction or there was not. Here, in contrast, we are to assess "the quality and nature of the [defendant's] activity in relation to the fair and orderly administration of the laws."[73]

We can plot the two variables on a chart. On the horizontal axis is the defendant's activity in the forum. The Court indicates that it might range from "casual" to "continuous and systematic." On the vertical axis is the relatedness of the claim asserted to the defendant's activity in the forum. The Court indicates that it might be "related" or "unrelated." The result is a chart with four boxes.

	Unrelated	
Relatedness	Box 2 NO	Box 3 MAYBE
Related	Box 4 MAYBE	Box 1 YES

Casual → Continuous and Systematic
Level of Activity

Box 1 is where the defendant has continuous and systematic activities in the forum and the claim arises from those activities. As the Court says, jurisdiction "has never been doubted" in such circumstances. An example would be a suit against Ford Motor Company in Michigan (where it has its world headquarters and manufactures many of its vehicles) on a claim arising from the manufacture of a vehicle in Michigan — for example, for an

---

[72] Though we may refer to the *International Shoe* test by the shorthand of "minimum contacts," remember that there are two components to it: contact *and* fairness. The relevant factors for each will become clearer through considering subsequent cases.

[73] 326 U.S. at 319.

alleged defect in a car manufactured in Detroit. Thus, Box 1 is labeled "yes," because the forum will have *in personam* jurisdiction in such cases.

Box 2 is where the defendant has limited contact with the forum and the claim does not arise from that activity in the forum. As the Court says, it is "generally recognized" that such casual contacts with the forum "are not enough to subject [the defendant] to suit on causes of action unconnected with the activities there."[74] So a defendant domiciliary of West Virginia, who has been to Hawaii once on vacation, could not be sued in Hawaii for a claim arising from her actions in West Virginia. Thus, Box 2 is labeled "no."

Box 3 involves a defendant with continuous and systematic activities in the forum, but who is sued on a claim unrelated to those activities. The Court indicates that cases go both ways in this area. Sometimes the activity is not so substantial as to permit suit on an unrelated claim. On the other hand, "there have been instances in which the continuous corporate operations within a state were thought so substantial and of such a nature as to justify suit against it on causes of action arising from dealings entirely distinct from those activities."[75] This is a recognition of what we call *general in personam jurisdiction* — that a defendant's contacts with the forum can be so substantial that the defendant can be sued there for a claim that arose anywhere in the world. An example might be a claim asserted against Ford Motor Company in Michigan for an alleged defect in a car built in Mexico. Another example is a suit against a West Virginia domiciliary in West Virginia involving a tort committed by her in Hawaii. The problem, of course, is determining when the contacts are so substantial as to justify jurisdiction for a claim unrelated to activities in the forum. Thus, because cases go both ways, Box 3 is labeled "maybe."

Box 4 involves a defendant with casual contact with the forum, being sued on a claim that arises from that contact. The Court indicates that this, like Box 3, is a "maybe" category. Some cases uphold jurisdiction and others do not. An example might be a suit in Hawaii against a West Virginia domiciliary for a tort allegedly committed in Hawaii. Again, because this is a "maybe" category, the difficulty is in determining what factors justify jurisdiction.

After going through these permutations, the Court in *International Shoe* finally addressed the facts of the case, and concluded easily that Shoe was subject to *in personam* jurisdiction in Washington. The Court saw the case as falling in Box 1. It concluded that Shoe's contacts with the forum "were neither irregular nor casual . . . [but] were systematic and continuous."[76] In addition, the claim (liability for unemployment compensation tax)

[74] *Id.* at 317.
[75] *Id.* at 318.
[76] *Id.* at 320. The Court gave no hint as to why this was true. Is it measured by an objective scale — say, for example, the generation of a certain number of dollars of revenue in

clearly arose from the activities in the forum. The Court also concluded that jurisdiction was fair on a *quid pro quo* basis — Shoe "received the benefits and protection of the laws of [Washington], including the right to resort to the courts for the enforcement of its rights."[77]

In sum, *International Shoe* was an easy case, and the Court could have addressed it in familiar terms. Instead, the Court went out of its way to inject new (and relatively uncertain) terms into the assessment of personal jurisdiction. Why? In all likelihood, the Justices determined that it was time to reassess the jurisdictional inquiry. It is always a good idea to look at the date of opinions you read, and to try to place the decision in a historical context. *International Shoe* was decided in 1945, toward the end of World War II. At the time, Americans were thinking of themselves more as Americans and less as Texans and Californians. Interstate travel and interstate business were vastly increased. In sum, state lines probably meant less than they had in the past. The Court already had recognized that service of process can cross state lines. And now it seems to want to free up the availability of personal jurisdiction. Rather than the rigid *Pennoyer* bases for *in personam* jurisdiction, the Court in *International Shoe* provides a grab-bag of flexible variables, to be assessed on the facts of each case.

It must have seemed quite clear, even in 1945, that the jurisdictional inquiry had just become more difficult to predict. Think of your job as a lawyer after the Court decided *International Shoe*. Suppose a client asked you how she can avoid being amenable to *in personam* jurisdiction in a particular state. Under *Pennoyer*, you could give fairly concrete advice: "Do not go to the state and do not appoint an agent for service of process there." After *International Shoe*, what can you tell your client? Something like this: "Do not establish such minimum contacts with that state so that the exercise of jurisdiction would not offend traditional notions of fair play and substantial justice." How helpful is that? Perhaps later cases can provide the lawyer and her client with more certainty.

§2.4.4 Progeny of *International Shoe* to the Present

In this section, we review the major cases in which the Supreme Court has applied *International Shoe*. It is helpful to think of each case as giving some hint — some relevant factor — for applying the test. It is also

---

a year? Or is it measured by a relative scale — say, for example, a certain percentage of the defendant's overall business activity? We still don't know for sure, as we see in §2.4.5.

[77] *Id.* at 319-320. Won't this factor always be met? Everyone has the right of access to the courts to assert a claim.

helpful to remember that the law is still unfolding. You need to understand at the outset, however, that there is never a point at which all uncertainty vanishes. There are many unanswered questions in personal jurisdiction law today. That is frustrating, but a fact.

Decisions in the 1950s

After deciding *International Shoe* in 1945, the Court stayed out of personal jurisdiction jurisprudence for over a decade. Perhaps it wanted to let the state courts and the lower federal courts try their hands at applying the new test. The Court's first important new pronouncement came in 1957, with *McGee v. International Life Ins. Co.*[78] There, a Californian (Insured) purchased a life insurance contract from an Arizona company. The Arizona company was acquired by a Texas corporation, which was required by law to honor the insurance contract held by Insured. It mailed a certificate of "reinsurance" to Insured, who continued to pay his premiums by mail from California to Texas. Thereafter, Insured died, and his mother (the beneficiary under the policy) made a demand for the insurance money. The insurance company refused to pay the claim; it argued that Insured had committed suicide, which voided the policy. The beneficiary sued the Texas insurance corporation in California to recover on the policy.

The Supreme Court held that California had *in personam* jurisdiction over the Texas insurance corporation, even though the defendant's only contact with California was this single insurance policy. The defendant never solicited or accepted any other business from California. Thus, the holding makes clear, jurisdiction can be based on a single contact with the forum. The Court emphasized three things. First, "the suit was based on a contract which had substantial connection with [the forum]." In discussing *International Shoe*, we referred to this as "relatedness" between that one contact and the claim — though the Texas corporation had only one contract in California, the suit involved an alleged breach of that very contract.[79] Second, "California has a manifest interest in providing effective means of redress for its residents." This was shown by California's having passed statutes aimed at regulating the insurance industry. Third, the balance of inconveniences favored allowing the plaintiff to sue in California. It would be far more difficult for the beneficiary (a widow

---

[78] 355 U.S. 220 (1957).

[79] This case falls within Box 4 in the *International Shoe* chart on page 72, because it involves casual contact with the forum, but a claim that arises from that contact. We labeled that box "maybe" for jurisdiction. On the facts of this case, though, *McGee* falls on the "yes" side of "maybe."

whose son has died) to go to Texas to sue than it would be for the Texas corporation to defend in California.[80]

With the expansive readings of *Pennoyer* in the early twentieth century (discussed in §2.4.2) and the expansive reading of *International Shoe* in *McGee*, some observers began to wonder if the Court would ever say no to an assertion of personal jurisdiction. It did so the following year in *Hanson v. Denckla*.[81] There, a wealthy Pennsylvania widow, Mrs. Donner, set up a trust in Delaware with a Delaware bank.[82] Under the trust, Mrs. Donner received periodic payments of the interest and reserved the right to designate the persons who would receive the property placed in trust.[83] She moved to Florida and continued to receive the periodic interest payments there and issued occasional orders to the Delaware bank from there. Mrs. Donner died in Florida. Her will designated (among other things) who should receive the trust assets.

Mrs. Donner's estate was probated in Florida and litigation ensued between siblings fighting over the assets of her estate. One question was whether the trustee (the Delaware bank) was subject to *in personam* jurisdiction in Florida. The Supreme Court held that it was not, and injected a new term into the *International Shoe* test: *purposeful availment.* To have a relevant contact under the minimum contacts test, the defendant must have "purposefully avail[ed] itself of the privilege of conducting activities within the forum State, thus invoking the benefits and protections of its laws."[84] The Delaware bank did not do so. Instead, its ties with Florida were caused by Mrs. Donner's moving there. This "unilateral activity of those who claim some relationship with a nonresident defendant cannot satisfy the requirement of contact with the forum State."[85] Thus, Florida lacked jurisdiction over the Delaware bank because that bank had done nothing to avail itself of the privilege of conducting activities in Florida.

---

[80] Interestingly, Justice Black wrote the opinion in *McGee*. Recall that he wrote a concurrence in *International Shoe* that criticized the open-ended methodology of that case. Here, he demonstrates that, as a judge, he realized that he lost on that issue and is now required to apply the test he did not favor adopting. Moreover, given his nervousness that the Court would use the new test to limit the jurisdictional reach of state courts, he may have been pleased to write the opinion upholding jurisdiction in this case.

[81] 357 U.S. 235 (1958).

[82] You will study trusts in an upper-division course on Wills and Trusts. A trust is a very handy vehicle for permitting someone with assets to provide for herself or others without having to take on the burden of investing the assets. The owner, known as the *settlor*, transfers legal title of the assets (usually money or stock) to the *trustee*, who is then under a legal duty to invest and care for the assets for the benefit of the *beneficiaries*. The settlor can be one of the beneficiaries.

[83] This is called the *corpus* of the trust. Remember from the preceding footnote that the settlor (Mrs. Donner) placed the corpus of the trust into the trust, and received only the interest during her life. That left the entire corpus to be distributed when Mrs. Donner died.

[84] 357 U.S. at 253.

[85] *Id.*

The Court contrasted the case with *McGee*. Though Mrs. Donner carried on some trust administration from Florida, the Delaware bank did nothing to reach out to Florida in the way the Texas insurance company reached into California in *McGee*. There, the Texas corporation solicited the contract of insurance from California (indeed, recall, it was required by law to honor the contract, which had been entered by a corporation it acquired).

Not everyone is convinced that the Court was right in *Hanson*. After all, the Delaware bank did send periodic interest payments to Mrs. Donner in Florida. This seems stronger than *McGee*, in which the periodic payments on the policy went the other way — from California to Texas. The Court did not discuss these points, however, and we have to be content to gain the notion of purposeful availment as part of the test for whether a defendant has a relevant contact with the forum.[86]

Ahead to 1980: World-Wide Volkswagen

The Supreme Court then left *in personam* jurisdiction alone for two decades.[87] It returned with the celebrated case of *World-Wide Volkswagen v. Woodson*.[88] The facts are tragic. The Robinson family decided to move from Massena, New York, to Tucson, largely for health reasons. To make the trip, they bought a new Audi from Seaway Volkswagen in Massena. While driving through Tulsa, the Audi was rear-ended by a vehicle driven by an uninsured drunk driver. The Audi burst into flames. Only the heroic efforts of a Good Samaritan saved the two family members who were in the Audi (the others were in another vehicle). Those two, particularly Mrs. Robinson, suffered horrible personal injuries in the fire.

---

[86] Some people feel that the Court strained to hold that there was no jurisdiction in *Hanson* because a contrary holding would have benefitted family members who seem to have struck the Court as greedy.

[87] The Court did decide an important QIR-2 case in 1977, *Shaffer v. Heitner*, addressed later in this section. In addition, it decided *Kulko v. Superior Court* in 1978, which we discuss while addressing *World-Wide Volkswagen*. It did not have a blockbuster *in personam* opinion, however, until *World-Wide*.

[88] 444 U.S. 286 (1980). The name "Woodson" in the case name refers to the state-court trial judge who held that Oklahoma did have personal jurisdiction. As discussed in Chapter 6, the defendants then had a choice — they could proceed to trial or seek "extraordinary relief" from an appellate court in the Oklahoma system. They attempted the latter, seeking a "writ of prohibition" from the Oklahoma Supreme Court. This is an original proceeding in the appellate court, and in Oklahoma practice, the trial-court judge is named as the respondent. (In other states, only the court (not the individual judge) is named.) That does not mean that they sued Judge Woodson as a defendant. Judges are absolutely immune from damages claims for acts taken in their judicial capacity. Rather, Woodson was just named as the respondent in the proceeding by which the defendants sought review by a higher court. See §6.3.

The injured persons sued in an Oklahoma state court. The principal theory of the case was that the gas tank of the car was positioned unsafely, in a way that led to the explosion when the car was hit from the rear. The plaintiffs sued four defendants: (1) the manufacturer of the car (Audi, a German corporation); (2) the North American importer (Volkswagen of North America); (3) the regional distributor (World-Wide Volkswagen), which distributed Audis in New York, Connecticut, and New Jersey; and (4) the dealer that sold the car (Seaway), which did business only in Massena, New York. By the time the matter got to the Supreme Court, the only issue was whether the third and fourth defendants (World-Wide and Seaway) were subject to *in personam* jurisdiction in Oklahoma. The other two defendants either did not contest jurisdiction or abandoned that defense by that time.

The Supreme Court held that World-Wide and Seaway were not subject to jurisdiction in Oklahoma.[89] The reason was essentially the same for finding no jurisdiction in *Hanson* — the defendants had no relevant contact with Oklahoma because they did not purposefully avail themselves of any benefit in Oklahoma. Along the way, however, the Court shed more light on the purpose of the *International Shoe* test. (The problem is that some of the light was then put out by a subsequent case. Again, remember, determining the state of the law today requires review of various ebbs and flows along the way.)

According to the majority opinion, written by Justice White and adopted by five other Justices, the minimum contacts test serves two purposes. First, it protects defendants from litigation in an unduly burdensome forum and, second, it ensures that states (through their courts) do not impinge upon the sovereignty of other states by overreaching their own jurisdictional power. He then explained that the minimum contacts test does (as we expected) consist of two parts: contact and fairness. And the two parts serve the respective purposes of the overall test. That is, the insistence on "fair play and substantial justice" is meant to protect the defendant from litigation in an inappropriate forum. And the insistence on "contact" between the defendant and the forum protects against the usurpation of power by one state over another.

This is a handy dichotomy — the constitutional test consists of two prongs, each of which works toward protecting one of two interests. Oddly, however, just two years later, in *Insurance Corp. v. Companie des Bauxites*,[90] the Court disagreed with the analysis in *World-wide*

---

[89] It thus reversed the decision of the Oklahoma Supreme Court, which had upheld jurisdiction over these two defendants. Remember from §1.2.2 that the Supreme Court can review decisions by the highest state court only on matters of federal law. Obviously, the question of whether jurisdiction in Oklahoma comports with the Constitution is a question of federal law.

[90] 456 U.S. 694 (1982).

Volkswagen in one particular. (More oddly, that opinion was also by Justice White.) In *Insurance Corp.*, he wrote for the Court that the minimum contacts test serves only one goal: "a function of the individual liberty interest preserved by the Due Process Clause."[91] Thus, the part about restraining states from overreaching is not a due process goal in itself, but merely part of the larger concern of protecting the defendant from litigation in an inappropriate forum. Though it is strange for the Court to change its mind (especially so quickly and in opinions by the same Justice) over the purpose of a test, we need not make too much of this. At the end of the day, the factors laid out by *World-Wide Volkswagen* are still the relevant points to address, even while keeping in mind that the Court changed its mind about *why* those factors are relevant.

The Fairness Factors. In *World-Wide Volkswagen*, the Court listed five factors as relevant to assessing the "fairness" part of the jurisdictional inquiry. The Court has consistently listed them ever since. They are

1. the burden on the defendant, which the Court calls "a primary concern";
2. the forum state's interest in adjudicating the dispute, for which the Court properly cites *McGee*;
3. the plaintiff's interest in obtaining convenient and effective relief;
4. "the interstate judicial system's interest in obtaining the most efficient resolution of controversies"; and
5. "the shared interest of the several States in furthering fundamental substantive social policies."

For the third and fifth factors, the Court cited *Kulko v. Superior Court.*[92] In that case, a New York couple obtained a divorce in that state. The ex-husband had custody of their two children and remained in New York. The ex-wife moved to California. Later, the children wanted to live with their mother. The father agreed and purchased a one-way ticket for one of the children to go to California. (The mother bought the ticket for the other child.) The mother then sued the father in California for child support. The Supreme Court held that the father was not subject to *in personam* jurisdiction in California, because sending the child to that state did not constitute a sufficient contact to support jurisdiction, even for a claim for child support. The father had not "purposefully availed" himself of the benefits and protections of California.

On the "substantive social policies" point, the Court concluded that permitting suit against the father in California would discourage parents from accommodating the interest of family harmony. Specifically, if the father knew that sending his children to California would subject him to personal

---

[91] *Id.* at 702-703 & n.10.
[92] 436 US. 84 (1978).

jurisdiction there, he might not have acquiesced in their desire to be with their mother. This is not persuasive. Imagine the case from the other viewpoint: If a mother who agrees to take on the responsibility for raising the children in California has to go to New York to sue for child support, how likely is it that she will accept the responsibility? Moreover, why does California not have a great interest in allowing the mother to sue in California? After all, if the children are not cared for, they will become a drain on the California welfare system. The Court did not address these points. The Court rarely discusses these sorts of social policies. Another example, seen below, is *Keeton v. Hustler Magazine.*

The Absolute Prerequisite: Relevant Contact. Back to *World-Wide Volkswagen.* After listing the relevant factors for assessing the fairness side of the *International Shoe* test, the Court made clear that fairness considerations were only relevant *after* the court found a relevant contact. No matter how overwhelming the showing of fairness in the forum might be, there can be no jurisdiction without an initial finding that the defendant has a relevant contact with the forum. The holding in *World-Wide Volkswagen* is based on this point: Oklahoma lacked personal jurisdiction over World-Wide and Seaway because the Court found "a total absence of those affiliating circumstances that are a necessary predicate to any exercise of state-court jurisdiction."[93]

The Court noted that the defendants did not sell or service cars in Oklahoma. They did not solicit business there or have salespeople there. Nor did they regularly sell cars to Oklahoma residents or seek to serve the Oklahoma market. There was only one tie between the defendants and Oklahoma: One car they sold in New York exploded when hit from the rear in Oklahoma. (Remember throughout this discussion that the only defendants relevant here are World-Wide Volkswagen, which distributed vehicles in New York, Connecticut, and New Jersey; and Seaway, which sold vehicles only in Massena, New York.) This tie, the Court concluded, was simply not sufficient. Indeed, like the tie between the Delaware bank and Florida in *Hanson v. Denckla*, the connection between the defendants and Oklahoma resulted from the "unilateral activities" of the plaintiffs — they drove the car to Oklahoma; the defendants did not reach out to Oklahoma.

The Court addressed the notion of foreseeability. The plaintiffs argued that it was foreseeable that a vehicle sold in Massena, New York, would be involved in an accident in Oklahoma. The Court agreed that it might be foreseeable that the automobile would get to Oklahoma. But if that sort of foreseeability were sufficient for personal jurisdiction, there would have been jurisdiction in *Hanson* and in *Kulko*. After all, the Court noted, it was foreseeable that Mrs. Donner would move to Florida and that Mr.

---

[93] 444 U.S. at 295.

Kulko might send his daughter to California. That sort of foreseeability is irrelevant. Rather, the Court held, it must be foreseeable "that the defendant's conduct and connection with the forum State are such that he should reasonably anticipate being haled into court there."[94] Based on the facts, the Court concluded, it was not.

Thus, as part of assessing whether the defendant has a relevant contact with the forum, the Court insists on purposeful availment by the defendant of the forum *resulting in* its being foreseeable that the defendant would get sued there. Again, foreseeability of the product's reaching the forum is not enough; it must be foreseeable that the defendant would be sued there. But this reasoning seems circular. If it is foreseeable that a product would get to State X, is it not foreseeable that if the product malfunctions, there will be a lawsuit there?

Justice Brennan wrote a lengthy dissent, much of which is included in most casebooks. He argued that the majority insists too much on a contact as a prerequisite to jurisdiction. He suggested that there be a sliding scale. If the showing of fairness is overwhelming, he suggests, there ought to be jurisdiction on a lesser showing of contact. He also made much of the interstate system of highways, and that the defendants benefitted from Oklahoma highways by selling the car in New York. Justice Marshall, joined by Justice Blackmun, ran with this ball in his dissent, arguing that the defendants sell more cars in New York because they can be driven to places such as Oklahoma. Thus, they argued, the majority erred when it held there was no relevant contact between the two defendants and Oklahoma.

Recap. *World-Wide Volkswagen* is helpful because it makes certain things clear. First, the *International Shoe* test does consist of two parts: contact and fairness. Second, a relevant contact is absolutely necessary before fairness is assessed. In other words, without a relevant contact, all the fairness in the world will not give a court personal jurisdiction. Third, in assessing contact, there must be purposeful availment and foreseeability. Purposeful availment, as we saw in *Hanson*, consists of the defendant's doing something to avail herself of the benefits of the forum in some way. Foreseeability means that it must be foreseeable that the defendant would get sued in the forum. Finally, the Court set out (albeit in dictum) five factors to be addressed in assessing whether the exercise of jurisdiction in the forum would be fair. On the other hand, there is something less than satisfying about *World-Wide Volkswagen*. Many readers cannot help but feel that the Court would have upheld jurisdiction over the defendants in a state closer to New York than Oklahoma — say, Pennsylvania or Kentucky. Still, it is impossible to point to language in the opinion that would justify such a conclusion.

---

[94] 444 U.S. at 297.

Two Defamation Cases in 1984: Keeton *and* Calder

In 1984, the Court decided two companion cases upholding personal jurisdiction in defamation cases. In one, *Keeton v. Hustler Magazine*,[95] the plaintiff, a New York citizen, sued the publisher of a magazine in New Hampshire, seeking to recover for damage to her reputation caused by an article published by the magazine. She sued in New Hampshire because it had a longer statute of limitations than any other state and the case would not be barred there. The Court upheld jurisdiction not only for a claim of damage caused by publication in New Hampshire, but also for injury suffered in any other state as a result of the distribution of the magazine. The case, like *Kulko*, then permitted the Court to comment on the shared substantive policies that might support the fairness of exercising personal jurisdiction. According to the Court, New Hampshire had a "substantial interest in cooperating with other States . . . to provide a forum for efficiently litigating all issues and damages claims arising out of a libel in a unitary proceeding."[96]

In *Calder v. Jones*,[97] the Court upheld jurisdiction in California over the writer and editor of a story that allegedly defamed the actress Shirley Jones.[98] The article was published in the National Enquirer and there was no question about personal jurisdiction over the magazine. The question was whether the writer and editor of the story — both of whom worked only in Florida — could be sued in California. The Court emphasized that these defendants "aimed" their efforts at California, which is where Jones lived and would suffer the greatest harm. *Calder* is significant because it makes obvious what most people considered likely before — that the relevant contact between the defendant and the forum can be established not only by the defendant's going to the forum and doing something there, but by her intentionally causing an effect there. Some people refer to this as the "*Calder*-effects" test.

---

[95] 465 U.S. 770 (1984).

[96] *Id.* at 777. The case involved the "single publication rule," which you might study in Torts. It stands for the proposition that a single publication of a defamatory utterance gives rise to only one claim, in which all damages suffered in all jurisdictions can be recovered. So when an issue of a magazine defames someone, the single publication rule impels the plaintiff to bring one case, seeking to recover for all the damage caused everywhere. The rule stands for the proposition that the plaintiff cannot sue 50 times — once in each state, for the harm caused in that state. This gives an example of cooperation among the states, as New Hampshire allows the plaintiff to recover for harm caused, say, in Florida, without having to burden the Florida courts with a suit. The Court elaborated that the single publication rule "reduces the potential serious drain of libel cases on judicial resources. It also serves to protect defendants from harassment resulting from multiple suits." 465 U.S. at 777.

[97] *Id.* at 783 (1984).

[98] Shirley Jones was an enormously successful star of movies, particularly musicals (including *Oklahoma*). In the 1970s and 80s she made a comeback on television as the mom in *The Partridge Family*, in which her real-life son David Cassidy also starred.

- *D* mails a package containing a bomb from New York to *P* in California. *P* opens the package in California, the bomb explodes, and *P* is injured. *P* sues in California for damages caused by the bomb. It seems obvious that *D* is subject to *in personam* jurisdiction in California. She directed a package there, intending that it have the injurious effect that it did. The case seems at least as strong for jurisdiction as *Calder*.
- But didn't Mr. Kulko "aim" his daughter at California when he sent her there? Didn't doing so clearly have the effect of imposing upon the California parent the expenses of raising and supporting the child? Yet in *Kulko* the Supreme Court held that Mr. Kulko was not subject to *in personam* jurisdiction for a child support case in California. Why should sending a bomb or sending a defamatory story at the forum support jurisdiction, while sending a child does not? Perhaps it seems clear that sending a bomb or a defamatory article will cause harm in the forum, while sending a child to a state does not necessarily result in a claim. On the other hand, the child has to be fed and housed and clothed, all of which are imposed by sending the child to live with the other parent.

Burger King

Burger King Corp. v. Rudzewicz[99] is interesting on several levels. First, it involves a contract dispute, while the others cases in the *International Shoe* line involved torts. This fact should make no difference, however, in delineating the due process test for personal jurisdiction. Second, it upheld personal jurisdiction, after a series of cases (*Hanson*, *Kulko*, and *World-Wide Volkswagen*) had found no jurisdiction. Third, because the elements of contact were overwhelming, the Court had a relatively rare opportunity to flesh out the fairness component of personal jurisdiction jurisprudence. And fourth, Justice Brennan wrote the majority opinion, while Justice White dissented. This is the opposite of *World-Wide*, in which White spoke for the majority and Brennan dissented.

In *Burger King*, two men in Michigan — Rudzewicz and MacShara — entered a franchise agreement with Burger King Corporation (BK).[100] The restaurant apparently never quite got off the ground, and BK sued Rudzewicz and MacShara in federal court in Miami concerning their alleged breach of the deal.[101] The question was whether there was personal jurisdiction over the two franchisees in Florida. One cannot help but

[99] 471 U.S. 462 (1985).

[100] Rudzewicz and MacShara are the franchisees. BK is the franchisor. Most fast-food restaurants are franchises, in which the franchisees are given permission to operate the store within carefully prescribed standards.

[101] As mentioned in §2.1, however, and discussed in detail in §2.5, the fact that the case was brought in federal court is irrelevant to the personal jurisdiction inquiry. A federal court has exactly the same personal jurisdiction power that a state court does. So personal jurisdiction was proper in *Burger King* in a federal court in Florida *because* it would have been proper in a state court in Florida. In terms of subject matter jurisdiction, the case was

see the relative equities here: A huge multinational corporation wants to litigate at home and to drag two "little guys" from Michigan to litigate in BK's hometown. The Supreme Court — in an opinion by Justice Brennan, long thought to be something of a champion of the "little guy" — upheld jurisdiction in Florida.[102]

The majority opinion emphasized that there are two components to the *International Shoe* inquiry: contact and fairness. (Consistent with *Insurance Corp.*, it explained that the two parts are there to protect the defendant's liberty interest in not being subject to jurisdiction in a state in which she has no ties.) The starting point, then, consistent with *World-Wide Volkswagen*, is whether there is a relevant contact between the defendant and the forum. The tie must result from the defendant's purposeful availment and render it foreseeable that the defendant could be sued there. Justice Brennan offers some helpful discussion of purposeful availment, and makes it clear that the defendant can engage in such availment without physically entering the state. "Once it has been decided that a defendant purposefully established minimum contacts within the forum State," he said, the contacts are to be considered in light of other factors to determine whether the exercise of jurisdiction is consistent with "fair play and substantial justice." He listed the same five fairness factors laid out in *World-Wide Volkswagen*. An especially strong showing of fairness might justify jurisdiction on a lesser showing of contact, but some relevant contact is absolutely required.

In Part I-B of the opinion, the Court applies the law to the facts of the case. The conclusion that Rudzewicz and MacShara have relevant contacts with Florida was easy. The Court looked at all the factors in the negotiation of the franchise agreement. Though Rudzewicz never set foot in Florida,[103] he reached out to Florida to negotiate a 20-year, million-dollar contract with a Florida entity. The defendants (who would rather be sued in Michigan) argued that their operation was overseen by the midwest regional authority for BK in Michigan, but the Court pointed out that the corporate headquarters in Miami called all the shots and approved the deal. Moreover, the contract expressly provided that disputes would be governed by Florida law, which is another example of the defendants' availing themselves of Florida. Indeed, "it reinforced [the] deliberate affiliation

---

properly brought in federal court because of diversity of citizenship jurisdiction, discussed in detail in §4.5.

[102] Be prepared for your professor's jokes about BK wanting to "have it your way" and about this being a "whopper of a case." Are they crummy jokes? Of course, but laugh anyway. You want your professor in a good mood.

[103] MacShara attended training in Florida, at Burger King University. After the trial court held for BK, MacShara did not appeal. Thus, only Rudzewicz took the case to the Supreme Court.

with the forum State and the reasonable foreseeability of possible litigation there."[104]

The more interesting discussion in *Burger King* concerns fairness. The Court makes several things clear. First, the burden is on the defendant to demonstrate the *unfairness* of the forum. Second, mere inconvenience is not enough. The defendant must show that the forum is *unconstitutional*. Due process does not guarantee the *best* forum or even a reasonably good forum. Rather, it protects the defendant against having to litigate in an unconstitutionally bad forum. The defendant must show that litigation in the forum is "so gravely difficult and inconvenient that a party unfairly is at a severe disadvantage in comparison to his opponent."[105] Though the defendants argued that it would be difficult for them to get Michigan witnesses to go to Miami to testify for them, the Court found no support in the record that the inconvenience was of constitutional magnitude. And third, in assessing whether the burden of litigating in Florida was unduly great, the relative wealth of the parties is irrelevant. "Absent compelling considerations, a defendant who has purposefully derived commercial benefit from his affiliations in a forum may not defeat jurisdiction there simply because of his adversary's greater wealth."[106]

Finally, the majority rejected the Court of Appeals' conclusion that the franchise contract was one of "adhesion,"[107] in which BK had essentially taken advantage of the franchisees. Justice Brennan made short work of this point, emphasizing that the trial judge had found no misrepresentations or duress, and that the record supported those findings. The dissent, by Justice Stevens, joined by Justice White, was based almost entirely on the contract of adhesion point and consisted mostly of quotations from the Court of Appeals.

Recap. *Burger King* is consistent with *World-Wide Volkswagen* in setting out the requirement of a relevant contact before assessing whether the exercise of jurisdiction would be fair. It constitutes the most important discussion to date on the substantial burden a defendant must shoulder to demonstrate that the forum is unfair.

---

[104] 471 U.S. at 482. Though there was this law selection clause, the contract did not contain a forum selection clause, by which the parties would have consented to personal jurisdiction in a particular location.

[105] *Id.* at 478 (internal quotations omitted), *quoting* The Bremen v. Zapata Off-Shore Co., 407 U.S. 1, 18 (1972).

[106] *Id.* at 484 n.25 (citation omitted).

[107] You will study contracts of adhesion in Contracts. They are not enforceable because they are the result of overreaching or unfair treatment by an unduly powerful party to the deal.

Asahi *and the Stream of Commerce*

One fact pattern has long vexed the courts under *International Shoe* — that involving the "stream of commerce." The classic stream of commerce involves the defendant's manufacturing something in State *A* and sending it to State *B*. Then someone in State *B* sends it to State *C*. The thing malfunctions in State *C*, injuring the plaintiff there. The question is whether the defendant, which manufactured only in State *A* and sent the thing only to State *B*, can be sued in State *C*. On the one hand, we might say no, because the defendant did not reach out to State *C*; the thing got to State *C* only because of the unilateral act of a third party (the one in State *B* who sent the thing to State *C*). Thus, under *Hanson* and *World-Wide Volkswagen*, we might argue that there is no purposeful availment by the defendant of State *C*. On the other hand, we might say yes, because the defendant probably makes money from the resale by the person in State *B* into State *C*. In other words, if the person in State *B* did not send the thing into State *C*, the defendant would not sell as many of these things. So, arguably, the defendant, at least indirectly, availed herself of the market in State *C*.

Courts have never known quite what to do in these cases. One famous state court opinion is *Gray v. American Radiator & Standard Sanitary Corp.*,[108] in which the Illinois Supreme Court upheld jurisdiction in such a scenario. In that case, the defendant manufactured valves in Ohio and sold them only to Pennsylvania. A Pennsylvania company then put those valves into its water heaters[109] and sold the water heaters nationwide. The plaintiff bought one in Illinois. The valve malfunctioned, causing an explosion that injured the plaintiff in Illinois. The court held that Illinois courts had *in personam* jurisdiction over the Ohio valve manufacturer. Along the way, the court engaged in outright speculation that there must have been many of the Ohio corporation's valves in Illinois (despite the lack of any evidence of this in the record). The court also concluded that the Ohio company's sale of valves to the company in Pennsylvania was "in contemplation of use" in Illinois. But the later Supreme Court decision in *World-Wide* says that foreseeability of the product's getting to the forum is not the relevant test. Rather, it must be foreseeable that the defendant would get sued there.[110] Though *Gray* can be criticized on these points, it was a leading state court effort in the area. It and other state court opinions pointed out the need for guidance from the Supreme Court.

---

[108] 176 N.E.2d 761 (Ill. 1961).

[109] Why do people say "hot water heaters"? If the water is hot, it does not need to be heated. So they should be called *water heaters*.

[110] In *World-Wide Volkswagen*, the Court rejected the idea that amenability to suit should travel with the product. Nonetheless, the Court cited *Gray* with favor.

The Supreme Court finally agreed to tackle the issue in 1987, in *Asahi Metal Industry Co. v. Superior Court.*[111] The case set up a classic stream-of-commerce fact pattern, albeit in an international context. Zurcher was injured when his motorcycle crashed in California. He alleged that the wreck was caused by a problem with the rear tire. The tube for that tire was manufactured by Cheng Shin, a Taiwanese corporation. Zurcher sued Cheng Shin in California. Cheng Shin admitted that it was subject to personal jurisdiction in California. Cheng Shin filed an "impleader" claim in the case to bring in Asahi,[112] a Japanese corporation that allegedly manufactured the valve on the tube. Cheng Shin claimed that the wreck was caused by the valve, and that Asahi was required to indemnify it if it lost to Zurcher. Asahi claimed that California did not have personal jurisdiction over it. Zurcher's claim against Cheng Shin was settled, so the only issue left in the litigation was the indemnity claim by Cheng Shin against Asahi. The question of whether Asahi had established minimum contacts with California is the same as it would have been had Zurcher sued Asahi.

So we have a nice stream-of-commerce fact pattern: Asahi manufactures valves in Japan and sells them to Cheng Shin in Taiwan; Cheng Shin puts the valves into its tires in Taiwan and sells the tires to the plaintiff in California. So the Asahi valve gets into California, but not because of any direct effort by Asahi. Has Asahi purposefully availed itself of California?

Asahi is a major disappointment because of the way the Justices split on the issue of whether Asahi had a relevant contact with California. In reading the opinion, note carefully how many Justices joined each opinion. You will find that there are two theories on whether Asahi established a relevant contact with California: one espoused by Justice O'Connor and the other by Justice Brennan. Neither theory commanded a majority of the Court; each was adopted by four Justices. As a result, there is no holding on the vital question of what constitutes a relevant contact in the stream-of-commerce fact pattern.

On the other hand, eight Justices agreed, in Part II-B of the opinion, that personal jurisdiction in California would not be fair under the unusual circumstances of the case. So the holding — that California lacks personal jurisdiction over Asahi — is based upon fairness (not contact) grounds. The fact that the Justices split four-to-four on the important question of contact leaves the issue open to further argument. To date, the Court has not revisited the question. The best we can say is that two theories on this issue each garnered the support of four Justices.

The O'Connor theory (joined by Chief Justice Rehnquist and Justices Powell and Scalia) is set out in Part II-A of the opinion. She asserts that merely putting a product into the stream of commerce, even with the knowledge that it will get to the forum, is not enough. To her, purposeful

---

[111] 480 U.S. 102 (1987).
[112] We study impleader in §12.6.2.

availment requires another factor — "additional conduct" — that indicates "an intent or purpose to serve the market in the forum State."[113] Examples, according to Justice O'Connor, would include designing the product for the forum-state market, advertising in the forum, establishing channels for giving advice to customers in the forum, or marketing through a distributor who agrees to serve as the sales agent in the forum. Because Asahi had no such additional conduct in California, the O'Connor group concluded, there was no relevant contact between Asahi and California.

The Brennan theory (joined by Justices Marshall, White, and Blackmun) is set forth at the beginning of Justice Brennan's separate opinion. To Justice Brennan, so long as the defendant places a product in the stream of commerce and is "aware that the final product is being marketed in the forum State, the possibility of a lawsuit there cannot come as a surprise." Nor, he continued, would the litigation impose a burden for which there was no benefit. The defendant has benefitted economically from the retail sale of the final product in the forum. (That is, Asahi sold more valves (and made more money) because Cheng Shin was able to sell its inner tubes in California. If Cheng Shin did not sell tubes in California, Asahi would have sold fewer valves to Cheng Shin.) Brennan would not require any additional factors. On the facts of the case, the Brennan group found that there was a sufficient contact between Asahi and California.

As noted, however, eight Justices[114] concluded in Part II-B of Justice O'Connor's opinion that the assertion of jurisdiction in California would not be fair. This is the only case in which the Supreme Court has rejected personal jurisdiction on the basis of unfairness. Remember that earlier cases finding no jurisdiction (such as *Hanson* and *World-Wide Volkswagen*) were based on the lack of a relevant contact with the forum.

But the facts of *Asahi* are unique: They involve a dispute between a Taiwanese corporation and a Japanese corporation, in which California would have no discernible interest. The Court set out the same five fairness factors we saw in *World-Wide Volkswagen* and *Burger King*. The burden on Asahi was severe, having to defend thousands of miles from home in a court of a foreign country. As the case stood when it got to the Supreme Court, the only issue was whether Asahi owed Cheng Shin indemnity. This issue had nothing to do with road safety in California, and would be determined not by reference to California law, but to the contracts between the two corporations. Moreover, Cheng Shin is not a California resident, making the state's interest even more attenuated. Finally, addressing the fourth and fifth fairness factors (the interests of the states in efficiency and in shared substantive policies), the Court found an interest in trying

---

[113] 480 U.S. at 112.

[114] Justice Scalia did not join this part of the opinion. For him, the conclusion that there was no contact rendered assessment of the fairness factors superfluous.

to keep American courts from determining a dispute between foreign corporations. Thus, dismissal was warranted.

We must mention the role of Justice Stevens in *Asahi*. He could have been the tie-breaker between the O'Connor theory and the Brennan theory. Stevens filed a concurring opinion in which he simply refused to take sides. He would not agree with O'Connor because he thought the issue not necessary to a decision. In view of the holding on fairness grounds, he simply did not need to address contact. In addition, he thought there was more on the facts than mere awareness that the valve got into California; though he "was inclined" to think there was a relevant contact, he would not join either camp. It is unfortunate that he thereby robbed the Court of the opportunity to give definitive guidance on this constitutional question.

Return to Quasi-in-Rem: Shaffer v. Heitner

We now consider a case out of its chronological order: *Shaffer v. Heitner*,[115] decided in 1977. We treat it here, however, so as not to interrupt the flow of *in personam* cases. Until *Shaffer*, the Supreme Court had decided only two major *quasi-in-rem* type 2 (QIR-2) decisions: *Pennoyer* itself in 1878 and *Harris v. Balk* in 1905 (discussed in §2.4.2). The upshot of those cases was that QIR-2 jurisdiction was constitutional if the property that served as the jurisdictional predicate was attached at the outset of the case and proper notice (including publication notice) was given. In *Harris*, the Court even expanded the use of QIR-2 to allow jurisdiction based on intangible property. With *Shaffer*, the Court reassessed these principles in light of *International Shoe* and its progeny.

In *Shaffer*, a shareholder of Greyhound Corporation brought a "derivative suit" against directors of the corporation.[116] The claim was that the directors breached fiduciary duties to the corporation by permitting it to engage in an antitrust violation that resulted in the corporation's losing a judgment of $12 million. The plaintiff sought recovery of that sum from the directors of the corporation. Plaintiff sued in a state court in Delaware and attempted to exercise QIR-2 jurisdiction over the defendant directors by asking the court to attach (Delaware law uses the word *sequester*) the

---

[115] 433 U.S. 186 (1977).

[116] In a derivative suit, a shareholder sues to vindicate a claim that actually belongs to the corporation (not to the shareholder personally). The corporation is an entity in the eyes of the law, and is managed by the board of directors. The directors owe fiduciary duties (e.g., a duty of care and a duty of loyalty) to the corporation. Most derivative suits are brought against directors and allege that they breached a fiduciary duty to the corporation. The law permits a shareholder to bring such a case because it is unlikely that the directors would authorize the corporation to sue themselves for breach of fiduciary duty. Do not let the procedural stance distract you: This is essentially a case against the people who ran Greyhound, arguing that they did not do their jobs well enough, and that their mistakes cost the corporation a lot of money.

shares of stock that the defendants held in Greyhound Corp. Shares of stock represent an ownership interest in a corporation. Though ownership of stock is usually represented by a stock certificate, the interest itself is intangible property. Directors of corporations generally are not required to own stock in the company, but often do, and the relevant defendants in *Shaffer* were stockholders. A Delaware statute provided that the ownership interest represented by stock in a Delaware corporation (such as Greyhound was at the time) was "present" in Delaware. The Delaware Supreme Court upheld QIR-2 jurisdiction over the defendants. The case seems indistinguishable from *Harris v. Balk*, in which (as discussed in §2.4.2) the Court permitted the seizure of intangible property to serve as the jurisdictional predicate for QIR-2 jurisdiction.

In *Shaffer*, the Supreme Court reversed the Delaware decision, and rejected the use of QIR-2 jurisdiction. The opinion has some very broad pronouncements, but also has language that seems to limit the reach of those pronouncements, at least in some circumstances. Not surprisingly, the ultimate impact of *Shaffer* is still debated. One enormously important question — which has an impact in the next case we study — is whether the Court in *Shaffer* determined that *International Shoe* supplanted *Pennoyer* or, on the other hand, whether the two can coexist.

In Part II of his opinion for the majority in *Shaffer*, Justice Marshall reviewed the evolution of *in personam* doctrine from *Pennoyer* to *International Shoe*. He concluded that "the relationship among the defendant, the forum, and the litigation, rather than the mutually exclusive sovereignty of the States on which the rules of *Pennoyer* rest, became the central concern of the inquiry into personal jurisdiction."[117] He then noted that "[n]o equally dramatic change has occurred in the law governing jurisdiction *in rem*." But, he said, there have been "intimations that the collapse of the *in personam* wing of *Pennoyer* has not left that decision unweakened as a foundation for *in rem* jurisdiction."[118]

Wait a minute. When and where did the "*in personam* wing of *Pennoyer*" collapse? True, *International Shoe* and later cases have looked at different factors than *Pennoyer*, as we have discussed. But the Court never expressly *overruled Pennoyer*. Indeed, in *International Shoe*, the Court laid out the minimum contacts test as relevant *for cases in which the defendant is not present in the forum*. The clear implication of that, as noted in §2.4.3, is that presence of the defendant in the forum (when served with process), in itself, would continue to support *in personam* jurisdiction.

At any rate, the Court in *Shaffer* was facing a QIR-2 matter. Part III of the opinion is the most important. Start with its conclusion. The last sentence of the section is widely cited and sweeping: "We therefore conclude that all assertions of state-court jurisdiction must be evaluated according

---

[117] 433 U.S. at 204.
[118] *Id.* at 205.

to the standards set forth in *International Shoe* and its progeny."[119] This seems clearly to mean, then, that in *in rem* and *quasi-in-rem* cases, the relevant inquiry is not simply whether the property serving as the jurisdictional predicate is attached at the outset, but, instead, whether the defendant has such minimum contacts with the forum that the exercise of jurisdiction would not offend traditional notions of fair play and substantial justice.[120]

Read Part III of the opinion carefully, however. It may be that the broad conclusory statement is not all that broad. In the second paragraph of Part III, the Court is careful to note that "the presence of property in a State may bear on the existence of jurisdiction by providing contacts among the forum State, the defendant, and the litigation."[121] It then discusses two important examples. First, "when claims to the property itself are the source of the underlying controversy, it would be unusual for the State where the property is located not to have jurisdiction."[122] In footnote 24, it makes clear that this sentence refers to *in rem* and QIR-1 cases. In such disputes, the Court says, the defendant's claim to the property would indicate that she expected to benefit from the state's protection of the interest. Thus, the state would have a strong interest in assuring that the property is marketable and that the dispute is resolved peacefully. In addition, the relevant evidence and witnesses will be present in the forum. Thus, in *in rem* and QIR-1 cases, *the presence of the property in the forum probably satisfies the requirement that the defendant meet the* International Shoe *test.*

Second, in the same paragraph, the Court indicates that the "presence of property may also favor jurisdiction in cases . . . where the defendant's ownership of the property is conceded but the cause of action is otherwise related to rights and duties growing out of that ownership."[123] This language refers to QIR-2 cases in which the property that is the jurisdictional predicate *caused* the injury to the plaintiff. The main example here, as the Court notes, is an injury on land owned by an absentee.

- ○ *D*, a citizen of New York, owns rental property in Florida. *P*, a citizen of Michigan, rents the property. While there, ceiling tiles in the rental property fall on *P*'s head, injuring her. Assuming there is no *in personam* jurisdiction, *P* may proceed with QIR-2 by having the rental property attached at the outset. The fact that *D* owns the property, and that the property

---

[119] *Id.* at 212.

[120] More broadly, some have asserted that this means literally that *all* cases, including *in personam* cases in which the defendant is served with process in the forum. The Court gets to that in a 1990 case, which is discussed starting at page 93.

[121] 433 U.S. at 207.

[122] *Id.*

[123] *Id.* at 208.

itself caused the injury, seem to satisfy the requirement that D's contacts with Florida satisfy the *International Shoe* test.

Third, in footnote 30, the Court indicates that other jurisdictional doctrines, such as that regarding adjudication of status, may also be consistent with *International Shoe*. Remember from §2.4.2 that *Pennoyer* treated questions of status — such as marriage and divorce — as not being *in personam*. Thus, it was not necessary to get *in personam* jurisdiction over the defendant. Surely, the state interest in determining such status questions is great. And it seems clear from this footnote that *Shaffer* has no effect on the jurisdictional rules concerning such cases.

After discussing these examples, the Court concludes that "jurisdiction over many types of actions which now are or might be brought *in rem* would not be affected by a holding that any assertion of State-court jurisdiction must satisfy the *International Shoe* standard."[124] Indeed, what change is wrought by *Shaffer*? The Court addresses it in the remainder of Part III of the opinion, where it discusses QIR-2 cases in which the property seized "is completely unrelated to the plaintiff's cause of action." Here, the Court (quite properly, it seems) concludes that seizure of the property is essentially a substitute for jurisdiction over the person. So if jurisdiction over the person would require satisfaction of *International Shoe*, so should QIR-2.

Thus, in *Shaffer*, Delaware could not have jurisdiction simply by seizing property owned by the defendants in Delaware. Rather, there must be a showing that the defendants' contacts with Delaware satisfy the *International Shoe* standard. In Part IV of the opinion, the Court concluded that they did not, and thus that Delaware lacked jurisdiction over the defendants. The Court recognized that Delaware might well have an interest in policing whether directors of Delaware corporations perform their fiduciary duties in accordance with state law. But Delaware had never based jurisdiction on the fiduciary capacity of these people. Instead, jurisdiction was based on ownership of stock, which has no necessary correlation with being a director. The Court concluded that the defendants lacked a relevant contact with Delaware.

The separate opinions of various Justices deserve attention. Justice Powell concurred in the holding that *International Shoe* should govern on the facts in *Shaffer*, but would not have reached the question of "whether the ownership of some forms of property whose situs is indisputably and permanently located within a State may, without more, provide the contacts necessary to subject a defendant to jurisdiction within the State to the extent of the value of the property." Thus, as to real property, he would have retained the traditional rule that seizure at the outset

---

[124] *Id.*

of the case is sufficient, at least in *in rem* and QIR-1 cases. Again, the majority seems to have admitted as much; Justice Powell probably wrote in an abundance of caution. Justice Brennan agreed that *International Shoe* should apply but thought the Delaware court should be given a chance to apply that test. He went on to conclude that the defendants' contacts would satisfy *International Shoe*.

So what are we to make of *Shaffer*? No doubt it overrules *Harris v. Balk* and that part of *Pennoyer* that would uphold QIR-2 jurisdiction simply on the basis of seizure of the property at the outset of the case. Clearly, in cases such as *Harris v. Balk* and *Mitchell v. Neff*, today the plaintiff must demonstrate that the defendant's contacts with the forum satisfy *International Shoe*. But the Court went out of its way to note that the presence of the property — by itself — will generally satisfy that standard in *in rem* and QIR-1 cases, in QIR-2 cases in which the property caused the injury suffered by the plaintiff, and in cases involving status. Thus, at the end of the day, the sweeping language — that all assertions of jurisdiction must be assessed under *International Shoe* — may really change only the way the world works in QIR-2 cases in which the property did not cause the injury.

Very shortly after the decision in *Shaffer*, the Delaware legislature passed a statute providing that every nonresident director of a Delaware corporation "shall be deemed" to have consented to the appointment of an agent for service of process and thus to *in personam* jurisdiction in Delaware.[125] No one has suggested that *Hess v. Pawloski* and the notion of implied consent is no longer valid, so such a statute would seem effective to grant *in personam* jurisdiction. On the other hand, however, *Shaffer* did say that "all assertions" of state-court jurisdiction must satisfy *International Shoe*. Does that mean that traditional bases, such as residence, consent, and presence in the forum when being served with process, are swept aside in favor of the *International Shoe* equation?

The Most Recent Word: The Burnham *Case*

The Court was forced to visit this question in 1990, in *Burnham v. Superior Court*,[126] which remains its most recent effort in personal jurisdiction. Dennis Burnham lived in New Jersey. His wife, Francie, lived in California with the couple's two children. The couple had separated and apparently agreed that Francie would file for divorce in California. But Dennis filed for divorce in New Jersey. Dennis went on a business trip to California and then went to visit his children in that state. When he returned

---

[125] 10 Del. Code §3114. The Delaware Supreme Court held that the statute is valid in *Armstrong v. Pomerance*, 423 A.2d 174 (Del. 1980).

[126] 495 U.S. 604 (1990).

to Francie's house after an outing with one child, he was served with process in a California action for divorce and monetary support.[127] Dennis claimed that California lacked *in personam* jurisdiction over him for that case.

The issue was thus set up perfectly — does service of process within the forum give *in personam* jurisdiction, or does jurisdiction have to be assessed under *International Shoe*? In other words, does service in the forum, called *transient* or *tag* jurisdiction — which was recognized in *Pennoyer* — exist as an independent basis of *in personam* jurisdiction? Or, instead, must the defendant have such contacts with the forum to satisfy *International Shoe*? Moreover, everyone agreed that the claim was unrelated to Dennis's presence in California. The claim arose in New Jersey. Because of this, the case required that California be able to assert "general jurisdiction," which we discussed in §2.4.2 and again in §2.4.5.

In *Burnham*, all nine Justices agreed that Dennis was subject to general *in personam* jurisdiction in California. They differed, however, as to why. And, just as in *Asahi*, the Justices split four-to-four on the key issue. So, just as with *Asahi*, the case fails to resolve the core issue definitively.

Justice Scalia, in an opinion joined by Chief Justice Rehnquist and Justices White and Kennedy, concluded that jurisdiction can be based on presence in the forum when the defendant was served with process — without assessment of the *International Shoe* standard. The conclusion is based in some measure on historical assessment — that service of process on the defendant in the forum was recognized by Roman law and at English common law. More important, courts in this country accepted the notion at the time the Fourteenth Amendment was ratified. Not until 1978, in the wake of the broad language of *Shaffer* (that "all assertions" of personal jurisdiction must be assessed under *International Shoe*) did a single U.S. court ever suggest that service in the forum was not sufficient to establish general jurisdiction. Since then, the overwhelming majority of courts has continued to apply jurisdiction based on service in the forum.

To this group of Justices, then, *International Shoe* permits exercises of jurisdiction that would not have been permitted under *Pennoyer*, but does not displace the *Pennoyer* bases, including in-forum service on the defendant. To them, service in-state is not *necessary* to the exercise of *in personam* jurisdiction, but certainly remains *sufficient* for the exercise of personal jurisdiction. And, as noted in §2.4.2, the Court in *International Shoe* set forth its minimum contacts test only after saying that "the defendant be not present in the forum." So *International Shoe* itself seemed clearly to recognize that presence when served is itself sufficient to establish general personal jurisdiction. Finally, these Justices asked, how can a

---

[127] If the case were simply for divorce, the Court could have discussed status as a basis of personal jurisdiction. Instead, the case involved a claim for monetary recovery (e.g., child support) and was for that reason an *in personam* case.

basis of jurisdiction that has been part of the legal landscape for centuries be antithetical to "traditional notions of fair play and substantial justice"? Three of the four Justices (not including Justice White) opined in Parts II-D and III of Justice Scalia's opinion that *Shaffer*'s broad pronouncement (that "all assertions of state court jurisdiction" be assessed under *International Shoe*) applied only to *in rem* and *quasi-in-rem* cases.

On the other hand, Justice Brennan, in an opinion joined by Justices Marshall, Blackmun, and O'Connor, concluded that the historical pedigree of jurisdiction based on service in the forum is not enough *by itself* to justify it. To them, *Shaffer* meant that *all* assertions of personal jurisdiction — even those set forth in *Pennoyer*, must be assessed by the *International Shoe* test. In other words, *International Shoe* replaced *Pennoyer* and does not exist alongside it. It is important to remember, however, that these Justices also agreed — based on the application of *International Shoe* — that Dennis Burnham was subject to general jurisdiction in California. Note, then, that Justice Brennan concludes that Dennis Burnham's spending a few days in California is sufficient purposeful availment to subject him to general jurisdiction there![128]

How does he reach this conclusion? Justice Brennan says that any transient defendant avails herself of "significant benefits provided by the State." He mentions three: (1) the health and safety of the transient are protected by the state's police and other services; (2) the transient is free to travel in the state; and (3) the transient "likely enjoys the fruits" of the state's economy as well. Moreover, because of privileges and immunities, the state cannot deny her privileges it accords citizens, including access to the courts. On the other hand, there are only slight burdens on the transient. Modern transportation and communications make it easier for her to defend herself in a distant state. Indeed, says Justice Brennan, the defendant has already journeyed to the forum at least once, so she can hardly complain about the burden. Accordingly, "as a rule the exercise of personal jurisdiction over a defendant based on his voluntary presence in the forum will satisfy the requirements of due process."[129]

It is difficult to understand how Justice Brennan's reasoning would not result in the exercise of general *in personam* jurisdiction over *anyone* who had spent a couple of days in California (or any other state). He seems to conclude that the benefits gained simply by being there outweigh the burden of having to defend in the forum. Indeed, as Justice Scalia points out in Part III of his opinion, Justice Brennan seems to say that California can

---

[128] Part III of Justice Scalia's opinion responds point by point to what Justice Brennan says on this score. Reasonable people can disagree, and you should draw your own conclusions. You should also be aware of what your professor thinks. I find Scalia's argument is far stronger.

[129] 495 U.S. at 639.

exercise general jurisdiction based on these contacts, regardless of whether the defendant was served with process there.

Whatever one thinks of Justice Brennan's reasoning in applying the *International Shoe* test, the bigger point is clear: The Justices split four-to-four on whether that case supplanted the *Pennoyer* bases of personal jurisdiction. Thus, there is no definitive ruling on this important point. As in *Asahi*, we must look at Justice Stevens's role. Again, he refused to adopt either approach espoused by his colleagues. In so doing, again, he ensured that the Court would not produce a clear holding.

In most instances, as in *Burnham* itself, the Scalia approach and the Brennan approach reach the same result. The choice of theory could become important — indeed, determinative — depending on the facts.

- *D* is a citizen of Georgia. She plans a vacation in California, and decides to drive from Atlanta to San Diego. On the way, she drives through Texas. She stays a night in a hotel in Dallas. *P* serves *D* with process in Dallas for a suit in Texas, concerning a claim that arose in Hawaii.
  - Under the Scalia approach, Texas would have jurisdiction because the defendant was served with process in the forum. Moreover, this traditional basis has always supported general jurisdiction, so the fact that the claim arose in Hawaii is irrelevant.
  - Under the Brennan approach, Texas would also have jurisdiction. Like Dennis Burnham in California, *D* here intended to go to Texas and gained some benefit from being there. It is not clear from Justice Brennan's opinion whether the defendant must be in the state a given time to avail herself of enough benefits to justify the exercise of jurisdiction. Here, *D* is only in Texas for a day or so. But she stayed in a hotel there and thus seems to have availed herself of the fruits of the economy of the state.
- Same facts, but instead of driving, *D* flies from Atlanta to San Diego. She has to change planes in Dallas, and is served with process in the airport in Dallas for the case in Texas (concerning the claim that arose in Hawaii).
  - Under the Scalia approach, Texas has jurisdiction, because *D* was served with process while in the forum.
  - Under the Brennan approach, perhaps Texas has jurisdiction. After all, *D* intentionally went to Texas. On the other hand, she was not there very long. Is a couple of hours in the Dallas airport sufficient availment to justify jurisdiction? Who knows?
- Same facts, but *D* books a nonstop flight from Atlanta to San Diego. The plane develops engine trouble over Texas and lands in Dallas to get mechanical attention. *D* is served with process while in the airport in Dallas for the action in Texas (concerning the claim that arose in Hawaii).
  - Under the Scalia approach, Texas probably has jurisdiction, because *D* was served with process in the forum. While she did not intend to go there, she was not forced or tricked into the forum.
  - Under the Brennan approach, this may be a tough case. Unlike the previous questions, here *D* did not intend to go to Texas. She did not

direct her actions toward that state. On the other hand, she may be in Texas longer than she would have been under the preceding hypothetical. (After all, it may take longer to fix the plane than to change planes.) While in the Dallas airport, is *D* availing herself of protections of Texas? Is she partaking of the fruits of the economy of Texas?

A Quick Recap

Pennoyer gave us the traditional bases for the exercise of *in personam* jurisdiction: (1) service of process on the defendant in the forum; (2) residence in the forum; (3) consent; and (4) service of process on the defendant's agent in the forum. *International Shoe* lays out an amorphous test involving assessment of the defendant's contact with the forum and an assessment of whether the exercise of jurisdiction would be fair. The *International Shoe* test has undergone significant refinement and clarification, but remains an amorphous undertaking.

Though *Shaffer* said that "all assertions of state court jurisdiction" must be assessed under *International Shoe*, the Court has never held that residence and consent are not sufficient in themselves. Indeed, given cases like *Milliken v. Meyer* and *Hess v. Pawloski*, it seems quite unlikely that one should have to assess minimum contacts when the defendant resides in the forum or consents to jurisdiction in the forum. As to presence, however, we have a four-to-four split on whether it is a basis for jurisdiction independent of *International Shoe*.

In the non-*in personam* arena, *Shaffer* clearly holds that *International Shoe* must be assessed. Rather than focus on seizure of the jurisdictional predicate at the outset of the case, the court must inquire whether the defendant has minimum contacts with the forum. On the other hand, though, the Court indicated that presence of the property — in itself — satisfies the requirement of *International Shoe* in *in rem*, QIR-1, and status cases, as well as in QIR-2 cases in which the property caused the plaintiff's injury.

§2.4.5 General Jurisdiction

We first saw the concept of general personal jurisdiction in the wake of *International Shoe* in §2.4.3. That case set out two variables: the defendant's level of activity in the forum and whether the plaintiff's claim is related to the defendant's activity in the forum. We placed those variables on a chart on page 72, which created four scenarios, which we labeled as Boxes 1, 2, 3, and 4. Box 3 addressed situations in which the defendant's activity in the forum is "continuous and systematic," but in which the claim is unrelated to that contact. That box was labeled "maybe," indicating that there are cases (as the Court recognized in *International Shoe*) in which the defendant's contacts with the forum may be so substantial that she can be sued there even on a claim that arose elsewhere.

Before *International Shoe* called our attention to this possibility, we had pretty much assumed that the forum had general personal jurisdiction. *Pennoyer* laid out the traditional bases of personal jurisdiction, without expressing concern about whether the claim arose from the defendant's contact with the forum. If anything, we probably assumed that service of process on the defendant in the forum gave the state personal jurisdiction to adjudicate *any* claim against the defendant. Indeed, it was not until *Hess v. Pawloski,* and its treatment of a nonresident motorist statute, discussed in §2.4.2, that we started talking about *specific* jurisdiction — that is, jurisdiction for a claim arising from or related to the defendant's contacts with the forum. That limitation was imposed by the Massachusetts statute being applied in *Hess*, probably because the state legislature was nervous about exercising jurisdiction based on implied consent.

The Supreme Court has decided only two cases based directly on the notion of general personal jurisdiction: *Perkins v. Benguet Consolidated Mining Co.*[130] in 1952 and *Helicópteros Nacionales de Columbia, S.A. v. Hall*[131] in 1984. In the former case, it upheld general *in personam* jurisdiction, and in the latter it rejected it. The opinions make clear that general jurisdiction is appropriate when the defendant's contacts with the forum are "continuous and systematic," but do not do much to help us assess what that phrase means.

In *Perkins*, the defendant was a corporation formed under Philippine law. Though the company was forced to suspend its gold mining operations in the Philippines during the Japanese occupation of that nation during World War II, the corporation continued to exist. Its president, general manager, and main shareholder set up an office and bank accounts in Ohio, from which the corporation paid salaries to office personnel and paid other company expenses. The Court upheld *in personam* jurisdiction over the corporation in Ohio on a claim arising in the Philippines. It noted that the corporation conducted a "continuous and systematic, but limited, part of its general business" in Ohio.[132] In *Perkins*, the president of the defendant corporation was served in the forum state while acting in his corporate officer capacity.[133] The Court did not make much of this traditional basis of *in personam* jurisdiction (service of process in the forum on the defendant's agent), and it is difficult to know if the fact of in-state service influenced the Court's decision.

---

[130] 342 U.S. 437 (1952).
[131] 466 U.S. 408 (1984).
[132] 342 U.S. at 438.
[133] 342 U.S. at 440.

In *Helicópteros*, the Court rejected general jurisdiction. There, representatives of four people killed in a helicopter crash in Peru sued a Columbian corporation in Texas. The parties stipulated that the claim did not arise from the defendant's activities in Texas,[134] so the courts assessed the case as an attempt to assert general *in personam* jurisdiction. The defendant had these contacts with Texas: (1) its chief executive officer visited Texas to negotiate the contract for the defendant to provide transportation services (the fatal crash occurred during provision of those services); (2) the defendant received more than $5 million in payments for the services, through a Texas bank; and (3) the defendant bought more than $4 million worth of helicopters from a Texas company, with which it provided its transportation services. The Court concluded that these did not constitute "continuous and systematic" contacts with Texas. Thus, it rejected the application of general *in personam* jurisdiction.

One way to reconcile the holdings in these two cases is to note that in *Perkins*, the actual *operation* of the corporation was centered in the forum, while in *Helicópteros*, the defendant engaged mainly in purchasing products in the forum. Perhaps the former constitutes continuous and systematic contact while the latter does not. Beyond this, it is difficult to discern what kinds of contacts are required to establish general jurisdiction.[135] The question of when general jurisdiction is proper has produced a great deal of academic commentary.[136] Many observers agree that there must be both a *quantitative* assessment of contact with the forum—perhaps measured in dollar value of business—and a *qualitative* assessment as well—perhaps measured by the percentage of business done in the forum. Though many cases address the issue, the decisions are simply impossible to reconcile.[137]

Perhaps it is fortunate that there is some other Supreme Court reasoning on the topic. Remember that in *Burnham* (see §2.4.4) the Court upheld jurisdiction over a man who visited California on business and was served with process there for a suit involving non-California activities. All nine Justices concluded that California had general *in personam* jurisdiction over Mr. Burnham. Four of the Justices, led by Justice Scalia, concluded

---

[134] Justice Brennan questioned this stipulation, and noted that the claims may have been at least "related to" the defendant's contacts with the forum of Texas. *See* 342 U.S. at 425 n.3 (Brennan, J., dissenting).

[135] And, again, it is possible that the result in *Perkins* was affected by the fact that there was in-state service of process on the defendant's president.

[136] *See, e.g.*, Patrick J. Borchers, *The Problem with General Jurisdiction*, 2001 U. Chi. Legal F. 119; B. Glenn George, *In Search of General Jurisdiction*, 64 Tul. L. Rev. 1097 (1990); Charles W. Rhodes, *Clarifying General Jurisdiction*, 34 Seton Hall L. Rev. 807 (2004); Mary Twitchell, *The Myth of General Jurisdiction*, 101 Harv. L. Rev. 610 (1988).

[137] *See, e.g.*, Severinsen v. Widener University, 768 A.2d 200, 203 (N.J. Super. Ct. App. Div. 2001) (cases "appear to summon one line of decisions and then another to support the varying moods of their opinions").

that presence in the forum when served with process was a traditional basis of general jurisdiction.[138]

Four other Justices, however, led by Justice Brennan, concluded that Mr. Burnham's being in California for several days, where he could conceivably invoke the protection of police and where he likely "enjoyed the fruits" of the state's economy constituted sufficient availment to justify jurisdiction for a claim that arose outside the forum. This is truly a remarkable conclusion. Nowhere did Justice Brennan explain *why* presence in the forum for a matter of days justified general *in personam* jurisdiction. He failed to assess why it constituted continuous and systematic contact with California. Remember, only four Justices signed that opinion. But if they are right, as we pointed out in discussing *Burnham*, it is difficult to see why *anyone* who has ever spent a couple of days in any state is not subject to general *in personam* jurisdiction there. Certainly, it is impossible to reconcile Justice Brennan's upholding general jurisdiction against Mr. Burnham with the holding in *Helicópteros* that a foreign corporation that had made $5 million from the Texas market and bought $4 million worth of products from Texas vendors was not subject to general jurisdiction.

Despite the uncertainty, we can draw some reasonable conclusions. It seems likely that service of process on the defendant in the forum supports general *in personam* jurisdiction — either because historically it always has or because of the Brennan conclusion that what seems like pretty minor contact with the forum supports it. It also seems clear that domicile in the forum supports general jurisdiction. This can be justified as a traditional basis, citing *Milliken v. Meyer* (see §2.4.2), or under the minimum contacts analysis. After all, one who is domiciled in a state has created what seems clearly to be such a substantial tie with the forum as to support jurisdiction for unrelated claims. Surely, if a domiciliary of New Hampshire committed a tort while on vacation in Hawaii, any plaintiff would expect to be able to sue the defendant in New Hampshire.

Beyond these traditional bases, we may be stuck with determining what constitutes continuous and systematic contact with the forum. For a corporation, this would seem clearly to encompass the state in which it is incorporated; that is the state that gave the corporation its very existence. It should also include the state in which the corporation has its principal place of business (which may be different from its state of incorporation). As an example, one would expect to be able to sue Ford Motor Company in Michigan for a claim arising anywhere in the world. Ford's main manufacturing activity takes place there, which should constitute such substantial and continuous activity as to support general jurisdiction. Similarly,

---

[138] They suggested, based on *Perkins* and *Helicópteros*, that the notion of general jurisdiction based on sufficient contacts might be limited to corporations. 495 U.S. at 610 (opinion of Scalia, J.).

one would expect to be able to sue the Coca-Cola Company in Georgia, for the same reasons. Courts have been inconsistent, however, about whether regional or smaller offices in the forum justify the exercise of general jurisdiction. As noted above, everyone seems to agree that there ought to be both a quantitative and a qualitative assessment as to whether contact is continuous and systematic, but the courts have not forged meaningful guideposts.

§2.4.6 Minimum Contacts in the Internet Age

All of the Supreme Court cases on personal jurisdiction predated the widespread use of the Internet. Still, in another context, the Court has recognized the Internet as "a unique and wholly new medium of worldwide human communication."[139] An increasingly important jurisdictional issue is how to analyze personal jurisdiction in cases involving use of this new medium. The Internet is everywhere (because anyone, anywhere, with a computer can gain access to it) and yet it is nowhere (because it is in cyberspace, not in one discrete physical location). So how does one assess personal jurisdiction in this context? Though modern technology has thrown new circumstances at the courts, it is not clear that it requires modification of long-established jurisdictional principles. Under *International Shoe*, there must still be some contact — caused by purposeful availment —by the defendant with the forum; and the exercise of jurisdiction must comport with the fairness factors espoused in the case law. In addition, if the plaintiff asserts specific (as opposed to general) jurisdiction, the claim must arise from or be related to the defendant's contact with the forum. If the plaintiff asserts general jurisdiction (discussed in §2.4.5), the defendant's contacts with the forum must be continuous and systematic.

Clearly, there are some easy cases involving the new technology.

- *D*, in Florida, sends an e-mail to *P*, in California. The e-mail contains outrageous statements intended to cause *P* to suffer emotional distress. *P* suffers emotional distress as a result of reading the e-mail. There is no reason to treat this case differently from one in which *D* had sent the message by regular mail or had used the telephone to convey the tortious message.[140]
- As we have seen, *International Shoe* embodies the clear possibility that a defendant can be subject to personal jurisdiction in a state without having set foot there. The Court recognized as much in *Burger King* and

---

[139] Reno v. ACLU, 521 U.S. 844, 850 (1997).

[140] *See* EDIAS Software Intl. v. Basis Intl. Ltd., 947 F. Supp. 413, 419 (D. Ariz. 1996) ("E-mail does not differ substantially from other recognizable forms of communication . . . where one person has an address or phone number to reach another person.").

with the *Calder*-effects test clearly envisioned that one can be haled into court in a state in which she has caused an effect, regardless of a lack of physical presence there.

A more difficult question is posed by the claims arising from the maintenance of a Web site. Specifically, when does the defendant's maintaining a Web site in State *A* constitute a contact with State *B*? As background, we should understand that the Internet is a global network of thousands of computer networks to which millions of people have access. Businesses, organizations, and individuals can post Web sites on the Internet, to which these millions of users around the world can gain access. The Internet thus has made it possible to do business anywhere in the world from a computer. There is a surprising paucity of state supreme court opinions addressing the constitutional questions concerning personal jurisdiction for claims arising from the defendant's maintaining a Web site. Moreover, because state trial and intermediate appellate courts rarely publish their opinions, there are relatively few state cases on the point. On the other hand, lower federal courts often do publish their opinions, so we find a considerable number of federal district and Court of Appeals opinions wrestling with the issues raised by the Internet.

One of these, *Zippo Manufacturing Co. v. Zippo Dot Com, Inc.*,[141] has been cited widely and is helpful in explaining that there are essentially three types of Web sites. The court intended this trifurcation to give basic rules of thumb, not to be the final word in all cases involving personal jurisdiction based on maintaining a Web site. The judge stressed that he envisioned a "sliding scale" for assessing contacts under *International Shoe* based on Web site activity. He said: "the likelihood that personal jurisdiction can be constitutionally exercised is directly proportionate to the nature and quality of commercial activity that an entity conducts over the Internet. This sliding scale is consistent with well-developed personal jurisdiction principles."[142]

- At one end of the spectrum is the "active" Web site — on which the defendant engages in activities such as transmitting files to the forum state over the Internet or entering contracts with residents of the forum. As a general rule, maintaining such a Web site in State *A* can establish a relevant contact with State *B*, at least if there is interaction with persons in State *B*. In such a case, the active Web site indicates a desire by the defendant to avail herself of the forum.
  - In *Zippo* itself, the defendant, a California corporation, set up a Web site, supported by seven Internet service providers (ISPs) in Pennsylvania; had 3,000 Pennsylvania subscribers; and "the intended object

---

[141] 952 F. Supp. 1119 (W.D. Pa. 1997).

[142] *Id.* at 1124. *See also* Mink v. AAAA Dev. LLC, 190 F.3d 333 (5th Cir. 1999) (adopting the sliding scale approach).

of these transactions has been the downloading of the electronic messages that form the basis of this suit in Pennsylvania."[143] The Web site contained information but was also interactive, and contained an application by which people anywhere could sign up for the defendant's service. The plaintiff, manufacturer of Zippo lighters, sued for violation of its trademark on the name Zippo. The court concluded that the defendant had sufficient contact with Pennsylvania to uphold personal jurisdiction in that state.

○ At the other end of the spectrum is the "passive" Web site — on which the defendant merely posts information. Even though people in other states may gain access to it, the passive Web site "that does little more than make information available to those who are interested in it is not grounds for the exercise [of] personal jurisdiction."[144]

  ○ A nightclub in Missouri established a Web site in that state to provide information concerning events at the club. The Web site was not interactive, and people desiring tickets for any of the club's shows were instructed to phone the club in Missouri or to buy tickets at the door. A New York nightclub sued the Missouri club in New York, asserting personal jurisdiction based on the Web site and alleging that the site infringed its trademark. The Missouri company did not reach out to New York to establish and maintain ties with New York customers and thus was not amenable to *in personam* jurisdiction in New York.[145]

○ In the middle, and clearly presenting the most difficult cases, is the "interactive" Web site — from which the defendant can send or receive information.

  ○ Some courts have concluded that merely maintaining a Web site accessible by persons in any state can constitute a relevant contact in any state. Because the Web communication can reach anyone, they reason, the defendant has purposefully availed herself of any state in which a plaintiff gains access to the site, and can be sued by one whose claim arises from accessing the information in State Z.[146]

  ○ Most courts disagree, however, and conclude that simply "creating a site, like placing a product into the stream of commerce, may be felt nationwide — or even worldwide — but, without more, . . . is not an act purposefully directed toward the forum state."[147] Only when the

---

[143] 952 F. Supp. at 1126.

[144] 952 F. Supp. at 1124.

[145] Bensusan Restaurant Corp. v. King, 126 F.3d 25 (2d Cir. 1997).

[146] *See, e.g.*, Inset Systems, Inc. v. Instruction Set, Inc., 937 F. Supp. 161, 162 (D. Conn. 1996) (jurisdiction in Connecticut over Massachusetts defendant concerning dispute over Web site domain name). The court in *Zippo* concluded that *Inset Systems* represented the "outer limits" of the constitutional exercise of personal jurisdiction. *Zippo*, 952 F. Supp. at 1125.

[147] *Bensusan Restaurant Corp.*, note 145 above, 126 F.3d at 29. An interesting case offering the flip side from the typical case (such as *Zippo*) involving personal jurisdiction over the operator of a Web site is CompuServe, Inc. v. Patterson, 89 F.3d 1257 (6th Cir. 1996). There, a Texas citizen entered into an agreement with an Ohio computer network service

> defendant has done something more to serve or exploit the forum — such as creating or maintaining the Web site in the forum, or encouraging persons in the forum to use the Web site, or conducting systematic business through the Web site — would jurisdiction be proper.

Of course, assessing when those contacts are sufficient under *International Shoe* can be vexing. But it should be familiar. In other words, there seems to be an emerging consensus that personal jurisdiction in the Internet context is assessed as it is in others. Even in the age of the Internet, state lines are not irrelevant. There must be some relevant contact with the forum. Technology merely increases the number of ways in which one can have contact with a distant forum. In addition, of course, the court must assess the fairness of exercising personal jurisdiction in the forum. Thus, the court in *Zippo*, after having found a relevant contact between the defendant and Pennsylvania, concluded that jurisdiction in that state was not unfair, and upheld specific jurisdiction over the California defendant.

Contrast this result with that in *Revell v. Lidov*,[148] in which the plaintiff sued in Texas for alleged defamation in an article posted by a professor on the Web site of a university in New York. The court, employing the sliding scale approach from *Zippo*, rejected jurisdiction. Although the bulletin board maintained by the university Web site was interactive, the allegedly defamatory posting was not directed at Texas; it concerned the plaintiff's activities when he was a government official in Washington. As such, the case differed from *Calder*, since here there was no intent to cause an effect in Texas. The court concluded that "[k]nowledge of the particular forum in which a potential plaintiff will bear the brunt of the harm forms an essential ingredient of the *Calder* test."[149]

What about general jurisdiction? When can Web site activities constitute such continuous and systematic activities in the forum as to subject the defendant to personal jurisdiction on a claim unrelated to those activities? It is clear that mere accessibility to the Web site — even 24 hours a

---

under which the service would market his software. After the Texan asserted that the network service had violated his trademark, the Ohio corporation sued in Ohio, seeking a declaratory judgment that it had not acted inappropriately. The court upheld personal jurisdiction over the Texan, concluding that he had availed himself of Ohio by entering the agreement by which the Ohio company would market his software. Further, jurisdiction in Ohio was fair because the Texan was an entrepreneur who anticipated a long-term relationship with an Ohio corporation; moreover, Ohio law governed the parties' agreement.

[148] 317 F.3d 467 (5th Cir. 2002).

[149] 317 F.3d at 475. The court also said: "we look to the geographic focus of the article, not the bite of the defamation. . . ." *Id.* at 476.

day — does not confer general jurisdiction.[150] There must be substantial and continuous interaction between the defendant and the forum. Of course, such substantial and continuous contact may consist of Web site activity *and other contacts*. A panel of the Ninth Circuit upheld personal jurisdiction in an interesting case in *Gator.com Corp. v. L.L. Bean, Inc.*[151] The panel's opinion was vacated, however, and oral argument set for the entire Ninth Circuit *en banc*.[152] Subsequently, the parties settled their dispute and the appeal was dismissed as moot.[153] Because the Ninth Circuit's original opinion was vacated, technically it does not exist. Nonetheless, the facts of the case and the panel's decision evoked significant interest, and are worth recounting here.

L.L. Bean is incorporated in Maine, where it also has its principal place of business, manufacturing facilities, and distribution centers. It mails over 200 million catalogues nationwide and maintains an interactive Web site over which customers around the world can make orders and payments. In 2000, about 16 percent of its sales (over $200 million) were consummated over the Internet. Gator.com, a Delaware corporation with all operations in California, created a "digital wallet" for customers using the Internet. It advertised with pop-up ads that appeared on the L.L. Bean Web site, and that contained coupons for a company that competes with L.L. Bean. Counsel for Bean wrote to Gator.com and demanded that it stop the use of such pop-up ads. The letter alleged that the ads infringed on Bean's trademark, appropriated goodwill, and constituted an unfair trade practice. In response, Gator.com sued Bean in California, seeking a declaratory judgment that its advertising did not infringe Bean's trademark and that it was otherwise proper. L.L. Bean moved to dismiss for lack of personal jurisdiction. The district court granted the motion, but the panel decision of the Ninth Circuit reversed.

---

[150] In *Revell*, cited in the two preceding notes, the court rejected an argument that a university was subject to general jurisdiction in Texas because its Web site allowed Internet users to subscribe to a journal, advertise on the Web site and in the journal, and to submit electronic applications for admission to the university. The court concluded that existing doctrine "is not well adapted to the general jurisdiction inquiry, because even repeated contacts with forum residents by [an out-of-state] defendant may not constitute the requisite substantial, continuous and systematic contacts required for a finding of general jurisdiction — in other words, while it may be doing business *with* Texas, it is not doing business *in* Texas." *Revell*, 317 F.3d at 471.

See Dagesse v. Plant Hotel N.V., 113 F. Supp. 2d 211 (D.N.H. 2000) (Aruba hotel Web site containing advertisements and permitting reservations to be made from New Hampshire did not support general jurisdiction in New Hampshire).

[151] 341 F.3d 1072 (9th Cir. 2003).

[152] 366 F.3d 789 (9th Cir. 2004).

[153] 2005 U.S. App. LEXIS 2521 (9th Cir. Feb. 15, 2005). *Moot* means that there is no live controversy remaining for the court to decide. Under Article III of the Constitution, the federal courts can only decide "cases" or "controversies." A dispute that has become moot is neither a case nor a controversy.

While L.L. Bean sends millions of catalogues to California, which generate millions of dollars' worth of business in that state, the court focused mostly on the Web-based activities. Relying in part on *Zippo*, the court held that L.L. Bean's active Web activities — including sending e-mails to California customers and accepting orders from California — constituted such commercial activity that it approximated physical presence in that state.[154] The court characterized the Web site as "clearly and deliberately structured to operate as a sophisticated virtual store in California."[155] Indeed, the tie between L.L. Bean and California was so extensive as to constitute a continuous and systematic contact that justified the exercise of general jurisdiction (which we study in the next subsection). That meant that the defendant could be sued in California on a claim unrelated to its California activities. As noted, this decision by the Ninth Circuit has been vacated. Nonetheless, it evoked some discussion, focusing on the questionability of basing general jurisdiction solely on the Web site activities. The conclusion would have been stronger — indeed, unassailable — had the court clearly based its finding of continuous and systematic activity in California on the other aspects of L.L. Bean's business there.

The Internet has given rise to the phenomenon of "cybersquatting." This occurs when someone registers a domain name that infringes on the trademark of an established business for the purpose of selling the name at an inflated price. Any well-known business wants domain names that bear, or at least resemble, the company name, their name, or any others so closely related to their name that customers might associate the site with it. Thus, the car manufacturer Porsche would want to hold the domain name *www.porsche.com* as well as *www.porsch.com*. In fact, the company registered the first name but found that some enterprising persons had already registered the misspelled domain name *www.porsch.com* and scores of others closely related to Porsche's name or the name of a Porsche product. Porsche sued under the Trademark Dilution Act, and sought *in rem* jurisdiction over the domains themselves (instead of *in personam* jurisdiction over those who registered the domain names). The district court rejected the claim, holding that the Trademark Dilution Act did not permit *in rem* proceedings.[156]

Around the same time, Congress passed the Anticybersquatting Consumer Protection Act (ACPA), which allows *in rem* proceedings against domain names created by a cybersquatter with the bad faith intent to gain

[154] 341 F.3d at 1079-1080. The court also relied on *Gorman v. Ameritrade Holding Corp.*, 293 F.3d 506, 512-513 (D.C. Cir. 2002), which upheld personal jurisdiction in the District of Columbia over an online brokerage service. That court noted that the defendant's Web site permitted persons in the District of Columbia to open accounts, to transmit funds into the accounts, to use the accounts to purchase securities, and to enter binding contracts.

[155] 341 F.3d at 1078.

[156] Porsche Cars North America, Inc. v. Porsche.com, 51 F. Supp. 2d 707 (E.D. Va. 1999), *vacated and remanded*, 215 F.3d 1320 (4th Cir. 2000).

monetary advantage. The Act has significant restrictions to ensure that the case proceeds *in rem* only if the persons responsible cannot be sued *in personam*.[157]

Though the Internet has thus introduced the new evil of cybersquatting and has changed the way in which defendants avail themselves of different fora, the opinions we have surveyed are remarkable for their undeniable tendency to treat the brave new world of the Internet within the paradigm already established by Supreme Court cases from earlier technological eras. Indeed, many opinions addressing personal jurisdiction in the Internet age so far seem to reflect the split between Justice O'Connor and Justice Brennan in *Asahi*, discussed in §2.4.4. This probably should not surprise us. Isn't the Internet simply a modern application of the stream of commerce? People release things onto the Internet in much the way they send products through the stream of commerce: They set them out there and see where the stream takes them. The stream may pass through many places, but may be acted upon only by persons in some of those places. When someone acts upon the passing of the thing through her state, is there a relevant contact between the defendant and that state? In the traditional stream-of-commerce case, Justice Brennan said there was a contact if the defendant could reasonably foresee the product's getting into the forum. Justice O'Connor, in contrast, asserted that such foreseeability was insufficient in itself; rather, there had to be "something more" — such as marketing for the forum — to establish a relevant contact with the forum.

In the big scheme of things, then, perhaps there is nothing unique about the Internet. Courts are using the same tools they use with regard to any other personal jurisdiction problem. This fact calls to mind Supreme Court language from 1958: "As technological progress has increased the flow of commerce between States, the need for jurisdiction has undergone a similar increase."[158] The Internet cases, then, have not pointed out a need for a new jurisdictional doctrine. Rather, they show the adaptability of the minimum contacts analysis.

---

[157] In the *Porsche* case, after plaintiffs asserted an *in rem* claim under the ACPA, some defendants submitted to *in personam* jurisdiction and argued that the ACPA thus did not apply. The Fourth Circuit rejected this argument, holding that the case was *in rem* when filed, and that the defendants could not manipulate jurisdiction by thereafter submitting to *in personam* jurisdiction. Porsche Cars North America, Inc. v. Porsche.net, 302 F.3d 248, 255-260.

[158] Hanson v. Denckla, 357 U.S. 235, 250-251 (1958).

§2.5 Statutory Analysis (Including Why Federal Courts Generally Look to State Statutes in Assessing Personal Jurisdiction)

The Need for a Statutory Basis

The fact that personal jurisdiction would be constitutional in a given case is not sufficient to permit a court to exercise personal jurisdiction. As noted in §2.3, the constitutional authority to exercise personal jurisdiction is not self-executing. Thus, *before addressing whether the exercise of jurisdiction would be constitutional,* one must find statutory authority for personal jurisdiction. Each state is free to determine how much or how little of the constitutional power of personal jurisdiction to grant to its courts. This is a political decision, made by the state legislature. It bears repeating, however, that even the clearest case of the constitutional exercise of personal jurisdiction cannot be made unless the forum state has passed a statute permitting it.

- ○ *P* sues *D* in State *X*. *D* is a domiciliary of State *X*. *D* was born in State *X* and has never been outside State *X*. The claim by *P* against *D* arose in State *X*. There is no question that State *X* can, constitutionally, exercise personal jurisdiction over *D*. But unless State *X* has passed a statute that grants personal jurisdiction in this sort of case, State *X* cannot exercise jurisdiction.

Statutes Relating to Traditional Bases of In Personam *Jurisdiction*

There is no doubt that State *X* would have a statute permitting jurisdiction in the hypothetical we just saw. Why? Each state has a series of statutes granting its courts personal jurisdiction. Some of these statutes seem to be ubiquitous. For example, each state apparently has a statute permitting *in personam* jurisdiction over persons who are domiciled or who reside in the state, which covers the hypothetical we just saw. In addition, each state has authority for exercising such jurisdiction over persons served with process in the state. (As we saw in discussing *Burnham* in §2.4, the question of whether personal jurisdiction in such a case is constitutional may depend on the facts, but the statutory basis is clear: There is statutory power if the defendant is served while in the state.) Similarly, each state has a statute granting *in personam* jurisdiction over corporations that are formed in the state.

Statutes Relating to Nonresidents

Beyond these typical statutes, each state authorizes its courts to exercise personal jurisdiction in some circumstances over nonresidents — defendants who are not domiciled or residing in the forum, and who are not served with process in the forum. Generally, states have two such statutes. First is the nonresident motorist statute. Apparently every state has one, and they tend to be similar to what we discussed in *Hess v. Pawloski* in §2.4.2. Such statutes are usually based on implied consent, and allow only specific jurisdiction. Thus, the statute grants jurisdiction only for assertion of the claim arising from the motor vehicle crash. The statutes usually permit personal jurisdiction over the operator and the owner of the vehicle that was involved in the crash.

The second type of statute permitting jurisdiction over nonresidents is generically called a *long-arm* statute — precisely because it permits the state to exercise its power outside the state lines. These statutes are quite similar to nonresident motorist statutes. Generally, they grant specific jurisdiction — the claim asserted against the nonresident must arise from something the defendant did in (or having an effect in) the forum. But they are broader than nonresident motorist statutes; that is, they cover more than the motor vehicle crash case. Historically, states passed nonresident motorist statutes in the 1920s and 30s, validated by *Hess v. Pawloski*. The more general long-arm statutes came along in the 1940s and 50s, in the wake of *International Shoe*.

Though long-arm statutes can differ substantially from state to state, most seem to be modeled on one of two general approaches. One is typified by the statute in California — it simply provides that the courts of the state can exercise jurisdiction over a nonresident to the full extent of the Constitution.[159] In such a state, the statutory analysis of personal jurisdiction is coextensive with the constitutional assessment. The second type of long-arm statute, which we can call a *laundry-list statute*, contains a list of activities that subject a nonresident to *in personam* jurisdiction. If your professor covered such a statute, beware on the exam. Many students get so focused on the constitutional test that they forget that there may be a serious statutory issue on the exam as well.

Laundry-list long-arm statutes usually provide for *in personam* jurisdiction over nonresidents who do particular things, such as transact business or commit a tortious act, in the forum. There are two important things to watch for in applying such statutes. First, study the language very carefully. There is a huge difference between a statute that permits jurisdiction over a nonresident who "transacts *substantial* business" in the state and one who "transacts *any* business" in the state. Second, remember that

---

[159] Cal. Code Civ. Proc. §410.10 ("A court of this state may exercise jurisdiction on any basis not inconsistent with the Constitution of this state or of the United States.").

courts may interpret the same language differently. If you studied such varying interpretations in your course, you should watch for them on the exam. One excellent example concerns language routinely found in long-arm statutes: that the courts of the forum have *in personam* jurisdiction over a nonresident "who commits a tortious act or omission" in the forum.[160] Note the careful drafting of including "act or omission." Without the reference to "omission," it would be arguable that the statute should apply only to intentional torts and not to torts based on omissions, such as some forms of negligence. Beyond that, however, would the statute apply in the following hypothetical?

- *D* manufactures widgets in State *A*. *P* orders a widget directly from *D*. *D* ships the widget to *P* in State *Z*. While *P* is using the widget in State *Z*, it explodes and injures *P*. *P* wants to sue *D* in State *Z*. The State *Z* long-arm statute grants *in personam* jurisdiction over nonresidents who "commit a tortious act or omission in State *Z*."[161] Does that statute grant jurisdiction over *D*? The answer depends on how the court construes whether there was tortious behavior *in State Z*. And, as you may have studied in class, courts can disagree on this point.
  - One interpretation is that the statute is *not* satisfied because the tortious act or omission, if any, occurred in State *A*. After all, that is where *D* manufactured the widget. So if *D* was negligent, that negligence took place in State *A*. The New York Court of Appeals reached this conclusion on similar language and facts in *Feathers v. McLucas*.[162]
  - The other conclusion is that the statute is satisfied because *P* was injured in State *Z*. The idea is that in whatever way *D* might have been negligent, it did not become tortious until it hurt somebody. And this widget did not hurt anyone until it blew up, which happened in State *Z*. The Illinois Supreme Court reached this conclusion on the same language in *Gray v. American Radiator & Standard Sanitary Corp.*[163]

---

[160] Some states except the tort of defamation from their long-arm statutes. *See, e.g.*, Code of Ga. Ann. §9-10-91. Thus, in defamation, the plaintiff may have to sue in the state where the defendant resides, unless some other basis for *in personam* jurisdiction can be found. Such legislative restriction does not seem required by the Constitution, in light of the Supreme Court's upholding jurisdiction in defamation cases such as *Keeton* and *Calder*, discussed in §2.4.4.

[161] There is something incongruous about this inquiry at this stage. It is not known whether the defendant is liable for a tort until the case is decided on the merits, which might be years after this jurisdictional assessment is made. Obviously, the court must avoid a mini-trial on the merits at this stage. Just as obviously, the conclusion that the court has jurisdiction does not predetermine the merits.

[162] 209 N.E.2d 68 (N.Y. 1965).

[163] 176 N.E.2d 761 (Ill. 1961). The Florida Supreme Court has held that a tortious e-mail sent from outside the state into Florida constitutes the commission of a tortious act in Florida. Wendt v. Horowitz, 822 So. 2d 1252 (Fla. 2002).

Each interpretation is defensible, and each emphasizes a different portion of the statutory language. The New York interpretation emphasizes the language *act or omission* — and insists that the defendant's behavior (not the effect or result of the behavior) must take place in the forum state. On the other hand, the Illinois interpretation emphasizes the word *tortious* — and emphasizes the effect of the defendant's behavior. The Illinois court reasoned that no behavior is tortious until someone is hurt. So if the injury takes place in the forum, the statute is satisfied. If you studied these (or similar) cases and saw a fact pattern like this on the exam, you would be foolish not to discuss both approaches. Then, of course, if you conclude that the statute is (or is arguably) satisfied, you must then go to the constitutional analysis and assess whether the exercise of personal jurisdiction on the facts would comport with due process. But that's a separate analytical step.

After the New York Court of Appeals decided *Feathers v. McLucas*, the New York legislature amended the long-arm statute by adding a provision to cover cases in which the tortious act or omission took place *outside* New York but the injury was suffered *in* New York. The legislature added a requirement in such cases, however, making jurisdiction proper *only* if the defendant engaged in a "persistent course of conduct" in New York or "derived substantial revenue" from activities in New York. Several states have adopted this language from the New York statute.

Thus, in several states, there are two long-arm provisions dealing with a nonresident's tortious act or omission. One provides for jurisdiction in the state if the nonresident committed the tortious act or omission *in* the state. The other provides for jurisdiction if the nonresident committed the tortious act or omission *outside* the state, but which injured the plaintiff in the state. This latter provision is satisfied, however, only if the plaintiff can make an additional showing — either that the defendant engaged in some persistent course of conduct in the forum or derived substantial revenue from activities in the forum.

When we think about it, in a state adopting such statutes, the legislature has in essence told its courts *not* to adopt the Illinois interpretation of the language "commits a tortious act or omission" in the forum. After all, if the Illinois interpretation is adopted, the tortious act or omission out of state is considered to be a tortious act or omission in the state (because the plaintiff was injured in the forum). Such an interpretation would render wholly superfluous the legislation addressing the case of the out-of-state tort harming the plaintiff in-state. Yet the Georgia Supreme Court somehow adopted the Illinois interpretation of the basic provision, at least for torts involving personal injury.[164] The same court rejected the

---

[164] *See* Coe & Payne Co. v. Wood-Mosaic Corp., 195 S.E.2d 399 (Ga. 1973).

Illinois interpretation, however, in a case involving fraud.[165] The inconsistency is indefensible, since the statute purports to make no distinction between torts involving personal injury and torts involving fraud. Indeed, the interpretation seems wholly antithetical to the interests of Georgia plaintiffs, since their state supreme court has concluded that it does not want them suing nonresident frauds in Georgia. That court later attempted to remedy the situation,[166] but the main point is simple: Each state's legislature passes the statutes it thinks best, and the interpretation of the statute is up to the state's courts. If the courts misinterpret the statutes, in theory the legislature should jump in and amend the statute. Legislatures are rarely so assiduous.

Given the divergent interpretations regarding statutes addressing tortious acts or omissions by nonresidents, let's do another hypothetical and think of how many things you could tell your professor *just on this statutory issue*.

- Defendant is a nonresident who has not engaged in a persistent course of conduct in the forum and has not derived substantial revenue from the forum. Thus that portion of the long-arm statute allowing jurisdiction over a nonresident who commits a tortious act or omission out of state that causes an injury in the forum does not apply. Defendant commits a tortious act out of state that causes an injury in the forum.
  - The most likely interpretation is that the statute is not satisfied. After all, the legislature dealt specially with defendants who committed a tortious act or omission out of state in that part of the statute requiring a showing of persistent course of conduct or deriving substantial revenue in the forum. Accordingly, the Illinois interpretation of the basic provision ("commits a tortious act or omission in" the forum) seems incorrect.
  - On the other hand, courts of each state are free to interpret their state's long-arm statutes as they see fit, and it is possible that a court would adopt the Illinois interpretation and find jurisdiction under the provision allowing jurisdiction over a nonresident who "commits a tortious act or omission" in the forum.
  - And if we are in Georgia, the court will adopt the Illinois interpretation if the tort involves personal injuries, but not if the tort is fraud.

In several states with laundry-list long-arm statutes, the courts have concluded that the legislature intended to extend personal jurisdiction to the full limits of the Constitution. This conclusion seems odd in the face of a

---

[165] *See* Gust v. Flint, 356 S.E.2d 513 (Ga. 1987).

[166] Clinical & Consulting Servs., LLC v. First Natl. Bank of Ames, 620 S.E.2d 352 (Ga. 2005).

detailed laundry-list statute. If the legislature intended to grant jurisdiction to the limit of due process, it could have passed a California-type statute in one sentence. But, again, it's up to the courts to interpret what the statute means.

- In *World-Wide Volkswagen*, the Supreme Court determined that Oklahoma did not have valid jurisdiction over two defendants. It noted the very detailed Oklahoma long-arm statute and also noted that the Oklahoma Supreme Court had held that the statute reached the constitutional limit. Could the United States Supreme Court have avoided the constitutional issue by holding that the Oklahoma *statute* did not extend to the facts of the case?
  - No. Remember from §1.2.3 that the U.S. Supreme Court can review state supreme court decisions only on matters of *federal* law. The Supreme Court has no business telling the sovereign state of Oklahoma what the Oklahoma statute means. It can only assess whether jurisdiction was appropriate under the (*federal*) Constitution.

Why would a state choose to give its courts less than the constitutional maximum power to exercise personal jurisdiction over nonresidents? This is a good question. It would seem that each state would want to allow its citizens the full constitutional reach of personal jurisdiction. Failing to do so may mean that the citizen will have to travel to a distant state to sue the defendant. Some have suggested that states may decide that exercise of the full constitutional power takes the courts too close to unfair assertions of jurisdiction. Remember, the Constitution does not require a convenient forum; it only prohibits a grossly inconvenient forum. As one scholar put it, "To say that a law does not violate the due process clause is to say the least possible good about it."[167]

The fact that courts may interpret their state's long-arm statute *not* to apply to a given fact pattern opens another important possibility: the exercise of QIR-2 jurisdiction. Way too many students (and some professors) assume that QIR-2 is a dead letter after *Shaffer v. Heitner* (discussed in §2.4.4). True, after that case, the exercise of jurisdiction in QIR-2 cases has to satisfy *International Shoe*. But that does not mean that QIR-2 jurisdiction has been subsumed by *in personam* jurisdiction. Suppose the nonresident defendant has sufficient contacts with the forum to satisfy *International Shoe* but that the state courts interpret the long-arm statute so narrowly that it does not apply in a given case. If the defendant has any property in the forum, which can be seized at the outset as a jurisdictional predicate, there is no reason for the plaintiff not to try to establish QIR-2 jurisdiction. For such cases, the long-arm statute is irrelevant. It grants *in*

[167] Elliott Cheatham, *Conflict of Laws: Some Developments and Some Questions*, 25 Ark. L. Rev. 9, 25 (1975).

personam jurisdiction. The proper statute, as we will see now, is an attachment statute.

Statutes Relating to In Rem *and* Quasi-in-Rem *Jurisdiction*

The statutory analysis for *in rem* and *quasi-in-rem* cases is usually a simple affair. Each state has an attachment statute, which permits attachment of property found in the forum state that a nonresident "owns or claims to own." In *in rem* and QIR-1 cases, of course, the nonresident claims to own the property. In QIR-2 cases, the nonresident clearly owns the property. The statute requires that the property be seized at the outset of the case, and provides methods for giving notice to the defendant.

Again, do not overlook the possibility of QIR-2 jurisdiction in a case in which *in personam* jurisdiction is impossible because the courts have interpreted the long-arm statute narrowly. If the long-arm statute does not apply, and thus *in personam* jurisdiction is not possible, but the defendant nonetheless has sufficient contacts with the forum to satisfy *International Shoe* (and has property in the forum that can be attached at the outset of the case as the jurisdictional predicate), the plaintiff should try QIR-2 jurisdiction.

Why Do Federal Courts Generally Look to State Law to Determine Personal Jurisdiction?

In §1.2.1, we noted that federal courts (as opposed to state courts) can only entertain certain types of cases (principally "diversity of citizenship" cases and "federal question" cases). We discuss this limited federal subject matter jurisdiction in detail in Chapter 4. State courts, as we see in §4.2, however, have general subject matter jurisdiction; with few exceptions, state courts can hear any cognizable claim. What about personal jurisdiction? As a general rule, the question of whether a court has personal jurisdiction over the defendant will almost always be the same in federal court as in state court. Thus, the assessment of whether a *federal* court in New York has personal jurisdiction over the defendant is generally the same as whether a *state* court in New York will have personal jurisdiction.

It is not obvious why this should be so. In fact, it seems wrong. The cases we read in our journey through the constitutional analysis of personal jurisdiction focused on contacts between the defendant and the *state* in which she was sued. This is entirely proper when a state court is exercising jurisdiction; the defendant must have the requisite contact with the government asserting jurisdiction — in state court, of course, that is the state government. But in federal court, it is the United States of America (not a state) that is asserting power over the defendant. Thus, it would seem appropriate to assess whether the defendant has the requisite contact with the United States — not with the state in which the federal court happens to sit.

Surely, as a matter of constitutional *power,* the federal courts do not have to be limited by state lines. Constitutionally, it is absolutely clear that the federal courts could be given personal jurisdiction over any defendant who has constitutionally sufficient contacts with the United States itself.[168] A federal court in Maine could be given the power to assert personal jurisdiction over a defendant domiciled in Hawaii — the defendant has sufficient contacts with the United States to justify the exercise of jurisdiction by a court of the United States (i.e., a federal court).

But have the federal courts actually been given such power? In some cases, the answer is yes. One, which is covered in most Civil Procedure courses, is "statutory interpleader," discussed at §13.2. When passing legislation allowing the federal courts to hear this specialized type of case, Congress expressly granted nationwide service of process. Thus, the federal court in Maine could exercise jurisdiction in such a case over a party who is served with process in Hawaii. Again, there is no constitutional problem with permitting the federal courts to have such power; they are part of the national government and can exercise authority throughout the nation.[169] There are other statutory claims created by Congress for which the legislature expressly permits nationwide service of process (most of which are rarely discussed in Civil Procedure courses); examples include

---

[168] Mississippi Publishing Corp. v. Murphree, 326 U.S. 438, 442-443 (1946).

[169] Some courts (wrongly it seems to me) conclude that, constitutionally, a defendant must have minimum contacts with the state in which the federal court sits. This conclusion ignores the fact that it is the *federal* court exercising jurisdiction. Thus, the better view is that the defendant merely must have minimum contacts with the United States as a whole. *See, e.g.,* In re Automotive Refinishing Paint Antitrust Litig., 358 F.3d 288, 293, 297-299 (3d Cir. 2004) (discussing nationwide service of process provision under federal antitrust law). Moreover, as discussed in §2.3, there are two Due Process Clauses: that in the Fifth Amendment (which limits the federal government), and that in the Fourteenth Amendment (which limits the state governments). Almost all of the cases we read interpreted the Fourteenth Amendment, and discussed the power of a *state* court to enter a binding judgment against the defendant.

When a federal court exercises jurisdiction, the Fifth Amendment is the relevant Due Process Clause. The better view, as just noted, is that the Due Process Clause of the Fifth Amendment requires an assessment of contacts between the defendant and the United States — not with any particular state in the United States. There is some debate over whether the fairness factors from the Fourteenth Amendment jurisdictional doctrine apply with equal force under the Fifth Amendment. Some courts conclude that fairness concerns in federal court can be accommodated by rules concerning venue and transfer of venue. *See, e.g.,* Oxford First Corp. v. PNC Liquidating Corp., 372 F. Supp. 191 (E.D. Pa. 1974) (concluding that Fifth Amendment includes fairness considerations for personal jurisdiction differing from Fourteenth Amendment limitations). *See generally* 4A Wright & Miller §1068.1; Wendy Perdue, *Aliens, the Internet, and "Purposeful Availment": A Reassessment of Fifth Amendment Limitations on Personal Jurisdiction,* 98 Nw.U.L.Rev. 455(2005).

some federal securities claims, antitrust claims, and claims concerning racketeering under RICO.

What happens, though, if there is no congressional grant of nationwide service of process? Here we might draw a distinction depending on the type of claim being asserted. As noted, the two main examples of cases in federal court are diversity of citizenship and federal question cases. In diversity of citizenship, the case goes to federal court because of the citizenship of the parties (and the amount in controversy in the dispute); as we study in Chapter 10, the underlying substantive claims are adjudicated under state (not federal) law. Thus, a citizen of Missouri might sue a citizen of Kentucky in federal court on a claim arising under state law — for example, in contract or tort. In these cases, because no federal law is being vindicated, it seems appropriate to assess personal jurisdiction in the same way we would in state court.

But in the other major type of federal court case — federal question cases — the underlying substantive claim being vindicated arises under *federal* law. There is a strong argument that a *federal* court asked to vindicate a *federal* law ought to have greater leeway in asserting personal jurisdiction than a state court would have. In other words, "it would be anomalous for a federal court adjudicating federally created rights and exercising the sovereign power of the United States to be bound by limitations developed under the Fourteenth Amendment, which by its own language applies only to the . . . states and is not a restraint on the federal government."[170] But does the relevant law support this argument?

Sometimes Congress creates a claim but does not provide for nationwide service of process. In such cases, the question of personal jurisdiction in federal court is informed by Federal Rule 4. Perhaps surprisingly, that Rule does little to distinguish between cases invoking diversity of citizenship jurisdiction (in which state jurisdictional limitations seem appropriate) and those invoking federal question jurisdiction (in which such limitations seem questionable). Rule 4(k)(1)(C) permits the exercise of personal jurisdiction as provided by federal statutes, including statutory interpleader. This simply tells the federal courts to apply nationwide service of process provisions when Congress has created them. Rule 4(k)(1)(B) creates what is usually called the "bulge rule," which allows special jurisdictional reach to join parties to litigation in very limited circumstances (see §3.3.4); these circumstances do not include the exercise of personal jurisdiction over the original defendant in the case (which is what we are dealing with).

So we are left with the fall-back provision in Rule 4(k)(1)(A), which permits personal jurisdiction when the defendant would be subject to personal jurisdiction in a *state* court in the state in which the federal court

---

[170] 4A Wright & Miller §1068.1, at 598.

sits. It is this provision that embodies the general rule that in *all cases in federal court* — diversity of citizenship and federal question cases included — we assess personal jurisdiction as we would in a state court in the state in which the federal court sits. Thus, Rule 4(k)(1)(A) does not distinguish between diversity of citizenship cases and federal question cases. The Rule may be best understood as embodying a policy of comity — that the federal courts, for instance in Louisiana, should be limited in exercising personal jurisdiction to the same power as the state courts in Louisiana. Again, this may not make great sense in cases in which the litigation focuses on vindication of federal rights, but that is the general rule.

On the other hand, Rule 4(k)(2) does expand the personal jurisdiction reach of federal courts in federal question cases. Specifically, it allows personal jurisdiction over a defendant to the full extent of the Constitution,[171] but only if (1) the claim asserted arises under federal law and (2) there is *no state court anywhere in the United States* that can exercise personal jurisdiction over the defendant. Thus, there must be no state court in which the defendant is subject to personal jurisdiction, yet the defendant has sufficient contacts with the United States as a whole to permit the exercise of jurisdiction. The provision was added in 1993 to avoid the result of a case in which a defendant was sued under federal law and who had constitutionally sufficient contacts with the United States, but who nonetheless did not fall within the long-arm statute of the state in which the federal court sat.[172] Obviously, Rule 4(k)(2) is of most use in cases involving defendants from outside the United States, and is fairly rare in application. Thus, even with the addition of that Rule, the general principle remains — in nearly every case, personal jurisdiction of the federal court is assessed in precisely the same way it would be assessed in state court.

§2.6 A Suggested Analytical Framework

What preceded was a lengthy discussion of the principles of the law of personal jurisdiction. Your job as a lawyer will be to apply these principles to a fact pattern given to you by a client to ascertain whether a court will have personal jurisdiction. Your job as a law student is to do the same with a fact pattern provided by your professor. Law school examinations

---

[171] Meaning, here, the Due Process Clause of the Fifth Amendment, because it is the federal government asserting jurisdiction. See footnote 169 above. In addition, the Rule will not allow personal jurisdiction if exercising it would violate some other federal law, such as a treaty to which the United States is a party.

[172] Omni Capital Intl. v. Rudolf Wolff & Co., 484 U.S. 97 (1987). *See generally* Oldfield v. Pueblo de Bahia Lora S.A., 2009 U.S. App. LEXIS 2657 (February 12, 2009)(applying Rule 4(k)(2) in an interesting fact pattern involving the Internet).

are not exercises in laying out the rules of law in the abstract. Rather, they require you to *apply* the rules of law to a given set of facts. As I say to all my students: You get zero points for *knowing* the rules. You get all your points by *applying* the rules to the facts and coming to a reasonable conclusion. That may be a frustrating reality, but reality it is. Thus, you need to be armed with an analytical framework with which to address a personal jurisdiction question. This section provides such a framework. It is certainly not sacrosanct. You may discern a better or more helpful framework on your own. Or your professor might suggest a framework. This is simply my effort to synthesize the material.

First: Statutory Bases for Personal Jurisdiction

The first analytical step is to determine whether a *statute* permits the exercise of personal jurisdiction. Even in federal court, this will be a *state* statute,[173] passed by the legislature of the forum state. If you are dealing with *in personam* jurisdiction, the statute might be one addressed to the traditional bases of jurisdiction. Each state has a provision granting *in personam* jurisdiction over persons served with process in the state or domiciled in the state. More likely, the fact pattern will involve purported jurisdiction over a nonresident, in which either a nonresident motorist act or a long-arm statute may apply.

In applying any statute — especially a long-arm statute — study the language very carefully. Among other things, look to see whether the statute expressly provides only for specific jurisdiction (which is likely) — that is, jurisdiction over the defendant only for some act or effect in the forum state. Watch for the difference between a requirement that the defendant transact "substantial" business in the forum versus transacting "any" business in the forum. Look for the difference between a defendant's committing a "tortious act" in the forum versus a "tortious act or omission" in the forum.

And always be aware that the same language may be interpreted differently. As discussed in §2.5, the classic example is the provision for jurisdiction over a nonresident who "commits a tortious act or omission" in the forum. As we saw there, some courts interpret this to require that the tort itself take place in the forum, while others require only that the injury occur in the forum. Many students have thrown away many points on many exams by failing to assess such differing interpretations of statutory bases for personal jurisdiction.[174]

---

[173] Except in those extremely rare situations, discussed at the end of §2.5, in which the federal courts have been given broader personal jurisdiction power than that of the state courts of the state in which they sit.

[174] Obviously, you must take all of these suggestions with a grain of salt, depending on what your professor covered. If your course did not address statutory materials at all, dis-

If the case involves *in rem* or *quasi-in-rem* jurisdiction, the relevant provision will be an attachment statute. These statutes do not vary much from state to state, and generally apply to permit attachment at the outset of the proceedings of property that the defendant "owns or claims to own." Usually, the statutory assessment in such a case is straightforward. And, as we emphasized in §2.5, be prepared to suggest that the plaintiff use QIR-2 jurisdiction if *in personam* is problematic because of a narrow interpretation of a long-arm statute. (Obviously, the defendant must have property in the forum that can be attached at the outset of litigation as the jurisdictional predicate for QIR-2.)

Second: Constitutional Analysis

If you find that there is a statutory basis for the exercise of personal jurisdiction — be it *in personam*, *in rem*, or *quasi-in-rem* — or even that there likely is a statutory basis,[175] the second part of the analysis is to assess whether the exercise of jurisdiction on the facts would be constitutional. In all likelihood, this will be worth far more points on the exam than the statutory analysis.

On the constitutional front, I suggest you first identify whether the case is *in personam*, *in rem*, or *quasi-in-rem*. (Remember that it might be more than one, as when the plaintiff seeks *in personam* jurisdiction under a long-arm statute and, in the alternative, QIR-2 under an attachment statute.) If it is an *in personam* case, you should then identify whether the case involves one of the traditional *Pennoyer* bases of jurisdiction — service of process on the defendant (or her agent) in the forum, consent, or residence in the forum. As to such bases, it is wise to identify it as a traditional basis and to note that under *Pennoyer* that basis would suffice. Then, however, you should recognize that *International Shoe* may have affected the traditional bases. True, nothing in *International Shoe* purported to overrule *Pennoyer*, but there is that broad language in *Shaffer v. Heitner* that "all assertions of state-court jurisdiction" must be assessed by *International Shoe*. As to the most traditional of bases (service of process on the defendant in the forum), the Justices split four-to-four in *Burnham* as to whether *Pennoyer* applied or whether *International Shoe* applied. We have no similar split regarding the other traditional bases of jurisdiction. Still, it may be argued — based upon

---

cussing them will not advance your cause. You must have a good sense of what your professor considers important in the analysis.

[175] I am always amazed that a student will conclude — based on one of two possible interpretations of statutory language — that there is no statutory basis for personal jurisdiction, and then say "so I don't have to assess constitutionality." Think. How likely is it that your professor would spend several weeks on the constitutionality of personal jurisdiction and then not have it on the exam?

Shaffer — that the court must undertake an *International Shoe* assessment as to those as well. For instance, we know that *Hess v. Pawloski* upheld a nonresident motorist statute on the basis of implied consent (and service of process on an agent in the forum). The Court has never overruled *Hess*, so it would seem to remain good law. But if *Shaffer* really meant that *all* cases must be assessed under *International Shoe*, a nonresident motorist case might not be justified solely on consent, but must be analyzed under minimum contacts too.[176]

And certainly you must apply *International Shoe* to assess the constitutionality of personal jurisdiction in cases involving nonresidents or others not falling within a traditional basis. For all the amorphousness of the terms in *International Shoe*, we do at least have a good understanding of the structure of the assessment to be made here.

Under the *International Shoe* test, there are two major components, as made clear from the famous language that the defendant must have "such minimum contacts with the forum" that "exercise of jurisdiction not offend traditional notions of fair play and substantial justice." First is the assessment of contact. Second is the assessment of fairness. A third element is implicit in the *International Shoe* equation, which addresses whether the claim asserted by the plaintiff arises from the defendant's contact with the forum. This factor addresses whether the case involves general or specific jurisdiction. You should get a sense of where your professor thinks this third implicit factor fits into the analysis.

Clearly, everyone agrees, the first thing to address under *International Shoe* is whether the defendant has established a relevant contact with the forum. We know from *World-Wide Volkswagen* and *Burger King* that such a contact is an absolute prerequisite to jurisdiction: All the fairness in the world will not establish jurisdiction if there is no relevant contact. This fact proves that state lines are not irrelevant. (Even in the Internet cases, we saw the importance of assessing contact between the defendant and the forum state.)

There are two elements in determining whether the defendant has established a relevant contact with the forum. First, the contact must result from defendant's *purposeful availment* of the forum. The contact between the defendant and the forum must not be fortuitous or accidental. It must relate in some way to the defendant's volition. This does not *require* that the defendant actually entered the forum. It can be satisfied by her intended *effects* in the forum, as we saw in *Calder*. Though purposeful availment is often shown by the defendant's desire to exploit a commercial market in the forum, purposeful availment does not necessarily require a desire for

---

[176] You should get a sense of what your professor thinks on this score — whether, for example, domicile is a basis for personal jurisdiction in itself (as *Milliken v. Meyer* held) or whether *Shaffer* means that even domicile cases must be assessed under *International Shoe*.

financial gain. For instance, a desire to use the forum's roads for pleasure driving may constitute purposeful availment.

Purposeful availment is a topic on which reasonable people often reach conflicting conclusions, so do not be fixated on getting the "right" answer. The key in most cases is to argue the matter both ways and come to a reasonable conclusion. Remember that there is especial uncertainty concerning purposeful availment in stream-of-commerce cases. In *Asahi*, the Justices split four-to-four in trying to define purposeful availment in the stream-of-commerce context. So if your professor gives you a stream-of-commerce hypothetical, you should be prepared to argue both the O'Connor view and the Brennan view (and any other reasonable view).

The second part of assessing whether the defendant has established a relevant contact with the forum is *foreseeability*. The Court emphasized in *World-Wide Volkswagen* that foreseeability does *not* mean asking whether it is foreseeable that the defendant's *product* would get into the state. Rather, it must be foreseeable that the defendant could get sued in this forum. We noted the circularity of this point, however, since a defendant who knows that her product is being used in the forum and knows that the product could hurt someone if it malfunctioned could foresee being sued there.

Thus, for the defendant to have a relevant contact with the forum under *International Shoe*, her connection with the forum (1) must result from the defendant's purposeful availment of the forum *and* (2) must render it foreseeable that the defendant could be sued in this forum.

Somewhere in your constitutional analysis, you should assess whether the case involves general or specific jurisdiction. I happen to think that this assessment belongs here — after the assessment of contact and before analysis of the fairness factors. Other professors disagree and put it elsewhere. To me, it is part of the *International Shoe* instruction that we look at the nature and quality of the defendant's contacts with the forum. With specific jurisdiction, of course, the claim arises from something the defendant has done in the forum or some effect she has had there. This "relatedness" may make up for a relatively low amount of contact between the defendant and the forum. In *McGee*, for example, the defendant had only one contact with the forum, but jurisdiction was upheld in part because the plaintiff's claim arose directly from that one contact. This relatedness is not required at all, of course, in cases of general jurisdiction — there, the defendant can be sued on a claim arising anywhere in the world.

Assuming there is a relevant contact (or if it's arguable that there is), and assuming that you assess relatedness (at some point), we shift to the assessment of the second major point in the *International Shoe* test: whether the exercise of jurisdiction is fair. More fully, we must determine whether the exercise of jurisdiction in this forum would comport with fair play and substantial justice. The Court routinely cites five factors as relevant to this inquiry, though it has offered more guidance on some than others.

The first fairness factor is the burden on the defendant. The defendant will usually complain that the forum is inconvenient, perhaps because it is far from her home or because it will be difficult to get her witnesses or her evidence to the forum. On this score, however, the Court established in *Burger King* that the defendant has a very high burden. She must establish not that the forum is inconvenient, but that it is *unconstitutionally unfair*. The standard is difficult — she must show that the forum is so "gravely inconvenient" that it puts her at a "severe disadvantage" in the litigation. And remember, in determining whether this is true, the relative wealth of the opposing party is not a factor. Thus, in *Burger King*, Justice Brennan's opinion concluded that two "little guy" franchisees in Michigan could be forced to litigate in Florida, in the backyard of the huge multinational corporate plaintiff.

The second fairness factor is the forum state's interest in adjudicating the dispute. In *McGee*, the Court noted that the forum state had an interest in providing a courtroom for its citizen in her case against a nonresident insurance company. The Court has never told us exactly how such an interest must be manifested. In *McGee*, California had passed statutes regulating the insurance industry and providing for jurisdiction in claims against it. At some level, it seems that every state has an interest in providing justice for its citizens, so it's not clear exactly what to make of this factor, other than to argue that it supports the fairness of jurisdiction, especially if the state has legislation concerning the particular type of dispute.

On law school exams, always be on the lookout for facts that may help make an argument. Get in the habit of reading aggressively — ask yourself why the professor told you this fact or that fact. For instance, suppose the plaintiff were a police officer harmed by the negligence of some nonresident defendant. It is worth arguing that the state has an especial interest in providing a forum for such public servants. If you ask yourself *why* each fact is in the hypothetical, arguments such as this will suggest themselves. Remember, success on law school exams is measured by how you *apply the facts to the law*. Knowing the law is not enough. You have to apply the facts to it.

The third fairness factor is the plaintiff's interest in obtaining convenient and effective relief. It is not clear how much weight this factor is accorded, though it is clearly less important than the burden on the defendant. The fourth and fifth fairness factors are, respectively, "the interstate judicial system's interest in obtaining the most efficient resolution of controversies" and "the shared interest of the several States in furthering fundamental substantive social policies." Very few cases discuss these factors.

Recall that *Kulko* spoke of the shared interest in family harmony and purported to further it by denying jurisdiction over a father who had acquiesced in his children's desire to live with their mother. In addition, in *Keeton*, the Court found a shared interstate interest in New Hampshire's exercising jurisdiction concerning the harm caused to the plaintiff in other states by an alleged defamation.

Again, in many jurisdiction problems (particularly those on law school exams), the "answer" will usually be something on which reasonable people can disagree. What you must do is discuss each relevant factor — such as purposeful availment, foreseeability, relatedness, the fairness factors — and come to a reasonable conclusion. Remember, though, it is *never* sufficient simply to list the relevant factors. And it is *never* sufficient simply to state your conclusion. You must *apply the relevant facts to the factors*. What facts support a finding of purposeful availment (and the other factors)? What facts augur against a finding of purposeful availment (and the other factors)? Argue the factors both ways — *based on the facts of the hypothetical* — and come to a reasonable conclusion. Show *why* you reached that conclusion. Showing how you reasoned based on the facts will be more important than the ultimate conclusion you reach.

Finally, if the case involves *in rem* or *quasi-in-rem* jurisdiction, the constitutional assessment must start with *Shaffer v. Heitner*. At the very least, that case means that the *Pennoyer* requirement that attachment of the property at the outset is not enough. *Shaffer* requires that *in rem* and *quasi-in-rem* jurisdiction cases be assessed under *International Shoe*. Specifically, that means that the defendant's contacts with the forum must satisfy *International Shoe*. It is important to remember, however, that the Court in *Shaffer* recognized that in several instances the presence of the property in the forum (attached at the outset) may satisfy this test. Specifically, in *in rem* and QIR-1 cases, the fact that the defendant claims to own the property in the forum almost always means that the defendant has minimum contacts with the forum. Similarly, in QIR-2 cases in which the property attached caused the injury of which the plaintiff complains, the presence of the property likely satisfies the requirement that the defendant's contacts with the forum satisfy *International Shoe*. Thus, when the dust settles, it seems that *Shaffer* really has its biggest effect in QIR-2 cases in which the property seized as the jurisdictional predicate does not cause the injuries to the plaintiff.

*******   *******   *******   *******

At this point, go back and re-read §2.1. There is a series of hypotheticals in that section, with suggested answers. Now that you have studied the cases and this suggested framework, and now that you know the relevant factors in analyzing personal jurisdiction, the hypotheticals in §2.1, which may have seemed so foreign and odd when we started, should be as comfortable as your favorite old sweatshirt.

Chapter *3*

Notice and Opportunity to Be Heard

§3.1   Defining the Issue

As we saw in Chapter 2, the constitutional concept of due process mandates that a judgment is valid only if the court entering it had personal jurisdiction over the defendant.[1] In this chapter, we see that due process also requires that the defendant be given notice and an opportunity to be heard before a judgment can be entered against her. Each jurisdiction prescribes rules by which the defendant is given notice and the opportunity to be heard. So, just as with personal jurisdiction, this topic entails a two-step inquiry. First, we must determine whether a rule or statute prescribes a method for giving notice and an opportunity to be heard. In most litigation, that method consists of "service of process," discussed in §3.3. And

---

[1] Recall that the Due Process Clause of the Fifth Amendment to the Constitution imposes various limits on the federal government, including the federal courts. The Fourteenth Amendment to the Constitution imposes like limits on the state governments, including the state courts.

second, we must assess whether that rule or statute, as applied in a specific case, comports with the requirements of due process, discussed as part of the constitutional requirements in §3.2.

In contrast to personal jurisdiction, however, here the constitutional step rarely presents problems. Why? Because the basic methods by which defendants are given notice and the chance to be heard are so well-established and universal, so time-tested, that their constitutionality is clear. Thus, although we must always be aware of the constitutional requirement, in most cases, the issue of whether appropriate notice and opportunity have been given is determined under state statutes or the Federal Rules. We focus on the Federal Rules, but contrast their provisions with some state practices as well.

In most suits, as we just said, the notice given to the defendant consists of "process," which includes a formal notification from the court that the defendant has been sued and must take certain steps to assert her defenses and avoid the imposition of liability. Proper service of process satisfies not only the requirement of notice, but also provides an opportunity to be heard, because it includes instructions to the defendant as to when and how she must respond to avoid entry of default judgment. Problems with the opportunity to be heard are relatively rare today, but can be encountered, for instance, in some commercial situations when a seller seeks to seize goods without providing a court hearing for the buyer who allegedly has failed to pay for them. We discuss such situations in §3.4.

Remember that the requirements of notice and opportunity to be heard are separate from personal jurisdiction. Giving notice to the defendant is never a substitute for having personal jurisdiction over her. Rather, it is the method by which the court *perfects* its personal jurisdiction over the defendant.

§3.2   The Constitutional Standard for Notice

The Due Process Clauses of the Constitution provide, among other things, that the government may not deprive someone of her property without giving that person "due process of law."[2] In the context discussed in this chapter, these words mean "that individuals whose property interests are at stake are entitled to 'notice and an opportunity to be heard.'"[3] The leading explication of the constitutional requirement for notice is found

---

[2] In §2.5, we noted that the Fourteenth Amendment requires state courts to provide due process, while the Fifth Amendment imposes the same requirement on federal courts.

[3] Dusenbery v. United States, 534 U.S. 161, 167 (2002), *quoting* United States v. James Daniel Good Real Property, 510 U.S. 43, 48 (1993).

in *Mullane v. Central Hanover Bank & Trust Co.*[4] That case involved a New York statute that allowed banks acting as trustees to pool relatively small trusts into one large account, to take advantage of economies of scale.[5] The statute required the trustee/bank to make periodic accountings to a court, demonstrating how it had invested the assets and what kind of return the investments had generated. If the court approved the accounting, it entered an order that (1) provided the trustee/bank with its fee (from trust assets) and (2) extinguished the beneficiaries' right to sue the trustee/bank for negligence or misfeasance in discharging its responsibilities. Beneficiaries were entitled to appear at the hearing on the accounting and to object to the trustee/bank's fee or to the way in which it did its job.

Obviously, though, beneficiaries could attend the hearing only if they knew about it. The New York statute allowed the trustee/bank to give notice to the beneficiaries of the pooled trusts by publication. That is precisely what the trustee/bank did in *Mullane*, publishing in a local newspaper its name and address, the name and date of the establishment of the common fund, and a list of the participating individual trusts. Representatives, appointed to protect the interests of the beneficiaries, objected that this form of notice did not provide due process to the beneficiaries. The New York courts disagreed, and upheld the accountings. The Supreme Court reversed, but, importantly, only with regard to some types of beneficiaries. In *Mullane*, the Court characterized the words of the Due Process Clauses as "cryptic and abstract," and emphasized that it had "not committed itself to any formula" for determining how much notice is sufficient in a given case.[6] Nonetheless, the Court did find some general principles, which it expressed in language that has become the classic statement of the constitutional requirement of notice:

> An elementary and fundamental requirement of due process in any proceeding which is to be accorded finality is notice reasonably calculated, under all the circumstances, to apprise interested parties of the pendency

---

[4] 339 U.S. 306 (1950).

[5] We encountered the trust in *Hanson v. Denckla*, §2.4.4. It is a device by which a person with money or other property (the settlor) transfers legal title of the property to a third party (the trustee), who is responsible for investing the property for the benefit of the beneficiaries specified by the settlor. Often, the trustee is a bank or other financial institution. The trustee is paid for its services. Some trusts may be so small that individual administration is not feasible, because the expenses are greater than investment potential. The New York statute in *Mullane* addressed exactly that situation and allowed the trustee to administer many small trusts together, as a single large trust, which is more economical. As the Court explained, under such pooling statutes, "income, capital gains, losses and expenses of the collective trust are shared by the constituent trusts in proportion to their contribution . . . [and] diversification of risk and economy of management can be extended to those whose capital standing alone would not obtain such advantage." *Mullane*, 339 U.S. at 308.

[6] *Id.* at 313-314.

of the action and afford them an opportunity to present their objections. The notice must be of such nature as reasonably to convey the required information, and it must afford a reasonable time for those interested to make their appearance. . . .

[W]hen notice is a person's due, process which is a mere gesture is not due process. The means employed must be such as one desirous of actually informing the absentee might reasonably adopt to accomplish it.[7]

This latter sentence, plus a reference in the opinion to providing the "best notice practicable,"[8] might seem to require individual notice to all interested persons in every case. If so, they overstate reality; there is no such blanket requirement. Remember that the reasonableness of notice in a given case is to be assessed *under all the circumstances*. Circumstances can differ from case to case, as shown in *Mullane* itself. Beneficiaries in *Mullane* fell into three groups, each of which was assessed to determine reasonableness of notice.

- ◦ One was a group of beneficiaries "whose interests or whereabouts could not with due diligence be ascertained."[9] These beneficiaries simply could not be identified. As to them, notice by publication was constitutionally permissible, and the Court upheld the New York judgment. Although there was a great possibility that the publication notice might not reach such unknown parties, it is "not much more likely to fail than any of the choices open to legislators endeavoring to prescribe the best notice practicable."[10] Publication was not, in other words, a mere gesture to give notice to these beneficiaries. The beneficiaries in this group were bound by the judgment in the accounting proceeding, even though they were not given individual notice.
- ◦ The second group consisted of beneficiaries whose whereabouts were not known in the ordinary course of business, but which "could be discovered upon investigation." With some effort (and at some expense) these beneficiaries could be identified and contacted. Here, too, the Court upheld the New York judgment and permitted notice by publication. The Court noted "the practical difficulties and costs that would be attendant on frequent investigations into the status of great numbers of beneficiaries, many of whose interests in the common fund are so remote as to be ephemeral."[11] It was simply unwilling to impose these burdens. Thus, publication notice was reasonable as to this group *under the circumstances*. This group, too, was bound by the judgment in the accounting proceeding, despite lack of individual notice.

---

[7] *Id.* at 314-315.

[8] *Id.* at 317.

[9] For example, suppose a trust provided for income to be given to grandchildren of the settlor who survive to the age of 21 or who survive a particular beneficiary. It may be impossible to identify all such contingent beneficiaries at a given time.

[10] *Mullane*, 339 U.S. at 317.

[11] *Id.* at 317.

○ Finally, a third group consisted of "present beneficiaries of known place of residence." As to them, notice by publication simply was not "reasonably calculated to reach them." Unlike the other two groups, here there was no excuse for failing to give individual notice. The Court reversed the New York Court of Appeals' judgment as to this group of beneficiaries.

But there are two important points to note with the Court's treatment of the latter group. First, it did not require individual notice to *every* identifiable beneficiary. Remember, the touchstone is reasonableness *under all the circumstances*. In *Mullane*, there were thousands of similarly situated beneficiaries, each with a relatively small interest. The right of one in the integrity of the fund and the trustee's management was shared by every other beneficiary. Accordingly, due process required "notice reasonably certain to reach *most* of those interested in objecting is likely to safeguard the interests of all, since any objection sustained would inure to the benefit of all."[12] Second, the Court did not require individual formal service of process (discussed at §3.3) on the known beneficiaries. Rather, delivery by regular mail was sufficient.

These things are not always true. For example, we will see that the Federal Rule on class action cases requires, at least in some situations, that individual notice be given to *each* member of the class who is reasonably identifiable.[13] Similarly, if the interests being extinguished in the accounting proceeding were substantial and unique to each beneficiary, the Court surely would have required individual notice to each.

In all instances, the requirement of appropriate notice serves not just the functional goal of informing the parties, but serves an important ceremonial function as well. Notice is provided by the judicial branch of the government, and the government must play by the rules. Thus, even if the trustee/bank could have shown that every known beneficiary in *Mullane* had actually read the notice published in the newspapers, the scheme would still have been unconstitutional.[14] As the Court explained, the publication notice to known beneficiaries was "inadequate, not because in fact it fail[ed] to reach everyone, but because under the circumstances it [was] not reasonably calculated to reach those who could easily be informed by other means at hand."[15] Notice of whatever type "is a ceremony whose performance assures that the termination of [one's] rights is not done in secret."[16]

---

[12] *Id.* at 319 (emphasis added).

[13] Fed. R. Civ. P. 23(c)(2)(B), requiring notice in a class action under Rule 23(b)(3). *See* §13.3.6.

[14] *See* Grand Entertainment Group Ltd. v. Star Media Sales, Inc., 988 F.2d 476, 492 (3d Cir. 1993) ("notice cannot by itself validate an otherwise defective service").

[15] *Mullane*, 339 U.S. at 319. The "other means at hand," of course, was mail.

[16] Restatement (Second) of Judgments §27, comment g.

It is important to see that *Mullane* does not necessarily require that the defendant *actually receive* the notice. This point was demonstrated in the 2002 decision in *Dusenbery v. United States*,[17] which involved a man (Mr. Dusenbery) convicted of federal drug charges. In executing a valid search warrant on the man's home, the FBI seized various property, including an automobile and $21,939 in cash. After Mr. Dusenbery was convicted and incarcerated in a federal penitentiary, the FBI started administrative proceedings to have the automobile and cash forfeited to the government. Pursuant to applicable federal law, the FBI sent written notice by certified mail to Mr. Dusenbery at the federal penitentiary, informing him of the pending forfeiture proceeding and indicating how he could oppose forfeiture. Because Mr. Dusenbery never responded to the notice, the property was forfeited.

Five years later, Mr. Dusenbery sought judicial relief and claimed that he had never received the notice of forfeiture. The Court rejected his contention that it should apply a cost-benefit analysis in place of *Mullane*, and found no reason to depart from the "well-settled practice" that *Mullane* governs "questions regarding the adequacy of the method used to give notice."[18] Thus, the question was whether the method of notice employed by the FBI — certified mail to Mr. Dusenbery at the penitentiary, where the Bureau of Prisons had a procedure for picking up mail each day, signing for all certified mail at the post office, transporting it to the prison, logging in certified mail at the mailroom, and assigning a staff member to deliver it — was, in the words of *Mullane*, "reasonably calculated, under all the circumstances, to apprise interested parties of the pendency of the action and afford them an opportunity to present their objections." The Court concluded that it was, even if Mr. Dusenbery never actually received it. The Court explained that due process does not require that the government "*must provide* actual notice"; rather, it requires "that it *must attempt to provide* actual notice."[19]

Mullane prescribes an *ad hoc* jurisprudence, one inevitably driven by the circumstances of each case. Clearly, *Mullane* has limited the availability of notice by publication in *in personam* cases; such notice may be

[17] 534 U.S. 161 (2002).

[18] *Id.* at 168.

[19] *Id.* at 170 (emphases original). Could the government have done more to ensure that Mr. Dusenbery actually received the document? Yes. Indeed, after the events giving rise to the case, the Bureau of Prisons imposed a requirement that prisoners acknowledge receipt of certified letters by signing a logbook. But these facts did not, to the majority in *Dusenbery*, make the practice followed in that case unconstitutional. *Id.* at 171-173. Due process does not require *the best* effort at notice — just one reasonably calculated under the circumstances to apprise the defendant of the proceedings. This is consistent with what we saw in discussing the *Burger King* case concerning personal jurisdiction; there, we saw that due process does not entitle the defendant to *the most convenient* forum — just one that is not egregiously inconvenient. See §2.4.4.

proper only when no other reasonable method of notice is practicable. The Court has given other clear guidance that has changed the practice for giving notice. For decades, many states have had statutes or rules permitting service of process on a defendant tenant in an eviction case by posting the process conspicuously on the premises from which the tenant was to be evicted. In *Greene v. Lindsay*,[20] the Court refused to enforce a judgment entered in a case in which service was made in this manner. Applying *Mullane*, the Court held that such notice was not reasonable under the circumstances because the papers could have been torn down by other people before the defendant saw them. In response to this and a subsequent suggestion by the Supreme Court, many states now permit such notice by posting only if it is followed by service on the defendant by mail.[21]

In *Jones v. Flowers*, the Supreme Court demonstrated again the importance of considering the specific facts at hand. In that case, the state sent a certified letter to a homeowner to inform him that he was delinquent in paying real property taxes and that failure to pay would result in public sale of his land. The letter was returned to the state agency as "unclaimed," after which the state took no additional steps to notify the owner. This inactivity in the face of knowledge that the owner had not received the letter violated due process. In other words, although sending a certified letter is usually reasonable and therefore comports with due process, things change when the state knows that the notice was not received. Due process requires that some additional step be taken to give notice.[22]

The flexibility of the *Mullane* standard invites courts to take advantage of technological advances. In one decision, upholding the constitutionality of serving process by e-mail, the Ninth Circuit explained that the "broad constitutional principle" of *Mullane* "unshackles the federal courts from anachronistic methods of service and permits them entry into the technological renaissance."[23]

---

[20] 456 U.S. 444 (1982).

[21] *See* Mennonite Board of Missions v. Adams, 462 U.S. 791 (1983) (suggesting that the additional step of mailing could render posting notice constitutional). For an example of a "nail and mail" statute, *see* Va. Code Ann. §8.01-296(2).

[22] 547 U.S. 220, 234-239 (2006). "What steps are reasonable in response to new information depends upon what the information reveals. The return of the certified letter marked 'unclaimed' meant either that Jones still lived at 717 North Bryan Street, but was not home when the postman called and did not retrieve the letter at the post office, or that Jones no longer resided at that address. One reasonable step primarily addressed to the former possibility would be for the State to resend the notice by regular mail, so that a signature was not required. . . . Following up with regular mail might also increase the chances of actual notice to Jones if — as it turned out — he had moved. Even occupants who ignored certified mail notice slips addressed to the owner (if any had been left) might scrawl the owner's new address on the notice packet and leave it for the postman to retrieve, or notify Jones directly." *Id.* at 235.

[23] Rio Properties, Inc. v. Rio Intl. Interlink, 284 F.3d 1007, 1017 (9th Cir. 2002).

Although the Supreme Court's *ad hoc* approach leads to uncertainty at the margin, relatively few cases raise constitutional problems of notice. In most litigation, it is clear that service of process on a defendant in accordance with Federal Rule 4 or a state counterpart is constitutional. In practice, then, the big question usually is not whether the rule for giving notice is constitutional, but whether the rule was satisfied on the facts of the case. In some ways, it is clear that the Federal Rules and state provisions regarding service of process have not "pushed the envelope" of permissible service. Despite authority upholding the constitutionality of e-mail service, for example, there is currently no general provision in the Federal Rules for serving process in that way. We now turn to the rules governing service of process.

§3.3   Service of Process

§3.3.1   Background

In the typical civil case, notice is given by the formal "service of process" on a defendant against whom a plaintiff asserts a claim.[24] "Service" refers to the methods for delivering process to the defendant. "Process," as generally used,[25] consists of two documents: a copy of the complaint and a summons. The complaint is drafted by the plaintiff's lawyer and sets forth the claims asserted against the defendant. See §7.3.1. Obviously, this document gives the defendant notice of the allegations against which she will have to defend. The summons stands on a different footing. It is an official document *from the court itself*, signed by the clerk of the court. It informs the defendant that she has been sued, that she has a particular period in which to respond, and that failure to make a timely response may lead to entry of default judgment against her.

The summons is the modern counterpart of the common law *capias ad respondendum*, which actually empowered the sheriff to arrest a civil defendant and incarcerate her pending trial. Today we do not feel the need to be so physical in demonstrating that the law is reaching out to the defendant, so the summons does not carry with it physical arrest. Although today the summons is often served by a civilian, remember that it is a symbol of the court's (and therefore the government's) power over the defendant.

---

[24] As seen in *Mullane*, however, notice can be important in other contexts too, such as the notice by mail to beneficiaries in that case of their right to object to the trustee's accounting. See §3.2.

[25] In federal court and in most states, process consists of the two documents discussed. In some states, the defendant is served only with the summons, and can gain access to the complaint at the courthouse, because, once filed, it is a public document.

The ceremonial importance of the summons and its service on the defendant, as we saw in §3.1, is shown by the fact that the defendant's independent actual knowledge of the pendency of suit does not suffice in the absence of proper service.[26]

Federal Rule 4(a)(1) sets forth the required contents of the summons in federal court. Note how the Rule ensures consistently worded notice to defendants, telling them that they have been sued, when they must respond, and what can happen if they do not take steps to defend themselves in the action. In practice, no lawyer really has to worry about drafting a summons containing these elements. Instead, she simply obtains a stack of blank summonses from the courthouse.[27] These forms contain all the required information except the names of the parties and counsel and the docket number. When filing a case, the plaintiff's lawyer drafts the complaint, fills in the blank portions of the summons, and takes both to the courthouse (along with the filing fee). The clerk of the court assigns a docket number to the case, stamps the complaint as filed, signs the summons and affixes her seal to it. The plaintiff then has this document and a copy of the complaint served on the defendant. Federal Rule 4(b) sets out these steps for the issuance of the summons.

In cases involving multiple defendants, each is named on the summons, but a separate summons is issued for each. Defendants not properly served are not brought before the jurisdiction of the court and thus cannot validly be subjected to a judgment.

Under Federal Rule 3, an action is commenced when the complaint is filed.[28] Federal Rule 4(m) then gives the plaintiff 120 days after filing in which to effect service of process on the defendant. If service is not effected within that period, the case will be dismissed without prejudice unless the plaintiff can show good cause for the delay.[29] This is a liberal provision, which effectively provides that service within 120 days after filing constitutes due diligence. Beyond that, the court has discretion to

---

[26] *See, e.g.*, McGuire v. Sigma Coatings, Inc., 48 F.3d 902 (5th Cir. 1994). This conclusion assumes that the defendant did not waive formal service of process.

[27] Behind the Federal Rules in your rules booklet is an Appendix of Forms. Form 3 shows what a summons looks like. The required contents of the summons in most state courts are substantially similar to those seen in Form 3.

[28] This is the rule in many states as well. In some states, however, actions are commenced when process is served on the defendant, even if this precedes filing of the complaint. The provision that an action is commenced when filed is superior, because it focuses on a clear, public event from which to compute various events, including the time in which to serve process.

[29] Courts have great discretion in determining what constitutes good cause. Most courts insist on a showing of diligence. A showing of repeated but futile attempts to locate the defendant or to determine her address might constitute a showing of good cause and justify the court's granting additional time to effect service. *See, e.g.*, DeFrancis v. Bush, 859 F. Supp. 1022 (E.D. Tex. 1994) (difficulty in locating defendant exacerbated by defendant's frequent moves).

determine good cause for extension. Some state rules are not nearly so liberal.[30]

Before 1983, the United States Marshal's Service usually served process in civil cases in federal court.[31] Today, in contrast, the marshals are rarely involved.[32] Instead, Federal Rule 4(c)(2) provides that service may be effected by "any person who is at least 18 years old and not a party." A civilian serving process need not be appointed by a court. This, too, is more liberal than the practice in some states, in which officers (typically the sheriff or a deputy) routinely serve process and civilians may do so only if appointed by a judge.[33]

The process server is supposed to file in court a "proof of service" (sometimes called a *return*), which explains what was done to effect service. Federal Rule 4(*l*)(1) is typical of such provisions. Under that Rule, a civilian process server must make proof of service by affidavit, which is a statement under penalty of perjury. Officers, however, need not make their proofs under oath. Failure to file a proof of service does not affect the validity of service, so a properly served defendant cannot have a case dismissed for this mere technical failure. The filing of a proof of service is prima facie evidence that the events stated occurred, and can be overcome only by strong evidence that service was not proper.[34] The defendant may be able to present such evidence, in which case an issue of fact is raised, which the trial court must resolve.

With this background about the definition of process, and about who serves process and when, we now turn to the question of *how* process is served.

---

[30] For example, in Georgia, service is to be effected within five days after filing the complaint. Ga. Code Ann. §9-11-4(c). Beyond that, service may be upheld, but only if the plaintiff shows due diligence. Bennett v. Matt Gay Chevrolet, 408 S.E.2d 111 (Ga. App. 1991).

[31] Whenever a marshal serves process, it is incumbent on the plaintiff to give instructions on where to find the defendant. For an amusing opinion, *see* Mayo v. Satan and His Staff, 54 F.R.D. 282 (W.D. Pa. 1971), in which the plaintiff sued the devil himself. The court dismissed the case when the plaintiff failed to tell the marshal how to serve process.

[32] *See* Fed. R. Civ. P. 4(c)(3) (marshals may serve process when plaintiff requests it and must do so in cases involving rare particular types of cases). Taking marshals out of the business of serving process in regular lawsuits reflected (1) funding cutbacks for the Marshal's Service and (2) a sense that the task did not require professional law enforcement personnel. In contrast, however, the Marshal's Service is involved in serving some other types of court documents, such as writs of execution. *See* Fed. R. Civ. P. 4.1(a).

[33] *See* Rule 4(c), Alaska R. Civ. P. (allowing service by a "person specially appointed by the Commissioner of Public Safety"); Ga. Code Ann. §9-11-4(c) (permitting service by a civilian only if she is "specially appointed by the court for that purpose" or "has been appointed as a permanent process server by the court in which the action is brought").

[34] *See, e.g.*, Howard Johnson International, Inc. v. Wang, 7 F. Supp. 2d 336 (S.D.N.Y. 1998); FROF, Inc. v. Harris, 695 F. Supp. 827 (E.D. Pa. 1988).

§3.3.2 Methods of Service of Process on a Human Defendant

Federal Rule 4(e)(2) provides three methods of service of process on an individual in the typical federal civil case:[35] personal service, substituted service, and service upon an agent. We will call these the *basic methods* for service. In addition, however, Rule 4(e)(1) allows a federal court to incorporate *state* law methods for service, and Rule 4(d) permits the defendant to waive service of process. At the outset, it is important to note that Rule 4(e)(2) does *not* prescribe a hierarchy; there is no preferred method for serving process — any of the three basic methods is permissible. In contrast, the practice in some states prescribes a "descending order" rule, in which a second method of service is proper only if the preferred method is not available on the facts of the case.[36] Now, we examine the three basic methods for serving process.

Personal Service

The first basic method of service, found in Rule 4(e)(2)(A) and which is permitted in every jurisdiction, is service on "the individual personally." Usually referred to as "personal service," this is effected when the process server delivers the process directly to the defendant. There is no question that personal service of process comports with due process. Indeed, it is the archetypal method for giving notice.

Note that Rule 4(e)(2)(A) does not require that personal service be effected at any particular place, such as the defendant's home or office. Personal service can be made *anywhere* within the forum state — at the ball park, at the opera, wherever the server happens to find the defendant. For example, one process server obtained a ticket to dance on a television special featuring singer Donny Osmond, who was the defendant in the action. The server danced up to Donny and served him with process on live television.[37] Sometimes, the defendant will see the process server and try to escape. In such instances, service is probably effected if the server does the best she can under the circumstances, even if the defendant does not take the documents into her hands. In one case, the defendant ducked into an automobile and locked the doors. The process server,

---

[35] We focus in the text on Rule 4(e), which governs the methods of service of process on individuals generally. Other provisions address service on individuals in specific situations. Federal Rule 4(g) governs service upon minors and incompetents, while Rule 4(i) governs service upon the federal government or an agency or officer thereof. Rule 4(j) concerns service upon other governments, including foreign and state governments.

[36] *See, e.g.,* Va. Code Ann. §8.01-296.

[37] *See* Martin Grayson & Bart Schwartz, *Adventures in Serving Process*, 11 Litigation 11, 12 (1985) (a very amusing article).

having already announced his intentions, left the process under the windshield wipers of the automobile. Service was upheld.[38]

In some circumstances, the law may recognize an immunity from personal service of process. In other words, even though the defendant is served with process in the forum state, there may be some reason for concluding that she has not been properly served and thus is not subject to personal jurisdiction. In §2.4.1, we discussed one such basis for immunity — recognized in federal and many state courts — when the defendant was forced or tricked into the forum. In addition, federal courts and many states recognize an immunity for parties, witnesses, and lawyers who enter a state to participate in another civil case.[39] Recognizing immunity for such persons encourages their appearance in that other proceeding and thus supports the administration of justice. There is a split of authority on whether a criminal defendant's presence in the forum to answer charges against her renders her immune from service of process in a civil suit.[40] Indeed, there is a good deal of variety among the states concerning when it is proper to recognize immunity from service. A few states, for instance, still recognize immunity from service of process on Sunday.[41] Whether a federal court recognizes immunity presents a question of federal law, on which state law is not binding.

Substituted Service

The second basic method for service of process on an individual, found at Rule 4(e)(2)(B), is service "at the individual's dwelling or usual place of abode with someone of suitable age and discretion who resides there." This method is often called *substituted service*, since it is made not on the defendant but on a substitute. The idea, clearly, is that a person of suitable age and discretion residing in the defendant's dwelling can be trusted to pass the documents along to the defendant. This rule reposes a good bit of faith in the suitable person. In essence, it appoints such a person as the defendant's agent for service of process. What if she does not bring the documents to the defendant's attention? In all likelihood, the answer is "tough luck" — the plaintiff had process served properly under

---

[38] Trujillo v. Trujillo, 71 Cal. App. 2d 257 (1945). Another well-known case is *Errion v. Connell*, 236 F.2d 447 (9th Cir. 1956), in which the defendant moved away from the door after determining a process server was knocking. The server slid the papers through a hole in the door. Service was upheld.

[39] See, e.g., Pointer v. Ghavam, 107 F.R.D. 262 (D. Ark. 1985); Lester v. Lester, 637 So. 2d 1374 (Ala. App. 1994).

[40] See 4 Wright & Miller §1081.

[41] See, e.g., Fla. Stat. §48.20; D.C. Code Ann. §13-303; Md. Cts. & Jud. Proc. Code Ann. §6-304; N.Y. Gen. Bus. Law §11.

the applicable Rule. Nothing in Rule 4(e)(2)(B) requires that the defendant actually receive it. As we saw in §3.2, the Constitution generally does not require actual notice.

The major issue in any case involving substituted service is likely to be whether the Rule itself was satisfied. The language of the provision presents three potentially troublesome issues. First, what is the defendant's "dwelling or usual place of abode"? For most of us, there is little uncertainty on this score; we have a house or apartment, and live there all year round. But what about persons who have two or more dwelling places throughout the year? For example, what about a student who resides in a dorm room in Madison, Wisconsin, during the school year but at home with her parents in Denver during the summer? Although Rule 4(e)(2)(B) does not expressly say so, courts generally conclude that one's "dwelling or usual place of abode" is the place she is living at *present* — when service is made. For our student, then, during the school year, this would be her dorm; in the summer, it would be her parents' house. (The concept is more flexible than the idea of "residence" for venue purposes, which we study at §5.4.1. For venue purposes, the student probably resides in the federal district where her parents live.)

Clearly, a place that was once the defendant's dwelling but that has been abandoned will not work. For example, where the defendant had graduated from high school and lived aboard a ship, his parents' house was no longer his dwelling or usual abode.[42] On the other hand, a person can have more than one dwelling or usual abode. Often, such people live the lifestyles of the rich and famous (because they are rich and famous). For instance, billionaire Adnan Khashoggi's New York apartment, one of 12 residences worldwide, had enough indicia of ownership to constitute an appropriate abode even though he resided there only one month of the year.[43] In that case, the court noted that the defendant was in New York when service was effected on his housekeeper at the New York apartment. There is some authority for upholding substituted service even when the defendant is temporarily away from the usual abode.[44]

The second difficulty comes from the requirement that the person on whom substituted service is made under Rule 4(e)(2)(B) be of "suitable age and discretion." The Rule does not prescribe a specific age. In contrast, the provisions in some states do.[45] Note also that the Federal Rule also does not require that the person on whom substituted service is made

---

[42] Cox v. Quigley, 141 F.R.D. 222 (D. Me. 1992).

[43] National Development Co. v. Triad Holding Corp., 930 F.2d 253 (2d Cir. 1991). Indicia of ownership included multimillion dollar remodeling and continuous employment of servants.

[44] *See, e.g.*, Jaffe & Asher v. Van Brunt, 158 F.R.D. 278, 280 (S.D.N.Y. 1994) (upholding service at abode in New York when defendant was temporarily in California).

[45] *See, e.g.*, Fla. Stat. §48.031 (age 15 or older); Va. Code Ann. §8.01-296 (age 16 or older).

be a member of the defendant's family. Thus, service on a doorman who controls access to a condominium building where the defendant resides may be proper.[46] In contrast, the provisions of some states prescribe that service must be on a family member.[47] Whether the person served is of suitable age and discretion is for the court to decide on a case-by-case basis. Many cases involve service on the defendant's spouse or child in mid-to-late teen years, and such service is usually upheld.[48]

The third source of some problems in substituted service is the requirement that the person on whom substituted service is made *reside* at the place where service is effected. Some state provisions adopt the same language, and some have equally unhelpful terms; for instance, the Virginia provision requires that this person is not "a guest or temporary sojourner."[49] The idea is clear enough — the person served should be someone with enough connection to the defendant's dwelling that we are reasonably certain she will forward the papers to the defendant. In practice, the issue is to be determined by the court on a case-by-case basis and it is sometimes difficult to draw a definitive line. Someone who is a guest for the weekend should not suffice. On the other hand, one of those in-laws who finds a way to stick around for a month at a time may qualify. In one case, the Tenth Circuit upheld substituted service of process made on the defendant's cook even though it appeared that the cook did not reside full-time at the defendant's house; the facts were ambiguous and the defendant failed to assert the issue properly, so the court upheld service.[50]

Service on an Agent

The third basic method of service on an individual, found in Rule 4(e)(2)(C), is service on "an agent authorized by appointment or by law to receive service of process." Virtually anything someone can do can be done by that person's agent; this includes receiving of service of process. But not all agents are authorized to receive service of process; it depends upon whether accepting service of process is within the scope of the agency. A defendant can specifically appoint someone to serve as her agent for service of process.[51] Or, as we saw in §2.4.2, a defendant may appoint an agent

---

[46] *See, e.g.,* Hartford Fire Ins. Co. v. Perinovic, 152 F.R.D. 128 (N.D. Ill. 1993).

[47] *See, e.g.,* Va. Code Ann. §8.01-296 (service on a member of defendant's family).

[48] *See, e.g.,* Resolution Trust Corp. v. Polmar Realty, Inc., 780 F. Supp. 177, 180 (S.D.N.Y. 1991) (spouse); Azuma N.V. v. Sinks, 646 F. Supp. 122, 124 (S.D.N.Y. 1986) (18-year-old son).

[49] Va. Code Ann. §8.01-296.

[50] Home-Stake Prod. Co. v. Talon Petroleum, 907 F.2d 1012, 1016-1017 (10th Cir. 1990).

[51] The leading case is *National Equipment Rental, Ltd. v. Szukhent,* 375 U.S. 311 (1964), in which parties to a contract appointed an individual as agent for service in New York. That person in fact gave prompt notice to the defendants after service. The Court upheld the service even though the contract did not require the agent to give such prompt notice.

for service of process by operation of law, as with a nonresident motorist statute. Such statutes permit service, for example, on the state registrar or commissioner of motor vehicles, and require that office to notify the defendant promptly, usually by registered mail.[52]

State Law on Methods of Service

We have seen the three basic methods of serving process under Federal Rule 4(e)(2). Federal Rule 4(e)(1) augments those methods by incorporating *state* provisions concerning service of process. Note, however, that this Rule may incorporate the law of *two* states: the state in which the action is pending and the state in which service is effected.

○ Assume that a civil case is filed in federal court for the Western District of New York. The defendant is in Pennsylvania but is subject to personal jurisdiction in New York and may, under applicable law, be served with process there. (See §3.3.4 for why this would be true.) What *methods* of service may be used to serve that defendant? There are three sets of rules that can be used: (1) any methods for service prescribed by the Federal Rules (the major ones of which we have just seen); (2) any methods for service prescribed by the law of New York; and (3) any methods for service prescribed by the law of Pennsylvania.

This incorporation of state laws helps to explain why Federal Rule 4(e)(2) has such a limited menu of methods for service of process and why it does *not* have a provision permitting service of process by mail. Rule 4(e)(1) makes up for the parsimony of Rule 4(e)(2) by incorporating state laws. Thus in situations in which the relevant state law allows service of process by mail (e.g., with a long-arm statute), the federal court can use that method. As a general rule, state provisions concerning methods of service of process are far more detailed than Federal Rule 4(e)(2). They may include, for example, posted notice (accompanied by mail notice) in actions seeking to dispossess a defendant of real property. They may also include publication notice (hopefully in accord with the constitutional requirements of *Mullane*, discussed in §3.2), service on agents under nonresident motorist acts and, often, out-of-state service by registered mail under a long-arm statute. Thus, when it comes to methods of service in a civil case in federal court, the Federal Rules are only the starting point.

---

[52] Remember *Hess v. Pawloski*, §2.4.2. *See also* Illinois C.G.R. Co. v. Hampton, 117 F.R.D. 588 (S.D. Miss. 1988) (Mississippi nonresident motorist statute).

Waiver of Formal Service

We have seen the three basic methods for serving process under Federal Rule 4(e)(2) and the incorporation in federal court of state law methods for serving process under Federal Rule 4(e)(1). These provisions are augmented still further by Federal Rule 4(d), which permits the defendant to waive formal service of process by mail. *This provision does not allow service of process by mail. Rather, it is a provision by which the defendant waives the requirement for formal service of process on her.* Why would a defendant ever make the plaintiff's life easier by waiving formal service? There are at least three reasons.

First, as Rule 4(d)(5) makes clear, the defendant preserves any objections to venue or personal or subject matter jurisdiction; so waiving formal service of process does not waive these important defenses. Second, the defendant who waives service gets extra time to answer the complaint. Under Rule 4(d)(3), she may answer up to 60 days after the plaintiff sends her the waiver form, instead of within 20 days after formal service of process on her.[53] Third, and most important, Rule 4(d)(1) imposes on the defendant "a duty to avoid unnecessary expenses of serving the summons." Then, Rule 4(d)(2) provides that if a defendant fails, without good cause, to sign and return the waiver, "the court must impose on the defendant" the expenses incurred by the plaintiff in undertaking formal service and the costs and attorneys' fees of any motion the plaintiff brings to collect those expenses.

How does this waiver work? The plaintiff sends to the defendant "by first-class mail or other reliable means" (Rule 4(d)(1)(G)) a form notifying the defendant of suit (Rule 4(d)(1)(D)), a copy of the complaint, two copies of a waiver form, and a "prepaid means for returning the [waiver] form" (Rule 4(d)(1)(C)).[54] In the Appendix of Forms found behind the Federal Rules in your rules booklet, Form 5 is a model of the notice to be given and Form 6 is a model of the waiver form. Under Rule 4(d)(1)(F), the notice must give the defendant a "reasonable time of at least 30 days after the request [for waiver] was sent" in which to return it. The usual "prepaid means" for returning the waiver form is a self-addressed stamped envelope, by which the defendant returns the executed waiver, usually to the plaintiff's lawyer. The plaintiff then files the waiver form with the court

---

[53] One part of Rule 4(d)(3) is curious. It provides that a defendant who returns the waiver in a timely way "need not serve an answer to the complaint until 60 days after the request was sent. . . ." As seen in Chapter 8, a defendant generally responds to being sued (1) by answer or (2) by motion. Literally, Rule 4(d)(3) makes the 60-day provision applicable only to the former, not the latter. In other words, it gives her 60 days in which to answer, but not in which to bring a motion. There is no good reason for making such a distinction, and the provision is probably the result of inadvertence in drafting.

[54] Other requirements are set forth throughout rule 4(d)(1).

and, under Rule 4(d)(4), the case proceeds "as if a summons and complaint had been served at the time of filing the waiver." Again, as seen in the preceding paragraph, if the defendant fails to return the waiver form, the plaintiff will take steps to have her served formally, and the defendant will have to pay the expenses of such service.

§3.3.3 Methods of Service of Process on Corporations and Associations

Not all litigants are individuals. Often, business associations such as corporations or partnerships are involved in litigation. Such associations do not have a corporeal existence; they exist through the people who run them and work for them. The question here, then, is what sort of person is deemed an agent of the business for purposes of receiving service of process? The key provision is Rule 4(h)(1)(B), which allows service of process on a business to be made upon "an officer, a managing or general agent, or any other agent authorized by appointment or by law to receive service of process."

Usually, there is little confusion about who is an "officer" of a corporation. Each corporation has at least one officer, and most have more than one. It is common for state corporation law to require the appointment of a president, a secretary, and a treasurer (although one person can usually serve in all three capacities). The corporation is required to file various information — including the identity of officers — with the state, so it is usually relatively easy to identify an appropriate officer for receiving service under Rule 4(h)(1)(B). Note that the Rule does not permit service on an "owner" of the corporation. Of course, an owner may also be an officer (or general or managing agent), in which case service would be proper because of the latter status.[55]

There can be significant uncertainty, however, as to who is a "managing or general agent" of a business association. The decision is very fact-specific. In addressing a given situation, the guiding principle should be the purpose of the Rule. The whole point is to find someone who can be said to *represent* the corporation or association, who understands the importance of the papers, and who is likely responsible enough to ensure that they are transmitted to those who can act upon them. Thus, courts look to the level of responsibility and authority exercised by the person

---

[55] An interesting case is *Fonar Corp. v. Tariq Contracting, Inc.*, 885 F. Supp. 56 (E.D.N.Y. 1995), in which service was made on a nonofficer whom the corporation held out to be an officer. The court upheld service, noting that this person regularly exercised discretion on the corporation's behalf. Thus, the person would seem to be a managing or general agent. Service would also seem proper because the corporation, by holding the person out as an officer, should be estopped from denying that the person was an officer.

receiving process.[56] It is an *ad hoc* assessment. For instance, in most corporations, one would expect that a receptionist would lack that degree of responsibility and discretion to be a managing or general agent.[57] In another corporation, however, a receptionist might have played a large role in setting up the structure of the business, and thus may be seen as a managing or general agent.[58]

Of course, as Rule 4(h)(1) expressly recognizes, a corporation (like an individual) may have an agent for service of process whom it appoints expressly or who is appointed by operation of law. If the agent is appointed by operation of law (as with a long-arm statute, for example), and if that law requires service by mail on the defendant itself (as long-arm statutes do), Rule 4(h)(1) requires that such service by mail be made.

Finally, as with service of process on individuals, the methods discussed are supplemented by provisions from state law of the state in which the federal court sits and in which service is effected. See Rule 4(d)(1)(A). Moreover, the provision in Federal Rule 4(d) for waiver of formal service of process that we saw with regard to individual defendants applies in suits against corporations or associations. This is made clear in the first phrase of Rule 4(h), which provides that the methods prescribed do not apply if "the defendant's waiver has been filed."

§3.3.4 Geographic Restrictions on Service of Process in the United States

Here we address where — in a geographic sense — service may be effected. More specifically, in what state can service be made? Remember from Chapter 2 that personal jurisdiction is assessed on a statewide basis. In other words, we assessed whether Oregon could assert personal jurisdiction over Marcus Neff or whether Washington could assert personal jurisdiction over the International Shoe Company. Because service of process is the means by which a court perfects its personal jurisdiction, it is clear that process may be served throughout the state asserting jurisdiction.

Thus, a state court in El Paso can permit service of process on a defendant who is found in Houston, which is over 750 miles away, because Houston is in the same state that is asserting jurisdiction. The same principle

---

[56] *See, e.g.,* United States v. Ayer, 857 F.2d 881, 888 (1st Cir. 1988); Allan v. Brown & Root, Inc., 491 F. Supp. 398, 403 (S.D. Tex. 1980).

[57] *See, e.g.,* Estate of Baratt v. Phoenix Mut. Life Ins. Co., 787 F. Supp. 333 (W.D.N.Y. 1992).

[58] This was the situation in *Direct Mail Specialists, Inc. v. Eclat Computerized Technologies, Inc.,* 840 F.2d 685 (9th Cir. 1988), in which the court upheld service on a receptionist as service on the corporation because of the receptionist's role in the business.

applies in federal court. The federal district in El Paso (the Western District of Texas) may permit the service of process on a defendant found in Houston (in the Eastern District of Texas). Lawyers and judges often capture this notion by saying that "process runs throughout the forum state."[59]

What happens, though, if the plaintiff wants to have process served on someone outside the forum state? A state may exercise personal jurisdiction over such a person only if (1) it has a statute that permits the exercise of personal jurisdiction on the facts of the case (such as a long-arm or nonresident motorist statute) and (2) the exercise of personal jurisdiction satisfies the constitutional requirements of due process. (These requirements were discussed in detail in Chapter 2.) The state statute providing the basis for personal jurisdiction will always have some provision for serving process outside the forum state. Recall from §2.5, for example, that the typical long-arm statute allows service of process outside the forum in various ways, such as personal service or service by registered mail. Thus, a state court in El Paso may permit service of process on a defendant in a town in New Mexico (say, only 25 miles from El Paso) *only* if a Texas long-arm statute (1) applies, (2) is constitutional on the facts of the case, and (3) if service is effected in a manner prescribed by the Texas statute.

Now, how is this issue of service outside the forum state handled in federal court? The situation is more complicated than it needs to be. For starters, remember that all the due process restrictions on personal jurisdiction that we studied in §2.4 are limitations on a *state's* power to exercise jurisdiction over the defendant. As a matter of constitutional law, a *federal* court, being an arm of the federal (not state) government, is not restricted by state boundaries; as long as the defendant has sufficient ties with the United States, a federal court can be given the power, constitutionally, to serve process on her, even if she is in Hawaii and the action is pending in federal court in Maine.

As we saw in §2.5, however, the federal courts have limited their personal jurisdiction in most civil cases. This limitation is found in Federal Rule 4(k)(1)(A), which provides that a federal court can serve process to establish personal jurisdiction *only if* the defendant would be subject to personal jurisdiction in a state court[60] in the state in which the federal court is located. In other words, this Rule says that a federal court can

---

[59] This principle is embodied in Federal Rule 4(k)(1)(A), which provides that service of process establishes personal jurisdiction in a federal district over a defendant who could be subjected to jurisdiction of a state court in the state in which the federal court sits.

[60] Rule 4(k)(1)(A) says a "court of general jurisdiction in the state where the district court is located." This reference to "general jurisdiction" is *not* general *personal* jurisdiction, which we discussed in §2.4.6. Rather, it is a reference to general *subject matter jurisdiction.* Thus, the rule is simply saying that the federal court can serve process if the state court that handles regular, run-of-the-mill civil cases (as opposed to specialized cases such as probate) could do so.

exercise personal jurisdiction and permit service of process outside the state in which it sits *only* if a state court in that state could do so. Though it may seem odd (as we argued in §2.5), this restriction applies regardless of the basis for federal subject matter jurisdiction. In other words, it applies not only in cases invoking diversity of citizenship jurisdiction (which are governed by state law) but even in cases in which the claim asserted arises under federal law.

- ○ The case is pending in the federal district court for the Western District of Texas, in El Paso. The plaintiff wishes to have that court exercise personal jurisdiction over, and permit service of process upon, a defendant who can be found in a town in New Mexico, just 25 miles from El Paso. Under Rule 4(k)(1)(A), the federal court in Texas can do so *only* if a state court in Texas could do so. Thus, the assessment of whether the New Mexico defendant is subject to personal jurisdiction in the federal court in El Paso is exactly the same as whether she would be subject to personal jurisdiction in a state court in El Paso; the issue will be determined by the Texas personal jurisdiction statutes and constitutional limits of due process.[61] If personal jurisdiction is proper, service may be effected in New Mexico pursuant to the terms of the Texas long-arm provision for out-of-state service.

That is the general rule. But it is subject to three exceptions (also discussed in §2.5). First, there are federal statutory exceptions. Rule 4(k)(1)(C) provides that a federal court can serve process outside the state in which it sits — regardless of state law — "when authorized by a federal statute." The best example is the Federal Interpleader Act, which, as discussed in §13.2.2, permits nationwide service of process. Such statutes are relatively rare and represent a congressional assessment that the federal courts ought to be empowered to serve process nationwide in particular kinds of cases.

The second exception — allowing service of process in a federal action outside the forum state regardless of state law — is commonly called the "bulge rule," found at Rule 4(k)(1)(B). The bulge rule is extremely narrow. First, it does not permit nationwide service of process. Rather, it

---

[61] This means, of course, that the New Mexico defendant must have such contacts with Texas as to render exercise of jurisdiction by Texas constitutional. Again, federal courts, constitutionally, could be empowered to exercise personal jurisdiction over any defendant having sufficient contacts with the United States, and to have nationwide service of process. Rule 4(k)(1)(A), however, stands for the proposition that the federal courts have, as a general rule, refused to exercise such power. They have chosen, instead, to limit themselves to the same jurisdictional power (and corresponding power to serve process out of state) as the state courts.

144

allows service out of state only if it is effected within 100 miles of the federal courthouse in which the action is pending.[62] Second, and more important, the bulge rule has absolutely nothing to do with serving process on a typical defendant. Rather, it is for serving process on persons not originally parties to the suit but who are brought in later, under Rule 14 (impleader) or Rule 19 (necessary parties).[63] Thus, for the basic task we are addressing — service of process on the *defendant* — the bulge rule is irrelevant.

- ○ Same facts as above, in which the case is pending in the federal district court in El Paso. The plaintiff wants to have the court exercise personal jurisdiction over a defendant found in a town in New Mexico, only 25 miles from El Paso, and to permit service of process on her there. Assume that no provision of Texas law would permit personal jurisdiction or service over this defendant. Can the defendant be served under Rule 4(k)(1)(B)? No. That Rule does not permit service of process on original defendants. It works only to allow service over persons joined later in the proceedings, under Rule 14 or 19.
- ○ And don't let the professor trick you with something like this: The case is pending in the federal district court in El Paso; one defendant can be found and served with process in Van Horn, Texas, which is 115 miles from El Paso. Can the federal court in El Paso allow service of process on the defendant? Yes. Why? Because the defendant is in the forum state in which the federal court sits, and service of process runs throughout the forum state. The mileage is irrelevant in such a situation.

The final exception allowing a federal court to exercise personal jurisdiction and serve process outside the state in which it sits (regardless of state law) is found in Rule 4(k)(2). It applies only to claims that invoke federal question jurisdiction (discussed at §4.6). Thus, it is of no use when other bases of federal subject matter jurisdiction, such as diversity of citizenship, are invoked. Unlike the bulge rule, however, Rule 4(k)(2) does permit service of process on an original defendant. It does so only when the defendant is not subject to personal jurisdiction of a state court, but when the exercise of personal jurisdiction would be *constitutionally* proper.[64] For example, if a defendant's contacts with a particular state are

---

[62] Obviously, if a long-arm statute in the state in which the federal court sits would permit personal jurisdiction over this person, and the exercise of personal jurisdiction would be constitutional, you would not need the bulge rule. It is needed only when forum state law does not permit the exercise of personal jurisdiction over the out-of-stater.

[63] We discuss these methods for joining new parties at §§12.6.1 and 12.6.2.

[64] The constitutional analysis would be pursuant to the Fifth Amendment (not the Fourteenth Amendment) because it is a federal court (not a state court) that is asserting personal jurisdiction. In §2.5, we noted that the better view under the Fifth Amendment is that the defendant have minimum contacts with the United States as a whole, and not with any particular state. When you review that section, pay especial attention to footnote 169.

not sufficient to support personal jurisdiction in that state, but her contacts with the United States generally support the exercise of personal jurisdiction over her, she may be served with process anywhere in the United States for a federal civil case invoking federal question jurisdiction. As one court has described it, the Rule "provides for what amounts to a federal long-arm statute in a narrow band of cases in which the United States serves as the relevant forum for a minimum contacts analysis."[65]

The use of Rule 4(k)(2) raises a potentially difficult issue of burden of proof on the "negation requirement" — that is, the requirement that the defendant is not subject to personal jurisdiction in any state. Is it incumbent on the plaintiff to show that the defendant is not subject to personal jurisdiction in each of the 50 states? Some courts conclude that it is, and require the plaintiff to show that there is no state in which the defendant can be subject to personal jurisdiction.[66] Other courts reject this approach as unwieldy. For example, the Seventh Circuit places the burden on the *defendant* to identify any state in which it *would* be subject to personal jurisdiction. "Naming a more appropriate state would amount to a consent to personal jurisdiction there. . . . If, however, the defendant contends that he cannot be sued in the forum state and refuses to identify any other [state] where suit is possible, then the federal court is entitled to use Rule 4(k)(2)."[67] The First Circuit uses a shifting-burden approach. Initially, the plaintiff pleads that there is no state in which the defendant can be sued. Then the burden shifts to the defendant, who must proffer evidence that shows there is a state in which she would be subject to personal jurisdiction.[68] Then the plaintiff may respond by showing that the state(s) identified by the defendant would not have personal jurisdiction.[69] Whatever the approach taken on the proof issue, it bears repeating that Rule 4(k)(2) works a very modest increase in the federal courts' power to exercise personal jurisdiction.

[65] Glencore Grain Rotterdam B.V. v. Shivnath Rai Harnarain Co., 284 F.3d 1114, 1126 (9th Cir. 2002). *See also* Graduate Management Admissions Council v. Raju, 2003 U.S. Dist. LEXIS 979 (E.D. Va. 2003) (Indian operator of Web site had insufficient contacts for personal jurisdiction in Virginia but had sufficient contacts with United States as a whole to satisfy Rule 4(k)(2) because Web-operated business targeted U.S. market).

[66] *See, e.g.*, Smith v. S&S Dundalk Engineering Works, Ltd., 139 F. Supp. 2d 610 (D.N.J. 2001).

[67] IST Intl., Inc. v. Borden Ladner Gervais LLP, 256 F.3d 548, 552 (7th Cir. 2001).

[68] Or, of course, the defendant could show that her overall contacts with the United States fail to establish personal jurisdiction under the Fifth Amendment.

[69] United States v. Swiss American Bank, Ltd., 191 F.3d 30, 41 (1st Cir. 1999).

§3.3.5 International Service of Process

In recent years, there has been a "substantial increase in the number of international transactions and events that are the subject of litigation in federal courts."[70] Accordingly, Federal Rule 4(f), which governs service of process in a foreign country, has become increasingly important.[71] As amended in 1993, that Rule no longer requires the express authorization of state or federal law to permit service outside the United States. Rather, the Rule itself is a grant of authority for such service. The Rule also recognizes that a defendant in a foreign country may waive formal service under Rule 4(d), just as a defendant in the United States may.[72]

Rule 4(f)(1) permits "any internationally agreed means of service that is reasonably calculated to give notice." The most important such means is provided by the Hague Convention on the Service Abroad of Judicial and Extrajudicial Documents, which the Rule expressly embraces. It applies only if the country in which service is sought is a signatory; in addition to the United States, about 40 countries have signed the convention, including Canada, China, France, Germany, Great Britain, Israel, Italy, Japan, Spain, and the United Kingdom. Under the Convention, each signatory designates a "Central Authority" to which requests for service from other signatory nations are sent. The documents to be served must be written in English, French, or an official language of the country from which the process emanates, although the Central Authority of any signatory nation may require translation into an official language of its country. If the documents are proper, the Central Authority effects service, although each country can make "declarations" that modify its obligations under the Convention. By the express terms of Rule 4(f)(1), service that is valid under the Convention is deemed to satisfy Rule 4. Thus, the fact that it might not conform to other provisions of Rule 4 is irrelevant.[73]

---

[70] 1993 Advisory Committee Notes to Fed. R. Civ. P. 4(f).

[71] Rule 4(h)(2) addresses service of process on a corporation or association outside the United States. It expressly embraces the methods of international service in Rule 4(f), except one subdivision of that Rule (Rule 4(f)(2)(C)(i)) that applies only to individual defendants. With that one exception, the permissibility of service on a corporation or association overseas is essentially coterminous with that on an individual.

[72] We discussed this in §3.3.2. The defendant waiving service in a foreign country, however, has 90 days (as opposed to 60) from the mailing of the documents in which to answer.

[73] It may be possible to avoid the requirements of the Hague Convention for service abroad by serving process on the defendant's agent in the forum. In *Volkswagenwerk v. Schlunk*, 486 U.S. 694 (1988), the Court upheld personal jurisdiction in Illinois over a German corporation by serving process on its subsidiary in Illinois. Illinois law authorized service on the German corporation by substituted service on its subsidiary without sending documents to Germany. Because that law was satisfied, and the exercise of jurisdiction over the German corporation was constitutional, the Court upheld jurisdiction despite the failure to satisfy the Hague Convention.

If there is no internationally agreed method for serving process internationally, as, for example, when service is to be effected in a country that has not signed the Hague Convention, Rule 4(f)(2) permits service abroad in several other ways. First, Rule 4(f)(2)(A) permits service in any manner permitted by the country in which service is effected, which requires the U.S. lawyer to research the issue under the foreign law. Second, Rule 4(f)(2)(B) permits the plaintiff to ask the foreign country for instructions on how to serve process. Such a request traditionally has been called a *letter rogatory* but today is also called a *letter of request*. Third, Rule 4(f)(2)(C) provides that unless the foreign law prohibits it, service may be effected (1) personally in the foreign country, or (2) by any form of mail that requires a signed receipt, sent by the clerk of the court to the defendant in the foreign country.

Finally, Rule 4(f)(3) allows service "by other means not prohibited by international agreement, as the court orders." This provision permits the court to order any method for serving process on a foreign defendant that does not violate "international agreement." Thus, any method that does not violate a treaty or other international compact is permitted, *even if* that method would violate the law of the country in which service is effected.[74] The Advisory Committee notes, while recognizing this breadth, counseled courts to be wary of violating such law. (And, of course, any method ordered by the court under Rule 4(f)(3) must satisfy the constitutional standard under *Mullane*.)

Moreover, it is clear that Rule 4(f)(3) is available in the alternative to the methods permitted by Rule 4(f)(2). One interesting case is *Rio Properties, Inc. v. Rio International Interlink*,[75] in which the operator of a Nevada casino sued a Costa Rica Internet gambling operation for trademark infringement. Unable to find an agent for service of process in the United States or in Costa Rica, the plaintiff sought a court order under Rule 4(f)(3) permitting service by e-mail to the defendant's e-mail address. In upholding the service, the Ninth Circuit rejected the argument that Rule 4(f) provides a hierarchy in which some other methods of service, including letters rogatory, must be exhausted before a court can order service under Rule 4(f)(3). The plaintiff "need not have attempted every permissible means of service of process before petitioning the court for alternative relief. Instead, [it] needed only to demonstrate that the facts

---

[74] *See* Mayoral-Amy v. BHI Corp., 180 F.R.D. 456, 459 n.4 (S.D. Fla. 1998). This provision is far broader than that in Rule 4(f)(2)(C), which does not permit use of methods that are prohibited "by the law of the foreign country" in which service is effected.

[75] 284 F.3d 1007 (9th Cir. 2002). The opinion was written by Judge Stephen Trott, who, before attending law school, was a member of a folk music band in the 1960s that had a number one hit record with its rendition of "Michael Row the Boat Ashore."

and circumstances of the present case necessitated the district court's intervention."[76]

The Ninth Circuit had no trouble upholding the constitutionality of e-mail service in *Rio Properties*. While recognizing that it "tread upon untrodden ground," since it was aware of no case in which a court of appeals had upheld e-mail service, the court found that e-mail satisfied the *Mullane* standard, discussed in §3.2. Not only was e-mail reasonably calculated under all the circumstances to apprise the defendant of the pendency of the case; on the facts of the case (which involved the defendant's attempts to evade service), "it was the method of service most likely to reach [the defendant]."[77]

Finally, note that Rule 4(f) provides methods for service if the defendant has not waived formal service under Rule 4(d). Rule 4(d) operates in the international context the same as domestically, with one minor exception. If the defendant is outside the United States, there are two minor adjustments to timing. First, under Rule 4(d)(1)(F), she must be given at least 60 days (instead of 30 days) to return the waiver form. And second, under Rule 4(d)(3), the international defendant who waives formal service has 90 days (instead of 60 days) from the sending of the waiver form to her in which to answer.

§3.3.6 Service of Subsequent Documents

The foregoing discussion, in §3.3.1 through §3.3.5, dealt with service of *process*. Of course, process includes the summons, which is a command emanating from the judicial branch of the government, commanding the defendant to appear. It is the symbol of the government's power over the defendant. Because the assertion of this power is such an important event, the law imposes the exacting requirements we have seen. But such a show of power need be made only once as to each defendant.

Thereafter, service of subsequent documents (and there may be many, including additional pleadings, motions, and discovery requests and responses) is not so formal. First, no summons is needed. Second, Rule

---

[76] *Id.* at 1016 ("We expressly agree with the district court's handling of this case and its use of Rule 4(f)(3) to ensure the smooth functioning of our courts of law.").

[77] *Id.* at 1017. The court relied on an earlier case that upheld service of process by telex on Iranian defendants. In that case, the court explained: "No longer do we live in a world where communications are conducted solely by mail carried by fast sailing clipper . . . ships. Electronic communication via satellite can and does provide instantaneous transmission of notice and information. No longer must process be mailed to a defendant's door when he can receive complete notice at an electronic terminal inside his very office, even when the door is steel and bolted shut." New England Merchants Natl. Bank v. Iran Power Generation & Transmission Co., 495 F. Supp. 73, 81 (S.D.N.Y. 1990).

5(b)(2) permits service of such subsequent documents by personal delivery, or by leaving them at the party's office, or by regular mail. If mail is used, Rule 5(b)(2)(C) provides that service of these documents is complete upon mailing. If the party consents in writing, Rule 5(b)(2)(E) permits service of these subsequent documents to be made by electronic transmission. In most cases, parties simply mail these documents to other parties. If the document served by mail or electronic transmission is one to which a response is required (such as discovery requests), Rule 6(d) gives the receiving party three extra days in which to respond.

§3.4 Problems with Opportunity to Be Heard

In addition to notice, due process guarantees a defendant a meaningful opportunity to be heard.[78] In most cases, this requirement poses no serious problem. Under Federal Rule 12(a), a defendant has at least 20 days after service of process in which to respond, either by answering or bringing a motion. The practice is at least that generous[79] in the state courts. Allowing this much time, especially following the clear notice provided by the summons, is usually sufficient to permit the defendant to respond and avoid entry of default judgment. If the defendant needs more time to respond, she may make a motion to "enlarge" the time in which to respond, under Federal Rule 6(b). So the typical case does not present a problem concerning opportunity to be heard.

So when do such problems arise? Generally, it's when the plaintiff seeks to have the defendant's property seized before the dispute is resolved on the merits. In a series of opinions, the Supreme Court addressed various procedures by which plaintiffs have attempted to do this and gave some guidance on the conditions under which such actions might be appropriate. Before looking at those cases, it is helpful to review some terminology. *Garnishment* usually refers to seizure of a defendant's wages. Creditors might want to garnish the wages of a debtor to ensure that they get paid. *Replevin* is a procedure by which a seller of goods seeks to recover the goods (because the buyer has not paid for them) or to recover the cash equivalent of the goods. For example, suppose a retailer sells a stereo system to the defendant on an installment plan, by which the buyer is to pay a given amount each month. If the buyer fails to make payments, the seller will want to get the stereo system back or to recover from the

---

[78] *Mullane*, 339 U.S. at 314 ("right to be heard has little reality or worth unless one is informed that the matter is pending and can choose for himself whether to appear or default, acquiesce or contest"). We discussed *Mullane* at §3.2.

[79] For example, Georgia allows the defendant 30 days from service of process in which to respond. Ga. Code Ann. §9-11-12.

buyer the cash value of the stereo. Because the buyer may not have enough money, however, getting the property back may become a priority.

Notice the clash of legitimate interests presented by such cases. The seller has a right to be paid or to get the property back. It does not want to wait through extended litigation to do so, because in the intervening months or years, the buyer may destroy the property or abscond with it, or it may simply become less valuable. On the other hand, the buyer wants a chance to present defenses, to explain why she has not paid for the goods. After all, maybe the stereo is defective, or maybe she claims that she has indeed paid for it in full. The question for the Supreme Court has been how to balance these conflicting legitimate expectations.

The first case in the modern treatment of these issues was *Sniadach v. Family Finance Corporation.*[80] There, the Court held unconstitutional a Wisconsin law that allowed a creditor to garnish a debtor's wages before any hearing on the merits of the creditor's claim. Without some protection for the debtor, such a seizure would "drive a wage-earning family to the wall"[81] and would violate the debtor's due process rights.

But what sorts of protections could be built into such statutes to render them constitutional? The Court gave some guidance (but not much) in *Fuentes v. Shevin,*[82] which invalidated replevin statutes in Pennsylvania and Florida. Those statutes permitted a seller to seize property before the court held a hearing on the merits of the dispute. They provided the buyer with some protection by allowing her to reclaim the property before trial by posting a bond. According to the Court, however, this protection was insufficient.

The Court was more forthcoming in *Mitchell v. W.T. Grant Company,*[83] in which it upheld a Louisiana practice that permitted pre-hearing sequestration (just a fancy word for seizure) of property when the plaintiff feared the defendant might remove or injure the property in the interim. The Louisiana statute, unlike that addressed in *Fuentes,* required that the writ (just a fancy word for order) allowing seizure of the property be issued by a judicial officer rather than by the sheriff. It also required the plaintiff to set forth reasons for sequestration under oath and in detail, rather than by simple conclusory statements. Moreover, the Louisiana law permitted the buyer to reclaim possession, pending litigation, without delay. Further, the plaintiff had a lien on the property.[84] These factors distinguished the case from *Fuentes* and satisfied due process. Note that the judicial involvement

---

[80] 395 U.S. 337 (1969).

[81] *Id.* at 341-342.

[82] 407 U.S. 67 (1972).

[83] 416 U.S. 600 (1974).

[84] A lien is a claim on the property. Remember from §2.2 that a valid *in personam* judgment creates a lien against the defendant's real property, which means that the property can be sold at public auction to raise the money to pay off the lien. In *Mitchell,* the plaintiff had a vendor's lien, which is a right against the property to collect for goods sold.

in the Louisiana law was not to conduct a hearing on the merits of the underlying claim (of whether the buyer had improperly failed to pay the seller). Rather, it was simply to determine, based upon the plaintiff's sworn statement, whether to issue the writ allowing seizure of the property before litigation.

In *North Georgia Finishing, Inc. v. DiChem, Inc.*,[85] the Court struck down a Georgia statute by which a creditor had garnished the defendant's bank accounts. Under that statute, such seizure was permitted based upon conclusory sworn statements by the plaintiff and the plaintiff's posting a bond of twice the amount claimed from the defendant. The writ allowing seizure was issued by a court clerk, not a judicial officer. Although the defendant could repossess the property by posting her own bond, there was no provision for an expedited hearing on the merits. These were insufficient protections for the defendant, and the statute violated due process.

A more recent case in the area is *Connecticut v. Doehr*,[86] which involved the plaintiff's seizure of the defendant's real property before judgment for the purpose of ensuring sufficient assets to satisfy a judgment on an underlying battery claim. The Court held the Connecticut statute unconstitutional because it permitted such seizures based upon the plaintiff's conclusory sworn statement that "there is probable cause to sustain the validity of the plaintiff's claims." Unlike the statute in *Mitchell*, the Connecticut law did not require the plaintiff to post a bond. Also unlike *Mitchell*, the plaintiff did not have a lien on the property. Thus, the plaintiff had no interest in the real property except the general interest all plaintiffs have in ensuring that the defendant has enough assets to pay a judgment. There was no evidence that the defendant was going to transfer the land or otherwise diminish his assets to avoid a judgment.

From these cases, we are left with a series of potential protections for the defendant in a pretrial seizure situation, including (1) involvement of a judicial officer in the determination of whether the seizure should be made; (2) notice to the defendant of the plaintiff's effort to make a prehearing seizure; (3) a requirement that the plaintiff post a bond; (4) a requirement that the plaintiff state under oath specific, particularized reasons for the seizure; and (5) a procedure by which the defendant may get the property back, perhaps by posting a bond, pending the trial on the merits. In addition, it seems clear that the plaintiff is on a better footing if she has a lien against the property to be seized.

But the ultimate question of how many of these safeguards must be present, and in what combination, is unclear. *Mitchell* is the only one of the cases in which the challenged statute was upheld,[87] so one is tempted

[85] 419 U.S. 601 (1975).
[86] 501 U.S. 1 (1991).
[87] In *D.H. Overmyer Co. v. Frick Co.*, 405 U.S. 174 (1972), the Court upheld the use of a "cognovit" provision in a contract. Such a clause authorizes a creditor to sue the debtor

to say that the factors present in that case would constitute the due process minimum. This conclusion is difficult to reach, however, because each case varies at least slightly on its facts. Perhaps all we can say is that a court must balance factors such as those listed, and the relative rights of the parties, in a flexible, case-by-case assessment to ensure appropriate protection to the defendant.

---

and automatically have "judgment by confession" entered against the defendant without notice. The Court emphasized that the provision was the result of good faith bargaining between parties of equal bargaining power, that the plaintiff had given good consideration for this right, and that relevant state law protected the defendant by permitting it to set aside the judgment if it had a valid defense. *Overmyer*, thus, is nothing more than a recognition that one can waive her due process right to an opportunity to be heard. Such waivers are not recognized, however, if the parties are of unequal bargaining power and are imposed upon the weaker party. Moreover, they are especially questionable if used against a debtor of limited financial means. *See* Swarb v. Lennox, 405 U.S. 191 (1972).

Chapter 4

Subject Matter Jurisdiction

§4.1 Defining the Issue

It is important to distinguish between personal jurisdiction and subject matter jurisdiction. Personal jurisdiction is a geographic question — it addresses whether the plaintiff may sue a defendant in a particular state (or states). As we studied in Chapter 2, a defendant may be sued in any state with which she has sufficient contacts to satisfy the statutory and constitutional tests for personal jurisdiction. The assessment of subject matter jurisdiction has nothing to do with geography. Instead, it concerns what court (in a state having personal jurisdiction) will hear the case. Recall from §1.2 that in each state there are two separate types of courts — those of the state court system and at least one (a trial court) of

155

the federal court system. Thus, the basic subject matter jurisdiction question is whether the case will be heard in a federal court or in a state court.

Stated another way, personal jurisdiction deals with the court's power over the *parties*. Subject matter jurisdiction deals with the court's power over the *case and the claims asserted in it*. To enter a valid judgment, a court must have both personal and subject matter jurisdiction.

Federal courts have *limited subject matter jurisdiction*, which means that they can only hear specific types of cases. Mostly, we are concerned with *original jurisdiction*, which, noted at §1.2.2, refers to cases filed and decided by trial courts (as opposed to *appellate jurisdiction*, which concerns appeals from trial courts to "higher" courts). There are rare subsets of cases invoking federal jurisdiction in which federal courts have *exclusive subject matter jurisdiction*, which means that no other court may entertain such cases.[1] State court systems, in contrast to the federal courts, have *general subject matter jurisdiction*, which means that they can hear any cognizable claim at all (except, of course, those over which the federal courts have exclusive subject matter jurisdiction). As you can tell from this brief discussion, in many instances, a case can be heard either by a federal or a state court. In such cases, the federal and state courts have *concurrent subject matter jurisdiction*.

The determination of whether a court has subject matter jurisdiction is made by reference to the state or federal constitution and statutes that implement the constitutional grants. In some cases, as we will see, there are also common law (court-made) rules that affect subject matter jurisdiction.

§4.2   The General Subject Matter Jurisdiction of State Court Systems

As we just noted, each state's judicial system has general subject matter jurisdiction — it can hear any claim (except those rare cases that invoke exclusive federal court jurisdiction). Each state is free to divide subject matter jurisdiction between whatever courts the state wishes to establish. There is enormous variety in the names that states use for their trial courts; common names include superior court, municipal court, circuit court, and district court. It is common to have more than one trial court in a state judicial system. In some states, for instance, there are specialized tribunals to address questions of probate law, family law, and the like. In some states, subject matter jurisdiction is divided along monetary lines; for

---

[1]Examples include admiralty (§1333), bankruptcy (§1334(a)), patent and copyright infringement and plant variety protection cases (§1338(a)), antitrust (15 U.S.C. §§15-26), and securities cases (15 U.S.C. §78a).

example, one court may hear claims involving $15,000 or less and another court may hear claims involving a greater amount.

The important points are simple. First, the allocation of cases within the state court system is purely a matter of state law. The state may, through constitution or through statute, determine what state courts will exist and what types of cases they will hear. Most civil procedure teachers do not spend much time on state court structure and subject matter jurisdiction. If yours does, you should know what provisions are relevant for that purpose. Second, every state judicial system — in the aggregate — has general subject matter jurisdiction. Thus, while not every court in a given state will be able to hear every case, a plaintiff will be able to find some court in any state in which to assert her case. Get used to thinking about the fact that state courts are "always there." If a case cannot invoke federal subject matter jurisdiction, it can always be taken to a state court.

§4.3   The Limited Subject Matter Jurisdiction of the Federal Courts

In the Constitution, the states cede powers to the central, or federal, government. The entire federal government is one of limited powers (although, as you will see in your course on Constitutional Law, the Supreme Court has interpreted many of these powers broadly). In Civil Procedure, we are concerned primarily with Article III of the Constitution. Article III, §2, provides nine categories (or "heads") of jurisdiction — that is, nine types of disputes that the federal court system may hear. The federal courts simply have no power to adjudicate cases that do not fall within these bases of jurisdiction. In reviewing the nine heads of federal jurisdiction, note that some are based upon the substantive law to be applied to the dispute[2] while others are given a federal forum because of the character of the parties.[3]

Interestingly, the jurisdiction listed in Article III, §2, is not automatically bestowed on the federal courts. Instead, it is incumbent on Congress to determine how much of the constitutional jurisdiction the federal courts

---

[2] The first one listed in Article III, §2, is cases arising under federal law; others include cases involving bankruptcies. The Framers apparently thought that federal courts would possess or develop especial expertise in these areas of federal law, or that they might be especially sensitive to the federal policies underlying such substantive laws.

[3] For example, cases involving ambassadors and consuls, disputes between states, and, most important for Civil Procedure courses, cases involving citizens of different states. With these, the Framers apparently concluded that the involvement of a particular type of litigant commanded the attention (or protection) of the federal courts.

are to exercise.[4] Indeed, as Article III, §1, of the Constitution makes clear, the Founders left it up to Congress to decide whether the country would have lower federal courts at all.[5] From the beginning, Congress has provided for such lower federal courts.[6] In setting their jurisdiction, Congress is not required to grant a particular constitutional head of jurisdiction to the full extent that it could. For example, Congress can impose an amount in controversy restriction. In general, as we will see, the statutory grants of federal subject matter jurisdiction are narrower than the Constitution would permit. Thus, the key issue in determining whether a federal court has jurisdiction usually is whether a *statute* has granted it; only rarely has Congress passed a jurisdictional statute that exceeded the Article III authority.[7]

Because federal courts can only hear limited kinds of cases, litigants whose dispute does not meet one of the bases of federal subject matter jurisdiction cannot consent to the jurisdiction of a federal court. There is a presumption against federal jurisdiction. Thus, a party initiating litigation in federal court bears a burden of establishing federal jurisdiction.[8] She must plead it and, if challenged, prove facts showing subject matter jurisdiction. We see in §6.2 that defendants must assert some defenses early in litigation, or else waive the right to raise that defense. This is not true, however, with lack of subject matter jurisdiction. A defect in subject matter jurisdiction cannot be waived by the parties or the court. The court is under an obligation to dismiss whenever it determines that a case before it lacks federal subject matter jurisdiction.[9] This rule may result in enormous waste of federal judicial resources, as when a case is litigated for years before the court determines that it did not belong in federal court.[10]

---

[4] There are exceptions to this principle, as Article III makes clear. Section 2, clause 2, provides that in cases affecting ambassadors and similar officers, and in which a state is a party, the Supreme Court has "original" (trial) jurisdiction. Congress has no power to abolish federal subject matter jurisdiction in these. But as to the other heads of jurisdiction, Congress has the authority to decide whether the federal courts should have jurisdiction.

[5] Article III, §1, requires the existence of only one federal court: the Supreme Court. Establishment of lower federal courts was a politically contentious issue, and the Founders decided to leave the decision to the Congress.

[6] In Chapter 1, we noted that the trial courts in the federal system are United States District Courts and the intermediate appellate courts are United States Courts of Appeals for the various circuits. See §1.2.2.

[7] Perhaps your casebook notes *Hodgson v. Bowerbank*, 9 U.S. 303 (1809), which dealt with just such a situation. Congress granted jurisdiction over cases in which a foreign citizen was a party. To the extent that this permitted jurisdiction over a case by an alien against an alien, it exceeded Article III. See §§4.5.3, 4.5.5.

[8] *See* Fed. R. Civ. P. 8(a)(1) (requiring complaint to contain "a short and plain statement of the grounds for the court's jurisdiction").

[9] *See* Fed. R. Civ. P. 12(h)(3) (lack of subject matter jurisdiction may be raised anytime).

[10] *See, e.g.*, Depex Reina 9 Partnership v. Texas Intl. Petroleum Corp., 987 F.2d 461 (10th Cir. 1990) (case dismissed for lack of subject matter jurisdiction after full trial, appeal, remand by the appellate court, and further proceedings in district court).

The two major grants of federal subject matter jurisdiction, which are staple parts of virtually every Civil Procedure course and of the daily work of the federal district court,[11] are diversity of citizenship jurisdiction under §1332(a)(1)[12] and federal question jurisdiction under §1332. One of these grants (diversity of citizenship) is based upon characteristics of the litigants, while the other (federal question) is based upon the substantive law to be applied to determine the outcome of the dispute. Before looking at them in detail, it is important to recognize why it may matter that a case can go to a federal, as opposed to a state, court.

§4.4 The Political Insulation of Federal Judges

Article III, §1, of the Constitution provides remarkable job security for federal judges, security not enjoyed by state court judges. First, a federal judge's pay cannot be reduced. Second, a federal judge serves during "good Behaviour," which means she serves for life and can never be forced to retire. Unless a federal judge dies or resigns, she can be removed only by impeachment (and only seven federal judges have been removed by impeachment in our nation's history). Third, under the Appointments Clause, federal judges are appointed by the President, but must be confirmed by vote of the Senate.[13] Thus, federal judges never face an electorate and do not stand for reappointments to specified terms.

In theory, as a result of these protections, federal judges are insulated from politics. The judges need not worry about offending Congress by interpreting or even striking legislation as unconstitutional, since Congress cannot reduce their pay. The judges need not worry about offending the public by making unpopular rulings, since the public does not get to vote them out of office. More specifically, the judges need not worry about ruling against a locally powerful figure or business, since that power broker cannot affect the judge's employment.

---

[11] We are concerned in Civil Procedure with the jurisdiction of the federal district courts, which are the main trial courts of the federal system. As we saw in §1.2.2, appeals from these courts go to the United States Court of Appeals. From there, review can be had by the Supreme Court of the United States (if it agrees to hear the case). Though this is beyond the scope of your course in Civil Procedure, note that there are other, specialized, federal courts, such as the Court of Federal Claims, and the Court of International Trade, the jurisdiction of which is quite specific. When a party erroneously files a case in the wrong federal court, it may be transferred to the appropriate court (one with subject matter jurisdiction) under §1631.

[12] Some courses address the related jurisdictional basis of alienage, §1332(a)(2). We address alienage at §4.5.5.

[13] U.S. Constitution, Article II, §2.

State judges are not so lucky. State judges have no federal constitutional guaranty that their salaries cannot be reduced. More important, however, most state judges, even at the state supreme court level, must face the electorate. Either they are elected to their post originally, or they must get voter approval for a new term, or both. Thus, state court judges who rule against popular opinion may find themselves without a job. In a dramatic example of this principle, California voters removed three justices from the California Supreme Court in the 1980s, after an intense campaign criticized particular opinions they had authored or joined (mostly about refusal to uphold sentences imposing the death penalty).

§4.5   Diversity of Citizenship and Alienage Jurisdiction

§4.5.1   Introduction

Diversity of citizenship jurisdiction is standard fare in most Civil Procedure courses. It is an important subject in the real world as well, accounting for about one-fifth of the civil cases filed in federal district courts. In law school, diversity jurisdiction permits the professor to test not only a variety of relatively mechanical rules, addressed in §4.5.3, but some interesting policy issues concerning the role of the federal courts, seen in §4.5.2.

Article III, §2, of the Constitution permits the federal courts to entertain cases "between citizens of different states."[14] Congress has enacted statutes granting this "diversity jurisdiction" to the federal courts since the first Judiciary Act of 1789. It has always included an amount in controversy requirement in the jurisdictional grant. Today, diversity jurisdiction is granted in §1332(a)(1), which mirrors the constitutional language by giving courts the power to hear cases "between citizens of different states," but adds the requirement that the amount in controversy in the case exceed $75,000. Thus, from the face of the statute, there are two requirements for a diversity case: It must involve "citizens of different States" and the amount in controversy must exceed $75,000. As we will see, there is more to these requirements than meets the eye.

Closely related to diversity of citizenship jurisdiction is alienage jurisdiction. The last "head" of jurisdiction listed in Article III, §2, is for cases "between a State, or Citizens thereof, and foreign States, Citizens, or Subjects." From this, *alienage*, as lawyers and judges use the term, includes

---

[14]This is the seventh of the nine heads of jurisdiction listed in Article III, §2. Do not confuse it with the two that precede it: "between two or more States" and "between a State and citizens of another State." Each of these bases involves litigation in which a State is actually a litigant. The latter basis was abrogated by the Eleventh Amendment.

disputes between a citizen of a state (of the United States), on one side, and an alien (i.e., a citizen or subject of a foreign country), on the other. Congress has always provided for this form of jurisdiction in federal courts. Today, it is found in §1332(a)(2),[15] which mirrors the constitutional language but also adds the same dollar requirement applicable in diversity cases: The amount in controversy must exceed $75,000. Alienage jurisdiction has never accounted for an appreciable percentage of the federal court docket and has never been controversial. No one argues that alienage jurisdiction ought to be abolished. That is not true, however, about diversity of citizenship. We discuss alienage in §4.5.5. Now we turn to the policy debate underlying diversity of citizenship cases — a discussion of why diversity jurisdiction is controversial.

§4.5.2 The Ongoing Debate Over Diversity of Citizenship Jurisdiction

Although the Founders provided for diversity of citizenship jurisdiction in the Constitution and the first Congress enacted it in the original Judiciary Act of 1789, it has always had its critics. Why? These cases go to federal court *not* because federal law applies, but because the litigants happen to be citizens of different states. These cases are governed by state substantive law.[16] Many people (including many law professors) see this as a misallocation of federal judicial resources. In an era of crowded federal court dockets, they argue, the federal courts should not be forced to spend valuable time interpreting and applying state law.

When engaging in this debate in class, remember this, however: State courts routinely must hear cases arising under federal law. Except in those rare instances in which federal question jurisdiction is exclusive, plaintiffs are free to take their federal law cases to state court. But there are two differences. First, under the Supremacy Clause of the Constitution, the state courts are required to apply governing federal law.[17] Second, when state courts interpret federal law, the cases may, at least in theory, be appealed to the Supreme Court of the United States.[18] So if the state

---

[15] Because the grant of alienage jurisdiction is found in the same statute as that for diversity of citizenship jurisdiction, some lawyers and judges refer to it as a type or species of diversity. Doing so does not cause harm, but it is preferable — especially in light of the divergent constitutional grants of the two — to keep them separate terminologically. So we refer to §1332(a)(1) as the grant of diversity jurisdiction and §1332(a)(2) as the grant of alienage jurisdiction.

[16] This is the upshot of the *Erie* doctrine, addressed in Chapter 10.

[17] U.S. Constitution, Article VI, §2. *See* Testa v. Katt, 330 U.S. 386 (1947) (Rhode Island must enforce Federal Emergency Price Control Act).

[18] Recall from §1.2.2 that the Supreme Court can hear appeals from a state's highest court, but only on matters of federal law. In fact, however, this might not be a great source of

courts make a mistake concerning the content of federal law, the ultimate federal court might be able to correct it. But if a federal court in a diversity case makes a mistake in interpreting state law, there is no way a state court can fix it, because there is no review of federal judgments by state courts.[19]

Why did the Founders provide for diversity of citizenship cases in federal court? The historic justification is that diversity jurisdiction provides a neutral forum for a litigant who might suffer from bias in the local courts of another state (or who might at least *fear* that she could suffer from local bias). Put more simply, in language lawyers use, the out-of-state litigant fears that she may get "hometowned" in a local court. Remember that state court judges are usually elected, and thus must answer to the members of the community. If a state court judge rules against local interests (and in favor of the out-of-state litigant), she might risk losing her job.

Before ratification of the Constitution, several states had enacted debtor-relief statutes that prevented creditors from collecting on their loans and other contracts. Thus, several scholars, including Felix Frankfurter,[20] suggest that the Founders' principal interest in providing for diversity jurisdiction was to assuage the apprehensions of the commercial class (some members of which sat in the Constitutional Convention, after all).[21] The prospect of a neutral forum, politically insulated from the state power structure, could encourage investment by out-of-state commercial interests. It seems to have worked. William Howard Taft concluded that diversity jurisdiction "was the single most important element in securing capital for the development of the southern and western United States."[22]

The question today is whether diversity jurisdiction has outlived its usefulness. Many believe that it has. They assert that modern travel and mass communication have so homogenized American culture that local and regional biases are no longer prevalent. Moreover, they point out, because

---

protection, because the Supreme Court can hear so few cases in a given year. Nonetheless, the system does have this potential protection.

[19] Occasionally, federal courts certainly do misinterpret state law in diversity cases. While the ruling binds the parties in that case, it does not establish precedent in the state court system. The state court system, in subsequent cases, is free to ignore the federal court's interpretation of state law (and even to point out the error of the federal court's ways). To avoid misapplication of state law, over half the states have "certification" statutes, which allow the federal court to ask the state supreme court for guidance on thorny issues of state law. We discuss such statutes at §10.8.

[20] Frankfurter was a Harvard law professor whom President Franklin Roosevelt appointed to the Supreme Court. He served as a Justice from 1939 to 1962.

[21] Felix Frankfurter & James Landis, The Business of the Supreme Court 8-9 (1928).

[22] William Howard Taft, *Possible and Needed Reforms in Administration of Justice in Federal Courts*, 8 A.B.A. J. 601, 604 (1922). Taft is the only person to have been President (1909-1913) and to have served on the Supreme Court (Chief Justice, 1921-1930).

federal courts in diversity cases must apply state substantive law, the existence of diversity jurisdiction does not result in a change of law. These anti-diversity commentators assert that the limited federal judicial resources ought to be spent on cases involving questions of federal law.[23] Thus, they urge Congress to abolish diversity jurisdiction.[24]

Others contend, however, that regional bias is not dead, and that the need for diversity jurisdiction continues today. They argue that even if bias against out-of-state litigants cannot be proved, the litigants' *apprehension* of local bias is not irrational. In this regard, consider the following statement from a justice of the West Virginia Supreme Court:

> As long as I am allowed to redistribute wealth from out-of-state companies to injured in-state plaintiffs, I shall continue to do so. Not only is my sleep enhanced when I give someone else's money away, but so is my job security, because the in-state plaintiffs, their families and their friends will re-elect me.[25]

Again, in theory, the out-of-state litigant has no such fears in federal court, since federal judges never face an electorate; they have lifetime tenure. See §4.4. Moreover, federal courts tend to sit in major cities, not in the rural hustings, and to draw their juries from a large region of the state, not simply from a single county. For all these reasons, a modern out-of-state litigant might still prefer to litigate against a local citizen in federal, not state, court. Further, abolition of diversity jurisdiction would simply funnel these cases back to already burdened state court systems.

In terms of practical political reality, Congress is unlikely ever to abolish diversity jurisdiction. Why? For the simple reason that the practicing bar supports diversity jurisdiction and is such a strong lobbying force. The anti-diversity voices tend to be those of law professors and some federal judges, none of whom has appreciable clout with Congress. Congress may, however, cut back on the number of diversity cases from time to time by increasing the amount in controversy requirement or by making narrow changes to §1332(a)(1). For example, even proponents of diversity jurisdiction recognize that its underlying rationale is not implicated when the

[23] *See, e.g.,* Larry Kramer, *Diversity Jurisdiction*, 1990 BYU L. Rev. 97; Report of Federal Courts Study Committee 38-43 (1990).

[24] The efforts to abolish diversity jurisdiction are aimed at §1332(a)(1). No one seems to want to abolish statutory interpleader jurisdiction under §1335, which is based upon diversity of citizenship but involves very specialized litigation (a dispute over ownership of property), discussed at §13.2.

[25] Richard Neely, The Product Liability Mess: How Business Can Be Rescued from the Politics of State Courts 4 (1988).

plaintiff invoking it is a citizen of the forum state.[26] Such a hometown plaintiff does not need the protection of the federal court, yet — under the current statute — is able to invoke it. In recent years, some members of Congress have suggested changing the diversity statute to remove jurisdiction in such a hometown plaintiff situation, but Congress has yet to do so.[27]

§4.5.3 Assessing Whether Diversity of Citizenship Jurisdiction Is Invoked

The Complete Diversity Rule

The most significant and well-known case involving diversity of citizenship jurisdiction is *Strawbridge v. Curtiss*,[28] which the Supreme Court decided in 1806. Chief Justice John Marshall's opinion is startlingly short — both in length and on reasoning. In *Strawbridge*, plaintiffs (called *complainants* in the syllabus of the opinion) were alleged to be citizens of Massachusetts; there were multiple defendants, most of whom were citizens of Massachusetts and one of whom was a citizen of Vermont. The Supreme Court held that the case did not invoke diversity jurisdiction, even though one of the plaintiffs was of diverse citizenship from one of the defendants. In the Court's view, "each distinct interest should be represented by persons, all of whom are entitled to sue, or be sued, in the federal courts."[29] In other words, each plaintiff must be of diverse citizenship from each defendant. This is the famous "complete diversity rule."

Nothing in the language of the Constitution or the diversity statute compels this rule. Indeed, a case by a citizen of Massachusetts against a citizen of Vermont and a citizen of Massachusetts would seem to be a case "between citizens of different states." Moreover, Marshall did not give any hint why the Court concluded that complete diversity was necessary. Some opine that because the Vermont citizen has a co-defendant who is a citizen of the same state as the plaintiff, she has no need to fear local bias.[30] On the other hand, though, the Vermont citizen, being the *only* "foreigner"

---

[26] *See* 15 Moore's Federal Practice §102.12.

[27] As we see in §4.8, however, the defendant may well be able to "remove" such a case from state to federal court on the basis of diversity jurisdiction. So prohibiting an in-state plaintiff from invoking diversity may not, in the long run, keep many cases out of federal court. It would, however, put the onus on the defendant — in such a case the one needing the protection of federal court — to get the case into that court.

[28] 7 U.S. 267 (1806).

[29] *Strawbridge*, 7 U.S. at 267.

[30] *See* David Currie, *The Federal Courts and the American Law Institute*, 36 U. Chi. L. Rev. 1, 18 (1968) ("the assumption apparently underlying *Strawbridge* is that the presence of Massachusetts people on both sides of a case will neutralize any possibility of bias affecting litigants from other states.").

in the case, would seem to have especial reason to fear being "home-towned" in a Massachusetts state court.

Despite the lack of a convincing rationale for it, the complete diversity rule of *Strawbridge* is good law to this day. Though the rule is difficult to justify (except as a docket control device to reduce the number of cases in the federal courts), it is easy to apply. The rule is extremely mechanical. Do not be sloppy in stating or applying the rule. Every Civil Procedure professor has read exams in which a student says that the rule means "every party must be diverse from every other party." That is simply not correct. The rule is that every *plaintiff* must be of diverse citizenship from every *defendant*. Parties on the same side of the dispute can be co-citizens.

- ○ Two plaintiffs, each a citizen of California, sue ten defendants, each of whom is a citizen of Arizona. This case satisfies the complete diversity rule. Even though there are co-citizens in the case (the plaintiffs are co-citizens with each other and the defendants are co-citizens with each other), every plaintiff is diverse from every defendant.

It is clear that the complete diversity rule is a *statutory*, and not a *constitutional*, requirement.[31] It applies to cases brought under §1332(a)(1).[32] The constitutional provision for diversity jurisdiction, in Article III, §2, requires only that there be "minimal" diversity — that at least one plaintiff be of diverse citizenship from one defendant. Accordingly, the facts of *Strawbridge* itself (Massachusetts plaintiff; Vermont and Massachusetts defendants) fall within the federal courts' *constitutional* power over diversity cases but not within the statutory grant of diversity jurisdiction under §1332(a)(1).

Two important consequences flow from the fact that the complete diversity rule is not constitutionally mandated. First, Congress could, constitutionally, amend §1332(a)(1) to overrule *Strawbridge* and permit

---

[31] This was established in *State Farm Fire & Cas. Co. v. Tashire*, 386 U.S. 523, 530-531 (1967), which upheld the constitutionality of jurisdiction in "statutory interpleader" cases (discussed in §13.2) based upon "minimal," as opposed to complete, diversity: "Article III poses no obstacle to the legislative extension of federal jurisdiction, founded on diversity, so long as any two adverse parties are not co-citizens." Most observers thought this conclusion was clear from *Strawbridge* itself, in which Marshall never mentioned the constitutional grant of diversity, but spoke only of "[t]he words of the act of Congress." *Strawbridge*, 7 U.S. at 267. But the Court did not expressly so hold until it decided *Tashire*.

[32] Interestingly, the complete diversity rule is not stated in §1332(a)(1). Courts frequently must interpret statutes, as the Supreme Court interpreted the precursor to §1332(a)(1) in *Strawbridge*. If Congress disagrees with the judicial interpretation, it is free to change it by amending the statute to reject the judicial "gloss." After *Strawbridge*, Congress has reenacted the general diversity statute on several occasions, without rejecting the Court's interpretation in that case. When that happens, we assume that Congress adopted the judicial interpretation.

jurisdiction based upon minimal diversity. In view of the burgeoning dockets of the federal courts and the ongoing debate over whether diversity of citizenship jurisdiction ought to be retained (see §4.5.2), such a move is politically unthinkable.

Second, even if it does not change §1332(a)(1), Congress can grant jurisdiction under *other statutes* based upon minimal diversity. Indeed, it has done so three times. One is statutory interpleader, under §1335. Interpleader is a very specialized kind of litigation, which we address at §13.2. Permitting its invocation on the basis of minimal diversity makes it more readily available but (because it is so specialized) without a risk of inundating the federal courts. More recently, Congress employed minimal diversity in the Multiparty, Multiforum Trial Jurisdiction Act, which became effective in January 2003. It grants jurisdiction, based upon minimal diversity between adverse parties, over any case "that arises from a single accident, where at least 75 natural persons have died in the accident at a discrete location," provided other requirements are also satisfied.[33] As with interpleader, there is little risk of docket overload from such cases, and the use of minimal diversity permits a federal court to resolve in one proceeding a dispute that might otherwise involve several state and federal courts. More recently, in the Class Action Fairness Act of 2005, Congress permitted the invocation of minimal diversity to facilitate federal court access for class actions; this controversial act is discussed in §13.3.8.

As a matter of policy, it makes sense to have the constitutional grant be broader than the statutory grant of jurisdiction. It is far easier to change a statute than to amend the Constitution. Thus, a broader constitutional provision gives Congress leeway in determining whether to impose the complete diversity restriction. What is odd, though, is that the constitutional provision for diversity jurisdiction and the statutory version in §1332(a)(1) are worded identically — each speaks of a case "between citizens of different states." This may be your introduction to something you will see throughout your legal career — situations in which the same words mean different things in different contexts. Until your studies get to these other statutes, however, the concept of minimal diversity will have no impact. In discussing diversity jurisdiction under §1332(a)(1), you must apply the complete diversity rule.

The Supreme Court drove home the importance of the complete diversity rule in *Exxon Mobil Corp. v. Allapattah Services, Inc.*[34] There, it held that federal subject matter jurisdiction simply cannot attach in a case in

---

[33] 28 U.S.C. §1369.
[34] 545 U.S. 546 (2005).

which there are co-citizens on both sides of the case.[35] What happens? Presumably, the plaintiff can drop the nondiverse parties[36] and thereby structure the case so as to invoke diversity jurisdiction. If she preferred the efficiency of packaging all parties in a single case, she could, of course, opt to sue in state court.

- ○ Plaintiffs are citizens of Oklahoma, Nebraska, and Texas. There are 28 defendants. Twenty-seven of them are citizens of California and one is a citizen of Nebraska. The case fails to invoke diversity of citizenship under §1332(a)(1) because it does not meet the complete diversity rule. That rule is met only if *all* plaintiffs are citizens of different states from *all* defendants. Here, there are Nebraska citizens on each side of the case. The plaintiff may drop the one Nebraska defendant from the case and thereby invoke diversity jurisdiction. Or she could, after the court dismisses the case, file a new proceeding (joining everyone — even the Nebraska citizen) in state court. Remember, state courts can hear basically any kind of case; the citizenship of the parties is irrelevant to state court subject matter jurisdiction.

Determining Citizenship of Various Litigants

We know that to invoke diversity of citizenship jurisdiction, the case must satisfy the complete diversity rule. But to apply the complete diversity rule, we must understand how to determine a litigant's citizenship. There are different types of litigants — humans, corporations, other business associations (such as partnerships and limited liability companies), fiduciaries suing to represent other persons — and the tests for determining their citizenship may differ. Terminology is extremely important. We are speaking here of diversity of *citizenship*. Though some courts (and, unfortunately, some professors) are sloppy about terminology, precision is a good lawyerly trait. Citizenship is a term of art; it is a specific, technical term. Understand what it means, and use it. It is not diversity of "residence"[37] or "domicile" or where the litigant is "from." It is diversity of *citizenship*.

Now, how do we determine the citizenship of various litigants?

---

[35] 545 U.S. 546, 562 (2005). The Court spoke of this as the "contamination theory" — that is, the presence of nondiverse parties on both sides of a lawsuit "contaminates" the case because it "eliminates the justification for providing a federal forum."

[36] *See* Fed. R. Civ. P. 21. *See* Newman-Green, Inc. v. Alfonzo-Larrain, 490 U.S. 826, 832 (1989) (even appellate court can drop nondiverse parties to preserve diversity, even after entry of judgment).

[37] Residence is an important notion in determining venue, which is an entirely different issue from subject matter jurisdiction. Do not mix the terms. If you attempt to invoke diversity of citizenship jurisdiction and allege the parties' residence, the court should dismiss the case.

Natural Persons (Humans). Before coming to law school, you used the word "person" to refer only to human beings. In the eyes of the law, however, there are different kinds of persons. While humans obviously are persons, so are some entities, such as corporations. So it is necessary to distinguish between them. Humans are "natural persons," as opposed to "artificial persons," such as corporations.

For general purposes in diversity of citizenship, Congress has never generally defined the citizenship of natural persons.[38] It has left the issue to the courts. According to the Supreme Court, to be a citizen of a state (meaning, a state of the United States) for diversity purposes, a human must be (1) a citizen of the United States[39] and (2) domiciled in that state.[40] In most instances, the first part of this requirement will be clear. But the second part can give rise to interesting problems.

Before defining domicile, it is important to understand that a person has only *one* domicile at a time. It is impossible to have more than one domicile at any given point. So, for diversity purposes, a human can only be a citizen of one state at a time. (We see shortly that this is not true of other kinds of litigants.) Minors are usually ascribed the domicile of their parents. At the age of majority, or at emancipation, however, they are able to establish their own domicile. Until surprisingly recently, a sexist common law rule provided that a married woman took the domicile of her husband.[41] In addition, a human *always* has a domicile.[42] You cannot lose your domicile. You retain the domicile ascribed at birth until you affirmatively change it. And you retain that new domicile until you affirmatively change it.

Now, what is a person's domicile? Courts have used different phrases, but one classic definition is that domicile is that place where a person "has [her] true, fixed, and permanent home and principal establishment, and to which [she] has the intention of returning whenever [she] is absent therefrom."[43] It is absolutely clear that changing one's domicile requires the two concurrent factors: (1) establishing physical presence in the new state with (2) the subjective intent to make that state her domicile. There are no

---

[38] It has, however, for narrow subsets of litigants. Permanent resident aliens are defined as citizens of the state in which they are domiciled, as we see below. Executors and other fiduciaries are defined as citizens of the person they represent, as we also see below.

[39] We deal with cases involving citizens of other countries below. Throughout the materials, however, unless the facts indicate that a party is a citizen of another country, assume that she is a citizen of the United States. This requirement is not stated in each hypothetical.

[40] Sun Printing & Publishing Assn. v. Edwards, 194 U.S. 377, 383 (1904); Brown v. Keene, 33 U.S. 112 (1834).

[41] This is one of many issues discussed in *Mas v. Perry*, 489 F.2d 1396 (5th Cir. 1974), a case found in most Civil Procedure casebooks, discussed at various points below.

[42] Katz v. Goodyear Tire & Rubber Co., 737 F.2d 238, 243 (2d Cir. 1984).

[43] Wright & Kane, Federal Courts 163 (paraphrasing Justice Story's famous definition in Story, Conflict of Laws, §41 (8th ed. 1883)).

papers to fill out. There is no official decree. It is a matter of establishing these two elements — one physical and one mental — concurrently. One element alone never suffices. All the intent in the world to change one's domicile doesn't effect a change until coupled with physical presence in the new state. Similarly, residence in the new state, even for an extended period, does not constitute a change of domicile unless the intent also is present. Thus, one's residence is not necessarily one's domicile.[44]

One popular case on this point is *Mas v. Perry*,[45] in which a married couple sued their landlord, alleging that he invaded their privacy by installing two-way mirrors that allowed him to spy on them in their bedroom and bathroom. The defendant was clearly a citizen of Louisiana. One key question was whether Mrs. Mas was also a citizen of Louisiana.[46] If so, obviously, there would be no diversity jurisdiction. Mrs. Mas had been born and raised in Mississippi, and thus started as a citizen of that state. She lived in Louisiana for several years to attend graduate school and to work as a graduate assistant. She and her husband moved to Illinois and intended to return to Louisiana for more schooling. She was undecided about where she would live after that. The court held that Mrs. Mas had never changed her domicile from Mississippi. Although present in Louisiana for years, she had never formed the subjective intent to make that her home. Thus, she was of diverse citizenship from the defendant.

- Ms. Robinson is a citizen of New York. She forms the intent to change her domicile to Arizona. She packs her belongings in her car and leaves New York, driving toward Arizona. On the way, however, she is involved in an auto wreck with *D* in Oklahoma. Ms. Robinson is still a citizen of New York. Even though she has satisfied the subjective intent requirement to establish an Arizona domicile, she has not satisfied the physical component, since she did not make it to Arizona. Thus, even though she has left New York, with no intent to return, she is still a domiciliary (and, therefore a citizen) of New York.
- Suppose Ms. Robinson, while in New York, formed the intent to make Arizona her permanent home. She packs her belongings in her car and drives to California without incident. As soon as she drives across the

---

[44] Do not fall into the habit of talking about residence when addressing diversity jurisdiction. Residence is relevant to venue, as we see in Chapter 5. It is irrelevant to subject matter jurisdiction. Here, we speak of *citizenship*, not of *residence*.

[45] 489 F.2d 1396 (5th Cir. 1974).

[46] *Mas* is a popular case because it discusses a host of important topics. Mr. Mas was a citizen of France, so his claim against the defendant invoked alienage jurisdiction. See §4.5.5. The case also demonstrates that the amount actually recovered by the plaintiff is irrelevant to whether the amount in controversy requirement for §1332 is met. See §4.5.3. It also shows that the requirements for subject matter jurisdiction are assessed at the time the case is commenced. Finally, it shows the abolition of the sexist rule ascribing to a married woman the domicile of her husband. So even though the case is over 30 years old, it is still popular in Civil Procedure courses.

state line into California, she is probably a domiciliary (and therefore a citizen) of California. Her intent was very clear and she is now present in California. There is probably no need to rent an apartment or buy a house before she is considered a domiciliary of California. In most cases, however, the expression of one's intent is not as clear as it was for Mrs. Robinson.

○ Travellin' Joe is a citizen of Texas. At age 18, he leaves Texas to attend college in Michigan. He knows he does not want to return to Texas, but is not sure where he wants to settle. After two years in Michigan, he transfers to a college in Oregon. After two more years, he graduates and attends medical school in Maryland. After four years there, he graduates and moves to Hawaii for a one-year internship. During his travels, he has never formed an intent to make any of these places his domicile, but he is certain that he does not want to go back to Texas. What is his citizenship for diversity purposes? Texas. Although Travellin' Joe now lives in Hawaii, and has resided in other states, he never formed the intent to make any of them his domicile.

The question of whether someone has formed the subjective intent to establish a new domicile can be difficult. Obviously, most of us do not jump up one day and cry out, "I have formed the intent to make this state my permanent home!" The issue is often litigated, and no single factor is determinative in establishing the intent to change one's domicile. Although the intent being tested is subjective, courts often must look to objective facts to determine it. They view all relevant information, including things such as voter registration, qualifying to pay in-state tuition, automobile registration, payment of real and personal property taxes, location of bank accounts[47] — as one court explained, a "grab-bag of indicia having to do with everyday life"[48] — that might indicate the intent to establish domicile.

One's reason for changing domicile is irrelevant. What if someone changes her domicile expressly to create diversity jurisdiction? As long as the two-part test for changing domicile is met, she can invoke diversity jurisdiction.[49] This result is consistent with the general rule, to be discussed at §4.5.3, that subject matter jurisdiction is assessed at the time the case is filed, not at the time the claim arose.

Three other issues deserve attention. First, several American political subdivisions — such as the District of Columbia, Puerto Rico, Guam, and the Virgin Islands — are not states. Nonetheless, §1332(e) provides that citizens of such places shall be treated as citizens of states for diversity

---

[47] *See, e.g.,* Lew v. Moss, 797 F.2d 747 (9th Cir. 1986).

[48] Simmons v. Skyway of Ocala, 592 F. Supp. 356, 366 (S.D. Ga. 1984).

[49] Williamson v. Osenton, 232 U.S. 619 (1914) (change of domicile to create diversity jurisdiction is permissible). In §4.5.4, we discuss "collusive joinder" and see that changing one's citizenship for the purpose of creating diversity jurisdiction is not "collusive."

purposes. Can Congress simply decree that a person who is not a citizen of a state be considered a citizen of a state? The statute is plainly contrary to an 1804 Supreme Court holding that a domiciliary of the District of Columbia is not a citizen of a state for diversity purposes.[50] Nonetheless, in 1949, the Supreme Court upheld §1332(e).[51] So the bottom line is simple enough: Treat the listed subdivisions as states, even though they are not.

Second, in 1990, Congress enacted the last sentence of §1332(a), which provides that foreign citizens or subjects (whom we refer to generically as *aliens*) who are admitted to the United States for permanent residence[52] shall be deemed citizens of the state in which they are domiciled. In other words, this statute ascribes to aliens a citizenship of a state of the United States. On its face, the statute is problematic, because the Supreme Court long ago held that one can be a citizen of a state only if she is a *citizen of the United States* and domiciled in the state.[53] According to some, Congress intended that the provision be used to *defeat* jurisdiction in a case involving a permanent resident alien and a U.S. citizen who were domiciled in the same state.[54] But nothing in the statute so limits its reach.

- *P* is a citizen of the United Kingdom, but is admitted to the United States for permanent residence. She has established her domicile in New Hampshire. She sues *D*, a citizen of New Hampshire, asserting a state law claim in excess of $75,000. Although this case would seem to invoke alienage jurisdiction (see §4.5.5), because it is between an alien and a citizen of a state (and exceeds $75,000), the last sentence of §1332(a) ascribes to *P* a New Hampshire citizenship. The result is that the case fails to invoke diversity of citizenship jurisdiction. Evidently, Congress intended that persons such as *P* would not be considered aliens, but as citizens of the state in which they established domicile.
- Now let's say *P*, the same person as in the preceding hypothetical, sues *D*, who is a citizen of Spain, on a state law claim exceeding $75,000. If we take the last sentence of §1332(a) on its face, this case invokes alienage jurisdiction, because it is between an alien and a citizen of a state (and exceeds $75,000). But there is a serious problem. This is a case by an

---

[50] Hepburn & Dundas v. Ellzey, 6 U.S. 445, 453 (1804).

[51] National Mutual Ins. Co. v. Tidewater Transfer Co., 337 U.S. 582 (1949). The opinion is quite unusual, since there is no majority rationale. Five Justices held the statute constitutional, but they did so for two mutually exclusive reasons, neither of which commanded a majority! The provision was codified as §1332(d) until 2005.

[52] In common parlance, permanent resident aliens are called *green card* aliens (although the card issued to them to confirm their status is no longer green). They are to be contrasted with aliens who are legally present in the United States on temporary or student visas and with illegal aliens. Section 1332(a)'s ascription of citizenship of the state in which domiciled applies only to green card aliens.

[53] See notes 40 and 41 above and text accompanying them.

[54] *See* Lee v. Trans-Am. Trucking Serv., 111 F. Supp. 2d 135 (E.D.N.Y. 1999); Arai v. Tachibana, 778 F. Supp. 1535 (D. Haw. 1991) (so interpreting the statute).

alien against an alien. As we noted in the paragraph preceding these hypotheticals, the Supreme Court has held that one cannot be a citizen of a state without also being a citizen of the United States. Thus *P* is an alien and this case is by an alien against an alien. Article III simply does not extend to cases by an alien against an alien, so the federal courts cannot have subject matter jurisdiction over such cases.[55] So far, courts have avoided the constitutional problem posed by this statutory provision of state citizenship to an alien.[56]

Third, a U.S. citizen can establish her domicile in a foreign country. Doing so does *not* make her a citizen of that country. Remember, a U.S. citizen's domicile *in a state of the United States* makes one a *citizen* of that state. Domicile in a foreign country does not make one a citizen of that country. Each country is sovereign to determine who its citizens are. Moreover, because such a person is not a citizen of a state (because not domiciled in a state), she cannot sue or be sued under diversity jurisdiction. Thus, U.S. citizens domiciled abroad fall through a "hole" in the diversity and alienage statutes.[57] Does that mean they are denied justice? No. It just means they cannot sue or be sued in federal court under diversity of citizenship or alienage jurisdiction. They can sue or be sued in state court and they can sue or be sued in federal court on some other basis of federal subject matter jurisdiction (such as federal question jurisdiction, see §4.6).

Corporations and Other Business Associations. Not all litigants are human beings. Various types of businesses and entities often litigate in federal court. To assess whether they can sue or be sued under diversity jurisdiction, obviously, we must be able to determine their citizenship. In an upper-division course on Business Associations, you will study the different forms that businesses can take — associations such as the corporation, the general partnership, the limited partnership, the limited liability company, the limited liability partnership, and others. For purposes of diversity jurisdiction, the law bifurcates business associations — every business either is (1) a corporation or (2) is not a corporation. Historically, for a variety of purposes (including taxation of income), the corporation has been seen as an entity — a distinct "artificial person."[58] But other forms of business — the "non-incorporated" forms — traditionally have been seen not as entities unto themselves, but as *aggregations* of the persons who run them.

---

[55] Hodgson v. Bowerbank, 9 U.S. 303 (1809). Alienage jurisdiction involves cases between an alien and a citizen of a state. See §4.5.5.

[56] *See, e.g.*, Singh v. Daimler-Benz, A.G., 9 F.3d 303 (3d Cir. 1993).

[57] This problem is seen again when discussing alienage in §4.5.5.

[58] As opposed to a "natural person," which, as we discussed above, is a human being.

This bifurcation affects the way courts determine the citizenship of the associations. Congress has defined the citizenship of a corporation by statute, and that definition (as we see in a moment) treats the corporation as a thing, separate from the people who run it. On the other hand, Congress has never defined the citizenship of non-incorporated businesses. Consistent with the law's general treatment of such businesses as aggregations rather than as entities, courts have assessed their citizenship by looking to the citizenships of the individual members of the business.

A corporation can be formed (lawyers usually say "incorporated" or "chartered") *only* by satisfying the corporate formation requirements established by state law. Each state has a corporation law prescribing these requirements. Though the particulars vary from state to state, in every jurisdiction those forming a corporation must file appropriate documents with a state agency. When the agency accepts those documents as proper, it decrees the corporation formed. It is a creature of the state in which it is formed, but can "qualify" to do business in other states without having to incorporate in those other states. The federal courts struggled for generations to determine the citizenship of corporations for diversity purposes. Our lives were made much easier when Congress stepped in and defined corporate citizenship by statute in 1958. That definition is now found in §1332(c)(1), which is an extremely important provision.

It is difficult to imagine a law school exam question dealing with diversity jurisdiction that does not involve the citizenship of a corporation. It is imperative to read §1332(c)(1) with care. It provides that a corporation is a citizen of "any State" (read that as plural) in which it is incorporated *and* of "the State" (read that as singular) in which it has its "principal place of business." As to the former, it is possible for a corporation to incorporate in more than one state. If it does, it is a citizen of each such state. As a practical matter, though, today it is almost impossible to find a corporation incorporated in more than one state.[59] This is because modern corporation law, as we just noted, allows a business to incorporate in one state and qualify to do business in others (without incorporating in the

---

[59] To the extent there are dual incorporations today, they tend to be bridge or turnpike authorities that operate thoroughfares between two states. For political reasons, they may incorporate in each state. Thus, the authority that operates bridges between Pennsylvania and New Jersey may be incorporated in each state. *See* Yancoskie v. Delaware River Port Auth., 528 F.2d 722 (3d Cir. 1975). Dual incorporation used to be quite common because states used to require corporations to charter there if they were to own realty in the state. Modern corporation laws regarding authorization to operate in a state in which a company is not incorporated, however, obviated the need and, thus, the practice of multiple incorporation.

others). As a practical matter, then, there is usually only one state of incorporation. And the professor simply cannot hide the ball on this; the exam question presumably must tell you the state of incorporation.[60]

But remember that a corporation is *also* a citizen of the one state in which it has its "principal place of business." So a corporation, unlike a human, can be a citizen of more than one state at a time. If a corporation is incorporated in Delaware and has its principal place of business in California, it is a citizen of Delaware *and* California.[61] But not all corporations are a citizen of two states. Many corporations have their principal place of business in the same state in which they are incorporated. Such a corporation is a citizen of only that one state. The fact that a corporation might have more than one citizenship, however, may make it more difficult to invoke diversity jurisdiction.

- Big Co., incorporated in Delaware and having its principal place of business in New York, sues *XYZ* Corporation, which is incorporated in New York with its principal place of business in California. Big Co. is a citizen of *both* Delaware and New York. *XYZ* Corporation is a citizen of *both* New York and California. Thus, there is no diversity jurisdiction because the plaintiff and the defendant are both citizens of New York. The case violates the complete diversity rule.

Note, however, that there is *only one principal place of business. No corporation can have more than one principal place of business under §1332(c)(1).*[62] Even if the corporation has a billion-dollar manufacturing plant in each of the 50 states, it is *not* a citizen of all 50 states. It is a citizen of the state in which it is incorporated and of the *one state* in which it has its principal place of business. So, assuming the corporation is not incorporated in more than one state (and that is a safe assumption, since such corporations are exceptionally rare), a corporation will be a citizen of at most two states — the state of incorporation and the state where it has its principal place of business.

---

[60] It could say, for example, that the corporation is formed under Pennsylvania law, or chartered in Pennsylvania, or is a Pennsylvania corporation. All of these would be telling you the same thing: that it is incorporated in Pennsylvania.

[61] Do not say Delaware *or* California. It is a citizen of *both* states, as §1332(c)(1) makes clear.

[62] Do not make the mistake that so many law students (and bar applicants) have made by saying that a corporation is a citizen of all states in which it does business. Although some people have proposed such a rule as a way of reducing the number of diversity cases, it is not and never has been the law. We see in §5.4.1 that, for venue purposes, a corporation might *reside* in all 50 states. But *citizenship*, not residence, is the relevant inquiry here.

◦   *P* Corporation is incorporated in Delaware, has its principal place of business in Illinois, and is qualified to do business in California, New York, Ohio, Michigan, and Virginia. Of what states is *P* Corporation a citizen?[63]

The assessment of what constitutes the principal place of business is very fact-specific (and very exam-worthy). Neither §1332(c)(1) nor any other statute defines the term, so it has been left to the courts. They have tended to look at two basic factors. Today, most courts put those two factors together in a "total activities" test. One factor is the *physical* aspect of the corporation's business. This sees the principal place of business as the state in which the corporation does more of whatever it does (manufacturing widgets, providing services, etc.) than anywhere else.[64] This emphasis is variously called the *place of activities*, or *bulk of activities*, or *center of activities*, or *muscle-center* test. The other main factor is the corporation's *decision-making activity*. This sees the principal place of business as the state from which the corporation directs its activity and makes its decisions.[65] This emphasis is sometimes called the *nerve center* approach. Under either factor — that focusing on activities or that focusing on decision making — it is a mistake to ascribe to a corporation's headquarters or executive offices or registered office any *presumptive* status as the "principal place of business."[66]

It is also a mistake to think of these two factors as somehow competing for the honor of being the corporation's principal place of business. As noted, most courts seem to look to the overall picture and determine, on the facts of the case, which *emphasis* — "muscle" or "nerve" — makes the most sense. Courts generally refer to this approach as the total activities test.[67] Using this approach, some rules of thumb have emerged. First, when a corporation's activity takes place in several states, courts generally conclude that the nerve center is the principal place of business. Second, if the corporate activity is localized in a single state, with the decisions made in another, there is a tendency to conclude that the muscle center is

[63] Only of Delaware (where incorporated) and Illinois (where it has its principal place of business). Qualifying to do business in a state does not make a corporation a citizen of that state.

[64] A leading example is *Kelly v. United States Steel Corp.*, 284 F.2d 850 (3d Cir. 1960). *See also* Topp v. CompAir, Inc., 814 F.2d 830, 834 (1st Cir. 1987) ("locus of operations").

[65] A leading example is Scot Typewriter Co. v. Underwood Corp., 170 F. Supp. 862 (S.D.N.Y. 1959). *See also* Danjeq S.A. v. Pathe Communications Corp., 972 F.2d 772, 776 (9th Cir. 1992) ("nerve center").

[66] *See* Randazzo v. Eagle-Picher Industries, Inc., 117 F.R.D. 558 (E.D. Pa. 1987) (plaintiff alleged registered office and other irrelevant points; court dismissed with prejudice and criticized "counsel whose familiarity with . . . §1332 could be no more than a friendly wave from a distance visible only through a powerful telescope.") If *Randazzo* is not in your casebook, you might look it up; it is short and extremely amusing.

[67] A leading example, found in several casebooks, is *J.A. Olson Co. v. City of Winona*, 818 F.2d 401 (5th Cir. 1987).

the principal place of business.[68] Third, if the corporation's activity is "passive," most courts conclude that the nerve center is the principal place of business, since passive activity simply does not bring the business into significant contact with the local populace so as to consider it a citizen where it undertakes its activity.

Be smart in approaching an exam question in this area. You can imagine what an exam fact pattern will look like.

> ○ Plaintiff, a California corporation with its principal place of business[69] in Darien, Connecticut, sues Widget Corp. Widget is incorporated in Delaware, has its headquarters and executive decision makers in Pennsylvania, and has manufacturing plants in California (which is the biggest plant, making 30 percent of the company's widgets), Georgia (which makes 25 percent of the widgets), Illinois (which makes 25 percent of the widgets), and Connecticut (which makes 20 percent of the widgets). Obviously, Plaintiff is a citizen of California and Connecticut. The question is whether Widget is also a citizen of either of those states.

Widget is a citizen of Delaware because it is incorporated there. But what is its principal place of business? If it is California or Connecticut, there is no diversity. If it is Georgia, Illinois, or Pennsylvania, there is diversity. Do not make the mistake of simply applying one test or another (e.g., muscle or nerve) and failing to argue the other way. You've learned different approaches to the issue; show the professor that you know them. Here, a strict application of the muscle test would yield a California principal place of business, because that is where the company manufactures *more* widgets than anywhere else. On the other hand, a strict application of the nerve test would yield a Pennsylvania principal place of business because that is where the decisions are made. But because this company does business in several states, and its activity is not localized in a single place, emphasis on the muscle test makes less sense. Most courts would conclude that the principal place of business is in Pennsylvania, and that diversity exists.

What about the myriad types of businesses that are not corporations? There are many such associations, as we noted above, including general and limited partnerships, limited liability companies, and limited liability partnerships. As we said, these forms are not seen by the law as entities separate from the people who run it, and Congress has never attempted to define their citizenship. Because they are not corporations, §1332(c)(1) is irrelevant; thus, the concept of "principal place of business" is irrelevant.

---

[68] *See generally* 15 Moore's Federal Practice §102.54.

[69] Here, the facts tell you the principal place of business, so there is no need to discuss the various approaches to that issue. Take what your professor gives you. As to Plaintiff, it is clear that the citizenship is California (where incorporated) and Connecticut (site of the principal place of business).

The job of defining the citizenship of unincorporated associations has been left to the courts. The rule is very simple and is consistent with the notion that these associations are seen not as entities but as aggregates of their members: Courts look to the citizenship of each *member* of the association.

The classic non-incorporated business is the partnership. It is an association of two or more persons to conduct a business for profit, and may be formed by conduct, without any documentation (though it is good practice to have a written partnership agreement). Forming a partnership — unlike forming a corporation — does not require filing documents with a state agency. Most partnerships are "general" partnerships, in which a group of partners each has equal authority to run the business, equal right to share in the profits, and equal liability for partnership losses.[70] It has always been the case that a court looks to the citizenship of all the general partners in assessing the partnership's citizenship. Thus, a law firm, formed as a general partnership with partners who are citizens of New York, New Jersey, Pennsylvania, and Florida, is deemed to be a citizen of New York, New Jersey, Pennsylvania, and Florida.

What about a limited partnership? In such an arrangement, only the "general" partner(s) usually have any right to run the business. Limited partners invest in the business but have no voice in management and no liability for partnership losses. In *Carden v. Arkoma Associates*,[71] the Supreme Court held that a court must look to the citizenship of all the partners — general and limited — in assessing the citizenship of the business. So a limited partnership whose general partners are citizens of New York and New Jersey, with limited partners who are citizens of Connecticut, Pennsylvania, and Ohio, is deemed to be a citizen of New York, New Jersey, Connecticut, Pennsylvania, and Ohio. Thus, under the complete diversity rule, if the opposing litigant is a citizen of any of those states, there can be no diversity of citizenship jurisdiction. Labor unions generally are not corporations. Thus, a national union such as the Teamsters, whose members are citizens of every state, is deemed for diversity purposes to be a citizen of every state. Thus, it can never sue or be sued under diversity jurisdiction.[72]

---

[70] All these things can be modified by agreement, but such an agreement would not affect the citizenship of the partnership for diversity of citizenship purposes.

[71] 494 U.S. 185 (1990).

[72] Don't panic over this fact, though. Obviously, such an association can sue or be sued in state court. Moreover, if the case arises under federal law (as may often be the case with a labor union, since there is pervasive federal legislation in the labor area), it can go to federal court under federal question jurisdiction. See §4.6.

One of the most significant developments in business law over the past two decades has been the emergence of a new business form — the limited liability company (LLC). It shares some characteristics of the traditional corporation — such as formation by filing certain documents with a state agency — with some of non-incorporated associations — such as the manner in which income taxation is handled. Because of its hybrid nature, there was some initial confusion about how the LLC should be treated for purposes of assessing its citizenship. Despite strong arguments that it should be treated as a corporation under §1332(c)(1),[73] the courts have concluded that the LLC should be treated as other non-incorporated associations.[74] Thus, the court looks to the citizenship of all members of the LLC.

As a bottom line, then, we have a very clear, mechanical, bright-line rule. Instead of engaging in a functional analysis, determining whether a particular business association is more or less like a corporation, courts look to one thing — whether the business is deemed to be a "corporation" under the law of the state in which it was formed. If it is, §1332(c)(1) applies; if it is not (even if it acts in many ways like a corporation), §1332(c)(1) does not apply and the court looks to the citizenship of all members. Thus, the court applied §1332(c)(1) to an electrical cooperative, despite the fact that it lacked some classic attributes of a corporation, when the applicable state law referred to it as a corporation.[75] And another court applied §1332(c)(1) to a "professional corporation" — again, despite the fact that it lacked some attributes normally associated with general business corporations — because the relevant state law labeled it a corporation.[76]

Now we complicate it a bit. It is possible for corporations to act as a partner in a partnership. When that happens, be careful to apply the rules we have seen.

○ Plaintiff, an LLC with members who are citizens of Arizona, New Mexico, and California, sues Defendant, a limited partnership. The general partner of Defendant is a citizen of New York, and the limited partner is a corporation, incorporated in Delaware with its principal place of business in California. There is no diversity jurisdiction. Why?

---

[73] The leading proponent of this approach is Professor Debra Cohen. *See* Debra R. Cohen, *Citizenship of Limited Liability Companies for Diversity Jurisdiction*, 6 J. of Small & Emerging Bus. Law 435 (2002). (I am proud to say that Professor Cohen was a student of mine.)

[74] *See, e.g.,* Rolling Hills MHP, LP v. Comcast SCH Holdings, LLC, 374 F.3d 1020 (11th Cir. 2004); GMAC Commercial Credit LLC v. Dillard Dept. Stores, Inc., 357 F.3d 827 (8th Cir. 2004); Belleville Catering Co. v. Champaign Market Place LLC, 350 F.3d 691 (7th Cir. 2003).

[75] Kuntz v. Lamar Corp. 385 F.3d 1177, 1182-1183 (9th Cir. 2004).

[76] Hoagland v. Sandberg, 385 F.3d 737, 740 (7th Cir. 2004).

○ For starters, note that both Plaintiff and Defendant are non-incorporated associations (an LLC and a limited partnership), so each will be deemed a citizen of each state of which its members are citizens. For Plaintiff, the members are citizens of Arizona, New Mexico, and California; those are Plaintiff's citizenships. For Defendant, under *Carden*, we look to the citizenship of both the general and the limited partners. The facts make it clear that the general partner is a citizen of New York. The limited partner is a corporation, for which §1332(c)(1) defines citizenship. Because it is incorporated in Delaware and has its principal place of business in California, it is a citizen of both. Thus, Defendant is a citizen of New York, Delaware, and California. Because both Plaintiff and Defendant are citizens of California, there is no diversity of citizenship jurisdiction.

Litigation Through Representatives. Not all persons with litigable interests have the capacity to sue or be sued. For example, minors and persons suffering a mental disability generally cannot represent their own interests in litigation. The minor lacks legal capacity and the person under a mental disability lacks mental (and therefore legal) capacity to sue. Litigation involving such persons — either for them or against them — is brought by or against a fiduciary who represents the minor or incompetent. Typically, the representative is a guardian, a guardian *ad litem*, or a committee.[77] Such a representative is charged with responsibility of representing the interests of the person who lacks capacity, and, as a fiduciary, owes a duty of utmost loyalty to the person represented. Similarly, when a person dies, there may be claims by or against her estate. A fiduciary, usually called an executor (if the decedent had a will) or administrator (if the decedent died without a will), represents the interests of the decedent's estate and is the proper party for litigation concerning the estate.

When a representative of a decedent, minor, or incompetent sues (or is sued) on behalf of the person she represents, whose citizenship is relevant for diversity of citizenship purposes? Does the court look to the citizenship of the representative or of the person being represented? The issue was subject to considerable debate and uncertainty until Congress provided a clear answer in §1332(c)(2). It provides that the representative of a decedent, an incompetent, or "an infant" (which simply means a minor — someone who has not reached the age of majority) "shall be deemed to be a citizen only of the same State as the decedent [minor or incompetent]." Accordingly, the court ignores the citizenship of the representative and uses the state of citizenship of the person *being represented*

---

[77] A general guardian is one who has daily, general control of the person lacking legal capacity. A guardian *ad litem* does not have general control, but represents the ward only "for the litigation." A committee (pronounced comb-ee-TAY) is one who essentially stands in the shoes of the litigant. The decision of which type of representative is chosen generally is made under the law of the state in which the federal court sits.

in the litigation. This is a nice mechanical rule that usually results in clear jurisdictional rulings.

> ○ Decedent, who was a citizen of Wyoming, dies in a Wyoming hospital. Her family members want the estate to sue the hospital, alleging that its medical malpractice resulted in Decedent's wrongful death. Decedent's executor is a citizen of Colorado. She, on behalf of Decedent's estate, sues the Wyoming hospital. Under §1332(c)(2), the court looks to Decedent's citizenship, not that of her representative. Thus, the executor's citizenship is irrelevant. The case is seen as Wyoming v. Wyoming, and does not invoke diversity of citizenship jurisdiction.

It does not matter whether the decedent, minor, or incompetent would be the plaintiff or the defendant; the definition is the same in either situation.

We should note two other points about §1332(c)(2). First, the statute provides that the representative shall be deemed to be a citizen "of the same State" as the person represented. When the word "State" is capitalized in §1332, it refers to a state of the United States (and not to a foreign country). When the word "state" is not capitalized in §1332 (as in §1332(a)(2)), it refers to a foreign country.[78] What if the person being represented is not a citizen of a state of the United States? For instance, suppose the decedent was an alien (say, a citizen of Costa Rica), and that the executor is a citizen of California. Suppose further the defendant is a citizen of California. Section 1332(c)(2) does not seem to apply here, because the decedent was not a citizen of a "State" (of the United States). Thus, apparently (because §1332(c)(2) does not apply), we would look to the citizenship of the executor. If we do that, there is no subject matter jurisdiction, because both the plaintiff (executor) and the defendant are citizens of California. So §1332(c)(2) does not appear to apply when the person being represented — the decedent, the minor, or the incompetent — was a citizen of a foreign country.[79]

Second, §1332(c)(2), as we have already seen, applies only to cases involving decedents, minors, and incompetents. It does not apply in the class action, which is litigation in which a representative sues on behalf of a group so large that the members cannot practicably be joined in a single case.[80] The issue of whose citizenship "counts" for diversity purposes has been left to the courts, which have concluded that *only* the citizenship of the representative is relevant.[81] Thus, in a class action, only the representative must be diverse from the defendant(s).

---

[78] This fact is not immediately discernable, but the courts have read the words this way.

[79] If it did, there might be alienage jurisdiction, discussed at §4.5.5.

[80] Fed. R. Civ. P. 23. We discuss the class action in §13.3.

[81] Supreme Tribe of Ben-Hur v. Cauble, 255 U.S. 356 (1921). We revisit this and related topics in §13.3.8.

° *P*, a citizen of Arizona, brings a class action on behalf of 1,000 class members, 990 of whom are citizens of California and 10 of whom are citizens of Arizona. The defendant is a citizen of California. There is diversity. Section 1332(c)(2) does not apply. Courts look only to the representative of the class, not the class members. Thus, the case is seen as Arizona v. California.

Alignment and Realignment

The alignment of parties set forth in the plaintiff's complaint is not sacrosanct. Indeed, the court has a duty to assess whether the true interests of any of the litigants lie with the other side of the litigation. If so, the court may realign a party to the other side of the litigation. This process may defeat diversity and result in dismissal for lack of subject matter jurisdiction.[82] In the leading case, *City of Indianapolis v. Chase National Bank*, the Supreme Court indicated that the trial court must determine whether there is an "actual, substantial controversy" or a "collision of interests" between citizens of different states.[83]

While the court will make this determination initially on the face of the pleadings, information discerned during the litigation may lead the court to conclude that it should realign the parties.[84] The inquiry is not whether a litigant changes her citizenship after the case is commenced; as we see below, the existence of jurisdiction is assessed only at the time the case is commenced. Rather, the court attempts to determine whether the plaintiff's initial alignment of the parties reflected the true dispute.

° *P* knows that *V* plans to sue her for tort damages. *P* feels that the tort to be alleged is covered by her insurance with Insco, and that if *V* wins, Insco should pay the damages (and defend *P* in the suit). *P* sues first, naming as defendants *V* and Insco, and seeking a declaratory judgment[85] that Insco must defend *P* and pay any damages. The court may realign *V* to the plaintiff's side of the litigation, since *V* and *P* have the same interest in having the declaration of insurance coverage.[86]

There is great uncertainty in how parties should be aligned in cases involving overlapping interests, some of which are consistent with one side

---

[82] *See, e.g.*, United States Fidelity & Guar. Co. v. Algernon-Blair, Inc., 705 F. Supp. 1507 (M.D. Ala. 1987).

[83] 314 U.S. 63, 69 (1941).

[84] *See* American Motorists Ins. Co. v. Trane Co., 657 F.2d 146, 151 (7th Cir. 1981) (subsequent events in litigation may show that original alignment was wrong).

[85] A plaintiff seeking declaratory judgment is seeking a court order describing the relative rights of the parties, as opposed to some form of "coercive" relief, such as damages or an injunction. For more detailed discussion, see §4.6.3.

[86] *See* Wright & Kane, Federal Courts 180.

and some with another.[87] The important point is to recognize that the court is the ultimate decision maker of whose interests lie on what side of the case, and that this assessment may affect diversity jurisdiction.

The Amount in Controversy Requirement

Satisfaction of the complete diversity requirement is only half the battle in invoking diversity of citizenship jurisdiction. The case must also meet the amount in controversy requirement. This aspect of diversity (and alienage jurisdiction, see §4.5.5) gives the professor a great many opportunities for exam questions. Let's divide the various rules into two groups. The first, the basic rules, are not difficult but simply must be kept in mind. The second, the aggregation rules, are more difficult conceptually and deserve separate treatment.

The Basic Rules. Nothing in the constitutional grant of diversity or alienage jurisdiction contains or requires an amount in controversy provision. Congress has always included one, however, and has increased it periodically. Obviously, the amount in controversy requirement is a docket control device. By mandating that only cases of a certain value invoke jurisdiction, Congress avoids inundating the federal courts. Similarly, the requirement attempts to ensure that federal courts not become small claims courts. Moreover, it may be that the fear of local bias that underlies diversity jurisdiction is greater in larger cases.

Effective in 1997, the amount in controversy of a diversity or alienage case must exceed $75,000. That provision followed a 1989 increase to an amount in excess of $50,000. Those who argue for the abolition of diversity jurisdiction, realizing that total abolition is unlikely, argue that the amount in controversy should be increased substantially. Some also argue that various types of damages, such as punitive damages, ought to be excluded from the equation. Lately, there has been some interest in a statute that would increase the amount in controversy automatically, by tying it to inflation indices. Currently, however, there is no such provision. Now, to the series of basic rules concerning amount in controversy.

First, the amount in controversy must *exceed* $75,000. The plaintiff bringing a diversity case need not set out an exact figure for damages, but must allege that the amount *exceeds* $75,000. More than one embarrassed lawyer has had a case dismissed for alleging that the amount in controversy was *exactly* $75,000. (Even if your professor is not picky enough to test this issue, some bar examiners are.)

Second, §1332(a) provides that the amount requirement is "exclusive of interest and costs." Thus, the starting point is that neither interest nor costs can be included in the amount claimed. The "interest" referred to is

---

[87] *See* 16 Moore's Federal Practice §102.20[3]-[5]; Wright & Kane, Federal Courts 180-183.

simply that which accrues because of delay in payment. In contrast, if the interest claimed "is itself the basis of the suit" — such as a claim to recover for coupons on a bond — it is included from the amount in controversy.[88] While this distinction is somewhat opaque, the meaning of "costs" is not, and is important. Costs is a term of art, and should be distinguished from attorneys' fees. The general rule is that the prevailing party in litigation recovers her costs from the loser.[89] But, under the American Rule, both sides bear their own attorneys' fees. Costs are virtually all the expenses of litigation *except* attorneys' fees and so include such things as filing fees, fees to compel the attendance of witnesses, mileage fees for witnesses, fees for expert witnesses, discovery costs, costs of photocopying documents, and the like. Though they can add up to a healthy sum, costs generated in a case are usually nowhere near as great as attorneys' fees. While costs cannot be included in the amount in controversy equation under §1332(a), attorneys' fees, if permitted to be recovered under an exception to the American Rule, can be.[90]

Third, the plaintiff's ultimate recovery is irrelevant. Suppose Plaintiff sues for $100,000 and wins a judgment of $7,000. Defendant may be tempted to argue that the court lacked subject matter jurisdiction because the amount in controversy, as it turns out, did not exceed $75,000. The argument will fail for the common-sense reason that the judicial system cannot allow cases to be in jurisdictional limbo. To accept the defendant's argument here would mean that no one would know whether there was subject matter jurisdiction until after the judgment was rendered, which may be years after the case was filed. Such uncertainty is untenable. The popular case of *Mas v. Perry*[91] demonstrates this point. The case was decided when the amount had to exceed $10,000. Both Mr. and Mrs. Mas claimed a proper amount, but Mr. Mas's recovery was only $5,000. The court properly upheld jurisdiction.

Fourth, if a plaintiff ultimately recovers less than $75,000, though jurisdiction is not affected, §1332(b) provides that the plaintiff may not recover her costs from the defendant and, indeed, that the plaintiff may have to pay the defendant's costs. This provision probably does not strike fear in the hearts of most plaintiffs. It deals only with costs, not attorneys' fees. Also, it does not *require* an assessment of costs against such a plaintiff. If

---

[88] Wright & Kane, Federal Courts 210.

[89] *See* Fed. R. Civ. P. 54(d).

[90] For example, attorneys' fees may be recoverable by contract or a statute may provide that the prevailing party shall recover attorneys' fees. If so, a reasonable claim for such fees may be included in the amount in controversy. *See, e.g.*, In re Abbott Laboratories, 51 F.3d 524 (5th Cir. 1995) (including statutory attorneys' fees in class action representative's claim). Plaintiff must allege that an exception to the American Rule applies. Department of Recreation v. World Boxing Assn., 942 F.2d 84, 89 (1st Cir. 1991).

[91] 489 F.2d 1396 (5th Cir. 1974). We saw other aspects of this case when discussing citizenship. See §4.5.3.

the plaintiff claimed the original amount in good faith, courts usually allow her to recover costs from the defendant, even if the ultimate recovery was less than the statutory amount in controversy.[92]

Fifth, the Supreme Court has established that the plaintiff's good faith allegation that the jurisdictional amount is satisfied controls *unless* it "appear[s] to be a legal certainty that the claim is really for less than the jurisdictional amount. . . ."[93] After the plaintiff alleges that the case involves the requisite amount, the defendant may challenge the allegation.[94] At that point, the plaintiff bears the burden of showing that it is *not* "clear to a legal certainty" that the jurisdictional amount is not involved.[95]

It is quite rare for a court to dismiss a case for failure to satisfy the amount in controversy requirement. One example is when the plaintiff seeks damages that are not allowed as a matter of law. Suppose, for example, that *P* sues for $50,000 breach of contract and $100,000 punitive damages, and that relevant law precludes punitive damages in contract cases. As a matter of law, *P* has claimed only $50,000 and thus has failed to invoke diversity jurisdiction.[96] Occasionally (but not often), a court will dismiss because it concludes that the harm alleged, while not precluded by law, simply is not substantial enough to meet the amount in controversy requirement. For example, one court considered a plaintiff's claim that a flight attendant had treated him so brusquely as to cause embarrassment as too trivial to meet the amount in controversy requirement.[97]

Such rulings are rare. In *Ortega v. Star-Kist Foods, Inc.*[98] the plaintiff asserted damages on behalf of a minor child who had cut her finger while opening a can of tuna. The plaintiff alleged damages in excess of $75,000, noting that the child had suffered severed tendons, and had to undergo multiple surgeries. The district court, applying Puerto Rico law (the case was brought in the District of Puerto Rico), dismissed for failure to meet the amount in controversy requirement. The Third Circuit (which hears

---

[92] *See* Dr. Franklin Perkins School v. Freeman, 741 F.2d 1503, 1523 (7th Cir. 1984) (costs imposed upon plaintiff only if plaintiff acted in bad faith). Regarding costs, see §9.3.

[93] St. Paul Mercury Indem. Co. v. Red Cab Co., 303 U.S. 283, 288 (1938).

[94] Courts rarely raise *sua sponte* the issue of whether the amount in controversy is met. *See* In re A.H. Robins Co., 880 F.2d 709, 724 (4th Cir. 1989) (no affirmative duty to inquire absent "apparent reason" to do so).

[95] Gibbs v. Buck, 307 U.S. 66 (1939).

[96] Similarly, if a statute, for example relating to liability of hotels for property damage, limits recovery to an amount not exceeding the amount in controversy, it is clear to a legal certainty that the claim does not involve the requisite amount. *See, e.g.,* Pachinger v. MGM Grand Hotel-Las Vegas, Inc., 802 F.2d 362 (9th Cir. 1986).

[97] Diefenthal v. Civil Aeronautics Board, 681 F.2d 1039 (5th Cir. 1982). This is an area in which lawyers speak of the "straight-face" test. No one could argue with a straight face that the harm alleged was serious enough to meet the requirement.

[98] 370 F.3d 124 (3d Cir. 2004). Though the Supreme Court reversed the decision in *Ortega*, it did so on grounds unrelated to the valuation of the plaintiff's individual claim. *See* Exxon Mobil Corp. v. Allapattah Servs, Inc., 545 U.S. 546 (2005).

appeals from, among others, the District of Puerto Rico) reversed. Though the district court had relied on decisions of the Puerto Rico Supreme Court (which is that Commonwealth's equivalent of a state supreme court) concerning damages awards, it failed to take into account the fact that in federal court the case would be tried to a jury, while in the Puerto Rico court system there would be no right to a jury trial. Noting that jury awards are usually larger than those awarded in "bench" trials (trials in which there is no jury), and noting the seriousness of the alleged injuries, the Third Circuit held that it was not "clear to a legal certainty" that the damages could not exceed $75,000.[99]

To this point, we have dealt with claims for damages. What is the amount in controversy, however, when the plaintiff seeks equitable relief, such as an injunction or declaratory judgment?[100] For example, suppose D erects a building that encroaches on P's property. P sues to have the building moved or modified to remove the encroachment. Clearly, the "value" of this injunction may differ depending upon whose viewpoint is assumed. If we look at this dispute from P's viewpoint, the damage caused by D's building may be small — it would depend upon how large the encroachment is and how much it interferes with P's enjoyment of her land. If we take D's viewpoint, however, the requested injunction would clearly be substantial, since it would require her to move a building (or part of it). Cases reflect these two viewpoints. Most courts seem to adopt the "plaintiff's viewpoint" test, and hold that the amount is met only if the defendant's act harms the plaintiff by the requisite amount.[101] There is a trend, however, that supports jurisdiction if the amount in controversy would be satisfied under either the plaintiff's or the defendant's viewpoint.[102] Still other courts look to the viewpoint of the party invoking diversity jurisdiction — plaintiff's in cases filed originally in federal court and defendant's in cases removed from state court.[103]

The Aggregation Problem(s). Many students find aggregation of claims a challenge. The key to success is to remember the definition of aggregation: It is the adding together of two or more claims to meet the amount in controversy requirement. For example, suppose P has two separate claims against D. One is a tort claim for $50,000 and the other is an unrelated contract claim for $30,000. Obviously, neither claim alone satisfies the amount in controversy requirement. The only way to meet the

[99] 370 F.3d at 128-129.

[100] We discussed the distinction between law and equity at §1.2.3. Damages are the classic remedy at law. Equity developed separate remedies, such as the injunction. The distinction is important in determining the right to a jury trial in federal civil cases. See §9.2.2.

[101] *See, e.g.,* Ericsson GE Mobile Communications v. Motorola Communications & Electronics, 120 F.3d 216, 218-220 (11th Cir. 1996). *See generally* Brittain Shaw, *The $75,000 Question: What Is the Value of Injunctive Relief?,* 6 Geo. Mason L. Rev. 1013 (1998).

[102] *See, e.g.,* Smith v. Washington, 593 F.2d 1097 (D.C. Cir. 1978).

[103] *See, e.g.,* McCarty v. Amoco Pipeline Co., 595 F.2d 389 (7th Cir. 1979).

requirement is to *aggregate* (which simply means add) the two claims. The rules governing aggregation are court-made. They are generally mechanical and easy to state, but not always easy to apply and often hard to justify.

The basic rule is: If the case involves a single plaintiff suing a single defendant, the plaintiff can aggregate as many claims as she has to satisfy the amount requirement. Thus, in the hypothetical in the previous paragraph, the plaintiff can aggregate the claims; the amount in controversy is $80,000. The claims can be aggregated even though completely unrelated legally and transactionally. And the plaintiff can aggregate as many claims as she has, so long as she is the sole plaintiff and there is only one defendant.

- *P* sues *D* and asserts 100 separate, totally unrelated claims, each worth $800. The amount in controversy is $80,000, because, with one plaintiff against one defendant, the plaintiff is permitted to add all claims she has against the defendant in determining the amount in controversy. The rule seems silly because it can inundate the federal courts with unrelated small claims, but the rule is clearly established.[104]

The corollary to this rule is: If there are multiple parties on either side of the case, aggregation is not allowed. The problem is that this corollary is said to be subject to an exception, which is: The courts permit aggregation in the multiple-parties scenario *if* the claims are "joint" or "common and undivided."[105] The thrust of the rule is to determine whether the liability of multiple defendants, or the rights of multiple plaintiffs, are "joint," as opposed to "several." You may become familiar with the concepts of joint and several liability in your Torts class. Although the terms *joint* and *several* are not self-explanatory, common sense goes a long way. (In addition, frankly, so does looking for the word "joint," which usually is a giveaway that the claim involved is joint.)

- *P-1* and *P-2* are injured in a car wreck with *D*. *P-1*'s personal injury claim is $50,000. *P-2*'s personal injury claim is $30,000. Can these two claims against *D* be aggregated? No. Because there are multiple plaintiffs, the basic rule allowing aggregation does not apply. Moreover, personal injury claims are distinct and separate, not joint, even when they arise from the same transaction or occurrence. This makes sense, since each person's interest in her bodily sanctity is separate from everyone else's. Another way to see it is to note that neither *P-1* nor *P-2* could recover more than $75,000 (because neither claims more than $75,000). Because the claims

---

[104] *See, e.g.*, Jones v. Teledyne, Inc., 690 F. Supp. 310 (D. Del. 1988) (aggregating 54 separate, relatively insignificant, claims). *See generally* 16 Moore's Federal Practice §102.108[1].

[105] Zahn v. International Paper Co., 414 U.S. 291, 294 (1973). An older case often cited for this proposition is *Pinel v. Pinel*, 240 U.S. 594 (1916).

cannot be aggregated, the case fails to meet the amount in controversy requirement.

○ *P* sues *D-1* and *D-2*, alleging that *D-1* owes *P* $50,000 under a contract to haul goods and that *D-2* owes him $30,000 under a separate contract to haul goods. Can these two claims by *P* be aggregated? No. Because there are multiple defendants, the basic rule allowing aggregation does not apply. Moreover, the claims arise under separate contracts and thus cannot be considered joint. Another way to see it is to note that neither of the defendants could ever be held liable for an amount in excess of $75,000 (because neither is sued for more than $75,000). Because the claims cannot be aggregated, the case fails to meet the amount in controversy requirement.

○ *P* sues *D-1* and *D-2* as joint tortfeasors, alleging that they attacked and beat him physically. *P* claims damages of $80,000. Is the amount in controversy satisfied? Yes! True, there are two defendants, but this is a joint claim. With a joint claim, the court looks to the total value of the claim. Here, that claim is $80,000, which exceeds $75,000, and thus meets the statutory requirement.

Because the theory of liability in the preceding hypothetical is *joint* liability, any tortfeasor may be held liable for the full amount of the claim. Thus, *D-1* could be sued and held liable for the full $80,000 *or D-2* could be sued and held liable for the full $80,000. It is not as though *P* has a $40,000 claim against *D-1* and a different $40,000 claim against *D-2*. There is only one claim—it is against both *D-1* and *D-2* jointly, and it exceeds $75,000. Viewed this way, we can see that joint claims do not really involve aggregation at all. To aggregate, one needs multiple claims. Here, there is only one claim (albeit against two persons), and it meets the amount in controversy requirement. The same reasoning works with the assertion of a jointly held right by more than one plaintiff:

○ *P-1* and *P-2* claim joint ownership of a parcel of real property that *D* also claims to own. *P-1* and *P-2* sue *D* to quiet title to the property. The property is worth $80,000. Does this case satisfy the amount requirement? Yes. The two plaintiffs are asserting a joint claim, so there is only one claim, and both *P-1* and *P-2* "own" it. Because it is one claim and it exceeds $75,000, the requirement is met. Again, it is not as though *P-1* has a $40,000 claim and *P-2* has a different $40,000 claim. Once we see the interest is joint, each plaintiff owns the $80,000 claim.

There are two minor points to complete our discussion of amount in controversy. First, one Supreme Court opinion may provide authority for the proposition that the value of a defendant's counterclaim against the plaintiff can be included in determining whether the *plaintiff's* claim meets the jurisdictional amount requirement.[106] Courts have not read the case expansively, however, and most observers feel that it was based on a peculiarity of Texas law.[107] Thus, most observers believe, a defendant's counterclaim is irrelevant to determining whether the plaintiff's case meets the amount in controversy. Second, there is considerable uncertainty about the standards for determining the amount in controversy for a class action invoking diversity jurisdiction. We address that issue at §12.8.4.

Timing the Assessment of Whether There Is Jurisdiction. As a general rule, the requirements of federal subject matter jurisdiction are assessed as of the time the plaintiff commences the case,[108] which means when she files her complaint.[109] Thus, courts look to the citizenship of the parties at the time the case is filed. If the requirements of diversity of citizenship jurisdiction are satisfied at that point, jurisdiction attaches and remains intact throughout the case. It is irrelevant that there may not have been diversity when the claim arose or a party changes her citizenship to destroy diversity after the case is filed.[110] This rule is consistent with the principle, discussed above, that the amount ultimately recovered in a diversity case is irrelevant. Jurisdiction attaches at the outset, with the plaintiff's good faith allegation that the amount in controversy exceeds $75,000.

- ○ *P*, a citizen of Minnesota, and *D*, also a citizen of Minnesota, are involved in an automobile wreck. *P* is injured in an amount over $75,000. After the wreck, but before suit is filed, *P* becomes a citizen of Wisconsin. *P* then files suit. Although there was no diversity when the claim arose, there was diversity when the case was filed. Because we measure jurisdiction at the time the case was filed, diversity jurisdiction is established.
- ○ *P*, a citizen of Washington, files a diversity of citizenship case against *D*, a citizen of Oregon, claiming damages in excess of $75,000. After filing, but before any appreciable litigation in the case, *P* becomes a citizen of Oregon. Although there is now no diversity, there was diversity when the case was filed. Because that is the relevant time for making the determination, diversity jurisdiction is established.[111]

---

[106] Horton v. Liberty Mutual Ins. Co., 367 U.S. 348 (1961). A counterclaim is a claim asserted by the defendant against the plaintiff in the pending suit. See §12.5.1.

[107] *See* Wright & Kane, Federal Courts 221-224. Under Texas law, a suit by a workers' compensation insurer to set aside part of an award opened the entire compensation award. Arguably, that makes the entire potential award the amount in controversy.

[108] Newman-Green, Inc. v. Alfonzo-Larrain, 490 U.S. 826, 830 (1989); Navarro Sav. Assn. v. Lee, 446 U.S. 458, 459 (1980).

[109] Fed. R. Civ. P. 3 (action "commenced" when complaint is filed).

[110] Faysound Ltd. v. United Coconut Chemicals, Inc., 878 F.2d 290, 296 (9th Cir. 1989); Field v. Volkswagenwerk AG, 626 F.2d 293, 304 (3d Cir. 1980).

[111] If *Mas v. Perry* is in your casebook, check footnote 2 of that case — it makes exactly this point.

The converse of this principle is also true: If the parties are not of diverse citizenship when the case is commenced, the defect cannot be cured. The Supreme Court demonstrated this principle in 2004 in *Grupo Dataflux v. Atlas Global Group, LP*.[112] There, a limited partnership sued a Mexican defendant. It attempted to invoke alienage jurisdiction by alleging that the plaintiff was a citizen of Texas and the defendant was a citizen of Mexico.[113] The case proceeded for years — all the way through trial — before it was discovered that at the time the case was filed the limited partnership had had a partner who was a citizen of Mexico. As we discussed above, the citizenship of a limited partnership is determined by looking to the citizenship of all its partners. Thus, at the time the case was filed, because of the Mexican limited partner, the plaintiff was a citizen of Mexico. That meant that there was no alienage jurisdiction at that point, because both the plaintiff and the defendant were citizens of Mexico. During the litigation, however, and before entry of final judgment in the trial court, the Mexican limited partners had left the partnership. So, at the time the judgment was entered, there *was* alienage, because the plaintiff was then solely a citizen of Texas. Notwithstanding that change, the Court held that there was no jurisdiction, and the case must be dismissed. *At the time the case was commenced*, there was no alienage, and a subsequent change in citizenship of one of the parties could not cure that defect.

This scenario — in which the citizenship of a party changed during litigation — must be distinguished from that in which a *party might be dropped* from litigation to save jurisdiction. In *Caterpillar Inc. v. Lewis*,[114] there was not complete diversity when a case was removed from state court to federal court (see §4.8), but the parties and the court failed to notice that fact. When the defect was discovered, and before entry of final judgment, the court dismissed the diversity-destroying party. The Supreme Court upheld the judgment and embraced this post-filing dismissal as a way to cure the jurisdictional defect. This principle is embodied in the second sentence of Federal Rule 21, which permits the court to drop parties at any stage of litigation "on terms that are just." Indeed, the Court has held that such jurisdiction-curing dropping of parties can be done on appeal.[115] Whether it is the trial court or the appellate court that cures the jurisdictional defect, however, it is critical that the party dropped be *dispensable*. This term refers to an assessment under Federal Rule 19 (discussed at §12.6.1). Under that Rule, some parties are indispensable to the

---

[112] 541 U.S. 567 (2004).

[113] An alienage case must be between a citizen of a state of the United States and a foreign citizen, and the amount in controversy must exceed $75,000. See §4.5.5.

[114] 519 U.S. 61 (1996). In a case removed from state to federal court, the general rule is that federal subject matter jurisdiction must exist not only when the case is filed in state court, but when it is removed as well. We discuss this point at §4.8.

[115] Newman-Green, Inc. v. Alfonzo-Larrain, 490 U.S. 826, 832 (1989). This should be done, however, only if it will cause no prejudice to any party. *Id.* at 838.

litigation and thus cannot be dropped. Only one who is not indispensable — who is "dispensable" — may be dropped to cure a litigation defect.

It is important to see the difference between *Grupo Dataflux* and *Caterpillar*. In the former, there was no jurisdiction when the case was commenced, but one of the parties to the case — which remained a party throughout the case — *changed its citizenship* during the litigation. This will not cure the jurisdictional defect. In the latter, there was no jurisdiction when the case was commenced, but the *jurisdiction-destroying party was dropped* from the case to cure that defect. This is permitted. The Court in *Grupo Dataflux* explained:

> The purported cure arose not from a change in the parties to the action, but from a change in the citizenship of a continuing party. Withdrawal of the Mexican partners from [the plaintiff limited partnership] did not change the fact that [the limited partnership], the single artificial entity created under Texas law, remained a party to the action. Thus, the composition of the partnership, and consequently its citizenship, changed. But allowing a citizenship change to cure the jurisdictional defect that existed at the time of filing would contravene the principle [of the time-of-commencement rule].

In sum, then, the general rule is that the court assesses subject matter jurisdiction at the time the case is commenced. A change in the citizenship of a party who remains in the case does not affect jurisdiction, either to create it or destroy it. But, as we saw earlier in this section, the court has the power to realign the parties according to what it finds their true interests to have been as of the time the case was commenced. If the court realigns a party and that realignment destroys diversity, the action will be dismissed. Beyond that, there may be a change in parties after the case is commenced, and that change may affect jurisdiction. First, as we just saw, a lack of diversity might be cured by dismissing dispensable nondiverse parties. Second, as we see in §12.6.1, in some circumstances, the court may order that a nonparty be brought into the case because she is "necessary," or "required." When this happens, the court assesses whether joinder of the absentee would destroy diversity. If so, the court might find the nonparty "indispensable" and dismiss the case at that time.

§4.5.4 Exceptions to Diversity of Citizenship Jurisdiction: Collusive Joinder, Domestic Relations, and Probate Cases

There are three areas in which federal courts will not exercise jurisdiction even though the requirements for diversity of citizenship or alienage jurisdiction are met.

Collusive Joinder Cases

Under §1359, the federal court has no jurisdiction in cases "in which any party, by assignment or otherwise, has been improperly or collusively made or joined to invoke the jurisdiction of such court."[116] For many years, courts took inconsistent positions on whether this statute applied to appointments of representatives, such as guardians, to create diversity. That issue is now moot, since, as we saw in §4.5.3, §1332(c)(2) provides that courts look to the citizenship of the person being represented in the litigation.

Today, §1359 is aimed mostly at efforts to create diversity by assignment of claims. For example, assume *P* and *D* are citizens of the same state but that *P* wants to sue *D* in federal court for $100,000. *P* assigns her claim to *T*, who is of diverse citizenship from *D*. *T* then sues *D* under diversity jurisdiction. In the leading case, *Kramer v. Caribbean Mills, Inc.*,[117] *T* (the assignee) agreed to remit to *P* (the assignor) 95 percent of any recovery. The Court concluded that this fact, coupled with *T*'s previous lack of connection with the dispute, compelled the application of §1359. *T* was essentially a collection agent for *P*. *Kramer* instructed courts to look to all relevant circumstances in assessing the application of §1359.[118] Some of these include whether there is an actual business purpose for the assignment, the character of any interest retained by the assignor, and the subjective intent of the parties, although courts have reached varying conclusions on the importance of the latter.[119]

The application of §1359 does not invalidate the assignment. Whether the assignment is valid is governed by the law under which it was made. Instead, application of §1359 merely requires the court to ignore the assignment in assessing whether there is subject matter jurisdiction. In a case like *Kramer*, then, §1359 counsels the court to look to *P*'s, not *T*'s, citizenship. Section 1359 is not implicated when a litigant changes her citizenship for the purpose of creating diversity. Such an act is unilateral, not collusive. If someone wants to go to all the trouble of changing her citizenship simply so she can invoke diversity jurisdiction, §1359 will not stand in her way. In other words, the motive for changing domicile is irrelevant.[120]

---

[116] 28 U.S.C. §1359.

[117] 394 U.S. 823 (1969).

[118] *Id.* at 827-828.

[119] *See generally* 15 Moore's Federal Practice §102.19[4][a].

[120] Morris v. Gilmer, 129 U.S. 315 (1889). Of course, the other party may argue that the one attempting to change domicile fails to satisfy the subjective intent requirement that she intends to make the new state her permanent home. See §4.5.3.

Domestic Relations Cases

Federal courts do not hear domestic relations cases. It is important to stress, however, that domestic relations for this purpose are defined narrowly; the exception does not apply simply because a case might be between or among family members. Rather, it applies only to cases "involving the issuance of a divorce, alimony, or child custody decree."[121] Outside that narrow area, federal courts can exercise diversity of citizenship jurisdiction to hear any intrafamily dispute.

This rule is rooted in history as well as policy. In the original Judiciary Act, Congress granted jurisdiction over cases "at common law or in equity" that were between citizens of different states. Historically, domestic relations cases were heard neither at law or at equity, but by ecclesiastical (church) courts. Accordingly, the statutory grant of diversity jurisdiction did not include domestic relations cases.[122] The fact that more recent versions of the diversity statute, including today's §1332(a)(1), speak not of "law" and "equity," but of "civil actions," does not change this result.[123] In terms of policy, the Supreme Court has noted that state courts have developed expertise in domestic relations cases and that there is an especial local interest in handling issues related to recognition of marriage and child custody issues.

Probate Cases

When someone dies, the law must provide some mechanism for winding up her affairs, paying her taxes and other debts, and distributing her assets to those she specified in her will (or, if she had no will, in accordance with intestacy statutes). This process is called *probate*. Federal courts do not probate wills or oversee the administration of a decedent's estate. The ultimate contours of this exception for "probate cases" are not clear.[124] For example, a federal court, sitting in diversity, can decide a case against an executor to assert a claim against an estate, but only if the federal court does not take general control over the estate or interfere with state probate proceedings.[125] This principle, created by the courts and not by statute, fosters finality by ensuring that any question about the validity

---

[121] Ankenbrandt v. Richards, 504 U.S. 689, 704 (1992). This opinion is the leading modern discussion of the domestic relations exception, though the discussion was dictum. The Court held that the exception did not apply on the facts of the case, which involved an alleged intrafamily tort.

[122] This rationale was first discussed in a dissent in *Barber v. Barber*, 62 U.S. 582, 603-605 (1859) (Daniel, J., dissenting).

[123] *Ankenbrandt*, 504 U.S. at 700. The Court noted that Congress could change the rule.

[124] Judge Posner refers to this as "one of the most mysterious and esoteric branches of the law of federal jurisdiction." Dragan v. Miller, 679 F.2d 712, 713 (7th Cir. 1982). For more detailed discussion, *see* 15 Moore's Federal Practice §102.92[3].

[125] *See* Markham v. Allen, 326 U.S. 490 (1946).

of a will be resolved with the probate proceedings in state court. It also is based upon the recognition that state courts have special expertise in these matters and that the federal courts should avoid interfering unnecessarily with state courts on issues of local concern.

Thinking back to Chapter 2, we can consider a probate proceeding (and a marriage, for that matter) as a "thing" over which the state court has *in rem* jurisdiction; the federal courts will not interfere with that jurisdiction. There is a common-sense general rule that no court will interfere with the jurisdiction of a court that has taken jurisdiction over property.

The Supreme Court's most recent effort in this area involved a case brought by Anna Nicole Smith and that was decided shortly before her death. Smith (whose married name was Marshall) was married to a wealthy man, who died before she did. She sued the son of her late husband, and alleged that the son had thwarted his father's efforts to execute documents necessary to provide a trust for Anna Nicole. She made the claim in a federal bankruptcy case and won a judgment of $449 million in compensatory and $25 million in punitive damages. The son claimed that there was no federal subject matter jurisdiction because of the probate exception. The Court disagreed, and emphasized the narrowness of the probate exception. It does not remove federal jurisdiction over cases involving alleged misconduct of those who administer estates. Anna Nicole's claim was a well-recognized tort, and did not did require the federal court to interfere with the state-court administration of the husband's estate. Thus, it did not fall within the probate exception.[126]

§4.5.5 Alienage Jurisdiction

As we discussed above, §1332(a)(1), which addresses cases "between citizens of different States," is the grant of diversity of citizenship jurisdiction. Section 1332(a)(2), in contrast, provides for jurisdiction over cases "between a citizen of a State and citizens or subjects of a foreign state."[127] This latter basis of jurisdiction is known technically as *alienage* jurisdiction; many people treat it as a subset of diversity jurisdiction. Though diversity jurisdiction has many critics, alienage jurisdiction is universally embraced. The Founders felt that two strong policies supported alienage, and observers agree that both remain vital today. First, aliens, at least as much as out-of-state citizens, might fear local bias when litigating in a state court. Second, the grant of alienage jurisdiction was a statement to foreign countries that litigation involving their nationals was so important to

---

[126] Marshall v. Marshall, 547 U.S. 293, 299 (2006).

[127] When capitalized, as in §1332(a)(1), the word "states" refers to states of the United States. When not capitalized, as in §1332(a)(2), the word refers to foreign countries.

the United States that it belonged in the national courts, and not the state courts. The Supreme Court has explained:

> Both during and after the Revolution, state courts were notoriously frosty to British creditors trying to collect debts from American citizens. . . . This penchant for state courts to disrupt international relations and discourage foreign investment led directly to the alienage jurisdiction provided by Article III of the Constitution.[128]

The statute defines an alien as a "citizen or subject" of a foreign country. This language reflects that persons with allegiance to a foreign country may have different relationships to that country. In *JPMorgan Chase v. Traffic Stream (BVI) Infrastructure, Ltd.*,[129] a corporation chartered in the British Virgin Islands claimed that it was not a "citizen" of the United Kingdom because, as a resident of a territory of that Kingdom, it had fewer rights than a citizen. The Supreme Court upheld alienage jurisdiction and emphasized the breadth of the phrase "citizen or subject." While it was true that the corporation was not a citizen of the United Kingdom, it certainly was a subject of that nation and thus was an alien for purposes of alienage jurisdiction. Thus, the Court concluded, "it is immaterial for our purposes that the law of the United Kingdom may provide different rights of abode for individuals in the territories."[130] The thrust of the inquiry is whether the litigant is a foreign national.

Be careful in applying §1332(a)(2). First, note that alienage requires the same amount in controversy as a diversity jurisdiction case. So all the rules discussed in §4.5.3 concerning amount in controversy apply in alienage. Second, alienage does *not* provide for jurisdiction simply because an alien is a party. Nor could it, since Article III of the Constitution does not permit jurisdiction simply on such a basis.[131] Thus, a case by a citizen of Spain against a citizen of Canada does not invoke alienage jurisdiction. Such a case must go to a state court (unless, of course, it arises under federal law and thus invokes federal question jurisdiction).

Third, to invoke alienage jurisdiction, the case must be between a citizen of a state (of the United States) and an alien (a foreigner, a non-U.S. person). It does not matter whether the alien is plaintiff or defendant — just that the litigant on the other side is a citizen of a state. In *Mas v. Perry*[132] (which we discussed concerning diversity jurisdiction, §4.5.3), recall that one plaintiff, Mr. Mas, was a citizen of France. His claim

---

[128] JPMorgan Chase Bank v. Traffic Stream (BVI) Infrastructure, Ltd., 536 U.S. 88, 94 (2002).
[129] *Id.*
[130] *Id.* at 99.
[131] Hodgson v. Bowerbank, 9 U.S. 303 (1809).
[132] 489 F.2d 1396 (5th Cir. 1974).

against a citizen of Louisiana thus invoked alienage, since it was between an alien and a citizen of a state.[133]

- ◦ *P*, a U.S. citizen domiciled in England, sues *D*, a citizen of Kansas, on a state law claim exceeding $75,000. There is no diversity, because *P* is not a citizen of a state of the United States. Though *P* is a citizen of the United States, and thus would be a citizen of the state in which he is domiciled (§4.5.3), *P* is not domiciled in a state. There is no alienage because *P* is not a citizen of England. Establishing domicile in a foreign *country* does not make one a citizen of that country. Only the foreign country can determine who its citizens are. Thus, although the amount in controversy would be satisfied for diversity of citizenship or for alienage, this case can invoke neither.

Finally, recall from §4.5.3 that §1332(c)(1) defines a corporation's citizenship as its state(s) of incorporation and the one state in which it has its principal place of business. The statute fails, however, to address a corporation that is either formed under the law of a foreign country or has its principal place of business in a foreign country. Though courts have not been consistent in these situations, and there is substantial uncertainty,[134] there seems to be a trend toward two rules: (1) a corporation formed in another country but with its principal place of business in the United States is considered a citizen of the state in which it has its principal place of business,[135] and (2) a corporation formed in the United States but having its principal place of business in a foreign country is considered a citizen of the state in which it was formed.[136]

§4.6 Federal Question Jurisdiction

§4.6.1 Introduction

The first head of jurisdiction provided for in Article III, §2, is cases "arising under the Constitution, laws, or treaties of the United States." Section 1331 grants jurisdiction to the federal district courts using exactly the same operative language. The reference to the Constitution, laws, or treaties of the United States is, of course, a reference to federal law. Thus, pursuant to §1331, cases arising under a federal law may be filed in federal court.

---

[133] In the last sentence of §1332(a), Congress ascribes to permanent resident aliens the citizenship of the state in which they are domiciled. See the discussion of this problematic statute at §4.5.3.

[134] *See* 13B Wright & Miller §3628.

[135] *See, e.g.*, Danjaq, S.A. v. Pathe Communications Corp., 979 F.2d 772 (9th Cir. 1992).

[136] *See, e.g.*, Cabalceta v. Standard Fruit Co., 883 F.2d 1553 (11th Cir. 1989).

This branch of federal subject matter jurisdiction is usually called *federal question jurisdiction*, though some call it *arising under* jurisdiction.

To be precise, §1331 is the *general* federal question statute. It grants jurisdiction over a case that arises under *any* federal law. There are other specialized federal question statutes that grant jurisdiction over claims arising under specific federal laws, such as federal antitrust (§1337), civil rights (§1343), and patent laws (§1338). While some of the specialized federal question statutes grant *exclusive federal question jurisdiction*,[137] meaning that a claim arising under them must be asserted only in federal court, §1331 does not. Any claim asserted under §1331 may, at the plaintiff's option, be asserted in state court instead.

Unlike diversity of citizenship cases, federal question cases go to federal court not because of any characteristics of the parties, but because of the substantive nature of the claim asserted. So in determining whether a case invokes federal question jurisdiction, citizenship is absolutely irrelevant, and there is no amount in controversy requirement. For many years §1331 did have an amount in controversy requirement, but that was abolished in 1980.[138] Thus, a citizen of Colorado may sue a citizen of Colorado for one penny in damages, and the federal court will have subject matter jurisdiction if the plaintiff's claim arises under federal law.

The policy justifications for federal question jurisdiction are clear and are not controversial. Federal judges may be expected to develop special expertise in matters of federal law, and might also be more sympathetic to the policies underlying federal law. Interestingly, however, from our earliest days as a nation, the state courts have been expected to decide cases arising under federal law.[139] This is shown by the fact that §1331 does not grant exclusive federal jurisdiction. It is also shown by the fact that (aside from a one-year exception[140]) there was no version of a general federal question statute until 1875. So until then a great many federal question cases could *only* go to state court. While it is usually quite clear when a federal law (e.g., the Constitution, federal statutes) is involved in a case, the tough issue will be to determine when a case "arises under" that federal law. As we will see, the constitutional grant is interpreted more

---

[137] Major examples are listed at note 1 above.

[138] For this reason, pre-1980 federal question cases you may read discuss amount in controversy. The fact that there is no amount in controversy requirement under §1331 does not mean that there is never a jurisdictional amount in federal question cases. Some specialized grants of federal question jurisdiction still carry an amount in controversy requirement. *See, e.g.,* 15 U.S.C. §2310(d) (claims under Moss-Magnuson Consumer Product Warranties Act must exceed $50,000).

[139] See §4.5.1 (discussion of federal courts deciding state law cases and vice versa).

[140] In 1801, the famous Midnight Judges Act included a general grant of federal question jurisdiction. It was repealed, however, in 1802.

broadly than the statutory grant, despite the fact that they use the same operative language.[141]

§4.6.2 The Constitutional Limits of Federal Question Jurisdiction

To arise under federal law, must *every aspect* of the case involve federal law? In *Osborn v. Bank of the United States*,[142] the Supreme Court gave a startlingly broad interpretation to the *constitutional* grant of federal question jurisdiction. Chief Justice John Marshall's opinion held that a case falls within Article III if federal law might "form an ingredient" in the overall case. Even if the federal issue is but a tiny part of a dispute dominated by state law issues, Article III would permit a federal court to decide the entire case. Indeed, Marshall went much further, saying that it does not matter whether the federal issue actually does arise in the litigation; the mere *potential* that a federal issue might be injected in the litigation is enough to conclude that the case arises under federal law for Article III purposes.

In *Osborn*, the Bank of the United States sued to stop a state official in Ohio from collecting taxes under an Ohio law that taxed non-Ohio banks. The bank contended that the Supremacy Clause of the Constitution, Article VI, §2, prohibited a state from imposing a tax upon it, since it was a federal instrumentality. The mere presence of this federal issue meant that the case arose under federal law for constitutional purposes. For example, Marshall continued, if the bank sued on a simple contract, one question that could be raised would be whether federal legislation forming the bank gave it capacity to bring suit.[143] Even if the capacity issue had been resolved definitively, it could at least potentially lurk in every contract case in which the bank was involved. That phantom presence of any such federal issue satisfied Article III. Thus, for example, any private state-law dispute over ownership of land, in which the title could be traced back to the United States, would satisfy the Article III requirement for federal question jurisdiction.

Obviously, it makes little sense to have the federal courts inundated with these and similar cases in which some federal issue might conceivably be

---

[141] We saw the same thing in §4.5.3 regarding diversity of citizenship jurisdiction, in which the interpretation of the Constitution's use of the phrase "between citizens of different states" is broader than the statutory use of the same phrase.

[142] 22 U.S. 738, 823 (1824).

[143] Marshall was actually speaking of a companion case, *Bank of the United States v. Planters' Bank of Georgia*, 22 U.S. 904 (1824).

relevant. Thus, Congress, in passing the statutory grant of federal question jurisdiction, might well be expected to narrow this broad constitutional power. But §1331 appears to contain no such limitations, since it mirrors the operative language of the constitutional grant. Nonetheless, as they did with diversity jurisdiction, the federal courts have long *interpreted* the language in the statute as narrower than the same language in the Constitution. They have imposed two such "statutory" limitations on the reach of §1331: the well-pleaded complaint rule, and a requirement that federal law be sufficiently central to the plaintiff's claim. Congress has never acted to undo either of these limitations, so they retain vitality.

§4.6.3 One Statutory Limitation: The Well-Pleaded Complaint Rule

Although the constitutional grant of federal question jurisdiction would permit jurisdiction if *any* federal issue *might potentially* be raised in the case, §1331 is not nearly so broad. To invoke jurisdiction under §1331, federal law must be part of the plaintiff's "well-pleaded" complaint. There are two important points to this rule. First, the court looks only to the plaintiff's complaint — not to the defendant's assertions of defenses[144] or to the defendant's filing of counterclaims against the plaintiff[145] — to determine whether there is federal question jurisdiction. Second, in looking at the plaintiff's complaint, the court assesses only the "well-pleaded" parts thereof. This is a terrible phrase. It sounds as though the court is judging sentence structure and syntax. In fact, well-pleaded refers to that part of the complaint supporting only the plaintiff's claim. In other words, the court ignores any extraneous material the plaintiff may have put in her complaint — material that does not relate to her *claim*. For example, if the plaintiff's complaint anticipates that the defendant might raise a particular defense and attempts to rebut it in advance, such allegations are ignored in assessing federal question jurisdiction. Why? Because they do not relate to the plaintiff's claim itself. Only if the plaintiff's *claim* (not plaintiff's discussion of things beyond her claim) arises under federal law will the case satisfy §1331.

[144] *See* Gully v. First Natl. Bank, 299 U.S. 109, 113 (1936).

[145] *See* Holmes Group, Inc. v. Vornado Air Circulation Sys., Inc., 535 U.S. 826, 831 (2002) (counterclaim is part of defendant's answer and therefore cannot be part of a well-pleaded complaint; "we decline to transform the longstanding well-pleaded complaint rule into the 'well-pleaded-complaint-or-counterclaim rule' urged by respondent"). The case involved jurisdiction under §1338(a), concerning patent claims. The well-pleaded complaint rule works the same way in that statute as it does under §1331.

The most famous example of the well-pleaded complaint rule is *Louisville & Nashville Railroad Co. v. Mottley*,[146] which involves the misadventures of a married couple, the Mottleys. It seems the Mottleys had been injured in 1871, many years before the case was filed, in an accident on the Louisville & Nashville Railroad (L&N). In settlement of their claim, the Mottleys accepted a pass that entitled them to free lifetime passage on the railroad.[147] They enjoyed this pass for decades, until Congress enacted a law forbidding railroads from giving free passes.[148] Because of this statute, the L&N refused to allow the Mottleys their customary free passage, and the Mottleys sued the railroad in federal court. In essence, the Mottleys' complaint said: (1) we have a contract with the railroad, pursuant to which we are to get free passage; (2) the railroad refuses to honor the pass, despite our full compliance with everything we were supposed to do; (3) we think the railroad is going to assert that this new federal statute precludes it from continuing to honor our pass; but (4) we think the statute does not apply to us; and (5) if the statute does apply to us, it violates our constitutional rights by depriving us of property without just compensation.

In the trial court, issues (1) and (2) were not really contested. After all, the railroad had to admit that it had a deal with the Mottleys and that it had breached the deal. The only contested issue was whether the railroad's defense (issue (3)) would prevail or whether the Mottleys' reasons for not following federal law (issues (4) and (5)) would obviate application of the federal law. In other words, the only issues to be contested at trial were issues relating to the application of the federal law. The trial court addressed the issues, and the Mottleys won.

The Supreme Court agreed to hear the case.[149] The only questions the railroad raised before the Supreme Court were issues (4) and (5). The Supreme Court refused to address them, however, because the case did not fall within §1331.[150] In other words, the federal trial court had no federal question jurisdiction over the case and, thus, the judgment entered by that court was void. Why? Because of the well-pleaded complaint rule.

---

[146] 211 U.S. 149 (1908).

[147] This fact makes you wonder a bit about the Mottleys. They wanted unlimited free rides on a railroad that allegedly injured them.

[148] Interestingly, this statute was an early form of campaign finance reform, since members of Congress had routinely accepted such free passes to go home to see their constituents. The law was an effort to show that members of Congress could not be bribed by railroads' giving them free passes.

[149] At the time, there was no intermediate appellate court in the federal system.

[150] Actually, the general federal question statute was then known by a different number, and had an amount in controversy requirement. But the operative "arising under" language interpreted in the Supreme Court opinion is the same as in §1331. Remember that it is incumbent on a federal court to dismiss *sua sponte* whenever it determines that there is no basis for subject matter jurisdiction. See §4.3.

The Mottleys' well-pleaded complaint — one that set forth only their claim, not extraneous material — would involve only issues (1) and (2). And neither of those issues implicated federal law in any way. Their claim was simply one for breach of contract under state law; there was nothing federal about it. The only way federal law was injected into the case was by the railroad's *defense* that the federal statute forbade it from honoring the pass. The Mottleys anticipated (correctly) that the railroad would raise the federal defense, *but an anticipated defense is not part of a well-pleaded complaint.* Thus, it must be disregarded in assessing whether the case arises under federal law.[151] The Supreme Court remanded to the lower court with instructions to dismiss the case.

Obviously, then, the fact that a plaintiff alleges something about federal law in her complaint does not mean that the case arises under federal law under §1331. The *claim itself* must be based upon federal law. One way to force yourself to apply the well-pleaded complaint rule is to apply this shorthand test. Ask yourself: Is the plaintiff attempting to vindicate some right given by federal law? In *Mottley*, the answer was no. The federal law involved in that case simply precluded the railroad from giving away free passes. It did not give the Mottleys any rights to vindicate in litigation. Indeed, the Mottleys' only allegation about the federal statute was that it *did not apply to them.* So, clearly, they were not trying to vindicate any right given to them by that (or any other) federal law.

The well-pleaded complaint rule has some harsh critics.[152] The most obvious criticism is that the rule clearly channels cases out of federal court in which the central issues to be resolved are purely federal. *Mottley* is an excellent example; the case cannot be filed in federal court even though only issues (4) and (5) — purely issues of federal law — were contested. Of course, the result is that such cases go to state court, and the state courts determine such issues of federal law. Only in the rare case in which the Supreme Court grants review of the case (and in which the parties pay to fight to the Supreme Court) does a federal court ever address the issues.[153] Indeed, this happened with the Mottleys. After the Supreme Court ordered dismissal of their case, the Mottleys filed anew in state court. The case was appealed through the state court system and the Supreme Court ultimately agreed to review the case *on exactly the same federal issues they attempted to raise in federal court in the first place!* Three years after issuance of the

---

[151] There is nothing ethically or professionally wrong with anticipating a defense in one's complaint. The well-pleaded complaint rule simply stands for the proposition that any such anticipated defense cannot be a basis for federal question jurisdiction.

[152] *See, e.g.*, Donald Doernberg, *There's No Reason for It; It's Just Our Policy: Why the Well-Pleaded Complaint Rule Sabotages the Purposes of Federal Question Jurisdiction*, 38 Hastings L.J. 597 (1987).

[153] Remember that only the Supreme Court can review state decisions, and then only decisions of the highest state court, and only as to issues of federal law. See §1.2.3.

Mottley opinion discussed above, the Supreme Court determined the federal issues (and the Mottleys lost).[154]

The well-pleaded complaint rule does create these problems. Nonetheless, it has the benefit of allowing an early decision on whether subject matter jurisdiction exists. The court need only look to the complaint, without awaiting the defendant's response. If jurisdiction could be based upon defenses, the court would be in limbo until the defendant actually raised the federal issue as a defense. Allowing jurisdiction based upon the plaintiff's anticipation of a defense is even more problematic, because there is no guarantee that the defendant will in fact raise the issue. In that situation, the case would be in federal court even though no federal issue is ever injected. Thus, despite the criticism of the well-pleaded complaint rule, it remains vital: "This bright-line rule prevents the disruption, to both the system and the litigants, of shifting a case between state and federal fora in the middle of an action as federal issues arise or fall out."[155]

In §12.5.1, we see that a defendant might assert a claim — called a counterclaim — against the plaintiff in the pending case. In assessing whether the plaintiff's complaint asserts a claim that arises under federal law, it would seem obvious that the court should not look to any counterclaim stated by the defendant. After all, if the defendant's assertion of a federal defense cannot be used to impart federal question jurisdiction to the plaintiff's complaint, it seems clear that her assertion of a claim would be equally unavailing. The Supreme Court so held in *Holmes Group v. Vornado Air Circulation*,[156] in which the plaintiff's claim did not arise under federal law but the defendant's counterclaim did. The case did not invoke federal question jurisdiction because the claim that did arise under federal law was not part of the plaintiff's well-pleaded complaint.

The well-pleaded complaint rule runs into especial problems in cases brought for declaratory judgment. We think of most plaintiffs as seeking

---

[154] 219 U.S. 467 (1911). The fact that the Supreme Court decided these issues proves that §1331 is narrower than the constitutional grant of federal question jurisdiction. The Supreme Court could only address the issues if they fell within Article III, because Article III limits the jurisdiction of all federal courts, including the Supreme Court. But, as the original *Mottley* opinion held, the issues did not satisfy §1331. Thus, §1331 is narrower than Article III.

[155] Arthur Miller, *Artful Pleading: A Doctrine in Search of Definition*, 76 Tex. L. Rev. 1781, 1783 (1998).

[156] 535 U.S. 826, 831 (2002) ("Our prior cases have only required us to address whether a federal defense, rather than a federal counterclaim, can establish 'arising under' jurisdiction. Nonetheless, those cases were decided on the principle that federal jurisdiction generally exists 'only when a federal question is presented on the fact of the plaintiff's properly pleaded complaint.' . . . It follows that a counterclaim — which appears as part of the defendant's answer — cannot serve as a basis for 'arising under' jurisdiction."). Though *Holmes Group* was decided under §1338 (dealing with patent infringement) and not §1331, the Court noted that the arising under language in both statutes is interpreted identically. There can be no doubt that the reasoning of *Holmes Group* applies to §1331.

what is usually called *coercive relief* — an order that the defendant pay her money (damages) or that she do or desist from doing something (injunction). With declaratory judgment, however, the plaintiff seeks a court order defining the relative rights among the parties. Because Article III, §2, provides that federal courts can only hear "cases" or "controversies," they cannot issue advisory opinions. To ensure that the declaratory judgment procedure does not permit the issuance of advisory opinions, Congress requires that a request for declaratory judgment be made only "in cases of actual controversy."[157]

How does the well-pleaded complaint rule work in a declaratory judgment case? After all, with declaratory judgment, the person who would not be suing for coercive relief might be the plaintiff. The late Professor Charles Alan Wright synthesized the cases by saying that "the declaratory action may be entertained in federal court only if the coercive action that would have been necessary, absent declaratory judgment procedure, might have been so brought."[158] Suppose, for example, that a patent holder seeks a declaration that her patent is valid and that defendant is infringing it. Her claim invokes federal question jurisdiction, since she could just as easily have brought a claim for damages or other coercive relief. Or suppose that the railroad in *Mottley* sued for a declaration that the federal statute under which it refused to honor the Mottleys' passes was valid. This case would not invoke federal question jurisdiction, since neither the Railroad's claim for declaratory judgment nor the Mottleys' claim for coercive relief would have arisen under federal law.[159]

Whatever the merits or demerits of the well-pleaded complaint rule, it remains a significant limitation on the ability to invoke federal question jurisdiction. It is not the only one, however.

§4.6.4   Another Statutory Limitation: The Centrality of the Federal Issue

Courts have imposed a second limitation on federal question jurisdiction under §1331. This one is more difficult to conceptualize than the well-pleaded complaint rule, and many professors do not cover it in the basic Civil Procedure course. It concerns what may be called the *centrality* of the federal law to the claim being asserted. This is a relatively amorphous inquiry, which requires us to review some Supreme Court decisions that

---

[157] Federal Declaratory Judgment Act, 28 U.S.C. §§2201, 2202. The Act provides only a remedy and not a basis of subject matter jurisdiction. Skelly Oil Co. v. Phillips Petroleum Co., 339 U.S. 667 (1950).

[158] Wright & Kane, Federal Courts 113.

[159] The railroad has no claim for relief based upon the federal statute. And, under the well-pleaded complaint rule, as discussed above, neither do the Mottleys.

are difficult to reconcile. As we will see, the problem arises because some claims are admixtures of state and federal law. More specifically, sometimes state law creates a right of action — a claim — that is measured by federal standards, and sometimes the converse is true.

The starting point is *American Well Works Co. v. Layne & Bowler Co.*,[160] in which Justice Holmes wrote the majority opinion. There, Company *A* manufactured a pump. Company *B* held a patent on a pump. (A patent is essentially a *federally* granted right to exclude others from making, using, selling, or offering to sell the patented item.) Company *B* apparently contended that Company *A*'s pump infringed its patent, but did not sue (though it was thinking of doing so). Instead, Company *A* sued Company *B*, alleging that Company *B* had wrongfully claimed that Company *A*'s pump violated Company *B*'s patent. Further, it alleged that Company *B* had driven away customers by threatening to sue anyone who bought a Company *A* pump. Company *A* based its claim on *state* trade libel law. Although state law created the cause of action being asserted, the litigation would focus on a federal issue: whether Company *A*'s pump violated Company *B*'s (federal) patent. The Court held that the case did *not* invoke federal question jurisdiction[161] and adopted a mechanical test: "A suit arises under the law that creates the cause of action."[162] Because the claim was created by state law, the case did not arise under federal law. This approach is sometimes called the *Holmes test* (for Justice Holmes) or the "creation test" (because it looks at what law created the claim.

Although the Holmes test is easy to apply, the Court seemed to forget about it just five years later. In *Smith v. Kansas City Title & Trust Co.*,[163] the plaintiff was a shareholder in a corporation, and sued to stop that corporation from investing in bonds issued under a federal statute (the Federal Farm Loan Act). He argued that the federal statute was unconstitutional and, therefore, that the corporation's investment would violate Missouri law (which forbade corporations from investing in unlawfully issued investments). The case seems indistinguishable from *Well Works* — state law created the claim, but the litigation would focus on the federal law (the constitutionality of a federal statute). Surprisingly, though, the Court upheld federal question jurisdiction. According to the majority opinion (predictably, Justice Holmes dissented), "where it appears from the [complaint] . . . that the right to relief depends upon the construction or application of the Constitution or laws of the United States, and that such federal claim . . . rests upon a reasonable foundation, the District

---

[160] 241 U.S. 257 (1916).

[161] The case involved a precursor to §1338, concerning patent cases, and not of §1331, the general federal question statute. Nonetheless, it is clear that the interpretation of "arising under" is the same in both.

[162] *American Well Works*, 241 U.S. at 260.

[163] 255 U.S. 180 (1921).

Court has jurisdiction."[164] The entire analysis seems antithetical to *Smith*, since the Court was willing to assess what might be called "litigation reality" — that is, what issues would actually arise if the case went to trial.

The Court confused things further 13 years later with *Moore v. Chesapeake & Ohio Railway*,[165] in which the plaintiff sued his employer under a state employer's liability law. Under that law, the employer could not claim that the plaintiff was guilty of contributory negligence if the employer had violated a statute "enacted for the safety of employees." The plaintiff claimed that his employer had violated the Federal Safety Appliance Act. Like *Well Works* and *Smith*, then, *Moore* involved a state-created claim in a case to be decided by the construction of federal law. In *Moore*, the Court held that there was no federal question jurisdiction.

Two years later, the Court decided *Gully v. First National Bank in Meridian*,[166] which featured some typically elegant language from Justice Frankfurter. There, a national bank transferred its rights and liabilities to another (successor) bank. By contract, the successor bank was liable for state taxes, which were assessed on the stock of the national bank. When it failed to pay them, a state officer sued the bank in state court. The successor bank removed the case to federal court. The lower courts upheld federal question jurisdiction. While recognizing that the claim was created by state contract law, the lower courts were impressed by the fact that the power to tax a national bank was based in a federal statute. The Supreme Court reversed, and rejected federal question jurisdiction. The analysis was similar to that in *Smith*, since the Court looked to litigation reality and concluded that the federal issue was merely "lurking" in the background and probably would not arise. In sum, then, *Gully* was pretty easy. It involved a state-law claim in which litigation would center on issues of state contract law. Clearly, there was no need for a federal forum.

The Court then left the area alone for 50 years, when it decided the vexing case of *Merrell Dow Pharmaceuticals, Inc. v. Thompson*.[167] That case involved claims for damages allegedly caused by the plaintiffs' mothers' ingestion of a drug (Bendectin) while the mothers were pregnant. The plaintiffs asserted a variety of state law claims, including negligence per se. They alleged that the defendant drug manufacturer was guilty of negligence per se because it allegedly violated the Federal Food, Drug, and Cosmetic Act (FDCA) by "misbranding" Bendectin. So once again, the Court faced a case in which state law created the claim, but in which the

[164] *Id.* at 199.
[165] 291 U.S. 205 (1934).
[166] 299 U.S. 109 (1936).
[167] 478 U.S. 804 (1986).

litigation would focus on interpretation of federal law.[168] The Court held that there was no federal question jurisdiction. Review these four cases in following chart. It would seem impossible for the Court to decide *Merrell Dow* without deciding whether the one aberrant case — *Smith* — is still good law.

Case	Law Creating Claim	Law to Be Interpreted	§1331 Jurisdiction?
Well Works	State	Federal	No
Smith	State	Federal	Yes
Moore	State	Federal	No
Gully	State	State	No
Merrell Dow	State	Federal	No

We need a bit of background before looking at *Merrell Dow* in detail. Sometimes Congress passes a statute proscribing certain behavior, but fails to create a cause of action to allow individuals harmed by such behavior to sue. In the vernacular, Congress fails to create "a private right of action." Instead, such statutes often permit administrative agencies of the federal government to undertake enforcement actions, or they permit the Attorney General to bring suits for injunctions or even criminal prosecutions against those violating the statutes. Occasionally, however, federal courts hold that Congress *did* create a private right of action even though the legislation failed to say so. These "implied rights of action" create controversy because they ascribe to Congress a goal that Congress did not expressly include in the statute's text. When courts find such implied rights of action, however, there is clearly a federally created claim. In such a case, the Holmes test would uphold the invocation of federal question jurisdiction (because federal law creates the claim).

In *Merrell Dow*, the parties stipulated that the FDCA *did not* create a private right of action — either express or implied — to sue for violations of its provisions. For this reason, *Merrell Dow* involved a state-created claim (for negligence per se). But, as noted, deciding whether the defendant's behavior constituted negligence per se would require application of a standard set out in federal law (the FDCA). Would the Court adopt *Smith* or would it adopt *Moore*? The majority (five Justices, in an opinion by Justice Stevens) spoke of the lack of "importance" of the federal law involved, and emphasized the fact that Congress had not created a federal right of action. The majority concluded that once Congress determined

---

[168] Plaintiffs filed the case in state court. It was the defendant who tried to invoke federal jurisdiction; it did so by "removing" the case to federal court. We discuss removal at §4.8.

there was no federal remedy, the Court was "not free to 'supplement' that decision in a way that makes [that decision] 'meaningless.'"[169]

There are at least two problems with this conclusion. First, it is a *non sequitur*. There is nothing inconsistent with Congress's decision not to create a right of action and a decision to permit a case arising under the law to invoke federal question jurisdiction. As one commentator notes, "[t]o provide federal *jurisdiction* for a state-created cause of action . . . does not itself 'supplement' the federal remedy; the *state* remedy itself has already done that."[170] Second, the Court's conclusion would seem to dictate that *Smith* be overruled, because the holding in that case clearly is inconsistent with what the Court says. Oddly, however, the majority opinion did not overrule *Smith*. Instead, it tried to reconcile *Smith* and *Moore* by saying that the "nature of the federal interest" in *Smith* was more important than that in *Moore*.[171]

The dissent by Justice Brennan (found compelling by most commentators)[172] concludes that *Smith* and *Moore* are irreconcilable, and that *Moore* (which has never generated much of a following) ought to be overruled.[173] In its view, the majority's reliance on the "importance" of the federal interest is so malleable as to be unworkable. Indeed, in the wake of *Merrell Dow*, lower courts were unclear as to whether the requirement of an important federal issue required a federal constitutional issue to be raised, rather than a federal statutory issue.

At a more fundamental level, the majority and dissenting opinions in *Merrell Dow* reflect different views of the role of federal question jurisdiction. The majority clearly sees the purpose of §1331 as providing a federal forum for the vindication of *federally created* remedies. If one adopts this view, the fact that Congress created no right of action means that a lower federal forum is not necessary — there is no federal right to vindicate. On the other hand, Justice Brennan clearly embraced a broader view. To him, §1331 has a role in ensuring uniformity of federal law. In this view, there should be lower federal court jurisdiction whenever, as in *Merrell Dow*, the outcome of the case depends upon an *interpretation* of federal law.[174]

---

[169] *Merrell Dow*, 478 U.S. at 812, n.10.

[170] 15 Moore's Federal Practice §103.31[4] (emphases original).

[171] *Merrell Dow*, 478 U.S. at 814, n.12. The entire debate over the continued vitality of *Smith* is set forth in footnotes.

[172] *See, e.g.,* 15 Moore's Federal Practice §103.31[4]; Patti Alleva, *Prerogative Lost: The Trouble with Statutory Federal Question Doctrine After* Merrell Dow, 52 Ohio St. L.J. 1477 (1991); Martin Redish, *Reassessing the Allocation of Judicial Business Between State and Federal Courts: Federal Jurisdiction and "The Martian Chronicles,"* 78 Va. L. Rev. 1769 (1992).

[173] *Merrell Dow*, 478 U.S. at 821, n.1 (Brennan, J., dissenting).

[174] Such lower court jurisdiction under §1331 would be necessary because the Supreme Court's discretionary review of cases decided by state courts can only be invoked rarely.

(For that matter, under this view, there should be federal question jurisdiction in cases such as *Mottley*. See §4.6.3. Yet even Justice Brennan would refuse to undo the venerable well-pleaded complaint rule established in that case.[175])

Luckily, *Merrell Dow* is not the last word. In 2005, the Supreme Court gave some much-needed guidance in *Grable & Sons Metal Products v. Darue*.[176] In that case, the Internal Revenue Service (IRS) seized *P*'s land for nonpayment of taxes. After *P* failed to redeem the property, it was sold at public auction to *D*. Thereafter, *P* sued *D* in state court, on a state-law claim for quiet title. *P*'s claim was that *D* did not receive valid title from the IRS because the IRS had failed to follow proper procedure for giving notice to *P* that it was in default on its taxes. *D* removed the case to federal court and a unanimous Supreme Court upheld federal question jurisdiction. In doing so, the Court revived *Smith* and rejected any notion that federal question jurisdiction required a federally created claim. Rather, a state-law claim can satisfy the centrality requirement by implicating sufficiently a federal law. Thus, federal question jurisdiction exists at least in part to provide lower federal courts for the interpretation of federal law. And that federal law need not be constitutional — federal statutory issues can suffice.

Moreover, the Court set forth three factors to consider in determining whether a state-law claim should be seen to arise under federal law. Specifically, if (1) the case necessarily raises a federal issue, (2) the federal issue is actually disputed and substantial, and (3) federal jurisdiction will not disturb "any congressionally approved balance of federal and state judicial responsibilities,"[177] the centrality requirement is satisfied. The test is remarkably pragmatic. It permits a court to look at litigation reality — to assess whether the federal issue will actually be litigated if the case proceeds to trial. The third factor also reflects pragmatism. The Court treated this factor as a "veto" that can keep cases out of the federal courts if recognizing federal question jurisdiction would swamp those courts.

On the facts of the case in *Grable*, the federal issue was actually disputed. Indeed, as a matter of litigation reality, whether the IRS had satisfied the notice requirement of federal law was the *only* disputed issue. It was also substantial. On this score, the Court noted the federal government's interest in prompt collection of taxes. Moreover, the exercise of federal jurisdiction would not affect the allocation of cases between state

---

[175] Franchise Tax Board v. Construction Laborers Vacation Trust, 463 U.S. 1 (1983). The facts of this case led the late Professor Wright to refer to it as "the Exam Question from Hell masquerading as a federal lawsuit." Wright & Kane, Federal Courts 110-111 n.3. Luckily, he was discussing the exam in the upper-division course on Federal Courts, not Civil Procedure.

[176] 545 U.S. 308 (2005).

[177] *Id.* at 313-314.

and federal courts; very few state-law cases involving title to realty will raise a serious federal issue. Thus, exercising jurisdiction will not swamp the federal courts. In contrast, the Court noted, recognizing federal question jurisdiction in *Merrell Dow* would have shifted an enormous number of tort cases from state to federal court.

This latter point can be seen in another way as well. By refusing to take cases that would swamp the federal courts, the *Grable* test also leaves to state courts the job of interpreting and developing state law. For instance, in *Merrell Dow*, the plaintiffs had asserted several cutting-edge common law tort theories under state law. Had the federal courts recognized federal question jurisdiction, many of those cases would have gone to federal court, which would have robbed the state courts to a degree of the ability to shape the development of state law.

The year after deciding *Grable*, the Court rejected federal question jurisdiction in *Empire Healthchoice Assurance, Inc. v. McVeigh*.[178] There, an insurance company sued under state contract law to be reimbursed for benefits it had paid to an insured under a federal law. By contract, the insured was required to refund payments received from another source to the insurance company. The suit did not invoke federal question jurisdiction in part because it presented no significant question of federal law. Moreover, as a matter of litigation reality, it is not clear that adjudication of the dispute required application of any federal law.

In sum, *Grable* is a welcome addition to the jurisprudence of federal question jurisdiction. Of course, the Holmes test will remain the first word on assessing centrality. Its hard-and-fast test will be determinative in most cases. But Holmes is not always the last word. In appropriate cases, *Grable* supplants its rule with a set of pragmatic standards.[179]

§4.7   Supplemental Jurisdiction

When You Need It; When You Don't Need It

Many students have trouble with supplemental jurisdiction. The trouble usually is caused by failing to understand the basic point of what supplemental jurisdiction does. To this point, the plaintiff has filed a claim that satisfies some basis of federal subject matter jurisdiction; she has filed a

---

[178] 547 U.S. 677 (2006).

[179] *See* Richard D. Freer, *Of Rules and Standards: Reconciling the Statutory Limitations on "Arising Under" Jurisdiction*, 82 Ind. L.J. 319 (2007).

claim that meets the requirements of either diversity of citizenship, alienage, or federal question jurisdiction.[180] We can say that this claim satisfies an "independent" basis of subject matter jurisdiction — it can get into federal court by itself. Because of this, the case is now in federal court. But (and this is crucial) there may be additional claims asserted in that case. The plaintiff herself may have additional claims in her original complaint (or may add some later by amendment). The defendant may assert claims in the pending case (maybe back against the plaintiff, maybe against a co-defendant, maybe even against someone who has not yet been joined in the case). Indeed, an absentee (a nonparty) may intervene into the case and assert a claim or have a claim asserted against her. And here is the key: *Every single claim asserted in a case in federal court (not just plaintiff's original claim that got the case into federal court) must satisfy a basis of federal subject matter jurisdiction.*

So let's distinguish between the original jurisdiction-invoking claim, by which the case gets into federal court, and all these additional claims. We can refer to these simply as the "original" or "jurisdiction-invoking" claim, on the one hand, and "additional" claims, on the other. All of them must have a basis of subject matter jurisdiction, or they simply cannot be asserted in federal court. Obviously, if an additional claim satisfies an independent basis of subject matter jurisdiction — such as diversity of citizenship, alienage, or federal question — it can be asserted in federal court.

But what if one of these additional claims does *not* satisfy an independent basis, such as diversity of citizenship, alienage, or federal question jurisdiction? In those instances, it is possible that the claim nonetheless can be heard in federal court under *supplemental jurisdiction.* So supplemental jurisdiction allows a federal court to hear claims that could not get into federal court by themselves — that is, claims that do not invoke diversity, alienage, or federal question.[181] But two points are critical here. First, supplemental jurisdiction is *never* available to get the original case itself into federal court; it is only available for additional claims. The plaintiff *absolutely must* assert at least one claim that meets diversity, alienage, or federal question (or some other basis of original federal subject matter jurisdiction) to get the *case* into federal court. After that happens, supplemental jurisdiction might be available to get *additional claims* into federal court. Second, supplemental jurisdiction is not needed if there is a standard independent basis of subject matter jurisdiction over the claim. In other words, supplemental jurisdiction is only necessary, and therefore

---

[180] Remember that there are other bases of federal subject matter jurisdiction, such as cases involving the United States as a party or disputes between an individual and a state. Civil Procedure courses rarely address such bases. The focus, as above in this chapter, is on diversity, alienage, and federal question.

[181] Or any other basis of original federal subject matter jurisdiction.

only relevant, if there is no diversity jurisdiction, alienage, and no federal question jurisdiction over the claim.

- *P*, a citizen of Minnesota, asserts a state law claim against *D*, also a Minnesota citizen. This case cannot go to federal court. There is no diversity of citizenship jurisdiction, and there is no federal question jurisdiction (because *P* is asserting a state law claim). Supplemental jurisdiction cannot apply here; it is not available until the case is properly in federal court because *P* asserts a claim that satisfies diversity, alienage, or federal question jurisdiction.

- *P*, a citizen of Minnesota, sues *D*, a citizen of Wisconsin, alleging (1) that *D* violated *P*'s rights under the federal securities law and (2) that *D* also violated *P*'s rights under state securities law. *P* claims damages of $400,000. Here, claim (1) invokes federal question jurisdiction, so the case gets into federal court. Claim (2) also invokes diversity of citizenship jurisdiction. So claim (2) has an independent basis of federal jurisdiction. It "belongs" in federal court by itself. Thus, supplemental jurisdiction is irrelevant (and discussing it would not impress your professor — at least, not favorably).

- *P*, a citizen of Minnesota, sues *D*, also a citizen of Minnesota, alleging (1) that *D* violated *P*'s rights under the federal securities law and (2) that *D* also violated *P*'s rights under state securities law. *P* claims damages of $400,000. Here, claim (1) invokes federal question jurisdiction, so the case gets into federal court. Claim (2), however, does not satisfy diversity of citizenship jurisdiction (because there is no diversity at all). Claim (2) also does not invoke federal question jurisdiction (because *P* is asserting a state law claim).

  - Supplemental jurisdiction may apply to get claim (2) into federal court. First, the case itself is already in federal court (because claim (1) invoked federal question jurisdiction), so we are talking here about jurisdiction over an additional claim. Second, this additional claim cannot invoke one of the basic, independent bases of subject matter jurisdiction.

The Constitutionality of Supplemental Jurisdiction: The Gibbs *Test*

So now we understand that supplemental jurisdiction gets nonfederal, nondiversity additional claims into federal court. But under what circumstances? To answer that, we need to ask an even more fundamental question: Why is this constitutional? After all, the federal courts have limited subject matter jurisdiction (basically, for our purposes, hearing diversity of citizenship, alienage, and federal question cases). And that limited subject matter jurisdiction is prescribed by the Constitution. So how can it be constitutional for a federal court to entertain claims that do not satisfy one of the limited bases of federal subject matter jurisdiction?

The answer: When the plaintiff files an original claim that invokes federal subject matter jurisdiction (e.g., a diversity, alienage, or federal question claim), the federal court takes jurisdiction over the entire "case" or "controversy" of which that claim is part. Article III grants subject matter jurisdiction over "cases" or "controversies" involving the various heads of federal jurisdiction.[182] Thus, the Supreme Court has long recognized that a federal court may take jurisdiction over claims (that do not, by themselves, satisfy an independent basis of federal subject matter jurisdiction) *if and only if* the claims are so closely related to the claim that invoked the federal court's jurisdiction as to be considered part of the same case or controversy as that claim. In other words, if the additional claim is so closely related to the plaintiff's original claim (which invoked diversity, alienage, or federal question) as to be part of the same overall dispute, the federal court can hear the additional claim.

Although the Supreme Court first recognized the concept of supplemental jurisdiction in 1861,[183] and had addressed the topic sporadically through the years,[184] its most important case in this area is *United Mine Workers v. Gibbs*,[185] decided in 1966. In that case, both the plaintiff and the defendant were citizens of Tennessee,[186] so there was no possibility of diversity jurisdiction. Simplifying the facts a bit, the plaintiff asserted two claims: (1) that defendant had violated his rights under federal labor laws and (2) that the same behavior by the defendant also violated the plaintiff's rights under state law. Obviously, claim (1) invoked federal question jurisdiction (because the claim arose under federal law). Just as obviously, claim (2) failed to invoke either diversity or federal question jurisdiction (the parties are co-citizens and the claim arises under state, not federal, law). Stated another way, claim (2), by itself, could not get into federal court; it did not have an independent basis of subject matter jurisdiction.

Nonetheless, the Supreme Court held that the federal courts had supplemental jurisdiction[187] over claim (2) because that claim "derive[d] from a

---

[182] In listing federal subject matter jurisdiction, Article III, §2, refers to "cases" involving some heads of jurisdiction and "controversies" involving others. There is no difference in the scope of a case and a controversy.

[183] Freeman v. Howe, 65 U.S. 450 (1861).

[184] *See, e.g.*, Hurn v. Oursler, 289 U.S. 238 (1933).

[185] 383 U.S. 715 (1966).

[186] The plaintiff was human. Why was he a citizen of Tennessee? The defendant was an unincorporated association. Why was it a citizen of Tennessee? Constantly test these points, so they become second nature to you. (The answers: Citizens of the United States are deemed citizens for diversity purposes of the state in which they are domiciled; unincorporated associations are deemed citizens of all states of which its members are citizens.) See §4.5.3.

[187] The Court spoke of "pendent" jurisdiction. Before the supplemental jurisdiction statute, §1367, was passed in 1990, courts spoke not of "supplemental" but of "pendent" and "ancillary" jurisdiction. (Largely, pendent referred to claims by plaintiffs while ancillary referred to claims by nonplaintiffs.) With §1367, Congress employed a generic

common nucleus of operative fact" with the claim that invoked federal subject matter jurisdiction.[188] Claims sharing such a common nucleus of operative fact, then, are part of the same constitutional case or controversy as the claim that invoked federal jurisdiction, and thus may be decided by the federal court. Through the years, courts and commentators agreed that the "common nucleus" test is always satisfied if claims arise from the same "transaction or occurrence" (indeed, we will see below, in the section starting on page 216, that "common nucleus" is even broader than "transaction or occurrence").[189] This is a nice equation, since many of the joinder rules under the Federal Rules (as we see throughout Chapter 12) use the "transaction or occurrence" label.

Gibbs presented another interesting problem. Before it got to the Supreme Court, the case had been tried, and the jury had returned a verdict for the plaintiff on both claim (1) and claim (2). But the trial judge threw out the verdict on claim (1) because he held, as a matter of law, that the evidence did not support such a claim.[190] So the *only* claim left in the case for final judgment was one over which there was only supplemental jurisdiction. The jurisdiction-invoking claim was now gone! Can a federal court enter a judgment on such a claim? The Supreme Court answered the question by distinguishing between a federal court's *power* and its *discretionary decision* to use supplemental jurisdiction.

If the nonfederal, nondiverse claim meets the common nucleus test, the federal court has *power* to hear it. Jurisdiction is proper. But, according to the Court, there is a series of discretionary factors under which a court with power to hear the claim might decide not to exercise it. We discuss these factors in detail below. For example, if the jurisdiction-invoking claim is dismissed early in the proceedings, or if the state law issues

---

rubric — supplemental jurisdiction — for the entire area. So don't let older cases' discussion of pendent or ancillary jurisdiction bother you; today, the entire area is known as supplemental jurisdiction.

[188] Stated more pragmatically, the Court said that supplemental jurisdiction would be proper over claims that one "would ordinarily . . . expect[] to try . . . all in one judicial proceeding." *Gibbs*, 383 U.S. at 726-727. Oddly, however, the quoted matter is preceded with "But if," as opposed to "And if." Realistically, however, the point quoted will rarely be all that meaningful. Obviously, if claims are transactionally related, one would expect to try them together, since evidence of one set of facts would underlie both claims. Moreover, as we see in §11.2, the doctrine of claim preclusion may require the plaintiff to assert transactionally related claims in a single case or else waive the right to assert them.

[189] Indeed, although the Federal Rules cannot expand the jurisdiction of the federal courts, Fed. R. Civ. P. 82, the Supreme Court in *Gibbs* recognized that the Rules' view of the appropriate joinder was entitled to respect. *Gibbs*, 383 U.S. at 725. *See generally* Richard Freer, *Avoiding Duplicative Litigation: Rethinking Plaintiff Autonomy and the Court's Role in Defining the Litigative Unit*, 50 U. Pitt. L. Rev. 809, 815-817 (1989).

[190] When *Gibbs* was decided, this procedure was called *judgment notwithstanding the verdict (JNOV)*. Now it's called a *renewed motion for judgment as a matter of law*. See §9.5.

predominate substantially in the litigation, or if trying the jurisdiction-invoking claim together with the additional claim would confuse the jury, the court may decline to exercise supplemental jurisdiction.[191] In *Gibbs*, the nonfederal, nondiverse claim satisfied the common nucleus test (because the same behavior was alleged to violate federal and state law) and was not dismissed until after trial (in other words, only after the federal court had invested a good deal of time and effort). Thus, there was power and none of the discretionary factors required declining it. The Supreme Court upheld the judgment of the trial court.

It is worth noting the practical consequences of exercising supplemental jurisdiction. Suppose the Court had not permitted supplemental jurisdiction over claim (2) in *Gibbs*. One of two things would have ensued, both of them bad. First, because the plaintiff could not bring claim (2) in federal court, she would proceed in federal court only on claim (1) and file a separate action based upon claim (2) in state court. This result is inefficient for the plaintiff, who now must pay for (and prosecute) two separate lawsuits. It is also inefficient for the judicial system, since it requires two cases in two systems to decide a dispute arising from a single set of facts. (Plus, it is conceivable that the two cases would be resolved inconsistently, which might erode public confidence in the judicial system.) Second, the plaintiff can avoid these problems only by filing both claims (1) and (2) in state court. This route is efficient, but requires the plaintiff to eschew a federal forum for her federal claim. Moreover, if the jurisdiction-invoking claim were within the exclusive jurisdiction of the federal courts, she could not do this, and would have to proceed with two cases.

Thus, supplemental jurisdiction fosters efficiency, convenience, and consistency of outcome. It permits a federal court to determine all claims that are transactionally related to a claim that invokes federal subject matter jurisdiction. But supplemental jurisdiction raises some problems. Notably, if extended to its limits in diversity cases, supplemental jurisdiction would eviscerate the complete diversity rule. For example, suppose *P*, a citizen of Maryland, sues *D-1*, a citizen of Virginia, on a state law claim for $400,000. This claim invokes diversity of citizenship jurisdiction. Now suppose *P* adds a transactionally related state law claim against *D-2*, a citizen of Maryland. This claim does not invoke either diversity or federal question. But because it arises from the same transaction as the claim against *D-1* (which is properly in federal court), it satisfies the common nucleus test of *Gibbs* and thus can be supported by supplemental jurisdiction. To do so, though, makes a mockery of the complete diversity rule of *Strawbridge* (§4.5.3). In addition, it would risk inundating the federal courts with too many cases. Thus, the Supreme Court tried to balance the desire for supplemental jurisdiction with the need to protect the complete diversity rule.[192]

---

[191] *Gibbs*, 383 U.S. at 727.

[192] *See, e.g.*, Owen Equipment & Erection Co. v. Kroger, 437 U.S. 365 (1978), which we refer to as *Kroger* and discuss in detail when we address impleader at §12.6.2.

Interestingly, from 1861 until 1990, the federal courts made the rules concerning supplemental jurisdiction with no general involvement from Congress.[193] This fact might create a constitutional problem, because the Constitution empowers Congress (not the courts) to prescribe the subject matter jurisdiction of the federal courts. Nonetheless, the Court continually indicated that supplemental jurisdiction was proper as long as the *Gibbs* test was met and as long as Congress had not *prohibited* it. Thus, the Court created a presumption that Congress approved supplemental jurisdiction over claims satisfying *Gibbs* unless Congress acted to reject such jurisdiction.[194] In other words, congressional silence was to be seen as congressional approval of supplemental jurisdiction. This presumption went unquestioned until 1989, when the Supreme Court rendered its unfortunate opinion in *Finley v. United States*.[195]

The Finley *Case Leads to the Supplemental Jurisdiction Statute*

In *Finley*, the plaintiff's husband and children were killed in the crash of a small airplane. She had two theories of liability. First, the Federal Aviation Administration (FAA) might be liable because of negligence in air traffic control and maintenance of runway lights. Second, the city and a utility company might be liable for maintaining electrical power lines too close to the airfield. The plaintiff sued the FAA,[196] asserting liability under the Federal Tort Claims Act (FTCA), which gives exclusive federal jurisdiction. She also joined a claim against the city and utility for liability under state tort law. The claim against the FAA invoked federal question jurisdiction, but the claim against the city and utility did not invoke federal question or diversity jurisdiction. Thus, the only way to have the latter heard in federal court was through supplemental jurisdiction.[197] Courts at the time spoke of such a case as involving "pendent parties" jurisdiction,

---

[193] Except, however, with regard to patent cases. Section 1338(b) permits supplemental jurisdiction over state law claims related to patent infringement actions even in the absence of diversity jurisdiction.

[194] In *Aldinger v. Howard*, 427 U.S. 1 (1976), the Court concluded that Congress had precluded supplemental jurisdiction in cases brought under 42 U.S.C. §1983, which permits civil actions against state actors for violation of federal constitutional rights. The Court found a clear congressional mandate to this effect despite the fact that Congress made absolutely no mention of supplemental jurisdiction in that statute or any of its legislative history. *See also Kroger*, 437 U.S. 365 (1978).

[195] 490 U.S. 545 (1989).

[196] Actually, because the FAA is a federal agency, the claim was against the United States, which has waived its sovereign immunity under the Federal Tort Claims Act.

[197] This version of supplemental jurisdiction was called *pendent parties jurisdiction*. It differs from pendent claim jurisdiction in *Gibbs* in that the nonfederal, nondiverse claim in *Finley* was asserted against a different defendant than the jurisdiction-invoking claim.

because the nonfederal, nondiverse claim involved a different party from the claim that invoked federal subject matter jurisdiction.[198]

Under *Gibbs*, supplemental jurisdiction was clearly constitutional, since the state law claim shared a common nucleus of operative fact with the jurisdiction-invoking FTCA claim; both claims arose from the same crash. But the Supreme Court, in a five-to-four decision, rejected supplemental jurisdiction. Along the way, the Court reversed the presumption in favor of supplemental jurisdiction in the absence of congressional action. Instead of presuming that supplemental jurisdiction applies if the *Gibbs* test is met and Congress has not precluded it, the Court held that there could be no supplemental jurisdiction unless Congress *affirmatively granted* it. Since Congress had never addressed the issue of supplemental jurisdiction under the FTCA, the Court reasoned, it did not exist.

The decision, which rejected the view of the majority of the Courts of Appeals, created a nightmare for the plaintiff. Mrs. Finley was forced to continue her case against the FAA in federal court (because federal courts have exclusive jurisdiction over FTCA cases) and to file her claims against the city and the utility in state court. Thus, she (and the taxpayers) had to pay for two suits and run the risk of inconsistent judgments, despite the obvious fact that there had been only one crash. Moreover, the Court's broad language reversing the historic presumption (in favor of supplemental jurisdiction in the absence of congressional action) may have threatened all supplemental jurisdiction.

Because of this, Congress responded to *Finley* with a statute that addressed the whole area, rather than simply overrule the result in *Finley*.[199] In short order, Congress passed, and the President signed, the supplemental jurisdiction statute, §1367. The stated aims of the statute were to overrule the result in *Finley* and, in other respects, to codify the practice that the courts had developed before *Finley*. This statute now governs all questions of supplemental jurisdiction in general civil cases.

The statute has accomplished some of the stated goals. It clarified the language by creating a generic term — *supplemental jurisdiction* — for what had previously been called *pendent* and *ancillary jurisdiction*. It also ensured that the wasteful result wrought by *Finley* would not befall other plaintiffs. But the statute also created problems that did not previously exist.[200] Rather than codify pre-*Finley* practice, it changed that

---

[198] In contrast, *Gibbs* involved "pendent claim" jurisdiction because the nonfederal, non-diversity claim involved the same party as the claim that invoked federal subject matter jurisdiction.

[199] Interestingly, the federal courts addressing the impact of *Finley* had basically limited it to its facts. *See, e.g.,* Alumax Mill Prods., Inc. v. Congress Fin. Corp., 912 F.2d 996 (8th Cir. 1990). Nonetheless, most observers concluded that a well-crafted universal supplemental jurisdiction statute would be a good idea.

[200] Section 1367 has generated a stunning amount of commentary. The first critical article was Richard D. Freer, *Compounding Confusion and Hampering Diversity: Life After*

practice overtly in some ways and inadvertently in others. Nonetheless, it is the law, and you must be able to work with it.

Applying the Supplemental Jurisdiction Statute: Jurisdictional Aspects

Before looking at the statute in detail, note the overall structure of §1367. Subsection (a) is the grant of supplemental jurisdiction. After *Finley*, Congress felt it necessary to make an affirmative grant of supplemental jurisdiction. Subsection (b) then withdraws supplemental jurisdiction in certain instances. Understanding those instances is critical to successful application of the statute. Subsection (c) is Congress's effort to codify the discretionary factors the Court set forth in *Gibbs*, in which the court might decline to exercise supplemental jurisdiction. Subsection (d) is a tolling provision, which stops the running of the statute of limitations in certain instances. Finally, subsection (e) defines "State" to include the District of Columbia and other political subdivisions, just as §1332(d) does. Nearly all Civil Procedure courses emphasize the first two subsections, the workings of which are critical.[201]

Subsection (a) grants supplemental jurisdiction in the broadest possible terms. Congress was quite clear that it intended to reach to the full extent of Article III in permitting federal courts to exercise supplemental jurisdiction. There is little doubt that §1367(a) is meant to codify the *Gibbs* common nucleus test.[202] Thus, §1367(a) grants supplemental jurisdiction over all claims asserted in a federal civil action if they share a common nucleus of operative fact with the claim that invoked federal subject

---

Finley and the Supplemental Jurisdiction Statute, 40 Emory L.J. 445 (1991). This was followed by a spirited debate between Professors Steven Burbank, Thomas Rowe, and Thomas Mengler, defending the statute, and Professor Freer and Professor Thomas Arthur, criticizing the statute. *See* 40 Emory L.J. 943 (1991). This colloquy was followed by an exchange of other commentators at 41 Emory L.J. 31 (1992). More recently, there was a symposium concerning possible amendments to §1367 at 74 Ind. L.J. 1 (1998). There are countless articles in between and after.

[201] Some professors may spend considerable time on §1367(c). Although Congress indicated that it intended to codify the factors set forth in *Gibbs*, the factors in §1367(c)(1) and (4) appear nowhere in *Gibbs*. Moreover, at least one *Gibbs* factor (avoidance of jury confusion) is not reflected in the statute.

[202] H.R. Rep. 734, 101st Cong., 2d Sess. (1990), *reprinted in* 1990 U.S.C.C.A.N. 6873, 6875 n.15. While everyone agrees that this test includes claims arising from the same transaction or occurrence as a jurisdiction-invoking claim, courts generally conclude that the statute is broader. One representative opinion concludes that the statute requires nothing more than some "loose factual connection" between the claims. *See, e.g.*, Jones v. Ford Motor Credit Co., 358 F.3d 205, 210-215 (2d Cir. 2004) (upholding supplemental jurisdiction over permissive counterclaim). The issue is discussed in more detail at §12.5.1.

matter jurisdiction in the case.[203] The last sentence of that subsection makes it clear that supplemental jurisdiction includes claims involving additional parties, which makes it clear that the statute overrules the result in *Finley*.

As we discussed above, though, such a grant of supplemental jurisdiction would eviscerate the complete diversity rule, unless Congress restrained it in some way. Congress addressed this problem in §1367(b). It is imperative that we understand three things about §1367(b). First, it prohibits supplemental jurisdiction. So although subsection (a) gives such jurisdiction, subsection (b) takes it away in certain circumstances. Second, §1367(b) *applies only in cases in which the jurisdiction-invoking claim was asserted under §1332*. In other words, §1367(b) is never applicable if the plaintiff's original claim — the one that got the case into federal court in the first place — invoked federal question jurisdiction. It applies only if that original claim was brought under diversity jurisdiction.[204]

Third, §1367(b)'s prohibition of supplemental jurisdiction in diversity cases applies only to claims asserted by plaintiffs or parties subsequently joined on the plaintiff's side of the litigation.[205] Note the language carefully. Although the statute does not delineate these categories specifically, it is handy to break the detailed provisions of §1367(b) into three parts. Doing so makes it clear that the section precludes supplemental jurisdiction over three categories of claims:

(1) "claims *by plaintiffs* against persons made parties under Rule 14, 19, 20, or 24 of the Federal Rules...";

(2) "claims by persons proposed to be joined *as plaintiffs* under Rule 19..."; and

(3) claims by persons "seeking to intervene *as plaintiffs* under Rule 24..." (emphasis added).

Note, then, that §1367(b) does not apply to claims asserted by parties other than plaintiffs. Thus, claims satisfying §1367(a) asserted in a diversity case *by a defendant (or a party joined on the defendant's side)* will invoke supplemental jurisdiction.

---

[203] The statute does not say this expressly. Rather, it speaks of granting supplemental jurisdiction to the extent of Article III. *Gibbs* is universally regarded as defining the Article III reach of supplemental jurisdiction.

[204] Apparently the restrictions of §1367(b) also apply if original jurisdiction were based upon alienage. This seems clear because §1367(b) refers to cases brought under §1332, not just under §1332(a)(1) (diversity). Some professors who assisted in drafting the legislation have indicated that they did not intend §1367(b) to apply in alienage cases, but the statute, on its face, seems to do so.

[205] As we see in Chapter 12, various joinder rules provide for addition of parties after the case has been filed.

In Chapter 12, we address these Federal Rules to which the statute refers, and we address the availability of supplemental jurisdiction over each kind of claim at that time. It is more effective to review the availability of supplemental jurisdiction for each type of claim when we study the procedural availability of each type of claim. For now, the important point is to note that §1367(b) only precludes supplemental jurisdiction claims (1) asserted in diversity jurisdiction cases (2) by plaintiffs. Even without knowing the intricacies of the various Federal Rules, we can apply the statute in the following fact patterns.

- *The* Gibbs *Scenario.* P, a citizen of Tennessee, sues D, a citizen of Tennessee, asserting (1) violation of federal labor law and (2) violation of state labor law. The two claims are based upon the same alleged actions by D. Claim (1) invokes federal question jurisdiction, but claim (2) does not satisfy diversity or federal question jurisdiction.[206] Claim (2) invokes supplemental jurisdiction under §1367(a) because it arises from a common nucleus of operative fact as claim (1) (the jurisdiction-invoking claim). Section 1367(b) does not apply at all, because the underlying basis of subject matter jurisdiction in the case (the reason the case is in federal court in the first place) is *not* §1332. (Rather, it is §1331 (federal question).) So supplemental jurisdiction supports claim (2).
- *The* Finley *Scenario.* P, a citizen of California, asserts (1) an FTCA claim against the FAA and (2) a state law negligence claim against D-2, who is a citizen of California. The claims arise from a single airplane crash. Claim (1) invokes federal question jurisdiction, but claim (2) does not satisfy diversity or federal question. Claim (2) invokes supplemental jurisdiction under §1367(a) because it arises from a common nucleus of operative fact as claim (1). Under the last sentence of §1367(a), it is irrelevant that supplemental jurisdiction is sought for a claim against an additional party, as in this hypothetical. Section 1367(b) does not apply, because the underlying basis of subject matter jurisdiction in the case is *not* §1332. (Again, it is §1331.) So supplemental jurisdiction applies to claim (2).
- P, a citizen of Michigan, sues D, a citizen of Iowa, on a state law claim for $400,000. D asserts a counterclaim (which is a claim against an opposing party) against P for $60,000; the counterclaim arises from the same transaction as P's claim. P's claim invokes diversity jurisdiction, but D's counterclaim does not satisfy diversity jurisdiction (because it does not exceed $75,000) and does not satisfy federal question (because it is based upon state law).[207] D's claim satisfies supplemental jurisdiction under §1367(a) because it arises from a common nucleus of operative fact as P's claim (which invoked federal subject matter jurisdiction by invoking

---

[206] There is no diversity because P and D are co-citizens. There is no federal question jurisdiction over claim (2) because it is based upon state, not federal, law.

[207] Remember that we only address supplemental jurisdiction if we need it. If the facts were the same but D's claim against P were for $80,000, D's claim would invoke diversity jurisdiction (since it would be by a citizen of Iowa against a citizen of Michigan and would exceed $75,000). In that instance, supplemental jurisdiction would be irrelevant.

diversity jurisdiction). But §1367(b) must be addressed, because the underlying basis of jurisdiction in the case is §1332. Here, however, the prohibition against supplemental jurisdiction does not apply, because this is not a claim by a plaintiff or by one joined on the plaintiff's side of the case. It is by a defendant. Thus, supplemental jurisdiction applies to claim (2).

Applying the Supplemental Jurisdiction Statute: Discretionary Aspects

We noted above that in *Gibbs*, the Supreme Court distinguished between the *power* to exercise supplemental jurisdiction and the *discretionary authority* to refuse to do so. According to *Gibbs*, a court that has supplemental jurisdiction over a claim might determine not to exercise that jurisdiction if any of these things were true: (1) the federal claims were dismissed early in the proceedings; (2) the state issues "substantially predominate, whether in terms of proof, of the scope of the issues raised, or of the comprehensiveness of the remedy sought"; or (3) if considerations of "judicial economy, convenience, and fairness to litigants" counseled such a refusal to exercise supplemental jurisdiction.[208] An example of the latter would be a "likelihood of jury confusion in treating divergent legal theories of relief . . . that would justify separating state and federal claims for trial."[209]

In passing the supplemental jurisdiction statute, Congress embraced the notion that the court should have discretion to decline to exercise supplemental jurisdiction. Rather than leave the discretionary factors to case law development, Congress codified them in §1367(c). That statute does not codify the *Gibbs* factors precisely. It provides that a court "may decline to exercise supplemental jurisdiction over a claim" on the basis of any of these factors: (1) the claim "raises a novel or complex issue of State law"; (2) the claim "substantially predominates" over the claim that invoked federal subject matter jurisdiction; (3) the court "has dismissed all claim over which it has original jurisdiction"; or (4) "in exceptional circumstances, there are other compelling reasons for declining jurisdiction."

The first two statutory factors relate to the *Gibbs* concern that the state law tail should not wag the federal dog. That is, if the major thrust of the case would be state law — either because the claims predominate or involve novel questions — the court may decline jurisdiction. The third statutory factor relates to the first *Gibbs* factor. These recognize the most obvious basis for declining supplemental jurisdiction — that the claims that got the case into federal court initially have been dismissed. When this happens early in the proceedings — before the federal court has

---

[208] *Gibbs*, 383 U.S. at 726-727.
[209] *Id.* at 727.

invested considerable time in the supplemental claim — it makes sense to dismiss and let the parties litigate the supplemental claim in federal court. On the other hand, if the jurisdiction-invoking claims are dismissed late — after the court has invested time and resources in the litigation of the supplemental claim — it makes sense to keep the supplemental claim for final decision in federal court. Indeed, this is exactly what happened in *Gibbs*, when the federal question claims were only dismissed after trial.

What is missing from the statutory equation is an express adoption of the *Gibbs* concern about judicial economy, convenience, and fairness to litigants. This omission is odd, because Congress indicated that it intended to codify prior practice, which would, of course, include the *Gibbs* discretionary factors. Moreover, an early draft of the statute contained an express direction to consider such factors; for some reason, it was removed before the final draft was approved.

Courts have taken two basic approaches. The clear majority view is that §1367(c) replaced *Gibbs* and limited the scope of discretion enjoyed under that case. Indeed, the Second, Third, Eighth, Ninth, and Eleventh Circuits[210] conclude that unless one of the factors of §1367(c) is met, the court must exercise supplemental jurisdiction. They and others agree, however, that once one of the statutory factors applies, the court may look to the full range of *Gibbs's* "animating values" of "judicial economy, convenience, and fairness to litigants" in deciding whether to decline jurisdiction.[211]

On the other hand, the Seventh and District of Columbia Circuits conclude that §1367(c) does not restrain the common law discretion of *Gibbs*.[212] These courts will not say that a court *must* exercise supplemental jurisdiction whenever a specific provision of §1367(c) does not apply. Indeed, they seem to conclude as a theoretical matter that the *Gibbs* discretionary factors operate independently of the statute. It is worth noting, however, that neither court seems to have permitted a discretionary decline of jurisdiction in the absence of a statutory factor under §1367(c).[213]

---

[210] Parker v. Scrap Metal Processors, Inc., 468 F.2d 733, 743 (11th Cir. 2006); Treglia v. Town of Manlius, 313 F.3d 713, 723 (2d Cir. 2002); McLaurin v. Prater, 30 F.3d 982, 984 (8th Cir. 1994); Executive Software North America, Inc. v. United States District Court, 24 F.3d 1545, 1555-1556 (9th Cir. 1994); Growth Horizons, Inc. v. Delaware County, Pa., 983 F.2d 1277, 1283 (3d Cir. 1993).

[211] *See, e.g.*, Annulli v. Panikkar, 200 F.3d 189, 202 (3d Cir. 1999); Musson Theatrical, Inc. v. Federal Export Corp., 89 F.3d 1244, 1255 (6th Cir. 1996); Gullickson v. Southwest Airlines Pilots' Assn., 87 F.3d 1176, 1187 (10th Cir. 1996); Roche v. John Hancock Mut. Life Ins. Co., 81 F.3d 249, 257 (1st Cir. 1996); Shanaghan v. Cahill, 58 F.3d 106, 110 (4th Cir. 1995).

[212] LaShawn A. v. Barry, 87 F.3d 1389, 1393 (D.C. Cir. 1996); Timm v. Mead Corp., 32 F.3d 273, 276-277 (7th Cir. 1994).

[213] Indeed, the Seventh Circuit may now require citation to a factor under that provision. Montano v. City of Chicago, 375 F.3d 593, 602 (7th Cir. 2004) (reversing rejection of supplemental jurisdiction, noting district court's failure to cite statutory basis for its decision).

Thus, the ultimate scope of discretion under §1367(c) is not entirely clear. For example, can a court decline supplemental jurisdiction (as it could under *Gibbs*) because it is likely that the jury will be confused if both the original jurisdiction-invoking claim and the supplemental claim are tried together? No factor in §1367(c) expressly addresses the issue. Perhaps, at least for some courts, such factors fall within the discretion accorded under §1367(c)(4), as an exceptional circumstance. If the court exercises its discretion under §1367(c) and declines supplemental jurisdiction, it dismisses only the supplemental claim. It does not dismiss the original claim that properly invoked federal subject matter jurisdiction.[214]

- *P* asserts two claims against *D*: (1) is for violation of federal antitrust laws and (2) is for violation of state antitrust laws. The two claims arise from a common nucleus of operative fact. *P* and *D* are co-citizens, so there is no diversity of citizenship jurisdiction. Claim (1) invokes federal question jurisdiction. Claim (2) does not (because it is based upon state law), and also does not invoke diversity of citizenship jurisdiction, as just noted.

Nonetheless, claim (2) invokes supplemental jurisdiction because it shares a common nucleus of operative fact with claim (1). Suppose the court makes the discretionary determination that it will decline supplemental jurisdiction because, for instance, claim (2) would predominate substantially and involves novel questions of law. The court will dismiss only claim (2). Claim (1) will continue through litigation in federal court.

When the court dismisses the state law claim under §1367(c), it does so without prejudice, so the plaintiff can assert the claim in state court.[215] The plaintiff might worry, however, about whether the statute of limitations has run on her claim. Section 1367(d) allays her fears by providing that the statute is tolled while the case is pending in federal court and for 30 days after dismissal. (It also provides that a state statute can extend tolling for a longer time.) In §7.6.3, we see that tolling a statute of limitations means to arrest or stop it from running.

- Return to the previous hypothetical. *P* filed the case one day before the statute of limitations would have run on her state law claim. Filing the case, and invoking supplemental jurisdiction over the state law claim, tolled the statute of limitations. Section 1367(d) tolls the statute of limitations for an additional 30 days after the court dismisses claim (2). Thus, if *P* asserts the claim in state court within 30 days of the dismissal in federal court, it will be timely.

---

[214] *See, e.g.,* Borough of West Mifflin v. Lancaster, 45 F.3d 780, 787 (3d Cir. 1995).
[215] *See, e.g.,* Gold v. Local 7 United Food & Commercial Workers Union, 159 F.3d 1307, 1311 (10th Cir. 1998).

It is clear that the tolling provision of §1367(d) applies when a claim is dismissed under §1367(c). By the better view, §1367(d) should apply only to such dismissals. Suppose instead the court dismisses a state law claim because it does not satisfy the requirements for supplemental jurisdiction. Section 1367(d) should not apply to this dismissed claim. Why? Because it provides for tolling for a "claim asserted under subsection (a)." A claim that did not properly invoke supplemental jurisdiction is not a claim under §1367(a).The Supreme Court has held that §1367(d) does not apply to toll the statute of limitations on a claim dismissed under the Eleventh Amendment, which provides states with immunity from suit in federal court.[216] The Court did not have to determine whether, as a general matter, §1367(d) would apply to refusals to exercise supplemental jurisdiction other than those involving discretionary refusal under §1367(c).

§4.8   Removal Jurisdiction

The Concepts of Removal and Remand

To this point, the decision to proceed in federal court has been made by the plaintiff. Removal is a remarkable procedure that gives the *defendant*, sued in state court, the right to "remove" the case to federal court. In other words, it allows the defendant to override the plaintiff's choice of forum. (Obviously, as discussed in detail below, this is only possible in a case that satisfies a basis of federal subject matter jurisdiction.) Removal is not mentioned in the Constitution, and is wholly the product of statutory law. Today, most provisions for removal jurisdiction and procedure in general civil cases are found in various provisions of §§1441, 1446, and 1447. The relevant provisions are best considered as a series of related, fairly mechanical, rules. While none of these is particularly difficult in itself, in the aggregate, there is a good deal to remember when approaching a removal question.

Removal is simply a mechanism to transfer a case, at the defendant's behest, from a *state* trial court to a *federal* trial court.[217] Although removal effects a transfer of the case, we do not call it *transfer*. *Transfer* is a term of art to lawyers and judges and, as we see in §5.5, refers to changing venue

---

[216] Raygor v. Regents of Univ. of Minnesota, 534 U.S. 533 (2002). The Eleventh Amendment removes jurisdiction of *federal* courts to entertain cases brought against a state (or an "arm" of a state). It does not prohibit suits against states in *state* court. Thus, the fact that the claim in *Raygor* could not be asserted in federal court did not mean that the plaintiff could not sue in state court. But, the Court held, the statute of limitations on the claim dismissed under the Eleventh Amendment was not tolled under §1367(d).

[217] Removal is not an appeal. Remember from §1.2.2 that one cannot appeal a general civil case from a state trial court to a federal court.

from one *federal* trial court to another *federal* trial court (or from one state trial court to another state trial court in the same state). What we deal with here — going from a state trial court to a federal trial court — is referred to with another term of art, *removal*. Remember that removal is a one-way street. A case can be removed *only* from state court to federal court. There is no provision for removing or transferring a case from federal court to state court. If a case is removed to federal court improperly (either because the defendant made a procedural mistake or because there is no federal subject matter jurisdiction), the federal court can *remand* the case to state court.

Procedural Issues

Only defendants can remove a case. Plaintiffs cannot. Even if the defendant has asserted a claim against the plaintiff in the pending case, so the plaintiff is a "defendant" on that claim, the plaintiff cannot remove the case to federal court.[218] After all, the plaintiff had the original choice of forum; if she wanted to be in federal court, she should have filed in federal court at the outset. And because §1441(a) grants the right to remove to "the defendant or the defendants," courts have concluded that *all* defendants must agree to remove a case.[219] If there are multiple defendants, and any of them refuses to join the notice of removal, the case cannot be removed.[220]

But when do we determine who all the defendants are? Suppose the plaintiff files a complaint in state court naming three defendants, but serves process on only two. The cases are clear that the rule of unanimity requires unanimous involvement in the notice of removal by all defendants who have been *served with process* in the case.[221] Thus, if the two who have been served remove the case to federal court, the removal is proper — because it was effected by all defendants who had been served in the state court action at that point.

We will see below that the defendants must remove the case to federal court within 30 days after being served with process. What happens if there is a gap in the times at which defendants are served? For example, suppose *P* sues two defendants (*D-1* and *D-2*) in state court, asserting a case that clearly is removable. *P* serves process immediately on *D-1* but not on *D-2* (for whatever reason — maybe *D-2* was out of the country for a while).

[218] Shamrock Oil & Gas Corp. v. Sheets, 313 U.S. 100 (1941).

[219] Chicago, R.I. & P. Ry. Co. v. Martin, 178 U.S. 245 (1900); Brown v. Demco, Inc., 792 F.2d 478, 481 (5th Cir. 1986).

[220] There is a narrow and somewhat vexing exception to this rule under §1441(c) for cases involving a "separate and independent" federal question claim against one of several defendants. We discuss that exception below.

[221] *See, e.g.,* Lewis v. Rego Co., 757 F.3d 66 (3d Cir. 1985) (named but unserved defendant need not join in removal).

D-1 fails to remove the case within 30 days after being served with process. Now *P* effects service on *D-2*. Can *D-2* remove? The statute gives no guidance in this scenario. Not surprisingly, courts have disagreed on what to do.

The early rule — which was undeniably the general rule for years — was that *D-2* could not remove unless she could show that *P* knew about her within the 30-day period for serving process on *D-1* and delayed joining her in bad faith. Obviously, it would be difficult to make such a showing. So the upshot of this approach was usually to deny *D-2*'s efforts to remove. In other words, the fact that *D-1* had not removed robbed *D-2* of the chance to try to get *D-1* to agree to remove. The Fifth Circuit adopted this view in 1986 in *Brown v. Demco, Inc.*[222] The Fourth Circuit and some district courts[223] followed the lead of that case and adopted the "first-served" rule for removability.

Over time, however, this rule has eroded. The majority view today is that the 30 days begins to run again when *D-2* is served with process. According to the courts adopting this "last-served" rule, *D-2* should have the opportunity to cajole *D-1* into agreeing to remove the case to federal court within 30 days after service on *D-2*.[224] Courts adopting this approach were concerned in part with the seeming unfairness of having *D-2* lose a chance to remove based upon the inaction of *D-1*.

The defendant need not get permission to remove the case. She starts the process by filing a "notice of removal" in the federal court. (The required contents of the notice are set forth in §1446(a).) After filing the notice in federal court, §1446(d) requires that the defendant give written notice of the removal to "all adverse parties" and that she file a copy of the notice in the state court. That filing of the copy in the state court "shall effect the removal and the State court shall proceed no further unless and until the case is remanded." In other words, that act divests the state court of jurisdiction over the case.

If removal is improper for some reason *other than* lack of subject matter jurisdiction — for example, if the defendant failed to include in the notice of removal all the information required by §1446(a) or if fewer than all defendants joined in the notice of removal — the plaintiff must move to remand within 30 days after the removal. §1447(c). If she does not, the procedural defect is waived, and the case will not be remanded. On the

---

[222] 792 F.2d 478 (5th Cir. 1986). *See also* Getty Oil Corp. v. Ins. Co. of North America, 841 F.2d 1254, 1262-1263 (reiterating the holding).

[223] The most amusing district court case on point, without doubt, is *Noble v. Bradford Marine, Inc.*, 789 F. Supp. 395 (S.D. Fla. 1992), which was written in "Wayne's World" language. It is short and very amusing. Take a look at it when you have a spare moment. It is no longer good law, since the Eleventh Circuit has since adopted the last-served rule, in a case cited in the next footnote.

[224] *See* Bailey v. Janssen Pharmaceutica, Inc., 536 F.3d 1202, 1205-1208 (11th Cir. 2008); Marano Enterprises of Kansas v. Z-Teca Restaurants, LP, 254 F.3d 753, 755 (8th Cir. 2001); Brierly v. Alussuisse Flexible Packaging, Inc., 184 F.3d 527 (6th Cir. 1999).

other hand, if there is no federal subject matter jurisdiction, there is no time limit for the plaintiff's moving to remand the case to state court. Indeed, as §1447(c) also makes clear, the court must remand *sua sponte* whenever it determines that subject matter jurisdiction is lacking.

Finally, it is possible for the defendant to waive the right to remove by taking some action in the state court that she is not required to take.[225] For example, filing a permissive counterclaim (as opposed to a compulsory counterclaim) in state court probably waives the right to remove.[226] Generally, however, filing an answer in state court that raises a defense that might conclusively determine the merits of the case does not result in such waiver.[227] In addition, it is clear that by removing a case to federal court, the defendant does not waive the defense of lack of personal jurisdiction.[228]

Issues of Jurisdiction and Venue

The most important (and most obvious) rule relating to removal is that the defendant can remove a case only if it "is one of which the district courts of the United States have original jurisdiction." §1441(a). That means, of course, that the case must satisfy a basis of federal subject matter jurisdiction. Here, we see one of the great attractions of removal for your professor. It enables her to test not only your mastery of the various rules relating to removal, but the requirements of federal subject matter jurisdiction as well. The rules for invoking federal subject matter jurisdiction addressed above (including, for example, the complete diversity rule in diversity cases and the well-pleaded complaint rule in federal question cases) apply in cases in which the defendant seeks to remove. As we see below, however, removal jurisdiction is actually narrower than the plaintiff's right to file in federal court, at least as to diversity cases; there are two important exceptions to the removability of a diversity of citizenship case.

Obviously, if the case does not satisfy a basis of federal subject matter jurisdiction, the federal court must remand to state court. Usually, the lack of jurisdiction will be clear immediately. Occasionally, however, a federal court will not appreciate that it lacks subject matter jurisdiction until long after removal. Even if the court has invested enormous time and resources,

---

[225] *See* 16 Moore's Federal Practice §107.18[3][a].

[226] *See, e.g.*, Isaacs v. Group Health, Inc., 668 F. Supp. 306, 308-309 (S.D.N.Y. 1987). Counterclaims are asserted by the defendant against the plaintiff. A permissive counterclaim is not transactionally related to the plaintiff's claim and does not have to be asserted in the pending case. A compulsory counterclaim is transactionally related to the plaintiff's claim and generally must be asserted in the pending case. See §12.5.1.

[227] *See, e.g.*, Miami Herald Publ. Co. v. Ferre, 606 F. Supp. 122, 124 (S.D. Fla. 1984).

[228] Lambert Run Coal Co. v. Baltimore & Ohio R.R. Co., 258 U.S. 377 (1922).

the case must be remanded *whenever* it is discovered that there is no subject matter jurisdiction. §1447(c). We saw this principle in §4.3, where we said that a case filed originally in federal court must be dismissed whenever it is determined that it does not invoke federal subject matter jurisdiction. Federal courts simply cannot seize the power to determine a case not invoking their jurisdiction. But note the difference in the operation of this principle. If the case in which jurisdiction is lacking was filed originally in federal court, the case is dismissed. If the case in which jurisdiction is lacking was filed originally in state court and removed to federal court, the case is *not* dismissed, but is remanded to the state court.

- Mottley, a citizen of Kentucky, sues Railroad, also a citizen of Kentucky, in state court for $80,000, alleging that Railroad has breached a contract by which it agreed to furnish her with a lifetime pass. Mottley also alleges that a federal statute prohibiting such passes does not apply to her and, if it does, that it is unconstitutional. Railroad removes the case to federal court and plaintiff moves to remand for lack of subject matter jurisdiction. How does the court rule? The court will grant the motion and remand to state court. First, obviously, there no diversity, since the plaintiff and defendant are co-citizens. Second, the case also fails to invoke federal subject matter jurisdiction. Why? Under the well-pleaded complaint rule, see §4.6.3, this claim does not arise under federal law; the federal provision mentioned is raised as an anticipated defense, and does not constitute part of her claim.

- Same facts, same claim, except here Mottley is a citizen of Illinois, Railroad is a citizen of Kentucky, and the claimed value of the railroad pass is $80,000. Railroad removes the case to federal court and plaintiff moves to remand for lack of subject matter jurisdiction. How does the court rule? The court will deny the motion to remand. This case is removable because it satisfies the requirements for diversity of citizenship jurisdiction.

- State sues Indian Tribe in state court, asserting that the Tribe owes various state taxes. The Tribe asserts the defense that federal law makes it immune to claims for state taxes. The Tribe removes the case to federal court and the plaintiff moves to remand for lack of subject matter jurisdiction. How does the court rule? The court will grant the motion and remand to state court. Even though the Tribe has raised a serious federal issue, it cannot remove because this case does not invoke federal question jurisdiction. The federal issue is being injected by way of defense, which violates the well-pleaded complaint rule. Only if the federal law is part of the plaintiff's well-pleaded complaint is there federal question jurisdiction. Since that is not the case here, defendant cannot remove.[229]

---

[229] Oklahoma Tax Commn. v. Graham, 489 U.S. 838 (1989). Although the Court recognized that it might make sense to jettison the well-pleaded complaint rule for removal, it concluded that only Congress could do so.

On the other hand, if the jurisdictional defect is cured before entry of judgment in federal court, removal might be upheld. The Supreme Court addressed such a situation in *Caterpillar, Inc. v. Lewis*.[230] There, when defendant removed the case, there was no basis for federal subject matter jurisdiction, but the federal court did not appreciate that fact. The case was litigated, during which the claim against the defendant who destroyed diversity jurisdiction was dismissed before judgment was entered. In this circumstance — although the case should not have been removed, but the defect was cured before entry of judgment — the Supreme Court upheld the judgment.[231]

In removed cases, the *defendant* is invoking the federal court's jurisdiction, and has the burden of establishing federal subject matter jurisdiction. She must do so, however, on the basis of the plaintiff's complaint. It is the plaintiff's case that must invoke federal subject matter jurisdiction. Because state pleading rules usually do not require the plaintiff to plead citizenship of the parties, the defendant often has to show, in the notice of removal, the existence of diversity of citizenship jurisdiction. The general rule is that removal is permitted on the basis of diversity jurisdiction only if the requirements for diversity are met *both* at the time the case was filed in state court *and* at the time the defendant removes the case.[232] Historically, the reason for this rule was to prevent the state court defendant from changing her citizenship after being sued and then removing on the basis of diversity.[233] That rule — invented to prevent manipulation of federal jurisdiction by the defendant — should not apply, however, where no such gamesmanship is possible. Accordingly, over time, the federal courts came to uphold removal if a case that was originally not removable *became removable by voluntary act of the plaintiff.*

- ○ Suppose *P*, a citizen of California, sues *D-1*, a citizen of Arizona, and *D-2*, a citizen of California, in a state court in Nevada[234] on a state law claim for $500,000. Obviously, there is no federal question (because the claim

---

[230] 519 U.S. 61 (1996).

[231] *See also* Barbara v. New York Stock Exch., Inc., 99 F.3d 49 (2d Cir. 1996) (federal judgment permitted although case lacked subject matter jurisdiction when removed; plaintiff amended complaint to set forth federal question claim). This situation is to be contrasted with that in *Grupo Dataflux v. Atlas Global LP*, note 112 above, in which the Court held that a jurisdictional defect at the date of invoking federal jurisdiction cannot be cured by the change of citizenship of a party during litigation. In *Caterpillar*, in contrast, the cure came from dropping a nondiverse party during litigation. (We discussed this distinction at §4.5.3.)

[232] Pullman Co. v. Jenkins, 305 U.S. 534, 537 (1939).

[233] *See* Wright & Kane, Federal Courts 233.

[234] Don't let this fact throw you. Whether *P* can sue these defendants in Nevada (state or federal court) is a question of personal jurisdiction. Maybe the defendants have sufficient contacts to justify personal jurisdiction in Nevada. If the defendants do not object, the defense of personal jurisdiction is waived.

is based upon state, not federal, law). Also, there is no diversity jurisdiction (because the plaintiff is a co-citizen with *D-2*). So, as it stands initially, the defendants cannot remove the case. After a few months, suppose the claim against *D-2* is dismissed. *Now there is diversity of citizenship jurisdiction*, because the nondiverse defendant has just been taken from the case. Can *D-1* remove now?

- ○ If the claim against *D-2* is dismissed by the plaintiff voluntarily,[235] yes, the case has become removable, and *D-1* may remove within 30 days.[236] If, however, the claim against *D-2* is dismissed involuntarily (e.g., the court finds there is no personal jurisdiction over *D-2*), *D-1* cannot remove the case.[237] The theory is that an involuntary dismissal may be overturned on appeal, in which case the claim will be reinstated and diversity destroyed. If the dismissal is voluntary, however, the plaintiff cannot appeal it, and it cannot be overturned.

After the case is removed on the basis of diversity, what happens if the plaintiff seeks to join additional defendants who destroy diversity? Under §1447(e), "the court may deny joinder, or permit joinder and remand the action to the State court."

Recall from §4.2 that state courts, at least in the aggregate, have general subject matter jurisdiction. Thus, almost every case removed from state to federal court will be one over which there is *concurrent subject matter jurisdiction*, which means that both the state and federal court systems can properly entertain the claim. This is not always the case, however, since there are some rare situations in which state courts lack subject matter jurisdiction because there is exclusive federal question jurisdiction.[238] Suppose the plaintiff files such a case — one falling within the exclusive jurisdiction of the federal courts — in state court. As the law stood for many years, the defendant could not remove the case to federal court. Removal was then thought to be "derivative," so it was proper only if the state court had subject matter jurisdiction. This was a pretty silly rule, because it meant the case had to be dismissed by the plaintiff in state court, and re-filed in federal court. In the interim, there might be problems with the statute of limitations. Even if that were not the case, the

---

[235] Fed. R. Civ. P. 41(a).

[236] The relevant statute provides that the defendant must remove "within thirty days after receipt by the defendant, through service or otherwise, of a copy of an amended pleading, motion, order or other paper from which it may first be ascertained that the case . . . is or has become removable. . . ." 28 U.S.C. §1446(b). In *Murphy Brothers, Inc. v. Michetti Pipe Stringing, Inc.*, 526 U.S. 344 (1999), the Court rejected a broad interpretation of "through service or otherwise." In that case, the plaintiff filed the complaint and faxed a copy of it to the defendant, but did not have process served on the defendant until a few days later. The Court held that the 30 days for removal ran from service of process, not from the informal sending of a copy of the complaint. We discuss service of process at §3.3.

[237] *See* Poulos v. Naas Foods, Inc., 959 F.2d 69, 72 (7th Cir. 1992); Insinga v. LaBella, 845 F.2d 249, 254 (11th Cir. 1988).

[238] We saw major examples at note 1 above.

procedure is wasteful. Congress did a good thing, then, when it passed §1441(e), which addresses exactly these situations. It rejects the notion that removal jurisdiction is "derivative" of state court jurisdiction, and provides that removal is proper regardless of whether the state court had subject matter jurisdiction over the case.

Cases removed from state court have their own venue provision, separate from cases filed initially by the plaintiff in federal court. Under §1441(a), a case can be removed only to the federal district "embracing the place where [the] action is pending." In other words, the only federal district court to which a case can be removed is the one that "embraces" — that means geographically — the state court in which the case is pending. Thus, the general venue provisions that govern which federal districts are appropriate in cases filed by the plaintiff directly in federal court (§1391, addressed in §5.4) do not apply to cases removed from state court. For example, a case filed in state court in Buffalo can only be removed to the United States District Court for the Western District of New York, since that is the district "embracing" Buffalo. This is true regardless of whether venue would have been proper there under the general venue statutes.

Suppose a plaintiff wants to litigate only in state court. Can she plead her state-court case in such a way as to thwart removal? As a general rule, the plaintiff is "master of her complaint," so if she pleads a case that cannot be removed, there is not much the defendant can do about it. But courts occasionally look beyond what is pleaded to see whether the case ought to be removed, so we need to refine the "master of her complaint" theory.

It is helpful to consider the three main ways in which the plaintiff might try to plead to thwart removal. First, assuming her claim is based upon state (not federal) law, the plaintiff might join a defendant whose citizenship prevents removal. For instance, she might join a defendant who is a co-citizen with her, thereby defeating complete diversity.[239] Here, the defendant can remove only if she can convince the court that joinder of the jurisdiction-defeating party is fraudulent. In this context, *fraudulent* is a term of art and does not impugn the integrity of the plaintiff or her lawyer. Rather, it means that there is no bona fide claim by or against that party.[240]

Second, also assuming the plaintiff's claim is based upon state (not federal) law, and assuming the case as structured would meet the complete

---

[239] Or she might join a defendant who is a citizen of the forum state, which would defeat removal on the basis of diversity even if the other requirements of diversity jurisdiction were met. We discuss this point below, in the last subpart of this section.

[240] Pete Rose sued the Commissioner of Major League Baseball (to challenge his banishment from baseball) in state court in his hometown of Cincinnati. He joined as a defendant the Cincinnati Reds, whose presence defeated diversity and precluded removal. The court found, however, that Rose had no real claim against the Reds, and permitted removal. Rose v. Giamatti, 721 F. Supp. 906 (S.D. Ohio 1989).

diversity rule, the plaintiff might sue for exactly $75,000 or less. Such a claim, the plaintiff will contend, cannot be removed because it does not meet the amount in controversy requirement for diversity jurisdiction. (Remember, for a diversity case, the amount must *exceed* $75,000.) We are tempted to say that the plaintiff has defeated removal, because she has limited herself to recovering less than the jurisdictional amount for a diversity case. But there is a problem. In many states, the plaintiff's demand for judgment in her complaint does not limit the amount she can recover. So a plaintiff who demands exactly $75,000 in her complaint might actually recover far more than that. In such cases, courts tend to permit the defendant to remove by making a clear showing that the plaintiff's claim in fact meets the jurisdictional amount requirement.[241] Again, the burden is on the defendant, so some courts make it clear they will remand unless the defendant shows to a legal certainty that the amount requirement is satisfied.[242] Federal jurisdiction is measured at the time the case is removed, and is not based upon subsequent events. So if the case involves more than $75,000 when removed, the plaintiff cannot then gain remand by stipulating to a recovery of a lesser amount.[243] On the other hand, if the plaintiff stipulates before removal that she will not recover more than $75,000, the case cannot be removed on the basis of diversity jurisdiction.

Third, we know that many real-world events give rise to a state-law claim and a federal-law claim. What happens if such a plaintiff chooses not to assert a federal question claim? Can she thwart an effort to remove by doing this?[244] Generally, the answer is yes. No one can be forced to assert a federal claim. Moreover, the defendant cannot convert a state law claim into a federal question by asserting a federal defense, because the federal question must be presented in a well-pleaded complaint, as we studied in §4.6.3. On the other hand, there is a narrow exception to this rule — though it is an exception rarely covered in Civil Procedure courses. It is this: If a substantive area has been "completely" preempted by federal law, there is no basis for a state-law claim. In such a situation, a plaintiff cannot avoid removal by purporting to assert a state-law claim.[245] Such areas of complete preemption are rare, and include the Labor Management Relations

---

[241] *See., e.g.,* Dunn v. Pepsi-Cola Metropolitan Bottling Co., 850 F. Supp. 853 (N.D. Cal. 1994) (denying remand where complaint sought less than jurisdictional amount but allegations showed plaintiff could recover more than enough to satisfy the requirement). *See generally* 16 Moore's Federal Practice §107.14[2][g].

[242] *See, e.g.,* Kliebert v. Upjohn Co., 915 F.2d 143 (5th Cir. 1990).

[243] In re Brand Name Prescription Drugs Antitrust Litigation, 248 F.3d 668, 670-671 (7th Cir. 2001) ("If the plaintiffs' original claim was worth more than [$75,000], removal was proper, the case was within federal jurisdiction, and the plaintiffs could not defeat that jurisdiction by scaling back their claim.").

[244] We are assuming here that there is no basis for diversity of citizenship jurisdiction.

[245] *See, e.g.,* Pilot Life Ins. Co. v. Dedeaux, 481 U.S. 41, 47-48 (1987) (ERISA preempts common law action by employee against insurer).

Act and ERISA. In those areas, because federal law has completely supplanted state law concerning certain claims, any claim is, by definition, a federal claim and invokes federal question jurisdiction. The courts thus permit removal in such cases even though the plaintiff's complaint does not mention a federal claim.[246]

Two Important Exceptions to Removal in Diversity of Citizenship Cases

As we noted above, removal is permitted only if the case is one over which the federal court has subject matter jurisdiction. There are two important exceptions to this general rule, each of which applies only in diversity of citizenship cases. First, there is no removal of a diversity case if any defendant is a citizen of the forum.[247] This rule is consistent with the traditional rationale for diversity of citizenship; if one of the defendants is a citizen of the forum, she has no need for the protection of the federal court. See §4.5.2.

Second, no case can be removed on the basis of diversity of citizenship jurisdiction more than one year after the case was filed in state court.[248] This rule rarely comes into play because, as we saw above, a case must be removed no later than 30 days after it becomes removable; because most cases will be removable, if at all, when filed, this one-year limit is not usually implicated. This rule becomes an obstacle for cases that are not removable when filed but subsequently become removable because of the plaintiff's voluntary act.

For example, *P*, a citizen of Florida, sues *D-1*, a citizen of Georgia, and *D-2*, a citizen of Alabama, on a state law claim for $200,000. *P* files the case in state court in Georgia. At that point, the case is not removable because (even though it satisfies the requirements for diversity jurisdiction) one of the defendants is a citizen of the forum. After a period of litigation, assume that *P* settles the claim with *D-1* and voluntarily dismisses the claim against *D-1*. At that moment, the case has become removable because (1) it meets the requirements for diversity jurisdiction and (2)

---

[246] Trying to avoid removal by stating only state-law claims in such cases is referred to as "artful pleading." *See* 16 Moore's Federal Practice §107.14[3][b]. The ultimate contours of the doctrine are not clear. *See* Arthur Miller, *Artful Pleading: A Doctrine in Search of Definition*, 76 Tex. L. Rev. 1781 (1998). Recently, the Supreme Court held that a defendant cannot remove on the basis of federal question jurisdiction when the defendant raises the preclusive effect of a prior federal judgment. Rivet v. Regions Bank, 522 U.S. 470 (1998).

[247] 28 U.S.C. §1441(b) provides that federal question cases "shall be removable without regard to the citizenship or residence of the parties." All other cases, obviously including diversity cases, "shall be removable only if none of the parties in interest properly joined and served as defendants is a citizen of the State in which such action is brought."

[248] 28 U.S.C. §1446(b) provides that "a case may not be removed on the basis of jurisdiction conferred by §1332 . . . more than one year after commencement of the action."

there is no longer a defendant who is a citizen of the forum. The remaining defendant, *D-2*, must remove the case within 30 days of the dismissal of *D-1*. However, if more than one year has elapsed since the case was filed in state court, removal is not allowed. This is a terrible rule, because it permits the plaintiff to join a defendant who defeats removal, wait a year, and then voluntarily dismiss the claim against the defendant who defeated removal. There is nothing the remaining defendant can do.

○ *P*, a citizen of Texas, sues *D*, also a citizen of Texas, for $45,000 in a Texas state court. *P*'s allegation is that *D* violated *P*'s rights under the federal securities law. Can *D* remove the case to federal court? Yes. Don't go for the fake here. This case invokes federal question jurisdiction. The rule precluding removal if any defendant is a citizen of the forum only applies in diversity cases, so it is irrelevant here.

The Separate and Independent Federal Question Claim Problem

Section 1441(c) has not had a happy life. It provides that if the plaintiff joins a "separate and independent" federal question claim "with one or more otherwise nonremovable claims," the defendants may remove the *entire case*, including the otherwise nonremovable matters. The provision vests the federal court with discretion to remand to state court "all matters in which State law predominates." Before 1990, the separate and independent claim that invoked federal subject matter jurisdiction did not have to be a federal question claim. The two cases that found their ways into more casebooks than any others involved removal of separate and independent diversity[249] and alienage[250] claims respectively. Neither could invoke §1441(c) today.

Applying §1441(c) presents several problems. First, the definition of "separate and independent" is very difficult to meet. The claims must be truly unrelated. As the Supreme Court explained, "where there is a single wrong to a plaintiff, for which relief is sought, arising from an interlocked series of transactions, there is no separate and independent claim under §1441(c)."[251] In most states, multiple defendants can be joined in a single case only if, *inter alia*, the claims against them arise from the same transaction. If the claims are transactionally related, it would seem difficult to

---

[249] American Fire & Cas. v. Finn, 341 U.S. 6 (1951).

[250] Twentieth Century-Fox Film Corp. v. Taylor, 239 F. Supp. 913 (S.D.N.Y. 1965). In this case, a studio sued Richard Burton and Elizabeth Taylor, alleging that they breached their contracts during the filming of *Cleopatra*. Burton removed under §1441(c) on the basis of alienage (he was Welsh, so a British subject) and included the otherwise non-removable claim against Taylor. The district court denied remand, despite the seemingly strong argument that the claims were not separate and independent.

[251] *Finn*, 341 U.S. at 14.

meet §1441(c). Second, taken at face value, the statute would seem to allow removal of nondiversity, nonfederal claims that do not qualify for supplemental jurisdiction (precisely because they are not transactionally related to the federal question claim). Obviously, such an interpretation raises serious constitutional questions, as it puts in a federal court claims not falling within Article III. Third, the remand provision quoted above is unclear. Some courts have concluded that it permits remand of the entire case, including the federal question claim.[252] For these and other reasons, the statute has been criticized by commentators and largely ignored in practice.[253] Professor Charles Alan Wright well concluded that the statute "is useless and ought to have been repealed."[254]

---

[252] *See, e.g.*, Moralez v. Meat Cutter Local 539, 778 F. Supp. 368, 370 (E.D. Mich. 1991).
[253] *See* 16 Moore's Federal Practice §107.14[6]; Wright & Kane, Federal Courts §39.
[254] Wright & Kane, Federal Courts 235.

Chapter 5

Venue

§5.1   Defining the Issue

It is helpful to think of venue as the third of three hurdles to be crossed in selecting a forum. First, rules of *personal jurisdiction* determine whether the plaintiff can sue the defendant in a particular state. Second, rules of *subject matter jurisdiction* determine whether the plaintiff can sue in state court or federal court in that state. Third, the question of *venue* asks where, *within the chosen court system*, the case will be filed. For example, suppose personal jurisdiction is proper in California and that the case could be brought in the state court system there. But where: San Diego? San Francisco? Los Angeles? Calexico? That is the venue consideration. Subject matter jurisdiction places the case within a judicial *system* (federal or state). Venue determines where — in a geographic sense — the case is filed within that system.

In state court systems, as we see in §5.3, venue is laid in political subdivisions, such as counties. In the federal system, as we discuss in §5.4, venue is laid in federal districts. Venue statutes, whether state or federal, give the plaintiff choices of where to bring suit. Generally, these choices reflect a legislative assessment of a convenient place for the litigation. The two most common choices permitted by venue statutes are (1) the place where the defendant resides and (2) the place where the claim arose. These choices recognize, as a general matter, that trial is convenient for defendants where they reside, and that the place where the claim arose is convenient because relevant witnesses and evidence may be found there and because both the plaintiff and the defendant have at least some connection with that locale. Only occasionally do statutes permit venue where the *plaintiff* resides, although obviously such a locale would be most convenient for her. One may legitimately ask why the venue statutes should be more solicitous of defendants than plaintiffs.[1]

Venue raises no federal *constitutional* issue. In other words, there is no federal constitutional right to have a case brought in a particular place.[2] Thus, the venue hurdle in federal court[3] involves only a statutory inquiry. And because the defense of improper venue does not involve the court's subject matter jurisdiction, the court generally does not raise a venue problem on its own motion. Rather, the defendant must assert the defense of improper venue in a timely fashion, or it will be waived, as we see in §6.2.[4]

All judicial systems (federal and state) provide for transfer of venue from one place to another *within that system*. Such transfers may be permitted to move a case from an improper venue to a proper one. Or transfer may be permitted from one proper venue to another, perhaps because the latter is far more convenient for the parties and witnesses or more desirable from the standpoint of judicial resources. See §5.5. Note, however, that transfer is possible only from one court within a judicial system to another in that same system. Thus, transfer is impossible if the more convenient and appropriate forum is in a different judicial system from the pending case. In such a case, the court cannot order transfer, but may dismiss under the doctrine of *forum non conveniens*, which then permits the plaintiff to pursue the case in the more convenient forum. See §5.6.

Finally, regardless of venue statutes, the parties generally are free to agree where a case is to be filed. This agreement may be made after the claim arises, by simple waiver of a venue objection. Or it may be made before litigation through a contractual "forum selection clause." Federal law, and the law of most states, permits parties to agree to the forum for their future litigation, so long as the agreement is not the product of fraud or overreaching, and as long as the selected forum is not unreasonable or

---

[1] This is especially so because we are assuming that the forum has personal jurisdiction. Thus, the defendant is being sued in a state with which she has constitutionally sufficient contacts to justify entry of a binding judgment.

[2] Neirbo Co. v. Bethlehem Shipbuilding Corp., 308 U.S. 165 (1939).

[3] This is also true in most state court systems. In some states, however, venue is a state constitutional matter. *See, e.g.*, Ga. Const. Art. VI, §II, para. III through VI (prescribing venue in specific cases).

[4] *See* Federal Rule 12(h)(1). There is some question, however, about whether this is true concerning venue of "local actions." See §5.2.

unjust.[5] Such clauses are relatively common in contracts concerning international or even interstate business transactions.

§5.2 Local Actions and Transitory Actions

Under most venue schemes, the first question to ask is whether the case is a *local action.* This is a term of art, the definition of which varies from state to state. But, in general, a local action is one directly involving title, possession, or injury to land.[6] More specifically, local actions include (1) *in rem* or *quasi-in-rem* cases in which the land is used as a basis for jurisdiction; (2) cases claiming a remedy in real property, such as a claim to foreclose on a mortgage or to quiet title or eject a tenant; and (3) cases involving damage to realty, including damage caused by trespass. Again, however, the definition can vary, and some states, for example, do not classify trespass cases as local actions.[7] All cases that are not local actions are, for venue purposes, called *transitory actions.* The vast majority of cases, then, are transitory. All states and the federal system have specific standards for venue of transitory actions, as we see at §§5.3, 5.4.

Although the definition of local action can vary, the rule concerning its venue seems universal: Venue may be laid *only* where the relevant real property is found. In state court systems, the plaintiff places venue in the county (or other relevant political subdivision) in which the land is located. In federal court, venue is proper in the federal district in which the land lies. In both the federal and state systems, if the subject realty lies in more than one county or federal district, venue is proper in the county or district in which any part of the land lies.[8]

Laying venue where the subject realty lies makes especial sense in *in rem* and *quasi-in-rem* cases. There, as discussed in §2.2, the property is the very basis of jurisdiction; it can only be attached in the venue where it is found.[9]

---

[5] The leading case is *M/S Bremen v. Zapata*, 407 U.S. 1, 15 (1972) (enforcing negotiated forum selection clause in admiralty). *See also* Carnival Cruise Lines, Inc. v. Shute, 499 U.S. 585 (1991) (enforcing boilerplate, nonnegotiated forum selection clause).

[6] Land is usually referred to as "real property" or "realty." Do not confuse real property with the concept of tangible property, which is any property that has a corporeal existence. A wristwatch is tangible property, but is not real property.

[7] *See, e.g.,* Reasor-Hill Corp. v. Harrison, 249 S.W.2d 994 (Ark. 1952); Ingram v. Great Lakes Pipe Line Co., 153 S.W.2d 547 (Mo. App. 1941). *See* Annotation, 30 A.L.R.2d 1219.

[8] *See, e.g.,* 28 U.S.C. §1392 (local action "involving property located in different districts in the same State, may be brought in any of such districts").

[9] Remember also that with *in rem* and *quasi-in-rem* jurisdiction, the property that serves as the jurisdictional predicate does not have to be land; it can be any property. The local action rule for venue, in contrast, deals only with real property.

In most jurisdictions, however, the definition of local action is broader than *in rem* and *quasi-in-rem* cases. As noted above, most states and the federal courts, for instance, hold that *in personam* cases involving trespass to real property are local actions. One court stated the justification as follows:

> The distinction between local and transitory actions is not fanciful or technical. It is founded on a keen sense of justice. An action at law involving essential characteristics of land ordinarily can be tried with a stronger likelihood of ascertaining the truth and doing right between the parties in a jurisdiction where the land is situated than in a foreign state. In the vicinity the nature of the land can be understood, the evidence bearing upon its title be conveniently presented, its properties and adaptability for valuable use comprehended, the elements of damage to it ascertained, its essential features recognized, and their accurate worth established in every and in all respects much better than at a distance.[10]

True, litigating in the venue where the land lies permits ready access to the land to determine what damage it sustained. But it is not apparent why the situs of the property (rather than, say, the residence of the defendant or the plaintiff) ought to be the *only* proper venue in an *in personam* trespass case. Nonetheless, the rule concerning trespass has been followed in many jurisdictions for generations.

In many states, the local action rule for venue is statutory.[11] In federal court, however, the general venue statute is silent on local actions.[12] The local action rule is well established, however, in common law, and traces back to the celebrated case of *Livingston v. Jefferson.*[13] There, the plaintiff sued Thomas Jefferson *in personam*, seeking damages for trespass to the plaintiff's land in Louisiana.[14] The plaintiff sued Jefferson in Virginia, because (in those early days, long before *International Shoe*) he could not establish personal jurisdiction over the former president in Louisiana. Jefferson objected that Virginia was not a proper venue. A decision that the case was a local action (in which venue had to be laid in Louisiana)

---

[10] Arizona Commercial Mining Co. v. Iron Cap Copper Co., 128 N.E. 4, 6 (Mass. 1920).

[11] *See, e.g.*, Md. Ann. Code §6-202(b). In some states, it is constitutional. *See, e.g.*, Ga. Const. Art. VI, §II, para. IV ("Cases respecting title to land shall be tried in the county where the land lies, except where a single tract is divided by a county line, in which case the superior court of either county shall have jurisdiction.").

[12] *See* 28 U.S.C. §1391. The sole reference to the concept in general federal venue statutes is in §1392, which concerns cases involving realty located in more than one district. See note 8 above.

[13] 15 Fed. Cas. 660 (C.D. Va. 1811).

[14] The plaintiff did not contend that Jefferson trespassed personally. Rather, the claim was that Jefferson instructed United States marshals to eject the plaintiff from his land abutting the Mississippi River in New Orleans. Jefferson thought, incorrectly, that the land belonged to the federal government.

would be tantamount to telling the plaintiff that he had a right without a remedy. And that's exactly what happened: The court held that, at least in the federal courts, trespass to land is a local action.[15] Although the court was inclined to limit local actions to *in rem* and *quasi-in-rem* cases, it felt obliged by English precedent to include trespass cases as well. That remains the rule to this day, although the unfairness suffered by the plaintiff in *Livingston v. Jefferson* would likely be avoided today, since commission of the tortious act in Louisiana would likely give that state *in personam* jurisdiction over the defendant.

There is some surprising uncertainty about whether the local action rule in federal court is simply a matter of venue or goes, instead, to the court's subject matter jurisdiction. The difference is important. If the rule is merely one of venue, it can be waived, and the defendant can consent to a venue other than where the land lies.[16] On the other hand, if the rule is one of subject matter jurisdiction, a defect cannot be waived. See §4.3. There is authority for both conclusions.[17] The view that the local action rule is jurisdictional is anachronistic, born of a mystical historical view of real property,[18] and should be jettisoned in favor of the view that the local action rule implicates only venue.

To the extent the jurisdictional theory should be followed, it should be limited to *in rem* and *quasi-in-rem* cases,[19] because in such disputes the property must be attached to give the court power over the case. (We discussed this point in §2.2.) But there is no reason to treat the rule as anything other than one of venue for *in personam* proceedings. A court with *in personam* jurisdiction over a defendant can compel her to execute a

---

[15] The judge deciding the case was John Marshall, who was, of course, Chief Justice of the United States. In those days, the Justices were required to "ride circuit," which meant, among other things, that they had to serve as judges in federal trial courts in the circuit for which they were responsible. (The Chief Justice has always been the Circuit Justice for the Fourth Circuit, since its headquarters, Richmond, is relatively close to Washington, D.C.) On a personal level, it must have rankled Marshall to rule as he did, since he and Jefferson were not at all friendly toward one another. For a lively account of the case and its background, *see* Ronan Degnan, *Livingston v. Jefferson — A Freestanding Footnote*, 75 Cal. L. Rev. 115 (1987).

[16] The consent can be voluntary or involuntary (e.g., by failing to make a timely objection on venue grounds). *See* Federal Rule 12(h)(1). See also §6.2.

[17] *See* Trust Co. Bank v. United States Gypsum Co., 950 F.2d 1144, 1149 n.7 (5th Cir. 1992) (noting split of authority and not taking position); Hayes v. Gulf Oil Corp., 821 F.2d 285, 287 (5th Cir. 1987) (local action rule jurisdictional).

[18] Throughout your time in law school, you will see examples of the law's presumption that all realty is unique. One consequence of this presumption is that a court can order specific performance of a contract to convey land. The common law judges who invented the notion that all land is unique (1) never saw a cluster-home development and (2) never flew over much of the United States.

[19] This demarcation was suggested in Note, *Local Actions in the Federal Courts*, 70 Harv. L. Rev. 708, 712-714 (1957).

deed conveying property in another state (or even another country).[20] In addition, there is no reason a court having *in personam* jurisdiction over the defendant cannot impose a judgment for damages for her trespass to land in another state. Again, the venue where the land lies may be especially convenient (because, for example, the jury could view the damage to the land). This fact might augur in favor of transferring the case to that venue, but should not defeat venue elsewhere.

§5.3 Venue for Transitory Actions in State Court

Assuming the case brought in state court is not a local action, see §5.2, the plaintiff must address the state law governing venue in a transitory action. In most states, this law is embodied in a statute (though some states address the topic constitutionally). And almost always, the statute consists of a "laundry list" of choices for laying venue in the appropriate political subdivision. These provisions vary greatly from state to state in terms of complexity and content, so counsel must read the relevant provisions with care. One common statutory model lists particular venues as permissible generally, and adds others for specific types of cases. For example, the general Maryland statute provides for venue where the defendant (1) resides, (2) carries on a regular business, (3) is employed, or (4) habitually engages in a vocation.[21] In addition, another provision permits venue in a tort negligence case in the county where the claim arose.[22]

Venue statutes represent the legislature's assessment of a convenient place for trial. The Maryland statute is typical in placing venue generally where the defendant resides or has significant ties, or where the claim arose. Thus, it is solicitous of defendants, permitting them to be sued "at home." Moreover, the venue where the claim arose is a place where both the defendant and plaintiff have been and is likely to be a place where witnesses may be found. Statutes occasionally permit venue where the *plaintiff* resides; for example, such a provision may be appropriate in divorce or alimony cases, or in claims against nonresidents.

---

[20] *See* Penn v. Lord Baltimore, 27 Eng. Rep. 1132 (1750), in which the English Court of Chancery ordered Lord Baltimore (over whom it had *in personam* jurisdiction) to abide by an agreement conveying land in the American Colonies (essentially what is now Delaware) to William Penn. Because the court had *in personam* jurisdiction over Lord Baltimore, it could enforce its decree by contempt citation if necessary.

[21] Md. Code Ann. §6-201(a).

[22] Md. Code Ann. §6-202(8). Most long-arm statutes and nonresident motorist statutes lay venue where the claim arose. In those instances, the defendant is a nonresident, so the place of the defendant's residence is not an option.

§5.4 Venue for Transitory Actions in Federal Court

§5.4.1 Cases Filed Originally in Federal Court

If the case in federal court is not a local action, see §5.2, it is, of course, "transitory." And the question becomes where venue is proper under the federal venue statutes. Venue in the federal courts is determined *solely* by federal law, no matter what the basis of federal subject matter jurisdiction. So state venue law is irrelevant in federal court. Although there are many special federal venue statutes addressing particular types of claims,[23] most cases (and certainly most law school courses) involve the general venue provisions of 28 U.S.C. §1391. Compared to many state venue provisions, §1391 is quite simple. At the same time, however, it is not particularly well drafted, so one must read it with care.

Section 1391(a) applies to cases "wherein jurisdiction is founded only on diversity of citizenship." Section 1391(b) applies to all other cases (including, obviously, federal question cases). The two subsections are identical in structure: They lay out the general venue choices in subsections (1) and (2), and then provide a fall-back alternative in subsection (3). Although these fall-back provisions — §1391(a)(3) and §1391(b)(3) — differ slightly, they are almost never relevant (for reasons discussed below). Thus, nearly every case will be governed by subparts (1) or (2) of the respective subsection. Fortunately, §1391(a)(1) is identical to §1391(b)(1) and §1391(a)(2) is identical to §1391(b)(2). In practice, then, the venue rules for diversity and federal question cases are the same in nearly every case. For simplicity, we discuss the basic rules for diversity of citizenship and other cases together; remember, however, that §1391(a) applies to the former and §1392(b) to cases in which the subject matter jurisdiction is not based "solely" on diversity of citizenship.[24]

These provisions give the plaintiff two basic venue options: one based upon residence of the defendants and one based upon the events underlying the claim.[25] By the plain language of the statute these are alternatives, and neither is favored. In other words, if one choice would permit venue in District *A* and the other would permit venue in District *B*, the plaintiff

---

[23] *See, e.g.*, 28 U.S.C. §1397 (venue in statutory interpleader cases).

[24] Why are there separate sections — §1391(a) and §1391(b)? For many years, venue was available more liberally in diversity of citizenship cases than in federal question cases, the statute long allowed venue in diversity cases in the district where the *plaintiff* resided. When Congress removed that provision and made §1391(a) and §1391(b) essentially identical, it should have simplified things by collapsing the provisions into a single section. Instead, it kept the separate sections.

[25] Sections 1391(a)(2) and (b)(2) also provide for venue in a district where "a substantial part of the property that is the subject of the action is situated." This provision is rarely invoked, and is relevant particularly in interpleader, discussed at §13.2.2.

can choose the one she prefers.[26] She is not required to choose the most convenient of different alternatives.[27]

Before looking at these choices, note that venue in the federal system is tied to federal *districts*. Congress has divided the country (and federal enclaves, such as the District of Columbia and Guam) into 94 districts, and has established a federal district court (with multiple judges) in each district. With one inconsequential exception (involving Yellowstone National Park), districts do not cross state lines.[28] In Arizona, New Jersey, Massachusetts, and several other states, the entire state comprises a single federal district. Other states, however, are subdivided into two, three, or even four federal districts. Only three states — California, New York, and Texas — have four districts. Congress legislates what counties go into each district and names each district. The names are geographical and not creative, for example, the District of Arizona, the Southern District of California, and so forth. We focus on laying venue in an appropriate federal district.[29]

Venue Based Upon Residence of Defendants

Under §1391(a)(1) and §1391(b)(1), the plaintiff may lay venue in any district where "any defendant resides, if all defendants reside in the same State."[30] This is poor drafting. The subsections should be redrafted to state clearly what they mean: Venue is proper (1) in any district in which all defendants reside, and (2) if all defendants reside in different districts of the same state, venue is proper in any district in which a defendant resides. Apply these principles to these hypotheticals.

- *P* sues *D-1*, who resides in the Northern District of Georgia, and *D-2*, who resides in the Central District of California. Neither of those districts is a proper venue. Although each is one in which "any defendant resides,"

---

[26] One federal judge has concluded that the statute is to be read hierarchically. Thus, if a district satisfies §1391(a)(1) or (b)(1), it must be chosen, even though another district satisfies §1391(a)(2) or (b)(2). *See, e.g.,* Cobra Partners L.P. v. Liegl, 990 F. Supp. 332 (S.D.N.Y. 1998). Such a reading is contrary to the language of the statute, and judges in the same district have not followed this hierarchical reading. *See, e.g.,* I.M.D. USA, Inc. v. Shalit, 92 F. Supp. 2d 315 (S.D.N.Y. 2000).

[27] *See, e.g.,* Susman v. Bank of Israel, 56 F.3d 450, 457 (2d Cir. 1995) (no sanctions can be imposed for selection of an inconvenient forum if the forum chosen is a proper venue).

[28] There are federal districts, of course, in each state. In addition, Congress has established federal districts in U.S. possessions that are not states, including the District of Columbia, Puerto Rico, the Virgin Islands, Guam, and the Northern Mariana Islands.

[29] For convenience, Congress subdivides some districts into divisions. For example, Minnesota is one district, but consists of six divisions, with at least one district judge sitting in each division. This means that people in more rural areas do not have to litigate only in the federal district court in Minneapolis.

[30] 28 U.S.C. §1391(a)(1) and §1391(b)(1).

the two defendants do not reside in the same state, so neither §1391(a)(1) nor §1391(b)(1) is satisfied.

○ *P* sues *D-1*, who resides in the Southern District of New York, and *D-2*, who also resides in the Southern District of New York. Venue is proper in the Southern District of New York, because all defendants reside there. Note, though, that venue would *not* be proper under these provisions in any other district in New York. So if *P* laid venue in the Eastern District of New York (or the Northern or Western Districts of New York), the defendants could challenge the choice as improper.

○ *P* sues *D-1*, who resides in the Northern District of Illinois, and *D-2*, who resides in the Southern District of Illinois. The case against the two defendants may be filed in either of those two districts. Even though neither is a district in which all defendants reside, all defendants reside in the same state. In that situation, venue is proper in either district.

○ Would the answer to any of the preceding three hypotheticals be different depending upon the basis of subject matter jurisdiction? In other words, does it matter whether the cases invoked diversity of citizenship or federal question jurisdiction? No. The language of §1391(a)(1) (for diversity of citizenship cases) and §1391(b)(1) (for all other kinds of cases) is identical.

Defining Residence for Venue Purposes

It is important to note that §1391(a)(1) and §1391(b)(1) provide for venue based upon the defendants' *residence*; the venue statutes do not refer to *citizenship* (citizenship may be relevant, of course, to subject matter jurisdiction; see §4.5).

○ Although some lawyers, professors, and even judges are sloppy, we should keep the language of subject matter jurisdiction and venue distinct. If you want to invoke diversity of citizenship jurisdiction, you must allege the parties' *citizenship*. If you allege the parties' *residence*, the case should be dismissed for lack of subject matter jurisdiction. Why? Because the Constitution and statutes grant diversity of *citizenship* jurisdiction, not diversity of *residence* jurisdiction. See §4.5.1. On the other hand, if you want to lay venue under §1391(a)(1) or §1391(b)(1), you must discuss the defendants' residence. Why? Because that's what the statute says.

Residence of Human Beings

As we will see, the federal venue statutes define the residence of some defendants, but not of others. Notably, they fail to define the residence of a human defendant. Where does a natural person *reside* for venue purposes? Long ago, the Supreme Court suggested that such a defendant resides in the district in which she is domiciled.[31] This interpretation basically equates the test for residence (for venue purposes) with that for a human's citizenship (for subject matter jurisdiction) purposes.[32] The overwhelming majority of lower courts agree with this interpretation,[33] which means, of course, that a human defendant has only one residence (since she can have only one domicile, as we saw in §4.5.3).

On the other hand, because venue rules are aimed at placing a case in a convenient forum, it seems preferable to adopt a more flexible approach. For instance, a college student, graduate student, or member of the military may live for long periods in a state that is not her domicile. It would be preferable to conclude that such a person "resides" there, and thus permit venue where she actually is living.

○ *D* is a citizen of the United States and was born and raised in Oklahoma. She left Oklahoma seven years ago to attend college, and then law school, in New York. She has never been back to Oklahoma, but has also never formed the intent to make New York her permanent home. Her domicile is still Oklahoma (so her citizenship is still Oklahoma). Equating one's residence for venue purposes as her domicile, she would be deemed to "reside" (under §1391(a)(1) and §1391(b)(1)) in the federal District of Oklahoma. In fact, however, because she has been living for seven years in the Southern District of New York, the latter would be a far more convenient venue, and should be considered to be the district in which she resides.

Notwithstanding this argument in favor of a flexible reading of "resident," most courts continue to equate one's district of residence with the district in which she is domiciled.

What if the defendant is an alien (i.e., a citizen or subject of a foreign country)? Section 1391(d) provides that an alien "may be sued in any district." Thus, if the defendant is an alien, there is no need to worry about where she resides; there is no need to worry about §1391(a) or (b) at all, because §1391(d) makes life much easier for the plaintiff. Section 1391(d) should apply even if the alien is admitted to the United States for permanent residence. As we discuss at §4.5.3, Congress has made a special

---

[31] Shaw v. Quincy Mining Co., 145 U.S. 444, 449 (1892).

[32] Recall that a citizen of the United States is deemed to be a citizen (for diversity of citizenship purposes) of the state in which she is domiciled. As we discussed in §4.5.3, domicile is established by presence plus the intent to make that place one's permanent home. Congress evidently intended to permit venue where the defendant was a "citizen" in this sense. Technically speaking, however, humans are citizens of *states*, not of federal districts. Because venue is placed in federal districts, and not states, Congress concluded that it could not use the word "citizen" in the venue statutes. Technically, there is no such thing as a citizen of a *district*; one is a citizen of a *state*. So Congress used the term *resides* instead.

[33] *See, e.g.,* Manley v. Engram, 755 F.2d 1463, 1466 n.3 (11th Cir. 1985) ("well established" that domicile "is the benchmark for determining proper venue").

provision concerning the citizenship of aliens admitted for permanent residence, found in 28 U.S.C. §1332(a). That provision indicates that it governs for particular purposes (including statutory interpleader and removal) but does not mention venue. Thus, permanent resident alien defendants are treated — for venue purposes — as any other alien, and §1391(d) governs.

Residence of Corporations

Congress did define the residence of a corporation for venue purposes. Pursuant to the first sentence of §1391(c), a corporate defendant resides in all districts in which it is "subject to personal jurisdiction when the case is commenced." This is potentially far broader than the definition of a corporation's citizenship for subject matter jurisdiction purposes.

- Big Motor Corporation is incorporated in Delaware and has its principal place of business in Michigan. It does business in every federal district in the United States, because it has at least one retail sales outlet in every district. What is Big Motor Corporation's citizenship?[34] Where does Big Motor Corporation reside?[35]
- *P*, a citizen of Wisconsin, sues *XYZ* Corporation, which is incorporated in Delaware and has its principal place of business in Michigan. The claim exceeds $75,000, so the case clearly invokes diversity of citizenship jurisdiction. *P* brings the case in the federal district court for the District of Wisconsin. *XYZ* Corporation moves to dismiss for lack of personal jurisdiction and improper venue. The court concludes that it has personal jurisdiction over *XYZ* Corporation, because it has sufficient contacts with that state. How should the court rule on the motion regarding venue?[36]
- Would the answer to the preceding hypothetical be different if the case had invoked federal question jurisdiction instead of diversity of citizenship jurisdiction?[37]

---

[34] It is a citizen of Delaware, because it is incorporated there, *and* of Michigan, because it has its principal place of business there. See §4.5.3. These facts are relevant for invoking diversity of citizenship jurisdiction.

[35] It resides in every district of the United States because (by virtue of having a retail outlet in each district) it is subject to personal jurisdiction in each district. This fact is relevant for laying venue under §1391(a)(1) or §1391(b)(1) in a case in which Big Motor Corporation is a defendant.

[36] It should deny the motion to dismiss. Venue is proper (under §1391(a)(1)) in a district where all defendants reside. Here, there is only one defendant, *XYZ* Corporation. A corporation resides (under §1391(c)) in all districts in which it is subject to personal jurisdiction when the case is commenced. Here, once the court held that it had personal jurisdiction over the defendant, because the defendant is a corporation, it also concluded that the defendant resides there.

[37] No. Under §1391(b)(1) — applicable in federal question cases — venue is proper in a district where all defendants reside, just as under §1391(a)(1). The definition of the corporate defendant's residence under §1391(c) is the same.

Of course, defining the corporate defendant's residence by reference to personal jurisdiction incorporates all the vagaries of personal jurisdiction law (which we saw in Chapter 2) into venue. But it also brings a true benefit — once the court assesses personal jurisdiction, it has also assessed the corporate defendant's residence; there is no separate, potentially vague test for that separate issue (as there used to be under prior law).[38] There is no distinction between general and specific personal jurisdiction. Evidently, the court is to assess whether the corporate defendant is subject to personal jurisdiction in this case — either on the basis of general or specific jurisdiction.

Note also that §1391(c) now dictates a clear time for assessing personal jurisdiction. It requires that the corporation has been subject to personal jurisdiction "at the time the action is commenced." This is a bit odd. Under Federal Rule 3, a case is commenced when the complaint is filed. The defendant will not be served with process until after the complaint is filed, as we saw in §3.3.1. Technically, then, personal jurisdiction is not actually exercised over the corporation in a particular case until after the case is commenced. Does this create a problem under §1391(c)? Generally, no. Courts have not been so technical in applying the statute. They tend to look at whether the corporation's contacts with the forum — assessed at the time the complaint is filed[39] — subject it to personal jurisdiction in the forum.

Life gets somewhat more complicated if the case is filed in a state having more than one federal district. Then, as the second sentence of §1391(c) provides, the corporation's residence is assessed with respect to each district, and not with regard to the state as a whole. In other words, the fact that the corporate defendant is subject to personal jurisdiction in California does not necessarily mean that it resides in each of the four federal districts in that state. Instead, the court treats each district as though it were a separate state to see if the corporation's contacts would justify personal jurisdiction there. Thus, a corporation subject to personal jurisdiction in California, but which has contacts only in the Northern District of

---

[38] The present version of §1391(c) was passed in 1988. Before that, the section defined corporate residence as districts in which the corporation was "incorporated" or "licensed to do business" or "doing business." While the first two phrases were fairly easy to determine, the effort to determine where a corporation was "doing business" was just as vague as the present statutory standard. In essence, many courts had read the older statute as defining the corporation's residence wherever it was subject to personal jurisdiction. Thus, the 1988 amendment was thought to codify what most courts were doing anyway.

[39] Before the "commenced" language was inserted into the statute in 1988, some courts concluded that the corporation must have been subject to personal jurisdiction when the claim arose. The current version of the statute is thus more precise about when the jurisdictional issue is measured.

California, resides in the Northern District of California. It does not reside in the Central, Eastern, or Southern Districts of California.[40]

Life gets more complicated, however, if a corporation is subject to personal jurisdiction in a particular state but lacks sufficient contacts to be subject in a specific single district in that state. The second sentence of §1391(c) also applies in such (hopefully rare) situations, and provides that the corporation resides in the district in which it has the "most significant contacts."

- ○ A corporate defendant has enough contacts, in the aggregate, to be subject to personal jurisdiction in California. But it does not have enough contacts with any of the four individual federal districts in California to be subject to personal jurisdiction in any one of them. But of the four districts in California, it has more contacts with the Southern District than any other. Under §1391(c), it would reside only in the Southern District of California.

Residence of Non-Incorporated Associations

As we saw in discussing diversity of citizenship jurisdiction in §4.5.3, businesses might be incorporated or non-incorporated. The incorporated business, of course, is a corporation. Congress defined its citizenship in §1331(c)(1) and its residence, as we have just seen, in §1391(c). The non-incorporated business may take many forms, including the partnership, the limited partnership, most labor unions, and the limited liability company (LLC). Congress has never defined the citizenship of such associations, nor has it defined their residence for venue purposes. So courts have been left to figure these things out on their own. As we discussed in §4.5.3, the courts have divined a test for the citizenship of such businesses, and the test is quite different from that prescribed by Congress for corporations. What about the residence of non-incorporated associations?

Happily, the courts have forged a consensus here: We define the non-incorporated association's residence the same as we do the corporation's residence.[41] That is, courts apply §1391(c) to non-incorporated associations (notwithstanding that statute's failure to refer to anything but corporations). Thus, non-incorporated associations in any form — partnership, labor union, limited partnership, LLC, whatever — "reside"

---

[40] Bicicletas Windsor, S.A. v. Bicycle Corp. of America, 783 F. Supp. 781, 785-786 (S.D.N.Y. 1992) (venue requires analysis of personal jurisdiction "confined to" district in which suit is filed).

[41] The Supreme Court did so regarding an earlier version of §1391(c). Denver & Rio Grande W.R.R. Co. v. Brotherhood of R.R. Trainmen, 387 U.S. 556, 562 (1967). Courts have embraced the same interpretation of the current version of §1391(c). *See* 15 Wright & Miller §3812.

for venue purposes in all districts in which they are subject to personal jurisdiction when the case is commenced.

Some Review

These questions are designed to review several of the issues we just addressed regarding venue based upon residence of defendants.

- ∘ *P*, a citizen of Oregon, sues *D-1*, an individual who is a citizen of Colorado but who is attending college in San Diego (in the Southern District of California), and *D-2*, a corporation incorporated in Georgia with its principal place of business in Nevada. The corporation also has a manufacturing plant (though not its principal place of business) in the Central District of California. The claim exceeds $75,000. Plaintiff lays venue in the Central District of California (which is where Los Angeles is). Is venue proper?[42]
- ∘ Same facts except *D-1* is domiciled in the Southern District of California and *P* brings suit in the Northern District of California. Is venue proper?[43]

Venue Based Upon Events

Under §1391(a)(2) and §1391(b)(2), plaintiff may lay venue in any district "in which a substantial part of the events or omissions giving rise to the claim occurred."[44] This is very good drafting, and avoids a problem found in an earlier version of the statute. The older version permitted venue in the district "where the claim arose." The Supreme Court held that this language — referring to the district where "the" claim arose — meant that

---

[42] This is a diversity of citizenship case, so venue is assessed under §1391(a). (Diversity is satisfied because the plaintiff (Oregon) is of diverse citizenship from both defendants (*D-1* is Colorado and *D-2* is Georgia and Nevada) and the amount in controversy exceeds $75,000.) Under §1391(a)(1), venue is proper in the Central District of California if all defendants reside there or if they all reside in different districts of the same state and one of them resides there. Here, *D-2* is a corporation, which, under §1391(c) resides in the Central District of California because it has a manufacturing plant there and thus clearly is subject to personal jurisdiction there. *D-1*, an individual, is going to college in the Southern District of California, but does he reside there? No. For an individual, residence is equated with domicile. For *D-1*, that is Colorado (as shown by the fact that he is a citizen of that state). Thus, *D-1* does not reside in California at all. So the rule allowing venue in the district in which any defendant resides — if all reside in the same state — does not apply here.

[43] No. Here, *D-1* resides in the Southern District of California and *D-2* resides in the Central District of California. When all defendants reside in different districts of the same state, any of those districts is a proper venue for all defendants. So both could be sued in either the Southern District or the Central District of California. Here, though, plaintiff has sued in the Northern District of California. No defendant resides there, so it is not a proper venue.

[44] Or, as that section says, in the district "where a substantial part of the property that is the subject of the action is situated." 28 U.S.C. §1391(a)(2) & (b)(2). Thus, for example, a suit regarding ownership of personal property could be filed in the district where the property (or a substantial part of it) is found.

there was only one such district.[45] But in many cases it is difficult to determine a single place where the claim arose. For example, assume a citizen of California and a citizen of Nebraska enter a contract. They negotiate the contract in Colorado and execute it in New Mexico. It calls for performance by the parties in Texas and in Arizona. When there is a dispute under the contract, where is the one place in which the claim arises? The answer, obviously, is subject to uncertainty. Is it where the decision was made that allegedly breached the contract? Was it where performance was to have been rendered? Tough to say.

Fortunately, such difficulties are largely avoided by the current version of the statute. No longer do we worry about the single place in which a claim arises. The statute clearly envisions multiple districts for venue. So long as a "substantial part" of the events giving rise to the claim took place in a district, it is appropriate under §1391(a)(2) and §1391(b)(2). The following scenario demonstrates this provision in action:

> ∘ Creditor sends a letter to Borrower, demanding payment and making threats. The letter violates federal debt collection laws. Creditor mails the letter from Pennsylvania to Borrower's home address in New York. But Debtor had moved to Arizona and the new occupant at the New York address forwards the letter to Borrower in Arizona, where Borrower reads it. Borrower sues Creditor under the federal debt collection laws, invoking federal question jurisdiction. Is venue proper in Arizona? Under the present version of the statute, the court need not engage in the difficult task of identifying the one district where "the claim" arose; clearly, a "substantial part" of the claim arose in Arizona, where the borrower read the letter, and received the threat. Venue is proper there.[46]

The underlying theory here, of course, is that the place where a substantial part of the claim arose will be convenient, since witnesses to any events are likely to be found there and, presumably, both plaintiff and defendant have been there, or done something having an effect there.

The Fall-Back Provisions

The provisions of §1391(a)(3) and §1391(b)(3) apply only when *no district anywhere in the United States* satisfies either of the two venue choices already discussed. Such a case will be rare. Such a case will almost

---

[45] Leroy v. Great Western United Corp., 443 U.S. 173 (1979).

[46] This fact pattern is adapted from *Bates v. C&S Adjusters, Inc.*, 980 F.2d 865 (2d Cir. 1992). There may be other districts in which a substantial part of the events giving rise to the claim arose. For example, the district in which Creditor drafted the offending letter would appear to be proper. The result would be the same, of course, if the case were brought under diversity of citizenship jurisdiction, since §1391(a)(2) (applicable in diversity) is identical to §1391(b)(2) (which applies in federal question cases).

always involve a claim that arose entirely outside the United States. Why? Because if any substantial part of the claim arose somewhere in the United States, there will be a federal district that satisfies §1391(a)(2) or §1391(b)(2). Even in a case in which the claim arose entirely outside the United States, §1391(a)(3) and (b)(3) will not apply if all defendants reside in a single state in the United States. If they do, venue will be proper in a district in which any defendant resides under §1391(a)(1) or §1391(b)(1).

In the rare cases in which a fall-back provision applies, the statute gives slightly different venue tests depending upon the basis of subject matter jurisdiction. In a case invoking "only" diversity of citizenship jurisdiction, §1391(a)(3) provides that venue is proper in any district "in which any defendant is subject to personal jurisdiction at the time the action is commenced." In all other cases, though, §1391(b)(3) permits venue in any district "in which any defendant may be found." It seems that the former is broader than the latter, which may require that the defendant actually be served with process in the district where venue is laid. Courts have not agreed on the significance of the different language used in §1391(a)(3) and §1391(b)(3).[47] No one seems to know why there is this difference between diversity and other cases when it comes to fall-back venue. Fortunately, the issue rarely arises, because so few cases involve the fall-back venue provisions. Be careful not to use the fall-back provision when it does not apply.

○ *P*'s claim against *D* arose overseas. The claim invokes diversity of citizenship jurisdiction. *D* resides in the District of Kansas but is subject to personal jurisdiction in the Middle District of Florida (where he has a house and lives a good part of the year). *P* sues in the Middle District of Florida and claims that venue is proper under §1391(a)(3) because *D* is subject to personal jurisdiction there. Venue is not proper. Section 1391(a)(3) (and §1391(b)(3) if it were a federal question case) applies *only* if there is no district *anywhere in the United States* that satisfies either §1391(a)(1) or (a)(2) (or §1391(b)(1) or (b)(2)). Here, the District of Kansas satisfies §1391(a)(1) (and §1391(b)(1)) because the sole defendant resides there. Accordingly, §1391(a)(3) (or §1391(b)(3)) simply cannot apply.

§5.4.2   Cases Removed from State Court

The venue rules discussed in the preceding subsections apply *only* when a plaintiff files a case in a federal district court. Section 1391 simply does not apply to cases filed in state court that the defendant removes to federal district court. Rather, in removed cases, as we saw in §4.8, venue is

---

[47]*See, e.g.,* 15 Wright & Miller §3802.1.

proper under 28 U.S.C. §1441(a) *only* in the federal district embracing the state court in which the case was filed.

- *P* sues *D* in state court in St. Louis. *D* removes the case to the federal district court for the Eastern District of Missouri (which embraces St. Louis). *D* does not reside in the Eastern District of Missouri. No part of the claim arose in the Eastern District of Missouri. In other words, the Eastern District of Missouri is not a proper venue under §1391(a)(1) or (2) or §1391(b)(1) or (2). Nonetheless, the Eastern District of Missouri is a proper venue. Why? Because in removed cases, venue is possible *only* in the federal district embracing the state court in which the case was originally filed. Section 1391 is totally irrelevant to cases removed from state to federal court.[48]

§5.5 Transfer of Venue

§5.5.1 Introduction

All states and the Federal Judicial Code have provisions allowing for transfer of cases. It is important to remember, though, that transfer can only be effected *within* a court system. Thus, a state court in Birmingham, Alabama, can transfer a case to a state court in Mobile, Alabama, since both courts are in the Alabama court system. But that court in Birmingham *cannot* transfer a case to a state court in Missouri, because those two courts are not in the same judicial system. Similarly, outside of removal jurisdiction,[49] there can be no transfer of a case from a state court to a federal court or vice versa. Within the federal system, cases can be transferred from one federal district to another; state lines are irrelevant. Why? Because the transfer, though crossing state lines, is from one court to another within the same (the federal) judicial system. Thus, a *federal* court in Alabama can transfer a case to a *federal* court in Missouri.

Obviously, an order of transfer overrides the plaintiff's choice of forum. Such a move is not to be taken lightly, so the party seeking transfer (usually, but not always, the defendant) has the burden of showing that the case should proceed in another place in the judicial system. The court ordering transfer is the *transferor court*. The one to which the case is transferred is the *transferee court*. The transferor court makes the decision; the transferee court does not have a voice in the matter. Under the basic

[48] Polizzi v. Cowles Magazines, Inc., 345 U.S. 663, 665-666 (1953).

[49] Recall that removal permits the defendant in a state court case to "remove" the case to the federal district embracing the state court. Removal is thus a species of transfer, but is so exceptional (in involving more than one court system) that it warrants discussion in the materials on subject matter jurisdiction. See §4.8.

transfer statutes discussed in §5.5.2, an order of transfer puts the entire case in the transferee court for all purposes; once the case is transferred, the transferor court has no jurisdiction over the case. The transferee court takes over the case at its present stage; it does not start the litigation over afresh.

The bases on which a party may seek a transfer of venue vary from state to state, but certain common themes emerge. First, virtually all judicial systems permit transfer when the transferor court does not satisfy venue rules; such a case can be transferred to a proper venue in the same judicial system. Second, even when the case is filed in a proper venue, statutes generally permit transfer based upon an assessment of the relative convenience to the parties and witnesses.[50] For instance, suppose Birmingham was a proper venue under Alabama law, because the defendant corporation did business there, but that the claim arose in Mobile, all the witnesses and evidence were in Mobile, and the corporation was headquartered in Mobile. The Birmingham court, in its discretion, might order transfer because the transferee court is the more convenient and logical place for the case to proceed.

It is usually the defendant who seeks transfer. She does so by making a motion to transfer under the appropriate statute. Occasionally, however, a plaintiff will move to transfer. This is rare, because, after all, the plaintiff chose the original forum. So it seems odd to have the plaintiff decide to forgo that forum for another. Nonetheless, it does happen, and there is generally nothing in the transfer statutes to prevent it.[51] Although the basic federal transfer statute, discussed below, does not impose time limits for making a motion to transfer, it behooves the moving party to move relatively early. As a practical matter, courts are less likely to order transfer after having invested time and resources in the matter. It is also appropriate for courts to order transfer on their own initiative — that is, without a motion from any party. In such a case, it is good practice for the judge to inform the parties of this possibility and hear their objections, if any, on the matter.[52]

Transfer must also be distinguished from dismissal under the doctrine of *forum non conveniens*. The latter, which we discuss in §5.6, is used when the case *cannot* be transferred. Why could a case *not* be transferred? Because the more convenient forum — the one in which the litigation should proceed — is in a *different judicial system*. The factors assessed

---

[50] In addition to these reasons, many states add other specific grounds for seeking transfer; for example, one party cannot receive a fair trial because of pretrial publicity in the original venue. One of the best is a Florida statute that permits transfer when the moving party "is so odious to the inhabitants of the county that he or she could not receive a fair trial" in the original venue. Fla. Stat. Ann. §47.101(b).

[51] *See, e.g.,* Coffey v. Van Dorn Iron Works, 796 F.2d 217, 219 (7th Cir. 1986) (under federal transfer statute §1404(a)).

[52] *See* Fort Knox Music, Inc. v. Baptiste, 139 F. Supp. 2d 505, 512 (S.D.N.Y. 2001).

in ordering transfer for convenience of the parties and witnesses are the same as those used to order a *forum non conveniens* dismissal. (And some people refer to a transfer of this type as a *"forum non conveniens* transfer."*)* Not surprisingly, however, because *forum non conveniens* results in dismissal, there must be an especially strong showing that the other forum is more convenient and appropriate.

§5.5.2 Basic Transfer Provisions in Federal Court

The Two Statutes

In federal court, there are two basic transfer statutes: §1404(a) and §1406(a). Lawyers and judges routinely refer to them by number, and speak of a "1404 transfer" or "1406 transfer."[53] The major difference between them is fairly apparent on the face of the two provisions: §1404(a) applies when the transferor court (the original federal court) is a proper venue, while §1406(a) applies when the transferor court is an improper venue. This fact explains why §1406(a) provides for transfer "in the interest of justice" or, in the alternative, for dismissal of the case. A case filed in an improper venue is subject to dismissal under Federal Rule 12(b)(3). Section 1404(a), on the other hand, does not permit dismissal, for the simple reason that the court in which the case was filed is a proper venue.

The assessment of which statute applies, then, requires an analysis of whether the transferor court — the *original federal district court* — is a proper venue. If it is, transfer (if made) will be under §1404(a). If it is not, transfer (if made) will be under §1406(a). The assessment of whether the original federal district court is a proper venue will be made by applying the provisions of §1391(a) (for diversity of citizenship cases) and §1391(b) (for other cases), as discussed in §5.4.1. The one exception is in cases removed from state court to federal court. In those instances, as we discussed in §5.4.2, §1391 is totally irrelevant.

    ◦   *P* sues *D* in state court in St. Louis and *D* removes the case to the federal district for the Eastern District of Missouri (which embraces St. Louis). Any transfer from the Eastern District of Missouri will be made under §1404(a), and not under §1406(a). Why? Because venue is proper in the

---

[53] These statutes effect transfer of the entire case from one federal district to another for all purposes. This is to be distinguished from Multidistrict Litigation (MDL) transfer under §1407, which transfers related cases to a single district for consolidated resolution of *pretrial* matters. In theory, after the pretrial proceedings are complete, the cases are then transferred back to the districts in which they were originally filed. MDL transfer is ordered not by the transferor judge, but by a panel of judges, appointed by the Chief Justice, sitting as the Judicial Panel for Multidistrict Litigation. The court to which the cases are transferred for consolidated pretrial proceedings may not invoke §1404(a) to transfer the cases to itself for trial. Lexecon Inc. v. Milberg Weiss Bershad Hynes & Lerach, 523 U.S. 26 (1998).

Eastern District of Missouri, regardless of whether it would have been proper under §1391. Section 1391 does not apply to removed cases. Venue is in the district embracing the state court in which the case was originally filed. Period. Again, see §5.4.2.

Some courts have muddied the waters by holding that venue is improper — even if the relevant venue provision is satisfied — if the transferor court lacks personal jurisdiction over the defendant. This interpretation confuses personal jurisdiction with venue. The statutes clearly speak only to whether the original court is a proper *venue*, not whether it has personal jurisdiction. Indeed, these courts confuse things further by disagreeing about which statute is invoked to transfer a case in which the transferor court is a proper venue but lacks personal jurisdiction over the defendant. Some courts hold that such a case may be transferred only under §1406(a),[54] while others conclude that transfer in such a case is proper under either §1404(a) or §1406(a).[55]

Fortunately, such situations — where venue is proper but the original court lacks personal jurisdiction — should be rare under the present general venue statutes. Earlier versions of §1391 permitted venue in diversity cases in the district where the *plaintiff* resided. If the defendant was not subject to personal jurisdiction there, one could easily encounter the problem discussed in the preceding paragraph. Today, however, §1391 does not permit venue where the *plaintiff* resides. Instead, as we saw in §5.4.1, venue is proper in any district where all defendants reside or where a substantial part of the claim arose. If either of those conditions is met, generally that court will have personal jurisdiction over the defendant. After all, either she resides in the district or committed a substantial part of the act or omission for which she is being sued there. So it is harder under the current §1391 to imagine a case in which venue would be proper but in which the court would not have personal jurisdiction over the defendant.

Harder, but not impossible. Don't forget about removal (your professor won't). In a case removed from state to federal court, venue is proper in the district embracing the state court in which the case was filed. If the defendant is not subject to personal jurisdiction there, we would then have the problem of no personal jurisdiction but proper venue. In such cases, the better view is that transfer is effected under §1404(a); venue in the original federal district was proper, which should mean that §1406(a) does not apply.

The issue of which statute applies — §1404(a) or §1406(a) — can be important, because it may determine the application of various transfer principles that come from three important Supreme Court cases, which

---

[54] *See, e.g.*, Pittock v. Otis Elevator Co., 8 F.3d 325, 329 (6th Cir. 1993).

[55] *See, e.g.*, Muldoon v. Tropitone Furniture Co., 1 F.3d 964, 967 (9th Cir. 1993); Roofing & Sheet Metal Services v. La Quinta Motor Inns, Inc., 689 F.2d 982, 992 n.16 (11th Cir. 1982).

we address below. First, however, let's look in more detail at those two statutes.

Applying §1404(a)

Section 1404(a) permits transfer for "the convenience of parties and witnesses, in the interest of justice." As noted above, any party may move for transfer (though usually it's the defendant), and the moving party bears the burden of showing that transfer is warranted. A court considering transfer has great discretion, as is reflected by the flexible terms in the statute. In general, the court considers the same sorts of public and private factors assessed in ruling on a *forum non conveniens* dismissal, which we see in §5.6. In essence, the court is trying to determine whether another district might be the "center of gravity" for the case — the place where the litigation makes more sense than the present venue. Under §1404(a), the case is presently in a proper venue; the question is whether there is another venue that is sufficiently more convenient that the court should override the plaintiff's choice and send the case there.

In making this assessment, the plaintiff's choice of forum must be given significant weight. Transfer is the exception, not the rule. In addition, the court considers such things as where the relevant events took place, whether one court could compel attendance of witnesses more readily, location of evidence and witnesses, relative court docket loads in the two courts, and familiarity with the applicable law. The court may also consider the existence of a forum selection clause, although such a clause is not automatically dispositive on whether the case should be transferred.[56]

Applying §1406(a)

Because cases involving §1406(a) are pending in an improper venue, the court may dismiss or, if it is "in the interest of justice," transfer. Earlier versions of the statute did not permit transfer. Thus, a court lacking venue had to dismiss, which is usually wasteful, because the plaintiff has to refile in a proper court and may run a risk that the statute of limitations has run in the meantime. Transfer is thus almost always the better option, because it obviates the need to file a new case. The same case simply proceeds in the new court, so if it was filed timely, there will be no statute of limitations problem. Still, a court may conclude that transfer is not in the interest of justice — for example, if it is futile because the case was time-barred when filed originally and cannot be brought within a statute of limitations — and dismiss for lack of venue.

---

[56] Stewart Organization, Inc. v. Ricoh Corp., 487 U.S. 22 (1988).

The Goldlawr *Case*

In *Goldlawr, Inc. v. Heiman*,[57] the Supreme Court upheld a §1406(a) transfer by a transferor court that lacked personal jurisdiction over the defendant. The clear majority of federal courts conclude that this rule ought to apply to §1404(a) transfers as well,[58] although some courts disagree and permit a §1404(a) transfer only if the transferor court has personal jurisdiction over the defendant.[59] The majority view is clearly correct, since it is consistent with *Goldlawr*. After all, in *Goldlawr*, the Supreme Court upheld transfer by a court that had *neither* personal jurisdiction nor venue (since it was a §1406(a) transfer, venue in the original forum was improper). It is difficult to fathom why a court lacking *only* personal jurisdiction over the defendant should not have the same power.

There is another statute, which we mentioned in §4.3, which may have tangential relevance here. Section 1631 allows transfer from one federal court to another to cure a "want of jurisdiction." Though the statute seems aimed at curing lack of subject matter jurisdiction,[60] there is some support for its invocation to cure a lack of personal jurisdiction.[61] It is not clear why §1630 would ever be used in such a way, however. After all, in view of the holding in *Goldlawr*, which, as noted, should apply in §1404(a) and §1406(a) transfers, courts have a common law power to order transfer even when they lack personal jurisdiction over the defendant. The better view is that §1631 applies only to transfers to cure a lack of subject matter jurisdiction.[62]

The Hoffman *Case*

Section 1404(a) permits transfer to a district where the action "might have been brought." In *Hoffman v. Blaski*,[63] the Supreme Court interpreted this language to mean that the transferee court must be a proper

[57] 369 U.S. 463, 466 (1962).

[58] *See, e.g.*, Muldoon v. Tropitone Furniture Co., 1 F.3d 964, 967 (9th Cir. 1993); Cote v. Wadel, 796 F.2d 981, 984 (7th Cir. 1986).

[59] *See, e.g.*, Ross v. Colorado Outward Bound School, Inc., 822 F.2d 1524, 1526 (10th Cir. 1987).

[60] *See* Carefirst of Md., Inc. v. Carefirst Urgent Care Center, LLC, 305 F.3d 253, 257 n.2 (discussing cases); Songbyrd, Inc. v. Estate of Grossman, 206 F.3d 172, 179 n.9 (2d Cir. 2000) (noting in dictum "legislative history of §1361 provides some reason to believe that this section authorizes transfers only to cure lack of subject matter jurisdiction"); Pedzewick v. Foe, 963 F. Supp. 48, 49-50 (D. Mass. 1997) (statute applies only regarding subject matter jurisdiction).

[61] *See, e.g.*, Mellon Bank (East) PSFS, N.A. v. DiVeronica Bros., Inc., 983 F.3d 551, 558 n.3 (3d Cir. 1993) (making the point in one sentence, without discussion); Ross v. Colorado Outward Bound School, Inc., 822 F.2d 1524, 1527 (10th Cir. 1987).

[62] *See* 15 Wright & Miller §3842, at 323 (Section 1631 "is concerned only with subject matter jurisdiction. It has nothing to do with personal jurisdiction or venue.").

[63] 363 U.S. 335, 343-344 (1960).

venue (see §§5.2, 5.4) and must have personal jurisdiction over the defendant. Although *Hoffman* was a §1404(a) case, there is no doubt that its holding applies in §1406(a) transfers as well, because the latter statute also permits transfer only to a district where the case "could have been brought."[64] Importantly, though, *Hoffman* held that these two requirements — venue and personal jurisdiction in the transferee court — must be met *independently*, without waiver by the defendant. The Court reasoned that a contrary rule would simply give the defendant too much power to overturn the plaintiff's choice of forum; the defendant could essentially decree that the case be transferred to a particular federal district by waiving objections to venue and personal jurisdiction. The plaintiff's venue choice should not be so readily overturned by the defendant.

○ *P* sues *D* in the District of Minnesota. *D* moves to have the case transferred to the District of Hawaii. Venue is not proper in the District of Hawaii, nor would Hawaii have personal jurisdiction over *D*. But *D* declares that she will waive both defenses and submit to the venue and personal jurisdiction of the federal court in Hawaii. Under *Hoffman*, the District of Minnesota cannot transfer to the District of Hawaii, because that latter court is not one in which venue and personal jurisdiction were independently proper. Waiver doesn't count. This is true for transfer under either §1404(a) or §1406(a).

So, under *Goldlawr* and *Hoffman*, transfer under either statute can only be made *to* a district that is a proper venue and has personal jurisdiction. But transfer can be made *from* a court that lacks venue (§1406(a)) and lacks personal jurisdiction over the defendant.

The Van Dusen *Case*

In *Van Dusen v. Barrack*,[65] the Supreme Court held that a transferee court in a §1404(a) transfer must apply the choice of law rules that the transferor (the original district) would have applied. It reasoned that the change of venue should simply change the courtroom, and not the law to be applied to the merits of the case. In a diversity of citizenship case, as we see in Chapter 10, federal courts must apply state *substantive* (as opposed to procedural) law. Choice of law provisions are substantive, so a federal court sitting in diversity must apply state choice of law rules.

---

[64] *See, e.g.*, Minnette v. Time Warner, 997 F.2d 1023, 1026 (2d Cir. 1993). It is odd that Congress did not use precisely the same language in this regard. In §1404(a), the transferee court is one where the case "might have been brought" and in §1406(a) it is one where the case "could have been brought." Nonetheless, courts interpret the phrases the same, and thus *Hoffman* applies to each.

[65] 376 U.S. 612 (1964).

Thus, a federal court in California must apply California's choice of law rules.

What are choice of law rules? They can vary dramatically from state to state, and are the subject of an upper-division law school course on Conflict of Laws. For present purposes, it is enough to understand that choice of law rules determine what law governs a particular dispute. For example, suppose a citizen of Massachusetts enters a contract with a citizen of Arizona. They negotiate the contract at a meeting in Texas. The contract calls for performance in California and Guam. When a dispute arises between the parties, what law will govern in determining whether a party breached the contract and, if so, what the appropriate remedy is? The answer to that question (thankfully) is not something we need to know in this class. What we do need to know is that choice of law rules will make that determination. If the case is filed in Texas, the judge will apply Texas choice of law rules to determine whether the dispute will be governed by the substantive contract law of Massachusetts or Arizona or Texas or California or Guam (or some other jurisdiction). If the case is filed in California, the judge will use California choice of law rules to determine whether the dispute will be governed by the contract law of Massachusetts or Arizona or Texas or California or Guam (or some other jurisdiction). And this is true regardless of whether the case is in federal or state court. The Texas federal judge will use Texas choice of law rules and the California federal judge will use California choice of law rules.

The point here is relatively simple: When a case is transferred under §1404(a), *Van Dusen* requires the transferee court (the one to which the case is transferred) to apply the choice of law rules that the transferor court (the original federal court) would have used. Thus, *Van Dusen* ensures that the choice of law rules do not change just because the venue has changed.

○ Plaintiff files a diversity case in the Northern District of California, but the case is transferred under §1404(a) to the Southern District of Florida. California choice of law rules would conclude that the merits of the dispute should be determined under the law of Singapore. Florida choice of law rules would conclude that the dispute should be decided under the law of Florida. The Florida federal judge must apply California choice of law rules and, thus, the merits will be decided under Singapore law.

In the unfortunate case of *Ferens v. John Deere Co.*,[66] the Supreme Court extended *Van Dusen* to a §1404(a) transfer initiated by the *plaintiff*. In that case, the plaintiff was injured while using an appliance manufactured by the defendant. The accident took place in Pennsylvania, which has a two-year statute of limitations for such claims. The plaintiff failed to

---

[66] 494 U.S. 516 (1990).

sue within two years. After two years, the plaintiff sued in federal court in Mississippi. Mississippi has a six-year statute of limitations for such claims, and the plaintiff sued within that time. Shortly after filing, however, the plaintiff moved to transfer to federal court in Pennsylvania. The court transferred under §1404(a), and the Mississippi choice of law rules (which dictated the application of the longer statute of limitations) went with the case (under *Van Dusen*). So the plaintiff ended up in Pennsylvania federal court able to assert a claim that would have been barred by the Pennsylvania statute of limitations had he sued there in the first place. In other words, the plaintiff, by suing in Mississippi, was allowed to "capture" the longer Mississippi statute of limitations (through application of Mississippi's choice of law rules) and use it even after the case was transferred to federal court in Pennsylvania. *Ferens* thus allowed the plaintiff to do indirectly what he could not do directly (i.e., sue in Pennsylvania).

Van Dusen was a §1404(a) case. Clearly, its holding should *not* apply to a §1406(a) transfer, since in such a case the transferor court is not a proper venue. Applying *Van Dusen* would allow the plaintiff to capture favorable choice of law rules from an improper venue. Courts properly conclude, then, that *Van Dusen* does not apply in a §1406(a) case;[67] the transferee court applies its own choice of law rules. This is clearly also the proper result in any *Goldlawr* transfer. In such cases, the transferor court lacks personal jurisdiction over the defendant. It would be outrageous to permit a plaintiff to sue a defendant where she is not subject to personal jurisdiction and capture favorable choice of law rules for determining the outcome of the case. Thus, the vast majority of courts properly reject such efforts, and hold that *Van Dusen* does not apply to *Goldlawr* transfers.[68]

The following chart summarizes the basic rules applicable to §1404(a) and §1406(a):

---

[67] *See, e.g.*, Davis v. Louisiana State University, 876 F.2d 412, 413 (5th Cir. 1989).

[68] *See, e.g.*, Muldoon v. Tropitone Furniture Co., 1 F.3d 964, 967 (9th Cir. 1993); Manley v. Engram, 755 F.2d 1463, 1467 n.10 (11th Cir. 1985). At least one court concluded to the contrary, though, and applied *Van Dusen* to a *Goldlawr* transfer. *See* Myelle v. American Cyanamid Co., 57 F.3d 411, 412 (4th Cir. 1995).

Transfer Statute	Transferor District	Transferee District	Hoffman Apply?	Goldlawr Apply?	Van Dusen Apply?
§1404(a)	Proper venue	Proper venue & personal jurisdiction independently	Yes	Yes	Yes[69]
§1406(a)	Improper venue	Proper venue & personal jurisdiction independently	Yes	Yes	No

§5.6   *Forum Non Conveniens*

Forum non conveniens is a Latin phrase that means, not surprisingly, that the "forum is not convenient." Some courts invoke the phrase when speaking of transfer under §1404(a), which, as we saw in §5.5, involves transfer from a proper venue to a more convenient proper venue. Using the phrase "*forum non conveniens* transfer" in such cases is appropriate. More commonly, though, the phrase is used to refer to a doctrine of *dismissal*: A case, though pending in an appropriate forum, is *dismissed* because there is another forum that is far more appropriate. But why would a court ever dismiss (as opposed to transfer)? The court dismisses because it *cannot* transfer. And why would that be true? Because the more appropriate court is in a different judicial system. Remember that transfers are possible *only within a judicial system*.

- Case is filed in a proper state court in Alabama. The court has personal jurisdiction, subject matter jurisdiction, and is a proper venue under Alabama law. Under the relevant factors (which we discuss in a moment), however, litigation in Indiana would make far more sense. The Alabama court cannot transfer to Indiana, because they are in different judicial systems.[70] If the showing is strong enough, the Alabama court might dismiss under the doctrine of *forum non conveniens* to permit litigation in Indiana.

- Case is filed in federal *or* state court in New York. The court has personal jurisdiction, subject matter jurisdiction, and is a proper venue. Under the relevant factors, however, litigation in Bolivia would make far more sense. Obviously, neither a federal nor a state court can transfer a case to Bolivia, because it is a separate sovereign. *If the showing is strong*

---

[69] Unless the transferor court lacks personal jurisdiction. In Goldlawr transfers (under either §1404(a) or §1406(a)), *Van Dusen* should not apply, as we discuss in the text immediately above the chart.

[70] As we discussed in §5.5.1, however, a federal court in Alabama could transfer to a federal court in Indiana. Federal courts are in the same judicial system, even though they may sit in different states.

enough, the federal or state court might dismiss under the doctrine of *forum non conveniens* to permit litigation in Bolivia.

Each state is free to develop its own rules for applying *forum non conveniens*. Many, but not all, states have adopted a version very similar to the federal law on the issue. The leading case on the federal principle of *forum non conveniens* is *Piper Aircraft Co. v. Reyno*,[71] the facts of which also afford a remarkable opportunity to review a great deal of material from Chapters 2, 4, and this chapter. We undertake that review in §5.7. Now, we discuss the aspect of *Piper* dealing with the federal standard for *forum non conveniens* dismissals.

Piper Aircraft Co. v. Reyno

Piper involved the crash of a small airplane that killed all six persons aboard. The crash was in Scotland. The five passengers and the pilot were Scottish. The company that owned and maintained the plane was Scottish. The company that operated the charter business using the plane was Scottish. The heirs and next of kin of those killed in the crash were Scottish. But the airplane involved was manufactured in Pennsylvania by Piper Aircraft Company, and the propellers on the plane were manufactured in Ohio by Hartzell Corporation. The plaintiff asserted that these manufacturers were liable for the wrongful deaths of the passengers under various tort theories, including negligence and strict products liability.

Gaynell Reyno was a U.S. citizen, domiciled in California. She was not related to any of the parties in the case, but was appointed by a state court in Los Angeles to serve as administratrix of the estates of the five passengers. (That means that she represented the estates of those decedents in the California court, and was entitled to assert the wrongful death claims on behalf of the passengers' estates.) Those estates had already filed wrongful death cases in Scotland, but stood to recover a far greater amount under the law of almost any U.S. state that recognizes strict products liability and permits recovery for anguish. (Scottish law does neither.) Reyno filed the case in state court in Los Angeles. She named only Piper and Hartzell as defendants. The Scottish owner and operators of the plane, as well as the estate of the pilot, were not subject to personal jurisdiction anywhere in the United States, and thus were not included as defendants. Piper and Hartzell removed the case to federal court for the Central District of California (which embraces Los Angeles). That court granted the defendants' motion to transfer to the federal district court for the Middle District of Pennsylvania (which is where Piper manufactures its airplanes). The details involved in the removal and transfer are discussed in the following section and provide an interesting story. The federal judge in

[71] 454 U.S. 235 (1981).

261

Pennsylvania dismissed the case under *forum non conveniens*. The Third Circuit reversed, and held that the case should not be dismissed. Then the Supreme Court took the case and reversed the Third Circuit. The Supreme Court upheld the district court's dismissal and clarified the federal standard for *forum non conveniens* dismissals.

A court has great discretion in applying the doctrine, and the result is always dictated by the specific facts of the case. But some general observations are possible. The starting point, as it is in cases in which a party seeks transfer under §1404(a), is that the plaintiff's choice of forum should rarely be disturbed.[72] Only if a party can demonstrate that an alternative forum is *clearly* more appropriate should either transfer or dismissal be ordered. In fact, because dismissal is harsher than transfer, the party seeking *forum non conveniens* dismissal must make an even stronger showing than would be required to support transfer. On the other hand, it will be relatively easier to gain dismissal if the *plaintiff* is a foreigner; in such a case, the ordinary bias in favor of the plaintiff's choice of forum is not as strong.[73]

The Court in *Piper*, in footnote 6, divided the relevant factors into two groups: "public interest factors" and "private interest factors."[74] The public factors include (1) administrative difficulties of keeping the case; (2) local interest in having localized controversies decided at home; (3) the desire to have a case tried in a forum well versed in the law that will apply; (4) avoiding undue problems with conflict of laws or in the application of foreign law; and (5) the unfairness of burdening citizens with jury duty in a case unrelated to the forum. The private factors focus on practical issues of convenience, relating to the expeditious and inexpensive trial of a case, including (1) relative ease of access to evidence; (2) ability to compel attendance of witnesses at trial through subpoena; and (3) expense of obtaining attendance of willing witnesses.

In *Piper*, all factors supported dismissal. The alternative forum in Scotland already had jurisdiction over related litigation involving all interested persons, including Piper and Hartzell. Administratively, the case would be very difficult for a Pennsylvania court, since (for reasons discussed in the next section), Scottish law applied to the claims against

---

[72] We are assuming, of course, that the court in which the case is pending has personal jurisdiction over the defendant and is a proper venue. If either of those is not the case, the litigation can be dismissed on either of those bases.

[73] As a further reflection of this point, some courts will simply never grant a *forum non conveniens* dismissal if the plaintiff resides in the forum. A resident plaintiff has an especially strong interest in litigating there.

[74] The Supreme Court had discussed these factors in *Gulf Oil Corp. v. Gilbert*, 330 U.S. 501 (1947), in which it upheld a *forum non conveniens* dismissal of a claim in federal court in New York when the more appropriate forum was a federal court in Virginia. At the time, the case could not have been transferred because there was no statute allowing it. Section 1404(a) was passed in reaction to *Gulf Oil*.

Piper and Pennsylvania law to the claims against Hartzell. This fact would force the court to rely upon experts in Scottish law. It could also confuse the jury, and burden the citizens of a community (in Pennsylvania) far removed from the events underlying the suit (in Scotland). In contrast, Scotland had a substantial stake in the outcome of the case. Because the owner and operator of the plane, and the estate of the pilot, could not be sued in the United States, permitting the case to go forward in the United States fostered inefficient, piecemeal litigation. In sum, then, the factors indicated that another court was available and more appropriate than the federal court in Pennsylvania.

But that is not the end of the inquiry. The other court must not be simply available — it must also be adequate. In cases such as *Piper* — in which dismissal is sought to facilitate litigation in a foreign country — the plaintiff routinely will argue that the foreign forum is not adequate because she cannot recover as much overseas as in the United States. That was undoubtedly true in *Piper*: The fact that Scottish law would govern in Scotland meant that plaintiffs could not avail themselves of progressive theories of tort liability and damages for anguish. But the Court in *Piper* established that such a change in the law was not dispositive. Only "if the remedy provided by the alternative forum is so clearly inadequate or unsatisfactory that it is no remedy at all"[75] should the unfavorable change in applicable law be given substantial weight. On the facts in *Piper*, the Court held, there was no such showing.

Forum non conveniens dismissals are often "conditional." That is, the court will grant the defendant's motion to dismiss *conditioned upon* the defendant's waiving certain defenses or agreeing to certain things. For instance, the defendants in *Piper* stipulated that they would not object to the personal jurisdiction of the Scottish courts. They also agreed to waive any statute of limitations defense in that action. As another example, a defendant agreed to allow the plaintiff to undertake American-style discovery even though such intrusive measures would not be allowed in the foreign tribunal.[76] Of course, defendants are usually all too happy to make such concessions. Why? Because these concessions are usually a small price to pay for avoiding litigation in the United States, with its relatively pro-plaintiff tort laws and remedies.[77] Thus, it is routine for defendants to move to dismiss on grounds of *forum non conveniens* while offering to submit to jurisdiction or to waive some defense in the overseas court.

---

[75] *Piper*, 454 U.S. at 254.

[76] This happened in litigation concerning a toxic tort disaster in Bhopal, India. *See* In re Union Carbide Corporation Gas Plant Disaster at Bhopal, India, 809 F.2d 195 (2d Cir. 1987).

[77] "As a moth is drawn to the light, so is a litigant drawn to the United States. If he can only get his case into their courts, he stands to win a fortune." Russell Weintraub, *International Litigation and Forum Non Conveniens*, 29 Tex. Intl. L.J. 321, 322 (1994) (*quoting* Lord Denning).

In an early *forum non conveniens* case, the Supreme Court had said that the doctrine "can never apply if there is absence of jurisdiction."[78] In reaction, some lower federal courts concluded that they could not dismiss under this doctrine until they had concluded that they had personal jurisdiction over the defendants. In 2007, the Court rejected this approach, and held that a court may, "when judicial economy so warrant[s]," bypass questions of personal and subject matter jurisdiction and dispose of a suit under the doctrine of *forum non conveniens*.[79]

§5.7 Using *Piper Aircraft Co. v. Reyno* to Review Forum Selection Issues (You Should Read This Section; It's a Good Review)

The facts of *Piper* are remarkable because they involve so many elements of forum selection we have already seen in Chapters 2, 4, and this chapter. As we recount various facts, the text asks questions that force you to remember aspects of the course. Use this as a review; the answers to the questions are in the footnotes to the text below.[80]

Reyno sued Piper Aircraft Company, which manufactured the airplane involved in the crash giving rise to the suit. Piper is headquartered and manufactures airplanes in Lock Haven, Pennsylvania, which is in the Middle District of Pennsylvania. Piper clearly did substantial business throughout the country, selling its planes through regional distributors. There is no question it was subject to personal jurisdiction in California. Hartzell manufactures aircraft propellers, including the propellers on the plane involved in the crash in this case. Its headquarters and plant are in Ohio. It sells many of its props to Piper in Pennsylvania. Everyone seemed to agree that there was no personal jurisdiction over Hartzell in California.[81]

Reyno sued in state court in Los Angeles. She was the executrix of the Scottish citizens killed in the crash. Reyno is a U.S. citizen domiciled in California. Piper is a Pennsylvania citizen; Hartzell is an Ohio citizen. The claims were for millions of dollars. We know that the state court in Los

---

[78] Gulf Oil Corp. v. Gilbert, 330 U.S. 501, 505 (1947). The case is discussed at footnote 73 above.

[79] Sinochem Intl. Co. Ltd. v. Malaysia Intl. Shipping, 127 S. Ct. 1184, 1192 (2007). See also §6.5.

[80] I wrote a slightly more involved version of what follows for law professors in an article that suggests that they can review a great deal of Civil Procedure by asking their classes 16 questions arising from the facts of *Piper*. Richard D. Freer, *Refracting Domestic and Global Choice-of-Forum Doctrine Through the Lens of a Single Case*, 2007 BYU L. Rev. 959.

[81] Perhaps you can construct a stream-of-commerce argument for jurisdiction over Hartzell in California. See §2.4.4.

Angeles had personal jurisdiction over Piper but not over Hartzell. Did the state court in Los Angeles have subject matter jurisdiction over the case?[82]

The defendants removed the case to the federal district court for the Central District of California. Why was there federal subject matter jurisdiction?[83] (Be careful with this one. Whose citizenship is relevant on the plaintiffs' side?[84]) That federal court transferred the case to the federal district court for the Middle District of Pennsylvania. Why *must* that transfer have been pursuant to §1404(a) and not §1406(a)?[85] In other words, why was the Central District of California a proper venue *even though* it would not have been a proper venue under §1391?[86] (By the way, why would the Central District of California not be a proper venue under §1391?[87] In other words, why did Hartzell not *reside* in the Central District?[88])

[82] Yes. State courts have general subject matter jurisdiction. They can hear any case not falling within exclusive federal question jurisdiction. This is a case for wrongful death, based upon various tort theories. There is no federal question at all, let alone an exclusive federal question. See §4.2.

[83] There is no federal question jurisdiction, since, as we said above, the claims do not arise under federal law. What about diversity or alienage? This is tough. Reyno was a citizen of California. The defendants were citizens of Pennsylvania and Ohio. The amount in controversy is clearly met. But Reyno represented Scottish citizens. Is it her citizenship or that of the decedents that controls? If it is hers, the case invokes diversity of citizenship jurisdiction. If it is the decedents', the case invokes alienage jurisdiction. We address the question of whether it's diversity or alienage in the next footnote.

[84] In §4.5.3, we saw a statute that provides that in cases involving decedents, minors, or incompetents represented in litigation by a fiduciary, the court looks to the citizenship of the decedent, minor, or incompetent, and not to that of the fiduciary. 28 U.S.C. §1332(c)(2). At first glance, then, that statute would seem to tell us that it is the decedents' citizenship (Scotland) and not the representative's (California) that governs. So the case would invoke alienage rather than diversity. But we need to be very careful. Section 1332(c)(2) provides that the representative is deemed to be a citizen of "the same State" as the decedent, minor, or incompetent. In the jurisdictional statutes, the capitalized word "State" means state of the United States. Because the decedents were not citizens of any state of the United States, arguably, §1332(c)(2) does not apply on this fact pattern. (We discussed this in §4.5.3.) Presumably, then, the court looks to the citizenship of the representative (California), so the case invokes diversity of citizenship jurisdiction and not alienage.

[85] Because §1404(a) applies to transfers *from* a proper venue. The Central District of California was a proper venue. If the reason for this is not clear, see the next footnote.

[86] Section 1391 is irrelevant in a case removed from state court. It applies only to cases filed by the plaintiff in federal court. In a removed case, venue is proper only in the federal district embracing the state court in which it was originally filed. 28 U.S.C. §1441(a). See §5.4.2. Los Angeles is in the Central District of California.

[87] The plane was manufactured in Pennsylvania and crashed in Scotland. Thus, no part of the claim arose in the Central District of California and venue was not proper there under §1391(a)(2). Moreover, the Central District is not one in which all defendants reside, so venue was not proper there under §1391(a)(1). One defendant (Piper) resided there, but not the other (Hartzell). If the reason for this is not clear, see the next footnote.

[88] Under §1391(c), a corporation resides in all districts in which it is subject to personal jurisdiction at the time the case is filed. Hartzell was not subject to personal jurisdiction in

The judge in the Central District of California transferred the case to the Middle District of Pennsylvania. Under *Hoffman v. Blaski*, what must be true about that transferee court?[89] In other words, (1) why does the Middle District of Pennsylvania have personal jurisdiction over the defendants,[90] and (2) why is it a proper venue under §1391?[91] But how could the Central District of California transfer as to Hartzell, when that court did not have personal jurisdiction over Hartzell?[92] After the case was transferred, why would the Middle District of Pennsylvania have to apply different choice of law rules to the two defendants[93] (In other words, why does *Van Dusen* apply to Piper but not to Hartzell?[94]) Thus, when the case got to the federal judge in Pennsylvania, he had to apply the choice of law rules of California as to Piper and the choice of law rules of Pennsylvania as to Hartzell. He concluded that California choice of law rules would dictate that Pennsylvania law apply to the claim against Piper. He also concluded that Pennsylvania choice of law rules would apply Scottish law to the claim against Hartzell.

_____

California. Note that Piper was, so it resided there for venue purposes, but venue is proper under §1391(a) only if all defendants reside in the district or in different districts of the same state.

[89] Under *Hoffman*, transfer is proper only to a court that has personal jurisdiction over the defendants and is a proper venue under §1391, absent waiver by the defendant. See §5.5.2.

[90] Because Piper has its headquarters and manufactures airplanes there, it clearly has minimum contacts. Hartzell manufactures its propellers in Ohio but ships a large percentage of them to Piper in Pennsylvania, pursuant to a long-term commercial relationship. Thus, it has minimum contacts with Pennsylvania. (Note that Hartzell's relationship with Pennsylvania is not through a stream-of-commerce theory. It ships these goods directly and purposefully to Pennsylvania; they are not carried there by the vagaries of the stream of commerce.) See §2.4.4.

[91] Because all defendants reside there, venue is proper under §1391(a)(1). A corporation resides in every district in which it is subject to personal jurisdiction when the case is filed. (This is provided by §1391(c).) Also, there is a strong argument that a substantial part of the claim arose there, because that is where the plane was manufactured, so venue would be proper under §1391(a)(2).

[92] Because *Goldlawr* permits transfer even by a court lacking personal jurisdiction over the defendant. See §5.5.2.

[93] Because under *Van Dusen*, the choice of law rules of California are transferred along with the case. This is so, however, only as to Piper, not Hartzell. See §5.5.2.

[94] Because *Van Dusen* does not apply to *Goldlawr* transfers, that is, to a transfer involving a defendant over whom the transferor court lacked personal jurisdiction. See §5.5.2. The Central District of California had personal jurisdiction over Piper, so *Van Dusen* applies to the transfer of the case against it; it did not have personal jurisdiction over Hartzell, however, so *Van Dusen* does not apply to the transfer of the claim against it.

Chapter 6

Challenging the Selection of Forum

§6.1   Defining the Issue

We have spent a good deal of time addressing the selection of a proper forum for litigation. The doctrines of personal jurisdiction, subject matter jurisdiction, and venue guide this selection. Here, we address how the defendant might challenge the plaintiff's selection of forum.[1]

The basis for the challenge affects how the challenge might be raised. Limitations on personal jurisdiction (including propriety of service of process) and venue, as we saw in Chapters 2, 3, and 5, give the defendant personal rights, which, like most personal rights, may be waived. Moreover, because they present a threshold issue of whether the litigation is in the proper court, it seems advisable to determine them as early as possible. It makes no sense to litigate for some lengthy period only to find out, after all that effort, that the case is not in a proper court. Such litigation wastes the parties' and the court's resources. Thus, a court might want to impose strict limits on when and how the defendant can challenge things like personal jurisdiction and venue, to ensure that they are raised early or else waived. In §6.2, we see that most judicial systems have done exactly

---

[1] In a case removed from state to federal court, see §4.8, it may be the plaintiff who challenges the defendant's selection of a federal forum; for example, through a motion to remand to state court.

that. In §6.3, we consider the factors relevant to a defendant's decision of whether to challenge personal jurisdiction directly or in a collateral proceeding.

But subject matter jurisdiction is a different proposition. True, it would be efficient to force the defendant to raise a subject matter jurisdiction objection early or else waive it. But, as we saw in §4.3, subject matter jurisdiction does not implicate a litigant's personal rights. Instead, principles of subject matter jurisdiction involve the proper allocation of litigation between federal and state courts. They are rules about the structure of government.[2] Thus, litigants cannot waive strictures on subject matter jurisdiction. Despite the possible inefficiency, it is clear, at least generally, that a court's lack of subject matter jurisdiction can be raised for the first time almost anytime — even after entry of judgment. There is a significant question, however, as to whether one can attack subject matter jurisdiction in a collateral proceeding, as we see in §6.4.

§6.2   Different Approaches to Challenging Personal Jurisdiction, Venue, and Process Issues (And How Rule 12 Works)

§6.2.1   *In Personam* Jurisdiction: Special Appearance and the Modern Approach Under Rule 12

Development of the Special Appearance

Consider the dilemma facing a defendant who wants to argue that the state in which she has been sued lacks personal jurisdiction. She will want to go to that state and make a motion to dismiss. But by going to that state, or even by sending her lawyer, has the defendant subjected herself to personal jurisdiction there? After all, is she not present in the forum when she raises the challenge? Or can it be said that she has consented to jurisdiction by going there? Understanding this dilemma, courts developed the "special appearance," which allows the defendant to appear in the forum for the sole purpose of arguing that the court lacks personal jurisdiction. The special appearance is to be contrasted with a "general appearance," which constitutes a submission to personal jurisdiction.

The special appearance method of questioning personal jurisdiction is not the majority view today; most states have adopted the modern approach, which we discuss below. It is important to remember, though, that a few states — including such populous states as California and

---

[2] Remember that federal courts can entertain only certain types of cases, because the Constitution says so. U.S. Const. art. III, §2. We discussed this point at §4.3.

Texas — still employ the special appearance. Though some special appearance states are stricter than others, it is important to keep in mind that the defendant making a special appearance ordinarily can raise *only* an objection to personal jurisdiction. Asserting another defense or filing an answer *before or even contemporaneously with* the personal jurisdiction defense may constitute a general appearance and thus a waiver of the personal jurisdiction objection.[3] The notion of the general appearance is that the defendant has at some point become so engaged in the proceedings that it is fair to say, essentially, that she has consented to the court's power over her.

The special appearance has the advantage of presenting a single, potentially dispositive issue to the court. If the court concludes that it lacks personal jurisdiction, early dismissal avoids meaningless litigation on the merits of the claim. On the other hand, though, it has the obvious disadvantage of forcing the defendant to put all the eggs in one basket, at least initially. Generally, in special appearance jurisdictions, the defendant may raise other possible defenses only after losing on the personal jurisdiction defense.[4]

Another problem is that the special appearance rule can be a trap for the unwary. Again, some states are stricter than others about what can be raised in a special appearance without waiving the personal jurisdiction defense. For example, in most states, a defendant may safely raise a lack of personal jurisdiction in the alternative with a motion to dismiss for *forum non conveniens* (which we discuss at §5.6). In especially strict states, however, the combination of the personal jurisdiction issue with the alternative motion can constitute a general appearance.[5] Counsel must

[3] *See generally* Clifford Plunkett, *Waiver and the Special Appearance in Arkansas*, 47 Ark. L. Rev. 883 (1994).

[4] A good example of this limitation is *Asahi v. Superior Court*, discussed at §2.4.4. There, the valve manufacturer, Asahi, made a special appearance to challenge California's assertion of jurisdiction. After losing that challenge, Asahi succeeded in getting appellate review of the personal jurisdiction issue by the California appellate courts and, ultimately, by the Supreme Court of the United States. During the lengthy delay caused by all the appellate involvement, Asahi's lawyers apparently discovered that it had not even manufactured the valve involved in the accident. But if it presented that fact to the court (e.g., through a motion for summary judgment), it would have been making a general appearance and would waive the personal jurisdiction objection.

[5] While nervously waiting to make his first oral argument in the practice of law, the author witnessed an oral argument in California Superior Court where exactly that happened. The defendant was deemed to have made a general appearance and thus to have waived its personal jurisdiction objection. Indeed, some courts have been so strict as to say that requesting a continuance (delay) of the hearing on the motion to dismiss for lack of personal jurisdiction constitutes a general appearance. *See, e.g.*, Bumgarner v. Federal Dep. Ins. Corp., 764 P.2d 1367 (Okla. App. 1988); Pfeiffer v. Ash, 206 P.2d 438 (Cal. App. 1949). On the other hand, challenging personal jurisdiction at the same time as removing a case to federal court is not a general appearance. Lambert Run Coal Co. v. Baltimore & Ohio R.R. Co., 258 U.S. 377 (1922).

be very careful in determining what defenses, if any, a given jurisdiction will allow a defendant to raise with her personal jurisdiction objection. Interestingly, some strict special appearance states appear to permit the defendant to challenge subject matter jurisdiction along with personal jurisdiction, without waiver.[6]

The Modern (Rule 12) Approach

The modern approach to challenging the selection of a forum is typified by Federal Rule 12. It applies (of course) in federal court, and also in the majority of states, since most states have modeled their rules on the Federal Rules. Federal Rule 12 abolishes the special appearance by allowing the defendant to raise several defenses, including personal jurisdiction, simultaneously. Doing so does not waive a personal jurisdiction objection. In the words of the third sentence of Rule 12(b), "[n]o defense or objection is waived by being joined with one or more other defenses or objections in a responsive pleading or motion."

How does Rule 12 work? For starters, it is important to remember that a defendant has a choice of how to respond to litigation against her: She either files and serves a *responsive pleading* (called an *answer*) or she brings a *motion*. (We discuss these options in detail at §7.4.) In the answer, the defendant responds to the plaintiff's complaint and raises affirmative defenses. With a motion, a party requests that the court enter a particular order. In the course of litigation, there may be hundreds of motions — for example, motions to amend pleadings, to compel discovery, for extension of time in which to respond, for summary judgment — the list is endless. Some of the most important motions are motions to dismiss because of some problem with the selection of the forum.

Here we focus on the seven defenses found in Federal Rule 12(b). (Not surprisingly, they are known as the "12(b) defenses.") Take a close look at these seven 12(b) defenses (and be sure to notice that the first five all relate to selection of a forum): (1) lack of subject matter jurisdiction; (2) lack of personal jurisdiction; (3) improper venue; (4) insufficient process; (5) insufficient service of process;[7] (6) failure to state a claim on which relief can be granted; and (7) failure to join an absentee under Rule 19.

---

[6] *See, e.g.,* Goodwine v. Superior Court, 407 P.2d 1 (Cal. 1965).

[7] What's the difference between 12(b)(4) and 12(b)(5)? The former is aimed at problems with the process itself — for example, failure to have both summons and a copy of the complaint. See §3.3.1 above. Such problems are rare. The latter is aimed at problems not with the documents, but with how they were served on the defendant — for example, that substituted service was not effected on a person of suitable age and discretion or on a proper corporate agent. See §§3.3.2 and 3.3.3. Such problems are more common.

Rule 12(b) provides that all seven of the 12(b) defenses may be raised *either* by motion or in the defendant's answer.[8]

The fact that the defendant has a choice of how to raise the Rule 12(b) defenses raises the possibility of inadvertent waiver of defenses. Be very careful about Rules 12(g) and (h). They impose timing requirements on raising the Rule 12(b) defenses, and contain many traps for the unwary lawyer (or careless law student). Rule 12(g)(2) requires a defendant who makes a *motion* under Rule 12[9] to join in that motion "a defense or objection that was available to the party but omitted from its earlier motion." If she does not do so, she "must not make another motion under this rule," with exceptions as provided in Rule 12(h)(2) and (h)(3). Thus, Rule 12(g) is concerned with a defendant's asserting two Rule 12 *motions*. If she omits from the first one some Rule 12 defense that is available to her at the time, she cannot make a second Rule 12 motion, unless she falls within the saving grace of Rule 12(h)(2) or (h)(3). In other words, as a general matter, omitting a Rule 12 defense from a Rule 12 motion waives the right to bring a second motion under Rule 12.

Rule 12(h) addresses waiver of all seven of the Rule 12(b) defenses, but clusters them into three groups for purposes of timing. Four of the five defenses relating to selection of a forum (lack of personal jurisdiction, improper venue, insufficient process, and insufficient service of process) are found in Rule 12(h)(1). That subsection provides that such defenses are waived if omitted from a Rule 12 motion *or* if omitted from a responsive pleading (or a pleading amended as a matter of course, which we see at §7.5.1). Notice, then, how (as to these four defenses) Rule 12(h)(1) supplements Rule 12(g) by providing for waiver not only if the defendant tries to bring two Rule 12 motions, but also if the defendant omits one of the defenses from *either* a motion or the answer and then tries to raise it with a subsequent motion or answer. This gets quite complicated, and we will make it simpler in a moment. Before we do, though, notice that Rule 12(h)(3) addresses timing of the other forum selection issue — lack of subject matter jurisdiction — and provides, essentially, that it can be raised anytime. And Rule 12(h)(2) addresses the two Rule 12(b) defenses that do not concern forum selection — the motion to dismiss for failure to state a claim and to dismiss for failure to join an absentee under Rule 19.

[8] Why, then, would a defendant raise any of these in her answer, rather than by motion? Putting the defense in the answer preserves it, so a defendant who thinks one of the 12(b) defenses *might* be plausible does not have to make a motion on it now, but can preserve it and push the issue later, when she has more factual grounding for it.

[9] A Rule 12 motion might be based upon any of the seven Rule 12(b) defenses, or it might be a Rule 12(e) motion for more definite statement or a Rule 12(f) motion to strike. See §7.4.1.

All of the timing issues in Rule 12(g) and (h) can be summarized in three principles.

Principle Number 1. The defenses in Rule 12(b)(2), (3), (4), and (5) must be put in the first defensive response under Rule 12 — whether that is a motion or an answer. If they are not, they are waived. This rule makes a great deal of sense, because these four defenses — lack of personal jurisdiction, improper venue, insufficiency of process, and insufficiency of service of process — are threshold issues, which ought to be determined at the outset. They are also waivable defenses, so the rule appropriately puts the burden on the defendant to raise them in her first Rule 12 response (motion or answer) or else lose them.

Principle Number 2. The defenses in Rule 12(b)(6) and (7) may be raised as late as "at trial," which means anytime before entry of judgment by the trial court. This result is dictated by Rule 12(h)(2), and also makes sense, because these defenses — failure to state a claim on which relief can be granted and failure to join an absentee under Rule 19 — may mature later in the litigation.[10] These two defenses do not have to be put in the defendant's *first* Rule 12 response. They are waived only if they are not raised sometime before judgment is entered at the trial court.

Principle Number 3. The defense in Rule 12(b)(1) may be raised anytime. This result is dictated by Rule 12(h)(3) and also makes sense, because the defense is lack of subject matter jurisdiction. As discussed in §4.3, the limited subject matter jurisdiction of the federal courts is a matter of governmental structure. If a case does not invoke federal subject matter jurisdiction, a federal court must dismiss, even if it has invested years in the case under the incorrect impression that it had subject matter jurisdiction. See §6.4.

These three principles allow you to resolve any fact pattern in this area.

- *P* sues *D*. Within the proper time, *D* makes a motion to dismiss for lack of personal jurisdiction. The court denies the motion. Then *D* makes a motion to dismiss for improper venue. She has waived the venue defense under Rule 12(g). Why?[11]
- *P* sues *D*. Within the proper time, *D* makes a motion to dismiss for lack of personal jurisdiction. The court denies the motion. Then *D* files an

[10] This is especially so with Rule 12(b)(7), which involves failure to join an absentee under Rule 19, often called a "necessary" party (although the rule calls it a "required" party). Often, the fact that such an absentee exists will not be ascertainable until the case unfolds a bit, perhaps in discovery. See §12.6.1.

[11] This is covered by Principle Number 1. *D* made a Rule 12 motion, followed by another Rule 12 motion raising one of the four "waivable" defenses; the waiver is effected by Rule 12(g).

answer, in which she asserts the defense of improper service of process. That defense is waived and may be stricken. Why?[12]

○ *P* sues *D*. Within the proper time, *D* serves and files an answer raising the defense of improper venue. Then she makes a motion to dismiss for lack of personal jurisdiction. She has waived the defense. Why?[13] (Your professor may add facts making it overwhelmingly clear that *D* had absolutely no contacts with the forum; still, personal jurisdiction there is proper because *D* waived the personal jurisdiction defense.)

○ *P* sues *D*. Within the proper time, *D* makes a motion to strike *P*'s pleading under Rule 12(f). The court denies the motion. Then *D* serves and files an answer (or makes a motion) raising lack of personal jurisdiction. Again, she has waived the latter defense. Why?[14]

○ *P* sues *D*. Within the proper time, *D* makes a motion to enlarge the time in which she may respond to the complaint. The court grants the motion, after which *D* files an answer (or makes a motion) raising lack of personal jurisdiction. Has she waived this defense? No! Why not?[15]

○ *P* sues *D*. *D* makes a motion to dismiss under the doctrine of *forum non conveniens* (which we discussed in §5.6). The court denies the motion, after which *D* moves to dismiss for lack of personal jurisdiction. Has she waived this defense? No. Why not?[16]

○ *P* sues *D*. Within the proper time, *D* serves and files an answer. The case proceeds to trial and the trial court enters judgment for *P*. On appeal, *D* asserts for the first time that the case should have been dismissed for failure to join an absentee under Rule 19. The defense is waived. Why?[17]

○ *P* sues *D*. Within the proper time, *D* serves and files an answer. The case proceeds to trial and the trial court enters judgment for *P*. On appeal, *D* asserts for the first time that the case should have been dismissed for

---

[12] This is also covered by Principle Number 1. *D* waived this defense under Rule 12(h)(1)(B). Rule 12(g) does not apply because that subsection addresses only the situation in which the defendant makes a Rule 12 motion followed by another Rule 12 motion. Here she made a motion followed by a pleading, but the timing principle is the same.

[13] Again, this is governed by Principle Number 1. It is not governed by Rule 12(g) because that applies only when *D* makes a motion followed by a motion. Here, she filed a pleading followed by a motion. The waiver is effected by Rule 12(h)(1)(B)(ii).

[14] Principle Number 1. Her original motion was one permitted under Rule 12(f), so it constitutes a "motion under this rule," as Rule 12(g) says.

[15] Principle Number 1. Under Rules 12(g) and 12(h)(1)(A), *D* must include the "waivable defenses" in a "motion under this rule," which means a motion made under Rule 12. A motion for enlargement of time is made under Rule 6(b), not Rule 12.

[16] Again, Principle Number 1 covers this situation. Though lack of personal jurisdiction is a waivable defense, that means it must be included in the first response under Rule 12. Most courts conclude that a motion to dismiss under *forum non conveniens* is not a Rule 12 response. The defendant raising the issue is not contesting jurisdiction or venue. Rather, she is arguing that *even though* the present forum is proper, there is another court in another judicial system in which litigation would make far more sense. *See, e.g.*, Abiola v. Abubakar, 267 F. Supp. 3d 907, 918 (N.D. Ill. 2003).

[17] This is governed by Principle Number 2. Waiver is under Rule 12(h)(2). This defense must be asserted for the first time no later than "at trial," which means no later than entry of judgment at the trial court. Here, *D* did not raise the defense until after judgment.

lack of federal subject matter jurisdiction. *D* has not waived the defense. Why not?[18]

§6.2.2 *In Rem* and *Quasi-in-Rem* Jurisdiction

What if the defendant wishes to challenge a court's *in rem* or *quasi-in-rem* jurisdiction? Such cases involve seizure of the defendant's property as the jurisdictional predicate. (If this is fuzzy, see §2.2.) The defendant's dilemma is whether she can go to the forum and challenge jurisdiction without thereby submitting to *in personam* jurisdiction.[19] States have taken different approaches to this issue. Most of the cases addressing the question are old, which reflects the decreasing importance of *in rem* and *quasi-in-rem* jurisdiction in an era of expanded *in personam* jurisdiction.

In some states, the defendant is allowed to appear and litigate the merits of the underlying claim without submitting to *in personam* jurisdiction if she makes a "limited appearance."[20] As with the special appearance, states may impose different technical requirements about how one makes a limited appearance. In fact, some states evidently do not permit a limited appearance.[21]

In federal court, the practice is not entirely clear. Federal Rule 4(n)(2), which addresses service of process, permits a federal court to seize a defendant's property in accordance with the law of the state in which the federal court sits. Neither it nor any other Federal Rule, however, mentions limited appearances. The cases are unclear on two points: whether to permit limited appearances in federal court[22] and, if so, whether the federal court is obligated to follow state law on the topic.[23] Because the issue simply does not come up much anymore, there will probably never

---

[18] This is governed by Principle Number 3. Rule 12(h)(1) makes it clear that the lack of subject matter jurisdiction can be raised "whenever" it becomes apparent. See §6.4.

[19] Remember, a judgment *in rem* or *quasi-in-rem* is valid only to the value of the property that serves as the jurisdictional predicate. In an *in personam* case, however, a valid judgment creates a personal obligation for the defendant to pay the amount of the judgment to the plaintiff. The plaintiff can enforce a valid *in personam* judgment in any state through full faith and credit.

[20] A classic case is *Cheshire Natl. Bank v. Jaynes*, 112 N.E. 500 (Mass. 1916). The legendary law professor Brainerd Currie was a proponent of the limited appearance. *See* Brainerd Currie, *Attachment and Garnishment in the Federal Courts*, 59 Mich. L. Rev. 337 (1961).

[21] *See, e.g.*, Johnson v. Holt's Administrator, 31 S.W.2d 895 (Ky. 1930) (act of contesting propriety of seizure converts case to *in personam*).

[22] *See, e.g.*, McQuillan v. National Cash Register Co., 112 F.2d 877 (4th Cir. 1940) (yes); Campbell v. Murdock, 90 F. Supp. 297 (N.D. Ohio 1950) (no).

[23] *See, e.g.*, Cargill, Inc. v. Sabine Trading & Shipping Co., 756 F.2d 224 (2d Cir. 1984); U.S. Industries, Inc. v. Gregg, 58 F.R.D. 469 (D. Del. 1973) (state law applied); Dry Clime Lamp Corp. v. Edwards, 389 F.2d 590 (5th Cir. 1968) (federal law applied).

be a Federal Rule on point. If there were, it would govern the practice in federal courts under the rule in *Hanna v. Plumer*, discussed in §10.6.

§6.3   Direct and Collateral Attacks on Personal Jurisdiction

Regardless of whether a particular jurisdiction employs the special appearance or Federal Rule 12 as its model, the defendant who wishes to challenge personal jurisdiction must decide whether to make a *direct* or a *collateral* attack on that issue. A *direct attack* is when the defendant seeks dismissal of the pending case for lack of personal jurisdiction by making an appropriate motion in that case.[24] As we have just seen in §6.2, such a motion must be made early in the proceedings. The whole idea is to have the issue cleared up at the outset, before the court and parties invest significant time and resources in litigating the merits of the case. If the motion is successful, of course, the case is dismissed and the defendant goes home happy (although the plaintiff may, of course, sue the defendant in her home state).

But the defendant has another option. She could simply refuse to appear in the case, and allow the court to enter default judgment against her.[25] Then she would wait for the plaintiff to seek to enforce that judgment — to collect on it — in the defendant's home state. That judgment is enforceable — entitled to full faith and credit — only if the first court had personal jurisdiction. So the defendant may argue *in this second case* that the first court did not have personal jurisdiction. This is called a *collateral attack*, since it takes place in a second, or collateral, suit.

- ° *P* sues *D* in Michigan. *D* is a citizen of Arizona,[26] and thinks that Michigan does not have personal jurisdiction over her. Rather than go to Michigan and make a direct attack there, *D* fails to appear in Michigan and

[24] In some states, particularly those using the special appearance practice, the motion is called a "motion to quash service of process." Under Rule 12, and in most states, it is simply a "motion to dismiss for lack of personal jurisdiction," or, sometimes, a "motion to dismiss for want of personal jurisdiction." All states permit some form of direct attack, although the Supreme Court long ago held that due process does not require the states to provide for such challenges. York v. Texas, 137 U.S. 15 (1890).

[25] We discuss default and default judgments at §7.5.

[26] When you hear these facts about citizenship, you may start thinking about diversity of citizenship jurisdiction. Remember, though, that diversity of citizenship is totally irrelevant to what we are discussing here. Diversity of citizenship is a basis for federal *subject matter jurisdiction*. See §4.5. What we're talking about here — personal jurisdiction — raises the same issues whether the case is in federal or state court. The fact that different states are involved here raises the question of whether a judgment in Michigan (state or federal court) would be enforceable in Arizona (state or federal court).

allows the court there to enter a default judgment against her. Now *P* takes that judgment to a court in Arizona (where there clearly is personal jurisdiction over *D*, and where *D* presumably has assets) for enforcement.[27] *D* may appear in the Arizona proceeding and argue that the Michigan judgment is not entitled to full faith and credit because Michigan did not have personal jurisdiction over her.

The collateral attack has some advantages over the direct attack. The defendant does not have to travel from Arizona to Michigan and does not have to retain a Michigan lawyer[28] to raise the direct jurisdictional challenge there. Instead, she gets to litigate "at home" in Arizona with her own lawyer in familiar surroundings. There is, however, one enormous drawback to the collateral attack: In it, the defendant may raise *only* the question of whether the first court had personal jurisdiction. If the Michigan court is held to have had personal jurisdiction, the defendant cannot litigate the underlying merits of the claim in the second action. In other words, by defaulting in Michigan, the defendant has waived any argument concerning the merits of the underlying claim,[29] at least if the Michigan court is held to have had personal jurisdiction.

   ◦ *P* sues *D* in Michigan on a claim for battery. On the merits of that claim, *D* admits that she slugged *P*, but wants to argue that she did so in self-defense, because *P* had attacked her. If the Arizona court determines that Michigan did have personal jurisdiction over *D*, the Michigan default judgment is entitled to full faith and credit, and *P* can enforce it in Arizona. *D* will have no opportunity to litigate the self-defense issue.[30]

In other words, if *D* relies on a collateral attack, she puts all the eggs in the personal jurisdiction basket. Obviously, then, if *D* has a strong defense to the claim on the merits (such as compelling evidence from witnesses

---

[27] In other words, to convert the judgment into money. *P* could do this wherever *D* has assets that can be seized and sold to satisfy the Michigan judgment (if that judgment is valid and therefore entitled to full faith and credit).

[28] As you probably know, lawyers are licensed by individual states. In all likelihood, a member of the Arizona bar will not also be a member of the Michigan bar (although she could be). A non-Michigan lawyer cannot appear in Michigan courts unless allowed to practice there for the purpose of a single case (called *pro hac vice* admission). Even then, most bars require that a local lawyer at least be associated on the case. So going to Michigan to litigate will involve the expense and delay of having to find a Michigan lawyer.

[29] The word "merits" refers to the facts concerning the claim itself. If *P* had sued *D* for battery, the decision on the merits would be whether *D* did commit battery and, if so, whether *D* had any excuse for doing so. It might be that *D* did punch out *P*, but that she did so in self-defense.

[30] Of course, if the Arizona court determines that Michigan did *not* have personal jurisdiction, the Arizona court will not enforce the Michigan judgment; it is not valid, and not entitled to full faith and credit. *P* might then attempt to sue *D* in Arizona, where there clearly is personal jurisdiction over *D*.

that she acted in self-defense), she will not want to take this route. Rather, she should opt for a direct attack. That avenue will allow D to raise the personal jurisdiction issue and then, if she loses on that, to litigate the claim on the merits.

There are some problems, however, with this approach too. Some of these problems are obvious: D will have to hire a Michigan lawyer and will have to litigate far from home, presumably on P's home turf. But one problem is less obvious: What happens if the Michigan court rules that it has personal jurisdiction? Can D appeal that ruling to the state appellate courts immediately?

In most states, the answer is no. The decision that the court has personal jurisdiction is not a "final judgment," and thus, under the general rule, is not appealable at this point in the proceedings. See §14.4. The issue can be taken to the appellate level only after a decision on the merits of the case. Thus, once the defendant loses on the personal jurisdiction issue, she should be prepared to stick around and litigate the merits of the underlying dispute. In some states, however, the defendant may seek immediate appellate review of the personal jurisdictional issue, either by an express exception to the final judgment rule or by extraordinary writ,[31] but this is the exception. The general rule is that the court's finding that it has personal jurisdiction is not subject to appeal until the merits of the case have been decided.

Notice, then, the range of factors an Arizona lawyer would have to consider in advising D whether to make a direct attack. She would have to assess at least these factors:

(1) how direct attacks are made in Michigan;
(2) the strength of the personal jurisdiction challenge;
(3) the strength of D's defense on the merits;
(4) whether Michigan permits immediate review in an appeals court from the personal jurisdiction ruling or, on the other hand, requires a decision on the merits of the claim;
(5) if Michigan permits interlocutory review, whether it is automatic or discretionary; and
(6) whether the personal jurisdiction issue can be raised on appeal from a decision on the merits.[32]

---

[31] We discussed this possibility in *World-Wide Volkswagen* and *Asahi*, §2.4.4. In each of those cases, the defendant was permitted to seek immediate appellate review of the personal jurisdiction issue through extraordinary writ. California is especially liberal in its review of jurisdictional issues by extraordinary writ. *See* Cal. Code Civ. Proc. §418.10(c).

[32] As a general rule, the defendant can raise the personal jurisdiction issue on appeal after trial on the merits, so long as she properly preserves her objection on the record. See §14.6. Certainly, that is the rule in federal practice. Toledo Ry. & Light Co. v. Hill, 244 U.S. 49 (1917).

The lawyer must be careful to explain to *D* that the decision to make a direct attack means that the personal jurisdiction issue will be decided by a Michigan court and appealed in Michigan. In a collateral attack, the question of whether Michigan had personal jurisdiction will be decided by an Arizona court and appealed in Arizona. And of course it is critical to explain that making a collateral attack means *D* will not be able to litigate the merits unless the Arizona court determines that Michigan had no jurisdiction.

- ○ Suppose *D*'s defense on the merits is very strong. She has independent witnesses who will testify that *P* attacked *D* without warning, and that *D* slugged *P* in self-defense. Suppose the question of whether Michigan has personal jurisdiction is close. What do you recommend to *D*? This seems to be a strong case for a direct attack. If personal jurisdiction is a toss-up, and since *D* is strong on the merits, there is little sense in putting all the eggs in the jurisdiction basket.
- ○ On the other hand, if jurisdiction is a toss-up and *D* has a weak case on the merits, *D* might as well make a collateral attack. That way, she litigates the jurisdiction issue at home and the waiver of the defense on the merits is not that big a deal, since the defense was weak anyway.

Whichever route the defendant chooses — direct or collateral attack — it is important to follow through with it, and not to mix approaches. Do not make the mistake made by the hapless defendant in *Baldwin v. Iowa State Traveling Men's Assn.*[33] There, the plaintiff brought suit in Missouri against an Iowa citizen. The defendant made a direct attack, going to Missouri to argue that that state did not have personal jurisdiction over it. After the parties argued the issue, the Missouri court held that it had personal jurisdiction. The defendant then refused to participate further in the Missouri proceedings. The court in Missouri then had no choice but to enter default judgment against the defendant. The plaintiff then sought to enforce the Missouri judgment in Iowa,[34] and the defendant raised a collateral attack there, asserting that the Missouri judgment was no good because Missouri had lacked personal jurisdiction.

The Supreme Court held that the Missouri judgment was entitled to enforcement. Under the doctrine of issue preclusion (or collateral estoppel),[35] a party gets one chance to litigate an issue. Once it has been litigated and determined, the disgruntled party may appeal the decision, but may not relitigate it in another court. In *Baldwin*, the defendant litigated the question of personal jurisdiction in a direct attack in Missouri. Thus, it

---

[33] 283 U.S. 522 (1931).

[34] Actually, the Missouri and Iowa proceedings were in federal court in those states. That fact, however, does not affect the personal jurisdiction issue.

[35] See §11.3. In fact, the Court used the term *res judicata*, but did so as a generic term that includes collateral estoppel. More modern terminology refers to collateral estoppel as issue preclusion.

could not relitigate that issue in a collateral attack in Iowa. It should have appealed the Missouri ruling in Missouri. The defendant in *Baldwin* mixed approaches. Having lost in a direct attack, it tried a collateral attack. The doctrine of issue preclusion prohibits this.

The lesson is clear: Once a defendant chooses to make a direct attack, she has to follow through in that state — either with an immediate appeal on the personal jurisdiction issue (if that is allowed) or with a decision on the merits followed by an appeal on the personal jurisdiction issue.[36] This lesson flows from the fact that every court has jurisdiction to determine whether it has jurisdiction. If a litigant does not like the determination made, it must appeal, and not attempt a collateral attack.[37]

§6.4   Challenging Subject Matter Jurisdiction

As with a challenge to personal jurisdiction, a challenge to subject matter jurisdiction can be direct or collateral. A defendant makes a direct attack under Rule 12(b)(1), usually through a motion to dismiss for lack of subject matter jurisdiction. In cases removed from state court to federal court, it is the *plaintiff*, if anyone, who asserts that the case does not belong in federal court. See §4.8. Under Rule 12(h)(3), the court must dismiss if it "determines at any time that it lacks subject-matter jurisdiction." See §6.2 (especially *Principle Number 3*). Indeed, that rule also makes it clear that the court has the duty to raise the issue of subject matter jurisdiction *sua sponte*. So even if a party fails to assert a lack of subject matter jurisdiction, the court must dismiss whenever it discovers that the case does not invoke such jurisdiction. See §4.3. Accordingly, it is clear that the defendant can assert a lack of subject matter jurisdiction for the first time after entry of judgment, either at the trial court or on appeal.[38] See §4.3.

These facts have led to this famous catechism: "Subject matter jurisdiction is not waivable; it can be raised for the first time anytime." This assertion is absolutely correct in direct attacks. It may require some

---

[36] The defendant in *Baldwin* would have been all right even if it had defaulted on the merits, so long as it had appealed the judgment in Missouri on the basis of the personal jurisdiction issue. The problem was that it submitted the issue for decision in Missouri and then failed to follow through.

[37] An appeal of the decision in the court in which the direct attack is made is not a collateral attack. It is considered part of the direct attack.

[38] Such a challenge is still a direct attack (as opposed to a collateral attack) because it takes place in the original action. There cannot be a collateral attack without a second (or collateral) litigation. An appeal is not a collateral attack. It is a continuation of the litigation, not a new litigation.

amendment, however, when we consider collateral attacks. Before doing that, however, consider how wasteful and inefficient the principle is.

Because subject matter jurisdiction is not a waivable defense, even the party who brought the case in federal court can appeal an adverse judgment after trial by asserting lack of subject matter jurisdiction. In the venerable case of *Capron v. Van Noorden*,[39] the plaintiff sued in federal court, allegedly invoking diversity of citizenship jurisdiction. After losing at trial, however, the plaintiff appealed, asserting that there never had been diversity of citizenship in the case. It turns out that the plaintiff was correct, and the Supreme Court held that the case had to be dismissed, notwithstanding that the judiciary (and parties) had invested considerable resources in trying the case. The result is the same with a defendant who removes a case to federal court. In *American Fire & Casualty Co. v. Finn*,[40] the defendant removed and lost at trial in federal court. It then appealed because, as it turns out, there was no federal subject matter jurisdiction. The Supreme Court again held that the case had to be remanded to state court because there was no federal subject matter jurisdiction.

In addition to wasting resources, this rule opens the door to some outrageous tactics. Suppose the plaintiff alleges that she and the defendant are of diverse citizenship. The defendant, however, knows that the plaintiff is incorrect about her citizenship and that, in fact, there is no diversity. The defendant fails to reveal this fact and tries the case. If she wins at trial, the defendant will say nothing about the jurisdictional problem. If she loses, however, the defendant may reveal her true citizenship and appeal because of the lack of subject matter jurisdiction. Although the concealment may create problems under professional ethics rules, or under Rule 11, see §7.6, the judgment will be set aside.[41] So too, some defendants have waited to assert a lack of subject matter jurisdiction until after the state statute of limitations has run. Even in such a case, if in fact the federal court lacked subject matter jurisdiction, it must dismiss the case, and the plaintiff might be left with no remedy in state court.[42]

Reacting to cases such as these, some commentators have argued that litigants should be estopped from raising a lack of subject matter jurisdiction, at least in cases involving bad faith.[43] Such arguments have gone

---

[39] 6 U.S. 126 (1804).

[40] 341 U.S. 6 (1951).

[41] *See, e.g.*, Mennen Co. v. Atlantic Mut. Ins. Co., 147 F.3d 287 (3d Cir. 1998); Rubin v. Buckman, 727 F.2d 71 (3d Cir. 1984).

[42] *See, e.g.*, Wojan v. General Motors Corp., 851 F.2d 969 (7th Cir. 1988).

[43] *See, e.g.*, Dan Dobbs, *Beyond Bootstrap: Foreclosing the Issue of Subject Matter Jurisdiction Before Final Judgment*, 51 Minn. L. Rev. 491 (1967); Comment, *Second Bites at the Jurisdictional Apple: A Proposal for Preventing False Assertions of Diversity of Citizenship*, 41 Hastings L.J. 1417 (1990).

nowhere, however, and the principle that a case must be dismissed "whenever" it appears that there is no subject matter jurisdiction remains vital for direct attacks.[44]

But what about collateral attacks on subject matter jurisdiction? Can a court's purported lack of subject matter jurisdiction provide a basis for attacking a judgment in a separate suit? Here, it is helpful to recognize that such collateral attacks on subject matter jurisdiction might come up in two ways: (1) cases in which the parties litigated the subject matter jurisdiction issue in the first suit and (2) cases in which the issue was not raised in the first case.

As to the former class of cases, the rule is basically the same as it is with challenges to personal jurisdiction. As we saw in §6.3, the Supreme Court held in *Baldwin v. Iowa State Traveling Men's Assn.*[45] that once the issue of a court's personal jurisdiction had been litigated and determined, it could not be attacked in a collateral proceeding. The reason was the doctrine of issue preclusion — the rule that a litigant has one chance to litigate an issue — either in a direct or collateral attack. Once it is litigated, the party cannot relitigate the question. See §11.3.

The analogous case concerning subject matter jurisdiction is *Durfee v. Duke*,[46] which involved a dispute over the ownership of land along the Missouri River, which forms the state line between Missouri and Nebraska. The dispute focused on whether the land was in Missouri or Nebraska. (The result would depend upon why the river had changed its course.[47]) In the initial case, Durfee sued Duke in state court in Nebraska. That court had subject matter jurisdiction *only* if the disputed land was in Nebraska. The parties litigated the issue and the court determined that the land was in Nebraska. The disgruntled Duke appealed to the Nebraska Supreme Court, which affirmed.

Duke did not, however, seek further review by the U.S. Supreme Court. Instead, he launched a collateral attack by bringing a second suit — against Durfee — in a Missouri state court. He sought an order of quiet title, arguing that the land was in Missouri. Durfee removed the case to the federal court. This case ultimately went to the U.S. Supreme Court, which held that Missouri had no authority to redetermine the question of Nebraska's

---

[44] Two cases seemed to demonstrate adoption of such an estoppel approach. *See* DiFrischia v. New York Cent. R.R., 279 F.2d 141 (3d Cir. 1960); Klee v. Pittsburgh & W. Va. Ry. Co., 22 F.R.D. 252 (W.D. Pa. 1958). The "trend" amounted to nothing. In fact, the Third Circuit later expressly rejected *DiFrischia*. Rubin v. Buckman, 727 F.2d 71 (3d Cir. 1984).

[45] 283 U.S. 522 (1931).

[46] 375 U.S. 106 (1963).

[47] This sort of thing happens more frequently than one might guess (especially, it seems, with regard to Nebraska borders). In §12.6.2, we see a dispute about whether a corporation's principal place of business (and therefore its citizenship) was in Nebraska or Iowa. The uncertainty, again, came from the Missouri River's changing course. Owen Equipment & Erection Co. v. Kroger, 437 U.S. 365, 373 n.5 (1978).

subject matter jurisdiction. The Nebraska judgment was entitled to full faith and credit on those issues "fully and fairly litigated and finally decided in the court which rendered the original judgment."[48] Just as we saw with regard to personal jurisdiction, §6.3, a court has jurisdiction to determine its own jurisdiction. A litigant who does not like the result must appeal the judgment, and not engage in a collateral attack.

The Supreme Court's opinion in *Durfee* recognized, however, that this principle of finality was not inflexible. There can be exceptions when that principle is simply overborne by other considerations.[49] For instance, a state court's determination that it had subject matter jurisdiction was subject to collateral attack in a federal bankruptcy court because Congress had given the federal bankruptcy court exclusive subject matter jurisdiction.[50] There, permitting the state court to determine the issue plainly violated the exclusive jurisdiction of the federal forum. Absent such a clear violation of an important policy, however, the principle of finality should prevail.

Now to the more difficult situation: What about a collateral attack on subject matter jurisdiction when the issue of subject matter jurisdiction was *not* litigated in the first case?[51] Can a party raise the issue for the first time in a collateral attack? Straightforward principles of issue preclusion would say yes; after all, the issue was not litigated and determined, and therefore cannot be the subject of issue preclusion. See §11.3.2.

But the answer from the Supreme Court seems to be that a party may *not* raise the issue in a collateral attack in such circumstances. In *Chicot County Drainage District v. Baxter State Bank*,[52] a statute purported to establish federal subject matter jurisdiction. No one had any reason to suspect a problem with the statute, so the parties litigated the merits of the dispute in federal court. Later, in a completely unrelated action, that statute was stricken as unconstitutional. So the party that lost the first case, understandably, mounted a collateral attack on the judgment. After all, the federal court in that case had exercised subject matter jurisdiction based upon a statute now declared unconstitutional. Surprisingly, however, in *Chicot County*, the Court did not permit the collateral attack.

---

[48] *Durfee*, 375 U.S. at 111.

[49] The principle of finality of a judgment (i.e., its res judicata or collateral estoppel effect) is always subject to being overridden by other factors. The Court noted this fact in *Durfee*, 375 U.S. at 114. See §11.4.

[50] Kalb v. Feuerstein, 308 U.S. 433 (1940). *Kalb* preceded *Durfee*. The Court in *Durfee* discussed *Kalb* as an exception to the principle of finality on which the holding in that case was based. It should be noted, however, that the subject matter jurisdiction issue in *Kalb* evidently was not litigated in the state court action. *Durfee*, 375 U.S. at 114 n.12.

[51] We know that a party could raise the subject matter jurisdiction issue for the first time on appeal from the first judgment, but that would be part of a direct attack. See §6.3.

[52] 308 U.S. 371 (1940). This case was decided the same day as *Kalb v. Feuerstein*, note 50 above.

According to the Court, the party should have challenged the constitutionality of the jurisdictional statute in the first case.[53] This result seems quite harsh, since there was no reason to suspect that there was no subject matter jurisdiction in the first case, but the Court has never questioned *Chicot County* since.

There is one final subset of this question. What if the first case ended in a default judgment, in which there was no litigation of anything related to the merits of the claim? It may be one thing to say — as *Chicot County* evidently does — that parties who litigated an underlying dispute in the initial case should have raised a problem with subject matter jurisdiction (even if doing so would have required prescience). But is it another thing to say that a defendant who defaults should be precluded from raising a subject matter jurisdiction defense? Such a defendant has litigated *nothing at all.*[54] Such a defendant would be permitted to raise a collateral attack on the issue of personal jurisdiction. Nonetheless, there is little support for a collateral attack on subject matter jurisdiction in this situation.[55]

But why should there be a difference in the treatment of personal and subject matter jurisdiction in default cases? Perhaps the answer lies in the profound difference between those two defenses. Personal jurisdiction protects defendants from litigation in an inappropriate place. It is a waivable defense. If the defendant does not raise it, the court need not address it. In a default case, the defendant has raised nothing, so the issue of personal jurisdiction is simply not before the judge. Subject matter jurisdiction is different, for reasons discussed in §6.1. A court is under a continuing obligation to determine whether it has subject matter jurisdiction — regardless of whether any party raises the question. Indeed, it should be the first thing the judge addresses, as soon as the complaint is filed. Perhaps, then, we engage in the supposition that the court has made a determination on this issue — even if the parties do not raise it, and even if the defendant defaults. Put bluntly, a court has no business

[53] Some may suggest that this result is proper because claim preclusion (also known as res judicata) precludes relitigation not only of issues actually litigated and determined in the first case, but also of those issues that could have been raised in the first case. This seems wrong, however, because the question here is one implicating issue preclusion (also known as collateral estoppel), not claim preclusion. And issue preclusion is proper only as to questions actually litigated and determined in the first case. See §11.3.2.

[54] In *Chicot County*, the claimants did not appear in the first case. *See* 103 F.2d 847 (8th Cir. 1939). Others did, however, and the underlying merits were litigated vigorously. The Supreme Court did not mention the claimants' absence or a default judgment. Nonetheless, Professor (now Judge) Karen Moore regards *Chicot County* as a default judgment case. *See* Karen Moore, *Collateral Attack on Subject Matter Jurisdiction: A Critique of the Restatement (Second) of Judgments*, 66 Cornell L. Rev. 534, 553 (1981).

[55] *See* Restatement (Second) of Judgments §12, comment f (1982). The Restatement (Second) of Judgments §66(2) would permit a collateral attack on a default judgment for lack of subject matter jurisdiction unless doing so "would impair another person's substantial interest of reliance on the judgment."

entering a default judgment unless it has already satisfied itself that it has subject matter jurisdiction. So maybe we are justified in assuming that the issue was, if not actively litigated, at least determined in the first case, and is therefore entitled to finality.

§6.5　Rejection of Hypothetical Jurisdiction

For many years, lower federal courts employed "hypothetical jurisdiction" to avoid difficult questions of subject matter jurisdiction. Under this doctrine, if the decision on the merits would be easy, and would be unfavorable to the party seeking to invoke federal subject matter jurisdiction, the court would bypass the difficult jurisdictional question and decide the case on the merits.[56] After all, if there were no jurisdiction, the same party would win anyway. In 1998, in *Steel Co. v. Citizens for a Better Environment*,[57] the Supreme Court disapproved of this practice. Speaking for the majority, Justice Scalia concluded: "We decline to endorse such an approach because it carries the courts beyond the bounds of authorized judicial action and thus offends fundamental principles of separation of power."[58] In other words, a court of limited subject matter jurisdiction cannot rule on the merits until it is convinced that it has power to speak — that is, until it is convinced that it has jurisdiction.

The following year, however, the Court held that while federal courts must determine jurisdictional questions before proceeding to the merits of the case, they do not necessarily have to determine subject matter jurisdiction before dismissing for lack of personal jurisdiction. In *Ruhrgas AG v. Marathon Oil Co.*,[59] the question of subject matter jurisdiction was especially difficult. Indeed, it was a question of first impression. The personal jurisdiction issue, in contrast, was relatively straightforward and did not raise a difficult question of state law, because the state long-arm statute

---

[56] *See, e.g.*, Isby v. Bayh, 75 F.3d 1191 (7th Cir. 1996) (because there would be no practical difference in the outcome of the case, court would disregard potentially difficult jurisdictional questions and proceed directly to the merits); Burlington Northern R.R. Co. v. Interstate Commerce Commn., 985 F.2d 589 (D.C. Cir. 1993) (when the merits of a case are clearly against the party seeking to invoke subject matter jurisdiction and the jurisdictional question is exceptionally difficult, the court of appeals would rule on the merits without addressing the jurisdictional issue).

[57] 523 U.S. 83 (1998).

[58] 523 U.S. at 93. On the other hand, "where the jurisdictional issue and substantive issues are so intertwined that the question of jurisdiction is dependent on the resolution of factual issues going to the merits, the jurisdictional determination should await a determination of the relevant facts on either a motion going to the merits or at trial." McGraw v. United States, 281 F.3d 997, 1001 (9th Cir. 2002), *quoting* Augustine v. United States, 704 F.2d 1074, 1077 (9th Cir. 1983), *amended on other grounds*, 298 F.3d 754 (9th Cir. 2002).

[59] 526 U.S. 574 (1999).

reached to the constitutional limit. Under these circumstances, the Court held, it was not an abuse of discretion to determine that the court lacked personal jurisdiction without addressing subject matter jurisdiction.

The Court may have retreated a bit from the strictness of *Steel Company* in its 2007 decision in *Sinochem International Co. Ltd. v. Malaysia International Shipping.*[60] In an early *forum non conveniens* case, the Supreme Court had said that that doctrine "can never apply if there is absence of jurisdiction."[61] In reaction, some lower federal courts concluded that they could not dismiss under *forum non conveniens* until they had concluded that they had personal jurisdiction over the defendants. In *Sinochem*, the Court rejected this approach, and held that a court may, "when judicial economy so warrant[s]," bypass questions of personal and subject matter jurisdiction and dispose of a suit under the doctrine of *forum non conveniens.*[62]

[60] 127 S. Ct. 1184 (2007).
[61] Gulf Oil Corp. v. Gilbert, 330 U.S. 501, 505 (1947).
[62] *Sinochem*, 127 S. Ct. at 1192.

Chapter 7

Pleadings, Amended Pleadings, and Judgments Based upon Pleadings

§7.1 Defining the Issue

In modern civil litigation, there are very few surprises at trial. Though depictions of trials in movies and on television often show surprise witnesses and shocking new revelations from the witness stand, such occurrences are extremely rare in the real world. Why? Modern procedure has abandoned the notion of "trial by ambush." Modern procedure is geared toward full disclosure, in an effort to ferret out the truth, rather than to reward clever lawyers who can seize upon surprise to their client's advantage. Generally, a case goes to trial only after months (indeed often years) of pretrial litigation. Much of that litigation constitutes an education process, in which each party learns every contention that each other party will make if the case does go to trial.

That education process starts with the pleading stage. Pleadings are documents in which claimants set forth their claims and defending parties respond to the claims and raise defenses. Though in earlier times pleadings were expected to perform several functions, as we will see in §7.2, today their principal role is to inform the other parties of each party's contentions. Under the Federal Rules, the pleading stage is relatively brief, and gives way to the discovery phase, which we study in Chapter 8. It is useful to consider pleadings and discovery as two phases of the education process for the parties. While pleadings set the basic boundaries and tenor of the litigation, in discovery the parties learn the details and find whether the real-world evidence supports the contentions they made in their pleadings.

Pleadings are the gatekeepers of the judicial system. The plaintiff must allege a cognizable claim in her pleading (usually called the *complaint*) to get the case into the litigation stream. If she cannot do this, the case can be dismissed at the pleading stage, without wasting litigant and judicial time in discovery and other aspects of litigation. Much of the historical development of pleading reflects a debate about how high the pleading barrier should be. Generally, older procedure systems used pleadings to erect a very high barrier to entry, sometimes thwarting efforts of deserving plaintiffs to obtain justice. Modern procedure has lowered that barrier considerably, and has made it easier for the plaintiff to get past the pleading stage and get to discovery. This policy choice is not without critics. Given the expense of the discovery phase of litigation, some commentators and judges believe that the pleading barrier should be raised to make it more difficult to state a claim and get the case into the litigation stream.

After being sued, the defendant must respond in a timely and proper fashion. She does so either by making a motion or by filing and serving a pleading (usually called the *answer*). Failure to make an appropriate response puts the defendant at risk of losing by default. Issues properly asserted by the plaintiff in her complaint and denied by the defendant in her answer are said to be "joined," and the case can go forward into the discovery phase of litigation on such issues.

Undeniably, pleading practice is less important than it was in earlier eras. And undeniably, pleading practice today is more forgiving than it was in earlier eras. For example, as we will see, modern procedure is generally liberal about allowing parties to amend their pleadings as the case evolves. But do not conclude that pleading practice is unimportant. Pleadings matter, and a lawyer can get her client (and herself) into serious trouble by neglecting the requirements of the pleading rules.

In §7.2, we see that there are two major approaches to pleading in the United States: "code" pleading and the Federal Rules. As always, the Federal Rules govern practice in the federal courts. States are free, of course, to adopt their own rules about all matters of procedure, including pleading, for use in their courts. The Federal Rules on pleadings have been influential, however, and most states have adopted the Federal Rules provisions in this regard. Some states, however, have rejected the Federal Rules approach, and others have not adopted all aspects of the Federal Rules on pleadings. As a result, pleading practice can vary substantially from state to state. Throughout this chapter, we focus on the Federal Rules, but also note dominant variations adopted in code states.

§7.2   Evolution of the Role of Pleading

Through the history of Anglo-American civil litigation, there have been three great theories of pleading: (1) common law pleading, (2) "code" pleading, and (3) Federal Rules pleading. Code and Federal Rules pleading are both vital in the United States today. Though no American jurisdiction uses common law pleading today, we need a bit of historical exposure to it for two reasons. First, vestiges of it remain and influence some of what we do today. Second, both code and Federal Rules pleading emerged in reaction to the untoward restrictions imposed by common law pleading.

Common law pleading held sway in England for centuries and dominated in the colonies and the first century of the United States. It was based for the most part on the "writ system." A plaintiff wishing to sue had to select the appropriate substantive writ for her claim. She asked the court to issue that writ for her type of case, and then had to plead the "form of action" for her kind of case. There was a different writ and form of action for assumpsit, trover, trespass — in short, for all the recognized claims. In common law practice, the parties had no plenary right to discovery. That is, there were no formal litigation mechanisms for finding out what relevant information the other party (or third parties) might have.[1]

That meant that the pleadings were the principal vehicle for developing facts and narrowing issues to be tried. With common law pleading, the parties went back and forth through round after round of allegations. This exercise was aimed at framing a single disputed factual issue, which was then tried. What happened, though, if that issue did not fit the writ the plaintiff chose at the outset of the case? This was a common occurrence, since the parties, without discovery, had to make an educated guess at what facts would be established at trial. Moreover, the writs were extremely narrow, and it was easy for a plaintiff to establish at trial a right to recovery that was different from the writ she had chosen. The price to pay for this "variance" was steep — the plaintiff lost.

○   The common law writ of "trespass" basically addressed intentional torts. The common law writ of "trespass on the case" basically addressed negligence. Plaintiff was injured when the carriage in which she was riding collided with another carriage. She sued the driver of the vehicle under the writ of trespass on the case; her theory was that the driver had been negligent and that the negligence caused the collision. At trial, however, the evidence established that the driver had collided with the other vehicle intentionally, in an effort to injure the driver of the other vehicle. Though Plaintiff was injured and the driver was clearly responsible for her injuries, it turns out that she sued under the wrong writ. She should have pursued a writ of trespass, not trespass on the case. The variance was fatal; Plaintiff lost the case.

Common law pleading put a premium on arcane niceties. It was an excruciating exercise, better calculated to lead to a decision based upon technicalities than on the merits. Pleading became something of a goal in itself, more important than the fact-finding to be done by the jury. Common law pleading elevated form over substance and often hindered the administration of justice.

There were many cries for reform both in England and the United States. The most extraordinary reformer on this side of the Atlantic was David Dudley Field,[2] a lawyer in Albany, New York. With remarkable diligence, he wrote a codification of reforms that was adopted in New York in 1848. To this day, the codification is known to some as the "Field Code," and is

---

[1] Modern litigation, in contrast, is characterized by broad discovery rights, as we see in Chapter 8.

[2] The Fields were a very impressive lot. David Dudley was the principal law reformer in the United States in the nineteenth century. His brother Henry was a world traveler and writer of widely read books on exotic places like Gibraltar. Another brother, Cyrus, played an important role in establishing the trans-Atlantic telegraph cable. And don't forget brother Stephen — he served as an Associate Justice on the United States Supreme Court for 34 years (and wrote the opinion in *Pennoyer v. Neff*, which we studied in detail in §2.4.1).

the basis for the phrase "code pleading." The starting point of Field's effort was to abolish the common law writs and forms of action. Then, Field limited the number of pleadings; instead of round after round, there would be a complaint by the plaintiff and an answer by the defendant (and sometimes a "reply" by the plaintiff). Most important, Field recognized that pleadings were a poor vehicle for determining what actually had happened in the real world. So his reform shifted the role of fact-development from the pleading stage to a discovery stage. Pleadings, Field thought, should state facts and should play one central role: putting the other parties on notice of one's contentions.

By the beginning of the twentieth century, code pleading had largely supplanted common law pleading in the United States. But some courts were unable to handle a better system. So steeped in the hypertechnical (and often silly) ways of common law pleading, some judges imported nonsense into code pleading. At worst, they stifled the reform effort by replacing one set of arcane rules with another. We see how they did this in §7.3.2. For now, it is sufficient to note that problems with implementing Field's vision led to another call for reform.

That call was answered by the Federal Rules in 1938. Federal Rules pleading is not a revolutionary departure from the Field approach. In fact, the Federal Rules largely refine the code-pleading approach. Again, there is a limited number of pleadings, pleadings are limited to the role of putting parties on notice, and fact development is accomplished by broad discovery provisions. The difference between Federal Rules pleading and code pleading is largely confined to the detail with which one is expected to plead. As discussed in §7.3.2, the code states — even today — generally require a statement of the *facts* underlying a claim, which generally entails slightly more detailed allegations than the Federal Rules. The Federal Rules do not require a statement of *facts* but merely a "short and plain statement of the claim, showing that the pleader is entitled to relief."[3] On the other hand, in 2007, the Supreme Court sent a discordant message with a decision in which it held that a claimant must state "facts" supporting a "plausible" claim. We discuss that case and its potential impact in §7.3.2.

Obviously, the Federal Rules apply to all civil litigation in the federal courts. Each state is free to determine its own pleading rules for its courts. Most states model their pleading provisions on the Federal Rules. A few states, however, including California, still use code pleading. The modern approach — whether under the Federal Rules or code pleading — avoids the silly arcane rules of common law pleading. It adopts a simplified approach to pleading and a limited role for it, which goes hand in hand with broad discovery mechanisms. It also embraces liberal amendment

---

[3] Bell Atlantic Corp. v. Twombly, 127 S. Ct. 1955 (2007).

rules, which we see in §7.6, to allow the parties to adjust and adapt to the facts as they develop throughout the litigation stream.

§7.3   The Pleadings in Modern Practice

§7.3.1   Matters of Form

Modern pleading rules — in both code states and under the Federal Rules (and, obviously, states that adopt the Federal Rules) — limit the number of pleadings each party may file in a case. Federal Rule 7(a) provides for only three basic pleadings: the complaint (in Rule 7(a)(1)), the answer (which may be filed in response to various claims, as seen in Rule 7(a)(2), (3), (4), and (6)), and the reply (in Rule 7(a)(7)), which will be filed only if the court orders a party to do so.[4] Thus, a "motion," by which a party asks the court to enter a particular order, is not a pleading. We revisit this point in §7.3.3.

Before looking at the individual pleadings (and related motions), note that Federal Rule 10 gives general guidance for the form of all pleadings. Rule 10(b) requires the party to set forth her allegations in "numbered paragraphs" (as opposed to lettered paragraphs), "each limited as far as practicable to a single set of circumstances." In addition, Rules 10(b) and 10(c) expressly allow incorporation by reference of paragraphs. Rule 10(c) also provides that parties may attach a written instrument as an exhibit to a pleading, and that the instrument thus is considered a part of the pleading for all purposes.

These provisions are helpful. If the case involves a dispute over a contract, the plaintiff may simply append a copy of the contract to the complaint. It is thus considered part of the complaint, without the make-work of having to retype the entire contract into the complaint. In addition, rather than reiterate allegations of a paragraph as needed in different parts of a pleading, the party simply incorporates the previous allegation by reference. For example:

- Plaintiff's complaint sets forth two claims against Defendant. In Paragraph 5 of the complaint, which was part of the first claim, Plaintiff made

---

[4] The Rule also allows the "third-party complaint," which is a mechanism by which another party may be added to the dispute in limited circumstances, as we see in §12.6.2. Aside from that, Rule 7(a) also talks of answers to various claims, such as the third-party claim and a cross-claim, which we study in §12.5.2. So we say there are three "basic" pleadings (complaint, answer, and reply) because those are the pleadings asserted by the plaintiff and defendant in a typical two-party case.

allegations that are also relevant to her second claim. In stating the second claim, say in Paragraph 10 of the complaint, she need not retype Paragraph 5, but may simply allege "Plaintiff here incorporates by reference the allegations of Paragraph 5."

Rule 10(a) concerns the form of all pleadings, and requires that each "must have a caption with the court's name, a title, a file number, and a Rule 7(a) designation." When a plaintiff files a civil action, the clerk of the court assigns a file number (or "case number" or "docket number") to the litigation. This number must appear on every document in that case. The file number usually is preceded by the designation "Civ.," showing that it is a civil (not a criminal) case. After that, the first number of the file number is a two-digit indication of the year in which the case was filed. That number is followed by the case's specific number, which is assigned in the order in which cases are filed in that district in that year. So the 305th case filed in the district in the year 2010 would have file number: "Civ. 10-00305." Following this number, the clerk will affix the initials of the district judge to whom the case is assigned. Assignments are made at random among the judges in the district.[5] The caption for the complaint in this fictitious case in the Southern District of New York would look like this:

United States District Court
Southern District of New York

Roger Sterling,	)	
Plaintiff,	)	
	)	Civ. 10-00305-JG[6]
vs.	)	
	)	COMPLAINT
Don Draper,	)	
Defendant.	)	

[5] Each district has a Local Rule providing that related litigation may be assigned to the district judge to whom the first related case was assigned. So if Judge Gooblatz was assigned the first case involving an airplane crash, all other cases in that district involving the same crash would not be assigned at random to other judges, but would be assigned to Judge Gooblatz. This process is often called *low-numbering*, because the subsequent cases are sent to the judge to whom the lowest numbered (that is, earliest filed) case was assigned.

[6] These are the judge's initials. In some districts, the clerk will also assign a magistrate judge to the case, whose initials may be shown in parentheses after the judge's initials. We discuss the role of magistrate judges in §8.6.

The body of the complaint would then set forth Sterling's claims in numbered paragraphs. The caption for the defendant's answer would look the same except for indicating "answer" instead of "complaint." It would set forth Draper's responses to the complaint and affirmative defenses in numbered paragraphs.

Rule 11(a) provides, *inter alia*, that "[u]nless a rule or statute specifically states otherwise, a pleading need not be verified or accompanied by an affidavit." A "verified" pleading is one executed under penalty of perjury (as is an affidavit). Thus, this provision of Rule 11(a) means that, generally, parties are not required to plead under oath. Pleadings can be executed on the basis of the best information and belief of the parties. As we see in §7.7, pleadings ordinarily are not even signed by the parties; they are signed by the lawyer. Only if a Rule or statute requires must the party execute a verified pleading. (One of the very few instances off verified pleading in federal court is found in Rule 23.1, which concerns a specialized kind of litigation known as a shareholder derivative suit.) Now we turn to the requirements of each pleading.

§7.3.2   The Complaint

Under the Federal Rules, and under the law of nearly every state, the principal pleading by the plaintiff — and the initial pleading in any case — is the *complaint*. A few states use different terms for this pleading, such as *petition* or *declaration*. Under Federal Rule 3, the case is commenced when the plaintiff files the complaint. (Recall from §3.3.1 that the plaintiff must then arrange to have a summons and a copy of the complaint (together, called *process*) served on the defendant.) Federal Rule 8(a) sets forth the three requirements of any complaint: (1) a statement of the grounds of subject matter jurisdiction, (2) a statement of the claim, and (3) a demand for the relief sought. A complaint lacking any of the three requirements will be dismissed, usually "without prejudice" (or "with leave to amend"), which means that the plaintiff will be permitted to file an amended complaint in which she corrects the problem. Of the three requirements, the second — the statement of the claim — is worthy of the most attention, because it is the part most frequently open to challenge as insufficient.

It is worth noting that Rule 8(a) is not limited to complaints. Indeed, the word "complaint" does not even appear in Rule 8(a). Rather, that Rule provides requirements for any "pleading that states a claim for relief." In other words, it gives the rules for the assertion of *any claim*. The complaint will set forth an original claim, and thus is subject to Rule 8(a). In Chapter 12, we discuss other documents in which a party asserts a claim — including the counterclaim, crossclaim, and third-party claim.

Each of these is asserted *after* the plaintiff has commenced the case with the filing of the complaint that invokes the subject matter jurisdiction of the federal court. When you see these claims in Chapter 12, remind yourself that the requirements of Rule 8(a) apply. For convenience, we discuss Rule 8(a) in the context of the complaint.

Rule 8(a)(1): Statement of Grounds of Subject Matter Jurisdiction

The requirement of Rule 8(a)(1) should not cause any trouble to the careful lawyer. The complaint must contain a "short and plain statement of the grounds for the court's jurisdiction. . . ."[7] The reference is to subject matter jurisdiction, not to personal jurisdiction.[8] As we studied in Chapter 4, federal courts are of limited subject matter jurisdiction, and the plaintiff has the burden of establishing that her claims can be heard by a federal court. For starters, she must satisfy Rule 8(a)(1). Though the Rule provides for a "short and plain" statement, counsel should not make it too short or conclusory. For instance, it would be insufficient simply to allege "there is diversity of citizenship jurisdiction over this dispute." How does one know how much detail to include?

At least a partial answer lies in the forms, which are found in an Appendix to the Federal Rules. You can find them in the Rules booklet you purchased for this course, behind the Rules themselves. The drafters of the Rules provide these forms as examples for lawyers and judges. Rule 84 says that the forms "suffice under these rules and illustrate the simplicity and brevity that these rules contemplate." Thus, you will never encounter trouble if you use one of the forms; by definition, they are sufficient.

Certainly, regarding allegations of subject matter jurisdiction, there is no good reason to make life more difficult than the forms allow. Form 7 provides appropriate allegations of subject matter jurisdiction. Note the simplicity of Form 7(b) for stating federal question jurisdiction. Form 7(a) addresses diversity of citizenship jurisdiction, and permits the allegation that the plaintiff is a citizen of a particular state, the defendant is a citizen of a particular state, and that the matter in controversy, not counting interest and costs, exceeds the sum specified in 28 U.S.C. §1332. Thus, there is

---

[7] The Rule provides an exception when the court already has subject matter jurisdiction. This exception will not apply to the complaint, because it is the pleading that first vests the court with subject matter jurisdiction.

[8] 2 Moore's Federal Practice §8.03[1]. Some state rules add a requirement that the plaintiff allege grounds of personal jurisdiction if the defendant is not a resident of the forum.

no need to allege *why* a party is a citizen of a particular state or *why* the matter in controversy exceeds $75,000.[9]

A word to the wise here: Use the proper terminology in pleading diversity of citizenship jurisdiction. The word "resides" should never appear here. It is the parties' *citizenship* that is relevant to diversity of citizenship; residence is relevant to venue, which you are not required to allege under Rule 8(a). In addition, in alleging a corporation's citizenship, you must allege both its state of incorporation *and* (*not "or"*) the one state in which it has its principal place of business. Do not allege things like "headquarters" or "licensed to do business" or any other irrelevant fact. Section 1332 is absolutely clear on what terms must be alleged (as is Form 7(a)). If any of this is fuzzy, review §4.5.3.

And if you don't believe me, read *Randazzo v. Eagle-Picher Industries, Inc.*[10] In that case, the district court took the admittedly harsh step of dismissing the case *with prejudice* (which means that the plaintiff cannot again assert the claim). The opinion, though amusing, is a chilling indictment of a lawyer who brazenly failed to take advantage of an opportunity to plead diversity of citizenship correctly. Criticizing counsel's failure to understand the difference between "and" and "or" in alleging the citizenship of a corporation, the judge concludes that the plaintiff's lawyer's "familiarity with . . . §1332 could be no more than a friendly wave from a distance visible only through a powerful telescope."[11] That is not a distinction you want to achieve.

Rule 8(a)(3): Demand for Relief Sought

Rule 8(a)(3) simply requires the plaintiff to make her "demand for the relief sought." This demand is often called the *prayer* for relief. When the plaintiff demands a monetary recovery (as opposed to equitable relief such as an injunction), the demand is sometimes called the *ad damnum* clause. By common practice, the plaintiff puts the demand for judgment at the end of the complaint, preceded by the word "Wherefore" or "Therefore." Form 10 in the Appendix of Forms to the Federal Rules contains a classic demand: "Therefore, the plaintiff demands judgment against defendant for $[____], plus interest and costs."

Damages usually are pleaded as a lump sum. In some circumstances, however, such as a demand for "special damages," the plaintiff must plead in detail. (We discuss pleading such special matters in §7.3.5.) There is nothing in Rule 8(a) (or anywhere else) that requires the plaintiff to plead

---

[9] Remember, under §1332, the amount in controversy must *exceed* $75,000, not including interest and costs. So an allegation for exactly $75,000 will fail to invoke diversity of citizenship jurisdiction. See §4.5.3.

[10] 117 F.R.D. 557 (E.D. Pa. 1987).

[11] *Id.* at 558.

damages in a particular amount. Often, a plaintiff will put a dollar figure in her complaint. But some plaintiffs simply demand "damages in an amount to be shown at trial." Of course, in a diversity of citizenship case, the plaintiff will have alleged in satisfying Rule 8(a)(1) that the amount in controversy exceeds $75,000. There is nothing wrong with doing that and then demanding judgment in an amount to be determined at trial.[12]

Of course, the plaintiff might not be limited to seeking damages. Instead (or perhaps in addition), she may seek equitable relief, such as an injunction, declaratory judgment, rescission, reformation, or specific performance. Forms 17, 19, and 20 provide examples of appropriate demands for such relief. As we see in §9.2.2, the relief sought will have a significant impact on whether there is a right to jury trial in federal court.

It is interesting, and perhaps surprising, that the plaintiff's recovery is not limited by what she seeks in her demand for judgment. Federal Rule 54(c) makes it clear that the plaintiff is entitled to recover whatever amount and whatever type of relief shown appropriate at trial, regardless of what she asked for in the demand. There is one exception to this rule, however, which is also set forth in Rule 54(c): In cases of default judgment (discussed in §7.5), the plaintiff cannot recover more (or a different kind of relief) than she sought in her demand for judgment.

- ° *P* files a proper complaint, in which she demands recovery of damages from *D* in an amount of $250,000. Based upon the evidence adduced at trial, the jury returns a verdict in favor of *P* for $350,000 and the judge determines, based upon the evidence presented at trial, that *P* is entitled to an injunction too. This relief — more damages than *P* demanded and a different type of relief than *P* demanded — is appropriate.
- ° On the other hand, if *P* won the same case by default judgment, she could recover no more than $250,000 in damages and could not be granted the injunction (because she did not demand an injunction in her complaint).

Rule 8(a)(2): Statement of the Claim

Under Rule 8(a)(2), the plaintiff must set forth "a short and plain statement of the claim showing that the pleader is entitled to relief." In code states, in contrast, a plaintiff must set forth "a statement of the facts constituting a cause of action." As we noted in §7.2, the Federal Rule provision was a reaction to what some courts in some code states did in applying the code requirement. They created a monster by encrusting the code requirement with arcane definitions of "facts" and "causes of action."

---

[12] Remember that the good faith claim that the amount in controversy exceeds $75,000 will satisfy that requirement of §1332 unless it is "clear to a legal certainty" that the plaintiff cannot recover that much. Such cases are rare. See §4.5.3.

In assessing whether the plaintiff has pleaded enough to satisfy Rule 8(a)(2) or the code requirement of facts constituting a cause of action, it is important to understand that the complaint can be attacked for two kinds of insufficiency: It might be *legally* insufficient or it might be *factually* insufficient. (The difference between the Federal Rules and code approaches is most significant with regard to *factual* sufficiency.) How does the defendant challenge either legal or factual sufficiency of the complaint? We need a bit of terminology here. In federal court, the defendant will make a motion to dismiss for failure to state a claim under Federal Rule 12(b)(6).[13] In many state courts (certainly those following code pleading), she will file a *demurrer*.[14] Technically, in most code states, if she is challenging *legal* sufficiency, she will file a *general demurrer*; and if she is challenging *factual* sufficiency, she will file a *special demurrer*. One more bit of technical jargon: A motion to dismiss under Rule 12(b)(6) in federal court is either "granted" or "denied"; in contrast, a demurrer in most state courts is either "sustained" or "overruled." Again, in federal court, the motion to challenge either factual or legal sufficiency is the motion to dismiss for failure to state a claim under Rule 12(b)(6); there is no such thing as a demurrer in federal court.

Legal Sufficiency. The complaint must state a claim (or, in code states, a "cause of action"). If it does not, the court may dismiss *sua sponte* (which means it may do so on its own, without a motion by a party) or may grant a motion to dismiss under Rule 12(b)(6) (or, in code states, may sustain a general demurrer). If the complaint sets forth several purported claims, only one of which is insufficient, the court may simply dismiss the defective claim. Dismissals of this sort are usually without prejudice, which allows the plaintiff another chance to try to state a legally sufficient claim. At some point, however, if it is clear that the plaintiff cannot state a legally sufficient claim, the court will dismiss with prejudice. Doing so makes perfect sense. If the plaintiff does not have a claim that the law recognizes, it is a complete waste of the defendant's time (and the court's time) to have the litigation go further.

In ruling on legal sufficiency of the complaint (or of an individual claim in the complaint), the court looks only to the face of the complaint. It does

---

[13] The defense of failure to state a claim can be raised anytime through trial (see Rule 12(h)(2)). Usually, the defendant will bring such a motion at the outset, under Rule 12(b)(6), in lieu of an answer. But she can make the motion after answering, in which case it is brought under Rule 12(c), and is called a *motion for judgment on the pleadings*. See §7.3.3.

[14] It is important that law students learn to talk like lawyers. "Demurrer" is pronounced with a short "u," such as that in "fur." It is *not* pronounced with a long "u," such as that in "demure." I learned this lesson the very first day of law school. One of my classmates pronounced the word "demyoorer." The professor said, "It's demurrer; to say demyoorer is the sign of a rank amateur." You don't want to sound like a rank amateur in front of your professor (or, worse yet, in front of a judge or a lawyer with whom you are interviewing for a job). See note 46 below.

not look at evidence. (In this regard, testing the legal sufficiency of the complaint is quite different from a motion for summary judgment under Rule 56, which we study in §9.4. With a motion for summary judgment, the court may look at evidence.[15]) When it looks at the face of the complaint, the court asks: "If the plaintiff proved everything she has alleged here, would she win?" In other words, does the law recognize a right to recover on the facts she has alleged?

If the answer is no, as we just noted, there is no point in having the litigation continue. If the answer is yes, the litigation should continue to see whether plaintiff indeed can demonstrate what she has alleged. Thus, if the court determines that the complaint is legally sufficient, it is *not* saying that the plaintiff wins. It is simply allowing the case to go forward to the next stages of the litigation stream. The plaintiff may ultimately fail to demonstrate the facts necessary to win a judgment. Or the defendant may have a valid defense to the claim. Those considerations — the merits of the case — are for another day. Right now, the court is simply determining whether the plaintiff gets "past the pleading stage" and can engage in further litigation. As the Supreme Court has said, "[T]he issue is not whether a plaintiff will ultimately prevail but whether [she] is entitled to offer evidence to support her claims."[16]

- Suppose relevant law defines *consortium* as "conjugal fellowship and sexual relations between spouses." *P*'s live-in lover is severely injured by the negligence of *D*. *P* sues *D*, seeking damages for loss of consortium. *P* alleges that *D* caused the injuries to the injured person and that the injuries have robbed *P* of conjugal fellowship and sexual relations with the injured person. *P* fails, however, to allege that *P* and the injured person are spouses. The court will grant *D*'s motion to dismiss under Rule 12(b)(6). Why? Because if *P* proved everything she alleged, the law would not allow recovery, because she has not alleged that she and the injured person were spouses. The law only allows recovery for consortium between spouses.

- The court would probably dismiss under Rule 12(b)(6) without prejudice, thus allowing *P* to try again to state a claim. Because *P* and the injured person in fact are not married, she cannot allege that they are spouses. She files an amended complaint, however, alleging what she had alleged in the original complaint and adding the allegation that *P* and the injured person are "live-in lovers." The court will grant *D*'s motion to dismiss under Rule 12(b)(6). Why? Again, if *P* demonstrated everything she has alleged, the law would not allow her to recover, because she and the injured person are not spouses. This time, the court would dismiss with prejudice, and enter final judgment for the defendant.

---

[15] Rule 12(d) provides that if a court does look at matters extraneous to the pleadings in a motion under Rule 12(b)(6), it can convert the motion into one for summary judgment.

[16] Scheuer v. Rhodes, 416 U.S. 232, 236 (1974).

At that point, *P* is free to appeal the final judgment to the court of appeals.[17] There, she can argue that the law ought to be changed to recognize a claim for loss of consortium between persons who are not spouses. In §1.2.2, we discussed the doctrine of precedent, or *stare decisis*. That doctrine provides that appellate courts' pronouncements on matters of law are binding on lower courts within that jurisdiction. The question of whether consortium should be recognized beyond the marital relationship is a question of law. The trial court is not free to change the law, but must apply it as declared by the appellate courts in its jurisdiction. On appeal, however, *P* may certainly attempt to convince the court of appeals to change the law. If so, the appellate court would reverse the judgment and remand the case to the trial court for appropriate proceedings, including trial on the consortium claim. Moreover, from that point on, trial courts in that jurisdiction would have to apply the "new" law.[18] If the appellate court failed to change the law, however, it would affirm the judgment against *P*.

Obviously, counsel for the plaintiff must do her homework on what claims are legally cognizable. She must hit the books — whether statutes or case law — to determine the elements of the claim, and, as we just saw, address the elements in her complaint. You are taking several "substantive" courses during the first year of law school, including Contracts, Torts, and Property. In those courses, you learn (among other things) the elements of various claims. Those are the elements that must be pleaded to satisfy the requirement that a complaint be legally sufficient.

Factual Sufficiency. We just saw that the substantive law erects barriers to entering the litigation stream. Here our focus is different. Assuming the law gives the plaintiff a right to relief, how much detail must she allege in stating her claim? As a general answer, the code-state requirement that the plaintiff plead "a statement of facts constituting a cause of action" mandates somewhat more detailed pleading than the Federal Rules requirement of "a short and plain statement of the claim showing that the pleader is entitled to relief." In recent times, code states have become more liberal in assessing factual sufficiency of the complaint, but it is a mistake to think that all code states are as liberal as the federal courts in this regard.

As discussed in §7.2, code pleading developed in the nineteenth century in response to the absurd technicalities that flourished in the earlier common law "writ" system of pleading. It was a liberal advance to have the plaintiff allege simply "a statement of facts constituting a cause of

---

[17] In the federal system, appeal is to the court of appeals for the circuit in which the federal district court sits. In state court systems, there may be an intermediate appellate court that can entertain the case. If not, *P* may be able to seek discretionary review by the state supreme court. See §§1.2.2, 14.2.

[18] There are circumstances (beyond our scope) in which an appellate pronouncement on a matter of law might be applied retroactively and thus be binding on cases filed before the appellate pronouncement. You may study that topic in Constitutional Law.

action." The problem was that old habits die hard, and many of the judges weaned on the technicalities of the common law system could not help but import silly subtleties into the new system. Though the code requirement of pleading "facts" seems clear enough, courts refined it to require a statement of the "ultimate facts" (whatever that means). If the plaintiff alleged too generally to suit the judge, she was said to be pleading "conclusions of law" rather than facts, and the court would sustain a demurrer and dismiss the case. On the other hand, if the plaintiff alleged with too much detail to please the judge, she was said to be pleading "evidentiary facts," and the court would sustain a demurrer and dismiss the case. The courts created an absurd game that was every bit as arcane and silly as the common law system had been. They lost track of the fact that at the pleading stage no one really knows what happened — there has been no chance to engage in discovery. Erecting formalistic barriers depending on the individual judge's conception of what constituted "ultimate facts" thwarted the administration of justice by keeping potentially deserving plaintiffs out of the litigation stream by promoting dismissal at the pleading stage.

There are many examples of this formalism. In one case, the plaintiff, a lineman, suffered serious personal injuries when he fell 30 feet from a power pole when a spike in the pole broke when he stepped on it. The defendant had put the spikes into the pole. The plaintiff alleged that the defendant "negligently caused said step to be driven and placed in said pole not far enough to make it reasonably safe." The trial court overruled the defendant's demurrer, and the case went to trial. The plaintiff won a substantial judgment. On appeal, however, the Missouri Supreme Court held that the trial court should have sustained the demurrer. The plaintiff's allegation, the court concluded, was too conclusory; it constituted a conclusion of law rather than the allegation of "facts constituting a cause of action."[19] Thus, the plaintiff was robbed of his victory because the verbal formulation of his claim did not meet the fancy of the reviewing court. The result is absurd. There was no chance that the defendant had been misled by the allegation. Reading it, the defendant clearly understood what plaintiff was charging. The judicial system and parties had invested great effort and expense litigating the matter. Yet it was all undone because of a petty technicality. The cases — particularly older cases — concerning factually sufficient allegations in code states cannot be reconciled. For almost any situation, there is a plausible argument that the plaintiff is alleging either too generally or with too much specificity.

- ○ *P* sues to eject *D* from real property. Under the applicable law, *P* must plead and prove several issues; one of them is that she has superior title

---

[19] Kramer v. Kansas City Power & Light Co., 279 S.W 43 (Mo. 1925).

to the disputed property. How does one allege the "ultimate fact" of superior title?

- An allegation that *P* "has superior title to the property" may be attacked as too general and thus as alleging a legal conclusion rather than facts.[20]
- Similarly, an allegation that *P* is "entitled to possession of the property" may be attacked on the same ground.[21]
- *P* alleges that she "paid for the property pursuant to contract and [that *D*] delivered to her a deed to the property." This allegation may be attacked as too specific — as pleading of evidence, and not of facts.[22]

I do not suggest that all code-state courts would find fault with these formulations. Nor do I deny that courts in many code-pleading states are more liberal today than they were in previous generations. I simply give a word to the wise: Some code-pleading courts can still require a verbal precision that is very difficult to divine or describe. In particular, some code-state courts still ignore what they see as conclusions of law in determining whether the plaintiff has stated a cause of action. In the 1990s, the Nebraska Supreme Court reminded lawyers that trial courts in that state will consider "the pleaded facts, as distinguished from legal conclusions."[23] (Interestingly, Nebraska has since abandoned code pleading and adopted the Federal Rules approach.)

There is no question that the Federal Rules were intended to liberalize pleading requirements for the plaintiff. Instead of worrying about what constitute "facts" (let alone "ultimate facts") that constitute a "cause of action," Rule 8(a)(2) requires a "short and plain statement of the claim showing that the pleader is entitled to relief." An indisputable goal of the drafters was to lower the formal barrier erected by the pleading rules to entering the litigation stream. This lowered barrier went hand in hand with expanded discovery provisions under the Federal Rules (as we will see in Chapter 8). The idea is that the plaintiff is not in a position to plead much detail at the outset of litigation, and pleading rules should not impose an unrealistic barrier to her getting to the discovery phase of litigation.

How much detail is required to satisfy Rule 8(a)(2)? Clearly, it is not enough simply to allege "*D* owes me $1,000,000." But how much more is needed? One old but famous case on the general question is *Dioguardi v.*

---

[20] Sheridan v. Jackson, 72 N.Y. 170, 173 (1878).

[21] *Id.*

[22] That was the result in *McCaughey v. Shuette*, 117 Cal. 223 (1896), on a very similar allegation.

[23] Gallion v. Woytassek, 504 N.W.2d 76, 79 (Neb. 1993). *See also* Papin Builders, Inc. v. Litz, 734 S.W.2d 853, 858 (Mo. Ct. App. 1987) (code pleading not as liberal as Federal Rules pleading).

Durning,[24] a Second Circuit opinion authored by Judge Charles Clark.[25] Clark had been the Dean of Yale Law School in the 1930s and was the principal drafter of the original Federal Rules, which were promulgated in 1938. This case, decided in 1944, gave Clark a chance to explain the Federal Rules' theory on the role of pleading and the type of detail required by Rule 8(a)(2). Despite its age, the case is still found in most Civil Procedure casebooks.

Mr. Dioguardi was an Italian immigrant with limited facility in English. A shipment of "tonics" was sent from Italy to Mr. Dioguardi, evidently under a consignment agreement; this meant that Mr. Dioguardi (the "consignee") was to sell the tonics and remit certain payments to the sender in Italy (the "consignor"). The customs officers in New York seized the tonics because the duty was not paid. Mr. Dioguardi claimed that the consignor was to have paid the duty. At any rate, the customs collector, acting under a federal statute, held the tonics for a year and then sold them at public auction. Apparently, Mr. Dioguardi bid $110 for the tonics, but someone else at the auction bid $120, and the sale was made to this other person. Mr. Dioguardi, eschewing a lawyer, sued the collector of customs. He drafted his own complaint, in which he alleged that the defendant "sold my merchandise to another bidder with my price of $110, and not of his price of $120." In addition, the complaint alleged that "three weeks before the sale, two cases, of 19 bottles each case, disappeared."[26]

The district court granted a motion to dismiss for failure "to state facts sufficient to constitute a cause of action." On appeal, Judge Clark patiently pointed out that the "new" Federal Rules, which had been in effect for some years before the district court ruled in *Dioguardi*, do not mention the phrase "facts sufficient to constitute a cause of action." He then proceeded to explain why Mr. Dioguardi's complaint satisfied the requirement of Rule 8(a)(2) that he make a "short and plain statement of the claim showing [he was] entitled to relief." In language that has been widely quoted, Judge Clark explained that

> however inartistically they may be stated, the plaintiff has disclosed his claims that the collector has converted or otherwise done away with two of

---

[24] 139 F.2d 774 (2d Cir. 1944).

[25] Clark's protege on the Yale faculty in the 1930s was J.W. Moore, who became a legendary figure in legal education and was the principal author of an important multivolume treatise that still bears his name, Moore's Federal Practice. Interestingly, Moore had a student who later served as law clerk for Clark, who also became a legendary figure in legal education and was the principal author of the other important multivolume treatise in the field. He was Charles Alan Wright, and the work is Wright & Miller's Federal Practice and Procedure. Clark was a mentor, then, to the two men who produced the two principal multivolume treatises on federal jurisdiction and practice. If you do any litigation in federal court, you will become familiar with both works.

[26] 139 F.2d at 774.

his cases of medicinal tonics and has sold the rest in a manner incompatible with the public auction he had announced. . . . [W]e do not see how the plaintiff may properly be deprived of his day in court to show what he obviously so firmly believes. . . .[27]

Some observers criticized the *Dioguardi* decision by pointing out that the plaintiff lost when the case went to trial. But that fact is irrelevant to the pleading question. The only issue under Rule 8(a)(2) is whether the plaintiff has alleged enough to justify having the case proceed in the litigation stream. Whether the plaintiff wins at trial is a different matter. Despite the criticism, *Dioguardi* long stood the test of time. In fact, the Supreme Court specifically endorsed Judge Clark's approach in *Conley v. Gibson*.[28]

In *Conley*, the Court said Rule 8 requires only that the plaintiff give the defendant "fair notice of what the plaintiff's claim is and the grounds upon which it rests."[29] This phrase gave rise to the shorthand expression that the Federal Rules use "notice pleading" — that all the plaintiff must do is put the defendant "on notice" of what the claim is. Details can be fleshed out in discovery. The Federal Rules operate on the assumption that there is nothing intrinsically so important about good pleading that it should cost a plaintiff a potentially meritorious claim for failure to meet the formal niceties. As one opinion explains, the Federal Rules "make a complaint just the starting point. Instead of lavishing attention on the complaint until the plaintiff gets it just right, a district court should keep the case moving. . . ."[30]

Judge Clark did not like the phrase "notice pleading," because it was not sufficiently precise.[31] Nonetheless, it is commonly used. Clark was quite pleased with the Forms contained in the Appendix to the Federal Rules. Indeed, he thought them the most important part of the Federal Rules on the topic of factual sufficiency of pleadings. It is worth the time to review some of the complaints in the Forms, such as those in Forms 11 through 15 (the Appendix is in your Federal Rules booklet, right behind the Rules). They show how little detail is required in federal court. As a matter of practice in the real world, however, it is clear that very few lawyers use the forms.

Another passage from *Conley* became standard fare for citation by any federal court entertaining a motion under Rule 12(b)(6) for failure to plead with appropriate factual sufficiency:

[27] *Id.* at 775.
[28] 355 U.S. 41 (1957).
[29] *Id.* at 46.
[30] Bennett v. Schmidt, 153 F.3d 516, 518 (7th Cir. 1998).
[31] Charles Clark, *Pleading Under the Federal Rules*, 12 Wyo. L. Rev. 177, 181 (1958).

In appraising the sufficiency of the complaint we follow, of course, the accepted rule that a complaint should not be dismissed for failure to state a claim unless it appears beyond doubt that the plaintiff can prove no set of facts in support of his claim which would entitle him to relief.[32]

This is pretty liberal, all right. Judge Posner, of the Seventh Circuit, concluded that "[a]lthough the exceedingly forgiving attitude toward pleading deficiencies evidenced that was expressed...in *Conley v. Gibson*...continues to be quoted with approval, it has never been taken literally."[33]

The* Twombly *Case. Judge Posner was on to something. In 2007, the Supreme Court threw a wrench in the gears of federal pleading with its decision in *Bell Atlantic Corporation v. Twombly.*[34] *Twombly* is a complicated case, and its ultimate impact on federal pleading standards is far from clear. Understanding it requires background concerning the operation of telephone companies. In 1984, American Telephone & Telegraph Co., which had held a virtual monopoly on telephone service in the United States, was required to give up local phone service. Regional businesses, known as Incumbent Local Exchange Carriers (ILECs), were set up to handle local phone service in various regions. They were expressly to be free of competition in their local markets, but could not provide long-distance phone service. In 1996, Congress tried to increase competition in the local telephone markets by passing a law that permitted the ILECs to provide long-distance service (which was very lucrative), but *only* if they permitted other ILECs to compete with them for their local phone service.

As expected, ILECs went into the long-distance business. Not as expected, however, ILECs did not attempt to do business in other local markets. They did not compete with one another in the local telephone markets. As a consequence, the prices for local telephone service did not go down (as they would with competition).

If the ILECs' failure to compete with each other in local markets was the result of a conspiracy (an agreement among the ILECs), it would violate federal antitrust law. Specifically, §1 of the Sherman Antitrust Act prohibits contracts "in restraint of trade," and there is no question that such an agreement among the ILECs would fall within the heart of that provision. A violation of the Sherman Act could lead to criminal indictment and would certainly lead to private damages cases by local telephone customers. On the other hand, if the ILECs' failure to compete in local markets

---

[32] *Id.* at 45-46.
[33] Sutliff, Inc. v. Donovan Cos., Inc., 727 F.2d 648, 654 (7th Cir. 1984).
[34] 127 S. Ct. 1955 (2007).

was *not* the result of an agreement — if, for instance, the ILECs thought independently "gee, I'll stay out of the other guy's market and maybe he'll stay out of mine" — there would be no violation of the antitrust laws.

In *Twombly*, the plaintiffs brought a class action on behalf of local telephone customers, seeking to allege a violation of §1 of the Sherman Act. They tried to allege that the ILECs had conspired not to compete with each other in local phone service. The plaintiffs had no direct proof of such an agreement. For instance, they had no witnesses to a meeting at which the ILECs conspired and no memoranda confirming an understanding among them. Obviously, the plaintiffs would like to get to the discovery phase of the litigation to see if they could find any such "smoking gun" evidence in the ILECs' files or by taking testimony from people who might know of any such deal. But to get to the discovery phase — indeed, to proceed in the litigation stream at all — the plaintiffs must survive a motion to dismiss for failure to state a claim under Rule 12(b)(6).

The plaintiffs attempted to allege a conspiracy by alleging "conscious parallel behavior." That means that they alleged the defendants were aware of what each other was doing — offering long-distance service but not competing outside its region in local service — and did the same thing. For example, if Company X is aware that Company Y is not trying to compete for local service in Company X's region, then Company X might let sleeping dogs lie by refusing to compete in Company Y's backyard. Under the substantive antitrust law, however, the plaintiffs must prove at trial that any conscious parallel behavior was the result of an agreement. Under the law, they can do this by showing conscious parallel behavior and some "plus factor" to demonstrate that the behavior was the result of agreement.

The question in *Twombly* was what the plaintiff must *plead* to satisfy Rule 8(a)(2). Remember that *Conley* had said the complaint was sufficient "unless it appears beyond doubt that the plaintiff can prove no set of facts in support of his claim which would entitle him to relief."[35] So the plaintiffs in *Twombly* probably felt they were on firm ground when they alleged that the defendant ILECs engaged in conscious parallel behavior as a result of agreement.

But the Court held that the plaintiffs failed to state a claim. In the course of its decision, the Court overruled the quoted language from *Conley*.[36] The plaintiffs in *Twombly* failed to allege facts that tended to rule out that the ILECs were simply acting independently. They failed to allege "enough

---

[35] See note 32 above.

[36] 127 S. Ct. at 1968-1969. The Court noted that the language had long been questioned and criticized, as the quotation from Judge Posner at note 33 above demonstrated. *Conley*'s "no set of facts" phrase had, according to the Court, "earned its retirement" after 50 years of confusing the profession. *Id.* at 1969. "The phrase is best forgotten as an incomplete, negative gloss on an accepted pleading standard: once a claim has been stated, it may be supported by showing any set of facts consistent with the allegations in the complaint." *Id.* Plaintiffs' problem in *Twombly*, according to the Court, is that they failed to state a claim.

factual matter ... to suggest that an agreement was made."[37] While there was of course a "possibility" that there had been an agreement, the plaintiffs must go beyond possibility and allege "plausibility." The core of *Twombly* is its statement of what is required to state a claim. According to Justice Souter, in his opinion for the majority: "[W]e ... require ... only enough facts to state a claim to relief that is plausible on its face. Because the plaintiffs here have not nudged their claims across the line from conceivable to plausible, their complaint must be dismissed."[38]

The most striking thing about this standard is that it finds no grounding in Rule 8(a)(2). Nowhere does that Rule — or any Rule — speak of "plausibility." And the focus on "facts" is surprising, given that the Rules were intended specifically to avoid that word and — hopefully — all the baggage that went with it in code-pleading states.

Twombly has unleashed an avalanche of litigation. Within 18 months of the decision, it had been cited in over 6,000 opinions. The bulk of these, we must presume, are decisions in motions to dismiss under Rule 12(b)(6), in which the defendants were inspired by what is clearly a higher pleading burden for plaintiffs. Some have argued that *Twombly* will be limited to antitrust cases, but it is difficult to escape the fact that the majority opinion spoke frequently about pleading under Rule 8(a)(2), and not about antitrust pleading. The majority opinion also strongly rejected the argument that it was imposing a "heightened pleading standard" for any case. On the other hand, in his nearly savage dissent, Justice Stevens accused the majority of "protecting antitrust defendants — who are some of the wealthiest corporations in our economy — from the burdens of pretrial litigation."[39]

The result of *Twombly*, of course, is that the plaintiffs will never get to the discovery phase and thus never search the files of the defendants for proof of conspiracy. Indeed, the majority recognized this effect of the holding. It said:

> [I]t is no answer to say that a claim just shy of a plausible entitlement to relief can, if groundless, be weeded out early in the discovery process ... given the common lament that the success of judicial supervision in checking discovery abuse has been on the modest side. And it is self-evident that ... the threat of discovery expense will push cost-conscious defendants to settle even anemic cases before reaching [trial]. Probably, then it is only by taking care to require allegations that reach the level suggesting conspiracy that we can hope to avoid the potentially enormous expense of discovery in cases with no reasonably founded hope that the [discovery] process will reveal relevant evidence to support a §1 claim.[40]

---

[37] *Id.* at 1965.
[38] *Id.* at 1974.
[39] *Id.* at 1989 (Stevens, J., dissenting).
[40] *Id.* at 1967 (quotations and citations omitted).

This passage reflects a sentiment expressed by many observers through the years — that the liberality of Federal Rules pleading is not entirely good. To the extent that those rules make it very easy to get through the pleadings gate, they make it easy to get into discovery. And discovery can be staggeringly expensive and intrusive. To the extent the Rules allow shaky claims to get through the gate and force the defendant to go through discovery, they tie up judicial resources and put the defendant to unfair expense.[41]

Twombly has injected considerable uncertainty into pleading doctrine. It is difficult to square the case with one decided just two weeks later. There, in *Erickson v. Pardus*,[42] the Court cited *Conley* with favor. In *Erickson*, a prisoner suffering from illness sued prison officials, and alleged that their deliberate indifference to his medical needs violated his constitutional rights. He alleged that the defendants had diagnosed his condition and put him in treatment, but then removed him from the treatment. The Supreme Court, reversing a dismissal, upheld the complaint, saying that "specific facts are not necessary; the statement need 'only give the defendant fair notice of what the . . . claim is and the grounds upon which it rests.'"[43] It is almost inconceivable that the same Court that wrote *Twombly* could make this statement two weeks later.

In 2008, the Court granted certiorari in a case that implicates *Twombly*.[44] The profession hopes that the Court will bring some clarity to an area in which it has not distinguished itself. In fairness to the Court, however, one cannot help but wonder if a Rules Advisory Committee that was focused on problems in the profession — and not on its obsessive "restyling" and other silly tinkering — might have made an ameliorative contribution by considering whether Rule 8(a)(2) could be improved.

The Common Counts. Courts have always allowed plaintiffs to assert certain claims in a sort of legal shorthand called the *common counts*. These are basically one-sentence statements of claims that have long been accepted in virtually every court, no matter how demanding or strict those courts might be about stating other claims. The common counts plainly do not satisfy the code-pleading requirement of a "statement of facts constituting a cause of action," and may just barely satisfy the Federal Rules

[41] Another, more hidden, potential cost of liberal pleading rules is that they may allow a plaintiff to proceed through litigation without sufficient focus on the elements she must plead at trial. The elements of a claim are determined by the substantive law. At trial, the plaintiff will have to prove those elements. All we are discussing here is how much detail she must plead with. At trial, there is no question that she has to prove all the elements, even if she could skate a bit in pleading them. Sloppy pleading may lead to sloppy case preparation — preparation that is insufficiently focused on gathering evidence to prove the elements at trial.

[42] 127 S. Ct. 2197 (2007).
[43] *Id.* at 2200, *quoting Conley*.
[44] Iqbal v. Hasty, 490 F.3d 143 (2d Cir. 2007), *cert. granted*, 128 U.S. 2931 (2008).

standards of stating a claim on which relief can be granted. Still, they are permitted just about everywhere. The classic common counts are things you probably studied in Contracts — *quantum meruit* (a claim for the value of labor performed), *quantum valebant* (a claim for the value of goods delivered), and *indebitatus assumpsit* (a claim for money owed). The Federal Rules do not refer to the term *common counts*. Nonetheless, Forms 10 and 15 in the Appendix of Forms following the Rules (in your Rules booklet) set forth some examples of what are basically common counts.

§7.3.3 Defendant's Response: Answer and Motions

The Choices and the Timing

In addition to filing her complaint, the plaintiff must arrange to have process served on the defendant under Rule 4 (or the defendant might waive formal service of process under Rule 4(d)). Under the rules of every jurisdiction, the defendant must respond to the complaint in a prescribed way within a given period, or else risk losing by default (which we address in §7.5).[45] Federal Rule 12(a)(1) imposes the general requirement that the defendant respond within 20 days after being served with process.[46] Most states seem to provide the same period, although some allow the defendant 30 days in which to respond.

Under Rule 12, the defendant has a choice of how to respond to the complaint. One choice is to serve and file a pleading called an *answer*, which we discuss in detail below. The other option is to bring a *motion*. These choices are reflected, respectively, in Rule 12(a)(1)(A) and Rule 12(a)(4). A motion is not a pleading. Rather, it is a request that the court order something. During the pendency of a case, there may be hundreds of motions. Some of them will be made in writing, such as a motion to dismiss for lack of personal jurisdiction or to transfer for improper venue. Others may be made orally, such as a motion to strike a witness's answer at trial. In this chapter, we focus on the classic defensive motions that might be brought in lieu of an answer. These are found in Rules 12(b), 12(e), and 12(f).

---

[45] Throughout, we refer to the defendant responding to the complaint. Remember, however, that every defending party must respond to a claim against her. Thus, for example, the plaintiff against whom a counterclaim is asserted and the party against whom a cross-claim is asserted must also respond under Rule 12 or risk default on that claim. *See* Rule 12(a)(2).

[46] If the defendant waives formal service of process under Rule 4(d), Rule 12(a)(1)(A)(ii) permits her "to serve an answer" within 60 days after the plaintiff sent the waiver form to the defendant.

The question of whether the defendant should respond by motion or by answer is a strategic one. A motion may result in dismissal of the case, thereby obviating the need to draft an answer at all. On the other hand, responding by answer may be more appropriate when the defendant needs more time to develop the facts supporting a particular motion to dismiss. Often, a defendant responds both by motion and answer. For example, upon being sued, the defendant might move[47] to dismiss (say, for lack of personal jurisdiction). If the court grants the motion, clearly, the case is over and the defendant never has to answer. But suppose the court denies the motion. At that point, the defendant must serve and file an answer. So in that instance, she will have responded both by motion and by answer. It is imperative, however, that one not run afoul of the important (and very exam-worthy) waiver provisions of Rule 12(g) and (h), which we discuss below.

Before discussing the two types of defensive responses in depth, we need to know how to compute the number of days. Specifically, how do we calculate the passage of 20 days from the service of process on the defendant? Rule 6(a) makes clear that the day of the event that triggers the relevant period (here service of process) is *not* included in that period. Unless the relevant time for response is fewer than 11 days, the computation of the period includes Saturdays, Sundays, and legal holidays.[48] If the last day of the period falls on a Saturday, Sunday, or a legal holiday, the act may be performed on the next business day.

> ○ *D* is served with process on June 2. She must respond by answer or motion within 20 days of service. June 2 does not count in the calculation of the 20 days. June 3 is Day 1, June 4 is Day 2, June 5 is Day 3, etc. That means June 22 is Day 20, and is the last day on which she can respond; so *D* must respond as prescribed by Rule 12 by the end of the business day on June 22. If June 22 is a Saturday, Sunday, or legal holiday, however, *D* may respond by the end of the next business day.

Under Rule 12(a)(1), the defendant must serve (not file) her "responsive pleading" no later than 20 days after being served with process. Because motions are not pleadings, the phrase "responsive pleading" refers only to the answer, as noted in Rule 12(a)(1)(A)(i). What if the defendant wants to respond by motion? Rule 12(a)(4) provides that "serving a motion under this rule" (meaning Rule 12 as a whole) changes the time in which to serve the answer. Specifically, under Rule 12(a)(4)(A), if the court

---

[47] Talk like a lawyer. Remember: Motion is *not* a verb. A party *moves* for something or *makes a motion*. No one "motions" the court. To use motion as a verb is the sign of a rank amateur. *See* note 13 (another example of sounding like a rank amateur).

[48] If the time being measured is fewer than 11 days, according to Rule 6(a)(2), one does *not* include Saturdays, Sundays, and legal holidays. Rule 6(a)(4) lists the recognized legal holidays.

denies the motion (or postpones its disposition), "the responsive pleading must be served within 10 days after notice of the court's action." Thus, within 20 days after being served with process, the defendant must either serve an answer or serve a motion under Rule 12. Either action will (at least for the time being) obviate the risk of default. If the defendant makes a motion and the court denies it (or postpones its disposition), the defendant must serve her answer within ten days after being informed of the court's ruling on the motion.

- *D* is served with process on June 2. She serves and files a motion to dismiss for lack of personal jurisdiction on June 20. The motion is timely, because it was served no later than 20 days after *D* was served with process. On July 10, the court denies *D*'s motion to dismiss and informs the parties of that fact. So now *D* will have to serve and file an answer. She must do so no later than July 20. Why? Because, under Rule 12(a)(4)(A), she must respond no later than ten days after being informed of the court's ruling on her motion to dismiss.

It bears noting that the court is free to order a different timetable. In addition, under Rule 6(b), a party may move for an extension of time in which she is required to do something. Moreover, the parties can (and often do) stipulate to extensions. In federal court, such stipulations do not take effect automatically. Rather, they are effective only if approved by the court and contained in an order. Thus, if the plaintiff agrees to allow the defendant 45 days from service in which to respond to the complaint, the parties will enter a written stipulation and prepare an order to that effect for the judge's signature. The stipulation is ineffective without the judge's signature. Also, notice the difference a single word can make. A plaintiff might be willing to stipulate to an extension of time in which the defendant may "answer" the complaint, but not in which she may "respond" to the complaint. Why? A stipulation allowing the defendant more time to "answer" allows the defendant only to serve and file an answer. It does not permit her more time in which to bring a *motion*. In contrast, a stipulation allowing the defendant more time in which to "respond" would include the option to answer or bring a motion.

Responding by Motion

Motions Under Rule 12(b). We just saw that the defendant might respond by answer or by a motion under Rule 12. What motions are possible under Rule 12? The major motions are based upon Rule 12(b), which lists seven defenses and provides that the defendant may choose either to raise them in her answer (as affirmative defenses) or by motion. Specifically, the Rule 12(b) defenses are (1) lack of subject matter jurisdiction,

(2) lack of personal jurisdiction, (3) improper venue, (4) insufficient process,[49] (5) insufficient service of process,[50] (6) failure to state a claim on which relief can be granted (discussed in §7.3.2), and (7) failure to join an absentee under Rule 19 (traditionally known as an "indispensable party") (which we will see in §12.6.1).

The most important thing to remember about the Rule 12(b) defenses are the waiver provisions of Rule 12(g) and (h). We discussed these in detail (and had some hypotheticals applying them) in §6.2.1. In a nutshell, those provisions require the defendant to assert any of four Rule 12(b) defenses — those relating to personal jurisdiction (12(b)(2)), venue (12(b)(3)), process (12(b)(4)), and service of process (12(b)(5)) — in her *first response* under Rule 12. Thus, if her first response is a Rule 12 motion, those four defenses must be included in it or else they are waived. If her first response is an answer, likewise, those four defenses must be included in it or else they are waived. On the other hand, the defenses of failure to state a claim (12(b)(6)) and failure to join an absentee under Rule 19 (12(b)(7)) need not be put in the first response. They can be raised anytime through the end of trial. And the defense of lack of subject matter jurisdiction, as we saw both in §6.2.1 and §6.4, may be raised anytime in the case, even for the first time on appeal.

Motion for Judgment on the Pleadings Under Rule 12(c). Rule 12(c) permits a motion for judgment on the pleadings. This is precisely the same as the motion to dismiss for failure to state a claim under Rule 12(b)(6). It is called a motion for judgment on the pleadings if it is brought after the defendant has served her answer. The standards for granting it are the same as we discussed in addressing the Rule 12(b)(6) motion in §7.3.2. Thus, the court will take all allegations of the complaint as true and determine whether they state a legally cognizable claim.

Motion for More Definite Statement Under Rule 12(e). Rule 12(e) permits the defendant to bring a motion for more definite statement, which addresses a complaint that "is so vague or ambiguous that the party cannot reasonably prepare a response." This motion does not address legal or factual insufficiency, as a Rule 12(b)(6) motion does (see §7.3.2). Rather, it is aimed at a complaint that simply cannot be understood. The motion for more definite statement must "point out the defects complained of and the details desired." The defendant must make the Rule 12(e) motion before answering. After all, she is saying that the complaint is so vague or

---

[49] This defense is pretty rare. It deals with a defect in the papers served upon the defendant. Recall from §3.3.1 that process consists of a summons and a copy of the complaint. If a copy of the complaint were not served, or if the summons did not comply with Rule 4(a), for example, the defendant would raise the issue under Rule 12(b)(4).

[50] This defense is far more common than that discussed in the previous footnote. Here, the papers constituting process are fine, but there was a problem with how they were served on the defendant.

ambiguous that she *cannot* respond. If the court grants the motion, the plaintiff has ten days in which to plead with more clarity. The defendant must respond to the (hopefully) clarified complaint within ten days after it is served on her.[51]

Note that a motion for more definite statement can only be used to challenge a pleading to which a "responsive pleading is allowed." Because, generally, no responsive pleading is allowed to an answer, the plaintiff cannot assert a Rule 12(e) motion against an *answer* she finds unintelligible. Rather, she might move to strike the answer under Rule 12(f).

Motion to Strike Under Rule 12(f). Though we consider Rule 12(f) among the motions available to a defendant, the Rule clearly permits any party to move to strike pleadings or portions thereof. Specifically, "the court may strike from a pleading an insufficient defense or any redundant, immaterial, impertinent, or scandalous matter." The Rule appears to be strict about the timing of this motion. Rule 12(f)(2) requires that the defendant make a motion to strike before responding to the complaint, and that the plaintiff move to strike within 20 days after being served with the defendant's response. Despite this, however, the Rule also provides that the court can strike "on its own." This phrase has been interpreted to allow the court to grant a party's untimely motion to strike.[52]

The motion to strike is disfavored because it is often used simply to delay proceedings. It is rarely granted. Indeed, even though Rule 12(f) says nothing about prejudice, courts simply will not grant the motion unless the moving party shows that the matter to be stricken will cause her some harm if left in the pleading. One example of such prejudice is when the pleadings may be given to the jury for review during their deliberations. The jury might be unduly swayed by inappropriate or immaterial allegations in a pleading, causing prejudice to a party. There are undoubtedly other examples of prejudice, and the matter is always vested in the discretion of the trial judge. As a practical matter, however, it seems clear that successful motions to strike are especially rare in cases to be tried to the court (without a jury). We have considerable confidence in a judge's ability not to be diverted or swayed by inappropriate allegations in a pleading.

Rule 12(f) specifically allows the court to strike "an insufficient defense." A defense might be insufficient as a matter of law or the defendant may have failed to allege it with sufficient factual detail (though not much detail is required). The court might grant the motion to strike with

---

[51] *See* Rules 12(a)(4)(B) and 12(e). Of course, the court is always free to change the time requirements.

[52] *See, e.g.,* Zeelan Indus., Inc. v. De Zeeuw, 706 F. Supp. 702, 704-705 (D. Minn. 1989) ("[E]ven if a party's motion to strike is not made within the time limits established by [Rule] 12(f), a district court has authority to consider the motion because a court may strike material from the pleadings on its own initiative.").

leave to amend, to allow the defendant to assert the defense appropriately. Rule 12(f) also allows the court to strike "redundant," "immaterial," and "impertinent" matter. Again, however, as a practical matter, the moving party must show prejudice, and it is usually difficult to point to any harm caused by the other party's prolixity. Unnecessary detailed allegations about jurisdiction or irrelevant allegations about venue do not belong in good pleadings, but, unless they cause harm to some party, it is difficult to see why a court would spend time pruning such things from pleadings. It is not clear that "impertinent" adds much to "immaterial."

On the other hand, sometimes a motion to strike can be used to determine an important issue early in the proceedings. For instance, suppose one party in federal court demands trial by jury, and the other party believes that the Seventh Amendment would not accord a jury in the case. She might raise the issue by a motion to strike the jury demand, and have the issue determined well in advance of trial.

Finally, the Rule allows the court to strike "scandalous" matter. Parties here have slightly more success in bringing a motion to strike, because scandalous allegations may hold them up to ridicule, either to the jury or to the public (because pleadings are usually considered public records). A party is not entitled to have all distasteful allegations about her stricken. It is not enough that the allegation is unfavorable or even that it offends the party about whom the allegation is made. After all, an allegation of outrageous behavior may be relevant to a claim for an intentional tort or for punitive damages. But unduly derogatory allegations may be stricken. For example, in a case for physical and emotional injuries allegedly suffered by employees at the hands of their employer, the court struck allegations that the defendant attempted to "brainwash" and "torture" the plaintiffs like "Chinese communists in Korea."[53]

Finally, we will see in §7.3.5 that some allegations must be made with particularity or specificity — that is, as to certain issues, the plaintiff must plead in relatively greater detail than general pleadings. If the plaintiff fails to plead the required detail on such matters, some courts permit the defendant to respond with a motion to strike the pleading under Rule 12(f).

Responding by Answer

Instead of responding by motion (or if her pre-answer motion was denied), the defendant may respond by answer. An answer is a pleading. (Remember, motions are not pleadings.) In the answer, the defendant must accomplish two primary goals: She must respond to the allegations in the

---

[53] Alvarado-Morales v. Digital Equip. Corp., 843 F.2d 613, 618 (1st Cir. 1988).

complaint and she must raise affirmative defenses. Responding to the allegations of the complaint is addressed in Federal Rule 8(b). Raising affirmative defenses is addressed in Federal Rules (c).

Responding to Allegations in the Complaint. Drafting a good answer takes considerable patience and attention to detail. The job is to respond to each allegation the plaintiff has made in her complaint. Careful lawyers go through the complaint word-by-word to ensure that they respond carefully. Rule 8(b)(1)(A) and Rule 8(b)(5) (along with common sense) instruct the defendant that there are three possible responses to the plaintiff's allegations. The defendant can (1) admit allegations, (2) deny allegations, or (3) say she lacks sufficient information on which to admit or deny. Rule 8(b)(5) makes clear that the third option (if properly employed) "has the effect of a denial."

These three options — admit, deny, or claim a lack of sufficient information to admit or deny — must be assessed against the serious consequence provided in Rule 8(b)(6): An allegation (except one regarding the amount of damage) "is admitted if a responsive pleading is required and the allegation is not denied." This is why lawyers are so careful here: The failure to deny an allegation in the complaint is considered an admission of that allegation. (As noted, though, a failure to deny does not constitute an admission of damages.) So Rule 8(b)(6) creates some nervousness.

> ° *P* alleges in a particular paragraph of her complaint that *D* drove her automobile in a reckless fashion, causing the accident and causing personal injuries to *P*. *D* fails to deny the allegations. *D* has admitted the allegations. There need be no adjudication on these points. They are deemed established for purposes of this case.

We discuss denials in more detail below. Now, we look at the two other possible responses. First, the defendant may simply admit various allegations. This may seem antithetical to the competition of litigation, but there are usually allegations that the defendant simply cannot deny in good faith. As we discuss in §7.7, Rule 11 and other norms of professionalism require that a party (and a lawyer) not make unsupportable assertions. It would be a violation of these norms to deny an allegation that the party (or lawyer) knows is true. Thus, the defendant may admit jurisdictional allegations because, for instance, she agrees that she is of diverse citizenship from the plaintiff and that the amount in controversy exceeds $75,000. Or the defendant may agree with the plaintiff's allegation that the two parties entered a contract on a certain date. Admitting such issues establishes these points as facts that do not need to be adjudicated. Obviously, admitting one fact does not admit another. So the defendant may well admit the existence of the contract and deny the allegation that she breached it.

Second, a defendant must be careful when invoking Rule 8(b)(5) to assert that she "lacks knowledge or information sufficient to form a belief about the truth of an allegation." The requirements of Rule 11 and professional responsibility mean that the defendant cannot use this approach if she is in possession of the relevant information or if the matter alleged is something of public record. Thus, for example, if the plaintiff alleges something as to which the defendant has no precise recollection, but which is contained in her files, she cannot simply respond by saying she is without sufficient information. She must attempt to find the answer and, if appropriate, deny the allegation. If she fails to do so, she will be deemed to have failed to deny the allegation. Under Rule 8(b)(6), this means that she will have admitted the allegation. On the other hand, if the matter alleged by the plaintiff is truly beyond the defendant's knowledge and information, she may say so, and such a statement acts as a denial.

Now, how does the defendant deny allegations contained in the complaint? Rule 8(b)(2) warns the defendant that "[a] denial must fairly respond to the substance of the allegation." This tells the defendant to keep it simple. Do not get argumentative. Do not inject new facts. Just deny.

- In Paragraph 6 of her complaint, P alleges that "On November 20, 2009, D negligently drove her motor vehicle on Wilshire Boulevard in Los Angeles and struck the plaintiff."
  - D should simply respond in her answer by alleging: "D denies the allegations of Paragraph 6 of the complaint." If she did so, the issues alleged by the plaintiff would be "joined," which means they would require adjudication.
  - Instead, D alleges in her answer: "D demands that P demonstrate the truth of her allegations by evidence at trial." D has just failed to deny the allegation and, under Rule 8(b), has admitted the allegation. If you want to deny an allegation, simply deny it.
  - Instead, D alleges in her answer: "On November 20, 2009, D was on vacation in Barbados." This is called an "argumentative denial." In code states, it may well be treated as an admission, because it does not directly deny the allegation made by P. In federal court, D will probably get away with this, but it is sloppy. Again, if you want to deny an allegation, simply deny it.
  - Instead, D alleges in her answer: "D denies that on November 20, 2009, she negligently drove her motor vehicle on Wilshire Boulevard in Los Angeles and struck the plaintiff." This literal denial is fraught with the possibility of the "negative pregnant." What is that? Some courts treat such allegations as a denial of the precise allegation made, but as an admission of other possibilities. Thus, D here has denied something very precisely, but the denial is "pregnant" with the admission that she drove recklessly (instead of negligently) on that date, or that she drove negligently on another date.[54]

---

[54] Another example: P alleges that the value of the damaged vehicle "exceeded" $80,000, to which the defendant "denies that the value of the vehicle exceeded $80,000." The defendant's response is "pregnant" with an admission that the vehicle was worth exactly $80,000.

The negative pregnant is an example of elevating form over substance. Federal courts are likely to be forgiving on these technicalities, but some courts in code states might not be. But why tempt fate? Why make an easy job hard? Wise counsel will avoid the problem by responding so as to avoid the negative pregnant.

One technique for drafting an answer is to respond in sequence to each paragraph of the complaint. For example, "*D* admits the allegations of Paragraph 1 of the complaint. *D* denies the allegations of Paragraph 2 of the complaint," and so forth. One need not do that, however. Instead, the defendant might list together those paragraphs she wishes to admit and those she wishes to deny. For example, "*D* admits the allegations of Paragraphs 1 and 6 of the complaint. *D* denies the allegations of each other paragraph of the complaint."

In reality, though, the task is usually more difficult, because each paragraph of the complaint may contain material the defendant wishes to deny *and* material she should admit. The preferred way to respond is to admit expressly what can be admitted and to deny the remainder of the paragraph. The second sentence of Rule 8(b)(3) instructs that when a party intends to deny only part of an allegation, she "must either specifically deny designated allegations or generally deny all except those specifically admitted." And Rule 8(b)(4) says that "[a] party that intends in good faith to deny only part of an allegation must admit the part that is true and deny the rest."

- In Paragraph 4 of her complaint, *P* alleges that "*D* is a corporation formed under the laws of Pennsylvania with its principal place of business in West Virginia." *D* is a Pennsylvania corporation, but its principal place of business is in New Jersey. In its answer, *D* should allege: "In response to Paragraph 4 of the complaint, *D* admits that it is a corporation formed under the laws of Pennsylvania and denies the remainder of the Paragraph."

Finally, there is the "general denial," which is a very short document. In it, the defendant simply alleges something like: "Defendant denies each and every allegation of the complaint." The first sentence of Rule 8(b)(3) recognizes the possibility of the general denial, and code states generally permit them, but one should be careful. In view of Rule 11 and other rules of professional responsibility, it is difficult to imagine a case in which a defendant can properly use a general denial. After all, if there is *anything* in the complaint that should be admitted, the defendant should admit it. It

---

See National Bank v. Northern Illinois Corp., 202 F.3d 601 (7th Cir. 1953). Another example from daily life: A recording in an airport lobby says "smoking, eating, *and* drinking are prohibited." Can you form an argument that doing any one or two of the three activities would be permitted? In other words, if I eat and drink in the lobby, am I in trouble? I would say no, because I am not smoking, eating, *and* drinking; I'm just eating and drinking.

is a rare case in which the defendant can, in good faith, deny every allegation of the complaint.

Raising Affirmative Defenses. In addition to responding to the allegations of the complaint, the defendant will assert affirmative defenses in her answer. As we just saw, the defendant, in responding to the plaintiff's allegations, will not (or at least should not) inject allegations of new facts. Instead, she simply admits or denies what the plaintiff has alleged. With affirmative defenses, however, the defendant does inject new facts into the dispute. An affirmative defense is material additional to that alleged by the plaintiff which, if true, entitles the defendant to judgment. The affirmative defense is the modern counterpart to what common law pleading called the "plea of confession and avoidance." That plea permitted a defendant to admit the facts pleaded by the plaintiff but to avoid liability by raising a new fact.

Federal Rule 8(c)(1) lists 19 classic affirmative defenses, but is not an exhaustive list. The Rule says that the defendant "must affirmatively state any avoidance or affirmative defense, including" the 19 that are listed. Review the list of 19. Each is an example of how a defendant may inject into the case a new fact in an effort to avoid liability. The most routinely invoked are probably statute of limitations, statute of frauds, contributory negligence, and assumption of risk. Notice that self-defense is not listed in Rule 8(c), but it certainly constitutes an affirmative defense.

> ◦ *P* sues *D* for battery, and alleges that *D* slugged her in the nose. If *D* denies that she hit *P*, she will simply deny this allegation. On the other hand, if *D* did actually slug *P*, but did so in self-defense, she will admit the allegation, but raise the affirmative defense of self-defense. It is an affirmative defense because it injects a new factual element into the case that, if correct, will result in judgment for *D*.

Failure to assert an affirmative defense can create a serious problem for the defendant. Unless she is permitted to amend to set forth the defense, she may not be able to present evidence of the defense at trial. If she attempts to put on evidence of an affirmative defense that she failed to plead, the plaintiff can object that the evidence is at "variance" with the pleading and the court should refuse to allow the evidence to be presented. The effect of this is that the affirmative defense is effectively waived.[55] As

---

[55] A court may in some situations raise an affirmative defense for the defendant. In *Day v. McDonough*, 547 U.S. 198 (2006), a prisoner sued for federal habeas corpus relief. He argued that he was being detained by the state illegally. In its response, the state indicated that its calculation of the timing showed that the plaintiff had sued in a timely fashion. The district court noted, however, that the state had erred. By the court's calculation, the plaintiff's case was filed outside the eligible window permitted by statute. The district court dismissed on its own, and the Supreme Court affirmed. The defense was not jurisdictional, so the court had no obligation to raise it. And the defendant had not deliberately waived the

we see in §7.6.2, however, it is possible for the defendant to seek leave to amend even at that late date. But a prudent lawyer will not put herself in this position; she will be assiduous in asserting affirmative defenses in the answer.

It is helpful to think of the elements of a claim and of affirmative defenses as setting up what Professor Edward Cleary long ago called a series of "conditional imperatives." Suppose, for example, that there are four elements to a claim. That is, the substantive law provides that the plaintiff will recover if A, B, C, and D are established.[56] At trial, the plaintiff attempts to persuade the fact-finder that A, B, C, and D are true. The defendant attempts to persuade the fact-finder that at least one of those elements is not true. But even if the plaintiff persuades the jury that all the elements of her claim are true, the defendant will win if she can establish an affirmative defense. For instance, the defendant might show that she struck the plaintiff in self-defense or that the plaintiff assumed the risk or that the statute of limitations has expired, etc.

Stated as an equation, then, the plaintiff will win *if A* plus *B* plus *C* plus *D* are true *unless* the defendant establishes an affirmative defense. Roughly speaking, the plaintiff has the burden of pleading and proving the *ifs* (i.e., the elements of her claim), and the defendant has the burden of pleading and proving the *unlesses* (i.e., the affirmative defenses).

There are, however, some cases that do not fit this allocation. Consider, for example, a claim for defamation. You may have studied defamation in Torts. It is the publication of an *untrue* statement about the plaintiff that holds the plaintiff up to scorn. Note that a statement is defamatory only if it is untrue. Another way to say the same thing is to invoke the well-known phrase that "truth is a defense." So the question becomes: Who (the plaintiff or the defendant) should have the burden of pleading and proving the issue of truth? In other words, does the plaintiff have to show that what was said about her was untrue, or does the defendant have to show that what she said about the plaintiff was true? Further, who should have the burden of proving the issue at trial? Usually, the burden of proof follows the burden of pleading, so if a party is required to plead an issue, she is usually required to prove it as well.

The situation of defamation is anomalous, however, because *both* the plaintiff and the defendant must make allegations concerning truth or falsity. Obviously, the plaintiff must allege that the defendant's statement was false. Instead of merely denying the allegation, however, the defendant

---

defense. Under the circumstances, the court's raising it was permitted. Obviously, though, a defendant should not expect the court to rescue her from a mistake or miscalculation.

[56] You are learning the elements for various claims in your other courses. In Torts, for example, you probably will cover the elements of a claim for battery, for assault, for negligence, and others. Likewise, in Contracts you will cover the elements of a claim for breach.

must allege the affirmative defense of truth. Why? Because, as a practical matter, the law recognizes that the defendant is in the best position to offer proof on the issue.

- *D* defamed *P* by stating to a group that *P* is a prostitute. *P* sues *D* for defamation, and alleges, *inter alia*, that the statement is untrue. *D*, however, believes that *P* is indeed a prostitute and thus that her statement about *P* is true. She alleges the affirmative defense of truth.
- As a practical matter, *D* must have the burden of proof on the issue. Why? Because it is virtually impossible for *P* to prove that she is *not* a prostitute. Think of it. How can anyone prove a negative? How can you demonstrate conclusively that you are not a prostitute or a traitor or anything else? Unless she could call everyone in the world to the witness stand at trial, she simply cannot prove the issue.
- On the other hand, putting the burden of proof on *D* makes sense. *D* simply has to produce a single witness to testify that the witness had sex with *P* for money to prove that *P* is a prostitute.

The law accommodates burdens of pleading and proof, then, in pragmatic ways. Though both *P* and *D* will plead the issue (*P* that the statement is false and *D* that it is true), *D* has the burden of proof. Defamation, then, is one of the few substantive areas in which the burden of proof does not follow the burden of pleading.

Another is nonpayment of a debt. Assume *P* sues *D* for failing to repay a loan. *P* must allege that *D* failed to repay the loan. *D* may not simply deny the allegation, but must raise the affirmative defense of repayment. Why? Because *D* has the burden of proving that she did repay the debt. The reason for this allocation is the same as in defamation — as a practical matter, it is impossible for *P* to show that *D* did not repay the loan. How does one prove that she has *not* received money? It makes far more sense to place the burden of proof on *D*, who may prevail by introducing into evidence a canceled check.

§7.3.4 The Reply

A reply is a pleading by the plaintiff made in response to the defendant's answer.[57] As Rule 7(a)(7) makes clear, this pleading is only required "if

---

[57] Until the Rules were "restyled" in 2007, Rule 7(a) recognized two completely different documents with the name "reply." One was the reply that survives and is discussed in the text here. The other was the defensive responsive pleading to a counterclaim. In §12.5.1, we see that a counterclaim is an affirmative claim for relief filed by the defendant against the plaintiff. Obviously, the plaintiff must respond to this claim or risk default. For some reason, the responsive pleading was called a "reply." This made no sense, and, as amended in 2007, Rule 7(a)(3) now simply refers to such a responsive pleading as "an answer to a

the court orders one." Courts rarely do so. A reply is simply not necessary, because other provisions protect the plaintiff from anything raised in the defendant's answer. For instance, the second sentence of Rule 8(b)(6) says that "[i]f a responsive pleading is not required, an allegation is considered denied or avoided." Because no responsive pleading is required to an answer, this means that any allegations by the defendant in her answer are automatically deemed denied by the plaintiff. The only exception is if the court, for some reason, orders the plaintiff to file a reply. This system avoids a further layer of documents that, in all likelihood, simply is not worth the effort.

In some states that do not follow the Federal Rules, a plaintiff must assert a reply if the defendant raises an affirmative defense in her answer that the plaintiff wants to avoid.

- *P* files a proper complaint against *D. D* responds with a proper answer in which she asserts the affirmative defense of the Statute of Frauds.[58] *P* feels that the Statute of Frauds defense does not apply in this case, because of partial performance of the contract.[59] In some states, *P* will have to file a "reply" in which she controverts the affirmative defense of the Statute of Frauds. No such filing is required in federal court, however, unless the court orders it.

§7.3.5 Special "Heightened" Pleading Requirements

We have seen, especially in §7.3.2, that the Federal Rules generally do not require a party to plead in great detail. This fact is typified by the Rule 8(a) requirement that a claimant state "a short and plain statement of the claim showing that the pleader is entitled to relief." In some substantive areas, however, the Federal Rules (and sometimes statutes) impose more rigorous pleading requirements. In other words, as to certain topics, merely satisfying the "notice" pleading regime of the Federal Rules is not enough. There are, instead, "heightened" pleading requirements, and the party must give more detailed factual allegations as to these topics.

What are these topics? Under Rule 9(b), "[i]n alleging fraud or mistake, a party must state with particularity the circumstances constituting fraud

---

counterclaim." Similarly, Rule 7(a)(4) now calls the responsive pleading to a crossclaim (seen in §12.5.2) "an answer to a crossclaim."

[58] You probably recall from Contracts that certain types of agreements must be put in writing under the Statute of Frauds and cannot be enforced if they are simply oral.

[59] This is a widely recognized situation in which a contract that otherwise would have to be in writing under the Statute of Frauds might be enforced even if not in writing.

or mistake." Similarly, Rule 9(g) provides that "an item of special damage . . . must be specifically stated." Together, then, these two provisions prescribed detailed pleading about three topics — fraud, mistake, and special damage. Of the three, the great majority of case law concerns allegations of the circumstances constituting fraud,[60] and there are several well-understood reasons for requiring detailed allegations as to that topic. Primarily, the requirement is intended to protect the other party (the party accused of fraud) from the reputational harm caused by imputation of fraudulent behavior. In addition, experience shows that assertions of fraud are often made for nuisance value or to increase the chances of a favorable settlement. Further, fraud comes in a huge variety of fact patterns, meaning that the party accused of it should be given a detailed charge to enable her to respond and defend.

The obvious purpose of a heightened pleading requirement is to make it more difficult for allegations to get past the pleading stage and into the litigation stream. Though fraud is often asserted as a *claim*, Rule 9(b) applies to all parties who assert fraud or mistake. For example, the defendant in a contract case may raise the affirmative defense of fraud in the inducement or of mistake. She must allege the circumstances of the fraud or mistake with particularity. As another example, a party may seek to set aside a judgment under Rule 60(b)(1) on the ground of mistake or under Rule 60(b)(3) on the ground of fraud. The party making such a motion must plead the circumstances of either with sufficient detail to satisfy Rule 9(b).

The vexing question, of course, is how much detail is required to satisfy Rule 9(b).[61] In this regard, it is important to remember that Rule 9(b) is to be read in conjunction with Rule 8(a)(2), which requires only a short and plain statement of the claim, and Rule 8(d)(1), which says that "[e]ach allegation must be simple, concise, and direct." The idea is to balance the need for detail in allegations of fraud and mistake with the desire for a simple pleading regime that facilitates decisions on the merits, rather than on technicalities. Decades of experience have not clarified things greatly. Indeed, the number of cases involving motions concerning pleading under

---

[60] Very few cases deal with failure to plead circumstances of mistake with sufficient detail. In *Bankers Trust Co. v. Old Republic Ins. Co.*, 959 F.2d 677, 683 (7th Cir. 1992), the court indicated that in over 50 years only two reported cases held that a complaint should be dismissed for insufficient allegation of mistake. Moreover, the court concluded that the reason for requiring detailed allegations regarding mistake was "a mystery." *See* 2 Moore's Federal Practice §9.03[2].

[61] Interestingly, Official Form 21, in the Appendix of Forms that is part of the Federal Rules, allows what appears to be a very conclusory allegation of fraud in a claim to set aside a fraudulent conveyance. Paragraph 4 of that Form alleges that on a particular date, the defendant conveyed property to the plaintiff "for the purpose of defrauding the plaintiff and hindering or delaying the collection of the debt."

Rule 9(b) has been "quite stunning," and leading commentators have concluded that "the costs of requiring particularized pleading of fraud and mistake outweigh the benefits."[62] Nonetheless, there is no indication that Rule 9(b) will be amended anytime soon.

The difficulty of striking the appropriate balance between simplicity and detail is demonstrated by the myriad approaches courts have adopted in attempting to enforce Rule 9(b). The appropriate approach for enforcing Rule 9(b) is to grant a motion to dismiss for failure to state a claim under Rule 12(b)(6)[63] or a motion to strike under Rule 12(f).[64] Curiously, though, some courts simply refuse to do either, and thus fail to enforce the heightened pleading requirement of Rule 9(b).[65] Others have held that insufficiently detailed pleadings of fraud and mistake are subject to a Rule 12(e) motion for more definite statement. This approach is wrong, since Rule 12(e) is aimed at pleadings so vague or ambiguous that the defending party cannot form a response. Nonetheless, some courts have granted Rule 12(e) motions aimed at providing more detailed allegations of fraud or mistake, even when the pleading was not so vague or ambiguous as to satisfy Rule 12(e).[66]

We can draw some general conclusions from the case law. First, the heightened pleading requirement of Rule 9(b) must be raised by the opposing party. Failure to raise the issue in some appropriate way clearly waives the requirement of particularity.[67] Second, conclusory allegations of fraud are not sufficient. For example, the allegation that the defendant "actively practiced fraud upon the plaintiffs" by failing to tell them about dangers of contamination was insufficient.[68] Third, an allegation of fraud should generally include the identity of the person making the statement, when and where the misrepresentation was made, how it was communicated, and the resulting injury.[69] As one court said, the plaintiff "must adequately specify the statements [she] claims were false or misleading, give particulars as to the respect in which the plaintiff contends the statements were

---

[62] 5 Wright & Miller 582, 581 (2d ed. Supp. 2005).

[63] *See, e.g.,* Caballero-Rivera v. Chase Manhattan Bank, N.A., 276 F.3d 85, 87 n.3 (1st Cir.), *cert. denied,* 536 U.S. 905 (2002). The motion to dismiss will generally be granted without prejudice, to allow the claimant another opportunity to assert the claim sufficiently.

[64] Because Rule 12(b)(6) can be used only to challenge claims (not defenses), the motion to strike is the only appropriate avenue when the insufficiently pleaded allegations of fraud are contained in a defensive pleading. *See, e.g.,* Dynasty Apparel Indus., Inc. v. Rentz, 206 F.R.D. 603, 606 (S.D. Ohio 2002) (motion for summary judgment denied; plaintiff should have moved to strike insufficient allegation of affirmative defense of fraud).

[65] *See* 5 Wright & Miller 667-669 (2d ed. Supp. 2005).

[66] *See, e.g.,* David K. Lindemuth Co. v. Shannon Fin. Corp., 637 F. Supp. 991, 993-994 (N.D. Cal. 1986).

[67] *See, e.g.,* Burton v. R.J. Reynolds Tobacco Co., 181 F. Supp. 2d 1256, 1263 n.5 (D. Kan. 2002).

[68] Coffey v. Foamex L.P., 2 F.3d 157, 162 (6th Cir. 1993).

[69] 2 Moore's Federal Practice §9.03[1][b].

fraudulent, state when and where the statements were made, and identify those responsible for the statements."[70] Finally, in some situations, statutes prescribe special pleading requirements. The Private Securities Litigation Reform Act of 1995 (PSLRA) imposes more stringent requirements than Rule 9(b). It applies in particular securities fraud cases and requires, *inter alia*, that the plaintiff "state with particularity facts giving rise to a strong inference that the defendant acted with the required state of mind."[71]

Rule 9(g), as noted above, requires that an "item of special damage" must be "specifically stated." Special damages are to be distinguished from "general damages." General damages are those that naturally flow from an event; they can be foreseen readily as the normal consequence of an act or omission. For example, a person injured in a car wreck could suffer such foreseeable damages as medical expenses, lost wages, and pain and suffering. Because such damages are general, they can be pleaded generally and demanded as a lump sum.

In contrast, special damages are those that do not normally flow from an event. In other words, they are "unusual for the type of claim in question."[72] For example, in a claim for false arrest, the plaintiff's demand for "great financial damage" constituted special damage.[73] While one normally expects false arrest to lead to pain, emotional suffering, and even humiliation, a claim that it inflicted financial harm generally does not follow. Similarly, most claims for attorneys' fees constitute special damage, because of the American Rule that each party is presumed to bear her own attorneys' fees.[74] Again, while it is difficult to describe exactly how much detail is enough in a given case, the requirement of a detailed pleading of special damages is intended to give the defending party sufficient notice to permit a response.

Some federal courts have imposed heightened pleading requirements in circumstances not covered by Rule 9 or by statute. Faced with burgeoning case loads, these courts have attempted to weed out cases by requiring the plaintiff to plead in detail in certain classes of cases. The main example is litigation brought under 42 U.S.C. §1983, which permits suit for actions "under color of state law" that result in a deprivation of the plaintiff's federal civil rights. Thousands of such cases are brought each year by state prisoners, and many of their claims lack merit.[75]

---

[70] Cosmas v. Hassett, 886 F.2d 8, 11 (2d Cir. 1992).

[71] 15 U.S.C. §78u-4(b)(1).

[72] Aviate v. Metro. Club, Inc., 49 F.3d 1219, 1226 (7th Cir. 1995). *See generally* 2 Moore's Federal Practice §9.08[1][a].

[73] Funk v. Cable, 251 F. Supp. 598, 601 (M.D. Pa. 1996).

[74] *See, e.g.*, National Liberty Corp. v. Wal-Mart Stores, Inc., 120 F.3d 913, 916 (8th Cir. 1997).

[75] One court, acknowledging congressional efforts to reduce the amount of such litigation, noted "the number of frivolous cases filed by imprisoned plaintiffs, who have little to

A municipality (such as a city or a county) is liable under §1983 only if the deprivation alleged was caused by an official policy, custom, or practice of the municipality.[76] Many lower courts required plaintiffs to allege such a policy, custom, or practice with particularity. The effort was understandable. Most cases of this type fail on the merits, and by imposing a heightened pleading requirement, these courts hoped to dismiss at the pleading stage those in which the plaintiff could not allege a city policy, custom, or practice in detail. The Supreme Court rejected the effort quite bluntly, however, in *Leatherman v. Tarrant County*.[77] The reasoning was quite simple and direct: Because nothing in Rule 9 or in any statute requires detailed pleading in a §1983 case, the courts have no authority to impose a heightened pleading requirement.

The Court had to send the same message to the lower courts nine years later in *Swierkiewicz v. Sorema N.A.*,[78] in which it rejected efforts to require detailed pleading in employment discrimination cases. Though the substantive federal law required a plaintiff to establish certain facts at trial to demonstrate a prima facie case, nothing in Rule 9 or in federal statute required the plaintiff to *plead* each element in detail. Again, the Court was blunt: Heightened pleading requirements can be imposed by Federal Rule or by statute, but not by judicial fiat. Notwithstanding this clear Supreme Court precedent, some interesting scholarship demonstrates that district courts have de facto continued to require greater specificity in certain types of cases.[79] It is worth noting that in the enigmatic *Twombly* decision, discussed in detail at §7.3.2, the Court in 2007 insisted that it was not imposing a heightened pleading requirement and reiterated the impropriety of doing so in the absence of a Rule or statute.[80]

In addition to heightened pleading requirements, Rule 9 contains other notable provisions about pleading. Rule 9(b) permits allegations of malice, intent, knowledge, and other "conditions of a person's mind may be alleged generally." This provision reflects the fact that one alleging such topics simply is not in a position to know another party's subjective intent. Thus, she cannot allege such things in detail. Rule 9(c) allows one to "allege

---

lose and excessive amounts of free time with which to pursue their complaints." Napier v. Priestlike, 314 F.3d 528, 531 (11th Cir. 2002).

[76] Monell v. New York City Dept. of Social Servs., 436 U.S. 658 (1978). In other words, a plaintiff whose civil rights were violated by a city officer may sue that officer for damages, but may sue the city for whom the officer worked only if the plaintiff can prove that the officer's acts toward the plaintiff were part of an official city policy, custom, or practice.

[77] 507 U.S. 163 (1993).

[78] 534 U.S. 506 (2002).

[79] Christopher Fairman, *The Myth of Notice Pleading*, 45 Ariz. L. Rev. 987 (2003); Christopher Fairman, *Heightened Pleading*, 81 Tex. L. Rev. 551 (2002).

[80] Bell Atlantic Corp. v. Twombly, 127 S. Ct. 1955, 1973-1974 (2007).

generally that all conditions precedent have occurred or have been performed." It also provides that "when denying that a condition precedent has occurred or been performed, a party must do so with particularity." These provisions recognize that a defending party in a contract case may be in the best position to raise which of several conditions precedent might not have been satisfied. The defendant would do so, of course, by asserting an affirmative defense. Similarly, Rule 9(a)(1)(A) provides that a plaintiff need not allege capacity to sue or be sued. This Rule, too, recognizes that a party claiming that a litigant lacks capacity may raise the issue as an affirmative defense.

§7.3.6   Hypothetical and Inconsistent Pleading

Under Rule 8(d)(2), any party "may set out 2 or more statements of a claim or defense alternatively or hypothetically, either in a single count or defense or in separate ones." Further, "[i]f a party makes alternative statements, the pleading is sufficient if any one of them is sufficient." And Rule 8(d)(3) allows a party to "state as many separate claims or defenses as it has, regardless of consistency." Of course, parties must keep in mind that their allegations are subject to Rule 11, which, as we discuss in §7.7, imposes professionalism standards of good faith.

Rules 8(d)(2) and (d)(3) mark a liberal advance over earlier practice under common law and the codes. Those systems generally did not permit pleading of inconsistent facts or theories. They required a party to adopt a theory and guess on a set of facts to be pursued throughout the case. If the facts, as adduced through discovery and at trial, differed from those pleaded, the party was generally out of luck. Even if the facts showed that the plaintiff was entitled to relief, if it was on a different theory or different set of facts from those alleged, she would lose. The Federal Rules approach is far superior. It recognizes that a party may not be in a position at the outset of the case to know what actually happened or what facts may be established at trial. It permits the parties to plead alternative and even inconsistent theories and facts, and recognizes that the parties will learn about the facts through discovery. As part of this liberal pleading practice, the Federal Rules recognize that pleadings may have to be amended as the litigation unfolds. We discuss amendment of pleadings in §7.6.

Today, many state systems have adopted the Federal Rules approach to hypothetical and inconsistent pleading. A good example is provided by an older case decided by the Illinois Court of Appeals, which is found in several of the Civil Procedure casebooks. In *McCormick v. Kopmann*,[81]

---

[81] 161 N.E.2d 720 (Ill. Ct. App. 1959).

Mrs. McCormick sued two sets of defendants in a single case, seeking recovery for the alleged wrongful death of her husband. Mr. McCormick was killed in a motor vehicle collision; he was driving his own vehicle after visiting a tavern. Mrs. McCormick sued Kopmann, who was the driver of the vehicle that collided with Mr. McCormick's car, and also sued the Hulses, who operated the tavern in which Mr. McCormick had been drinking.

The claim against Kopmann (Count I) alleged that Kopmann was negligent in driving his truck, and that the negligence caused the death of Mr. McCormick. As part of this claim, the plaintiff alleged that Mr. McCormick was free from contributory negligence. In the claim against the Hulses (Count IV), the plaintiff alleged a violation of the dram shop law — in other words, that the Hulses had served alcohol to Mr. McCormick even though he was intoxicated. Obviously, the allegation in Count I that Mr. McCormick was free from negligence is inconsistent with the allegation in Count IV that he was drunk when the collision took place. At trial, the jury concluded that Mr. McCormick had not been drunk and that Kopmann was negligent. The court entered judgment in favor of the plaintiff against Kopmann for $15,500.

On appeal, Kopmann renewed an argument he had made at the trial court — that the inconsistency in the plaintiff's pleading required dismissal of the claim against him. The court disagreed, and affirmed the judgment against Kopmann. After citing the relevant Illinois provision, which mirrored Rule 8(d)(2), the court reviewed the situation from Mrs. McCormick's standpoint:

> There is nothing in the record before us to indicate that the plaintiff knew in advance of trial, that the averments of Count I, and not Count IV, were true. In fact, at the trial, Kopmann attempted to establish the truth of the allegations of Count IV that McCormick was intoxicated at the time of the collision and that his intoxication caused his death. He can hardly be heard now to say that before the trial, the plaintiff should have known that these were not the facts. Where . . . the injured party is still living and able to recollect the events surrounding the accident, pleading in the alternative may not be justified, but where, as in the case at bar, the key witness is deceased, pleading alternative sets of facts is often the only feasible way to proceed.[82]

Think of Mrs. McCormick's plight if she were not permitted to plead in the alternative. She would have to choose a theory at the outset and proceed against only one defendant at a time. If she sued the Hulses and lost, she would have to bring a second suit against Kopmann. And there is no guaranty that she would win that case. It is conceivable that the jury in the case against the Hulses would conclude that Kopmann was liable, and

---

[82]*Id.* at 728 (citations omitted).

that the jury in the case against Kopmann would conclude that the Hulses were liable. Alternative pleading allows the claims against both to go forward in a single case, and allows that plaintiff to avoid the possibility of being left out in the cold if she has to sue the defendants in separate suits.

Again, however, a lawyer in federal court must sign pleadings under Rule 11. As we discuss in §7.7, the lawyer's signature constitutes a certification, *inter alia*, that she has read the document, has made a reasonable investigation, and has in good faith concluded that the allegations are grounded in fact and law. There may be cases in which the state of the party's knowledge will rule out alternative pleading. On the other hand, a party is not required to adopt a single theory if she is in doubt about the factual background or legal theories underlying her claim or defense.

Inconsistent pleading is not limited to plaintiffs. As we discuss in §12.5.1, the defendant may assert a counterclaim against the plaintiff in the pending case, rather than suing on her claim separately. It is not uncommon for a defendant to adopt alternative theories in her defenses, on the one hand, and her counterclaim, on the other. For example, a defendant sued for breach of contract may assert as a defense that the parties never entered a contract while at the same time asserting a counterclaim seeking recovery from the plaintiff on the contract.[83] Again, the defendant is freed from the burden of having to guess which set of facts will be established at trial, and the judicial system is empowered to determine the overall dispute in a single case.

§7.4　Voluntary and Involuntary Dismissal

Rule 41(a) addresses voluntary dismissal and Rule 41(b) addresses the effect of an involuntary dismissal. Whenever a case is dismissed — voluntarily or involuntarily — the plaintiff will be very concerned with whether the dismissal is "without prejudice." Such a dismissal means that the plaintiff may assert the claim again (assuming the statute of limitations has not run). Another way to say the same thing is that the dismissal is "not on the merits." In contrast, a dismissal "with prejudice" (or "on the merits") means that the plaintiff may not assert the claim again. The claim is extinguished.

---

[83] *See, e.g.*, Olympia Hotels Corp. v. Johnson Wax Dev. Corp., 908 F.2d 1363 (7th Cir. 1990).

§7.4.1 Voluntary Dismissal (Rule 41(a))

Voluntary dismissal is exactly what it says — the plaintiff has filed a case and now wants to dismiss it. Perhaps the plaintiff has had a change of heart. Or perhaps the parties have settled the case and entered into an agreement that requires the plaintiff to dismiss the proceeding. Whatever the plaintiff's reason, note that Rule 41(a)(1)(A) limits her ability to take a voluntary dismissal without a court order. In fact, she can do so in only two situations, by two mechanisms. First, under Rule 41(a)(1)(A)(i), the plaintiff, unilaterally, may file a notice of dismissal. The requirement that the notice be *filed* makes it clear that it cannot be an oral notice — it must be in writing. The notice of dismissal may be filed, however, *only* before the adverse party "serves either an answer or a motion for summary judgment." Second, under Rule 41(a)(1)(A)(ii), the plaintiff may dismiss by stipulation of dismissal "signed by all parties who have appeared." Note that this second option does not permit unilateral action by the plaintiff — she must get the signed agreement of all parties who have appeared.

- *P* sues *D*. *D* files and serves her answer. Now *P* wants to take a voluntary dismissal. May she do so unilaterally by filing a notice of dismissal? No. Why? Because under Rule 41(a)(1)(A)(i), she may do that only before *D* served her answer. She may dismiss voluntarily without court order only if she gets a written stipulation that she and *D* sign.
- *P* sues *D*. *D* files and serves a motion to dismiss for failure to state a claim under Rule 12(b)(6). Now *P* wants to take a voluntary dismissal. May she do so unilaterally, by filing a notice of dismissal? Yes. Why? Because she has a right to do so anytime before *D* "serves either an answer or a motion for summary judgment." *D* in this hypothetical has done neither. A motion to dismiss for failure to state a claim is neither an answer nor a motion for summary judgment.

Rule 41(a)(1)(B) makes it clear that dismissal by either method — notice of dismissal or by stipulation of parties — is generally without prejudice. Thus, the plaintiff can file her claim again, with one exception, found in the second sentence of Rule 41(a)(1)(B): "But if the plaintiff previously dismissed any federal- or state-court action based on or including the same claim, a notice of dismissal operates as an adjudication on the merits." In other words, the first voluntary dismissal is without prejudice. But if the plaintiff refiles the case and then dismisses *by filing a notice of dismissal* (not by stipulation), that second dismissal operates as an adjudication on the merits (which means it is with prejudice, and the claim is extinguished). Importantly, as the Rule makes clear, this is true regardless of whether the first case was in federal or state court. So long as the second case is in federal court and is dismissed by filing a notice of dismissal, that dismissal is with prejudice.

- *P* sues *D* in state (or federal) court. *P* takes a voluntary dismissal of that case. It is without prejudice. *P* then sues *D* in federal court, asserting the same claim (and invoking federal subject matter jurisdiction). Now *P* files notice of dismissal. The dismissal caused by that filing is with prejudice.
- *P* sues *D* in state (or federal) court. *P* takes a voluntary dismissal of that case. It is without prejudice. *P* then sues *D* in federal court, asserting the same claim (and invoking federal subject matter jurisdiction). Now *P* dismisses this second case by stipulation of the parties. This dismissal is *without* prejudice. The language of Rule 41(a)(1)(B) clearly provides that the second dismissal operates on the merits *only* if it is effected by notice of dismissal, not by stipulation.[84]

It makes sense to limit the number of times a plaintiff can take a unilateral voluntary dismissal without prejudice. Otherwise, the plaintiff could harass the defendant by repeatedly suing and dismissing the claim. It also makes sense to limit the plaintiff's right to take a unilateral voluntary dismissal to a time early in the litigation. That way, it is unlikely that a case will be dismissed after the defendant or the court have invested substantial resources in it. Because Rule 41(a)(1)(A)(i) permits unilateral voluntary dismissal only before the defendant has served an answer or a motion for summary judgment, it is unlikely that dismissal will have wasted substantial resources.

On the other hand, there are cases in which the defendant and the court will have invested significant time and resources before the defendant has served an answer or motion for summary judgment. In such cases, should the plaintiff nonetheless have the right to dismiss under Rule 41(a)(1)(A)(i)? The answer appears to be yes. In *American Soccer Co. v. Score First Enterprises*,[85] the parties litigated the difficult issue of whether the plaintiff was entitled to a preliminary injunction for two months after the case was filed. The defendant and the court invested a great deal of time and effort on the matter. On the other hand, however, the defendant had not served an answer or a motion for summary judgment. After two months, the plaintiff filed a notice of dismissal. The court held that the plaintiff had a right to do so, because the terms of Rule 41(a)(1)(A)(i) were satisfied. The wasted effort by the defendant and the court was irrelevant.

Our discussion of voluntary dismissal to this point has not involved action by the court. Rule 41(a)(2) addresses voluntary dismissal by court order. It provides that in any situation not covered by Rule 41(a)(1), the court may grant a plaintiff's motion for voluntary dismissal. The Rule

[84] *See* Sutton Place Level. Co. v. Abacus Mortg. Inv. Co., 826 F.2d 637 (7th Cir. 1987).
[85] 187 F.3d 1108 (9th Cir. 1999).

makes clear that the court may impose whatever terms and conditions it deems proper.

- *P* sues *D*. *D* files and serves her answer. *P* wants to dismiss voluntarily, but *D* does not agree to the dismissal. *P* cannot act unilaterally under Rule 41(a)(1)(A)(i), because *D* has served an answer. *P* cannot dismiss under Rule 41(a)(1)(A)(ii), because D will not stipulate to the dismissal. *P* can have the case dismissed only if the court orders dismissal under Rule 41(a)(2).

Unless the court says otherwise in the order, the court's dismissal is presumed to be without prejudice. Under what circumstances would a court grant a motion for voluntary dismissal *with* prejudice? After all, doing so extinguishes the plaintiff's claim; she may not reassert it. One example is provided by *Grover v. Eli Lilly Co.*,[86] in which the Sixth Circuit held that the district court abused its discretion in entering a dismissal without prejudice. The case invoked diversity of citizenship jurisdiction and involved a claim alleged under Ohio law. Because Ohio law on the question of liability was not clear, the district court certified the question to the Ohio Supreme Court for clarification (we see that procedure in §10.8). That court held, four to three, that the plaintiff did not have a claim. The district court entered an order of dismissal *without* prejudice, reasoning that the Ohio court might change its mind or that the Ohio legislature might provide a remedy for persons such as the plaintiff. The Sixth Circuit reversed and explained that the "primary purpose" of requiring court approval for dismissal under Rule 41(a)(2) "is to protect the nonmoving party [the defendant] from unfair treatment."[87] Such unfair treatment consisted of the "plain legal prejudice" caused by dismissing without prejudice and leaving the defendant open to potential liability based upon a subsequent change in the law. It concluded: "At the point when the law clearly dictates a result for the defendant, it is unfair to subject him to continued exposure to potential liability by dismissing the case without prejudice."[88]

Finally, Rule 41(a)(2) expressly addresses dismissal of the case if a counterclaim is pending. (In other words, if the defendant has asserted a claim against the plaintiff in the pending case before the plaintiff moves to dismiss the case.) In such a situation, the court should dismiss against the defendant's objection "only if the counterclaim can remain pending for independent adjudication." Thus, if the counterclaim cannot remain in

---

[86] 33 F.3d 716 (6th Cir. 1994).
[87] *Id.* at 718.
[88] *Id.* at 719.

court (e.g., because there is no subject matter jurisdiction[89]), the court should not allow the plaintiff to dismiss her claim. If the counterclaim can remain in court for independent adjudication, the court may allow the plaintiff to dismiss her claim. This rule is intended to ensure that the defendant's claim against the plaintiff remain on the court's docket if the defendant so desires.

§7.4.2   Involuntary Dismissal (Rule 41(b))

Rule 41(b) provides for dismissal in three situations: for failure of the plaintiff (1) to prosecute the case, (2) to comply with the Federal Rules, or (3) to comply with a court order. Three initial points are important. First, Rule 41(b) is not exclusive. We already know that there are several ways in which a case may be dismissed against the plaintiff's wishes. For instance, all the defenses in Rule 12(b) — including lack of personal jurisdiction, lack of subject matter jurisdiction, or improper venue — may result in an involuntary dismissal. In addition, as we see in §7.7, a serious violation of ethical rules may also result in dismissal. In §8.4, we see that dismissal is possible as a discovery sanction in extreme cases as well. So Rule 41(b) augments other provisions that permit involuntary dismissal. Second, Rule 41(b) permits dismissal "of the action or any claim." There may be circumstances in which dismissal of less than the entire case is appropriate, such as when the plaintiff fails to comply with a court order concerning a particular claim. Third, though Rule 41(b) expressly provides that "a defendant may move to dismiss" for any of the enumerated reasons, the Supreme Court concluded in *Link v. Wabash Railway Co.*[90] that the Rule permits a district court to dismiss *sua sponte*, without a motion by the defendant.

Link is a widely cited case on involuntary dismissal.[91] In that case, the plaintiff filed suit in August 1954. The case was dismissed without having gone to trial in October 1960, which meant that this relatively simple personal injury case lingered on the docket for six years without going to trial.

[89] An example would be a counterclaim that failed to invoke diversity of citizenship or federal question or supplemental jurisdiction. *See* 8 Moore's Federal Practice §41.40[8]. Moreover, a court will usually not dismiss if the claim to be dismissed is inextricably linked to a pending counterclaim. *See, e.g.,* Bosteve Ltd. v. Marauszwki, 110 F.R.D. 257, 259 (E.D.N.Y. 1986).

[90] 370 U.S. 626 (1962).

[91] There are others. The Supreme Court seems to issue such an opinion every so often as a reminder to plaintiffs' lawyers that they must play by the rules and prosecute their cases with appropriate diligence. *See, e.g.,* Henderson v. United States, 517 U.S. 654, 662 (1996) ("Rule 41(b) [provides] for dismissal 'for failure of plaintiff to prosecute,' and could be invoked as a check against unreasonable delay."); Roadway Exp., Inc. v. Piper, 447 U.S. 752 (1980); National Hockey League v. Metropolitan Hockey Club, Inc., 427 U.S. 639 (1976).

How did that happen? Sixteen months were spent in the plaintiff's securing reversal of the district judge's erroneous dismissal of the case. Beyond that, though, the reason for the delay was the plaintiff's lawyer's seeking extensions in which to complete discovery. The precipitous event, though, was when the plaintiff's lawyer failed to attend a pretrial conference (something we discuss in §8.5) in October 1960. The lawyer called the judge's chambers on the day of the hearing and reported that he was busy working on a state-court case and could not attend the conference. The district judge's patience was exhausted, and he dismissed the case "for failure of the plaintiff's counsel to appear at the pretrial, for failure to prosecute this action."

The Supreme Court affirmed, and held that the district judge did not abuse his discretion by dismissing. Justice Black wrote a spirited dissent, and criticized the Court's willingness to punish the plaintiff for the misdeeds of his lawyer. The majority opinion, by Justice Harlan, concluded that the plaintiff had retained the lawyer, and thus had to live with the consequences.[92] By implication, the majority seems to be saying that a reasonable client would figure out that there is a problem when his (relatively simple) case has not gone to trial in six years. Clearly, each viewpoint creates problems. Justice Black's view would seem to make it impossible to dismiss, no matter how dilatory a lawyer has been, if the client did not participate in the delay. On the other hand, Justice Harlan's view that the docket may be cleared of such cases may ignore the fact that the dismissal may result in the plaintiff's filing of a malpractice case against the lawyer.

In *Link*, the district judge did not warn the plaintiff or his lawyer that failure to attend the pretrial conference could result in dismissal. Moreover, the court did not provide the lawyer a hearing at which the lawyer could explain why he did not attend. On the record of the case, however, the Supreme Court concluded that it was clear that the lawyer knew how serious the situation was. Still, it is clearly preferable for a court to provide a warning and an opportunity to explain dilatory behavior before entering dismissal. As we discuss in §7.7, Rule 11 now expressly requires notice and an opportunity to be heard before a court may impose sanctions less drastic than dismissal.

Federal Rule 83(a) permits each federal district to adopt Local Rules that augment the Federal Rules. (It is crucial in the real world that you consult the relevant Local Rules; never let any of the provisions in those

---

[92] This theory — that the client has hired the attorney and thus is bound by the mistakes of her "agent" — is a pervasive one. We see it again in §9.7, concerning motions to set aside a judgment. When an attorney's errors have resulted in a default judgment against a defendant, the defendant might attempt to set aside the judgment under Rule 60(b)(6) for extraordinary circumstances. Though the traditional view has been that the attorney's mistakes do not justify setting aside a judgment, some courts will accord relief if the attorney was guilty of gross negligence.

rules sneak up on you.) Some districts have a Local Rule providing for involuntary dismissal if the docket sheet shows that there has been no activity in the case for a given period, say, for one year. In such circumstance, the court will issue an Order to Show Cause (an O.S.C.[93]), which requires the plaintiff to demonstrate why the court should not dismiss the case for lack of prosecution.[94] Even in the absence of a Local Rule, the court certainly has the inherent authority to issue an O.S.C. when it thinks the plaintiff has not been diligent in prosecuting the case. In §8.5, we see that the Federal Rules seek to avoid such lulls in the case by imposing several scheduling requirements and conferences to keep the parties' feet to the fire.

The second sentence of Rule 41(b) addresses whether an involuntary dismissal is with prejudice (or "operates as an adjudication on the merits"). The general answer is yes — an involuntary dismissal is considered on the merits, and thus the claim is extinguished. But Rule 41(b) recognizes exceptions to this general rule. First, the court may provide to the contrary in its order of dismissal. Thus, if the court dismisses the case "without prejudice," it does *not* act as an adjudication on the merits. Second, if the dismissal is based upon lack of jurisdiction (personal or subject matter), improper venue, or failure to join a party under Rule 19, the dismissal is not considered to be on the merits. This provision recognizes that such dismissals — essentially for the court's lack of power over the case — do not address the merits in any way and thus should not bar the plaintiff from reasserting the claim.

On the other hand, this provision means that a dismissal for failure to prosecute would (absent court order to the contrary) act as an adjudication on the merits and thus bar refiling. This seems odd. When the court dismisses on this basis, there has been no adjudication on the merits in fact. But Rule 41(b) says that an involuntary dismissal "operates as an adjudication on the merits." We revisit this topic in Chapter 11, when we discuss claim and issue preclusion. It will be of enormous importance there whether a judgment is considered "on the merits." We also see (in §11.2.2)

---

[93] In some states, the O.S.C. is referred to by the ancient term *rule nisi* (pronounced nigh-sigh). Courts may issue an O.S.C. (or *rule nisi*) for any number of reasons; for example, it may want a party to explain why the court should not enter sanctions against it. Here we are concerned with an O.S.C. for failure to prosecute the case.

[94] Many states have similar provisions. California has stronger medicine. By statute, the trial court loses jurisdiction over the case if trial has not commenced within five years after the case was filed. Cal. Code Civ. Proc. §583.360.

that the Supreme Court has opened the door to limiting the preclusive effect of Rule 41(b). For now, though, the general rule is straightforward: Any involuntary dismissal except one based upon jurisdiction, venue, or indispensable parties is deemed to be with prejudice.

§7.5 Failure to Respond: Default and Default Judgment

§7.5.1 The Difference Between Default and Default Judgment

In §7.4, we saw that a case might be dismissed for the plaintiff's failure to play by the rules — for her failure to prosecute the case, to abide by the Federal Rules, or to obey a court order. In this section, we consider a bad fate that can befall the defendant — specifically, default and default judgment under Federal Rule 55. It bears note that Rule 55 is not the only provision that can result in entry of default judgment against the defendant. We see in §8.4 that the court may in extreme cases order default judgment against a defendant for failure to abide by the discovery provisions of the Federal Rules. Here, however, we are concerned with default caused by the defendant's failure to respond appropriately to a suit against her. This situation raises conflicting policies. For one, we prefer to decide cases on their merits, rather than on procedural technicalities. On the other hand, though, the plaintiff should not be put to undue delay, and the defendant should be required to play by the rules.

At the outset, it is important to distinguish a "default" from a "default judgment." A default is simply a notation made by the court clerk's office on the docket sheet for the case, indicating that the defendant has failed to respond within the time required by Rule 12. The entry of default, however, does not entitle the plaintiff to relief. To recover relief on her claim, the plaintiff must obtain a default *judgment*, which can then be enforced like any other judgment. Under Rule 55, in limited circumstances, the clerk of the court may enter the judgment. In other circumstances, however, the judgment can only be entered by the court itself. The entry of default is an absolute prerequisite to obtaining a default judgment. Thus, the first step when the defendant fails to respond timely under Rule 12 is for the plaintiff to seek entry of the default. When that is done, she can seek entry of default judgment.

§7.5.2   Entry of Default (Rule 55(a))

The default is usually entered by the clerk of the court,[95] and not by the judge.[96] Under Rule 55(a), the clerk has no discretion in the matter. If the plaintiff shows "by affidavit or otherwise" that the defendant[97] has failed "to plead or otherwise defend as provided by these rules," the clerk "shall" enter the defendant's default. On the other hand, Rule 55(a) does not provide for the automatic entry of default once the defendant's time for responding has run. The practice is to the contrary in some state courts, in which entry of default is automatic when the time for responding has expired. Rule 55(a), though, clearly requires that the plaintiff do something to have the default entered.

In §7.4.1, we saw that the defendant generally must respond under Rule 12 within 20 days after being served with process. The person who served process on the defendant is required to make a report to the court indicating when service was effective. (We discussed this requirement in §3.3.) The clerk's office records this information on the docket sheet for the case. Even if the server failed to make the report to the court, the plaintiff can present proof of when service was effected, and show the clerk that more than 20 days has elapsed. Any response filed by the defendant is recorded on the docket sheet for the case, so the clerk can quickly determine whether the defendant has responded under Rule 12.

Though the entry of the default does not entitle the plaintiff to relief (she needs a judgment for that), it does one important thing — it cuts off the defendant's right to file a response to the complaint. What happens if the defendant wants to serve and file her answer more than 20 days after she was served with process? If the plaintiff has already had the default entered, the defendant cannot file the answer, and will have to make a motion to set aside the default (which we address in §7.5.4). If the plaintiff has *not* had the default entered, technically the defendant should move for an extension of time in which to respond under Rule 6(b). In practice,

---

[95] Do not confuse clerks of the court with law clerks. The former are employees of the court system, who are required to oversee the filing of documents and maintenance of files and other administrative tasks. The latter are recent law school graduates hired by a judge (or by the court itself) to provide research and drafting assistance for the judge. Judicial clerkships are prestigious and provide invaluable experience to anyone interested in practicing litigation. Do not overlook them as an employment opportunity when you graduate from law school.

[96] Technically, though Rule 55(a) permits entry of default by the clerk, it does not prohibit the court (judge) from doing so. So the judge certainly has the authority to enter a default, but generally there is no reason to go to anyone but the clerk for entry of default.

[97] Actually, any defending party. Remember, a plaintiff might be sued by the defendant on a counterclaim. The plaintiff is a defending party on the counterclaim, and must respond to it under Rule 12. Here we assume that the defaulting party is the defendant.

however, some courts have permitted the defendant simply to respond anytime before the clerk enters the default, even without making a motion for extension of time.[98] Thus the plaintiff will want to get the default on the books as soon as possible, since it will preclude the defendant from responding; she will have to make a motion to set aside the default.

- ° *P* files her complaint against *D* and has process served on June 1. Under Rule 12(a)(1)(A)(i), *D* must respond no later than June 21. She fails to do so. On June 22, *P* demonstrates to the clerk of the court that *D* has not responded in a timely fashion. The clerk enters the default on the record. *D* cannot now answer or otherwise respond to the complaint unless she convinces the court to set aside the default.
- ° Same facts except here *P* fails to request entry of default. On June 24, *D* serves and files an answer in the case. The answer is not timely, because it is not served within 20 days after *D* was served with process. On the other hand, though, *P* has not had the clerk enter a default. In all likelihood, the clerk will allow *D* to answer. The more appropriate course for *D* would have been to make a motion for extension of time in which to respond under Rule 6(b). But many courts seem willing to let the defendant respond late rather than go to the trouble of making such a motion. After all, *P* could have cut off *D*'s right to respond by having the default entered as soon as *D* was late.

§7.5.3 Entry of Default Judgment (Rule 55(b))

Once the plaintiff gets the default, she will want to obtain the default judgment, which she can enforce to recover relief. Entry of default judgment in federal court is governed by Rule 55(b). It provides that the clerk of the court can enter default judgment in very limited circumstances. Outside those circumstances, however, the clerk cannot act and the plaintiff must seek the default judgment from the court itself (meaning from a judge). It is appropriate to limit the situations in which a clerk can enter judgment. After all, a judgment is an order — issued under the authority of the court — that creates a legal obligation from the defendant to the plaintiff. We are understandably reluctant to allow a bureaucratic officer to enter such an order, and thus limit the types of cases in which this can be done. Indeed, under the procedural provisions of some states, the clerk is never empowered to enter a judgment; in such states, judicial involvement is always required for entry of a default judgment.

Under Rule 55(b)(1), the clerk can enter default judgment at the behest of the plaintiff *only* if four things are true. First, the claim must be for a

---

[98] *See, e.g.*, Bach v. Mason, 190 F.R.D. 567, 574 (D. Idaho 1999); Barnsley v. Runyon, 1997 U.S. Dist. LEXIS 23551 (S.D. Ohio 1997), *aff'd*, 1999 U.S. App. LEXIS 4009 (6th Cir. 1999); DeTore v. Local No. 245, 511 F. Supp. 171 (D.N.J. 1981).

sum certain or for an amount that can be made certain by calculation. Second, the plaintiff must provide an affidavit (which is a sworn statement, executed under penalty of perjury) of the damages due. Third, the defendant must have failed to appear in the case. (We see in a moment (two hypotheticals down) that it is possible to default after having made an appearance. Default judgment from the clerk is available only if the defendant has failed to appear at all.) Fourth, the defendant cannot be a minor or an incompetent.[99] If these requirements are satisfied, the clerk has no discretion, but "shall enter judgment for [the amount shown in the affidavit] and costs against the defendant." In sum, then, the clerk enters the judgment only in those cases in which there is no need for judicial discretion: The claim is for a sum certain, and the defendant has shown no interest in responding, let alone litigating the merits or the question of damages.

- P sues D for $100,000 damages from breach of a contract. D is served with process on June 1. D failed to respond in any way within the 20 days permitted for response under Rule 12. On June 22, P has the clerk enter the default. P can ask the clerk to enter the judgment under Rule 55(b)(1), so long as D is neither an infant nor an incompetent, and provided P provides an affidavit that the $100,000 is the sum of damage she has suffered. The clerk can enter the default judgment because this case is for a sum certain and D has made no response whatsoever.

On the other hand, if any of the four requirements mentioned above is not satisfied, the clerk cannot enter the judgment under Rule 55(b)(1). Then, the plaintiff must seek entry of default judgment from the judge under Rule 55(b)(2). She does so by making what the Rule calls an "application" for default judgment.

- Same facts as in the preceding hypothetical, but here D responds to the complaint by making a timely motion to dismiss for lack of personal jurisdiction. The court denies the motion. D then fails to serve and file an answer within the appropriate time. P again asks the clerk to enter default. Here, however, P cannot ask the clerk for entry of default judgment. Why? Because here, D has made an appearance in the case — the motion to dismiss — and thus the requirements of Rule 55(b)(1) are not all satisfied. P can obtain a judgment only from the court.

---

[99] Though Rule 55(b) speaks only of the defendant's being neither an infant or incompetent, provisions of the Soldiers' and Sailors' Civil Relief Act, 50 U.S.C. App. §501 et seq., also impose certain requirements for obtaining a default judgment when a defendant is a member of the Armed Services.

The court will almost always hold a hearing on the application for default judgment.[100] In these cases, it is important to understand that the plaintiff has no *right* to a default judgment under Rule 55(b)(2), even though the defendant is clearly in default.[101] Why? Because, as we have said before, our system of justice prefers to resolve disputes on the merits rather than on technicalities. The matter is in the district judge's discretion, and she may ask for evidence on any relevant matter, including the strength of the plaintiff's claim on the merits and the viability of any defense the defendant might have. Courts generally will determine whether to grant a motion for entry of default judgment based upon (1) whether the defendant's failure to respond is willful, (2) whether the plaintiff has been harmed, and (3) whether the defendant has a meritorious defense to the underlying case.[102] The judge might refuse to enter judgment when it is clear that the merits are disputed and the potential liability is large.[103] On the other hand, if the defendant's contentions on the merits are weak, or if the delay has harmed the plaintiff, or if the defendant has acted in bad faith, the court would be inclined to enter default judgment.[104] In one case, the court entered judgment even though the defendants had a meritorious defense, because the defendants had been willful in failing to communicate with their lawyers and had simply not taken the suit seriously until after default, and the resulting delay prejudiced the plaintiff by leaving unresolved an important issue of whether the plaintiff's patent on a product was invalid.[105]

Does the defendant get notice of the hearing on the application for a default judgment under Rule 55(b)(2)? The Rule clearly requires written notice to the defendant, served at least three days before the hearing on the application, but *only* if the defendant has "appeared personally or by a representative" in the case.[106] The most obvious examples of an appearance are the defendant's making a motion or answering in the case. But courts are fairly liberal here in defining what constitutes an appearance.

---

[100] There are, however, clear cases in which no hearing is required. *See, e.g.,* United States v. Cabrera-Diaz, 106 F. Supp. 2d 234 (D.P.R. 2000).

[101] *See* Ganther v. Ingle, 75 F.3d 207, 209 (5th Cir. 1996).

[102] *See* Jackson v. Beech, 636 F.2d 831, 836 (D.C. Cir. 1986). At this point, according to some courts, it is not necessary that the defendant show that the defense is likely to win. Rather, merely alleging a colorable defense is sufficient. *Id.* at 837.

[103] *See, e.g.,* Pinaud v. County of Suffolk, 52 F.3d 1139 (2d Cir. 1995).

[104] *See, e.g.,* Bambu Sales v. Ozak Trading, 58 F.3d 849 (2d Cir. 1995).

[105] Honda Power Equip. Mfg., Inc. v. Woodhouse, 219 F.R.D. 2, 9-13 (D.D.C. 2003). Mere delay in obtaining relief ordinarily does not constitute the kind of "prejudice" relevant under Rule 55(b). *Id.* at 12-13. In *Honda Power,* however, the delay caused harm to the plaintiff because it left hanging over its head the allegation that a patent it held might be invalid.

[106] Whether the defendant appeared in the case was also important for another reason. If she has appeared, the clerk cannot enter default judgment under Rule 55(b)(1). (Just as if the claim were not for a sum certain or if the case were against an infant or incompetent, the clerk could not enter judgment.)

There is even support for finding that a defendant can make an appearance without submitting anything to the court. In one case, the defendant's lawyer did not file anything with the court, but wrote a letter to plaintiff's counsel noting the defendant's lack of money and expressing a desire to settle the case and to avoid default.[107]

If the court decides to enter default judgment, how does it determine the relief to be granted to the plaintiff? As we saw above, when the clerk enters the default judgment under Rule 55(b)(1), the judgment is for the sum claimed in the plaintiff's affidavit. Under Rule 55(b)(2), if the plaintiff has sued for a sum certain and the defendant does not contest that sum, the court may enter judgment for that amount without the need for further inquiry. But when the sum is not readily calculable, or if the defendant contests the amount, the court will hold a hearing to determine the appropriate remedy. Though a defaulting defendant has basically conceded her liability, a default generally does not concede the amount of damage.[108] The court essentially holds a trial on the question of damages, at which there may be a right to trial by jury (discussed at §9.2.2). In this regard, however, note that Rule 54(c) provides that the judgment can never exceed the amount of damages the plaintiff demanded in the complaint, nor can it include a type of relief that she did not seek in the complaint.[109] These limitations reflect uneasiness about default judgments. The defendant should not be subjected to greater loss than that for which she was given notice.

- ° *P* sues *D* for damages of $100,000 in federal court, properly invoking subject matter jurisdiction and stating a claim. Within 20 days after being served with process, *D* moves to dismiss for lack of personal jurisdiction. The court denies the motion and orders *D* to respond to the complaint within ten days. *D* fails to do so. *P* has the clerk enter the default under Rule 55(a), but cannot have the clerk enter the default judgment under Rule 55(b)(1). Why not? Because here, *D* made an appearance in the case, so the requirement of Rule 55(b)(1) that *D* have defaulted for failure to appear cannot be met.

- ° That means that *P* must apply to the court for entry of default judgment. *D* will get notice of the hearing because she appeared in the case. If, after the hearing, the court enters default judgment, it will do so in an amount shown appropriate at the hearing *except* that it cannot exceed $100,000, because that is the amount claimed in the complaint. P cannot be given a different type of relief than that which she demanded in her complaint.

---

[107] *See* Key Bank of Maine v. Tablecloth Textile Co., 74 F.3d 349 (1st Cir. 1996).

[108] *See, e.g.,* Gowen, Inc. v. F/V Quality One, 244 F.3d 64 (1st Cir. 2001), *cert. denied,* 534 U.S. 886 (defendant who did not oppose entry of default judgment entitled to contest damages).

[109] Neither of these limitations applies in nondefault cases. As we see in §9.2.4 (and mentioned in §7.3.2), in nondefault cases, in which the defendant's liability is adjudicated, the plaintiff can recover any and all relief to which the evidence shows she is entitled.

Thus, even if the facts adduced at the hearing demonstrated that she was entitled to an injunction against *D*, she cannot get the injunction. Judgment by default is limited to the type of relief sought in the complaint. *P* will, however, recover from *D* the costs *P* incurred in the case.[110]

§7.5.4 Motions to Set Aside (Rule 55(c) and Rule 60(b))

A defendant who has suffered a default or a default judgment may move to set it aside. It is important, however, to distinguish the two situations. Rule 55(c) provides that the defaulting party may move to set aside a default "for good cause." Regarding a default *judgment*, however, the rule refers to Rule 60(b) as the appropriate vehicle for relief. Rule 60(b) applies to a motion to set aside any judgment, not just default judgments, and we discuss it in §9.7. For present purposes, it is enough to note that courts are usually more willing to set aside a default than a default judgment. This general rule makes sense. A default is merely an interlocutory (nonfinal) ruling in the course of the case. A judgment, in contrast, is the official judicial order that the plaintiff is entitled to recover from the defendant. Thus, "[w]hile a default judgment may be vacated only by satisfying the stricter standards applied to final, appealable orders under [Rule] 60(b), an entry of default may be set aside for 'good cause shown.'"[111]

A defendant is not entitled to have the default or default judgment set aside merely for the asking. The matter is entrusted to the district court's discretion. In ruling on a motion to set aside, the court must be mindful of two conflicting policies (which we identified in §5.7.1). One, of course, is that the plaintiff's quest for justice should not be delayed unduly by the defendant's failure to play by the rules. The other is that our system of justice prefers to resolve disputes on their merits, and not on technicalities.

Motion to Set Aside a Default. To accommodate these policies, Rule 55(c) requires that the defendant moving to set aside the default show "good cause" for her failure to defend in a timely fashion. Good cause means a reasonable excuse. For example, if default resulted from a misunderstanding between the lawyers for the respective parties,[112] or from an error by the defendant's lawyer (as opposed to the defendant herself),[113] or

---

[110] This is consistent with the general rule that the winner in litigation recovers her costs from the loser. Costs, remember, do not include attorneys' fees. See §§1.1, 9.3.

[111] Berthelsen v. Kane, 907 F.2d 617, 620 (6th Cir. 1990). When this case was decided, Rule 55(c) spoke of "good cause shown." Now, as restyled in 2007, it speaks of "good cause."

[112] *See, e.g.*, Shepard Claims Serv., Inc. v. William Darrah & Assocs., 796 F.2d 190 (6th Cir. 1986) (misinterpretation of extension of time granted by plaintiff's lawyer).

[113] *See, e.g.*, Augusta Fiberglass Coatings, Inc. v. Fodor Contracting Corp., 843 F.2d 808 (4th Cir. 1988).

an inability to communicate with counsel,[114] or illness,[115] or from some honest oversight by the defendant, the court may find that the defendant has shown good cause. This will be especially likely if the court is convinced that the defendant is acting in good faith.

Although Rule 55(c) does not mention timing, courts will insist that the motion to set aside the default be made within a "reasonable time." As a practical matter, the longer the defendant waits to bring her motion to set aside the default, the tougher it will be to convince the court that she is acting in good faith, or even that she has "good cause." Each case is decided on its own facts, so the wise defendant, obviously, will make the motion as soon as possible. The district court has authority to require the defendant to post a bond or other security as a condition of setting aside the default.

But there is an important second requirement. Though Rule 55(c) does not mention it, the court may well insist that the defendant show that she has a viable defense.[116] It makes no sense to set aside a default, and thus to put the case back in the litigation stream, if the defendant has no colorable defense on the merits.[117] Because the issue is addressed to the discretion of the court, there is no uniform approach to how strong a showing the defendant must make. Most courts seem to insist at least that the defendant allege specific facts, as opposed to conclusory allegations, that constitute a defense on the merits. Some courts are more demanding, and insist that the defendant demonstrate not merely the existence of a meritorious defense, but a "fair probability of success on the merits."[118] It is not easy to reconcile the case law regarding setting aside a default. In some opinions, courts seem unwilling to set aside a default if the defendant was culpable in some way in her failure to respond in a timely fashion, regardless of the presence of a viable defense.[119] In other cases, courts have set aside a default despite the defendant's culpability when there was no showing of prejudice to the plaintiff and when the defendant had a viable defense.[120]

Motion to Set Aside Default Judgment. As we see in §9.7, any judgment — including a default judgment — is subject to being vacated by the court that entered it under Rule 60(b). That Rule states several

---

[114] *See, e.g.,* Biton v. Palestinian Interim Self Govt. Auth., 233 F. Supp. 2d 31, 33 (D.D.C. 2002) (defendants involved in Palestinian-Israeli conflict unable to communicate with lawyers in the United States).

[115] *See, e.g.,* Leshore v. County of Worcester, 945 F.2d 471 (1st Cir. 1991).

[116] *Berthesen, supra,* 907 F.2d at 620-621.

[117] The defense must be on the merits of the case. The mere recitation that European defendants lacked resources to obtain counsel in the United States "[did] not address the merits of [the plaintiff's] claims in a substantive way." Honda Power Equip. Mfg., Inc. v. Woodhouse, 219 F.R.D. 2, 10 (D.D.C. 2003).

[118] FSLIC v. Kroenke, 858 F.2d 1067, 1071 (5th Cir. 1988).

[119] *See, e.g.,* Albright v. Alan Neuman Prods., Inc., 862 F.2d 1388, 1391-1392 (9th Cir. 1988).

[120] *See, e.g.,* Berthelsen v. Kane, 907 F.2d 617, 621 (6th Cir. 1990).

possible grounds for setting aside a judgment, including, in Rule 60(b)(4), that the judgment is void. For example, if the court entering the default judgment lacked personal jurisdiction or subject matter jurisdiction, the judgment can be attacked on that ground.

A more likely possibility in the default judgment situation is Rule 60(b)(1), in which the motion to set aside is based upon "mistake, inadvertence, surprise, or excusable neglect." The defendant moving under this ground must convince the court that she was guilty of a mistake or of excusable neglect that should be forgiven by setting aside the judgment. There is a split of authority as to whether "mistake" under this part of the Rule refers to legal errors committed by the court. Some courts permit relief from judicial mistakes under Rule 60(b)(1), at least under some circumstances,[121] while others do not.[122] Even if the defendant succeeds in establishing good cause under Rule 60(b)(1), however, she must show the existence of a viable defense.[123] The district court has great discretion in determining whether the defendant has made the required showings, and how to weigh factors such as prejudice to the plaintiff and good faith of the defendant. In addition, a court granting a motion to set aside a default judgment may require the defendant to post a bond or other security.

Many opinions make the general assertion that default judgments are not favored because our system of justice prefers to resolve disputes on the merits rather than technicalities.[124] Interestingly, however, in the wake of large caseloads in the federal courts, there may be a trend toward taking a harder line toward defendants. The Seventh Circuit, rather baldly, has "moved away from the traditional position" of leniency and is "increasingly reluctant to reverse refusals to set aside [default judgments]." As the court elaborated: "The entry of a default judgment is becoming — without interference from this court — a common sanction for late filings by defendants. . . . At a time of unprecedented caseloads, federal judges are unwilling to allow the processes of the federal courts to be used for purposes of delaying the payment of debts."[125]

§7.6 Amended and Supplemental Pleadings

Modern pleading provisions, as exemplified by the Federal Rules, are quite liberal in allowing parties to amend their pleadings. This liberality

[121] *See, e.g.,* International Controls Corp. v. Vesco, 556 F.2d 665, 669 (2d Cir. 1977) (holding, however, that a motion for relief from the judgment on this ground must be made before the time for appeal runs).

[122] *See, e.g.,* Parke-Chaptley Constr. Co. v. Cherrington, 865 F.2d 907, 914-915 n.7 (7th Cir. 1989); Page v. Schweiker, 786 F.2d 150, 154-155 (3d Cir. 1986).

[123] *See* 12 Moore's Federal Practice, §60.24.

[124] *See, e.g.,* Adriana Intl. Corp. v. Thoronen, 913 F.2d 1406, 1412-1413 (9th Cir. 1990).

[125] In re State Exch. Fin. Co., 896 F.2d 1104, 1106 (7th Cir. 1990).

makes sense. Often, as the case goes on, parties will learn things that make it necessary or desirable to change what they asserted earlier. Federal Rule 15 governs amendments in federal practice, and is broad-ranging. It is helpful to see that each subpart addresses a different factual scenario. It is helpful to divide the discussion or Rule 15 into four subparts, one for each of its subsections — Rule 15(a) through Rule 15(d).

§7.6.1 Amendments of Right and Leave to Amend (Rule 15(a))

Rule 15(a) addresses two kinds of amendments — "as a matter of course" (in Rule 15(a)(1)) and what are usually called "permissive" amendments (in Rule 15(a)(2). When a party has a right to amend, obviously, she need not get court approval. She simply files and serves the amended pleading. If the other party feels that there was no right to amend, she may file a motion to strike the pleading under Rule 12(f). Permissive amendment applies in all cases in which there is no right to amend. Under permissive amendment, the party may amend only if the opposing party consents in writing or if the court grants "leave" to amend. Granting "leave" to amend is just another way of saying the court allows the party to amend.

Rule 15(a)(1)(A) defines when a plaintiff[126] has a right to amend; Rule 15(a)(1)(B) defines when a defendant has a right to amend. The plaintiff has a right to amend *once* "before being served with a responsive pleading." Be careful with this language in three particulars. First, there is no day limitation; the right to amend is cut off by the act of the defendant. Second, there is a right to amend only *once*; a second amendment, even if attempted before the defendant responds, can be made only with court permission. Third, it is the service of a "responsive pleading" that cuts off the right to amend. Remember from §7.3.3 that "responsive pleading" refers to the defendant's answer. A motion is not a pleading. This gives rise to a great exam question.

○ *P* files her complaint and has process served on *D* the same day. Eighteen days later, *D* makes a motion to dismiss under Rule 12(b)(6), asserting that *P* had failed to allege an element of the claim. The court sets the motion for hearing three weeks later. In the meantime, ten days after *D* moved to dismiss (and 28 days after *P* served process on *D*), *P* files and serves an amended complaint, in which she includes the element *D* raised in the motion to dismiss. Did *P* have a *right* to amend her complaint? Yes, because *D* has still not served a "responsive pleading." True, *D* has

---

[126] Actually, any claimant. Thus, a defendant who asserts a counterclaim against the plaintiff would have a right to amend in the circumstances indicated in the Rule. For present purposes, we simply consider the claimant to be the plaintiff.

properly responded to the complaint by making a motion. But Rule 15(a)(1)(A) gives *P* a right to amend before *D* serves a responsive pleading, and a motion is not a pleading.

Often, perhaps usually, the amended pleading will set forth an additional claim against the same defendant who was named in the original complaint. But the plaintiff may wish to amend to add new parties to (or drop extant parties from) the case. Some courts conclude that amendment of right does not cover such a situation, and that the plaintiff must make a motion (and thus get court permission) to add or drop parties under Rule 21.[127] Most courts seem to conclude, however, that the right to amend — being able to amend "as a matter of course" — includes the right to add or drop parties without court permission.[128]

Under Rule 15(a)(1)(B), the defendant[129] has a right to amend *once* "within 20 days after serving" her answer. Note two things about this provision. First, as with the plaintiff's right to amend, it can only be exercised once; the second time defendant wants to amend, even if within the 20 days, she must seek leave of court. Second, the right is cut off by the passage of days, and not by the act of another party. So if the defendant acts within 20 days of serving her answer (the one she wants to amend), she has a right to amend, and can avert disaster that might have been caused by her original answer.

- ∘ *P* files her complaint and has process served on *D* the same day. Within the appropriate time, *D* files and serves her answer. Eighteen days after serving her answer, *D* realizes that she failed to assert lack of personal jurisdiction as an affirmative defense in the answer. If she acts within two days (before the end of 20 days from when she served her answer), she has a right to amend and thus can save the personal jurisdiction defense.

What happens if the time in which there is a right to amend (for either party) has expired? Then Rule 15(a)(2) applies. It provides that the party seeking permission to amend must get court permission or written consent of the adverse party to amend. To obtain court permission, the party makes a "motion for leave to amend." The liberality of the Federal Rules is suggested by the phrase that "[t]he court should freely give leave when

---

[127] *See, e.g.,* Moore v. Indiana, 999 F.2d 1125 (7th Cir. 1993).

[128] *See, e.g.,* United States ex rel. Precision Co. v. Koch Indus., Inc., 31 F.3d 1015 (10th Cir. 1994).

[129] Actually, any defending party. For instance, a defendant may assert a counterclaim against the plaintiff; the plaintiff would be a defending party on that claim and technically would be known as "plaintiff and counter-defendant." She would have to respond to the counterclaim just as the defendant has to respond to the complaint. For present purposes, we simply consider the defendant to be the defending party.

justice so requires." This standard both reposes great discretion in the district judge and indicates a preference for permitting amendment. Consistent with that preference, the Supreme Court made it clear in the leading case of *Foman v. Davis*[130] that the district court must state its reasons for *denying* a motion for leave to amend.

Each case is decided on its own facts, and courts tend to balance the same factors in reaching their decisions. In *Foman v. Davis*, the Court listed the relevant factors and emphasized the need to balance harm to the moving party if she is not permitted to amend against prejudice caused to the other party if leave to amend is granted. It instructed courts to consider other factors as well: whether the moving party has delayed unduly in seeking leave to amend, bad faith or dilatory purpose of the moving party, whether the moving party has failed to fix deficiencies in previous amendments, and whether amendment would be futile.[131] Obviously, if amendment would be futile — for example, if a claim to be added by amendment is not legally cognizable[132] — the court should deny leave to amend. Just as obviously, a court will likely deny leave to amend if the amendment sought would prejudice the other party.[133]

Whenever the plaintiff amends (either of right or by permissive amendment), Rule 15(a)(3) says that the defending party must respond (unless the court orders otherwise) "within the time remaining to respond to the original pleading or within 10 days after service of the amended pleading, whichever is later." The time remaining for response to the original pleading refers to the time set forth in Rule 12 for defensive responses. Ordinarily, as we saw in §7.3.3, this period is 20 days from the date of service. Thus, unless the court orders otherwise, the defendant will never have fewer than ten days after service of the amended complaint in which to respond.

§7.6.2   Amendments During and After Trial — "Variance" (Rule 15(b))

Rule 15(b) becomes relevant, if ever, *only at trial*. More specifically, it comes up only when a party seeks to introduce evidence at trial of a claim or defense *that she did not plead*. Though the Rule does not use the word, you should know that this is a "variance" — somebody is trying to put on

---

[130] 371 U.S. 178, 182 (1962).

[131] *Id.*

[132] *See, e.g.*, Sinay v. Lamson & Sessions Co., 948 F.2d 1037 (9th Cir. 1991).

[133] *See, e.g.*, McKnight v. Kimberly Clark Corp., 149 F.3d 1125, 1130 (10th Cir. 1998) (if amendment were granted, defense witnesses would have to be deposed again, causing prejudice to the defendant; denial is especially appropriate because of delay by plaintiff in seeking amendment despite being aware of facts underlying the newly asserted claim).

evidence of something she did not plead. It may be the plaintiff, seeking to put on evidence of a claim she did not include in her complaint. Or it may be the defendant, seeking to put on evidence of an affirmative defense she did not include in her answer.[134]

At common law and under some codes, variance could be fatal if the other party objected to it. An example is *Wabash Western Railway v. Friedman*,[135] in which the plaintiff sued for personal injuries sustained when the train on which he was a passenger derailed. He had purchased a ticket to travel from Moberly to Ottumwa, and he boarded at Moberly. The train derailed between two intermediate stops on the route — between Kirksville and Glenwood Junction — and there is no question the plaintiff was on the train when it derailed and that he was hurt badly. The jury returned a verdict of $30,000 and the trial court entered judgment for the plaintiff in that amount. On appeal, though, the defendant pointed out that the plaintiff had alleged that he had boarded the train at Kirksville to travel to Glenwood Junction. The Illinois Supreme Court reversed because what the plaintiff alleged (that he boarded at Kirksville, bound for Glenwood Junction) was at variance from what he proved (that he boarded at Moberly, bound for Ottumwa). The result is preposterous. The issue of where the plaintiff boarded the train does not change the fact that he was onboard when it derailed and that he was badly injured. The railroad certainly understood that it was being sued over a derailment between Kirksville and Glenwood Junction. Yet the plaintiff lost his recovery because of the variance on the inconsequential matter of where he boarded the train.

Rule 15(b) represents the modern way of treating variance. Even in code states, today it is doubtful that any court would come to the conclusion reached in *Wabash Western*. Today, variance is a basis for objection by the other party *at trial*. In other words, when a party seeks to introduce evidence at trial that goes beyond the scope of her pleadings, the other party may object and ask the court to exclude the evidence, so it will not be part of the trial record the fact-finder considers in reaching a conclusion. But variance should not be a basis for upsetting a trial judgment.

It is crucial to see that Rule 15(b) addresses two possible variance scenarios — one under Rule 15(b)(1) and the other under Rule 15(b)(2). The scenarios depend upon what the other party does in the face of a variance. The other party may do one of two things: (1) she might agree to allow the variance, or (2) she might object to the variance. In situation

---

[134] Throughout this subsection, we speak of amendments to the complaint or the answer. In fact, it is likely that the operative document to be amended is the pretrial conference order. In §8.5, we see that the pretrial conference order takes the place of the pleadings — it supersedes the pleadings. Because problems of variance, by definition, come up at trial, it is likely that the amendment to conform to the evidence will amend that document.

[135] 30 N.E. 353 (Ill. 1892).

(1), the court applies Rule 15(b)(2), and we are concerned with conforming the pleadings to the evidence. In situation (2), the court applies Rule 15(b)(1), and we are concerned with the possibility of amending the pleadings at trial.

First, assume Party *A* (it does not matter whether she is the plaintiff or defendant) introduces evidence at trial that goes beyond the scope of her pleadings. As we know, the opposing party (Party *B*) may object to that evidence on the ground of variance with the pleadings and ask the court to deny its introduction at trial. But Party *B* might acquiesce and allow the introduction of the evidence either by failing to object to it or by expressly consenting to it. When Party *B* acquiesces in allowing the evidence, the first sentence of Rule 15(b)(2) provides that the issues addressed in that evidence "must be treated in all respects as if raised in the pleadings." Thus, the variance is ignored, the evidence is admitted at trial, and we treat the pleadings as though they included the issues raised by the evidence.

In addition, the second sentence of Rule 15(b)(2) provides that "[a] party may move — at any time — even after judgment — to amend the pleadings to conform them to the evidence and to raise an unpleaded issue." Failure to do so, the next sentence provides, does not affect the outcome of the trial. In other words, when Party *A* introduced evidence beyond the scope of the pleadings and Party *B* either did not object or expressly consented to its admission at trial, the evidence is received and Party *A* can move to amend the pleadings to conform to that evidence — to mirror what was actually litigated at trial. Amendment to conform to the evidence is a housekeeping measure. It ensures that the pleadings will mirror what actually was tried and decided.[136]

- *P* sues *D* for breach of contract, and alleges only a claim for damages. At trial, however, *P* introduces evidence not only of damages, but of evidence that would support the grant of equitable relief, such as rescission of the contract. *D* does not object to introduction of the evidence. That means the evidence is admitted at trial and the court will treat *P*'s complaint as though it asserted the claim for equitable relief. Assume *P* wins, and the court awards damages as well as rescission. *P* may make a motion (even after judgment) to amend her complaint to conform to the evidence — to show the equitable claim. Regardless of whether she does so, however, the judgment on the equitable claim will stand.[137]
- *P* sues *D* for battery. In her complaint, *D* fails to raise the affirmative defense of self-defense. At trial, however, *D* introduces evidence that she hit *P* in self-defense. *P* does not object to the evidence. That means the evidence is admitted at trial and the court will treat *D*'s answer as though

---

[136] This fact may be helpful to clarify the record on appeal or to determine the preclusive effect (e.g., issue preclusion) of the judgment in this case.

[137] *See, e.g.*, D. Federico Co. v. New Bedford Redev. Auth., 723 F.2d 122 (1st Cir. 1983).

it had raised that affirmative defense. *D* may move to amend her answer to reflect the affirmative defense.

The second possibility is that a party facing variance will object to it. Here, when Party *A* introduces evidence beyond the scope of her pleading, Party *B* objects and asserts that the evidence should be excluded at trial. If the court agrees that one party's proffered evidence goes beyond the scope of the pleadings, it will uphold the other party's objection and bar the introduction of the evidence.

At that point, however, Rule 15(b)(1) permits the party proffering the evidence to move to amend! As the Rule says, when Party *B* objects to the introduction of evidence by Party *A* on the ground of variance, "the court may permit the pleadings to be amended." Thus, even though the variance points out a deficiency in Party *A*'s pleading at a very late stage (we are at trial, remember), Party *A* may still be able to amend her pleading to cover the issues raised by the evidence she is proffering at trial. The standard for being allowed to amend is found in the second sentence of Rule 15(b)(1): "The court should freely permit an amendment when doing so will aid in presenting the merits and the objecting party fails to satisfy the court that the evidence would prejudice that party's action or defense on the merits." This provision demonstrates how liberal the Federal Rules can be about amendment. Even though Party *A*'s pleading is deficient and even though the issue does not come to light until the case is in trial, the burden is *on the other party* to show prejudice. The final sentence in Rule 15(b)(1) furthers the liberal pleading ethos by reminding the court that it can enter a continuance of the trial to allow Party *B* to do what she has to do to respond to the evidence.

Though there is no denying the liberality of Rule 15(b)(1), such amendment at trial is rare. Again, the case is in trial; discovery has been completed. The parties have spent months (probably even years) to get to this point. Especially if there is a jury, a court will be reluctant to stay the trial to allow Party *B* to engage in discovery or do what she must to respond to this new evidence. After all, it is Party *A*'s fault that she did not include the allegation relating to this evidence. In most such instances, then, we would expect the court to deny admission of the evidence and to deny Party *A*'s motion to amend. In rare cases, though, if the proffered evidence truly advances the decision on the merits and there is little if any prejudice, an amendment would be appropriate.

° *P* sues *D*, alleging only a claim for fraud. At trial, *P* seeks to introduce evidence that would support *D*'s liability on the basis of vicarious liability. Though *P* did not plead vicarious liability, it is essentially just another theory on which *P* might win recovery for the same harm caused by the fraud. Because it is directly related to the fraud claim, and because the defendant had a full opportunity to present evidence to avoid liability, the court might permit amendment at trial.

§7.6.3   Amendments and the Statute of Limitations — "Relation Back" (Rule 15(c))

Rule 15(c) deals with amendment of pleadings after the statute of limitations has run. The problem can come up in two ways. First, the plaintiff may seek leave to amend her complaint to add a new claim (or the defendant to raise a new defense) after the statute has run. This scenario is addressed in Rule 15(c)(1)(B). Second, the plaintiff may seek leave to amend to join a new defendant after the statute has run. This scenario is addressed in Rule 15(c)(1)(C). In each case, there is an obvious clash of important policies. On the one hand, we favor resolution of disputes on the merits, and thus favor a liberal amendment policy. On the other hand, the statute of limitations protects the defendant from the assertion of stale claims; she should be protected by that policy from an unfair lengthening of the time for which she may remain subject to suit.

The Federal Rules balance these two policies through the doctrine of "relation back." Rule 15(c) provides that an amended pleading — asserted after the statute of limitations has run — "relates back" to a pleading that was filed before the statute of limitations ran. This simply means that the amended pleading is treated as though it was filed when an earlier, timely pleading was filed. Relation back thus avoids the bar of the statute of limitations.[138]

We start with some background on statutes of limitations. For every claim, whether created by statute or by common law, there is a period of limitations, which sets the outer temporal boundary in which the claimant must commence her action. These periods vary from state to state and from claim to claim. Generally, the statute for tort cases is shorter than that for contract cases. A typical statute would allow the plaintiff two years in which to assert a tort claim. That means that the plaintiff would have two years from "accrual" of her claim in which to "commence" her suit. When the claim "accrues,"[139] the statute starts to "run."[140] That means the

---

[138] Relation back is an example of treating something *nunc pro tunc*. That Latin phrase creeps into lawyerly discussions from time to time and you should be familiar with it. It means "now as then." So with relation back, an amended pleading *now* is treated as though it had been filed when the original pleading was filed — *then*.

[139] This is another term on which jurisdictions may adopt different definitions. The majority rule is that the claim accrues when the defendant breached a duty to the plaintiff.

[140] This should not be confused with "tolling" of the statute, which refers to events that stop the ticking of the statute of limitations. For instance, if the plaintiff is a minor, the statute of limitations is tolled until she reaches the age of majority. That just means the

clock starts ticking on the two years (or whatever other period is prescribed by the statute). If the plaintiff fails to commence suit before the clock expires, her claim will be barred by the statute of limitations.

With this background, we can more readily appreciate the importance of the doctrine of relation back under Rule 15(c).

- *P* files her complaint against *D* on May 10, and has process served on *D* the same day. The relevant statute of limitations expires on July 30. Thus, *P*'s complaint was timely — she commenced the case before the statute ran. *P* seeks leave to amend her complaint (maybe to add a new claim or to add a new defendant) on September 24. The problem, of course, is that September 24 would be too late if she were filing her complaint now (because the statute of limitations ran on July 30). But if the amendment satisfies the requirements of Rule 15(c), her September amended complaint — even though filed after the statute ran — will relate back to the original complaint. That means it will be treated as though the amended complaint had been filed when the original was filed. This was May 10, so *P* avoids the bar of the statute of limitations.

In this hypothetical, of course, the defendant will not be pleased with the application of relation back. To her, it extends the time for which she can be sued and vitiates the protection of the statute of limitations. Because of the seriousness of the issue, Rule 15(c) permits relation back in limited circumstances — circumstances in which the defendant will not be prejudiced. What are those circumstances? For our purposes, one can be dismissed quickly. Rule 15(c)(1)(A) provides that relation back applies when "the law that provides the applicable statute of limitations allows relation back." Thus, if the statute providing the period of limitations also expressly allows relation back of amendments, there will be relation back.

Far more important for our purposes are the provisions of Rules 15(c)(1)(B) and (c)(1)(C). Rule 15(c)(1)(A), as we noted above, deals with amendment *to add a new claim* after the statute has expired. It makes no sense for the court to allow such an amendment if the claim to be added is barred by the statute of limitations. The standard under Rule 15(c)(1)(A) is clear: Relation back is permitted if the amended pleading "arose out of the conduct, transaction, or occurrence set out — or attempted to be set out — in the original pleading." The rationale of the Rule is also clear: If the amended pleading arises from the same real-world events as the original pleading, the defendant was put on notice of her potential liability before the statute expired. This notice — of potential culpability from some conduct, transaction, or occurrence — satisfies the statute of limitations.

---

statute does not start to run until she turns age 18 (or whatever the relevant age of majority is). Tolling is relevant to an issue we discuss in §10.5.

Thus, courts routinely permit amendment with relation back when the claim being added simply espouses a new theory of liability arising from the same real-world events alleged in the original complaint. Likewise, if the amendment merely fixed a defective jurisdictional allegation from the original complaint, but concerns the same real-world events as the original, relation back is appropriate. Only if the amendment raises new matter for which the defendant was not fairly put on notice by the original complaint would relation back not be appropriate. For example, in one case, when the amended complaint alleged an injury on a date earlier than that alleged in the original complaint, relation back was inappropriate.[141]

Rule 15(c)(1)(C) addresses a more difficult situation—amendment after the statute of limitations has expired *to add a new defendant*. Here, we are understandably concerned that the new defendant is not brought into the case until after the statutory period. Rule 15(c)(1)(C) permits relation back in this context only if three requirements are satisfied: (1) the claim arises from the same conduct, transaction, or occurrence as that stated in the original complaint;[142] (2) within 120 days after *filing* of the original complaint, the new defendant has received such notice of the suit that she will not be prejudiced in defending (Rule 15(c)(1)(C)(i)); and (3) within the same period, the new defendant "knew or should have known that the action would have been brought against it, but for a mistake concerning the proper party's identity" (Rule 15(c)(1)(C)(ii)).

There is basically one class of cases that satisfies these requirements—one in which the plaintiff sued the "wrong" defendant originally, but the "right" defendant knew about the case and knew that, but for a mistake, she would have been named originally.

- *P* is injured in a slip and fall at Joe's Supermarket. On March 1, she filed her original complaint, in which she names "Joe's Supermarket" as the defendant. In fact, there is no such legal entity as "Joe's Supermarket." The store was operated by Joeco, Inc. Joe is the president of Joeco, Inc. On March 10, the statute of limitations on *P*'s claim expired. On March 20, *P* had process served on Joe, as agent for the defendant. On April 15, *P* seeks leave to amend her complaint to name Joeco, Inc. as the defendant.
- The amendment would bring Joeco, Inc. into the suit after the statute of limitations had run. Nonetheless, Rule 15(c)(1)(C) would permit the amended complaint to relate back to the date of the original. Thus, the case would be treated as though it had been filed against Joeco, Inc. on March 1, which is timely. Why does relation back apply here?
- First, the amended complaint concerns the same slip and fall as the original complaint. Second, Joeco, Inc. was on notice of the suit on March 20

---

[141] O'Loughlin v. National R.R. Passenger Corp., 928 F.2d 24 (1st Cir. 1991).

[142] Of course, we just saw this requirement in Rule 15(c)(1)(B); it is incorporated by reference in Rule 15(c)(1)(C).

(when Joe was served with process), which is within 120 days of the filing of the original complaint on March 10. Third, Joeco, Inc. is charged with notice on March 20 (when Joe was served with process) that "but for a mistake concerning the identity of the proper party," the action would have been brought against it. That is, when Joe received service of process on March 20, he saw that *P* named a defendant that did not exist and understood that *P* should have named Joeco, Inc.

One point deserves especial attention in applying Rule 15(c)(1)(C). Note that the second and third requirements — that the proper defendant be on notice of the case and that she know that but for a mistake in identity she would have been sued — must be met "within the period provided by Rule 4(m) for serving the summons and complaint." Rule 4(m) provides that service should be effected within 120 days after filing of the complaint. Thus, the only thing that absolutely must occur before the statute of limitations expires is the filing of the complaint. The new defendant does not have to be put on notice before the statute expired. As long as the new defendant is put on notice within 120 days after the filing of the complaint, the Rule is satisfied.[143]

§7.6.4   Supplemental Pleadings (Rule 15(d))

Supplemental pleadings differ from amended pleadings in a fundamental way: They concern the assertion of things that *occurred* after the pleading was filed. As Rule 15(d) says, a supplemental pleading "set[s] out any transaction, occurrence, or event that happened after the date of the pleading to be supplemented." Amendment, on the other hand, concerns setting forth matters that *occurred* before the pleading was filed, but that were not discovered (or at least not asserted) until after pleading. Supplemental pleadings thus serve to update the parties and the court on the dispute by bringing to their attention facts that had not occurred when the pleading was filed. They may, among other things, add new claims or even new parties.

Though there is a right to *amend* pleadings in certain instances, as we saw in §7.6.1, there is no right to supplement pleadings. The matter must be raised on motion by the party seeking leave to supplement, and the district judge has great discretion in determining whether to grant the motion. Based upon the same policies that underlie the federal courts' liberal approach to amendment, most courts allow supplementation unless

---

[143] The Rule was amended to make this clear in 1991. That amendment was in reaction to the decision in *Schiavone v. Fortune*, 477 U.S. 21 (1986), in which the Supreme Court held under the earlier version of Rule 15(c) that the new defendant had to be on notice before the statute of limitations expired. The Rule was amended because this holding was considered too harsh.

it will cause undue delay or prejudice, or if the party seeking leave to supplement is guilty of bad faith. Note too that Rule 15(d) permits supplemental pleadings even if the original pleading was defective — for example, if it failed to state a claim. When the plaintiff is permitted to supplement her complaint, it seems likely that the court will allow the defendant to respond.

> ◦ *P* has a contract with Manufacturing Corp. (MC), under which MC is to deliver widgets to *P* each month. MC fails to deliver the widgets for January 2009, and *P* sues MC in February 2009 concerning the failure. In September 2009, while the case is in the discovery phase, MC fails to deliver widgets for that month. If *P* wants to sue MC for the September 2009 failure to deliver, and to assert the claim in the pending case, it will seek leave to supplement its complaint. If the court feels that the pleading can be supplemented by adding this matter without causing undue delay and without prejudicing MC, it will grant the motion.[144]

§7.7   Professional Responsibility — Rule 11 and Other Sanctions

Even in your first year of law studies, you have heard a lot of lawyer jokes. Most of them paint the profession as money-hungry and willing to do anything to win. Unfortunately, the profession has asked for some of that treatment (though we know most of the criticism simply reflects jealousy). The vast majority of lawyers, of course, are honest, decent professionals. But a few bad apples can tarnish the profession's reputation. In reality, the profession is to be credited for its awareness of the problem and for taking steps to increase professionalism. One of the most important classes you will take is Professional Responsibility. Be sure, however, not to limit what you study there to that class. Dedication to the highest ideals of the profession should affect everything you do.

In Civil Procedure, we address one particularly important tool of professionalism: Federal Rule 11. Even states that have not adopted the Federal Rules generally have a counterpart to Rule 11, the aim of which is to ensure veracity in pleading and other elements of litigation practice. The

---

[144] *Twin Disc, Inc. v. Big Bud Tractor, Inc.*, 772 F.2d 1329 (7th Cir. 1985), involved facts along these lines. In this case, however, the plaintiff did not seek leave to supplement its complaint until one week before trial. The court denied the motion to supplement because of the plaintiff's delay and because the defendant could not be expected to prepare for trial on the new facts. It refused to delay the trial to permit inclusion of the new facts. The Court of Appeals affirmed, concluding that the district judge did not abuse his discretion in denying the motion to supplement.

history of Rule 11 reflects cycles of concern. The original Rule, promulgated when the Federal Rules were adopted in 1938, simply required that a lawyer have "good grounds to support" her contentions in pleadings. In over 40 years, fewer than one dozen reported cases applied the Rule.

In 1983, the Supreme Court amended the Rule to toughen it dramatically. There is no doubt that the amendments were fueled by the perception of a "litigation explosion," caused at least in part by frivolous litigation. The amended Rule 11 applied not only to pleadings but to all documents in the case, and imposed a certification requirement. The lawyer's signature on a document constituted a certification of various things, aimed primarily at ensuring that the lawyer had made an investigation and in good faith could support the assertions made. Interestingly, the 1983 version of Rule 11 *required* the imposition of sanctions for violations. The invigorated Rule led to a stunning amount of litigation over sanctions for alleged violations of Rule 11. This, in turn, led to a stunning amount of academic commentary on the Rule, including criticism that the required sanctions chilled the assertion of viable claims and created a debilitating amount of satellite litigation.

Reacting to such criticism, the Supreme Court amended Rule 11 to its present basic form in 1993. (Rule 11, like all the Rules, was "restyled" in 2007.) The amendment clearly took some of the bite out of Rule 11 in an effort both to reduce the amount of litigation over sanctions and to ensure that the fear of sanctions not inhibit creative lawyering. Rule 11(a) imposes a signature requirement on the attorney of record for a party.[145] It also makes clear that Rule 11 applies to "[e]very pleading, written motion, and other paper." At the same time, Rule 11(d) makes it clear that the Rule does not apply to discovery documents. (As we see in §8.4, there is a similar certification for discovery documents, found in Rule 26(g).) Thus, pleadings, motions, briefs—all documents except discovery documents—are to be signed under Rule 11. The last sentence of Rule 11(a) makes clear that the court "must strike" any document that is unsigned, unless the omission is promptly corrected.

What does the signature represent? Under Rule 11(b), it is a *certification to the court* of several important things. Though it is natural to focus on the four specific numbered items listed in Rule 11(b), there is some important prefatory language. Specifically, the Rule says that by signing, the person "certifies that to the best of the person's knowledge, information, and belief, formed after an inquiry reasonable under the circumstances," the four specific items are true. Thus, the Rule presumes that the lawyer signing the document has made an "inquiry reasonable under

---

[145] If there is no attorney of record — that is, if the party is litigating *pro se* (representing herself) — the Rule imposes the signature requirement on the party herself. In most cases, of course, the parties are represented by counsel, which means that in most cases the parties never sign the documents. Their lawyers do.

the circumstances" and has satisfied herself that the listed things are true. What constitutes a reasonable inquiry depends on the facts of the case. It also depends on timing. For instance, a lawyer consulted the day before the statute of limitations will run simply cannot undertake the kind of detailed investigation that is possible if she is not laboring under such a time constraint. The main point is simple, though: The Rule imposes a duty of reasonable inquiry before signing a document to be filed with the court.

Importantly, Rule 11(b) imposes a continuing certification. Specifically, the certification under Rule 11(b) is made not just when the lawyer signs the document, but every time she *presents* a document to the court. The first sentence indicates that "presenting" includes "signing, filing, submitting, or later advocating" something asserted in the document. Before 1993, the certification was simply as of the time of signing. The difference is stark.

> ○ Lawyer drafts, signs, and files a complaint on behalf of Plaintiff. She satisfies Rule 11(b) in so doing, because she has made a reasonable inquiry and has a good faith belief that the thing stated in the complaint satisfies Rule 11(b). Six months later, she advocates to the court a position set forth in the complaint. At that point — even though it is six months after she signed and filed the complaint — Lawyer is "re-certifying" that the certification under Rule 11(b) is still true. If she can no longer make that certification, she violates Rule 11 by presenting the issue to the court.

What are the items certified in Rule 11(b)? In the aggregate, they are aimed at ensuring that there are reasonable bases for the version of the facts and law asserted. First, under Rule 11(b)(1), the signer certifies that the document is not presented for an improper purpose, such as delay or harassment. Second, under Rule 11(b)(2), she certifies that the legal contentions are warranted by law or "by a nonfrivolous argument for extending, modifying, or reversing existing law or for establishing new law." This is intended to protect creative lawyering and the assertion of novel theories of the law; the only limitation is that they not be frivolous. The third and fourth items specified relate to allegations of fact, as opposed to allegations of law. Specifically, under Rule 11(b)(3), the signer certifies that the factual contentions "have evidentiary support or, if specifically so identified, will likely have evidentiary support after a reasonable opportunity for further investigation or discovery." This is good language and protects the lawyer who believes that evidence will be found to support a factual assertion. Finally, Rule 11(b)(4) provides in like terms for the *denials* of factual allegations. Obviously, then, Rule 11(b)(3) is aimed at parties asserting a claim and Rule 11(b)(4) is aimed at parties defending against a claim.

Purported violations of Rule 11 may be raised in two ways. First, of course, the court may raise them on its own. Under Rule 11(c)(1)(B), the court will enter an order to show cause (O.S.C.) requiring a party, attorney, or law firm to show cause why specified behavior did not violate Rule 11(b). Second, a party may move for sanctions against another party or her attorney or law firm under Rule 11(c)(2). The motion must state specifically what conduct allegedly violated Rule 11(b) and must be brought separately from any other motions. It is important to note, however, that Rule 11(c)(2) has a "safe harbor" of 21 days for the party allegedly violating Rule 11.

- Plaintiff believes that Defendant (or her lawyer or law firm) has violated Rule 11. Plaintiff's lawyer drafts a motion for sanctions under Rule 11(c)(2), specifying the alleged violations by Defendant (or her lawyer or law firm). Plaintiff's lawyer serves the motion on Defendant, *but does not file the motion with the court*. Defendant then has 21 days in which to fix the problem. If Defendant fixes the problem, there are no sanctions. If Defendant does not fix the problem within 21 days, however, then Plaintiff may file the motion. Note, though, that the motion cannot be filed immediately upon violation of Rule 11. Rather, the moving party must give the other side 21 days in which to fix the problem. This safe harbor provision is intended to save the court from becoming embroiled in Rule 11 sanction motions.

Regardless of how the matter gets to the court — on the court's initiative or by motion after the safe harbor period — what sanctions are available? First, sanctions are no longer required, but are to be imposed in the discretion of the court. Second, the purpose of sanctions is *not* to punish wrongful behavior, but to deter such behavior in the future. As Rule 11(c)(4) states, "A sanction imposed under this rule must be limited to what suffices to deter repetition of the conduct or comparable conduct by others similarly situated."

Rule 11(c)(4) suggests that nonmonetary sanctions are appropriate. These can include directives to the person violating the Rule to do some act. The court may order the offender to "pay a penalty into court." Also, if imposed on motion and "warranted for effective deterrence," the court may require the offender to pay all or part of the expenses — expressly including attorneys' fees — incurred by the moving party as a direct result of the violation of Rule 11. Note that under Rule 11(c)(5)(A), a party represented by counsel cannot be held liable for a monetary sanction for violating Rule 11(b)(2). This makes sense, because that certification relates to the legal contentions; a party represented by a lawyer cannot be presumed to know the law sufficiently to satisfy that certification item.

Of course, Rule 11 is not the only provision aimed at litigation behavior. Rule 3.1 of the Model Rules of Professional Conduct, for example, provides that "[a] lawyer shall not bring or defend a proceeding, or assert or controvert an issue therein, unless there is a basis for doing so that is not frivolous." In addition, 28 U.S.C. §1927, which applies in federal court, provides that an attorney who "multiplies the proceeding in any case unreasonably and vexatiously may be required ... to satisfy personally the excess costs, expenses, and attorneys' fees reasonably incurred because of such conduct."

Further, it is clear the federal courts have "inherent power" to sanction bad faith litigation conduct by lawyers or litigants. One chilling reminder of this power is *Chambers v. NASCO, Inc.,*[146] in which the Supreme Court upheld a district court order requiring the losing party to pay just under $1 million in attorneys' fees to the plaintiff. It was the defendant, and not its attorney, who acted inappropriately in the conduct of the litigation. Some of the sanctioned conduct did not violate Rule 11 or §1927. Nonetheless, the Court upheld the entire award, invoking the inherent authority of courts to punish inappropriate litigation behavior.

In one case, lawyers failed to assess appropriately whether there was subject matter jurisdiction over the dispute. The district court also failed to address the issue, and the case went through trial, resulting in a judgment for the plaintiff. On appeal, the Seventh Circuit vacated the judgment, because, as it turned out, there was no subject matter jurisdiction. Despite the lack of subject matter jurisdiction, the appellate court required the lawyers to re-litigate the case in state court without charging their clients. The court explained:

> The costs of a doomed foray into federal court should fall on the lawyers who failed to do their homework, not on the hapless clients. Although we lack jurisdiction to resolve the merits, we have ample authority to govern the practice of counsel in the litigation. . . . The best way for counsel to make the litigants whole is to perform, without additional fees, any further services that are necessary to bring this suit to a conclusion in state court, or via settlement. That way the clients will pay just once for the litigation. This is intended not as a sanction, but simply to ensure that clients need not pay for lawyers' time that has been wasted for reasons beyond the clients' control.[147]

Finally, any lawyer must distinguish between costs and attorneys' fees. Costs are the expenses of litigation, such as filing fees, fees for serving process, discovery costs, fees paid to witnesses, including expert witnesses, costs of giving notice to class members when required in class action litigation, etc. In short, costs generally consist of litigation expenses *other than* attorneys' fees. Federal Rule 54(d)(1) provides that such costs "should be allowed to the prevailing party" unless the court directs otherwise. In other words, generally, the losing party pays the winning party's

---

[146] 501 U.S. 32 (1991).

[147] Belleville Catering Co. v. Champaign Market Place LLC, 350 F.3d 691, 694 (7th Cir. 2003).

costs. Such costs are "taxed" by the court clerk to the losing party and are included in the judgment. See §9.3.

What about attorneys' fees? In almost every case, they are likely to amount to a far greater expense than costs. The American Rule is that each party bears her own attorneys' fees. In other words, generally, the loser does *not* pay the winner's attorneys' fees. This rule is controversial, and many people have proposed that litigation in the United States be run as it is in Great Britain, where the loser does pay the winner's attorneys' fees. Despite ongoing debate, the American Rule seems destined to remain in force here, largely because of the belief that the contrary rule would chill meritorious litigation. That is, a person with a legitimate claim, but who (like most litigants) is not assured of victory, will not take the chance of incurring liability for the defendant's attorneys' fees should she lose. Thus, in the United States, each party bears her own attorneys' fees *unless* there is an exception.

As we saw above, §1927 provides an exception, as does the inherent power of the court to punish wrongful behavior in the conduct of litigation. And, as we also saw, Rule 11 also permits such "fee shifting" in certain circumstances. There are other statutory and common law exceptions to the American Rule, and lawyers are careful to research the issue in every case.

Chapter *8*

Discovery and Judicial Management of Litigation

§8.1 Defining the Issue

Discovery is an extremely important phase of litigation, but you would not know that from movies and television programs about lawyers. Those shows focus on trials and courtroom scenes. Long before a case comes to trial, however, the discovery phase has reduced the possibility that there will be any surprises at trial. Through discovery, each party has the opportunity to learn relevant information from each other party. Done correctly, discovery is supervised mostly by the parties themselves. The court oversees the discovery phase generally, but gets involved more directly only when the parties have a disagreement.

The Federal Rules clearly adopt the philosophy that more information is better than less, and that each side should — before going to trial — know virtually every relevant thing the other side knows. This philosophy, in turn, promotes the search for truth and can provide a "reality check" for the parties, which may foster settlement instead of trial. For example, a party may find through discovery that her position is not as well supported by the evidence as she had thought. Learning this gives the party an incentive to settle, and perhaps a realistic view of what to seek in settlement. And the free exchange of information may hone issues for trial, by pointing out questions on which there is no dispute and questions on which the parties truly desire adjudication. It avoids "trial by ambush" and ensures that the adjudication phase can be based upon the presentation of evidence that everyone knows is coming, rather than on the ability of a lawyer to pull a surprise witness or surprise evidence out of the hat.

People with no exposure to the discovery process are usually surprised at the breadth of the Federal Rules provisions and how intrusive and time-consuming discovery can be. One important criticism of litigation today is that it is too expensive and time-consuming, and this criticism is often aimed at discovery. As we will see, the drafters have amended the Federal Rules periodically in an effort to limit overly burdensome discovery, and judges have great discretion to protect parties (and nonparties who may be subject to discovery) from overly intrusive or overly expensive discovery requests. Still, the Rules are very broad and the discovery phase of litigation can be an expensive proposition.[1]

Broad discovery was not born in a vacuum. It is part of the Federal Rules' vision that ascribes relatively little importance to pleadings. As we saw in §7.3, pleadings in federal court historically have not been required to do much more than put other parties on notice of the various claims and defenses. Experience at common law and with the Codes taught that pleadings were not effective tools for ferreting out the facts underlying claims and defenses. The Federal Rules' narrow role for pleadings is complemented by the broad discovery provisions. Through discovery, the parties find out what the other side's claims or defenses are *really* all about and what facts they are based upon. Although the Federal Rules apply only in federal court, most states have adopted most of the Federal Rules provisions on discovery.

Throughout the study of discovery, keep in mind how expensive the process can become — not only in terms of dollars but in terms of hours. Worries about that expense and burden of discovery have led some to argue that the pleading standards in federal court ought to be bolstered. As we saw in §7.3, the argument is that the plaintiff ought to have to do

---

[1] It is a mistake to think that *every* case involves enormous expenditures of effort and money on discovery. Some data suggest that parties use extensive discovery in relatively few cases. *See, e.g.*, Linda Mullenix, *The Pervasive Myth of Pervasive Discovery Abuse and the Consequences for Unfounded Rulemaking*, 46 Stan. L. Rev. 1393 (1994). The ultimate value of the case guides the lawyers in assessing the needs of discovery; clearly, for instance, the lawyers will not undertake $100,000 worth of discovery in a case involving a $10,000 claim.

more than make conclusory allegations to subject the defendant to the discovery phase of litigation. Indeed, the Supreme Court's 2007 opinion in *Bell Atlantic Corporation v. Twombly*,[2] which was discussed at §7.3.2, reflected this concern. In the eyes of many, the Court raised the bar for stating a claim, rather pointedly to avoid the expense and burden of discovery.

In §8.2 we survey the tools available for discovery. The Federal Rules permit parties to employ five traditional discovery tools (which are also available in virtually every state court system). As we will see, while all five allow a party to obtain information from another party to the case, two of them also permit discovery from nonparties. In addition, the Federal Rules have since 1993 provided for "required disclosures," which, as the name makes clear, mandate that each party disclose information even in the absence of a request. The required disclosure provisions of the Federal Rules have proven somewhat controversial, and states generally have not been keen to adopt them.

In §8.3, we discuss the scope of discovery. Knowing what tools can be used, here we determine how broadly each party can inquire. Various principles — including "relevance" and "privilege" — limit the scope of inquiry. Ultimately, we find that the scope of discovery is quite broad and understand why the process can be so expensive. Accordingly, the court is empowered to limit overzealous use of discovery.

Section 8.4 addresses the court's role when a party does not "play by the rules." The sanction available depends upon the nature of the transgression, but it is clear that the court has plenty of tools to coerce compliance and to deal with the problem of discovery abuse.

In §§8.5 and 8.6, we consider topics relevant far beyond the discovery phase of the litigation. Together, they address the role of the judge in the modern procedural world. As we see in §8.5, she plays an increasingly bureaucratic role, as she is responsible for "keeping the case moving" and for ensuring that the parties keep litigating actively. The Federal Rules impose rather remarkable duties on the parties to avoid letting the case languish; the significant costs of complying with these duties may, over time, increase the incentive to settle the case. But the Rules also impose significant case-management duties on the judge. The federal judicial system's caseload is heavy,[3] and judges are under considerable pressure to keep litigation moving through the system.[4]

---

[2] 127 S. Ct. 1955 (2007).

[3] Congress, which sets the number of federal judges, has resisted various calls to increase dramatically the number of federal judgeships. Many state-court systems face even more daunting caseloads.

[4] Detailed discussion is beyond our scope, but it is worth noting that much of the pressure on federal judges comes from very large criminal caseloads. Criminal defendants have

Even with this pressure, it is the norm that years will pass between filing the case and trial. Much of that time is spent in discovery, under the watchful eye (and occasional goading) of the judge. In discovery and other phases of litigation, the increasing caseload has led to increasing use of adjunct judicial personnel in the federal system, including "magistrate judges" and "masters." We discuss their roles in §8.6. It is important to note that their usefulness to the system is not limited to discovery matters. They may be employed to help the judge in a variety of ways. Their increased use is one of the earmarks of the modern federal judicial system.

§8.2   Tools Available for Conducting Discovery

Each party has six tools in her discovery arsenal. Five of these — depositions, interrogatories, requests for production, medical examinations, and requests for admission — have long been part of civil litigation in federal and state courts. As we see in this section, each party determines (within a time frame set by the Federal Rules) whether and when to use these tools. Those five traditional discovery tools are augmented in federal court by "required disclosures."

§8.2.1   Required Disclosures

Since 1993, the Federal Rules have provided for required disclosures under Rule 26(a). These are exactly what the name implies: disclosures that each party must make *even though* nobody asks for them. They are controversial, largely because they are antithetical to the adversary system and because they take away parties' autonomy to determine how and when to use the discovery tools. In fact, three Justices dissented from the Supreme Court's promulgation of the required disclosure regime in 1993.[5] For the most part, though, Rule 26(a) largely requires the production of what good lawyers would have requested anyway, so some resistance to the Rule has died away in the wake of experience with it. Rule 26 mandates that each party produce information at three stages of the litigation.

---

a right to a speedy trial, while civil litigants do not. Thus, criminal trials often take precedence over civil trials. State-court judges face similar pressures.

[5] 507 U.S. 1099-1100 (1993) (dissenting statement of Justice Scalia, joined by Justices Thomas and Souter) ("By placing upon lawyers the obligation to disclose information damaging to their clients — on their own initiative . . . — the new Rule would place intolerable strain upon lawyers' ethical duty to represent their clients and not to assist the opposing side.").

Each of the three sets of required disclosures must be written and signed and served on the other parties.[6] Only the final set of disclosures, however, must be filed with the court.

Required Initial Disclosures. Rule 26(a)(1)(A) requires parties to provide the following information to each other party: (1) the name, address, and telephone number of each person "likely to have discoverable information — along with the subjects of that information — that the disclosing party may use to support its claims or defenses, unless the use would be solely for impeachment"[7]; (2) a copy (or a description by category and location) of all documents, electronically stored information, and tangible things in the possession or control of the disclosing party that she may use to support her claims or defenses (again, unless solely for impeachment); (3) the plaintiff must provide a computation of damages claimed, and evidentiary material on which the computation is based; and (4) the defendant must identify (and make available for copying) any insurance agreement under which an insurer may be liable to satisfy all or part of the judgment.

We discuss the timing of these disclosures in §8.5. For now, it is sufficient to understand that a party is under an obligation to produce these things quite early in the litigation. Again, no one need request them; production is required. And the requirement makes sense — these are the sorts of preliminary things that competent counsel would seek in any case anyway. Gaining access to this information early in the litigation also may jump-start the discovery process and assist the parties in determining how to proceed.

Rule 26(a)(1)(B) exempts certain kinds of cases from the required initial disclosures. The cases listed are quite specialized; most civil cases of the type addressed in the course on Civil Procedure will *not* be exempted. Rule 26(a)(1)(A) permits a court order or stipulation of the parties to vary the timing and scope of the initial disclosures. As promulgated in 1993, the Rule permitted each federal district court to pass a Local Rule rejecting initial disclosures in all cases. The result was an unfortunate balkanization of practice, with some courts requiring initial disclosures and some not. The Rule was amended in 2000 to remove the right of district courts to opt out of the requirement by Local Rule. Thus, the initial disclosures apply unless the case falls within Rule 26(a)(1)(B) or there is a court order or stipulation to the contrary.

---

[6] They can simply be served by mail under Rule 5. See §3.3.6.

[7] *Impeachment* here does not refer to the process of removing a federal officer from office. Rather, it is a term you will learn in a course on Evidence, and refers to the process of discrediting a witness on the stand. For example, a party can impeach a witness by pointing out that her testimony at trial is contrary to testimony given in deposition. Information one expects to use solely for impeachment does not have to be produced as part of the initial required disclosures under Rule 26(a)(1).

It bears repeating that Rule 26 applies only in federal court, and that though the other Federal Rules concerning discovery have been widely adopted by state courts, states generally have not adopted required disclosures.

Required Disclosures Concerning Expert Witnesses. The second set of required disclosures, under Rule 26(a)(2), concern "expert" testimony. These disclosures become relevant much later in the case, after discovery through the traditional discovery devices (which we review in §8.2.2) has largely run its course and the parties have focused on whether they will have expert testimony at trial. Rule 26(a)(2) provides that this disclosure generally is to be made at least 90 days before trial. Commonly, this issue will not come to the fore until the case has been pending for many months or even a couple of years. Unlike the initial disclosure under Rule 26(a)(1), here there is no provision for exempted cases and there is no general provision for avoiding the requirement by court order or stipulation of the parties.

Not all cases involve expert testimony, which is testimony from someone with professional expertise relevant to the case and who is entitled to testify as to her professional opinions. As a general rule, anyone testifying at trial (called a *witness*) is not permitted to give her opinions. Rather, she is to testify about facts she observed or perceived. Experts, however, as we see in more detail in §8.3.3, are often hired precisely to testify as to their professional opinions. Their testimony can be very helpful to the jury. For example, a psychiatrist, testifying as an expert witness, may give her opinion that a party to the case was suffering from delusions at the time of an accident. In an antitrust case, an economist, testifying as an expert witness, may opine that the defendant's commercial practices caused a restraint of trade in the market. A nonexpert witness (or "lay witness") could testify to what she perceived, but could not offer such opinions.

To avoid surprise by expert testimony at trial, Rule 26(a)(2) requires each party to disclose to each other party the identity of anyone who may be used at trial to present expert testimony. In addition, the party must provide a written report of the expert, containing her statement of all opinions to be expressed and the basis for them, the information used by the expert to form these opinions, the qualifications of the expert and how much she is being paid by the party, and a list of cases in which she has testified as an expert in the past four years. By court order or stipulation, the requirements mentioned in the last sentence might be obviated or amended. This required disclosure augments other provisions about discovery concerning experts, which we discuss at §8.3.3.

Required Pretrial Disclosures. The final set of required disclosures becomes relevant as the case nears trial. Under Rule 26(a)(3)(A), each party must serve on each other party detailed information about evidence she anticipates presenting at trial (except solely for impeachment). At this stage, the parties may have been litigating for years — through pleadings, motions of various types, and discovery — and now have honed the issues remaining to be adjudicated.

The information required under Rule 26(a)(3)(A) includes the name, address, and telephone number of each witness to be called by that party (and those who may be called if the need arises at trial), designation of those witnesses whose testimony will be presented by deposition transcript rather than by live testimony, and the identification of each document or other exhibit to be offered at trial. Long before required disclosures became part of the Federal Rules in 1993, virtually every district had a Local Rule requiring the exchange of this sort of information. This exchange of information facilitates the final pretrial conference order, which serves as a blueprint for trial, and which we discuss at §8.5. Under Rule 26(a)(3)(A), the party not only serves the information on other parties, but files it with the court as well. Thus, the pretrial required disclosures are the only ones that must be filed. The court does not get copies of the other required disclosures.

§8.2.2 Traditional Discovery Devices

The addition of required disclosures to the Federal Rules in 1993 did not change the traditional discovery devices. These tools have always been part of litigation under the Federal Rules. Though professors take varying approaches to covering this material, many agree that it is important to understand what each tool is, how it is used, what information is best obtained with it, and whether it can be used to get information from a nonparty. As we will see, each can be used to obtain information from a party; only two can be used generally to get information directly from a nonparty. Absent court order or stipulation of the parties, these tools may not be used until after the Rule 26(f) conference. See §8.5.

You may read some older cases (such as the famous *Hickman v. Taylor*, discussed in §8.3.2) that refer to parties' *filing* discovery responses with the court. It used to be required that parties file the deposition transcripts, answers to interrogatories, etc. This requirement never made much sense, and simply wasted space in the federal courthouse. Moreover, it is incumbent on the parties — not the court — to determine what portions of the discovery responses will be relevant for motions or trial. Thus, the Federal Rules no longer require filing of the traditional discovery devices. Rather, responses (like discovery requests) are served on each party. We address the discovery tools in the order in which they are found in the Rules. This does not correspond, however, with the order in which they are used in most cases, as we discuss.

Depositions. It is difficult to imagine a case of any importance in which parties will not use depositions. In a deposition, the person being deposed (called the *deponent*) is asked questions, to which she responds orally. Her testimony is recorded[8] and can later be transcribed into book-like form.[9] The deponent may request the opportunity to review the deposition testimony and correct any errors before signing it under penalty of perjury.[10] At the outset, the court reporter administers an oath to the deponent, who thus affirms that the testimony she will give is the truth, under penalty of perjury.[11] In some ways, a deposition looks like testimony at trial. The deponent is "sworn in" and then responds to questions "live." In some ways, though, it is not like a trial. Depositions, for instance, do not take place in a courtroom, and no judge is present. Instead, the parties and their lawyers are entitled to attend; the lawyer for each party has a right to ask questions.[12] The only other person usually present is the court reporter, who administers the oath and records the deposition.

A party wishing to depose someone must "notice" the deposition, which means she must give written notice to all parties of the deposition. Under Rule 30(b)(1), the notice (usually one page) must name the person to be deposed and indicate the date, time, and place of the deposition.[13] Importantly, a party can depose *anyone* who has discoverable information — even nonparties.[14] A nonparty deponent should be *subpoenaed* to attend the deposition. Otherwise, the nonparty is under no obligation to attend

---

[8] Traditionally, the recording is done by a court reporter on a stenographic machine. Rule 30(b)(3) allows recording by sound or video/sound mechanisms as well. The party taking the deposition must arrange to have a court reporter attend and record the deposition. Each city has court reporting firms that provide these services. *See also* Rule 30(b)(4) (allowing court order or stipulation for depositions by telephone or other remote means).

[9] If a deposition (or any part of it) will be offered for evidence at trial, it (or the portions offered) must be transcribed. Fed. R. Civ. P. 32(c).

[10] Rule 30(e)(1) permits the deponent or a party to request that the deponent have 30 days after being notified by the court reporter that the transcript is available in which to review it. If she makes changes "in form or substance," the deponent must sign a statement reciting the changes and why they were made. The court reporter must note whether any such review was requested and, if so, append any changes to the transcript.

[11] Rule 28(a)(1) requires that depositions be taken before an officer authorized to administer a valid oath. Court reporters are licensed to do so.

[12] A party who is not represented by an attorney — called a *pro se* party — is entitled to attend and ask questions. The nonparty deponent may have her lawyer present.

[13] The notice of deposition is served on all parties under Rule 5, which allows service, *inter alia*, by mail or by delivery to a party's attorney. See §3.3.6. Rule 27(a) addresses depositions taken before a case is filed. The purpose of such a deposition is to preserve evidence (or "perpetuate testimony") for the case. For instance, if a key eyewitness was seriously ill, a potential party might want to take a deposition pre-filing to perpetuate the witness's testimony. A court order is required for such depositions, upon showing satisfying the standards in Rule 27(a)(1).

[14] Rules 30(a)(1) and 31(a)(1) permit the deposition of "any person, including a party."

the deposition.[15] A subpoena, issued under Rule 45, emanates from the court and commands a person to attend an event (such as a deposition or a trial) and give testimony.[16] To take a deposition of a party to the litigation, however, no subpoena is required; the properly served notice of deposition suffices to require the party to attend her own deposition. This distinction makes sense. A party has already been brought before the jurisdiction of the court (the plaintiff by suing; the defendant by being served with process), so no further order of the court is necessary. A nonparty, in contrast, has never been brought before the jurisdiction of the court, so this exercise of "power" over her is necessary to compel her attendance.[17] A subpoena can require the nonparty not only to attend and be deposed, but to bring documents or things with her; such an order is called a *subpoena duces tecum*.[18]

The deponent is required to testify based upon her present knowledge and recollection. If she knows that the answer to a particular question would be contained in files in her office, but does not remember what the documents say, she simply indicates her lack of recollection; she is under no obligation to review all relevant files before being deposed. Because they are "live," and because lawyers can adjust their questioning in response to what the deponent says, depositions can become very tense, even dramatic. Sometimes, for instance, a deponent may lose her composure or admit something important. Occasionally, the lawyer for the deponent may object and instruct the deponent not to answer.[19] Rule 30(c)(2) limits the types of objections that are properly raised in depositions. Ultimately, the judge may be required to determine whether the objections are proper.

Obviously, depositions are very useful. But they are also very expensive. Lawyers prepare a good deal in advance of each deposition, studying relevant documents and devising lines of questioning. Under Rule 30(a)(2)(A)(ii), no one can be deposed more than once in a case unless the court orders an additional deposition. Because parties only have one

---

[15] If a party notices the deposition of a nonparty and fails to subpoena her, and she does not show up because of the lack of a subpoena, that party is liable for costs and attorneys' fees incurred by other parties that showed up for the deposition. Fed. R. Civ. P. 30(g). So *always* subpoena a nonparty deponent.

[16] Rule 45(a) provides that a subpoena compelling attendance at a deposition issues from the court in the district in which the deposition is to be held. Rule 45(c) protects nonparty deponents from undue burden or expense by limiting where the nonparty can be deposed.

[17] Of course, a nonparty who has not been subpoenaed is free to show up and be deposed if she so chooses. Without a subpoena, though, she cannot be sanctioned for failing to do so.

[18] "Duces tecum" is Latin for (roughly) "bring with you."

[19] For example, counsel might do so to preserve an evidentiary privilege, as we discuss in §8.3.1.

chance at a deposition, then, they must be fully prepared to take advantage of each deposition. This fact counsels assiduous use of all discovery devices in a coordinated way. Rarely will the deposition be used first. Usually, it makes more sense to serve interrogatories (discussed below) first, to get helpful background information, before deciding whom to depose and what lines of questioning to pursue.

Suppose a party wants to depose someone but does not know the person's name. For example, suppose the design of an automobile's gas tank is relevant. A party may wish to depose the engineer responsible for that design. If the manufacturer for which this person works is a party to the litigation, the best course might be to serve interrogatories on the manufacturer, asking it to identify the engineer. Once she is identified, her deposition can be taken. But what if the manufacturer is not a party (and thus (as we see below) cannot be served with interrogatories)? Rule 30(b)(6) permits the party to name the manufacturer as the deponent and to describe the matters on which discovery is sought. The manufacturer then is required to identify and produce the appropriate person for the deposition.

Responding to discovery abuses, the drafters of the Rules in 1993 imposed presumptive limits on depositions. Unless a court order or stipulation of the parties[20] permits, Rule 30(a)(2)(A)(i) limits each party to no more than ten depositions in the case. Also, unless a court order or stipulation permits, Rule 30(d)(1) limits each deposition to a single day of no more than seven hours. In 2000, the Rule was amended to take away each district's ability to alter these limitations by Local Rule. Again, the court can make an order increasing the number of depositions or allowing a person to be deposed more than once or to extend the length of the deposition (or the parties can so stipulate) — but the court order must be made on a case-specific basis, and not as a standing Local Rule.

Finally, most depositions are taken under Rule 30, which allows deposition on oral examination. That means that the questions put to the deponent are asked orally by the lawyers for each party. Rule 31, however, permits a deposition on written questions. These are fairly rare. They work in all ways as an oral deposition, with one exception — the questions are not asked orally by counsel for a party. Instead, they are submitted in advance and are read by the court reporter, who then records the deponent's oral responses. Rule 31 depositions are cheaper than Rule 30 depositions, because the party taking the deposition need not have her

---

[20] Rule 29(b) permits parties to stipulate to various aspects of discovery procedure. The one area on which parties cannot stipulate under that Rule is the time for responding *if* an extension would interfere with the time already set for completing discovery or for hearing a motion or commencing trial. In such a situation, a stipulation will work only if approved by the court. Outside that, the parties have a good deal of leeway in working out the scheduling and scope of discovery. See §8.5.

attorney attend and ask questions. They suffer a significant and obvious drawback, though, in that the questions are pre-scripted and cannot be changed to account for responses by the deponent. Most lawyers want to take oral depositions, so they can watch the deponent as well as listen to her responses. This enables the lawyer to sense weaknesses in the deponent's position, and to hone in with appropriate follow-up questions.

Interrogatories. This tool is used in virtually every case. Interrogatories, which are governed by Rule 33, are written questions, to which the responding party must respond in writing within 30 days of being served with the questions.[21] Unlike depositions, then, interrogatories are rarely going to uncover a "smoking gun." Someone under the pressure of a deposition might "crack under the strain" and blurt out something damaging to her case. But interrogatories rarely lead to such dramatic moments, in part because of the temporal interlude between the question and the answer and in part because a party's lawyer will assist the party in drafting her answers. Answers to interrogatories are signed by the responding party under oath, under penalty of perjury. The responding party may object to an interrogatory, for example, because it calls for material that is protected by an evidentiary privilege; if she does, she must expressly invoke the relevant privilege, which we discuss in §8.3.1.

Interrogatories can be invaluable to discover background facts — names and addresses of relevant persons, dates of contracts, the number of contacts between the parties — any objective data relevant to the claims or defenses of any party. They also are helpful to clarify a party's pleadings. Recall that federal court pleadings can be fairly conclusory. A defendant sued for negligence will want to send interrogatories to the plaintiff to force her to detail the allegedly negligent behavior. Parties often use such "contention interrogatories" to force the other side to take a position, by asking something like: "Do you contend that the plaintiff was contributorily negligent?" Usually, parties use answers to interrogatories to prepare for the deposition of the other party. So responses to interrogatories and initial required disclosures usually provide valuable information for deciding whom to depose and what sorts of questions to ask her.

As we just saw, a party can take the deposition of a nonparty. Interrogatories, in contrast, can only be sent to other parties.[22] There is no provision for sending interrogatories to nonparties. Another difference concerns the type of information the responding party must assess before responding. Recall that the deponent is required to testify only as to her present knowledge or recollection. In responding to interrogatories, however, the party must give information reasonably available to her. Thus, if

---

[21] The responses are served on all parties under Rule 5(b). If the interrogatories were served by mail, the responding party is allowed an extra three days from the date on which they were mailed. Fed. R. Civ. P. 6(d). See §3.3.6.

[22] Rule 33(a)(1) provides that interrogatories may be served on "any other party."

an interrogatory asks for information the party does not recall, but that is contained in her files, she must to go through the files and find that answer.

In this regard, however, Rule 33(d) provides the "business records option." Suppose Party *A* sends an interrogatory to Party *B*, the answer to which is contained in Party *B*'s business records (including electronically stored information). If the burden of finding the answer to the interrogatory would be substantially the same for both parties, Party *B* (instead of finding the answer herself) can simply give Party *A* access to the business records so she can find the answer.

In response to abusive discovery, in which parties would send massive sets of interrogatories to each other, Rule 33(a)(1) imposes a presumptive limit: Each party can serve one set of a maximum of 25 interrogatories (including subparts) on each other party in the case. District courts may not change this limitation by Local Rule. On the other hand, the court may make a case-specific order increasing the number of interrogatories allowed, or the parties may stipulate to a larger number.[23]

Requests for Production. This tool, in Rule 34, is also used in nearly every case of significance. It permits one party to request that another party produce documents, electronically stored information, or tangible things, or allow entry upon land to permit various acts, such as testing. The materials must be "in the possession, custody, or control" of the party to whom the request is made. The most common use of Rule 34 is to gain access to documents, which the requesting party may then inspect and copy. The Rule is useful far beyond that, however. For instance, where Plaintiff sues Defendant for infringing Plaintiff's patent on a widget, Rule 34 would permit Plaintiff to gain access to Defendant's widget and to inspect it (or have her consultants inspect it). In a case involving damages to Plaintiff's house, Defendant can gain access to the property to inspect it (or have her consultants inspect it).

Effective in 2006, Rule 34 specifically includes "electronically stored information" (ESI). In §8.3.5, we discuss generally the 2006 amendments to the rules to adapt to recent developments in technology. One area of especial concern has been discovery of e-mails. Before 2006, many people argued that e-mails were discoverable as "documents" under Rule 34. Often, however, e-mails exist only on a server and not in hard-copy format. The specific reference to discovery of ESI removes any doubt — ESI is discoverable. Rule 34(b)(1)(C) permits a party sending a request for production of ESI to specify the form in which ESI is to be produced. For example, a party may ask for hard copies of such information. Under Rule 34(b)(2)(D), the responding party may object to the requested form for producing ESI. She may then indicate what form she intends to use in

---

[23] Rule 29(b) permits the parties to stipulate to many issues concerning the scheduling and scope of discovery. See note 20.

producing the information. For example, she may prefer to produce such information in a form that can be searched electronically.

The party making the request drafts a request under Rule 34(b)(1) and serves it on all parties.[24] The request must set forth the documents or things desired "with reasonable particularity." It can specify documents individually (e.g., "the letter from *A* to *B* dated November 4, 2008") or by categories (e.g., "sales receipts from October 1, 2009, to January 5, 2010"). The responding party must respond within 30 days of service of the request[25] and must either indicate that the inspection will be allowed or assert objections to the inspection. Rule 34(b)(2)(E) provides that "[a] party must produce documents as they are kept in the usual course of business or must organize and label them to correspond to the categories in the request." This requirement is intended to make it difficult for the responding party to bury a key document in a mountain of unimportant material.

Frequently, a party will want to discover documents (or things) from a party whose deposition will be taken. It is possible to have the request for production accompany the notice of deposition, in which case the party will have to show up for her deposition with the requested documents (or things). On the other hand, it might be more useful to obtain the documents and review them before taking the other party's deposition. So counsel might prefer to use the requests for production before taking the deposition. In practice, there is a great deal of cooperation between counsel to schedule the exchange of documents and depositions of the parties.[26]

Rules 34(a) and (b) speak only of making requests for production from parties; they do not permit requests for production from nonparties. Rule 34(c), however, reminds us that nonparties can be compelled to produce documents or things under Rule 45, which governs subpoenas. Rule 45(a)(1)(A), in turn, makes it clear that a nonparty can be compelled to produce documents, electronically stored information, and tangible things for inspection or to allow access to property.[27] Accordingly, a nonparty can be required to produce things, just as a party can be, but the nonparty is not required to comply with the request unless she is served with a subpoena.

The availability of a subpoena solely to gain the production of documents and things from a nonparty is handy. Before this could be done under Rule 34(c), a party seeking documents from a nonparty had to notice the

[24] The requests are served on parties under Rule 5(b), usually by mail. See §3.3.6.

[25] The responses are also served on all parties under Rule 5(b). If the requests were served by mail, the responding party is allowed an extra three days from the date on which they were mailed. Fed. R. Civ. P. 6(d).

[26] Rule 29(b) permits the parties to stipulate to many issues concerning the scheduling and scope of discovery. See note 20.

[27] Notice how Rule 45(a)(1)(A)(iii) speaks of commanding a "person" as opposed to a "party." Thus the target of a subpoena need not be a party to the litigation.

nonparty's deposition and serve the nonparty with a *subpoena duces tecum* (which required the nonparty's attendance and required her to bring specified documents or things with her). The nonparty would then be sworn in for the deposition and asked if she brought the requested documents with her. Once she identified the documents, the deposition would end and the parties would inspect the documents. Now, if one simply wants documents or things (and no deposition) from the nonparty, she need merely serve the nonparty with a subpoena for production of the materials; there is no need to go through the inconvenience of noticing her deposition.

Medical Examinations. This discovery tool is unique because, as Rule 35(a)(2)(A) makes plain, it is only available if the court grants a party's motion to subject someone to a physical or mental examination (which we will simply call a *medical exam*). The party seeking the order must demonstrate two things. First, under Rule 35(a)(1), she must show that a person's "mental or physical condition — including blood group — is in controversy." Second, under Rule 35(a)(2)(A), she must demonstrate good cause for the examination. Upon such a showing, the court can order someone to undergo a medical exam before a "suitably licensed or certified examiner." The motion (and the court order, if granted) must state the time, place, manner, and scope of the exam, and give the name of the person who will perform it. The requirement of a court order makes sense; without it, this tool could easily be used to harass or oppress other parties.[28]

The Supreme Court has emphasized that conclusory allegations are not sufficient to justify an order of a medical exam. Rather, the party seeking the examination must make "an affirmative showing . . . that each condition as to which the examination is sought is really and genuinely in controversy and that good cause exists for ordering each particular examination."[29] Moreover, the ability to obtain the desired information in some less intrusive fashion is relevant to whether the party establishes good cause for the order.

Rule 35(a)(1) permits an order for a medical exam only of "a party," but also permits the court to order a party to "produce for examination a person who is in its custody or control." Courts have interpreted this latter phrase narrowly. It includes, for example, a child of a party, because a child is (at least in theory) in the custody and control of her parent.[30] It does not include an employee.[31]

---

[28] On the other hand, Florida has long permitted some medical examinations without court orders, seemingly without substantial abuse. *See* Fla. R. Civ. P. 1.360 (2004).

[29] Schlagenhauf v. Holder, 379 U.S. 104, 118 (1964).

[30] *See, e.g.,* Schempp v. Reniker, 809 F.2d 541, 542-543 (8th Cir. 1987) (parental custody or legal control of minor child).

[31] From time to time, there have been proposals to expand Rule 35 to cover an employee or agent of a party, but all such efforts have failed. *See* 7 Moore's Federal Practice §35.06.

- A bus operated by BusCo and driven by Driver collides with another vehicle. Plaintiff, a passenger on the bus, was injured and sues BusCo. Plaintiff believes that Driver's poor eyesight contributed to the wreck, and seeks a court order that Driver have her eyesight examined by a suitably licensed professional. Obviously, if Driver were a party, Plaintiff could seek the order. But in this case, Plaintiff sued only BusCo. Plaintiff cannot get the order, because Driver, though an employee of a party (BusCo), is not considered to be "in the legal control or custody" of BusCo. That being the case, can you think of a discovery plan to get information about Driver's eyesight?

- For one thing, Plaintiff can take the deposition of Driver. She would have to secure Driver's attendance with a subpoena. At the deposition, Plaintiff can inquire about Driver's eyesight. For example, she can ask Driver about how often she has her eyes checked, whether she wears glasses, etc.

- Another approach would be to require Driver, through a subpoena *duces tecum* (either before or concurrent with the deposition), to produce her glasses for examination by Plaintiff's experts. Plaintiff can also gain production of any documents relating to Driver's glasses or prescriptions. Moreover, in deposition, Plaintiff could ask Driver to identify her doctor and then depose the doctor about Driver's eyesight.[32]

The medical exam will often be performed by a medical doctor, but note that Rule 35 envisions an exam by any suitably licensed or certified person. Many such people do not hold the M.D. degree. The Rule is intended to facilitate examinations by any suitable health care professional. Thus, exams can be performed by chiropractors, podiatrists, physical therapists, and other such professionals. Of course, the professional is compensated for performing the medical exam. The party requesting the exam pays for it, and that expense becomes a "cost" of the litigation. (Remember from §1.1 that, generally, the prevailing party recovers her costs (which do not include attorneys' fees) from the loser.)

After the medical exam has been performed, the examining professional sends her report to the party who sought the exam. The person who was examined has a right to receive a copy of the report. All she has to do is request it from the party who sought the order of examination. Under Rule 35(b)(1), that party must deliver it to the person making the request. But requesting the report carries a price. Under Rule 35(b)(4), by requesting and obtaining the report, the person who was examined "waives any privilege it may have — in that action or any other action involving the same controversy — concerning testimony about all examinations of the same condition." In other words, the person examined waives any privilege in the reports of other professionals concerning the same condition. Indeed,

---

[32] We see in §8.3.1 that confidential communications between Driver and her doctor would be privileged and thus could not be discovered.

under Rule 35(b)(3), once the person examined receives the report from the court-ordered examination, she must (upon request of the other party) produce reports of her own doctors concerning that medical condition.

Requests for Admission. This tool can be very useful; don't forget about it when you are in the "real world." Rule 36(a)(1)(A) permits a party to force another party to admit or deny any discoverable matter relating to "facts, the application of law to fact, or opinions about either." And Rule 36(a)(1)(B) permits the same regarding "the genuineness of any described documents." As you will study in a course on Evidence, documents can only be admitted for consideration at trial if they are authenticated — that is, established as genuine. Litigants should cooperate in admitting the genuineness of documents whenever possible, to avoid the expense of going through the exercise of finding the author of each document and asking her under oath whether she wrote it.

Rule 36 is not so much a discovery tool as it is a device to force a party to take a position on specific issues. Requests for admission can put a party's feet to the fire and may narrow the scope of issues to be tried. Though Rule 36 does not impose a presumptive limit on the number of requests to be served in a case, Rule 26(b)(1) empowers the court to impose such restrictions by order or by Local Rule.

Requests for admission can only be served on parties.[33] There is no provision for sending them to nonparties. The responding party has 30 days from the service of the requests in which to serve on all parties her written and signed response to the requests.[34] In the response, she must either specifically deny the matter or "state in detail" why she is unable to admit or deny; as to the latter, she cannot say that she lacks knowledge on the matter unless she states that she has made a reasonable inquiry and that the information obtainable is insufficient to permit her to admit or deny. (Of course, a party may object to any request for admission that asks for improper matter, such as irrelevant or privileged material. See §8.3.1.) If the responding party fails to deny a request to admit, the matter is deemed admitted. Rule 36(b) provides that a matter admitted under Rule 36 "is conclusively established unless the court, on motion, permits the admission to be withdrawn or amended." Rule 36(a)(1) makes clear that admissions are binding only in the pending case and thus cannot be used in other litigation.

The word to the wise here is simple: If you can honestly deny the request for admission, deny it. Do not respond with argument. Simply

---

[33] Rule 36(a)(1) states that requests for admission may be served on "any other party." Service is usually done by mail under Rule 5. See §3.3.6.

[34] The responses are also served on all parties under Rule 5. If the requests were served by mail, the responding party is allowed an extra three days from the date on which they were mailed. Fed. R. Civ. P. 6(d).

reply that the party "denies this request for admission." Doing anything else may run the risk of failing to deny, which, as we have seen, constitutes an admission.

- ○ Plaintiff serves a set of requests for admission on Defendant. One of them states "Defendant drank alcohol within 30 minutes before the automobile collision." In her response, Defendant states "whether Defendant was drinking alcohol within 30 minutes before the automobile collision is a disputed fact to be determined at trial." Defendant has failed to deny the request, and therefore is considered to have admitted it. Unless the court allows withdrawal or amendment, it is now established as a fact that Defendant drank alcohol within 30 minutes of the collision. Note that the tenth sentence of Rule 36(a) (the last sentence of the second paragraph of Rule 36(a)) specifically addresses this issue, and states that a party may not object simply on the ground that the request raises a triable issue of fact.

§8.2.3 Duty to Supplement Responses

We must remember that the litigation process often takes years to complete. It is quite possible that a party's response to discovery that was fully accurate when made months or years ago might not be accurate after further facts are uncovered. On the other hand, it is quite possible, given the passage of time and the rigors of law practice, that the party or lawyer would not realize that discovery of new facts rendered earlier responses inaccurate.

In 1993, Rule 26(e) was amended to address these concerns. As currently written, Rule 26(e)(1) imposes a duty on each party to "supplement or correct" any required disclosure and any responses to interrogatories, requests for production, and requests for admission. The duty attaches under Rule 26(e)(1)(A) only "if the party learns that in some material respect the disclosure or response is incomplete or incorrect."[35] And even then, the duty applies only "if the additional or corrective information has not otherwise been made known to the other parties during the discovery process or in writing."

These supplemental responses are required even though no party asks for them. Thus, Rule 26(e)(1) requires each party to police itself to ensure that responses previously made have not become misleading or inaccurate as the case unfolds. Thus, it is incumbent on each party (guided by her lawyer) to review the responses to required disclosures to ensure that they are accurate as the case unfolds.

---

[35] Rule 26(e)(1)(B) requires supplemental responses if the court orders them. The more important self-policing provision in Rule 26(e)(1)(A) is discussed in text.

Rule 26(e)(2) addresses only the very specific case of required disclosures about expert witnesses, which are found in Rule 26(a)(1)(B). It requires a party to supplement or correct not only the information included in the expert's report but also information given during her deposition.

§8.3   Scope of Discovery

§8.3.1   Relevant, Nonprivileged Matter, and the Concept of Proportionality

Discoverable Versus Admissible Information. We have just reviewed the tools available for gaining information in the discovery phase of litigation. In this section, we address what kinds of information a litigant can seek with those tools. The basic standard for discoverable information is set forth in Rule 26(b)(1): Unless the court orders otherwise, parties may discover "any nonprivileged matter that is relevant to any party's claim or defense." The key word in this standard is *relevant*. The Rule does not define it. In common parlance, the term means essentially *pertinent*. The third sentence of Rule 26(b)(1) helps by providing that "Relevant information need not be admissible at the trial if the discovery appears reasonably calculated to lead to the discovery of admissible evidence." So relevant information may be discovered even if it is not admissible at trial. Stated another way, the concept of discoverability is broader than the concept of admissibility.

You will study admissibility in detail in a course on Evidence. For now, it is sufficient to know that there are limitations on what evidence can be presented at trial for consideration by the fact-finder (which might be a jury or might be the judge). One of the most important restrictions concerns "hearsay" evidence. Hearsay is information that the witness (the person testifying at trial) has encountered, but which she did not observe or otherwise perceive firsthand. Suppose, for instance, your roommate tells you that she cheated on an exam. If you relate that information to someone, your report is hearsay. It may be true, but you don't know it to be true; you have no independent knowledge on the subject. The general rule is that hearsay evidence is not admissible at trial. (The rule is subject, though, to a stunning number of exceptions, which need not concern us here.)

So if the issue to be determined at trial were whether your roommate had cheated on an exam, as a general matter, your testimony might well be inadmissible to prove the point. The fact that information is inadmissible, however, does not necessarily mean that it cannot be the subject of discovery. Again, this is because the third sentence of Rule 26(b)(1) provides that information is discoverable if it is "reasonably calculated to lead to the discovery of admissible evidence." So, assuming the issue were relevant in the litigation, if you were asked in a deposition whether your roommate told you she cheated on an exam, you would be required to relate what she told you. The fact that it would not be admissible at trial is irrelevant to discovery.

- In an automobile collision case, W could testify at trial that she heard brakes screech shortly before hearing the sound of the collision. The evidence is admissible because it is within W's personal perception. But W could not testify at trial that her boyfriend told her that he had heard the screeching brakes and the collision. The evidence is inadmissible because it is hearsay; she is testifying about something someone told her rather than something she perceived.
  - Nonetheless, W's hearsay testimony is *relevant*. The information is reasonably calculated to lead to the discovery of admissible evidence because it will lead the party asking the question to W's boyfriend, who actually heard the screeching brakes and the collision. So a party can ask W (in a deposition, for instance) about her boyfriend's telling her what he had heard. But the same party could not ask W to testify at trial about what her boyfriend told her. Again, the information is relevant, but not admissible at trial.[36]
- P sues D, her supervisor at work, for sexual harassment. She seeks discovery of evaluations of D as a supervisor at different times, when D oversaw other employees. While this evidence is probably not admissible to show sexual harassment of P, it is discoverable.[37]

Rule 26(b)(1) requires that the information be relevant "to any party's claim or defense." Until December 2000, the Rule had allowed discovery of information relevant "to the subject matter involved in the action." The current standard is narrower, and reflects concern that discovery had become too wide-ranging. Some observers are skeptical that the current standard — relevant to a claim or defense — is narrower in any definable way than the older standard.[38] Indeed, it is impossible to quantify any difference in the two. Maybe all that can be said is that the new standard constituted an attempt by the Advisory Committee (which drafts the Rules

---

[36] Another example may be the requirement in Rule 26(a)(1)(iv) that a defendant divulge in required disclosures the amount of insurance coverage she has for the claims asserted against her. The existence of insurance is not admissible at trial but, obviously, is subject to discovery, even without a showing that it would lead to discovery of admissible evidence.

[37] *See* Jones v. Commander, Kansas Army Ammunitions Plant, 147 F.R.D. 248, 251 (D. Kan. 1993).

[38] The Advisory Committee, which drafts the Federal Rules for the Supreme Court, has been criticized in recent years for making too many changes of little import. The result, according to critics, is the imposition of busy work. An interesting example involves the

for the Supreme Court) to send a message to judges to monitor the scope of discovery, with a keen eye to what the parties have pleaded.

The second sentence of Rule 26(b)(1) permits the court, for good cause, to order discovery along broader lines: "relevant to the subject matter involved in the action." The circumstances warranting such expansion (like the determination of what information is relevant) vary with the facts of each case, and the matter is committed to the sound discretion of the district judge.

- ○ P sues D for personal injuries, alleging that she was injured by D's negligence. She seeks compensatory damages of $100,000. P wants to discover information concerning D's net worth. Is the requested information discoverable? The answer should be no, because the information is not relevant to a claim or defense in the case. P seeks compensatory damages. Such damages are intended to compensate the plaintiff for harm caused. Whether D has $1 or $1,000,000 in the bank does not affect the calculation of how much money is needed to make P whole.[39]

- ○ P sues D for personal injuries allegedly caused by D's wanton conduct and for punitive damages, which are permitted under applicable law for wantonly caused harm. She seeks compensatory damages of $100,000 and punitive damages of $1,000,000. P wants to discover information concerning D's net worth. Is the requested information discoverable? The answer here should be yes, because D's net worth is relevant to the question of punitive damages. Such damages are intended to punish a defendant for egregious conduct. They simply cannot be assessed without knowing the defendant's net worth. Stated bluntly, it would take a far larger punitive damages award to punish a billionaire than it would to punish someone of modest means. Until the court knows the net worth of the defendant, it cannot know how large a punitive damages award will suffice.[40]

---

change in definition of discoverability, which, as noted in text, went into effect in December 2000. In a motion decided March 29, 2001, a district judge applied the old standard, which may have showed that the amendment promulgated in December 2000 had not been well publicized. Anderson v. Hale, 2001 U.S. Dist. LEXIS 3774 (N.D. Ill. Mar. 29, 2001). When the new standard was brought to the court's attention, it rendered a second opinion, in which it concluded the answer was the same under it and the older provision. Anderson v. Hale, 2001 U.S. Dist. LEXIS 7538 (N.D. Ill. June 1, 2001). At the end of the day, it is not clear how "relevant" to a "claim or defense" is much different from "relevant" to the "subject matter of the action."

[39] See, e.g., Henderson v. Zurn, 131 F.R.D. 560, 562 (S.D. Ind. 1990) (because the financial status of defendant is irrelevant to compensatory damages, defendant's tax returns are not relevant). But see Baker v. CNA Ins. Co., 123 F.R.D. 322, 329-330 (D. Mont. 1988) (permitting discovery in similar circumstances).

[40] See, e.g., Caruso v. Coleman Co., 157 F.R.D. 344, 348 (E.D. Pa. 1994). Most courts, like the one in Caruso, permit discovery even in the absence of a prima facie showing that the circumstances exist for the imposition of punitive damages. Though some courts delay discovery until liability for punitive damages has been established, the relevant point is the same — a claim for punitive damages implicates the defendant's net worth.

Privileged Matter. Assuming the matter sought is "relevant to any party's claim or defense," Rule 26(b)(1) permits discovery only if that matter is "nonprivileged." The concept of *privilege* is another topic you will study in the course on Evidence. The term refers to a privilege to keep something secret. If something is privileged in this sense, the person holding the privilege cannot be forced to divulge it — either in discovery or at trial.

Privileges of this type protect *confidential communications between particular people.* For example, confidential communications between lawyer and client, between doctor and patient, between clergy member and parishioner, and between spouses, might be privileged (depending on the applicable law). Communications between others are not privileged, no matter how confidential and "secret" the people may have intended them to be. So if the defendant admits in a confidential communication to her lawyer, her priest, or her husband that she was speeding at the time of the accident, she cannot be made to divulge that statement, either in discovery or at trial.[41] And, if she asserts her privilege, her lawyer, priest, or husband cannot be made to divulge the statement. It is privileged. The privilege is said to be "absolute," meaning that no party can make a showing strong enough to overcome the protection. As long as the privilege is asserted and not waived, it protects — absolutely — against disclosure. But the communication must be between persons having one of the specific relationships recognized as raising a privilege. For example, if the woman were not married, and told her boyfriend — in "strict confidence" — that she was speeding, that communication would not be privileged. There is a spousal privilege; there is not a "significant other" privilege.

As you will study in Evidence, the concept of privilege embodies a policy determination that particular relationships would be harmed if parties to confidential communications were forced to divulge the content of those communications. Clearly, all privileges (including the constitutional privilege against self-incrimination) inhibit the truth-seeking function. Society abides this hindrance because it values these relationships. If the truth-seeking function of litigation were the only relevant goal, there would be no privileges. But we want people to speak freely to their lawyers, their spouses, their clergyperson, etc., without fear that the confidential communications will later be divulged.

Notwithstanding the value society puts on such relationships, privileges can be waived. Those seeking the protection of a privilege in discovery

---

[41] Assuming, of course, that the relevant law recognizes privileges for confidential communications between these people. Nearly every jurisdiction recognizes the ones listed in the text, though it is worth noting that federal law generally does not recognize a physician-patient privilege. *See, e.g.,* Patterson v. Caterpillar, Inc., 70 F.3d 503, 506 (7th Cir. 1995). In federal-court cases involving state law, however, a state physician-patient privilege may be applied.

must assert it. If a discovery request would require a party to divulge privileged material, the party must claim the privilege when withholding the information. As Rule 26(b)(5)(A) provides, the party withholding information on the basis of privilege must "expressly make the claim" and "describe the nature of the documents, communications, or tangible things not produced or disclosed — and do so in a manner that, without revealing information itself privileged or protected, will enable other parties to assess the claim." Failure to assert the privilege results in waiving it.

Remember that privileges only attach to *confidential* communications. So if a client tells her lawyer something in a crowded elevator, it is not privileged. Also, the confidential communication with a professional, like a lawyer, must have been made in furtherance of providing professional services. Something said in confidence to a lawyer as part of an initial interview to see whether she will retain the lawyer will be privileged, even if she does not ultimately hire that lawyer. But something said in confidence to a lawyer on a golf course, without knowledge that the person is a lawyer and without relating to retention of her legal services, will not be privileged.

The Concept of Proportionality. Does a party have a right to discover *all* relevant, nonprivileged matter? We have seen that Rule 30(a)(2)(i) sets presumptive limits on the number and length of depositions and that Rule 33(a)(1) sets a similar limit on the number of interrogatories. In addition, Rule 26(b)(2)(C) permits the court to limit, by order or by Local Rule, the number of requests for admissions to be sent in each case. Beyond these mechanical points, Rule 26(b)(2)(C) requires the court to limit discovery based upon what might be called a general sense of *proportionality*.[42] Specifically, the court "must limit the frequency or extent of discovery" in any of three situations (discussed in the next three paragraphs). In any such case, the court may limit discovery either by entering a protective order (discussed in more detail in §8.3.4) or by acting on its own, after giving notice to the affected parties.

The first circumstance requiring limitation of discovery — found in Rule 26(b)(2)(C)(i) — is when the "discovery sought is unreasonably cumulative or duplicative, can be obtained from some other source that is more convenient, less burdensome, or less expensive." Here, it is not enough that there is some overlap or duplication of request. The court must determine whether the requests — in light of other circumstances and the claims involved — are "unreasonably" redundant. For example, when material already produced contained sufficient information to determine whether there was ethnic bias against a group of employees, the court refused to

---

[42] *See* Convergent Tech. Securities Litigation, 108 F.R.D. 328, 331 (N.D. Cal. 1985) (amendments to discovery rules, particularly Rule 26(b)(2), hailed as "superimposing the concept of proportionality on all behavior in the discovery arena").

require the defendant/employer to review 1,700 personnel files for additional information.[43] Moreover, the mere fact that information may be obtained from another source does not preclude discovery from a party. The court must assess the situation on a case-by-case basis.[44]

The second circumstance requiring limitation of discovery — found in Rule 26(b)(2)(C)(ii) — is when "the party seeking discovery has had ample opportunity to obtain the information by discovery in the action." This provision conveys a strong anti-dilatory message. If a party has a chance to discover something, it should do so promptly and not risk running afoul of this provision by delaying its efforts unduly.

The final circumstance requiring limitation of discovery — found in Rule 26(b)(2)(C)(iii) — is when "the burden or expense of the proposed discovery outweighs its likely benefit." The court is instructed to take into account such fact-specific things as the needs of the case, the amount in controversy, the importance of the issues, and the parties' resources. Obviously, the court has enormous discretion here in determining whether the cost imposed by discovery requests simply is not worth it in view of what will be gained. Many observers had high hopes that the amendments that forced courts to consider such questions of proportionality would curb discovery abuses. By 2000, many felt that courts had failed to implement the limitations in Rule 26(b)(2)(C) with sufficient care. In that year, Rule 26(b)(1), which states the general scope of discovery, was amended by adding a new last sentence expressly to remind courts of their authority to limit discovery under Rule 26(b)(2)(C).

To review, Rule 26(b)(1) thus defines *discoverable* information as that which is relevant (to any party's claim or defense) and which is not protected by a privilege. But there is no right to discover every bit of discoverable information. The court has significant discretion to limit discovery in accord with the proportionality concerns of Rule 26(b)(2)(C).

Limitations Concerning Electronically Stored Information (ESI). In discussing the request for production in §8.2.2, we noted that Rule 34 was amended in 2006 to permit discovery (among other things) of ESI. We also noted that one particular concern had been discovery of e-mails and other ESI that may exist on a server but may not have been reduced to hard copy. As part of a set of 2006 amendments addressing ESI, the Advisory Committee added Rule 26(b)(2)(B). It provides that a party need not provide ESI from a source that it identifies as "not reasonably accessible because of undue burden or cost." For instance, if ESI is kept on a server maintained by a nonparty, and it would be unreasonably expensive or burdensome to gain access to it, the party must say so and can then refuse to proffer discovery.

---

[43] Aramburu v. Boeing Co., 885 F. Supp. 1434, 1444 (D. Kan. 1995).
[44] *See generally* 6 Moore's Federal Practice §26.60.

Obviously, the other party may disagree. She may move for an order to compel the discovery (which we will address in §8.4). The party from whom the discovery is sought has the burden of demonstrating that complying with the request would be unduly burdensome or expensive. Even if the party makes that showing, though, the party seeking discovery may get it upon a showing of good cause. The court may then specify conditions for the discovery.

§8.3.2   Work Product

In §8.3.1, we saw that the law of privilege protects confidential communications between particular people from being divulged. The law also affords protection for "work product." We should speak of a work product "protection" and not a work product "privilege." Work product protection is different from privilege in two important ways: (1) it does not necessarily consist of confidential communications, and (2) its protection is often not absolute. The concept of work product in federal court is governed by Rule 26(b)(3), which was promulgated in 1970 and which, interestingly, does not use the term *work product*. Instead, it refers to "trial preparation materials."[45] Notwithstanding the language used in the Rule, just about everybody calls it *work product*.

What is it? Rule 26(b)(3)(A) defines work product as "documents and tangible things that are prepared in anticipation of litigation or for trial." Why should such materials be protected from discovery? The Supreme Court discussed the issue in the famous case of *Hickman v. Taylor*,[46] which was decided before the Federal Rules addressed the topic. Today, work product issues in federal court are governed by Rule 26(b)(3), which in some ways is broader than the common law doctrine established in *Hickman* and in some ways may be narrower. The starting point, however, is the common law discussion in *Hickman*, a case found in virtually every Civil Procedure casebook.

The case involved the sinking of a tug boat that was towing a car ferry across the Delaware River near Philadelphia. Five of the nine crew members of the tug drowned. Shortly after the disaster, the owners of the tug (and their insurance company) employed a lawyer named Fortenbaugh to defend them against potential suits for wrongful death and to sue the railroad for which the tug was pulling the car ferry. Fortenbaugh interviewed the surviving crew members and had their statements recorded and

---

[45] This title is misleadingly narrow. The protection covers materials generated in anticipation of *litigation*, not of *trial*. As we see in Chapter 9, very few cases that start in the litigation stream (by filing of the complaint) end up in trial.

[46] 329 U.S. 495 (1947).

signed.[47] In a wrongful death action against the tug owners and the rail-road, brought by relatives of one of crew members who drowned, the plaintiff attempted to discover the witness statements taken by Fortenbaugh.[48]

Everyone agreed that the statements were not protected by the attorney-client privilege, because they were not confidential communications between a lawyer and her client. These were conversations between Fortenbaugh and third parties. Because at the time there was no Federal Rule concerning work product, the plaintiff argued that the materials were not protected and thus had to be produced. The Supreme Court disagreed. While recognizing the Federal Rules' policy of liberal discovery, the Court found a countervailing policy protecting material prepared "with an eye toward . . . anticipated litigation."[49] Such material "falls outside the arena of discovery and contravenes the public policy underlying the orderly prosecution and defense of legal claims. Not even the most liberal of discovery theories can justify unwarranted inquiries into the files and the mental impressions of an attorney."[50] Absent a showing of necessity, or that "denial of such production would unduly prejudice the preparation of [a party's] case or cause him any hardship or injustice," a court should not permit discovery of such material.[51]

Hickman v. Taylor led to the adoption of Rule 26(b)(3), which differs in important ways from the common law rule announced in that case. There are seven important points to make regarding Rule 26(b)(3).

First, as noted, work product consists of materials "prepared in anticipation of litigation or for trial." That phrase is important. Work product must be generated, in the words of *Hickman v. Taylor*, "with an eye toward litigation," even if no case has yet been filed. So long as the party-to-be prepares the material *because she anticipates that there will be litigation,* the requirement is met. On the other hand, "materials assembled in the ordinary course of business, or pursuant to public requirements unrelated to litigation, or for other nonlitigation purposes" are not protected.[52]

---

[47] These witness statements were informal; they were not depositions.

[48] There was a serious problem with the effort to get *any* information from Fortenbaugh. The plaintiff sought information from him through an interrogatory asking for the content of the witness statements. As we saw in §8.2.2, interrogatories cannot be used to get information from nonparties. Fortenbaugh was not a party and thus could not have been subject to any discovery by interrogatory. The Supreme Court noted this fact, but, under the circumstances, "deem[ed] it unnecessary and unwise to rest [its] decision upon this procedural irregularity." 329 U.S. at 505. Because the issue of work product protection was so important, the Court went on to address it.

[49] *Id.* at 498.

[50] *Id.* at 510.

[51] *Id.* at 509.

[52] Fed. R. Civ. P. 26(b)(3), advisory committee's note (1970).

Accordingly, if a manufacturer routinely creates a report about each accident involving one of its products, those reports might not be protected as work product.[53]

Second, Rule 26(b)(3)(A) provides that "[o]rdinarily, a party may not discover" work product. So the starting point is clear — once we identify something as work product, as a general matter, it is protected from discovery.[54] This rule makes sense. If Party *A* engages in investigation in anticipation of litigation (like the investigation done by Fortenbaugh in *Hickman v. Taylor*), Party *B* should not be able to gain access to it. To allow Party *B* easy access to the material would reward freeloading. If Party *B* wants the benefit of investigation, she should do her own investigating (or hire someone to investigate).[55] As with privilege, however, the party asserting work product protection has the burden of raising the issue.[56] Failure to do so will waive the protection.

Third, Rule 26(b)(3)(A) defines work product as only "documents and tangible things" prepared in anticipation of litigation. Technically, this language would seem to allow Party *B* to send interrogatories to Party *A* in which she asks about the content of interviews with witnesses. After all, the interrogatory does not seek the discovery of the document or tangible thing. Courts have long rejected such an end-run around work product protection. As one court explained shortly after the adoption of Rule 26(b)(3), the "discovery of a detailed description of the contents of

[53] *See, e.g.,* Soeder v. General Dynamics Corp., 90 F.R.D. 253, 255 (D. Nev. 1980). This interpretation seems overly parsimonious, since accidents lead almost inevitably to litigation. In another case, a consumer complained to a manufacturer that its product was defective. The manufacturer generated internal memoranda discussing the possible defect in the product. Later, the consumer sued the manufacturer. The court permitted discovery of the memoranda and held that they were prepared in an effort to maintain good customer relations and not with an eye toward litigation. Scott Paper Co. v. Ceilcote Co., 103 F.R.D. 591, 596 (D. Me. 1984). Another court drew the distinction between investigating the *accident* (which does not create work product) and investigating a potential *claim* (which does). Spaulding v. Denton, 68 F.R.D. 342, 346 (D. Del. 1975). Such decisions reflect the fact that work product protection (like privileges) thwart the truth-finding function of litigation and thus will be interpreted narrowly.

[54] Noting that work product protection robs the parties of useful information, Professor Thornburg has concluded that this cost outweighs its benefits. Elizabeth Thornburg, *Rethinking Work Product*, 77 Va. L. Rev. 1515 (1991).

[55] While a professor at the University of Chicago (before he became a judge on the Seventh Circuit), Frank Easterbrook questioned whether we ought to encourage independent investigation by all parties. "To say . . . that a restriction of the scope of the attorney-client and work product privileges would reduce the investment in information in litigation may be to praise that result, not to condemn it." Frank Easterbrook, *Insider Trading, Secret Agents, Evidentiary Privileges, and the Production of Information*, 1981 Sup. Ct. Rev. 309, 361.

[56] Rule 26(b)(5)(A)(i) requires the party claiming privilege or work product protection "expressly make the claim."

documents through interrogatories is equivalent to discovery of the documents themselves" and should not be permitted.[57]

Fourth, under Rule 26(b)(3)(A)(ii), the work product protection can be overcome if the party seeking the information (Party *B* in our example) shows two things: (1) "substantial need for the materials to prepare [her] case" and (2) that she "cannot, without undue hardship, obtain their substantial equivalent by other means."[58] In other words, she needs this material and basically cannot get it elsewhere. In such circumstances, the work product protection is overcome. Obviously, then, work product protection is not absolute. If Party *B* makes the specified showing (which we call the *exception to work product* for shorthand) as to Party *A*'s work product, she can obtain that material. This rule also makes sense because, if Party *B* can make that showing, there is no danger of her being a freeloader.

- ○ After an accident, and in anticipation of litigation concerning the accident, *A*'s agent investigates the accident scene and interviews Joe, who was a witness to the accident. *A*'s agent records Joe's statement. Suppose *B* sues *A* concerning the litigation and seeks discovery of Joe's statement. For starters, the statement is work product, because it was prepared in anticipation of litigation, so (assuming *A* asserts the protection) *B* cannot get it. If *B* wants information from Joe, *B* can interview Joe or take his deposition.
- ○ Suppose, though, that Joe is unavailable. He is a citizen of Brazil and has returned home. Now *B* will be able to overcome *A*'s work product protection. First, she has substantial need of Joe's statement, because he was a witness. Second, she is unable without undue hardship (traveling to Brazil and finding Joe) to obtain the information. So *A* will have to produce the statement for *B*. It is work product, but *B* has overcome the protection ordinarily accorded it by invoking the exception to work product.

Fifth, some types of work product appear to be absolutely protected. Rule 26(b)(3)(B) provides that the court, in ordering the production of materials as to which the exception to work product has been invoked, "must protect against disclosure" of certain things: "mental impressions, conclusions, opinions, or legal theories. . . ." Many lawyers and judges refer to such nondiscoverable matter as "opinion work product," which is a fine shorthand as long as we remember that the quoted list covers more than opinions. The directive that the court "must protect against disclosure" of such materials seems absolute, and some courts have concluded that no showing can overcome the protection.[59] On the other hand, other courts

---

[57] Peterson v. United States, 52 F.R.D. 317, 320 (S.D. Ill. 1971).

[58] Rule 26(b)(3)(A)(i) simply says that the material sought must be discoverable under Rule 26(b)(1), which means that it is relevant and not privileged, as we saw in §8.3.1.

[59] *See, e.g.*, In re Grand Jury Investigation, 412 F. Supp. 943, 949 (E.D. Pa. 1976).

will permit discovery of opinion work product, but only on a showing of extraordinary circumstances.[60]

If a single document contains discoverable work product (such as Joe's witness statement) and nondiscoverable work product (such as a conclusion of counsel that Joe seems trustworthy and would be a good witness at trial), the court should order production with the nondiscoverable material *redacted*. That means the protected material would be blocked out from the copy given to the party seeking discovery.

Sixth, it is important to understand that work product under Rule 26(b)(3) is *not* limited to material generated by a lawyer. Many people (quite sloppily) refer to this topic as "attorney work product,"[61] which is inaccurate.[62] Rule 26(b)(3)(A) protects material generated in anticipation of litigation "by or for [a] party or its representative (including [her] attorney, consultant, surety, indemnitor, insurer, or agent)." This language is quite broad. Work product can be generated by a party's attorney, *but need not be*. So long as it is generated in anticipation of litigation — by the party herself, her lawyer, her private investigator, her insurer, or any other agent of hers — it is protected under Rule 26(b)(3)(A). Even "opinion work product" — consisting of things like legal theories — does not have to be generated by a lawyer. Rule 26(b)(3)(B) plainly provides protection for opinion work product generated by "the attorney or *other representative*."

Seventh, Rule 26(b)(3)(C) gives anyone (regardless of whether she is a party) a right to obtain her "own previous statement about the action or its subject matter." Thus, for example, anyone who made a witness statement that was taken down by a party or her representative can obtain a copy of the statement without making any showing. If she requests it, she has a right to get it.

---

[60] *See, e.g.*, Loftis v. Amica Mut. Ins. Co., 175 F.R.D. 5, 11-12 (D. Conn. 1997) (discovery of opinion work product is not favored and is permissible only in extraordinary cases). It seems clear that a party waives opinion work product by putting those opinions directly in issue in the litigation, as by designating the person who made the opinions an expert witness. *See, e.g.*, Hager v. Bluefield Reg. Med. Ctr., Inc., 170 F.R.D. 70, 78 (D.D.C. 1997). Such cases are rare.

[61] They may get this term from *Hickman v. Taylor*, which discussed work product created by a lawyer and thus used the term *attorney work product*.

[62] Obviously, Rule 26(b)(3), like all Federal Rules, applies only in federal courts. States are free to define work product in any way they like, or, alternatively, not to protect work product at all. *See, e.g.*, Pa. R. Civ. P. 4003.3 (permitting discovery of most materials prepared in anticipation of litigation). States may limit the concept of opinion work product to materials generated by lawyers. For example, in California, work product must be generated by an attorney or her agent. Cal. Code Civ. Proc. §2018.020.

§8.3.3 Expert Witnesses and Consultants

Different Types of Experts. In many (but certainly not all) cases, parties will find it worthwhile to retain experts, possibly for two reasons. First, an expert in a relevant field may serve as a consultant to a party, to assist her in preparing the case. For example, in a medical malpractice case, both sides might find it helpful to consult a medical expert. Second, of course, parties may retain experts to testify for them at trial. Expert witnesses, whether testifying at trial or in deposition before trial, are permitted to offer their opinions on matters within their expertise. (We noted this point in §8.2.1, discussing required disclosures concerning expert witnesses.) Rule 702 of the Federal Rules of Evidence allows qualified experts to offer opinions if "scientific, technical, or other specialized knowledge will assist the trier of fact to understand the evidence or to determine a fact in evidence." For example, in antitrust cases involving the allegedly anticompetitive effect on a market of a business arrangement, it is common for both sides to have expert economists testify, both to educate the jury about the dynamics of the market and to render their opinion as to whether and how the deal under scrutiny affected competition. Non-expert (or "lay") witnesses, in contrast, generally are not permitted to give their opinions on matters in the litigation.

Obviously, parties want to discover whatever they can about each other's plans to call experts as trial witnesses, about the expert's qualifications, and about the expert's opinions. From a common-sense standpoint, it ought to be easier to get discovery concerning experts another party expects to call as a witness at trial, rather than experts who may have served as consultants but who will not be called to testify at trial. After all, the expert who testifies is in a position to affect the outcome of the case more readily than one who will never be seen by the fact-finder at trial. We use "expert witness" to refer to an expert who is expected to testify at trial and "consulting expert" to refer to one who is not expected to testify at trial.

Expert Witnesses. Discovery concerning expert witnesses is greatly simplified in federal practice by required disclosure under Rule 26(a)(2). Specifically, Rule 26(a)(2)(A) provides that each party must identify any witness it "may use at trial" to present evidence under various provisions of the Federal Rules of Evidence. These provisions are the ones that permit experts to express their opinions. So, in sum, Rule 26(a)(2)(A) is aimed at those experts who may testify as experts at trial.

Rule 26(a)(2)(B) requires that each such witness prepare a written report, which she must sign. The report must be given to other parties as part of the required disclosure. It is an important document. The report contains detailed information, as listed in that subsection. Principal among the information are (1) a "complete statement of all opinions the witness will express and the basis and reasons for them"; (2) the data considered in forming those opinions; (3) the exhibits to be used to support or summarize her opinions; (4) the witness's qualifications, including a list of publications within the past ten years; (5) a list of other cases in which she has served as an expert within the past four years; and (6) the compensation the expert is to be paid for her work on this case.

Ordinarily, the court will direct the parties when to exchange this information concerning expert witnesses. Absent a court order or stipulation to the contrary, Rule 26(a)(2)(C)(i) requires that the information must be produced at least 90 days before the trial date. Of course, failure to produce the required information can result in sanctions, as discussed in §8.4 below. (Suffice it to say here that one possible sanction is an order that one's expert not be allowed to testify at trial.[63])

After the parties make the required disclosures under Rule 26(a)(2), pursuant to Rule 26(b)(4)(A) the other parties have a right to take the expert witness's deposition. It is inconceivable that a party would not take advantage of this right. No one would want to go to trial without having deposed the other side's expert witness. The deposition not only permits discovery of relevant information and elucidation of the expert's opinions, but also gives the lawyers a good chance to assess whether the expert will be effective in front of a jury. Under Rule 26(b)(4)(C)(i), unless "manifest injustice" would result, the court will require the party seeking discovery to "pay the expert a reasonable fee for time spent in responding to discovery."

Consulting Experts. The required disclosure under Rule 26(a)(2) and the provision for depositions in Rule 26(b)(4)(A) apply only to expert *witnesses*. What about discovery concerning an expert who was consulted but who will *not* be testifying at trial? Opposing parties would love to get this material because the fact that the expert will not be testifying may mean that she had bad news for the party who retained her. After all, if what the expert says favors the party who hired her, why wouldn't the expert be testifying at trial? Unfettered access to this information, however, would make parties less likely to retain experts for consulting purposes and, in turn, less likely to get "reality checks" from consultants. Accordingly, the Federal Rules impose limits on such discovery in this situation. The matter is addressed in Rule 26(b)(4)(B), which raises some interesting issues.

First, that Rule applies only if a consulting expert was "retained or specially employed by another party in anticipation of litigation or to prepare for trial." The phrase "anticipation of litigation" is interpreted as it is with regard to work product, which we saw in §8.3.2. The phrase "retained or

---

[63] *See, e.g.*, China Resource Prod. v. FAYDA Intl., 856 F. Supp. 856, 866-867 (D. Del. 1994).

specially employed" does not include an expert who was consulted informally, even if the informal consultation concerned the litigation at issue. Courts have looked to various factors to determine whether an expert was retained or merely informally consulted, including the manner in which the consultation was initiated, the extent of information or material provided to the expert, and the duration of the relationship. The matter is considered on a case-by-case basis.[64] If the court concludes that the expert was not actually retained, but was informally consulted, there can be no discovery concerning the expert — not even of her identity.[65]

Second, assuming the expert was retained in anticipation of litigation, Rule 26(b)(4)(B) permits discovery only if the expert is an examining health care professional under Rule 35[66] or (more important) if the party seeking the information can show "exceptional circumstances under which it is impracticable for the party seeking discovery to obtain facts or opinions on the same subject by other means." This standard imposes a high burden and courts are reluctant to find that it is satisfied.[67] Among the relatively rare fact patterns that might satisfy it is a case in which a consulting expert examined a machine or piece of equipment before it was destroyed or lost or rendered inoperative. The information from the party's consulting expert's tests might be discoverable because there is effectively no other way other parties can gain access to such information.[68]

Third, the party making the showing is entitled to "discover facts known or opinions held" by the consulting expert. Rule 26(b)(4)(B) does not impose any special requirement, however, for discovery of the consulting expert's *name*. Some courts thus have permitted the discovery of the consulting expert's identity without any special showing.[69] But if the identity of consulting experts were freely discoverable, the protection accorded by this Rule would be illusory. A party could simply ask another party to identify any experts consulted but who will not be testifying at trial. Armed with the expert's identity, the discovering party could then simply talk to that expert or take her deposition. Accordingly, other courts have concluded, rightly it seems, that the showing discussed in the preceding

---

[64] One well-known case discussing this and other issues under Rule 26(b)(4)(B) (and included in several Civil Procedure casebooks) is *Ager v. Jane C. Stormont Hospital & Training School for Nurses*, 622 F.2d 496, 501 (10th Cir. 1980).

[65] *Id.*

[66] We saw Rule 35 in §8.2.2. It requires a court order for a party to force another party to undergo a medical examination. By requesting a copy of the report, the party examined waives any privilege concerning that condition regarding any other health care professionals who examined her. Those professionals are thus subject to nonparty discovery, such as depositions.

[67] Wright & Kane, Federal Courts 589 ("Most cases have refused to find the exceptional circumstances that will justify this discovery.").

[68] *See Ager*, note 64 above, 622 F.2d at 503 n.8 (giving this example).

[69] *See, e.g.*, Roesberg v. Johns-Manville Corp., 85 F.R.D. 292, 303 (E.D. Pa. 1980).

paragraph — exceptional circumstances — must be satisfied even to gain discovery of the consultant's identity,[70] as well as her facts known and opinions held.

§8.3.4 Protective Orders

As we have seen, the Federal Rules envision broad discovery.[71] The Rules seek to facilitate each party's efforts to learn what truly happened. If the parties know each others' contentions and the facts, they can, in theory, either resolve their differences without trial or focus on truly disputed facts to expedite adjudication. But the benefits of discovery exact several prices.

First, as we've said, discovery is expensive and time-consuming. Second, discovery can intrude into people's privacy significantly. Responding to a sense of the overuse of discovery, the drafters of the Federal Rules have through the years imposed notable restrictions, including presumptive limits on the number of depositions and interrogatories (discussed in §8.2.4), the certification requirement of Rule 26(g) (discussed in §8.4), and the limits in Rule 26(b)(2) based upon proportionality (discussed in §8.3.1). They have not, however, abandoned the general theme of broad discovery.[72]

The Rules also reflect concern about discovery costs by allowing the judge, in the context of each case, to protect parties (or nonparties from whom discovery is sought) from overly expensive and overly intrusive discovery. Rule 26(c)(1) permits the judge to enter a "protective order" to shield from "annoyance, embarrassment, oppression, or undue burden or expense." The Rule details eight situations in which protective orders might be appropriate. This list is not exhaustive and the court has great discretion in entering protective orders. We already discussed one apt area for imposition of a protective order — to facilitate the proportionality limitations of Rule 26(b)(2), discussed in §8.3.1. In addition, when complying with a request for discovery of electronically stored information would be unduly burdensome or expensive, the responding party may seek a protective order, as noted in Rule 26(b)(2)(B). In this section, we focus on other key uses of the protective order.

---

[70] See Ager, note 64 above, 622 F.2d at 502-504.

[71] It is worth noting that no other country seems to embrace such broad discovery as the United States. See Stephen N. Subrin, Discovery in Global Perspective: Are We Nuts?, 52 DePaul L. Rev. 299 (2002).

[72] For a discussion of periodic shifts in thrust of the discovery provisions of the Federal Rules, see Richard L. Marcus, Only Yesterday: Reflections on Rulemaking Responses to E-Discovery, 73 Fordham L. Rev. 1, 1-7 (2004).

Rule 26(c) crafts a nice balance between the broad thrust of the discovery provisions and the needs of individual litigants. It does not permit the judge to exempt parties from discovery or to re-write the discovery provisions. But it does permit her to protect when necessary. Rule 26(c)(1) permits the person seeking protection to make a motion for protective order, in which she must certify that she has endeavored in good faith to confer with other parties to resolve the dispute without court involvement.

Many circumstances might justify a request for a protective order. For example, a discovery request might be overburdensome in that it seeks production of documents covering a period far greater than necessary for discovery of relevant material. The party receiving such a request may simply object under Rule 34(b)(2)(B). If the propounding party disagrees with the assertion that the request is overburdensome, she will make a motion to compel the discovery (as we discuss in §8.4). At the hearing on that motion, the court will determine whether the request was overburdensome and, if so, what materials are appropriately discoverable. On the other hand, the party from whom the request was made may strike first by moving for a protective order on the basis that the request is overburdensome. The opposing party may oppose the motion, and the court will decide the issue. It might, of course, grant the motion and enter an order protecting the responding party from having to produce the materials sought by the other side.

In rare cases, the court might order a protective order under Rule 26(c)(1)(E) that discovery proceed with only limited persons present. For instance, suppose a party will take the deposition of a child. The court might limit the number of persons in the room in an effort to make the child more comfortable. In other cases, the court may, under Rule 26(c)(1)(D), limit the scope of questioning in discovery to ensure that a deponent or party is not badgered or embarrassed. Again, however, the court must weigh the need to protect with the duty to permit discovery as envisioned by the discovery provisions.

In commercial cases, the parties may fight over protective orders concerning trade secrets. As you may discuss in your Torts class, trade secrets are things that are not patented or otherwise protected by law, but that companies expend great effort to protect from public disclosure. Examples include the formula for Coca-Cola and the recipe for Kentucky Fried Chicken. If the corporations patented these things, they would have a federally granted right to exclude others from exploiting them, but only for a limited period. By retaining them as trade secrets, companies seek to exploit them forever. Obviously, they will fight hard to keep competitors from obtaining trade secret information. Nonetheless, if discovery is proper, the company may be compelled to produce the information. On the other hand, the court might, under Rule 26(c)(1)(G), order that disclosure be made only in particular ways that might protect competitive advantage. You may study protective orders in great detail in a course on Complex Litigation.

In §8.4, we see what happens when parties do not abide by the discovery rules. In one situation, resorting to a protective order is the only recourse available. When a party fails completely to respond to a notice of its own deposition, to respond to interrogatories, or to respond to a request to produce, the propounding party can seek an award of sanctions. In response to such a motion for sanctions, the party who failed to respond cannot simply assert that the requests were objectionable. Rather, as provided in Rule 37(d)(2), she must move for a protective order.

§8.3.5   A Note About Discovery of Electronically Stored Information

The technological revolution of the past generation has been astonishing. When many of your (older) professors were studying Civil Procedure, the big deal was a self-correcting electric typewriter, which is now found only in museums. The fax machine, personal computers, the Internet, cell phones, pdf-format documents, CDs, optical scanners, e-mail, instant messaging, hand-held communication devices, and many other staples of daily life now were simply unknown then. One important question is how (if at all) the technology revolution should affect our discovery provisions. The Federal Rules generally have been adapted to earlier advancements in technology. For instance, the widespread use of (and advances in) photocopying machines clearly increased dramatically the number of documents that could be discovered. A relatively minor change to Rule 34 — permitting requests for production without a court order — sufficed to accommodate that development.[73]

Increasingly, courts and litigants have become concerned with issues about discovery of electronically stored information (ESI), especially e-mails. Some observers felt that the Federal Rules did not have to be amended to account for such issues; rather, they argued, provisions allowing discovery of "documents" should be interpreted to include discovery of ESI. The Rules Advisory Committee, to the surprise of some, promulgated changes to the discovery rules in 2006 to address concerns about ESI. We already saw some of these changes above. As noted in §8.2.1, initial required disclosures under Rule 26(a)(1) now require a party to identify ESI as well as other relevant information. And as seen in §8.2.2,

---

[73] *Id.* at 4.

provisions about traditional discovery tools now address ESI. For one, under Rule 33(d), a party responding to an interrogatory can refer the requesting party to business records to find the answer; business records now include ESI. For another, Rule 34 expressly includes ESI as a form of discovery. In addition, as seen in the discussion of Rule 34, Rule 26(b)(2)(B) permits a party may refuse to produce ESI if obtaining it from other sources is unreasonably expensive or burdensome.

Other major provisions concerning ESI will be seen below. Specifically, in the Rule 26(f) meeting, discussed in §8.5, the parties must discuss a litany of issues, including those raised by discovery of ESI, including the form in which ESI should be produced. And, as seen in the next section, Rule 37(e) creates a "safe harbor" that forbids sanctions against parties who failed to produce ESI because it was lost in the routine, good-faith operation of an ESI system.

§8.4 Sanctions for Discovery Abuse

The Federal Rules have always envisioned that parties will cooperate and conduct discovery in good faith. Within the relatively broad confines of the scheduling provisions (discussed in §8.5) and with the exception of required disclosures (discussed in §8.2.1), the parties have considerable leeway to determine what discovery tools to use and when to use them. They also have the responsibility to play by the rules. The court gets involved when the cooperative system breaks down. Sometimes the parties simply have a reasonable disagreement about whether a particular discovery request is appropriate. Other times, someone simply refuses to do what she is required to do. In this section, we are concerned with what the court can do to compel discovery and to punish those who do not participate appropriately.

Rule 37 is the repository of most of the court's power to force the parties to abide by the discovery rules. In general, as Rule 37(a)(2) makes clear, sanctions against a party are to be sought in the court in which the action is pending, while sanctions against nonparties are sought in the court for the district in which discovery was sought. Overall, Rule 37 may be best viewed as setting out specific sanctions for certain behavior and as establishing a two-part approach to what we can consider the most common discovery abuses. We start with that provision.

The One-Step Versus Two-Step Approach to Common Discovery Abuses. Rule 37 draws an important distinction between what we will call a *partial failure* to comply, on the one hand, and a *total failure* to comply, on the other, with basic discovery provisions.[74] For partial failures (defined below), the Rule envisions the parties' going through two steps before the party failing to play by the rules is subject to significant sanctions. In contrast, a party guilty of a total failure to abide by basic discovery provisions is subject to an immediate imposition of serious sanctions.

Partial Failures and the First Step: The Motion to Compel. Partial failures to comply with the basic discovery provisions are listed in Rule 37(a)(3)(B) and consist of (1) failure to answer a question at a deposition; (2) failure of an entity to designate a proper person for a deposition under Rule 30(b)(6); (3) failure to answer an interrogatory; and (4) failure to state in response to a request for production under Rule 34 that inspection will be permitted or to permit the actual inspection. We call these *partial failures* because the party did comply in part (maybe even for the most part). For instance, she might have answered every question at her deposition except one, or every interrogatory except one. Such situations are contrasted with situations in which the party simply does not respond.

> ∘ A party whose deposition is properly noticed shows up at the deposition. She answers some of the questions asked, but refuses to answer some. Or a party on whom interrogatories are properly served answers some of the interrogatories, but not others. At most, these are partial failures, because the party did respond, just not fully.

It is important to understand, though, that the failure to answer some of the questions might not be a "failure" at all. Sometimes, a failure to answer particular questions is justified. For example, perhaps the party claims that the question would invade a privilege or is protected as work product. In such situations, the party seeking discovery has no right to it, and the party from whom it is requested has every right to refuse to answer and raise the appropriate objection. But we will not know whether the responding party's claim of privilege or of work product (or other excuse) is justified until a court rules on the issue.

How does the court get involved? Rule 37(a) makes it clear that the *only* sanction available at this stage for the partial failures listed above is a court order compelling the responding party to answer the unanswered questions. Thus, the party seeking discovery will make a motion to compel answers under Rule 37(a)(1). This Rule requires the moving party to certify to the court that she has tried in good faith to get the information without

---

[74] Neither the Rules nor anyone else uses the terms *partial failure* and *total failure* as we use them here. This is just our shorthand way of distinguishing between different sets of sanctions. So if you use the phrases "partial" and "total" violations in class or with people who are not studying from this book, they might not understand what you're talking about.

court involvement.[75] In briefing and arguing the motion, the responding party may try to convince the judge that the material is privileged or otherwise protected from discovery. The court will consider the parties' contentions and rule — either granting or denying the motion to compel. The motion to compel discovery, then, is the first step in the two-step trip toward serious sanctions for failure to abide by the discovery provisions.

Along these lines, note that under Rule 37(a)(4), an evasive answer is treated as a failure to respond. So if a party, in her deposition testimony, hems and haws or is otherwise nonresponsive to a question, she has failed to respond to that question. Similarly, an incomplete answer to an interrogatory is treated as a failure to respond to that question. The party seeking discovery might make a motion to compel answers to such questions.

If the court grants the motion to compel, the party making the motion may be able to recover from the other party her expenses, including attorneys' fees, incurred in making the motion.[76] The party against whom the order was entered then is permitted to answer the unanswered questions. If she does so, the matter is resolved and the case moves on. Put another way, the sanction for a partial failure is an order to compel the party to answer the unanswered questions (and, perhaps, to pay the moving party's expenses and attorneys' fees incurred in bringing the motion).

Partial Failures and the Second Step: Violation of the Order Compelling Responses. What happens, though, if a party disobeys an order under Rule 37(a) compelling her to answer question(s)? The answer is found in Rule 37(b)(2)(A), which permits the court to impose significant sanctions on the recalcitrant party. That Rule empowers the court to make orders that are "just," and sets forth a list of possibilities in Rule 37(b)(2)(A)(i) through (vii). One of these, found at Rule 37(b)(2)(A)(i), is often called an *establishment order*, which simply establishes facts for purposes of this litigation.

- ○ Defendant claimed that she was not subject to personal jurisdiction. In interrogatories and in her deposition, Plaintiff asked Defendant about her contacts with the forum. Defendant refused to answer these questions. After the court ordered Defendant to answer, she still refused. As a sanction, the court may enter an order establishing that Defendant is subject to personal jurisdiction.

---

[75] This requirement, which was added in 1993, is aimed at forcing the parties to try to work out discovery squabbles before coming to court with them, and thus to cut down on the number of motions to compel discovery.

[76] This matter is controlled by Rule 37(a)(5)(A), which provides, *inter alia*, that the court may deny recovery of such expenses if the moving party failed to attempt to resolve the dispute without going to court or if the responding party's failure to respond to the question(s) was "substantially justified."

Another possible sanction, under Rule 37(b)(2)(A)(ii), is to refuse to allow the disobedient party to introduce evidence at trial on issues relevant to the discovery. Under Rule 37(b)(2)(A)(iii), the court can strike the disobedient party's pleadings as to matters relating to the discovery. Rule 37(b)(2)(A)(v) and (vi) are the ultimate sanctions — dismissal against the plaintiff or default judgment against the defendant. These should be reserved for extreme cases, involving bad faith. We saw such involuntary dismissals at §7.4.2 and default judgment at §7.5.3.

In addition (or in lieu of the foregoing), Rule 37(b)(2)(A)(vii) permits the court to hold the recalcitrant party in contempt. A court has discretion to find a party in contempt anytime she violates a court order, which, of course, is the situation here because the party is violating an order compelling her to respond to discovery. A contempt citation is appealable. See §§14.5.2, 14.6.

The court is required to enter any of the listed sanctions. Under Rule 37(b)(2)(A)(iv), the judge may simply stay proceedings until the recalcitrant party complies with the earlier order compelling responses. In sum, the sanctions listed in Rule 37(b)(2)(A) are not exclusive. The matter is left to the judge's discretion. In any event, Rule 37(b)(2)(C) allows the court to require the nonresponsive party to pay expenses and attorneys' fees of the moving party.

So, in the partial failure situations listed above, we need to go through two steps before a party can be subject to serious sanctions. First, there must be an order compelling her to answer the specific unanswered questions; that order is only appropriate if the responding party's excuse (such as a claim of privilege) is rejected. Second, the party against whom the order is entered must violate that order. That, as we just saw, opens the party up to serious sanctions and a contempt citation.

Total Failures and Sanctions. The "total failure" situation is addressed in Rule 37(d). Here, instead of simply refusing to answer some questions at a deposition or in interrogatories, the party is guilty of one of the misdeeds listed in Rule 37(d)(1)(A): (1) failure to appear for her deposition; (2) failure to serve answers or objections to interrogatories; or (3) failure to serve a written response to a request for production. In these situations, there is no need for the party requesting discovery to seek an order compelling discovery. Instead, she can move immediately for sanctions.

Rule 37(d)(3) incorporates by reference the sanctions we already saw at Rule 37(b)(2)(A), with one exception. It does not permit an order of contempt.[77] Why not? Because here, the recalcitrant party has not violated a court order. When we considered contempt as a sanction under Rule 37(b)(2)(A)(vii), it was because a party had violated a court order to respond to discovery. The permitted sanctions, as we just saw, include

---

[77] This is clear by the reference in Rule 37(d)(3) to the sanctions in Rule 37(b)(2)(A)(i) through (vi). This list omits Rule 37(b)(2)(A)(vii), which is the sanction of contempt.

the establishment order, refusal to allow the recalcitrant party to introduce evidence at trial, and striking her pleadings. In addition, under Rule 37(d)(3), the court can order that the jury (if the case goes to trial before a jury) be informed of the disobedient party's failure. And, under Rule 37(b)(2)(C), the party sanctioned can be required to pay the expenses, including attorneys' fees, that the other party incurred in seeking the sanctions.

There are two other points to emphasize with Rule 37(d). First, Rule 37(d)(1)(B) provides if the failure concerned interrogatories or a request for production (not a deposition), the party seeking sanctions must certify that she tried in good faith to obtain the discovery without court intervention. The moving party need not make this certification if the other party did not show up for her deposition.[78]

Second, Rule 37(d)(2) tells us that the party failing to respond cannot escape sanctions by arguing that the discovery request was objectionable. Rather, she must invoke her objection by seeking a protective order under Rule 26(c), which we discussed in §8.3.4. This is quite different from the partial failure situation under Rule 37(b). There, the party responded to the discovery request, but raised objections to specific questions. That procedure is sufficient there because the party has made some response to the discovery request. In the total failure situation, in contrast, because the party from whom discovery is sought was a "no-show," the Rule places the burden on her to seek protection (under Rule 26(c)) from the discovery request.

Sanctions Concerning Required Disclosures. In §8.2.1, we discussed the Rule 26(a) required disclosures. Rule 37(a)(3)(A) deals with a party's failure "to make a disclosure required under Rule 26(a)." This provision apparently is aimed at parties who file something as required disclosures, but whose disclosures are not complete. In that regard, this situation is like the partial failure scenario discussed above. Under Rule 37(a)(3)(A), any other party may make a motion "to compel disclosure and for appropriate sanctions." The party making this motion to compel must certify that she has attempted to confer with the party failing to make the disclosures in an effort to resolve the issue without court involvement. If a party violates an order compelling her to make required disclosures, Rule 37(b)(2)(A) then allows the court to enter the significant sanctions listed there, including contempt, as discussed above.

---

[78] You have to read Rule 37(d)(1)(B) carefully to catch this. It requires certification only when the motion for sanctions concerns "failing to answer or respond." This phrase refers to Rule 37(d)(1)(A)(ii), which addresses failure to answer interrogatories or to respond to a request for production. It does not apply to Rule 37(d)(1)(A)(i), which is aimed at failure to "appear" at a deposition.

In addition, Rule 37(c) addresses a party who "fails to provide information or identify a witness as required by Rule 26(a)." This provision apparently is intended to deal with the total failure to provide any of the three required disclosures. The Rule provides that such a party will not be permitted to use at trial any evidence that should have been provided under Rule 26(a), unless the failure was substantially justified or is harmless. In addition to that sanction, the court may, upon motion and upon affording the party an opportunity to be heard, impose other appropriate sanctions, including attorneys' fees caused by the failure and including sanctions listed in Rule 37(b)(2)(A)(i) through (vii). Further, at trial, the jury may be informed of the party's failure to abide by Rule 26(a). The incorporation of the listed sanctions from Rule 37(b)(2)(A) mirrors those for the total failure with regard to other discovery devices discussed above. Because a party in this position will not have violated a court order at this point, contempt is not an available sanction. In sum, then, required disclosures are treated like interrogatories — a partial failure leads to a motion to compel and, if violated, serious sanctions; while a total failure leads immediately to serious sanctions.

Sanctions Concerning the Duty to Supplement. In §8.2.3, we saw that Rule 26(e) imposes a duty on parties, under certain circumstances, to supplement, correct, or amend their responses to various forms of discovery. What sanctions are available if a party fails to discharge this duty? Rule 37(c)(1) addresses this situation and permits the court to impose the same sanctions we saw in the preceding paragraph concerning failure to make required disclosures.

Sanctions Concerning Medical Examinations. In §8.2.2, we discussed Rule 35, which allows a court, upon proper showing by a party, to order another party or someone in that party's "custody or legal control" to undergo a medical examination. If a party is ordered to undergo an exam and fails to do so, she can incur sanctions under Rule 37(b)(2)(A).[79] That Rule provides for whatever sanctions the court considers just and lists specific significant sanctions from Rule 37(b)(2)(A)(i) through (vi). These, as we have seen, include an establishment order, an order refusing to allow that party to support or defend against claims by prohibiting the production of evidence at trial, and an order striking the disobedient party's pleadings. In addition to the listed sanctions, under Rule 37(b)(2)(C), the court can also order the disobedient party to pay the moving party's expenses, including attorneys' fees, incurred in seeking sanctions.

---

[79] Rule 37(a)(1), which permits the party requesting discovery to move for an order compelling another party to respond, is not relevant in this situation. Under Rule 35, there is already a court order compelling the party to attend her medical exam (or to produce someone in her custody or legal control for a medical exam). So violation of that order invokes Rule 37(b)(2).

Rule 37(b)(2)(B) makes clear that a party who is ordered to produce for examination someone in her "custody or legal control," and who fails to do so, is subject to the same sanctions. She is excused, however, if she can show that she is unable to obey the order. For example, perhaps the person ostensibly under her custody or legal control is out of the jurisdiction.

Because violation of a Rule 35 order involves failure to obey a court order, we would expect to find an order of contempt as an available sanction. On this score, however, Rule 37(b)(2)(A)(vii) expressly provides that contempt is not to be imposed as a sanction for failing to comply with an order to submit to a medical examination. And in listing sanctions for failure to produce someone in one's "custody or legal control" for a medical exam, Rule 37(b)(2)(B) does not include the sanction of contempt.[80]

Sanctions Concerning Requests for Admission. In §8.2.2, we discussed Rule 36, which permits a party to require another party to admit discoverable matter. As we saw there, the responding party's failure to deny a request of this sort may be treated as an admission of the fact for purposes of the litigation.

What happens, though, if the responding party denies a request for admission, but the propounding party later establishes at trial that the matter was true? Rule 37(c)(2) provides that the party who propounded the request for admission may move for an order that the recalcitrant party "pay the reasonable expenses, including attorney's fees, incurred" in proving the issue at trial. If the moving party makes this showing, the court "must" make such an order, unless one of the factors listed in Rule 37(c)(2)(A) through (D) is satisfied. For example, such an order would be excused if the court finds that the party failing to admit had a reasonable ground to believe that it would prevail on that issue.

○ *P* was injured when involved in a collision with a truck owned by *D*, Inc. The truck was being driven by *X*. *P* claims that *D*, Inc., is vicariously liable for the tort of *X*, and alleges that *P* was the agent of *D*, Inc., and was acting within the scope of her employment at the time of the collision. *D*, Inc., claims that *X* was not acting within the scope of her employment, but was on a "frolic," and therefore that *D*, Inc., is not vicariously liable for any tort committed by *X*. *P* sends a request for admission to *D*, Inc., asking it to admit "that *X* was acting in the course of her employment with *D*, Inc., at the time of the collision." *D*, Inc., specifically denies the request. At trial, *P* establishes to the jury's satisfaction that *X* was acting within the scope of her employment at the time of the collision. Under Rule 37(c)(2), *P* may seek to recover all expenses, including attorneys' fees, incurred in proving at trial that this was true. The court may deny that sanction, however, if it finds that *D*, Inc., had reasonable ground to

---

[80] This fact is shown by its reference to Rule 37(b)(2)(A)(i) through (vi), which does not include contempt (which is found at 37(b)(2)(A)(vii)).

conclude that it would prevail on the issue at trial or other good reason to fail to admit.

Certification Under Rule 26(g). Rule 11, which we discussed at §7.7, requires attorneys (or, if there is no lawyer, by the *pro se* herself[81]) to certify that various documents are, essentially, justified in law and fact. They make the certification initially by signing the document. But Rule 11, as we noted there, does not apply to discovery documents. Instead, Rule 26(g) applies. It is divided into three parts. First, Rule 26(g)(1) imposes a certification requirement regarding certain required disclosures and other discovery requests and responses. As with Rule 11, the certification is made by signing the document. Second, Rule 26(g)(2) says that parties need not respond to an unsigned disclosure, request, response, or objection. Only when the document is signed by counsel does a party have a duty to act with regard to it. Third, Rule 26(g)(3) lists the sanctions for improper certification. The first and third aspects of Rule 26(g) require further discussion.

Required disclosures under Rule 26(a)(1) and (a)(3) must be signed by at least one lawyer of record in her individual name and must include her address (or by a *pro se* party). The Rule simply does not apply as to required disclosures under Rule 26(a)(2). Under Rule 26(g)(1)(A), the signature on disclosures under Rule 26(a)(1) and (a)(3) constitutes a certification that "to the best of the person's knowledge, information, and belief, formed after a reasonable inquiry," the disclosure "is complete and correct as of the time it is made." The first quoted part of this requirement mirrors language from Rule 11, and imposes a duty to make a reasonable inquiry.

As for the other traditional discovery devices, Rule 26(g)(2)(B) requires that "[e]very discovery request, response, or objection" must be signed, which constitutes a certification — again, as to the best of the signer's knowledge, information, and belief, formed after a reasonable inquiry — that various things are true. Specifically, the signer certifies that the request, response, or objection is (1) consistent with the Federal Rules and warranted by existing law or a good faith argument for change in the law; (2) not interposed for an improper purpose (such as to harass or delay); and (3) not unreasonably or unduly burdensome. This provision is quite broad. It applies to both parties — the party making the request and the responding party — and it applies to responses and to objections asserted to the discovery requests.[82]

---

[81] *Pro se* means that a party is representing herself in the proceeding, without a lawyer. Occasionally, such a party is said to be acting *in propria persona* (or in *pro per*), which means in her own stead.

[82] Remember that the party herself must sign the substantive answers to interrogatories and her deposition testimony under oath, as we saw in §8.2.2.

Rule 26(g)(3) provides that a court may sanction a violation of the certification requirement, either on motion of a party or on its own. It applies to violations of the certification requirement concerning required disclosures (in Rule 26(g)(1)(A)) and concerning the traditional discovery devices (in Rule 26(g)(2)(B)). Sanctions are permitted if a party violates the Rule "without substantial justification." The Rule calls for "an appropriate sanction," which may include an assessment of the expenses, including attorneys' fees, incurred by another party because of the violation of the Rule. The sanction may be levied against the lawyer making the certification or upon the party on whose behalf the disclosure, request, response, or objection was made.

Safe Harbor Regarding Electronically Stored Information (ESI). Section 8.3.5 discussed the 2006 amendments to the Rules to address various issues encountered with discovery of ESI. Part of those amendments was a safe harbor found at Rule 37(e). It establishes that — absent exceptional circumstances — a court "may not impose sanctions" for a party's failure to provide ESI that was lost "as a result of the routine, good-faith operation of an electronic information system." This protection was thought essential because many information systems routinely delete certain ESI. For example, it is common to have e-mail systems delete e-mails after six months. As long as such a deletion was in good faith and occurred routinely because of the way the system operates, a party should not be sanctioned for failing to produce the deleted information.

This safe harbor will not avail a party, however, if the court has ordered retention of various ESI. It is common for courts to instruct litigants to avoid routine deletion of ESI, such as by printing hard copies before the information is deleted. A party who violates such an order cannot rely on Rule 37(e), and may be sanctioned for violating the court's information-retention order.

§8.5 Scheduling of Discovery and Other Phases of the Case

This section addresses scheduling of a civil case under the Federal Rules. It addresses far more than just the discovery phase of the litigation. There are two important themes to keep in mind throughout this material. First, note how the Federal Rules — particularly Rules 16 and 26 — impose significant burdens on the parties to keep the case moving. Many of these provisions are relatively new and reflect a conscious decision that the Rules ought to keep the parties' feet to the fire. In earlier days, the Rules left more of the timing issues to the discretion of the parties. Second, note how the judge is involved in managing the progress of the case. This is one of the significant developments of the past generation, which has seen the role of the judge change from that of passive umpire, reacting to the parties, to active case manager. Some federal judges complain that the job has become too bureaucratic. The Administrative Office of the federal courts requires each judge to report caseloads and the progress of each case periodically. This requirement creates at least implicit pressure on the judge to keep things rolling along expeditiously. In §8.6, we discuss the concomitant increase in the use of judicial adjuncts to help reduce case backlog.

It is helpful to address Rules 16 and 26 together to see the timeline they create. The driving point at the early stage is Rule 16(b)(1), which provides, with some exceptions, that the court must enter a scheduling order mapping out the progress of the litigation from that point until trial. As we have mentioned, this may cover a good bit of time. It would be almost unheard of to have this window open for less than a year; more typically, it would be longer, even substantially longer. It is critical to note how much the parties must do before that scheduling order is entered, and how little time they have in which to do it. Under Rule 16(b)(2), the scheduling order is to be entered no more than 120 days after the defendant is served with process.

What must be done in those 120 days?[83] In a given case, these requirements and the timing may be altered by court order or stipulation, but we will outline the timeline as modeled in the Rules, assuming no exceptions. First, at least 21 days before the scheduling order, the parties must have the Rule 26(f) conference. This event, attended by the parties and their lawyers, requires significant preparation. Under Rule 26(f)(2), the parties must confer to consider their claims and defenses and the possibility that the case might be settled or otherwise resolved promptly. In addition, they must arrange for their Rule 26(a)(1) required disclosures and, significantly, "develop a proposed discovery plan." This plan is quite detailed, as shown by Rule 26(f)(3), and requires the parties to express their "views and proposals" concerning various issues. Among the issues addressed are any changes that should be made for required disclosures, the subjects on which discovery may be needed, when discovery should be completed, whether it should be conducted in phases, and the form in which electronically stored information should be produced.

Second, no later than 14 days after the Rule 26(f) conference, the parties must agree on a proposed discovery plan for the litigation, and submit to the court a written report outlining the plan. So there may be a good deal of work after the Rule 26(f) conference, since the parties must agree

---

[83] In a given case, it could be fewer than 120 days; remember, Rule 16(b)(2) provides that 120 days is the *longest* time that can elapse between service of process on the defendant and the scheduling order.

on a discovery plan and submit a jointly crafted written report laying out the plan.

Third, also no later than 14 days after the Rule 26(f) conference, the parties must make their required disclosures under Rule 26(a)(1), which we discussed in §8.2.1. Obviously, complying with that Rule requires further effort.

In sum, these provisions require a significant investment of time and effort for each party in the first 120 days after the defendant is served with process. The days when a plaintiff could file a case and sit back for a few months are gone, at least in federal court.[84] This intense activity costs the parties a good bit of money because the lawyers will be billing for their time.[85] One implicit goal of these requirements is to make the litigants do a reality check on how expensive the case may get and thus to become more amenable to settling the dispute. So the time frame for the first phase of a typical suit looks like this:

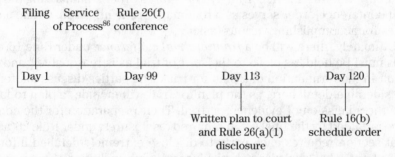

And, of course, this is just the beginning. After these tasks are completed, the parties still must actually undertake all the discovery in the case. Employing and responding to each discovery tool requires time and effort from each party and her lawyer. As the months and years go on, and discovery is completed, the case will become ripe for adjudication. If the case involves expert witnesses, as discussed in §8.3.3, the parties will have required disclosures under Rule 26(a)(2) and will depose the other parties' experts.

---

[84] Some states impose similar responsibilities, though it is worth noting that required disclosures under Rule 26(a) have not been widely adopted in state courts.

[85] This is invariably true on the defense side. On the plaintiff side, the lawyer may have taken the case on a contingent fee basis, in which case the plaintiff does not "pay as she goes," but shares a percentage of any recovery (whether achieved through adjudication or settlement) with her lawyer. Even in such a case, though the plaintiff is not paying attorneys' fees, she will be paying the various litigation costs, such as filing fees and discovery costs.

[86] Recall from §3.3.1 that process generally must be served within 120 days of filing of the complaint.

Somewhere along the way, most cases are disposed of without trial. Most of these are settled, with the parties agreeing to terms of the settlement and the plaintiff taking a voluntary dismissal of her case under Rule 41(a)(1), as we addressed in §7.3.5. Other cases may be disposed of on motion or by default judgment.

In those cases that go to trial, Rules 16 and 26 impose further tasks on the parties. Rule 16(a) permits *pretrial conferences* in the court's discretion for a variety of purposes, such as expediting disposition of the action and "establishing early and continuing control" of the case.[87] Rule 16(c)(2) lists various topics that can be considered at any such conference. Courts sometimes will call a conference simply to assess where the parties are and why the case seems not to be moving as well as the judge expects; these are often called *status conferences*. Under Rule 16(d), all pretrial conferences result in entry of an order "reciting the action taken." That Rule also provides that this order "controls the course of the action unless the court modifies it." Accordingly, the court's order summarizing the pretrial conference order serves as a roadmap for the litigation. Often, it sets dates for accomplishing various tasks.

Ultimately, there will be a *final pretrial conference* under Rule 16(e).[88] This must be held "as close to the start of trial as is reasonable," and will result in the formulation of a plan for trial. The parties discuss matters in considerable detail here, as the plan for trial will include "a plan to facilitate the admission of evidence" at trial. Their preparation for the conference is guided by the final set of required disclosures, under Rule 26(a)(3). That section requires each party to disclose extremely detailed information about what she plans to produce at trial, including the name and address of each witness to be called (and those who may be called if the need arises at trial[89]) and the identification of each document and exhibit to be introduced at trial.[90] These disclosures require a great deal of work and must be made as directed by the court, but in no event fewer than 30 days before trial.[91]

After the final pretrial conference, the court will enter an order (not surprisingly, the *final pretrial conference order*). This order is lengthy and

---

[87] Under Rule 16(f), the court has access to a serious panoply of sanctions to punish parties and lawyers who do not participate appropriately in such conferences.

[88] In many cases, this may be the *only* pretrial conference.

[89] For example, perhaps a party has a witness who will testify to counteract testimony from a witness another party may call. Only if that other witness actually testifies will the need arise.

[90] Before the required disclosures were promulgated in 1993, most federal districts required this sort of detailed disclosure by Local Rule. Thus, Rule 26(a)(3) was not all that revolutionary.

[91] Within 14 days after disclosure of the materials required by Rule 26(a)(3), each party must raise various objections to the proposed evidence of other parties, risking waiver of certain evidentiary objections if she fails to do so.

detailed and lists the contentions of the parties, the witnesses and evidence to be proffered by each party, and other information required by Rule 26(a)(3) or by the court. Pursuant to Rule 16(d), this document then controls subsequent events, which means it becomes the roadmap for the trial itself. Essentially, the document supersedes the pleadings.

Thus, a party who raised an issue in pleadings must ensure that it is preserved and presented in the final pretrial conference order, or risk losing the right to present evidence on that point at trial. Similarly, a party who forgets to list a witness may encounter a serious problem when she attempts to call that witness at trial. Rule 16(f) makes it clear that the "court may modify the order issued after a final pretrial conference only to prevent manifest injustice."[92] The party seeking amendment bears the burden of proof, and, generally, a court will allow amendment only if refusing to do so would result in injustice to the party seeking amendment, the party opposing the amendment will not be substantially harmed by the amendment, and the court will not be inconvenienced thereby.[93]

Many courts are quite strict on this score. In *Walker v. Anderson Electric Connectors*,[94] the plaintiff sued for sexual harassment, seeking damages and equitable relief, including a declaratory judgment that the defendants had engaged in such harassment. At the final pretrial conference, though, the plaintiff abandoned the equitable claims and proceeded to trial seeking only damages. The jury found that the defendants had indeed committed sexual harassment, but also found that the plaintiff had suffered no monetary harm. Plaintiff sought to amend the pretrial order to reinstate her claim for equitable relief, including an order that the defendants had engaged in prohibited conduct. She did this because a "prevailing party" could, under a federal statute, seek recovery of attorneys' fees. Without the equitable relief, she could not argue that she was a "prevailing party." The court refused to amend the pretrial conference order and the Eleventh Circuit affirmed, holding that modification would work injustice on the defendants. The plaintiff had chosen her litigation strategy and had to live with the consequences of that choice.

---

[92] By way of review, suppose a party presents evidence at trial on a matter not reflected in the final pretrial conference order, and the other side does not object. What might happen? Under Rule 15(b)(2), the evidence might be admitted (because there was no objection) and might then form the basis for amending the final pretrial conference order to conform to the evidence. *See, e.g.*, Kirkland v. District of Columbia, 70 F.3d 629 (D.C. Cir. 1995). We discussed this possibility in §7.5.2.

[93] *See, e.g.*, DP Solutions, Inc. v. Rollins, Inc., 353 F.3d 421, 435 (5th Cir. 2003).

[94] 944 F.2d 841, 844 (11th Cir. 1991).

§8.6   Use of Judicial Adjuncts

In the preceding section, we saw that the role of the judge (especially, perhaps, the federal judge) has become more bureaucratic or administrative in recent decades. She is responsible not only for deciding motions and overseeing trials and other traditional "judicial" roles, but, increasingly, for managing the court's caseload. For example, Rule 16(a)(2) expressly envisions the judge's "establishing early and continuing control" of the case. As the tasks have increased, so has a movement toward use of adjuncts to assist the federal district judge.

The principal adjunct player in the federal court system is the United States Magistrate Judge. There are approximately as many such officers as there are United States District Judges. Magistrate judges are not Article III judges. Thus, they are not appointed by the President with the advice and consent of the Senate, nor do they enjoy constitutional grants of lifetime tenure and protection against salary reduction.[95] Rather, magistrate judges serve a term of years and are selected by the federal district judges for each district.

Congress first provided for magistrate judges in 1968, in response to a glut of complex cases in federal courts growing out of a huge series of antitrust cases. From the beginning, Congress intended that magistrate judges would assist federal district judges in processing cases. Though magistrates may perform duties regarding criminal cases, our focus is on what they do in civil litigation. The authority of these adjunct judicial officers is defined in 28 U.S.C. §636 and is reflected as well in Rules 72 and 73. Magistrates perform a variety of functions in criminal and civil cases, at the behest of the district judge, who "refers" matters to the magistrate by order. It is difficult to imagine how the courts could handle their present caseloads without magistrates. Among other tasks in civil cases, they often oversee the progress of discovery, preside over scheduling and pretrial conferences, and become involved in attempts to settle cases.

The division of labor between district judges, on the one hand, and magistrates, on the other, must be clear. Because magistrate judges are not Article III judges, they cannot be given authority to rule dispositively in a case unless the parties waive their right to an Article III judge. Under §636(b)(1)(A) and Rule 72(a), a district judge may (without consent of the parties) refer *nondispositive pretrial* matters (such as motions to compel discovery) to be heard by a magistrate judge.[96] The magistrate's orders

---

[95] We discussed Article III judges, and the extraordinary protections accorded them by the Constitution, in §4.4.

[96] Section 636(b)(1)(A) does not use the term *nondispositive*. Rather, it permits the district judge to refer "any pretrial matter" to the magistrate and then lists exceptions — including motions for injunctive relief, motions for certification of a class action, and motions for summary judgment. Lawyers and judges routinely refer to what is left as

on such issues are subject to review by the district judge. Such review is on the record created by the magistrate judge (so the district judge does not have to hold a new hearing). Moreover, the district judge is deferential in reviewing such matters; she will uphold the magistrate judge's orders unless there was "clear error."

Under §636(b)(1)(B) and Rule 72(b), a district judge may (also without consent of the parties) refer to the magistrate judge *dispositive pretrial* matters.[97] For example, she could refer a motion for summary judgment to the magistrate judge. The magistrate enters findings and recommendations on such dispositive matters under §636(b)(1)(C), which are subject to review by the district judge. Because the issue is dispositive, however, the district judge must review the magistrate judge's decision de novo. This standard of review (which we address regarding appeals at §14.7) means that the district judge does not defer to what the magistrate decided, but applies the legal standard to the facts on her own.

What about trial? Section 636(c)(1) expressly provides that a magistrate can preside over a civil trial (jury or nonjury) *only* if all parties consent to it. By doing so, they waive the right to have an Article III judge determine their case. In *Roell v. Withrow*,[98] the Supreme Court held that such consent need not be express, but can be inferred from the conduct of the parties. There, the magistrate repeatedly told the parties that they could object to trial before her and insist on trial before the district judge. No one objected and the case proceeded. No one objected when the magistrate indicated her belief that all parties had consented to her trying the case. Only after an adverse verdict and judgment did defendants object to trial before the magistrate. In light of their voluntary participation in the entire litigation and failure to voice objection, however, the Court found that the defendants had consented to trial before the magistrate. When the parties consent to trial by the magistrate judge, the final judgment is not reviewed by the district judge; it is appealed directly to the court of appeals. Section 636 ensures that the court will not exert undue pressure on parties in an effort to get them to waive their right to trial by an Article III judge.

Often, magistrates are used very effectively to preside over pretrial conferences and to manage the progress of the case. They may also be important in trying to settle a case. The district judge who will preside over trial is reluctant to become too closely involved with settlement efforts, because she might become aware of something that would not be admissible at trial and that might jeopardize her impartiality. The magistrate,

---

"nondispositive." Rule 72(a), on the other hand, does speak of referring "nondispositive matters" to the magistrate judge.

[97] Section 636(b)(1)(B) does not use the term *dispositive*, but Rule 72(b) does.
[98] 538 U.S. 580 (2003).

however, who will probably not preside over the trial, may be more willing and able to cajole the parties into settlement.

Another judicial adjunct is the "master," who is usually a well-regarded member of the local bar who is appointed by the district judge to perform various tasks, as provided in Rule 53. Reflecting the fact that they are appointed to a single matter at a time, they are almost universally referred to as "special masters." They may be employed to address pre- or post-trial matters when district judges and magistrates are so overburdened that they cannot address them in a timely way. Perhaps the most common use for special masters, however, is to perform an accounting or to resolve a difficult computation of damages for the court, as reflected in Rule 53(a)(1)(B).

Chapter 9

Adjudication and Related Motions

§9.1   Defining the Issue

We saw in Chapter 7 that a case enters the litigation stream when the plaintiff files her complaint. There are many ways the case might leave the litigation stream. For one, the defendant may move to dismiss based upon any of a variety of factors — including failure to state a claim or a problem with forum selection, such as personal jurisdiction, subject matter jurisdiction, or venue. If the court grants a motion to dismiss, the case will end. That ending might be temporary, though, if the court granted the motion to dismiss "without prejudice" or "with leave to amend." In such a situation, the plaintiff can re-file the case. On the other hand, if the dismissal were "with prejudice," judgment would be entered for the defendant and the case at the trial court would end.[1] For another possibility, the defendant might fail to respond at all, and the court might enter default

---

[1] The plaintiff might appeal, as discussed in Chapter 14, but the case at the trial court would be ended.

judgment in favor of the plaintiff. Or perhaps the parties engaged in alternative dispute resolution, such as arbitration or mediation, as we saw in §1.3. The most likely way for a case to leave the litigation stream is settlement — the parties, perhaps after a "reality check" provided by the discovery phase, resolve the dispute, and the plaintiff voluntarily dismisses the case.[2]

In this chapter, we address what happens to cases that are not taken from the litigation stream by court order, alternative dispute resolution, or settlement. Such a case will usually progress through the pleading stage, through various motions, through discovery, and eventually become ripe for adjudication. Adjudication means that there will be a judicial resolution of the merits of the dispute. The merits, of course, involve the underlying dispute, including such questions as: Did the defendant breach the contract? Did the defendant commit a tort? Was the plaintiff contributorily negligent? How fast was the car going? How serious are the injuries suffered? Who is telling the truth? Throughout the litigation stream, these issues have been asserted and "joined" and now are ready to be decided.

In adjudicating the merits, the judicial system must accomplish two tasks. First, it must have a mechanism for determining what the facts actually were. This is the "fact-finding" function. Second, it must apply the law to those facts to determine who should win the judgment.

The typical model for adjudication is trial, which we address in §9.2. This is the phase of litigation usually depicted in movies and television shows. It is the courtroom drama — witnesses testifying under oath, counsel objecting, the judge rapping her gavel for order in the courtroom (which doesn't really happen all that often). The trial is the ultimate litigation experience. After months (more likely years) of pretrial litigation — through pleadings, motions, discovery, etc. — the parties and their lawyers are ready to do battle in the courtroom. You will study about trials in your course on Evidence and in "hands-on" classes such as Trial Techniques.

For present purposes, we focus on several points regarding adjudication by trial. In §9.2.1, we discuss the relative roles of the judge and the jury at trial. When we use a jury, it is the fact-finder. Its function is to determine what happened in the "real world." This function involves considering the evidence presented at trial and making judgments about the credibility of witnesses. The judge instructs the jury on the law to apply to those facts. In §9.2.2, we see that there is a constitutional right to have a jury make these fact determinations in some (but not all) civil disputes in

---

[2] Attorneys who litigate must also be skilled at contract negotiation and drafting. Settling a case involves having the parties enter a contract — with terms well spelled out. Generally, the plaintiff agrees to accept money from the defendant, in return for which the plaintiff signs a release of all claims and of any right to sue the defendant concerning the same matter. When the money is paid, usually the plaintiff will then take a voluntary dismissal, as we saw in §7.4.1.

federal court. (Even then, the parties may waive the right to jury trial and have the facts determined by the judge.)

And even in civil cases in which there is a right to a jury, the judge serves an important gatekeeping function. A motion for "judgment as a matter of law" permits the judge essentially to circumvent the jury and to determine facts herself, but only when the facts are susceptible of but one reasonable interpretation. Given the importance of the right of jury trial, this motion must be used with great care, so as not to usurp the jury function. In some limited circumstances, the judge may actually "un-do" what the jury decided by granting a "renewed motion for judgment as a matter of law," or by ordering a new trial, or by setting aside the judgment. We address these motions in §§9.5, 9.6, and 9.7.

Though the trial is the typical model for adjudication, not all cases are adjudicated at trial. In some cases, the court may enter summary judgment, which adjudicates the case without going to trial at all. Again, in view of the importance of the right of trial by jury, summary judgment must be handled with care. The court might grant summary judgment before trial for precisely the same reason it might not let the case "go to the jury" at trial: There is no dispute as to the material facts. This fact allows the judge to rule in the case as a matter of law. We study summary judgment in §9.4.

§9.2 The Trial

§9.2.1 The Purpose and Conduct of Trial and the Roles of Judge and Jury

We said above that adjudication requires fact-finding and application of the law to the facts as determined. The only reason to use trial as the mode of adjudication is to resolve a dispute of material fact. If there is no genuine dispute of material fact, there is no need for trial (as we see in §9.4, regarding summary judgment). In this section, because we are dealing with trial, obviously, there is a disputed material fact (or, more likely, more than one) to be resolved. Remember how disputed facts arise. The plaintiff alleged things in her complaint, which the defendant either admitted or denied. If she admitted them, they are deemed established and are not in dispute. Those issues the defendant denied, however, are "joined," or disputed. Perhaps during discovery the parties were able to hone the number of disputed facts. The final pretrial conference order lists the issues to be decided at trial. The parties are well aware of what these issues are and have planned carefully about what evidence to introduce at trial to prove their version of the disputed facts. In addition to the facts relating to the elements of the plaintiff's claims and the defendant's affirmative defenses (if any), the trial will resolve, often by implication, the credibility of various witnesses. Specifically, when witnesses have given opposing testimony on a fact, the outcome will hinge in part on which witness the fact-finder believes.

Who resolves these disputed facts? In other words, who is the "fact-finder"? In many cases, the parties will have a choice: Either the judge can do it (in a "bench trial") or the jury[3] can do it (in, not surprisingly, a "jury trial"). The jury is not always available for this function. In §9.2.2, we see when the right to jury trial attaches in federal civil cases. In all trials — bench or jury — the judge is responsible for discerning the applicable law. In jury cases, the judge will instruct the jury as to what the law is, to guide the jury in its determination of the facts. We discuss this process in §9.2.4. In bench trials, the judge uses the applicable law to guide her own determination of the facts.

Also, in all trials, the judge oversees the presentation of the evidence and the behavior of the participants. She must resolve the inevitable disagreements about what evidence is admissible (a critical topic, which you will study in your course on Evidence). She must ensure that the trial moves along expeditiously, while allowing each party a fair opportunity to present her evidence. In jury trials, she will be especially diligent in policing the admission of evidence and behavior of the parties and lawyers, to ensure that the jurors are not exposed to matters that might prejudice them or make it difficult for them to discharge their fact-finding responsibility dispassionately.

At the outset of trial (after selection of the jury, if there is one), the lawyers for each party usually will make an opening statement. This oral statement is intended to acquaint the judge and jury with background of the dispute and with that lawyer's assessment of what the evidence will show. During the jury selection process (discussed in §9.2.3), the jurors will have learned about the case only in the most general terms. The opening statement is the first chance they have to hear about the details of the case. Opening statements may be accompanied by charts and diagrams, but do not involve the introduction of evidence. The plaintiff's lawyer gives her opening statement first, followed by the defendant's lawyer.[4] Lawyers

---

[3] Throughout our materials, technically we are speaking of a "petit" (pronounced "petty") jury, members of which sit as fact-finders in trials. These jurors are to be contrasted with "grand" jurors, who are also drawn from the citizenry, but whose job is far different. Grand jurors work in secrecy, and hear evidence of alleged crimes, presented by appropriate law enforcement officials. In the federal system, a lawyer for the United States Attorney for the local district presents the evidence. The grand jury is to determine whether there is sufficient evidence for an indictment. If so, it "returns" an indictment.

[4] Sometimes, the defendant's lawyer may choose to delay her opening until after the plaintiff's presentation of evidence. Usually, however, the defense lawyer wants to make

understand the importance of the opening statement in educating the jury and starting the process of winning the confidence of the jurors.

After opening statements, the plaintiff presents her "case-in-chief." She does this by calling witnesses, who are "sworn in" and thus testify under oath before the judge and the jury. Witnesses testify in response to questions by the lawyers, rather than holding forth with soliloquies. After the plaintiff's lawyer examines each of her witnesses, the defendant's lawyer is allowed to cross-examine the witness. In cross-examination, the lawyer often attempts to create doubt about the witness's recollection or to expose inconsistencies between her testimony and that of other witnesses. This process is repeated for each of the plaintiff's witnesses. The plaintiff may present documentary and other evidence in addition to the oral testimony of the witnesses. Generally, a witness will have to establish the authenticity of documentary evidence, and each piece of evidence is marked as an "exhibit." These are marked sequentially, and may be referred to, for example, as "plaintiff's exhibit A" when asking witnesses about a particular piece of evidence. When she has presented her case, the plaintiff "rests," which closes the presentation of the plaintiff's case-in-chief.

As we see in §9.5, at this point the defendant may make a motion for judgment as a matter of law (JMOL), which, if granted, would obviate the rest of the trial and result in judgment for the defendant.[5] If such a motion is not made or is denied, the defendant then puts on her case-in-chief.[6] She does this just as the plaintiff did — witness by witness, asking questions to elicit testimony under oath. The plaintiff's lawyer may cross-examine each defense witness. The defendant may also introduce documentary and other evidence. When she has presented her case, the defendant "rests," which closes the presentation of her case.

At that point, the plaintiff may move for JMOL, which, if granted, would obviate the rest of the trial and result in judgment for the plaintiff. If such a motion is not made or is denied, the plaintiff may then present "rebuttal" evidence. This is done in the same way as the case-in-chief, but consists of testimony and other evidence designed to rebut evidence the defendant presented. The defendant then may also present rebuttal evidence. At some point, the parties will have presented all of their cases-in-chief and rebuttal evidence, and the court will "close all the evidence."

---

the opening statement immediately after the plaintiff's lawyer, to blunt the impact of the plaintiff's lawyer's statement.

[5] This motion, as we see in §9.5, can only be made after the other side "has been fully heard," which is satisfied after she has had a chance to present evidence.

[6] At common law, the defendant who moved for judgment as a matter of law (then called *directed verdict*), waived the right to present evidence if the motion were denied. That is no longer true, as we see in §9.5.

At that point, both parties might move for JMOL. If granted, the court will decide the case, dismiss the jury, and enter judgment. If no such motion is made, or if it is denied, the judge will then instruct the jury (if there is one) on the law, and the jury will retire to deliberate and determine the facts. The jury is to do so based upon the "record evidence" — that is, the evidence that the judge admitted into evidence in the trial. The jurors are to disregard any evidence to which they might have been exposed in trial but which the court found inadmissible.[7] The jury will announce its result in a "verdict," which the court will embody in its "judgment." Even then, as we see in §§9.5 and 9.6, parties may make motions to avoid or un-do the judgment. If there is no jury, of course, the judge will determine the facts and announce her judgment in the case.

§9.2.2 The Right to a Jury Trial

The Seventh Amendment

In federal court, the right to a jury trial in civil cases[8] is embodied in the Seventh Amendment, which provides that "[i]n suits at common law, where the value in controversy shall exceed twenty dollars, the right of trial by jury shall be preserved...." Federal Rule 38(a)(1) echoes the importance of this constitutional guarantee by providing that the right to jury trial under the Seventh Amendment "is preserved to the parties inviolate."

We imported the civil jury from England. Though Great Britain abolished the right to jury trial in most civil cases in 1920, Americans continue to embrace the jury trial as one of their most cherished, almost sacred, rights. The jury is praised for bringing the wisdom of the common person to bear in the legal system. The jury is the voice of the community, a repository of democratic values and virtue. There are critics, however, who see the jury trial as expensive and cumbersome, and who would rather entrust the outcome of litigation to the learned trial judge than to the layperson jury. Whatever the merits of the debate, in the United States, the jury system is here to stay. For one thing, wholesale eradication of the right to jury trial in the federal system would require constitutional amendment. For another, the Supreme Court generally has embraced the right broadly.

---

[7] This might happen, for example, when a witness testifies that someone told him that X, Y, and Z happened. Upon objection, the court might declare that this statement is inadmissible because it is "hearsay" (which you will study in depth in your course on Evidence). The judge will then instruct the jury to disregard what the witness said about X, Y, and Z, because it is inadmissible. (Of course, as all trial lawyers know, it may be difficult for people to disregard something after they have heard it.)

[8] The Sixth Amendment, in contrast, addresses the right to jury trial in criminal cases. The Sixth Amendment is beyond our scope.

Importantly, the Seventh Amendment applies only to civil cases in federal court. It is one of the provisions of the Bill of Rights that has *not* been incorporated to apply to the states through the Fourteenth Amendment. Thus, the Seventh Amendment simply does not apply in state courts. States are free, therefore, to determine when and if a jury trial will be provided in civil cases in their courts. In many (probably most) states, the state constitution or a state statute guarantees a right of jury trial and usually does so in terms quite similar to those in the Seventh Amendment. We focus on the right to jury trial in federal civil cases. Our understanding of the right to jury trial under the Seventh Amendment must note two phrases in particular. First, the Amendment does not "create" or "grant" a right of jury trial; instead, the right is "preserved." Second, the Amendment does not apply in all civil cases; instead, the right attaches only to "suits at common law," as opposed to cases in equity. This fact poses no great problem in some simple cases, but makes life difficult in more complex cases, which can easily involve aspects of both law and equity. (We discussed the evolution of law and equity courts in §1.2.3.)

The fact that the Seventh Amendment *preserves* the right to jury trial locks the federal courts into a historical test. Because the states ratified the Seventh Amendment in 1791, the federal courts have concluded that the opening inquiry is whether there would have been a right to jury trial in that year. Moreover, because the right attaches only to suits at common law, the more precise question becomes whether there would have been a jury trial in 1791 in the common law courts. To take it a step further, the relevant common law is that of England! Justice Story determined this point in 1812, in a case in which he was sitting as a circuit judge.[9] He concluded:

> Beyond all question, the common law here alluded to is not the common law of any individual state (for it probably differs in all), but it is the common law of England, the grand reservoir of all our jurisprudence. It cannot be necessary for me to expound the grounds of this opinion, because they must be obvious to every person acquainted with the history of the law.[10]

---

[9] For many years after the formation of the United States, Justices of the Supreme Court were required to "ride circuit." This meant that they sat as trial judges at the circuit courts, in addition to their duties on the Supreme Court. At that time, the circuit court was the trial court in the federal system. Now, of course, the trial court is the district court. The practice of making Supreme Court Justices sit as trial judges was abolished long ago. What survives, however, is the assignment of Justices to serve as Circuit Justices for each circuit of the U.S. Court of Appeals. Some extraordinary matters, such as requests for a stay of execution in a death penalty case, may be addressed to the Circuit Justice. The Chief Justice has always been the Circuit Justice for the Fourth Circuit, and the reason goes back to the circuit-riding days. The Fourth Circuit sits in Richmond, Virginia, which is the circuit seat closest to Washington, D.C. Thus, the Chief Justice was required to travel a shorter distance than the other Justices.

[10] United States v. Wonson, 28 F. Cas. 745, 750 (No. 16,750) (C.C.D. Mass. 1812).

Regardless of whether this conclusion was obvious, no one has doubted it seriously since. Think of what this means: To determine — now, in the twenty-first century — whether one is entitled to a jury in a civil case in federal court, the court must assess whether there would have been a right to jury trial in 1791 under English common law. (If this strikes you as a bizarre exercise, you are not alone, as we see below.) In the real world, many (probably most) cases are not difficult.[11] Why? Because many cases involve traditional claims that clearly existed in 1791. For example, claims based upon historically recognized tort and contract theories — negligence, battery, conversion, fraud, trespass, breach of contract, and many others — were unquestionably part of the docket in 1791. The question of whether they would be on the common law docket (and therefore entitled to a jury) or the equity docket (and not entitled to a jury) would be determined by the remedy sought.

Legal and Equitable Remedies

The classic common law (or "legal") remedy is damages, which is a monetary recovery to *compensate* the plaintiff for harm suffered; this explains why they are often called compensatory damages. You undoubtedly study these damages in your courses on Contracts, Torts, and Property. For instance, a plaintiff in contract may sue to recover damages representing her "benefit of the bargain" — to make her whole because of the other side's breach. In a typical case, if the defendant breaches a contract, the plaintiff is expected to "cover" the breach by obtaining the equivalent from another source. The plaintiff may then recover from the defendant the amount by which this "cover" exceeded the amount she would have paid under the contract. Similarly, in tort, a plaintiff may recover damages to compensate her for lost wages, medical expenses, and pain and suffering inflicted as a result of the defendant's tortious act or omission. As noted, there is no question that assessment of such damages is a fact issue at the heart of the jury function.

Punitive damages, in contrast, are intended to punish the defendant for egregious behavior. They are sometimes called *exemplary damages*, because an award of them is to make an example of the defendant. Jurisdictions can take different approaches to the level of behavior necessary to uphold an award of punitive damages. For instance, some states require that the defendant have engaged in malicious, oppressive, or fraudulent behavior to be subject to such an award. The assessment of punitive

---

[11] "[T]he number of cases in which existence of a jury right will be difficult to determine is very small. . . . [T]he vast and controversial literature that has developed about the scope of the jury right is, fortunately, not in proportion to the practical importance of the problem in the actual working of the courts." Wright & Kane, Federal Courts 657.

damages — the decision of how large an award is necessary to punish a defendant — is also a jury question.[12]

As we saw in §1.2.3, equity developed a panoply of remedies intended to provide relief when the legal remedy was inadequate. The classic equitable remedies include (1) the injunction (by which a court orders a party to do something or to refrain from doing something); (2) specific performance (by which the court commands a party to do something she has a duty to do); (3) rescission of a contract; and (4) reformation of a contract. In 1791, common law courts were separate from equity courts, so the assessment of whether one had a right to a jury was relatively easy — jury trials could be had in the law courts, but not in the equity courts.[13] Today, however, law and equity are merged in the federal system and in almost all states.[14]

But it is true to this day, in all court systems (federal and state), that one cannot obtain equitable relief until she has shown that damages are inadequate to remedy her situation. And it is also true that the key issue in determining the right to a jury trial in federal court is whether the plaintiff seeks legal or equitable relief.

- *A* and *B* enter a contract under which *B* is to deliver certain products to *A* at set times. *B* fails to deliver goods as required by the contract. *A* sues *B* for specific performance — that is, for an order requiring her to deliver the goods pursuant to the agreement. *A* cannot seek this equitable remedy, however, until she establishes that her legal remedy of damages is inadequate. In the ordinary case, for example, the court would expect *A* to go out and "cover" — get the goods from another source, and then to seek damages from *B* for the extra amount she had to pay the third party for the goods. Absent extraordinary circumstances, then, *A*'s claim would be for damages and she would be unable to avail herself of equitable remedies such as specific performance. Because damages are legal relief, the right to jury trial would attach.

- *P* owns real property. *D* trespasses across the property each day. If *P* sues at common law, her legal remedy will be damages (say *X* dollars

---

[12] Professor Murphy argues persuasively that the assessment of punitive damages should be entrusted to the judge, not the jury. She likens punitive damages to the assessment of civil penalties, which, as we see below, are assessed by the court, not a jury. *See* Colleen Murphy, *Integrating the Constitutional Authority of Civil and Criminal Juries*, 61 Geo. Wash. L. Rev. 723, 739-782 (1993).

[13] Occasionally, the chancellor at equity would empanel an advisory jury, to assist in deciding a case. There was, however, no general right to a jury trial in equity. (We discussed the development of equity as a separate system of justice in §1.2.3.)

[14] The promulgation of the Federal Rules of Civil Procedure in 1938, which we discuss in §10.6, accomplished this merger in federal courts. Before 1938, the federal district courts maintained separate law and equity dockets. Most state court systems long maintained separate law and equity dockets; almost all have since merged law and equity.

per day), calculated to compensate her for the harm done by *D*'s trespassing. *D* may happily pay *P* the damages of *X* dollars per day and continue trespassing. *P* has a strong argument that her legal remedy is inadequate. She does not want *X* dollars per day. She wants *D* to stop trespassing. She wants an injunction — a court order to *D*, telling her to stop trespassing on *X*'s property.

- ∘   If the court entered an injunction against *D*, and *D* violated the injunction, she would be in contempt of the injunction. The court could fine *D* or could order her incarcerated until she agreed to stop trespassing on *P*'s land. An equitable decree is enforceable through such a contempt citation, which is usually very effective. If she failed to abide by the injunction, it would encourage her to modify her behavior by putting her in jail until she agreed not to trespass.

These cases are pretty easy, because they involve claims either for entirely legal relief or entirely equitable relief. If *P* seeks only equitable relief, there would be no right to a jury trial under the Seventh Amendment. But if *P* seeks only damages, the Seventh Amendment would grant a jury trial on all questions of fact, including the question of how large a recovery of damages would be required to compensate the plaintiff for the harm done her by the defendant.

Hybrid Cases: Law and Equity

Your professor is likely interested in more complicated matters. Specifically, what happens if a single case involves both issues of law and issues of equity? In England, historically, courts were guided by what they considered to be the primary thrust of the case. For example, if the court considered the case to be mainly about an equitable remedy — if the center of gravity of the case, the most important part of the case, was equitable — the entire case would be heard in the equity court. The equity courts in England developed the "clean-up doctrine," which allowed the equity court to provide limited, or "incidental," legal relief. The clean-up doctrine thus avoided the need for two cases, one at law and one at equity. On the other hand, because the case was in equity, there was no jury, *even as to the incidental legal issues decided.* Because of the clean-up doctrine, then, a plaintiff might lose access to a jury trial on a legal remedy. Equity would determine the entire dispute. In contrast, the law courts had no such clean-up power. A law court, in which the plaintiff sought damages, had no authority to grant equitable relief.

- ∘   Let's return to the fact pattern above. *P* sues *D* for an injunction (equitable relief) to stop *D*'s trespassing on *P*'s land. In addition, *P* seeks damages (legal relief) to compensate her for past trespasses on the land.
- ∘   The basic tenor of the case — the center of gravity — is equity, because (as we discussed above) *P* is most interested in the injunctive relief. The

damages *P* seeks are merely incidental to the injunction — they flow naturally from the fact that there has been trespassing in the past. Historically, the entire case — for injunction and for damages — would be heard at equity. The claim for the injunction would invoke equity jurisdiction and the claim for damages could be heard at equity without a jury under the clean-up doctrine.

All of this changed dramatically in 1959, when the Supreme Court decided *Beacon Theatres, Inc. v. Westover.*[15] *Beacon Theatres* is one of the pivotal cases in the development of the Seventh Amendment and established important new perspectives on the Seventh Amendment. First, according to the Court, the historical test used to determine a right to jury trial is not static. The inquiry is not *entirely* how the case would have been handled in England in 1791. Rather, courts today are to take account of modern procedural reforms, including the Federal Rules of Civil Procedure.[16] Remember that equity acts only when one's legal remedy is inadequate. Modern procedure — including liberal joinder provisions under the Federal Rules — allows the assertion of more claims in a single case than the common law rules did. Accordingly, cases seeking legal relief (to which a jury trial would attach) may be joined with claims for equitable relief.

Second, this reassessment spelled the end of the center-of-gravity theory and the clean-up doctrine. Those doctrines "must be re-evaluated in the light of the liberal joinder provisions of the Federal Rules, which allow legal and equitable causes to be brought and resolved in one civil action."[17] After *Beacon Theatres*, then, federal courts do not assess whether the main thrust of the case was equitable or legal and thus whether the case as a whole is tried with a jury. Instead, they are to assess the availability of a jury on an issue-by-issue basis. The mere presence of equitable issues cannot rob a party of the right to a jury on legal issues. The Court established these rules:

- ○ If an issue of fact underlies a claim for legal relief, it must be tried to a jury, without regard to whether the overall thrust or tenor of the case is equitable.
- ○ If an issue of fact underlies both a claim for legal relief and equitable relief, it must be tried to a jury.
- ○ Only if an issue of fact underlies a purely equitable matter is it tried to the judge without a jury.

---

[15] 359 U.S. 500 (1959).

[16] The Court also cited the Declaratory Judgment Act, 28 U.S.C. §§2201, 2202, as such a procedural development. That Act permits a federal court to declare the relative rights of the parties when there is an actual dispute. For example, an insurance company might seek a declaration that a particular event is not covered under a policy with the insured.

[17] *Beacon Theatres*, 359 U.S. at 510.

○ Finally, unless there are "imperative circumstances, circumstances which in view of the flexible procedures of the Federal Rules we cannot now anticipate" to the contrary, the jury issues shall be tried before the equity issues. This order of trial ensures that the judge will be bound by the jury's determination of the facts, rather than vice versa.

Beacon Theatres vastly expanded the right to jury trial in federal civil cases. Instead of looking to the main thrust of the case, the Seventh Amendment right is seen to attach to *issues*, not to *claims*. And every doubt is resolved in favor of jury determinations — from the jury trial for issues underlying claims that are both legal and equitable to the trial of jury issues before equitable issues.

○ Let's return to the fact pattern we saw above — in which *P* sues for an injunction to stop *D* from trespassing on her land and also seeks damages for *D*'s past trespasses. As we saw above, before *Beacon Theatres*, no issue would have been determined by a jury, because the central thrust of the case was equitable and the equity court, under the clean-up doctrine, would be permitted to determine the issues related to legal relief (damages).

○ Under *Beacon Theatres*, however, the court would consider the Seventh Amendment issue by issue. The issue of whether *D* has trespassed underlies the claim for damages (legal relief), so a jury would decide that issue. The issue of damage caused by the past trespass underlies the legal claim, so a jury would decide that issue as well. Only the question of whether *P* is entitled to an injunction (equitable relief) would be decided by the judge. And on that question, the judge is guided by what the jury found regarding past trespass, which may affect the need for an injunction.

Moreover, the order in which the legal and equitable issues are asserted in the case is irrelevant.

○ *P* sues *D*. Both are parties to a contract. *P* claims that the contract should be rescinded because he was induced to enter it by *D*'s fraudulent misrepresentations. *D* claims that the contract is valid, should not be rescinded, and that *P* has breached the contract and owes her damages. *P* sues *D* for rescission, which is classic equitable relief. *D* answers and asserts a counterclaim[18] against *P* for breach of the contract damages. The counterclaim obviously states a claim for legal relief (damages).

○ Before *Beacon Theatres*, there would have been no jury in this case. *P*'s claim for rescission would have invoked equity jurisdiction, and the equity court, under the clean-up doctrine, could have determined whether *D* was entitled to damages if the contract were valid.

---

[18] A counterclaim is a claim asserted by the defendant against the plaintiff in the pending case. See §12.5.1.

○ After *Beacon Theatres*, however, the jury question is assessed issue by issue, regardless of the order in which the claims are asserted. *D*'s counterclaim for damages states a claim for legal relief. Obviously, every issue underlying that claim — including whether the contract was valid and whether it was breached — would be decided by a jury. Thus, much of the equitable claim for rescission would be affected by the jury determination, because its determination of the validity of the contract would affect the judge's determination of whether rescission is proper. In other words, if the jury determined that the contract is valid, it would be very difficult for the judge to order rescission.

In 1962, the Supreme Court reinforced *Beacon Theatres* with *Dairy Queen, Inc. v. Wood*.[19] In that case, the plaintiff sought an injunction to stop the defendant from using its trade name and also sought an "accounting" for the past improper use of the name. The latter claim was essentially for damages, but by using the phrase "accounting" — which was historically a proceeding in equity — the plaintiff hoped to defeat any claim for a jury trial. The case presented a classic example of what in the old days would have been handled by the clean-up doctrine in equity. Seeking the injunction invoked equity jurisdiction and the claim for accounting — even if seen as damages — could be decided by equity as incidental to the injunction. Thus, in the old days there would have been no jury trial on any issue. Despite *Beacon Theatres*, the lower courts applied the clean-up doctrine and struck the defendant's demand for a jury trial.

The Supreme Court used the occasion in *Dairy Queen* to drive home what it said in *Beacon Theatres*. First, it does not matter whether a claim to legal relief is seen as "incidental" — the right to a jury trial on such issues cannot be deprived by the fact that it is asserted in a case that also contains a claim for equitable relief. Whether the equitable claim is somehow more important is irrelevant. Second, the jury issues are to be tried first, absent exceptional circumstances that the Court could not foresee.

That left the question of whether the claim for accounting was equitable or legal. Again, the Court was willing to consider modern procedural developments in making the assessment. Historically, claims for an accounting were handled in equity precisely so there would be no jury. The theory was that complicated matters of calculation were beyond the capacity of lay jurors, so such claims should be tried at equity and not at law. The Court in *Dairy Queen* noted, however, that Federal Rule 53(b) permits a district court to appoint a special master to aid the jury in calculating damages. (We discussed the use of special masters in §8.6.) Because of the availability of a special master, it was more difficult for the plaintiff to show that her legal remedy of damages was inadequate. Thus, it was

[19] 369 U.S. 469 (1962).

more difficult to show that she needed the equitable remedy of an accounting. Only in rare situations, not presented in *Dairy Queen*, will a party be able to show that damages are inadequate.

In the end, then, the defendant was entitled to a jury trial on all issues underlying the plaintiff's claim for damages. Those issues also underlay the plaintiff's claim for an injunction, so the jury would determine all important issues in the case. The judge would determine the propriety of an injunction, but would be bound to follow the jury's determination of the facts concerning whether the defendant had used the plaintiff's trade name inappropriately.

In the decades since *Beacon Theatres* and *Dairy Queen*, the Supreme Court has largely continued to embrace a broad interpretation of the Seventh Amendment. For example, it has found a right to jury trial in some circumstances in cases arising in procedural settings that evolved in equity. Specifically, class actions, interpleader, and shareholder derivative suits (all of which we see in Chapter 13) developed in equity. Does that mean that there is no jury right in such cases? No. The court is to look at the claims asserted in the proceeding to determine whether a jury trial right attaches.[20] The fact that the claim is asserted in a procedural device having its roots in equity is irrelevant.[21] Thus, if the plaintiff in a class action or a shareholder derivative suit seeks damages, there is a right to a jury just as there is in the assertion of any legal claim.

Application of Seventh Amendment to More Recently Recognized Claims

The examples we have seen thus far have involved claims that clearly were recognized in the eighteenth century. But a great deal of substantive law has developed since then. The law has developed claims for intentional infliction of emotional distress, virtually the entire field of labor law and civil rights law, as well as securities fraud and antitrust statutes. How does a federal court assess the Seventh Amendment right to jury trial for substantive claims that did not exist in 1791? Consistent with its generally liberal view toward the right to jury trial, the Court has not required that the claim asserted be one that existed in 1791. Such an requirement, obviously, would ensure that there is no right to jury trial in many cases brought under modern statutory and common law theories. Instead, the Supreme

---

[20] The leading case is *Ross v. Bernhard*, 396 U.S. 531 (1970), which was a shareholder derivative suit, in which the Court concluded that the underlying claims asserted by the shareholder on behalf of the corporation were legal, and thus entitled to jury trial.

[21] The same is true with declaratory judgment cases. Though declaratory judgment developed largely in equity, the remedy of a declaration of rights is neither equitable nor legal. The court must look to the underlying assertion in the case to see if the jury trial right attaches. In other words, the court looks to see how the dispute would arise if it were asserted as a traditional case, not as one in which the claimant seeks a declaration.

Court has adopted a two-pronged test, looking both to the common law of 1791 and to the remedy sought.

A good example is *Chauffeurs, Teamsters & Helpers, Local No. 391 v. Terry*,[22] which involved suit by workers against the local of their labor union. The plaintiffs in *Terry* worked for a trucking company that was a party to a collective bargaining contract with the local. The plaintiffs were members of the local. The trucking company downsized its facilities and the plaintiffs were laid off. They filed a grievance with their local union, which refused to refer their charges to the grievance committee (which is the way the grievance was to be adjudicated under the collective bargaining agreement). They sued the trucking company and the local. The trucking company went bankrupt, however, and was dismissed from the suit. The case proceeded against the local union. The plaintiffs alleged that the union breached a duty of fair representation that it clearly owed to them. They sought reinstatement and compensatory damages for back pay and lost health benefits. The plaintiffs sought trial by jury, which the defendant opposed.

The claim for breach of the duty of fair dealing did not exist in 1791. Indeed, labor unions were illegal in 1791! Nonetheless, the Court in *Terry* upheld the right to jury trial and applied a now-familiar two-part test. First, the federal court is to determine whether the claim asserted — though of recent origin — has an eighteenth-century analog in the common law. If there clearly is not (a rare event), there is no right to a jury under the Seventh Amendment. If there may be, the court applies the second part of the test, which is to "examine the remedy sought and determine whether it is legal or equitable in nature."[23] The Court has expressly recognized the second step as the more important.

Finding a common law analog for the claim asserted is more art than science. The party wishing to defeat the jury claim will posit analogs from equity practice of 1791, while the party seeking a jury will posit analogs from law practice of 1791. The Supreme Court has addressed this sort of thing several times, but *Terry* is an especially helpful opinion (which is why it is in so many casebooks) because the Court roams around inconclusively through a series of possibilities proffered by the parties. It shows just how malleable this part of the test is. The claim for breach of the duty of fair representation is not akin to a suit to vacate an arbitration award, says the majority, but it is similar to an action by a beneficiary against a trustee for breach of fiduciary obligation. The fact that this was an equity claim in the eighteenth century counsels against a jury right. The case is somewhat akin to an attorney malpractice action, which was heard at law in the eighteenth century, but not really, says the majority. So it concludes

---

[22] 494 U.S. 558 (1990).
[23] *Id.* at 565.

(sort of) that the trustee analogy is the best, which seems to say there is no right to a jury.

But then the majority, consistent with cases like *Beacon Theatres*, looked to the *issues* to be addressed, rather than the overall claim. Here, the Court noted that the plaintiffs must prove two things: (1) that the *trucking company* breached the collective bargaining agreement,[24] and (2) that the union breached the duty of fair representation. Though issue (2) was analogous to a fiduciary claim, which is equitable, issue (1) was more like breach of contract, which is legal. So at the end of Part III(A) of the opinion, the Justices in the majority throw up their hands and say they are left in "equipoise" — equally unsure about whether this kind of case would have gone to law or equity in 1791.

That being the case, the majority then looks, in Part III(B) of the opinion, at the remedy. The plaintiffs wanted back pay and benefits. The Court concludes quite readily (without the wandering that characterizes Part III(A) of the opinion) that the claim is for damages, which, of course, is legal (not equitable).[25] In sum, then, the Court concludes that the plaintiffs were entitled to a jury on all issues in the case.

Justice Brennan concurred but argued that the Court should jettison the first part of the inquiry. Finding a historical analog for a modern claim is inexact and needlessly difficult. Moreover, he argued, judges are not trained in legal history. Though many professors disagree, I certainly think there is much to what Justice Brennan says. Indeed, the malleability of the analogue test is shown by the majority opinion. Essentially, one can argue for almost any outcome in almost any case. The real crux of the matter boils down to how the court characterizes the remedy. Justice Brennan was careful to say that *some* historical analysis is required by the Seventh Amendment. The requirement is met, however, when the court analyzes whether the remedy is essentially legal or equitable.

---

[24] They must show this even though the trucking company was no longer a party to the case. The union could not be liable for breach of its duty of fair representation if the trucking company had not acted in violation of the collective bargaining agreement.

[25] The Court distinguished between damages, which compensate for harm, and restitution, which is the forced return of an unjust benefit. Damages are legal relief; restitution generally is equitable. If a toll collector charges you $2.00 instead of $1.50, he has been unjustly enriched by 50 cents. Your claim for return of that sum would be restitution, not damages. The Court suggested in *Terry* that restitution was entirely equitable. Professor Murphy concludes, however, that most claims for restitution historically would have been tried at law. Colleen Murphy, *Misclassifying Monetary Restitution*, 55 SMU L. Rev. 1577, 1598-1607, 1626-1628 (2002).

Can the Seventh Amendment Right Be Overridden by Various Concerns?

One lingering question is whether the Seventh Amendment right can be obviated in cases of surpassing complexity. In other words, are some cases just so difficult that a jury cannot be expected to discharge its function? From time to time, the Court has said (at least in footnotes) that "the practical abilities and limitations of juries" are relevant considerations under the Seventh Amendment.[26] The common law of 1791 did recognize a "complexity exception" to the right to jury trial.[27] There may also be an argument that requiring a jury to determine facts in a case beyond its capacity violates the due process rights of litigants. But lower courts have been reluctant to find such an exception, even in cases that might cry out for one. In *In re U.S. Financial Securities Litigation*,[28] the district court refused to allow a jury trial, because the case involved complex issues, would tie up the jury for two years, and involved evidence that was "the equivalent of reading the first 90 volumes of the Federal Reporter, Second Series."[29] The Ninth Circuit reversed, and relied upon the fact that the Supreme Court has never actually embraced a "complexity exception." The court also noted that there is no reason to believe that a judge has any greater background in complex issues of electronics or economics, for example, than jurors would.

The Supreme Court raised a few eyebrows in *Markman v. Westview Instruments, Inc.*,[30] when it held that the judge, rather than a jury, should determine the issue of the scope of a patent. Thus, though there is a right to a jury in patent infringement cases, the issue of how to construe the patent was up to the judge. In reaching this decision, the Court employed a functional analysis, and was impressed by the relative ability of the judge, as opposed to the jury, to determine the question. *Markman* has not supported a movement toward embracing a general "complexity exception." First, the Court did not speak in expansive terms, but expressly limited its holding to the interpretation of "terms of art in patent cases."[31] Second, it did not refer to any of its previous footnotes mentioning the practical abilities of jurors. Third, historic practice was not clear as to whether the issue of the interpretation of the patent was for the judge or jury. In sum, *Markman* is probably best interpreted narrowly.

The Supreme Court does not always uphold a right of jury trial. In Chapter 11, we discuss how a valid judgment entered in one case may have a

---

[26] *See, e.g., Terry*, 494 U.S. 558, 565 n.4 (1990); *Ross*, 396 U.S. at 538 n.10.

[27] *See generally* Roger Kirst, *The Jury's Historic Domain in Complex Cases*, 58 Wash. L. Rev. 1 (1982).

[28] 609 F.2d 411 (9th Cir.), *cert. denied*, 446 U.S. 929 (1979).

[29] *Id.* at 416 n.13.

[30] 517 U.S. 370 (1996).

[31] *Id.* at 384 n.9.

binding effect on subsequent litigation, through the "preclusion doctrines." In *Parklane Hosiery Co. v. Shore*,[32] which we discuss in §11.3.5, the Court held that these doctrines may legitimately deprive one of having a jury determine fact issues. There, the first case was litigated before an administrative body, before which there is never a right to jury trial. The second case was a civil proceeding in federal court, in which a jury trial would have been proper. The first case determined issues that were relevant in the second case, and the Court held that those determinations bound the parties in the second case. This was true even though the result was to remove those issues from the jury's purview in the second case. Another way to view the result is to say that because of preclusion law, there was no issue of fact remaining to be tried in the case in federal court.

As suggested in the preceding paragraph, it is clear that Congress can create claims and provide for their enforcement before administrative tribunals that are not Article III courts. The congressional power to do this is beyond our scope; you will study it in detail in an upper-division course on Federal Courts. Suffice it to say for present purposes that the Supreme Court generally has recognized Congress's power to do this, at least when the case involves "public rights" (meaning rights between citizens and the government).[33] What about cases involving private rights — that is, disputes between private citizens? Occasionally, Congress creates a substantive right to be enforced in the federal courts, and expresses a preference that the issues be decided by the judge, without a jury. Of course, provisions of the Constitution are supreme over contrary provisions in legislation. So if the Seventh Amendment would recognize a right to jury trial in federal court, Congress has no power to override that right.[34] As to the converse situation, it has long been clear that Congress can grant a jury trial right by statute even as to matters that would not fall within the Seventh Amendment.[35] Thus, if Congress expressly provides for a jury trial — or if a statute is silent but is interpreted as giving a right of jury trial — the court need not determine whether the Seventh Amendment applies.

---

[32] 439 U.S. 322 (1979).

[33] *See* Atlas Roofing Co. v. Occupational Safety & Health Review Commn., 430 U.S. 442, 460 (1977).

[34] *See, e.g.*, Granfinanciera, S.A. v. Nordberg, 492 U.S. 33, 52-53 (1989) (Congress "lacks the power to strip parties contesting matters of private right of their constitutional right to a trial by jury"); Curtis v. Loether, 415 U.S. 189 (1974) (statutory claim for damages for racial discrimination invoked Seventh Amendment right to jury trial, notwithstanding congressional ambivalence on whether the case should be tried to a jury). *See generally* Mary Kay Kane, *Civil Jury Trial: The Case for Reasoned Iconoclasm*, 28 Hastings L.J. 1, 20-27 (1976).

[35] *See generally* 9 Wright & Miller §2302.2.

Problems with Some Monetary Remedies

Not all monetary recoveries constitute damages and, thus, legal relief. We noted in footnote 25 above that "restitution" — though monetary — is not necessarily legal relief. In *Tull v. United States*,[36] the federal government sought civil penalties under the Clean Water Act, alleging that the defendant had violated the Act by dumping material on wetlands. Under the Act, the government sought civil penalties of $10,000 per day, totaling $22 million. The Court refused to rely on an "abstruse historical search for the nearest 18th-century analog,"[37] and focused instead on the remedy. Because the penalties were intended to deter and punish (rather than restore the status quo), they were analogous to damages, which, traditionally, was available at law. Interestingly, while the Court concluded that the Seventh Amendment thus required a jury determination on the question of the defendant's *liability*, the determination of the civil penalty was not for the jury. According to the Court, the assessment of the civil penalty was largely unconstrained by meaningful standards and thus entrusted to the discretion of the judge; the assessment was simply not a "fundamental element" of jury trial.[38]

On the other hand, *Feltner v. Columbia Pictures Television, Inc.*[39] upheld the right to have a jury determine the amount of statutory damages to be awarded for violation of the Copyright Act. Under that Act, the plaintiff has a choice of showing actual damages or recovering statutory damages of at least $500 and no more than $20,000, "as the court considers just." Though the Act clearly envisioned that the judge would set the amount of statutory damages, the Court concluded that the Seventh Amendment required a jury determination. The Court found "overwhelming evidence that the consistent practice at common law was for juries to award damages."[40] It distinguished *Tull* by noting that there was "no evidence that juries had historically determined the amount of civil penalties to be paid to the Government."[41]

The lesson from these cases is that one should not assume that a monetary recovery automatically constitutes damages. Civil penalties and restitution are examples of such relief that may not qualify as legal relief, and thus may not trigger the Seventh Amendment right to jury trial. On the other hand, an award aimed at compensating the claimant for harm done,

---

[36] 481 U.S. 412 (1987).

[37] *Id.* at 421. The defendant argued that the claim was akin to an action in debt, which was at law. The government claimed it was more like an action to abate a public nuisance, which would historically have been heard at equity.

[38] *Id.* at 426 n.9.

[39] 523 U.S. 340 (1998).

[40] *Id.* at 353.

[41] *Id.* at 355.

or at punishing the defendant for egregious behavior, constitutes classic legal relief, for which a jury may be demanded to assess the damages figure.

Requirement of Written Demand for Jury

A jury is not automatically empaneled in those cases in which the Seventh Amendment allows a jury trial. Under Rule 38(b)(1), a party must demand a jury trial in writing "no later than 10 days after the last pleading directed to the [jury-triable] issue is served." The demand can be made in a pleading or in a separate document, but must be in writing. A party who fails to make such a written demand and serve it on the other parties waives her right to a jury trial and the case is tried to the judge, as Rule 38(d) makes clear. On the other hand, Rule 39(b) provides that the court has discretion to grant a motion for jury trial on proper issues even when a party failed to make a proper demand.

Under Rule 38(d), a party who demands a jury and then changes her mind can withdraw the jury demand only with the consent of all other parties. Moreover, it is worth noting that there is no right *not* to have a jury. If one party does not want a jury but another party does — and makes a timely, proper written demand for it on jury-triable issues — there will be a jury.

§9.2.3   Selecting the Jury

The Voir Dire Process

Lawyers take jury selection very seriously. Each trial lawyer has things she looks for in potential jurors, and develops a "sixth sense" about potential jurors who will be sympathetic and those who will not. Jury selection has become a cottage industry for consultants, who are often employed by lawyers, at least in high-profile cases, to help select the jury. We focus here on the process by which the jury is selected. In federal and state judicial systems, court administrators generate a "master roll" of potential jurors from a variety of public sources. Rosters of registered voters, licensed drivers, taxpayers, and welfare recipients are common sources of this list. For much of our history, certain groups were systematically excluded from the master rolls in various communities. The Supreme Court struck down such exclusions, and established that the Constitution requires that the master roll reflect a reasonable cross-section of the local population.[42] The jury is the voice of the community, and the master roll must represent a reasonable cross-section of that community. There is no

---

[42] *See, e.g.,* Taylor v. Louisiana, 419 U.S. 522 (1975) (reversing defendant's conviction because jury excluded women and was not a fair cross-section of the community).

right to have the jury itself "composed in whole or in part of persons of [one's] own race," but a litigant "does have the right to be tried by a jury whose members are selected pursuant to nondiscriminatory criteria."[43]

The court administrator summons citizens as needed to report for jury duty. A group of those summoned each day is sent to a courtroom in which a jury is needed. They constitute the *venire* from which the jury itself will be chosen. The members of the venire — perhaps a couple dozen persons — then go through the *voir dire* process, which consists of a series of questions. "Voir dire" means "to speak the truth" or "to see what is said." The goal is to empanel a jury of unbiased persons who have no independent knowledge of the transaction in question.[44] Thus, the questions are aimed at determining whether any potential juror has a bias, personal knowledge of the facts, or a relationship with one of the parties or the lawyers. In federal court, Federal Rule 47(a) permits the judge to conduct the voir dire questioning, or to allow the parties or their lawyers to do so. The judge has great discretion in running the voir dire, and may, for example, use written questionnaires in conjunction with oral questioning. Invariably, when the judge conducts the voir dire, she will allow the parties and lawyers to suggest lines of questioning. The lawyers for each party watch each potential juror closely, study the responses to the various questions carefully, and try to pick up clues about which way that person might "lean" in the case.

In every judicial system, each side in the litigation has two methods for disqualifying potential jurors from serving on the case. These challenges (also called *strikes*) can be "for cause" (also known as "for favor") or "peremptory." A strike for cause is based upon the potential juror's bias or relationship with a party or lawyer. For example, the plaintiff's sister could be challenged for cause, as could an employee of the defendant corporation or a potential juror who was an eyewitness to the events that are the subject of the litigation. The court determines whether a party's challenge for cause should be granted.

In contrast to this type of challenge, a peremptory strike is exercised without statement of a reason. Such challenges date to the thirteenth-century English practice (at least in criminal cases). In this country, peremptory strikes have been recognized in civil cases from colonial times. Many lawyers and commentators defend the use of peremptory challenges as permitting the lawyer who suspects bias, but who cannot elicit evidence

---

[43] Batson v. Kentucky, 476 U.S. 79, 85 (1986).

[44] The jury's verdict is to be based upon the evidence introduced at trial. A juror who was an eyewitness or who otherwise had independent knowledge of the facts might base her decision on that independent knowledge. Moreover, other jurors might be swayed by the independent knowledge of this one juror. So such persons are weeded out in the voir dire process.

of it in voir dire, to remove a potential juror. Some commentators have also argued that the ability to strike potential jurors without stating a reason legitimizes the resulting verdict.[45]

Each judicial system permits unlimited strikes for cause but limits the number of peremptory challenges. In federal civil cases, 28 U.S.C. §1870 provides that each party shall have three peremptory strikes.[46] As noted, a peremptory strike is one that does not have to be explained. The lawyer may act on her intuition, "psychic" abilities, or even a hunch in using a peremptory strike. Does that mean, however, that a lawyer can engage in racial discrimination in exercising peremptory challenges? The Supreme Court said no in *Batson v. Kentucky.*[47] There, the Court held that a prosecutor's use of peremptory strikes on the basis of race violated constitutional principles of equal protection. Because *Batson* was based upon federal constitutional provisions applicable to the states under the Fourteenth Amendment, its holding affected practice in state as well as in federal courts. All courts have gained experience in holding "*Batson* hearings" to determine whether the use of peremptory strikes is racially discriminatory.

But *Batson* was a criminal case, in which the prosecutor — a government actor — engaged in racially discriminatory conduct. What about civil cases between private parties, in which there is no government actor? As you know from your course in Constitutional Law, the Constitution protects persons from deprivation of equal protection of the laws, but the deprivation must be caused by "state action." Purely private discrimination is not unconstitutional (though it may violate statutes). In the important 1991 case of *Edmonson v. Leesville Concrete Co.,*[48] the Supreme Court extended *Batson* to civil cases between private parties. The majority opinion emphasized that the government (either federal or state) sets up the court system that permits the use of peremptory strikes. It concluded that the use of those strikes — even in litigation involving nongovernmental parties — constitutes state action.

---

[45] The legendary English legal scholar Blackstone made this point by saying that a party "should have a good opinion of his jury, the want of which might totally disconcert him, the law wills not that he should be tried by any one man against whom he has conceived a prejudice, even without being able to assign a reason for such . . . dislike." 4 William Blackstone, Commentaries * 353 (1859).

[46] It also provides that in cases of multiple plaintiffs or defendants, the court may consider the multiple parties "as a single party" for this purpose. Thus, each side — the plaintiff side and the defendant side — would have a total of three peremptory strikes. The same statute goes on, however, to allow the court to permit additional peremptory strikes.

[47] 476 U.S. 79 (1986).

[48] 500 U.S. 614, 631 (1991).

The Court extended its conclusion in *Edmonson* to the gender-based discrimination three years later in *J.E.B. v. Alabama*.[49] In that case, Alabama, acting on behalf of the mother of a minor child, sued a man for paternity and child-support payments. The suit was in state court, and Alabama used nine of its ten peremptory strikes (under state law) to remove potential male jurors. As a result, the jury was entirely female. The defendant objected to the state's use of peremptory strikes based on gender, and claimed that it violated his rights of equal protection. The case was much easier than *Edmonson* on the question of state action; it was, after all, a *state* that was using the peremptory challenges. The tougher issue was whether discrimination on the basis of *gender* violated equal protection. The Court concluded that it did, in ways similar to racial discrimination. It also painted with a broad brush in determining whose rights were violated:

> Discrimination in jury selection, whether based on race or on gender, causes harm to the litigants, the community, and the individual jurors who are wrongfully excluded from participation in the judicial process. The litigants are harmed by the risk that the prejudice which motivated the discriminatory selection of the jury will infect the entire proceedings. . . . The community is harmed by the State's participation in the perpetuation of invidious group stereotypes and the inevitable loss of confidence in our judicial system that such state-sanctioned discrimination in the courtroom engenders. When state actors exercise peremptory challenges in reliance on gender stereotypes, they ratify and reinforce prejudicial views of the relative abilities of men and women. . . . [I]ndividual jurors themselves have a right to nondiscriminatory jury selection procedures. . . . Striking individual jurors on the assumption that they hold particular views simply because of their gender . . . denigrates the dignity of the excluded juror. . . .[50]

There is no question that the holding in *J.E.B.* will apply in wholly private litigation as well. *Edmonson* commands that result. And it is also absolutely clear that both *Edmonson* and *J.E.B.* apply equally in state and federal courts. The holdings are based upon equal protection guarantees applicable to the federal government and applicable to the states through the Fourteenth Amendment.

There are some notable problems in the wake of *Edmonson* and *J.E.B.* First, what classes of potential jurors are protected? We can say with certainty that a litigant may not use her peremptory challenges to strike potential jurors because of their race or their gender. What about national origin? What about sexual preference? What about religion? The Supreme Court has not addressed the question with regard to such groups, and lower federal courts and state courts are having difficulty discerning where to draw

[49] 511 U.S. 127 (1994).
[50] *Id.* at 140-142 (footnotes and citations omitted).

the line. One state appellate court concluded that it is permissible to use a peremptory strike to remove a potential juror on the basis of her religion. It reasoned that one's religion imparted to her certain beliefs, and that it has always been permissible to strike jurors because of their beliefs. On the other hand, membership in a racial or gender group does not say anything about one's beliefs.[51]

The second troublesome issue after *Edmonson* and *J.E.B.* is the procedure the court should use for determining whether a litigant is using peremptory challenges in an unconstitutional way. As noted above, though there is no right to a jury composed of one's own race, there is a right to be tried by a jury selected through nondiscriminatory criteria. In her concurrence in *J.E.B.*, Justice O'Connor lamented that the Court's "further constitutionalizing jury selection procedures . . . increases the number of cases in which jury selection — once a sideshow — will become part of the main event."[52] Though the steps in this "sideshow" are clear, the standards have not been applied consistently.

It is absolutely clear that a party challenging another party's use of a peremptory strike must raise the issue promptly — specifically, at the time the challenge is used. The court has no duty to raise the issue on its own motion, and a party's failure to object in a timely fashion waives the objection.[53] The court must then inquire into the matter in what is routinely called a *Batson hearing*. There, the objecting party must make a prima facie showing that the would-be juror was a member of a relevant group and was removed *because* of her membership in that group. Courts have had great difficulty determining what constitutes a prima facie showing.[54]

If the objector makes a prima facie showing of discrimination, the burden shifts to the other party to show a neutral reason for her use of the peremptory challenge to strike this particular juror. The objecting party is then allowed to present rebuttal evidence in an effort to show that the other party's "neutral" reason is actually a pretext for improper discriminatory behavior. The burden of persuading the court lies with the party objecting to the use of the peremptory strike. Because the issue involves subjective matters, the trial court's decision on whether to uphold the peremptory challenge is rarely disturbed on appeal.

In his concurring opinion in *Batson*, Justice Marshall argued that peremptory challenges should be eliminated. He was concerned that any

[51] Casarez v. Texas, 913 S.W.2d 468, 495 (Tex. Ct. Crim. App. 1995).

[52] *J.E.B.*, 511 U.S. at 147 (O'Connor, J., concurring).

[53] *See, e.g.*, Dawson v. Wal-Mart Stores, Inc., 978 F.2d 205, 210 (5th Cir. 1992) (objection after trial was untimely); Clark v. Newport News Shipbuilding & Dry Dock Co., 937 F.2d 934, 939 (4th Cir. 1991) (court under no obligation to raise *Batson* issue).

[54] *Compare* Byram v. Ozmint, 339 F.3d 203 (4th Cir. 2003) (use of nine of ten peremptory strikes and four additional challenges to exclude white jurors not a prima facie showing) *with* Mahaffey v. Page, 162 F.3d 481 (7th Cir. 1998) (use of peremptory strikes to exclude every juror of the defendant's race made a prima facie showing).

trial lawyer worth her salt would be able to state a "neutral" reason for her exercise of a peremptory strike. For example, if a lawyer's assertion that a potential juror was "uncommunicative" or "never cracked a smile" constituted a legitimate nondiscriminatory reason for exercising the peremptory strike, "the protection erected by the Court today may be illusory."[55] Some people feel that it is. In addition, it is not clear what a court should do if race or gender is one of multiple reasons for striking a potential juror. The Second Circuit has concluded that "*Batson* challenges may be brought by [parties] who can show that racial discrimination was a *substantial part* of the motivation for a . . . peremptory challenge[]."[56]

Size of the Jury

The voir dire process winnows the venire to the jury itself (sometimes called the jury *panel*). Historically, courts empaneled 12 jurors in civil (and criminal) cases, and employed "alternate jurors." The alternate jurors (usually two) would sit in the jury box with the other jurors, but would play a role only if one of the original jurors was excused during the case. Jurors can always be excused, even during the trial, for "good cause." Such cause includes things such as illness or a family emergency.[57] If an original juror is taken off the case for such a reason, an alternate juror takes her place and participates in deliberations and in rendering the verdict. If no original juror was excused, the alternate jurors play no role in the deliberations and verdict.

This is still the system in most state courts. In the federal system, however, things have changed. Though, as noted, tradition supported 12-person juries, some federal district courts experimented with smaller juries, mostly as a way to reduce costs. The Supreme Court upheld the use of a six-person jury in a civil case in *Colgrove v. Battin*.[58] Though the Seventh Amendment preserves jury trial as it existed at "common law," as we discussed in §9.2.2, that reference is to the *right* that existed at common law, and not to "the various incidents of trial by jury."[59] The size of the jury is simply an "incident" of jury trial, and thus the federal courts today are not locked into the common law practice of using 12 jurors.

The size of the civil jury in federal court is governed by Federal Rule 48, which allows juries of not fewer than six and not more than twelve members. For economic reasons, federal judges routinely empanel smaller juries; the use of six jurors is common. In 1991, Rule 47 was amended to

---

[55] *Batson*, 476 U.S. at 106 (Marshall, J., concurring).

[56] Howard v. Senkowski, 986 F.2d 24, 30 (2d Cir. 1993) (emphasis added).

[57] One interesting case is *Bondie v. Bic Corp.*, 947 F.2d 1531, 1535 (6th Cir. 1991), in which the court dismissed the juror for chronic tardiness.

[58] 413 U.S. 149 (1973).

[59] *Id.* at 156.

abolish the alternate juror in civil cases in federal court. Every juror empaneled participates in the trial, deliberation, and verdict unless excused under Rule 47(c) for "good cause." Rule 48 requires, unless the parties stipulate to the contrary, that the verdict must be "returned by a jury of at least 6 members." That means that a prudent judge in a case involving a lengthy trial will empanel at least seven jurors. Then, if one is excused for cause, the remaining six can return a verdict.

§9.2.4 Jury Instructions, Deliberation, and Verdict

Jury Instructions and Deliberation

After all parties have presented their evidence at trial — at the "close of all evidence" — the lawyer for each party makes her "closing statement" (or "summation"). As with the opening statement, the plaintiff goes first. The lawyers summarize the evidence in a light most favorable to their clients and urge the jurors to find the facts in favor of their client. Then the case is ready for submission to the jury.[60]

We noted in §9.2.1 that the jury's job is to determine the *facts*, while the judge determines the *law*. When the case is submitted to the jury, the court instructs the jury on the applicable law through "jury instructions."[61] Jury instructions are delivered by the judge orally. The parties submit proposed jury instructions to the judge in advance of this occasion.[62] The judge determines which jury instructions to give, either from the parties' suggestions or on her own. Under Federal Rule 51(c)(1), a party objecting to a jury instruction must make her objection "distinctly" and state the grounds for objection. Rule 51(c)(2) endeavors to ensure that objections to jury instructions are made before the jury retires to deliberate, which gives the judge a chance to correct any errors in the instructions.

Obviously, the reading of jury instructions (also called *charging the jury*) is rarely a scintillating event. Imagine listening as the judge reads

---

[60] This assumes that the case did not involve a bench trial. In a bench trial, the lawyers give their summations to the judge. We also assume here that the court allows the case to go to the jury. We discuss in §9.5 that the court in a civil case has the power in some circumstances to direct a verdict (or, in current federal parlance, to grant a "motion for judgment as a matter of law"), which means that the judge enters judgment, without allowing the jury any role. Obviously, given the importance of the right to jury trial, such a course is taken only when the evidence clearly does not justify sending the case to the jury.

[61] Traditionally, jury instructions have been read to the jury immediately before the jury retires to deliberate. In some rare situations, a court might give at least some jury instructions at the outset of the trial, to allow jurors to hear the evidence at trial against the background of the law.

[62] In most jurisdictions, there are books of "form jury instructions," from which counsel and the court may pick and choose. The use of such forms probably contributes to the stilted nature of jury instructions.

(or drones) on about the elements of a claim, such as negligence, the definition of proximate cause, the elements of defenses such as assumption of risk, and the like. In addition to stating the law, at least in federal practice, the judge may also comment on the evidence. This authority, which comes from the common law, has been abolished in many state courts. Though she can thus discuss the evidence, the federal judge should make it clear that the ultimate decision of what the facts *are* is for the jury. She must also be careful not to argue a particular point of view to the jury. Outside that, however, the federal judge certainly may "clear away false issues and lead the jury to a proper understanding of the facts."[63]

After the court instructs the jury, the jurors "retire from the bar" to deliberate the case. Jury deliberations are always conducted in utmost secrecy, in the privacy of the jury room. In large measure, how a jury works is one of the great unknowns in the law. The jury is instructed to select a foreperson, who can communicate with the judge if there is a problem or question during the deliberations, and who will be called upon to announce the jury's verdict. It is up to each jury to determine how to select its own foreperson. And how the jury proceeds from that point is up to the jurors. Sometimes the jury takes a "straw poll" at the outset, to see if there is much disagreement. There is no rule book for how the jury is to discharge its function.

One of the most important things on which the judge instructs the jury is the burden of persuasion. We discussed this burden, along with the burdens of pleading and proof, in §7.3.3. There we said that (as a general rule) the party that must plead a particular issue must also offer evidence on it and must also persuade the trier of fact that it is true. In civil cases, the burden of persuasion is to establish a fact "by a preponderance of the evidence." That means that the party with the burden must persuade the fact-finder that something is "more likely than not." The burden of persuasion is important as a tie-breaker.

For example, suppose the parties present evidence on the existence of Issue A. This issue could be anything — whether the parties entered a contract, whether the defendant owed the plaintiff a duty, whether a vehicle's brakes were defective. One party introduces evidence to show that A is true. The other party introduces evidence to show that A is not true. If the jury concludes that the issue is just as likely as not — that is, that neither scenario is more likely than the other — the evidence is said to be in "equipoise." In that instance, the party with the burden of persuading the fact-finder on Issue A will lose. If the burden was on the plaintiff, she will lose for failing to persuade the jury that A was true. If the burden was on the defendant, she will lose for failing to persuade the jury that A was *not* true. In assessing the facts, the jury determines how much weight to ascribe to

---

[63] Wright & Kane, Federal Courts 676.

various pieces of evidence and whether various witnesses are credible. The jury, in essence, has this chart in mind, by which it weighs the evidence:

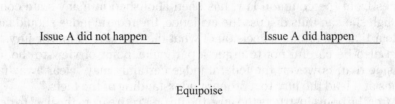

Some cases involve a greater burden of persuasion. In criminal cases, the government must prove the defendant's guilt "beyond a reasonable doubt." Obviously, if the government simply showed that the defendant's guilt was more likely than not (but not that it was true beyond a reasonable doubt), the prosecution will fail. In civil cases, there can occasionally be an intermediate standard for the burden of persuasion. For example, plaintiffs often are required to prove a right to punitive damages by "clear and convincing" evidence. This is a greater showing than "preponderance of the evidence," but less than "beyond a reasonable doubt."

The Jury's Decision: The Verdict

The jury's decision is the *verdict*. The court's decision is the *judgment*. The form of the verdict is usually quite simple. In most cases, the jury is asked to return a "general verdict," which simply says which party won and, if the plaintiff won, what the recovery will be. There are other verdict forms, however, that a court might employ in its discretion. One is the "special verdict," found in Federal Rule 49(a). With this procedure, the jury does not return a general verdict, but responds in writing to a series of questions posed by the judge. Usually, there is one question for each issue of fact presented in the trial. The questions are submitted when the jury commences its deliberations. Obviously, there is a risk that the jury might reach inconsistent positions. It might answer the question "did the defendant owe the plaintiff a duty?" negatively, and then answer the question "did the defendant breach the duty owed to the plaintiff?" affirmatively. Even when such problems do not arise, some commentators criticize the use of the special verdict because it makes the process of fact-finding too precise and scientific, robbing it of the sense of the common person as the general decisionmaker.[64]

---

[64] *See, e.g., id.* at 678-679.

A middle course for verdict forms is provided by Rule 49(b), which has the jury return a general verdict *and* answer specific questions.[65] The questions relate to disputed facts on which the verdict will depend. This avenue may focus the jury's attention on the important factual questions and thus permit jurors to ensure that its general verdict is proper.

Whatever the form of the verdict, Rule 48 provides, unless the parties stipulate to the contrary, that "the verdict must be unanimous." Generally, then, the jury is required to deliberate on and on until the members are unanimous in the verdict. This is not the case, of course, if the parties have stipulated, for example, that the decision of five jurors will constitute the verdict. If the jury is hopelessly deadlocked (which happens more in criminal than in civil cases), at some point the judge can declare a mistrial and order the case retried to a new jury.

In assessing damages, the jury is not limited by the demand for relief sought in the claimant's pleading, which we studied at §7.3.2. Rule 8(a)(3) requires a claimant to make a demand, but there is no requirement that the demand state a particular dollar figure. Some claimants, however, do make specific dollar demands. In federal court, these demands do not limit the amount of damages a jury may grant.[66] Neither does the demand for judgment limit the type of recovery that may be awarded by the court's judgment.

○ *P* sues *D*, and seeks $100,000 in damages, plus costs of litigation.[67] At trial, *P*'s evidence demonstrated that she had suffered damage of $150,000 and that *P* would be entitled to an injunction to stop *D* from acting in a particular way. The jury returns a verdict of $150,000 and the judge enters a judgment for that amount and imposes an injunction on *D*. The judgment is valid. Even though *P* only asked for damages (and only for $100,000), a greater recovery and recovery of a different form of relief is permitted.[68]

---

[65] The specific questions are referred to as "interrogatories" to the jury. These are not to be confused with the interrogatories under Rule 33, which are discovery tools sent by one party to another, discussed in §8.2.2.

[66] The only exception to this statement in federal court is the default judgment. As we discussed in §7.5.3, in a default case, the plaintiff cannot recover more than she demanded in her complaint. Moreover, in some states, the demand for judgment does limit the plaintiff's ultimate recovery even in cases that are tried. *See, e.g.,* Va. Code Ann. §8.01-421.

[67] We've noted before the general rule that the prevailing party recovers her costs from the losing party, and that costs do not include attorneys' fees.

[68] The court, not the jury, would determine the equitable relief applicable. See §9.2.2.

§9.3   Entry of Judgment and Award of Costs and (Maybe) Attorneys' Fees

The Judgment

While the jury's determination is embodied in the verdict, the court's determination is embodied in a judgment. Under Rule 54(a), a judgment constitutes "any order from which an appeal lies." We see in §14.4 that an appeal ordinarily lies from a "final judgment," which is the trial court's ultimate conclusion of the merits of the entire case.[69] Thus, the court's grant of a motion to dismiss for failure to state a claim — granted with leave to amend to attempt again to state a claim — will not constitute a judgment. Why? Because the order does not finally adjudicate the case; the plaintiff may replead her complaint.

No matter how a case is adjudicated — whether by jury trial, bench trial, motion for summary judgment, or otherwise, the final outcome will be embodied in a judgment. Thus, while not all cases will involve jury verdicts (because, for example, there is no right to a jury trial or a motion of JMOL has been granted), every case that is finally resolved in the trial court will result in a judgment. The judgment is a very short document, the operative language of which can often be contained in a single sentence. For example, it might say "judgment is entered for the plaintiff in the amount of $100,000, plus costs" or "judgment is entered for the defendant, plus costs." Indeed, Federal Rule 54(a) counsels that the document be kept short by saying that the judgment "should not include" extraneous things such as a recital of pleadings or the record of proceedings.

Rule 58(a) mandates that every judgment "must be set out in a separate document."[70] The clerk of the court generally prepares this document.[71] The purpose of the separate document requirement is to avoid uncertainty about whether an order or ruling is intended to be a judgment. If the court

---

[69] There are also situations, studied in §14.5, in which a nonfinal, or interlocutory, order can be appealed. The court's ruling on such an appealable order would also be embodied in a judgment under Rule 54(a).

[70] The rule also says that a separate document is not required for an order disposing of five specific motions, including orders granting or denying various post-trial motions, including those we see in §§9.5, 9.6, and 9.7. Note that Rule 54(b) permits a court to enter separate judgments for separate claims or regarding different parties in a single case. We discuss this Rule in conjunction with when a party may take an appeal in §14.4.3.

[71] Rule 58(b)(1) details the execution of the judgment by the clerk. In certain instances, such as the return of a general verdict, the clerk of the court prepares, signs, and enters the judgment without any order from the judge. In more complex cases, such as the jury's returning a special verdict, the judge must approve the form of the judgment under Rule 58(b)(2) before the clerk enters it. In exceptional cases, the court might ask counsel to submit a draft judgment for the court's consideration. *See, e.g.*, Gold v. United States, 552 F. Supp. 66, 72-73 (D. Colo. 1982) (because of counsel's familiarity with complex calculations in a tax case, the court asked counsel to draft judgment).

intends a judgment, it must say so in a separate document. In addition, the clerk of the court is required to note the judgment on the docket sheet promptly.[72]

Together, these two acts — rendition of the judgment on a separate document and its notation on the docket sheet — constitute "entry" of the judgment. This is a very important event, because it starts the clock for bringing post-judgment motions such as the motion for renewed JMOL, motion for new trial, and motion to set aside the judgment. In addition, as we see in Chapter 14, it starts the clock running for filing one's notice of appeal. None of these clocks starts to run, however, until the judgment is entered in accordance with the Rules.

The provisions regarding entry of judgment are extremely mechanical and are salutary for that reason. In federal court, because of these requirements, there can be no doubt when a judgment is entered and when the periods for seeking post-judgment relief or for appeal start to run.

- ○ After a verdict, the clerk drafts the judgment and stamps it "filed." The judgment has not been entered. Not until the clerk makes the notation of judgment on the docket sheet for the case has the judgment been entered.
- ○ After a verdict, the clerk marks judgment on the docket sheet, but fails to draft a separate document embodying the judgment. The judgment has not been entered. Both rendition of judgment on a separate document and entry on the docket sheet are required to enter the judgment.

Award of Costs and (Maybe) Attorneys' Fees

In §1.1, we noted that each party in litigation pays her own costs and attorneys' fees as the case progresses. We also saw the important difference between costs and attorneys' fees. Once judgment is entered — once there is a prevailing party — the prevailing party will seek to "shift" her costs (and maybe her attorneys' fees) to the other party. Under the "American Rule," embodied in Rule 54(d), the winner generally is entitled to recover her *costs* from the loser.[73] The general rule, though, is that she is not entitled to recover her *attorneys' fees* from the other side. Only if some

---

[72] In every case, Rule 79(a) requires the clerk's office to maintain a "civil docket" on which it marks various events briefly and in chronological order. Thus, the docket sheet will indicate the dates on which the complaint was filed, when process was served, when the defendant appeared, the filing and results of motions, etc. One thing the clerk's office must record, as a ministerial duty, is the entry of judgment.

[73] There are a couple of exceptions to this. First, under Rule 68, a defendant may offer to allow judgment to be entered against her on stated terms. If the plaintiff rejects the offer and fails ultimately to recover a more favorable judgment, the plaintiff may be required to pay the defendant's costs incurred after the offer was made. Second, as we saw in §4.5.3, the plaintiff in a diversity of citizenship case who recovers less than $75,000 may be required to pay the defendant's costs.

exception applies (some of which we observed in §1.1), will the law permit the shifting of attorneys' fees.

Under Rule 58(e), ordinarily, a motion for "taxation" (which just means "recovery") of costs or the award of attorneys' fees will not delay the entry of judgment in the case. We see in §14.4 that a losing party has 30 days from entry of judgment in which to file a notice of appeal. That 30 days runs from entry of the judgment, and not 30 days from when the court rules on the motion for taxation of costs or attorneys' fees. (We discuss this at §14.4.2.)

An award of costs does not necessarily make the prevailing party whole for all out-of-pocket expenditures incurred in the litigation. The taxable costs are listed in §1920 of the Judicial Code, which imposes statutory caps on some allowances. Strangely, the expenses of paying a private process server to serve process on the defendant generally are not taxable, and thus cannot be recovered.[74]

Rule 54(d)(1) imposes no time limit for moving to tax costs. Many districts impose a limit by Local Rule. Without such a provision, the motion must simply be made within a reasonable time. The prevailing party's "bill of costs" must be verified — meaning that it must be executed under oath — either by the party, her agent, or her attorney. The clerk of the court has the initial responsibility for determining what costs will be recovered. The other party may then object to the clerk's taxation of costs, in which case the district judge reviews the matter de novo.

§9.4   No Need for Trial: Summary Judgment (Federal Rule 56)

Background and Standard

In §9.2.1, we noted that adjudication consists of determination of the facts and application of the law to those facts. We also said that the only reason to have a trial is to resolve genuine disputes of material fact. So if the court determines before trial that there is no genuine dispute as to any material fact, it may enter judgment as a matter of law, without a trial. The vehicle for adjudicating in this fashion is summary judgment, which, in federal practice, is governed by Rule 56. The summary judgment provisions in most states mirror Rule 56.

---

[74] *See* 10 Moore's Federal Practice §54.191. Moreover, the court has general equitable authority to limit or deny an award of taxable costs to the prevailing party, though such denial is rare outside the circumstances discussed in the preceding footnote. *Id.* at 54.101[1][b].

Do not confuse a motion for summary judgment with a motion to dismiss for failure to state a claim under Rule 12(b)(6). The latter motion, as we discussed in §7.3.2, is aimed at the claimant's[75] *allegations*. It is a device to test whether the plaintiff alleged enough to get past the pleading stage and to have the case remain in the litigation stream. It is not concerned with what actually happened in the real world and, accordingly, the court addressing a Rule 12(b)(6) motion does not look beyond the face of the pleadings. In entertaining a Rule 12(b)(6) motion, the court assumes that the plaintiff's allegations are true and inquires whether the allegations state a claim that the law recognizes. It does not look at evidence that might be admitted at trial.

With summary judgment, the plaintiff has stated a claim. The case is in the litigation stream. Perhaps the parties have gone through pleadings and motions and discovery. At some point, however, one of the parties asserts that there is no need for a trial. Why? The standard for granting the motion is buried in the third sentence of Rule 56(c): "there is no genuine issue as to any material fact and . . . the movant is entitled to a judgment as a matter of law." The first phrase in that quote is the most important, because it indicates *why* there is no need for a trial. If there is no "genuine issue as to any material fact," no dispute of fact needs to be resolved at trial. If that is true, the second part of the quote generally will follow — if there is no dispute on a material issue of fact, the court can enter judgment as a matter of law. There being no dispute of fact, all that remains is a question of law, which the judge may decide without trial.

Importantly, in ruling on a motion for summary judgment, the court may go beyond the pleadings and consider *evidence*. That is, it may view sworn statements that might be proffered if a trial were held. This fact drives home the thrust of summary judgment — the motion can "pierce" the pleadings and look to what actually happened in the real world. Though the parties alleged various disputes in their pleadings, now — looking at evidence proffered by the parties — it turns out there is no real-world dispute as to what happened. Thus, the court may conclude, no trial is needed, it can rule as a matter of law, and summary judgment is appropriate.

Though the court may view evidence in ruling on summary judgment, the motion is not a vehicle for the court to try the facts. Instead, it is a vehicle by which the court may determine whether there is a dispute as to the material facts. Whenever the papers proffered in a summary judgment motion show that there *is* a genuine dispute on a material issue of fact, summary judgment must be denied, and the matter must go to trial.

Any party may move for summary judgment. So, for instance, a claimant may seek summary judgment on her claim or a defendant may seek it

---

[75] A claimant is anyone asserting a claim. In every case, of course, the plaintiff is a claimant. But other parties may be claimants, as when the defendant asserts a counterclaim against the plaintiff. For simplicity, we refer to the claimant here as the plaintiff.

on an affirmative defense. Moreover, the moving party need not seek summary judgment on the entire case. Rule 56(d)(1) makes it clear that the court can determine specific *issues* in the case on summary judgment. The case can then proceed to trial on the contested issues of material fact, with the jury instructed that the undisputed facts are taken as established.[76]

- ○ Plaintiff sues Defendant on a claim that has four elements: *A, B, C,* and *D.* Though Defendant's answer denied Plaintiff's allegations on all four issues, as the litigation proceeded it became clear (perhaps in discovery) that there is actually no dispute that *A* is true. Plaintiff's motion for partial summary judgment — to establish that *A* is true — can be granted. If it is, the case will then proceed to trial to determine whether *B, C,* and *D* are true (as well as any affirmative defense asserted by Defendant). If that case is tried to a jury, the judge will instruct the jury that *A* is true and that Plaintiff will prevail if she establishes *B, C,* and *D.*

Materials Used in Summary Judgment

How does the court determine whether there is no "genuine issue of material fact"? The third sentence of Rule 56(c) provides that in ruling on the motion the court may consider: (1) pleadings, (2) discovery, (3) disclosure materials on file, and (4) affidavits.

Though Rule 56(c) does not *require* the use of affidavits, they are commonly used in summary judgment motions. An affidavit is a written statement executed under oath, meaning under penalty of perjury. In addition, the first sentence of Rule 56(e)(1) requires that affidavits be (1) based on personal knowledge, (2) "set out facts that would be admissible in evidence," and (3) demonstrate that the affiant "is competent to testify on the matters stated." These requirements reflect an important point — in ruling on summary judgment, the court may go beyond the pleadings and look at evidence. The requirements of Rule 56(e)(1) are aimed at ensuring that affidavits contain the sort of information — under oath, based upon personal knowledge — that might be admitted at trial.[77]

---

[76] Everyone calls this *partial summary judgment,* but the name is a bit misleading. As we saw in §9.3, the word "judgment" should be used only to refer to an appealable order — that is, one that disposes of the entire case, not just part of it.

[77] In fact, affidavits themselves might not be admissible at trial, because they constitute hearsay if they would be used to establish the truth of what they assert. The concepts of admissibility and hearsay are beyond our scope. Just realize that Rule 56 allows the court to address evidence proffered in affidavits that satisfy Rule 56(e) in assessing what the parties or their witnesses will be able to say at trial (if there is one). This is relevant in ruling on the motion for summary judgment. Professor Duane has written extensively about the relationship between Rule 56 and the rules of evidence. One especially helpful article is James Duane, *The Four Greatest Myths About Summary Judgment,* 52 Wash. & Lee L. Rev. 1523, 1523-1533 (1996).

The parties' lawyers usually draft the affidavits of their party and witnesses who support their party. The affidavits can be targeted at specific issues, and be "tailor-made" to support (or oppose) a motion for summary judgment. The lawyer drafts the affidavits based upon discussions with the affiant, and must be careful to ensure that the affidavit reflects the affiant's true recollection. Because the affiant signs the affidavit under penalty of perjury, the lawyer must tell her of the seriousness of that fact. The second sentence of Rule 56(e)(1) permits affidavits to refer to documents, but requires that the document be attached or served with the affidavit.

Anytime the court considers documentary evidence, the document must be "authenticated," which means that the party proffering the document must provide admissible evidence from a person with firsthand knowledge sufficient to allow that person to have the document admitted into evidence. Otherwise, the documentary evidence cannot be considered.

- In a wrongful death case, Plaintiff had to prove that the company leasing a helicopter to her husband was responsible for placing the fuel in the copter. She moved for summary judgment based upon fuel invoices showing that the company had purchased the fuel. Because the invoices were unauthenticated, however, they could not be used, and summary judgment was denied.[78]

The court may look at "discovery and disclosure materials on file." Discovery, of course, includes depositions and answers to interrogatories. These documents, like affidavits, are executed under penalty of perjury and may be considered in ruling on a motion for summary judgment. (See §8.2.2.) To be used in summary judgment, deposition testimony and interrogatory answers must satisfy the requirements listed above for affidavits — they must be based upon personal knowledge, set forth admissible facts, and demonstrate that the person making the statement is competent to testify to the issues.[79]

Note also that the list of materials available in Rule 56(c) includes documents that do not necessarily constitute evidence. Specifically, it allows the court to look at "pleadings." Pleadings, as we know from §7.3.1, usually are not executed under oath. Thus, they cannot be considered evidence. In extremely rare situations, parties may file "verified pleadings,"

---

[78] Canada v. Blain's Helicopters, Inc., 831 F.2d 920, 925 (9th Cir. 1987). *See also* Hoffman v. Applicators Sales & Services, Inc., 439 F.3d 9 (1st Cir. 2006) (chart purporting to show number of employees and their ages could not be considered because it was based on data that was not authenticated).

[79] *See, e.g.,* Hoover v. Switlik Parachute Co., 663 F.2d 964, 965-967 (9th Cir. 1981) (deposition). *See generally* 11 Moore's Federal Practice §56.14[2][a] & [b].

which are executed under penalty of perjury.[80] If they satisfy the requirements of the first sentence of Rule 56(e)(1), such pleadings are considered the functional equivalent of affidavits. But nonverified pleading may
also be relevant on summary judgment — not because they constitute evidence, but because they contain an admission.

○ Plaintiff sues Defendant, and alleges the requisite elements of a claim: *A*,
  B, *C*, and *D*. In her answer, Defendant denies the allegations of *A*, *B*, and
  D, but fails to deny *C*. On the face of the pleadings, then, the court is
  justified in concluding that there is no dispute as to issue *C*. Defendant
  failed to deny it, and thus can be taken as having admitted it. (We discussed this in §7.4.2.) The court might enter partial summary judgment
  on that issue, because there is no genuine dispute as to that factual issue.

Similarly, the court may consider admissions under Rule 36 (which we
saw in §8.2.2) or admissions made at any point during the case, as in the
pleadings, in open court, in stipulations of the parties, or even in correspondence with the court.[81] The court may take those matters as admitted and, thus, not subject to genuine dispute. If such admissions permit
the court to rule as a matter of law, it may enter summary judgment.

○ Government brought a civil action against Taxpayer to establish liability
  for taxes, based upon an allegation that Taxpayer fraudulently transferred
  property to another in a sham effort to evade tax. Government sent
  requests to admit to Taxpayer, asserting that Taxpayer's conveyance of
  property was a sham, intended as tax evasion. Taxpayer failed to deny
  the request to admit. On the Government's motion for summary judgment,
  the "fact" that Taxpayer made a fraudulent conveyance to evade tax liability is established.

Rule 43(c) provides that when a motion relies on facts not in the record,
the court may hear the evidence by live testimony. Despite this provision,
it is extremely rare for a court to permit such testimony in considering a
motion for summary judgment.[82] The very purpose of summary judgment
is to *avoid* a trial; having live witness testimony would essentially turn the
hearing on the motion into at least a minitrial.

Rule 56(e)(2) is important, but should also be obvious. It says that when
a motion for summary judgment is made and supported with evidence,
"an opposing party may not rely merely on allegations or denials in its own

---

[80] In federal court, under Rule 23.1, a complaint in a shareholder derivative suit (defined
in §13.1) must be verified.

[81] *See* 11 Moore's Federal Practice §56.14[2][d][iii].

[82] *See, e.g.,* Seamons v. Snow, 206 F.3d 1021, 1025 (10th Cir. 2000) (oral testimony should
rarely be used in motion for summary judgment).

pleading." Rather, she must set forth facts, by affidavit or otherwise, showing a genuine dispute on a material issue of fact. This sentence means that one cannot oppose a summary judgment motion based upon evidence by merely relying on her pleadings. If she could, Rule 56 would have no efficacy.

∘ Plaintiff sues Defendant on a promissory note, alleging that Defendant borrowed $100,000, which he agreed to repay with interest by a particular date. Plaintiff alleged that the date has come and gone, and Defendant has failed to pay. Defendant files an unverified answer in which she alleges that she never signed the note. Plaintiff moves for summary judgment, based upon affidavits of two witnesses who aver under oath that they saw Defendant sign the agreement. Defendant opposes the motion by relying on her answer, in which she denied signing the note.

The court should grant summary judgment for Plaintiff here. In ruling on the motion, the court looks to the admissible evidence proffered by the parties — in the form, for example, of affidavits, deposition testimony, answers to interrogatories — in addition to admissions (including any admissions from the pleadings). The judge then asks herself this question: Based upon these things, is there a *genuine* dispute as to a *material* issue of fact? If the answer is no, there is no need for a trial, the court may apply the law to the established facts and enter summary judgment. And that is the case here. The only evidence proffered to the court is the affidavits in favor of Plaintiff's position. Defendant has attempted to rely on her unverified pleading to rebut evidence. To allow her to do so would be contrary to Rule 56(e)(2) and, more important, contravene the very purpose of summary judgment. If Defendant wants to oppose the motion, she should proffer evidence showing that she did not sign the agreement (or, perhaps, that she did, but under duress). If Defendant proffered such evidence, the motion for summary judgment would be denied.

Of course, if the party moving for summary judgment fails to demonstrate that there is no genuine issue of material fact and that she is entitled to judgment as a matter of law, she should lose. This is true even if the opposing party presented nothing.[83] The party opposing summary judgment need respond only if the moving party has satisfied the standard set forth in the third sentence of Rule 56(c).

---

[83] A famous example is *Adickes v. S.H. Kress & Co.*, 398 U.S. 144 (1970), in which a white woman sued a store for alleged violation of her civil rights. She alleged that the store refused to serve her because she was in the company of black people. One issue in the case was whether the store employees operated in agreement with the police officer who was present at the time plaintiff was refused service. (Such involvement of a state officer was required for the claim.) The defendant moved for summary judgment based upon the affidavit of its store manager that he had not communicated with the police officer. Plaintiff presented in response no evidence that would satisfy Rule 56(e)(2). Nonetheless, the

What Constitutes a "Genuine" Dispute as to a "Material" Fact?

Summary judgment is not defeated by a mere dispute as to some facts. Rather, the dispute must be "genuine" and must concern a "material" fact. Materiality is determined by the substantive law creating the claim or defense. A material fact is one that might affect the outcome of the case under the governing law. Thus, "[f]actual disputes that are irrelevant or unnecessary will not be counted."[84] What constitutes a material fact is often obvious. In the hypothetical in the preceding paragraph, the fact of whether Defendant signed the promissory note was obviously material.

What constitutes a "genuine" dispute on such a material fact? The Supreme Court addressed this issue in *Anderson v. Liberty Lobby*,[85] which is one of three cases decided the same day in 1986. In the aggregate, these three cases sent an unequivocal message to the lower federal courts: Loosen up and grant summary judgment more readily. Obviously, the message was not a license to ignore the requirements of Rule 56. But the Court clearly was saying that lower courts should not invent reasons *not* to grant summary judgment. With these three cases, "summary judgment went from being seen as a motion reluctantly granted only in rare cases to being viewed as a fulcrum for adjudicating the heavy caseload facing federal courts."[86]

Among others, Professor Arthur Miller laments the movement toward more vigorous us of summary judgment. He asserts that largely unfounded assumptions about a "litigation explosion" and clichés about efficiency have been used to justify what he sees as a dangerous modern trend in favor of summary judgment and concomitant erosion of the right to trial.[87] His work may cause some rethinking about the thrust of the trilogy of summary judgment cases. It is likely that at least one of the trilogy cases is in your casebook. We review the three cases now. It is helpful to see each as a rejection of a lower court's raising a non–text-based barrier to summary judgment.

***The* Anderson *Case*.** *Anderson* is important for two reasons. First, it made clear that the summary judgment inquiry is functionally similar to that made in ruling on a motion for directed verdict (which is now called

---

Supreme Court held, the defendants' motion for summary judgment had to be denied. The defendant failed to present evidence foreclosing the possibility that the police officer and some store employee had reached an agreement that plaintiff not be served.

[84] Anderson v. Liberty Lobby, 477 U.S. 242, 248 (1986).

[85] 477 U.S. 242 (1986).

[86] 11 Moore's Federal Practice §56-26.

[87] Arthur Miller, *The Pretrial Rush to Judgment: Are the "Litigation Explosion," "Liability Crisis," and Efficiency Cliches Eroding Our Day in Court and Jury Trial Commitments?*, 78 N.Y.U. L. Rev. 982 (2003) [hereinafter *Pretrial Rush to Judgment*].

a motion for judgment as a matter of law, or JMOL, which we address in §9.5). Second, it clarified the standard for considering evidence from the nonmoving party to create a "genuine" issue of material fact and thus to defeat a motion for summary judgment. *Anderson* is a difficult case because it involves defamation law, with which you may not yet be familiar.

The Court established in 1964 that a "public figure" can sue for defamation only if she can show that the defendant acted with "actual malice," which means that she acted with knowledge that the defamatory statement was false or with reckless disregard for whether it was false.[88] In addition, the plaintiff must establish such malice by "clear and convincing evidence." In *Anderson*, public figures sued for defamation over articles that characterized them as racist, anti-Semitic, and neo-Nazi. The defendants moved for summary judgment based largely upon an affidavit by the author of some of the allegedly defamatory articles. The affidavit stated that the author had researched the articles exhaustively, and that he believed the statements made about the plaintiffs to be true. The plaintiffs opposed the motion for summary judgment by asserting that the defendants had failed to verify their information and that an editor of the magazine in which the articles were published characterized them as "ridiculous."

The Court addressed whether this opposition by the plaintiffs had created a "genuine" dispute on a material issue of fact. Some courts had held that summary judgment should be denied if the nonmoving party (the plaintiffs in *Anderson*) produced even a "scintilla" of evidence in support of her position. In *Anderson*, the Court clearly rejected this approach and held that the nonmoving party must produce sufficient evidence from which a reasonable jury could find in favor of the nonmoving party. Moreover, importantly, the "clear and convincing" requirement is relevant in determining whether the plaintiff could avoid summary judgment. In other words, the plaintiff was required to produce sufficient evidence in opposition to the summary judgment motion from which a reasonable jury could conclude that the plaintiff showed actual malice by clear and convincing evidence. Because the lower courts did not apply this standard, the Court remanded for reconsideration of the motion for summary judgment.

The Celotex Case. The second of the three cases decided in 1986 is *Celotex Corp. v. Catrett*,[89] which involved a wrongful death claim brought against several manufacturers of asbestos. One defendant moved for summary judgment not by producing evidence but by pointing out that the plaintiff lacked evidence showing that the decedent had been exposed to asbestos that it (as opposed to other manufacturers) had manufactured. The moving party used its motion to establish that the plaintiff's responses to interrogatories and other discovery failed to reveal any evidence that

---

[88] New York Times v. Sullivan, 376 U.S. 254, 279-280 (1964).
[89] 477 U.S. 317 (1986).

the decedent had been exposed to its products. The district court granted the motion, but the court of appeals reversed. According to the appellate court, an earlier Supreme Court case, *Adickes v. S.H. Kress & Co.*,[90] required a party making a motion for summary judgment to support its motion with *evidence*.

The Supreme Court reversed and concluded that nothing in *Adickes* supported the court of appeals' reasoning. Thus, after *Celotex*, it is clear that a party who does not have the burden of proof at trial may move for summary judgment without producing evidence. Such a party may simply point out that the record is devoid of evidence supporting the other party's position. Once the moving party makes such a showing, the burden shifts to the party with the burden at trial to produce evidence supporting its position. Obviously, *Celotex* is especially helpful to defendants, and allows them to move for summary judgment on the basis of an absence of record evidence supporting an element of the plaintiff's claim. By doing so, the defendant can force the plaintiff to "put her cards on the table" and produce evidence supporting that aspect of her claim. Though finding "mixed signals" in the opinion, Professor Miller concludes that it is "not surprising that *Celotex* has been read as an instruction to the lower courts to increase the disposition of cases under Rule 56 either to protect defendants or to achieve systemic efficiency."[91]

The **Matsushita** *Case.* The third of the 1986 cases was *Matsushita Electric Industrial Co. v. Zenith Radio Corp.*,[92] which was a complex antitrust case. Speaking quite generally, antitrust law concerns anticompetitive business behavior. In *Matsushita*, U.S. manufacturers of televisions sued several Japanese manufacturers, and alleged that the Japanese companies had conspired to keep prices of their products sold in the United States artificially low. Such "predatory pricing" could support a claim for violation of the antitrust laws of the United States.

The Supreme Court upheld the defendants' motion for summary judgment. It noted that the plaintiffs' theory of predatory pricing was "implausible" because it would have required the defendants to endure many years of losses to drive the U.S. manufacturers out of business. Because their theory was implausible, the Court held, the plaintiffs were required to come forward with more persuasive evidence than would otherwise be required to defeat summary judgment. Courts routinely say that the party opposing the motion for summary judgment is to receive the benefit of all reasonable doubts as to whether there is a genuine issue of fact.[93] But the

---

[90] 398 U.S. 144, 159 (1970).

[91] Arthur Miller, *Pretrial Rush to Judgment*, note 87 above, at 1133.

[92] 477 U.S. 574 (1986).

[93] *See generally* Wright & Kane, Federal Courts 712.

doubts must be reasonable, and courts should "not slip into sheer speculation"[94] when assessing the nonmoving party's position. *Matsushita* indicates that the courts will insist on especially strong evidence when the nonmoving party is the plaintiff and has espoused an implausible theory of liability.

Inspired by *Matsushita*, the defendant in a later case, *Kodak Co. v. Image Technical Services, Inc.*,[95] moved for summary judgment in an antitrust case by arguing that the plaintiff's theory was economically implausible. The Supreme Court rejected the effort because it found the plaintiff's theory plausible. Because a reasonable jury might accept the plaintiff's theory of antitrust violation, *Matsushita* did not apply. It is difficult to know whether *Kodak* speaks more to summary judgment law or to antitrust law. At the very least, however, *Matsushita* demonstrates two things. First, it is worth noting that summary judgment can be appropriate in large complex litigation. Second, a court may properly assess plausibility of a theory in determining how much evidence a nonmoving party must produce to defeat a motion for summary judgment.

Credibility Issues and the Court's Discretion

Even if the standard for summary judgment is met, the court is not *required* to grant a motion for summary judgment. It has discretion to conclude that it would be more appropriate to go to trial rather than to grant the motion.[96] Of course, the 1986 Supreme Court decisions discussed above counsel that the court should not invent reasons not to grant summary judgment. But it is completely legitimate to resolve reasonable doubts against entering summary judgment. One source of doubt may be the credibility of a person giving evidence. Answers to interrogatories and affidavits can be crafted with care, with the assistance of counsel, and are given without cross-examination. Deposition testimony, on the other hand, is given "live" and lawyers for each party are entitled to ask questions. These characteristics may make courts less nervous about accepting deposition testimony at face value.

This does not mean that affidavits and answers to interrogatories cannot be taken at face value. It is simply to raise the possibility that true doubts about credibility may make summary judgment inappropriate. The 1963 advisory committee notes to Rule 56(e) specifically warn that "[w]here an issue as to a material fact cannot be resolved without observation of the demeanor of witnesses in order to evaluate their credibility, summary judgment is not appropriate." On the other hand, this cannot

---

[94] Gibson v. Old Town Trolley Tours, 160 F.3d 177, 181 (4th Cir. 1998).
[95] 504 U.S. 451 (1992).
[96] *See, e.g.*, Lind v. United Parcel Serv., Inc., 254 F.3d 1281 (1st Cir. 2001) (despite lack of dispute as to material fact, court may conclude the case should be tried).

mean that the party opposing summary judgment should be able to defeat the motion simply by saying, in essence "the affiant has motivation to lie." Instead, courts generally look for specific facts from which a legitimate question is raised concerning credibility.[97]

A good example is *Thomas v. Great Atlantic & Pacific Tea Co.*,[98] in which the plaintiff, representing a pedestrian killed when hit by a motor vehicle, sued a supermarket under a dram shop theory. The plaintiff alleged that the supermarket had sold beer to the driver of the vehicle, in violation of dram shop provisions because the driver was visibly intoxicated. The supermarket moved for summary judgment, supported in part by the affidavit of the driver of the vehicle, in which she stated that she had not consumed the beer she bought at the supermarket before hitting the pedestrian. The court denied summary judgment, noting that the affiant's credibility could be questioned because any contrary statement in the affidavit would have harmed her position in her pending criminal case.

Other circumstances may counsel a court to deny summary judgment in a given case. For example, though circumstantial evidence is admissible and can provide the basis for a judgment, a court might conclude that plenary trial should be held. Moreover, even though Rule 56 applies to all cases, as a practical matter, summary judgment seems more likely in certain types of litigation than others. There is a widespread sense that summary judgment is more often applied in cases on debts and notes than in negligence cases. Indeed, "particular deference has been accorded the jury in [negligence] cases in light of its supposedly unique competence in applying the reasonable person standard to a given fact situation."[99] In addition, some courts seem reluctant to enter summary judgment in cases involving matters of subjective intent (though *Anderson* may be read as rejecting any blanket rule against summary judgment in such cases).

When Summary Judgment Must Be Denied

The court has no discretion — and must deny summary judgment — if the admissible evidence shows a genuine dispute as to a material issue of fact. As an easy example, suppose one party produced admissible evidence showing that the traffic light was green at the time of the accident, and the other party produced admissible evidence that the traffic light was red. The court *must* deny a motion for summary judgment for the simple reason that here, admissible evidence creates a genuine dispute as to a material issue of fact: the color of the light at the time of the accident. That is precisely the situation in which we need a trial — to resolve a dispute of fact.

[97] *See* 10A Wright & Miller 446 ("specific bases for possible impeachment").
[98] 233 F.3d 326 (5th Cir. 2000).
[99] 10A Wright & Miller 533.

The court should not *decide* credibility — that is, who is lying and who is telling the truth — on a motion for summary judgment. Put another way, credibility of the affiants is a genuine question of fact.[100] The question of which affiant is telling the truth — the one who said the light was red or the one who said it was green — cannot be judged without the fact-finder's seeing the two testify at trial. Similarly, the court should not grant summary judgment simply because the moving party produces more affidavits than the opposing party. So if the party claiming the light was green had five affidavits to that effect and the party claiming it was red had one, summary judgment would still be denied. The evidence showed a genuine dispute on a material issue of fact, making summary judgment improper. Remember that the denial of a motion for summary judgment does not result in victory for the nonmoving party. It simply results in having the dispute go to trial for resolution.

Timing of the Motion

Though in rare cases a court may enter summary judgment on its own motion, ordinarily a party will make a motion for summary judgment. Under Rule 56(a), a claimant may not move until at least 20 days after filing of the case (unless the defendant moves for summary judgment in the interim). This window allows the defending party to respond to the complaint. Rule 56(b) provides that a defending party may move anytime. These provisions are not usually important, because summary judgment normally becomes an option later, after the parties have engaged in discovery and the lack of a genuine dispute on a material fact has become obvious. Rule 56(c) provides that a motion for summary judgment must be served no fewer than ten days before the time set for the hearing on the motion. It allows the opposing party to serve affidavits "before the hearing day." The court has great discretion in setting the timing for hearings and responses to motions for summary judgment and will usually be quite generous with time limits. For example, when appropriate, it may allow the responding party time to conduct discovery on issues subject to the motion.

The motion will include a brief, arguing to the court why summary judgment is appropriate, supported by affidavits and other documents used to support the motion. The opposing party will also file a brief and should also append affidavits and other documents in opposition to the motion. It is incumbent on the parties to put the relevant evidence and other documents in the judge's hands with the motion papers. As one court explained:

[100] This statement is not inconsistent with our discussion immediately preceding. There, we said that a court might deny summary judgment if it has reason to question the credibility of an affiant. Here we are saying that the court should not grant summary judgment based upon its conclusion that one set of affiants is more believable than another.

"District judges are not archaeologists. They need not excavate masses of papers in search of revealing tidbits — not only because the rules of procedure place the burden on the litigants, but also because their time is scarce."[101]

§9.5   Motion for Judgment as a Matter of Law (and the "Renewed" Motion) (Federal Rules 50(a) and 50(b))

Background and Comparison to Motion for Summary Judgment

We saw in the preceding section that a grant of summary judgment averts trial altogether. We also saw that summary judgment is appropriate only when evidence and admissions proffered before trial show that there is no genuine dispute as to a material issue of fact. In such a case, no trial is required, and the court can rule as a matter of law.

In this section, we address motions that are functionally similar to the motion for summary judgment, but which are made at (or even after) trial. Here, the court did not enter summary judgment (perhaps because nobody moved for it), and the case went to jury trial. Now, *at trial*, and based upon evidence adduced at trial, the judge concludes that the jury should not be permitted to determine the facts — that the case should not "go to the jury." Why? Because there is insufficient evidence to justify having the jury consider it. Put another way, the evidence at trial shows, essentially, that there is no dispute on a material issue of fact — reasonable people could conclude only one way. That being the situation, there is no need to have the jury deliberate, and the court can simply enter judgment as a matter of law. Historically, this has been called a *directed verdict*, which is a very good name, because the judge indeed directs the outcome of the case, without jury involvement. Today, in the federal system, under Rule 50(a)(1), it is called *judgment as a matter of law* (or, as abbreviated, JMOL).[102] Most state courts still refer to it by its classical name, directed verdict.

In fact, there is another motion that comes up even later. With this second motion, the judge has let the case go to the jury for deliberation, and the jury has reached a conclusion that reasonable people simply could

---

[101] Postscript Enterprises v. City of Bridgeton, 905 F.2d 223, 226-227 (8th Cir. 1990).

[102] Rule 50(a) was amended in 1991 to change the name from directed verdict to JMOL. It was a silly amendment, which simply ensured that the terminology for this motion would differ in federal and state courts. Many lawyers and judges still routinely use the older terminology.

not have reached. Here, the court may be able to take the victory away from the winner (as chosen by the jury) and enter judgment for the other party! Historically, this has been called judgment notwithstanding the verdict, or JNOV, which is an abbreviation of the Latin words for that phrase (judgment *non obstante veredicto*). This is also a very good name, because the court is doing exactly that — entering judgment for one side notwithstanding the verdict for the other side. But today, in the federal system, under Rule 50(b), this is called the *renewed motion for judgment as a matter of law* (or RJMOL).[103] Here too, generally, state courts use the older terminology.

These devices — JMOL and RJMOL — seem disrespectful of the jury. In one, the judge refuses to let the jury play a role. In the other, the judge ignores what the jury has done and enters judgment for the other party. Why are these procedures not unconstitutional encroachments on the Seventh Amendment right to jury trial? The answer is that there is no absolute right to a jury trial — even under the Seventh Amendment — in a civil case in federal court. The situation is different for criminal law. In a criminal case, the defendant has an absolute right to have her case go to the jury. Even if she has no defense and even if the evidence of guilt is overwhelming and unassailable, the criminal defendant can force the prosecution to put on evidence and to persuade the jury of her guilt beyond a reasonable doubt.

Moreover, the jury in a criminal case has a right to acquit the criminal defendant even when the evidence of guilt is undoubted. This is called *jury nullification* — the jury, as the conscience of the community, can allow a "guilty" defendant to walk away. Jurors might acquit someone who is clearly guilty because they feel the government acted wrongly or because they think the law is senseless, or for any reason at all. The jury does not have to justify its decision, and the prosecution cannot appeal a verdict of not guilty.

Civil cases are different. In civil cases, the judge has always played a gatekeeping function. The jury will be allowed to deliberate only if there is sufficient evidence to warrant the submission of the case to it. The judge makes this determination in ruling on a motion for JMOL. The standard, as stated in Rule 50(a)(1), is that "a reasonable jury would not have a legally sufficient evidentiary basis to find for the party on that issue." When the court grants JMOL, it is saying, essentially, that there is no dispute as to a material issue of fact. When that is true, as in summary judgment, all that remains is a question of law as to who should prevail, which the court can decide. The difference from summary judgment, then, is largely timing. A motion for summary judgment is brought before trial (based mostly on evidence proffered by the parties); granting it obviates the need for trial.

---

[103] Again, many lawyers and judges in federal court still call this JNOV.

A motion for JMOL is brought at trial (based on trial evidence); granting it obviates the need to have the jury deliberate. The Supreme Court emphasized the similarity between the motions in *Anderson v. Liberty Lobby*, discussed above, in which it noted that "the inquiry under each is the same: whether the evidence presents a sufficient disagreement to require submission to a jury or whether it is so one-sided that one party must prevail as a matter of law."[104]

Timing of the Motion

Under Rule 50(a)(1), any party may move for JMOL, but only after the other party "has been fully heard on an issue in a jury trial." In determining whether this requirement was met, we must understand the order of trial in a civil case, which we addressed in §9.2.1. The plaintiff puts on her evidence and then rests. This point is the close of the plaintiff's case. At that point, the defendant may move for JMOL, because the plaintiff has been fully heard (she has presented her case-in-chief). The plaintiff may not move for JMOL at this point, because the defendant has not been heard yet (she has cross-examined the plaintiff's witnesses but has not yet presented her own evidence).

At common law, the defendant faced a difficult choice here: If she moved for JMOL, and the motion was denied, she waived the right to put on her evidence. That draconian rule is no longer followed. If the defendant's motion is denied, the case then proceeds to the next phase of trial: presentation of evidence by the defendant. After the defendant has presented her case, and the parties have presented any rebuttal evidence, the court will close all the evidence. At that point, both sides — plaintiff and defendant — may move for JMOL. Why? Because at that point, each side has been "fully heard."

Thus, the defendant might move for JMOL twice — typically, once at the close of the plaintiff's case and again at the close of all the evidence. Or she might simply move at the close of all the evidence. There is no requirement that she move at the close of the plaintiff's case. Generally, the plaintiff will move only at the close of all evidence, because it is usually at that point that the defendant has been fully heard. There is no

---

[104] 477 U.S. 242, 251-252 (1986). Professor Miller criticizes this equation of the motions as having permitted entry of summary judgment too readily. He notes that JMOL motions arise at trial and involve better developed evidence than motions for summary judgment, which are, of course, brought before trial and based largely upon untested evidence. "One would expect that some significant attention would have been devoted to adjusting the trial motion practice to the pretrial motion context. That does not appear to have happened, however; at least there is no evidence of it in judicial opinions." Arthur Miller, *Pretrial Rush to Judgment*, note 87 above, at 1062. Professor Mullenix has made similar arguments in advocating a more limited role for summary judgment. Linda Mullenix, *Summary Judgment: Taming the Beast of Burdens*, 10 Am. J. Trial Advoc. 433 (1987).

requirement that a party move for summary judgment before trial to preserve the right to move for JMOL at trial.

- ○ Plaintiff sues Defendant on a claim that has four elements. Thus, for Plaintiff to win, she must establish elements *A*, *B*, *C*, and *D*. She properly pleads the elements in her complaint, and Defendant properly denies them in his answer. Neither party moves for summary judgment. At trial, Plaintiff puts on her evidence and rests. Defendant believes that Plaintiff presented evidence on elements *A*, *B*, and *D*, but that Plaintiff presented no evidence on element *C*. Defendant should move for JMOL. On this state of the record, the court should agree that "a reasonable jury would not have a legally sufficient evidentiary basis to find for [Plaintiff] on that issue," and can grant Defendant's motion for JMOL. Defendant thus will win the case.

- ○ If Defendant failed to move for JMOL at the close of Plaintiff's case — or if her motion was denied — she is *not* estopped from moving again at the close of all the evidence. Again, if there is a "hole" in Plaintiff's evidence — if she failed to put on evidence of one of the elements of her claim — there is no need for the court to allow the jury to deliberate. On the state of the record, no reasonable jury could find for Plaintiff, and the court may enter judgment for Defendant as a matter of law.

Suppose, however, that the court let this case go to the jury. Some judges are reluctant to grant JMOL, because doing so robs the parties of any jury deliberation.[105] And if the facts are as we just indicated — with Plaintiff lacking evidence to support one of the elements of her claim — the odds are quite good that the jury will get it right and return a verdict for Defendant. But what if the jury returns a verdict for Plaintiff? Here, Defendant may be able to seek RJMOL, which, if granted, would do an extraordinary thing. It would take the victory away from Plaintiff and give it to Defendant. (Remember the historical name for this — Defendant would win "judgment notwithstanding the verdict.")

Granting RJMOL is a serious slap in the face to the jury. Worse than not letting the jury hear the case, RJMOL literally undoes what the jury concluded and enters judgment for the other side. What can justify this extraordinary action? The standard is the same as with JMOL — the court must conclude, based on the evidence at trial, that there was no "legally sufficient evidentiary basis to find for [the party who won the jury's verdict]." In other words, the jury reached a conclusion that reasonable people could

---

[105] For a candid assessment, *see* Konik v. Champlain Valley Physicians Hosp., 733 F.2d 1007, 1013 n.4 (2d Cir. 1984): It is preferable "to refrain from granting a motion for [JMOL] and instead allow the case to be decided — at least in the first instance — by the jury.... [I]f the jury reaches what the judge considers to be an irrational verdict, the judge may grant [RJMOL]. If this ruling is reversed on appeal, the jury's verdict may simply be reinstated. If, however, [the trial court granted JMOL], and that ruling is reversed on appeal, an entire new trial must be held."

not have reached. In the facts we've dealt with — where Plaintiff failed to introduce evidence on one of the elements of her claim — that standard clearly would be met. As with summary judgment, however, the fact that the standard for granting RJMOL is met does not compel the court to grant it. It might instead enter an order for the lesser remedy of a new trial, which we discuss in §9.6.

But there is an important prerequisite to moving for RJMOL. Part of the Seventh Amendment (known as the "reexamination clause") provides that federal courts may not reexamine facts determined by juries "otherwise . . . than according to the rules of the common law." The common law recognized RJMOL (then known as judgment notwithstanding the verdict), *but permitted it only if* the party seeking it had moved for JMOL (then called directed verdict) *at the close of all the evidence*.[106] In such a situation, the post-trial RJMOL could be seen as an extension of the JMOL motion made at trial and thus would not constitute an improper reexamination of the facts. If, on the other hand, the party moving for RJMOL after trial failed to move for JMOL at the close of all the evidence at trial, the RJMOL would constitute an improper reexamination of facts determined by the jury, and could not be granted. This requirement was carried forward in Rule 50(b), which long permitted RJMOL *only* when "the court does not grant a motion for judgment as a matter of law made at the close of all the evidence."[107]

But that changed on December 1, 2006, when Rule 50(b) was amended to require only that the party seeking RJMOL have moved for JMOL at trial. In other words, it is no longer required that a party move for JMOL *at the close of all evidence*. To preserve the right to seek RJMOL, now all that is required is that a party move for JMOL appropriately at trial.

- *P* puts on all of her evidence at trial and rests. *D* then moves for JMOL under Rule 50(a)(1). The court denies the motion. *D* then puts on her evidence at trial and rests. The evidence is then closed. The jury returns a verdict for *P*, and the court enters judgment for *P* on the basis of that verdict. Now *D* moves for RJMOL.
  - Under Rule 50(b), as it existed for generations, *D* had waived the right to make the RJMOL motion. Why? Because she failed to move for JMOL at the close of all evidence.

---

[106] Baltimore & Carolina Line v. Redman, 295 U.S. 654 (1935). In this case, the Court recognized that the common law permitted submission of a case to a jury subject to the court's reservation that it may later rule on legal questions raised in motion for directed verdict. Rule 50(b) does not require the court to make such an express reservation. It creates the inference that when a motion for JMOL is made and not rejected, the court submits the case to the jury subject to later determination of the motion.

[107] In addition, even if a party has properly preserved the right to make the motion for RJMOL, Rule 50(b) requires that she make the motion no later than ten days after entry of the judgment. We discussed entry of the judgment at §9.3.

- Today, however, Rule 50(b) permits D to make the RJMOL motion. The Rule requires only that the party bringing RJMOL have moved for JMOL at an appropriate time[108] at trial — not necessarily at the close of all the evidence. D did move for JMOL at an appropriate time at trial (after P had been fully heard), so she has preserved the right to bring the RJMOL motion.
- P puts on all of her evidence at trial and rests. D does not move for JMOL under Rule 50(a)(1). D then puts on her evidence at trial and rests. The evidence is then closed. Again, D fails to move for JMOL. The jury returns a verdict for P, and the court enters judgment for P on the basis of that verdict. Now D moves for RJMOL.
  - D is out of luck. By failing to seek JMOL at trial, she has waived the right to seek RJMOL. To preserve her RJMOL motion, a party must move for JMOL at an appropriate time at trial. Here, D never did.

As we have seen, RJMOL is strong medicine — it takes victory away from one party and gives victory to the other party. In contrast, the motion for new trial — which we see in §9.6 — is less radical. It results in taking victory away from one party but then in starting over with a new trial; so the same party might ultimately win. A party that waived the right to seek RJMOL (for example, as D did in the last hypothetical, by failing to move for JMOL at trial) might seek the lesser remedy of a new trial. And even a party who did preserve her right to seek RJMOL might move for a new trial in the alternative. Then, if the court denies RJMOL, she might still obtain the lesser relief of an order of new trial. We see these alternative motions in §9.6. (These alternative motions are popular on exams, because they allow the professor to test you on both RJMOL and new trial.)

Sufficiency of Evidence Required to Avoid JMOL

The examples we've seen so far have been fairly easy. In each, the plaintiff failed to produce evidence as to one of the elements of her claim. There is no doubt in such a case that the standard for JMOL (and RJMOL) would be satisfied because there is no dispute as to the facts and, as a matter of law, the defendant is entitled to judgment. Most JMOL motions involve subtler situations, and many (including most of those in Civil Procedure casebooks) raise the question of how much evidence the plaintiff must set forth to overcome a defense motion for JMOL and, thus, to get the case to the jury.

One older but helpful case is *Lavender v. Kurn*,[109] in which the plaintiff sued under the Federal Employers' Liability Act (FELA). That Act

---

[108] By "appropriate time," we simply mean that the party move, as Rule 50(a)(1) requires, after the other party has been "fully heard" at trial.

[109] 327 U.S. 645 (1946).

allows recovery for personal injuries to (and wrongful death of) employees of railroads (and others) engaged in interstate commerce, if the injuries result from negligence of the employer. The employee (or her representative) may sue in state or federal court.[110] In *Lavender*, a railroad employee (Mr. Haney) was killed by a blow to the back of the head while working as a switchman in the railroad terminal in Memphis. Haney worked for Illinois Central Railroad. When he was killed, he was throwing a switch to allow a train operated by the St. Louis-San Francisco (Frisco) Railroad to travel on a spur track to the station. There were no eyewitnesses, and no one knew what had struck Haney's head. The parties, of course, had different theories. Haney's personal representative sued both railroad lines, on alternative theories. As to Frisco, he asserted that the train had a mail hook that dangled from the train and, while negotiating a curve, swung out from the car and struck Haney. As to Illinois Central, the theory was that it had failed to provide Haney with a safe working environment; it was dark and he was permitted to work so close to the track that the mail hook could hit him. The railroads argued that they were not liable, because someone murdered Haney.

The suit, filed in state court in Missouri,[111] went to trial. The defendants moved for a directed verdict (now called JMOL in federal court). The trial court denied the motion and let the case go to the jury, which returned a $30,000 verdict against both defendants. The defendants moved for judgment notwithstanding the verdict (now called RJMOL in federal court). On appeal, the Missouri Supreme Court reversed, and held that the case should not have been submitted to the jury, because the plaintiff had failed to produce sufficient evidence to overcome the defendant's motion for directed verdict. The United States Supreme Court reversed; the plaintiff had produced sufficient evidence to get to the jury. Because the plaintiff won at trial, the Court noted that it was required to consider the facts in the light most favorable to him. The evidence showed that it was possible, given Haney's height and the height of the ground near where he was struck — and the height of the mail hook from the car and the distance it could swing out — that the mail hook hit Haney.

---

[110] Congressional policy on some aspects of procedure in such cases is so strong that a state court will have to follow the federal directive. We study this point (often called reverse *Erie*) in §10.8.

[111] Always review matters of forum selection. First, Missouri would undoubtedly have personal jurisdiction over two national railroads. Second, by statute, state courts have subject matter jurisdiction to hear FELA cases. Also by statute, the defendants cannot remove a FELA case to federal court. 28 U.S.C. §1445. Third, the vexing issue is venue. Haney was killed in Memphis. The suit was filed in St. Louis. Don't refer to 28 U.S.C. §1391, which we addressed in Chapter 3. That prescribes venue for civil cases in *federal* court. This case was brought in state court. We don't know what the Missouri venue rules are, but it is interesting that Haney's representative did not sue in Memphis, where Haney must have lived and where the railroads would also be subject to personal jurisdiction.

As to the defendants' theory that Haney was murdered, this was also possible. But the Court observed that Haney had not been robbed; his watch was on his body, and his wallet was later found nearby (with no cash, but Mrs. Haney testified that her husband never carried much cash). No one will ever know what or who killed Mr. Haney. The jury determined that it was the mail hook, and thus the negligence of the defendants. The question is whether there was sufficient evidence from which a jury could make that finding. If not, the jury engaged in mere speculation, and the judgment should not stand.

The Supreme Court concluded a jury verdict may be set aside on RJMOL "[o]nly when there is a complete absence of probative facts to support the conclusion reached. . . ."[112] Because there was evidence from which a reasonable jury could find that Haney was killed by the mail hook, the jury verdict should be respected. Some people have read *Lavender* as adopting a "scintilla" test — that is, that JMOL (and RJMOL) must be denied if the nonmoving party has produced a scintilla of evidence supporting her claim. The Court never used the word, but the language just quoted does seem to argue for such an approach. Remember, however, that the Supreme Court rejected the scintilla test in *Anderson v. Liberty Lobby*,[113] which we discussed in §9.4. *Anderson* was a summary judgment case, but the Court emphasized that summary judgment and JMOL should be decided by the same standard. If *Lavender* indeed embraced a scintilla test, it may be limited to FELA cases.[114]

From *Anderson*, we should conclude that one produces sufficient evidence to overcome a motion for JMOL if she shows enough that a reasonable jury could find for her.[115] Courts routinely refer to the need for "substantial evidence" from the nonmoving party.[116] This is said to mean "evidence of such quality and weight that reasonable and fair-minded jurors may reach different conclusions."[117] In other words, a court "should not be satisfied by evidence that establishes only the mere theoretical possibility that the nonmovant could prevail."[118] More recently, the Supreme Court held that, in ruling on the motion, the court should look to *all* evidence — that supporting the nonmoving party and unfavorable evidence as well.[119] Courts routinely say that they will make all "legitimate"

---

[112] 327 U.S. at 653.

[113] 477 U.S. 242 (1986).

[114] *See, e.g.*, Boeing Co. v. Shipman, 411 U.S. 365, 370-373 (1969).

[115] If her claim requires a showing of "clear and convincing" evidence (as opposed to the usual "preponderance of the evidence" test), which is rare, and which we discussed in §9.2.4 above, the burden is greater — she must produce evidence from which a reasonable jury could conclude that she has met that standard.

[116] *See, e.g.*, Konkel v. Bob Evans Farms, Inc., 165 F.3d 275, 279 (4th Cir. 1999).

[117] 9 Moore's Federal Practice at 50-91.

[118] *Id.* at 50-92.

[119] Reeves v. Sanderson Plumbing Prods., Inc., 530 U.S. 133 (2000).

inferences from that evidence in favor of the nonmoving party.[120] But what inferences are "legitimate" may be debated on the facts of each case.

Like it or not, there is no precise mathematical formula for ruling on such motions. We must recognize forthrightly that juries are required to speculate to a degree. The question — and the focus for the court — is whether the speculation would be so far fetched as to result in an unfair, unfounded verdict. Is there enough evidence in the record from which a reasonable juror could infer that the nonmoving party should win? Or is the evidence so lopsided that a reasonable jury could only come out one way? In the final analysis, much is in the eye of the beholder.

○ Plaintiff's prize bull got onto a train track, was hit by a train and killed. The train track and right-of-way is fenced, and Railroad is responsible for maintaining the fence. If the bull got onto the track through a hole in the fence, Railroad would be liable. If the bull got onto the track through a gate left open, Railroad is not liable. The bull was struck next to the gate, a mile from a point where there was a hole in the fence. After the plaintiff introduces this evidence, Railroad moves for JMOL. How should the court rule?

○ As in *Lavender*, nobody knows how the underlying events occurred. The question is whether the jury is left simply to speculate — which is not permissible — or whether there is sufficient evidence to allow the jury to determine how the bull got on the tracks. The federal courts routinely say that the evidence should be viewed in the light most favorable to the nonmoving party and that that party should be given the benefit of legitimate inferences from the facts.[121]

○ Here, it seems likely that the bull went through the gate. But a reasonable person could, it seems, conclude that the bull went through the hole in the fence and walked a mile before being hit.[122] Some courts would thus deny the motion for JMOL. On the other hand, it is certainly possible that some courts would find the hole-in-the-fence theory so implausible that they would grant the motion.

One important function of the jury is to assess credibility of witnesses at trial. If witness testimony produces enough evidence to get to the jury, the judge should not grant JMOL because she thinks the witness is not trustworthy. The questions of what witnesses are to be believed, and of

---

[120] *See* Wright & Kane, Federal Courts 687.

[121] *See, e.g.,* Simblest v. Maynard, 427 F.2d 1, 4 (2d Cir. 1970) ("whether the evidence is such that, without weighing the credibility of the witnesses or otherwise considering the weight of the evidence, there can be but one conclusion as to the verdict that reasonable [people] could have reached.").

[122] The facts here are taken from an old case — *Reid v. San Pedro, Los Angeles & Salt Lake R.R.,* 118 P. 1009 (Utah 1911) — in which the Utah Supreme Court held that the case should not have been submitted to the jury because the plaintiff had failed to put forth enough evidence from which the jury could conclude that it was more likely than not that the bull went through the hole in the fence.

how much weight to accord the testimony of each, are for the jury. Thus, "credibility of witnesses and weight of the evidence... are not the concern of the court on a motion for [JMOL or RJMOL]."[123]

Finally, the court does not have the power to enter JMOL or RJMOL on its own. A party must make a motion for such relief. On the other hand, the court does have inherent authority to enter the less drastic order of new trial. Indeed, Rule 50(b) instructs the court to which a RJMOL motion is made to consider this alternative. We now consider new trial.

§9.6 Motion for New Trial (Federal Rule 59)

Background and Comparison to RJMOL

Though a motion for new trial under Federal Rule 59(a) is made at the same time as a motion for RJMOL — no later than ten days after entry of the judgment[124] (which we defined in §9.3) — it is a radically different motion. As we just saw, when a court grants RJMOL, the effect is (1) to take the judgment away from the party whom the jury declared the winner and (2) to enter judgment for the other party. In contrast, when a court grants a motion for new trial, the effect is (1) to take the judgment away from the party whom the jury declared the winner, and (2) to start over with a new trial. Clearly, then, an order of new trial is less drastic than the grant of a motion for RJMOL. The party declared the winner by the jury has her victory taken away, but she still has a chance to win, because there will be a new trial.

A motion for new trial must state the grounds for the new trial. Under Rule 59(d), however, the court is free to grant a new trial on any ground, even one not stated in the motion. This salutary provision can rescue a party when the court has difficulty determining the basis on which counsel is seeking a new trial. Indeed, as Rule 59(d) also makes clear, the court can order a new trial on its own — without a motion from a party.

Grounds for Ordering New Trial

Interestingly, Rule 59 does not provide specific grounds on which a new trial can be ordered. Rather, Rule 59(a)(1)(A) provides that a new trial can be ordered in a jury case "for any reason for which a new trial has heretofore been granted in an action at law in federal court." In general, the motion is based upon some error that may have tainted the result of the trial. In ruling on a motion for new trial — as opposed to a RJMOL — the

---

[123] Wright & Kane, Federal Courts 687.
[124] This timing requirement is found in Rule 59(b).

court *may* consider credibility of the witnesses and the weight of the evidence. Moreover, in ruling on the motion for new trial, the court is not required to view the evidence in the light most favorable to the party who won at trial.[125]

Many grounds may support a motion for new trial. For instance, perhaps the judge made some mistake — such as putting the burden of persuasion on the wrong party, giving an erroneous jury instruction, or wrongfully allowing the introduction of improper evidence — that leads her to believe that justice would be served by having the parties re-try the case before a new jury. Or maybe there is probative new evidence, which could not have been discovered with due diligence in time for trial.[126] Or perhaps a party or lawyer engaged in misconduct that justifies a new trial. Whoever made the mistake or acted inappropriately, however, the error or misconduct will not justify an order for new trial unless it was *prejudicial*. If the error or misconduct was harmless, and did not infect the outcome of the case, new trial is inappropriate.[127]

One interesting question is whether a motion for new trial may be based upon juror misconduct. At common law, a juror could not be heard to "impeach" the verdict rendered.[128] This rule enhanced the stability of verdicts and the finality of judgments, and also protected jurors from possible harassment by the losing litigant. There is a trend, however, toward permitting impeachment of a jury verdict based upon "extrinsic" (as opposed to "intrinsic") influences on jurors. Extrinsic influences are things that can be verified objectively. For example, if the jurors based their decision on an independent investigation of the facts outside the courtroom, or upon being bribed by a party, such "extrinsic" factors can be considered in ordering a new trial. Intrinsic factors are those that are inherent to reaching the verdict, and are not objectively verifiable. This distinction protects the verdict from the judge's intrusion into the jurors' thought processes.[129]

[125] Holzapfel v. Town of Newburgh, 950 F. Supp. 1267, 1272 (S.D.N.Y. 1997).

[126] We consider this basis for setting aside a judgment under Rule 60(b) in §9.7. The standard for seeking a new trial on this basis is the same as that under Rule 60(b). *See* 12 Moore's Federal Practice §60-113.

[127] *See, e.g.*, Patrolmen's Benevolent Assn. of N.Y. v. City of New York, 310 F.3d 43 (2d Cir. 2002) (affirming denial of motion for new trial because error in jury instruction was harmless); Crowley v. L.L. Bean, Inc., 303 F.3d 387 (1st Cir. 2002) (affirming denial of motion for new trial because jury's possible error in concluding there was systematic sexual discrimination was harmless).

[128] Technically, the common law rule was a one of evidence: A juror's testimony regarding misconduct was not admissible. Because jurors themselves will be the only witnesses to most examples of juror misconduct, however, the rule had the effect of shielding juror activity from review.

[129] Federal Rule of Evidence 606(b) provides that "a juror may not testify as to any matter or statement occurring during . . . deliberations . . . , except that a juror may testify on the question whether extraneous prejudicial information was improperly brought to the

In *Tanner v. United States*,[130] the Supreme Court held that evidence that some jurors drank alcohol during lunch breaks and that two jurors ingested cocaine during the trial was not admissible to impeach the verdict. The Court refused to see such evidence as "extrinsic," and likened it, rather, to such intrinsic factors as illness or lack of sleep. In *McDonough Power Equipment, Inc. v. Greenwood*,[131] the Court addressed whether a juror's incorrect answer during the voir dire process could serve as a basis for new trial. It concluded that the party seeking new trial must demonstrate (1) that the juror failed to answer a material question on voir dire, and (2) that a correct response to the question would have provided a valid basis for striking the juror for cause. This is a very difficult standard, and new trials are rarely granted on this basis.

One controversial ground for a new trial motion is that the verdict was against the weight of the evidence adduced at trial. It is controversial because, at least potentially, it seems to invite the judge to substitute her fact-finding for that of the jury. The trial judge should respect the jury's assessment, even if she would have decided the case differently, unless doing so essentially leads to an unjust result. A helpful statement of the standard for granting a new trial on this ground is: "If, having given full respect to the jury's findings, the judge on the entire evidence is left with the definite and firm conviction that a mistake has been committed, it is to be expected that he or she will grant a new trial."[132] Consequently, most courts will say that this ground for new trial is that the verdict is against the "*great* weight" of the evidence.

This ground for a new trial should be kept in mind in cases in which a party entitled to RJMOL has waived the right to bring that motion by failing to seek JMOL at the close of all the evidence. As discussed in §9.5, RJMOL allows the court to take victory away from one party and enter judgment in favor of another party. This path is proper, however, only when the jury reached a conclusion that reasonable people could not have reached *and* when the party seeking RJMOL moved for JMOL at the close of all the evidence. Let's return to an example we saw above.

  ○ Plaintiff sues Defendant on a claim with elements *A*, *B*, *C*, and *D*. Plaintiff presents her evidence at trial and presents evidence supporting elements *A*, *B*, and *D*. She presents nothing to support element *C*. Defendant presents her evidence and the court closes all the evidence. Defendant fails to move for JMOL at trial (though she certainly had grounds to

---

jury's attention or whether any outside influence was improperly brought to bear upon any juror."

[130] 483 U.S. 107 (1987).

[131] 464 U.S. 548 (1984).

[132] Wright & Kane, Federal Courts 681.

do so[133]). The jury returns a verdict for Plaintiff and the court enters judgment on the basis of that verdict.

○ Defendant cannot move for RJMOL. As we saw in §9.5, she waived the right to bring that motion by failing to move for JMOL at an appropriate time at trial. But Defendant certainly can move for a new trial on the basis that the verdict was against the great weight of the evidence. Obviously, Defendant would rather have gotten RJMOL, because that order would result in entry of a judgment in her favor. Having waived that, though, she should be thrilled with an order of new trial. She will escape the judgment in favor of Plaintiff and have a chance to prevail at that new trial.

Another troublesome basis for an order of new trial is that the damages awarded in the verdict were excessive or inadequate. Again, the judge cannot simply supplant the jury's decision with her sense of what the damages should be. On the other hand, if the jury's determination of damages is sufficiently off the mark, the judge can order a new trial. How far off the mark must the determination be? Though Rule 59 does not say so, federal courts apply a "shock the conscience" test; the jury's assessment of damages may be the basis for a new trial order if it shocks the judge's conscience. On the other hand, in *Gasperini v. Center for Humanities, Inc.*,[134] the Supreme Court held that a federal court in a diversity of citizenship case may be required to apply a state-law standard for assessing whether damages are excessive or inadequate. In *Gasperini*, the New York legislature passed a statute allowing judges to order a new trial when a jury's verdict "deviates materially" from verdicts returned in similar cases. This standard permits a judge to intervene more permissively than the ordinary federal "shocks the conscience" standard.

Partial and Conditional Orders of New Trial

Suppose the trial judge considers the jury's finding of liability clearly supported by the evidence, but is shocked by the size of the verdict (either high or low). Instead of ordering a new trial on all issues, she might grant a partial new trial — as to damages only. Thus, at the new trial, liability would be deemed established, and the parties would try the damages issue afresh to a new jury.

Or the judge might consider a *conditional* order of new trial. This order would grant a new trial on damages (or on all issues, as appropriate) *only* if a party rejects the condition the court puts on the order. In federal court, this is the method by which the court attempts *remittitur* of an excessive verdict.

---

[133] Why? Because *P*'s failure to present evidence on one of the elements of her claim meant, as a matter of law, that *D* should win the case. A reasonable jury could not conclude that *P* should win under these circumstances. See §9.5.

[134] 518 U.S. 415 (1996). We discuss *Gasperini* in detail in §10.6.4.

○ *P* sues *D* for personal injuries. At trial, *P* produces substantial evidence of *D*'s liability but the evidence of damages shows minimal harm. The jury returns a verdict in favor of *P*, and against *D*, for $750,000. The court finds the award shockingly excessive, because the evidence clearly supported only relatively minor damages. *D* moves for a new trial on the ground of excessive damages. The court may grant the motion and order a new trial on damages.

○ Instead, however, the court may avoid the new trial by ordering *remittitur* to $40,000. This is a way in which the court plays "hardball" with the plaintiff. It is saying, in essence, "unless you, plaintiff, agree to accept $40,000 instead of the $750,000 the jury gave you, I'm going to order a new trial on damages (and you might not even get that much)."

This use of the conditional new trial through remittitur, obviously, is a way the court might play hardball with the plaintiff. The court tries to pressure the plaintiff to remit what the court believes is excessive damages. Remittitur is permitted in most state courts. It is permitted in federal court, but *only* if the court allows the plaintiff the option of accepting either (1) the figure set by the court or (2) the order of new trial. In other words, the Seventh Amendment prohibits a federal court from entering an order for the lesser amount.[135] All the court can do is give the plaintiff the option.

The converse situation — when the jury's damages determination is shockingly low — raises the question of whether *additur* might be appropriate. Here the court would play hardball with the defendant.

○ *P* sues *D* for personal injuries and produces substantial evidence of *D*'s liability and of the very serious harm caused by the event. The jury returns a verdict in favor of *P*, and against *D*, but for only $40,000. The low figure shocks the conscience of the judge. *P* moves for new trial on the ground of the inadequate verdict. The court may grant the motion and order new trial on damages.

○ But may the court avoid the new trial by giving the defendant a choice? The choice would be either to pay an augmented amount in damages, say $500,000, or face a new trial. This would be playing hardball with the defendant — saying "either pay this poor plaintiff $500,000 or I'll order a new trial (in which you might get hit for a more substantial verdict)."

This latter course is not permitted in federal court. In *Dimick v. Scheidt*,[136] the Supreme Court held that a conditional new trial based upon *additur* violates the Seventh Amendment. *Dimick* has no friends today, and the Supreme Court has hinted that the case's days may be numbered.[137] But it remains vital at the moment, and thus *additur* cannot be

---

[135] Hetzel v. Prince William County, 523 U.S. 208 (1998).

[136] 293 U.S. 474 (1935).

[137] Gasperini v. Center for Humanities, Inc., 518 U.S. 415, 433 n.16 (1996).

used in federal court. Because the Seventh Amendment does not apply to the states, as we saw in §9.2.2, state courts are not bound by *Dimick*. Accordingly, *additur* is permitted in many state courts.

Moving for New Trial and RJMOL in the Alternative

A party often will move for RJMOL and new trial in the alternative (assuming, of course, that the party preserved the right to move for RJMOL by moving for JMOL at an appropriate time at trial, as we saw in §9.5). Rule 50(c)(1) allows a party whose motion for RJMOL is granted to ask the court to rule "conditionally" on the motion for new trial as well. At first this seems silly, because the entry of RJMOL obviates the need for new trial. But asking for the conditional ruling on the new trial motion actually makes great sense. Why? The entry of RJMOL is appealable.[138] If the court of appeals were to vacate the RJMOL as improper, the case would have to be remanded to the district court for a ruling on the new trial motion. To save this step, Rule 50(c)(1) tells the district court to rule on both motions. Under Rule 50(c)(2), the conditional grant of the motion for new trial does not affect finality (and therefore appealability), and if the RJMOL is reversed on appeal, the case is remanded to the trial court for the new trial.

There is some authority that a litigant waives the right to move for new trial if she does not seek a conditional ruling on the alternative motions. In *Arenson v. Southern University Law Center*,[139] the plaintiff won at trial. The defendant moved for RJMOL and new trial in the alternative. The court granted the RJMOL and did not rule on the motion for new trial. The court of appeals reversed the entry of RJMOL and remanded to the district court. The defendant renewed his motion for new trial, which was granted. The defendant won at the second trial. The plaintiff appealed, arguing that the grant of new trial was improper. The Fifth Circuit reversed the order of new trial. It held that Rule 50(c)(1) creates a "use-it-or-lose-it" option. By failing to have the district judge rule conditionally on the original new trial motion, the defendant waived its right to seek new trial on remand. The district court had no authority to grant the new trial after remand from the court of appeals.

[138] As we see in §14.4.1, this ruling would constitute a final judgment and could be appealed.
[139] 43 F.3d 194 (5th Cir. 1995).

§9.7   Motion to Set Aside a Judgment or Order (Federal Rule 60)

Rule 60 permits a party to seek relief from a judgment or order. It consists of two parts. First, Rule 60(a) allows a court to correct "a clerical mistake or a mistake arising from oversight or omission" that is found "in a judgment, order, or other part of the record." The court can act on its own or pursuant to a motion of any party. A "clerical mistake" is one that misrepresents what the court actually intended to order. Such a mistake might be inconsequential, such as misnumbering paragraphs in findings of fact. Or the error might be of considerable moment, such as a transposition of numbers in a judgment,[140] misnaming a party,[141] or a mistake regarding the amount of attorneys' fees awarded.[142] The thrust of Rule 60(a) is to clarify a judgment to ensure that the court's original intent is implemented; it is aimed at errors resulting from inadvertence, not from mistaken judgment.

Second, Rule 60(b) permits the trial court to correct substantive errors that cannot be addressed under Rule 60(a). As one court explained:

> The basic distinction between "clerical mistakes" and mistakes that cannot be corrected pursuant to Rule 60(a) is that the former consist of "blunders in execution" whereas the latter consist of instances where the court *changes its mind,* either because of a legal or factual mistake in making its original determination, or because on second thought it has decided to exercise its discretion in a manner different from the way it was exercised in the original determination.[143]

Rule 60(b) lists six bases on which the court may grant relief from "a final judgment, order or proceeding": (1) mistake, inadvertence, surprise, or excusable neglect; (2) newly discovered evidence; (3) fraud, misrepresentation, or other misconduct of an adverse party; (4) the judgment is void; (5) the judgment has been satisfied, or a prior judgment upon which it is based has been reversed or vacated; and (6) "any other reason that justifies relief." The relief sought, almost always, is an order setting aside a judgment. The Rule requires that a party move for relief, and provides that it may be granted on terms that are "just."

[140] *See, e.g.,* Esquire Radio & Electronics, Inc. v. Montgomery Ward & Co., 804 F.2d 787, 795-796 (2d Cir. 1986) (changing judgment from $269,000 to $296,000).

[141] *See, e.g.,* McNamara v. City of Chicago, 138 F.3d 1219, 1221 (7th Cir. 1998) (changing "Chicago Police Department" to "Chicago Fire Department" in opinion).

[142] *See, e.g.,* Dura-Wood Treating Co. v. Century Forest Industries, 624 F.2d 112, 114 (5th Cir. 1982).

[143] United States v. Griffin, 782 F.2d 1393, 1397 (7th Cir. 1986) (citation omitted) (emphasis original).

Under Rule 60(c)(1), a motion under Rule 60(b) must be made "within a reasonable time." Moreover, if the motion is based upon grounds (1), (2), or (3) listed above, the motion cannot be made more than one year after entry of the judgment or order or date of the proceeding. Note that on those three grounds, the moving party does not necessarily have one year in which to make the motion. One year is the *absolute limit*; the court may determine that a period of less than a year violated the requirement that the motion be brought "within a reasonable time."

Except for judgments that are void (addressed by Rule 60(b)(4)), the decision of whether to grant the motion is always vested in the court's discretion. In other words, outside the situation of a void judgment, there is no *right* to have a judgment set aside.[144] Our judicial system ascribes great importance to finality of judgments, so a judgment should not be set aside lightly. In addition, a party who failed to prosecute a timely appeal ordinarily should not be allowed to use a Rule 60(b) motion to raise grounds that could have been raised on appeal. Further, the system of justice favors decisions based upon the merits rather than on technicalities, so default judgments may be more readily set aside than those entered after full litigation.[145] And, unless the judgment is void, the party seeking to set aside a judgment must show that she has a meritorious claim or defense. It makes no sense to set aside a judgment against a party if that party has either no claim to assert or no defense to a claim.

Rule 60(b)(1) is often the basis for a motion to set aside a default judgment (which we saw in §7.5.3). There, the defendant who defaulted will attempt to convince the court that she was guilty of a mistake or of excusable neglect that should be "forgiven" by setting aside the judgment. There is a split of authority as to whether "mistake" under this part of the Rule refers to legal errors committed by the court. Some courts permit relief under Rule 60(b)(1) from judicial mistakes, at least under some circumstances,[146] while others do not.[147]

Rule 60(b)(2) expressly limits the use of newly discovered evidence to that which "with reasonable diligence, could not have been discovered in time to move for a new trial under Rule 59(b)." A Rule 59 motion, as we saw in §9.6, must be brought within ten days of entry of judgment, so the Rule 60(c)(1) timing requirement for bringing a Rule 60(b) motion is considerably more liberal. Courts require essentially the same showing for a

---

[144] *See, e.g.*, UMWA 1974 Pension v. Pittston Co., 984 F.2d 469, 476 (D.C. Cir. 1993).

[145] *See* 12 Moore's Federal Practice §60.22[3][a].

[146] *See, e.g.*, International Controls Corp. v. Vesco, 556 F.2d 665, 669 (2d Cir. 1977) (holding, however, that a motion for relief from the judgment on this ground must be made before the time for appeal runs out).

[147] *See, e.g.*, Parke-Chaptley Constr. Co. v. Cherrington, 865 F.2d 907, 914-915 n.7 (7th Cir. 1989); Page v. Schweiker, 786 F.2d 150, 154-155 (3d Cir. 1986).

motion for new trial and a motion to set aside based upon newly discovered evidence.[148] Although cases discuss various factors, for the most part, the moving party will have to show that the evidence existed at the time of the original adjudication, that it could not have been discovered, even with reasonable diligence, in time for the first adjudication, *and* that the new evidence is so important that it would likely change the outcome of the case.[149] Obviously, this is a difficult standard.

Under Rule 60(b)(3), the court may set aside a judgment for fraud or other misconduct by an adverse party. This provision addresses a wide variety of misdeeds. For example, a party's failure to respond to discovery requests, which hindered the moving party's ability to prepare for trial, might be sufficient.[150]

Rule 60(b)(5) permits setting aside a judgment for various reasons, including that the judgment "is based on an earlier judgment that has been reversed or vacated." There has been some uncertainty about what the drafters intended by the word "based." Courts generally interpret this provision to mean that one judgment is so closely related to another that it has a preclusive effect on it.[151] The Rule thus is not implicated when a judgment relies on an earlier judgment as legal precedent and it is reversed or vacated.[152]

Rule 60(b)(6) is a catch-all provision allowing relief for "any other reason that justifies relief." This Rule can be invoked *only* when two things are established. One, the case must not satisfy any of the other bases for relief under Rule 60(b). Thus, Rule 60(b)(6) cannot save a party who failed to move for relief within a reasonable time, or failed to move on the bases in Rule 60(b)(1), (2), or (3) within the absolute one-year limit.[153] Two, the moving party must establish "extraordinary circumstances" for relief.[154] In the typically colorful language of Judge Richard Posner, "The first five subsections [of Rule 60(b)] seem to cover the waterfront. The only work left for (6) to do is to allow judgments to be set aside, without limitation of time, when the circumstances of its invocation are 'extraordinary.'"[155]

---

[148] *See generally* 12 Moore's Federal Practice §60.42[2].

[149] *See, e.g.*, Jones v. Aero/Chem Corp., 921 F.2d 875, 878 (9th Cir. 1990).

[150] *See, e.g.*, Schultz v. Butcher, 24 F.3d 626, 630-631 (4th Cir. 1994).

[151] *See, e.g.*, Tomlin v. McDaniel, 865 F.2d 209, 210-211 (9th Cir. 1989). We discuss preclusive effects — claim preclusion and issue preclusion — in Chapter 11.

[152] *See, e.g.*, *Tomlin*, 865 F.2d at 211.

[153] *See* Pioneer Investment Servs. Co. v. Brunswick Assocs. LP, 507 U.S. 380, 393 (1993) ("A party who failed to take timely action due to 'excusable neglect' may not seek relief more than a year after the judgment by resorting to section (6).").

[154] *See* 12 Moore's Federal Practice §60.48[1] & [2].

[155] Lowe v. McGraw-Hill Cos., 361 F.3d 335, 342 (7th Cir. 2004).

One interesting question is whether misconduct by one's lawyer can justify relief under Rule 60(b)(6). In cases such as *Link v. Wabash Ry. Co.*,[156] the Supreme Court has indicated that the lawyer is the agent of the client, and the client must suffer the consequences of her lawyer's misdeeds. After all, the reasoning goes, the client hired the lawyer, and thus must pay the price if she hired a poor lawyer. The issue is often presented under Rule 60(b)(6) in a default judgment situation

- ○ Defendant's lawyer failed to plead or otherwise defend her client, and the court entered default judgment against Defendant. Now Defendant moves to set aside the judgment under Rule 60(b)(6). Is the lawyer's negligence an "extraordinary" circumstance that justifies relief?

The general rule is no; certainly if the lawyer is guilty of simple malpractice, courts will not set aside the judgment. There is a split of authority, however, when the client can show *gross negligence* by the lawyer. While some courts refuse relief even under these circumstances,[157] others will set aside a judgment on such grounds. An example is *Community Dental Services v. Tani*,[158] in which the defendant's counsel filed an answer (albeit late) but never served it on the plaintiff, despite a court order to do so, and failed to abide by other court orders, all the while telling the defendant that things were proceeding smoothly. Because the lawyer was guilty of "extreme negligence or egregious conduct,"[159] the Ninth Circuit ordered the district court to set aside its default judgment and allow the case to proceed.

As noted above, Rule 60(b)(4) is unique. It provides for relief from a void judgment. Unlike the other bases for relief under Rule 60(b), here the court has no discretion; if the court determines that a judgment is void (as opposed to simply wrong), it *must* set aside the judgment.[160] Why? Because a void judgment is a nullity; it does not exist. Put another way, a void judgment is one that is beyond the court's power. Most often, "void" means that the court lacked personal jurisdiction or subject matter jurisdiction.[161] It certainly does not include an erroneous decision by the court. Indeed, the vast majority of errors committed by trial courts that could be

---

[156] 370 U.S. 626 (1962) (upholding involuntary dismissal of case based upon counsel's failures to prosecute case and follow court orders). We discussed *Link* at §7.4.2.

[157] *See, e.g.,* Dickerson v. Bd. of Educ., 32 F.3d 1114, 1118 (7th Cir. 1994); Heim v. Commissioner, 872 F.2d 245, 248 (8th Cir. 1989).

[158] 282 F.3d 1164 (9th Cir. 2002).

[159] *Id.* at 1168. *See also* William Darrah & Assocs., 796 F.2d 190, 195 (6th Cir. 1986); Boughner v. Secretary of Health, Educ. & Welfare, 572 F.2d 976, 978 (3d Cir. 1978) (granting relief in cases involving grossly negligent attorney).

[160] *See, e.g.,* Bally Export Co. v. Balicar, Ltd., 804 F.2d 646, 649 (7th Cir. 1995).

[161] *See, e.g.,* Farm Credit Bank v. Ferrera-Goitia, 316 F.3d 62, 67 (1st Cir. 2003); Garcia Fin. Group, Inc. v. Virginia Accelerators Corp., 3 Fed. Appx. 86, 88 (4th Cir. 2001).

reversed on appeal do not render the judgment void and therefore cannot provide a basis for a motion under Rule 60(b)(4).

Finally, it bears emphasis that the motion for relief under Rule 60 — like the motion for RJMOL (discussed in §9.5) and the motion for new trial (discussed in §9.6) — is addressed to the trial court that entered the judgment or order from which relief is sought. In other words, no appellate review is sought here. A losing litigant might be able to seek review by an appellate court, as we discuss in Chapter 14.

Chapter *10*

The Erie *Doctrine(s)*

§10.1   Defining the Issue

It is rare to have one word impart so much to so many people as the simple word *Erie*. Law students, law professors, judges, and lawyers know that the word refers to one of the most important cases ever decided by the Supreme Court: *Erie Railroad Co. v. Tompkins*.[1] Many students (and professors) consider *Erie* the most difficult material in Civil Procedure. Part of the problem is that what we call *Erie* (or "the *Erie* doctrine") is

---

[1] 304 U.S. 64 (1938).

really two doctrines. Before we get to that, though, the initial task is simply to recognize what the material is about. *Erie* problems arise only in federal court, and concern the choice between federal and state law. Specifically, when does a federal court apply state law?

The issue generally arises in diversity of citizenship cases. After all, in a federal question case, the claim arises under federal law, and federal law will most likely provide the rules for deciding the case. In a diversity of citizenship case, however, the litigation is in federal court simply because the parties happen to be of diverse citizenship (and, of course, the amount in controversy requirement is met). Because the claim asserted in a diversity of citizenship case does not arise under federal law, there is room for the application of state law. Indeed, as we will see, the Constitution *requires* the application of state law to some aspects of the case.

Two words of caution are important about *Erie*. First, more than with most topics in Civil Procedure, professors have a variety of views in this area; many disagree on the interpretation and importance of particular cases. What is presented here certainly is not gospel and, obviously, you should strive to understand the material as your professor does. The material is rich and can offer a springboard for discussion of deep jurisprudential themes, as we will see. Some professors make much of such things; some do little with such things. Second, it is impossible simply to jump into *Erie*. Understanding and applying current doctrine requires background, including historical development through a series of Supreme Court cases. After reviewing that development in §§10.4 through 10.6, I suggest in §10.7 a mode of analysis for addressing any *Erie* issue. Before getting to the cases, however, we discuss why *Erie* raises a "vertical" (as opposed to a "horizontal") choice of law issue.

§10.2 Vertical Choice of Law Versus Horizontal Choice of Law

It may seem strange, but courts routinely apply the laws of other jurisdictions. A California court may apply the law of New York or a Florida court may apply the law of Colorado to determine the outcome of a dispute. The question of which state's law governs raises a *horizontal choice of law* inquiry. That is, the choice of applicable laws is between equal political entities (states). Courts make this determination based upon doctrines of "choice of law," which constitutes a large part of an upper-division course called Conflict of Laws. For our purposes in Civil Procedure, we only need to know that this body of law exists and that each state is free to adopt its own rules for determining horizontal choice of law issues.

For example, in contract cases, a common (but not universal) horizontal choice of law approach is to apply the law of the state in which the parties entered the contract. In addition, parties generally are free to provide by contract that the law of a particular state will govern their dispute; such a provision is called a *law selection clause*,[2] and most states enforce them so long as they are reasonable and not the product of overreaching. In tort cases, one common (but not universal) approach provides that the court should apply the law of the place of the injury.

○ *P*, a citizen of Ohio, and *D*, a citizen of New Mexico, do not know each other. Each is on vacation in Hawaii. *D*, driving a rental car there, negligently hits *P*, who was walking by the side of the road. *P* sues *D* to recover for personal injuries in New Mexico. (For review, why New Mexico?[3]) The court in New Mexico, applying New Mexico's "choice of law" rules, will probably conclude that Hawaii tort law governs, because the injury was suffered in Hawaii. Thus, the New Mexico court will look to Hawaii law to determine the elements of *P*'s claim and of *D*'s defenses.

The *Erie* doctrine (which *is* important in our course in Civil Procedure) addresses a different choice of law issue. Here, the question is not whether the law of State *A* or State *B* will apply, but whether the federal court should apply state law at all. The choice here is between *state* law and *federal* law. If the court decides that an issue should be determined by state (rather than federal) law, it will *then* undertake the horizontal choice of law inquiry to determine which state's law applies. But this antecedent question — the focus of this chapter — is a *vertical choice of law* inquiry.

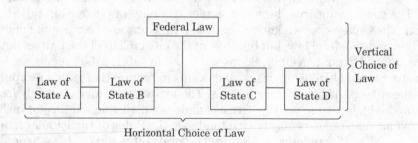

---

[2] Remember the *Burger King* case from personal jurisdiction (§2.4.4)? There, the Michigan franchisees entered a contract with Burger King that contained a law selection clause that provided for the application of Florida law to any dispute under the contract.

[3] Because she can get personal jurisdiction over *D* in New Mexico; *D* is domiciled in that state. It is doubtful that *P* could sue in Ohio (her home state) unless *D* for some reason had sufficient contacts to be subject to personal jurisdiction there. Of course, *P* might also sue in Hawaii, where there would be personal jurisdiction over *D* because the accident occurred there. For this hypothetical, assume *P* sues in New Mexico.

§10.3   The Rules of Decision Act and the Regime of *Swift v. Tyson*

The starting point in studying vertical choice of law is the Rules of Decision Act, which has been part of the Judicial Code since 1789. Today it is codified at 28 U.S.C. §1652.[4] Look carefully at the language, which provides in full:

> The laws of the several states, except where the Constitution or treaties of the United States or Acts of Congress otherwise require or provide, shall be regarded as rules of decision in civil actions in the courts of the United States, in cases where they apply.

This is an awkward provision. It seems to say: State law provides the rules of decision in civil cases in federal court, except where federal law applies, in cases in which state law applies. However poorly drafted, the statute indicates that federal courts must apply state law as the rules of decision in civil cases, except where federal law applies. It is important to understand why the statute carves out the exception for cases in which *federal* law requires that state law not apply. Under the Supremacy Clause of the Constitution, federal law is "the supreme law of the land."[5] Thus, for example, when Congress legislates in an area in which the Constitution gives it authority, that legislation becomes supreme, and is binding in federal and state courts. That is why the Rules of Decision Act does not generally create problems in federal question cases. By definition, the claim in such a case arises under federal law, which, under the Supremacy Clause, must govern. There is no role for state law in defining such a claim.

The same is not true, however, under diversity of citizenship jurisdiction. Those cases, as we know, are in federal court not because the claim arises under federal law, but because of the citizenship of the parties (and the amount in controversy). So, as we noted in §10.1, §1652 seems aimed at diversity of citizenship cases, and seems to require that state law apply as the rules of decision in such cases. The matter may not be entirely free from doubt, but what we say here certainly is a plausible interpretation.[6]

Whatever Congress may have intended in the Rules of Decision Act, the Supreme Court concluded in 1842 that federal courts did *not* have to apply state law on *all* aspects of a diversity case. The famous decision in which

---

[4]The statute was §34 of the original Judiciary Act of 1789. Some of the cases you read — including *Swift v. Tyson* and *Erie* itself — refer to it as "§34." Don't be confused by that; it is the same statute that you have in your statutory supplement as 28 U.S.C. §1652.

[5]U.S. Const. art. VI, cl. 2.

[6]*See* Patrick Borchers, *The Origins of Diversity Jurisdiction, the Rise of Legal Positivism, and a Brave New World for* Erie *and* Klaxon, 72 Tex. L. Rev. 79, 79-81 (1993).

it did so, *Swift v. Tyson*,[7] stood for 96 years, until it was overruled by *Erie* itself. *Erie* simply cannot be understood without background in *Swift*. In that old case, the question was one of contract law — whether discharge of a debt constituted consideration for a contract. It was an issue on which courts of various states had reached different conclusions. The traditional view was that discharge of a debt did not constitute consideration, but a then-modern trend reached the opposite conclusion.

Swift was a diversity of citizenship case brought in federal court in New York. The New York state courts clearly adhered to the traditional rule that discharge of a debt was not consideration. The Supreme Court held that the federal courts sitting in diversity need not follow New York precedent on this issue. The Court then embraced the then-modern principle that discharge of a debt *was* consideration. How did the Court justify ignoring state law? It interpreted the phrase "laws of the several States" in the Rules of Decision Act to include only state *statutes* and state common law of *local concern* (e.g., perhaps, land). As to common law matters of *general* concern (e.g., basic principles of torts and contract, including what constitutes consideration for a contract), the Court concluded, federal courts in diversity cases were free to apply their own conception of "general" common law.[8] Interpreting "laws of the several states" in the Rules of Decision Act, Justice Story's opinion in *Swift* said:

> In the ordinary use of language, it will hardly be contended that the decisions of courts constitute laws. They are, at most, only evidence of what the laws are; and are not, of themselves, laws.... The laws of a state are more usually understood to mean the rules and enactments promulgated by the legislative authority thereof, as long-established customs having the force of laws.... It never has been supposed by us, that the [Rules of Decision Act] did apply, or was designed to apply, to questions of a more general nature ... as, for example, ... questions of general commercial law.

There are several problems with *Swift*. First, the notion that decisions of courts do not constitute "laws" should strike you as odd. We are used to seeing judicial opinions as "law" today. Remember that *Swift* was decided over a century and a half ago. It was not until the early twentieth century, with the advent of the "legal realist" school of jurisprudence, that there was widespread acceptance of the notion that judges make "laws" just as surely as legislatures make laws. Throughout your law school career, you have become comfortable with this notion. For example, in your Torts class, you see the common law development of negligence and strict liability doctrines. We consider those to be "laws" even though they

---

[7] 41 U.S. 1 (1842).

[8] *Id.* at 18-19. Common law, as we discussed in §1.1, consists of judicial opinions. Statutory law, in contrast, is legislation.

were decreed by courts rather than legislatures. So there is something strange to the modern lawyer about Justice Story's considering state court decisions as something less than "law."

Second, *Swift* was based upon a notion, widespread in the nineteenth century, that there was only one true common law. Justice Story expressed this belief with a colorful phrase from Cicero that the law cannot mean one thing in Rome and another in Athens.[9] To him, and most legal philosophers of the day, judges would "discover" that one true approach, and someday all courts would come to see the wisdom of it and to embrace it. This notion, like the one that state court decisions are not law, is foreign to us today. We are quite comfortable with the idea that the common law can vary from state to state. Again, you have seen examples in your other classes, as when some states embrace certain tort theories that others do not.

Third, *Swift* assigned the job of determining the content of the one true common law to the *federal* bench. *Swift* reflects a doctrine of enormous arrogance: Only the federal judges were able to divine the true general common law. They would set it forth in diversity of citizenship cases in an effort not only to decide those cases but to educate the state courts on what the general common law ought to be. The state judges, so the theory went, would see the wisdom of the approach taken by their federal brethren and conform state decisions to it.

But the state courts were not compelled by *Swift* to adopt the federal courts' reasoning on matters of general common law. They could persist in applying a different version of the general common law in their decisions. This fact led to the most devastating shortcoming of the *Swift* doctrine: The general common law to be applied depended upon what court — state or federal — was hearing the case. For example, after *Swift*, the New York courts continued to embrace the traditional rule that discharge of a debt was not consideration for a contract. Federal courts, guided by *Swift*, decreed that discharge of a debt was consideration to support a contract. So where did that leave the citizens of New York? What would a New York lawyer tell a client for whom the issue of consideration for a contract was important? The lawyer would have to explain that there were two sets of law in New York: One would apply if litigation took place in state court and a completely different rule would apply if litigation ensued in federal court. Put more bluntly, New York citizens were subject to two antithetical laws on this point. Some commentators refer to this phenomenon as "vertical disuniformity" — the law is different *within a single state* depending upon whether the issue is addressed in

[9] 41 U.S. at 19.

federal or state court. Obviously, vertical disuniformity makes it very difficult for people in New York (or people dealing with New York citizens) to plan their commercial activities.

In addition, vertical disuniformity creates enormous incentives for forum shopping. After all, the only people who can avoid New York law and avail themselves of the federal courts' version of the general common law are those who can invoke diversity of citizenship jurisdiction. A New York citizen in a dispute with another New York citizen will not be able to gain access to federal court (because there is no diversity) and to the federal general common law. When a New York citizen entered a contract with a citizen of another state, however, a dispute could go either to state or federal court (assuming, of course, that the amount in controversy requirement for a diversity case was satisfied). Thus, when a dispute arose, a litigant could choose the court likely to apply a version of general common law more to her liking. And even if a dispute raised an issue on which the federal courts had not expressed an opinion, one invoking diversity of citizenship jurisdiction at least had the opportunity to persuade the federal court to adopt a view of some general common law different from that adopted by the state courts.

The most egregious example of forum shopping to exploit vertical disuniformity is *Black & White Taxicab Co. v. Brown & Yellow Taxicab Co.*[10] There, Brown & Yellow, a taxicab operator, entered an exclusive dealing contract with Railroad. Under the contract, Railroad's passengers at the station in Bowling Green, Kentucky, could *only* use taxicabs provided by Brown & Yellow. Obviously, other taxicab companies — including one called Black & White — opposed this contract, because it froze them out of serving Railroad's passengers. The Kentucky courts had clearly held that exclusive dealing contracts such as this were void. Because of that, Black & White continued to serve passengers at the Bowling Green station, secure in the knowledge that the contract purporting to exclude it was void under state common law.

Brown & Yellow, meantime, wanted to sue Black & White in federal court, to argue that there should be an enlightened federal general common law that would enforce such exclusive contracts. The problem was that Brown & Yellow and Black & White were both citizens of Kentucky, so there was no way to invoke diversity of citizenship jurisdiction. The enterprising proprietors of Brown & Yellow then dissolved the corporation and reincorporated in Tennessee, thus making the corporation a citizen of Tennessee.[11] That corporation then sued Black & White (a citizen

---

[10] 276 U.S. 518 (1928).

[11] Recall that under §1332(c)(1), a corporation is a citizen of both the state of incorporation and the state of its principal place of business. See §4.5.3. That statutory definition did not come into existence until 1959, long after the *Black & White Taxicab* case was decided. At the time of the case, a corporation was deemed to be a citizen *only* of the state of its

of Kentucky) in federal court under diversity of citizenship jurisdiction. Brown & Yellow sought an injunction prohibiting Black & White from competing with it at the Bowling Green train station. The federal court held that federal general common law permitted exclusive dealing contracts and entered an injunction that prohibited Black & White from competing with Brown & Yellow. The Supreme Court upheld the injunction.

The result is outrageous.[12] The proprietors of Brown & Yellow clearly manufactured diversity of citizenship jurisdiction for the sole purpose of exploiting the vertical disuniformity made possible by *Swift*. After the Supreme Court opinion in *Black & White Taxicab*, what was the law of Kentucky concerning the enforceability of exclusive dealing contracts? The answer depended upon what court would decide the case. It makes life in Kentucky difficult, because its citizens are subject to two irreconcilable laws on the topic. There was considerable criticism of the *Black & White Taxicab* case and, thus, of the regime of *Swift v. Tyson*. No one knew it at the time, but *Swift* would be overruled a decade later.

Before getting to that point, we should note one other problem created by *Swift*. As noted, the case established a dividing line between common law of "local" concern — as to which a federal court must follow state court pronouncements — and common law of "general" concern — which a federal court may ignore. The federal courts wrestled unsuccessfully throughout the near-century reign of *Swift* to define where that line was. Many matters were obvious, such as basic issues of contract and tort law — things like offer, acceptance, and consideration for a contract and duty and breach for negligence. Those were clearly matters of general common law, as to which *Swift* permitted the federal courts to decree their own interpretation. What constituted local common law was far less clear, but it was usually thought to include interpretation of state statutes and issues relating to land.[13] But the *Erie* case itself involved an issue that was neither plainly local nor general. The parties argued the case at the Supreme Court on that basis but, as we will see, the decision rendered the distinction meaningless.

---

incorporation. Thus the reincorporation created diversity of citizenship. Today, if Brown & Yellow's principal place of business was in Kentucky, it would also be a citizen of Kentucky, and there would be no diversity between it and Black & White. Also, §1359, discussed at §4.5.4, which addresses the collusive creation of diversity of citizenship jurisdiction, was not on the books at the time the case was decided.

[12] Justice Oliver Wendell Holmes wrote a memorable dissent in the case, which the Court quoted extensively when it overruled *Swift v. Tyson* in *Erie*. See §10.4.

[13] *See, e.g.*, Kuhn v. Fairmont Coal Co., 215 U.S. 349 (1910) (following local common law on questions of land, unless state law unsettled). One commentator of the day noted that there were hundreds of cases involving the distinction between local and general common law under *Swift*, but "these rules and their application are notoriously far from clear." Armistead Dobie, Federal Procedure 558 (1928).

§10.4   The *Erie* Case Itself

§10.4.1   The Facts

It is interesting that such an important and at times difficult doctrine derived from a case with such simple facts. Harry Tompkins, a citizen of Pennsylvania, was walking along a path next to a train track, "on a dark night" near Hughestown, Pennsylvania. A freight train operated by the Erie Railroad (Erie) passed by from behind Mr. Tompkins. Something — perhaps an open door — protruded from one of the cars and hit Mr. Tompkins in the head. He suffered serious personal injuries. He sued the railroad in federal court in New York. Erie was a citizen of New York, and the claim met the amount in controversy requirement, so the case invoked diversity of citizenship jurisdiction.

The path on which Mr. Tompkins was walking was on the railroad's right-of-way, which is a strip of land astride the tracks. Tompkins contended that the path was openly and commonly used by members of the public and that the railroad was aware of this fact. That, argued Tompkins, made him an "invitee" on the property. When one is an invitee, the owner of the property owes him a duty, which is breached by simple negligence. Thus, asserted Tompkins, he could sue the railroad for its negligence in having the object protrude from the train and hit him. On the other side, the railroad contended that Tompkins was not an invitee, but a trespasser. If he were a trespasser, the railroad would not be liable for simple negligence. The only duty owed to a trespasser is to not cause him harm willfully or wantonly. Tompkins could probably prove that the railroad was negligent, but there was no way he could prove willful or wanton behavior. So, ultimately, if Tompkins was an invitee, the railroad could be held liable to him for simple negligence; if Tompkins was a trespasser, though, the railroad could not be held liable to him for simple negligence.

On this score, state law[14] was absolutely clear: Tompkins was a trespasser and, therefore, would lose. That is why Tompkins's lawyer sued in federal court — he wanted the federal court, under *Swift v. Tyson*, to apply federal general common law and hold that Tompkins was an invitee, who could win by showing mere negligence. The federal district court agreed with Tompkins and applied general federal common law; based upon a jury verdict, that court entered judgment for Tompkins for $30,000. The

---

[14] Though the case was litigated in federal court in New York, the relevant state law was that of Pennsylvania. Why? Remember from §10.2 that the doctrine of horizontal choice of law determines whether the law of State *A* or State *B* shall apply. We see below that horizontal choice of law is an issue on which state (not federal) law will govern. Under the New York choice of law rules, the law of Pennsylvania would govern (because the accident took place there). Don't lose sleep over this fact. Remember, how courts make the horizontal choice of law decision is covered in a different course — that on Conflict of Laws.

Court of Appeals for the Second Circuit affirmed, and the Supreme Court agreed to hear the case.

Why did the Supreme Court agree to hear the case? Ostensibly, the reason was to determine whether Tompkins's status — as invitee or trespasser — was a matter of general or local common law. Under *Swift v. Tyson*, as we saw in the preceding section, the federal court could apply its own view of the common law *only* if this was a general (and not a local) matter. That was the issue on which the parties briefed and argued the case at the Supreme Court. Imagine everyone's shock, then, when the first sentence of Justice Brandeis's opinion in *Erie* announced: "[T]he question for decision is whether the oft-challenged doctrine of *Swift v. Tyson* shall now be disapproved." No one involved in the case had argued that *Swift* should be overruled. The parties, the lower courts, and seemingly the Supreme Court at oral argument all assumed that *Swift* was good law. Imagine the further shock when the Court declared in *Erie* not only that it was overruling *Swift*, but that because of *Swift* the federal courts had been violating the Constitution for nearly a century!

§10.4.2   The Opinion and Its Two Themes: Litigant Equality and the Tenth Amendment

The Court's opinion, written by Justice Brandeis, is divided into four parts (of which the third is the real bombshell). In the first section, the Court noted that "more recent research of a competent scholar" suggested that *Swift* was wrongly decided. The research was by Professor Charles Warren, a legendary Harvard Law School professor,[15] who concluded, after reviewing the text of the original Rules of Decision Act, that the drafters intended that federal courts would apply state law — statutory and common law — as rules of decision in matters in which federal law does not apply.[16] Regardless of whether Professor Warren was correct,[17] the Court also noted widespread criticism of the vertical disuniformity caused by *Swift*, particularly after the decision in the *Black & White Taxicab* case,[18] discussed in §10.3.

In the second section of the opinion, the Court recognized forthrightly that the theory of *Swift* — that the federal courts would divine the one

---

[15] Many people believe that Professor Warren was the model for Professor Kingsfield in the movie *The Paper Chase*. If you've never seen that film, you might want to rent it. If you can get past the 1970s clothes and hairstyles, it's a timeless portrayal of the first year of law school.

[16] Charles Warren, *New Light on the History of the Federal Judiciary Act of 1789*, 37 Harv. L. Rev. 49, 51-52, 81-88, 108 (1923).

[17] Some disagree with Warren's conclusion. *See, e.g.*, Wilfred J. Ritz, *Rewriting the History of the Judiciary Act of 1789*, 148 (1990).

[18] We discussed that case above. See text accompanying notes 10-12.

true general common law for the states to follow — had failed in practice. State courts had persisted in their own views on matters of general common law, and the hoped-for transcendental, universal general common law had not emerged. That fact created the problem of vertical disuniformity and what the Court called the "mischievous" result of *Swift*: "In attempting to promote uniformity of law throughout the United States, the doctrine had prevented uniformity in the administration of the law of the State."[19] Because those with access to federal court had access to a different body of general common law, *Swift*

> introduced grave discrimination by non-citizens against citizens. It made rights enjoyed under the unwritten "general law" vary according to whether enforcement was sought in the state or in the federal court; and the privilege of selecting the court in which the right should be determined was conferred upon the non-citizen. Thus the doctrine *rendered impossible equal protection of the law*.[20]

By referring to "equal protection of the law," the Court was not speaking of the Equal Protection Clause of the Constitution. Rather, as the context of the statement made clear, the Court was concerned with the sort of unfairness caused by vertical disuniformity — specifically, that those who can invoke diversity of citizenship jurisdiction get access to law (in federal court) that those in state court cannot. I have referred to this concern as one for "litigant equality."[21] It is a basic notion that similarly situated persons ought to be treated alike: If exclusive dealing contracts are void in state court in Kentucky, they should be void in federal court too; if discharge of a debt is not good consideration for a contract in state court in New York it should not be good consideration in federal court. *Swift* violated this important tenet.

In the last paragraph of the second part of its opinion in *Erie*, the Court clearly seems to be leading up to overruling *Swift*. To do so, of course, all the Court needed to do was hold that the phrase "laws of the several states" in the Rules of Decision Act includes state decisional law of the general common law type. Such a holding would have rid the justice system of the "injustice and confusion incident to the doctrine of *Swift v. Tyson*."[22] But then the Court took a surprising turn: "If only a question of statutory construction were involved, we should not be prepared to abandon a doctrine so widely applied throughout nearly a century."[23] In other words, the

[19] 304 U.S. 75 (1938). The Court is discussing what we have called *vertical disuniformity*.

[20] *Id.* (emphasis added).

[21] Richard D. Freer, *Some Thoughts on the State of* Erie *After* Gasperini, 76 Tex. L. Rev. 1637, 1645 (1998).

[22] 304 U.S. at 77.

[23] *Id.*

Court would be reluctant to overrule *Swift* simply to fix that case's interpretation of the phrase "laws of the several states" in the Rules of Decision Act.

Then, in the last sentence of the second part of the opinion, the Court says something stunning: "But the *unconstitutionality* of the course pursued has now been made clear and compels us to [overrule *Swift*]."[24] Thus, in a case in which no party argued that *Swift* should be overruled, the Court overrules *Swift* — and not just as a matter of the construction of the Rules of Decision Act, but as a matter of constitutional law. Not only had *Swift* misinterpreted the Rules of Decision Act, but — according to the last sentence of the second part and the entire third part of the opinion — the *Swift* doctrine was unconstitutional!

Part three of the opinion discusses the constitutional basis of the holding, which we address in detail below. Part four of the opinion remanded the case to the Second Circuit for further proceedings. Obviously, this required the Second Circuit to remand the case to the district court, which was then required to apply state law on the underlying issue of what duty the railroad owed to Mr. Tompkins. As we know, state law provided that Tompkins was merely a trespasser and thus that the railroad owed him no duty beyond that not to inflict willful or wanton harm upon him. Because Tompkins could not show willful or wanton action by the railroad, the application of state law dictated that he lost the case.

In law school, of course, it is important to learn the principles established by the cases we study. But it is also a good idea to keep an eye on the human story involved in litigation. Law school gives you a vicarious view of hundreds — maybe thousands — of real-world struggles and, sometimes, heartaches. Mr. Tompkins had won a judgment of $30,000 at trial. On appeal, the railroad offered him $7,500 to settle the case. This would have been a significant sum in the 1930s, especially for an unemployed married man with a young child. One study of the background of the case notes that Tompkins leaned toward accepting the settlement, but that his lawyer — who wanted to appear in a Supreme Court case — urged him not to do so. The lawyer had Tompkins stay with him at his New York house for two weeks during the appellate process, until the railroad withdrew the settlement offer. As it turns out, the lawyer realized his dream of litigating at the Supreme Court. The result, unfortunately, was that Mr. Tompkins did not recover a penny for his injuries.[25] Now, let's look at the most important part of the *Erie* opinion — the third section.

Many observers have wondered why the Court based its holding in *Erie* on the Constitution, as opposed to the Rules of Decision Act. (After all, the Court could simply have overruled *Swift* by holding that the phrase "laws of the several states" in that statute included general common law

---

[24] *Id.* (emphasis added).

[25] *See* Irving Younger, *What Happened in* Erie, 56 Tex. L. Rev. 1011, 1021-1022 (1978).

decisions by state courts (and not just statutes and local common law decisions).) Ordinarily, the Court decides a case on statutory grounds when it can thus avoid a constitutional question. Yet, in *Erie*, the Court seemed to go out of its way to base its holding on the Constitution. As noted, the Court said it would be reluctant to overrule a 96-year-old precedent simply on statutory grounds. Ultimately, then, the Justices felt compelled to hold that the Rules of Decision Act itself was constitutional but that the *Swift application* of that statute was unconstitutional.

The Court's constitutional discussion is curious for this reason: Though making a constitutional holding, the Court never expressly identifies which part of the Constitution was violated by the regime of *Swift v. Tyson*. Despite this strange omission, everyone seems to agree that the holding is based upon the Tenth Amendment, which provides that "[t]he powers not delegated to the United States by the Constitution, nor prohibited by it to the States, are reserved to the States respectively, or to the people." The Tenth Amendment embodies the important principle of federalism — the states retain those powers that they did not cede to the federal government in the Constitution.[26] So *Erie* is an important statement of federalism. As the Court said in part three of the opinion:

> Except in matters governed by the Federal Constitution or by Acts of Congress, the law to be applied in any case is the law of the State. And whether the law of the State shall be declared by its Legislature in a statute or by its highest court in a decision is not a matter of federal concern. *There is no federal general common law. Congress has no power to declare substantive rules of common law applicable in a State, whether they be local in their nature or "general," be they commercial law or a part of the law of torts. And no clause of the Constitution purports to confer such a power on the federal courts.*[27]

In other words, *Swift* was an unconstitutional grab — by the federal courts — of power vested in the states. Put powerfully: "It is impossible to overstate the importance of the *Erie* decision. It announces no technical doctrine of procedure or jurisdiction, but goes to the heart of the relations between the federal government and the states and returns to the

---

[26] Justice Brandeis's majority opinion in *Erie* relied upon a lengthy quotation from Justice Field's dissent in *Baltimore & Ohio R. Co. v. Baugh*, 149 U.S. 368, 401 (1893), in which he rather clearly asserted that *Swift* violated the Tenth Amendment. He spoke of that part of the Constitution that "recognizes and preserves the autonomy and independence of the States" and of *Swift* as "an invasion of the authority of the State." We have met Justice Field before — he wrote the majority opinion in *Pennoyer v. Neff*, discussed at §2.4.1. See also §1.2.1 concerning creation of the federal government by states' ceding power to it.

[27] 304 U.S. at 78 (emphasis added).

states a power that had for nearly a century been exercised by the federal government."[28]

The three italicized sentences from the indented quotation above make two significant points. One point (made in the last two sentences) is structural: Nowhere does the Constitution give the federal government — either the legislature or the courts — authority to declare substantive rules of common law. The second point, made in the first italicized sentence, concludes that there is no such thing as "federal general common law." Of course, *Swift* was based upon the search for the one true general common law, which was to be declared by the *federal* courts. Now, 96 years later, it turns out *Swift* sent the federal courts in search of something that does not exist — indeed, cannot exist. Let's look more closely at these two points.

Many people probably come to law school believing that the federal government can do pretty much whatever it wants. In Constitutional Law, however, you learn that the federal government's powers are enumerated in the Constitution. So when the Court said that "Congress has no power to declare substantive rules of common law applicable in a State," it was not saying that Congress can *never* pass legislation that displaces state law. Of course it can — but *only* as to those matters which the Constitution entrusts to the federal legislature. So could Congress pass a statute declaring the duty owed by a railroad to a person walking along the railroad's right-of-way (the core issue in *Erie*)? Yes, you will see in Constitutional Law — but *only* if it had a constitutional basis for using its federal legislative power. For instance, Congress's power to regulate interstate commerce would undoubtedly give it the power to pass such a statute.

Though Congress could have legislated on the topic raised in *Erie*, it had not. There was no legislation mandating the application of federal law. Then the Court added the last sentence of the quoted material above, in which it reminded the country that nothing in the Constitution gives the federal *judiciary* any general power to make common law. Thus there was no *judicial* authority for the application of federal law. Because there was no federal law (legislative or judicial) on-point, the Tenth Amendment (and the Rules of Decision Act) commanded the application of state law.

But why does the federal *judiciary* not have the power to make common law in all areas in which the federal legislature can pass legislation? The answer seems to be this: The federal *judicial* authority is not as broad as the federal *legislative* authority. This fact reflects the concept of separation of powers, which circumscribes the courts' role vis-à-vis the legislature. It also reflects federalism in two ways. First, as provided in the Tenth Amendment, power not expressly given to the federal government

---

[28] Wright & Kane, Federal Courts 378.

is reserved to the states or to the people. Second, while the states' interests are represented in Congress (because the citizens of the states elect members of the House and the Senate[29]), those interests are not necessarily represented by members of the federal judiciary (who are not elected at all).

In addition to the constitutional basis for the *Erie* holding, there is no question that the case represented a different jurisprudential model than that reflected in *Swift*. The opinion quotes from Justice Holmes's famous statement that *Swift* was based upon the assumption that there was one true general common law — "a transcendental body of law outside of any particular State but obligatory within it unless and until changed by statute."[30] By the early twentieth century, judges, lawyers, and scholars — influenced by the legal realists — more readily understood that the common law was whatever the highest court of each state said it was. As Justice Frankfurter later explained:

> In overruling *Swift* ... *Erie* ... did not merely overrule a venerable case. It overruled a particular way of looking at law which dominated the judicial process long after its inadequacies had been laid bare. Law was conceived as a "brooding omnipresence" of Reason, of which decisions [by state courts] were merely evidence and not themselves the controlling formulations.[31]

Legal realists such as Holmes and Brandeis embraced the idea that "law" consists not only of statutes but of judicial declarations of the law. (As noted in §10.3, we in the twenty-first century are completely comfortable with this idea.) In a famous law review article, Holmes said, "[T]he prophecies of what the courts will do in fact, and nothing more pretentious, are what I mean by the law."[32] Another jurisprudential school in the ascendancy at the time of *Erie* was positivism. One tenet of positivism is that law is not some abstract and transcendental truth, but, rather, simply the command of a sovereign. Thus, to a positivist, all law must be either commanded by the federal or by the state government. The two schools together support the conclusions in *Erie* that (1) common law is what judges say it is; and (2) there is no overarching, general federal common law; each state is free to decree its own. From there, the Tenth Amendment makes the commandment quite clear: State common law is to govern in diversity of citizenship cases.

---

[29] Originally, members of the Senate were elected by the state legislatures. Not until 1913, with the ratification of the Seventeenth Amendment, were members of the Senate elected directly by the people of the state.

[30] 304 U.S. at 79, *quoting* Black & White Taxicab Co. v. Brown & Yellow Taxicab Co., 276 U.S. 518 (Holmes, J., dissenting) (we discussed this case in §10.3).

[31] Guaranty Trust Co. v. York, 326 U.S. 99, 101-102 (1945).

[32] Oliver Wendell Holmes, Jr., *The Path of the Law*, 10 Harv. L. Rev. 457, 461 (1897).

Though *Erie* was startling, its importance escaped the popular press. Felix Frankfurter, then a professor at Harvard Law School, wrote a letter to President Roosevelt, saying "I certainly didn't expect to live to see the day when the Court would announce, as they did Monday, that it itself has usurped power for nearly a hundred years. And think of not a single New York paper — at least none that I saw — having a nose for the significance of such a decision."[33] Justice Stone was so distraught over the lack of coverage that he wrote a letter to a columnist of the New York Times, prodding him to bring the "momentous decision" to the attention of the public.[34]

To recap, then, *Erie* overruled *Swift* and identified two major themes for doing so. The plainly constitutional theme, of course, is the Tenth Amendment — that state law must govern on matters of general common law. The other theme, which is not based in the Constitution, but in policy, is the notion of litigant equality. This is the idea that similarly situated persons should be treated alike — that the governing law should not differ depending upon whether the case is in federal or state court. In later cases, the Court sometimes emphasizes one of these themes over the other.

§10.4.3 Birth of the Dichotomy Between Substance and Procedure

Justice Stanley Reed concurred in the result in *Erie* and wrote an important separate opinion.[35] He agreed that *Swift v. Tyson* should be overruled, and he agreed with Justice Brandeis's reasoning *except* as to holding *Swift* unconstitutional. He would have based the holding on the Rules of Decision Act alone, and would have held that "the laws of the several states," as used in that statute, should include all decisions of the state courts. (We noted above that many have questioned why the majority felt compelled to base the *Erie* holding on constitutional grounds.)

Justice Reed suggested that Article III of the Constitution, together with the Necessary and Proper Clause, might empower Congress to pass "rules of substantive law" to be applied in federal court. Certainly, he asserted, *Erie* did not compel the federal courts to comply with every provision of state law. After all, "no one doubts federal power over procedure."[36] Here,

---

[33] Roosevelt and Frankfurter: Their Correspondence 1928-1945, at 456 (Max Freedman ed., 1967).

[34] Wright & Kane, Federal Courts, at 378 n.13. Interestingly, Chief Justice Stone later referred to the constitutional holding in *Erie* as "unfortunate dicta." *Id.* at 383 n.4.

[35] Justice Cardozo took no part in the *Erie* decision because he was quite ill at that time. Of the eight Justices participating, Brandeis and four others joined the majority opinion, and Justice Reed concurred. Two Justices — Butler and McReynolds — dissented from overruling *Swift v. Tyson*.

[36] 304 U.S. at 92 (Reed, J., concurring).

Reed addressed an issue the majority did not: whether *Erie* left the federal courts free to ignore state law on any points. His concurring opinion gave rise to labels that you will undoubtedly hear in law school: that in a diversity of citizenship case, the federal court must apply state "substantive" law but may apply federal "procedural" law. At one level, the distinction is harmless, and there is nothing wrong with using "substance" as a label for those rules as to which a federal court must follow state law and "procedure" for those as to which the federal court need not follow state law. As we see in subsequent sections, however, the labels should not be used as substitutes for analysis.

The distinction between substance and procedure seems clear from the Rules of Decision Act itself. That Act requires application of state law (as does *Erie*) *only* as to "rules of decision." Clearly, purely procedural matters would not seem to constitute rules of *decision*, and thus a federal court in a diversity of citizenship case may be free to "do its own thing" as to such matters.

§10.4.4 The Remarkable Year of 1938

Erie was not the only engine of change in 1938. That year also saw the promulgation of the original Federal Rules of Civil Procedure. Those rules, which we now take for granted, were made possible by the Rules Enabling Act, passed in 1934, and now codified at 28 U.S.C. §2072. The Rules Enabling Act is a delegation from Congress to the Supreme Court of the authority to promulgate uniform rules of procedure for the federal courts. After its passage, it took four years to get the initial Rules drafted, approved by the Court, and accepted by Congress. Before 1938, the Conformity Act required federal district courts to apply the procedural law of the state in which the court sat. So think of the changes thrust upon the federal courts in diversity of citizenship cases in 1938. Until then, federal judges applied state procedural law and invented their own general common law. After that year, in contrast, they applied uniform federal rules of procedure but adhered to state common law. In other words, there was a diametric change in each area — substance and procedure.

The events of 1938 must also be seen in the overall political context of Franklin Roosevelt's New Deal, which marked a massive expansion of federal power, unquestionably at the expense of state autonomy. The Court, after initial reluctance, ultimately upheld and thus legitimated most of these federal assertions of power. *Erie* seems out of step with the tenor of such times, because it embraces the importance of the state pronouncements of law. On the other hand, diversity of citizenship jurisdiction under the regime of *Swift v. Tyson* was widely thought to create a favorable litigation climate in federal courts for large corporate interests, often at the

expense of the "little guy."[37] *Erie*, which stripped the federal court of its
power to make up general common law, may be seen as a decision against
corporate interests and thus as more consistent with some thrusts of the
New Deal.[38]

§10.5   Progeny of *Erie* Until 1965: *Klaxon* Through *Byrd*

After *Erie*, of course, federal courts must apply state law (including
common law) as the rules of decision (or, in shorthand, on law of *substance*) in diversity of citizenship cases. Whatever "substance" means —
whatever "rules of decision" are — clearly, the bottom-line issue in *Erie*
fell within both. The issue in that case was Mr. Tompkins's status as a trespasser or invitee and the resultant duty owed to him. Without doubt, those
issues define the very circumstances under which one party is liable to
another and thus constitute rules of substance.

In the wake of *Erie*, the Court was forced to decide whether a variety
of topics constituted substance as to which state law must govern in diversity of citizenship cases. The Court had to make that determination as to
topics that are hard to characterize — such as choice of law, statutes of
limitations, whether the statute of limitations should be tolled, and the burden of proof at trial. For nearly three decades, the Court addressed such
issues in vertical choice of law, and seemed to establish different tests for
determining when a federal court in diversity must apply state law. Our
job in this section is to review those cases and the tests they formulated.
Though the Court will make a dramatic discovery in 1965, as we see in
§10.6, the cases we study here have never been overruled. Ultimately, we
will have to decide how they fit into an overall, integrated approach to
vertical choice of law.

Four years after *Erie*, the Court decided *Klaxon v. Stentor Electric
Manufacturing Co.*,[39] in which it held that a federal court in diversity must
apply *state* choice of law rules. Stated in a conclusory way, then, choice
of law rules are substantive; they constitute rules of decision, as to which
state law must govern. We discussed choice of law rules in §10.2. They
are the rules for determining "horizontal choice of law" issues — that is,
whether the law of State *A* or of State *B* will govern a dispute. *Klaxon*
holds that a federal court in diversity must apply the choice of law rules
of the state in which that federal court sits. The Court had done this by

---

[37] *See* Edward Purcell, Jr., Litigation and Inequality: Federal Diversity Jurisdiction in
Industrial America, 1870-1958 (1992).
[38] Ironically, and unfortunately for Mr. Tompkins, the decision in *Erie* itself favored the
corporate defendant.
[39] 313 U.S. 487 (1941).

implication in *Erie* itself. That case was tried in a federal district court in New York. New York choice of law doctrine dictated that the law of Pennsylvania would govern the dispute (because the injury was suffered in Pennsylvania).[40] Though commentators have criticized *Klaxon*, the Court has reaffirmed the holding of the case, and it is undoubtedly good law today.[41]

Guaranty Trust

In 1945, the Court decided a significant case in *Guaranty Trust Co. v. York*.[42] The plaintiff's claim, asserted in federal court under diversity of citizenship jurisdiction, was barred by the state statute of limitations. But it was an equitable claim. Traditionally, equity courts applied the doctrine of "laches" to determine whether a plaintiff should be barred for having "slumbered on his rights" too long; laches could trump a statute of limitations in a case involving the assertion of an equity claim. In *Guaranty Trust*, the federal district court recognized that the state statute of limitations barred the claim. Nonetheless, as a court of equity, it determined that the plaintiff was not guilty of laches and thus should be able to proceed. The Supreme Court held that the district court was wrong, and that *Erie* required it to apply the state statute of limitations. Justice Frankfurter's opinion recognized that courts and commentators talked a great deal about how *Erie* set up a "great divide cutting across the whole domain of law" — a divide between "substance" and "procedure."[43]

The Court refused to apply a labeling test, however, and instead analyzed the problem functionally. Justice Frankfurter's opinion recognized that federal courts should be free to prescribe the way in which substantive rights are enforced. Thus, he said, "the forms and mode of enforcing [a] right may at time, naturally enough, vary because the two judicial systems are not identic."[44] On the other hand, the Court noted "since a federal court adjudicating a State-created right solely because of diversity of citizenship of the parties is for that purpose, in effect, only another court

---

[40] See note 14 above. This inquiry can get convoluted. In one case, a judge noted, "Our principal task . . . is to determine what New York courts would think California courts would think on an issue about which neither has thought." Nolan v. Transocean Air Lines, 276 F.2d 280, 281 (2d Cir. 1960). Again, though, choice of law is an important topic in a different law school course — Conflict of Laws.

[41] Day & Zimmerman, Inc. v. Challoner, 423 U.S. 3, 4 (1975). We saw an issue regarding this point in discussing transfer of venue in §5.5.2. There, we noted that a case transferred under §1404(a) would carry with it the choice of law rules of the transferor court.

[42] 326 U.S. 99 (1945). The opinion was written by Justice Frankfurter. Recall from note 33 that when he was a professor at Harvard he had written to President Roosevelt concerning the popular press's lack of appreciation for the importance of *Erie*.

[43] 326 U.S. at 109.

[44] *Id.* at 108.

of the State, it cannot afford recovery if the right to recover is made unavailable by the State...."[45] Ultimately, the Court posited: "[T]he outcome of the litigation in the federal court should be substantially the same, so far as legal rules determine the outcome of a litigation, as it would be if tried in a State court."[46] The state law (the statute of limitations) required dismissal of the case. The district court's ignoring that law under the doctrine of laches would permit the case to proceed. Because ignoring state law would thus lead to a different "outcome" than applying state law, it would violate the command of *Erie*.

In §10.4.2, we discussed the two underlying themes of *Erie*. One, of course, is the constitutional provision protecting state sovereignty in the Tenth Amendment. The other was the nonconstitutional notion of "litigant equality" — that similarly situated persons should be treated alike. *Guaranty Trust*, as applied, seemed to say that *Erie* requires that the *outcome* of litigation in federal court be the same as it would have been in state court. Nothing in *Erie* said that. Thus, some criticize *Guaranty Trust* as adopting an overly wooden approach to the litigant equality theme from *Erie*. This criticism is unfair to a degree. Justice Frankfurter's opinion was more subtle than later cases that applied it. As noted above, Justice Frankfurter actually said that the outcome should be the same in federal and in state court "so far as *legal rules* determine the outcome of a litigation."[47]

But later cases — particularly in the lower courts — missed this nuance in *Guaranty Trust*. These cases interpreted *Guaranty Trust* as prescribing an "outcome determinative" test, which indeed requires the federal court to ensure that the *outcome* — who wins and who loses — not differ from the result in state court. This reading is unfortunate, because it led to the view that federal courts in diversity cases were simply to be clones of the state courts. The federal courts comprise a system of justice separate from that in the states, and that system must have the authority to prescribe its own rules except for rules of decision. There is no rule — no matter how plainly nonsubstantive — that does not become "outcome determinative" at some point. And reading *Guaranty Trust* woodenly seems to require the federal court to adopt the state rule even on such points.

- ° Suppose state courts require that pleadings be filed on 14-inch paper. The federal court, however, requires that pleadings be on 11-inch paper. There is nothing even remotely "substantive" about the length of paper on which one drafts her pleadings. There is no chance that the size of the paper on which pleadings are asserted is a "rule of decision." Still, a wooden application of *Guaranty Trust* might proceed this way when a plaintiff files

---

[45] *Id.* at 108-109.
[46] *Id.* at 109.
[47] *Id.* (emphasis added).

in federal court on 14-inch paper: (1) the 14-inch document would be accepted in state court, so the case could proceed; (2) if the clerk's office in federal court does not accept the 14-inch paper, the case will not proceed; (3) therefore, the rule about 14-inch paper is outcome determinative; and (4) the federal court must follow state law and permit the filing on 14-inch paper.

Such a result would be absurd. Obviously, the federal judicial system must be able to prescribe such rules for itself. As Justice Frankfurter said in *Guaranty Trust*, "the forms and mode of enforcing the right may at times, naturally enough, vary because the two judicial systems are not identical."[48] Even the Supreme Court seemed to forget this point in the years following *Guaranty Trust*. It transformed a concern with litigant equality into an inflexible rule of "outcome equality." Nowhere was this more obvious than in what are known as the "triple play" cases.

The "Triple Play" Cases

On one day in 1949, the Supreme Court decided three cases that signaled to many observers that *Erie* might eviscerate the Federal Rules of Civil Procedure. All three seemed to require a federal diversity court to apply what clearly seemed to be state "procedural" rules. In *Ragan v. Merchants Transfer & Warehouse Co.*,[49] the question was when an action is "commenced" for purposes of tolling the statute of limitations. Understanding the case requires some background in the application of statutes of limitations. Such statutes allow a claimant no more than a specified period — say two years[50] — in which to commence the action. The period starts to "run" from "accrual" of the claim. That means the clock starts ticking on the plaintiff's two years (or whatever the period is) when her claim accrues. Jurisdictions adopt different standards for when a claim accrues. One typical approach is that accrual occurs on the date the defendant allegedly breached a duty or caused harm, even if the claimant is unaware of the breach or harm. The other major approach is that accrual occurs when a reasonable claimant would have discovered that she had been harmed. At any rate, *commencing* the action before the limitations period expires is said to "toll" the running of the statute. Tolling simply means that the ticking of the limitations clock is stopped.[51] The bottom

---

[48] *Id.* at 108.

[49] 337 U.S. 530 (1949).

[50] Statutes of limitations vary greatly from state to state and for various claims even within a state. Typically, tort claims have a shorter statute of limitations than contract or property claims. Defamation usually has a short limitations period, often one year from accrual of the claim.

[51] Other things can toll the running of the statute of limitations. For example, lack of mental or legal capacity generally tolls the statute. Suppose *D* commits a tort that injures *P*,

line is simple: The claimant must "commence" the action before the limitations period expires.

In *Ragan*, the statute of limitations expired after the plaintiff filed the case but before the defendant was served with process. (Recall from §3.3.1 that there is often a delay between the date on which the complaint is filed and the date on which the defendant is served with process.) State law provided that the statute was tolled from the date on which the defendant was served with process — *not* the date on which the complaint was filed. Thus, under state law, the plaintiff would be barred by the statute of limitations. On the other hand, Federal Rule 3 provides that "a civil action is commenced by filing a complaint with the court." The plaintiff in *Ragan* argued that, under Rule 3, the statute of limitations was tolled from the date on which the complaint was filed. The Supreme Court rejected this argument, and held that state law governed the question of tolling. Why? Because of "outcome determination." If state law were applied, the case would be dismissed. If state law were ignored, the case would proceed. As in *Guaranty Trust*, the Court felt it inappropriate to have a different "outcome" in federal court than there would have been in state court.

The second case decided that day was *Woods v. Interstate Realty Co.*[52] There, a Mississippi statute provided that corporations formed in other states must register with the state before doing business in Mississippi. Under the statute, failure to do so waives that corporation's right to sue in Mississippi courts. (Such a provision is called a *door-closing statute*, for the obvious reason that it closes the (state) courthouse door to such a corporation.) A non-Mississippi corporation commenced suit in federal court under diversity of citizenship jurisdiction, and the question was whether the state door-closing statute should be followed by the federal court. The Supreme Court held that it should. Again, it invoked outcome determination as the test. If state law were applied, the case would be dismissed. If it were ignored, the case would proceed. This different outcome — like that in *Guaranty Trust* — dictated that the federal court must apply state law and dismiss the case.

---

who is 14 years old. Let's say the relevant statute of limitations is two years. But *P* lacks legal capacity because she is a minor at the time the claim accrued. The statute is tolled (and therefore does not start to run) until *P* reaches age 18 (the age of majority, when she has legal capacity). Accordingly, the two-year statute would start to run when *P* turned 18. She can sue until she turns age 20.

[52] 337 U.S. 535 (1949). This does not mean that federal courts must follow every state door-closing statute. The one involved in *Woods* served a state purpose (requiring out-of-state corporations to register and pay fees) that would be subverted if the federal courts allowed them to sue. A door-closing statute aimed merely at reducing state court caseload would not be violated by entertaining a diversity case. *See* Szantay v. Beech Aircraft Corp., 348 F.2d 60 (4th Cir. 1965).

The third case was *Cohen v. Beneficial Industrial Loan Co.*,[53] which involved a specialized kind of litigation called a *shareholder derivative suit*.[54] Federal Rule 23.1 enumerates prerequisites for bringing a derivative suit in federal court. It does *not* require the plaintiff in such a case to post a bond with the court. The law of some states, including New York (which was the relevant state in *Cohen*), does require that the plaintiff post a bond as a prerequisite to the derivative suit. The purpose of such a requirement is to deter "strike" or "nuisance" suits. A shareholder who has to post a bond (which is money from which the corporation can recover its litigation expenses if the suit is frivolous) is less likely to bring a bogus derivative suit than one who does not have such a financial stake in the case. In *Cohen*, the Supreme Court held that a federal court must apply the state-law bond requirement, even though, as noted, Federal Rule 23.1 does not include such a requirement.

Though it was decided earlier (and so is not technically one of the "triple play" cases), *Palmer v. Hoffman*[55] should be mentioned here. The case concerned which party assumes the burden of proof at trial on the issue of the plaintiff's contributory negligence. In some states, the defendant must prove that the plaintiff was negligent; in others, the plaintiff must prove her own lack of negligence. Federal Rule 8(c)(1) lists contributory negligence as an affirmative defense that the defendant must plead. In *Palmer*, the Supreme Court held that notwithstanding Rule 8(c)(1) (which was then simply Rule 8(c)), a federal court sitting in diversity jurisdiction must apply state law concerning burden of proof at trial. That law placed the burden of proof on the plaintiff, and thus governed in *Palmer*.

Many influential observers saw these cases as a serious threat to the authority of the federal courts to apply their own rules even as to clearly procedural aspects of a case. One famous law review article characterized the 1949 cases as a "triple play" on the Federal Rules of Civil Procedure.[56] Charles Clark himself — who was the principal drafter of the Federal Rules — concluded that few of the Rules could "be considered safe from attack" after the triple play cases.[57]

Was this nervousness justified? Yes. On the face of things, *Ragan* seemed to eviscerate Rule 3. After all, that Rule clearly provided that a case is commenced when filed, yet the case held that a federal court must apply the state-law definition of when a case was commenced. *Palmer* seemed to make light of Federal Rule 8(c)(1) by requiring the plaintiff to

---

[53] *Id.* at 541.

[54] We discuss this type of litigation briefly in §13.1.

[55] 318 U.S. 109 (1943).

[56] Edward Merrigan, Erie *to* York *to* Ragan: *A Triple Play on the Federal Rules*, 3 Vand. L. Rev. 711 (1950). "Triple play" is a baseball reference. In a triple play, three outs are recorded on a single play. The batting team thus loses its at-bat in one fell swoop. It is a bad thing (for the batting team).

[57] Charles Clark, *Book Review*, 36 Cornell L.Q. 181, 183 (1950).

prove her lack of contributory negligence. Similarly, *Cohen* seemed to eviscerate Rule 23.1 by requiring federal courts to engraft on its list of pre-requisites for a derivative suit the state-law requirement of a bond. In some ways, however, *Woods* seems most threatening to the federal judicial system. It held that a *state* statute could require the *federal* judicial system to close its doors, and to refuse to exercise its validly invoked diversity of citizenship jurisdiction.

Together, these cases show that the pendulum had swung too far toward the "state" side of things, and away from the "federal" side. The fixation on outcome equality — itself a perversion of one theme of *Erie* — seemed destined to relegate the federal courts to the status of mere clones of the state judicial systems. It was time for the Supreme Court to reassert that the federal judicial system has legitimate interests that do not have to bow to state law. It did so nine years after the triple play cases in *Byrd v. Blue Ridge Rural Electrical Cooperative, Inc.*[58]

Byrd v. Blue Ridge

Mr. Byrd was injured while working for a construction company. The construction company was part of the Blue Ridge Rural Electrical Cooperative ("Co-op"), which sold electric power in rural South Carolina. Mr. Byrd could not sue his immediate employer (the construction company) because of workers' compensation laws. Those laws provide that an employee cannot sue her employer for work-related injuries. Rather, the employer is strictly liable and must compensate the employee for injuries according to a statutory schedule. On the one hand, this is a disadvantage to the seriously injured employee, because she cannot sue and recover more than the statutory schedule permits. On the other hand, this is an advantage to the employee, because she does not have to sue at all; she is entitled to the workers' compensation benefits automatically, and does not have to waste time litigating anything.

Lawyers for Mr. Byrd brought a diversity of citizenship case against the Co-op,[59] on the theory that Byrd was not an employee of the Co-op and thus was not limited to workers' compensation recovery. The Co-op argued that Byrd was a "statutory employee," which meant that he would be treated as an employee of the Co-op and thus was limited to workers' compensation benefits from it. Obviously, the question of whether Byrd was a statutory employee of the Co-op was the crucial issue. If he was, he had no right to sue, and his case would be dismissed. Just as obviously, the question was one of fact — someone had to determine, based upon the evidence, whether Byrd was a statutory employee of the Co-op. And the fight

---

[58] 356 U.S. 525 (1958).

[59] Byrd was a citizen of North Carolina, the Co-op was a citizen of South Carolina, and the amount in controversy requirement was satisfied.

that went to the Supreme Court was over who was to make that factual decision — the judge or a jury.

Under South Carolina case law, the judge, without a jury, would make the decision. Though the South Carolina Supreme Court had clearly held this to be the law, it had not explained *why* the judge, and not a jury, was to make the decision. Byrd's lawyers argued that the South Carolina law was not binding on the federal court sitting in diversity of citizenship jurisdiction, and thus that the issue should be determined by a jury.[60]

The Court held that *Erie* did *not* require the federal court to follow state law on this issue.[61] Note, then, *Byrd* is the first case after *Swift v. Tyson* was overruled in which the Court upheld a federal court prerogative in the face of a contrary state law. The Court's interpretation of *Erie* is found in Part II of the opinion, drafted by a young Justice Brennan. That part of the opinion is subdivided into three sections. Before assessing them, another word of caution. I consider *Byrd* to be the Court's finest hour in laying out a test for determining when *Erie* requires federal courts to apply state law. Not all professors agree. Even those of us who are fans of *Byrd* have to admit that its usefulness has been limited because the Supreme Court has largely ignored it in the succeeding decades. Your professor will undoubtedly have her own thoughts about the importance of *Byrd* and the other cases, and you should be aware of what she thinks.

In the first sentence of the first subsection of Part II, the Court says, "It was decided in [*Erie*] that the federal courts ... *must* respect the definition of state-created rights and obligations by the state courts."[62] Notice the word "must" — connoting that there is no discretion. This is a command to the federal courts and thus obviously emanates from the Tenth Amendment. Also notice that the "must" attaches to the "definition of state-created rights and obligations." This phrase seems to refer to matters all would agree are purely substantive — the elements of a claim or defense, for example. As to them, *Erie* commands federal courts to respect state law, which makes sense. After all, elements of a claim or defense, without question, constitute rules of decision for a case and, thus, the Rules of Decision Act requires application of state law. We can refer to these issues as raising questions of "pure substance."

---

[60] Think about why Byrd wanted a jury and the Co-op did not. Byrd was seriously hurt. A jury would presumably be more sympathetic to him and less sympathetic to the large Co-op's argument that Byrd should be limited to the (relatively paltry) remedies provided by workers' compensation law. As we saw in §9.2.2, parties are willing to spend a great deal of time and money in litigating the issue of who will be the fact-finder on a particular issue.

[61] The Court addressed this question after holding, in Part I of the *Byrd* opinion, that the lower courts erred by not permitting Byrd to present evidence on the statutory employee issue. Because the case had to be remanded for fact-finding on that question, the Court had to determine who (judge or jury) would make that determination.

[62] 356 U.S. at 535 (emphasis added).

The following sentence is equally interesting. "We must, therefore, first examine the rule in [the South Carolina case holding that the judge is to decide the statutory employee issue] to determine whether it is *bound up* with these rights and obligations in such a way that its application in the federal court is required."[63] Notice the phrase "bound up," which the Court fails to define. Clearly, though, it must mean that there are some state rules that are so closely related to matters of pure substance that the Tenth Amendment requires federal courts to respect them; they fall within the Tenth Amendment command.

Unfortunately, the Court has never defined "bound up." It seems, though, that the phrase encompasses things that refine the state's assessment of when someone is entitled to recover from another. We have seen examples. *Klaxon* required a federal diversity court to apply state choice of law rules. Such rules do not define the elements of a claim or defense, but do serve to refine the state-law assessment of when a claimant can recover. They instruct the court which state's law to apply and thus seem bound up with "rights and obligations" defined by state law. In addition, *Palmer v. Hoffman* held that a federal diversity court must apply state law on the burden of proof at trial. Again, the burden of proof does not exactly define when a party may recover, but is closely related to it. It seems bound up with the definition of when a claimant can recover because it determines the winner when no proof is introduced on a particular issue.[64]

In *Byrd*, the Court then launches into a lengthy paragraph in which it determines that the South Carolina rule does not define state-created rights and obligations and is not bound up with such rules. Instead, it is "merely a form and mode of enforcing the immunity."[65] What happens with issues of "form and mode"? The Court explains in the second subsection of Part II. The first sentence is long but interesting:

> But cases following *Erie* have evinced a *broader policy* to the effect that the federal courts should conform as near as may be — in the absence of other considerations — to state rules even of form and mode where the state rules may bear substantially on the question whether the litigation would come out one way in the federal court and another way in the state court if the federal court failed to apply a particular local rule.[66]

---

[63] *Id.* (emphasis added).

[64] I think statute of limitations would be another example. Such statutes do not define the rights and obligations, but put a temporal limitation on the claimant's ability to assert a right of pure substance. Given the holding in *Guaranty Trust*, however, in which the Court described the statute of limitations as a matter of the "form and mode" of enforcing a right, perhaps such rules are not bound up.

[65] 356 U.S. at 536. *Guaranty Trust* had first used the term *form and mode* to describe the statute of limitations.

[66] *Id.* at 536-537 (emphasis added).

This sentence is a gold mine. The term *broader policy* refers to *Erie*'s theme about litigant equality. Recall from our discussion in §10.4.2 that *Erie* embodied not only the constitutional basis of the Tenth Amendment but the nonconstitutional policy underpinning of a concern that similarly situated parties be treated alike. *Guaranty Trust*, at least as it came to be applied, had perverted this interest in *litigant* equality into one of *outcome* equality. Here, in *Byrd*, the Court for the first time explains that this policy applies to cases in which the state law issue is not purely substantive or bound up with pure substance. This policy counsels — *but does not compel* — the federal courts to apply state law *in cases in which* failure to apply state law will be outcome determinative. It thus gives a context for the *Guaranty Trust* analysis: As to issues of form and mode, and when failure to apply state law would be outcome determinative, the federal court will apply state law "in the absence of other considerations." The Court opens the door to the possibility that "other considerations" might override outcome determination and permit a federal court to refuse to follow state law.

Indeed, *Byrd* itself is such a case. The Court makes the very important point that the federal courts, as an independent system for the administration of justice, have an interest in keeping "essential characteristic[s]" of that system free from interference by state law. Such an interest constitutes an "affirmative countervailing consideration[]"[67] that justifies a federal court's ignoring state law. In *Byrd*, the federal systemic interest is in the division of labor between judge and jury, which is influenced by the Seventh Amendment.[68] State law — at least state law that is not pure substance or bound up with it — "cannot in every case exact compliance with a state rule . . . which disrupts the federal system of allocating functions between judge and jury."[69] Because the state system had articulated no reason for its rule, while the federal system had a strong interest in allocating fact-finding functions between judge and jury, the federal courts were justified in ignoring the state rule about having the judge decide the issue of whether Byrd was a statutory employee.

In the third subsection of Part II of the opinion, the Court notes that its preceding analysis was based upon the supposition that the question of who decided whether Mr. Byrd was a statutory employee was "outcome determinative" in the *Guaranty Trust* sense. Here, it hints that the issue is probably not outcome determinative. That being the case, it is possible that much of what the Court said in the second subpart of Part II is dicta.

---

[67] *Id.* at 537.

[68] It is curious that the Court did not simply hold that the issue of whether Mr. Byrd was a statutory employee was one as to which the Seventh Amendment applied to grant a right to jury trial in federal court. Had it done so, the Supremacy Clause would render *Erie* inapplicable.

[69] *Id.* at 538.

One hopes, however, that it is not, because that part of the opinion makes so much sense. It told us that on matters of form and mode — as to which the Tenth Amendment does not command the federal court to apply state law — the federal court can nonetheless be conscripted to apply state law. It will do so if failing to do so would be outcome determinative *and* if no federal system interest in the allocation of duties outweighs the state interest. *Byrd* is famous for bringing "balancing" into the *Erie* equation, but it is important to see that it did so only in the limited circumstances summarized in this paragraph.

Byrd thus sets up a helpful linear model, diagrammed below. At one polar extreme are things that all would agree are purely substantive (like the elements of a claim), which the Court characterized as rules "respect-[ing] the definition of state-created rights and obligations." At the other polar extreme are things that all would agree are purely procedural (like the length of paper on which pleadings are to be filed). Clearly, the federal court can "do its own thing" on purely procedural matters. Nothing in the Rules of Decision Act or *Erie* requires the federal court to apply state law there. Just as clearly, the Tenth Amendment commands the federal court to apply state law on matters of pure substance. As one moves away from pure substance, however, there are rules that are so bound up with the definition of rights and obligations as to be treated as pure substance under *Erie*. The Tenth Amendment requires the federal diversity court to follow such state rules, such as choice of law and burden of proof rules.

Further removed from pure substance are rules of form and mode (which may be a fancy way of saying "procedure"). Here, *Byrd* establishes, the Tenth Amendment does not apply. But the policy of litigant equality espoused in *Erie* does. If ignoring the state law on this point will be outcome determinative, the federal court will — as a matter of comity, to avoid differing outcomes in the two systems — apply state law. *But* it will not do this if it would violate some interest of the federal courts as a separate judicial system. Here, it will balance the relative interests of the systems. In *Byrd*, the federal systemic interest was great, while the state gave no reason for its rule and thus had little interest in it. The federal interest outweighed the state's and the federal court was justified in ignoring state law.

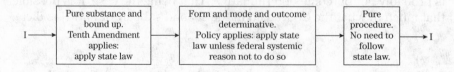

In sum, *Byrd* is not perfect (it does not define "bound up" and does not tell us how to weigh truly competing federal and state interests), but it is far better than anything we've seen so far. It permitted the federal courts to avoid the application of state law that would disrupt the operation of the federal system, and told us what part of *Erie* is commanded by the Tenth Amendment and what part is counseled by policy. It also gave us a context for application of the outcome-determination test of *Guaranty Trust*. Sadly, the Court has done next to nothing with *Byrd* since it was decided.

§10.6   The *Erie* Doctrine Splits: *Hanna v. Plumer* and Subsequent Developments

§10.6.1   *Hanna*'s Establishment of Two Levels of Vertical Choice of Law: The *Hanna* Prong and the *Erie* Prong

The Background. The next important case was a giant — *Hanna v. Plumer*,[70] which was decided in 1965. In that case, the plaintiff brought a diversity case in federal court in Massachusetts. The defendant was the executor of a deceased person. He was served with process under a provision now found in Federal Rule 4(e)(2)(B), which allows for "substituted" service of process by serving someone of suitable age and discretion who resides at the defendant's dwelling or usual abode.[71] Under Massachusetts law, however, service on a representative of a decedent, such as an executor, had to be effected personally; substituted service was not permitted. The question was clear: Did *Erie* require the federal court to apply state law in this instance, or was the federal court free to ignore state law and apply Rule 4?

Based upon what we have seen (especially *Byrd*), we would expect a federal court to look at whether the state rule requiring personal service of process was part of the definition of state-created rights and obligations or was bound up with such a definition. If (as seems likely) it was not — but was merely a rule of form and mode — the court would next look to whether it was outcome determinative under *Guaranty Trust*. It certainly seems so: If state law were applied, the case would be dismissed; if state law were ignored, the case would proceed. Thus, we would expect the court to apply state law unless there was a federal systemic interest

---

[70] 380 U.S. 460 (1965).

[71] At the time the case was decided, the "substituted" service of process rule was found in Federal Rule 4(d)(1), so the opinion refers to that. We discussed substituted service at §3.3.2.

that outweighed the state interest in its rule. No such interest seems obvious, so we might expect *Erie*, as we have seen it, to require the application of state law. Indeed, the lower courts concluded that state law should govern and held that service of process was improper because it was not effected in the way required by state law. At the Supreme Court, the defendant (who had won in the lower courts) argued that the lower courts were right under *Guaranty Trust* because the rule was outcome determinative.

So what did the Court do? It did not purport to approach the case under the *Byrd* scheme. Thus, it did not discuss whether the state law was part of the definition of state-created rights or bound up with such a definition. It did, however, discuss *Guaranty Trust* and outcome determination. Consistent with *Byrd*, it seemed to discuss outcome determination as something that applies only to state rules of form and mode. But *Hanna* proposed a fundamentally different way to look at outcome determination. Chief Justice Warren's opinion noted that "[o]utcome-determination analysis was never intended to serve as a talisman.[72] Indeed, the message of [*Guaranty Trust*] itself is that choices between state and federal law are to be made not by application of any automatic 'litmus paper' criterion, but rather by reference to the policies underlying the *Erie* rule."[73] This is important language because it recognizes that courts had come to apply *Guaranty Trust* woodenly. In fact, the Court noted (as we did in §10.5) that at some point *every* procedural variation between the federal and state courts will be outcome determinative in the sense that the courts had come to apply that test.

The Twin Aims of Erie. The Court then posited that outcome determination, while relevant to a Rules of Decision Act inquiry, should be guided by what it called the *twin aims* of *Erie*: (1) discouragement of forum shopping and (2) avoidance of the inequitable administration of the laws. This is the first time the Court identified these twin aims as such. It traced them not to the Tenth Amendment basis of *Erie*, but to what we have called the litigant equality theme from that case: "a realization that it would be unfair for the character or result of a litigation to differ materially because the suit had been brought in a federal court."[74] According to the Court, *Erie* was based (at least in part) upon a reaction to the forum shopping that was inspired by *Swift v. Tyson*, which we discussed in §10.3. Guided by these principles, the outcome-determination test should focus not at the point in litigation where compliance with the state rule becomes a problem, but at the *outset* of the case. The question should be whether

---

[72] At this point, the Court cited *Byrd*, which was the only time the Supreme Court cited *Byrd* between 1958 and 1996. It failed, however, to discuss *Byrd* in any way.

[73] 380 U.S. at 467.

[74] *Id.* In his concurring opinion, which we discuss toward the end of this subsection, Justice Harlan decried the majority's focus on litigant equality. *Erie*, to Justice Harlan, was more about the Tenth Amendment than about forum shopping.

the difference between applying state law and ignoring state law would influence the plaintiff in choosing the federal forum. If so, the federal court should lean toward applying state law.

This new outcome-determination analysis from *Hanna* is known as the "modified-outcome-determination" test or the "twin aims" test. It appears to be far more sensitive and consistent with what Justice Frankfurter implied in *Guaranty Trust* than the wooden test that courts evolved from that case. Moreover, it seems consistent with *Byrd* in treating the outcome-determination analysis as part of the policy of litigant equality rather than the Tenth Amendment core of *Erie*.[75]

Some commentators have questioned, however, whether there really are two aims in the twin aims test. Instead, it seems that the Court was worried about only one thing — avoidance of forum shopping. If there is forum shopping, it seems that the "inequitable administration of the laws" follows automatically. Stated another way, if ignoring a state law will cause litigants to flock to federal court, this will automatically result in the inequitable administration of the laws. Why? Because only citizens of another state will be able to gain access to the federal court (because only they can invoke diversity jurisdiction). An example proves the point.

> ○ Assume the law of State *A* requires plaintiffs in a medical malpractice suit to file with their complaint an affidavit of a health care professional stating her professional conclusion that malpractice was likely to have occurred. Plaintiffs do not like this requirement because it makes it more expensive and difficult simply to initiate such a suit. Plaintiff, a citizen of State *B*, sues Doctor, a citizen of State *A*, in federal court for medical malpractice. If the federal court does not follow state law, Plaintiff will be able to sue without an affidavit. This undoubtedly would cause forum shopping — every plaintiff who could go to federal court would do so, because she would thus evade the affidavit requirement. *Because only citizens of states other than State* A *can go to federal court (because only they can invoke diversity of citizenship against a doctor who is a citizen of State* A), *the federal court's failure to follow state law would automatically create the inequitable administration of the laws.*

Whether the test really has one aim or two, it is important to see how the *Hanna* approach differs — in focus and result — from that of *Guaranty Trust*. The issue in *Hanna* (whether service of process was proper) certainly was outcome determinative in the wooden *Guaranty Trust* sense. Why? Because, as we already noted, if state law applied, the case would be dismissed; if state law were ignored, the case would proceed. This is exactly the scenario the Court found to be outcome determinative

---

[75] It is odd that *Hanna* cites *Byrd* only once, and does not discuss *Byrd*'s overall approach to vertical choice of law.

in *Guaranty Trust*. But the facts of *Hanna* were not outcome determinative in the new twin aims sense. Why? Because no litigant — in assessing where to sue *at the outset of litigation* — would sue in federal court just to avoid the personal service of process requirement of state law. The plaintiff in *Hanna* probably had every intention of effecting personal service on the defendant. Not until service was attempted did the need for substituted service arise.

Thus, the question of how one serves process upon the defendant is not "outcome determinative" in the new sense of that phrase as reflected in *Hanna*. Because the issue was not outcome determinative, state law need not be applied. At this point in the opinion, then, the Court seems to be modifying the outcome-determination test and to be on the verge of holding, under *Erie*, that state law did not govern. Instead of doing so, however, the Court suddenly informs us that its new twin aims analysis is irrelevant to the issue before it! In fact, everything we have read so far is irrelevant. Why? Because everything we have read so far deals with the Rules of Decision Act, and that statute is irrelevant to the issue before the Court in *Hanna*. Instead, the Court explains, the vertical choice of law issue in *Hanna* implicates an entirely different statute: the Rules Enabling Act.

The Rules Enabling Act and the Supremacy Clause. The *Hanna* Court stuns the reader by saying that the defendant's argument — that the *Guaranty Trust* test should apply — is subject to a "fundamental flaw" — namely, "the incorrect assumption that the rule of *Erie* constitutes the appropriate test of the validity and therefore the applicability of a Federal Rule [of Civil Procedure]."[76] When a Federal Rule of Civil Procedure applies, one does not apply *Erie* at all! In such a case, the question "is a far cry from the typical, relatively unguided *Erie* choice."[77] Instead, the Federal Rule constitutes an instruction by Congress to apply that provision, so long as the provision is valid. And to determine whether the Rule is valid, the Court must analyze it under the Rules Enabling Act.

As we noted in §10.2.4, the Rules Enabling Act — 28 U.S.C. §2072 — made possible the promulgation of the Federal Rules of Civil Procedure. Under §2072(a), Congress has delegated to the Supreme Court the congressional authority to promulgate rules of "practice and procedure" for the federal courts. Through the years, the Supreme Court has empaneled an Advisory Committee to draft the Rules and consider amendments to them. The Advisory Committee historically has published its proposed amendments and new rules for public comment, after which the Supreme Court decides whether to propose them for adoption. If so, the Court sends the proposed Rules to Congress. If Congress does not amend or reject any of the proposals within a given period, they become effective. Thus, by

[76] 380 U.S. at 469-470.
[77] *Id.* at 471.

the time a Federal Rule goes into effect, it has been reviewed (at least in theory) by the Advisory Committee, the public, the Supreme Court, and the Congress.

These layers of review are intended to ensure not only that any amendment or new Federal Rule is well drafted, but to ensure that the proposal does not violate §2072(b). That subsection provides that the Federal Rules "shall not abridge, enlarge, or modify any substantive right." This is an important limitation, designed to ensure that the federal government does not use the guise of a rule of procedure to encroach on state substantive law. Thus, it embodies the concern of the Tenth Amendment — that the states retain powers not ceded to the federal government.

Hanna sets forth the assessment of whether a Federal Rule is valid under the Rules Enabling Act. The Court explained that Congress's *constitutional* power to establish the lower federal courts includes the power to prescribe rules of procedure for use in those courts. According to the Court in *Hanna*, this power enables Congress to prescribe any rule that is "rationally capable of classification" as procedural. Many people refer to this as the "arguably procedural" test — a Federal Rule falls within Congress's constitutional power to regulate procedure in the federal courts if the rule is "arguably procedural." This is not much of a test, as the Court in *Hanna* recognized. It is unthinkable that the Supreme Court would propose, and the Congress would approve, a Federal Rule of Civil Procedure that was not even arguably procedural. So the constitutional standard for validity of a Federal Rule is not much of a hurdle.

But there is another test. As we just saw, §2072(b) provides that the Federal Rules "shall not abridge, enlarge, or modify any substantive right." Thus, a Rule is valid only if it falls within Congress's constitutional authority and within the scope of the delegation of the Rules Enabling Act. The Court has never struck down a Rule as violative of §2072(b). Indeed, the process by which the Rules are promulgated gives them "presumptive validity under both the constitutional and statutory constraints."[78] The Court has gone so far as to say that "Rules which incidentally affect litigants' substantive rights do not violate this provision if reasonably necessary to maintain the integrity of that system of rules."[79] In *Hanna*, the Court had no trouble concluding that Federal Rule 4 was both constitutional and fell within §2072(b). The provision concerned giving notice to a defendant and thus dealt with an issue of procedure and practice. It did not affect any substantive right. Thus, Rule 4 governed and trumped state law.

Why does federal law govern? Why does it trump state law? Though the Court did not make the point as clearly as it could have, the answer is dictated by the Supremacy Clause of the Constitution. That clause, in Article VI of the Constitution, provides that federal law is "the supreme

---

[78] Burlington Northern R.R. Co. v. Woods, 480 U.S. 1, 6 (1987).
[79] *Id.* at 5.

law of the land." The holding in *Hanna* is simply an application of the Supremacy Clause. So once a court determines that a federal directive (such as a Federal Rule of Civil Procedure) (1) applies to the facts of the case and (2) is valid, the Supremacy Clause requires that it be applied. In such circumstances, the federal directive has trumped state law on the point.

And that was the holding in *Hanna*. Federal Rule 4 applied to the facts of the case and was valid both under the Constitution and the Rules Enabling Act. Thus, it applied. Under the Supremacy Clause, then, Rule 4 must govern. It trumps state law. There is no analysis of *Erie* at all. No outcome determination. No twin aims. No *Byrd*. Those are all relevant to analysis under the Rules of Decision Act, but do not apply when there is a valid federal directive on-point.

Two Prongs of Analysis. It is difficult to overstate the importance of *Hanna*. The case establishes that what we had thought of as a single doctrine — the *Erie* doctrine — is actually two. Before applying the "typical, relatively unguided" *Erie* inquiry we have seen in all the cases from *Erie* through *Byrd*, a court must ask whether there is a federal directive on-point. If so, the federal directive applies, so long as it is valid. We call this the *Hanna prong* of vertical choice of law doctrine. *It is always the first step in vertical choice of law.* Though in *Hanna* the federal directive was a Federal Rule of Civil Procedure, the *Hanna* directive clearly applies to *any* federal provision — including a federal constitutional provision or a federal statute. If it is on-point and valid, the Supremacy Clause dictates that it will govern.

So when does *Erie* come up? Only when there is *no federal directive on-point*. In such situations, the federal government has not prescribed a rule to apply, so the court must apply the *Erie*, or the Rules of Decision Act, inquiry of vertical choice of law. We call this the *Erie* prong of vertical choice of law. And as we already know, it is a confused analysis. *Hanna* added to the confusion by suggesting its twin aims amendment to the outcome-determination test. Because the Court based its holding in *Hanna* on the Rules Enabling Act, however, its discussion of outcome determination — the twin aims material — was dicta. It was not necessary to the holding of the case. Nonetheless, subsequent cases have adopted twin aims as part of the *Erie* prong of the analysis.[80]

Lower courts, however, have been quite unclear about whether the twin aims test completely displaces the wooden outcome-determination test of *Guaranty Trust*. Many courts continue to apply the wooden approach, some instead of twin aims and some in conjunction with twin aims. The confusion simply points out that the Court has not been good at integrating the various factors in the *Erie* prong analysis. This makes your life

[80] *See, e.g.,* Walker v. Armco Steel Corp., 446 U.S. 740, 753 (1980).

difficult for exam purposes. Try to get a sense of whether your professor believes that the twin aims approach of *Hanna* has displaced the outcome-determination analysis of *Guaranty Trust*. Many professors believe that it has. In my view, these professors overlook what the lower courts have done. Despite *Hanna*, many lower courts continue to use the wooden *Guaranty Trust* approach. So, in my suggested synthesis of the materials in §10.7, I recommend applying both *Guaranty Trust* and the twin aims test.

Since deciding *Hanna*, the Supreme Court has addressed vertical choice of law several times. Most of those efforts have involved the *Hanna* prong of the analysis and a determination of whether a federal directive covers the issue in question. The Court has had very little to say about the *Erie* prong of vertical choice of law. Its most meaningful opportunity to clarify the law in that area came in 1996, with *Gasperini v. Center for Humanities, Inc.*,[81] which we discuss in §10.6.5. Unfortunately, as we will see, the Court did not take advantage of the opportunity to provide clarity.

Justice Harlan's Concurrence. Justice Harlan concurred with the result in *Hanna*. His reasoning, however, was quite different from that of the majority. The Harlan opinion is worth studying, and many professors spend some time on it in class. Justice Harlan forthrightly admitted that the Court had not articulated a workable doctrine under *Erie* but worried that the majority opinion in *Hanna* was simplistic. In particular, he decried the majority's focus on the litigant equality theme; to Justice Harlan, *Erie* was far more than a case that expressed worry about forum shopping. It was about the Tenth Amendment, and the majority in *Hanna* gave short shrift to that part of the analysis. To Justice Harlan, the primary question should be whether state law must govern when the issue is one that "would substantially affect those primary decisions respecting human conduct."[82] If it does, state law must govern. If it does not, state law can be ignored. On the facts in *Hanna*, he concluded, no one would structure her real-world human conduct on the method for serving process in a wrongful death case. Therefore, state law would not control.

The Harlan equation — that state law governs those "primary decisions respecting human conduct" — has strong appeal to many commentators and professors, especially as a proxy for determining whether a Federal Rule violates the Rules Enabling Act. As we saw above, §2072(b) provides that a Federal Rule cannot affect a substantive right. A Federal Rule that purported to govern a "primary decision[] respecting human conduct" would, it seems clear, affect substantive rights and thus violate §2072(b).

Tough Questions. While *Hanna* drew distinct lines between the *Hanna* prong and the *Erie* prong of vertical choice of law, it left open

---

[81] 518 U.S. 415 (1996).
[82] *Hanna*, 380 U.S. at 475 (Harlan, J., concurring).

several questions. Under *Hanna*, courts must first assess whether a federal directive is on-point — whether it covers the question before the court. This was easy on the facts of *Hanna* — Rule 4 clearly applied to the question of how to serve process. The question is not always that clear. As we see in the next subsection, the Court has been inconsistent in whether federal directives are to be read narrowly or broadly. The inconsistency gives rise to uncertainty (and to some great exam possibilities for your professor). In addition, if a court finds that there is a federal directive on-point, the court must apply the federal law *if it is valid.* Thus, we must know how to assess the validity of federal directives. We discuss that issue in §10.6.4. Finally, of course, we have the uncertainty we have always had in applying the Rules of Decision Act in the *Erie* prong. For example, how does one deal with *Byrd*, especially in light of the Court's inattention to it? We hoped to get an answer in 1996, when the Supreme Court decided *Gasperini.* As we see in §10.6.5, though, that case left open nearly as many questions as it answered. In addition, as we saw, there is the question of whether twin aims replaces or exists alongside the *Guaranty Trust* outcome-determination test. We address these topics when we suggest an overall approach to vertical choice of law in §10.7.

§10.6.2 Applying the *Hanna* Prong: Determining When a Federal Directive Is On-Point

According to the Court, its decision in *Hanna* was the first occasion on which a Federal Rule of Civil Procedure conflicted directly with a state provision. This suggestion seems belied, however, by cases such as *Ragan* and *Cohen*,[83] in which the Court appeared to eviscerate a Federal Rule. The majority opinion in *Hanna* explained, though, that those cases did not hold that a Federal Rule was displaced by state law. Instead — and this is an important point — they held that the Federal Rule *was not sufficiently broad to cover the issue in dispute.* For example, in *Palmer v. Hoffman*,[84] in which the issue was burden of proof at trial, the Court held that Rule 8(c) required that the defendant assert an affirmative defense. As explained in *Hanna*, though, Rule 8(c) addressed only pleading the affirmative defense; it did not address the issue of which party had the burden of proof at trial. Because there was no federal directive on-point, then, the Court was justified in treating the issue of burden of proof under the *Erie* prong of vertical choice of law.

Justice Harlan's concurring opinion in *Hanna*, which we discussed toward the end of the preceding subsection, noted skepticism on this issue. Specifically, he could not understand how *Ragan* — in which the Court

---

[83] These are two of the "triple play" cases discussed in §10.5.
[84] This case is also discussed in §10.5.

held that a federal diversity court must apply state law concerning tolling of the statute of limitations — could survive *Hanna*. He concluded that Federal Rule 3 — which provides that an action is commenced when filed — covers the tolling issue and thus must trump state law. The Court returned to this issue in 1980, long after Justice Harlan had died. The facts of *Walker v. Armco Steel Corp.*[85] were indistinguishable from those in *Ragan*. The Court upheld *Ragan* by concluding that Federal Rule 3 did not address tolling at all. Rather, it defines the commencement of a suit *only* for purposes of applying the Federal Rules and not for purposes of whether the statute of limitations is tolled. Because there is no federal directive on-point, the Court addressed the issue of tolling under the Rules of Decision Act prong and concluded that state law must govern.

Through the years, the Court has stated the *Hanna* prong inquiry in different ways. In *Hanna* it asked whether the federal directive "covers the point in dispute."[86] In two cases, it asked whether the federal directive was "sufficiently broad to control the issue before the Court."[87] The important point in parsing the language is to determine whether the Court is of the opinion that the federal directive should be read broadly or narrowly. Though many of the cases involve interpretations of Federal Rules, remember that the federal directive might be any federal law — the Constitution, a statute, or a Federal Rule.

It seems appropriate that federal courts should read federal directives narrowly in applying the *Hanna* prong. In other words, *Hanna* should be invoked only if the federal directive clearly does cover the point in dispute. Doubts should be resolved by refusing to invoke *Hanna*. Why? Because applying *Hanna* means that the federal directive will govern the situation (assuming, of course, that the federal law is valid). Federal law trumps state law in such circumstances, without any assessment of outcome determination, twin aims of *Erie*, or any balancing of the relative interests of the federal and state judicial systems. *Hanna* is heavy-handed and hard-hearted. A sensitive concern for state interests dictates that federal courts should counsel a narrow interpretation of federal directives, and thus undertake the more flexible and state-sensitive *Erie* prong analysis.

What has the Court done in this regard? It has been inconsistent. In *Walker v. Armco Steel*, discussed above in this subsection, the Court indicated that it would give Federal Rule 3 its "plain meaning" in applying the *Hanna* prong.[88] It seems that the Court read Rule 3 quite narrowly, however, in finding that it governed "commencement" of an action for purposes *other than* tolling the statute of limitations. It did so, clearly, to avoid

[85] 446 U.S. 740 (1980).
[86] 380 U.S. at 470.
[87] Burlington N. R.R. v. Woods, 480 U.S. 1, 5 (1986); *Walker*, 446 U.S. at 750 n.9.
[88] 446 U.S. at 750 n.9.

a conflict between the Federal Rule and state law on the topic, which seems appropriate. Again, reading the federal directive narrowly gives the court a chance to find, as the Court did in *Walker*, that state law should govern.[89] Moreover, a narrow reading of a Federal Rule will avoid potentially thorny questions of whether the Rule is valid under the Rules Enabling Act. For instance, if Rule 3 had been interpreted to lengthen the statute of limitations, it might well have violated the dictate of the Rules Enabling Act, §2072(b), that a Federal Rule "not abridge, enlarge, or modify any substantive right."

The Court did something similar in *Semtek Intl. Inc. v. Lockheed Martin Corp.*,[90] in which it interpreted Federal Rule 41(b). That Rule, as we saw in §7.4.2, governs involuntary dismissals and provides that — with some exceptions — such dismissals are to operate as adjudications on the merits. That is, they are to be considered dismissals "with prejudice." That phrase, in turn, means that the claim is dismissed and cannot be refiled; it is extinguished. In *Semtek*, however, the Court read Rule 41(b) in a painfully narrow way — holding that it meant only that the case could not be refiled in another *federal* court, but that the dismissal did not bar refiling in state court. In his opinion for the Court, Justice Scalia expressed concern that a broader interpretation of Rule 41(b) — one that would bar refiling of a claim even in state court — would run afoul of the Rules Enabling Act by modifying a substantive right. To avoid that possibility, the Court interpreted the rule narrowly, avoided the *Hanna* hatchet, and applied the *Erie* prong.

In other cases, however, the Court has interpreted federal directives more broadly. *Burlington Northern R.R. v. Woods*[91] involved the possible application of Rule 38 of the Federal Rules of Appellate Procedure.[92] That Rule permits (but does not require) a Court of Appeals to impose an award of double costs if it finds that an appeal was frivolous. State law, on the other hand, required that an appellant be fined 10 percent of the judgment if the appellant had obtained a stay of the trial court judgment and lost on appeal. The Court concluded that Rule 38 covered the matter in question

---

[89] Oddly, however, the Court found that Rule 3 had a different "plain meaning" in *West v. Conrail*, 481 U.S. 35, 39 (1987). There, in a federal question case, the Court concluded that Rule 3 *did* cover tolling of the statute of limitations. It distinguished *Walker* by noting that the latter was a diversity of citizenship case. Again, however, a narrower reading of the federal directive is most appropriate when it can avoid overriding state law, as in *Walker*.

[90] 531 U.S. 497 (2001).

[91] 480 U.S. 1, 4-8 (1987).

[92] Note, this is not one of the Federal Rules of *Civil* Procedure, which govern in federal district courts and on which we spend so much time in Civil Procedure. This was a provision of the Federal Rules of *Appellate* Procedure, which govern in federal courts of appeals. They are also adopted under the Rules Enabling Act, in the same fashion as the Federal Rules of Civil Procedure. They are included in your Rules pamphlet.

by permitting only permissive sanctions and prohibiting mandatory sanctions. This interpretation of Rule 38 seems quite broad, since there is nothing on the face of that Rule indicating an intent to preclude a mandatory penalty in the circumstances covered by the state rule. In other words, it seems that Rule 38, with its discretionary sanctions, could have coexisted with state law mandating a sanction in certain circumstances.

The best example of the danger of overzealous use of *Hanna* is *Stewart Organization, Inc. v. Ricoh Corp.*[93] In that case, an Alabama citizen entered a contract with a New York citizen. The contract contained a forum selection clause that provided that litigation arising from the contract would take place in New York. Alabama law prohibited the enforcement of forum selection clauses, while New York law permitted such clauses.[94] The Alabama citizen sued the New York citizen in state court in Alabama. The defendant removed the case to federal court and sought enforcement of the forum selection clause by transfer to federal court in New York. The Supreme Court held that the venue-transfer statute, 28 U.S.C. §1404(a),[95] was on-point and directed federal courts to consider the existence of a forum selection clause as a factor in favor of transfer under the statute. The Court considered this "a straightforward exercise in statutory interpretation to determine if the statute covers the point in dispute."[96] It thus upheld enforcement of the clause by transfer of the case to federal court in New York.

There are two significant problems with the holding in *Stewart*. First, nowhere in the language of §1404(a) did Congress indicate that the existence of a forum selection clause was relevant to a transfer, nor did the legislative history indicate any congressional conclusion that such clauses be made enforceable. Indeed, such a conclusion would be unthinkable because §1404(a) was adopted at a time when virtually no states enforced such clauses. Second, and far more important, consider the result of the holding: In Alabama, the enforceability of forum selection clauses now depends upon whether the issue is addressed in state or federal court. In federal courts they are enforceable; in state courts they are not. This is exactly the vertical disuniformity caused by *Swift v. Tyson* and so criticized by *Erie*. By holding that the federal directive was on-point, the Court ran roughshod over legitimate state interests. Under the *Hanna* prong, there is no opportunity to assess outcome determination, twin aims, or to balance the relative state and federal interests.

---

[93] 487 U.S. 22 (1988).

[94] Parties to such a clause agree that litigation concerning a contractual matter will be held in a particular forum. While the modern trend is clearly to enforce such clauses so long as they are not the product of overreaching, some states will not enforce them.

[95] We discussed transfer of venue under this statute at §5.5.2.

[96] 487 U.S. at 30.

The Court's most important recent effort in vertical choice of law is *Gasperini v. Center for Humanities, Inc.*[97] It may signal a more sensitive approach to the application of the *Hanna* prong. It did little, however, to improve our understanding of the *Erie* prong of vertical choice of law. Though the case is in all of the Civil Procedure casebooks, some professors do not cover it. It is a relatively tough case on the facts, and, at least in the opinion of most commentators, does not provide clear legal exposition. Before looking at *Gasperini*, we need to discuss how one determines whether a federal directive is valid.

- Remember the different approaches adopted in cases like *Walker* and *Semtek*, on the one hand, and *Burlington Northern and Stewart*, on the other. There is nothing obvious on the face of the Rules interpreted in those cases to compel the answers that the Court reached. Sometimes it has interpreted Rules narrowly (as in *Walker* and *Semtek*) and sometimes it has interpreted them broadly (as in *Burlington Northern and Stewart*). On an exam, if the professor gives you a Federal Rule (or a proposed Federal Rule), you should be ready to argue both for a narrow interpretation of it and a broad interpretation. A narrow interpretation would probably lead to the conclusion that the provision is not on-point and thus that *Hanna* does not apply. When *Hanna* does not apply, the student should then assess the case under the *Erie* prong. On the other hand, a broad interpretation will probably lead to the conclusion that *Hanna* does apply and the need to assess whether the provision is valid (which we see in the next subsection).
- The language of the federal directives addressed in *Walker, Semtek, Burlington Northern,* and *Stewart* could have been interpreted either way — either as applying to the facts at hand or as not applying. You should be prepared to make such arguments on the exam.
  - Do not throw away points by failing to argue both ways. I have read too many exams in which a student has concluded that the directive is broad enough to cover the case and therefore that *Hanna* governs. While such students often do a good job of assessing validity of the federal directive, they throw away all points for the opposite conclusion — that *Hanna* does not apply and thus that the case should be assessed under the *Erie* prong.

§10.6.3 Applying *the Hanna* Prong: Determining Whether the Federal Directive Is Valid

We just saw that determining whether a federal directive is on-point can be a difficult task. Assuming the federal directive is on-point, the next step under *Hanna* is to assess whether the directive is valid. If it is, it will apply

---

[97] 518 U.S. 415 (1996).

and trump state law, under the Supremacy Clause. If it is not valid, obviously, it cannot be applied. It is important to remember that the federal directive will not always be a Federal Rule of Civil Procedure. As we saw three paragraphs above, in *Stewart*, the federal directive was a statute. Or it might be a constitutional provision. What are the tests for validity of the various directives?

Clearly, a constitutional provision is always valid. So if a federal constitutional provision is on-point, it applies. Period. An example, mentioned in footnote 68 above, could have come from the facts in *Byrd*. There, the Court might have concluded, quite simply, that the Seventh Amendment applied and mandated that a jury (not the judge) determine the facts surrounding the question of whether Mr. Byrd was a statutory employee. Had the Court done so, the Seventh Amendment would have trumped state law, and the Court would not have had to assess *Erie* at all.

What about statutes? Congressional authority to legislate is enumerated in the Constitution. In §10.4.2, we noted that Congress could pass a valid statute declaring the duty owed by railroads to persons such as Mr. Tompkins in the *Erie* case. The statute would have come within Congress's power to regulate interstate commerce, which is one of the most expansive bases of federal legislative power. Few Civil Procedure courses delve into the issue of the constitutional validity of congressional legislation. Rather, you will study the topic in detail in your course on Constitutional Law.

If the federal directive is a Federal Rule, we must assess validity as the Court did in *Hanna*. As we saw in detail in §10.6.1, the Court indicated that a Federal Rule was valid if two things were true. First, it had to fall within the constitutional authority of Congress to prescribe procedural rules for the federal courts. This test required only that the provision be "arguably procedural." Second, it had to fall within the Rules Enabling Act. Under §2072(a), it must be a provision dealing with "practice or procedure" in the federal courts. Under §2072(b), it "shall not abridge, enlarge or modify any substantive right." As we also noted in §10.6.1, some professors believe that Justice Harlan's concurring opinion in *Hanna* gave a nice proxy for determining when a provision would affect a substantive right. Such a provision would be one dealing with "primary decisions respecting human conduct."[98] A provision masquerading as a Federal Rule of Civil Procedure but dealing with such primary decisions of human conduct would violate §2072(b) because it would modify a substantive right. No Federal Rule has ever been held to violate §2072(b).

---

[98] *Hanna*, 380 U.S. at 475 (Harlan, J., concurring).

§10.6.4   The *Gasperini* Case

In *Gasperini v. Center for Humanities, Inc.*,[99] the plaintiff invoked
diversity of citizenship jurisdiction in a federal court in New York. The
defendant admitted liability and the case went to trial solely to determine
damages; the jury returned a verdict of $450,000. The defendant moved
for new trial under what is now Rule 59(a)(1)(A), which permits such
orders "for any reason for which a new trial has heretofore been granted
in an action at law in federal court."

The defendant contended that the verdict was excessive, which is a traditional basis for an order of new trial. Rule 59 does not prescribe a standard for determining when a verdict is to be considered excessive. Federal
courts had established a standard in case law: They would order a new
trial if the verdict "shocks the conscience" of the court. On the other hand,
under New York tort reform law, state courts applied a more intrusive test
and were to assess whether a verdict "deviates materially from what would
be reasonable compensation." In addition, the New York tort reform statute required appellate courts to assess the question of whether a verdict
was excessive de novo; in other words, the appellate court would not defer
to the trial court assessment, but would apply the "deviates materially"
standard independently. The New York legislature was clear in stating its
goals. The deviates materially standard was intended to invite more careful judicial scrutiny of verdicts. The state concluded that the "shocks the
conscience" test was an insufficient protection against excessive verdicts.
The state wanted to influence the outcome of litigation by limiting the
range of jury awards.

The vertical choice of law issues were clear: Must a federal diversity
court (1) apply the state provision defining when a new trial is to be granted
for an excessive verdict, and, if so, (2) apply the state provision providing
that the appellate court applies that standard de novo? The Supreme Court
concluded that the federal court must apply the New York deviates materially standard for granting new trial, but not the provision for de novo
appellate review.

On the *Hanna* prong, the Court concluded that Rule 59 was not on-point.
It explained that federal courts "have interpreted the Federal Rules . . . with
sensitivity to important state interests and regulatory policies."[100] The
statement is not exactly accurate. Though it is consistent with cases in
which the Court had interpreted federal directives narrowly — such as
Walker — it cannot be squared with the broad interpretations of *Burlington Northern* and *Stewart*. Still, one hopes the Court meant what it said,
and that *Gasperini* signals a new sensitivity to the need to interpret federal directives narrowly and thus to avoid overzealous application of

[99] 518 U.S. 415 (1996).
[100] *Id.* at 421 n.7.

Hanna. The Court properly concluded that Rule 59 did not apply to the issue at hand. Though that Rule does permit new trials for various reasons, including excessive verdicts, it simply gives no standard for determining when a verdict is excessive. Thus, there was no federal directive on-point, and the Court had to apply the *Erie* prong of vertical choice of law analysis.

As to that analysis, *Gasperini* is the first Supreme Court case since *Byrd* to discuss *Byrd*. (*Hanna* contained a citation to *Byrd*, without discussion.) Yet, surprisingly, the Court fails to discuss *Byrd* with regard to the issue of whether the federal court must apply the New York standard for new trial. It makes no effort to assess whether the state deviates materially standard is part of the state's definition of rights and obligations or is bound up with such a definition. Instead, the Court goes to the twin aims test of *Hanna*, which raised the question of whether a federal court's refusal to apply state law would lead to forum shopping. The answer would seem to be yes — a plaintiff would prefer to avoid the deviates materially standard because it permits the judge to meddle with the plaintiff's verdict readily. But after setting up the issue, the Court then fails to apply the twin aims test. Instead, it jumps to a point not debated by the parties — that a statutory *cap* on damages would be "substantive" under *Erie*. It then analogizes the deviates materially standard to such a cap, saying that it has the same purpose to limit recoveries. Thus, the Court concludes, the deviates materially standard must be substantive. Having concluded this, the Court *then* applies the twin aims test and concludes that ignoring state law would cause plaintiffs to flock to federal court. This is a strange application of twin aims, because it comes *after* determining that the rule is substantive, rather than as *part of* the assessment of whether it is substantive.

As noted, the Court concluded that the New York provision requiring appellate application of the deviates materially standard was not binding on the federal courts. It is here that the Court discusses *Byrd* for the first time in nearly four decades. According to the Court, *Byrd* established that *Guaranty Trust* had provided insufficient protection for "countervailing" federal interests. In *Byrd*, the countervailing federal interest was the Seventh Amendment right to jury trial for the determination of issues of fact in cases at law. In *Gasperini*, it was another part of the Seventh Amendment — the "reexamination clause." That clause provides that "no fact tried by a jury, shall be otherwise reexamined in any Court of the United States, than according to the rules of the common law."

It is not at all clear, however, whether the Court bases its holding in this regard on *Erie* or on the Seventh Amendment. If it is based upon the Seventh Amendment — if the Seventh Amendment commands that appellate courts may not apply a de novo standard — no discussion of *Erie* factors would be relevant. Why? Because a federal directive would be on-point on this issue and, under the Supremacy Clause, would prevail without assessment of state concerns.[101] If it is based upon *Erie*, however, the Court's effort is vexing. When applying *Erie* as to the deviates materially standard, as we just saw, the Court used the twin aims test (sort of). Here, however, the Court fails even to mention twin aims.

The bottom line of *Gasperini* is clearly right: The state-law allocation of authority between trial and appellate courts should not affect how that allocation is made in the federal courts. The federal judicial system certainly has a strong interest in deciding for itself how to assign the functions of trial and appellate courts — just as it did in assigning functions between judge and jury in *Byrd*. The Court's path to that conclusion in *Gasperini* is not clear, and does not shed much light on how one goes about making the *Erie* assessment.[102]

§10.7   A Suggested Synthesis

Lawyers, judges, and law students have to apply the lines of cases discussed in §§10.4, 10.5, and 10.6, to the facts of a given case and make a determination about whether state law will govern. In this section, I synthesize the lines of cases and suggest a method for analyzing any vertical choice of law problem.[103] Throughout, we assume that state law provides a particular rule. The question is whether a federal court, hearing a diversity of citizenship case, must apply that state rule.

The first question *always* is whether there is a federal directive on-point. In other words, is there some federal provision (from the Constitution, federal statutes, Federal Rules — any federal source) that governs the matter addressed by the state law? If the answer is yes, the case is governed by *Hanna* and does not implicate *Erie* or the Rules of Decision Act. When a federal directive is on-point, it applies, so long as it is valid. We discussed the tests for assessing validity of various federal directives in §10.6.3.

---

[101] Remember from §9.2.2 that the Seventh Amendment applies only in federal court civil cases. It does not apply to the states.

[102] Commentators generally have not had good things to say about the Court's effort in *Gasperini. See, e.g.,* C. Douglas Floyd, Erie *Awry: A Comment on* Gasperini v. Center for Humanities, Inc., 1997 BYU L. Rev. 267; Richard D. Freer, *Some Thoughts on the State of* Erie *After* Gasperini, 76 Tex. L. Rev. 1637 (1998); Wendy Collins Perdue, *The Sources and Scope of Federal Procedural Common Law: Some Reflections on* Erie *and* Gasperini, 46 U. Kan. L. Rev. 751 (1998). Even the positive comments have been less than fulsomely embracing. *See* Thomas D. Rowe, *Not Bad for Government Work: Does Anyone Else Think the Supreme Court Is Doing a Halfway Decent Job in Its* Erie-Hanna *Jurisprudence?,* 73 Notre Dame L. Rev. 963 (1998).

[103] The approach suggested here is my best interpretation of the cases. Your professor may have a different approach. By all means, follow the approach your professor gives you.

On your exam, do not give the *Hanna* prong short shrift. Remember that the Court has taken inconsistent approaches to how broadly one should read the federal directives. Though the most recent effort, *Gasperini*, counsels a narrow interpretation, other cases, such as *Burlington Northern* and *Stewart*, are still on the books and adopted very broad readings of the federal provisions. The point for law school examinations is simple: Be prepared to argue that any federal directive is broad enough to cover the point covered by the state law, and also be prepared to argue that it is not broad enough to be on-point with the state law.

If the federal directive is *not* on-point, the *second* step in vertical choice of law is to apply the *Erie*, or the Rules of Decision Act, analysis. This analysis is especially difficult, because, as we have seen, the Court has thrown different factors into the equation at different times. Moreover, the case that arguably does the best job of integrating various factors — *Byrd* — has suffered from neglect. Still, the starting point under *Byrd* makes great sense: Is the state law part of that state's definition of rights or obligations? Examples include the elements of a claim or defense. If so, the Tenth Amendment *requires* the federal court to apply the state law in a diversity case. If not, we must ask whether the state rule is bound up with the state's definition of rights or obligations. Such rules are so closely related to matters of pure substance that here, too, the Tenth Amendment *requires* the federal court to follow state law in a diversity case. Though the Court has never defined "bound up," the phrase seems to apply to matters such as choice of law rules and the burden of proof and may well explain the results of *Klaxon* and *Palmer v. Hoffman*.

If the state law is neither pure substance nor bound up with it, then, in the parlance of *Byrd*, we are facing an issue concerning "form and mode." As to such rules, we ask whether ignoring the state law in federal court would be outcome determinative. Here we have a dilemma, because we have two outcome-determination tests. The *Guaranty Trust* version is rough-hewn and asks whether the case would come out differently if we ignore the state law than if we apply it. Thus, in *Guaranty Trust* itself, applying state law meant the case must be dismissed, while ignoring state law meant that it could proceed. This was deemed outcome determinative. But we also have the "modified outcome determination" or twin aims test of *Hanna*. That requires us to ask whether ignoring state law on this point would cause litigants to flock to federal court. To avoid such forum shopping, the federal court ought to apply state law.

But that opens two large questions. First, which version of outcome determination do we use? Second, how does it fit in with *Byrd*? The Court has never answered either question, though *Gasperini* certainly implies on the first one that the modified version of outcome determination is preferred. On the other hand, *Gasperini* was not altogether clear in its application of the twin aims test, so we are left to do what prudent lawyers and judges would do. A prudent person, faced with two tests, would employ both of them. So I encourage you to apply both the *Guaranty Trust* version of outcome determination and the *Hanna* twin aims version. Be careful, though, because many professors conclude that the *Hanna* twin aims test has completely replaced the *Guaranty Trust* model. If your professor is among these, you should adopt your professor's approach.[104] I also conclude that they should be incorporated into the *Byrd* test. Thus, if ignoring state law will either lead to a different outcome or encourage litigants to shop for federal court, *Byrd* teaches that the federal court is to apply state law *unless* there is a good reason not to do so. Importantly, this conclusion is *not* mandated by the Tenth Amendment, but is counseled in *Erie*'s theme of litigant equality.

What is a good reason not to apply state law? We have two examples. In *Byrd*, it was the federal judicial system's interest in allocating responsibility between judge and jury. In *Gasperini*, it was the federal judicial system's interest in allocating responsibility between trial and appellate courts. In both cases, the federal interest in its systemic integrity outweighed any state interest to the contrary.

Let's try some hypotheticals.

- *Number 1.* In a diversity case, Plaintiff seeks to have her case certified as a class action. Under the state class action rule, the case would not be certified. Under Federal Rule 23 (the federal class action rule, which we discuss in §13.3), the case would be certified as a class action. Which provision does the federal court apply?
  - Is there a federal directive on-point? Yes. The issue in question is what standards must be met to qualify as a class action. Federal Rule 23 covers the issue in question. Thus, under *Hanna*, Federal Rule 23 applies, so long as it is valid. Federal Rules of Civil Procedure are valid so long as they are "arguably procedural." Because the Rule defines the procedural requisites for a class, and is not affected by the substantive law applied, the Rule is plainly procedural. It thus trumps state law. The case is governed by the Rules Enabling Act and *Hanna*. *Erie* and the Rules of Decision Act play no role.
- *Number 2.* P sues D in state court. D moves for summary judgment. Applying state law, the state court denies the motion. D removes in timely fashion to federal court, invoking diversity of citizenship jurisdiction. D moves for summary judgment in federal court. Though the state-court standard for summary judgment was not met, the standard under Federal Rule 56 (which governs summary judgment in federal court, and which we addressed in §9.4) would be met. Should the federal court grant the motion for summary judgment under Rule 56?

---

[104] With all due respect, professors who conclude that *Hanna* has replaced the rough-cut outcome-determination test of *Guaranty Trust* have not read enough lower court opinions. For whatever reason, many lower courts continue to employ *Guaranty Trust*, unaffected by *Hanna*.

- ○ Yes. The reasoning is the same as in Number 1. There is a federal directive on-point. The case is in federal court now, and valid provisions of the Federal Rules govern.[105]
- ○ *Number 3.* The legislature of State *A* is concerned about rising medical insurance rates, and passes a statute aimed at reducing the verdicts recovered in medical malpractice cases. The statute requires that such cases be heard by an arbitration panel consisting of health care professionals and lawyers. The panel is to render its decision. The plaintiff may accept that decision or continue to jury trial. If she goes to trial, the arbitration panel's decision is admissible in evidence. Plaintiffs do not like the arbitration process, because they believe that panels of doctors and lawyers are less likely to hold for plaintiffs (and less likely to award large damages) than juries. A citizen of State *B* is treated by a doctor who is a citizen of State *A* in State *A*. She claims malpractice and sues the doctor in federal court in State *A*, invoking diversity of citizenship jurisdiction. Is the federal court in State *A* required to apply the arbitration procedure, or can the case simply proceed through discovery to jury trial in federal court?
    - ○ First, there is no federal directive on-point. There is no provision in the Federal Rules concerning medical malpractice arbitration cases, and no federal statute addresses the issue. So this case does not invoke *Hanna.* It is an *Erie* or Rules of Decision Act problem.
    - ○ Second, is the state law part of the definition of rights and obligations? It seems not, since the arbitration provision does not say anything about the standard to be applied for finding liability. Is it bound up with such a rule? Perhaps one can make a reasonable argument that the arbitration panel proceeding is closely related to the standards for who wins a medical malpractice action, but that seems unlikely. Thus, the state rule seems a matter of form and mode.
- ○ Would ignoring the state provision in federal court be outcome determinative?
    - ○ It is not clear that it is outcome determinative in the *Guaranty Trust* sense. After all, the panel and the jury might reach the same conclusion. On the other hand, the panel provision seems calculated to reduce recovery by plaintiffs.
    - ○ What about modified outcome determination, or twin aims? Would ignoring the state law in federal court lead litigants to "shop" for federal court? Absolutely. Every plaintiff who could go to federal court would do so, to avoid the arbitration panel.
    - ○ Because only noncitizens of State *A* can go to federal court (by invoking diversity of citizenship jurisdiction), failure to apply state law in federal court would lead to the inequitable administration of the laws. State *A* citizens would be stuck with the arbitration panel, while other citizens would not.

---

[105] Fairbank v. Wunderman Cato Johnson, 212 F.3d 528 (9th Cir. 2000).

- Because this rule of form and mode is outcome determinative, the federal court should apply state law unless there is a good federal systemic reason not to do so.
- The federal courts have an interest in trial by jury. But, unlike the situation in *Byrd*, this state law provision does not vitiate that right. It merely delays it until after the arbitration hearing. Also unlike the situation in *Byrd*, here the state has a compelling interest in its rule. It is attempting to reduce medical malpractice judgments in an effort to reduce medical expenses, which is clearly an important state interest.

Finally, let's summarize this suggested approach to vertical choice of law with a flowchart, which is set out on page 523.

§10.8   Other Issues: Determining the Content of State Law and "Reverse *Erie*"

In this section, we address two ancillary issues raised by vertical choice of law. One of these issues affects federal courts and one affects state courts. Specifically, how does a federal court determine what state law is? And are state courts ever required to apply federal "procedural" law?

Assume that a federal court has determined that an issue is one on which it must apply state law. Where does the court look to find that law? Obviously, some matters clearly may be governed by state statutory provisions. If not, and the court has to look to common law or to judicial interpretations of statutes, what are the rules? In *Erie*, Justice Brandeis indicated that federal courts must follow state law as determined by the "highest court"[106] of the state. Often, however, there is no state high court pronouncement on an issue. For many years, the federal courts concluded that they were compelled to apply *whatever* appellate authority they found from that state. In one case, the federal court held that it was bound to follow an unpublished opinion by a state intermediate court of appeals — even though the opinion had no precedential value in the state court system![107]

Now, however, it is clear that the federal court is not required to do this. Instead, it should apply the law that *it believes* the state high court would apply. In blunt terms, the federal judge has to make her best guess at what the state high court would rule on the question. It looks to all available data to make this assessment, including trends in the law in other states and the particular state's high court practice in the past of adopting

---

[106] *Erie*, 304 U.S. at 78.
[107] Gustin v. Sun Life Assurance Co., 154 F.2d 961 (6th Cir. 1946).

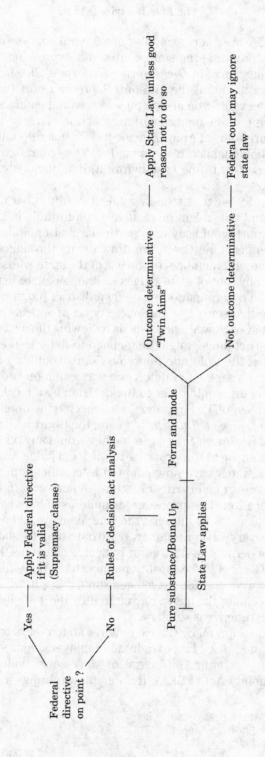

Federal
directive
on point ?

Yes —— Apply Federal directive
if it is valid
(Supremacy clause)

No —— Rules of decision act analysis

Pure substance/Bound Up

State Law applies

Form and mode

Outcome determinative
"Twin Aims"

Apply State Law unless good
reason not to do so

Not outcome determinative

Federal court may ignore
state law

such trends. There are many examples of a federal court's guessing incorrectly, and thus prodding the state courts into expressing their view on the matter. For instance, in *Dick Proctor Imports v. Sumitomo Corp.*,[108] the federal judge held that the Missouri Supreme Court (which had not spoken on the relevant issue in over 80 years) would embrace the modern trend permitting enforcement of forum selection clauses. The following year, the Missouri Court of Appeals made it clear that the state would cling to the old law holding such clauses void.[109] The federal court's guess is binding on the parties to the case before it, but, obviously, cannot bind the state courts.

A federal district judge is usually a member of the bar of the state in which she sits and thus might be relatively comfortable in guessing what the state high court would say on a particular matter. Judges of the federal courts of appeals, however, are drawn from throughout the circuit and frequently are not members of the bar of the state whose law is being assessed. Naturally, out-of-state judges on the appellate bench might be deferential to the determination made by a district judge who is a member of the bar of that state. For instance, a court of appeals judge who is a member of the bar of New Mexico, who is reviewing the decision of a Colorado federal district judge, might be inclined to defer to the local judge's guess about what the Colorado Supreme Court would say on a question of law. For many years, such deference was common on the courts of appeals — that court would defer to the decision by a local district judge at the trial court level. The Supreme Court rejected the practice, however, in *Salve Regina College v. Russell.*[110] There, the Court held that the court of appeals must review an *Erie* guess as they would any other question of law, without deferring to the expertise of the local judge.

Over half the states have now adopted a "certification" procedure by which a federal court can certify questions of state law to the state high court for clarification. This procedure is quite useful, and avoids making the federal judge guess about what the state court would do. The certification statutes vary in important ways from state to state. Some, for instance, do not permit the state court to decide questions that depend on issues of fact. Generally, the most populous states do not have certification statutes. Moreover, there have been some cases in which the federal court cannot decipher the answer given to it by the state high court. Still, the certification practice is salutary.

Of course, the Supremacy Clause requires state courts to follow applicable federal law. For instance, railroad employees injured at work can sue their employers either in federal or state court under the Federal Employees' Liability Act (FELA). If an employee brings a FELA case in

---

[108] 486 F. Supp. 815 (E.D. Mo. 1980).
[109] 619 S.W.2d 928, 930 (Mo. App. 1981).
[110] 499 U.S. 225 (1991).

state court, federal law creates the claim and governs concerning the railroad's liability. The presumption is that the state court will apply its own rules of procedure. On the other hand, the Supreme Court has held that some procedures are "essential to effectuate" the purposes behind the federal substantive law. Such procedures, which are "part and parcel of the [federal] remedy afforded," must be followed in state court. Accordingly, in *Dice v. Akron, Canton & Youngstown R.R.*[111] (from which these quotations are taken), the Court required state courts to grant a right of jury trial, even when such a right would not be available under state law. This result is sometimes referred to as "reverse *Erie*," and applies only to such procedural issues that are closely related to the underlying federal claim. Thus, state courts in FELA cases must also follow federal law concerning the sufficiency of evidence to sustain a verdict.[112]

§10.9   Federal Common Law

Erie did not hold that there is no federal common law. It held that there is no *general* federal common law. The same day the Court decided *Erie*, it also decided *Hinderlider v. La Plata River & Cherry Creek Ditch Co.*,[113] in which it concluded that federal common law controlled the issue of whether an interstate stream must be apportioned between two states. The holding makes great sense. After all, the dispute was between two states; we can predict that the law of State *A* would declare State *A* the winner and the law of State *B* would declare State *B* the winner. Such interstate disputes must be determined by federal law. Because there is no constitutional or statutory provision on-point, the only federal law available is federal common law.

Obviously, then, there can be circumstances in which the creation of federal common law is appropriate. Through the years, the Supreme Court has not always been clear in stating the justifications for federal common law or in defining the circumstances in which it is appropriate. Most observers conclude that federal common law is justified either to effectuate some congressional policy, in which Congress left gaps in a statutory scheme, or to protect federal interests.[114] In a concurring opinion, Justice Jackson echoed these considerations in helpful (and widely cited) terms:

> The federal courts have no *general* common law, as in a sense they have no general or comprehensive jurisprudence of any kind, because many subjects

---

[111] 342 U.S. 359, 361.

[112] Brady v. Southern Ry., 320 U.S. 476 (1943).

[113] 304 U.S. 92 (1938).

[114] *See generally* Richard D. Freer & Martin H. Redish, Federal Courts 357-370 (2004).

of private law which bulk large in the traditional common law are ordinarily within the province of the states and not of the federal government. But this is not to say that wherever we have occasion to decide a federal question which cannot be answered from federal statutes alone we may not resort to all of the source materials of the common law, or that when we have fashioned an answer it does not become a part of the federal non-statutory or common law.[115]

Detailed consideration of federal common law usually awaits an upper-division course on Federal Courts. Few Civil Procedure courses deal with the topic in depth. For our purposes, we note some of the general areas in which it has been found appropriate. One, as noted, is when Congress has left "gaps" in statutory schemes. For example, Congress may enact a general regulatory scheme and provide that the federal courts are to develop rules for effectuating it. The best example is §301 of the Labor Management Relations Act, which granted federal subject matter jurisdiction over suits for violation of collective bargaining (labor union) contracts. Congress failed to provide any rules for adjudicating the dispute. In *Textile Workers Union v. Lincoln Mills*, the Supreme Court held that the statute "authorizes federal courts to fashion a body of federal law for the enforcement of these collective bargaining agreements. . . ."[116]

In addition, there are various substantive areas in which the Supreme Court has upheld federal common law even in the absence of a statutory gap. One involves the federal government's acting in a "proprietary" role. The government does this in many ways — by entering contracts, overseeing regulatory programs, issuing commercial paper, etc. Any dispute involving these activities involves an undeniable federal interest. Sometimes the Court finds such interests so "uniquely federal" that federal law — including federal common law — will apply and preempt state law. The best example is *Clearfield Trust Co. v. United States*.[117] There, the United States issued a check that was thereafter stolen and cashed. The Supreme Court concluded that federal common law — and not state law — governed the liability for the funds. The Court emphasized that the federal government's authority to issue the check originated with the Constitution and federal statutes. It then concluded that it was important to have a uniform standard for determining liability on such commercial paper, and that the United States thus not be subject to law that differed from state to state.[118]

---

[115] D'Oench, Duhme & Co. v. Federal Deposit Ins. Corp., 315 U.S. 447, 469 (1942) (emphasis original).

[116] 353 U.S. 448, 451 (1957).

[117] 318 U.S. 363 (1943).

[118] In contrast, in Empire HealthChoice Assurance, Inc. v. McVeigh, 547 U.S. 677 (2006), the Court concluded that the Federal Employees Health Benefits Act of 1959 — under which the federal government negotiates and regulates health benefits plans for federal

The Court has sometimes held that federal common law applies, but that the content of the federal common law should mirror state law — in other words, that federal common law should adopt state law as the federal common law. One example is *United States v. Yazell*,[119] in which the Court held that federal common law governed the issue of whether a wife was legally obligated on her husband's Small Business Administration (SBA) loan. Because the SBA loan — unlike the check in *Clearfield Trust* — was not part of a nationwide program, and because Texas had a strong interest in applying its law of domestic relations, the Court held that federal common law adopted Texas law as its own. Another example, discussed in detail on this point in §11.2.2, is *Semtek International, Inc. v. Lockheed Martin Corp.*[120] There, the Court held that the preclusive effect of a judgment entered by a federal court in a diversity of citizenship case is to be determined by federal common law. On the facts of the case, however, that Court held that federal common law would adopt California law.

Another substantive area in which federal common law applies is international relations. Again, the need for federal law is obvious, because it is the federal government that engages in international affairs. The nation must speak in one voice and have one set of laws for determining international relations. Thus, issues involving relations of the United States with foreign countries are determined by federal common law. Admiralty law can also raise issues in which a federal standard is desirable. Admiralty is a fascinating topic and addresses all manner of concerns occurring on navigable waters. In some of these areas, application of state laws could be awkward, so the Court has used a balancing test to determine whether federal common law should supersede state law on various admiralty topics. In *Bivens v. Six Unknown Named Agents of Federal Bureau of Narcotics*,[121] the Supreme Court recognized a private right of action against federal officers for damages violations of the Fourth Amendment prohibition against unreasonable searches and seizures. The Amendment itself is silent on any such remedy, and Congress has never provided one for such deprivations by federal officers.[122] The Court nonetheless concluded that the issue was proper for treatment by federal common law.

---

employees — did not require the generation of federal common law. The contractual claim for reimbursement in that case did not threaten an identifiable federal interest. *Id.* at 692-693.

[119] 382 U.S. 341 (1966). The Court discussed the "prudent course" as being "to adopt the readymade body of state law as the federal rule of decision until Congress strikes a different accommodation" in *United States v. Kimbell Foods, Inc.*, 440 U.S. 715, 740 (1979).

[120] 531 U.S. 497 (2001).

[121] 403 U.S. 388 (1971).

[122] Congress has provided a very important remedy — 42 U.S.C. §1983 — for deprivation of federal rights under color of *state* law, for example, by state officers.

Whenever federal common law is allowed, it commands the same deference under the Supremacy Clause as other federal law.[123] Thus, it can displace state law in the particular substantive area. Moreover, claims asserted under federal common law invoke federal question jurisdiction under §1331.[124] Congress can undo federal common law by legislating in the area.[125]

---

[123] Banco Nacional de Cuba v. Sabbatino, 376 U.S. 398 (1964).
[124] Illinois v. City of Milwaukee, 406 U.S. 91 (1972).
[125] New Jersey v. New York, 283 U.S. 336 (1931).

Chapter 11

The Preclusion Doctrines

§11.1   Defining the Issue

The material covered in this chapter is known by a variety of names. Your casebook may refer to it as the "doctrine of former adjudication" or "res judicata" or "claim and issue preclusion" or "effect of judgments" or the "preclusion doctrines." The Supreme Court tends to refer to the individual doctrines as claim preclusion and issue preclusion, and to the general topic as res judicata.[1] Whatever the terminology, however, this

---

[1] "The preclusive effect of a judgment is defined by claim preclusion and issue preclusion, which are collectively referred to as 'res judicata.'" Taylor v. Sturgell, 128 S. Ct. 2161, 2171 (2008).

material can be raised only when the fact pattern involves at least two cases. The first case (which we call Case 1) has ended, and a judgment has been entered. Now the question is whether that judgment from Case 1 precludes anyone from litigating anything in Case 2, which is pending.[2] It might do so through the operation of either of two doctrines: claim preclusion or issue preclusion.

Claim preclusion is the modern terminology for "res judicata" (which literally means "the thing has been decided"); it is also sometimes called the *rule against splitting a claim*. The modern terminology is influenced by the Restatement (Second) of Judgments.[3] Both "claim preclusion" and "res judicata" are currently in use and they are interchangeable. We address claim preclusion in detail in §11.2. It stands for the proposition that a claimant only gets one opportunity to assert a claim. If you have one claim, you get one suit to vindicate it. You get "one bite at the apple." If you sue a second time on the same claim, the case will be dismissed under claim preclusion. That means that the claimant must be careful to seek all rights to relief encompassed in a single claim in Case 1. If she does not, she cannot seek the other rights to relief in Case 2. Jurisdictions can define the scope of one's claim in different ways.

- ○ *P* is involved in an auto collision with *D*. *P* suffers personal injuries and her car is damaged. In Case 1, she seeks only damages for the personal injuries. After judgment is entered in that case, she brings Case 2, seeking to recover for property damage to her car from the same collision. If the law defines her "claim" as all rights to relief arising from a single transaction (which we explore in §11.2.3), Case 2 will be dismissed under claim preclusion, because she is suing twice on the same claim. If, however, the law defines her claims as the individual rights invaded (also explored in §11.2.3), Case 2 will not be dismissed under claim preclusion, because there she is vindicating a different right (and therefore a different claim) from that vindicated in Case 1.

---

[2] Throughout the chapter, we refer to Case 1 and Case 2. The designations do not necessarily reflect the order in which the cases were filed. Rather, Case 1 is Case 1 because it has gone to judgment first. Preclusion — either claim or issue preclusion flows from entry of a final judgment that meets certain criteria. See §§11.2.2 and 11.3.1.

[3] Restatements of the law are promulgated by the American Law Institute (ALI), a prestigious group of lawyers, judges, and academics with about 3,000 members. The ALI periodically focuses on specific areas of the law, appointing a Reporter for each project. The Reporter is assisted by a small group of Advisers and by a Members Consultative Group. The Reporter presents the project to the full membership of the ALI for a vote to determine whether the Institute adopts the project. The Restatements have been very influential, and you will undoubtedly encounter Restatements in various courses throughout law school. For our purposes here, the Restatements of Judgments are particularly important. There have been two: The original Restatement of Judgments was promulgated in 1942 and the Restatement (Second) was published in 1982.

Issue preclusion is the modern terminology (influenced by the Restatement (Second) of Judgments) for "collateral estoppel." Both terms are currently in use and they are interchangeable. We address issue preclusion in detail in §11.3. In an important way, it is narrower than claim preclusion — it precludes relitigation in Case 2 of a particular *issue* that was litigated and determined in Case 1. The focus, then, is not on something relatively broad — the scope of a "claim" — but on something fairly narrow — an *issue* that was litigated and decided in Case 1. If issue preclusion applies, that issue is deemed established in Case 2. It will not be relitigated; the fact-finder in Case 2 will be instructed that that issue is established. Issue preclusion, then, does not necessarily result in dismissal of Case 2. Rather, it may simply narrow the scope of what must be litigated in Case 2.

- In Case 1, *P* sues *D* on a claim that requires *P* to establish four issues: *A*, *B*, *C*, and *D*. After trial, *P* wins, and judgment is entered in her favor. Now *P* sues *D* in Case 2, asserting a different claim (so there's no claim preclusion). The claim in Case 2 requires *P* to establish five issues: *W*, *X*, *Y*, *Z*, and *A*. If issue preclusion applies, issue *A* will be deemed established in Case 2. *P* need not put on evidence on that issue, and *D* cannot relitigate it. At trial, *P* will be required only to establish issues *W*, *X*, *Y*, and *Z*.

When reading cases about preclusion, keep in mind another source of terminological confusion. Some courts (particularly in older cases) use "res judicata" in a generic sense to refer to both claim and issue preclusion. So you may read a case in which the court talks about res judicata but is actually applying issue preclusion.[4]

Both claim and issue preclusion are affirmative defenses under Federal Rule 8(c)(1).[5] Thus, it is incumbent on the defendant to raise them or risk waiving them. And once the defendant raises a defense of claim or issue preclusion, she bears the burden of proof on the issue.[6] Reflecting the contemporary concern with crowded judicial dockets, some courts seem willing to raise preclusion on their own motion.[7]

---

[4] An example is the famous case of *Cromwell v. County of Sac*, 94 U.S. 351 (1877), which we discuss in §11.3.2.

[5] Rule 8(c)(1) lists both "estoppel" and "res judicata" as affirmative defenses. There is no question that these references encompass both claim and issue preclusion. Simi Inv. Co. v. Harris County, Texas, 236 F.3d 240, 252 n.16 (5th Cir. 2000); Mozingo v. Correct Mfg. Corp., 752 F.2d 168, 172 (5th Cir. 1985) (reference to res judicata in Rule 8(c) includes issue preclusion). We saw affirmative defenses at §7.3.3.

[6] Taylor v. Sturgell, 128 S. Ct. 2161, 2179-2180 (2008) (defendant bears burden of proof on all elements of affirmative defense).

[7] *See, e.g.*, Doe v. Pfrommer, 148 F.3d 73, 80 (2d Cir. 1998). *But see* Scherer v. Equitable Life Assur. Soc. of America, 347 F.3d 394 (2d Cir. 2003) (trial court erred in raising preclusive effect of prior state court; defendant waived preclusion defense by failing to assert it).

531

While the rules of claim and issue preclusion can be treated rather mechanically, it is important to realize that these are not just procedural technicalities. Several closely related and important policies support these doctrines. First, there is a legitimate interest in *finality*. At some point, litigation must be declared finished. It is not productive for the parties or for society to allow serial relitigation of a claim already asserted or an issue already decided by a competent court. Second, at some point a defendant has a right to *repose* — to know that she cannot be sued repeatedly on the same claim. Third, there is an interest in *consistency*. If the same issue were to be relitigated several times, there is a chance that it would be resolved differently in different cases — one jury might find that the defendant was driving her car recklessly while another jury, determining the same issue, might find to the contrary. Such inconsistency may erode the public's confidence in the judicial system by making that system seem more like a lottery than an orderly mechanism for resolving disputes. Fourth, the community has a legitimate interest in *efficiency*. Litigation is publicly funded dispute resolution, and the public has a right to expect that the resources of the judicial system not be wasted. The use of preclusion reflects confidence in the judicial system — one opportunity to litigate a claim or an issue suffices to ensure each party of her "day in court."[8]

While courts may emphasize one or another of these policy bases in a given case, the underlying precepts are significant. Thus, the Supreme Court has said that preclusion embodies "public policy and private peace"[9] and serves "vital public interests."[10] Leading commentators have referred to preclusion as a "pillar of modern judicial philosophy."[11] On the other hand, the preclusion doctrines must be flexible. There are occasions — rare, but they do exist — in which the use of preclusion would not be fair, or when the policies underlying preclusion should give way to some other policy. We see such situations in §11.4. The narrowness of these exceptions again manifests the seriousness with which the judicial system takes the preclusion doctrines.

In addition, there is the sometimes vexing question of what preclusion law to apply when Case 1 and Case 2 are litigated in courts of different jurisdictions. If Case 1 was decided in a Kansas state court and Case 2 is pending in a Massachusetts court, what preclusion law applies — that of Kansas or that of Massachusetts? Each state is free to determine its own preclusion rules, so long as they do not violate due process, and states have adopted different approaches to various issues. This question becomes more complicated when a federal court is involved, particularly

---

[8] Of course, if the trial court errs in its resolution of a case, the proper avenue is not to file a new case to relitigate the dispute, but to appeal. See §14.2.

[9] Hart Steel Co. v. Railroad Supply Co., 244 U.S. 294, 299 (1917).

[10] Federated Dept. Stores, Inc. v. Moitie, 452 U.S. 394, 401 (1981).

[11] 18 Moore's Federal Practice 131-21.

if the federal court is exercising diversity of citizenship jurisdiction. These situations implicate constitutional and statutory notions of full faith and credit and related doctrines. We study them in §11.5.

Before addressing claim preclusion and issue preclusion, we should contrast them with some other, similar concepts you may encounter. *Double jeopardy* is the criminal law analogue to claim preclusion; it ensures that no criminal defendant is made to answer twice for the same crime. Because it is a doctrine of criminal law, we do not encounter it in Civil Procedure.

Stare decisis, as we discussed in §1.2.2, is the doctrine of precedent. It requires that courts of a jurisdiction adhere to the legal pronouncements by appellate courts of that jurisdiction. Such pronouncements potentially affect all citizens; res judicata and collateral estoppel, in contrast, only bind those who were litigants in Case 1 (or in privity with a litigant in Case 1).

Law of the case establishes that issues decided in a suit will not be relitigated later in the same case. It is different from issue preclusion because the issues are raised in a single case. With issue preclusion, a judgment has been entered in Case 1, and the question is whether that judgment affects one's ability to relitigate issues in Case 2.

Finally, *judicial estoppel* prevents a litigant from taking inconsistent positions in different cases. It is a doctrine of equity, for which there are no immutable rules. An example is *New Hampshire v. Maine*,[12] which involved a dispute over the boundary between those two states. The Court noted that New Hampshire had taken a different position regarding the point of the boundary in litigation some three decades earlier, and invoked judicial estoppel to reject the state's different position in the more recent case.

§11.2 Claim Preclusion (Res Judicata)

As noted in §11.1, claim preclusion provides that a claimant may sue only once to vindicate a claim. What constitutes a claim is a matter of some debate, as we see in §11.2.3. Suffice it to say now that a single claim might include more than one right to recover. For example, as we showed in §11.1, a single claim arising from an automobile accident may include the right to recover both for personal injuries and for property damage. Because the claimant only gets to sue on the claim once, she must be careful to seek recovery for all rights to relief in that one case. If she does not, her second bite at the apple — her second case — will be dismissed under claim preclusion, which historically has been called *res judicata*. We noted

---

[12] 532 U.S. 742 (2001).

above that both terms are in use currently, though we tend to use the modern terminology. In addition, older cases tend to refer to the doctrine as prohibiting two cases based on the same *cause of action*, while more modern cases talk about cases based on the same *claim*. Those terms also are interchangeable, but we tend to use the modern terminology.

Courts occasionally state the requirements of res judicata in different ways. When push comes to shove, however, there are three requirements for the operation of claim preclusion. First, both Case 1 and Case 2 must have been brought by the same claimant against the same defendant. Second, Case 1 must have ended in a valid, final judgment on the merits. And third, both Case 1 and Case 2 must be based upon the same "claim."[13]

One more bit of terminology. Some courts refer to claim preclusion as resulting either in *merger* or *bar*. Do not let these terms give you any trouble. Merger is simply claim preclusion when the claimant *won* Case 1. The claim she attempts to set forth in Case 2 is "merged" with the judgment from Case 1 and thereby precluded. Bar is claim preclusion when the claimant *lost* Case 1. That claimant is said to be "barred" from proceeding with Case 2. These terms do not mean a great deal, and the requirements for claim preclusion are the same whether the case is one of merger or bar. Now we turn to the individual requirements for claim preclusion.

§11.2.1   Case 1 and Case 2 Were Asserted by the Same Claimant Against the Same Defendant

Claim preclusion applies only if Case 1 and Case 2 are brought by the same claimant against the same defendant.[14] Resist the temptation to say, as some students (and courts) do, that the requirement is simply that both Case 1 and Case 2 "involve the same parties." That statement is not sufficiently precise. Remember, claim preclusion tells *claimants* that they have only one bite at the apple — that they only get to sue on a claim one time. So unless the same party is *asserting a claim* in both cases, claim preclusion simply cannot apply.

  ○ *A* and *Z* are involved in an automobile collision, and each is injured. In Case 1, *A* sues *Z*. The case is litigated and judgment is entered. Now, in Case 2, *Z* sues *A*. Is *Z* barred by res judicata? No! *Z* has never been a claimant before, so it is impossible for her to be suing on the same claim twice.

---

[13] *See, e.g.*, Kale v. Combined Ins. Co., 924 F.2d 1161 (1st Cir. 1991).

[14] Actually, as we see later in the text of this subsection, it would be sufficient if Case 2 was brought by one who was in privity with the claimant in Case 1 or against one who was in privity with the defendant in Case 1. We discuss these concepts in detail at §§11.3.4 and 11.3.5.

- Still, it does not seem right that Z should be able to file a separate case about this accident. What could lead us to conclude that Z should not be able to bring this suit? The compulsory counterclaim rule! Under Federal Rule 13(a)(1), which we discuss at §12.5.1 (and which is adopted in many states), if a defendant has a claim against the plaintiff, and the claim arises from the same transaction or occurrence as the plaintiff's claim, she must assert it in the pending case. Failure to do so waives the claim. But this preclusion of Z's claim comes from the operation of the compulsory counterclaim rule, and not from claim preclusion.

We should also resist the temptation to say that claim preclusion requires that Case 1 and Case 2 be brought by the same "plaintiff" against the same defendant. As we see in the materials in Chapter 12, a defendant can assert claims against the plaintiff in a pending case. If she does so, she could be subject to claim preclusion in a second case. Claim preclusion applies to parties who assert the same claim twice; thus, it applies to "claimants" and not just "plaintiffs."[15]

- A and Z are involved in a business deal. Independent of their business deal, A and Z, each driving her own car, collide; each is injured and each car is damaged. In Case 1, A sues Z for a problem arising from their business deal. Z files a permissive counterclaim[16] against A in Case 1, seeking recovery for personal injuries from the auto collision. The entire case goes to judgment. Now, in Case 2, Z sues A to recover for property damage to her car from the collision. If the applicable law adopts a transactional test for claim (discussed at §11.2.3), Case 2 will be dismissed under claim preclusion.
- Why? Because Z has sued twice on the same claim (first in Case 1 by the counterclaim and second in Case 2 as plaintiff). She was a claimant in both cases, even though she was only a plaintiff in Case 2. And under a transactional test for claim, both assertions by Z involved the same claim (because they involved the same transaction — the car wreck).[17]

The requirement that claim preclusion applies only when Case 1 and Case 2 are brought by the same claimant against the same defendant reflects an important constitutional precept. Due process provides that one may be bound by a judgment only if she was a party to the case in which that judgment was entered. This requirement is satisfied by our definition of claim preclusion, since it may be asserted only *against* one who was a claimant in Case 1. We discuss this point in detail at §11.3.4.

---

[15] All plaintiffs are claimants, but not all claimants are plaintiffs.

[16] Fed. R. Civ. P. 13(b). This rule allows a defendant to assert any claim she has against the plaintiff in the pending case, even if it has no relation to the plaintiff's claim. We discuss the permissive counterclaim at §12.5.1.

[17] If the applicable law adopted the "primary rights" theory for defining claims (which we see in §11.2.3), however, Case 2 will not be dismissed under claim preclusion.

Finally, claim preclusion does not necessarily require that the claimant and defendants be exactly the same persons in Case 1 and Case 2. There is some flexibility, to reflect the fact that some people or entities are so closely related that litigation by one ought to bind the other. In other words, under some circumstances, preclusion might affect someone who was not a party to Case 1. This "nonparty preclusion" is often said to apply when the nonparty is in "privity" with one who was a party to Case 1. Accordingly, claim preclusion will apply if Case 1 and Case 2 are brought by the same claimant (or someone in "privity" with the claimant) against the same defendant (or someone in "privity" with the defendant). Although the leading case on the meaning of "privity" arose in the context of claim preclusion,[18] the issue usually arises in cases involving issue preclusion. We discuss it (and the leading case) in detail at §11.3.4.

§11.2.2   Case 1 Ended in a Valid Final Judgment on the Merits

Preclusion (either claim preclusion or issue preclusion) does not attach to every judicial order. Only a particular kind of judicial order is entitled to preclusive effect — one that has three characteristics: (1) it must be valid, (2) it must be a final judgment, and (3) it must be on the merits. If the order by the court in Case 1 has these characteristics, it has enough safeguards to justify according it a preclusive effect. Stated another way, only such an order is worthy of such respect as to preclude parties from subsequent litigation.[19]

Validity

First, the order must be *valid*. This requirement addresses the competence of the court in Case 1. That inquiry typically focuses on whether the court in Case 1 had subject matter jurisdiction over the case and personal jurisdiction over the parties. If it did, the judgment is considered valid.[20]

---

[18] That case is *Taylor v. Sturgell*, 128 S. Ct. 2161 (2008).

[19] Almost always, the valid final judgment in Case 1 will be entered by a court. It is possible, however, that the litigation in Case 1 took place before an administrative tribunal, an arbitrator, or an arbitration board. Their judgments can give rise to claim and issue preclusion in subsequent judicial cases, subject to considerations beyond our scope. For a detailed discussion, *see* 18B Wright & Miller §4475.

[20] Today, there appears to be a trend toward recognizing judgments as preclusive in some circumstances even if the court in Case 1 lacked jurisdiction. *See* 18A Wright & Miller §§4428 & 4430. This trend reflects a contemporary sense that courts are so crowded that society cannot afford to allow Case 2 to proceed if the only problem with Case 1 was a technical lack of jurisdiction. This trend balances the interests in finality and efficiency (recognized in preclusion law) against the concern with jurisdictional limitations on courts (reflected

The assessment of whether an order is valid has nothing to do with whether it was right in its resolution of the merits of the underlying claim. A judgment may be valid even though it is incorrect. If the judgment was wrong on the merits, the losing party should have appealed the judgment in Case 1 to the appropriate appellate court. In the words of the Supreme Court, "[T]he res judicata consequences of a final, unappealed judgment on the merits [are not] altered by the fact that the judgment may have been wrong or rested on a legal principle subsequently overruled in another case."[21]

Final Judgment

Second, the order must be a *final judgment*. As we see in §14.4, this is the same basic requirement most judicial systems impose for determining whether an order can be appealed.[22] A final judgment is one that "ends the litigation on the merits and leaves nothing for the [trial] court to do but execute the judgment."[23] It wraps up the case; it announces who won and, if the claimant won, what relief is appropriate. Every other order in a case is "interlocutory," which just means that it is not final. During litigation, the court may make hundreds of interlocutory rulings before entering the one final judgment. It makes sense that only the final judgment is appealable, and that only the final judgment is entitled to claim preclusive or issue preclusive effect. An interlocutory order may be amended during the course of the litigation. It would be wasteful to allow an appeal from such an order or to give it preclusive effect, because the order might not stand the test of time;[24] it might be changed or abandoned as the litigation develops.[25]

---

in the requirements of personal and subject matter jurisdiction). Increasingly, courts seem tempted to find the balance to favor preclusion.

[21] Federated Dept. Stores, Inc. v. Moitie, 452 U.S. 494, 398 (1981).

[22] The analogy is not perfect, because sometimes "definitions of finality cannot automatically be carried over from appeals cases to preclusion problems," 18A Wright & Miller 55, but the analogy is appropriate for most cases and for our purposes.

[23] Catlin v. United States, 324 U.S. 229, 233 (1949).

[24] Even though interlocutory orders are not entitled to claim preclusive or issue preclusive effect, the court may decide to defer to such rulings under the "law of the case" doctrine, which we mentioned briefly in §11.1.

[25] We see at §14.5 that there are exceptions to the final judgment rule, in which a party is allowed to appeal even though the court has not entered final judgment; these exceptions are relatively rare, though. In addition, we saw in §9.7 that a final judgment may be attacked in the court in which it was entered by a motion to set aside the judgment. The existence of this procedure, however, does not vitiate the preclusive effect of the judgment. Obviously, if the court later sets aside the judgment, it may no longer be worthy of carrying a preclusive effect; until that happens, though, the judgment is entitled to preclusive effect.

What happens, though, if the final judgment in Case 1 is appealed? The appellate process will certainly take months (and perhaps years) to complete. Obviously, if the appellate court reverses or vacates the final judgment of the trial court, that judgment is no longer entitled to preclusive effect — it simply no longer exists in the same form in which it was entered. Just as obviously, if the appellate court affirms the trial court's final judgment, it is entitled to continued preclusive effect.

But what is the status of things during the pendency of the appeal? Before the appellate court has acted, is the final judgment entitled to preclusive effect or is it held in abeyance until the resolution of the appeal? Federal law on the subject says that the judgment is entitled to preclusive effect,[26] and most states agree.[27] In some states, however, the fact that an appeal is pending means that the final trial court judgment does not create preclusion.[28] As a policy matter, the majority rule accords with the reality that most appeals result in affirming the trial court's judgment.

On the Merits

The third characteristic of an order entitled to preclusion is that it be *on the merits*. The term *merits* refers to the underlying dispute — whether the claimant has shown that she is entitled to judgment because, for example, the defendant breached a contract or committed a tort, and if so, what damage befell the claimant. So for a valid final judgment to be entitled to preclusive effect, it must have been based upon the merits — that is, on the underlying dispute, the question of who did what. In contrast, a judgment based upon something unrelated to the underlying dispute — say, for example, on some procedural or jurisdictional basis — should not be given preclusive effect.

Having said that, however, as we will see, many judgments are accorded preclusive effect even though there has been no true assessment of the merits of the case at all. For this reason, some commentators have argued

[26] *See, e.g.,* Smith v. Securities & Exch. Commn., 129 F.3d 356, 362 n.7 (6th Cir. 1997) ("The fact that Smith has an appeal of that judgment pending does not deprive the judgment of res judicata effect."). *See also* 18A Wright & Miller §4433.

[27] *See, e.g.,* Phelps v. Hamilton, 122 F.3d 1309, 1318 (10th Cir. 1997) ("Kansas courts have adopted the now-majority view regarding the pendency of appeals which provides that the fact that an appeal is pending in a case does not generally vitiate the res judicata effect of the judgment."); Cully v. Lutheran Med. Ctr., 523 N.E.2d 531, 532 (Ohio App. 1987) ("It is well-settled that the pendency of an appeal does not prevent the judgment's effect as res judicata."); Jones v. American Family Mut. Ins. Co., 489 N.E.2d 160, 166 (Ind. App. 1986) ("an appeal from the judgment of the trial court does not have the effect of vacating the judgment of the trial court").

[28] *See, e.g.,* Faison v. Hudson, 417 S.E.2d 302, 305 (Va. 1992) ("[T]he better rule . . . is that a judgment is not final for the purposes of res judicata or collateral estoppel when it is being appealed or when the limits fixed for perfecting the appeal have not expired.").

that the phrase "on the merits" should be jettisoned.[29] Courts continue to use the phrase, however, and it is important that we review what it means as applied. For starters, it is helpful to recognize that preclusion does not require that the judgment in Case 1 be determined *literally* on the merits. Rather, it is more accurate to think of the requirement as one that the court had the *opportunity* to get to the merits of the case, even if it did not actually do so. A review of the relevant situations should demonstrate the point.

Let's start with the easiest situation. If Case 1 went to trial, the resultant valid final judgment is undoubtedly on the merits. This example, in fact, is the archetype of what it means for a judgment to be on the merits. But "on the merits" does not require that there be a trial. For example, suppose a valid final judgment is entered on summary judgment (which we discussed at §9.4). Recall that summary judgment allows a court to rule as a matter of law without trial, because there is no dispute on a material issue of fact. Such a judgment is entitled to preclusive effect. It is on the merits for these purposes. It is an adjudication that a party is entitled to prevail as a matter of law.[30]

Obviously, then, "on the merits" is not tantamount to "litigated at trial." But how far can we push this concept? Suppose the plaintiff wins on default judgment (discussed at §7.4.3). With default, the defendant has failed to respond within the prescribed time. Can a default judgment be on the merits for preclusion purposes? The general answer is yes,[31] because default does establish (albeit by defendant's failure to respond) that the plaintiff's claim is substantively valid.

But what about dismissals that seem to have nothing to do with the underlying substantive claim? For example, with a voluntary dismissal (discussed at §7.4.1), the plaintiff simply pulls the plug on the case. Is that dismissal on the merits for preclusion purposes? Federal Rule 41(a) provides that such a dismissal is "without prejudice," which means that it is not deemed on the merits, unless the notice or stipulation or order of dismissal provides otherwise.[32]

That brings us to *involuntary* dismissals, which can be entered for an almost infinite number of reasons. Are they on the merits for preclusion purposes? Here the starting point is Rule 41(b), which bears careful scrutiny and envisions three scenarios. First, if the involuntary dismissal is

---

[29] The Restatement (Second) of Judgments does not use the phrase. *See* Restatement (Second) of Judgments §§24, 25, and 26.

[30] *See, e.g.,* Campanelli v. Allstate Ins. Co., 119 F. Supp. 2d 1073, 1076 (C.D. Cal. 2000) ("Summary judgment constitutes a final adjudication on the merits" and is entitled to claim preclusive effect).

[31] *See, e.g.,* Morris v. Jones, 329 U.S. 545, 550-551 (1947) (Missouri default judgment res judicata against Illinois insurance company).

[32] Or, you will recall, unless it is a second voluntary dismissal and is by notice. See §7.4.3.

based upon lack of jurisdiction (meaning either personal or subject matter[33]), improper venue, or failure to join a party under Rule 19 (the indispensable party issue, discussed at §12.6.1), the Rule provides that the dismissal does *not* "operate[] as an adjudication on the merits." That means, of course, that such a dismissal is not entitled to preclusive effect. This rule makes sense: A judgment based upon any of these three defenses truly does not involve an investigation of the underlying merits of the case.

Second, for "failure of the plaintiff to prosecute or to comply with these rules or any order of court," a dismissal "operates as an adjudication on the merits" unless the court says otherwise in its dismissal order. Note how broadly this provision can sweep. The reference to failure to prosecute is fairly precise,[34] as is the failure to comply with a court order. Beyond that, though, dismissals for failure to comply "with these rules" obviously means dismissals for failure to comply with *any* of the Federal Rules. For example, a court might dismiss the plaintiff's case as a penalty for abusing the discovery provision. Unless the court indicates otherwise in its order of dismissal, such a dismissal "operates as an adjudication on the merits" and bars a second action on the same claim.[35] This rule also makes sense, because a plaintiff who is guilty of failing to prosecute the action or of failing to comply with the Federal Rules has had an *opportunity* to present her case for consideration of the merits, but has failed to do so properly. The legal system has given her a chance, and has an interest in enforcing its own rules for how cases are to proceed. Thus, unless the court provides otherwise in its order of dismissal, Rule 41(b) treats such a judgment as on the merits for purposes of claim and issue preclusion.

Third, under Rule 41(b), unless the court orders otherwise, "any dismissal not under this rule . . . operates as an adjudication on the merits." Literally, this provision requires that every involuntary dismissal (other than those based upon jurisdiction, venue, or Rule 19) is to be treated as on the merits. But the Supreme Court decision in *Semtek International, Inc. v. Lockheed Martin Corp.*[36] makes it clear that the Rule is not always to be read literally in this regard. In *Semtek*, the plaintiff filed Case 1 in a California state court and the defendant removed it to federal court on the basis of diversity of citizenship jurisdiction. The federal court dismissed the case as barred under California's two-year statute of limitations.[37] The order of dismissal stated expressly that the dismissal was "on

---

[33] *See* American Natl. Bank v. FDIC, 710 F.2d 1528, 1535-1536 (11th Cir. 1983). *See generally* 18A Wright & Miller 149.

[34] We discussed dismissals for failure to prosecute at §7.4.2.

[35] *See, e.g.,* In re Reed, 861 F.2d 1381 (5th Cir. 1988).

[36] 531 U.S. 497 (2001).

[37] Recall that under the *Erie* doctrine a federal court sitting in diversity applies state statute of limitations law. See §10.5.

the merits and with prejudice." The plaintiff filed Case 2, on the same claim, in state court in Maryland, a state where the statute of limitations (three years) would not bar the claim.[38] Was Case 2 barred by claim preclusion? More specifically, was the judgment in Case 1 on the merits for purposes of preclusion? Again, the court in Case 1 expressly said that its judgment was on the merits. And even without that statement, Rule 41(b) declares that such a dismissal will operate as an adjudication on the merits (because it was a "dismissal not provided for in this rule").

Nonetheless, the Supreme Court held (unanimously) that the California federal judgment was not entitled to a claim-preclusive effect. Accordingly, the plaintiff could proceed with suit in Maryland. Why? First, the Court concluded, Rule 41(b) is not aimed at claim preclusion at all. Its provision that a dismissal "operates as an adjudication on the merits" means only that the plaintiff cannot refile the same claim *in the same federal district court that entered the judgment of dismissal*. According to the Court, the Rule does not purport to establish federal law on claim preclusion. As the opinion explained, it would be "highly peculiar" to find a rule on claim preclusion "ensconced in rules governing the internal procedures of the rendering court itself."[39]

Second, because the Federal Rule was not on-point, the Court then determined whether a federal court was required to apply state law on the issue. The Court determined that the topic should be governed by federal common law,[40] but that federal common law in this instance — where Case 1 was in federal court under diversity of citizenship jurisdiction — would adopt the law of the state in which that federal court sat.[41] The Court then decided that California law would not have ascribed claim preclusion to a dismissal based upon the statute of limitations. That is, a California state court would have dismissed the plaintiff's case but would not have objected to the plaintiff's suing in Maryland to take advantage of Maryland's longer statute of limitations.

---

[38] Defendant removed that case to federal court in Maryland, which remanded to the state court. Though the requirements of diversity of citizenship jurisdiction were satisfied, the case could not be removed because the defendant was a citizen of the forum. (We saw this limitation on removal jurisdiction at §4.8.) So the litigation proceeded in state court in Maryland.

[39] *Semtek*, 531 U.S. at 503. Indeed, if Rule 41(b) *did* prescribe the requirements for claim preclusion, the Court indicated, the rule might run afoul of the Rules Enabling Act by prescribing a substantive rule.

[40] In §10.9, we saw that there are narrow areas in which federal common law operates to provide the rule of decision. The *Erie* doctrine established that there is no *general* federal common law, but did not rule out the possibility of federal common law in specialized areas. *Semtek* involves one such area — the question of the preclusive effect of a federal court judgment. The Court reiterated the point in *Taylor v. Sturgell*, 128 S. Ct. 2161, 2171 (2008).

[41] *Semtek*, 531 U.S. at 507-508. See §11.5.4.

Semtek thus makes it clear that the language of Rule 41(b) — that an involuntary dismissal other than under that rule (and other than one based upon jurisdiction, venue, or Rule 19) "operates as an adjudication on the merits" — does not state a universal truth for purposes of preclusion. True, the rule stops the plaintiff from refiling in the same federal court that dismissed the action. But whether the first court's dismissal is on the merits for claim preclusion and issue preclusion in other courts requires an analysis of federal common law, which, in turn, in a diversity case usually will look to the law of the state in which the federal court deciding Case 1 sat. So ultimately, the question of whether the California federal judgment should result in claim preclusion in a Maryland court will depend upon whether a California state court would have treated it as on the merits for preclusion purposes.

§11.2.3   Case 1 and Case 2 Were Based on the Same Claim

Even if Cases 1 and 2 are brought by the same claimant against the same defendant and Case 1 ended in a valid final judgment on the merits, claim preclusion applies only if the two cases are based upon the same claim. The essence of claim preclusion is that a claimant gets one chance — meaning one suit — to vindicate her claim. Unfortunately, "claim" is not a self-defining word. It might mean different things in different contexts.[42] More important for present purposes, even in the claim preclusion context, the word can mean different things in different jurisdictions. The differing definitions reflect policy choices each state is free to weigh for itself. It is likely that your casebook contains cases applying different definitions of claim.

While there is thus some variation in approach among jurisdictions, the undeniable trend has been toward a broader definition of claim. This broader definition has not been created in a vacuum. Rather, it reflects developments in related areas of the law. In earlier procedural regimes, pleading and joinder rules imposed severe restrictions on the plaintiff's

---

[42] For example, what constitutes a "claim" for pleading purposes under Federal Rule 12(b)(6) might not be the same as what constitutes a claim (or "cause of action") for claim preclusion purposes. In the words of Justice Cardozo:

A "cause of action" may mean one thing for one purpose and something different for another. It may mean one thing when the question is whether it is good upon demurrer, and something different when there is a question of the amendment of a pleading or of the application of the principle of res judicata. . . . At times and in certain contexts, it is identified with the infringement of a right or the violation of a duty. At other times and in other contexts, it is a concept of the law of remedies. . . . Another aspect reveals it as . . . the group of operative facts out of which a grievance has developed.

United States v. Memphis Cotton Oil Co., 288 U.S. 62, 67-68 (1933).

ability to assert rights of action and join parties in a single case. Consequently, the law of claim preclusion defined the scope of the claim narrowly, reflecting the fact that the plaintiff might need Case 2, in which to seek something that was unavailable under the joinder rules in Case 1. The generally broader definition of claim today reflects the more liberal rules of pleading and joinder. Because those rules permit the plaintiff to package a great deal into Case 1, there is less need for the legal system to provide the plaintiff with an opportunity to bring Case 2.

Two Major Themes: Focus on Transaction or on Primary Rights Invaded

Federal law and the law of most states today adopt a transactional test for defining one's claim.[43] This transactional focus has been stated in different ways, including whether the two cases involve the same "operative facts,"[44] "transaction or occurrence,"[45] "basic factual situation,"[46] "defendant's wrongdoing,"[47] or "a single core of operative facts."[48] The most influential articulation comes from the Restatement (Second) of Judgments, which provides that a claim encompasses all rights to relief "with respect to all or any part of the transaction, or series of connected transactions, out of which the action arose."[49]

But not all jurisdictions have adopted a transactional test for defining the scope of a claim. Another school of thought focuses on the rights allegedly invaded by the defendant's behavior. Under this approach—often called the *primary rights* theory—the claimant has a separate claim (and therefore can file a separate case) for each right violated by the defendant.

There are other approaches to the question as well, some of which are mentioned below. Most jurisdictions seem, however, to adopt some form of one of these two approaches—one focusing on the underlying *transaction* and the other on the *rights* invaded. The difference in scope between these two is aptly demonstrated by a hypothetical first raised as an example in §11.1:

---

[43] *See, e.g.,* Mitchell v. City of Moore, 218 F.3d 1190, 1202 (10th Cir. 2000) ("We employ the transactional approach of the Restatement (Second) of Judgments"); River Park, Inc. v. City of Highland Park, 703 N.E.2d 883, 893 (Ill. 1998); O'Brien v. City of Syracuse, 429 N.E.2d 1158, 1159 (N.Y. 1981); Rush v. City of Maple Heights, 147 N.E.2d 599, 607 (Ohio 1958); Adape v. Akins, 668 P.2d 130, 134-135 (Idaho App. 1983).

[44] *See, e.g.,* Landscape Properties, Inc. v. Whisenhunt, 127 F.3d 678, 683 (8th Cir. 1997).

[45] *See, e.g.,* Great Lakes Trucking Co. v. Black, 477 N.W.2d 65, 68 (Wis. App. 1991).

[46] Gasbarra v. Park-Ohio Indus., 655 F.2d 119, 121 (7th Cir. 1981).

[47] Plotner v. AT&T, 224 F.3d 1161, 1170 (10th Cir. 2000).

[48] Mandarino v. Pollard, 718 F.2d 845, 849 (7th Cir. 1983).

[49] Restatement (Second) of Judgments §24(1).

○ *P* is involved in an auto collision with *D*. *P* suffers personal injuries and property damage to her car. In Case 1, she seeks only damages for the personal injuries. After judgment is entered in that case, she brings Case 2, seeking to recover for property damage from the same collision.

Is Case 2 barred by claim preclusion? The answer depends entirely on the definition of claim adopted by the jurisdiction. If the law defines her "claim" transactionally — as all rights to relief arising from a transaction — Case 2 will be dismissed under claim preclusion. Why? Because *P* is suing twice about the same transaction; thus, she is suing twice on the same claim. On the other hand, if the law defines her claims as the individual rights invaded, Case 2 will not be dismissed under claim preclusion, because there she is vindicating a different right from that vindicated in Case 1.

Policy and Efficiency Considerations

A transactional definition of claim is clearly more efficient than a focus on the rights invaded. It coerces the plaintiff to join her personal injury and property damage assertions in a single case. If she fails to do so, her second case will be dismissed under claim preclusion. Thus, the judicial system deals with only one suit for what is, defined in transactional terms, one event. Moreover, the transactional test comports broadly with tests for joinder and for supplemental jurisdiction. In Chapter 12 we discuss various joinder devices — including the compulsory counterclaim, cross-claim, and various claims under Federal Rule 14(a) — that adopt the "same transaction or occurrence" test. In §4.7, we saw how supplemental jurisdiction also adopts a largely transactional test for determining when claims failing to satisfy an independent basis of subject matter jurisdiction may nonetheless be asserted in federal court. The transactional test for claim reflects and complements these developments in other areas of the law.[50]

Of course, the system can only allow its claim preclusion doctrine to demand a claimant to assert all transactionally related claims in a single suit if the procedural rules for joinder allow the claimant to do so in Case 1. Because Federal Rules are liberal (especially regarding claim joinder, as we see in §12.3), and permit a claimant to assert all claims — even those not transactionally related — in a single suit, it is fair to impose a claim preclusion rule requiring her to assert all transactionally related claims in Case 1.

---

[50] For a discussion of how the rules of joinder, preclusion, and supplemental jurisdiction can operate together to facilitate efficient packaging of litigation, *see* Richard D. Freer, *Avoiding Duplicative Litigation: Rethinking Plaintiff Autonomy and the Court's Role in Defining the Litigative Unit*, 50 U. Pitt. L. Rev. 809, 813-837 (1989).

In contrast, the primary rights approach seems potentially wasteful of judicial resources. It allows the plaintiff in the hypothetical above to bring two suits over what the parties probably view as one real-world event.[51] Witnesses can be required to testify at two trials. The defendant is made to go through the trauma of being sued twice. And, of course the judicial system is made to accommodate two cases. Given contemporary concern with crowded judicial dockets, it is no surprise to see an increasing number of jurisdictions adopting the broader transactional test for claim.

One federal district court, applying Illinois law, expressed frustration with the fact that Illinois had not yet embraced a transactional test:

> Because of crowded dockets, it is difficult for courts to give litigants the one day in court they deserve. The Plaintiff in this case insists on having three. Thus, we press on in the hope that Illinois courts will eventually see fit to follow the current trend among state courts to follow the approach of the Restatement.[52]

Despite such criticism, the primary rights theory still has its adherents. California has never repudiated its embrace of that standard.[53] In Georgia, the primary rights theory is prescribed by statute in motor vehicle crash cases.[54] The experience in Virginia is especially interesting. In 1949, in the well-known case of *Carter v. Hinkle*,[55] the Virginia Supreme Court expressly rejected a transactional test and embraced primary rights in a case involving facts similar to the hypothetical above. In *Carter*, Case 1 was for property damage and Case 2 for personal injuries from a single collision. After reviewing the arguments in favor of both approaches, the court adopted the primary rights theory, which it described as the "less practical but...more logical path."[56] The court thus recognized that a transactional test was more efficient, but concluded that primary rights

[51] Just because a claimant *can* bring two separate cases does not mean that she will. In the hypothetical above, *P* could join the personal injury and property damage assertions in Case 1. But the primary rights theory — unlike a transactional theory — does not require her to do so.

[52] Salaymeh v. St. Vincent Memorial Hosp. Corp., 706 F. Supp. 643, 646-647 (C.D. Ill. 1989).

[53] *See* Holmes v. Bricker, 452 P.2d 647, 649 (Cal. 1969). The California primary rights definition of claim is criticized in Walter Heiser, *California's Unpredictable Res Judicata (Claim Preclusion) Doctrine*, 35 San Diego L. Rev. 599 (1998).

[54] Ga. Code Ann. §51-1-32. There is a special argument in favor of the primary rights theory in such cases. Suppose an insured driver is involved in an auto crash and suffers personal injury and property damage. Her insurance company may pay her for the property damage and then (as "subrogee" — which means as someone to whom the claim is assigned by operation of law) sue the other driver. If the insured has already sued that other driver for personal injuries, there is a risk in a transactional state that the insured driver and the insurance company (which stands in her shoes as subrogee) have split the claim. *See* Smith v. Hutchins, 566 P.2d 1136, 1137 (Nev. 1977).

[55] 52 S.E.2d 135 (Va. 1949).

[56] *Carter*, 52 S.E.2d at 138.

was more consistent with other aspects of the law. For example, as pointed out, the statutes of limitations are different for personal injury and property damage causes; a property damage claim can be assigned and does not abate at the plaintiff's death, while one for personal injuries cannot be assigned and does abate at death.

In 2006, the Virginia Supreme Court promulgated a Rule of Court adopting the transactional test for defining a claim.[57] Interestingly, though, the rule contains an express exception for cases in which one event causes both personal injuries and property damage.[58] Accordingly, despite this new Rule of Court in Virginia, a case like *Carter* would be decided as it was in 1949.

Experience in states adopting primary rights suggests that the theory might not be as inefficient as we might think. Though the theory would allow the plaintiff in *Carter* to bring Case 2 to recover for personal injuries, it does not require her to do so. She is free to package both claims in a single case. Indeed, many claimants undoubtedly do so, simply to avoid having to sue twice. Moreover, even if the claimant does bring two cases, the litigation in Case 2 will likely be rendered simpler by the use of *issue* preclusion. For instance, if the court in Case 1 found that the defendant was not negligent, Case 2 will be decided against the plaintiff on summary judgment. Why? Because *issue* preclusion will establish for Case 2 the issue that the defendant was not negligent in causing the wreck. If the court in Case 1 found for the plaintiff, including a finding that the defendant was negligent, Case 2 is streamlined because issue preclusion results in the establishment of the defendant's negligence for that case.

In addition, the findings from Case 1 may influence the parties to settle Case 2, in which situation Case 2 does not impose a significant burden on the court system. One court explained the effect of issue preclusion, even in a primary rights claim preclusion jurisdiction, this way:

> The total judicial time consumed, even if both parts are actually tried, may not be significantly greater than trying them together. In fact, it is likely that both will not be tried. If the decision in the property damage case is against

---

[57] Va. Sup. Ct. R. 1.6(a), which applies to judgments entered in Virginia in civil actions commenced after July 1, 2006, provides: "A party whose claim for relief arising from identified conduct, a transaction, or an occurrence, is decided on the merits by a final judgment, shall be forever barred from prosecuting any second or subsequent civil action against the same opposing party or parties on any claim or cause of action that arises from the same conduct, transaction or occurrence. . . ."

[58] Va. Sup. Ct. R. 1.6(c) provides: "The provisions of this Rule shall not bar a party or a party's insurer from prosecuting separate personal injury and property damage suits arising out of the same conduct, transaction or occurrence. . . ."

the plaintiff, there can be no second trial. If it is in favor of the plaintiff, the parties may well settle the damages claim.[59]

Applications

The examples above were relatively easy — personal injury and property damage clearly flowed from a single transaction. Not all cases are so easy.

- ∘ *P* and *D*, each driving her own automobile, collide, and each suffers personal injuries and property damage. Immediately after the collision, *D* jumps from her car, runs to *P*'s car, reaches through the window and punches *P* in the face. *D* then screams obscenities at *P*, threatens to kill *P*, and defames *P* by shouting to the crowd of onlookers various libelous falsehoods about *P*.

How many claims are involved here? Under a primary rights approach, *P* would seem to have these separate claims: (1) property damage to her automobile; (2) personal injuries from the accident and the punching;[60] (3) emotional injuries from the threats and obscenities; and (4) slander for the libelous falsehoods. Why? Because it seems that four rights have been invaded: (1) right to have her property free from injury; (2) right to have her person free from injury; (3) right to have her psyche free from injury; and (4) right to have her reputation free from injury.

What about under a transactional test? How many transactions were there here? Did one transaction end at the collision and another one start when *D* got out of her car, approached *P* and struck her? Did another transaction occur with the obscenities and threats, and yet another with the defamation? It is hard to say.[61] But remember, as we saw above, that the Restatement (Second) also instructs us to look at transactions or a "series

[59] Andrews v. Christenson, 692 P.2d 687, 690 n.1 (Or. App. 1984). Oregon subsequently adopted the transactional test for defining a claim. Peterson v. Temple, 918 P.2d 413 (Or. 1996) (rule that personal and property damage arising from a single accident constitute one claim to be applied prospectively).

[60] Could these injuries be subdivided into two claims — one for personal injuries from the wreck and another for personal injuries from the punching? Primary rights focuses on the harm caused, so perhaps not. *But see* Wood v. Allison Apparel Marketing, Inc., 398 S.E.2d 110 (Va. App. 1990) (administrative holding that plaintiff failed to show that carpal tunnel syndrome was caused by industrial accident did not bar subsequent workers' compensation claim that the same injury was caused by an industrial disease).

[61] We encounter similar problems under the "single wrongful act" test. Was the collision the result of one wrongful act, the battery the result of another, and the defamation of yet a third? The Restatement (Second) approach counsels us to address the situation in commonsense, real-world terms.

of connected transactions."[62] The Restatement (Second) adds to this definition an instruction to adopt a pragmatic approach, with a focus on whether facts are connected closely "in time, space, origin, or motivation [and] whether, taken together, they form a convenient unit for trial purposes," as well as whether treating them as a single claim will be consistent with the expectations of parties and businesses.[63] Thus, the inquiry becomes a practical one, guided by experience with particular kinds of cases, sensitive to the relevant policies.

On the facts of this hypothetical, it is at least arguable that everything was the result of a series of connected transactions. Considered pragmatically, should the judicial system countenance separate suits in this hypothetical? Should the defendant have to defend more than one action? Should the plaintiff be expected to package all of these claims into a single case? Arguably, based on such considerations, the hypothetical seems to present a single claim. The participants might well consider all the events as a single episode. Everything occurred in a relatively small area and within a relatively short time. Thus, the witnesses to one aspect of the episode — say, for example, the collision — were probably witnesses to the punching and the oral tirade as well. Having more than one case could burden the witnesses to testify more than once,[64] and having redundant testimony in multiple cases would waste judicial resources.

The point, of course, is that determining whether Case 1 and Case 2 involve the same claim is more art than science. It is imperative, though, that counsel be aware of whether the jurisdiction adopts a transactional or a rights-based approach to the issue. In her research, counsel may be surprised to find multiple tests adopted by a single state.[65] The lawyer who is aware of these cases may be equipped with multiple arguments in favor of a particular result. (And the law student who is aware of the various tests covered in her course materials will be able to demonstrate their application on the exam.)

Other Formulations of "Claim"

Courts can employ other formulations for defining the scope of a claim, but it is not clear that these are anything more than variations on the two

---

[62] Restatement (Second) of Judgments §24(1).

[63] Restatement (Second) of Judgments §24, cmt. b.

[64] And we should not forget that if all assertions were packaged in a single case, the trial court has the discretion to order separate trials of various issues to avoid confusion or embarrassment. See §12.4.

[65] For example, in Virginia, before adoption of the Rule of Court cited and discussed at note 57 above, that state's supreme court had embraced at least three definitions of claim. *See* Flora, Flora & Montague, Inc. v. Saunders, 367 S.E.2d 493, 495-496 (Va. 1988) (sameness of evidence); Brown v. Haley, 355 S.E.2d 563, 568-569 (Va. 1987) (transactional test); Carter v. Hinkle, 52 S.E.2d 135 (Va. 1949) (primary rights).

major approaches we have just seen. It may be that your professor does not address these other formulations, and that this discussion will not be relevant to your class. Some professors do address these other definitions of claim, however, so let's survey the main ones.

Some courts espouse a "sameness of the evidence" test, under which claims are the same if "the evidence needed to sustain the second action would have sustained the first."[66] This is an essentially meaningless test, as we see if we apply it to the facts in *Carter*, in which plaintiff sued in Case 1 for property damage and in Case 2 for personal injuries, both caused in the same wreck. If the sameness of the evidence test means all the evidence in the entire action, Case 2 should be allowed to proceed. Why? Because in Case 2, the plaintiff must produce evidence of personal injuries that was not required in Case 1. But if by sameness of the evidence this test refers only to the evidence necessary to establish liability, Case 2 should be dismissed. Why? Because the showing required to establish that the defendant was liable for the wreck is exactly the same in Case 1 as in Case 2 — her negligence is not affected by the type of damage claimed. Most courts seem to apply the test in this latter fashion.[67] As such, in focusing on liability, this test seems to add nothing to a transactional test, which focuses on the transaction that gives rise to defendant's liability.

Under another formulation, one's claim consists of all rights to relief arising from the defendant's "single wrongful act." This test obviously relates to a transactional inquiry, but may be narrower than the Restatement (Second) approach. Some commentators conclude that the single-wrong phrase should be discarded "because it may lead to unsound results by inviting abstract speculation about the number of rights that can dance on the head of a single transaction."[68]

An antiquated approach provides that a claimant has different claims for "different legal theories," even if they arise from a single transaction. This approach was a product of the narrow pleading rules imposed by the common law. Under common law pleading, a claimant could pursue only one legal theory in a case. Accordingly, preclusion law could not "punish" her for failing to assert more than one theory in the first case. Because such common law restrictions on pleading are now relegated to the history books, the "different legal theories" should be similarly interred.

- ◦ Plaintiff sues her employer in Case 1 for damages from alleged discrimination under state law and contract principles. After judgment is entered, she brings Case 2 against the employer, alleging that the same acts described in Case 1 also violated federal antidiscrimination law. Under a

[66] *See, e.g.*, Agriserve, Inc. v. Belden, 643 N.E.2d 1193, 1195 (Ill. App. 1999).

[67] *See, e.g.*, Sure-Snap Corp. v. State Street Bank & Trust Co., 948 F.2d 869, 874-875 (2d Cir. 1991); Kent County Bd. of Educ. v. Billbrough, 525 A.2d 232, 236-237 (Md. 1987).

[68] 18 Wright & Miller 167.

"different legal theories" test, Case 2 involves a different claim and would proceed. Today, however, it is likely that Case 2 would be dismissed under claim preclusion, because it involves the same transaction — and therefore the same claim — as Case 1.[69]

○ Similarly, an offer to produce different evidence in Case 2 should not defeat claim preclusion.[70] The point of claim preclusion is that the claimant gets one shot at a claim, and thus cannot blame anyone but herself for leaving out some element of recovery or for failing to marshal facts in an effective way.

Claim as Personal to Holder

A claim — no matter how defined — is personal to its holder. Suppose Louise and Patti are passengers on a bus that is involved in a wreck. Both Louise and Patti suffer personal injuries and property damage (to their luggage). Suppose further that the jurisdiction adopts a transactional test for claim. That test will coerce Louise to sue the bus company for personal injuries and property damage in a single case. (Both personal injuries and property damage are elements of a single claim, because both were caused in a single transaction.) Similarly, the transactional test will coerce Patti to sue for personal injuries and property damage in a single case. *But the definition of claim does not coerce Louise and Patti to join together as co-plaintiffs in a single case.* Louise's claim is hers and Patti's is hers. Claim preclusion does not force every person injured in a single case to join together in one suit. It simply forces each claimant to join the various elements of damage and legal theories arising from a claim into a single case.[71]

Contract Cases

There are some well-established general rules governing the scope of a claim in contract and similar cases. First, a claim, at least with regard to a single contract, is usually deemed to consist of all breaches that have occurred to the time of filing Case 1.

○ *D* leases a farm, including farm implements, from *P*. The lease provides that *D* will pay monthly rent and, upon failure to pay rent, will return the

---

[69] *See, e.g.*, Boateng v. InterAmerican Univ., 210 F.3d 56, 62 (1st Cir. 2000) (Case 1 based upon Puerto Rico and contract law; Case 2 based upon Title VII of the Americans with Disabilities Act).

[70] *See, e.g.*, New York Life Ins. Co. v. Gillespie, 203 F.3d 384, 387-388 (5th Cir. 2000).

[71] In §12.4, we discuss how Louise and Patti *may* join together as co-plaintiffs in a single proceeding. Whether they do so, however, is a choice given by the joinder rules, and has nothing to do with claim preclusion.

farm implements to *P*. *D* fails to pay rent and fails to return the equipment. *P* sues *D* in Case 1 for conversion of property (the farm implements). A valid final judgment is entered. Now *P* brings Case 2, seeking to recover the unpaid rent. Case 2 is barred by claim preclusion, because both rights to recover — the right to recover the property and the right to recover the rent — existed at the time Case 1 was filed, so they both constituted part of the same claim.

○ *P* and *D* enter an installment contract, under which *D* is to make monthly payments to *P*. *D* makes the payments for January and February, but fails to pay for March, April, and May. If *P* sues at that point, the claim consists of the failure to pay for those three months. If she sues only for the payment due for March, she would be prohibited by claim preclusion from ever seeking the payments for April and May.

Second, these hypotheticals assume that there is only one contract. If there are separate contracts, they generally are treated as separate claims. Thus, if *D* breached Contract #1 and Contract #2 in similar ways, *P* would probably have two claims — one for each contract. This rule is usually applied even if Contract #2 is identical in every way to Contract #1.[72]

Effect of Claim Preclusion

Remember that the effect of claim preclusion generally is to "rob" a claimant of getting into court for some right to relief. Unless some exception to claim preclusion applies (see §11.4), a claimant in a jurisdiction adopting a transactional definition of claim makes an enormous mistake if she sues only for property damage, and not personal injuries (or vice versa), in Case 1. If she commits this mistake, Case 2 will be dismissed and she never gets her day in court for personal injuries. But it's her own fault (or her lawyer's). The judicial system has given her one opportunity to vindicate her claim. It is up to her (or her lawyer) to know what that "claim" includes.

§11.3 Issue Preclusion (Collateral Estoppel)

Issue preclusion is the modern terminology for the doctrine historically known as collateral estoppel. Both terms are widely used today. Whatever we call it, the focus of issue preclusion is narrower than that of claim preclusion. As we saw immediately above, the application of claim preclusion usually prohibits the claimant from asserting a right to relief that she *could* have raised in Case 1 but failed to; it results in the dismissal of Case 2. Issue preclusion, in contrast, applies only to preclude *relitigation* of an

---

[72] *See* Gonzales v. Lopez, 52 P.3d 418, 424 (N.M. App. 2002).

issue that the parties *actually did litigate and the court determined* in Case 1; it generally does not in itself cause dismissal of Case 2. Rather, issue preclusion streamlines the number of issues to be litigated in Case 2, as noted in §11.1.[73]

On the other hand, in a way, issue preclusion is broader than claim preclusion, because its operation is not tied to transactional relatedness. That is, an issue determined in Case 1 may be deemed established in Case 2 even though the cases involve radically different real-world events. For example, a determination in Case 1 that a drug causes a particular side effect may be used to establish that issue in other cases involving different persons, hurt at different times in different places.

Courts occasionally state the requirements for issue preclusion in different ways. The standard definition contains five requisites. First, as with claim preclusion, Case 1 must have ended in a valid final judgment on the merits. Second, the same issue presented in Case 2 must have been litigated and determined in Case 1. Third, that issue must have been essential to the judgment in Case 1. Fourth, as a matter of due process, issue preclusion can only be asserted against one who was a party to Case 1 (or in "privity" with a party to Case 1). And fifth, the court in Case 2 must assess "mutuality," which concerns the question of who may assert issue preclusion. As we will see, the modern trend is to reject the traditional view that only parties to Case 1 may assert issue preclusion in Case 2. Now we turn to these individual requirements.

§11.3.1   Case 1 Ended in a Valid Final Judgment on the Merits

Preclusion — either claim preclusion or issue preclusion — flows from entry of a valid final judgment on the merits. The requirements discussed on this point for claim preclusion in §11.2.2 apply with equal force to issue preclusion.

---

[73] In some circumstances, however, the establishment of a single issue in Case 2 through issue preclusion may actually be determinative. Suppose, for example, that the jurisdiction recognizes the doctrine of contributory negligence. Suppose also that in Case 1, a litigant, Z, was found negligent. Now Z brings Case 2 as plaintiff, concerning the same event. If issue preclusion is used to establish in Case 2 that Z was negligent, it would result, ultimately, in dismissal of Case 2.

§11.3.2 The Same Issue Was Litigated and Determined in Case 1

While claim preclusion can operate to preclude a claimant from ever presenting evidence on a right to relief, issue preclusion can only apply to an issue that was actually litigated and determined in Case 1. Thus, it allows the judicial system to avoid the burden — and the concomitant risk of inconsistent results — caused by relitigating an issue that has already been decided. Innumerable cases discuss this point.[74] None is more famous, however, than *Cromwell v. County of Sac.*[75]

In *Cromwell*, the plaintiff sued to recover on bonds issued by a county. (Bonds are simply IOUs. People lend money to the county (in *Cromwell* they did so to build a new courthouse) and the county issues a bond — a piece of paper saying that the county will pay back the loan amount within a set period with specified interest.) The bond issuance in *Cromwell*, however, was fraudulent. It was set up by crooks who absconded with the money. Under the law of negotiable instruments, the county would not have to pay on the bonds if the bond issuance was fraudulent, with one exception: If the bond is in the hands of a "holder in due course" (HDC), the county must pay on the bond even though the issuance was fraudulent. An HDC is somebody who paid value for the bond and was unaware of the fraudulent issuance. (In some other contexts, the concept is referred to as being a "bona fide purchaser.")

In Case 1, Cromwell sued the county to recover on certain claims for interest on particular bonds.[76] The county proved that the bond issuance was fraudulent. Cromwell did not attempt to show that he was an HDC. In Case 2, Cromwell sued the county to recover on different claims for interest on the bonds. The county was entitled to issue preclusion on the issue that the bond issuance was fraudulent; so it was deemed established in Case 2 that the bond issuance was fraudulent. (Why?[77]) But Cromwell then

---

[74] There are a few opinions in which a court has permitted issue preclusion on an issue not actually litigated in Case 1. *See*, *e.g.*, Sutphin v. Speik, 15 Cal. 2d 195, 203-204 (1940). Such cases are aberrational; the overwhelming majority of courts hold that an issue cannot be the subject of issue preclusion unless it was litigated and determined in Case 1.

[75] 94 U.S. 351 (1877). This classic opinion, included in many casebooks, was written by our old friend Justice Stephen Field, who wrote the majority opinion in *Pennoyer v. Neff.*

[76] Actually, Case 1 was brought by someone named Smith and Case 2 was brought by Cromwell. The opinion makes clear, however, that Smith was acting as an agent for Cromwell and thus was in "privity" with him. So we treat the two cases as having been brought by Cromwell. We will see this concept in §11.3.4. *See also* Nestorio v. Assocs. Commercial Corp., 250 B.R. 50, 55 (D. Md. 2000). As you will study in an upper-level course on Business Associations, an agent is someone who acts for someone else (called the principal). The agent's acts, at least if done within the scope of the agency, will bind the principal. So Smith's litigation in Case 1 bound Cromwell in Case 2.

[77] Because that issue was litigated and determined in Case 1 and the other requirements of issue preclusion were met as well.

wanted to put on evidence in Case 2 that he was an HDC. The Supreme Court held that he was entitled to do so. The fact that Cromwell *could have* asserted the HDC issue in Case 1 was irrelevant. The HDC issue had not been litigated and determined in Case 1, and thus was not subject to issue preclusion.[78]

Though stated as a single requirement of issue preclusion — that the same issue must have been litigated and determined in Case 1 — this phrase actually contains three requisites. First, the issue must have been "litigated" in Case 1. Second, even though litigated, the issue must also have been "determined" in Case 1. And third, of course, we must be speaking of the "same issue" in both cases.

Determining Whether the Issue Was Litigated in Case 1

The situation is easy if Case 1 went to trial and evidence was presented on the particular issue. Then, clearly, the issue was litigated for purposes of issue preclusion. Even if the evidence presented was not sufficient to meet a party's burden at trial, the issue was litigated in Case 1.[79] Indeed, there is even support for the position that an issue framed by the pleadings, but as to which no evidence was presented at trial, was litigated.[80]

But what if Case 1 was decided without trial, or without a hearing on the particular issue? For example, as we saw in §11.2.2, a voluntary dismissal with prejudice will have a claim preclusive effect; because no issue was litigated in such a dismissal, however, it will not have an issue preclusive effect.[81] Similarly, though a default judgment can have a claim preclusive effect, it will probably not carry issue preclusion consequences, because no issue was actually litigated in the default.[82] So too, facts that

---

[78] The case was decided long before the terms *claim preclusion* and *issue preclusion* were coined. In *Cromwell*, the Court never actually says "collateral estoppel." This is a case in which the Court uses "res judicata" in a generic sense — to discuss both claim and issue preclusion. In reading the opinion, note especially two paragraphs. One, a lengthy one, starts "In considering the operation of this judgment, it should be borne in mind, as stated by counsel, that there is a difference. . . ." That sentence goes on to draw the distinction between what we would call claim preclusion and issue preclusion. The following paragraph (which starts "But where the second action . . .") is about issue preclusion, and makes the point that the issue must be litigated and determined in Case 1.

[79] *See, e.g.,* Peck v. Commissioner, 904 F.2d 525, 530 (9th Cir. 1990) (failure to satisfy burden of persuasion in Case 1 establishes the nonexistence of a fact for issue preclusion purposes).

[80] *See* 18 Wright & Miller 500-503.

[81] St. Vincent's Hosp. v. Div. of Human Rights, 553 F. Supp. 375, 379 (S.D.N.Y. 1982).

[82] The Court noted this point in *Cromwell*, 94 U.S. at 356-357 ("It could hardly be pretended that a judgment by default . . . would make the several statements evidence in any other proceeding."). *See also* In re Biselow, 271 B.R. 178, 185 (B.A.P. 9th Cir. 2001) (applying Washington law); Baron v. Bryant, 556 F. Supp. 531, 538 (D. Haw. 1983) (adopting "the preponderant view that a default judgment should not be given conclusive effect under the

are admitted in pleadings or an admission for failure to respond to a request under Federal Rule 36 are not litigated and should not support issue preclusion in a subsequent case.[83]

On the other hand, a judgment based upon summary judgment can carry issue preclusive effect. Recall (as we saw in §9.4) that summary judgment entails a judicial determination that there is no dispute on a material issue of fact and that the moving party is entitled to judgment as a matter of law. The determination that there is no material factual dispute is an adjudication on what facts exist and constitutes "litigation."[84]

Determining Whether the Issue Was Determined in Case 1

Not every issue litigated in a case will be determined. For example, a claimant may present alternative theories of recovery at trial. The fact-finder may base its decision on one of the alternatives and ignore the other. Similarly, a defendant may present alternative defenses. Once the fact-finder determines that one such theory is established, it may ignore the others. Or the parties may present evidence on an issue and then withdraw the issue before submission to the fact-finder. Because issue preclusion applies only to issues that are litigated *and* determined in Case 1, it will not apply to such issues.

In most cases, the issues that have been determined will be clear. In nonjury trials, the judge will enter findings of fact and conclusions of law, which ought to make clear what issues were actually determined. In jury trials, the jury can be pinned down on specific determinations through the use of special verdicts or interrogatories to the jury. See §9.2.4. In some cases, however, the issues actually litigated and determined will not be clear. Bench trials occasionally result in less-than-full findings and conclusions. More frequently, the problem will arise in a jury trial in which

---

doctrine of collateral estoppel."). Some courts have held to the contrary, though, seeing the default judgment as a confession of the material allegations and justifying issue preclusion on those allegations. *See, e.g.,* In re Calvert, 105 F.3d 315, 318 (3d Cir. 1997) (applying California law and finding that "a party who permits a default to be entered confesses the truth of all the material allegations in the complaint. A default judgment is as conclusive upon the issues tendered by the complaint as if rendered after an answer is filed and a trial is held. . . ."). Also, as we saw in §7.5.3, some issues, such as damages, may actually be litigated in a default judgment case; such litigated issues should be subject to issue preclusion.

[83] *See* United States v. Young, 804 F.2d 116, 118 (8th Cir. 1986). Rule 36 expressly provides that admissions thereunder are limited to the pending case only.

[84] *See* Roskam Baking Co. v. Lanham Machinery Co., 288 F.3d 895, 905 (6th Cir. 2002) ("Michigan law permits preclusion of issues decided by a judge as part of summary disposition"); Matosantos Comm. Corp. v. Applebee's Intl., Inc., 245 F.3d 1203, 1211 (10th Cir. 2001); Exhibitors Poster Exch., Inc. v. National Screen Serv. Corp., 421 F.2d 1313, 1319 (5th Cir. 1970).

neither special verdicts nor interrogatories were used. If it is not clear what issues were litigated and determined in Case 1, how should the court in Case 2 proceed? The party asserting issue preclusion bears the burden of establishing that the requirements are met; this burden includes presenting to the court in Case 2 an adequate record from Case 1 to support the assertion.[85] The court in Case 2 may have to review the trial record (including the transcript) from Case 1, to determine what issues were actually litigated, and whether any of those issues are presented in Case 2.

An example of the difficulty is provided in *O'Connor v. G&R Packing Co.*,[86] in which a teenaged boy was injured while trespassing on railroad property. Defendants won Case 1, with the judge finding that the boy "disobeyed ... statutes which were enacted for the benefit of the public" and "deliberately and needlessly exposed himself to a known danger." In Case 2, a different defendant sought to establish issue preclusion on the boy's contributory negligence. The New York Court of Appeals reviewed the transcript of the trial judge's ruling in Case 1. Though the quoted language is consistent with a finding of contributory negligence, in the context of the entire transcript, that court concluded, the trial judge in Case 1 had not ruled on contributory negligence at all.[87]

The following hypotheticals show how the form of a verdict can affect the assessment of what issues were determined in Case 1. For each question, assume that the applicable law recognizes contributory negligence as a bar to recovery in a negligence case. To win a case for negligence, then, (1) the claimant must have been free from negligence and (2) the defendant must have been negligent. We also assume that both of these issues were raised and litigated — that the parties put on evidence at trial concerning the possible negligence of each other. So the question in these hypotheticals is simply what issue(s) were determined in the case.

- *A* sues *Z* for negligence. The case is tried to a jury.[88] The jury returns a *general verdict* in favor of *A*. Do we know what issues were determined in this case? Yes. A general verdict in favor of the claimant is never ambiguous. The only way *A* could win is if the jury found *both* that *A* was not negligent and *Z* was negligent. So in a second case, there can be issue preclusion on either issue, since both issues actually were determined by the jury in Case 1.

[85] *See, e.g.*, Matter of King, 103 F.3d 17, 19 (5th Cir. 1997) (party failed to satisfy burden of proving requisites for issue preclusion).
[86] 423 N.E.2d 397 (N.Y. 1981).
[87] *O'Connor*, 423 N.E.2d at 399 ("litigation [in Case 2] of the contributory negligence issue is not precluded by such a nonspecific nonfactual determination").
[88] Or the case could have been a bench trial in which the judge made findings of fact, either because no right to jury trial existed or because the parties waived their right to jury trial. See §9.2.2.

○ *A* sues *Z* for negligence. The case is tried to a jury. The jury returns a general verdict in favor of *Z*. Can we know what issues were determined in this case? No. A general verdict in favor of the defendant is ambiguous. Why? Because it might be that the jury found (1) that *A* was negligent, *or* (2) that *Z* was not negligent, *or* (3) both of the above. But we do not know. So in a second case, there cannot be issue preclusion because we do not know what issue(s) actually were determined by the jury in Case 1.

○ *A* sues *Z* for negligence. The case is tried to a jury. The jury returns a special verdict finding that *A* was negligent. The court, accordingly, enters judgment for *Z*. Can we know what issue was determined in this case? Of course, because the jury told us exactly what issue it determined — the negligence of *A*. In a second case, the negligence of *A* could be established by issue preclusion. What about the negligence (or freedom from negligence) of *Z*? There can be no issue preclusion on that issue, because it simply was not determined in Case 1; the jury said nothing about it.

○ *A* sues *Z* for negligence. The case is tried to a jury. The jury returns a special verdict finding (1) that *Z* was negligent and (2) that *A* was not negligent. The court enters judgment, accordingly, in favor of *A*. Do we know what issues were determined here? Certainly. There is no doubt here. (This case is just like the first hypothetical in this series, but here the two facts that justify judgment in favor of the claimant are stated expressly, rather than embodied in a general verdict.) So in a second case, there could be issue preclusion on either of the issues.

Determining Whether the Cases Involve the Same Issue

Of course, issue preclusion is appropriate only when the same issue is presented in both Case 1 and Case 2. The entire thrust of issue preclusion is to ensure that we not *relitigate* something that has already been determined by a competent court. Sometimes, a party will try to justify relitigating an issue in Case 2 by asserting that she has new evidence supporting an assertion that was rejected in Case 1. While discovery of new evidence may justify setting aside a judgment under Federal Rule 60(b)(2) (but only in limited circumstances (see §9.7)), it does not avoid the operation of issue preclusion.[89] The party had her chance to litigate that issue; she does not get another.

Serious problems can arise concerning the characterization in Case 2 of just what "issue" was litigated and determined in Case 1. For example, if the claimant in Case 1 pursued a particular theory of negligence, is she precluded from raising a different theory in Case 2? If the defendant in Case 1 raised a defense that was rejected, is she precluded from raising a

---

[89] *See, e.g.*, Heim v. United States, 2001 U.S. Claims LEXIS 158 (Ct. Fed. Cl. August 10, 2001); Harline v. Barker, 912 P.2d 433, 443 (Utah 1996).

different defense in Case 2? The assessment of the scope of the issue determined in Case 1 may differ depending upon the party against whom preclusion is asserted.

○ *P* and *D*, each driving her own car, collide at an intersection. *P* suffers personal injuries and property damage to her car. In Case 1, *P* sues *D* for damages for the personal injuries, alleging that *D* was negligent because *D* was speeding into the intersection where the collision took place. After trial, judgment is entered for *D*, with a specific finding that *D* had not been speeding. In Case 2, *P* sues *D* for property damage arising from the same crash. Assume that the litigation is in a primary rights jurisdiction, so *D* cannot have the case dismissed under claim preclusion.[90] Clearly *P* cannot reassert that *D* was speeding. But can *P* assert that *D* was negligent in another way? For example, can *P* claim that *D* failed to keep a proper lookout, or that *D* ran a red light to come into the intersection?

The answer to these questions depends upon how the court in Case 2 characterizes the issue decided in Case 1. If it sees the issue narrowly — as the factual issue of whether *D* was speeding — Case 2 does not present the same issue, and issue preclusion will be rejected. On the other hand, if the court sees the issue broadly — as the legal conclusion about whether *D* was negligent — Case 2 does present the same issue, and issue preclusion will be allowed. There are problems with either of these two approaches. First, the narrow reading of the issue permits *P* to vex *D* with a theory of negligence that could have been asserted in Case 1; it also creates the risk of inconsistent results in Case 1 and Case 2, which reflects ill on the system of justice. Second, the broad reading of the issue precludes *P* from litigating specific questions that truly have never been before a court; this result seems to violate the requirement that issue preclusion apply only to questions actually litigated and determined.

So what does a court do? The Restatement (Second) of Judgments urges a pragmatic course (as it did in defining the scope of claim in claim preclusion, §11.2.3). Specifically, it instructs the court to look at such things as the degree of overlap between the evidence or arguments made in Case 1 and Case 2; whether new evidence or argument in Case 2 involves the same rule of law as that in Case 1; whether pretrial preparation (including discovery) in Case 1 could reasonably have embraced the new evidence or argument in Case 2; and whether there is a close relationship between the claims asserted in Case 1 and Case 2.[91]

On the facts of our hypothetical, the Restatement (Second) of Judgments counsels a finding of issue preclusion in Case 2.[92] First, there is

---

[90] If this does not ring a bell, review §11.2.3.

[91] Restatement (Second) of Judgments §27, cmt. c.

[92] Restatement (Second) of Judgments §27, cmt. c, illustration 4 is similar to the facts of our hypothetical.

substantial overlap between the evidence in Case 1 and the new evidence of liability in Case 2; both deal directly with how D's car got into the intersection and, presumably, will entail testimony from the same eyewitnesses. Second, the evidence of liability in Case 1 and in Case 2 seems to implicate the same rules of negligence law. Third, it seems likely that pretrial preparation of Case 1 would have uncovered any issue of D's failure to keep proper lookout or running a red light. Finally, the claims asserted in Case 1 and Case 2 are quite closely related. Indeed, for claim preclusion purposes, most jurisdictions would have concluded that both cases assert the very same claim. Let's try a hypothetical about defenses.

○ P and D enter a contract that requires D to make periodic payments for goods sold. In Case 1, P sues D, alleging that D has defaulted on three periodic payments. D defends by claiming that the contract violated the statute of frauds. The parties litigate in Case 1, and P wins, with the court expressly rejecting the statute of frauds defense. D subsequently fails to make other payments under the same contract. P brings Case 2 to recover these later defaults in payment. (Because these defaults came after Case 1 was filed, they are not part of the same claim as Case 1; so there can be no claim preclusion.[93]) Clearly, D cannot raise the defense of statute of frauds. But can D raise a different defense to the contract? Can he claim, for instance, that the contract violated fundamental public policy, or usury laws, or antitrust laws, etc.?

Using the pragmatic factors listed above, the Restatement (Second) here suggests that D should be able to raise the new defense.[94] Stated another way, it views the "issue" determined in Case 1 narrowly, as statute of frauds. In the preceding hypothetical, the Restatement (Second) viewed the "issue" litigated in Case 1 broadly, as negligence. The lesson is clear. The drafters of the Restatement (Second) deem it appropriate to expect a *claimant* to assert every possible basis for recovery in Case 1, but tend to allow a *defendant* to pick and choose among potential defenses, retaining others for another day. It is not clear why the issue preclusion rules ought to be more solicitous of defendants than of claimants on this score.

Of course, the application of the factors suggested by the Restatement (Second) will not always lead to a clear answer. As we saw with defining a claim in claim preclusion, this is an area of more art than science. We are well counseled, however, by these words from leading commentators:

> In the end, it may prove best to find that identical issues are involved only on a strong showing that relitigation would present matters that clearly bore

---

[93] If this does not ring a bell, review §11.2.3.

[94] Restatement (Second) of Judgments §27, cmt. c, illustration 6 is similar to the facts in this hypothetical.

on ultimate issues that were raised in the first action or that would jeopardize significant interests of justifiable reliance or repose. As with claim . . . preclusion, such showings must be tailored to the distinctive considerations that arise from litigating and living under different rules of substantive law.[95]

Almost always, a party will seek to invoke issue preclusion as to a question of fact that was litigated and determined in Case 1. But does issue preclusion apply to rulings of law from Case 1? The general answer (assuming the other requirements for issue preclusion are satisfied) is yes. For example, a court's determination that a claim for wrongful discharge of employment was preempted by federal law — clearly a question of law as applied to a given set of facts — was entitled to issue preclusive effect.[96] The Supreme Court has indicated that issue preclusion might not be available, however, for "unmixed" or "pure" questions of law that arise in successive cases "involving unrelated subject matter."[97] The scope and even the purpose of this exception are not terribly clear.[98]

§11.3.3   That Issue Was Essential to the Judgment in Case 1

The Concept of Essentiality

As we just saw, the issue on which someone wants issue preclusion must have been litigated and determined in Case 1. But that is not enough. The issue must also have been *essential* to the outcome of Case 1. The assessment of essentiality forces us to focus on the difference between the *issue* decided and the *judgment* entered in the case. The issue, of course, is relatively narrow — for example, whether *D* was driving her car too fast. The judgment is broader — it focuses on who won the case, not on why she won. The requirement of essentiality is illustrated by *Rios v. Davis*,[99] a case found in some Civil Procedure casebooks. We simplify the facts slightly in demonstrating the point.

- ∘ Rios and Davis, each driving a vehicle, collide. Each vehicle is damaged. In Case 1, Davis sues Rios to recover for damage to his vehicle. The case is litigated and the jury expressly finds that *both* Davis and Rios were negligent in causing the collision. Thus, two issues were litigated and determined — Davis was negligent and Rios was negligent. Under the doctrine of contributory negligence, as you know from Torts, a claimant

---

[95] 18 Wright & Miller 432.

[96] Jarvis v. Nobel/Sysco Food Servs. Co., 985 F.2d 1419, 1424-1425 (10th Cir. 1993).

[97] United States v. Stauffer Chem. Co., 464 U.S. 165, 169-170 (1984).

[98] For a helpful discussion of this and the related exception for "separable facts," *see* 18 Moore's Federal Practice §132.02[5].

[99] 373 S.W.2d 386 (Tex. Ct. Civ. App. 1963).

loses if she is shown to have been negligent. Applying that doctrine, the court entered judgment for Rios (because Davis, the plaintiff, was negligent).

◦ In Case 2, Rios sues Davis to recover for his injuries from the same collision. (There can be no claim preclusion. Why?[100]) Davis seeks to have issue preclusion applied concerning the finding in Case 1 that Rios was negligent. Indeed, that issue had been litigated and determined in Case 1. But issue preclusion should not apply to that issue because it was not *essential* to the judgment in Case 1.[101] Why not?

To determine essentiality, we ask: If the finding on this issue had come out the other way, would the judgment be the same? If so, the finding is not essential to the judgment, because the judgment does not rest on the finding on that issue. Let's try that test regarding the two findings in *Rios* — one that Davis was negligent and one that Rios was negligent.

◦ If the finding (in Case 1) that Rios was negligent had been instead that he was *not* negligent, would the judgment in Case 1 have been the same? Yes. Because of contributory negligence, once Davis (the claimant) was found negligent, the judgment could only come out one way — it must be in favor of the defendant (Rios). Rios's behavior — whether he was negligent or not negligent — is irrelevant to the judgment. Because changing the finding on this issue would not change the judgment, the finding is not essential to the judgment.

◦ If the finding (in Case 1) that Davis was negligent had been instead that he was *not* negligent, would the judgment in Case 1 have been the same? No! If Davis were not negligent, he would have won the judgment in Case 1. Why? Because then there would be findings (1) that the claimant was not negligent and (2) that the defendant was negligent. In such a case, the judgment would have been in favor of the claimant. Because changing the finding on this issue would change the judgment, the finding is essential to the judgment.

There are two main policy supports for refusing to accord issue preclusive effect to the finding in Case 1 that Rios was negligent. First, because Rios won the judgment in that case, he would not have been able to appeal the finding that he was negligent.[102] The right to appeal is from the *judgment*, not from an individual finding. The party losing the *judgment* has a

---

[100] Claim preclusion requires, among other things, that Case 1 and Case 2 be asserted by the same claimant against the same defendant (see §11.2.1). Rios was not a claimant in Case 1. He has never asserted a claim before, and thus cannot be guilty of trying to assert the same claim twice.

[101] *See* Kloth v. Microsoft Corp., 355 F.3d 322, 328 (4th Cir. 2004) (issue preclusion does not apply to findings that "support" a judgment; rather, they must be "critical and necessary" to the judgment).

[102] *Rios*, 373 S.W.2d at 387-388 ("the finding . . . that Rios was negligent proximately causing the accident would, if it had been controlling, have led to a different result").

right to appeal. Because Rios would have had no opportunity to have the finding of his negligence reviewed on appeal, that finding was not subject to full judicial scrutiny and thus is not worthy of issue preclusion. Second, because the finding on Rios's negligence was irrelevant to the outcome (Rios had to win once Davis was found contributorily negligent), there is a sense that the jury may not have devoted sufficient attention on the issue.[103] For these two reasons, courts conclude that they should accord issue preclusive effect only to those findings that mattered in the ultimate judgment.

Now let's try some other hypotheticals to test our understanding of essentiality.

- Suppose in Case 1 P in a negligence case wins a general jury verdict. In Case 2, what issues were essential to the judgment in Case 1? We know from §11.3.2 that a general verdict in favor of P in a negligence case is not ambiguous. Such a verdict is possible in a contributory negligence state only if two things are true: (1) D is negligent and (2) P is not negligent. Thus, we know those two issues were litigated and determined in Case 1. But which (if either) was *essential* to the judgment in favor of P?
  - Both are essential, and thus entitled to issue preclusive effect in subsequent litigation. Why? Because if either issue were decided differently, the judgment would be different.
  - First, if the finding that D was negligent were different, the judgment could not be in favor of P. If the finding were that D was not negligent, the judgment would have to be for D.
  - Second, if the finding that P was not negligent were different, the judgment could not be in favor of P. If the finding were that P was negligent, the judgment would have to be for D.

The Problem of Alternative Determinations

What happens if the court enters findings on more than one issue, each of which is consistent with the judgment? This possibility raises the problem of "alternative" determinations — that is, findings on issues, any one of which would be sufficient to compel the judgment that was entered. The following hypothetical is a good example.

- A sues Z for negligence. The case is tried to a jury. The jury returns a special verdict finding (1) that Z is not negligent and (2) that A is negligent. The court enters judgment, accordingly, in favor of Z.

---

[103] *See* Northgate Motors, Inc. v. General Motors Corp., 111 F. Supp. 2d 1071, 1078 (D. Wis. 2000) (fact-finder "may have devoted less care to determining an issue that did not affect the result").

These are alternative findings because *either* one of the two —
alone — would result in judgment for Z. If you take away either one of the
two findings, the judgment in favor of Z would still stand. For instance, if
all the jury in Case 1 did was decide that Z was not negligent, Z would win
regardless of whether A was negligent. Likewise, if all the jury in Case 1
did was decide that A was negligent, Z would win (because of the finding
that A was contributorily negligent). Alternative findings, then, offer two
reasons for the same conclusion.

Courts have not agreed on whether to consider alternative findings
essential for issue preclusion purposes. The traditional approach to the
problem, reflected in the first Restatement of Judgments, holds that *both*
of the alternative findings are essential.[104] Thus, both the finding that Z
was not negligent and that A was negligent would be entitled to issue preclusion in Case 2.[105] This view has been criticized, however, and when the
American Law Institute reconsidered the question in the Restatement (Second) of Judgments, it took the opposite approach. Under the Restatement
(Second), alternative determinations are deemed *not* to be essential to the
judgment in Case 1 and thus neither one is entitled to issue preclusion in
Case 2.[106] Thus, under this more modern approach, *neither* of the issues
determined in our hypothetical would be entitled to issue preclusion in
Case 2 unless it was expressly upheld on appeal. (There is an exception,
however, that provides for issue preclusion on one or both of the alternative determinations if they are upheld expressly on appeal.[107])

The Restatement (Second) approach is odd. It seems to punish a litigant for doing too well. That is, if Z had proved simply that she was not
negligent, that finding would be entitled to issue preclusion; by proving
not only that she was not negligent but that A was negligent, however, she
loses an issue preclusive effect for either finding. Why did the Restatement (Second) take this approach? There were two main reasons. First,
because the alternative determination is not necessary to the decision, it
might not have been considered as fully by the fact-finder. In other words,
once the fact-finder determined that A was negligent, it might not have
paid all that much attention to the determination of whether Z was negligent, because the ruling on that issue would not affect the outcome. Second, the losing litigant, faced with two negative findings, might be

---

[104] Restatement of Judgments §68, cmt. n (1942).

[105] Case 2 here might be brought by Z against A concerning the wreck (assuming the
jurisdiction did not have a compulsory counterclaim rule that required her to assert this
claim in Case 1; see §12.3.1). Or perhaps a third party injured in the same wreck (maybe a
passenger in one of the vehicles) brings Case 2 and seeks to assert nonmutual collateral
estoppel, which we address in §11.3.5. Or perhaps we are in a primary rights jurisdiction
and A will sue Z again, this time for property damage as opposed to personal injuries, see
§11.2.3.

[106] Restatement (Second) of Judgments §27, cmt. i.

[107] Restatement (Second) of Judgments §27, cmt. o.

dissuaded from seeking appellate review. On appeal, she would still lose even if the appellate court affirmed on just one of the two issues. Forcing her to appeal to avoid the effect of issue preclusion would increase the burdens on courts and litigants. To avoid that burden, the drafters decided to free the losing litigant from the effects of issue preclusion altogether (unless there is an appeal that results in affirming either or both of the issues).[108]

These reasons for the Restatement (Second) approach to alternative findings are not persuasive. The concerns could be accommodated, it seems, by careful attention to the requirement that the issue must be litigated and determined in Case 1 (which we saw in §11.3.2). For instance, in our hypothetical, suppose the court in Case 2 looked at the record and determined that the fact-finder in Case 1 really did focus on one of the two issues, so that the second issue was basically an afterthought. Rather than deny preclusive effect to both findings, the court in Case 2 should hold that the first issue is entitled to preclusive effect and the second is not. But not because of essentiality. The second issue would not be subject to preclusion because it was not actually litigated and decided in Case 1. Some courts have adopted this flexible approach to the problem.[109]

It is important to be able to recognize alternative determinations in a fact pattern. It is also important to remember that courts disagree on how to treat them.[110]

Moreover, be careful not to confuse alternative determinations — in which *either* of two findings would dictate the same judgment — with the situation in which *both* findings are necessary to a result. For example, let's return to a hypothetical we saw in §11.3.2.

> ○ *A* sues *Z* for negligence. The case is tried to a jury. The jury returns a special verdict finding (1) that *Z* was negligent and (2) that *A* was not negligent. The court enters judgment, accordingly, in favor of *A*.

These two findings are *not* alternative determinations. With alternative determinations, remember, *either* finding would dictate the judgment. That is not the case here. If all the court in Case 1 determined was that *Z*

---

[108] Restatement (Second) of Judgments §27, cmt. i.

[109] *Cf.* Malloy v. Trombley, 405 N.E.2d 213, 216 (N.Y. 1980) (though fact-finder in Case 1 said that a finding on contributory negligence was not necessary to the decision, the court in Case 2 gave the finding issue preclusive effect because it was convinced that the alternative determination was the product of "thorough and careful deliberation").

[110] Here's some advice for law school examinations. Whenever your class has covered an area on which courts disagree, be prepared to discuss the approaches taken by the courts. I cannot tell you how many exams I have read in which the student recognizes the problem of alternative determinations and then applies only one of the approaches — either the original Restatement or the Restatement (Second). The professor puts topics such as this on an exam precisely so you can demonstrate that you know the different approaches.

was negligent, that finding alone would not justify the judgment in favor of *A*. Why not? Because in a contributory negligence state, the claimant can win only if two things are established: that the defendant was negligent and that the claimant was free from negligence. In this fact pattern, *both* of the findings are necessary to get a judgment for *A*. Stated another way, if you took away either of the findings, the judgment in favor of *A* could not stand. So here, both issues are essential to the judgment and both are entitled to issue preclusive effect in Case 2.

§11.3.4 Due Process: Against Whom Is Preclusion Asserted?

Distinguishing Between Due Process and Mutuality

In addition to the requirements already discussed, assessment of issue preclusion requires that we address two other issues: due process and mutuality. Many students confuse these two topics. The key here, frankly, is to be mechanical. The due process inquiry concerns the question of *against whom* preclusion may be asserted; it is the topic of this subsection. The mutuality inquiry concerns the question of *by whom* preclusion may be asserted; it is addressed in §11.3.5. Due process ensures that one can only be bound by a judgment from Case 1 if she had a full and fair opportunity to litigate in Case 1.[111] So preclusion can only be asserted against someone who had a full and fair opportunity to litigate in Case 1.[112] Because this precept is commanded by constitutional principles of due process, it must apply in all cases, in whatever court system — federal or state. And though we discuss it here, in a section concerning issue preclusion, it also applies in claim preclusion.[113]

The Starting Point: Parties to Case 1 Can Be Bound

Preclusion, as just noted, can only be asserted against one who had a full and fair opportunity to litigate in Case 1. Although the concept of a

---

[111] Allen v. McCurry, 449 U.S. 90, 95 (1980) ("the concept of collateral estoppel cannot apply when the party against whom the earlier decision is asserted did not have a 'full and fair opportunity' to litigate that issue in the earlier case"); Blonder-Tongue Laboratories, Inc. v. University of Ill. Found., 402 U.S. 313, 317-320 (1971).

[112] Though this section deals with issue preclusion, this rule holds true in claim preclusion as well. Recall from §11.2.1 that one requirement of claim preclusion was that Case 1 and Case 2 be brought by the same claimant against the same defendant. We refine this point a bit, as we will with issue preclusion, below.

[113] We noted this in §11.2.1. Accordingly, claim preclusion can only be asserted against one who had a full and fair opportunity to litigate in Case 1.

full and fair opportunity to be heard is flexible, it certainly includes someone who was a properly joined *party* to Case 1.[114] Conversely, a *nonparty* to Case 1 generally will not be bound by the judgment in Case 1.

- In Case 1, *P-1* sues Airline, alleging that she was injured in a crash of a plane operated by Airline, and that Airline's negligence caused the crash. The case goes to trial and Airline wins because the jury makes an express determination that Airline was not negligent. In Case 2, *P-2* (who was not a party to Case 1) sues Airline to recover for her injuries suffered in the same crash. Clearly, Airline cannot invoke claim preclusion against *P-2*. (Why?[115]) But can Airline assert issue preclusion on the finding that it was not negligent? (It's the same issue, it was litigated and determined in Case 1, and Case 1 ended in a valid final judgment on the merits.)
- Based upon what we have seen so far, the answer is clear: Airline cannot use issue preclusion. *P-2*, the party in Case 2 against whom preclusion is sought, was not a party to Case 1 and thus cannot be said to have had a full and fair opportunity to litigate in Case 1. Many commentators and courts would say that *P-2* has never had her "day in court" and cannot be bound by issue preclusion.

Note, by the way, how difficult due process makes things for Airline. Suppose 100 persons were injured in the crash, and that they bring 100 separate suits against Airline. Even if Airline wins 50 cases in a row, with each case resulting in an express finding that Airline was not negligent, Airline cannot assert issue preclusion against the next plaintiff because no plaintiff was a party to a preceding case.

Expanding the Realm of Who Can Be Bound: "Privity"

It is clear, then, that the judgment from Case 1 binds parties to Case 1. But can it ever bind litigants in Case 2 who were *not* technically joined as parties to Case 1? The answer is yes, though the circumstances in which this is true are not always clear. The judgment in Case 1 binds not only parties, but persons deemed to be in "privity" with parties to Case 1.[116] "Privity" is a slippery word, encrusted with historical baggage. Originally, it was limited to arcane notions of property rights, and no opinion dealing

---

[114] *See generally* 18 Moore's Federal Practice §132.04[1][a]. This assumes that any defending party is properly brought before the personal jurisdiction of the court by appropriate service of process.

[115] Because claim preclusion only applies if Case 1 and Case 2 were brought by the same claimant against the same defendant. See §11.2.1. Here, Case 1 was brought by *P-1* and Case 2 was brought by *P-2*.

[116] Parklane Hosiery Co. v. Shore, 439 U.S. 322, 327 n.7 ("It is a violation of due process for a judgment to be binding on a litigant who was not a party nor a privy and therefore has never had an opportunity to be heard.").

with privity seemed complete without citation to Lord Coke's discussion of the classes of privies at common law.[117]

Over time, courts expanded the circumstances in which nonparties to Case 1 can be bound by the judgment in that case. Though those circumstances no longer are limited to common law privity, many courts continue to use the word. Today, it is simply a label that expresses "the conclusion that nonparty preclusion is appropriate...."[118] The term refers to a *relationship* between a nonparty to Case 1 and a party to Case 1. When that relationship is sufficiently close, courts justify binding the nonparty to the judgment. The idea is that the nonparty is so closely aligned with one who was a party to Case 1 that she has, in effect, been accorded her day in court.

In 2008, the Supreme Court clarified the circumstances in which someone who was not a party to Case 1 might nonetheless be bound by the judgment there. In *Taylor v. Sturgell*, the Court concluded that there were six such circumstances.[119] They are:

1. *Nonparty agrees to be bound.* Sometimes, someone who is not a party to a case will agree to be bound by the outcome of a case. The best example is the "test case."

- ○ Six sets of cases are pending, brought by six groups of plaintiffs against the same defendant, seeking tort damages for an allegedly defective product. All of the parties to the six cases agree that one of the six cases will proceed to trial first, and that the result of that trial will bind all others — win or lose — on the issue of defendant's liability.

2. *Nonparty is bound by a pre-existing substantive legal relationship with a party.* The best example here is successive holders of an interest in real property. For instance, a nonparty to Case 1 may be bound by the judgment in that case if she succeeds to a property interest held by someone who was a party in Case 1. The relationship of successor-in-interest closely approximates the common law definition of privity. The succession might be effected in any way — including sale or inheritance — and the property may be real or personal. Recognizing that the successor-in-interest is bound by the judgment involving her predecessor protects the other party from repetitive litigation and thus also avoids potentially inconsistent results.

---

[117] *See, e.g.*, Stacy v. Thrasher, 47 U.S. 44, 59 (1849). Incidentally, you will encounter the great Lord Coke in many classes. Please be aware that it is pronounced "Cook," and not like the author's favorite soft drink.

[118] Taylor v. Sturgell, 128 S. Ct. 2161, 2172 n.8 (2008). The Court in this case said that it would eschew use of the word "privity" in an effort "[t]o ward off confusion." *Id.*

[119] *Id.* at 2172-2173.

- In Case 1, *P* sues *D-1*, who owns the lot and house next door to *P*'s, concerning a boundary dispute. The court enters a valid final judgment on the merits, based upon its finding that the boundary runs over a particular course. *D-1* sells his property to *D-2*, who now claims that that boundary is incorrect. In Case 2, *P* sues *D-2* to enforce the boundary as determined in Case 1. Though *D-2* was not a party to Case 1, she is bound by the judgment. She is a successor-in-interest to the property and is thus bound.[120]

- In Case 1, *P-1* sues *D*, asserting that she (and not *D*) owns certain securities. The court enters a valid final judgment on the merits in favor of *D*. *P-1* dies and *P-2* inherits everything that *P-1* owned. In Case 2, *P-2* sues *D* for a declaratory judgment that she owns the same securities. *P-2* is bound by the judgment in Case 1.

In a 1974 case, the Supreme Court may have expanded this notion of binding a successor-in-interest. In that case, Corporation 1 was held to have violated federal labor law by firing an employee. Corporation 2 bought Corporation 1. The Supreme Court held that Corporation 2 was bound by the judgment that the employee's labor law rights had been violated and thus could be ordered to reinstate the worker. Allowing Corporation 2 to escape the import of the judgment could create repetitive litigation and threaten labor law policy.[121] Even if this case can be seen as expanding the concept of binding a successor-in-interest, this particular theory of binding a nonparty is, in the big scheme, fairly narrow.

3. *Nonparty is bound because she was adequately represented by one who was a party in Case 1.* Stated generally, a nonparty to Case 1 can be bound by the judgment in that case if her interests were adequately represented by a party to Case 1. Such representation can arise in a variety of ways.[122] The clearest example is the class action. As we see in §13.3, in a class action a representative sues expressly on behalf of class members.[123] Though the class members thus are not technically parties, they will be bound by the judgment in a case certified to proceed as a class action.[124]

---

[120] In Oklahoma v. Texas, 256 U.S. 70 (1921), Case 1 was between the United States and Texas and set the boundary between Texas and federal land. After judgment, the United States transferred the property to the new state of Oklahoma. In Case 2, Oklahoma sued Texas concerning the boundary. Oklahoma, as successor-in-interest to the property, and Texas, as litigant in Case 1, were held bound to the judgment in Case 1.

[121] Golden State Bottling Co. v. National Labor Rel. Bd., 414 U.S. 168 (1974).

[122] We deal with the major examples of binding through representation. There are several that we do not address here, such as whether litigation by a trade association or labor union binds its members and whether litigation by a governmental entity or agency binds other parts of the government or individuals. For detailed discussion of such points, *see* 18A Wright & Miller §§4456, 4458, and 4458.1.

[123] As we see in §13.3.5, there can be defendant classes, in which the representative is sued on behalf of a group.

[124] A case can only be certified as a class action in federal court if the court finds that the requirements set forth in Federal Rule 23(a) are satisfied. These requirements are aimed

Indeed, the very utility of the class action is that it can bind the numerous class members.

In a certain type of class action, members of the class are permitted to "opt out" of the proceeding; those who do so properly will not be bound by the judgment.[125] Generally speaking, though, those who do not opt out of such a class, and members of other types of class actions, are bound by the judgment. As the Supreme Court explained: "There is of course no dispute that under elementary principles of prior adjudication a judgment in a properly entertained class action is binding on class members in any subsequent litigation."[126]

Another clear example of binding representation involves litigation by or against fiduciaries. Some people cannot litigate in their own names because they lack legal capacity (this group includes minors and people under a mental disability). Litigation by or against such people can be conducted by a fiduciary, such as a guardian, guardian ad litem, conservator, or committee, whose express function is to represent the interest of the person lacking legal capacity. So long as the fiduciary is validly appointed, acts within the scope of the appointment, and is not guilty of prejudicial misconduct or conflict of interest, a judgment will bind the person represented.[127] Similarly, when a trustee litigates on behalf of beneficiaries to the trust, or an executor litigates on behalf of beneficiaries of the estate,[128] those beneficiaries will be bound by the result, even though they are not parties to the case.[129]

Some lower federal courts attempted to expand nonparty preclusion through a doctrine of "virtual representation." In 2008, the Supreme Court rejected this effort, as will be discussed following the sixth example of nonparty preclusion below.

4. *Nonparty controlled the litigation in Case 1.* The best-known example of this form of nonparty preclusion is *Montana v. United States*,[130] which grew out of a federal dam project in Montana. The United States hired a contractor to build the dam. The state of Montana imposed a tax on the contractor's gross receipts. The contractor and the federal government felt that this tax discriminated unconstitutionally against contractors dealing with the federal government. In Case 1, the contractor

---

expressly at ensuring that the representative will represent the class members adequately. See §13.3.4.

[125] *See, e.g.,* Robinson v. Sheriff of Cook County, 167 F.3d 1155, 1157 (7th Cir. 1999); In re Corrugated Container Antitrust Litigation, 756 F.2d 411, 418-419 (5th Cir. 1985).

[126] Cooper v. Federal Reserve Bank of Richmond, 467 U.S. 867, 874 (1984).

[127] *See generally* 18A Wright & Miller §4454.

[128] *See* Restatement (Second) §§41(1)(a) and (c).

[129] Sea-Land Services v. Gaudet, 414 U.S. 573, 593-594 (beneficiaries "are bound by the judgment with respect to the interest which was the subject of the fiduciary relationship").

[130] 440 U.S. 147 (1979).

sued Montana. Though the United States was not a party to that case, it controlled almost every detail of the litigation for the contractor. It urged the contractor to file the case, reviewed the pleadings, paid the attorneys' fees and litigation costs, directed that the contractor appeal an adverse judgment in the Montana court system, and submitted an amicus curiae[131] brief on the appeal.

The contractor lost Case 1, with the final judgment coming from the Montana Supreme Court. Thereafter, the United States filed Case 2, in which it raised the same challenge to the state tax. The Supreme Court held that the federal government was bound by the judgment in Case 1. While recognizing that the relationship between the United States and the contractor was not technically privity, two factors led the Court to conclude that the government should be bound. First, as a practical matter, the United States had run the litigation in Case 1. In the Court's famous phrase, the United States "plainly had a sufficient 'laboring oar' in the conduct of the state-court litigation to actuate principles of estoppel."[132] Second, the United States also had "a direct financial or proprietary interest" in the litigation.[133]

While courts often mention both factors in addressing whether to bind a nonparty to a judgment, clearly the first factor is the most important. Indeed, as a practical matter, it seems extremely unlikely that any nonparty would take control of litigation if it had no interest in the case. Thus, commentators urge that the "direct financial or proprietary interest" requirement be jettisoned.[134] Perhaps it has been; although the discussion was dicta, the Supreme Court's catalogue of nonparty preclusion in *Taylor v. Sturgell* did not mention any requirement beyond controlling the litigation.[135]

Courts have not read *Montana* expansively. They tend to require some combination or aggregate of factors such as those in *Montana* itself. No single factor by itself — such as paying for counsel or financing the litigation or filing an amicus curiae brief — will suffice. In the final analysis, the inquiry always depends on the specific facts of the case. The court in Case 2 must be satisfied that the nonparty, as a practical matter, controlled the litigation and the opportunity for review to such an extent that it ought to be treated as having been a party in Case 1. At the end of the day, this fact pattern applies in a narrow range of cases.

---

[131] Amicus curiae is Latin for "friend of the court." Sometimes, nonparties to litigation — such as a governmental entity, interest group, organization, or interested citizen — will want to brief issues of import to assist the court (often the Supreme Court) in assessing an issue. Generally, one must receive permission of the court to file such a brief.

[132] *Montana*, 440 U.S. at 155, *citing* Drummond v. United States, 324 U.S. 316, 318 (1945).

[133] *Montana*, 440 U.S. at 155. *See also* 18 Moore's Federal Practice §132.04[1][b].

[134] 18A Wright & Miller 384. The Restatement (Second) §39, cmt. a, also concluded that any interest requirement be dropped.

[135] *Taylor*, 128 S. Ct. at 2173.

5. *Nonparty litigates through a proxy.* It is clear that one cannot avoid the preclusive effect of a judgment by litigating through an agent or proxy. We saw an example of this in *Cromwell v. County of Sac*, which is discussed in §11.3.2 (especially, see note 76 above). There, Case 1 was brought by Smith, who was litigating as an agent for Cromwell. Case 2 was brought by Cromwell. To the extent that Case 1 was entitled to preclusive effect, Cromwell was bound by its judgment. Though he was not a party to Case 1, he was bound by the acts of his agent. Similarly, if a party litigates and loses in Case 1, she cannot try to escape the binding effect of that judgment by having someone else sue in a separate case on her behalf.

6. *Nonparty may be bound by litigation under special statutory schemes.* This form of nonparty preclusion is very narrow. Occasionally, legislatures pass statutory schemes under which successive litigation is not permitted. Generally, a single case can be brought on behalf of the public at large, and the world must live with the result, without the opportunity to litigate afresh. For example, federal bankruptcy proceedings are unitary events that foreclose separate litigation. State probate proceedings are another example.

In its 2008 decision in Taylor v. Sturgell,[136] the Court affirmed that a nonparty can be bound by a judgment in any of the six preceding ways. Importantly, in the same case, the Court rejected the efforts of some lower courts to expand nonparty preclusion through what they called "virtual representation." The lower courts never agreed on a universal definition of virtual representation.[137] The general idea, though, was that a nonparty to Case 1 should be bound if she asserted a legal position in Case 2 that had been asserted by a party in Case 1. At its extreme, virtual representation would justify preclusion based upon identical legal theory; a court would say, in essence: "This idea has been litigated before, and there is no good reason to relitigate it, even with a different party." The nonparty is bound because the party litigating that position in Case 1 "virtually" represented her. (The theory assumed, of course, that the party litigating in Case 1 had a full and fair opportunity to do so. See §§11.4.1 and 11.4.3.)

The emergence of virtual representation was understandable in an era of crowded courts and torts that can affect thousands of people. Courts were frustrated by having to relitigate the same issues over and over; virtual representation was a manifestation of this frustration. Ultimately, though, the theory was an unseemly attempt to deal with contemporary

---

[136] See note 119 above.

[137] Indeed, in *Taylor*, the Court noted that several lower court cases purporting to invoke virtual representation in fact merely applied one of the six permissible types of nonparty preclusion discussed above. "Some Circuits use the label, but define 'virtual representation' so that it is no broader than the recognized exception for adequate representation." 128 S. Ct. at 2173.

litigation reality and threatens due process protection. Let's return to a hypothetical we saw earlier:

- In Case 1, *P-1* sues Airline, alleging that she was injured in a crash of a plane operated by Airline, and that Airline's negligence caused the crash. The case goes to trial and Airline wins because the jury makes an express determination that Airline was not negligent. In Case 2, *P-2* (who was not a party to Case 1) sues Airline to recover for her injuries suffered in the same crash.

We saw before that Airline cannot invoke issue preclusion against *P-2* because *P-2* was not a party to Case 1. We also noted the frustration that Airline would encounter if there had been 100 injured passengers on the flight. If Airline litigated and won the first 50 cases against it, it would still have to litigate the next 50 cases. Due process gives each successive plaintiff her day in court. Now consider the added frustration of the judicial system. Judges have to preside over all of these cases, each rehashing the same issue. Over and over the system runs its wheels over the same ground.

One way to avoid the repetitive litigation in this scenario, of course, would be to have a class action on behalf of the 100 passengers. For any of several reasons, however, a plaintiff might choose not to pursue a class action. (One reason is litigant autonomy — why litigate as part of a class of 100 if you can get more personal focus by suing individually?) Virtual representation was essentially an effort to gain the efficiency of the class action by providing that once litigated, an issue cannot be relitigated by similarly situated nonparties. The problem, of course, is that the class action procedure contains safeguards to protect due process rights of class members; virtual representation does not.

The Fifth Circuit was the birthplace of the virtual representation theory. It got the ball rolling with *Aerojet-General Corp. v. Askew*.[138] In that case, Corporation entered a deal with two state agencies (Agencies) that owned land in Dade County, Florida. The deal gave Corporation a ten-year lease on the land and an option to buy the land at any time during the lease. Four years into the lease, before Corporation exercised the option to buy the land, Florida passed a statute providing that no state agency could sell land to anyone without first offering to sell it to the county in which it was situated. After that law went into effect, Corporation exercised its option to buy the land. But Dade County also wanted to buy the land and asserted that it had a right to do so under the new statute.

In Case 1, Corporation sued the Agencies, seeking specific performance of the contract. Strangely, the defendants did not rely on the defense that the statute required them to offer the land to Dade County; they never mentioned the statute at all. In addition, Dade County was not joined as a party.

---

[138] 511 F.2d 710 (5th Cir. 1975).

Corporation won on summary judgment, and the court ordered the defendants to transfer the land to Corporation. At this point, Dade County went to the Florida Supreme Court to seek an extraordinary writ of mandamus that the Agencies convey the land to it. (We discuss such writs at §14.6.) The claim was based entirely on the new statute. The defendants here did not contest such an order, and the Florida Supreme Court granted the writ.

Corporation then filed Case 2 against the Agencies and Dade County. It sought an order to stop interference with its judgment from Case 1 and to stop further prosecution of the writ of mandamus from the Florida Supreme Court. The case was appealed to the Fifth Circuit, where Corporation won on alternative grounds. First, the court held that the statute could not be applied retroactively to the contract entered by Corporation. (Indeed, if the statute were deemed to apply to this contract, it would violate the Contract Clause of the Constitution.[139]) Second, in the influential part of the opinion, the court held that Dade County was bound by the judgment from Case 1. Though the county had not been a party to Case 1, the Agencies were its "virtual representatives" in that litigation. In famous language, the court said, "[A] person may be bound by a judgment even though not a party if one of the parties to the suit is so closely aligned with his interests as to be his virtual representative"[140]; Dade County and the Agencies were sufficiently closely related for the latter to bind the former.

The facts of *Aerojet-General* should have ensured that the holding had limited impact. First, the county and the state agencies are related as political entities in ways that private litigants rarely are. It is often the case that state agencies are deemed to represent counties and other political entities in litigation.[141] Second, there was some sense that the Agencies had been playing games by not contesting Dade County's request for a writ of mandamus; the court wondered whether the Agencies weren't trying to undo the judgment in Case 1.[142] Third, of course, there was an alternative basis for the conclusion — that the statute did not apply at all to the contract. Indeed, Judge Roney concurred in the judgment in the case only because of this statutory issue.[143]

Thereafter, the Fifth Circuit moderated its approach to virtual representation.[144] One example was the well-known case of *Hardy v. Johns-Manville Sales Corp.*[145] *Hardy* involved claims for personal injuries

---

[139] *Id.* at 722-723.

[140] *Id.* at 719 (citations omitted).

[141] See note 122 above.

[142] *Aerojet-General*, 511 F.2d at 721.

[143] *Id.* at 723 (Roney, J., concurring) (agreeing on statutory issue "makes my difference as to the res judicata effect of the first lawsuit of no consequence").

[144] Pollard v. Cockrell, 578 F.2d 1002, 1008 (5th Cir. 1978). There, Case 1 was brought by a group of massage parlor owners, challenging a local ordinance. After they lost, Case 2 was brought by a different group of massage parlor owners, challenging the same ordinance.

allegedly caused by exposure to asbestos.[146] It was actually Case 2 in a scenario we can simplify as follows. (Keep in mind that many different companies manufactured asbestos through the years.)

In Case 1 (called the *Borel* case), plaintiffs sued six manufacturers of asbestos (Manufacturers 1-6) for personal injuries allegedly caused by exposure to asbestos. Plaintiffs won, and the court in Case 1 made a series of specific findings, including a finding that the defendants had failed to warn workers of the dangers of asbestos. In Case 2 (*Hardy*), different plaintiffs sued Manufacturers 1-6 and a second group of manufacturers (Manufacturers 7-14). The trial court allowed the plaintiffs to use issue preclusion against all 14 manufacturers. There is no question from a due process standpoint that the court in Case 2 can invoke issue preclusion against Manufacturers 1-6. After all, they were parties to Case 1 and are clearly bound by the judgment in that case. But how did the trial court justify use of issue preclusion against Manufacturers 7-14, who were not parties to Case 1? It did so through virtual representation. According to the trial court, all 14 manufacturers shared an "identity of interests," which constituted privity. They all manufactured the same product. They raised the same legal issues as Manufacturers 1-6 had in Case 1. One gets the feeling that the trial court — inundated with similar cases — simply concluded that the system should not be expected to facilitate litigation of the same issues about the same products presented in the same way over and over.

But the Fifth Circuit reversed. It held that Manufacturers 7-14 could not be bound by the judgment in Case 1 and chastised the trial court for stretching the notion of privity "beyond meaningful limits."[147] The fact that all 14 manufacturers are engaged in the manufacture of the same product does not create privity. The fact that all defendants assert similar defenses does

---

Though the two groups of plaintiffs employed the same lawyers and had nearly identical pleadings, the court refused to apply virtual representation. Thus, the second group was not bound by the judgment in Case 1. The court inserted a requirement of accountability — virtual representation would be possible only if there was "an express or implied legal relationship in which parties to the first suit are accountable to nonparties who file a subsequent suit raising identical issues." As examples of such relationships, the court listed only the classic examples of representative litigation we saw above, such as executors and trustees litigating on behalf of beneficiaries.

[145] 681 F.2d 334 (5th Cir. 1982).

[146] Asbestos is a fireproof building material used in innumerable structures over several decades. In the 1970s it became apparent that breathing asbestos fibers could cause potentially deadly lung diseases, including mesothelioma. Plaintiffs brought thousands of cases for personal injuries. In addition, there were thousands of cases regarding the expenses incurred in satisfying a federal mandate to remove asbestos from structures. There were also thousands of cases involving insurance coverage. Managing these asbestos-related cases was a judicial nightmare.

[147] *Hardy*, 681 F.2d at 339.

not create privity. As in *Pollard*, the defendants in Case 1 (Manufacturers 1-6) were not accountable to the nonparties (Manufacturers 7-14). They had no right or responsibility to represent them. The court even minimized its holding in *Aerojet-General* by characterizing that case as involving one governmental entity litigating on behalf of another, which "appears to be an unexceptional [situation of nonparty preclusion]."[148]

Other courts, however, expanded the notion of virtual representation. For instance, in *Tyus v. Schoemehl*,[149] the Eighth Circuit held that a group of plaintiffs who had dropped out of Case 1 were bound by the judgment in that case because they had been "virtually represented" by the plaintiff who remained. The court set forth a seven-factor test that counseled when the relationship between the party and nonparty was sufficiently close to justify preclusion. Other courts followed suit, with equally flexible and unpredictable multi-factor balancing tests.

The Supreme Court put an end to virtual representation in *Taylor v. Sturgell*. There, Plaintiff, an antique aircraft enthusiast used the Freedom of Information Act to attempt to gain access to documents concerning a vintage airplane. He wanted the information to help him restore his airplane to its original condition. The Federal Aviation Administration (FAA) rejected the request on the basis that the materials were exempt from disclosure because they were trade secrets. Plaintiff sued the FAA in federal court. The case was litigated, and Plaintiff lost. Thereafter, a friend of Plaintiff made a similar request for the same information. When the FAA refused to release, this second plaintiff sued the FAA. The question was whether this second plaintiff should be bound by the judgment in Plaintiff's case. The District of Columbia Circuit applied virtual representation to hold the second plaintiff bound.[150] The Supreme Court reversed, and ended the experimentation into virtual representation. Outside the six examples discussed above, the Court concluded, nonparties cannot be bound.

Taylor manifests that due process is deeply rooted in our sense of justice. It is simply unfair to bind someone who has not had an opportunity to litigate either in person or through an appropriate representative. The question is what constitutes an appropriate representative. The fact that

---

[148] *Hardy*, 681 F.2d at 340 ("two government entities were so closely aligned that a prior judgment against one entity bound the other."). The court cited Restatement (Second) §41(1) for this proposition; that section contains classic examples of nonparty preclusion, including the case of an "agency invested by law with authority to represent" another person's interest.

[149] 93 F.3d 449 (8th Cir. 1996).

[150] *Taylor* was a claim preclusion case. That is, the lower court concluded that because the second plaintiff was virtually represented by Plaintiff in the first case, the second plaintiff could not assert his claim to the documents. The question at hand — whether a stranger to Case 1 may be bound by the judgment in Case 1 — arises in both claim and issue preclusion. See §11.2.1.

the Court will not permit virtual representation — in view of the tremendous cost of relitigation — demonstrates just how important the concept is. If we are willing to allow similarly situated litigants to raise the same issues in the same pleadings, using the same lawyers over and over, we must be protecting something very important.

§11.3.5   Mutuality: By Whom Is Preclusion Asserted?

Distinguishing Again Between Due Process and Mutuality

In the preceding subsection, we saw that preclusion may only be asserted *against* one who was a party (or in privity with a party) to Case 1. We saw some expansion of the concept of privity, but the expansion was relatively minimal.

In this subsection, we deal with a completely separate question: *By* (not against) whom can preclusion be asserted? This question involves the ancient concept of *mutuality*. Because mutuality is not rooted in due process (or any other constitutional principle), courts are not compelled to apply it. Thus, jurisdictions may take different approaches to mutuality; and they have. Indeed, the most significant developments in preclusion law over the past generation have concerned the abandonment of the historic insistence on mutuality.

The Starting Point: Mutuality of Estoppel and Exceptions to It

Mutuality of estoppel is a very simple idea: The only people who can *use* preclusion in Case 2 are people who would be *bound* by the judgment in Case 1. The rule is based upon some basic sense of fairness — one should not be able to take advantage of the judgment from Case 1 if she would not be burdened by that judgment. Thus, under the traditional mutuality approach, the only people who can assert preclusion in Case 2 are those who were parties (or in "privity" with a party[151]) to Case 1.

But fairness can cut the other way. Why should one who has already litigated and lost in Case 1 get to relitigate the same issue against a different party in Case 2? True, the "new" litigant in Case 2 has not yet been burdened with litigation, so there is no harm to the interest of repose. But systemic interests are relevant. Relitigation burdens the courts at least to some degree by forcing them to repeat a task. Moreover, relitigation creates the possibility of inconsistent outcomes. Almost two centuries ago, Jeremy Bentham criticized mutuality for creating the "aura of the gaming table" precisely because it allowed someone to try again and again to seek

---

[151] We discussed privity at §11.3.4.

a different outcome from Case 1.[152] Thus, many critics through the years have urged the rejection of the mutuality requirement.

Because mutuality of estoppel is not rooted in any constitutional provision, courts are free to jettison it. The most important development in preclusion law over the past two generations has been the move to permit "nonmutual" assertion of issue preclusion. "Nonmutual" simply means that issue preclusion is being used by someone who was not a party to Case 1. This process of permitting nonmutual issue preclusion began not with outright rejection of the mutuality, but with recognition of *exceptions* to its operation.

The common law developed these exceptions long ago. They apply, however, only in cases involving an indemnification relationship. A good example involves vicarious liability, a concept you have probably covered in Torts. It is a concept that one is liable for the tort of another because of a relationship between the two. For instance, assume that Driver borrows Owner's car, with Owner's permission. Driver is negligent in driving the car, and her negligence injures P. Of course, P can sue Driver, who is *primarily* liable (because she caused the wreck that harmed P). But P can also sue Owner, who is *vicariously* (or *secondarily*) liable for what Driver does. The law imposes such vicarious liability on persons, such as Owner, who lend their cars to someone who then causes negligent injury with it.

Though the law imposes this vicarious liability on Owner, it also provides Owner with a right to be indemnified by Driver. In other words, the ultimate loss should be borne by the primarily liable person (Driver). So if P sues Owner and wins, Owner will have to pay the judgment to P. But Owner then has the right to sue Driver for indemnification. If Owner wins this indemnification claim, Driver must make Owner whole for the judgment she lost to P. In this roundabout way, then, Driver ends up reimbursing Owner for her vicarious liability. This result is appropriate, because Driver is the one who caused the harm to begin with.[153]

- In Case 1, P sues Driver. The parties litigate and Driver wins a valid final judgment on the merits, because the fact-finder expressly finds that Driver was *not* negligent. In Case 2, P sues Owner, asserting that Owner is vicariously liable for Driver's negligence. Owner cannot have Case 2 dismissed under *claim* preclusion. (Why?[154]) But wait a minute! P is saying that Owner is vicariously liable for Driver's negligence, but in Case 1 Driver was found *not* negligent! Can Owner assert issue preclusion against P on the issue of Driver's not being negligent? Let's see:

---

[152] 3 Jeremy Bentham, Rationale of Judicial Evidence 579 (1827).

[153] Of course, P could avoid this merry-go-round by suing both A and Z as defendants in a single case. But, as we see in §12.4, the joinder rules do not require P to do so. Here we will proceed on the assumption that P sues only one defendant in Case 1.

[154] Because one requirement for claim preclusion is that Case 1 and Case 2 be brought by the same claimant against the same defendant. See §11.2.1.

- ○ All the basic requirements for issue preclusion are satisfied: (1) Case 1 ended in a valid final judgment on the merits; (2) in Case 1, the issue of Driver's negligence was litigated and determined; and (3) the finding on that issue was essential to the judgment in Case 1. So far, so good.

- ○ In addition, the invocation of issue preclusion would not violate due process. Owner is asserting issue preclusion against *P*, and *P* was a party to Case 1, so due process is satisfied.

- ○ The problem is mutuality. Issue preclusion here is being asserted *by* Owner, who was not a party to Case 1. Under the mutuality doctrine, Owner cannot use issue preclusion, so Case 2 would go forward. Let's run with this a bit further and assume that Case 2 proceeds.

- ○ There are two possible outcomes of Case 2. For one, Owner might win, by convincing the fact-finder that Driver was not negligent. If this happens, the system will have accommodated two suits about the same issue, but the results of Case 1 and Case 2 would be consistent.

- ○ But the other possibility is that Owner loses, because the fact-finder in Case 2 finds that Driver was negligent and that Owner is vicariously liable for it. Now what happens? Nothing good. Presumably, Owner pays the judgment to *P* and then sues Driver to get indemnified for the loss. If she wins, Driver ends up paying for damage in an accident that, according to Case 1, she did not cause. If she loses, however, Owner ends up paying for a judgment the law says is not her primary responsibility.

This latter scenario is a disaster. Failing to allow Owner to use issue preclusion in Case 2 can lead only to two undesirable outcomes: Either (1) Driver's victory in Case 1 is rendered meaningless, or (2) Owner's right to indemnification is rendered meaningless. To avoid these bad outcomes, common law courts felt compelled to recognize what is usually called the *narrow exception* to the mutuality rule. The narrow exception is truly narrow. *It applies only in a vicarious liability situation in which the primarily liable party is found not negligent in Case 1.* Only in that instance does Case 2 lead to the two undesirable outcomes that may be avoided by allowing Owner to use issue preclusion in Case 2. Today, while there are states that have not outrightly *rejected* the mutuality doctrine, apparently every state will allow nonmutual issue preclusion in this situation.

Common law courts developed another exception to mutuality, also applicable only in vicarious liability cases. It involves a variation on the fact pattern above.

- ○ In Case 1, *P* sues Owner, the vicariously liable party. After litigation, Owner wins a valid final judgment on the merits, because the fact-finder expressly finds that Driver was not negligent and thus that Owner cannot be vicariously liable. In Case 2, *P* sues Driver, asserting that Driver's negligence injured her. As in the previous hypothetical, Driver cannot assert claim preclusion.[155] What about issue preclusion? After all, the issue of her negligence was litigated and determined in Case 1 and satisfies all the requirements for issue preclusion. In addition, because *P* was a party to Case 1, issue preclusion would not violate due process. The problem, as above, is mutuality. Under the mutuality doctrine, Driver could not assert issue preclusion, because she was not a party to Case 1.

Recognizing an exception to mutuality in this fact pattern is not as compelling as it was in the preceding hypothetical. There, failing to allow issue preclusion led to additional litigation concerning Owner's right to indemnification from Driver. Here, failing to allow issue preclusion will not create such additional litigation. If Driver is not allowed to assert issue preclusion, she will lose Case 2 at trial and be held liable. But that will be the end of the matter. Driver will not be able to sue Owner, because Owner does not owe indemnification to Driver. Accordingly, the policy that compelled the narrow exception does not apply here. Nonetheless, some courts have recognized what is usually called the *broad exception* to mutuality and permitted Owner to assert issue preclusion in Case 2. Such courts thus will not insist on mutuality in vicarious liability cases, even if Case 1 was against the primarily liable party and that person was found not negligent.

It is important to remember two things about the narrow and broad exceptions to mutuality. First, they are just that — *exceptions* to the general rule that mutuality is required. Second, they apply only in cases involving indemnification rights. Thus, they do not touch the majority of cases. In the mid-twentieth century, some courts took the next step. Instead of searching for an exception to mutuality, they would simply reject the requirement, at least in certain circumstances.

Rejection of Mutuality for Defendants (Nonmutual Defensive Issue Preclusion)

The California Supreme Court led the way in the rejection of mutuality with the landmark opinion by Justice Roger Traynor in *Bernhard v. Bank of America*.[156] The case involved the estate of an elderly woman who died. For some time before her death, the woman lived with a married couple named Cook. She gave Mr. Cook authority to write checks on her behalf from one of her accounts. Mr. Cook wrote a large check to himself (and his wife) from the account and put the money in his personal account. After the woman died, Mr. Cook became the executor of the woman's estate. In Case 1, the woman's relatives sued to challenge his accounting

---

[155] See note 154 above.

[156] 122 P.2d 892 (Cal. 1942). The late Professor Charles Alan Wright considered *Bernhard* to be one of the rare cases in which "a major change in established legal doctrine can be identified with a single decision and judge." Wright & Kane, Federal Courts 732.

of the estate, insisting that he return the money he had taken from her account. After litigation, the court expressly found that Mr. Cook had had the woman's permission to take the money as a gift. It entered judgment in his favor.

Later, Mr. Cook resigned as executor and one of the woman's daughters was appointed executrix of the estate. In Case 2, she sued the bank that had handled the woman's checking account. She asserted that her mother had never authorized Mr. Cook's taking money from the account, and thus that the bank was liable to the estate for that amount. The question was whether the bank could assert issue preclusion on the finding that the woman had given the money to the Cooks as a gift. Under the mutuality doctrine, of course, issue preclusion could not be invoked, because it was being asserted by the bank, which was not a party to Case 1. Issue preclusion was likewise impossible under the exceptions we just saw, because those only apply in vicarious liability cases.

Nonetheless, the California Supreme Court let the bank assert issue preclusion. Justice Traynor said, "No satisfactory rationalization has been advanced for the requirement of mutuality. Just why a party who was not bound by a previous action should be precluded from asserting it as res judicata[157] against a party who was bound by it is difficult to comprehend."[158] Again, the court did not try to find an exception to mutuality; it just rejected it. Thus, nonmutual preclusion was available beyond the vicarious liability cases.

But is issue preclusion *always* available to someone in Case 2, regardless of whether she was a party (or in privity with a party) in Case 1? No. For starters, remember that every state is free to determine its own preclusion rules, so long as those rules do not violate constitutional guarantees. Beyond this caveat, courts have emphasized that preclusion of any sort, including nonmutual preclusion, requires that the person against whom it is asserted had a full and fair opportunity to litigate in Case 1. See §§11.4.1 and 11.4.3.

The Supreme Court embraced *Bernhard* in its explication of federal law of issue preclusion in *Blonder-Tongue Laboratories, Inc. v. University of Illinois Foundation*.[159] *Blonder-Tongue* involved the alleged infringement of a patent (which is a federally granted monopoly to use one's invention). In Case 1, the plaintiff sued one defendant (*D-1*), alleging that *D-1* infringed the plaintiff's patent. After litigation, the court entered a valid final judgment on the merits in favor of *D-1*, based upon its express finding that the

---

[157] Remember that courts often use "res judicata" in a generic sense to refer to preclusion. See §11.1.

[158] *Bernhard*, 122 P.2d at 895.

[159] 402 U.S. 313 (1971). In addition to each state's having its own preclusion law, there is a federal common law of preclusion. For discussion of when it applies, see §§11.5.1, 11.5.4, and 11.5.5.

plaintiff's patent was invalid. In Case 2, the plaintiff sued a different defendant (*D-2*), alleging that it had infringed the same patent. Obviously, *D-2* wanted to assert issue preclusion on the finding in Case 1 that the patent was invalid. Just as obviously, though the basic requirements for issue preclusion were met, the mutuality rule would not permit *D-2* to use it. *D-2* had not been a party to Case 1. Moreover, the exceptions to mutuality would not apply, because the case did not involve vicarious liability.

The Supreme Court permitted *D-2* to use issue preclusion. The opinion relied in considerable part on *Bernhard*, and rejected mutuality while employing an express safeguard. The Court recognized that relitigation imposes a burden on the judicial system and raised the possibility that avoiding that burden might justify jettisoning the mutuality rule.[160] Importantly, however, the Court then noted, "it is clear that more than crowded dockets is involved."[161]

> The broader question is whether it is any longer tenable to afford a litigant more than one full and fair opportunity for judicial resolution of the same issue. . . . Permitting repeated litigation of the same issue as long as the supply of unrelated defendants holds out reflects either the aura of the gaming table or "a lack of discipline and of disinterestedness on the part of the lower courts, hardly a worthy or wise basis for fashioning rules of procedure." Though neither judges, the parties, nor the adversary system performs perfectly in all cases, the requirement of determining whether the party against whom an estoppel is asserted had a full and fair opportunity to litigate [in Case 1] is a most significant safeguard.[162]

Thus, the Court concluded that the system of justice affords a litigant one full and fair opportunity to litigate an issue. Once that protection has been afforded, the litigant may be bound by the finding on that issue in subsequent litigation, even by persons who were not parties (or in privity with a party) to Case 1. Though some observers suggested that the holding in *Blonder-Tongue* should be limited to patent cases, lower courts have not limited the holding in that way.[163]

Bernhard and *Blonder-Tongue* are examples of "nonmutual defensive issue preclusion." "Nonmutual" means that issue preclusion is being used by one who was not a party to Case 1. "Defensive" means that the person using issue preclusion in Case 2 is the defendant. (Some people refer to it as using nonmutual issue preclusion "as a shield," because it is being used

---

[160] Later in the opinion, the Court seemed to conclude that any saving to the judicial system was "an incidental matter" and merely "de minimis." *Blonder-Tongue*, 402 U.S. at 348, 349.

[161] *Id.* at 328-329.

[162] *Id.* at 329, *quoting* Kerotest Mfg. Co. v. C-O Two Co., 342 U.S. 180, 185 (1952).

[163] *See, e.g.*, Miller Brewing Co. v. Joseph Schlitz Brewing Co., 605 F.2d 990, 995 (7th Cir. 1979); Hallal v. Hopkins, 947 F. Supp. 978, 989-990 (S.D. Miss. 1995).

by a defendant.) Federal law (through *Blonder-Tongue*) and the law of most (but apparently not all) states allows nonmutual defensive issue preclusion, as long as the party against whom it is used in Case 2 was afforded a full and fair opportunity to litigate in Case 1.

But neither the *Bernhard* nor the *Blonder-Tongue* opinion expressly limited its holding to the nonmutual defensive situation. They thus left open the possibility that a *claimant* ought to be permitted to use nonmutual issue preclusion. That is the next, and most controversial, step in the development of this area of the law.

Rejection of Mutuality for Claimants (Nonmutual Offensive Issue Preclusion)

In the wake of cases embracing nonmutual defensive issue preclusion, some commentators started to consider problems that might arise if *claimants* were permitted to use nonmutual issue preclusion. Such use is usually called *nonmutual offensive issue preclusion*. "Nonmutual," as we know, means the person using issue preclusion was not a party to Case 1. "Offensive" means that the person using issue preclusion in Case 2 is a claimant (usually, of course, the plaintiff).[164]

The problems came to light especially in mass tort cases.

- A commercial airplane operated by Airline crashes, injuring 100 passengers. In Case 1, one of the passengers (*P-1*) sued Airline. The case was litigated, and a valid final judgment on the merits was entered in favor of Airline; the fact-finder expressly found that Airline was not negligent. In Case 2, another passenger (*P-2*) sued Airline regarding her injuries from the crash. Can Airline use issue preclusion on the finding that it was not negligent? The answer is no. Why? Because of due process! Airline is attempting to use issue preclusion *against P-2*, who was not a party to Case 1 (and was not in privity with *P-1* by any of the definitions we saw in §11.3.4). This hypothetical raises no problem of mutuality; issue preclusion is being asserted *by* Airline, which was a party to Case 1.

This hypothetical points out, as we saw in §11.3.4, that due process imposes a huge burden upon the defendant. To escape liability, Airline would have to win all 100 cases involving the 100 passengers. Because of due process, it can never use issue preclusion against a successive plaintiff.

- Assume the same facts about the plane crash and that in Case 1, *P-1* sues Airline. The case is litigated and a valid final judgment on the merits was entered in favor of *P-1*; the fact-finder expressly found that Airline was negligent and that its negligence was the proximate cause of *P-1*'s negligence. In Case 2, *P-2* sues Airline. Can *P-2* use issue preclusion on the

---

[164] See note 15 above.

finding that Airline was negligent? All the basic requirements are satisfied, and issue preclusion is being asserted against Airline, which was a party to Case 1, so due process is satisfied. The problem here is mutuality — issue preclusion is being asserted *by* someone who was not a party to Case 1.

Notice the policy choices raised by this hypothetical. If the court follows the mutuality rule, each of the 100 plaintiffs will be required to prove Airline's negligence. The same issue will be litigated, in theory, 100 separate times. Inconsistent results seem inescapable — that is, some plaintiffs will win and some plaintiffs will lose — fostering the sense that the judicial system is little more than a gaming table. Thus, permitting *P-2* to use issue preclusion will foster efficiency and consistency. But at what cost?

Allowing a claimant to use nonmutual issue preclusion means that Airline can be held negligent in 100 separate cases simply by losing Case 1. If *P-1* proves that Airline was negligent and subsequent plaintiffs can use issue preclusion on that finding, *P-2* through *P-100* will not have to prove negligence in their cases.[165] It is the worst of all worlds for Airline: If it loses in Case 1, 99 other plaintiffs can use the finding of its negligence against it; if it wins, however, none of these 99 plaintiffs is bound. Airline can be hurt by issue preclusion but cannot be helped by it. Should the judicial system force Airline to face potentially massive liability on the strength of one adverse finding? The problem can be refined by changing some facts.

∘ Suppose the first ten passengers bring individual suits against Airline. Airline wins all ten, with the fact-finder in each case expressly finding that Airline was not negligent. Now *P-11* sues Airline. Because of due process, as we have seen, Airline cannot use issue preclusion against *P-11*, so all issues are litigated. Assume *P-11* wins a valid final judgment on the merits, with an express finding that Airline was negligent. Now, can *P-12* through *P-100* use issue preclusion against Airline in their cases? After all, *P-11* won by establishing an issue that *P-12* through *P-100* must establish.

Allowing nonmutual issue preclusion by these claimants seems especially problematic. Why? Because in 10 of 11 cases, Airline was found not negligent. So the finding that Airline was negligent seems like a fluke — an

---

[165] Presumably, at least in a contributory negligence state, the issue of whether the individual plaintiff was negligent would have to be litigated in each case. But issue preclusion on Airline's negligence would be a huge step toward each plaintiff's recovering against Airline.

aberration. Why should the legal system repose great faith in it? On the other hand, if *P-1* won, how can we be sure it was not a fluke?[166]

Courts have had these sorts of issues in mind when they addressed whether to permit nonmutual offensive issue preclusion. The leading opinion on the topic is *Parklane Hosiery Co. v. Shore*,[167] in which the Supreme Court adopted nonmutual offensive issue preclusion, with several safeguards, as federal law. *Parklane* involved the violation of federal securities laws by a corporation and some of its managers and stockholders. In Case 1, the Securities and Exchange Commission (SEC) filed suit against the various defendants, alleging that they had issued a materially false and misleading proxy statement in connection with a merger. The SEC sought only equitable relief. After trial, the court entered a valid final judgment on the merits for the SEC, based upon its express finding that the proxy statement was materially false and misleading as alleged. In Case 2, private plaintiffs sued the same defendants on the same basic claim concerning the same proxy statement. They sought damages. The plaintiffs in Case 2 wanted issue preclusion on the finding that the defendants had issued a materially false and misleading proxy statement. Under the mutuality doctrine, of course, they could not use issue preclusion, because they were not parties to Case 1.

In the course of its opinion, the Court contrasted the potential efficiency of nonmutual *defensive* issue preclusion with the potential inefficiency of nonmutual *offensive* issue preclusion. The defensive use of issue preclusion (as in *Bernhard* and *Blonder-Tongue*) gives the claimant an incentive to join all potential defendants in Case 1. After all, if the claimant fails to do so, and loses Case 1, the defendant in Case 2 can use the adverse finding against the claimant in Case 2. Thus, recognizing nonmutual defensive issue preclusion probably promotes efficient joinder of Case 1 — the claimant will probably join all potential defendants in that case.

But the offensive version creates the opposite effect. It counsels potential claimants *not* to join in as a party to Case 1. Why? Because by staying out of Case 1, a potential claimant risks nothing and may gain something. If *P-1* loses in Case 1, *P-2* is not bound by the judgment in that case (because of due process). But if *P-1* wins in Case 1, and the court recognizes nonmutual offensive issue preclusion, *P-2* can use *P-1*'s victory to her own advantage in Case 2. Thus, this type of preclusion "will likely increase rather than decrease the total amount of litigation, since potential [claimants] will have everything to gain and nothing to lose" by not joining in Case 1.[168] The answer is not to prohibit the use of nonmutual

---

[166] The classic article raising such concerns in the wake of *Bernhard* is Brainerd Currie, *Mutuality of Estoppel: Limits on the* Bernhard *Doctrine*, 9 Stan. L. Rev. 281 (1957).

[167] 439 U.S. 322 (1979).

[168] *Id.* at 330.

offensive issue preclusion, but to apply it only in cases in which it will not "reward a private plaintiff who could have joined in [Case 1]."[169]

Moreover, the Court expressed concern that nonmutual offensive issue preclusion might be unfair to a defendant in various circumstances. It provided three examples. First, a defendant who is sued in Case 1 for a small amount of money might have little incentive to defend with vigor, especially if she foresees no other litigation concerning the event. If she lost Case 1, it would be unfair to allow issue preclusion in Case 2 where the claimant seeks a large recovery.[170] Second, if there had been multiple judgments concerning the underlying events, it would be unfair to allow a claimant to get issue preclusion from one in which the defendant was found liable and to ignore another in which the defendant won. And third, preclusion would be unfair if the defendant in Case 1 did not have a full and fair opportunity to litigate in Case 1. This latter point is consistent with a safeguard we saw in nonmutual defensive issue preclusion. (Indeed, no preclusion of any sort ought to be accorded if the person against whom it is sought did not have such an opportunity in Case 1. See §§11.4.1 and 11.4.3.)

In the final analysis, the Court in *Parklane* embraced nonmutual offensive issue preclusion, but only in cases in which these concerns could be allayed. And such was the case in *Parklane* itself. First, it was not a case in which allowing preclusion would promote inefficient litigation. The plaintiffs in Case 2 could not have joined in Case 1 because Case 1 was brought by the SEC and private plaintiffs would not have been permitted. Second, none of the three examples of unfairness was present. One, given the seriousness of the allegations in Case 1, and the clear foreseeability that private plaintiffs would sue if the SEC won Case 1, the defendants had every incentive to litigate vigorously in Case 1. Two, there were no inconsistent judgments on the books; the only judgment was unfavorable to the defendants. And three, there were no procedural opportunities available in Case 2 that were not available to the defendants in Case 1. Thus, the Court concluded, "none of the considerations that would justify a refusal to allow the use of offensive collateral estoppel is present in this case."[171]

Interestingly, the Court saw no unfairness in the fact that the use of issue preclusion in *Parklane* robbed the defendant of a right to jury trial on the issue of whether its proxy statement was misleading. That issue was decided in an administrative proceeding before a government agency, in which there is no right to jury trial. In the ensuing civil case in federal court, the defendant would have had a Seventh Amendment right to jury trial on that question. Employing issue preclusion to establish the issue meant that the defendant was never entitled to have a jury determine the

---

[169] *Id.* at 331-332.
[170] *See* 18 Moore's Federal Practice 132-144.
[171] *Parklane*, 439 U.S. at 332.

facts. Again, the Court did not consider this to be a procedural unfairness that rendered issue preclusion unavailable.

Parklane stands for the proposition that nonmutual offensive issue preclusion is appropriate, but only if the court in Case 2 is convinced (1) that the party using issue preclusion could not "easily have joined in the earlier action" and (2) that use of issue preclusion is not unfair to the defendant. While these are reasonable and sensible safeguards limiting the wholesale use of nonmutual offensive issue preclusion, it is unfortunate that the Supreme Court has not revisited the topic to give further guidance. Suppose, for instance, that the claimant in Case 2 could have intervened into Case 1 but did not do so. Does that failure result in forfeiting the privilege of seeking issue preclusion? The *Parklane* opinion characterized it as a "general rule" that one who could have joined easily in Case 1 should not be able to use issue preclusion in Case 2. But the Court gave no guidance on exceptions to this "general rule."

Moreover, exactly what did the Court mean when it spoke of whether the claimant in Case 2 could have joined easily in Case 1? In the usual private civil litigation context, Case 1 will not be brought by a government agency like the SEC, but by a private plaintiff. Presumably, any other potential plaintiff could intervene into that case if she desired. But what if Case 1 is pending in Baltimore and the other potential plaintiff lives in Indianapolis? She could intervene, but it might not be convenient. Does this matter? Again, the Court did not say.

The judicial acceptance of nonmutual offensive issue preclusion — with the limits laid out in *Parklane* — has led to a litigation strategy that might be called *plaintiff shopping*. The attorneys for numerous potential claimants might agree to have the strongest case go to judgment first, so the subsequent claimants can "ride" the successful judgment through nonmutual offensive issue preclusion.[172]

Though *Parklane* has been on the books for more than a generation, it is a mistake to assume that it reflects the majority view. It reflects federal law and the law of several states,[173] but apparently most states have not embraced nonmutual offensive issue preclusion.[174] In many states, it is difficult to determine the present state of the law, because the state supreme court has not addressed the topic in several decades.

---

[172] Though lawyers adopted this strategy in some of the asbestos litigation in the 1970s and 80s, courts did not permit preclusion to the extent some had predicted. *See* Michael Green, *The Inability of Offensive Collateral Estoppel to Fulfill Its Promise: An Examination of Estoppel in Asbestos Litigation*, 70 Iowa L. Rev. 141 (1984).

[173] *See, e.g.,* Briggs v. Newton, 984 P.2d 1113, 1120 (Alaska 1999); Property & Cas. Inc. Guar. Assn. v. Walmart Stores, Inc., 403 S.E.2d 625, 629 (S.C. 1999); Silva v. State, 745 P.2d 380, 384 (N.M. 1987); Oates v. Safeco Ins. Co., 583 S.W.2d 713, 719 (Mo. 1979).

[174] *See, e.g.,* Beaty v. McGraw, 15 S.W.3d 819, 825 (Tenn. App. 1998); Trappell v. Sysco Food Servs., 850 S.W.2d 529, 543 (Tex. App. 1992).

Let's wrap up this section by returning to a couple of hypotheticals we raised earlier.

- ° A commercial airplane operated by Airline crashes, injuring 100 passengers. In Case 1, one passenger (*P-1*) sues Airline. The case is litigated and a valid final judgment on the merits is entered in favor of *P-1*; the fact-finder expressly found that Airline was negligent and that its negligence was the proximate cause of *P-1*'s injuries. In Case 2, a second passenger (*P-2*) sues Airline. Can *P-2* use issue preclusion on the finding that Airline was negligent?

For starters, the basic requirements for issue preclusion (Case 1 ended in a valid final judgment on the merits, the issue of Airline's negligence was litigated and determined, and the finding on that issue was essential to the judgment in Case 1) are all satisfied. Next, there is no problem with due process, because preclusion is being asserted against Airline, which was a party to Case 1. But the assertion of preclusion here is nonmutual — it is being made by someone (*P-2*) who was not a party to Case 1. And it is offensive — it is being asserted by a claimant in Case 2. Should nonmutual offensive issue preclusion be permitted?

The answer depends upon the applicable law. If we are applying the law of a state that adopts only the exceptions to mutuality, this assertion will not be permitted. Why? Because the exceptions apply only in vicarious liability situations (not so here) and, even then, only to assertions of issue preclusion by a defendant. If we are applying the law of a state that adopts only *Bernhard* or *Blonder-Tongue*, the answer is also no. Why? Because those cases permit only nonmutual *defensive* issue preclusion. So only if we are in a jurisdiction that adopts the *Parklane* approach is there any chance to have preclusion here.

Now, if we are in a *Parklane* jurisdiction, we must assess the factors given in that case. First, if *P-2* could have joined in Case 1, the Court indicated, she should not be permitted to use preclusion. To let her do so would reward a "wait and see" attitude that fosters inefficient litigation. On the other hand, as noted, the Court did not say that failure to join always led to forfeiture of issue preclusion. Moreover, it did not say whether this factor alone would obviate preclusion even if the other factors counseled in favor of preclusion. And here the other factors seem to do just that. One, Case 1 was for a serious claim, and Airline knew that the crash injured 100 people, so it is clear that it had every incentive to litigate vigorously and could foresee future litigation by the other passengers. Two, there are no inconsistent judgments on the books here, so *P-2* is not simply picking a finding she likes and ignoring those that hurt her cause. And three, there is no indication that Airline did not have a full and fair opportunity to litigate in Case 1. So where does that leave us? Again, it depends upon how one weighs the factors.

○ Suppose the first ten passengers bring individual suits against Airline. Airline wins all ten, with the fact-finder in each case expressly finding that Airline was not negligent. Now *P-11* sues Airline. Because of due process, as we have seen, Airline cannot use issue preclusion against *P-11*, so all issues are litigated. Assume *P-11* wins a valid final judgment on the merits, with an express finding that Airline was negligent. Now, can *P-12* through *P-100* get issue preclusion against Airline in their cases?

Here, the preliminary analyses are the same as above regarding the basic requirements of issue preclusion, due process, and whether nonmutual offensive issue preclusion would be permitted. Only in a *Parklane* jurisdiction is it even arguable. Under *Parklane*, would such preclusion be allowed? Again, we have the problem of not knowing exactly what the Court meant when it assessed whether a later claimant could have joined in an earlier case. Beyond that, however, here we have inconsistent judgments. Airline has won ten times. It has lost only once. It seems grossly unfair to allow *P-12* through *P-100* to take advantage of this one holding. The second of the three "fairness" factors seems clearly to counsel against use of preclusion here. This case is fairly easy because it seems that the judgment in the eleventh case was an aberration. We should not repose much confidence in it.

That fact leaves unanswered the big question, however. Assume *P-1* wins in Case 1. Because it is first, there are no inconsistent judgments on the books, and the argument in favor of applying preclusion is stronger under *Parklane*. But how do we know that this judgment is not the fluke? Maybe, if all 100 cases were litigated separately, Airline would win the other 99. *Parklane* does not tell us why we should repose such great confidence in a single judgment. Perhaps nervousness over this point explains why some jurisdictions have never embraced nonmutual offensive issue preclusion. One way around the problem would be to have a test case (or group of test cases) go through trial to see which way the wind is blowing, as a means of ultimately settling the overall disputes. We discussed the test case as part of the consideration of *Taylor v. Sturgell* on page 567.

§11.4 Exceptions to the Operation of Preclusion

§11.4.1 In General

Even when the requirements of claim preclusion or issue preclusion are satisfied, there may be situations in which preclusion should not be applied. Courts have recognized some exceptions to the application of each doctrine. As we will see, most of these exceptions are fairly narrow and well established. It is inherent in the operation of both claim and issue preclusion that the party against whom preclusion is to be applied in Case 2 had a full and fair opportunity to present its position in Case 1. Thus, the most obvious exception to the operation of preclusion arises in those relatively rare cases in which a party was not accorded a full and fair opportunity to litigate in Case 1. Examples include failure to give appropriate notice to a party in Case 1, gross misconduct (often referred to as "fraud on the court") by another litigant or participant, and egregious error by the court itself in Case 1.[175] Such things may obviate the operation of claim and issue preclusion. More frequently, however, it would seem appropriate to raise these sorts of issues in a motion to set aside the judgment in Case 1.[176]

Suppose the controlling principles of law are changed between the entry of judgment in Case 1 and the resolution of Case 2. Should the change in law weaken the application of preclusion, or should the judgment in Case 1 have preclusive consequences in Case 2? The quick answer, subject to a narrow exception discussed below with regard to issue preclusion, is that the change in law does not excuse the operation of claim or issue preclusion.

Courts occasionally are tempted to recognize some ad hoc exception to the operation of preclusion in the general interest of "fairness," "simple justice," "private justice," or some similar amorphous notion. As a general rule (and as emphasized by the Supreme Court), such open-ended exceptions are less appropriate with claim preclusion than with issue preclusion. Why? Because the cost to the judicial system is greater when there is an exception to claim preclusion. Recall that claim preclusion is the broader of the two preclusion doctrines and that invocation of claim preclusion results in dismissal of Case 2. Thus, recognizing an exception to claim preclusion results in the filing of a case that otherwise would not have been filed. On the other hand, issue preclusion operates to foreclose the litigation only of an issue in Case 2; it streamlines the scope of litigation of a case that will be filed anyway. So recognizing an exception to issue preclusion will not cause the filing of a case that would otherwise not be filed.[177]

§11.4.2   Claim Preclusion

The principal exceptions to claim preclusion are catalogued in §26(1) of the Restatement (Second) of Judgments. One set of exceptions applies

---

[175] *See, e.g.,* United States v. Pueblo of Taos, 515 F.2d 1404, 1407 (Ct. Cl. 1975) (decision by administrative agency concerning Indian lands "probably was tainted" by failing to give a full and fair opportunity to litigate).

[176] We discussed such motions, made under Federal Rule 60(b), at §9.7.

[177] *See* 18 Wright & Miller 385 ("exceptions to issue preclusion may be justified by correspondingly reduced showing of public interest or private justice").

when either the defendant or the court in Case 1 agrees to allow the claimant to split her claim. Thus, courts generally allow parties to Case 1 to consent that the claimant will split her claim without claim preclusive effect.[178] This recognition allows parties, for example, to simplify litigation by limiting it to one aspect of a claim, while negotiating settlement to the remainder of the claim pending outcome. Obviously, a defendant who consents to such splitting cannot complain that she has lost the protection from multiple litigation that claim preclusion is designed to give her. Express consent of this sort is usually expressed in a settlement agreement or in a consent decree, and common principles of contract interpretation govern to determine the parties' intent. Consent may be implied as well. Because preclusion is an affirmative defense,[179] the defendant might waive a claim preclusion objection by acquiescing in multiple suits on the same claim.[180] Moreover, though the preclusive effect of a judgment is to be determined by the court in Case 2, the court in Case 1 might expressly reserve a claimant's right to split her claim.[181]

Another exception applies if the claimant in Case 1 could not have sought all rights to relief for her claim because of limitations imposed on the court in Case 1.[182] For instance, if the applicable joinder rules did not permit the claimant to seek damages and injunctive relief in a single case, it would not be fair to impose claim preclusion when the claimant sought one form of relief in Case 1 and a different form in Case 2. More commonly, such limitations on the court in Case 1 will be subject matter jurisdiction rules in a state court.

○ *P*, riding her bicycle, was struck by a car driven by *D*. *P* suffered personal injuries and her bike, worth $300, was ruined. In Case 1, *P* sues *D* for property damage, in a state small claims court, which by state law cannot entertain claims exceeding $1,500. *P* wins a judgment for $300. In Case 2, *P* sues *D* to recover $15,000 damages for her personal injuries from the wreck. She files Case 2 in a different state trial court, this one having jurisdiction of claims exceeding $1,500. *D* asserts that Case 2 should be dismissed under the doctrine of claim preclusion, properly noting that the jurisdiction has adopted a transactional test for claim preclusion. The requirements for claim preclusion are met, but can *P* avoid dismissal by invoking an exception to claim preclusion?

---

[178] Restatement (Second) of Judgments §26(1)(a).

[179] Fed. R. Civ. P. 8(c)(1) lists "res judicata" as an affirmative defense. This reference clearly encompasses both claim and issue preclusion, and the defendant has the burden of pleading and proving the affirmative defense. See notes 5 and 6 above.

[180] 18 Moore's Federal Practice §131.24[1].

[181] Restatement (Second) of Judgments §26(1)(b).

[182] Restatement (Second) of Judgments §26(1)(c).

On the face of it, the argument for an exception seems appropriate. After all, because of limitations on subject matter jurisdiction, the court in Case 1 could not have entertained the assertion for damages for personal injuries; the claim would have exceeded the amount in controversy that could be heard in the small claims court. But suppose *P* could have sought relief for both personal injuries and property damage in a single case in the court having jurisdiction of claims exceeding $1,500. Thus, *P* could have achieved efficient joinder in one case in that court. Instead, she chose an inefficient route, one that would force *D* to defend twice. Some courts faced with such a situation reject the argument for an exception and dismiss Case 2 under claim preclusion.[183] Only if state law would not have allowed *P* to bring both assertions in a single case in some court should the exception be recognized.

Closely related to this notion is an exception that recognizes that claim preclusion would be contrary to the appropriate implementation of a constitutional or statutory scheme.[184] Under the Bankruptcy Code, for instance, only certain matters qualify for expedited hearing. The courts have concluded that a claimant proceeding in an expedited hearing on such a matter is not precluded from bringing a separate action regarding related matters.[185] The scheme established by the Bankruptcy Code envisioned bifurcation of matters in this way. Courts have reached a similar conclusion concerning cases brought under the Declaratory Judgment Act, which we discussed at §4.6.3. A claimant seeking declaratory judgment is asking the court to declare the relative rights of the parties; she is not asking for "coercive" relief, such as damages or an injunction. Seeking declaratory judgment, as a general rule, will not preclude the claimant's later action for coercive relief.[186] (Remember, though, that even if claim preclusion might not bar a second case, issue preclusion from Case 1 might preclude relitigation of particular issues in Case 2.[187])

Suppose that when the claimant files Case 1 she is unaware of the full extent of her injuries. Suppose further that this ignorance causes her to seek only some of the aspects of her claim in Case 1. Can she bring Case 2

---

[183] *See, e.g.,* Mells v. Billops, 482 A.2d 759, 761 (Del. Super. 1984) (plaintiff "voluntarily chose a court of limited jurisdiction when he could have presented all of his claims . . . had he brought the original action in this Court").

[184] Restatement (Second) of Judgments, §26(1)(d).

[185] In re Hooker Investments, Inc., 131 B.R. 922, 929-930 (Bankr. S.D.N.Y. 1991).

[186] *See, e.g.,* Harborside Refrigerated Servs., Inc. v. Vogel, 959 F.2d 368, 373 (2d Cir. 1992). This rule assumes that the claimant did not seek coercive relief in the same action with the request for declaratory judgment. If she did, any subsequent effort to seek coercive relief would be subject to claim preclusion.

[187] And issue preclusion might prove determinative of Case 2. Suppose, for example, that in Case 1, for declaratory judgment, the parties litigate and the court determines that the defendant did nothing wrong and that the claimant was at fault. Though Case 2 may not be dismissed under claim preclusion, the findings on these issues, established through issue preclusion, will be determinative of Case 2; the defendant will win.

to seek recovery for those harms of which she was ignorant in Case 1, or does claim preclusion bar her from a second proceeding? There is some support for the conclusion that claim preclusion should not apply here. In 1978, the Hawaii Supreme Court opined that the majority of jurisdictions "will not bar claims of which the plaintiff was ignorant . . . unless plaintiff's ignorance was due to her own negligence."[188] The opinion relied upon cases that were several decades old, however, and it is arguable that none of those opinions actually established such a liberal rule.[189] The majority view seems to require more of the claimant who is attempting to avoid claim preclusion; she must show that "fraud, concealment, or misrepresentation . . . cause[d] the [claimant] to fail to include a claim in a former action."[190] This tougher approach reflects the modern concern with the policies underlying claim preclusion in an era of crowded dockets.[191]

Beyond these relatively specific exceptions to the operation of claim preclusion, some courts have attempted to create an exception based upon broad concepts of fairness. The Supreme Court slammed the door on the development of open-ended exceptions, however, in *Federated Department Stores, Inc. v. Moitie*.[192] In that case, purchasers brought several actions against operators of department stores, alleging that the defendants violated federal antitrust law by agreeing to fix prices to be charged to retail customers. In Case 1,[193] the district court dismissed because the plaintiffs could not demonstrate that they suffered a harm recognized by the antitrust laws. The disappointed plaintiffs reacted in different ways. Some of them (Group 1) appealed the judgment of dismissal to the Ninth Circuit. Others, however (Group 2), brought Case 2, which simply reasserted their original claim in state court; the defendants removed to federal court, and the federal court dismissed under claim preclusion — after all, the Group 2 plaintiffs were asserting the same claim as they did in

---

[188] Bolte v. Aits, Inc., 587 P.2d 810, 813-814 (Haw. 1978).

[189] *See, e.g.*, McVay v. Castenara, 152 Miss. 106, 113-114 (1928) (noting lack of pleading of issues on applicability of claim preclusion and exception); Badger v. Badger, 69 Utah 784, 300-301 (1927) (refusing to apply an exception to claim preclusion; appellant).

[190] Harnett v. Billman, 800 F.2d 1308, 1313 (4th Cir. 1986). This helpful opinion was written by Judge Dickson Phillips, who taught Civil Procedure for years at the University of North Carolina School of Law, where he also served as Dean. The position espoused in *Harnett* is reflected in Restatement (Second) of Judgments §26, cmt j.

[191] In one of the old cases espousing the more liberal view about allowing an exception to claim preclusion for the claimant's ignorance, the court said that "[t]he rule applying to splitting a cause of action is one of practice merely, and is not without exception." McVay v. Castenara, 152 Miss. 106, 113 (1928). That view of claim preclusion is quite different from the less flexible view today. See the discussion of policies in §11.1 and the Supreme Court's view as discussed immediately below.

[192] 452 U.S. 394 (1981).

[193] Actually, there were multiple suits. We can treat them in the aggregate, however, and refer to the dismissal as a singular Case 1.

Case 1. The Group 2 plaintiffs then appealed the dismissal of Case 2 to the Ninth Circuit.

While both sets of cases were on appeal to the Ninth Circuit, the Supreme Court decided a different case that changed the rules about anti-trust injury; under the law established in this opinion, the plaintiffs in Groups 1 and 2 would be able to show sufficient injury to invoke the anti-trust laws. How should this change in the law affect Groups 1 and 2? The Ninth Circuit reversed the judgment as to Group 1 and remanded to the district court, instructing it to reconsider the case in light of the new Supreme Court opinion. That court also concluded that the Group 2 plaintiffs, even though they did not appeal their loss in Case 1, should not be barred by claim preclusion. The court recognized an exception to claim preclusion for "public policy" and "simple justice," and concluded that the Group 2 plaintiffs should be able to proceed.

The Supreme Court reversed and held that the Group 2 plaintiffs were barred by claim preclusion. In unmistakable terms, it rejected open-ended exceptions to claim preclusion. The Court reasserted the importance of claim preclusion as a key principle of justice. The Court said:

> [W]e do not see the grave injustice which would be done by the application of accepted principles of res judicata. "Simple justice" is achieved when a complex body of law developed over a period of years is evenhandedly applied. The doctrine of res judicata serves vital public interests beyond any individual judge's ad hoc determination of the equities in a particular case. There is simply "no principle of law or equity which sanctions the rejection by a federal court of the salutary principle of res judicata." The Court of Appeals' reliance on "public policy" is similarly misplaced. This Court has long recognized that "[p]ublic policy dictates that there be an end of litiga-tion; that those who have contested an issue shall be bound by the result of the contest, and that matters once tried shall be considered forever settled as between the parties." We have stressed that "[the] doctrine of res judicata is not a mere matter of practice or procedure inherited from a more techni-cal time than ours. It is a rule of fundamental and substantial justice. . . ."[194]

Finally, as we saw earlier, there is a strong argument in favor of apply-ing the primary rights definition of claim in motor vehicle crash cases involving subrogation of an insurance company.[195] Even in states that oth-erwise would apply a transactional test to claim preclusion, there may be an exception in such cases to ensure that the driver's insurance company is not barred in seeking damages from another driver involved in a colli-sion with its insured.

---

[194] *Moitie*, 452 U.S. at 400 (citations omitted).
[195] See note 54 above.

§11.4.3   Issue Preclusion

As discussed in §11.4.1, the invocation of preclusion of either type requires that the party against whom it is applied had a full and fair opportunity to litigate in Case 1. Just as failure to give notice, or fraud on the court, or other violations of this fair hearing requirement may vitiate claim preclusion, so will they vitiate issue preclusion. In addition, several of the basic requirements of imposing issue preclusion act to ensure that its use is fair. Specifically, issue preclusion can only be used for an issue actually litigated and determined in Case 1. Moreover, that issue must have been essential to the judgment in Case 1, which tends to ensure that the fact-finder truly focused on the issue before deciding it. Moreover, the court in Case 2 has a good deal of discretion in defining what issue was actually litigated and determined in Case 1. This discretion might be shaped in Case 2 to avoid results that seem unfair to the court.

The principal exceptions to issue preclusion are catalogued in §28 of the Restatement (Second) of Judgments. Some provisions of that section mirror those we saw for claim preclusion in §11.4.2. So issue preclusion might be avoided if the party against whom it is asserted could not have obtained review of the judgment in Case 1,[196] or if a new determination of the issue is needed because of "differences in the quality or extensiveness of the procedures followed by the two courts or by factors relating to the allocation of jurisdiction between them."[197]

Sometimes the court in Case 2 will be required to assess whether a difference in burden of persuasion should affect application of issue preclusion.[198] For example, in a criminal case, the defendant must be proved guilty "beyond a reasonable doubt." In a civil case, in contrast, the claimant must prove the elements of her claim only by "a preponderance of the evidence," which is an easier standard to satisfy. Often, an issue in a criminal case may be raised in a civil case for damages by the victim of the crime. For example, if *D* breaks into *P*'s house and steals *P*'s stereo, *D* might be prosecuted by the state for committing a crime and *P* might sue *D* in a civil case to recover damages caused by the theft.

  ◦ In Case 1, the state successfully prosecutes *D* for the theft. In Case 2, *P* sues for damages from the theft. Can *P* use issue preclusion on the issue of whether *D* stole the stereo? Yes, because the state in Case 1 proved that issue and proved it to a higher degree of certainty than *P*

---

[196] Restatement (Second) of Judgments §28(1) (party against whom issue preclusion is sought "could not, as a matter of law, have obtained review of the judgment in the initial proceeding").

[197] Restatement (Second) of Judgments §28(3).

[198] Restatement (Second) of Judgments §28(4).

needs to satisfy. Thus, assuming the other requirements for issue preclusion are met,[199] *P* would not have to prove the theft in Case 2.

○ In Case 1, *P* sues *D* for damages from the theft and wins (which includes, of course, a determination that *D* stole the stereo). In Case 2, the state prosecutes *D* for the theft. Can the state use issue preclusion on the issue of whether *D* stole the stuff? No, because *P* proved the theft to a lesser degree of certainty than the state needs to satisfy in the criminal case.

Suppose the defendant pleads guilty in the criminal case. Then the person whose things were stolen sues that person in a civil case, seeking damages for the theft. Can the plaintiff in the civil case use issue preclusion on the question of whether the defendant stole the stuff? The quick answer must be no, because the issue of theft was not litigated and determined in Case 1. After all, that case ended in a guilty plea, and was not resolved by litigation. On the other hand, allowing the defendant to litigate an issue on which he admitted criminal guilt is more than some courts can accept. They will refuse to let the defendant change his tune. Courts doing so are probably applying *judicial estoppel*. As we discussed at page 533, that doctrine does not permit a party to take disparate positions in separate litigation.

Occasionally (but rarely), an intervening change in the controlling law might justify an exception to issue preclusion.[200] A famous example is *Commissioner of Internal Revenue v. Sunnen*,[201] which concerned taxability of income from a royalty agreement. An inventor patented his invention and entered a contract with a manufacturer, under which the latter made the machines and paid a royalty to the inventor's wife. The IRS took the position that the income should be taxed to the inventor, not the wife (which was bad news for the inventor, because he was in a higher tax bracket than his wife). In Case 1, the parties litigated the issue, and the inventor won.

After expiration of the contract, the inventor entered another deal with the manufacturer, again providing that the royalty be paid to the inventor's wife. The IRS sued again (Case 2), in an effort to establish that the royalty income should be taxed to the inventor, not his wife.[202] The inventor tried to assert issue preclusion; after all, this very issue had been litigated and determined in Case 1. The Supreme Court held that issue preclusion should not apply, because of an intervening change in the law,

---

[199] This would be nonmutual offensive issue preclusion, because the claimant in Case 2 was not a party to Case 1 and is asserting the claim.

[200] Restatement (Second) of Judgments §28(2)(b) (a new determination is warranted on a question of law "to take account of an intervening change in the applicable legal context or otherwise to avoid inequitable administration of the laws").

[201] 333 U.S. 591 (1948).

[202] There was no claim preclusion because each taxable year constitutes a different claim.

which made it clear that the income should be taxed to the inventor.[203] The Court refused to allow the inventor to use issue preclusion on this question. Because of the intervening change in the law, it would not be proper to allow the inventor to use issue preclusion to lock in for him advantageous tax treatment not available to fellow citizens.

Finally, the Supreme Court has held that nonmutual offensive issue preclusion cannot be used in litigation against the United States.[204] The federal government may litigate the same issue in many cases throughout the country. As a matter of policy, the Court concluded, it should not be required to appeal every adverse ruling in an effort to avoid imposition of issue preclusion.

§11.5   Full Faith and Credit and Related Topics

§11.5.1   In General

In this section we deal with preclusion when Case 1 and Case 2 are decided in different judicial systems; this topic has become known as "interjurisdictional preclusion."[205] For example, if the judgment in Case 1 is entered by a state court in Arizona and Case 2 is brought in a state court in Florida, which state's law determines the preclusive effect of the judgment? Similarly, if Case 1 were decided in a federal court and Case 2 in a state court (or vice versa), does federal or state law determine the preclusion effect of the judgment? Moreover, does it matter whether Case 1 was in federal court under diversity of citizenship jurisdiction, instead of federal question? Such questions are important because each state is free to determine its own preclusion law, so long as that law does not violate due process,[206] and because there is also federal law on preclusion, which may differ from state law.

---

[203] The Court also opined that even though the contracts between the inventor and the manufacturer were identical, Case 2 did not involve exactly the same facts as Case 1. Instead, the facts in Case 2 were "separable" even though they were the same facts! *Sunnen,* 333 U.S. at 599-600. Thus, the basic requirement that the two cases must involve the same facts was not satisfied. This "separable facts" notion is of uncertain present vitality. *See* 18 Moore's Federal Practice §132.02[5][c]. *Sunnen* may demonstrate the occasional difficulty encountered with issue preclusion on rulings of law. See §11.3.2.

[204] United States v. Mendoza, 464 U.S. 14 (1984).

[205] *See, e.g.,* 18 Moore's Federal Practice §133; Howard Erichson, *Interjurisdictional Preclusion,* 96 Mich. L. Rev. 945 (1998). Professor Erichson's article builds on a groundbreaking piece by the late Professor Ronan Degnan, *Federalized Res Judicata,* 85 Yale L.J. 741 (1976).

[206] Richards v. Jefferson County, 517 U.S. 793 (1996).

Interjurisdictional preclusion problems can arise in four general scenarios. First is when Case 1 and Case 2 are decided in state courts of different states; we call this situation "state-to-state preclusion." Second is when Case 1 is decided in a state court and Case 2 is filed in federal court; we call this situation "state-to-federal preclusion." Third is when Case 1 is decided in a federal court and Case 2 is filed in a state court; we call this "federal-to-state preclusion." And, finally, we have the situation in which Cases 1 and 2 are in federal courts; not surprisingly, we call this "federal-to-federal preclusion."

We first encountered the concept of full faith and credit in our discussion of personal jurisdiction, §2.2, where we saw that a valid judgment was entitled to full faith and credit in states other than the one that entered it. We spoke there of being able to sue in the second state to enforce a judgment from the first state. Here we are concerned with a different issue: In determining whether the judgment from Case 1 is entitled to claim or issue preclusive effect in Case 2, what preclusion law does the court in Case 2 use? Full faith and credit plays a role here. As the Supreme Court said in *Durfee v. Duke*: "Full faith and credit thus generally requires every State to give to a judgment at least the res judicata effect which the judgment would be accorded in the State which rendered it."[207] Thus, full faith and credit applies not only to the enforcement of a judgment in a second action but to determining the preclusive effect of a judgment.

There are two sources of full faith and credit law: The Full Faith and Credit Clause of the Constitution (Article IV, §1) and the full faith and credit statute, now codified at 28 U.S.C. §1738. The constitutional provision is quite narrow. It requires that each *state* give full faith and credit to (among other things) "judicial proceedings of every other State" and thus applies only in the state-to-state preclusion scenario. The full faith and credit statute is broader. It applies not only in the state-to-state preclusion scenario, but in the state-to-federal situation as well. It provides that a state or federal court in Case 2 must give "the same full faith and credit" as would be given by the state court that entered judgment in Case 1. Interestingly, then, full faith and credit law applies directly only in the first two of our four scenarios. As we will see, however, courts have fashioned similar principles to cover the other two scenarios, though the precise source of those principles is unclear.

§11.5.2   State-to-State Preclusion

∘ Case 1 is litigated in state court in Texas and results in a valid final judgment on the merits. Case 2 is brought by the same claimant against the

---

[207]375 U.S. 106, 109 (1963). We discussed *Durfee* at §6.4, concerning collateral attacks on subject matter jurisdiction.

same defendant in a state court in Louisiana. Louisiana preclusion law would permit the second suit but Texas preclusion law would not. What does the Louisiana court do in Case 2?

The answer seems straightforward: Both the constitutional provision for full faith and credit and §1738 require the courts of a second state to honor the judgments, including the preclusion rules, of the courts of the state that decided Case 1. So the Louisiana court should apply Texas law and dismiss Case 2 under claim preclusion.

Our hypothetical is similar to *Magnolia Petroleum Co. v. Hunt.*[208] In that case, a Texas worker was injured on the job. In Case 1, he recovered an award for his injuries in an administrative proceeding in Texas. Texas law clearly provided that such a worker was not entitled to bring a second proceeding to recover additional compensation from his employer. So the worker brought Case 2 in Louisiana, seeking additional compensation. The Supreme Court held that the Louisiana court should have dismissed Case 2 because under Texas law, the judgment in Case 1 was the end of the matter. Similarly, in another case, the Oregon Supreme Court concluded that an Ohio judgment precluded a second action on the same claim even though Oregon law might have allowed a second case to proceed.[209]

Thus, we seem to have a clear black-letter principle: The court in Case 2 must apply the preclusion law of the state whose court decided Case 1. After all, §1738 requires the court in Case 2 to give the judgment "the same" effect it would have in the state that decided Case 1. Indeed, the Restatement (Second) of Judgments takes the position that the requirement in §1738 that one state accord another state's judgment "the same" effect that it would have in the judgment-rendering state mandates the court in Case 2 "to give to the state judgment the same effect — *no more and no less* — than the court [deciding Case 1] would give it."[210]

But things are not as clear as they seem here. The famous quote from *Durfee v. Duke* above said that full faith and credit "generally requires every State to give to a judgment *at least* the res judicata effect which the judgment would be accorded in the State which rendered it."[211] This language seems to recognize that the court in Case 2 might give a *greater* preclusive effect than the state in Case 1 would, but also seems to rule out the possibility of its giving a *lesser* preclusive effect. Commentators have long debated, however, whether the court deciding Case 2 might be free to accord the judgment from Case 1 a lesser effect than it would have in the judgment-rendering state. Professors Wright and Miller, for example,

---

[208] 320 U.S. 430 (1943).
[209] Benjamin v. S.R. Smith Co., 632 P.2d 13 (Or. 1981).
[210] Restatement (Second) of Judgments §86 cmt. g (emphasis added).
[211] 375 U.S. 106, 109 (1963) (emphasis added).

contend that full faith and credit enshrines only the "central" or "core" principles of claim and issue preclusion — those that "support the core values of finality, repose, and reliance, as well as some of the rules that facilitate control by the first court over its own procedure" — and not "every minute detail" of preclusion doctrine.[212] Specifically, they assert that the nonmutual employment of issue preclusion "is not so central a component of res judicata to be swept into full faith and credit."[213] To them, then, the court in Case 2 should not always be forced to accept every aspect of the preclusion law of the jurisdiction that decided Case 1.

Can "The Same" Mean "Less"? The Supreme Court has never held that the court in Case 2 can accord the judgment from Case 1 a *lesser* preclusive effect than would the state in which Case 1 was decided. There is an especial paucity of case law from other courts on this point. The issue raised by Professors Wright and Miller can be illustrated in this hypothetical:

- *P* sues Pharmaceutical Co. (*PC*) in California. After full trial, *P* wins a judgment, based upon the finding that *PC*'s product was unfit and caused serious physical harm to persons who used it. Now thousands of persons around the country plan to sue *PC* for the same harm. *P-2* sues in Virginia, on the same theory used by *P*, and asks the court to employ nonmutual offensive issue preclusion on the question of whether the product is unfit and causes the physical harm alleged.

Does §1738 require Virginia to apply nonmutual offensive issue preclusion? If the statutory mandate is absolute — that Virginia is to give the judgment "the same" effect as California — the answer would seem to be yes. But if commentators are correct that full faith and credit only embodies the central aspects of preclusion law — principally those supporting the principles of finality — the determination will be considerably more nuanced. Specifically, full faith and credit should not "demand obeisance to . . . aspects of preclusion doctrine that are incidental to the central role of preclusion and that may intrude on substantial interests of later courts."[214] In our hypothetical, then, it would be proper to assess whether Virginia ought to be forced to accept nonmutual offensive issue preclusion. California's interest in allowing such preclusion might not be damaged if Virginia does not follow California law on this point. After all, California is still free to use nonmutual estoppel in its own courts. On the other hand, what if Virginia's adherence to mutuality in the mass tort situation was its response to the concerns we discussed in §11.3.5? The state

---

[212] 18B Wright & Miller 33-34 ("[F]ull faith and credit embraces the central doctrines of res judicata. No other result could be tolerated in a federalistic society as mobile and litigious as ours. . . . None of these decisions, however, compels the conclusion that full faith and credit incorporates every minute detail of res judicata doctrine.").

[213] 18B Wright & Miller 44.

[214] Wright & Kane, Federal Courts 736.

could have concluded that no defendant should be subjected to massive liability essentially on the basis of losing one case. Is this interest to be swept away through obedience to every tenet of California's preclusion law? The argument that it is not seems especially strong. But the issue is left mostly to the world of academic surmise.

Can "The Same" Mean "More"? There is some case support for the notion that the court in Case 2 can accord a judgment from Case 1 *greater* preclusive effect than the state deciding Case 1 would. Clearly, the court in Case 2 cannot be *required* to give the judgment greater effect than it would have in the state deciding Case 1.[215] But may it choose to do so? Let's see how this issue might come up.

- *P* is involved in a car wreck and suffers personal injuries and property damage. She brings Case 1 in Georgia, seeking recovery only for personal injuries. In motor vehicle crash cases, Georgia adopts the primary rights definition of claim, meaning that *P* has separate claims for personal injuries and for property damage. The court in Georgia enters a valid final judgment on the merits. Now *P* brings Case 2 against the same defendant, seeking to recover for the property damage from the same crash. Case 2 is filed, however, in Nevada, which employs a transactional test for claim preclusion.

If the Nevada court uses the preclusion law of Georgia, there is no claim preclusion, and *P* can proceed in Case 2. Doing so, however, requires Nevada to entertain litigation that its own rules of preclusion would hold barred. Should Nevada be able to dismiss Case 2 under claim preclusion? In other words, should Nevada be permitted to accord the Georgia judgment greater preclusive effect than it would have in Georgia? If so, *P* is "robbed" of the right given her by Georgia law to proceed in separate actions. Given the clash between upsetting *P*'s legitimate expectation that she can proceed separately and Nevada's interest in docket control, which should prevail? Reasonable people may disagree on this point, but there is a strong argument that Nevada ought to be able to dismiss without prejudice to *P*'s right to bring Case 2 in Georgia (or any other state that would allow the suit to proceed).[216]

The problem may arise as well in the issue preclusion context.

---

[215] *See* In re Attorney Discipline Matter, 98 F.3d 1082 (8th Cir. 1996). Illinois entered judgment in Case 1 acquitting a lawyer of perjury. Case 2 was in Missouri, and was a discipline proceeding against the same lawyer for suborning perjury. Illinois law would not give issue-preclusive effect to the finding from Case 1, because a criminal case has a higher burden of persuasion than a disciplinary proceeding. Missouri could not be required to give the finding preclusive effect because it cannot be required to give a judgment greater effect than it would have in the rendering state.

[216] 18B Wright & Miller 46-48.

○ In Case 1, *P-1* sues *D* in state court in Virginia. The case goes to trial and the court determines that *D* was negligent and that her negligence proximately caused tortious damage to *P*. In Case 2, *P-2*, who was injured in the same episode but who was not a party in Case 1, sues *D* in state court in California. *P-2* wishes to employ nonmutual offensive issue preclusion to establish *D*'s negligence in Case 2.[217] Virginia does not recognize nonmutual offensive issue preclusion but California does. Assuming the requirements for such preclusion are satisfied, should California apply it?

If the California court in Case 2 applies Virginia law, it will not apply issue preclusion, and the parties will litigate the issues of *D*'s negligence and causation afresh. The California court will bear the burden of that litigation. The justice system runs the risk that this second litigation of the same issue will result in an inconsistent finding, with concomitant erosion in the respect accorded that system.

But should the California court be free to give the Virginia judgment a *greater* preclusive effect than it would have in Virginia?[218] The Supreme Court has never addressed the issue in this context. Other courts have reached different conclusions, but there is considerable support for allowing California to apply nonmutual offensive issue preclusion against *D*.[219] Again, reasonable people may disagree, but allowing California to employ preclusion here can be criticized on at least two bases. First, it is possible that in Case 1, *D* relied upon Virginia's adherence to the mutuality rule to conclude that she would not try to join *P-2* in Case 1. It would seem unfair now to tell *D* that, having lost to *P-1*, she will probably lose to *P-2* by preclusion. Second, the California courts have not previously litigated any issue in the case, so the burden imposed upon them is not as great as it would be if Case 1 had been in California. It seems doubtful that the California interest in avoiding judicial effort outweighs Virginia's interest in its preclusion standards.

§11.5.3 State-to-Federal Preclusion

○ Case 1 is litigated in a state court in Kansas and results in a valid final judgment on the merits. Case 2 is brought in federal court in New York. Does that federal court apply the preclusion law of Kansas, or New York, or is it free to apply federal law of preclusion?

[217] Or Case 2 could have been brought *by D* against *X*, who was not a party to Case 1. *X* would want to assert nonmutual defensive issue preclusion on the finding from Case 1 that *D* was negligent.
[218] 18B Wright & Miller 49-50 nn.81-82.
[219] *Id.* at 49-50 ("There is substantial support for the view that a second court should be able to rest nonmutual preclusion on the judgment of a court that would deny it. The contrary view is better.") (footnotes omitted).

This situation is handled in the same manner as the previous one. Why? Because just as it requires a state court to give "the same full faith and credit" to the state court judgment in Case 1 as that court would, so the full faith and credit statute also requires a *federal* court to do the same.[220] As the Supreme Court explains: "Congress has specifically required all federal courts to give preclusive effect to state court judgments whenever the courts of the State from which the judgments emerged would do so."[221] In our hypothetical, then, the federal court in New York would apply the preclusion law of Kansas to determine whether the judgment in Case 1 is entitled to claim preclusion or issue preclusive effect in Case 2.

The concerns discussed in §11.5.2, about whether the court in Case 2 can give greater or lesser preclusive effect to the judgment from Case 1, also arise here. Thus, for example, if Case 1 is decided in a state that does not embrace nonmutual offensive issue preclusion, the federal court in Case 2, it seems, should not apply such preclusion.[222] But there are two special situations deserving attention.

First is the case of *Baker v. General Motors Corp.*,[223] in which the Supreme Court indicated that the full faith and credit statute does not require the court in Case 2 to apply the same methods of enforcing a judgment that the state court in Case 1 would use. In *Baker*, Case 1 involved an employment claim against General Motors (GM), brought by a GM engineering analyst (Elwell) in a Michigan state court. That court entered an injunction that prohibited Elwell from testifying as an expert witness against the corporation in other cases. Case 2 was brought in a federal court in Missouri by a different plaintiff, claiming that GM was liable on various tort theories for wrongful death. The plaintiff in Case 2 called Elwell as an expert witness. GM insisted that the Michigan injunction was entitled to full faith and credit in Case 2, and that it precluded Elwell from testifying.

The Supreme Court held that the federal court in Case 2 was not required to honor the injunction. It relied on two points. First, full faith and credit does not require the court in Case 2 to "adopt the practices of other states regarding the time, manner, and mechanisms for enforcing judgments."[224] Second, the orders of one court "commanding action or inaction" cannot

---

[220] As discussed in §11.5.1, however, the full faith and credit provision of the Constitution does not cover the state-to-federal preclusion situation.

[221] Allen v. McCurry, 449 U.S. 90, 96 (1980). *See also* San Remo Hotel v. County of San Francisco, 545 U.S. 323, 342-343 (2005) (refusing to recognize exception to §1738).

[222] *See, e.g.,* Kuehn v. Garcia, 608 F.2d 1143, 1146-1147 (8th Cir. 1979) (judgment in Case 1 entered by North Dakota state court; federal court in Case 2 rejects use of nonmutual offensive issue preclusion because North Dakota does not recognize that doctrine).

[223] 522 U.S. 222 (1998).

[224] *Id.* at 235.

be allowed to interfere with litigation before a different judicial system.[225] In other words, a Michigan order will not be allowed to prohibit a federal (or state[226]) court in Missouri to permit someone to testify as an expert witness. The Court in *Baker* emphasized that its holding was narrow and stated that it did not intend to create a "general exception to the full faith and credit command."[227] Surely, said the Court, its holding "does not permit a State court to refuse to honor a sister State judgment based on the forum's choice of law or policy preferences."[228]

Does that mean that GM had no recourse? No. The Court made it clear that GM could have enforced the Michigan order in Michigan (by holding Elwell in contempt if he testified in Missouri) or that GM could have sued Elwell in Missouri to enforce the injunction against him personally.[229] Though *Baker* arose in a state-to-federal scenario, it would apply in the state-to-state situation.

The second special situation can only arise when Case 2 is in a federal court, under exclusive federal jurisdiction. In such a case, the rule that the federal court gives full faith and credit to the judgment in Case 1, including preclusion rules, can create some odd inquiries. For example, in *Marrese v. American Academy of Orthopaedic Surgeons*,[230] a group of physicians sued a professional association in an Illinois state court in Case 1. They claimed that the association excluded the plaintiffs from membership in violation of a variety of state laws. The court entered a valid final judgment on the merits against them. Then the physicians brought Case 2 against the association, this time in federal court and this time alleging violations of federal antitrust law. The antitrust claims are among those rare cases in which federal courts have exclusive federal question jurisdiction, as we discussed at §§4.1 and 4.6.1, so those claims could not have been asserted in state court in Case 1. On the other hand, all claims — federal antitrust and state claims — could have been asserted in Case 1 had Case 1 been filed in federal court.[231]

Should the federal court in Case 2 dismiss under claim preclusion? All the requirements were satisfied, but the question became whether an

---

[225] *Id.* A Michigan order should not "interfere[] with litigation over which [it] had no authority." *Id.* at 239.

[226] Though *Baker* arose in a state-to-federal scenario, it would also apply in the state-to-state situation.

[227] *Id.*

[228] *Id.* at 239.

[229] *Id.* at 239-240. GM apparently erred by seeking to force the Missouri federal court to give full faith and credit to the Michigan order in the context of the litigation there rather than simply suing Elwell directly.

[230] 470 U.S. 373 (1985).

[231] Why? Because the federal antitrust claims would have invoked federal question jurisdiction. The state claims either would have invoked diversity of citizenship jurisdiction or, failing that, supplemental jurisdiction. Why the latter? Because the claims arose from the same transaction or occurrence as the federal question claim. See §4.7.

exception should be recognized because the state court in Case 1 could not have entertained the federal antitrust claims. The federal district court and court of appeals held that Case 2 should be dismissed, and noted that the plaintiffs could have brought federal and state claims together in federal court. The Supreme Court reversed and remanded, instructing the district court to apply the preclusion law of Illinois. In so doing, the Court was instructing the lower court to do something that seems fruitless — to determine what Illinois law would say about whether there should be preclusion of an action that could never have been asserted in Illinois courts. As the district judge recognized on remand, its "task is an exercise in extrapolation because, of course, the Illinois courts never address issues pertaining to exclusively federal lawsuits."[232]

The Supreme Court reached the same conclusion in *Matsushita Electric Industrial Co. v. Epstein*,[233] which involved allegations of fraudulent behavior in a securities transaction. Case 1 was a class action in Delaware state court, and asserted only state law claims. It resulted in a valid final judgment on the merits. Case 2 was a class action in a federal court in California, and asserted federal securities law claims involving the same transaction. The federal securities claims, like the antitrust claims in *Marrese*, invoke exclusive federal question jurisdiction and thus could not have been asserted in Case 1. The Supreme Court held that Delaware law governed the question of whether Case 2 should be dismissed under claim preclusion. The Court was even more forthright than it had been in *Marrese* in recognizing that the inquiry was difficult — the court had to determine whether Delaware would apply claim preclusion as to assertions that simply cannot be made in state court. There is unlikely to be state law on such a question; nonetheless, full faith and credit commands the court in Case 2 to undertake the inquiry. The Court also rejected the notion that the grant of exclusive federal jurisdiction created an exception to the full faith and credit statute and ultimately concluded that the federal action had to be dismissed under the claim preclusive effect of the Delaware judgment.

Marrese and *Matsushita Electric* indicate that the Supreme Court sees the full faith and credit statute as a strict command to give the judgment from Case 1 truly "the same" full faith and credit it would receive in the state courts that decided Case 1.[234] The cases may also constitute persuasive evidence that the Supreme Court does not believe that the court in

[232] Marrese v. American Academy of Orthopaedic Surgeons, 628 F. Supp. 918, 919 (N.D. Ill. 1986). The district court refused to apply claim preclusion, and allowed Case 2 to proceed.
[233] 516 U.S. 367 (1996).
[234] These cases also constitute rejection of the position taken in §26(1)(c) of the Restatement (Second) of Judgments, which provides that a state court judgment in Case 1 should have claim preclusive effect in Case 2, when Case 2 is brought in federal court and invokes exclusive federal jurisdiction.

Case 2 can give a lesser preclusive effect than the courts deciding Case 1, even when exclusive federal jurisdiction is at stake. The interest in preserving a federal forum for those with claims invoking exclusive federal jurisdiction might counsel rejection of claim preclusion in these situations, but the Court permitted the state judgments to preclude the federal claim.[235]

§11.5.4 Federal-to-State Preclusion

o Case 1 is litigated in federal court in Indiana, and that court enters a valid final judgment on the merits. Case 2 is filed in state court in Florida. In determining the preclusive effect of the judgment in Case 1, does the Florida court apply federal law, Indiana law, or Florida law?

The general answer is clear: The Florida court will apply federal preclusion law, which is federal common law.[236] Some courts say that the result is dictated by full faith and credit.[237] In fact, however, neither the constitutional nor statutory provisions for full faith and credit apply when the judgment in Case 1 is entered by a federal court.[238] So what is the source of the rule that compels the court in Case 2 to apply federal preclusion law? Some have argued that the notion of "case or controversy" in Article III of the Constitution carries with it the authority to define the scope of the judgments entered in federal courts. In addition, the Supremacy Clause of the Constitution operates to make the federal judgments binding.[239]

Whatever the precise source of the compulsion to apply federal preclusion law, the conclusion must be correct. After all, if both state and federal courts must apply the preclusion law of a state court that entered judgment in Case 1, how can principles of federalism demand less when a

---

[235] Again, maybe the result is good from an efficiency viewpoint. The plaintiffs could have had all claims — federal and state — determined in a single case had Case 1 been in federal court. It would have invoked federal question jurisdiction for the federal claims and diversity of citizenship or supplemental jurisdiction for the state claims. Efficient joinder of all claims in one case could have been achieved — but only in federal court. When plaintiffs decided to go to state court first, they ran the risk of losing a federal forum for their federal claims.

[236] Though *Erie* held that there was no *general* federal common law, it left the federal courts able to fashion common law in discrete areas; preclusion is one. See §10.9.

[237] *See, e.g.,* Levy v. Cohen, 561 P.2d 252, 257 (Cal. 1977).

[238] The language of each provision speaks only of giving full faith and credit to *state court* judgments. The Supreme Court recognized this fact expressly in *Semtek Intl., Inc. v. Lockheed Martin Corp.*, 531 U.S. 497, 506 (2001) ("Neither the Full Faith and Credit Clause . . . nor the full faith and credit statute . . . addresses the question. By their terms they govern the effects to be given only to state-court judgments.").

[239] 18B Wright & Miller 51-55.

federal court enters the judgment in Case 1? The idea seems so obvious "that the rule requiring state courts to honor the res judicata effects of federal court judgments has been stated in an unbroken line of cases that do not offer any clear judicial thought or explanation."[240]

Does it matter, however, whether the federal court in Case 1 determined questions of federal law or questions of state law? The easier case for concluding that federal preclusion law governs is when Case 1 involved questions of federal law. In such a case, there is no arguable state interest in determining the scope of preclusion to be accorded the judgment. If Case 1 involved litigation of state law claims, however (e.g., under diversity of citizenship or supplemental jurisdiction), do different considerations govern? Though some commentators argued that state law ought to govern the question of preclusion in such a case, most courts disagreed. The Second Circuit once said:

> One of the strongest policies a court can have is that of determining the scope of its own judgments.... It would be destructive of the basic principles of the Federal Rules of Civil Procedure to say that the effect of a judgment of a federal court was governed by the law of the state where court sits because the source of federal jurisdiction is diversity.[241]

The Supreme Court spoke to the issue in *Semtek International, Inc. v. Lockheed Martin Corp.*[242] In *Semtek*, the plaintiff filed Case 1 in a California state court and the defendant removed to federal court on the basis of diversity of citizenship jurisdiction. The federal court dismissed the case as barred under California's two-year statute of limitations. The plaintiff filed Case 2, on the same claim, in state court in Maryland, a state whose longer statute of limitations (three years) would not bar the claim.[243]

The Supreme Court held unanimously that the Maryland court in Case 2 must apply federal common law to determine whether Case 2 ought to be dismissed under claim preclusion.[244] Thus, federal law governs to determine the preclusive effect of a judgment entered by a federal court but

---

[240] 18B Wright & Miller 52.

[241] Kern v. Hettinger, 303 F.2d 333, 340 (2d Cir. 1962). The Restatement (Second) of Judgments §87 took the same position. The leading academic proponent of the view was the late Professor Ronan Degnan, *Federalized Res Judicata*, 85 Yale L.J. 741 (1976).

[242] 531 U.S. 497 (2001). We discussed another aspect of *Semtek*, dealing with whether a judgment is "on the merits," in §11.2.2.

[243] The defendant removed that case to federal court in Maryland, which remanded to the state court. Though the requirements of diversity of citizenship jurisdiction were satisfied, the case could not be removed because the defendant was a citizen of the forum. (We saw this limitation on removal jurisdiction at §4.8.) So Case 2 proceeded in state court in Maryland.

[244] The Court said that no "federal textual provision" — either in the Constitution or any statute — "addresses the claim-preclusive effect of a judgment in a federal diversity action." *Semtek*, 531 U.S. at 507. The statement is interesting in view of the efforts of commentators

based upon state law. The Court did something very interesting, however, in determining the *content* of federal common law on this point. It held that federal common law would usually adopt the preclusion law of the *state* in which the federal court sat in Case 1.

Indeed, the facts of *Semtek* dictated such adoption of California law as federal law, for several reasons. First, because Case 1 was dismissed on the basis of the California statute of limitations, it makes considerable sense to look to California law to determine the effect of a dismissal on such grounds. Second, this conclusion is especially sound in a case, such as *Semtek*, in which there is no need for a uniform federal rule. Third, the Court invoked *Erie* doctrine principles in finding that use of the state rule would reduce the incentive for litigants to shop for a federal forum, in hopes of gaining access to different preclusion rules.[245] Thus, in the final analysis, the Maryland court in Case 2 should dismiss under claim preclusion only if California law would dictate that result.

Though on the facts of *Semtek* the Court found it appropriate to adopt state law as the content for the federal common law of preclusion, the Court left open the possibility that federal law would ignore state law. According to the Court, it could do so when there is a federal interest justifying the crafting of a federal rule. As an example, the Court noted that a willful violation of the discovery provisions of the Federal Rules might properly result in preclusion under federal law, regardless of state law.[246] Beyond that example, the Court gave little guidance as to when federal law would ignore state law. Thus, the Court ensured maximum flexibility; the court in Case 2 can ignore state law when it concludes that there is a good reason to do so.

§11.5.5 Federal-to-Federal Preclusion

There is every reason to conclude that preclusion questions in this scenario are handled the same as those in the federal-to-state situation discussed in the preceding subsection. Here, as there, neither the constitutional nor statutory provision for full faith and credit applies; those, as we have seen, apply only when Case 1 is decided in a state court. Here, as there, the general answer is that federal law will govern the preclusive effect of the judgment entered in Case 1. And here, as there, it is not entirely clear whether a particular constitutional provision — such as Article III or the Supremacy Clause — dictates this result.

---

to root the rule that federal law governs to Article III and the Supremacy Clause of the Constitution. See note 238 and accompanying text.

[245] *Semtek*, 531 U.S. at 508-509.
[246] *Id.* at 509.

No one has ever doubted that federal common law governs the preclu-sive effect if Case 1 were decided in federal court and involved a decision based upon federal law.[247] This result is correct regardless of whether the dispute in Case 2 is governed by federal or state law.[248] But what if Case 1 were decided on the basis of state law (as, for example, under diversity of citizenship or supplemental jurisdiction)? Though the Supreme Court decision in *Semtek*, discussed in the preceding subsection, technically involved the federal-to-state scenario, its approach should be followed here. Thus, the federal court in Case 2 would apply federal common law to determine the preclusive effect of the judgment from Case 1. Federal common law, however, will often incorporate state law of the state in which the federal court in Case 1 sat. The court in Case 2 has consider-able flexibility in determining the content of the governing federal common law.

---

[247] *See, e.g.*, Gunter v. Atlantic Coast Line R.R., 200 U.S. 273, 284-289 (1906).
[248] *See, e.g.*, Seven Elves, Inc. v. Eskenazi, 704 F.2d 241, 243-244 n.2 (5th Cir. 1983).

Chapter 12

Defining the Scope of Litigation: Joinder Rules and Subject Matter Jurisdiction

§12.1   Defining the Issue

In this chapter we define the scope of a civil action. Specifically, we are concerned with how many parties can be joined and how many claims they can assert in a single case. Each jurisdiction addresses these topics through its rules on "joinder." Historically, joinder rules were quite restrictive. At common law, for example, the writ system, which we discussed in §7.2, permitted the plaintiff to assert only a single, narrowly defined claim. The concept of a case was, correspondingly, quite narrow. Equity practice was broader, and expressed the goal of resolving an entire overall dispute, rather than narrow pieces. Modern joinder rules build largely on the equity practice, and expand the concept of a single civil action further. The Federal Rules ushered in the modern era of joinder. Of course, the Federal Rules apply to litigation in federal court. While each state is free to prescribe its own joinder provisions, the Federal Rules have been quite influential in this area. Many states have adopted the Federal Rules on joinder.

The Federal Rules approach focuses mainly on the "transaction or occurrence" giving rise to alleged liability. Many (though not all) joinder rules permit joinder of parties and claims along transactional lines. The drafters' goal was to allow resolution of transactionally related disputes in a single case, rather than foster piecemeal litigation arising from a single real-world event. This trend toward "packaging" transactionally related parties and claims into a single case is driven at least in part by a desire to promote efficiency and consistency. One case burdens the justice system less than multiple cases. It also avoids the possibility of inconsistent outcomes, which can erode public confidence in the justice system. Of course, the emphasis on packaging, and avoiding duplicative litigation, is heightened in an era of crowded dockets and litigation delay.[1]

We saw a similar focus on the transactional test in discussing claim preclusion in §11.2.3. There, the modern approach defines one's claim as all rights to relief arising from a transaction or occurrence (or series of related transactions or occurrences). That definition forces claimants to package all transactionally related assertions into a single case (or risk claim preclusion). Not surprisingly, we saw similar policy justifications concerning claim preclusion — the coercive effect of the transactional test for claim preclusion fostered efficiency and consistency, just as the Federal Rules joinder provisions do. Most of the joinder provisions are *permissive*, however, which means that litigants may take advantage of their packaging potential, but are not required to do so. The Rules thus embody a policy of litigant autonomy — that is, they tend to defer to the plaintiff's structuring of the case. Throughout our discussion of joinder, appreciate the tension between the urge to package the litigation efficiently and this sense that the plaintiff ought to be entitled to structure the case as she sees fit. There is significant debate over whether litigant autonomy should not be sacrificed, at least to a degree, in the interest of packaging disputes more comprehensively.[2]

---

[1] The classic discussion of the benefits of packaging is John McCoid, *A Single Package for Multiparty Disputes*, 27 Stan. L. Rev. 707 (1976).

[2] Some commentators conclude that litigant autonomy should give way to greater efficiency. *See, e.g.*, Richard D. Freer, *Avoiding Duplicative Litigation: Rethinking Plaintiff Autonomy and the Court's Role in Defining the Litigative Unit*, 50 U. Pitt. L. Rev. 809, 833 (1989) ("The plaintiff is entitled to due process, to a fair and convenient forum, but has no right to exclusive possession of center stage regardless of the consequences on scarce judicial resources"); and Martin H. Redish, *Intersystemic Redundancy and Federal Court Power: Proposing a Zero Tolerance Solution to the Duplicative Litigation Problem*, 75 Notre Dame L. Rev. 1347 (2000) (the traditional preference given to plaintiff's choice of forum does not justify the burdens and waste of duplicative litigation). On the other hand, others assert the need for plaintiffs, particularly in tort cases, to control the structure of their cases. *See, e.g.*, Roger Transgrud, *Joinder Alternatives in Mass Tort Litigation*, 70 Cornell L. Rev. 779, 848 (1985) (aggregation of litigation "adversely affects the traditional right of tort litigants to control the individual prosecution of their liability claims and unpredictably skews the fairness of the trial process").

In this chapter, then, we survey the joinder provisions of the Federal Rules. But mastery of the various joinder rules is not enough. The joinder rules provide the *procedural* tools for joining parties and asserting claims in a single case. They do not (in fact, under Federal Rule 82, they *cannot*[3]) affect the requirements for personal jurisdiction, subject matter jurisdiction, or venue. Thus, *every time* a joinder provision is used in federal court, it raises the need to assess jurisdiction and venue. We do not spend much time on personal jurisdiction in this chapter, beyond stating that when a party is joined in a defensive capacity, the court must have personal jurisdiction over her. (If a new party is joined in an offensive capacity (to assert a claim), she has submitted herself to the personal jurisdiction of the court and waives any objection on this score.) Likewise, we do not have a lot to say about venue in this chapter, except to note when venue might be affected by joinder.[4]

On the other hand, we have a great deal to say about subject matter jurisdiction. Remember, as we saw in §4.1, *every claim joined in federal court must be supported by federal subject matter jurisdiction*. Thus (assuming, as we do, that the case is in federal court), for every claim asserted, we must assess whether the claim invokes diversity of citizenship, alienage, or federal question jurisdiction. In the context of each joinder rule, then, we have occasion to review much of what we saw in Chapter 4 concerning subject matter jurisdiction. If a given claim does invoke an "independent basis" of subject matter jurisdiction — meaning it invokes diversity of citizenship, alienage, or federal question jurisdiction — obviously, it can be asserted in the pending case.

But what happens if we have a claim — properly asserted in the pending case under the joinder rules — that does not invoke diversity of citizenship, alienage, or federal question jurisdiction? It might still be asserted in federal court through *supplemental jurisdiction*. As discussed in §4.7, supplemental jurisdiction permits a federal court to hear a claim over which it does not have one of the three major independent bases of subject matter jurisdiction. It is available, however, only if the claim meets the requirements of the supplemental jurisdiction statute, 28 U.S.C. §1367. Because joinder can so easily raise questions of supplemental jurisdiction, you should be familiar with the materials in §4.7, particularly that subsection entitled "Applying the Supplemental Jurisdiction Statute: Jurisdictional Aspects."

---

[3] Rule 82 provides that the Federal Rules "do not extend or limit the jurisdiction of the district courts or the venue in those courts."

[4] If venue was laid in a district in which significant events occurred, under §1391(a)(2) and (b)(2), venue will probably be proper in that district for all claims related transactionally to those events. Similarly, if venue was laid in a district where defendants reside, under §1391(a)(1) and (b)(1), venue will probably be proper in that district for all claims against those defendants.

Remember, however, that supplemental jurisdiction is only relevant for claims over which there is *no* diversity of citizenship, alienage, or federal question jurisdiction. It is wise to be quite mechanical in approaching issues of joinder and subject matter jurisdiction. Whether a claim can be asserted (or a party joined) requires us to address three steps:

- First, is there a joinder provision in the Federal Rules that allows assertion of this claim (or joinder of this party)?
- Second, if so, does this claim invoke diversity of citizenship, alienage, or federal question jurisdiction? If so, it may be asserted in the pending case.
- If not, the third issue is whether the claim can nonetheless be asserted in federal court because it invokes supplemental jurisdiction. Again, the discussion in this chapter assumes that you understand the basic operation of the supplemental jurisdiction statute, particularly §1367(a) and (b).

§12.2 Real Party in Interest, Capacity, and Related Issues

Our legal system does not permit everyone who happens to be displeased about something to sue. Various legal doctrines address the question of who may sue. One limitation on the right to assert a claim is the doctrine of *standing*. Though detailed discussion of standing is beyond the scope of our course,[5] this doctrine requires that the claimant have suffered some "injury in fact" because of the defendant's behavior.[6] Standing often becomes an important consideration in public interest litigation, for example, when a citizen seeks to challenge governmental action. Suppose, for instance, that a group interested in environmental issues seeks to stop the federal government from building a dam or military base that might endanger some species of wildlife. By limiting the right to sue to those who are actually harmed by the government action, standing minimizes friction between the judicial branch and other branches of the government.

---

[5] Standing and other topics of "justiciability," such as mootness, ripeness, and the political question doctrine, are considered in detail in courses on Constitutional Law and Federal Courts.

[6] In addition to this requirement, there must also be a causal connection between that injury and the defendant's action, and it must be likely that a favorable judicial decision will remedy the harm suffered by the plaintiff. Lujan v. Defenders of Wildlife, 504 U.S. 555, 560-561 (1992).

Real Parties in Interest

More central to our focus is a concept embodied in Federal Rule 17(a)(1): "An action must be prosecuted in the name of the real party in interest." The real party in interest (RPI) is the person or entity "possessing the right or interest to be enforced through the litigation."[7] It serves a function similar to that served by standing — to ensure that the one who has the legal right being vindicated is the named claimant. While standing tends to be a problem in public interest litigation, the RPI question is not so limited.

Sometimes the RPI is not one who would receive the benefit if the litigation were successful. As the second sentence of Rule 17(a)(1) makes clear, a fiduciary may be the RPI, suing on behalf of others. For example, a trustee suing on behalf of trust beneficiaries is the RPI. Her success (or failure) will bind the beneficiaries for whom she sues. She is the RPI even though any benefit from a successful judgment would go to the beneficiaries.

Assignment of claims can create RPI problems. (You may be familiar with the concept of assignment from your course on Contracts.)

- Suppose *A* and *Z* are parties to a contract, and that *A* has a right to be paid by *Z* under the contract (because, for example, he delivered the widgets as required by the contract). *A* may be able to assign that right to be paid to *P*.[8] (Why would she want to do this? Maybe *A* owes money to *P* and does not have enough cash to pay, so assigning the right to this payment may be a way to pay *P*.) Suppose she does so. (*A* is the assignor and *Z* is the assignee.) Now *P* is the holder of the right to receive payment from *Z*. *P* is the RPI, and it is *P* who would bring suit if *Z* refused to pay.[9]

Unlike assignment, "subrogation" is one of those words one rarely hears before entering law school. Subrogation is simply an assignment, but it is effected by operation of law. It usually comes up in insurance cases.

- Suppose *P* has automobile insurance with Insco Corp. *P*'s car is damaged in the amount of $5,000 by the negligence of *D*. Because of the insurance, Insco Corp. will pay *P* the $5,000 (or it might just pay the repair shop

---

[7] 4 Moore's Federal Practice 17-10 to 17-11.

[8] We addressed assignment of claims at §4.5.4. The concern there was that someone might assign a claim to create diversity of citizenship jurisdiction, in violation of 28 U.S.C. §1359.

[9] Life was tougher in the old days. Common law refused to recognize assignments such as this. So after *A* assigned her claim to *P*, the common law would insist that *A* bring the suit (because the assignment would not be recognized). This rule makes no sense, because *A* no longer has any interest in the matter and will be unlikely to sue. Equity avoided the harshness of the common law on this score (as in others, as we discussed at §1.2.3) by recognizing the assignment and adopting the common-sense view that *P* was now the RPI. Rule 17(a) handles the situation as equity did.

directly, on behalf of *P*). Insco Corp. is now said to be "subrogated" to *P*'s right to sue *D*. (*P* is the subrogor and Insco Corp. is the subrogee.) All this means is that *P*'s right to sue *D* for damage to her car has now been assigned — automatically — to Insco Corp. This result makes sense, because *P* has been made whole; her car is fixed and she is out of pocket nothing. Insco Corp., on the other hand, is out of pocket $5,000 and now has the right to vindicate *P*'s claim against *D*, so the ultimate loss ends up on *D*. After the subrogation, Insco Corp. is the RPI of the claim. It works just like assignment.

So far we have assumed that the assignment or subrogation was total — that the entire claim was transferred to the assignee or subrogee. But assignment and subrogation can be partial. For example, *A* might assign to *P* a portion of the right to receive payment under the contract with *Z*. Let's say that *A* assigns to *P* the right to receive 75 percent of the payment owed by *Z*. Who's the RPI? They both are. *A* is an RPI to the tune of 25 percent of the contract amount; *P* is an RPI to the tune of 75 percent of the contract amount. Subrogation often will be partial because the insurance policy has a "deductible." With a deductible, the insured person agrees to pay a set amount (the deductible amount) of any covered damage to her property. In the example above, in which *P* had automobile insurance with Insco Corp., it is likely that the policy had a deductible — say, of $500. This means that *P* agrees that she will pay $500 of damage done to her property, and Insco Corp. will pay the rest.[10] In that case, who's the RPI? As with the partial assignment, they both are. *P* is an RPI to the tune of $500 and Insco Corp. is an RPI to the tune of $4,500.

Rule 17(a)(3) makes it clear that the court should not dismiss a case that is brought by someone other than the RPI until it has provided a "reasonable time" for the plaintiff to fix (courts often say "cure") the defect (usually by substituting the RPI for the person who brought suit[11]). Thus, if someone who is not an RPI asserts a claim (a fact that can be noted by the defendant or by the court on its own motion), the court may not grant dismissal immediately. If the matter is cured within a reasonable time, Rule 17(a)(3) provides that the RPI is treated as though she had been joined

[10] Deductibles can vary. Obviously, the higher the deductible, the lower the cost of the insurance (because the insured has agreed to absorb more of the loss personally). Conversely, the lower the deductible, the more expensive the insurance. When you buy such insurance, you have the option of choosing a particular deductible.

[11] Such substitution is effected by Rule 17(a)(3) and is distinguished from substitution under Federal Rule 25. Substitution of an RPI is mandated by the fact that the original claimant is not a proper RPI. In cases under Rule 25, on the other hand, the original parties were proper but substitution is required because of a change in capacity (e.g., a litigant died, and her executor must be substituted for her) or because of a transfer of interest during the litigation.

from the outset of the case. On the other hand, if the RPI defect is not cured within a reasonable time, the court may dismiss on that ground.[12]

Although a case brought by someone other than an RPI cannot be dismissed immediately on that basis, always be alert to the possibility that substitution of the RPI may make it impossible to invoke federal subject matter jurisdiction.

- *A* and *Z* are parties to a contract, under which *A* has a right to be paid $100,000 by *Z*. *A* assigns her right to receive that payment to *P*. *A* is a citizen of Florida. *P* and *Z* are citizens of Kentucky. *A* sues *Z* in federal court, seeking recovery of the $100,000 under the contract. The case appears to invoke diversity of citizenship jurisdiction, because it is brought by a citizen of Florida against a citizen of Kentucky, and the amount in controversy exceeds $75,000. The problem, of course, is that after the assignment, *A* is not an RPI. *Z* cannot seek immediate dismissal on that basis. But notice what happens when the RPI (*P*) is substituted for *A*. At that point, there is no diversity of citizenship jurisdiction, because the case is now by a citizen of Kentucky against a citizen of Kentucky. So *Z* will make a motion to substitute *P* as the RPI and will also move to dismiss for lack of subject matter jurisdiction. She should make the motions simultaneously.

- Take the same fact pattern and assume that the assignment from *A* to *P* was not total. Rather, it was an assignment to *P* of 25 percent of the value of the contract right. As we saw above, that means that *A* is an RPI in the amount of $75,000 and *P* is an RPI in the amount of $25,000. Can either of them sue *Z* under diversity of citizenship jurisdiction? No. Let's see why.

  - As we just saw, *P* cannot sue *Z* under diversity of citizenship jurisdiction because they are co-citizens (Kentucky). Not only that, but *P*'s claim is for only $25,000, so it does not meet the amount in controversy requirement.

  - What about *A*? She (a citizen of Florida) is of diverse citizenship from *Z* (a citizen of Kentucky). But she cannot invoke diversity of citizenship jurisdiction because her claim does not meet the amount in controversy. Why not? Because it is for exactly $75,000. For a diversity case, the amount must *exceed* $75,000. This claim is a penny short. See §4.5.3.

  - Moreover, *A* and *Z* cannot aggregate their claims for jurisdictional purposes. They are not joint claims and aggregation is permitted only

---

[12] *See, e.g.*, Weissman v. Weener, 12 F.3d 84, 86 (7th Cir. 1993) (case dismissed after plaintiff failed to remedy RPI defect). At some point, it seems that the RPI rule adds little of value. After all, if someone other than the RPI sues, the substantive law should prevent her from recovering. For this and other reasons, including the "loan receipt" problem discussed below in this subsection, some have advocated that Rule 17(a) be repealed. Essentially, critics argue, the rule is more trouble than it is worth. The most famous plea for abolition came from Thomas Atkinson (who was a leading scholar of wills and trusts), *The Real Party in Interest Rule: A Plea for Its Abolition*, 32 N.Y.U. L. Rev. 926 (1957).

when there is one plaintiff suing one defendant. Again, see §4.5.3. Finally, supplemental jurisdiction is of no help. It applies only when there is a claim that has invoked federal subject matter jurisdiction independently. Here, neither A nor P's claim has. See §4.7.

The same issues can arise, of course, in the subrogation context. Insurance companies occasionally try to avoid the operation of subrogation through use of a "loan receipt." Here's how it works.

- P, a citizen of New Hampshire, has homeowner's insurance with Insco Corp., a citizen of Delaware and of California. P's house is damaged by the negligence of D, a citizen of Vermont, to the tune of \$100,000. P's policy with Insco Corp. has a \$1,000 deductible. If Insco Corp. pays P \$99,000 under the policy, it is subrogated to her right to sue D. Insco Corp. is an RPI in the amount of \$99,000 and could invoke diversity of citizenship jurisdiction against D. P is an RPI in the amount of only \$1,000 and thus cannot invoke diversity jurisdiction because her claim does not meet the amount in controversy requirement.

- Often, however, an insurance company would prefer not to sue in its own name. Why? It fears jury prejudice, because many jurors have had problems with their insurance carriers, and because insurance companies are seen as deep pockets that can get along without beating up on little people. So some insurance companies may take the position that the \$99,000 it gave to P was not payment under the policy, but merely a "loan." Thus, they argue, they are not subrogated to P's right to sue. P remains the RPI for all \$100,000 and the suit should be brought by P. (And on our facts here, P could invoke diversity of citizenship jurisdiction if her claim were for \$100,000.) They add a stipulation to the "loan," of course — that P must repay the loan if P wins the litigation. Who is the RPI of \$99,000 in such a "loan receipt" situation? Courts have been inconsistent. Some hold (properly, it seems) that the insurance company is the RPI for the \$99,000; other courts see the insured as the RPI for the full policy amount.[13]

Capacity to Sue and Be Sued

Federal Rule 17(b) addresses capacity to sue or be sued, which is a broader concept than RPI. While RPI determines whether one holds the legal right to bring a claim in a particular case, capacity is aimed at whether one has the general ability to function as a litigant at all. Some persons are under a "legal disability," which means that they cannot function legally. For example, minors and persons adjudged insane (or "under a disability") usually lack the legal power or authority to litigate or undertake other legal acts, such as entering a binding contract. Rule 17(b) seeks

---

[13] *See* June Entman, *More Reasons for Abolishing Federal Rule of Civil Procedure 17(a): The Problem of the Proper Plaintiff and Insurance Subrogation*, 68 N.C. L. Rev. 893 (1990).

to ensure that the interests of such persons are adequately represented in litigation. Thus, litigation by or against such a person should be brought by or against a representative. A person under a disability may have someone who is responsible for her in a day-to-day sense — perhaps a general guardian, conservator, or committee. That person may act as the disabled person's representative in litigation. Or a court may appoint a "guardian ad litem," which means guardian for the purposes of this litigation, who will represent the person in the particular suit.

Under Rule 17(b)(1), the federal court assesses a human's capacity to sue or be sued by looking to the law of her domicile. Rule 17(b) also addresses the capacity of a business to litigate in its own behalf. For example, under Rule 17(b)(2), the capacity of a *corporation* is determined by the law of the state where the corporation was formed. Today, it is universal in corporation law that corporations have the power to sue and be sued. As we discussed in §4.5.3, concerning diversity of citizenship jurisdiction, however, not all business is conducted by corporations. *Non-incorporated businesses*, such as partnerships and limited liability companies (LLCs), are also addressed by Rule 17(b)(3), which gives the general rule that the capacity of such associations is determined by the law of the state in which the federal court sits. Though a few states still may not permit a partnership to sue or be sued in its common (partnership) name, most states do.[14] Regardless of state law on this point, Rule 17(b)(3)(A) permits a partnership or LLC to sue in its own name in federal court if it is asserting a federal question claim.

§12.3   Claim Joinder by a Claimant (Rule 18(a))

Procedural and Policy Issues

Federal Rule 18(a) governs the question of what claims[15] the plaintiff can assert in a single case. The rule essentially has no requirements. It

---

[14] The law has always regarded the corporation as an entity, separate from those who own and run it. Historically, however, the law saw a partnership as an aggregate of its members, rather than as a separate entity. Under this "aggregate" view, the common law (and some states today) require suit by or against every member of the partnership, rather than in the partnership's name. Allowing it to sue or be sued in its partnership name would be to treat it as an entity, contrary to the historical view. The aggregate view is waning, and, increasingly, the law considers partnerships to be entities for various purposes. LLCs, in contrast, are universally allowed to sue and to be sued.

[15] The word "claims," as used in Rule 18(a), is not necessarily synonymous with the definition of "claims" for claim preclusion purposes. In discussing the latter, we noted that this word might mean different things in different contexts. See §11.2.3. In Rule 18(a), the word refers to assertions or bases of liability. Multiple assertions of liability might, however, comprise a single claim for claim preclusion purposes.

allows the assertion of all claims the plaintiff may have against the defendant. The claims do not have to be related in any way. They can be completely unrelated transactionally, legally, and in terms of the remedy sought. They can be independent or alternate claims; they can be legal or equitable. There are simply no procedural restrictions. The rule can be characterized as saying "anything goes" or it is "open season" on the defendant. While the provision is fairly simple, it raises several points.

First, why should the Federal Rules countenance joinder of unrelated claims? Though many states have adopted the Federal Rules on joinder, some states have rejected the "open season" approach of Rule 18(a) and limit joinder to claims that arise from the same transaction or occurrence.[16] Such a limitation makes sense when the case goes to trial, because it means that the jury may focus only on transactionally related issues. The Federal Rule, on the other hand, can result in the assertion of disparate and unrelated claims, which runs the risk of confusing the jury. The drafters of the Federal Rules understood this possibility, and addressed it by permitting the trial judge to order separate trials, among other reasons, to avoid such confusion.[17] As a matter of policy, then, the Federal Rules choose to permit the plaintiff to put the entire dispute between the parties into a single case. It may be that such open claim joinder allows the parties to settle all their overall disputes by allowing packaging of all claims in a single proceeding. If the matter goes to trial, the trial judge is armed with tools to keep things manageable for the trier of fact.

Second, the rule provides that the plaintiff "may" join as many claims as she has against the defendant. The word "may" makes this rule "permissive," which means it does not *require* the plaintiff to assert all claims in a single case.[18] The plaintiff thus may choose how many assertions to include in a single case. Don't forget, however, that another doctrine — claim preclusion — might affect the plaintiff's choices.

○ *P* and *D*, each driving her own car, collide; each is injured and each car is damaged. *P* sues *D* and asserts only a claim for personal injuries from the collision; she does not seek recovery for property damage. There is nothing wrong with this course of action under Rule 18(a), because it is permissive and does not require her to pack all claims into a single case. Suppose, however, that this case results in a valid final judgment on the merits and that *P* files a second case against *D*, to recover for property damage from the crash. In a jurisdiction adopting a transactional definition of claim, this second case will be dismissed under claim preclusion. See §11.2.3. As a consequence, although Rule 18(a) is permissive, the

---

[16] *See, e.g.*, Va. Code Ann. §8.01-272 ("[A] party may plead as many matters, whether of law or fact, as he shall think necessary. A party may join a claim in tort with one in contract provided that all claims so joined arise out of the same transaction or occurrence. . . .").

[17] *See* Fed. R. Civ. P. 20(b) and 42(b), discussed at §12.4.

[18] "May" is to be contrasted with "must," which, of course, states a command. See §12.5.1.

majority view on claim preclusion operates to force the plaintiff to join all transactionally related assertions in a single case.

Third, though we speak in this section of "claim joinder by the plaintiff," Rule 18(a) does not apply only to plaintiffs. Instead, it permits any party asserting a claim for relief to join "as many claims as it has against an opposing party." This language recognizes (as we did in discussing claim preclusion in §11.2.1) that plaintiffs are not the only claimants. Defendants can become plaintiffs by asserting counterclaims, crossclaims, or third-party claims. Note, however, that Rule 18(a) does not apply to them *until* they become claimants by asserting one of the listed claims.

- We see in §12.5.2 that a crossclaim is asserted against a co-party, and must arise from the same transaction or occurrence as the underlying dispute. Suppose *P* sues two defendants, *D-1* and *D-2*, concerning a contract dispute. Suppose further that *D-1* has a claim against *D-2* that is completely unrelated to that contract dispute. *D-1 cannot* use Rule 18(a) to assert that unrelated claim *until* she has asserted a crossclaim against *D-1*. Why? Look again at the Rule: The "you-can-assert-any-claim-you-want" part of the Rule only applies to a party who is "asserting a claim" (such as a crossclaim).
- So if *D-1* has a claim against *D-2* that arises from the underlying contract dispute, she may assert it as a crossclaim and then use Rule 18(a) to join the unrelated claim. Without the crossclaim, however, *D-1* cannot assert the unrelated claim in the pending case.

Subject Matter Jurisdiction

Rule 18(a), like other joinder provisions of the Federal Rules, simply creates a procedure for asserting a claim. Even if a party satisfies this Rule, the claim can be asserted in federal court *only* if it invokes federal subject matter jurisdiction.

- *P*, a citizen of California, sues *D*, a citizen of Nevada, and uses Rule 18(a) to join two claims: (1) that *D* had violated federal employment law in firing *P* and (2) that *D* had breached an unrelated contract between the two, causing damage to *P* of $100,000. Joinder of the claims is procedurally proper under Rule 18(a). Is there subject matter jurisdiction over the claims? Yes. Claim (1) invokes federal question jurisdiction because it arises under federal employment law. Claim (2) invokes diversity of citizenship jurisdiction because it is asserted by a citizen of California against a citizen of Nevada and the amount in controversy exceeds $75,000.
- *P*, a citizen of Massachusetts, sues *D*, a citizen of Arizona, and uses Rule 18(a) to join two state law claims: (1) that *D* breached a contract between the two, causing damage of $45,000 to *P*; and (2) that *D* committed an unrelated tort, causing damage of $50,000 to *P*. Joinder of the claims is

procedurally proper under Rule 18(a). Is there subject matter jurisdiction over the claims? Yes. The case invokes diversity of citizenship jurisdiction. It is brought by a citizen of Massachusetts against a citizen of Arizona, and the amount in controversy exceeds $75,000. Why? The concept of *aggregation* permits a single plaintiff to add the value of all claims that she asserts against a single defendant. So here the amount in controversy is $95,000. (We discussed aggregation at §4.5.3.)

  ○ *P*, a citizen of Tennessee, sues *D*, a citizen of Tennessee, and uses Rule 18(a) to join two claims: (1) that *D* violated federal labor laws in a labor dispute and (2) that *D* violated state law in the same labor dispute. Joinder of the claims is procedurally proper under Rule 18(a). Is there subject matter jurisdiction over the claims? Yes. Claim (1) invokes federal question jurisdiction, because it arises under federal labor laws. Claim (2) does not invoke federal question jurisdiction (because it arises under state, not federal, law). Claim (2) also does not invoke diversity of citizenship jurisdiction, because the plaintiff and defendant are co-citizens. But Claim (2) does invoke supplemental jurisdiction. Why?

  ○ Section 1367(a) grants supplemental jurisdiction over claims that are part of the same "case or controversy" as a claim that properly invoked federal subject matter jurisdiction. As explicated by the Supreme Court, this requirement is satisfied if the claims share a "common nucleus of operative fact." As we discussed in §4.7, this test is broader than transaction or occurrence. Here, the two claims asserted by *P* do arise from the same factual nexus. Section 1367(b), which removes supplemental jurisdiction over certain claims, applies only in cases that invoked diversity of citizenship jurisdiction. This case invoked federal question jurisdiction, so §1367(b) does not apply. (If any of this material is fuzzy, review §4.7; this fact pattern is the same as the famous *Gibbs* case, which is codified in §1367(a).)

§12.4 Permissive Party Joinder (Rule 20(a))

Procedural and Policy Issues

Many cases involve a single plaintiff suing a single defendant. On the other hand, many cases involve multiple parties — either co-plaintiffs or co-defendants (or both). Here, we address the question of "proper parties" to a civil case, meaning those who *may* be joined in a single case. The issue is governed in federal court by Federal Rule 20(a). This Rule is available to the plaintiff when she is structuring the case. She decides whether to have multiple parties either on the plaintiff or defendant side and, if so, who those parties will be. As we see in this section, various considerations, including litigation strategy and jurisdictional limitations, may affect her choice. And as we see in §12.6, though the judicial system allows the plaintiff the first choice in determining who the parties will be, other litigants, third parties, and the court itself may override the plaintiff's party structure, at least in certain circumstances.

Rule 20(a)(1) defines who may be joined as co-plaintiffs. Rule 20(a)(2) defines who may be joined as co-defendants. In each, the Rule prescribes the same two-part test. Put in simple terms, two or more may join together as co-plaintiffs if their claims (1) arise "out of the same transaction, occurrence, or series of transactions or occurrences" and (2) raise at least one common question (of law *or* fact). Similarly, two or more may be joined as co-defendants if the claims *against them* (1) arise from the same transaction or occurrence and (2) raise at least one common question (of law *or* fact). Few, if any, cases raise problems with the second requirement. The Rule requires the *existence* of *only one* common question, and it can be a question of law or fact. That common question need not be of predominant importance in the case; it simply must exist, which will be obvious in most instances. The difficulties encountered with Rule 20(a) usually involve the requirement that the claims by or against multiple parties must be transactionally related.

Before exploring that issue, it is important to note that Rule 20(a) continues a theme we see throughout modern procedure: the packaging in a single case of claims arising from, and parties involved in, a "transaction or occurrence." This focus on the transaction — on the real-world grouping of facts — underlies the modern definition of claim for claim preclusion purposes, as we saw in §11.2.3. It also underlies several claim joinder devices we see in §12.5. And, as we will continue to see, the concept of transactional relatedness defines the general availability of supplemental jurisdiction.

As elsewhere, the concept of "transaction or occurrence" is somewhat elastic. There are many easy cases, of course, such as when there are persons hurt in a single motor vehicle accident or when there are multiple parties to a contract that has been breached. At the margin, however, some courts have been remarkably inventive in stretching the concept of the transaction to allow joinder of parties. Perhaps these courts have been especially liberal because Rule 20(a) (unlike other transaction-based joinder rules[19]) speaks not only of claims arising from the same transaction or occurrence, but of a "series of transactions or occurrences."[20] On its face, this language seems broader than rules that speak only of a transaction or occurrence. Few opinions, however, justify a broad reading of the Rule on the basis of this additional language. What seems more influential are various theories of liability asserted by the plaintiff, particularly in tort

[19] *See, e.g.*, Rule 13(a)(1) (compulsory counterclaim); Rule 13(g) (crossclaim), discussed in §12.5.
[20] This language is also reflected in the Restatement (Second) of Judgments definition of claim for claim preclusion purposes. See §11.2.3.

cases. Many of the opinions in this area, though ostensibly interpreting Rule 20(a), read like cases that would appear in a casebook on torts.

One example is *Poster v. Central Gulf Steamship Corp.*,[21] which involved a seaman, Mr. Poster, who contracted a painful gastrointestinal malady, amebiasis, while working on a ship operated by Sinclair. He claimed that he was stricken because that company hired local workers to help the ship's galley staff prepare food while the ship was in the Suez Canal. These local workers, he alleged, used unsanitary food handling practices, which resulted in his infection. Months later, the unlucky sailor was working for a different shipping line, Gulf. This ship also went through the Suez Canal and the company also hired local workers to help prepare food. And, again, the plaintiff was stricken with amebiasis. He sued both shipping companies as co-defendants in a single case. Though the court recognized that the two voyages were separate "occurrences," it upheld joinder. Significantly, the plaintiff was careful to allege that his present condition was the result of *both* episodes. In other words, he did not say that he was injured once on the first voyage and a second time on the second voyage. Instead, his present state of health resulted from *both* exposures to unsanitary practices. It was impossible to say what percentage of his condition was attributable to which company. As a matter of tort law, then, the way the plaintiff alleged his claim, both companies could be concurrently liable. Thus, the court properly concluded that the two companies could be joined as co-defendants in a single case.

Imagine the problems Mr. Poster would have faced had the court not been willing to consider the substantive theory of concurrent liability in assessing whether joinder was proper under Rule 20(a). First, Mr. Poster would have had to pay for and prosecute two separate suits — one against each shipping company. Second, if the cases went to trial separately, he could be "whipsawed."[22] That means that in each case, the defendant could say to the jury, in essence: "We feel terrible that Mr. Poster is hurt, but it's not our fault. He sailed on another vessel for another company, and it is that company that hurt Mr. Poster." By focusing attention on the other shipping company, each defendant might be able to escape liability. Third, if Mr. Poster won in his litigation against one shipping company, he could not use issue preclusion from that case in the case against the other company. (Why?[23]) On the other hand, if Mr. Poster lost in the first case to go

[21] 25 F.R.D. 18 (E.D. Pa. 1960).

[22] *See* Thomas Rowe & Kenneth Sibley, *Beyond Diversity: Federal Multiparty, Multiforum Jurisdiction*, 135 U. Pa. L. Rev. 7, 15 (1985).

[23] Because issue preclusion can only be asserted against one who was a party to a case. Gulf was not a party to the case by Poster against Sinclair and thus could not be bound by a judgment from that case. See §11.3.4.

to judgment, depending on the issues decided, the other company might be able to assert issue preclusion against him in the other case. (Why?[24])

Some notable cases have involved plaintiffs injured by accidents at different times. Court have been appropriately liberal in permitting joinder of the defendants in a single case when the plaintiff alleges that her present condition is the result of the combined effects of the wrecks, or that the second wreck exacerbated the injuries from the first, or that the injuries inflicted by each cannot be identified separately. An example is *Schwartz v. Swan*, in which a bad-luck plaintiff was injured in completely separate automobile accidents ten days apart.[25] The court upheld joinder of the drivers involved in the two collisions in a single case, and emphasized that joinder was appropriate when "it appears that the *cumulative effect* of the acts of which plaintiff complains is a single indivisible injury, or that it is unlikely that it can be ascertained to a reasonable degree of medical certainty which occurrence caused the injuries."[26]

No case strains the concept of transactional relatedness more than *Hall v. E.I. DuPont de Nemours Co.*,[27] which involved injuries sustained by about a dozen children while playing with blasting caps. At the time, six companies manufactured all of the blasting caps in the United States. The injured children were not related to each other. They were injured in separate explosions in ten states over four years. Because the explosions destroyed the blasting caps, no child (or parent) could be certain which company had manufactured the cap that injured her. All of the injured children (actually, their representatives — why?[28]) sued as co-plaintiffs against all blasting cap manufacturers and their trade association as co-defendants. The theory of the suit was that the defendants failed properly to warn by labeling that blasting caps may be harmful.

Despite the obvious fact that the injuries were inflicted in unrelated events at different times and in different places, the court upheld joinder of all parties under Rule 20(a). The court's opinion focused mainly on theories of tort liability. These theories, such as "enterprise liability," move the

[24] Because most jurisdictions allow nonmutual defensive issue preclusion. For example, if in the first case the court found that Mr. Poster assumed the risk by eating the native-prepared food when he did not have to do so, the defendant in the second case might be able to use that issue against him in the second case.

[25] 211 N.E.2d 122 (Ill. App. 1965). Talk about having a bad day: The plaintiff in *Watts v. Smith*, 134 N.W.2d 194 (Mich. 1965), was injured in separate collisions on the same day; he was allowed to join the other drivers in a single case.

[26] *Schwartz*, 211 N.E.2d at 126 (emphasis added).

[27] 345 F. Supp. 353 (E.D.N.Y. 1972). The opinion was written by Judge Jack Weinstein, a well-respected jurist and Civil Procedure scholar who, before being named to the bench, was a full-time professor at Columbia University School of Law.

[28] Because minors lack legal capacity to sue or be sued, so litigation by or against them should be brought by or against the minors' representative. See §12.2.

attention away from separate transactions and toward the overall culpability of the blasting cap industry. The court concluded, "[t]he allegations in this case suggest that the entire blasting cap industry and its trade association provide the logical locus at which precautions should be taken and liability imposed."[29] Thus, the substantive tort theory adopted by the plaintiffs allowed the court to stretch the concept of transactional relatedness by concluding, in essence, that the case was not about 12 separate explosions but, rather, one culpable industry. Not every court would have been so liberal in upholding joinder on such facts.[30]

These cases demonstrate the tension inherent in addressing the propriety of joinder of multiple parties. On the one hand, courts are mindful of the salutary policy of inclusive joinder — of deciding whole disputes in the context of a single case. On the other hand, however, they must be careful not to create an unmanageable and confusing morass. Imagine the difficulties, for example, of going to trial in the *Hall* case: Twelve plaintiffs, putting on evidence of injuries from separate explosions over various states at different times, questions of what state's law will govern which case, several defendants, each trying to prove that it did not manufacture the particular cap involved. The court in *Hall* recognized that it had created a fairly unwieldy case, and planned to transfer individual claims to the federal district in which the explosions occurred, after making pretrial rulings.[31] Especially in light of the need for such unusual contortions, the opinion in *Hall* seems less a court's effort to apply the language of Rule 20(a) and more an attempt to pressure settlement of multiple claims. This goal may be laudable, but it's not clear that Rule 20(a) is intended to be a tool for realizing it.[32]

---

[29] *Hall*, 345 F. Supp. at 378.

[30] *See, e.g.*, Saval v. BL Ltd., 710 F.2d 1027 (4th Cir. 1983) (allegations of similar warranty claims on automobiles did not arise from same transaction or occurrence); Demboski v. CSX Transp. Inc., 157 F.R.D. 28 (S.D. Miss. 1994) (personal injuries incurred in different accidents at different times but alleging safety of railroad crossings did not meet transactional test for joinder).

[31] Functionally, the court thus attempted to replicate the treatment that would have been accorded by multidistrict litigation treatment under 28 U.S.C. §1407. In such an "MDL" transfer, as we saw at §5.5.1, cases originally filed in different districts are transferred by the Judicial Panel on Multidistrict Litigation to a transferee district for consolidated pretrial proceedings. In *Hall*, in contrast, only one case was filed.

[32] Moreover, although this problem may not have arisen in *Hall*, straining to sustain joinder can sweep into the case some defendants whose involvement in the underlying dispute is marginal. Courts should be mindful that doing so can be extremely expensive to such "bystander" defendants, who now, presumably, have to participate in discovery and other aspects of involved and expensive litigation. Just as pusillanimous use of Rule 20(a) can hurt plaintiffs, so can overzealous use hurt defendants.

Strategic Issues

As we know, joinder of parties under Rule 20(a) is permissive. Because the Rule gives the plaintiff the option to take or leave the joinder opportunity it provides, it allows the plaintiff to engage in strategic choices.

- *P-1* and *P-2* take a ride in a taxi cab. The driver is negligent and causes a crash that injures both *P-1* and *P-2*. Those two *may* join together in a suit against the cab driver under Rule 20(a)(1). Why? Because their claims against the cab driver (1) arise from the same transaction or occurrence (the crash) and (2) raise at least one common question (whether the cab driver was negligent). They do not have to do so. Each may file a separate action against the cab driver if she prefers.
- Could *P-1* (or *P-2* or both together) sue two defendants — the cab driver and the company for which the cab driver works — in the same case? Yes, joinder would be proper under Rule 20(a)(2) because the claims against those two (1) arise from the same transaction or occurrence (the crash) and (2) raise at least one common question (again, whether the cab driver was negligent). Again, the Rule is permissive, so the plaintiff can choose to sue both defendants in a single case or to sue them in separate actions.

These two scenarios beg the question: Why would a plaintiff ever fail to join all possible plaintiffs and defendants under Rule 20(a)? Depending on the facts, there may be jurisdictional limitations on doing so. For example, perhaps the court cannot get personal jurisdiction over one of the potential defendants or perhaps joining all the parties will make it impossible to invoke diversity of citizenship jurisdiction. Our focus here, however, is on the sorts of litigation strategies that might animate the plaintiff's selective use of Rule 20(a).

Speaking very generally, plaintiffs prefer to have all potential defendants — everyone who might potentially be liable for her harm — joined in a single case. We touched on the reasons for this in discussing the *Poster* case above. First, it is less expensive and less burdensome to sue once than to file a separate case against each potential defendant. Second, the advent of nonmutual defensive issue preclusion gives the plaintiff an incentive to sue several defendants at once; if she sued separately and lost against one defendant, the defendant in another suit may be able to use issue preclusion against the plaintiff on any negative findings. (If this point is fuzzy, review §11.3.5.) Third, the plaintiff can often benefit from each co-defendant's effort in the litigation to shift the blame from itself to other co-defendants. Fourth, and quite important as a practical matter, as we saw in discussing the *Poster* case, suing individual defendants allows them to whipsaw the plaintiff. That is, the defendant in one case might convince the jury that the harm to the plaintiff is not her fault, but the fault of someone who is not a party in this case. The defendant in the other case can do the same, leaving a plaintiff who may have convinced two juries that she is entitled to relief, but who recovers nothing because each jury thinks the fault lies with an absentee.

Similarly, as a general matter, plaintiffs prefer not to have co-plaintiffs suing with them. First, suing alone may allow the plaintiff to recover from a defendant first, before other plaintiffs can get at the defendant's assets. Second, she may conclude that her case is more compelling than those of the other potential plaintiffs, and that adding a co-plaintiff would tarnish her luster and divert the jury's attention from her. Third, even if the case settles without going to trial, there is a widely held view that a single plaintiff fares better simply because she does not have to share a recovery with others. Thus, as a general strategic matter, we expect to see plaintiffs use Rule 20(a)(2) to join all potential defendants into a single case, but to keep center stage to themselves on the plaintiff's side.[33]

What Are Misjoinder, Severance, Separate Trials, and Consolidation?

What happens if the plaintiff structures the case in violation of Rule 20(a)? Rule 21 provides that such "misjoinder of parties" is *not* a basis for dismissal of the suit. Instead, the court may "sever any claim against a party." Severance results in two or more completely separate suits. Each will have its own docket number and will result in its own judgment. This concept of severance is different from a court's ordering a separate trial under Rule 20(b) or 42(b). A separate trial is just that — a separate adjudication of a claim (or claims) that are part of an individual case.

- *P-1* and *P-2*, properly joined as co-plaintiffs under Rule 20(a)(1), sue *D* on a claim that *D* breached a contract between the three. In addition, *P-1* asserts an unrelated claim against *D*, concerning an entirely separate event. *P-1* has the right to assert this unrelated claim under Rule 18(a)(1), as we saw in §12.3. Although those claims are part of one case, the court may order a separate trial on the unrelated claim asserted by *P-1* against *D*. After all, it involves different facts from the main claim, and might distract or confuse the jury hearing that main claim. So the two claims will be tried separately. But ultimately, they will be determined in a single judgment, because they are part of a single case.[34]
- Contrast that situation with this: *P* sues two defendants, *D-1* and *D-2*, alleging that they caused him tortious harm. The court concludes, however, that joinder of the two defendants violates Rule 20(a)(2), because

---

[33] For more detailed discussion of such litigation strategies in structuring a suit, *see* the articles cited at note 2 above.

[34] In §14.5.1, we see that the court might ultimately treat the separate claims as separate "cases" for purposes of appeal under Rule 54(c). But that's for later. The point here is that these claims, although tried separately, are properly joined in a single case.

they caused harm to P, if at all, in separate transactions. Here, under Rule 21, the court will order severance. The result of that order is to create two cases: (1) by P against D-1 and (2) by P against D-2. (Actually, the court will simply drop D-2 as a defendant, and P will have to file the second case (against D-2) and pay the filing fee for that case.) But there are now two separate cases, which will result in two separate judgments. This result is dictated by the fact that D-1 and D-2 were not properly joined in a single case because the claims against them did not satisfy Rule 20(a)(2).[35]

In this latter scenario, there is another procedural device that might come into play: consolidation under Federal Rule 42(a). That Rule permits a court in which two (or more) separate cases are pending to consolidate the cases for any or all purposes. The only requirement is that the separate cases involve at least one common question of law or fact.[36] Consolidation simply means that those separate cases will be treated together for whatever purposes the court deems appropriate. For example, the court might order consolidation for purposes of discovery, or for motions, or for trial, or even for all purposes. Consolidation does not merge the separate cases; they are still separate cases and will result in separate judgments, even if consolidated for all purposes.[37]

As we noted above, plaintiffs often attempt to join multiple defendants in a single case to ensure that they will be tried before the same jury. That way, as we said above, the plaintiff avoids the risk of having the jury conclude that the real "bad guy" is someone who is not in the court. If such a plaintiff loses the battle of joinder under Rule 20(a) — probably because the court concludes that the claims against the two do not arise from the same transaction or occurrence — she might still win the war at trial if the court orders consolidation for trial.

That is exactly what happened in *Stanford v. Tennessee Valley Authority*,[38] an older but still-instructive case. The plaintiff owned property in Tennessee and claimed that it was damaged by chemicals poured into the air by two chemical plants. The plants were operated by different companies. The plaintiff joined both companies as co-defendants. The court

---

[35] The same thing would happen if two plaintiffs were misjoined under Rule 20(a)(1).

[36] As noted above, it is also required that the separate cases be pending in the same federal district (or division within a district). Thus, a case pending in the Southern District of New York cannot be consolidated with a case pending in the Eastern District of Pennsylvania. Remember, however, that cases can, in appropriate circumstances, be transferred from one federal district to another. If the case in the Southern District of New York were transferred to the Eastern District of Pennsylvania, the two cases could be consolidated. But transfer and consolidation are separate steps.

[37] Johnson v. Manhattan Ry. Co., 289 U.S. 479 (1933).

[38] 18 F.R.D. 152 (M.D. Tenn. 1955).

rejected the joinder, however, because it concluded that what each company did was a separate transaction or occurrence.[39] It ordered severance, after which the plaintiff had two separate cases, one against each chemical company. In the same opinion, however, the court ordered that the now-separate cases be consolidated for trial. Thus, the plaintiff would get the advantage of having the two defendants before the same jury at the same time.

Subject Matter Jurisdiction

The plaintiff uses Rule 20(a) to determine how many plaintiffs and how many defendants will be joined in a single case. Once she does so, she must ensure that the case as structured can be brought in the court she chooses. Thus, she must assess whether the court has personal jurisdiction over the defendants and whether venue is proper. And, of course, she must determine that the case will invoke subject matter jurisdiction. Let's assume plaintiff wants to sue in federal court.

- ○ *P* sues two defendants, *D-1* and *D-2*, properly joining them under Rule 20(a)(2). All three litigants are citizens of California. *P*'s claim against *D-1* alleges that *D-1* violated *P*'s rights under a federal statute. *P*'s claim against *D-2* alleges that *D-2* breached a state law duty to *P*. The claims against the two obviously (given one of the requirements of Rule 20(a)) arise from the same transaction or occurrence. Is there federal subject matter jurisdiction as the case is structured?
  - ○ The claim against *D-1* invokes federal question jurisdiction, because it is for violation of a right created by a federal statute.
  - ○ The claim against *D-2* does not invoke federal question jurisdiction, because it arises under state, not federal, law. Further, the claim does not invoke diversity of citizenship jurisdiction, because *P* and *D-2* are co-citizens.
  - ○ The claim against *D-2* does, however, invoke supplemental jurisdiction. First, §1367(a) grants supplemental jurisdiction because the claim against *D-2* involves the same "case or controversy" as the claim that invoked federal subject matter jurisdiction (the claim asserted by *P* v. *D-1*). Why? Because it meets the *Gibbs* "common nucleus of operative fact" test. As we saw in §4.7, §1367(a) codifies *Gibbs* and the *Gibbs* test is actually broader than "transaction or occurrence." So any claim, such as the claim here, that arises from the same transaction or occurrence as a claim that invokes an independent basis of federal subject matter jurisdiction will always meet *Gibbs* and, therefore, invoke jurisdiction under §1367(a). Second, §1367(b) does not

---

[39] This holding seems very stingy. Perhaps the plaintiff should have argued that his harm was caused by the combined effect of the acts of the two companies, as was done in cases such as *Poster*, discussed above.

remove the grant of supplemental jurisdiction, because that subsection applies only in cases that invoked diversity of citizenship jurisdiction. This case invoked federal question jurisdiction, so §1367(b) does not apply.

The fact pattern we just saw is similar to the *Finley* case, the holding in which led to passage of the supplemental jurisdiction statute. (If any of this material does not ring a bell, review §4.7.) Now let's push farther with three important hypotheticals.

- **One.** Two plaintiffs, *P-1* and *P-2*, properly joined under Rule 20(a)(1), assert state law claims against a single defendant (*D*). *P-1* is a citizen of California. *P-2* is a citizen of Arizona. *D* is a citizen of Nevada. *P-1*'s claim is for $100,000 but *P-2*'s claim is for $60,000. As structured, is there federal subject matter jurisdiction? Because the claims arise under state law, there is no federal question jurisdiction. What about diversity of citizenship jurisdiction? Certainly there is no problem with citizenship, because the two plaintiffs are citizens of different states from the defendant. But there is trouble with the amount in controversy. *P-1*'s claim meets that requirement, because it exceeds $75,000 and thus invokes diversity of citizenship jurisdiction. But *P-2*'s claim does not satisfy the amount in controversy requirement, since it does not exceed $75,000. And when there are multiple parties such as this, they may not aggregate their claims to meet the amount in controversy requirement, as we discussed in §4.5.3. So it seems that the court should drop the claim asserted by *P-2* from the case. But might the supplemental jurisdiction statute change this result?
  - The claim asserted by *P-1* against *D* invokes diversity of citizenship jurisdiction. The claim asserted by *P-2* against *D* does not. But because the two claims arise from the same transaction or occurrence, §1367(a) grants supplemental jurisdiction over the claim by *P-2*. Obviously, §1367(b) *should* remove supplemental jurisdiction over this claim, or else the amount in controversy requirement will be eviscerated. But does it? Again, look carefully at its terms. Section 1367(b) applies only in cases that invoke diversity of citizenship jurisdiction (which *P-1* v. *D* does). And it removes jurisdiction over claims brought *"by plaintiffs against persons made parties under Rule . . . 20."* That is not the situation in this hypothetical. Here, the claim is asserted *by persons made parties under Rule 20 against a defendant.* Nowhere does §1367(b) remove the grant of supplemental jurisdiction.

This result (apparently not intended by the drafters of §1367) is inconsistent with *Clark v. Paul Gray, Inc.*,[40] in which the Supreme Court held

---

[40] 306 U.S. 583 (1939).

that each plaintiff's claim must satisfy the amount in controversy requirement to invoke diversity of citizenship jurisdiction. Lower courts generally held that the supplemental jurisdiction statute had overruled *Clark*,[41] and commentators generally conclude that this result makes sense.[42] In *Exxon Mobil Corp. v. Allapattah Services*,[43] the Supreme Court embraced this interpretation, and upheld supplemental jurisdiction over jurisdictionally sufficient claims by plaintiffs, so long as they arose from a common nucleus of operative fact with the claim of a plaintiff that did satisfy the amount in controversy requirement.

- ○ **Two.** A single plaintiff, *P*, a citizen of California, sues two defendants, *D-1* and *D-2*, properly joining them under Rule 20(a)(2). *D-1* and *D-2* are citizens of Kansas. *P*'s claims against *D-1* and *D-2* arise under state law. The claim against D-1 is for $100,000 and the claim against *D-2* is for $60,000. Here, the claim by *P* against *D-1* obviously invokes diversity of citizenship jurisdiction. The claim by *P* against *D-2* does not, however, because even though it is by a citizen of California against a citizen of Kansas, it does not exceed $75,000.
- ○ Based upon the preceding hypothetical, however, we would expect the claim by *P* against *D-2* to invoke supplemental jurisdiction. Indeed, the claim does satisfy §1367(a), as in hypothetical One. But look carefully at §1367(b). It applies in diversity cases, such as this case. And it removes supplemental jurisdiction over claims by plaintiffs against persons joined under Rule 20. That is exactly what we have here! *D-1* and *D-2* were joined under Rule 20, so §1367(b), on its face, removes supplemental jurisdiction over this claim.

This result makes no sense. Why should supplemental jurisdiction be proper to overcome an amount in controversy problem in a diversity case when there are multiple plaintiffs but not when there are multiple defendants? The Court did not address this "multiple defendants problem" in *Allapattah*. And as yet there is no definitive interpretation in the lower courts. Perhaps they can find a way to avoid what the statute seems to command. The hypothetical simply manifests one of many problems caused by a very poorly drafted statute.

- ○ **Three.** Two plaintiffs, *P-1* and *P-2*, properly joined under Rule 20(a)(1), assert state law claims against a single defendant (*D*). *P-1* is a citizen of California. *P-2* is a citizen of Arizona. *D* is a citizen of Arizona. *P-1*'s claim is for $100,000, and *P-2*'s claim is for $200,000. As structured, is there

---

[41] *See, e.g.,* Stromberg Metal Works v. Press Mech., Inc., 77 F.3d 928, 932 (7th Cir. 1996).

[42] *See* Thomas Rowe, *1367 and All That: Recodifying Federal Supplemental Jurisdiction,* 74 Ind. L.J. 53 (1998). The American Law Institute proposed a revision of §1367 that would expressly embrace this result. American Law Institute, Federal Judicial Code Revision Project (2004).

[43] 545 U.S. 546 (2005).

federal subject matter jurisdiction? Because the claims arise under state law, there is no federal question jurisdiction. What about diversity of citizenship jurisdiction? On the face of it, no. *P-1* is diverse from *D*, but *P-2* is not diverse from *D*. The structure of the case violates the complete diversity rule. But could §1367 affect this outcome?

○ Applying the statute literally, it seems the answer should be the same as in hypothetical One above. Here, as there, it appears that the claim asserted by *P-1* against *D* invokes diversity of citizenship jurisdiction. The claim asserted by *P-2* against *D* does not. But because the two claims arise from the same transaction or occurrence, §1367(a) grants supplemental jurisdiction over the claim by *P-2*. Obviously, §1367(b) *should* remove supplemental jurisdiction over this claim, or else the complete diversity rule is rendered meaningless. But does it? Again, look carefully at its terms. Section 1367(b) applies only in cases that invoke diversity of citizenship jurisdiction (which *P-1* v. *D* arguably does). And it removes jurisdiction over claims brought *"by plaintiffs against persons made parties under Rule . . . 20."* That is not the situation in this hypothetical. Here, the claim is asserted *by persons made parties under Rule 20 against a defendant.* Nowhere does §1367(b) remove the grant of supplemental jurisdiction.

Logically, there is no reason that the outcome here, in hypothetical Three, should be any different from that in hypothetical One. There, supplemental jurisdiction made up for a lack of amount in controversy in a diversity case. Here, it would make up for a lack of complete diversity in a diversity case. Both the complete diversity rule and the amount in controversy requirement are merely *statutory* (not constitutional) provisions of the grant of diversity of citizenship jurisdiction under §1332. As such, each should be equally amenable to change by §1367. On the other hand, concluding that the parties may use supplemental jurisdiction to overcome the complete diversity rule would threaten to inundate the federal courts with more cases than they could hope to handle.

In *Allapattah*, the Court found a way to avoid such inundation. As discussed in §4.5.3, the Court in that case clarified how jurisdiction attaches in diversity cases. If there is complete diversity, the presence of a single claim in excess of $75,000 invokes diversity of citizenship jurisdiction. In other words, as in hypothethical One above, the claim by *P-1* against *D* constituted a diversity of citizenship case in the federal courts, to which the claim by *P-2* could be supplemental. In contrast, the Court said in dictum, if there is not complete diversity of citizenship between all plaintiffs and all defendants, there is no diversity case at all, and nothing to which supplemental jurisdiction can attach.[44] So in hypothetical Three, the claim by P-1 against D failed to invoke diversity of citizenship jurisdiction, so there was no case in which to exercise supplemental jurisdiction. Stated

[44] *Id.* at 552-553.

another way, the Court concluded, the amount in controversy requirement is "claim-specific" while the complete diversity requirement is "action-specific." (If this does not ring a bell, see §4.5.3.)

This reasoning in *Allapattah* brings a significant change to the practice. Before that case, in a fact pattern such as hypothetical Three, a federal court would simply drop the nondiverse party (*P-2*) and permit the case to proceed with *P-1* against *D*. Because *Allapattah* concludes that the failure to satisfy the complete diversity rule obviates diversity jurisdiction altogether, however, now the entire case must be dismissed.

§12.5　Claim Joinder by a Defendant

As we discussed in §11.2.1, parties other than the plaintiff can be "claimants," meaning that they can assert claims for relief in the pending case. In this section, we look at claims that may be asserted by defendants. These claims should not be confused with the defensive responses we discussed at §7.4. There, the defendant's concern was avoiding the imposition of liability on her. Here, the interest is in *suing* somebody — asserting a claim against another party. As we see in detail below, the *counterclaim* is asserted against an "opposing party" (by the defendant against the plaintiff, for example), and the *crossclaim* is asserted against a "co-party" (by one defendant against another defendant, for example).[45]

Of course, it is never enough simply to satisfy one of the Federal Rules allowing joinder. In addition (assuming the case is in federal court), the claim must invoke federal subject matter jurisdiction. Thus, after discussing each joinder device, we address how such claims might invoke subject matter jurisdiction. For claim joinder by the defendant, we assume that the court has personal jurisdiction over the defendant. (If it did not, the defendant should be attempting to get the case dismissed on that basis rather than asserting a claim.) Moreover, venue is not a problem here. The venue statutes, discussed at §5.4, speak of where an action may be "brought," meaning that they dictate the place where the plaintiff can sue the defendant; they simply do not require venue for counterclaims and crossclaims.[46]

Rule 13(h) provides that a defendant asserting a counterclaim or crossclaim can join new parties to the claim so long as these newcomers are joined in accordance with the provisions of Rules 19 or 20, which deal

---

[45] The defendant can also assert a claim against a third party under certain circumstances by invoking Rule 14(a)(1). Because such "impleader" claims involve joinder of a new party to the pending case, however, we address it in a different part of the chapter. See §12.6.2.

[46] *See, e.g.,* Scott v. Fancher, 369 F.2d 842 (5th Cir. 1966) (crossclaim); Schoot v. United States, 664 F. Supp. 293, 295 (N.D. Ill. 1987) (counterclaim).

with joinder of parties. We discussed Rule 20 in §12.4, and discuss Rule 19 in §12.6.1. Rule 13(h) thus puts a defendant asserting a counterclaim or crossclaim on the same footing for party joinder as the plaintiff in originally structuring the suit. We see an example of the use of Rule 13(h) in §12.6.1.

Because the counterclaim and crossclaim are claims for relief, the party against whom they are asserted must respond just as the defendant had to respond to the original complaint. As discussed in §7.4, the defending party may respond under Rule 12 either by motion or by answer.

§12.5.1 Counterclaims (Rule 13(a) and Rule 13(b))

In General

Federal Rule 13 contains several subsections governing counterclaims in federal court. We see below that there are two types of counterclaims: "compulsory" (under Rule 13(a)) and "permissive" (under Rule 13(b)). Here, we look at general issues common to both types of counterclaims. For starters, a counterclaim is asserted against an "opposing party." In this context, "opposing party" means somebody who has asserted a claim against the party. So if the defendant has a claim against the plaintiff (who has obviously sued the defendant), it must be denominated a counterclaim. Almost all counterclaims in the real world (and on law school exams) will be by the defendant against the plaintiff. But realize that *any* party against whom a claim is made may have a counterclaim back against that party. For example, suppose a defendant (*D-1*) asserts a crossclaim (addressed in §12.5.2) against a co-defendant (*D-2*). If *D-2* has a claim back against *D-1*, it will be a counterclaim. Once *D-1* asserted the crossclaim against *D-2*, the two were "opposing parties," making *D-2*'s claim against *D-1* a counterclaim.

It also bears repeating that a counterclaim is a *claim*, not a defense. Thus, it does not attempt to "diminish or defeat the recovery sought by the opposing party."[47] That function is handled by responsive pleadings and motions, as we saw in §7.3.3. Instead, with a counterclaim, the defendant is suing the plaintiff. At common law, a defendant was permitted to raise defenses that would offset the plaintiff's recovery, but could not, as a general rule, win a recovery against the plaintiff. Rule 13(c) changes that practice by providing expressly that the counterclaim may exceed the plaintiff's claim. In addition, the counterclaim can be for a different type of relief than the plaintiff's original claim. For instance, if the plaintiff

---

[47] Fed. R. Civ. P. 13(c).

sues for damages, the defendant may counterclaim for an injunction. Similarly, if the plaintiff sues for $80,000, the defendant can counterclaim for $8 million.

Under Rule 13(a) and (b), a counterclaim is to be asserted in "[a] pleading." Because the defendant asserting the counterclaim has already been sued, the pleading will be an answer. So the counterclaim should be asserted in one's answer. If the party fails to assert the counterclaim "through oversight, inadvertence, or excusable neglect," Rule 13(f) allows her to seek leave of court to assert the counterclaim by amending her answer to include it. Under that Rule, the court will permit the defendant to do so "if justice so requires."

What happens, however, if the defendant's counterclaim does not mature — does not arise — until after the defendant has already answered? That situation is addressed by Rule 13(e), which allows the defendant to assert the claim by "supplemental pleading." This provision is consistent with our discussion of supplemental pleadings at §7.5.4. As you will recall, a supplemental pleading involves events occurring after a pleading has been filed.

The Compulsory Counterclaim

Procedural and Policy Issues. As already noted, there are two kinds of counterclaims. The compulsory counterclaim is created and governed in federal practice by Federal Rule 13(a). Of course, a counterclaim is always asserted against an "opposing party." The compulsory counterclaim, according to Rule 13(a)(1)(A), arises from the "same transaction or occurrence" as the opposing party's claim. In the usual context, then, it is a claim asserted by the defendant against the plaintiff, and it arises from the same transaction or occurrence as the plaintiff's claim against the defendant. The compulsory counterclaim is so named because Rule 13(a) says that the claim "must" be asserted in the pending case. "Must" is a mandatory word; it commands that the act be done. Interestingly, the Rule does not expressly state the consequences of violating the command. Nonetheless, those consequences are clear: The party failing to assert a compulsory counterclaim loses the claim and cannot assert it in another proceeding.[48]

○ *A* and *Z*, each driving her own car, collide. Each suffers personal injuries. In Case 1, in federal court, *A* sues *Z* to recover for her personal injuries. *Z* answers and defends that suit, which is litigated to conclusion. In Case 2, *Z* sues *A* to recover for her personal injuries from the collision. Case 2 should be dismissed. *Z*'s claim was a compulsory counterclaim in

---

[48] "It is entirely accepted that the failure to assert a claim as a compulsory counterclaim precludes the party from later bringing an independent action on the claim." Wright & Kane, Federal Courts 570.

the original case, because it was against an opposing party and arose from the same transaction or occurrence as A's claim in that case. Z failed to assert the claim in the then-pending case, so cannot assert it anywhere.

When we say "anywhere," we mean not only that Z cannot assert her claim in a separate action in a federal court. The compulsory counterclaim rule should operate to bar a subsequent case in state court as well (even if that state does not have a compulsory counterclaim rule). As we discuss momentarily, the compulsory counterclaim rule, properly understood, should be seen as establishing an estoppel against the defendant from asserting her claim in a second case. There is no reason the estoppel should not follow the defendant and preclude the later litigation in any court. Although there are some older decisions to the contrary, most state courts addressing the issue have reached this conclusion.[49] The converse should also be true: Failure to assert a compulsory counterclaim in Case 1 in state court (in a state that has such a rule) should bar the defendant from instituting Case 2 on that claim in federal court.[50]

Some courts inject needless confusion in their discussions of *why* Case 2 should be dismissed. Some have used the language of claim preclusion to say why D is barred from bringing suit.[51] This leads some courts into difficulty when the first case (in which the defendant did not assert a compulsory counterclaim, but should have) is settled rather than adjudicated. But claim preclusion plays no role here.[52] Remember from §11.2.1 that claim preclusion applies only when two actions are brought *by the same claimant against the same defendant*. Here, Case 1 was brought by A against Z. Case 2 was brought by Z against A. Thus, Z had never been a claimant before and is not suing twice on the same claim. Other courts use the language of waiver, which is more accurate.[53] Case 2 is dismissed because Z,

---

[49] *See, e.g.*, Nottingham v. Weld, 377 S.E.2d 621 (Va. 1989); Jocie Motor Lines, Inc. v. Johnson, 57 S.E.2d 388 (N.C. 1950).

[50] *See, e.g.*, Carnation Co. v. T.U. Parks Constr. Co., 816 F.2d 1099, 1103 (6th Cir. 1987); Chapman v. Aetna Fin. Co., 615 F.2d 361 (5th Cir. 1980) (although the result is not required by the full faith and credit statute (see §11.5.3), as a matter of comity, federal court should bar claim that would be barred by defendant's failure to assert compulsory counterclaim in state court action).

[51] *See, e.g.*, Dragor Shipping Corp. v. Union Tank Car Co., 378 F.2d 241 (9th Cir. 1967).

[52] *See* United States Fid. & Guar. Co. v. Maish, 908 P.2d 1329, 1340, 1341 (Kan. 1995) ("We conclude that the doctrine of res judicata is not applicable in this case. We believe these facts are more in tune with the estoppel theory, and we adopt that theory as the philosophical basis for the enforcement of the counterclaim bar in the instant matter.... [T]he fact that the previous action was settled rather than litigated on the merits does not avoid the compulsory counterclaim bar in this case.").

[53] *See, e.g.*, Martino v. McDonald's Sys., Inc., 598 F.2d 1079 (7th Cir. 1979); Dindo v. Whitney, 451 F.2d 1, 3 (1st Cir. 1971).

by failing to assert the claim in Case 1, has waived the claim. Some speak of the compulsory counterclaim rule as working "rule preclusion."[54]

The appropriate way to deal with the issue is that espoused by the late Professor Charles Alan Wright decades ago: *D* cannot proceed with a separate case because of "estoppel by rule."[55] Failure to assert the claim in Case 1 estops *D* from asserting the claim elsewhere. Because estoppel is an equitable principle, it can be applied with a heart. For example, let's return to the hypothetical we just saw. Suppose that in Case 1, *Z*'s insurance company took over the defense (as would normally be the case[56]) and failed to inform *Z* of the compulsory counterclaim rule. If, through no fault or lack of diligence of her own, *Z* was not informed of her right (let alone obligation) to assert the claim, perhaps she should not be estopped from bringing the separate action.[57]

Commentators have noted that there are surprisingly few published opinions in which courts discuss the nature of the bar worked by the compulsory counterclaim rule.[58] In all likelihood, the paucity of such cases simply reflects the fact that very few defendants fail to assert compulsory counterclaims. The rule is well ingrained in federal practice, and most states also have a compulsory counterclaim rule. Interestingly, however, not all states do. Virginia, for example, does not require the assertion of any counterclaims — even those transactionally related to the plaintiff's claim — in the pending case.[59]

Though the operation of the compulsory counterclaim rule is not the same as claim preclusion, it serves the same function as the modern approach to that doctrine. Both serve to force the joinder of transactionally related rights to relief into a single case.[60] Doing so is efficient and

[54] *See, e.g.*, Harris v. Huffco Petroleum Corp., 633 F. Supp. 250, 255 (S.D. Ala. 1986).

[55] The classic treatment is Wright, *Estoppel by Rule: The Compulsory Counterclaim Under Modern Pleading*, 38 Minn. L. Rev. 423, 428-436 (1954).

[56] Usually, a liability insurer is required not only to indemnify its insured for covered events, but to afford its insured a defense as well.

[57] *See* Dindo v. Whitney, 451 F.2d 1, 3 (1st Cir. 1971) ("Other courts have viewed the [compulsory counterclaim] rule . . . as creating an estoppel or waiver. The latter approach seems more appropriate, at least when the case is settled rather than tried. . . . If a case has been tried, protection both of the court and the parties dictates that there should be no further directly related litigation. But if the case is settled, normally the court has not been greatly burdened, and the parties can protect themselves by demanding cross-releases. In such circumstances, absent a release, better-tailored justice seems obtainable by applying principles of equitable estoppel."); United States Fid. & Guar. Co. v. Maish, 908 P.2d 1329, 1340 (Kan. 1995).

[58] *See, e.g.*, Wright & Kane, Federal Courts 571.

[59] Va. Rules of Court 3:8 (defendant "may, at his option, plead . . . a counterclaim. . . ."). Thus, in Virginia, all counterclaims are "permissive" — the party has the option of asserting it in the pending case or of suing on the claim in a separate case.

[60] Recall that the modern approach to claim preclusion defines one's "claim" as all rights to relief arising from a transaction or occurrence. See §11.2.3.

relatively convenient for the fact-finder, which may wrap up all claims arising from what the parties will generally consider a single real-world event. Moreover, the focus on the transaction is generally consistent with the exercise of supplemental jurisdiction, as we saw in §4.7. To be sure, the definition of "transaction or occurrence" can be troublesome at the margin (as we saw in §11.2.3), but in most cases the lines will be fairly easy to draw.

At this point, we need to refine our definition of compulsory counterclaim a bit. So far we have seen it as a claim against an opposing party that arises from the same transaction or occurrence as that party's claim. The refinement is necessary to reflect two situations in which the drafters of the Rule concluded that the defendant should *not* be estopped from bringing a separate action. First, if an otherwise compulsory counterclaim would "require adding another party over whom the court cannot acquire jurisdiction," Rule 13(a)(1)(B) provides that the claim is simply not considered compulsory. In other words, if the counterclaim implicates non-parties who should be joined but cannot be joined because, for example, there is no personal jurisdiction over them, it is not a compulsory counterclaim. This provision implements the policies of Rule 19, concerning joinder of "required," or "necessary," parties, which we see in §12.6.1.

Second, if the defendant has already asserted the claim by the time she is sued, Rule 13(a)(2) provides that her claim need not be asserted when the plaintiff sues her. Thus, in the hypothetical we saw above, suppose *Z* has already filed suit against *A* before *A* sued *Z*. In such a situation, *Z* need not assert the counterclaim against *A* when *A* sues her.[61] This exception makes sense; it simply tells someone who has already asserted her claim that she does not have to do so again.[62]

Related to these exceptions to the operation of the compulsory counterclaim rule, remember (as we discussed above in this subsection) that a counterclaim is to be asserted in a "pleading," which means with the defendant's answer.[63] If the case is resolved without the defendant's having to answer, the compulsory counterclaim rule will not apply.

---

[61] Of course, when *Z* sued *A*, *A*'s claim against *Z* would be a compulsory counterclaim in that case (assuming the jurisdiction has a compulsory counterclaim rule like Rule 13(a)).

[62] A third exception to the operation of the compulsory counterclaim rule is found in Rule 13(a)(2)(B), and should be quite rare. Under that subsection, if the plaintiff's claim is asserted *in rem* or *quasi-in-rem*, and the court did not acquire *in personam* jurisdiction over the defendant, the defendant's claim is not compulsory. The reason for this rule is to avoid forcing the defendant to do something that might subject her to *in personam* jurisdiction. Given the rarity of *in rem* and *quasi-in-rem* cases, however, this provision has seen little action through the years.

[63] Recall also, as discussed immediately before this subsection on the compulsory counterclaim, that if the defendant's claim matures after the plaintiff sues the defendant, it is not a counterclaim. *See* Rule 13(e).

○ In Case 1, *A* sues *Z* for injuries sustained in an auto collision between the two. *Z* does not answer, but files a motion to dismiss for improper service of process. The motion is granted and the case is dismissed. In Case 2, *Z* sues *A* to recover for her personal injuries from the collision. Case 2 will not be dismissed, because the compulsory counterclaim rule never attached in Case 1. *Z* never answered in Case 1, so she could not have asserted a counterclaim.[64]

Subject Matter Jurisdiction. Rule 13(a) simply provides a procedural mechanism for asserting a claim. The claim must invoke federal subject matter jurisdiction, however, or else it cannot be asserted in federal court. As always, this jurisdictional inquiry is a separate step, undertaken after determining that the claim is properly asserted under Rule 13(a).

○ *A*, a citizen of Maryland, sues *Z*, a citizen of Delaware, asserting a state law claim of $500,000. *Z* has a claim against *A* that arises from the same transaction or occurrence as *A*'s claim. It is based upon state law and *Z* claims damages of $100,000. Is there subject matter jurisdiction over *Z*'s compulsory counterclaim? Yes. Because the facts state that all claims in this case arise under state law, there is no federal question jurisdiction. Obviously, though, *A*'s original claim invokes diversity of citizenship jurisdiction — it is asserted by a citizen of Maryland against a citizen of Delaware, and it exceeds $75,000. *Z*'s claim against *A* is a compulsory counterclaim, because it arises from the same transaction or occurrence as *A*'s claim. It also invokes diversity of citizenship jurisdiction, because the litigants are of diverse citizenship and the claim exceeds $75,000.

○ Same facts as the previous hypothetical, except that the compulsory counterclaim by *Z* is for $45,000. As above, the original claim asserted by *A* against *Z* invokes diversity of citizenship jurisdiction.

　○ Again, the compulsory counterclaim arises under state law, and thus cannot invoke federal question jurisdiction. Here, the compulsory counterclaim does not invoke diversity of citizenship jurisdiction, because it does not meet the amount in controversy requirement; it is a claim for $45,000 and thus does not exceed $75,000.

　○ Nonetheless, the federal court can entertain *Z*'s counterclaim under supplemental jurisdiction. Why? Section 1367(a) grants supplemental jurisdiction over claims that are part of the same "case or controversy" as the claim that invoked federal subject matter jurisdiction (the claim asserted by *A* against *Z*). As interpreted, that requirement embraces the *Gibbs* standard and is met if the claims share a common nucleus of operative fact. As we saw in §4.7, this test is always met by claims that arise from the same transaction or occurrence as the claim that got the case into federal court initially. Thus, the compulsory counterclaim always meets this test. By definition, it arises from the same

[64] *See, e.g.*, United States v. Snider, 779 F.2d 1151, 1157 (6th Cir. 1985).

transaction or occurrence as the underlying case by *A* against *Z*. Section 1367(b) applies in cases that invoke diversity of citizenship jurisdiction (such as the claim asserted by *A* against *Z*), but removes supplemental jurisdiction only over claims asserted by *plaintiffs*. This is a claim asserted by a defendant, so §1367(b) does not remove the supplemental jurisdiction. (If any of this material is fuzzy, see §4.7.)

The Permissive Counterclaim

Procedural and Policy Issues. The second kind of counterclaim is the permissive counterclaim, created and governed in federal practice by Federal Rule 13(b). Any counterclaim, as we know, is asserted against an "opposing party." The permissive counterclaim is one that is not compulsory. In other words, it does *not* arise from the same "transaction or occurrence" as the opposing party's claim. In the usual context, then, it is a claim asserted by the defendant against the plaintiff, and is transactionally *unrelated* to the plaintiff's claim against the defendant.

The Rule 13(b) claim is called *permissive* precisely because the defendant is not *required* to assert it in the pending case. How do we know? The Rule provides that the claim "may" be asserted (not "must" be asserted) in the pending case. Thus, the defendant may assert it in that case if she so desires, but she may just as readily sue on the claim in a separate case. Rule 13(b) allows the defendant to join in the pending case any and all claims she may have against the plaintiff, regardless of the fact that they are unrelated to the plaintiff's claim against her. This provision mirrors the plaintiff's unlimited right to join claims under Rule 18(a), which we addressed at §12.3. The same policy applies here as there: The idea is to allow the parties to put their entire dispute(s) before the court in one case. We noted in discussing Rule 18(a) that this unlimited joinder might result in a confusing mix of claims in a single case. The permissive counterclaim rule can multiply the confusion. The antidote, as it was with Rule 18(a), is to equip the court with the discretionary authority to order separate trials of the various claims.[65]

In §12.3, we also noted that Rule 18(a) — which allows the assertion in a single case of any and all claims, regardless of transactional or legal relatedness — applies not only to plaintiffs, but to any claimant, including one who asserts a counterclaim. But Rule 18(a) is meaningless in the counterclaim situation. If the defendant has claims against the plaintiff that do arise from the same transaction or occurrence as the plaintiff's claim, she will assert them under Rule 13(a)(1); if she also has unrelated claims, she can assert them under Rule 13(b). Rule 18(a) gives such a defendant nothing that Rule 13(b) does not already give her.

---

[65] *See* Federal Rules 13(f), 20(b), and 42(b).

Subject Matter Jurisdiction. Of course, Rule 13(b) simply provides a procedural mechanism for asserting a claim. The claim must invoke federal subject matter jurisdiction, however, or else it cannot be asserted in federal court. As always, this jurisdictional inquiry is a separate step, undertaken after determining that the claim is properly asserted under Rule 13(b).

> ○   *A*, a citizen of Wyoming, sues *Z*, a citizen of Colorado, in federal court, asserting a state law claim for $200,000. *Z* has a permissive counterclaim against *A*, arising under state law, for $400,000. Is there subject matter jurisdiction? Yes. Because the claims arise under state law, there is no basis for federal question jurisdiction. But *Z*'s claim invokes diversity of citizenship jurisdiction. It is by a citizen of Wyoming against a citizen of Colorado and exceeds $75,000. The permissive counterclaim also invokes diversity of citizenship jurisdiction. It is by a citizen of Colorado against a citizen of Wyoming and exceeds $75,000.

In the preceding hypothetical, there was no need for supplemental jurisdiction, because the permissive counterclaim invoked diversity of citizenship. What happens, though, when a permissive counterclaim does not invoke federal question or diversity of citizenship jurisdiction? We would then inquire whether it could invoke supplemental jurisdiction. And here we may well encounter a problem.

Why? The fact that a permissive counterclaim does not arise from the same transaction or occurrence as the underlying dispute means that it generally will not invoke supplemental jurisdiction. Under §1367(a), supplemental jurisdiction attaches only to those claims that are part of the same "case or controversy" as an underlying claim that did invoke federal subject matter jurisdiction. As interpreted, that requirement incorporates the *Gibbs* standard and means that the claim must involve a common nucleus of operative fact as the underlying claim. As we discussed in §4.7, some courts equated the "common nucleus" test with "transaction or occurrence." Such courts thus state as boilerplate that permissive counterclaims, which by definition do *not* arise from the same transaction or occurrence as the underlying claim, cannot invoke supplemental jurisdiction under §1367(a).[66]

But, again as seen in §4.7, courts increasingly recognize that the test for supplemental jurisdiction under §1367(a) is broader than "same transaction or occurrence." One influential case is *Jones v. Ford Motor Credit Co.*,[67] which is the basis for the following hypothetical.

---

[66] *See, e.g.*, Lehman v. Revolution Portfolio LLC, 116 F.3d 389, 393 ("Only compulsory counterclaims can rely upon supplemental jurisdiction; permissive counterclaims require their own jurisdictional basis").

[67] 358 F.3d 205 (2d Cir. 2004).

○ Plaintiffs borrowed money from Defendant to finance their purchase of automobiles. Plaintiffs asserted that Defendant engaged in racial discrimination in making the loans, thereby violating federal law. Plaintiffs sued for violation of the federal law, thereby invoking federal question jurisdiction. Defendant asserted a counterclaim for the unpaid balance on the car loan. The court concluded that the counterclaim was permissive, and not compulsory, because it did not arise from the same transaction or occurrence as Plaintiffs' claim of racial discrimination. Nonetheless, the court concluded, §1367(a) requires only that there be a "loose factual connection" between the supplemental claim and the underlying suit. Although the permissive counterclaim obviously did not arise from the same transaction or occurrence as Plaintiffs' claim, it did share sufficient factual overlap to invoke supplemental jurisdiction under §1367(a).[68]

It seems clear that many — undoubtedly most — permissive counterclaims will be so factually unrelated from the underlying claim that they will not invoke supplemental jurisdiction. But *Jones* and similar cases[69] teach two important lessons — (1) that §1367(a) is broader than "transaction or occurrence" and (2) that supplemental jurisdiction should be assessed on the individual facts of each case.

§12.5.2   Crossclaims (Rule 13(g))

Procedural and Policy Issues. The crossclaim[70] is created and governed in federal practice by Federal Rule 13(g). It has two important

---

[68] *Id.* at 210-225. And §1367(b) did not remove that grant. Because Plaintiffs' claim invoked federal question jurisdiction, §1367(b) did not apply at all. Remember that §1367(b) does not apply in cases that got into federal court initially through federal question jurisdiction. Even if the underlying claim by Plaintiffs invoked only diversity of citizenship, on these facts, §1367(b) would not remove supplemental jurisdiction. Why? Although that subsection applies in diversity of citizenship cases such as *Jones*, it removes supplemental jurisdiction only over claims by plaintiffs. Because the counterclaim was not asserted by the plaintiff, §1367(b) did not remove supplemental jurisdiction. If any of this is fuzzy, review §4.7.

[69] *See, e.g.,* Channell v. Citicorp National Servs., Inc., 89 F.3d 379, 385-386 (7th Cir. 1996); Campos v. Western Dental Servs., Inc., 404 F. Supp. 2d 1164, 1168 (N.D. Cal. 2005) ("The test for supplemental jurisdiction under section 1367 appears to be broad enough to encompass some permissive counterclaims").

[70] From the initial promulgation of the Federal Rules in 1938 until December 2007, this word was hyphenated: cross-claim. When the Rules were restyled effective December 2007, the hyphen was removed: crossclaim. For whatever reason, the Advisory Committee thought this was an advance worth imposing on bench, bar, and academy. It makes research difficult, since on-line searches for "cross-claim" will not retrieve "crossclaim" and vice versa. I am not alone when I express the hope that the Advisory Committee on the Civil Rules will eschew such meaningless busy-work (or is it busywork?) in the future.

requirements. First, the crossclaim is a claim against a "coparty."[71] The existence of co-parties depends upon the plaintiff's original structuring of the suit using Rule 20(a). As we discussed in §12.4, the plaintiff, when instituting suit, may determine that there should be multiple plaintiffs or multiple defendants. Rule 20(a) defines when such multiple parties may be joined. If there are multiple parties on either side of the case, they are co-parties with each other. Thus, suppose two plaintiffs, *P-1* and *P-2*, are joined in a case against three defendants, *D-1*, *D-2*, and *D-3*. The two plaintiffs are co-parties. The three defendants are co-parties. Although a plaintiff may assert a crossclaim against a co-plaintiff (assuming the other requirement of Rule 13(g) is satisfied and that there is subject matter jurisdiction over the claim), more typically, crossclaims are asserted on the defendant side.[72]

Second, to be a crossclaim, the claim against the co-party must arise from the same "transaction or occurrence" as the "original action or of a counterclaim therein." Thus, to be a crossclaim, the claim must be transactionally related to the underlying dispute between the plaintiff and the defendant. The "transaction or occurrence" provision is familiar language. It serves the same function as in the compulsory counterclaim — to facilitate the joinder of all transactionally related claims in a single proceeding. Such joinder is also consistent with the modern view on claim preclusion, as we saw in §11.2.3 and with the general transactional packaging facilitated by supplemental jurisdiction, as we saw in §4.7.

Rule 13(g) is permissive. Because it says that the claim "may" be asserted, the party is not required to file the crossclaim in the pending case. She may if she wishes to, or she may choose to assert it in a separate case. In other words, there is no such thing as a compulsory crossclaim. This fact is odd because the goal, like that of the compulsory counterclaim, should be not just to facilitate but to *force* joinder of transactionally related claims into a single case. Why should there be an option to assert transactionally related claims against a co-party but a command to assert such claims against an opposing party? Recognizing that there is no good reason to treat the claims differently, some states have made the crossclaim compulsory.[73] Though some commentators have urged that

[71] Until December 2007, this word, like crossclaim, was hyphenated: co-party. See note 70 above.

[72] There is some (scant) authority for the proposition that a plaintiff can assert a crossclaim against a co-plaintiff only if the defendant has asserted a counterclaim against the co-plaintiffs. *See* Danner v. Anskis, 256 F.2d 123 (3d Cir. 1958). There is nothing in Rule 13(g) to suggest that this reading is right. Nowhere does the Rule suggest that *only* a party in a defensive capacity (like a plaintiff who has been sued in a counterclaim) can assert a crossclaim. So *P-1* ought to be able to assert a crossclaim against *P-2* (or vice versa), regardless of whether a defendant files a counterclaim against the plaintiffs.

[73] *See, e.g.,* Kan. Civ. Proc. Code Ann. §60-213(g); Citizens Exch. Bank of Pearson v. Kirkland, 344 S.E.2d 409 (Ga. 1986) (though Georgia's crossclaim provision mirrors Federal

Federal Rule 13(g) be made compulsory, the Rules Advisory Committee has not been persuaded. In all likelihood, few litigants fail to assert cross-claims, so the permissive nature of the Rule does not create much duplicative litigation. On the other hand, surely some parties burden the judicial system by filing separate cases after eschewing the right to assert a cross-claim.[74] And the burden created might not be remedied by issue preclusion. Remember that issue preclusion (like claim preclusion) flows from entry of a valid *final judgment* on the merits, as we saw at §11.2.2. Suppose a defendant in Case 1 refuses to file a crossclaim, but files Case 2 instead. Case 1 might not go to final judgment for years. Thus, issue preclusion cannot streamline the litigation in Case 2 in the meantime, meaning that both cases may proceed in litigation. We end up with two cases where one would do.[75]

The last sentence of Rule 13(g) provides that a crossclaim may include an assertion that the co-party is or may be liable for all or part of the claim against the party asserting the crossclaim. This sentence means that a crossclaim can include a claim against a co-party that that co-party is liable for indemnity or contribution on the plaintiff's claim.[76] This sentence does no harm, but is surplusage; a claim for indemnity or contribution would seem clearly to satisfy the "transaction or occurrence" test of Rule 13(g) anyway.

Remember that Rule 18(a), which we saw at §12.3, allows a litigant who asserts a crossclaim (among others) to assert any claim she may also have against that co-party, regardless of transactional or legal relatedness.

Let's review the principal characteristics of the crossclaim in a hypothetical. It will also demonstrate that crossclaims may come up in tandem with compulsory counterclaims.

- ○ *P*, driving her own car, is involved with a collision with *D-1*, who is driving a car owned by *D-2*. Under applicable law, *D-2* (as owner of the second car) is vicariously liable for the acts of the person to whom she lent the car (*D-1*).[77] *P* brings a single case against both *D-1* and *D-2*. (So *D-1*

Rule 13(g), it is treated as compulsory because of a state statute providing that a judgment is conclusive as to matters that could have been raised in a case).

[74] *See, e.g.*, Davis & Cox v. Summa Corp., 751 F.2d 1507 (9th Cir. 1986) (defendant in earlier case refused to assert crossclaim against co-defendant, but asserted the claim in separate action; permitted because Rule 13(g) is permissive).

[75] One avenue for avoiding overlapping litigation would be for a court to enjoin parties from litigating the dispute in another proceeding in another court. Such injunctions are difficult to get, especially if one seeks a federal court order enjoining parties from litigating in state court. The anti-injunction statute, 28 U.S.C. §2283, reflects an interest in federalism by prohibiting such injunctions outside of three narrow exceptions. The upshot is that it is difficult to stop overlapping *in personam* litigation in federal and state courts.

[76] We discuss these concepts in detail in §12.6.2.

[77] We saw vicarious liability in a similar context at §11.3.5.

and *D-2* are co-parties; why is this okay?[78]) Assume that you represent *D-2*. You don't know who was at fault in the crash. It could have been *P* or it could have been *D-2*. What claims must/may you file in the pending case?

- First, you will have *D-1* answer and file a compulsory counterclaim against *P*. The latter is a claim (for damage to *D-2*'s car) against an opposing party and it arises from the same transaction or occurrence as *P*'s claim against *D-2*. Indeed, as we saw in §12.5.1, *D-2* *must* assert this claim in the pending case or else she is estopped from ever asserting it.

- Second, you may file a crossclaim against *D-1*. This is a claim against a co-party and it arises from the same transaction or occurrence as the underlying case. Note that there will be two aspects to the cross-claim. First, you will claim that *D-1* owes *D-2* indemnity on *P*'s claim. Thus, if *P* wins against *D-2*, this indemnity claim will shift that liability from *D-2* to *D-1*. That protects *D-2* from liability on *P*'s claim. But, if the wreck was *D-1*'s fault, *D-2* will want to recover from *D-1* for damage to her car. So the second aspect of the crossclaim is to recover for the property damage. Both are part of the crossclaim, because both arise from the same transaction or occurrence as the underlying suit.

- In sum, by filing these claims, *D-2* has protected herself either way — whether the wreck was *P*'s fault or *D-1*'s fault. If it was *P*'s fault, *D-2* will recover on the compulsory counterclaim. If it was *D-1*'s fault, *D-2* has done two things: (1) ensured that *D-1* (not *D-2*) is ultimately liable to pay for the judgment (through indemnity) and (2) asserted a claim against *P-1* to recover for the damage to *D-2*'s car. Again, both of these functions are performed by the crossclaim.

- By the way, if *D-2* asserted a crossclaim against *D-1* *only* for indemnity on the claim asserted by *P* (and not for property damage to *D-2*'s car), what problem might *D-2* run into down the road? Claim preclusion! If *D-2* did this, and the jurisdiction adopted a transactional definition of claim, *D-2* would be splitting her claim. (If this point is fuzzy, review §11.2.)

- Now let's take another step. Suppose *D-2* files both the compulsory counterclaim against *P* and the crossclaim for indemnity and for property damage against *D-1*. In addition, suppose *D-2* has a totally unrelated claim against *D-1* (say, for past-due rent). Can she assert that claim in the pending case too? Yes. Rule 18(a) provides that, *once D-2 asserted the crossclaim*, she may join to it any claim she has against that party.[79]

---

[78] Because Rule 20(a) permits joinder of co-defendants if the claim against them arises from the same transaction or occurrence and raises as least one common question. We discussed this in §12.4.

[79] In the absence of the crossclaim, *D-2* could not use Rule 18(a) to assert the rent claim against *D-1*. Remember, Rule 18(a) only applies if a party has already asserted a claim, such as a crossclaim. See §12.3.

∘ Again, suppose *D-2* files both the compulsory counterclaim against *P* and the crossclaim for indemnity and for property damage against *D-1*. Suppose also that *D-1* has a claim against *D-2* arising from the same accident (say, that *D-2*'s car had defective brakes, which caused the wreck). Can *D-1* assert that claim in the pending case? Yes. In fact, arguably she *must* or else lose the claim. Why? We are tempted to say that the claim asserted by *D-1* against *D-2* is a crossclaim, because the two are co-parties. But once *D-2* asserts a crossclaim against *D-1*, the two have become "opposing parties." Thus, the claim back against *D-2* is a counterclaim. Because it arises from the same transaction or occurrence as *D-2*'s claim against *D-1*, it is a compulsory counterclaim.

Subject Matter Jurisdiction. Rule 13(g) simply provides a procedural mechanism for asserting a claim. The claim must invoke federal subject matter jurisdiction, however, or else it cannot be asserted in federal court. As always, this jurisdictional inquiry is a separate step, undertaken after determining that the claim is properly asserted under Rule 13(g).

∘ *A*, *B*, and *C*, each driving her own car, collide, and each is injured. Each suffered damages in excess of $75,000. *A* is a citizen of New York. *B* and *C* are both citizens of New Jersey. *A* sues *B* and *C*, as co-defendants, in federal court. There is no basis for federal question jurisdiction, but *A*'s case does invoke diversity of citizenship jurisdiction. (Why?[80]) *B* asserts a compulsory counterclaim against *A* to recover for her injuries from the wreck. (Why is it a compulsory counterclaim?[81]) *B* also asserts a crossclaim against *C* for those injuries. It is a crossclaim because it is against a co-party and arises from the same transaction or occurrence as the underlying suit. Now, is there subject matter jurisdiction over the counterclaim and the crossclaim? Assume that all claims arise under state law, so there is no basis for the assertion of federal question jurisdiction.

   ∘ *B*'s compulsory counterclaim against *A* invokes diversity of citizenship jurisdiction. It is by a citizen of New Jersey against a citizen of New York and the facts indicate that it exceeds $75,000. (Because it invokes diversity jurisdiction, supplemental jurisdiction is irrelevant; we don't need it.)

   ∘ But the crossclaim does *not* invoke diversity of citizenship jurisdiction. Even though it would satisfy the amount in controversy for diversity (because it exceeds $75,000), there is no diversity between *B* and *C*. The crossclaim is by a citizen of New Jersey against a citizen of New Jersey. So the only way the crossclaim can get into federal court is through supplemental jurisdiction. Does that work here?

   ∘ Section 1367(a) grants supplemental jurisdiction over claims that are part of the same "case or controversy" as the underlying claim that

---

[80] Because the plaintiff is not a co-citizen with either defendant, and the amount in controversy exceeds $75,000. See §4.5.3.

[81] Because it is against an opposing party and it arises from the same transaction or occurrence as that party's claim against *B*.

did invoke subject matter jurisdiction (*P*'s original claim). Claims meet that test if they satisfy the *Gibbs* standard of sharing a "common nucleus of operative fact" with the underlying claim. This standard is always met if the claim arises from the same transaction or occurrence as the underlying claim.[82] By definition, a crossclaim does, because Rule 13(g) requires that they arise from the same transaction or occurrence as the underlying dispute.

- ○ Section 1367(b) applies in cases that invoked diversity of citizenship jurisdiction (as the claim asserted by *A* against *B* and *C* did). It then operates to remove supplemental jurisdiction over certain claims; but that section only removes supplemental jurisdiction over claims asserted by *plaintiffs*. The claim in this case is asserted by a defendant, so §1367(b) does not remove the grant of supplemental jurisdiction. (If any of this material is fuzzy, see §4.7.)

- ○ One last hypothetical in this area, and this one will surprise you. Let's use the same facts as in the previous hypothetical, with the three-way car crash between *A*, *B*, and *C*. All claims are based upon state law, and all claims exceed $75,000. But here, *B* and *C*, as *co-plaintiffs*, sue *A*. *A* is a citizen of New York. *B* and *C* are citizens of New Jersey. As structured — with the two New Jersey plaintiffs against the one New York defendant and with the claims exceeding $75,000 — this case invokes diversity of citizenship jurisdiction. Obviously, *A* will have a compulsory counterclaim against the two plaintiffs. But here's the focus: Suppose *B* asserts a crossclaim for her injuries against *C*. It is a crossclaim because it's against a co-party (a co-plaintiff here), and it arises from the same transaction or occurrence as the underlying diversity of citizenship claim. Is there subject matter jurisdiction over this crossclaim?

  - ○ The crossclaim arises under state law, so it cannot invoke federal question jurisdiction. It also cannot invoke diversity of citizenship jurisdiction, because the crossclaim is asserted by a New Jersey citizen against a New Jersey citizen. Now, can the claim invoke supplemental jurisdiction? The answer should certainly be yes. But apply the supplemental jurisdiction statute. Clearly, §1367(a) grants supplemental jurisdiction, for the same reason as in the previous hypothetical. But look carefully at §1367(b). It applies in cases that invoke diversity of citizenship jurisdiction (as the claims by *B* and *C* against *A* did). And it removes jurisdiction over claims "by plaintiffs against persons made parties under Rule . . . 20." The claim by *B* against *C* is a claim asserted by a plaintiff against someone joined under Rule 20.[83] Thus, under a literal interpretation of the statute, there cannot be supplemental jurisdiction over this claim.

---

[82] Indeed, as we saw in §4.7, §1367(a) requires only that the supplemental claim have some "loose factual connection" with the jurisdiction-invoking claim. See the discussion at pages 641-642 above.

[83] As we saw in §12.4, the only way *B* and *C* could have sued together as co-plaintiffs was to have joined as co-parties under Rule 20(a)(1).

This result is absurd. It means that all other claims (by B and C against A; by A against B and C) will be heard in federal court but that this cross-claim by B against C cannot be; it must be asserted in state court. Thus, the parties and the judicial system are robbed of the efficiency promoted by the joinder rules and supplemental jurisdiction. This result — denying supplemental jurisdiction to a crossclaim by a plaintiff — is contrary to practice in federal courts before the enactment of §1367. In passing the statute, Congress indicated (as discussed in §4.7) that it intended to codify that earlier practice. In this area, however, as in others, the plain language of the statute changes prior practice. The result of a literal interpretation of the statute in this context is also contrary to the underlying premise of diversity of citizenship jurisdiction. After all, in our hypothetical here, each plaintiff remains diverse from each defendant, so there is no sense that permitting supplemental jurisdiction over $P\text{-}1$'s crossclaim will eviscerate the complete diversity rule. There is no clear case authority on this issue, but in view of the literal interpretations accorded §1367 in other contexts, it seems the unfortunate result suggested above may be difficult to avoid.

§12.6   Overriding Plaintiff's Party Joinder Choices

In §12.4, we discussed "proper" parties under Rule 20(a) — those who *may* be joined in a single civil case in federal court. If everyone who could be joined under Rule 20(a) were joined in a single case, there would be no risk of subsequent duplicative or inconsistent litigation; all interested parties would be joined in a single case, and the judgment in that case would bind them all. But as we also saw in §12.4, Rule 20(a) is permissive, so the plaintiff does not have to employ it to the fullest. For a variety of reasons, including jurisdictional limitations and litigation strategy, a plaintiff may often eschew full use of the provision and leave out persons who might have been joined under Rule 20(a). We refer to such nonparties as "absentees."

The question for us now is whether anyone can override the plaintiff's structuring of the case by forcing the joinder of absentees. The answer is yes — at least in certain circumstances. Three joinder devices — compulsory party joinder under Rule 19 (discussed in §12.6.1), impleader under Rule 14 (discussed in §12.6.2), and intervention under Rule 24 (discussed in §12.6.3) — can be used to restructure the party joinder of the case. Throughout our discussion of these devices, it is important to appreciate the effort to accommodate competing policies. On the one hand, our justice system accords great deference to the plaintiff's choices on party structuring; we value litigant autonomy. On the other hand, the plaintiff's party joinder choices may lead to inefficiency and inconsistent outcomes by promoting multiple litigation; it may also subject the interest of the absentee or of the defendant to possible harm. The Federal Rules take the position that the plaintiff's autonomy must give way in such circumstances. Thus, they recognize three policy interests that will justify overriding the plaintiff's party structuring: (1) efficiency, (2) avoiding harm to the absentee, and (3) avoiding harm to the defendant.

As we will see, compulsory party joinder under Rule 19 embraces all three of these policies. Impleader is based mostly on the first and third policies, and intervention embodies the first two policies. As we also will see, these devices might be invoked by different persons. Rule 19 issues are usually raised by a defendant, although the judge has the power to raise them on her own. Impleader is invoked by a defending party. Intervention is invoked by the absentee herself. Thus, these three devices empower different persons to assert that one of three policies ought to override the plaintiff's autonomy in structuring the suit.

§12.6.1 Compulsory Party Joinder (Rule 19)

"Proper," "Required" (or "Necessary"), and "Indispensable" Absentees

Remember, the issue here (and throughout §12.6) is whether an absentee (someone the plaintiff did not join in the pending case) should be forced into the suit. Federal Rule 19 is the most comprehensive provision providing for overriding the plaintiff's joinder choices. While it, like all Federal Rules, governs practice in federal court, most states have adopted a "compulsory joinder" rule modeled on Rule 19. Before looking at that Rule, however, we must tackle some traditional terminology and concepts (which are reflected today in Rule 19).

Parties and potential parties to a civil case fall into one of three traditional categories, which can be viewed as concentric circles. First, the outer (largest) circle reflects "proper" parties to the case. These are persons who *may* be joined, at the option of the plaintiff, because they have sufficient connection to the dispute. Today, such persons are defined in Rule 20(a), discussed at §12.4. Second, inside that circle, as a subset of proper parties, are "required" (or "necessary") parties. These are persons whom the plaintiff did not join in the case, but whose presence is so desirable that the court will override the plaintiff's choice by requiring them to be joined if joinder is possible. Today, such persons are defined in Rule 19(a). Third, inside this circle, as a subset both of necessary and of proper parties, are what have for generations been called "indispensable" parties. These are persons whom the plaintiff did not join, and who (because "necessary") should be joined, but who cannot be joined (e.g., because the court cannot get personal jurisdiction over them). And in their absence, the court has decided that it will dismiss the pending case rather than proceed without such absentees.

The Supreme Court set out famous formulations for necessary and indispensable absentees in the classic 1855 case of *Shields v. Barrow*.[84] The Court defined necessary absentees as "persons having an interest in the controversy, and who ought to be made parties, in order that the court may act."[85] It defined indispensable absentees as those "who not only have an interest in the controversy, but an interest of such a nature that a final decree cannot be made without either affecting that interest, or leaving the controversy in such a condition that its final termination may be wholly inconsistent with equity and good conscience."[86]

You see the problem. These phrases are hardly self-defining. In the wake of *Shields* and other cases, courts and lawyers began to seize on labels rather than analysis. They focused on notions of "joint" versus "severable" interests, and concluded that the label applied was determinative of whether an absentee was merely necessary or indispensable. As one scholar noted, opinions came to show "a ready reliance on labels for solutions of particular cases [and] a thoughtless reiteration — instead of a critical reexamination — of the basic principles of required joinder."[87]

The original version of Rule 19, promulgated in 1938, continued this focus on labels, and proved inflexible in practice. "There seemed to be a sense that absentees in particular kinds of cases automatically fell into one or anther category, without looking at the facts of the case."[88] Scholars criticized that Rule and suggested a more pragmatic and flexible approach to the issues.[89] In 1966, the Rules Advisory Committee, in response to this criticism, rewrote Rule 19. That amendment coincided with amendments to the Rules governing intervention of right[90] and class actions,[91] and emphasized the interplay between those concepts and compulsory joinder of parties. Importantly, the 1966 amendments shifted the focus away from labels toward a step-by-step practical assessment of when and why a court should override the plaintiff's structuring of a case by forcing joinder of a new party and, if that party cannot be joined, when and why the court might either proceed without the absentee or dismiss the pending case. The 2007 restyling of the Federal Rules tinkered with

---

[84] 58 U.S. 130, 139 (1855).

[85] *Id.* at 139.

[86] *Id.*

[87] John Reed, *Compulsory Joinder of Parties in Civil Actions (Pt. 1)*, 55 Mich. L. Rev. 327, 329 (1957).

[88] 4 Moore's Federal Practice 19-13.

[89] The two most influential were Geoffrey Hazard, *Indispensable Party: The Historical Origin of a Procedural Phantom*, 61 Colum. L. Rev. 1254 (1961); John Reed, note 87 above, and *Compulsory Joinder of Parties in Civil Actions (Pt. 2)*, 55 Mich. L. Rev. 483 (1957).

[90] Federal Rule 24(a)(2), which we discuss at §12.6.3.

[91] Federal Rule 23, which we discuss at §13.3.

terminology and, more irksomely, with subheadings. So cases predating the restyled Rule 19 (including those likely to be in your casebook) will refer to subsections that no longer exist, and have been superseded by the restyled subsections. This confusion is courtesy of the Civil Rules Advisory Committee, which spent years on this busy-work, none of which is supposed to change the operation of any of the Rules.

We turn now to the Rule, and emphasize at the outset that the Rule 19 inquiry is always case-specific. Avoid the temptation to reach an answer by knee-jerk reaction; apply Rule 19 in a pragmatic way — sensitive to the underlying policies of *why* the court might override the plaintiff's party structure.

Applying Rule 19

Rule 19 is somewhat tough to decipher. As Justice (then-Judge)[92] Clarence Thomas noted, Rule 19 prescribes a three-step process, "although this fact is obscured by its language."[93]

- First, the court must assess whether the absentee is a "required party" under Rule 19(a). Lawyers and judges have always called such an absentee "necessary." Although the retinkered 2007 version of Rule 19 avoids that word, it is likely that bench and bar will use "necessary" as much as "required." We will use both interchangeably.
- Second, if the absentee is required, the court then asks whether she can be joined in the pending case. Using the word used in Rule 19(b), the court assesses whether joinder is "feasible." This assessment requires the court to determine whether (1) the absentee is subject to personal jurisdiction; (2) whether the absentee can be joined without affecting diversity of citizenship jurisdiction; and (3) whether the absentee, once joined, would have a valid objection to venue. If joinder is feasible in light of these three inquiries, the absentee is ordered joined to the case.[94]
- If joinder of the absentee is *not* feasible, the court must determine whether, in "equity and good conscience," the court should (1) allow the case to proceed without the absentee or, on the other hand, (2) dismiss the case. This assessment is made based upon factors in Rule 19(b). If the court decides to dismiss the pending case rather than to proceed without the absentee, the absentee has always been labeled "indispensable." As noted, though, the 2007 restyling of the Rule deletes this word; nonetheless, bench and bar are accustomed to using it.

---

[92] Before Justice Thomas was appointed to the Supreme Court, he served on the United States Court of Appeals for the District of Columbia Circuit. In the federal system, judicial officers on the Supreme Court are called justices, and those at the court of appeals and district court level are called judges.

[93] Western Md. R. Co. v. Harbor Ins. Co., 910 F.2d 960, 968 n.5 (D.C. Cir. 1990).

[94] Normally, the court will permit the plaintiff to amend her complaint to join the absentee as a party in the case.

Recall that Rule 12(b)(7) permits a court to dismiss a case for failure to join a party under Rule 19. That motion will be granted only if the court goes through all of these steps and concludes that the case should be dismissed.

Now we look in detail at each of the steps involved in the application of Rule 19.

Inquiry Number One: Is the Absentee Required (or Necessary)? Remember, the question is whether an absentee ought to be forced into the case. The absentee will be required if the present party structure of the case satisfies any of the three situations prescribed in Rule 19(a). In addition to learning those three situations, it is important to understand the policies underlying them; each gives a policy basis for overriding the plaintiff's structuring of the case. Of the three bases for forcing joinder of the absentee, one is found in Rule 19(a)(1)(A), and the other two are found in Rule 19(a)(1)(B). The difference between the two subdivisions of the Rule is significant, as a careful reading of the Rule will demonstrate.

Rule 19(a)(1)(B) requires that the absentee claim "an interest relating to the subject of the suit." To qualify, the interest must be "legally protected, [and] not merely a financial interest or interest of convenience."[95] The absentee "must have a direct stake in the pending litigation; an interest in related subject matter is not sufficient to be defined as a necessary party."[96] We will see examples below. Beyond this interest, Rule 19(a)(1)(B) requires that the *failure* to join the absentee (in view of the absentee's interest) will harm someone — either the absentee (in Rule 19(a)(1)(B)(i)) or the defendant (in Rule 19(a)(1)(B)(ii)). Thus, Rule 19(a)(1)(B) can be called the *prejudice* prong of the compulsory joinder rule, because joinder is effected expressly to avoid prejudice to someone — either the absentee or the defendant.

Rule 19(a)(1)(A), in contrast, does not require that the absentee have any interest in the pending case. It mandates joinder not to avoid harm to anyone, but to achieve efficiency. It can be called the *complete relief* prong of the compulsory joinder rule.

In theory, if the absentee satisfies any of the three situations defined by Rule 19(a)(1)(A) and 19(a)(1)(B), the court should order her joinder if joinder is feasible. Now we address these three definitions of a necessary absentee in more detail.

Rule 19(a)(1)(A). Under Rule 19(a)(1)(A), the absentee should be joined if, without her, "the court cannot accord complete relief among existing parties." This clause reflects the traditional aim of equity to decide

---

[95] Northrop Corp. v. McDonnell Douglas Corp., 705 F.2d 1030, 1043 (9th Cir.), *cert. denied*, 464 U.S. 840 (1983).

[96] 4 Moore's Federal Practice 19-47 to 19-48.

disputes by the whole, rather than bit by bit.[97] Joinder under this provision is said to ensure that a court will not enter a "hollow" or "partial" judgment, one that fails effectively to resolve the overall dispute.[98] Joining the absentee obviates the need for other suits and binds the absentee to the judgment in the pending case; this, in turn, avoids the inconsistent results that could arise from multiple litigation.

Although these goals are undeniably laudable, Rule 19(a)(1)(A), as a practical matter, is pretty worthless. Why? It is capable of being interpreted in two ways, one of which is always satisfied and the other of which is never satisfied. (A rule that is either always or never met is not much of a rule.)

First, the Rule may mean that the absentee must be joined whenever leaving the absentee out will fail to resolve the overall dispute — will fail to "do justice" in some grand sense among all potentially affected persons. The problem is that this interpretation is satisfied *every time* there is an absentee who will sue (or will be sued) after resolution of the pending case. A few courts have adopted this interpretation of Rule 19(a)(1)(A), which amounts to holding that the absentee must be joined to avoid multiple litigation.[99] The archetypal case is said to involve a case by the plaintiff against an "excess insurer," which is an insurance company that agrees to cover losses *over* a particular amount.

> ○ *P*'s warehouse burns down. *P* had insurance on the warehouse and its contents with two companies: Primary Ins. Co. (Primary) contracted to cover losses through $200,000, and Excess Insurance Co. (Excess) insured losses over $200,000. *P* sues only Excess, asserting that the damage from loss of the warehouse was $350,000 (and thus that Excess owes *P* $150,000[100]). Some courts and commentators argue that Primary is required under Rule 19(a)(1)(A), because if the court in this case (by *P* against Excess) finds that the damage to *P* was only $195,000, its judgment will be "hollow." Why? Two reasons: (1) it could not be enforced against Excess (because Excess is not liable for amounts of $200,000 and

---

[97] Much of what is reflected today in the joinder provisions of the Federal Rules came from equity practice and from the Federal Equity Rules, which predated the Federal Rules of Civil Procedure. It is a common theme of equity that the court desired to resolve the entire dispute in one suit, rather than permit the litigants to sue serially over one dispute. We discussed the development of equity courts and procedure at §1.2.3.

[98] *See, e.g.*, Northrop Corp. v. McDonnell Douglas Corp., 705 F.2d 1030, 1043 (9th Cir.), *cert. denied*, 464 U.S. 849 (1983) ("This factor is concerned with consummate rather than partial or hollow relief as to those already parties."); Southern Union Co. v. Southwest Gas Corp., 165 F. Supp. 2d 1010 (D. Ariz. 2001).

[99] *See, e.g.*, Walsh v. Centeio, 692 F.2d 1239, 1243 (9th Cir. 1989) (failure to join absentees "would subject trustees to multiple litigation"); Whyham v. Piper Aircraft Corp., 96 F.R.D. 557, 560 (M.D. Pa. 1982); Davila Mendez v. Vatican Shrimp Co., 43 F.R.D. 294, 298 (S.D. Tex. 1966).

[100] Because Excess is liable only for the losses of over $200,000.

less), and (2) it could not be asserted against Primary (because Primary was not a party to the case and thus, under due process, cannot be bound by the judgment (as we discussed in §11.3.4)).

While there is no doubt that such a judgment would be hollow in the ways described, that does not mean that Rule 19(a)(1)(A) should apply to compel joinder of Primary. Such an interpretation of the Rule is contrary to its language. The Rule does not require joinder whenever failure to join the absentee will result in the court's not resolving all disputes among everybody in the world. Instead, it says that joinder is required only when nonjoinder of the absentee means that the court cannot accord complete relief "among existing parties." The judgment in the above hypothetical *does* resolve the entire dispute between those who are already parties, because it tells Excess that it owes *P* nothing. More basically, such a broad reading of Rule 19(a)(1)(A) would swamp all other joinder devices. Remember that Rule 19(a)(1)(A), unlike Rule 19(a)(1)(B), does not require that the absentee have an interest in the pending case. So if this provision is interpreted to require the joinder of any absentee whose nonjoinder threatens to create multiple litigation down the road, there is no need for impleader or for intervention.

Focusing on the specific language of Rule 19(a)(1)(A) thus leads to the second possible interpretation of Rule 19(a)(1)(A) — that it is invoked only when nonjoinder of the absentee means that the court in the pending case cannot wrap things up completely among those who are presently parties. And, as we just saw, it is hard to conceive of a case in which this test will be met. Either the defendant will owe something to the plaintiff or she won't. No matter what the judgment, it will wrap up the dispute *among existing parties* once and for all. So read, then, the Rule never applies.

In view of these problems with determining the proper scope of Rule 19(a)(1)(A), it is not surprising that courts have shied away from doing much with it. Courts seem never to rely on Rule 19(a)(1)(A) *exclusively* to order the joinder of an absentee. Instead, to the extent that courts pay attention to the subdivision at all, they use it in conjunction with one of the bases for joinder laid out in Rule 19(a)(1)(B).[101] Thus, Rule 19(a)(1)(A) has had little impact on compulsory joinder doctrine. Does that mean that its policy of efficient joinder is meaningless? No. The policy is important, but is limited in impact to those cases satisfying one of the prejudice bases for joinder under Rule 19(a)(1)(B). Every time joinder is effected under Rule 19(a)(1)(B), it fosters the efficiency and consistency we desire. It does so, however, in a way that does not simply run roughshod over plaintiff autonomy and render meaningless the other joinder provisions of the Federal Rules.

[101] *See* 4 Moore's Federal Practice §19.03[2][c].

Rule 19(a)(1)(B)(i). As we saw above, both bases for compelling joinder of the absentee under Rule 19(a)(1)(B) — 19(a)(1)(B)(i) and 19(a)(1)(B)(ii) — require that the absentee have some interest in the underlying dispute *and* that somebody (either the absentee or the defendant) stand to be harmed if the litigation proceeds without the absentee. Rule 19(a)(1)(B)(i) focuses on the potential harm to the *absentee's* interest if she is not joined in the pending case. Specifically, the court assesses whether the absentee is so situated that litigating without her "may as a practical matter impair or impede [her] ability to protect the interest." The policy basis for joinder here is clear: We should not allow the plaintiff's leaving the absentee out of the case to harm the absentee. We see in §12.6.3 that this same policy underlies intervention of right.

Notice that this provision focuses on *practical* harm to the absentee's ability to protect her interest. This language reflects the fact that the absentee generally could not suffer "legal" harm if the case proceeded as originally structured. As we discussed in §§11.2.1 and 11.3.5, absentees (unless in privity with a party, which is rare) cannot be bound legally by the judgment in a case. In many circumstances, however, an absentee not bound legally might be adversely affected in a practical way by the judgment. Suppose, for example, that *P* sues a Trustee, seeking to recover trust funds held by the Trustee. Absentee claims to be the proper beneficiary of the trust. If *P* wins the pending case, *A* is not bound by the judgment. But, as a practical matter, *A*'s ability to protect her interest may be impaired, because the money will be in *A*'s pocket, and may be squandered or removed from the country before *A* can sue *P*.

One interesting question is whether the absentee's ability to protect her interest might be harmed by the *stare decisis* effect of the judgment in the pending case. *Stare decisis* is the doctrine of precedent, which stands for the proposition that an appellate decree on a question of law binds all lower courts within that jurisdiction. As commonly understood, *stare decisis* cannot emanate from a trial court determination of issues of fact. Occasionally, but rarely, *stare decisis* can constitute a relevant harm under Rule 19(a)(1)(B)(i).

A good example of the proper use of *stare decisis*-as-relevant-harm involved disputed ownership of reefs near Florida.[102] Two private parties claimed ownership. If the reefs were part of the outer continental shelf, however, they would be owned by the United States. The case was brought by the United States against one of the private claimants to the reefs. The other private claimant to the reefs was the absentee. The court recognized that the issue was important enough to the parties to ensure that it would be appealed to the court of appeals for a determination of the legal question of government ownership. That ruling would result in precedent that

---

[102] Atlantis Dev. Corp. v. United States, 379 F.2d 818 (5th Cir. 1967).

would be very difficult for the absentee to undo in subsequent litigation.[103] In such circumstances, the court properly concluded, the precedential effect of the case could constitute a harm justifying joinder of the absentee.[104] Some other opinions have not been nearly as careful, and have invoked the "stare decisis" label to justify finding a harm to absentees from what seem to be nothing more than findings of fact by a trial court.[105]

Rule 19(a)(1)(B)(ii). Again, with Rule 19(a)(1)(B)(ii), the absentee has an interest in the pending case. But here the absentee must be joined to prevent potential harm to an existing party in that case. Specifically, as in Rule 19(a)(1)(B)(i), the absentee must have "an interest relating to the subject of the action" and must be so situated that not joining her might subject a party "to a substantial risk of incurring double, multiple, or otherwise inconsistent obligations." The policy basis for forcing joinder here is also clear: It is not to avoid harm to the absentee, but to a present party. The litigation is structured in such a way that going forward without the absentee involved puts a party at risk of being hit with double or inconsistent obligations.

We must note two points here. First, although the Rule focuses on harm to anyone who is already a party in the pending case, in fact it is concerned about harm to a *defending party*; in most cases, of course, this means the defendant.[106] If the plaintiff has so structured the case as to subject herself to harm, it is not clear why the judicial system should try to help her. But if she has so structured the case as to cause harm to a party haled into court in a defensive position, the system should try to ameliorate the situation. Second, note that the Rule is aimed at a specific kind of harm to the defendant: the risk of being put to "double, multiple, or otherwise inconsistent *obligations*" because of the absentee's interest.[107] The Rule does not say the joinder is required to avoid subjecting the defendant to

---

[103] Specifically, if the United States won the first case, the Fifth Circuit would have decreed as a matter of law that the reefs were part of the outer continental shelf. For the absentee to press its claim of private ownership in a separate case, it would have to get the Fifth Circuit to overrule that holding *en banc* or to get the Supreme Court to overrule it. Either was a long shot. *Atlantis*, 379 F.2d at 828.

[104] Actually, the case involved intervention of right under Rule 24(a)(2). As we see in §12.6.3, however, the operative test for harm to the absentee is the same in that Rule as it is in Rule 19(a)(1)(B)(i).

[105] *See, e.g.,* Ranger Ins. Co. v. United Housing of N.M., Inc., 488 F.2d 682, 684 (5th Cir. 1974) (holding in declaratory judgment case brought by insurance company concerning whether its coverage responsibilities under a policy might bind absentees through *stare decisis*).

[106] Remember, though, a plaintiff can be a defending party if the defendant has asserted a counterclaim against her.

[107] Because "double" is a form of "multiple," reference to the former seems unnecessary. The Rule should simply express concern about "multiple or otherwise inconsistent obligations." The word "double" adds nothing to the phrase.

multiple *litigation*. Thus, if the party structure merely threatens the defendant with potential multiple suits, that is not enough. This fact is another factor that counsels a narrow reading of Rule 19(a)(1)(A), as we saw above.

- ○ Busline provides bus transportation. One of its buses is involved in a wreck, injuring six passengers. Passenger #1 sues Busline for personal injury damages. Are Passengers #2 through #6 necessary under Rule 19(a)(1)(B)(ii)? No. Although the litigation as structured certainly threatens Busline with multiple litigation, it does not subject Busline to potential multiple or inconsistent *obligations*.

As envisioned by Rule 19(a)(1)(B)(i), inconsistent obligations are created when two (or more) orders put the defendant in a position in which she cannot satisfy one order without violating the other. Such problems usually arise in claims for equitable relief (like an injunction or declaratory judgment) and not in claims for damages. For example, the Rule would be invoked if one judgment ordered a corporation to issue stock in one person's name while another judgment ordered the corporation to issue stock in a different person's name. There, the corporation cannot honor one judgment without violating the other. This problem is not faced with monetary damages. If Passenger #1 wins, the court will order Busline to pay money to her. Then, if Passenger #2 loses, the court will order that Busline does not have to pay money to her.[108] These are not inconsistent obligations. There is nothing inconsistent in Busline's having to write a check to one passenger and not to another.[109]

Applying Rule 19(a). Let's try some hypotheticals, based upon cases that may be in your casebook.

- ○ *P* has surgery in which a metal "plate and screw device" is implanted in her spine. The surgery was performed by Doctor at Hospital; the device was manufactured by Corporation. *P* sues only Corporation, and does not join Doctor or Hospital. (Quick review question: Could *P* have joined Doctor and Hospital with Corporation as three co-defendants?[110]) Are Doctor or Hospital necessary under Rule 19(a)?

---

[108] In this case, perhaps Passenger #2 could have won if she could have used nonmutual offensive issue preclusion against Busline, on the issue of Busline's negligence (assuming that issue was litigated and determined in the first case). But many jurisdictions do not recognize nonmutual offensive issue preclusion. See §11.3.5.

[109] We revisit this point in discussing class actions under Rule 23(b)(1)(B), at §13.3.5.

[110] Yes. This question is covered by Rule 20(a). Joinder of co-defendants is proper when the claims against them arise from the same transaction or occurrence and raise at least one common question of law or fact. Here, the claims against all three arise from implanting the device in *P*'s spine, and all present the common question of who, if anyone, was negligent. (If any of this material is fuzzy, see §12.4.)

These are the facts of *Temple v. Synthes Corp.*,[111] in which a unanimous Supreme Court answered emphatically: No. According to the Court, joint tortfeasors are not necessary parties. Period. The Court simply says, "It has long been the rule that it is not necessary for all joint tortfeasors to be named as defendants in a single lawsuit. Nothing in the 1966 revision to Rule 19 changed that principle."[112] Thus, if a party wants to force the joinder of additional joint tortfeasors, she must find some joinder device other than Rule 19 (we see below that the appropriate action is for the defendant to implead the absentees).

○   *D* operates a shopping mall. It leases a space to *P*, who will operate a jewelry store. *D* now plans to lease another store in the same mall to *A*, who will also operate a jewelry store. *P* claims that this deal with *A* violates a clause in her lease that says that *D* would not allow another jewelry store to operate in the mall. *P* sues *D*, seeking an injunction to stop *D* from signing the lease with *A*. Is *A* necessary?

These are the facts of *Helzberg's Diamond Shops, Inc. v. Valley West Des Moines Shopping Center, Inc.*[113] Rather than reacting to the question intuitively, apply Rule 19(a) pragmatically. Because Rule 19(a)(1)(A) has had little independent impact, let's start with Rule 19(a)(1)(B). (Remember that anytime the court orders joinder of an absentee under Rule 19(a)(1)(B), the efficiency and consistency goals of Rule 19(a)(1)(A) are realized.)

First, *A* does have an interest in the pending suit, because *A* has negotiated a lease in the same mall. (Remember, under both parts of Rule 19(a)(1)(B), the absentee must have such an interest.) Second, the present joinder scheme threatens to harm *A*'s interest, because if *P* wins the pending suit, the court will issue an injunction stopping *D* from leasing the store to *A*. Thus, *A* satisfies Rule 19(a)(1)(B)(i) because failure to join *A* may *as a practical matter* impair or impede *A*'s ability to protect her interest.[114] Third, this case also satisfies Rule 19(a)(1)(B)(ii) because the present party structure threatens *D* with inconsistent obligations. If *P* wins the present case, the court will order *D* not to sign the lease with *A*. Then *A* will sue *D* in a separate case, seeking an injunction to force *D* to sign the lease. If *A*

---

[111] 498 U.S. 5 (1990).

[112] *Temple*, 498 U.S. at 7. The opinion is extraordinary because the Supreme Court granted certiorari and issued the opinion (reversing the Fifth Circuit's holding that the absentees were necessary) without oral argument. This procedural background is undoubtedly a sign that the Court considered the issue to be obvious.

[113] 564 F.2d 816 (8th Cir. 1977).

[114] The judgment in the case by *P* against *D* will not bind *A* as a legal matter. She is not a party, nor in privity with a party to that case, and thus, as a matter of due process, cannot be bound. See §§11.2.1; 11.3.4. Rather, the harm to *A*'s interest is practical — *D* won't sign the lease to her.

657

wins that case, *D* is put in an untenable situation: One decree tells it not to sign the lease with *A*, and another tells it to sign the lease with *A*. Rule 19(a)(1)(B)(ii) is aimed at avoiding exactly that sort of inconsistent obligation by forcing the joinder of *A* in the present case.

> ○ *A* owns 1,000 shares of stock in Corporation, in her own name. *P* claims that she and *A* had bought the stock together and that the stock was supposed to have issued in both names as joint owners. *P* sues Corporation, seeking to have *A*'s stock canceled and the shares reissued in the joint names of *P* and *A*. Is *A* necessary?

This hypothetical is similar to the preceding one, and is similar to the facts in *Haas v. Jefferson National Bank*.[115] First, *A* obviously has an interest in the pending suit, since the fight is about stock she presently owns outright. Second, the present joinder scheme threatens harm to *A*'s interest, because if *P* wins, *A*'s stock is canceled and reissued to him and *P* jointly. *A* goes from being sole owner of the stock to joint owner of the stock. Although *A* would not be bound legally by the judgment (because she was not a party to the case), as a practical matter, her interest would be worth demonstrably less than it is now. Third, the present party structure also satisfies Rule 19(a)(1)(B)(ii) because it threatens Corporation with inconsistent obligations. If *P* wins this case, the court will order Corporation to cancel *A*'s stock and reissue the shares in the joint names of *P* and *A*. Then *A* will sue Corporation. If *A* wins that case, the court will order Corporation to issue the same shares in the name of *A* only. Corporation cannot satisfy one decree without violating the other.

> ○ *P* represents the estate of a decedent who was killed in the crash of a chartered airplane. *P* sues the manufacturer of the airplane. Are any of these absentees necessary: the company that owned and operated the plane, the company that serviced the plane, the estate of the pilot?

The quick answer to this case is no, based upon the Supreme Court decision in *Temple v. Synthes Corp.*, which we saw above.[116] That case held that joint tortfeasors are not necessary parties. The case on which this hypothetical is based — *Whyham v. Piper Aircraft Corp.*[117] was decided before *Temple* — and is a good example of sloppy Rule 19 analysis.

The court in *Whyham* held that all three bases of Rule 19(a) were satisfied. First, it concluded that Rule 19(a)(1)(A) was met because the failure

---

[115] 442 F.2d 394 (5th Cir. 1971). Throughout our discussion of cases applying Rule 19, keep in mind that the restyling of the Rules in 2007 affected the subheadings of the provision. What is today Rule 19(a)(1)(A) was Rule 19(a)(1). What is today Rule 19(a)(1)(B)(i) was Rule 19(a)(2)(i). What is today Rule 19(a)(1)(B)(ii) was Rule 19(a)(2)(ii).

[116] See note 111 above.

[117] 96 F.R.D. 557 (M.D. Pa. 1982).

to join the absentees would result in multiple litigation. We discussed above why this conclusion is an erroneous interpretation of the Rule. Second, it concluded that Rule 19(a)(1)(B)(i) was met because the absentees somehow would be harmed by the judgment in the pending case. It is impossible to see how that can be the case, however. If the court orders the manufacturer to write a check to P, how does that harm the absentees? True, the manufacturer may now sue the absentees for contribution or indemnification, but the judgment in this case does nothing to the absentees. Finally, the court concluded that Rule 19(a)(1)(B)(ii) was met because the manufacturer would be subjected to multiple or inconsistent obligations. The argument is this: If the manufacturer loses this case and then sues the absentees for contribution or indemnity and loses, the manufacturer will have to pay the entire loss. Here, finally, the court is on solid ground. Such a scenario does seem to subject the defendant to multiple obligations as envisioned by Rule 19(a)(1)(B)(ii). In most cases, however, the defendant will be able to protect itself by impleading the absentee under Rule 14(a)(1) (see §12.6.2).[118]

To this point, we have determined that the absentees are necessary.

Inquiry Number Two: Is Joinder of the Absentee Feasible? Assuming the absentee is required the next focus is whether the absentee can feasibly be joined to the pending case. If the answer is yes, the court will force joinder of the absentee under Rule 19(a)(2).

Three factors are relevant to the feasibility inquiry. First, for joinder to be feasible, the absentee must be "subject to service of process," which means she must be subject to personal jurisdiction in the pending case. As we discussed at §2.5, the federal court in which the case is pending may use any long-arm statute available to state courts in the state in which it sits. In addition, the "bulge rule" allows for service outside the forum state, regardless of state law, within 100 miles of the federal courthouse.[119] In addition, the absentee may waive any personal jurisdiction objection by agreeing to be joined in the pending case.

Second, Rule 19(a)(3) also provides that if the absentee "objects to venue and the joinder [of the absentee] would make venue improper," the court must dismiss the absentee from the case. Such an absentee is treated as one whose joinder is not feasible.[120] Again, however, the absentee may simply waive a venue objection and be joined if she prefers.

---

[118] In *Whyham*, the defendant manufacturer could not use impleader, because the persons it would implead were not subject to personal jurisdiction. Thus, Rule 19 was the only vehicle for raising the potential harm to the defendant in that case.

[119] Federal Rule 4(k)(1)(B). The bulge rule is not available for service upon an original defendant, but may be used to serve process on a necessary absentee. See §3.3.4.

[120] 4 Moore's Federal Practice 19-74.

Third, and most important, Rule 19(a) provides that joinder will be feasible if "joinder [of the absentee] will not deprive the court of subject matter jurisdiction." As we have seen over and over, every claim asserted in federal court must be supported by federal subject matter jurisdiction. The subject matter limitations on federal jurisdiction are not waivable and the parties cannot avoid them by stipulation. The Federal Rules *cannot* affect the jurisdiction of the federal courts.[121] It is also important to remember that subject matter jurisdiction attaches to claims, not to parties.[122] Thus, the *claim asserted by or against the necessary party* must be assessed for subject matter jurisdiction. Obviously, if the claim asserted by or against the absentee arises under federal law, it invokes federal question jurisdiction and can be asserted in the pending case. Joinder is feasible and the court will order it. Most problems in this area concern state law claims asserted by or against the absentee, and the effect of joinder on diversity of citizenship jurisdiction.

In such cases, a crucial step in assessing subject matter jurisdiction is the *alignment* of the necessary party. Once the court determines that the absentee should be joined, it must then align the absentee in the pending litigation, which means it must determine whether the absentee should be joined as a plaintiff or as a defendant. The parties (and perhaps even the absentee) will brief this issue for the court, but the decision is made by the court itself. The court must determine, on the basis of the facts of the individual case, whether the absentee's interest is more closely aligned with the plaintiff or the defendant. The decision can have important ramifications for subject matter jurisdiction.

- *P*, a citizen of Oregon, sues *D*, a citizen of Colorado, on a state law claim (so there is no federal question jurisdiction) for $200,000. The claim invokes diversity of citizenship jurisdiction and is properly filed in federal court. *A*, the absentee, is a necessary party and is a citizen of Colorado. If *A* is joined as a defendant, against whom *P* will then assert a state law claim of more than $75,000, joinder is feasible. Why? Because there is diversity of citizenship jurisdiction over the claim asserted by *P* against *A*. In other words, joining *A* does not harm subject matter jurisdiction. Because joinder is feasible, the court would order that *A* be joined.
  - But suppose instead that the court aligns *A* as a plaintiff to assert a state law claim of more than $75,000 against *D*. Because *A* and *D* are co-citizens, the claim asserted by *A* against *D* cannot invoke diversity of citizenship jurisdiction. Unless supplemental jurisdiction can be used (which we address momentarily), joinder is not feasible, and the court would then go to Inquiry Number Three (below) of determining whether to proceed in the litigation without *A* or dismiss the case.

---

[121] Federal Rule 82 (Federal Rules "shall not be construed to extend or limit the jurisdiction of the United States district courts or the venue of actions therein.").

[122] Personal jurisdiction is exercised over parties, not claims.

The problem encountered in this last hypothetical is not limited to situations in which the absentee is brought in as a plaintiff. The same problem would be encountered if *A* in our hypothetical were a citizen of Oregon aligned as a defendant. In that case, the claim asserted by *P* against *A* would lack diversity of citizenship jurisdiction (because it would be by an Oregon citizen against an Oregon citizen). As another example, even if there were diversity of citizenship between the absentee and the party on the opposite side of the litigation, if the state law claim did satisfy the amount in controversy requirement for diversity cases, the claim could not invoke diversity of citizenship jurisdiction and joinder would not be feasible.

Can supplemental jurisdiction support the claim asserted by or against a necessary party? Supplemental jurisdiction, as we have seen repeatedly, allows federal courts to entertain claims that by themselves do not invoke an "independent" basis of federal subject matter jurisdiction — in other words, claims that do not invoke diversity of citizenship, alienage, or federal question jurisdiction. If supplemental jurisdiction will support claims by or against necessary parties, it will render joinder feasible because it will allow the claim to be joined in the pending case. (If any of this material is fuzzy, review §4.7; the remainder of the discussion here builds on that material.)

Historically, before the supplemental jurisdiction statute became law in 1990, courts refused to exercise supplemental jurisdiction over claims by or against necessary parties. Several commentators criticized the lack of supplemental jurisdiction in this context. First, it made inclusive joinder less feasible in federal court. Second, it was completely inconsistent with the view the courts had taken concerning supplemental jurisdiction over claims by and against intervenors of right under Rule 24(a)(2) (which we address in §12.6.3). For now, it is sufficient to note that the test for a necessary party under Rule 19(a)(1)(B)(i) and the test for intervention of right under Rule 24(a)(2) are functionally identical. Stated another way, an absentee who qualifies for intervention of right under Rule 24(a)(2) will also be a necessary party under Rule 19(a)(1)(B)(i). Yet, inconsistently, the courts would exercise supplemental jurisdiction in one situation — regarding intervention of right[123] — but not the other — regarding necessary parties. This inconsistency can be called the *Rule 19/Rule 24 anomaly.*

Every commentator who expressed a view on the Rule 19/Rule 24 anomaly urged that it be fixed by making supplemental jurisdiction available in both situations.[124] Not one commentator suggested that the

---

[123] *See, e.g.,* Curtis v. Sears, Roebuck & Co., 754 F.2d 781, 783 (8th Cir. 1985); Burger King Corp. v. American Natl. Bank & Trust Co., 119 F.R.D. 672, 678 (N.D. Ill. 1988).

[124] George Fraser, *Ancillary Jurisdiction of Federal Courts of Persons Whose Interest May Be Impaired If Not Joined,* 62 F.R.D. 483, 485-487; Richard D. Freer, *Rethinking*

anomaly should be fixed by removing supplemental jurisdiction over claims by and against an intervenor of right. Yet, that is exactly what Congress did in the supplemental jurisdiction statute. Thus, Congress, having declared its intention to codify familiar practice in §1367,[125] actually changed it with regard to supplemental jurisdiction involving intervention of right — and changed it in a way not one person had advocated! As to Rule 19, the statute evidently retains the historic rule rejecting supplemental jurisdiction. Because drafters of the statute have argued that it actually expanded supplemental jurisdiction in this area, however, we must review the application of §1367 to claims by and against absentees joined under Rule 19.

Section 1367(a) grants supplemental jurisdiction over claims that comprise part of the same "case or controversy" as a claim that invokes an independent basis of federal subject matter jurisdiction. As commonly interpreted, this means supplemental jurisdiction attaches to claims that arise from a common nucleus of operative fact (or from the same transaction or occurrence) as a claim that invoked federal question or diversity of citizenship jurisdiction. There has never been serious doubt that claims by and against necessary parties satisfy this test.[126] By definition, such an absentee has an interest in the case and is so closely related to it that either her interest may be impaired or her nonjoinder threatens the defendant with multiple or inconsistent obligations. Thus, §1367(a) clearly grants supplemental jurisdiction over claims by or against a necessary party.

The problems arise with the application of §1367(b), which cuts back on the grant of supplemental jurisdiction. Section 1367(b) applies only in cases that invoked diversity of citizenship jurisdiction and then removes supplemental jurisdiction over specific listed claims. Those claims fall into three categories, two of which are relevant here. Specifically, there is no supplemental jurisdiction in a diversity of citizenship case "over claims by plaintiffs against persons made parties under Rule . . . 19 . . . of the Federal Rules" or "over claims by persons proposed to be joined as plaintiffs under Rule 19 of such rules." Thus, supplemental jurisdiction is *not* available in a diversity of citizenship case for claims (1) asserted by the plaintiff against a necessary party joined as a defendant or (2) asserted by the necessary party if she is joined as a plaintiff.

Compulsory Joinder: A Proposal to Restructure Federal Rule 19, 60 N.Y.U. L. Rev. 1061, 1085-1088 (1985); John Kennedy, *Let's All Join In: Intervention Under Federal Rule 24*, 57 Ky. L.J. 329, 362-363 (1969); Joan Steinman, *Postremoval Changes in the Party Structure of Diversity Cases: The Old Law, the New Law, and Rule 19*, 38 U. Kan. L. Rev. 864, 950 (1990).

[125] The express goals of Congress were (1) to overrule the result of the *Finley* case and (2) in all other respects to "codify pre-*Finley* practice." See §4.7. Pre-*Finley* practice recognized supplemental jurisdiction over claims by and against intervenors of right. As we see in §12.6.3, however, §1367 changed that practice.

[126] *See* 4 Moore's Federal Practice, §19.04[1][b].

- ○ Assume that all claims are based upon state law and that they exceed $75,000. *P*, a citizen of Texas, sues *D*, a citizen of Missouri. The claim invokes diversity of citizenship jurisdiction and is properly filed in federal court. *A* is a necessary party and is a citizen of Missouri. If *A* is joined as a plaintiff, her claim against *D* does not invoke diversity of citizenship jurisdiction, because *A* and *D* are co-citizens. Supplemental jurisdiction is not available (even though the claim asserted by *A* against *D* satisfies §1367(a)) because this is a claim asserted by a person proposed to be joined as a plaintiff under Rule 19; §1367(b) prohibits supplemental jurisdiction.

- ○ Same facts except here *A* is a citizen of Texas and will be joined as a defendant. Here, there is no diversity of citizenship over the claim asserted by *P* against *A*, because each is a citizen of Texas. Does supplemental jurisdiction help? Again, the claim by *P* against *A* will satisfy §1367(a). But §1367(b) precludes supplemental jurisdiction over the claim by *P* against *A* because it is a claim asserted by a plaintiff against a person joined under Rule 19; section 1367(b) prohibits supplemental jurisdiction over that claim.[127]

On the other hand, the Fifth Circuit has employed supplemental jurisdiction in the Rule 19 context. It did so on a claim asserted by a defendant under Rule 13(h). As we saw in §12.5.1, that Rule permits a defendant to join a new party to its counterclaim or crossclaim, so long as the party joined satisfied either Rule 19 or 20. In *State National Insurance Co. v. Yates*,[128] a diversity of citizenship case, the defendant asserted a compulsory counterclaim against the plaintiff. The counterclaim independently satisfied the requirements of diversity of citizenship jurisdiction. The defendant used Rule 13(h) to assert the counterclaim against an absentee, who was a necessary party under Rule 19. The absentee was a co-citizen

---

[127] Although the statute precludes supplemental jurisdiction over the claims asserted there, some commentators have argued that nothing in §1367 prohibits *joining* the absentee as a defendant. They argue that *A* could be brought into the case as a defendant consistent with §1367(b) and go on to hail the statute for having expanded the availability of supplemental jurisdiction in the necessary parties context. Thomas Rowe, Stephen Burbank, & Thomas Mengler, *Compounding Confusion and Hampering Diversity? A Reply to Professor Freer*, 40 Emory L.J. 943, 955-959 (1991). The assertion is odd. The reason *A* is aligned as a defendant, presumably, is that *P* has a claim against her; she is joined precisely because *P* has a claim against her. Yet, §1367(b) makes it clear that there is no supplemental jurisdiction over that claim. So it is not at all clear what is gained by joining *A* in this scenario. *A* becomes a party but *P* cannot assert a claim against her. Why bother?

The commentators seem to be advocating the exercise of supplemental jurisdiction over a *party*, which is a fundamental misconception. Supplemental jurisdiction, like all subject matter jurisdiction, is exercised over *claims*, not parties. The First Circuit rejected the argument made by the commentators cited above in Picciotto v. Continental Cas. Co., 512 F.3d 9, 23 (1st Cir. 2008) ("[W]e fail to see how supplemental jurisdiction, which supports the addition of related claims, could be helpful to the [plaintiffs] in their argument for the joinder of a party against whom no claims would be asserted.").

[128] 391 F.3d 577, 579-581 (5th Cir. 2004).

of the defendant, however, which meant that counterclaim failed to invoke diversity (neither did it invoke federal question or alienage jurisdiction). The court held that the claim invoked supplemental jurisdiction. First, it fell within the grant of §1367(a) because it was sufficiently related to the underlying dispute to satisfy *Gibbs*. Second, though §1367(b) applies in diversity cases, nothing in that subsection removed supplemental jurisdiction. Specifically, the provision removes jurisdiction over claims by plaintiffs under specific Federal Rules. The claim in *Yates* was asserted by a defendant under Rule 13(h), which is not mentioned in §1367(b).[129]

So, ultimately the supplemental jurisdiction statute may help facilitate joinder of absentees under Rule 19, at least if they are brought in as additional parties to a counterclaim or crossclaim. It does not seem to help, however, when the absentee is brought in directly under Rule 19. Don't forget, though, that §1367(b) only applies in diversity of citizenship cases.

- ∘ *P*, a citizen of Tennessee, sues *D*, a citizen of Tennessee, for violating her rights under a federal statute. The claim invokes federal question jurisdiction and is properly filed in federal court. *A*, the absentee, is a necessary party and is also a citizen of Tennessee. She is joined as a plaintiff and asserts a state law claim against *D*. This claim is not supported by federal question jurisdiction (because it's based on state law) or by diversity of citizenship jurisdiction (because *A* and *D* are co-citizens). Does it invoke supplemental jurisdiction? Yes. First, §1367(a) grants supplemental jurisdiction because the claim derives from a common nucleus of operative fact from the underlying case. Second, §1367(b) does not apply, so it cannot remove this supplemental jurisdiction. Remember, §1367(b) only applies in cases that invoke diversity of citizenship jurisdiction. The original claim here invoked federal question jurisdiction.

To this point, then, the court has determined that the absentee is necessary and has assessed whether her joinder is feasible. If joinder is feasible, the court ordinarily allows the plaintiff an opportunity to add the absentee. Should the plaintiff fail to do so, Rule 19(a)(2) provides that the court "must order that [the absentee] be made a party." The court may order joinder as a defendant or as a plaintiff. If she is joined as a defendant, ordinarily the plaintiff will then amend her complaint to state a claim against the absentee. If she is joined as a plaintiff, she will file an appropriate pleading setting forth her claim.[130]

---

[129] *Id.* at 578-581.

[130] If a necessary absentee should be aligned as a plaintiff but refuses to participate, the court may order her joinder as a defendant and then realign her as a plaintiff. In rare cases, such an absentee can be joined as an "involuntary plaintiff," who will be bound by the judgment even if she refuses to participate in the case. Courts have applied the involuntary plaintiff doctrine only when the absentee and the plaintiff are so closely related that the absentee must allow the use of her name to allow the existing plaintiff to secure relief. These are

What happens, though, if the court finds that the absentee cannot feasibly be joined? Then, the court must move to the third step of the analysis.

Inquiry Number Three: If Joinder Is Not Feasible, Should the Court Proceed Without the Absentee or Dismiss the Pending Case? To this point, the court has concluded that the absentee ought to be joined but that her joinder is not feasible. Now, the court must either (1) proceed with the present litigation, without joining the absentee, or (2) dismiss the present case. Each choice is troublesome. If the court proceeds, it risks subjecting either the absentee or the defendant to the kind of harm Rule 19 is intended to avoid. On the other hand, if the court dismisses the case, it denies the plaintiff the forum she selected. If it chooses this latter course, the absentee has long been called "indispensable," and the case is dismissed under Rule 12(b)(7). The restyling of Rule 19 in 2007 removed the word "indispensable," but it seems likely judges and lawyers will continue to use it.

How does the court decide which way to go? The choice is governed by Rule 19(b), which starts by saying that the court should consider whether dismissal is appropriate "in equity and good conscience."[131] Beyond this open-ended phrase, Rule 19(b) lists four nonexclusive factors for guiding the decision. The factors are not listed in hierarchical order. At first blush, the factors do not seem original; they echo the sorts of concerns addressed under Rule 19(a) in determining whether the absentee was required in the first place. Importantly, however, the thrust of the Rule 19(b) assessment is different. While Rule 19(a) asks the court to determine whether the sorts of harm envisioned by that Rule *might* occur[132] if the absentee is not joined, here the assessment is whether such harm *really will* occur. "There is a difference in degrees. The decision of whether to proceed or dismiss the case requires a closer look at the real probability and severity of prejudice caused by nonjoinder versus prejudice caused by dismissal."[133]

Reflecting this emphasis on *probability* rather than *possibility*, Rule 19(b)(1) instructs the court to consider "the extent to which a judgment rendered in the person's absence might prejudice that person or the existing parties." Here, the court may sneak a peek at the merits and determine whether the plaintiff's claim is likely to result in harm of either type. In addition, the court should consider whether either the absentee or the defendant might be able to avoid harm by taking some action. For instance,

---

rare cases, and include suits by an exclusive licensee of a patent; the patent holder might be joined as an involuntary plaintiff. *See* 4 Moore's Federal Practice §19.04[4][b].

[131] This phrase comes from the classic case of *Shields v. Barrow*, 58 U.S. 130, 139 (1855), and is adopted verbatim in Rule 19(b).

[132] Rule 19(a)(1)(B) requires only that one of the relevant harms "may" occur; it does not require that such harm must or necessarily will occur.

[133] 4 Moore's Federal Practice 19-82.

the absentee might be able to intervene; her refusing to do so may indicate that the absentee does not consider the potential harm to be great. Likewise, the defendant may be able to avoid multiple or inconsistent obligations by impleading the absentee or, if the dispute concerns ownership of property, by instituting interpleader.

Rule 19(b)(2) calls for the court to be creative and to consider "protective provisions in the judgment," "shaping the relief," and other measures to avoid or lessen potential harm to the absentee or the defendant. Some people refer to this power as the court's "molding the decree" to let the case go forward while protecting the absentee and defendant from potential harm. For example, if the plaintiff sues for rescission of a contract to which the absentee is a party, the court might avoid the harm that rescission would cause by having the successful plaintiff recover damages.[134] Or, as the Supreme Court suggested in *Provident Tradesmens Bank & Trust Co. v. Patterson*,[135] in litigation concerning conflicting claims to a fund, the court might order that some of the fund remain undistributed, so it is available to satisfy a subsequent claim asserted by the absentee.

Rule 19(b)(3) instructs the court to address whether the judgment can be adequate if the case proceeds without joinder of the absentee. This factor implicates both the goal of avoiding harm to absentee and defendant and also "the interest of courts and the public in complete, consistent, and efficient settlement of controversies."[136] Again, the court looks to whether the harm that is the center of compulsory joinder doctrine will actually result if the case proceeds and not just that it is a theoretical possibility.

Finally, Rule 19(b)(4) counsels the court to address the flip side of the coin — "whether the plaintiff would have an adequate remedy if the action were dismissed for nonjoinder." In other words, if the court dismisses the pending case, will the plaintiff be able to get justice? In assessing this issue, most courts look to whether the plaintiff would have an adequate alternative forum in the event of dismissal. If there is a forum in which all interested persons — including the absentee — can be joined in a single proceeding, dismissal of the pending case may make great sense: It can result in a single case in another court that binds all interested persons, thus avoiding duplicative litigation and any potential harm either to the absentee or the defendant. As we saw in the second step in applying Rule 19, often the reason the absentee cannot be joined is that her presence in the case would destroy diversity of citizenship jurisdiction. When that is the case, there may well be a state court in which all parties are subject to

---

[134] *See, e.g.*, Campbell v. Triangle Corp., 56 F.R.D. 480, 482 (E.D. Pa. 1972) ("prejudice to [the absentee's] interests can be avoided by limiting relief to money damages should plaintiff prevail").

[135] 390 U.S. 102, 115 (1968).

[136] *Id.* at 111 ("We read the Rule's third criterion . . . to refer to this public stake in settling disputes by wholes, whenever possible.").

personal jurisdiction and can be joined in a single proceeding. The result of invoking Rule 19, then, may be that the plaintiff is induced to give up her federal forum for a state court.

- *P*, a citizen of Louisiana, sues *D*, a citizen of Texas, in a federal court in Texas, properly invoking diversity of citizenship jurisdiction. Absentee (*A*) is a necessary party, and is a citizen of Texas. The court concludes that *A* should be joined in the pending case as a plaintiff. Her claim against *D*, however, cannot invoke diversity of citizenship jurisdiction (because *A* and *D* are co-citizens), so joinder is not feasible. In determining whether to proceed without *A* or to dismiss the case, the court might well note whether all three parties can be joined in a single case in a state court in Texas (or elsewhere). This inquiry will include an assessment of whether Texas would have personal jurisdiction. If so, dismissing the federal court case can result in the most efficient litigation package possible. If the court dismisses, essentially it will be telling *P* that she must give up her federal forum in the interest of an efficient litigation package that will avoid harm to *D* and to *A*.

The Supreme Court applied Rule 19(b) in an unusual context in the 2008 case of *Republic of Philippines v. Pimentel.*[137] Ferdinand Marcos was a stunningly corrupt and brutal leader in the Philippines. While in power, he stole billions of dollars in assets and placed them in various places for the rainy day when he would be forced from power. The holder of most of those assets, a corporation founded by Marcos, instituted an interpleader case concerning the assets. In §13.2, we study interpleader, which allows the holder of property to force claimants to the property to litigate ownership in a single proceeding. Among the many claimants to these assets were the Republic of the Philippines and a commission created by it. Other claimants included thousands who sued for human rights violations by Marcos.

The Republic of the Philippines and the commission it created could not be joined to the interpleader case because they enjoyed sovereign immunity. The question was whether the interpleader could proceed without them. The Court concluded that it could not, and that it had to be dismissed under Rule 12(b)(7). First, the Philippines and its commission were necessary under Rule 19(a)(1)(B)(i); if they were not joined, the assets would be distributed to others and lost to these claimants. Second, under Rule 19(b), the case had to be dismissed. The Court confirmed that judges routinely must peek at the merits of claims and defenses in applying Rule 19. But the lower courts erred in dismissing as frivolous the claims to the money by the Philippines and its commission. In equity and good conscience — and to allow a sovereign nation to determine in its own

---

[137] 128 S. Ct. 2180 (2008).

courts who owns the assets absconded by its former leader — the Court held that the interpleader in federal court must be dismissed.

Raising Rule 19 Issues

Almost always, the defendant raises Rule 19 concerns, either in a motion to join a necessary party or a motion to dismiss the case under Rule 12(b)(7). The plaintiff will rarely do so, because the structuring of the case was the plaintiff's idea. It would be unusual for the plaintiff to change her mind and call to the court's attention that she failed to join someone who satisfies Rule 19. Why would the defendant do so? Obviously, in cases satisfying Rule 19(a)(1)(B)(ii), the defendant's self-interest dictates that she raise the issue. In those cases, the present structure threatens the defendant with multiple or inconsistent obligations; she will want to avoid those by forcing joinder of the absentee. Or, if joinder is infeasible, she will want to argue that the case should be dismissed under Rule 12(b)(7).

What about cases that satisfy only Rule 19(a)(1)(B)(i)? Here, the threatened harm from the present structure is to the *absentee*. Why would the defendant raise this issue to the court? First, she might do so out of altruism. Second, and more likely, she may do so if joinder of the absentee is not feasible and thus the case might be dismissed. In the absence of possible dismissal, it is difficult to see why the defendant would be worried about potential harm to the absentee. She simply has nothing to gain unless she can get the case dismissed. Thus, the absentee may be most threatened in precisely the case in which she could feasibly be joined. In such a case, the defendant cannot get the case dismissed under Rule 12(b)(7), so it is not clear why anyone will be looking out for the absentee's interest.

In theory, there are two protections for the absentee in such a case. One is Rule 19(c), which requires a party asserting a claim to "state the name, if known, of any person who is required to be joined if feasible but is not joined" as well as the "reasons for not joining that person." The idea is to put the court in a position to raise necessary parties issues. In practice, this Rule provides little protection, because it seems to be ignored as much or more than it is honored. The requirement of Rule 19(c) should be expanded to require all parties (not just claimants) to inform the court of Rule 19 absentees and should be given teeth by being included in the certification made under Rule 11.

The other protection theoretically available to the absentee is intervention. We see in §12.6.3 that intervention of right is available essentially to those absentees who would be found necessary under Rule 19(a)(1)(B)(i). Such an absentee can join the case of her own volition. But the right to intervene is worthless if the absentee is not aware of the pending case. The advisory committee that drafted the 1966 amendments to Rule 19 relied here upon Rule 19(c). The drafters opined that once the court knew of absentees who satisfied Rule 19, it could contact the absentees and inform them of their right to intervene.[138] Again, however, this protection suffers from the lack of respect accorded Rule 19(c).

§12.6.2 Impleader, or Third-Party Practice (Rule 14)

Procedural and Policy Issues

Third-party practice, which is more commonly known as impleader, is an important tool in the panoply of joinder devices. It is governed in federal practice by Rule 14(a)[139] and results in overriding the plaintiff's party structure in the pending case by allowing the joinder of an absentee in limited circumstances. Importantly, only a "defending party" can join an absentee through impleader. Obviously, a defending party is one against whom a claim has been asserted. Usually, of course, that party will be the defendant. But a plaintiff can be a defending party if, for example, another party has asserted a counterclaim or crossclaim against her. Rule 14(b) makes this point clear, by providing that a plaintiff who has been hit with a claim can implead. The provision is unnecessary, because Rule 14(a) already provides that only a "defending party" can implead. In fact, even someone who is impleaded is a defending party, and may, if she has a proper impleader claim, implead someone else.[140]

The defending party asserting impleader is known as the "third-party plaintiff," and the absentee joined by impleader is the "third-party defendant" (which we will abbreviate TPD). So, in the usual case, in which the defendant uses impleader, the defendant will be called *defendant and third-party plaintiff.* The pleading seeking relief from the TPD is the "third-party complaint." Rule 14(a)(1) establishes that a defending party has a right to implead within ten days after she serves her original answer to the plaintiff's complaint. Beyond ten days, she must make a motion seeking court permission to implead. Such motions are routinely granted unless doing so will unduly delay resolution of the case on the merits. Is a defending party *required* to implead? No. Rule 14(a)(1) is clearly permissive; the first sentence provides that the defending party "may" (not "must") implead.

---

[138] 1966 Advisory Committee Notes to Rule 19(c).

[139] As we see below in this paragraph of text, Rule 14(b) is irrelevant. Rule 14(c) applies only in admiralty or maritime cases, and thus is beyond our scope. Although Rule 14 applies only in federal court, many states have impleader rules patterned on it.

[140] When a third party is impleaded and then impleads another absentee, some courts call the latter claim a "fourth-party claim." *See, e.g.,* Interstate Power Co. v. Kansas City Power & Light Co., 992 F.2d 804, 806 (8th Cir. 1993). In fact, there can be successive impleaders; the record appears to be five. Bevemet Metais, Ltd. v. Gallie Corp., 3 F.R.D. 352 (S.D.N.Y. 1942).

The fact that only a "defending party" can assert an impleader claim becomes obvious when we see what kind of claim is asserted in impleader. The claim must be against an absentee "who is or may be liable to the [defending party] for all or part of the claim against it." This limitation is extremely important. The defending party is not permitted to join an absentee just because she has a claim against that absentee or because the plaintiff may have a claim against the absentee. Rather, the claim against the absentee reflects that the absentee owes the defending party for all or part of the claim that has been asserted against that defending party. Such claims are almost always for indemnity or contribution. In the usual case, then, the defendant impleads an absentee (TPD) who owes indemnity or contribution to the defendant for all or part of the plaintiff's claim against the defendant.

We discussed indemnification at §11.3.5, concerning issue preclusion. The duty to indemnify is a duty to hold someone harmless — to "pick up the tab" for that person's liability in full. For example, if you lend a classmate (*D*) your car, and *D* runs your car into *P*, you are vicariously liable for *D*'s act. *P* can sue you. If she does, and recovers a judgment against you, however, you can sue your classmate, *D*, because she (as the primarily liable actor) owes *indemnification* to you (the vicariously liable party). Another example is insurance coverage. If you drive your car negligently and injure someone who then sues you and recovers, the insurance company will have to pay that judgment on your behalf.[141]

Contribution is similar, but usually involves a pro rata payment by another person. A good example is contribution among joint tortfeasors.

○ *X*, *Y*, and *Z* are joint tortfeasors who injure the plaintiff. As a matter of joinder, the plaintiff can sue all three in a single case. (Why?[142]) But the plaintiff does not have to do so. (Why?[143]) Assume the plaintiff sues only *X*. Accordingly, *Y* and *Z* are absentees. They cannot be forced to join the pending case as necessary parties under Rule 19. (Why?[144]) But *X* can implead *Y* and *Z* because they, as joint tortfeasors, owe her a duty of contribution, which means that they each owe their pro rata share of the liability. If the plaintiff won a judgment against *X* for $150,000, *Y* would owe contribution for $50,000 (one-third of the liability) and *Z* would also owe contribution of $50,000 (one-third of the liability).

[141] Assuming, of course, that the event was within the coverage of your insurance policy and was within the policy limits. If your policy limit is $100,000 and the plaintiff recovers a judgment against you of $130,000, the insurance company is only on the hook for $100,000. You pay the rest.

[142] Because under Rule 20(a)(2), the claims against all three arise from the same transaction or occurrence and raise at least one common question. See §12.4.

[143] Because Rule 20(a) is permissive. See §12.4.

[144] Because the Supreme Court held that joint tortfeasors are not necessary parties in *Temple v. Synthes Corp.*, 498 U.S. 5 (1998). See §12.6.1.

Without impleader, X would have to litigate the pending case and, if she lost, would have to pay the entire judgment, say $150,000, to P. Then, in a separate action, she would sue Y and Z and hope to win her claims for contribution from them. She might lose that case, because, after all, Y and Z would not be bound by the judgment in the case by P against X. (Why?[145]) If she lost that case, she would absorb the entire $150,000 loss. Even if she wins the case against Y and Z, however, she would have had to pay the entire judgment in the interim and would have to pay for a second litigation to perfect her right to contribution.

Impleader, then, overrides the plaintiff's party structure of the case to avoid potential harm to the defendant. Without impleader, the defendant (X in our hypothetical above) runs the risk of losing to P and then losing in a separate case against her alleged joint tortfeasors. Avoiding such a loss is akin to the goal of Rule 19(a)(1)(B)(ii), which compels joinder of an absentee to avoid the defendant's being saddled with multiple or inconsistent obligations. (See §12.6.1.) Thus, impleader fosters efficiency, consistency, and fairness to the defendant. These benefits outweigh the interest in plaintiff autonomy, and justify allowing the defendant to restructure the case.

In some states, the substantive law provides that one may not sue for indemnity or contribution until she has already paid a judgment in full. In other words, in our hypothetical above, the law may provide that X may not sue Y and Z for contribution until after X has lost to P and paid the entire judgment. In such states, can X use Rule 14(a)(1) in federal court to implead Y and Z as TPDs in the pending case? Yes. Rule 14(a)(1) merely *accelerates the assertion* of the claim.[146] That is, X can file the claim against Y and Z in the pending case, but the claim does not come to fruition, does not ripen, until P wins the underlying case; then the court can go ahead and determine whether X is entitled to contribution from Y and Z. Rule 14(a)(1), then, allows the "early" filing of the claim to ensure that all related issues can be determined in a single case. Obviously, however, Rule 14(a)(1) does not (and could not) create a claim for contribution or indemnity that does not otherwise exist. So if the relevant state law does not allow contribution among joint tortfeasors, Rule 14(a)(1) will not permit impleader.[147]

---

[145] Because Y and Z were not parties to the case by P against X, and thus, as a matter of due process, cannot be bound by the judgment in that case. See §§11.2.1 and 11.3.4. Thus, for example, Y and Z could argue that they were not joint tortfeasors with X, and thus that they do not owe contribution to her.

[146] *See, e.g.,* Hiatt v. Mazda Motor Corp., 75 F.3d 1252, 1255 (8th Cir. 1996); Markvicka v. Brodhead-Garrett Co., 76 F.R.D. 205, 207 (D. Neb. 1977).

[147] This issue is governed by *Hanna v. Plumer,* which we discussed at §10.6. Under *Hanna,* if there is a federal directive on point (such as Rule 14(a)(1) here), it controls the issue in federal court, so long as it is valid. For a Federal Rule to be valid under the Rules Enabling Act, it must be "arguably procedural" and not "abridge, enlarge, or modify any

Do not confuse impleader with the crossclaim under Rule 13(g), which we discussed at §12.5.2. The crossclaim is asserted by a party against a co-party. The impleader claim is asserted by a party against an absentee. Moreover, the crossclaim arises from the same transaction or occurrence as the underlying case. The impleader claim, as we have seen, is narrower — it is for indemnity or contribution on that underlying claim.

We can review these and other points about Rule 14(a)(1) with a hypothetical. This is a great fact pattern, and it will review a good bit of ground. Before working on it, read Rule 14(a) with great care.

- *T* has permission from *D* to drive *D*'s truck. While doing so, he strikes *P*, a pedestrian. *D* is vicariously liable for *T*'s acts. By the same token, *D* will have a right of indemnity from *T*. *P* sues only *D*. *D* may implead *T* in the pending case, because *T* is or may be liable to *D* for all or part of the underlying claim by *P*. Why? Because, as we said, *T* owes a duty of indemnification to *D*. *This is not a crossclaim. A crossclaim is asserted against a co-party.* D *and* T *are not co-parties, because* P *did not sue the two of them as co-defendants under Rule 20(a).*[148] Indeed, *T* is an absentee, a nonparty, until *D* joins him through impleader. Let's assume that *D* properly impleads *T*.

- When we think about it, *T* now is hoping that *D* wins the underlying claim. If *D* wins against *P*, *T* cannot be held liable; there would be no judgment for which he would have to indemnify *D*. Suppose *T* notices that *D* failed to raise an important defense to the underlying claim by *P* against *D*. Say, for example, *D* forgot to raise the statute of limitations as an affirmative defense. Can *T* raise this defense, even though it is a defense that *D* should have raised? The answer is yes. Exactly what part of Rule 14(a) makes this clear?[149]

- What if *T* thinks he has a defense against *D*'s impleader claim? What part of Rule 14(a) allows him to raise that defense in the pending case?[150]

- After *D* impleads *T*, suppose *T* has a *claim* against *D* that arises from the same transaction or occurrence as the impleader claim. Suppose, for instance, that *T* feels the accident was caused by faulty brakes in

---

substantive right." 28 U.S.C. §2072(b). Again, here, Rule 14(a)(1) merely accelerates the filing of a claim that exists under state law. If the claim did not exist under state law, Rule 14(a)(1) could not allow its assertion. To do so would be to enlarge a substantive right, and would violate the Rules Enabling Act. *See* Connors v. Suburban Propane Co., 916 F. Supp. 73, 76 (D.N.H. 1996) ("Rule 14 does not operate to create causes of action; it merely prescribes a method for bringing causes of action already recognized under applicable statutory or common law.").

[148] P could have joined them as co-defendants under Rule 20(a), but in this hypothetical did not do so.

[149] The answer here is governed by Rule 14(a)(2)(C), which allows *T* to raise against *P* any defenses that *D* could have raised.

[150] It is Rule 14(a)(2)(A). Once *D* impleads *T*, *T* is a defending party, and, like any defending party, must respond within 20 days of service under Rule 12.

the truck. *T* was injured in the same wreck and wants to recover against *D*. Not only may *T* assert this claim in the pending case, he probably *must* do so. Why?[151] Do *not* call this claim a crossclaim. Why is it not a crossclaim?[152]

◦ Go back to the stage in which *D* impleads *T*. Suppose (as is likely) that *D* wants to recover from *T* for two things. First, he wants indemnification, so if *P* wins against *D*, *T* has to pick up the tab on that judgment. Second, if the wreck was really *T*'s fault, *D* wants to recover from *T* for the damage to his truck. We know that he can seek the first of these things through impleader, because this is exactly the kind of claim for which impleader is designed. Why can *D* *not* seek the recovery for property damage through impleader?[153]

◦ So if *D* impleads *T*, and asserts the indemnification claim there, can he also assert the claim for damage to his truck in the pending case? Yes. How does he do that?[154]

◦ Indeed, not only *may D* assert the property damage claim against *T* in the pending case, but arguably he *should* do so. Why? What risk does he run if he impleads *T* without also joining the property damage claim?[155]

The foregoing concerned the basic impleader claim under Rule 14(a)(1) as well as some other joinder provisions and a review of some preclusion materials from Chapter 11. Now we take one more step, pursuing other claims for which Rule 14(a) provides.

◦ Assume the same basic facts as in the preceding hypothetical: *T* borrows *D*'s truck with *D*'s permission, and runs into *P*, a pedestrian. *D* is vicariously liable for *T*'s acts and *D* has a right of indemnity from *T*. *P* sues

[151] The claim by *T* against *D* is a compulsory counterclaim under Rule 13(a)(1), which we saw in §12.5.1. Why? A counterclaim is a claim against an "opposing party." Once *D* impleaded *T*, he became an opposing party. This claim by *T* arises from the same transaction or occurrence as the impleader claim, so it is compulsory under Rule 13(a)(1). If *T* does not assert it here, he will be estopped from suing on the claim anywhere.

[152] A crossclaim is asserted against a co-party. *D* and *T* are not co-parties; *P* did not sue the two of them as co-defendants under Rule 20(a)(2).

[153] Because Rule 14(a)(1) impleader only allows recovery against the TPD for all or part of the plaintiff's claim against the defending party who institutes impleader. It does *not* allow recovery for all things that arise from the same transaction or occurrence as the underlying dispute, so it is narrower than the crossclaim under Rule 13(g).

[154] By using Rule 18(a)(1), which we discussed in §12.3. Remember, it allows a claimant who has asserted one of the listed claims to join any other claim — regardless of relatedness — against that person. One of the listed claims is an impleader claim under Rule 14(a)(1).

[155] He runs the risk of claim preclusion. Because the indemnity claim and the property damage claim arise from the same transaction or occurrence, they are part of the same "claim" for claim preclusion purposes in most jurisdictions. So if the pending case goes to a valid final judgment on the merits, and *D* does not seek property damage, he may be precluded from asserting the property damage claim in a separate case. See §11.2.

only *D*. *D* then impleads *T* for indemnification and joins a Rule 18(a)(1)[156] claim for damage to his truck. *T* files a compulsory counterclaim against *D*, asserting that *D* lent him a truck with defective brakes, which caused the wreck and personal injuries to *T*.[157]

○ Now that *T* has been joined in the case, *P* wants to assert a claim *against* T, arguing that *T* is also liable for *P*'s injuries. May *P* assert such a claim in the pending case? Yes. Why?[158]

  ○ Does anything *require* *P* to assert this claim against *T* in the pending case? No. Why?[159]

  ○ Assume that *P* does assert the claim against *T*. Oddly, this claim under Rule 14(a)(3) does not have a commonly accepted name. It is not a counterclaim, since *P* and *T* are not yet opposing parties; it is not a crossclaim, because *P* and *T* are certainly not co-parties. Based upon the diagram of the case, one good suggestion for a name is an "upsloping 14(a) claim."[160]

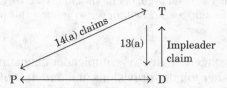

  ○ After *P* asserts the upsloping 14(a) claim against *T*, suppose *T* has a claim against *P* — say, that *P* somehow caused the wreck by acting negligently, and that *T* was injured. *T* wants to recover from *P* for these injuries. *T* may assert that claim in the pending case. In this scenario, however, Rule 14(a)(1) is irrelevant to her doing so. Why?[161]

○ Now go back to the stage where *P* has sued *D*, *D* has impleaded *T*, and *T* has asserted a compulsory counterclaim against *D*.

  ○ Now suppose *T* wants to assert a claim against *P* in the pending case. He asserts that the wreck was all *P*'s fault, and that he (*T*) was injured

---

[156] See note 154 above.

[157] See note 151 above.

[158] Rule 14(a)(3) permits the plaintiff to assert a claim against the TPD if it arises from the same transaction or occurrence as the plaintiff's underlying claim. This claim by *P* against the TPD does arise from the same wreck that forms the basis of the case, so it meets this test and may be asserted.

[159] Rule 14(a)(3) says the plaintiff "may" assert the claim, not that she "must" assert it. Thus, the claim is permissive. Also, there is nothing to fear from claim preclusion, because *P* has never asserted another claim against *T*, so cannot be guilty of splitting a claim.

[160] *See* 3 Moore's Federal Practice §14.06.

[161] The claim by *T* against *P* here is a compulsory counterclaim. Once *P* sued *T*, she became an "opposing party" to *T*. *T*'s claim arises from the same transaction or occurrence as *P*'s upsloping 14(a)(1) claim, and thus must be asserted in the pending case under Rule 13(a)(1).

because of it. May T assert such a claim in the pending case? Yes. Why?[162] *Must* he assert the claim in the pending case? No. Why?[163]

- This claim by T against P also does not have a commonly accepted name. Based again on the diagram of the case, a good suggestion is that we call this a "downsloping 14(a) claim."
- After T asserts this downsloping 14(a) claim against P, assume that P wants to assert a claim against T in the pending case. What is the claim?[164]

Thus, Rule 14(a) creates three claims: (1) the impleader claim under Rule 14(a)(1) asserted by a defending party against an absentee (the TPD) who may owe her indemnity or contribution on the underlying claim against her; (2) the upsloping 14(a) claim asserted by the plaintiff against the TPD, under Rule 14(a)(3); and (3) the downsloping 14(a) claim asserted by the TPD against the plaintiff, under Rule 14(a)(2)(D). The latter two claims must arise from the same transaction or occurrence as the underlying dispute. Having mastered the procedural propriety of these claims, now the fun begins, as we assess jurisdictional and related issues.

Jurisdictional and Related Issues

Impleader joins a new party (the TPD) to the case. The TPD is brought in, moreover, in a defensive capacity, meaning that she faces possible liability. Accordingly, the TPD must be subject to personal jurisdiction in the forum. Indeed, the first sentence of Rule 14(a)(1) assumes as much, since it requires that the TPD be served with summons and the third-party complaint. In most cases, the federal court obtains personal jurisdiction over the TPD just the way it does over an original defendant. Recall from our discussion at §2.3 that the personal jurisdiction inquiry in federal court usually is the same as it is in the state courts in the state in which the federal court sits. The first step is to consult jurisdictional statutes of that state, such as long-arm statutes, to see whether jurisdiction is possible.[165] There is, however, an additional method of exercising personal jurisdiction in the impleader situation. Under the "bulge rule" of Federal Rule 4(k)(1)(B), the TPD can be served outside the forum state — even in the

---

[162] Rule 14(a)(2)(D) permits the TPD to assert a claim against P if it arises from the same transaction or occurrence as the underlying dispute.

[163] Rule 14(a)(2)(D) says the TPD "may" (not "must") assert the claim. It is permissive. And there is no risk of claim preclusion against T here, because T has not been a claimant against P in another proceeding.

[164] It is a compulsory counterclaim. Once T asserted the claim against P, he became an "opposing party" to P. So any claim by P against T is a counterclaim, because it arises from the same transaction or occurrence as T's downsloping 14(a) claim, it is a compulsory counterclaim under Rule 13(a)(1) and must be asserted in the pending case.

[165] The second step, of course, is to assess whether the exercise of personal jurisdiction under that statute on the facts of the case comports with due process. See §2.4.

absence of a state long-arm statute — so long as she is served within 100 miles of the federal courthouse in which the case is pending. Thus, assume the case is pending in the Eastern District of Pennsylvania, in Philadelphia, and that the TPD is in New Jersey. Ordinarily, the federal court would look first to Pennsylvania law for a statutory provision allowing the exercise of jurisdiction out of state. If there is no such provision, but the TPD can be served in New Jersey within 100 miles of the Philadelphia federal courthouse, the bulge rule allows exercise of personal jurisdiction over the TPD.[166]

Venue provisions do not create barriers to joining the TPD. For starters, it is likely that the general venue statutes — §§1404(a) and 1406(a) — apply only to the initial claims against the defendant, and not to subsequent claims. Beyond this, the impleader claim is so closely related to the underlying case (after all, it is for indemnity or contribution *on* the underlying claim) that courts routinely recognize "ancillary venue." In other words, as long as venue is proper in the underlying case, the TPD has no right to object that venue is not proper as to her.[167] This practice makes great sense. As we are about to see, the impleader claim is so closely related to the underlying case that it will invoke supplemental jurisdiction, so there is no need for an independent basis of subject matter jurisdiction. That being so with regard to subject matter jurisdiction — which is not waivable — it must also be available for the concept of venue — which is waivable. For the remainder of this discussion, we assume that the court has personal jurisdiction over the TPD and that venue is proper.

The big question usually will be subject matter jurisdiction. Remember, there are three potential claims: the impleader claim, the upsloping 14(a) claim under Rule 14(a)(3), and the downsloping 14(a) claim under Rule 14(a)(2)(D). Of course, there must be subject matter jurisdiction over each that is asserted in federal court. As always, any of these might invoke an "independent" basis of subject matter jurisdiction (diversity of citizenship, alienage, or federal question jurisdiction) or it may invoke supplemental jurisdiction. Failing all of these, the claim must be asserted, if at all, in state court.

We will use the same fact pattern discussed above, in which T drives D's truck, with D's permission, and hits P, a pedestrian. D is vicariously liable for T's acts, and T owes a duty to indemnify D. We worked through the various procedural aspects to this scenario earlier in this subsection. Now we look at subject matter jurisdiction. The discussion gets pretty

---

[166] Remember that the bulge rule applies only to join TPDs in impleader and necessary parties under Rule 19. It is not available to join original defendants to the case. See §§3.3.4 and 12.6.1.

[167] *See* 3 Moore's Federal Practice §14.42.

involved, as we deal with several different claims and address more problems raised by the supplemental jurisdiction statute. We deal with several factual scenarios.

- **One**   *P* is a citizen of California and *D* is a citizen of Arizona. All claims in this hypothetical are based upon state (not federal) law and all claims exceed $75,000. *P* sues *D*, properly invoking diversity of citizenship jurisdiction. *D* impleads *T*. *T* is a citizen of Utah. Is there subject matter jurisdiction over the impleader claim? Yes. That claim invokes diversity of citizenship jurisdiction, because it is asserted by a citizen of Arizona against a citizen of Utah, and it exceeds $75,000. So it invokes diversity of citizenship jurisdiction and can be asserted in the pending case.
- **Two**   Same facts as in One except here *T* is a citizen of Arizona. The impleader claim thus cannot invoke diversity of citizenship jurisdiction because it is asserted by an Arizona citizen against an Arizona citizen.[168] And there is no federal question jurisdiction because the claim is based upon state law. Does the claim invoke supplemental jurisdiction? Yes. There has never been any question that the impleader claim satisfies the *Gibbs* test for supplemental jurisdiction.[169] As discussed in §4.7, *Gibbs* always allows supplemental jurisdiction over claims arising from the same transaction or occurrence as the underlying case. The impleader claim is even *narrower* than that: It is for indemnity or contribution on that underlying claim.
  - Section 1367(a) grants supplemental jurisdiction, precisely because that section adopts the *Gibbs* test. (See §4.7.) Section 1367(b) applies in cases that invoked diversity of citizenship jurisdiction (as *P* v. *D* does), but removes supplemental jurisdiction only over claims asserted by *plaintiffs*. Here, the impleader claim was asserted by the defendant, so §1367(b) does not remove the grant of supplemental jurisdiction. The impleader claim can be joined in the pending case.[170] (If any of this material is fuzzy, see §12.4.)
- **Three**   Same facts as in Two except that here *D* impleads *T* and joins with the impleader claim a claim under Rule 18(a)(1) for the property damage to his truck. (If this point is fuzzy, see note 154 above.) As in Two, *T* is a citizen of Arizona, so again there is no diversity of citizenship or federal question jurisdiction. We saw in Two that the impleader claim will invoke supplemental jurisdiction. What about the Rule 18(a) claim for property damage? The answer is yes.
  - Again, §1367(a) grants supplemental jurisdiction over this claim because it meets *Gibbs* — it shares a common nucleus of operative

---

[168] Remember we could raise the same issue by having *T* be a citizen of a state other than Arizona and the claim fail to exceed $75,000. Such a claim would fail to invoke diversity of citizenship jurisdiction because it fails to meet the amount in controversy requirement. See §4.5.3.

[169] *See, e.g.,* Alumax Mill Prods., Inc. v. Congress Fin. Corp., 912 F.2d 996, 1005 (8th Cir. 1990) (impleader claim satisfies *Gibbs* constitutional test for supplemental jurisdiction).

[170] *See generally* 3 Moore's Federal Practice §14.41[4][d].

fact with the underlying claim (the collision with *P*) that did invoke federal subject matter jurisdiction (the claim by *P* against *D*). Just because Rule 18(a) does not *require* that a claim be transactionally related to the underlying case does not mean that a claim asserted under that Rule cannot satisfy the *Gibbs* test. Section 1367(b) applies in cases that invoked diversity of citizenship jurisdiction (as *P* v. *D* does), but removes supplemental jurisdiction only over claims asserted by plaintiffs. This claim is asserted by a defendant, so §1367(b) does not remove the grant of supplemental jurisdiction. The claim can be asserted in the pending action.[171]

- **Four** Same facts as in Three, except here *T* is a citizen of California. So *D*, a citizen of Arizona, is impleading a citizen of California. And, remember, the plaintiff is a citizen of California. Is there subject matter jurisdiction over *D*'s impleader claim (and property damage claim) against *T*? Yes — diversity of citizenship! This is a claim by a citizen of Arizona against a citizen of California, and it exceeds $75,000. The fact that *T* is a co-citizen of *P* is absolutely irrelevant *to this point*. *P*'s citizenship is irrelevant in assessing this claim; *P* is not a party to this claim.
  - Now it gets tough. *P* now asserts an upsloping 14(a) claim against *T*, to recover for the personal injuries she suffered when *T* drove *D*'s truck into her. We know that this claim is procedurally proper under Rule 14(a)(3) because it arises from the same transaction or occurrence as the underlying case. But is there subject matter jurisdiction over *this* claim? There is no diversity of citizenship, because this claim is asserted by a California citizen (*P*) against a California citizen (*T*). There is no federal question jurisdiction because the claim is based upon state law. So what about supplemental jurisdiction?

This question — whether there is supplemental jurisdiction over an upsloping 14(a) claim (under Rule 14(a)(3)[172]) — requires us to discuss the important but lamentable case of *Owen Equipment & Erection Co. v. Kroger*.[173] The Supreme Court decided *Kroger* more than a decade before the supplemental jurisdiction statute was passed; the decision clearly influenced the drafters of that statute. In *Kroger*, a citizen of Iowa sued a citizen of Nebraska, properly invoking diversity of citizenship jurisdiction. The defendant impleaded a TPD, and the plaintiff asserted an upsloping 14(a) claim, based upon state law, against the TPD. At the time the plaintiff asserted the upsloping 14(a) claim, there appeared to be diversity of citizenship between the plaintiff and the TPD. Only during trial did the

---

[171] *See id.* at §14.41[4][c].

[172] When you read *Kroger*, you will find no reference to Rule 14(a)(3). There was no such subsection until the Rules were restyled in 2007. Before that, the upsloping 14(a) claim was found in the seventh sentence of Rule 14(a).

[173] 437 U.S. 365 (1977).

court and the plaintiff discover that the TPD was a co-citizen of the plaintiff.[174] Thus, there was no diversity of citizenship jurisdiction over the upsloping 14(a) claim. And because that claim arose under state law, it did not invoke federal question jurisdiction either.

Although the district court and the Eighth Circuit concluded that the claim was supported by supplemental (then called *ancillary*) jurisdiction, the Supreme Court reversed and held that supplemental jurisdiction was absolutely precluded. The Court assumed that the upsloping 14(a) claim satisfied the *Gibbs* constitutional test for supplemental jurisdiction.[175] Nonetheless, it was unwilling to permit supplemental jurisdiction over an upsloping 14(a) claim because doing so could open the door for a scheming plaintiff to avoid the complete diversity requirement (which we discussed at §4.5.3). For example, a plaintiff might sue a diverse defendant, invoking diversity of citizenship jurisdiction, knowing that the defendant would implead a TPD who is a co-citizen of the plaintiff. If the plaintiff can then assert an upsloping 14(a) claim against that nondiverse TPD, she would be permitted to sue a nondiverse party in federal court. Stated another way, the plaintiff could not have sued those two (the defendant and the TPD) as co-defendants initially, because such joinder would have violated the complete diversity rule. The Court concluded that the plaintiff was trying to do by indirection what she could not do directly and thus slammed the door by rejecting supplemental jurisdiction over the upsloping 14(a) claim.

While there is some appeal to the Court's reasoning, there are significant problems with it. For instance, there was no hint that the plaintiff in *Kroger* had engaged in such scheming. Indeed, given the confusion about the citizenship of the TPD, such gamesmanship would have been impossible. Moreover, a plaintiff who did engage in such a scheme to create diversity of citizenship jurisdiction would violate §1359, which prohibits collusive joinder to manufacture subject matter jurisdiction. (We discussed §1359 in §4.5.4.)

In the course of its opinion, the Court seized upon two factors to justify its conclusion that Congress, in passing the diversity of citizenship statute, intended not to grant supplemental jurisdiction over upsloping 14(a)

---

[174] The TPD was a corporation. A corporation is a citizen of the state in which it is incorporated and of the state in which it has its principal place of business. See §4.5.3. The TPD was incorporated in Nebraska and most folks assumed its principal place of business was there as well, because it was on the "Nebraska side" of the Missouri River. But there had been a change in the course of the Missouri River. As it turns out, the principal place of business was actually in Iowa, even though it was on the "Nebraska side" of the river. This fact did not become generally appreciated until a few days into trial. If the case is in your casebook (it probably is), read footnote 5 of the opinion.

[175] It had to assume this fact. After all, by definition, Rule 14(a) claims — both upsloping and downsloping — must arise from the same transaction or occurrence as the underlying dispute. As such, they satisfy the *Gibbs* test. See §4.7.

claims.[176] First, the claim in *Kroger* was not "logically dependent" to the underlying case.[177] The Court discussed the impleader claim as the archetype of a logically related claim, and indeed it is. If the plaintiff's underlying claim against the defendant fails, the impleader claim becomes irrelevant. On the other hand, if the plaintiff prevails on the underlying claim against the defendant, the court must assess the impleader claim to see whether the loss should be shifted from the defendant to the TPD. In contrast, the upsloping 14(a) claim is not logically dependent — its outcome is not necessarily affected by the resolution of the underlying claim between the plaintiff and the defendant.[178] While this is true, it is not clear why it matters. Supplemental jurisdiction has always been tied to *transactional relatedness* of the claims, not their logical dependence. A strict insistence on logical dependence would mean that only impleader claims may invoke supplemental jurisdiction. And that has never been the rule. Indeed, the *Kroger* opinion undid much of its argument here by recognizing the universal acceptance of supplemental jurisdiction over compulsory counterclaims, crossclaims, and claims by and against intervenors of right,[179] even though none of those is necessarily logically dependent on the underlying claims.[180]

Second, the Court noted that the claim requiring supplemental jurisdiction was asserted by the plaintiff, and not by a party in a defensive posture.[181] Apparently, the Court felt, true supplemental claims must be asserted by parties who are reacting to having been sued. It is difficult, however, to reconcile this statement with *Gibbs* itself, in which the Court upheld supplemental jurisdiction over a claim asserted by a plaintiff. The difference, of course, was that *Gibbs* was a federal question case. So perhaps the Court simply meant to limit the requirement of defensive invocation to diversity of citizenship cases.

The lower courts interpreted *Kroger* narrowly. Indeed, they limited its effect to the facts of the case. Thus, *Kroger* meant that there was no supplemental jurisdiction over upsloping 14(a) claims, but it meant nothing else. The "logical dependence" language did not lead courts to cut back on the use of supplemental jurisdiction over all manner of transactionally related claims, regardless of logical dependence. After *Kroger*, courts continued to allow supplemental jurisdiction over downsloping 14(a) claims by the

---

[176] This holding was quite a stretch. There is no evidence that Congress ever considered supplemental jurisdiction in any way — let alone as to upsloping 14(a) claims — in passing the diversity of citizenship statute, §1332.

[177] *Kroger*, 437 U.S. at 376.

[178] That is, whether the plaintiff wins against the defendant has absolutely no bearing on how the plaintiff's claim against the TPD will come out.

[179] *Kroger*, 437 U.S. at 375 n.18.

[180] *See* 13 Wright & Miller §3523.

[181] *Kroger*, 437 U.S. at 376.

TPD against the plaintiff.[182] The narrowness of *Kroger* is best demonstrated by this scenario: After the TPD asserts a downsloping 14(a) claim against the nondiverse plaintiff, the plaintiff files a compulsory counterclaim right back against the TPD. Had the plaintiff filed this claim before the TPD filed her downsloping 14(a) claim, *Kroger* would have defeated supplemental jurisdiction. But by waiting, the plaintiff is now acting in a defensive capacity and supplemental jurisdiction attaches.[183]

We have discussed before that Congress's expressed intent in passing the supplemental jurisdiction statute was (1) to overrule the unfortunate *Finley* decision and (2) to codify the use of supplemental jurisdiction recognized by the federal courts before *Finley*.[184] Obviously, then, it was incumbent upon Congress to codify the result in *Kroger*. Congress did so. Section 1367(a) clearly grants supplemental jurisdiction to all Rule 14(a) claims. As we have seen several times, that section codified *Gibbs*, which permits supplemental jurisdiction over all claims that constitute part of the same "case or controversy" as the claim that invoked federal subject matter jurisdiction. As interpreted, this means the claim must share a nucleus of operative fact as the underlying claim. Upsloping (and downsloping) 14(a) claims always meet this test, because Rule 14(a) permits them to be asserted only if they arise from the same transaction or occurrence as the underlying claim.[185] Section 1367(b) applies only in cases that invoked diversity of citizenship jurisdiction (such as *Kroger* and Scenario Four). It removes supplemental jurisdiction over several claims, including those by "plaintiffs against persons made parties under Rule 14." The claim asserted by the plaintiff in *Kroger* (and in Scenario Four) was precisely that — a claim against a TPD, brought into the case under Rule 14(a)(1). Clearly, then, the result in this hypothetical is the same under §1367 as it was under *Kroger*.

If Congress truly was attempting to codify pre-*Finley* practice, it was incumbent on the drafters to embrace the courts limiting *Kroger* to its facts. Unfortunately, they failed to do so. Section 1367(b) goes beyond the holding in *Kroger* and removes supplemental jurisdiction in situations in

---

[182] *See, e.g.,* Revere Copper & Brass Inc. v. Aetna Cas. & Sur. Co., 426 F.2d 709 (5th Cir. 1970).

[183] Courts reached this result even though the plaintiff in this scenario might be as devious as the plaintiff so feared by the Court in *Kroger*. That is, the plaintiff might have sued only the diverse defendant, knowing that the defendant would implead the TPD and that the TPD would assert a downsloping 14(a) claim against her. Now she can achieve by indirection — a compulsory counterclaim in response to a downsloping 14(a) claim — what she could not have achieved directly.

[184] See §§4.7, 12.5.2.

[185] *See* Rule 14(a)(2)(D) and Rule 14(a)(3). The common nucleus of operative fact test of *Gibbs* is broader than "same transaction or occurrence." Therefore, claims that arise from the same transaction or occurrence as a jurisdiction-invoking claim will always invoke supplemental jurisdiction under §1367(a).

which it had always been used. By doing so, the statute maims efficient joinder in diversity of citizenship cases. The statute embodies a disquieting anti-diversity bias.

- **Five**   *P*, a citizen of Missouri sues *D*, a citizen of Kansas. All claims are based upon state law and all exceed $75,000. So this original claim invokes diversity of citizenship jurisdiction and is properly filed in federal court. *D* files a counterclaim against *P*, which also invokes diversity of citizenship jurisdiction. Now *P* impleads *T*, who, *P* asserts, owes her indemnity or contribution for the counterclaim by *D* against *P*. *T* is a citizen of Missouri. Thus, the impleader claim is asserted by a citizen of Missouri against a citizen of Missouri. Obviously, then, this claim cannot invoke diversity of citizenship jurisdiction. And because it arises under state law, the claim also cannot invoke federal question jurisdiction. Is there supplemental jurisdiction over this impleader claim by *P*?

  - The impleader claim, as we discussed in Scenario Two above, certainly meets the *Gibbs* test. Moreover, because the claim is asserted by one acting in a defensive capacity, *Kroger* did not counsel rejection of supplemental jurisdiction. Thus, before adoption of the supplemental jurisdiction statute in 1990, the answer was quite clear: Supplemental (then called *ancillary*) jurisdiction applied to impleader claims asserted by the plaintiff.[186]

  - But what does the supplemental jurisdiction statute do? Section 1367(a) clearly grants supplemental jurisdiction over the impleader claim because, as we just said and as we saw in Scenario Two, it satisfies *Gibbs*. Section 1367(b) applies in cases that invoked diversity of citizenship jurisdiction (as *P* v. *D* does) and removes jurisdiction over certain claims, including claims asserted by "plaintiffs against persons made parties under Rule 14." The claim in this hypothetical is exactly such a claim — it is asserted by a plaintiff against someone impleaded under Rule 14. Thus, on its face, the statute *prohibits* supplemental jurisdiction over this claim.

This result is unfortunate. It changes jurisdictional law that was well established before passage of the statute. Moreover, it means that the underlying claim by *P* against *D* and the counterclaim by *D* against *P* will proceed in federal court, while the impleader claim by *P* against TPD must go to state court. This subjects *P* to precisely the kinds of harm impleader is intended to avoid. It burdens *P* with the risk of unfair loss and burdens the judicial systems with two cases over what is clearly one transactionally related dispute.

Moreover, the result in the hypothetical is apparently unintended by the drafters of the statute. Three professors who were involved in drafting the

---

[186] *See, e.g.*, Brown & Caldwell v. Institute for Energy Funding, Ltd., 617 F. Supp. 649, 651 (C.D. Cal. 1985) (exercising "ancillary" jurisdiction over impleader claim by plaintiff filed in response to counterclaim against the plaintiff).

statute have argued that the statutory interpretation described above is too wooden, that courts will be able to apply the "spirit of *Kroger*" to permit supplemental jurisdiction over claims asserted by a plaintiff in a defensive capacity.[187] They point to the last phrase of §1367(b) — which provides that supplemental jurisdiction is removed from various claims "when exercising supplemental jurisdiction ... would be inconsistent with the jurisdictional requirements of §1332" — and argue that it incorporates the flexible "spirit of *Kroger*."[188]

No doubt there *should* be supplemental jurisdiction over these claims. But courts are stuck with the language of the statute, and that language makes no express exception for claims asserted by plaintiffs in a defensive capacity. Predictably, courts have interpreted the statute to *prohibit* supplemental jurisdiction in this fact pattern.[189] Is it possible that other courts will hold the other way? Yes, which simply creates another area in which this statute has created great uncertainty.

○ **Six** *P*, a citizen of South Carolina, sues *D*, a citizen of Kentucky. All claims are based upon state law and exceed $75,000. The case thus invokes diversity of citizenship jurisdiction and is properly filed in federal court. *D* impleads *T*, a citizen of South Carolina. As in Scenarios One and Four above, this claim invokes diversity of citizenship jurisdiction. Now, *T* asserts a downsloping 14(a) claim against *P*. That claim does not invoke diversity of citizenship jurisdiction, because *T* and *P* are co-citizens. It does not invoke federal question jurisdiction, because the claim arises under state law. Does it invoke supplemental jurisdiction?

  ○ Yes. Section 1367(a) grants supplemental jurisdiction because 14(a) claims, by definition, must arise from the same transaction or occurrence as the underlying case; thus, they satisfy *Gibbs*. Section 1367(b) applies in cases that invoked diversity of citizenship jurisdiction (such as this) but only removes supplemental jurisdiction over claims by plaintiffs. This is a claim asserted by the TPD, so §1367(b) does not remove the grant of supplemental jurisdiction. The claim can be joined in federal court. (This result is consistent with the law before enactment of §1367.)

  ○ Now one more step. Suppose *P* now asserts a compulsory counterclaim against *T*. Once *T* asserted the downsloping 14(a) claim against *P*, *T* became an "opposing party," so *P*'s claim back is a counterclaim. This one arises from the same transaction or occurrence as *T*'s claim,

---

[187] Thomas Rowe, Stephen Burbank & Thomas Mengler, *Compounding or Creating Confusion About Supplemental Jurisdiction? A Reply to Professor Freer*, 40 Emory L.J. 943 (1991).

[188] *Id.*

[189] *See, e.g.*, Chase Manhattan Bank v. Aldridge, 906 F. Supp. 866, 868-869 (S.D.N.Y. 1995) (terms of statute dictate this result); Guaranteed Sys., Inc. v. American Natl. Can Co., 842 F. Supp. 855, 856-858 (M.D.N.C. 1994) (recognizing the unfortunate result but "bound by the plain terms of the statute").

so it is a compulsory counterclaim under Rule 13(a). Is there subject matter jurisdiction over this claim? Obviously, there is no diversity of citizenship or federal question jurisdiction; the two are co-citizens and the claim arises under state law.

- ○ Is there supplemental jurisdiction? Before Congress enacted §1367 there was.[190] But the statute creates the same problem we saw in Scenario Five. The compulsory counterclaim would clearly invoke supplemental jurisdiction under §1367(a) because it arises from the same transaction or occurrence as the underlying claim that invoked subject matter jurisdiction. The problem, again, comes from §1367(b), which applies in cases that invoked diversity of citizenship jurisdiction (such as this), and removes supplemental jurisdiction over claims by "plaintiffs against persons made parties under Rule 14." This claim is exactly that. Obviously, there should be supplemental jurisdiction, because *P* is acting in a defensive capacity and, in fact, is filing a *compulsory* counterclaim. But, just as obviously, this statute fails to address this situation, and creates uncertainty as to the viability of supplemental jurisdiction in this scenario.

- ○ **Seven**   *P*, a citizen of Wisconsin, asserts a federal question claim against *D*, a citizen of Delaware, properly invoking federal question jurisdiction. All other claims are based upon state law and exceed $75,000. *D* impleads *T*, a corporation that is incorporated in Delaware with its principal place of business in Wisconsin. (So, as we saw in §4.5.3, the corporation is a citizen of both of those states.) *P* asserts an upsloping 14(a) claim under Rule 14(a)(3) against *T*. Neither the impleader claim nor the upsloping 14(a) claim invokes diversity of citizenship or federal question jurisdiction. Does either claim invoke supplemental jurisdiction?

  - ○ Yes — they both do. Why? First, §1367(a) grants supplemental jurisdiction over both, because both satisfy *Gibbs*. Second, §1367(b) does not apply, and thus cannot remove the grant of supplemental jurisdiction over those claims. Remember, §1367(b) applies only in cases that invoked diversity of citizenship jurisdiction. This case did not, so §1367(b) does not apply and does not remove the grant of supplemental jurisdiction.

§12.6.3   Intervention (Rule 24)

Procedural and Policy Issues

Intervention is exactly what it sounds like — an absentee intervenes, brings herself into, a pending case. By doing so, obviously, the absentee

---

[190] *See, e.g.*, Finkle v. Gulf & Western Mfg. Co., 744 F.2d 1015, 1018-1019 (3d Cir. 1984); Berel Co. v. Sencit F/G McKinley Assoc., 125 F.R.D. 100, 102-103 (D.N.J. 1989) (both cases exercising "ancillary" jurisdiction over a compulsory counterclaim by the plaintiff against the third-party defendant).

overrides the plaintiff's party structure of the case. Intervention is governed in federal practice by Federal Rule 24, which recognizes both intervention of right (under Rule 24(a)) and permissive intervention (under Rule 24(b)).[191] The difference between these two types of intervention is also clear from the names. With the former, the court (at least theoretically) must allow the absentee to join; with the latter, the court has the discretion to permit the absentee to join.

Intervention of Right. An absentee may qualify for intervention of right in one of two ways. First, Rule 24(a)(1) notes that a federal statute might confer such a right. A good example is 28 U.S.C. §2403, which requires that the Attorney General of the United States be notified whenever a case calls into question "the constitutionality of any Act of Congress affecting the public interest."[192] After notification to the Attorney General, the United States has a right to intervene.

Rule 24(a)(2) is more important. It provides for intervention of right in the absence of a statute, if the absentee can establish (1) that she "claims an interest relating to the property or transaction that is the subject of the action" and (2) that she is "so situated that disposing of the action may as a practical matter impair or impede the [intervenor's] ability to protect its interest." But there is a third requirement. Notice that the Rule makes clear that the absentee will not have a right to intervene if an existing party adequately represents her interest.[193] On its face, then, Rule 24 seems to suggest that the party opposing intervention would have the burden of showing that an existing party adequately represented the would-be intervenor's interest. But the courts have made it clear that the intervenor has the burden on all three requirements, including, then, that the extant parties do not adequately represent her interests.

This test for intervention of right should ring a bell. The two basic requirements are the same as the two requirements for finding an absentee necessary under Rule 19(a)(1)(B)(i). We discussed those factors in detail in §12.6.1, and need not repeat that discussion here. Suffice to say that an absentee who would be found necessary under Rule 19(a)(1)(B)(i) will have a right to intervene under Rule 24(a)(2), provided she can also show that existing parties do not adequately represent her interest. This latter point has no counterpart in Rule 19. The Supreme Court has made clear that the burden of showing that no party adequately represents the

---

[191] As with other Federal Rules joinder provisions, most states have adopted a provision modeled on Rule 24.

[192] Many people have noted that this statute (actually its predecessor) was not followed in *Erie*, in which the Supreme Court questioned the constitutionality of the Rules of Decision Act.

[193] Trbovich v. United Mine Workers of Am., 404 U.S. 528, 538 (1972).

intervenor's interest is "minimal," and is satisfied by showing that the existing parties have some interest that differs from that of the absentee.[194] Thus, while it cannot be ignored, observers seem to agree that this factor has not had great independent significance. In the words of some, the absentee "should be treated as the best judge of whether the existing parties adequately represent . . . her interests, and . . . any doubt regarding adequacy of representation should be resolved in favor of the proposed intervenors."[195]

> ∘   *A* owns 1,000 shares of stock in Corporation, in her own name. *P* claims that she and *A* had bought the stock together and that the stock was supposed to have been issued in both names as joint owners. *P* sues Corporation, seeking to have *A*'s stock canceled and the shares reissued in the joint names of *P* and *A*. Does *A* have a right to intervene?

We saw the same fact pattern in §12.6.1, in which the question was whether *A* was a required party under Rule 19. The answer to that question and to the question asked here is yes. *A* has a right to intervene under Rule 24(a)(2) for essentially the same reasons that she was necessary under Rule 19(a)(1)(B)(i). First, she has an interest in the pending litigation; *P* is currently the sole owner of the stock at issue in the litigation. Second, she is so situated that litigation without her joinder might impair or impede her ability to protect that interest; if *P* wins the pending case, *A*'s stock is canceled and reissued to make her merely a joint owner, instead of outright owner. These two facts meant that *A* was necessary under Rule 19(a)(1)(B)(i). With Rule 24(a)(2) we must also assess the third factor — that *A*'s interest is not adequately represented by any of the present parties. This certainly seems to be the case; *P* wants to take away *A*'s present sole ownership of the stock. *D* is probably ambivalent on the issue; at least, it is not clear why the corporation cares who owns the 1,000 shares. Accordingly, *A* has a right to intervene under Rule 24(a)(2).

We are left, then, with two Rules — 19(a)(1)(B)(i) and 24(a)(2) — that overlap significantly. Indeed, they were revised together in 1966 to emphasize their interrelatedness.[196] Both Rules are aimed at overriding the plaintiff's party structure for one reason: to protect an interested absentee from harm to her ability to protect her interest. Why would two Rules do the same thing? The answer is that the two Rules empower different persons to force the joinder of the absentee. Rule 19 is invoked principally by the defendant, although the court may also raise Rule 19 issues on its own

---

[194] *Id.* at 538 n.10.

[195] 6 Moore's Federal Practice 24-42.

[196] The Supreme Court emphasized the relationship between Rules 19 and 24 in *Martin v. Wilks*, 490 U.S. 755, 765 (1989). An entertaining discussion of the overlap between the two Rules is Atlantis Dev. Corp. v. United States, 379 F.2d 818 (5th Cir. 1967). The case was decided within months of the effective date of the 1966 revisions to the two Rules.

(assuming that it knows about interested absentees). In contrast, the absentee herself invokes Rule 24. Thus, she is given a mechanism by which to override the plaintiff's structuring of the case expressly to protect herself.[197]

An absentee who qualifies to intervene of right is not required to do so. Rule 24(a)(2) makes it clear that the absentee "may" intervene, but does not require that she do so. Nonetheless, Justice Harlan once suggested that an absentee who eschews the opportunity to assert a claim in intervention under Rule 24(a)(2) should be barred from asserting a claim in another action.[198] The Supreme Court rejected this suggestion and confirmed the voluntary nature of intervention of right in *Martin v. Wilks*.[199] There, African-American firefighters sued a city, alleging racial discrimination in promotion. The resulting consent decree gave the plaintiffs relief that moved them ahead of white firefighters on the promotion list. Those white firefighters then sued the city. Although they were aware of the original case and satisfied the basic test for intervention of right under Rule 24(a)(2),[200] the district court rejected their petition to intervene as untimely.[201] That failure to join the white firefighters created duplicative litigation and put the city in a difficult position.[202] Nonetheless, the Court held, Rule 24(a)(2) is voluntary; the absentees had not been joined in the earlier case and thus could not be bound by the judgment in that case.[203]

Permissive Intervention. The second type of intervention — permissive intervention — is not available of right. Instead, whether to permit the

---

[197] Of course, an absentee can only intervene if she is aware of the pending case. Rule 19(c) is a feeble attempt to put the court in a position to know of absentees who might have a right to intervene under Rule 24(a)(2). The drafters of that Rule foresaw the possibility that the court might then inform absentees of their right to intervene. We discussed this point in detail at §12.6.1.

[198] Provident Tradesmens Bank & Trust Co. v. Patterson, 390 U.S. 102, 114 (1968).

[199] 490 U.S. 755 (1989).

[200] Remember why: Because they had an interest in that case, and were so situated that their ability to protect that interest may be impaired or impeded, and their interest was not adequately represented by an existing party. If plaintiffs won the first case, the absentees' relative places on the promotion ladder would have been lowered; the plaintiffs would have been put above them.

[201] As noted, under Rule 24, any application to intervene must be "timely." Contrast this requirement with the timing requirement for Rule 19. Under Rule 12(h)(2), a motion to dismiss for failure to join an indispensable party may be made anytime before entry of judgment at trial; in other words, indispensability under Rule 19 could be raised at the trial on the merits.

[202] The city was subject to multiple or inconsistent obligations. The judgment in one case might have told the city to promote certain firefighters and the judgment in a second case might have told the city to promote different firefighters to the same positions. For this reason, the white firefighters were necessary under Rule 19(a)(1)(B)(ii) in the original case.

[203] *Martin*, 490 U.S. at 765 ("Joinder as a party, rather than knowledge of a lawsuit and an opportunity to intervene, is the method by which potential parties are subject to the jurisdiction of the court and bound by a judgment.").

absentee to intervene is addressed to the discretion of the district court. A permissive intervenor generally is not as closely related to the pending case as an intervenor of right. She does not have a statutory right to come into the case and her nonjoinder does not threaten her interest with harm. Accordingly, there is less need for allowing her to join the case, and the trial judge may look at a wide range of factors relating to fairness and convenience in deciding whether to allow permissive intervention. Permissive intervention should be granted only if the court determines that its benefits outweigh the burdens it creates.

Like intervention of right, there are two provisions concerning permissive intervention. First, under Rule 24(b)(1)(A), the absentee may seek to intervene if a federal statute confers "a conditional right to intervene." There is such a statutory provision in the Bankruptcy Code, for example, which allows a party in interest to seek to intervene.[204] Such statutes do not confer a *right* to intervene, and even those who fall within them must submit their intervention fate to the discretion of the trial judge.

Rule 24(b)(2) is more significant and allows permissive intervention when the absentee "has a claim or defense that shares with the main action a common question of law or fact." The reference to "claim or defense" recognizes that an intervenor might come in on either side of the case — as a plaintiff or as a defendant. The requirement of a common question is not very demanding. Recall that it would take more than that for persons to be joined together as co-parties. Under Rule 20(a)(1), as we discussed in §12.4, persons can join as co-plaintiffs, for instance, only if their claims (1) arise from the same transaction or occurrence and (2) raise at least one common question. Here, the showing required for permissive intervention is merely the second of those two tests.

The common-question standard is the same as we saw for consolidation under Rule 42(b), which we also discussed in §12.4. It is quite broad. Note that it does not require that the absentee have any interest in the pending case. Further, it does not require that the common question predominate in the case; there simply has to be at least one common question presented both by the pending case and the absentee's claim or defense. Demonstrating that there is such a common question is no guaranty that permissive intervention will be granted. Again, permissive intervention (like consolidation) is a discretionary call for the trial judge. The court usually looks to such things as (1) whether the absentee has delayed unduly in seeking to intervene; (2) whether intervention might prejudice any existing parties; and (3) the status of the pending proceedings. For instance, if the pending case is nearing completion, and intervention would

---

[204] *See* 11 U.S.C. §1109(b).

introduce collateral issues that would delay resolution, the court should probably deny the application to intervene.[205]

Allowing permissive intervention overrides the plaintiff's structuring of the suit and can be disruptive to the existing parties. Accordingly, many courts will permit it only if they are convinced that the absentee will make some useful contribution to the development of the case or issues in the case. As Professor Edward Brunet has said, "[C]ourts should welcome unique input, . . . especially on subjects within the special expertise of the intervenor."[206] Thus, one court allowed intervention by the NAACP in a redistricting case, noting that the organization could bring a useful perspective to the court's constitutional inquiry.[207] In a case involving a challenge to election procedures under the Voting Rights Act, however, a county was not permitted to intervene; the court concluded that the county's involvement would not contribute to development of the relevant issues.[208] Moreover, intervention can be sought for limited purposes, for example, to litigate only on specific issues. For example, when the court in a civil rights case ordered that the settlement terms be kept confidential, it should have granted the motion of newspapers to intervene to challenge the order of confidentiality.[209]

Procedure and Timing. Under Rule 24(c), the absentee seeking to intervene must serve on all parties (1) a motion to intervene and (2) her pleading in intervention. Even when the case involves intervention of right, she must make the motion to intervene and does not become a party until the motion is granted. Thus, the absentee must choose to participate on one side of the dispute. The plaintiff-intervenor will offer a complaint in intervention, which states her claim against the defendant. The defendant-intervenor will offer an answer in intervention, which responds to the plaintiff's anticipated claim against her once intervention is granted. She makes this decision by determining which side is more consistent with her position. Often, there will not be a perfect match of interests, so she must decide which side offers less conflict with her position. The court has the discretion to look beyond the absentee's characterization and realign her according to what the court sees as the interests of the parties. This realignment may have serious consequences for subject matter jurisdiction, as we will see shortly.

---

[205] *See, e.g.*, Southmark Corp. v. Cagan, 950 F.2d 416, 419 (7th Cir. 1991) (intervention denied while dispositive motion pending); Sellers v. United States, 709 F.2d 1469, 1472 (11th Cir. 1982) (intervention would introduce collateral issues).

[206] 6 Moore's Federal Practice 24-55.

[207] Johnson v. Mortham, 915 F. Supp. 1529, 1538-1539 (N.D. Fla. 1995).

[208] League of Latin Am. Citizens v. Clements, 884 F.2d 185, 189 (5th Cir. 1989). As an alternative to permissive intervention, a court might permit the absentee to participate as *amicus curiae*, or "friend of the court," to brief issues and even present oral argument and, in some cases, to cross-examine witnesses. *See* 6 Moore's Federal Practice §24.23[2].

[209] Pansy v. Borough of Stroudsburg, 23 F.3d 772, 778 (3d Cir. 1994).

Both Rule 24(a) and (b) begin with the words "on timely application," meaning that any motion to intervene — whether of right or permissive — must be timely. Rule 24 does not define what that means. There is no magic time frame. In one case, intervention was untimely when made four months after a case was filed.[210] In another, intervention was timely although made four years after a case was filed.[211] The question is addressed to the discretion of the district judge, who must assess not simply the passage of time since the case was filed, but all relevant circumstances.[212] While there is no single exhaustive list of such factors, many courts look to these: (1) how long the absentee knew of her interest (or, with reasonable diligence, should have known of her interest) before seeking to intervene; (2) the extent of prejudice caused to existing parties by the absentee's delay; (3) the extent to which denial of intervention might prejudice the absentee; and (4) unusual facts that augur for or against a finding of timeliness.[213] Although it is unusual, there are cases in which courts have granted intervention after entry of judgment. For instance, an absentee whose interests are affected by the judgment might wish to intervene to prosecute an appeal when the original parties have refused to appeal.[214]

As a general rule, courts are more likely to find the effort to intervene "timely" with intervention of right under Rule 24(a)(2) than with permissive intervention.[215] The reason is clear: With intervention of right under that Rule, the absentee's ability to protect her interest will be impaired by the pending litigation. Joinder is required to avoid such potential harm to the absentee.

Jurisdictional and Related Issues

Because an intervenor voluntarily enters a pending case, she has no basis on which to object to a lack of personal jurisdiction over her; she has waived any personal jurisdiction objection she might have had. Similarly, an intervenor has no basis on which to complain about venue; she has objected to any venue objection she might have had as well.

---

[210] NAACP v. New York, 413 U.S. 345 (1973).

[211] Mountain Top Condominium Assn. v. Dave Stabbert Master Builder, 72 F.3d 361, 369 (3d Cir. 1995).

[212] NAACP v. New York, 413 U.S. 345, 366 (1973).

[213] See, e.g., Edwards v. City of Houston, 37 F.3d 1097, 1105 (5th Cir. 1994); Farmland Dairies v. Commissioner of the N.Y. State Dept. of Agric. & Mkts., 847 F.2d 1038, 1044 (2d Cir. 1988).

[214] See, e.g., NL Industries, Inc. v. Secretary of the Interior, 777 F.2d 433, 436 (9th Cir. 1985).

[215] See, e.g., Fiandaca v. Cunningham, 827 F.2d 825, 832 (1st Cir. 1987).

But, as we know, parties cannot waive or stipulate around limits on federal subject matter jurisdiction. Every claim in federal court must be supported by a basis of subject matter jurisdiction. Thus, the court must assess whether intervention can be accomplished consistent with the restrictions on federal subject matter jurisdiction. Some courts and commentators have been sloppy in discussing this issue, by framing the inquiry as whether the court would have subject matter jurisdiction over the *intervenor*. Remember, though, that the intervenor comes into the case either to assert a claim (as a plaintiff) or to have a claim asserted against her (as a defendant). Subject matter jurisdiction is exercised over *claims*, not over *parties*.[216] So the appropriate focus is whether the *claim asserted by or against the intervenor* invokes federal subject matter jurisdiction.

- ∘ *P*, a citizen of Delaware, asserts a state law claim of $100,000 against *D*, a citizen of Illinois. The claim invokes diversity of citizenship jurisdiction and is properly filed in federal court. *A*, an intervenor of right who is a citizen of California, intervenes as a plaintiff to assert a $100,000 state law claim against *D*. *A*'s claim invokes diversity of citizenship jurisdiction and thus is properly asserted in this case.
- ∘ Same facts as in the preceding hypothetical, but here the intervenor is a citizen of Illinois. Obviously, *A*'s claim against *D* does not invoke diversity of citizenship, because *A* and *D* are co-citizens. Also, there is no federal question jurisdiction, because *A*'s claim arises under state law. Can *A*'s claim invoke supplemental jurisdiction?

This is an important question. As with the discussions of supplemental jurisdiction for each of the joinder devices addressed in this chapter, you must be familiar with the operation of §1367, which we covered in §4.7. In addition, because of the functional identity between Rule 24(a)(2) and Rule 19(a)(1)(B)(ii), we addressed the issue of supplemental jurisdiction over claims asserted by or against intervenors of right in §12.6.1. That discussion is summarized briefly here. Before 1990, when Congress enacted §1367, the federal courts agreed that claims by or against intervenors of right under Rule 24(a)(2) invoked supplemental jurisdiction.[217] An intervenor of right, as we have seen, is an absentee with an interest in the pending case who is so situated that litigation may impair or impede her ability to protect that interest. Everyone agreed then, and seems to agree today, that a claim asserted by or against such a person is so closely related to the underlying claim to constitute part of the same case or controversy as that claim and thus to fall within supplemental jurisdiction recognized by the *Gibbs* case.[218] (If any of this material is fuzzy, review §4.7.)

---

[216] Personal jurisdiction is exercised over parties, not claims.

[217] *See, e.g.*, Curtis v. Sears, Roebuck & Co., 754 F.2d 781, 784 (8th Cir. 1985).

[218] There is a quick aside to this assertion. Courts recognized supplemental jurisdiction over claims by or against intervenors of right, but some then often added that such

The recognition of supplemental jurisdiction in the intervention of right context, however, created an anomaly. Why? Because claims by or against necessary parties under Rule 19(a)(1)(b)(ii) did not invoke supplemental jurisdiction. This result is odd, because, as we discussed above, the absentee who satisfies Rule 19(a)(1)(B)(ii) will also satisfy Rule 24(a)(2).[219] Thus, under the law before enactment of the supplemental jurisdiction statute, these absentees, though identically situated, were treated differently when it came to supplemental jurisdiction. If they intervened, there would be supplemental jurisdiction; if they were joined under Rule 19, there would not. Commentators have referred to this as the "Rule 19/Rule 24 anomaly."

Every commentator discussing the issue opined that the anomaly should be removed by extending supplemental jurisdiction to the necessary party situation. Instead, with the supplemental jurisdiction statute in 1990, Congress "fixed" the anomaly by removing supplemental jurisdiction in the intervention situation. Not one commentator had ever suggested that this be done, and the move is contrary to Congress's assertion that the supplemental jurisdiction statute was intended to codify practice as it had existed. Predictably, then, a chorus of commentators has criticized the statute on this point.[220] Among other things, by removing supplemental jurisdiction over claims asserted by and against intervenors of right, §1367 makes inclusive joinder more difficult in diversity of citizenship cases.

---

jurisdiction would not attach if the absentee would have been held indispensable under Rule 19. Commentators have criticized this latter proviso as part of an antiquated view that failure to join such an absentee is a jurisdictional defect. Moreover, under the 1966 amendments to Rule 19, this proviso makes little sense. Remember that under Rule 19 an "indispensable" absentee is one who is (1) necessary, but (2) cannot feasibly be joined in the pending case and (3) as to whom the court has decided to dismiss rather than proceed. That third step was determined based upon an assessment of flexible factors under Rule 19(b). One relevant factor was whether the absentee can protect her interest in the absence of dismissal. Because the absentee satisfying Rule 19(a)(1)(B)(i) can intervene under Rule 24(a)(2), she can protect herself and thus the court should not dismiss. In other words, the court should not find the absentee (to use a term no longer found in Rule 19, but widely used) "indispensable."

[219] The basic tests for the two Rules are the same, with one addition in Rule 24(a)(2) that the absentee show that her interest is not adequately represented by extant litigants. As we discussed above, however, this latter requirement imposes a minimal burden on the absentee.

[220] See, e.g., 7C Wright & Miller §1917; Wright & Kane, Federal Courts 548-549; Christopher Fairman, Abdication to Academia: The Case of the Supplemental Jurisdiction Statute, 19 Seton Hall Legis. J. 157, 185-188 (1994); Richard D. Freer, Compounding Confusion and Hampering Diversity: Life After Finley and the Supplemental Jurisdiction Statute, 40 Emory L.J. 445, 475-487 (1991); Marilyn Ireland, Supplemental Jurisdiction over Claims in Intervention, 23 N.M. L. Rev. 57, 72-74 (1993); Denis McLaughlin, The Federal Supplemental Jurisdiction Statute — A Constitutional and Statutory Analysis, 24 Ariz. St. L.J. 849, 860 (1992); John Oakley, Recent Statutory Changes in the Law of Federal Jurisdiction

Let's return to the hypothetical. Before adoption of the supplemental jurisdiction statute, the claim by *A* against *D* would be permitted in the pending case because it would invoke supplemental jurisdiction. What about today? Under §1367(a), *A*'s claim against *D* would invoke supplemental jurisdiction, because it does satisfy the *Gibbs* test, as we saw above. But §1367(b) applies in cases that invoked diversity of citizenship jurisdiction (such as our hypothetical) and removes supplemental jurisdiction over certain claims. Among them are claims by persons "seeking to intervene as plaintiffs under Rule 24." *A* is such a person, so §1367(b) removes supplemental jurisdiction over that claim. This means, of course, that *P*'s claim against *D*, and any counterclaim by *D* against *P*, will be litigated in federal court, while *A*'s claim against *D* must be litigated in state court. The supplemental jurisdiction statute robs the federal court of the ability to resolve the overall dispute. As noted earlier, because §1367(b) only applies in diversity of citizenship cases, and because it increased the situations in which courts would not have supplemental jurisdiction, the statute reflects an anti-diversity jurisdiction bias.

The language of §1367(b) is problematic in another way. Because the subsection applies to those "seeking to intervene as plaintiffs," does it include someone who seeks to intervene as a defendant, but who is realigned as a plaintiff? The uncertainty on this point simply creates more confusion. Some courts have been willing to realign an intervening plaintiff as a defendant, expressly to save jurisdiction.[221] Others have not done so, feeling bound by the absentee's choice to intervene on the plaintiff's side.[222] Some litigants have even tried to exploit this language by intervening as defendants when their interests are more closely aligned with the plaintiff.[223]

- *A* holds a stock certificate for 1,000 shares of Corporation, issued in *A*'s name. *P* claims that she and *A* had agreed to buy the stock together, each paying half, and that the stock should have been issued in their joint names. *P*, a citizen of Alabama, sues Corporation, a citizen of Delaware, seeking to have *A*'s stock canceled and then reissued in the joint names of *P* and *A*. The stock is worth $500,000. *P*'s claim against Corporation

and Venue: The Judicial Improvement Acts of 1988 and 1990, 24 U.C. Davis L. Rev. 735, 764-766 (1991).

[221] *See, e.g.,* Development Fin. Corp. v. Alpha Hous. & Health Care, Inc., 54 F.3d 156, 159-160 (3d Cir. 1995).

[222] *See, e.g.,* Maryland Cas. Co. v. W.R. Grace & Co., 1996 U.S. Dist. LEXIS 868 (S.D.N.Y. Jan. 30, 1996).

[223] *See, e.g.,* Atherton v. Casey, 1992 U.S. Dist. LEXIS 9976 (E.D. La. June 24, 1992). The court realigned the intervenor as a plaintiff to reject supplemental jurisdiction.

invokes diversity of citizenship jurisdiction and is properly filed in federal
court. A is required under Rule 19(a)(1)(B)(i) and has a right to intervene under Rule 24(a)(2).[224] Will there be subject matter jurisdiction if
she intervenes?

- In all likelihood, A will choose to intervene as a defendant. Her interest is antithetical to that of P. After all, P wants to dilute A's interest
  in the stock. Corporation is probably ambivalent about who owns the
  stock and may be satisfied with the status quo. A wants to keep the
  status quo. So let's say A would intervene as a defendant. She is a citizen of Alabama, so P's claim against A does not invoke diversity of
  citizenship jurisdiction (because they are co-citizens). The claim likewise does not invoke federal question jurisdiction because it arises
  under state law. So is there supplemental jurisdiction?
- As we saw above, §1367(a) will grant supplemental jurisdiction over
  the claim, because of its close relationship with the pending case. But
  does §1367(b) remove that grant? It applies only in cases that invoked
  diversity of citizenship jurisdiction, such as this, and removes jurisdiction over particular claims.

Some people have argued that joinder is proper in this case because
nothing in §1367(b) precludes it.[225] After all, there is no claim here asserted
by a person "seeking to intervene as a plaintiff under Rule 24." So that
prohibition does not apply. The problem with the argument, as we also
saw with regard to Rule 19(a)(1)(B)(i) in §12.6.1, is that it assumes that
subject matter jurisdiction is granted over *parties*. Why did A intervene as
a defendant? Presumably so she could defend against P's claim to her
stock. So she intervened as a defendant to defend a claim by P against
her. Notice, however, that §1367(b) expressly removes supplemental jurisdiction over claims asserted by a plaintiff against "persons made parties
under Rule . . . 24." This provision applies to A in this hypothetical. So the
claim by P against A — which was the very reason for A's intervening —
cannot be asserted in the pending case.

Finally, claims asserted by or against a permissive intervenor will rarely
invoke supplemental jurisdiction. Permissive intervention under Rule
24(b)(2) requires only that the intervenor's claim or defense have at least
one question in common with the pending case. There is thus no requirement that the claim or defense be so closely related to the pending case
as to arise from a common nucleus of operative fact; thus, satisfying the
requirement of Rule 24(b)(2) does not necessarily satisfy the degree of
relatedness required for supplemental jurisdiction under §1367(a). There

---

[224] Remember why: A has an interest in the pending case; her ability to protect that interest may be impaired or impeded by the pending case, and (for Rule 24(a)(2)) her interest is
not adequately protected by those who are presently parties.

[225] Rowe, Burbank & Mengler, note 127 above.

may be cases, however, in which the claims asserted by or against a permissive intervenor will share enough factual overlap with the underlying dispute to invoke supplemental jurisdiction, but they are unusual.[226] In most cases, claims involving permissive intervenors have to invoke diversity of citizenship, alienage, or federal question jurisdiction to be heard in federal court.

---

[226] *See, e.g.,* Beckham Indus., Inc. v. International Ins. Co., 966 F.2d 470, 473 (9th Cir.), *cert. denied,* 506 U.S. 868 (1992). Recall that there is authority that the grant is even broader than this, and requires only that the claims have some "loose factual connection." Jones v. Ford Motor Credit Co., 358 F.3d 205, 210-215 (2d Cir. 2004). Such a broad interpretation of the grant of supplemental jurisdiction might encompass claims involving permissive intervenors.

Chapter 13

Special Multiparty Litigation

§13.1   Defining the Issue

In this chapter we study two specialized kinds of multiparty litigation: interpleader and the class action. With each, we revisit some policy themes we saw in Chapter 12. Specifically, in §12.6, we noted three policy bases that justified overriding the plaintiff's structuring of a case: efficiency, avoidance of harm to the absentee, and avoidance of harm to the defendant. Each of these policies makes appearances in this chapter. Here, though, we are not overriding the plaintiff's party structure of the case. Instead, we are structuring a multiparty case at the outset, employing those policies.

Though interpleader and the class action share some policy underpinnings — particularly a desire for efficient resolution of multiple claims — they are fundamentally different forms of litigation. Interpleader allows resolution of competing claims to property in a single case. It is thus limited to the question of who owns specific property. The class action permits a representative (or multiple representatives) to assert or to defend claims on behalf of a group whose members are similarly situated. The claim might be any claim shared by the class, such as harm from a mass tort or the effects of discrimination. Properly executed, class litigation by the representative(s) will bind all class members.

Before embarking on our discussion, it is useful to distinguish the litigation we see here from a *shareholder derivative suit*. Though most Civil Procedure courses do not cover this type of litigation, you will encounter it in some of your readings and should know what it is. Indeed, two classic Civil Procedure cases — *Shaffer v. Heitner* (concerning *quasi-in-rem* jurisdiction, discussed at §2.4.4) and *Cohen v. Beneficial Industrial Loan Co.* (an *Erie* case, discussed at §10.5) — were derivative suits. Such a case is filed by a shareholder of a corporation to vindicate a claim that belongs to the corporation. Almost always, the claim is against corporate managers for violating duties that they owe to the corporation. (A good example is when corporate directors steal corporate assets; that breaches their duty of loyalty to the corporation.) Though the corporation has a right to sue the bad managers, often it will not (because the bad corporate managers usually make the decision of whether the corporation should sue). If the corporation does not file suit, a shareholder is permitted to assert the claim *on its behalf*. The claim is "derivative" because the right asserted by the shareholder "derives" from the corporation's right to sue. If the case is successful, generally the corporation receives the proceeds of the judgment. So while a class action seeks to vindicate the individual claims of numerous class members, the derivative suit asserts a claim that belongs to a corporation.

§13.2   Interpleader

§13.2.1   What Interpleader Is and How It Works

Policy and Terminology

Interpleader is a procedural device that allows someone in possession of property or money to force all adverse claimants to that property to litigate the ownership of that property in a single proceeding. It has existed in some form for nearly seven centuries, and is the model of efficient litigation: The question of ownership is litigated once, with all claimants and the present possessor of the property being bound by the judgment.

- ○ Insurance Co. issued a $250,000 life insurance policy. The insured died, and Insurance Co. must now pay out the benefit. Three people — *A*, *B*, and C — each claim to be the beneficiary of the entire policy amount. Consider how difficult things would be for Insurance Co. if it could not force A, B, and C to assert their claims to the policy in a single interpleader case.

° Suppose A sued Insurance Co. and won. The court would enter a judgment requiring the company to pay the policy amount to A. Then suppose B sued Insurance Co. The judgment in the case by A against Insurance Co. would not be binding on B, so B is free to assert her claim that she should get the money. (By the way, why is the judgment in the case by A v. Insurance Co. not binding on B?[1]) Suppose B wins. The court would enter a judgment requiring the company to pay the policy amount to B. Insurance Co. would now be subject to inconsistent obligations: It could not satisfy the judgment from the first case without violating the judgment from the second case. If it has to pay both, it will pay out twice as much in insurance proceeds as it contracted to do. And things might get even more complicated when C sues to claim that she should get the insurance money.

Interpleader avoids these problems by allowing Insurance Co. (or anyone in a similar situation) to join in a single case all the persons who claim to own the property. Thus, it is supported by the same policy interest we saw undergirding joinder of necessary parties under Rule 19(a)(1)(B)(ii)[2] and impleader under Rule 14(a)(1).[3] And because interpleader resolves the conflicting claims in a single proceeding, it saves judicial resources and avoids the inconsistent results that can erode confidence in the system of justice. In summary,

a many-sided dispute can be resolved economically and expeditiously in a proceeding, and the stakeholder can be relieved from the obligation of determining who has the rightful claim to the money or property. In addition, the stakeholder avoids possible multiple liability resulting from inconsistent judgements for different claimants in different suits. Even if multiple liability is unlikely, both the stakeholder and the judicial system avoid the expense and delay of multiple litigation. Conflicting claimants to the stake also may benefit from interpleader, since all conflicting claims are resolved in a single

---

[1] Because due process provides that a judgment cannot be binding against one who was not a party, in an earlier case. See §11.3.4. B was not a party in A v. Insurance Co., nor was any party representing B's interest. So B is not bound.

[2] That rule permits overriding the plaintiff's structuring of a suit expressly to avoid subjecting a party to double, multiple, or inconsistent obligations such as those seen here. See §12.6.1.

[3] Impleader permits a defending party to join in an absentee who owes her indemnity or contribution. Doing so protects the defendant from the possibility of losing in the pending case and then failing in a separate case to collect indemnity of contributions. Thus, impleader, like joinder of necessary parties under Rule 19(a)(1)(B)(ii) and interpleader, avoids imposition of multiple liability. See §12.6.2.

action and a limited fund can be distributed equitably. Furthermore, interpleader frequently eliminated the need to find and execute on the debtor's assets. The contested stake generally will be on deposit with the court.[4]

As suggested in this quotation, interpleader litigation involves specialized terminology.

○ The property to which the litigants have conflicting claims of ownership is the *stake* or *res*.[5]
○ The person in possession of the property is the *stakeholder*.
○ The persons who are joined in the interpleader proceeding, whose conflicting claims of ownership will be adjudicated, are the *claimants*.

Historically, interpleader was possible only if the stakeholder did not claim to own the stake — that is, if the stakeholder was *disinterested*. Traditionally, then, the stakeholder was one who found herself in possession of property, did not know to whom it belonged, knew that various people claimed to own it, but who did not claim ownership herself. Interpleader invoked by such a disinterested stakeholder is called *true* (or sometimes *strict*) *interpleader*. Over time, courts relaxed the requirement that the stakeholder not claim to own the stake and permitted an *interested stakeholder* to institute interpleader. Such a proceeding was (and is) known as *in the nature of interpleader*. (As we see in §13.2.2, the question of whether the stakeholder is interested may have a profound impact on the invocation of subject matter jurisdiction.)

○ *S* finds an expensive wristwatch in the basement of the house she buys. The previous owner of the house (*O*) claims to own it, and argues that she left it in the basement by mistake. A contractor (*C*) also claims to own it, and argues that she left it in the basement while doing renovation work. *S* is the stakeholder. *O* and *C* are the claimants. If *S* does not claim to own the wristwatch, she is a disinterested stakeholder, and the proceeding will be a true (or strict) interpleader.
○ If, however, *S* claims that she should be able to keep the wristwatch (because, for example, of a finders' statute), she will be an interested stakeholder, and the proceeding will be in the nature of the interpleader.

Two Types of Interpleader in Federal Court

Interpleader practice in the federal courts is complicated because there are two types of interpleader. Rule 22 permits interpleader. This is known as *Rule interpleader*. Because no Federal Rule can affect federal subject

---

[4] 4 Moore's Federal Practice at 22-9 to 22-11.
[5] "Res" is the Latin word for "thing," as we saw when we studied *in rem* personal jurisdiction in §2.2.

matter jurisdiction or venue, Rule 22 provides only a procedural mechanism for interpleader. It can only be used if some basis for federal subject matter jurisdiction (discussed in Chapter 4) and some basis for federal venue (discussed in Chapter 5) apply. Typically, Rule interpleader cases invoke diversity of citizenship jurisdiction under 28 U.S.C. §1332(a)(1). In addition, however, there are also three statutes — 28 U.S.C. §§1335, 1391, and 2361 — that create a different right to interplead and a separate basis of federal subject matter jurisdiction as well as provisions for venue and service of process. These three statutes together create what is known as *statutory interpleader*. The jurisdictional and venue differences between Rule and statutory interpleader are important, and are addressed in detail in §13.2.2. Other differences are discussed in the remainder of this subsection. Throughout your consideration of this topic, keep in mind that there are two completely separate vehicles — Rule interpleader and statutory interpleader — for invoking interpleader in federal court.

Claims That Exceed the Stake and Prospective Claims

In the examples we have seen so far, each adverse claimant claimed to own the entire take — either the wristwatch in the previous hypothetical or the $250,000 life insurance fund in the first example. But interpleader is also appropriate when the total claimed by the claimants exceeds the value of the stake. Such cases usually involve competing claims to a liability insurance fund.

° *D* has automobile insurance that covers her against liability to a total of $300,000 per occurrence. She is involved in an automobile crash that severely injures five people. Each of the five (*P-1* through *P-5*) files a case against *D* for personal injuries from the crash. The total demand in the five separate cases is $1,500,000. Thus, the claims exceed five-fold the amount of insurance coverage. *D*'s insurance company may wish to interplead the $300,000 fund and join the five claimants. There are three important points to note here.

First, interpleader litigation deals *only* with who is entitled to recover the *stake*; it involves *only* adverse claims *to* the stake. In this hypothetical, we do not know yet whether the claims by each of the five individual tort plaintiffs will result in judgments that exceed the $300,000 insurance coverage. The five tort claims are "unliquidated," because we do not know whether they will actually become claims against the insurance fund and, if so, for how much. The individual tort cases by *P-1* through *P-5* against *D* are *not* part of the interpleader. Those claims are asserted against *D* to impose upon *D* personal liability; they are not claims against the stake.[6] As those cases are litigated (or settled), the claim of each plaintiff will become "liquidated," which simply means that a dollar figure will be attached to it. Then, each plaintiff will have a claim against the stake, because each will want to recover her judgment from the insurance money. (If the stake is exhausted without compensating the claimants fully, the claimants will attempt to recover the shortfall from *D* personally.)

Second, if the claims of the various tort plaintiffs in this case are not yet liquidated (and might not be liquidated for years because they are in litigation in separate cases), how can the insurance company interplead *now*? Some states have "direct action" statutes, which allow claimants to sue insurance companies before winning a judgment against the person insured. In such a state, there is no problem with allowing interpleader at this stage, because *P-1* through *P-5* can sue the insurer in advance of winning a judgment against *D*. But many states do not permit such direct actions, and permit suit against the insurance company only after one has won a judgment against the insured. Is interpleader possible at this stage? Though the answer was debated for some time, it is now clear, at least in federal court, that the answer is yes. Under Rule interpleader by Rule 22, the stakeholder may proceed if separate claims "may expose [the stakeholder] to double or multiple liability . . . ." Under statutory interpleader, the stakeholder may join any who "are claiming or *may* claim to be entitled to the stake."[7] Thus, even if the applicable substantive law does not permit a direct action in the absence of a judgment against the insured, interpleader is proper at the outset.[8]

Third, what happens if the claims of the five plaintiffs, as finally liquidated, exceed the value of the stake? Suppose, for example, that *P-1* wins a judgment of $50,000; *P-2* wins a judgment of $100,000; *P-3* wins a judgment of $150,000; *P-4* wins a judgment of $200,000; and *P-5* wins a judgment of $400,000. That is a total of $900,000 in judgments against *D*. The available insurance fund is $300,000. If interpleader were not available,

---

[6] In all likelihood, *D*'s insurance company will have the duty to defend *D* in each of those cases, regardless of what the ultimate recoveries by each plaintiff may be. It usually is part of a liability insurer's contractual obligation not only to provide the policy coverage from which claimants can recover but also to defend the insured in litigation against her.

[7] 28 U.S.C. §1335(a)(1) (emphasis added).

[8] State Farm Fire & Cas. Co. v. Tashire, 386 U.S. 523, 533 (1967) ("Were an insurance company required to await reduction of claims to judgment, the first claimant to obtain such a judgment or to negotiate a settlement might appropriate all or a disproportionate slice of the fund before his fellow claimants were able to establish their claims. The difficulties such a race to judgment pose for the insurer, and the unfairness which may result to some claimants, were among the principal evils the interpleader device was intended to remedy."). Though this case involved statutory interpleader, there is no serious doubt that Rule 22 also permits interpleader of prospective claims, as shown by the language that separate claims "may" expose the stakeholder to harm. *See* 6247 Atlas Corp. v. Marine Ins. Co., 155 F.R.D. 454, 463 (S.D.N.Y. 1994).

we would have a race to recover from the insurance fund. The race might leave the tardy claimants with nothing. Thus, in addition to the policy advantages discussed above, allowing interpleader in this situation also serves the same principle addressed by Rule 19(a)(1)(B)(i) (discussed in §12.6) — avoiding harm to an absentee.

○ In this situation, interpleader serves to "slice the pie" equitably among the five claimants. As noted, their liquidated claims total $900,000, which is three times as large as the insurance fund. Accordingly, the interpleader court will allow each claimant to recover one-third of her claim. Thus, *P-1* will recover $16,666.66 from the fund; *P-2* will get $33,333.33; *P-3* will get $50,000; *P-4* will get $66,666.67; and *P-5* will get $133,333.33. None recovers her amount in full, but, more important, none is left out altogether. (Each one is now free to try to enforce her judgment against *D* personally for the two-thirds not covered by insurance.)

Injunctions Against Other Proceedings; Limitations of Interpleader

The efficacy of interpleader would be lost if the claimants were free to assert their rights to the stake in separate litigation. For instance, assume *S* institutes interpleader and joins *O* and *C* as claimants. If *C* can sue *S* in a separate suit in another court to recover the stake from *S*, the advantages of interpleader will be lost. To avoid such duplicative litigation, it would behoove the interpleader court to issue an injunction against the claimants, prohibiting them from suing for the stake in another case. In the federal system, interpleader courts certainly have the authority to enter such injunctions.

Section 2361, which is part of statutory interpleader, expressly provides that the federal court overseeing an interpleader case may "enter its order restraining [the claimants] from instituting or prosecuting any proceeding in any State or United States court affecting the [stake]."[9] Note that the language permits the federal court to issue an injunction against claimants from proceeding either in another federal court *or* in any state court.[10] But §2361 does not apply to Rule interpleader cases.[11] As to such cases, then, there is no express grant of injunctive power. Nonetheless, the interpleader court can issue an injunction, though getting to that conclusion is

---

[9] 28 U.S.C. §2361.

[10] It is important to note that such an injunction is not issued to the other courts. It would be unseemly for one court to order another court not to proceed with a matter; such orders are extremely rare. Instead, the injunction is against the claimants personally, forbidding them from litigating in another court. If a claimant violates the injunction, the federal court issuing it can hold the claimant in contempt, which means that the court can fine that party or even order her jailed until she agrees to abide by the injunction.

[11] United States Indus., Inc. v. Laborde, 794 F. Supp. 454, 459 (D.P.R. 1992).

more complicated. For starters, it is well established that the interpleader court may issue an injunction against overlapping litigation in another *federal* court.[12] This result is dictated by the "first-filed rule," which provides, as a general matter, that the court in which a matter is first filed has the power to enjoin litigants from proceeding in another federal court on the same matter.

What if the overlapping litigation is in a state court? Here, things get more complicated because of the Anti-Injunction Act, 28 U.S.C. §2283, which provides that a federal court may not issue an injunction against litigants proceeding in a state court, unless one of three exceptions applies. This statute recognizes an important policy of federalism — that it is generally inappropriate for the courts of the federal government to interfere with the courts of a sovereign state government.[13] Thus, a federal Rule interpleader court can issue an injunction against a pending state action only if one of the exceptions to the Anti-Injunction Act applies.[14] The exceptions are: (1) when Congress provides that the federal court may enjoin litigants from proceeding in state court;[15] (2) when an injunction is "necessary in aid" of the jurisdiction of the court; and (3) when an injunction is necessary to enable the court to effectuate a judgment it has entered.[16] Courts have concluded that the second exception applies in Rule interpleader cases.[17] In other words, the federal court in Rule interpleader can issue an injunction "in aid of its jurisdiction," because simultaneous litigation in state court would interfere with the interpleader court's efforts to distribute the stake.[18]

---

[12] One classic opinion is *Pan Am. Fire & Cas. Co. v. Revere*, 188 F. Supp. 474, 483 n.46 (E.D. La. 1960).

[13] This federalism concern is not present, of course, when the overlapping cases are both in federal court. In such cases, the first-filed rule can apply, because the different courts involved are in the same judicial system.

[14] If the claimant has not yet instituted a state court action, the Anti-Injunction Act does not apply and the federal court thus may issue the injunction. Why? The Act applies only to injunctions against pending state court proceedings, and not to state court actions that have not yet been filed. Dombrowski v. Pfister, 380 U.S. 479, 484 n.2 (1965) (Act does "not preclude injunctions against the institution of state court proceedings, but only bar stays of suits already instituted").

[15] This exception applies with *statutory* interpleader, because §2361 makes such an express provision.

[16] 28 U.S.C. §2283.

[17] *See, e.g.*, General Ry. Signal Co. v. Corcoran, 921 F.2d 700, 707 (7th Cir. 1991).

[18] In addition, once the interpleader judgment is entered, the Rule interpleader court can issue an injunction against state court proceedings that would seek to undo the result of the interpleader. Such an injunction satisfied the third exception to the Anti-Injunction Act, that the injunction enable the court to effectuate its judgments. *See, e.g.*, Truck-A-Tune v. Re, 856 F. Supp. 77, 81 n.10 (D. Conn. 1993), *aff'd on other grounds*, 23 F.3d 60 (2d Cir. 1993).

Any injunction prohibiting a claimant from litigating outside the interpleader proceeding must be properly limited. Specifically, it can only prohibit other claims *to the stake itself*. This fact drives home the limitation of interpleader: It is a device for placing in one proceeding claims to specific property; it is not a device that allows a court to force all potential tort claimants into a single case. *The interpleader case must involve only claims to the stake.*

The leading case on the scope of interpleader is *State Farm Fire & Casualty Co. v. Tashire*,[19] which involved a horrible collision between a Greyhound bus and a truck. The truck was driven by Clark and owned by Glasgow (who was a passenger in the truck at the time of the collision). The Greyhound bus was driven by Nauta. The collision killed two passengers on the bus and injured 33 other passengers, as well as Clark, Glasgow, and Nauta. Clark carried insurance with State Farm. The policy covered Clark (the driver of the truck) for claims up to $10,000 per person for bodily injury, with a maximum of $20,000 per occurrence. It was obvious that the claims against Clark for the collision would exceed the policy limit. State Farm filed an interpleader action. As claimants, it joined Clark, Glasgow, Nauta, Greyhound Lines, and each passenger (or, if deceased, the passenger's estate). The district court permitted the interpleader to proceed and entered an injunction requiring that all claims against State Farm, Clark, Greyhound, and Nauta be prosecuted in the interpleader proceeding. Thus, tort claims against the insurer and insured, as well as those against others involved in the wreck, could be asserted only in the interpleader case.

The Supreme Court drastically modified the injunction to reflect the proper scope of interpleader. Interpleader is limited to claims to the fund. In many cases, the Court noted, such claims will constitute the entire dispute, and there will be no collateral litigation. For example, in our hypothetical above concerning the wristwatch, the interpleader case would resolve the entire dispute between the homeowner, the previous owner, and the contractor; the only controversy was ownership of the watch.

In cases like *Tashire*, however, there are more assertions of liability than the mere claims to the fund of insurance money. In that case, there were tort claims against Greyhound, Nauta, Glasgow, and Clark. None of these tort claims constituted property brought within the interpleader proceeding. The interpleader could determine *only* who gets the $20,000 of State Farm insurance money for claims against Clark. Thus, anyone who had *already recovered* a judgment against Clark could seek to recover it from the State Farm fund. Those claims were properly asserted *only* in the interpleader case. But the underlying tort claims against Clark (and against the others) are not part of the interpleader case; quite simply, they

---

[19] 386 U.S. 523 (1967).

are not claims against the stake until one tries to enforce a judgment against the insurance fund. As the Court summarized:

> State Farm's interest in this case, which is the fulcrum of the interpleader procedure, is confined to its $20,000 fund. That interest receives full vindication when the court restrains claimants from seeking to enforce against the insurance company any judgment obtained against its insured, except in the interpleader proceeding itself. To the extent that the District Court sought to control claimants' lawsuits against the insured and other alleged tortfeasors, it exceeded the powers granted to it by the [interpleader] scheme.[20]

The court recognized that its holding meant that interpleader "cannot be used to solve all the vexing problems of multiparty litigation arising out of a mass tort. But interpleader was never intended to perform such a function, to be an all-purpose 'bill of peace.'"[21] The bill of peace was a tool of equity that permitted a court to join all interested parties in a single case, in an effort to resolve an overall dispute. There is no modern counterpart to the bill of peace. The lack of such a tool is frustrating, but this is part of the price we pay for the value we place on litigant autonomy. As the Court emphasized in *Tashire*, had interpleader been intended as a bill of peace, "careful provision would necessarily have been made to insure that a party with little or no interest in the outcome of a complex controversy [like State Farm] should not strip truly interested parties of substantial rights — such as the right to choose the forum in which to establish their claims. . . ."[22]

Invocation of Interpleader

Interpleader is odd because it reverses the normal role of plaintiff and defendant. Usually, when a plaintiff sues a defendant, it is to impose liability on the defendant. In interpleader, however, the stakeholder, as plaintiff, sues the claimants not to impose liability on them, but to force them to assert their claims to the property in the interpleader proceeding. In essence, she sues them to force them to sue her! She does so, however, because interpleader allows her to avoid being sued multiple times by the various claimants.

What happens, though, if one of the claimants sues the stakeholder before she institutes interpleader? Can there be *defensive invocation of interpleader*? Yes. Let's return to the fact pattern we saw above, about ownership of the wristwatch found in a house. Here, though, assume that

[20] *Id.* at 535.
[21] *Id.*
[22] *Id.* at 536.

O has sued S, seeking to recover the wristwatch. S is the defendant, but is also the stakeholder, and wants to invoke interpleader by bringing C into the case as well, so all the claimants can litigate the ownership question in a single proceeding. What does she do? She files a compulsory counterclaim against O, invoking interpleader and naming O as one of the claimants.[23] Rule 13(h) (see §12.5) permits S to join as additional parties to the counterclaim any absentee (such as C) who satisfies Rule 19 or Rule 20.[24] By definition, absentee claimants in interpleader (here, C) satisfy Rule 19 and thus can be joined under Rule 13(h).[25]

Stages of Interpleader Litigation

Assuming the court has personal jurisdiction over the parties and subject matter jurisdiction over the interpleader claim (which we discuss in §13.2.2), interpleader litigation proceeds in two stages. First, the court determines whether the case is appropriate for interpleader at all — whether the litigation concerns claims to property that meet the various requirements for interpleader. If so, the case proceeds to the second stage, in which the claimants litigate the question of who owns the stake. In true interpleader (where the stakeholder has no claim to the stake), the stakeholder does not participate in the second stage of the litigation; she is discharged from the case at the close of the first stage.[26] If, on the other hand, the proceeding is in the nature of interpleader (where the stakeholder claims to own the property), the stakeholder will participate in the second stage of the litigation. In essence, she is one of the claimants and must battle it out with the others. The result of the second stage of the litigation is a judgment as to who the rightful owner is. The judgment will bind all claimants who were joined in the case.

One important issue is what happens to the stake during the litigation. In federal court, there are different approaches under Rule interpleader

---

[23] The claim against O is a compulsory counterclaim because it is against an opposing party and arises from the same transaction or occurrence as that party's claim. Here, O's claim against S is for ownership of the wristwatch. S's counterclaim is for interpleader as to the same property; thus, it obviously arises from the same transaction or occurrence as O's claim. We discussed the compulsory counterclaim at §12.5.1. *See* Fed. R. Civ. P. 22(a)(2): "A defendant exposed to similar liability may seek interpleader through a crossclaim or counterclaim."

[24] Rule 20 concerns permissive joinder of parties. See §12.4. Rule 19 concerns joinder of necessary parties. See §12.6.1.

[25] An absentee stakeholder satisfied Rule 19(a)(1)(B)(ii) because her nonjoinder subjects a party (the stakeholder) to the possibility of multiple or inconsistent obligations. As we noted above, if the claimants sue individually, in separate litigation, the stakeholder may be subjected to inconsistent obligations, such as one judgment that C is the owner and another that O is the owner. Avoiding such potential harm underlies Rule 19(a)(1)(B)(i) and is the basic underlying reason for interpleader.

[26] Commercial Natl. Bank v. Demos, 18 F.3d 485, 487 (7th Cir. 1994).

and statutory interpleader. Under the latter, the stakeholder must deposit the stake with the court or post a bond with the clerk of the court in an amount determined by the court.[27] Indeed, under statutory interpleader, such deposit of the stake or a bond is a jurisdictional prerequisite, so failure to abide by the requirement deprives the court of jurisdiction to proceed.[28] If a claimant asserts that the value of the stake is higher than the stakeholder contends, the stakeholder must deposit the higher amount.[29] Rule 22, on the other hand, does not expressly require deposit of the stake or of a bond. Obviously, then, such deposit is not a jurisdictional requirement for Rule interpleader.[30] Nonetheless, the court in a Rule interpleader case can order the stakeholder to deposit the stake with it.[31] Such an order is routine.

Deposit of the stake with the court is a salutary event. It ensures that the property cannot be lost, transferred, stolen, or squandered while the litigation is ongoing. It also ensures that the property is present for distribution at the end of the case; there is no need to track down the possessor and get an order requiring her to deposit the property for distribution.

Another important question in interpleader litigation in federal court is whether there is a right to jury trial. Interpleader developed mostly at equity, but also had roots in the common law courts of England. As we know from §9.2.2, the Seventh Amendment preserves the right to jury trial in actions at law, but not in suits at equity. What does this mean for interpleader? The availability of a jury trial depends upon the stage of litigation involved. The first stage of interpleader — in which the question is whether the case meets the requirements for interpleader — is tried to the judge; there is no right to jury trial at this stage.[32] The second stage of interpleader — in which the question is who rightfully owns the stake — is tried to a jury under the Seventh Amendment if there would be a right to a jury trial if the same issues were raised in "regular" civil litigation.[33] In this stage, then, it is irrelevant that interpleader developed largely in equity. One makes the jury trial assessment in federal court just as she would if the case were in federal court without the interpleader proceeding.

---

[27] 28 U.S.C. §1335(a)(2).

[28] See, e.g., In re Sinking of the M/V Ukola, 806 F.2d 1, 5 (1st Cir. 1986).

[29] See, e.g., Nationwide Mut. Ins. Co. v. Eckman, 555 F. Supp. 775, 778 (D. Del. 1983). This requirement affects the determination of the amount in controversy for purposes of subject matter jurisdiction, which we address in §13.2.2.

[30] Gelfgren v. Republic Natl. Life Ins. Co., 680 F.2d 79, 82 (9th Cir. 1982).

[31] Central Bank v. United States, 838 F. Supp. 564, 566 (M.D. Fla. 1993). Federal Rule 67 authorizes the court to order such a deposit.

[32] See 4 Moore's Federal Practice §22.03[3].

[33] See, e.g., Hyde Props. v. McCoy, 507 F.2d 301, 305 (6th Cir. 1974).

Historic Equitable Restrictions on Interpleader

This subsection is of relevance only if your professor covered the historical development of interpleader; many professors do not. The procedure had a convoluted history in England. It originated in the common law courts and then "crossed over" into equity. Much of the interpleader practice therefore developed in the equity courts.[34] Those courts, and subsequently the equity courts in the United States, imposed four restrictions on the right to invoke interpleader. All four unduly limit the availability of interpleader and serve no redeeming purpose. In federal court — under both Rule interpleader and statutory interpleader — three of the four restrictions are jettisoned expressly, and most courts addressing the question conclude that the fourth also ought to be. Of course, states are free to permit interpleader on whatever terms they see fit. While most states have followed the federal lead and removed these historic equitable restrictions on interpleader, no doubt some states still adhere to at least some of them.[35] We review the four restrictions and how they are treated in federal practice.

The first is the one we have already mentioned: that the stakeholder must be disinterested and not make a claim of ownership of the disputed property. In other words, classic equitable practice did not permit actions "in the nature of interpleader." This requirement is rejected in Rule interpleader by the provision in Federal Rule 22(a)(1)(B) that no one may object if the stakeholder "denies liability in whole or in part to any or all of the claimants." In statutory interpleader, the rejection of this historical restriction is more direct, with the provision in §1335(a) that the stakeholder may proceed with an action "in the nature of interpleader."

The second and third equitable restrictions on interpleader are closely related. The second is that claimants must be claiming the same thing or debt, and the third is that their adverse claims to the property are dependent on or derived from a common source. Rule 22(a)(1)(A) expressly rejects both of these requirements for Rule interpleader in federal court. Similarly, §1335(b) expressly rejects both for statutory interpleader in federal court.

The final equitable restriction is that the stakeholder have no independent liability to any claimant. Oddly, neither Rule interpleader nor statutory interpleader expressly addresses this requirement. Nonetheless, most federal courts conclude, correctly, that the requirement is no longer relevant and should not be followed.[36] This restriction no longer makes sense.

---

[34] *See generally* Geoffrey Hazard & Myron Moskovitz, *An Historical and Critical Analysis of Interpleader*, 52 Cal. L. Rev. 706 (1964).

[35] *See, e.g.*, Midland Natl. Life Ins. Co. v. Emerson, 174 S.E.2d 211, 212 (Ga. Ct. App. 1970) (refusing to allow interested stakeholder to invoke interpleader at equity; led to legislative rejection of the rule).

[36] *See* Libby, McNeill & Libby v. City Natl. Bank, 592 F.2d 504 (9th Cir. 1978); Companion Life Ins. Co. v. Schaffer, 442 F. Supp. 826, 829 (S.D.N.Y. 1977).

It was imposed in an era when claimants had no procedural mechanism for asserting a claim against the stakeholder in an interpleader case; at the time interpleader developed, there was no counterclaim in equity practice. Thus, the courts of the day determined that permitting interpleader in such a case would be unfair to the claimant who had a separate claim against the stakeholder. Today, because the claimant in interpleader can assert a counterclaim against the stakeholder, there is simply no need for this restriction. Still, there are occasional opinions in which a court will deny interpleader because the stakeholder has an independent liability to one of the claimants.[37]

- Return to one of our hypotheticals above, in which *S* claims ownership of a wristwatch she found in the house she just bought. *O*, the previous owner of the house, also claims to own the watch, as does *C*, a contractor who had done work on the house. *S* institutes a proceeding in the nature of interpleader, joining *O* and *C*. Suppose *C* has a claim against *S* arising from the work *C* had done on the house; she claims that *S* did not pay her for various work done. The existence of this independent ground of potential liability of *S* to *C* violates the fourth equitable restriction on interpleader, and, if followed, would render interpleader impossible. Most federal courts recognize, however, that *C* can simply assert a counterclaim against *S* in the pending interpleader case; thus they ignore the fourth equitable restriction and allow the interpleader to proceed.

§13.2.2   Personal Jurisdiction, Subject Matter Jurisdiction, and Venue

The Development of Two Types of Interpleader

We already have noted that there are two types of interpleader in the federal court system: Rule interpleader under Federal Rule 22 and statutory interpleader under 28 U.S.C. §§1335, 1397, and 2361. One understandable question is: Why do we have two separate vehicles for doing the same thing? To a degree, it is a historical fluke. The original Federal Rules of Civil Procedure, promulgated in 1938, adopted as Rule 22 a provision that had been included in the earlier Federal Equity Rules. When the Federal Rules merged what had been separate law and equity practice in the federal courts, it was natural to include the interpleader provision. As we studied in detail in Chapter 12, however, the Federal Rules cannot affect the jurisdiction of the federal courts. Thus, Rule 22 interpleader — then and now — can be invoked only if the case brought under it invokes a basis of federal subject matter jurisdiction. As we know from Chapter 4, the main

---

[37] *See, e.g.,* Nevada Eighty-Eight, Inc. v. Title Ins. Co. of Minn., 753 F. Supp. 1516, 1527 (D. Nev. 1990).

bases of such jurisdiction are diversity of citizenship and federal question. Very few Rule interpleader cases invoke federal question jurisdiction. Nearly all such cases invoke diversity of citizenship jurisdiction (which we review in detail later in this subsection). Similarly, whether venue is proper is determined for Rule interpleader, just as it is for any diversity of citizenship case, under §1391(a). And, finally, personal jurisdiction over the claimants must be asserted as it would in any diversity of citizenship case. In sum, then, Rule interpleader is — for purposes of jurisdiction, venue, and service of process — just a diversity of citizenship case.

But statutory interpleader is a completely different proposition. Congress enacted statutory interpleader — again, today codified at §§1335, 1397, and 2361 — in 1917, in response to a Supreme Court case we will discuss in a moment. The three statutes, respectively, (1) create the claim for interpleader and grant subject matter jurisdiction therefor, (2) create a special venue provision for statutory interpleader claims, and (3) permit nationwide service of process for statutory interpleader cases. Rule 22 is completely irrelevant to statutory interpleader. And statutory interpleader is completely irrelevant to Rule 22. If a stakeholder proceeds under statutory interpleader, she is invoking subject matter jurisdiction under §1335, and not under the general diversity of citizenship statute, §1332(a)(1). Now we compare Rule interpleader and statutory interpleader in terms of personal jurisdiction, subject matter jurisdiction, and venue. Keep in mind that Rule interpleader is simply a diversity of citizenship case, while statutory interpleader has its own special provisions for personal jurisdiction, subject matter jurisdiction, and venue.

Personal Jurisdiction

In the 1916 case of *New York Life Insurance Co. v. Dunlevy*, the Supreme Court held that interpleader proceedings are *in personam* actions and, thus, the interpleader court must have *in personam* jurisdiction over the claimants.[38] This holding was not a foregone conclusion. Indeed, it seems wrong. An interpleader proceeding quite clearly appears to be a *quasi-in-rem* action of the first type, because it involves the issue of ownership of a stake placed in the court's possession.[39] Under the established doctrine of the day, judgments in such *quasi-in-rem* cases were valid if the court had jurisdiction over the disputed property and the parties

[38] 241 U.S. 518 (1916).

[39] We discussed *quasi-in-rem* actions of the first type at §2.2. They concern ownership of specific property, and the property itself is the basis of jurisdiction. These cases are contrasted with *quasi-in-rem* of the second type, in which property is used as the basis of jurisdiction, but the claim in litigation is unrelated to ownership thereof.

were given notice of the proceeding.[40] Nonetheless, the parties and the Court seemed simply to assume that the proceeding was *in personam*. And it has been so considered ever since.

The facts of *Dunlevy* demonstrate the importance of its holding. An insurance company held $2,500 under an insurance policy, to which there were three claimants. First, the insured, Joseph Gould, claimed that the money was his. Second, his daughter, Effie Dunlevy, claimed that her dad had assigned the proceeds to her. Third, a department store claimed the money because it had a judgment against Effie; so if Effie were entitled to the money, the store asserted that it should get it. The insurance company interpleaded the three claimants in a state court in Pittsburgh. Joseph and the department store were served with process and thus brought before the jurisdiction of the court. Effie, however, had moved to California, and the court did not have *in personam* jurisdiction over her. The interpleader court held that Joseph was entitled to the money, and ordered that it be paid to him. Then Effie brought a separate case against the insurance company in California. The Supreme Court upheld judgment in her favor. Because the interpleader court in Pittsburgh did not have *in personam* jurisdiction over Effie, she was not bound by its judgment. Thus, nothing precluded her from suing the insurance company.

The result, of course, was that the insurance company had to pay the policy amount twice. In other words, it suffered exactly the kind of harm — double liability — that interpleader is intended to avoid. In the wake of the holding in *Dunlevy*, every insurance company had cause to worry: Unless it could get *in personam* jurisdiction over all claimants in a single court, it could not bind all claimants to the interpleader judgment.

What could the insurance companies do to avoid this risk? Not much if they were left to litigate in state courts. Though a state court's *in personam* jurisdictional reach is far greater today than it was when *Dunlevy* was decided, absent consent no state court can bind anyone who lacks minimum contacts with the forum.[41] In contrast, though, federal courts can be empowered to exercise *in personam* jurisdiction over anyone with minimum contacts with the United States itself (and not just with a particular state).[42] In other words, federal courts can be given power to serve process nationwide. Insurance companies lobbied Congress to address the

---

[40] Indeed, even after *Shaffer v. Heitner*, it is arguable that the court's jurisdiction over the disputed property satisfies due process. See §2.4.4. At any rate, it's difficult to figure out why *Dunlevy* was not treated as a *quasi-in-rem* case. It may be that the lawyers simply did not think of it. There is also some possibility that no one ever gave notice of the interpleader proceeding to one of the claimants, who was in another state.

[41] By "minimum contacts," we mean satisfaction of the *International Shoe* test. See §2.4.3.

[42] If this point is fuzzy, see §2.4. Remember, the cases we studied, starting with *Pennoyer*, concern due process limitations on a *state's* power to exercise personal jurisdiction. The federal government can exercise jurisdiction over anyone having minimum contacts

problem presented by the holding in *Dunlevy* by providing for interpleader jurisdiction in federal court, and to permit nationwide service of process in such cases. The lobbying was instrumental in passage of the Federal Interpleader Act, or what we call *statutory interpleader*. The aspect of statutory interpleader allowing nationwide service of process on claimants is now found in §2361.

In contrast, Rule interpleader does not have its own separate statutory basis for service of process and personal jurisdiction. A Rule interpleader case is treated just as any other case in the federal court. Thus, as we discussed in §3.3.4, personal jurisdiction and service of process outside the state in which the federal court sits are possible only if they would be proper in a state court there.

- Trustee holds a fund of $100,000, to which there are three claimants, *C-1*, *C-2*, and *C-3*. Trustee institutes interpleader in federal court in California. Assume that subject matter jurisdiction and venue are proper. *C-1* is a citizen of California and can be served with process there. *C-2* is a citizen of Arizona but clearly has sufficient minimum contacts with California to be subject to *in personam* jurisdiction there. *C-3* is a citizen of Florida and has absolutely no contact with California.
- If the case is brought under Rule interpleader, the federal court in California will have *in personam* jurisdiction (and can serve process outside state lines) to the same extent as a California state court. Thus, *C-1* and *C-2* can be brought before the jurisdiction of the court, because they clearly have sufficient contacts with California. But *C-3* cannot be brought before the jurisdiction of the federal court in California, because she lacks minimum contacts with California. Because a California state court could not exercise *in personam* jurisdiction over *C-3*, neither can a federal court under Rule interpleader.
- If the same case were brought under statutory interpleader, however, *C-3* could be brought before the jurisdiction of the federal court in California. Under §2361, *C-3* is subject to nationwide service of process. Anyone found anywhere in the United States can be served with process for a statutory interpleader proceeding in a federal court anywhere in the country.

---

with the country, even if she does not have minimum contacts with the state in which the federal court sits. As a matter of comity, the Federal Rules have adopted the general notion that a federal court will exercise personal jurisdiction outside the state in which it sits only if a state court in that state could do so. See §3.3.4. Constitutionally, however, Congress can empower the federal courts to exercise nationwide service of process and thus to have personal jurisdiction over anyone who can be served anywhere within the United States. Statutory interpleader is one of the rare instances in which Congress has done so.

Subject Matter Jurisdiction

As we noted above, Rule 22 simply provides a procedural device for joining claimants in an interpleader case. It does not and cannot affect subject matter jurisdiction requirements. So Rule interpleader is proper only if the case invokes one of the independent bases of federal subject matter jurisdiction: diversity of citizenship, alienage, or federal question. On the other hand, statutory interpleader has its own legislative basis of subject matter jurisdiction, separate from the general grants of diversity of citizenship, alienage, and federal question jurisdiction.

Federal Question Jurisdiction. Whether interpleader arises under federal law can be difficult to assess. For one thing, as we have seen, interpleader is an odd kind of "claim" — it is really a device by which the stakeholder demands that others assert their claims *against* her. So it is difficult as a conceptual matter to characterize whether interpleader involves a federal right.[43] Moreover, interpleader can present the same problem we encountered with deciding whether declaratory judgment cases arise under federal law. In those cases, discussed at §4.6.3, courts look to whether coercive action by the stakeholder would invoke federal question jurisdiction.[44] When all is said and done, very few Rule interpleader cases invoke federal question jurisdiction. Examples include interpleader concerning an escrow account claimed under the Small Business Act[45] and funds ostensibly subject to federal tax liens.[46]

Subject Matter Jurisdiction Based upon Citizenship and Amount in Controversy. The vast majority of Rule interpleader cases invoke diversity of citizenship jurisdiction. Because Rule 22 cannot affect jurisdictional requirements, Rule interpleader cases are treated simply as diversity of citizenship cases under §1332(a)(1).[47] So all principles about invoking diversity of citizenship jurisdiction, which we discussed at §4.5, apply in Rule interpleader. Statutory interpleader is a completely different proposition. Though as a constitutional matter, the subject matter basis for statutory interpleader is diversity of citizenship, as a statutory matter, it does not rely on the general diversity statute, §1332(a)(1). Instead, §1335 applies. The requirements for subject matter jurisdiction for Rule and statutory interpleader differ markedly.

To Determine Diversity. Rule and statutory interpleader differ in two fundamental ways: (1) whose citizenships are relevant, and (2) what kind of diversity (complete or minimal) is required. Rule interpleader is just a regular diversity of citizenship case under §1332(a)(1). Accordingly, the courts look to the citizenship of the stakeholder, on the one hand, and the

---

[43] *See, e.g.,* Commercial Union Ins. Co. v. United States, 999 F.2d 581, 585 (D.C. Cir. 1993).

[44] Bell & Beckwith v. United States, 766 F.2d 910, 913 (6th Cir. 1985).

[45] Kim v. Kang, 154 F.3d 996, 999 (9th Cir. 1998).

[46] Amoco Prod. Co. v. Aspen Group, 8 F. Supp. 2d 1249, 1252 (D. Colo. 1998).

[47] Or, of course, they could invoke alienage jurisdiction under §1332(a)(2).

citizenships of the claimants, on the other. In addition, in keeping with the complete diversity rule of *Strawbridge v. Curtiss*,[48] the stakeholder must be diverse from every claimant.

With statutory interpleader, however, §1335 requires only that one claimant be of diverse citizenship from any other claimant. In general, then, the stakeholder's citizenship is irrelevant in statutory interpleader — we look only to the citizenship of the claimants. Moreover, the statute requires only "minimal" diversity — the statute is satisfied if *any one* claimant is of diverse citizenship *from any other claimant.*

- ◦ Stakeholder is a corporation, incorporated in Delaware with its principal place of business in Illinois. There are four claimants: *C-1* is a citizen of Illinois; *C-2* is a citizen of Ohio; *C-3* is a citizen of Ohio; and *C-4* is a citizen of Minnesota.
  - ◦ This case cannot invoke Rule interpleader, because the stakeholder is not of diverse citizenship from every claimant. Stakeholder is a citizen of Illinois, and so is *C-1*. Thus, the case does not satisfy the complete diversity rule applicable in Rule interpleader.
  - ◦ This case can invoke statutory interpleader. The stakeholder's citizenship is irrelevant. So the fact that Stakeholder and one of the claimants, *C-1*, are co-citizens (Illinois) does not matter.[49] In looking at citizenships of the claimants, all that is required is that one be diverse from at least one other. Here, the stakeholders are citizens of Illinois, Ohio, and Minnesota, so the requirement is satisfied. The fact that there are two claimants who are citizens of Ohio is irrelevant. Statutory interpleader is based upon minimal diversity; complete diversity is not required.

There is no doubt that Congress, in enacting statutory interpleader in 1917, intended to permit invocation of jurisdiction based upon minimal diversity. The only question was whether the statute was constitutional. Another way to state the issue was whether the holding in *Strawbridge v. Curtiss* — requiring complete diversity — was based upon the statutory grant (now found in §1332(a)(2)). The Supreme Court upheld the statute in *State Farm Fire & Casualty v. Tashire*,[50] in which it established that the Article III grant of diversity of citizenship jurisdiction is satisfied so long as any two adverse parties are not co-citizens.

Students often ask, quite rightly, why anyone would ever use Rule interpleader. Statutory interpleader offers considerable advantages (such as lower amount in controversy and nationwide service of process). So

---

[48] 7 U.S. 267 (1806). We discussed the case in detail at §4.5.3.

[49] Treinies v. Sunshine Mining Co., 308 U.S. 66, 72 (1939).

[50] 386 U.S. 523, 531 (1967) ("Article III poses no obstacle to the legislative extension of federal jurisdiction, founded on diversity, so long as any two adverse parties are not co-citizens.").

why does Rule interpleader ever get used? There is one fact pattern in which Rule interpleader is possible but statutory interpleader does not appear to be.

- Stakeholder is a citizen of Texas. All claimants are citizens of Louisiana. Obviously, this arrangement would satisfy the citizenship requirements for Rule interpleader, because Stakeholder is of diverse citizenship from all claimants. But it does not meet the citizenship requirements for statutory interpleader. Why? Because the statute requires at least one claimant to be diverse from at least one other claimant. Here, they are all co-citizens. So the statute appears unavailable.
- Suppose, however, on this fact pattern that the amount in controversy requirement for Rule interpleader (in excess of $75,000) is not satisfied, but that the amount requirement for statutory interpleader ($500 or more) is satisfied.
  - Stakeholder cannot invoke Rule interpleader here because the jurisdictional amount in controversy requirement is not met.
  - On the face of things, it appears that Stakeholder cannot invoke statutory interpleader either, because there is no minimal diversity among the claimants; all claimants are co-citizens.
- But what if the case involves an *interested stakeholder*? That is, as discussed in §13.2.1, what if Stakeholder in this case claims she is entitled to the stake?[51]

The better rule in this situation is that the stakeholder should be considered as one of the claimants, and thus that her citizenship should be relevant.[52] On the facts of this case, that would mean that statutory interpleader is invoked, because now one plaintiff is a citizen of Texas while the others are citizens of Louisiana. This result makes sense, because the stakeholder, after all, truly is a claimant, and will participate in the second stage of the interpleader litigation. Most courts addressing the issue appear to have adopted this view.[53] On the other hand, some courts refuse to consider the stakeholder's citizenship, and deny jurisdiction on these facts.[54] A word to the wise student: If you covered this fact pattern in class,

---

[51] An exam question might simply say that the case was "in the nature of interpleader," which means that the stakeholder makes a claim to the stake. See §13.2.1.

[52] Remember, by "this situation" we are referring to a case in which the stakeholder is making a claim to the stake — in which we have an interested stakeholder. If the stakeholder is disinterested (not making a claim to the stake), her citizenship is absolutely irrelevant in determining whether a statutory interpleader case invokes federal subject matter jurisdiction. Treinies v. Sunshine Mining Co., 308 U.S. 66, 72 (1939).

[53] See, e.g., Lummis v. White, 629 F.2d 397, 403 (5th Cir. 1980), *rev'd on other grounds sub nom.* Cory v. White, 457 U.S. 85 (1982); Mt. Hawley Ins. Co. v. Fed. Sav. & Loan Ins. Corp., 695 F. Supp. 469, 473 (C.D. Cal. 1987).

[54] See, e.g., American Family Mut. Ins. Co. v. Roche, 830 F. Supp. 1241, 1248 (E.D. Wis. 1993).

watch for it on the exam and be prepared to argue both ways for application of statutory interpleader.

To Determine the Amount in Controversy. Because Rule interpleader is treated as any other civil case, there is no special provision for amount in controversy. Thus, to invoke diversity of citizenship jurisdiction, in addition to satisfying the complete diversity rule as discussed above, the amount in controversy must exceed $75,000. In statutory interpleader, however, §1335 provides that amount must merely be $500 or more.

In addition, Rule and statutory interpleader differ radically in how the amount in controversy is determined. As we saw in §13.2.1, statutory interpleader requires that the stakeholder deposit the stake with the court or else post a bond. Rule interpleader does not require a deposit, though the court is empowered to order it (and often does). In determining the stake, in Rule interpleader, the stakeholder may deposit the amount it believes is disputed.[55] In statutory interpleader, however, the stake must equal the highest amount claimed by any of the claimants. The stakeholder must deposit that amount even if she asserts that a lesser amount is actually in controversy. Depositing the larger amount does not waive that assertion.[56]

Supplemental Jurisdiction. There is some uncertainty concerning the operation of supplemental jurisdiction in interpleader cases. We discussed supplemental jurisdiction in detail at §4.7. Section 1367(a) grants to the federal courts supplemental jurisdiction over claims so closely related to a claim that invokes federal subject matter jurisdiction as to be considered part of the same case or controversy as that claim. It seems clear that an interpleader claim should satisfy §1367(a). After all, the claimants are asserting a right to the same thing.[57]

Section 1367(b) applies to remove supplemental jurisdiction, but does so only in cases brought under §1332. Thus, §1367(b) does not apply to statutory interpleader cases, because such cases are not brought not under §1332, but under §1335.[58] Section 1367(b) would apply, however, to a Rule interpleader case that invoked diversity of citizenship jurisdiction (under §1332), but would not remove any grant of supplemental jurisdiction. Why? Recall that §1367(b) lists various claims that will not invoke supplemental jurisdiction in diversity cases; Rule 22 is *not* included in the list. In sum, then, if the interpleader claim invokes supplemental jurisdiction under §1367(a), nothing in §1367(b) should remove it. The exercise, however, seems to be more work that it is worth, since any case involving supplemental jurisdiction would seem to invoke statutory interpleader.

---

[55] *See, e.g.,* United Benefit Life Ins. Co. v. Leech, 326 F. Supp. 598, 600 (E.D. Pa. 1971).

[56] Nationwide Mut. Ins. Co. v. Eckman, 555 F. Supp. 775, 777 (D. Del. 1983).

[57] There is very little case law concerning supplemental jurisdiction in interpleader, and almost all of it predates the enactment of §1367.

[58] Statutory interpleader cases are brought under §1335.

○ Stakeholder is a citizen of Missouri, and there are three claimants: *C-1* is a citizen of Kansas, *C-2* is a citizen of Colorado, and *C-3* is a citizen of Missouri. On the face of things, Rule interpleader is not possible, because the stakeholder is not of diverse citizenship from every claimant. But it is arguable that Stakeholder could assert interpleader against *C-1* and *C-2*, invoking diversity of citizenship, then join *C-3* and argue that the interpleader claim against *C-3* invokes supplemental jurisdiction. As noted immediately above, the claim against *C-3* surely satisfies the relatedness requirement of §1367(a); and nothing in §1367(b) removes that grant. But why bother with this approach? The case as structured satisfies the requirements for statutory interpleader without jumping through these supplemental jurisdiction hoops. (The same would be true with defensive invocation of interpleader through a counterclaim.)

Venue

Rule Interpleader. Again, a Rule interpleader case is treated simply as a "regular" case — either federal question or diversity of citizenship. Thus, venue is governed by §1391(a) (for diversity) and §1391(b) (for federal question).[59] Those statutes provide for venue, basically, in either of two places: (1) any district where all the defendants reside or (2) any district in which a substantial part of the claim arose.[60] As to the second of these choices, there is little meaningful case law guidance on where an interpleader claim (or a substantial part thereof) arises. In practice, then, that statutory choice offers no help. Thus, the stakeholder/plaintiff is left with one basic choice — she must lay venue in a district where all defendants (claimants) reside. If they reside in different districts of the same state, remember, she may lay venue in any of the districts in which one resides, as we saw in §5.4.1. Thus, for Rule interpleader, venue can be a significant (and frustrating) restriction.

○ Stakeholder, a citizen of Iowa, wants to interplead two claimants, *C-1*, who is a citizen of Illinois and resides in the Northern District of Illinois, and *C-2*, who is a citizen of Michigan and resides in the Eastern District of Michigan. There is no district in which venue is proper based upon the residence of the defendants. They do not reside in the same district, nor do they reside in different districts of the same state. And because no one seems to know where an interpleader claim arises, §1391(a)(1) gives no help.

But let's take a closer look at §1391(a)(2) and (b)(2). Each contains an underused provision permitting venue in a district where "a substantial

---

[59] Leader Natl. Ins. Co. v. Shaw, 901 F. Supp. 316, 320 (W.D. Okla. 1995).

[60] We discussed these choices, and what happens if there is no district in the United States satisfying either choice, at §5.4.1.

part of property that is the subject of the action is situated." This seems perfectly suited to interpleader. Under it, in the preceding hypothetical, stakeholder could lay venue in the district in which the property is found. If it is movable property, she can take it to whatever district she prefers for venue. She might, for instance, lay venue in the district in Iowa in which she resides; certainly that would be most convenient for her. Though this provision thus allows the stakeholder to manipulate venue, leading scholars conclude that this fact will not create grave unfairness; after all, the venue chosen will still have to have personal jurisdiction over the claimants.[61]

What if the interpleader is asserted defensively? We discussed this possibility in §13.2.1. The scenario is usually this: A claimant sues the stakeholder to recover the stake, and the stakeholder files a counterclaim against the claimant, to which she joins additional claimants under Rule 13(h). How is the venue handled in such a case? Most courts adopt the idea of "ancillary venue" in such circumstances. As long as venue was proper in the original case by the claimant against the stakeholder, venue is proper even as to additional claims involving joinder of additional parties.[62] Some courts reach this conclusion by noting that the venue statute, §1391, speaks only of the district in which an action is "brought." Thus, the statute only addresses venue as to the original claim by the plaintiff against the defendant, and does not apply to subsequent claims involving additional joinder of parties.[63]

Statutory Interpleader. Statutory interpleader includes its own section for venue. Section 1397 provides that venue may be laid in any district where *any* claimant resides. The courts have determined that this provision is exclusive in statutory interpleader cases; in other words, §1397 replaces, and does not augment, §1391.[64] They reason that §1391 provides for venue only in cases in which there is no statutory provision to the contrary; §1397 provides the contrary legislation. In most cases, the exclusivity of §1397 will not create a problem, because it is easier to satisfy than §1391(a)(1).

○ Stakeholder interpleads three claimants, *C-1*, *C-2*, and *C-3*. Assume that personal jurisdiction and subject matter jurisdiction are proper. *C-1* resides in the Eastern District of Pennsylvania. *C-2* resides in the Western District of Pennsylvania. *C-3* resides in the Northern District of Illinois.

[61] *See* 7 Wright & Miller §1712, at 612.
[62] *See, e.g.,* Bredberg v. Long, 778 F.2d 1285, 1288 (8th Cir. 1985).
[63] *See, e.g.,* Nine Point Mesa of Nashville, Inc. v. Nine Point Mesa of Lexington, Inc., 769 F. Supp. 259, 263 (M.D. Tenn. 1991).
[64] *See* 4 Moore's Federal Practice §22.04[4][b].

o   If the case invokes Rule interpleader, no district is a proper venue under §1391(a)(1), because there is no district in which all claimants reside.[65]

o   If the case invokes statutory interpleader, venue may be laid against all three claimants in any of three districts: The Eastern District of Pennsylvania, the Western District of Pennsylvania, or the Northern District of Illinois. Why? Because §1397 (applicable only in statutory interpleader) permits venue in any district where *any* claimant resides.

Summary. This chart should be helpful in summarizing the major differences between Rule interpleader (invoking diversity of citizenship jurisdiction) and statutory interpleader.

Type	Personal Jurisdiction	Venue	Diversity	Jurisdictional Amount
Statutory	Nationwide service of process	District where any claimant resides	Minimal diversity between any two claimants	$500 or more
Rule	Same as state court in state in which situated; service per Rule 4	Per §1391(a) (where D's residence or property located)	Complete diversity between stakeholder, on one hand, and all claimants, on the other	In excess of $75,000

§13.3   The Class Action

§13.3.1   Overview of the Class Action and of Underlying Policy Issues

A class action is brought by or against a representative (or multiple representatives) on behalf of a group. If it's done correctly, the group is bound by the result of the litigation. This procedure obviously promotes efficiency, because it means that the individual members of the group do not litigate. In addition, the class action can promote the same policies of

---

[65] Of course, the provision in §1391(a)(2) permitting venue in a district where the property subject to litigation is found — which we discussed in the text above — would provide venue in this case.

avoiding harm that underlie Rule 19. Class actions are not exclusively good, however. They raise significant due process issues, precisely because they do bind persons who are not technically parties. In addition, the class action is subject to abuse, and raises significant ethical issues, as we will see. Concern with such abuse in some state courts led to passage of the Class Action Fairness Act of 2005, which, as we will also see, raises significant issues of federalism — about the proper roles of the federal and state courts.

Development of Federal Rule 23

Federal Rule 23 governs class action practice in federal court. The Supreme Court amended the Rule to its basic present form in 1966, along with Rules 19 and 24. Recall from Chapter 12 that Rules 19 and 24 govern, respectively, joinder of necessary (or "required") parties and intervention. Recall further that there was great overlap in the functions of Rules 19 and 24 and in the language used to determine when an absentee ought to be joined in a pending case. The amendments to all three Rules prescribed pragmatic assessments of the circumstances of a case under those two Rules. The focus is on practicality — on fact patterns rather than on legal relationships.

The 1966 drafters made a clean break from the original Rule 23, promulgated with the Federal Rules in 1938. The older rule had proved unworkable, in large part because it relied on arcane labels. It recognized different types of class actions, based upon legal relationships among parties and class members that are difficult to fathom. For instance, it defined the "true" class action as one in which the class right was "joint" or "common." The "hybrid" class action was one in which the class members asserted "several" rights to common property. The "spurious" class action also involved the assertion of "several" rights, but involved common questions and common relief. None of these terms is self-defining and none is very helpful.

The 1966 version of Rule 23 jettisoned the barnacle-encrusted language relating to legal relationships and provided instead a practical, step-by-step method for analyzing when class litigation is appropriate. The Rule is not without problems, as we will see, but is vastly superior to the original version. Indeed, the overwhelming majority of states have adopted the 1966 version of Rule 23 to govern their state class action practice. The federal version, which we study, has been amended in several ways since 1966, but the central requirements have remained the same.

Most class actions involve a *plaintiff class*, in which the class is asserting a claim (or claims) against a defendant (or defendants). It is possible under Rule 23 to have a *defendant class action*, in which a plaintiff (or plaintiffs) seeks to impose liability upon a group represented by a named defendant. It is even possible to have a plaintiff class sue a defendant class. Throughout these materials, except when we specifically address defendant class actions, we assume that the class is on the plaintiff side.

Class Representatives and Class Members

The person (or persons) suing on behalf of a plaintiff class (or being sued on behalf of a defendant class) is called the *named representative*, or just the representative. There is no doubt she is a party to the litigation. Thus, all Federal Rules provisions relating to parties apply to her. For instance, some of the discovery rules apply *only* to parties. The named representative is a party, and thus must comply with those Rules.

What about the other[66] class *members* — are they parties to the case? The quick answer is no. Emphasizing this fact, some courts refer to them as *absentee* class members. Though they are technically not parties, these class members can be bound by the judgment. How can that happen? Through representation. Recall from our discussion of the preclusion doctrines in Chapter 11 that a valid final judgment on the merits binds only those who were parties to the case *or who were in "privity" with a party*. Though "privity" is sometimes difficult to define, it clearly includes the notion of representation. So a valid final judgment on the merits binds parties to the case and those who were represented by parties to the case. Thus, one important focus of the procedural rule concerning class actions is that the members' interests be adequately represented, precisely so they can be bound by the outcome of the case.

Because class members are not parties, they are not subject to various Federal Rules directed at parties. For example, the adverse party has no right to serve interrogatories to class members. (Interrogatories can only be served on parties.) On the other hand, the party opposing the class may have a legitimate interest in obtaining information from class members. Courts have balanced this need against the fact that a class member is not a party, and have, on occasion, allowed limited discovery from class members. One instructive case is *Brennan v. Midwestern United Life Ins. Co.*,[67] in which the court approved an order requiring that a cross-section of the class be required to answer questions under oath. Some class members took the position that they could not be required to give any information. They refused to comply with the court's order, despite warnings that

---

[66] We say "other" class members because the named representative is a member of the class as well. Here we are speaking of class members other than the named representative.

[67] 450 F.2d 999, 1004-1005 (7th Cir. 1971). *See also* Redmond v. Moody's Investor Serv., 1995 U.S. Dist. LEXIS 6277 (S.D.N.Y. 1995) (limiting discovery from absent class members to interrogatories and depositions); Transamerican Refining Corp. v. Dravo Corp., 139 F.R.D. 619 (S.D. Tex. 1991) (granting defendants' motions requesting discovery from class members).

the court would dismiss them from the class if they did not answer the questions. Upon further intransigence, the court dismissed them from the class. The Seventh Circuit affirmed the dismissal. Though class members are not parties, they have no license to ignore court orders. In the usual case, however, class members will not be subjected to discovery requests. They are, in almost every case, "along for the ride." They are passive (indeed, sometimes they don't even know about the pendency of the case). They hope that the representative wins and that some benefit will trickle down to them.

Class Attorneys and the Potential for Abuse

In reality, often (certainly not always) the class members may feel that their interests have taken a back seat to those of the lawyers for the class. This fact underscores significant policy issues related to the class action.

- ° Suppose a chain of retail stores has been overcharging on some product in violation of some law. Each customer is overcharged an average of $5. Obviously, if there were no class action device, there would be no civil litigation about this overcharge. Why? Because no individual customer would sue to recover $5. Even if a particular consumer were overcharged 20 times, she will not sue for $100; the effort is greater than the return to be gotten. And, obviously, no lawyer will take the case of a potential plaintiff who has been harmed to the tune of $5, or even $100.
- ° This lack of civil litigation does not necessarily mean that the retail store is "getting away" with its bad behavior. If the overcharge violates the criminal law or some regulation, there may be a criminal prosecution or administrative fine. But it is unlikely that there will be any compensatory damages to the injured consumers.

What happens, though, if we do have a class action device? And let's assume that there are 500,000 consumers in the same boat. Now as a class action, there are 500,000 class members, each harmed by an average of $8. In the aggregate, that is a "claim" of $4 million. That claim is large enough that a lawyer will be attracted to take the case. This fact leads us to an interesting irony of the class action. The device is hailed for its efficiency because it permits one (large) case to take the place of thousands of (smaller) cases. But in this sort of case, a class action will create litigation that otherwise would not exist at all!

Is that a good thing? Is that a bad thing? The answer depends on one's point of view. If we emphasize the fact that the class action empowers a group to sue when individually they would not, we might hail the class action as "one of the most socially useful remedies in history."[68] The Supreme Court has explained: "Where it is not economically feasible to obtain relief within the traditional framework of a multiplicity of small individual suits for damages, aggrieved persons may be without any effective redress unless they may employ the class-action device."[69] More recently, Judge Posner said:

> The *realistic* alternative to a class action is not 17 million individual suits, but zero individual suits, as only a lunatic or a fanatic sues for $30. But a class action has to be unwieldy indeed before it can be pronounced an inferior alternative — no matter how massive the fraud or other wrongdoing that will go unpunished if class treatment is denied — to no litigation at all.[70]

On the other hand, the class action is enormously coercive, even if the claim on the underlying merits is weak. Precisely because the class action permits the assertion of huge potential liability in a single case, it creates overwhelming pressure on the defendant to settle. Rather than proceed to trial and take a chance on losing $4 million in our hypothetical above, the defendant might see the wisdom of writing a check to settle the case. Even a defendant convinced that it has done nothing wrong will be reluctant to roll the dice and go to trial with its entire financial future at stake. In fact, some empirical studies suggest that class claims (at least in certain substantive areas) are settled regardless of the strength of the class claim on the merits.[71] In other words, even weak claims may coerce a sizeable settlement out of a defendant who wants to avoid the potential devastation of a class action judgment. Emphasizing these facts, some have characterized the class action as "legalized blackmail."[72]

Obviously, neither side has a monopoly on virtue. For us, it is well to keep in mind that the class action is both an important device for achieving justice and a powerful weapon subject to abuse. But what drives the class action? One possibility is the representative. What is her interest? Though some courts allow the representative to recover some sort of bonus for vindicating the group's claim, in general there is no financial reason for the representative to take on the responsibility of the position. As we see in §13.3.6, she may be required to advance a significant amount

---

[68] Abraham Pomerantz, *New Developments in Class Actions — Has Their Death Knell Been Sounded?*, 25 Bus. Law. 1259, 1259 (1970).

[69] Deposit Guaranty Natl. Bank v. Roper, 445 U.S. 326, 339 (1980).

[70] Carnegie v. Household Intl., Inc., 376 F.3d 656, 661 (7th Cir. 2004) (emphasis original).

[71] Most of the studies seem to be in the securities fraud area. *See, e.g.*, Janet Cooper Alexander, *Do the Merits Matter? A Study of Settlements in Securities Class Actions*, 43 Stan. L. Rev. 497 (1991); John Coffee, Jr., *The Regulation of Entrepreneurial Litigation: Balancing Fairness and Efficiency in the Large Class Action*, 54 U. Chi. L. Rev. 877 (1987).

[72] Milton Handler, *The Shift from Substantive to Procedural Innovations in Antitrust Suits*, 71 Colum. L. Rev. 1, 9 (1971).

of money to give notice to class members. And in the usual case she does not recover anything other than her personal damages. Thus, in our hypothetical, the named representative will recover $8 (or whatever her damages were). Why would anyone take on the responsibilities of class representation to recover that amount? Usually, the representative is motivated by principle — by a desire to "get justice" for the class.

It is possible, though, that the real moving force behind the class action is not the representative at all, but her lawyer. Most plaintiff class actions are taken on a contingent fee basis, which means the lawyer is paid a percentage of what the class recovers. This arrangement is praised precisely because it permits prosecution of actions that otherwise could not be brought if the plaintiff had to pay an attorney by the hour. But the fee structure may create incentives for the lawyer that can conflict with her professional duties to her clients.[73] For example, suppose the defendant offers to settle the case on terms that include a substantial payment of attorneys' fees to the class lawyer. Going to trial, however, might lead to a better result for the class. The lawyer has a conflict of interest and must resist the temptation to put her own interest ahead of that of the class.

One common contemporary criticism of the class action — which has percolated to the forefront in recent debate — is the emergence of "sweetheart" deals or "coupon" settlements. Here, the defendant offers to settle the class action by paying large fees to the class lawyer and to compensate class members by providing them with coupons for discounts on future purchases of products from the defendant. Class counsel may be tempted by such an offer, because it provides her with a substantial payment without the risk of going to trial (where she might lose). The defendant finds such a deal advantageous, because it avoids both the expense of litigation and the risk of devastating liability at trial. The persons whose interests may be lost in the shuffle are the class members, for whom coupons for discounted products from a defendant who has wronged them may provide little compensation. Indeed, it is likely in such a case that many of the coupons will go unused, which further reduces the defendant's ultimate outlay to settle the case.[74]

---

[73] By the way, who is the client in a class action? Is it the named representative (who hired the attorney) or is it the class? The answer to this question has profound ramifications for various matters of professional responsibility, including the application of the attorney/client privilege and the question of whether the lawyer is justified in recommending terms of a settlement over the objections of her client. These issues may be considered in detail in an upper-division course on Professional Responsibility or Complex Litigation. In general, the client is the representative until the court "certifies" the case to proceed as a class action. At that point, the class itself is seen as the client.

[74] See generally Bruce Hay & David Rosenberg, "Sweetheart" and "Blackmail" Settlements in Class Actions: Reality and Remedy, 75 Notre Dame L. Rev. 1377 (2000).

The Role of the Court

In cases of abuse — such as that described in the preceding paragraph — who looks out for the interest of the class members? We are tempted to say that the representative herself is charged with this responsibility. In reality, though, most class representatives are ill-equipped for the task; they are lay people, unfamiliar with the law and with civil procedure. Increasingly, we realize that the only person who can protect the class from overreaching by lawyers is the court — the judge who oversees the class action. Rule 23(e) provides that no certified class action may be settled or voluntarily dismissed without court approval. We discuss this role of the court in reviewing settlements and dismissals in §13.3.6. For present purposes, it is sufficient to note that the court is thus required to protect the class members from an unscrupulous deal. Critics complain that courts are not in a good position to discharge this role, and that they may have incentives to "rubber stamp" settlements agreed to by the lawyers for both sides.

The notion that the court must protect class members from overreaching by class counsel seems inconsistent to the traditional view of the court's role. Historically, the court has been seen as neutral and essentially passive; it reacts to the arguments and evidence presented by the litigants, but does not undertake to help either side do its job. The need for protection of class members, and the emergence of complex forms of litigation generally, has fostered the contemporary view of the judge as a case manager. The job of the judge has become increasingly bureaucratic, focused on getting cases through the large queue, and involved, of necessity, in ensuring that class members do not get left behind. The metamorphosis from the traditional model to that of the "managerial judge" is a fact. We saw some aspects of this bureaucratization in §§8.5 and 8.6, concerning judicial oversight of litigation and use of adjunct personnel to assist in that task.

Class Action Fairness Act of 2005

Concerns about perceived abuses of the class action came to a head in early 2005, when Congress passed and President Bush signed the Class Action Fairness Act of 2005 (CAFA). Major corporate interests had long lobbied for such a bill, the purpose of which is to channel large interstate class actions from state to federal courts. It does so principally by relaxing federal subject matter jurisdiction requirements and by providing defendants with liberal rights to remove class actions from state to federal court. We discuss these jurisdictional details in §13.3.8. Here we address the motivation for and controversy surrounding CAFA. Some background is relevant.

Speaking very, very generally, there is a widespread impression it is relatively more difficult to pursue class litigation in federal court than in some state courts. Even though most state courts have adopted the core of Federal Rule 23 as their class rule, various factors may impel a plaintiff class lawyer to file in state court. First, in decisions such as *Amchem Products, Inc. v. Windsor*, which we discuss at §13.3.7, and *Ortiz v. Fibreboard Corp.*, which we see in §13.3.5, the Supreme Court appears to have imposed the Rule 23 requirements with particular strictness.[75] State courts are not bound to interpret their class rule in the same way. Second, as we see in §13.3.3, in federal court, Rule 23(f) provides for the possibility of immediate appellate review of class certification decisions. Thus, an order allowing a case to proceed as a class action may be reviewed (and reversed) before the case proceeds further. Few state courts have adopted this provision, meaning that a class certification order ordinarily will not be reviewed on appeal in state systems. Third, there is a sense that summary judgment is more readily available in federal court than in state court, based in large measure on cases decided by the Supreme Court in 1986, which we saw in §9.4. Again, state courts are not bound to apply these decisions to cases under the state summary judgment rule. Fourth, as a matter of proof at trial, in cases involving expert evidence (which includes many class actions), federal courts appear less hospitable to plaintiffs than some state courts.[76] State courts do not have to follow the federal precedent on this point either.

These hurdles in federal court undoubtedly made state court more attractive for some lawyers bringing class actions. Some state courts developed the reputation of being very pro-plaintiff and for certifying class cases quite freely. No matter what one's conclusion regarding the wisdom of CAFA, there is no question that some state courts permitted abuse in class actions and in other mass tort cases. The abuse commonly involved sweetheart deals and coupon settlements, which, as discussed above, lined the pockets of plaintiff's counsel while affording little relief for the class members. These deals permitted the defendant to buy peace essentially by paying off the plaintiff's lawyers. The courts failed to provide meaningful judicial oversight. There is debate over how widespread the abuse is, but there is no doubt that it occurs.

---

[75] In *Amchem*, 521 U.S. 521 (1997), the Court required full compliance with Rule 23(a) and (b) even in a class formed for settlement purposes. In *Ortiz*, 527 U.S. 815 (1999), the Court rendered it particularly difficult to satisfy the requirements of a particular type of class action. For an excellent discussion of these factors and CAFA, *see* Georgene M. Vairo, *Class Action Fairness Act of 2005* (LexisNexis 2005).

[76] This impression is based upon *Daubert v. Merrell Dow Pharmaceuticals*, 509 U.S. 579 (1993), which imposed strict requirements for the admission of expert scientific testimony in federal court. The holding has since been expanded to cover all expert witnesses — not just those presenting scientific evidence. Kumho Tire Co. v. Carmichael, 526 U.S. 137 (1999).

In passing CAFA, Congress made express findings that some state court handling of class suits had "harmed class members with legitimate claims and defendants that have acted responsibly," and had "undermined public respect for our judicial system."[77] Thus, it opened the doors to federal court to an unprecedented degree — not only for class actions but for "mass actions," which are non-class cases joined for trial and involving 100 or more plaintiffs.[78]

Proponents of the Act praise it as a vehicle to have the federal courts take over large interstate disputes and, *inter alia*, "to assure fairer outcomes for class members and defendants."[79] Critics decry the Act as fundamentally inimical to the interests of federalism. Specifically, they assert, the Act embodies an assumption that state courts cannot handle class action litigation fairly. Moreover, critics argue, CAFA is a naked pro-defendant effort to get class actions funneled into federal court, where they are more difficult to maintain and in which it is more difficult for plaintiffs to prevail. The fear is that many state-court class cases will be removed to federal court, where class certification will be denied and the case thus will essentially fizzle out. Thus, CAFA is seen not as providing a mere change of forum for class suits, but as a means of effectively denying access to the class device.

If the critics are right that such cases face higher hurdles in federal court, CAFA may have the effect of tort reform. That is, it will end class actions that would have proceeded in state court (many of which assert tort claims). It does so in the guise of "mere" jurisdictional legislation — legislation that purports merely to change the courtroom, not the result. Both sides in the debate base arguments on generalizations. In fact, very few (if any) state judges are overtly pro-plaintiff and irresponsible about certifying and overseeing class litigation. And in fact, very few (if any) federal judges are overtly pro-business and irresponsibly parsimonious in certifying large classes. Whatever one thinks of CAFA, though, there can be no denying this: It works a profound reallocation of judicial authority in large interstate cases and ensures that state courts will play a less important role in such disputes than they have historically.

---

[77] 28 U.S.C. §1711(a)(2).

[78] 28 U.S.C. §1332(d)(11). This section treats such mass actions as class actions, and is based upon the practice of some state courts to allow hundreds of plaintiffs to join in a single case. *See* Vairo, note 75 above, at 32-33.

[79] CAFA, Sen. 5, 109th Cong. (2005), *quoted in* Vairo, note 75 above, at 4.

§13.3.2 Due Process: How Can Class Members Be Bound by a Class Judgment?

The fact that class members are not parties to the litigation, but will nonetheless be bound by the judgment, raises obvious due process issues. The most important case on the due process requirements for a class action is *Hansberry v. Lee*,[80] which concerned the enforcement of a racially restrictive covenant in a subdivision in Chicago. The covenant forbade homeowners in the subdivision (all of whom were white) from renting or selling their property to non-whites. The case was decided eight years before *Shelley v. Kramer*, which declared such restrictions unconstitutional.[81] Thus, when the Court decided *Hansberry*, such covenants were generally enforceable. The covenant in *Hansberry* provided that it would be effective only if the owners of 95 percent of the frontage in the development signed it.

The outcome in *Hansberry* depended upon the validity of a judgment in the earlier case of *Burke v. Kleiman*.[82] In *Burke*, a white homeowner named Kleiman, who did not favor the racially restrictive covenant, rented property in the subdivision to an African American named Hall. Other property owners, led by Burke, sued for an injunction to stop Kleiman's renting to Hall. At the trial in that case, the parties stipulated that the covenant had been signed by the requisite 95 percent of owners of frontage in the subdivision and thus had become effective. In fact, though, only 54 percent of the relevant owners had actually signed the covenant, and thus it never should have gone into effect. Nonetheless, because of the parties' stipulation, the court upheld the covenant and stopped the proposed rental to the African-American family. The Illinois Court of Appeals affirmed. *Burke* was a class action, and thus, arguably, bound all owners in the subdivision.

A few years later, a white homeowner in the subdivision entered a contract to sell his house to the Hansberry family, who were African American.[83] Lee, another white homeowner in the subdivision, sued in state court to stop the sale. At trial, the Hansberrys proved that only 54 percent of the relevant homeowners had ever signed the covenant. The court recognized this fact, but nonetheless concluded that the judgment in *Burke v. Kleiman* bound the people who were trying to sell to the Hansberrys. The people selling to the Hansberrys had been represented by the homeowner

[80] 311 U.S. 32 (1940).
[81] 334 U.S. 1 (1948).
[82] 277 Ill. App. 519 (1934).
[83] One of the children of the Hansberry family was the playwright Lorraine Hansberry, who wrote *A Raisin in the Sun*, which was a successful play and movie. It was based in part upon the family's experiences in Chicago. For an interesting discussion of the case and the persons involved, *see* Allen Kamp, *The History Behind* Hansberry v. Lee, 20 U.C. Davis L. Rev. 481 (1987).

in the class action in *Burke* and were bound by the outcome — that the covenant was effective. (By way of review, why — as a matter of preclusion law — should the stipulation from *Burke* (that 95 percent of the homeowners had signed the covenant) not have been entitled to issue preclusion?[84]) The Illinois Supreme Court affirmed.

The United States Supreme Court reversed, and held that the people selling to the Hansberrys were *not* bound by the class action judgment in *Burke v. Kleiman*. The Court started by recognizing that, generally, one cannot be bound by a judgment unless she is a party to the case in which the judgment is entered. It further noted, however, that "to an extent not precisely defined by judicial opinion," a judgment in a class action "may bind members of the class or those represented who were not made parties to it."[85] For this proposition, the Court cited *Smith v. Swormstead*[86] and *Supreme Tribe of Ben-Hur v. Cauble.*[87] In *Smith*, a class of one group of clergymembers of the Methodist Episcopal Church sued another group to recover its share of a book fund established by the church. The clergymembers had split into two factions — North and South — over slavery. Though 5,000 preachers were not joined as parties, all were bound by the class litigation, because "the parties interested are numerous, and the suit is for an object common to them all. . . ."[88] In *Ben-Hur*, a class action on behalf of the members of a fraternal benefits organization bound all 70,000 members. As in *Smith*, the class members shared identical and nonseparable interests.

In *Hansberry*, however, the claims of the class members were different, because they were not held jointly. Rather, each person who signed the covenant entered an agreement with the others who signed the agreement. The claims were not held jointly, but were "several" (separate) obligations. The Court recognized that a judgment may bind class members even when those members do not hold joint claims — even "when the only circumstance defining the class is that the determination of the rights of its members turns upon a single issue of fact or law. . . ."[89] To do so, however, those represented must be members of the same class as those purporting to represent them. The plaintiff class in *Burke* sought to *enforce* the restrictive covenant. While the judgment in that case would bind all members of that class, it could not bind those homeowners (like Kleiman) who *opposed* enforcement of the covenant. Put simply, those in favor of

---

[84] Because issue preclusion only applies to issues that were actually litigated and determined in the earlier case. Because of the stipulation, the question of how many homeowners had signed the covenant was not litigated in *Burke v. Kleiman*. See §11.3.2.

[85] *Hansberry*, 311 U.S. at 41.

[86] 57 U.S. 288 (1853).

[87] 255 U.S. 356 (1921).

[88] *Smith*, 57 U.S. at 302.

[89] *Hansberry*, 311 U.S. at 43. This type of class action is now found in Federal Rule 23(b)(3). See §13.3.4.

the covenant and those opposed to it are not members of the same class. So a representative from one camp cannot bind someone in the other. As the Court explained:

> Those who sought to secure [the] benefits [of the covenant] by enforcing it could not be said to be in the same class with or represent those whose interest was in resisting performance, for the agreement by its terms imposes obligations and confers rights on the owner of each plot of land who signs it. If those who thus seek to secure the benefits of the agreement were rightly regarded by the state Supreme Court as a constituting class, it is evident that those signers or their successors who are interested in challenging the validity of the agreement and resisting its performance are not of the same class in the sense that their interests are identical so that any group who had elected to enforce rights conferred by the agreement could be said to be acting in the interest of any others who were free to deny its obligation.... [A] selection of representatives for purposes of litigation, whose substantial interests are not necessarily or even probably the same as those whom they are deemed to represent, does not afford that protection to absent parties which due process requires.... In seeking to enforce the agreement the plaintiffs in [*Burke*] were not representing the petitioners here whose substantial interest is in resisting performance.[90]

Under *Hansberry*, then, due process provides that class members can be bound by a judgment *only* if they are truly members of the same class as the representative. Stated another way, if the representative and the class members disagree on the key issue in the litigation, they are not members of the same class; the representative cannot represent people who disagree with her on that key issue. In *Hansberry*, the disagreement was clear — the representative in *Burke v. Kleiman* wanted to enforce the covenant and thus could not be allowed to bind those homeowners who opposed the covenant. Importantly, *Hansberry* does *not* stand for the proposition that there can be no disagreement between the representative and class members. There may be disagreements on matters of strategy and remedy. So long as the class members and the representative are united on the core issues in litigation, there will be no constitutional problem with the judgment's binding all class members.

Thus, *Hansberry* recognizes that class members can be bound if they are *adequately represented*. They do not need to be joined as parties. But do they need to be given notice of the proceeding? *Hansberry* says nothing about it. The later case of *Mullane v. Central Hanover Bank*,[91] which we discussed at §3.2, held that nonparties could be bound if given appropriate notice of the proceeding. *Mullane* did not involve a class action,

---

[90] *Hansberry*, 311 U.S. at 44, 45-46.
[91] 339 U.S. 306 (1950).

but concerned numerous beneficiaries to a pooled trust. The Court concluded that "notice reasonably certain to reach most of those interested in objecting is likely to safeguard the interest of all, since any objection sustained would inure to the benefit of all."[92]

Do *Hansberry* and *Mullane* together require that class members in a class action be adequately represented *and* be given notice of the proceedings? Apparently not. As we see in the next subsection, Federal Rule 23, which has never been successfully challenged on due process grounds, requires notice of the pendency of the class action in only one type of class action. In all class cases, however, the representation must be adequate.

§13.3.3　Filing and Certification of a Class Action Under Rule 23

The Difference Between a Putative Class and a Certified Class

In *Hansberry v. Lee*, which we discussed immediately above, the Supreme Court was required to determine the class membership and adequacy of representation of a class action that had already been litigated. This after-the-fact analysis is difficult. The drafters of Federal Rule 23 envisioned that the assessments of class membership and adequacy of representation are best made before the fact. Thus, the Rule prescribes specific factors for determining *at the outset* whether a case should proceed as a class action. Satisfaction of the requirements of Rule 23 will avoid any constitutional problems of the type encountered in *Hansberry*.[93] We noted in §13.3.1 that the drafters revised Rule 23 substantially in 1966. The Rule was also amended substantially in 2003; those recent amendments, which we discuss below, did not affect the basic prerequisites and definitions of class actions. Rather, they made significant changes in some procedural aspects of administering class actions. Though most states have adopted Rule 23 as their basic model for class actions, states have not rushed to adopt the 2003 amendments. In addition, in 2007, all Federal Rules were "restyled" in ways that are not supposed to affect the way they operate. To date, no state has adopted the "restyled" Rule 23.

A class action is commenced as any action — by filing the complaint. The class representative's complaint contains all the elements of any complaint under Rule 8(a). In addition, she alleges that the case is brought as

---

[92] *Mullane*, 311 U.S. at 319.

[93] As we saw above, in *Hansberry*, the "class" involved in the antecedent litigation of *Burke v. Kleiman* should never have been permitted to proceed. The representative (who wanted to enforce the restrictive covenant) had no business representing a group that sought exactly the opposite result. Under Rule 23, the case would not have proceeded as structured. Under the Illinois rule of that era, however, the court was simply not required to undertake a meaningful before-the-fact analysis.

a class action, and usually states that she is suing "on behalf of a class of persons (or entities) similarly situated." In the complaint, the representative will define the class. As we see below, it is important that the definition strike the court as a manageable group. There is no need to list the individual members of the class. (Indeed, in many cases that would be impossible.) Defining the group by salient characteristics is sufficient. For example, in a securities fraud case, the class might consist of "all persons who (or entities which) purchased common stock of the *XYZ* Corporation after June 15, 2009, and before September 30, 2009."

The case is not automatically deemed a class action. Indeed, at this point, it is generally referred to as a "putative class action" and the class as a "putative class." The label points out that the case does not technically become a class action until the court enters an order "certifying" it as such. Thus, at some point after filing the case (and after the defendant has responded to the complaint), the plaintiff class representative will make a motion to certify the case as a class action. Rule 23(a) and (b) guide the determination of whether the court will certify a class action. Rule 23(a) sets forth four express requirements that must be satisfied in *every* class action. There is no option; all four of these prerequisites must be satisfied. If they are, the court looks to Rule 23(b), which recognizes three (actually four) types of class actions. The case must fit within at least one of these types. Thus, while the case must satisfy all four requirements of Rule 23(a), it need satisfy only one of the types of class actions in Rule 23(b).

Under Rule 23(c)(1)(A), the court must make the certification determination "[a]t an early practicable time." (Before 2003, the Rule required the court to rule "as soon as practicable" after filing.) The parties may have to undertake discovery to determine whether the requirements for class certification have been met. The representative may determine during this interval that the class definition set forth in the complaint can be honed or refined in ways to increase the likelihood that the court will find the group manageable. Indeed, it is quite common for the class definition in the motion to certify to differ from that set forth in the complaint.

When the representative makes her motion for class certification, she and the defendant will brief the certification issues for the court, and the court undoubtedly will entertain oral argument on the motion. The certification decision is usually the watershed event in the litigation. If the court certifies the class, the defendant's incentive to settle the case will raise exponentially. Why? Because once the class is certified, the defendant faces potentially enormous aggregate liability to the entire class. On the other hand, if the court denies certification, the case may simply go away. Why? When the court denies certification, the representative's claim remains before the court. The case reverts to being a "regular" case in which the representative is the only plaintiff and in which her claim is the only one asserted. If the representative's claim is sizeable, that individual litigation will proceed. If, however, the class was to have consisted of numerous persons who suffered relatively small harm (such as in a typical consumer class action, where each person has a claim of a few dollars), the case will probably be dismissed voluntarily; nobody will litigate over a few dollars. Accordingly, the certification decision often is the real battleground in the litigation. Not surprisingly, then, the parties throw great resources into litigating the class certification issue.

Definition of the Class and Appointment of Class Counsel

If the court grants certification, it enters an order that, under Rule 23(c)(1)(B), must "define the class and the class claims, issues, or defenses, and must appoint class counsel under Rule 23(g)." The order certifying a class is not necessarily permanent. Rule 23(c)(1)(C) expressly recognizes that an order regarding certification "may be altered or amended before final judgment." Thus, the order is conditional, and may be revisited as the case progresses. The court is able to react as the litigation unfolds, perhaps to alter the definition of the class or perhaps to "decertify" and forgo the class action altogether. This fact emphasizes a point made in §13.3.1 — that the court constantly monitors the class action, both to ensure that the interests of class members are adequately represented and to consider the continuing viability of class action status. For instance, maybe discovery will reveal that there are so few members in the class that a class action is not needed, and that each individual should sue on her own.

Unless a statute provides otherwise, the court certifying a class action must appoint class counsel. We see in §13.3.4 that one requirement of any class action is that the representative be able to provide fair and adequate representation of the class interests. For years, courts routinely also required that the lawyer for the class be an adequate representative. This requirement is now "codified" in Rule 23(g)(4), which provides that "[c]lass counsel must fairly and adequately represent the interests of the class."

Rule 23(g)(1)(A) lists various factors the court must consider in making the finding, including work undertaken by the lawyer in identifying and investigating the class claims, her experience in handling complex litigation, her knowledge of the applicable law, and the resources she will commit to representing the class. Rule 23(b)(1)(B) counsels the court to look to any other facts pertinent to the lawyer's ability to represent the class interests fairly and adequately. In practice, even before Rule 23 listed factors to be considered, courts had long looked to matters such as the lawyer's experience in naming class counsel.[94]

---

[94] *See, e.g.,* In re Asbestos Litig., 90 F.3d 963, 977 (5th Cir. 1996).

Some observers criticize this focus on the lawyer's experience, because it makes it difficult for new lawyers to "break in" to what seems to be a "closed shop." In other words, how is one to get the experience necessary to be a class counsel unless the court allows her to be class counsel? In fact, the same handful of law firms with great expertise in plaintiff class litigation seem to show up in cases around the country. Still, though the focus on expertise may make it difficult for newcomers to get experience, the focus is appropriate. Remember, the class will be bound by the outcome of the case, and that outcome will be determined more by the actions of the lawyer than those of the representative herself.

Rule 23(g)(2) provides detailed procedures for the appointment of class counsel.[95] Obviously, lawyers will covet this appointment, because class counsel (1) gets to call the shots in the litigation on behalf of the class and (2) will be paid — often a significant amount. If more than one lawyer applies for the appointment as class counsel, Rule 23(g)(2)(B) provides that "the court must appoint the applicant best able to represent the interests of the class." Even if there is only one applicant, the court must ensure that she satisfies the Rule 23(g)(1) and 23(g)(4) standard of fairly and adequately representing the interests of the class. The order of appointment may include any relevant "provisions about the award of attorney's fees or nontaxable costs under Rule 23(h)."[96]

As we address in detail in Chapter 14, parties have a right to appellate review of "final" judgments. The court's determination of whether to certify the class is not "final" because it does not conclude the trial court's assessments of the merits of the case. Thus, the order is not appealable of right. Because the order is of such practical importance, however, courts of appeals long struggled to find some exception to the final judgment rule to permit appellate review of the order. The effort did not lead to consistent treatment of the issue. The Supreme Court remedied the situation in 1998 by promulgating Rule 23(f), which grants courts of appeals the discretion to review orders either granting or denying class certification. We consider that provision in §14.5.1.

Some people fear that this possibility of appellate review of the class certification decision gives the federal courts an additional chance to deny class treatment. That is, a district court's decision to certify may be reversed immediately, without the class proceeding to judgment or settlement. Interestingly, few states have adopted Rule 23(f), a fact that makes the Class Action Fairness Act of 2005 more difficult for some to swallow.

[95] Rule 23(g)(3) permits the court to appoint interim class counsel before determining whether to certify the class.

[96] Fed. R. Civ. P. 23(g)(1)(D). Rule 23(h) provides procedures for moving for an award of attorneys' fees and nontaxable costs. Importantly, it does not create any substantive rights to recover these things. Thus, for example, attorneys' fees are recoverable only if there is some exception to the general rule that each side bears her own attorneys' fees.

As we discuss in §13.3.8, that Act is aimed at funneling class actions out of state court and into federal court. We noted in §13.3.1 that class actions may face more hurdles in federal than in many state courts. Rule 23(f) — and the prospect of appellate reversal of class certification — is one of those hurdles.

Certification on Fewer Than All Issues; Subclasses

Not every issue in a class case must be litigated on a class basis. Significant economy of scale can be realized if some issues are determined *en masse.* For instance, it might be possible to have a class determination of the defendant's liability. If successful, the court might permit individual proof of damages. Similarly, the court might employ *subclasses.* Suppose a class asserts a claim on which the standard of liability varies slightly from state to state.

- ◦ Suppose the class seeks punitive damages (which, as we discuss in §13.3.5, are intended to punish the defendant for egregious behavior). Each state is free to determine the kinds of behavior that will give rise to a claim for punitive damages. In some, the plaintiff may have to show "willful misconduct." In others, perhaps the standard is "reckless disregard of the consequences of her actions." How can there be a class action if different plaintiffs must satisfy different substantive standards? For starters, the court might have an overall determination of the facts applicable to everyone — for example, whether the defendant in fact did certain things. If the court finds that the defendant did nothing of the sort alleged, the entire class claim would fail. If, on the other hand, it finds that the defendant did X, Y, and Z, the court might divide the group into subclasses. For one, the litigation would focus on whether the defendant's actions constituted "willful misconduct." For the other, the question would be whether the acts showed "reckless disregard," and so forth.

Courts have always had the discretion to entertain class actions on particular issues or to maintain subclasses. Rule 23(c)(4) expressly permits such actions.

When a Class Might Be Treated as Such Even Before Certification

We know that a case is not technically a class action until the court certifies it as such. Nonetheless, for some purposes, courts will treat the putative class as a class. The best example is the statute of limitations.

- ◦ Representative files a class action on June 1. The relevant statute of limitations would run and bar the assertion of claims on June 15. Thus, the case was filed timely. The court denies class certification, however, in

September. Now Connie, a member of the putative class, wants to assert her claim. Is she barred by the statute of limitations?

The answer depends upon whether Representative's filing of the class action on June 1 tolled (stopped) the running of the statute of limitations on June 1. Certainly, it did for Representative's personal claim, so that claim is timely. But what about the claims of class members? On the one hand, we might say the filing should not toll their claims, because the class certification was rejected. On the other hand, if the courts do not recognize tolling, all class members in our hypothetical would have to file individual suits before June 15 simply to protect their claims. Impressed by this latter practical point, the Supreme Court has held that filing of a class action tolls the statute of limitations for all class members, even if class certification is later rejected.[97] Thus, in our hypothetical, Connie has 14 days after the denial of class certification in which to file her individual case.[98]

§13.3.4 Prerequisites of Any Class Action Under Rule 23(a)

Before listing four express prerequisites, Rule 23(a) refers to the existence of a "class." We noted above that the plaintiff class representative will define the class in her complaint and her motion for certification. The wise lawyer will be aware of the need to convince the court — as a practical matter — that a "class" does indeed exist. Thus, counsel will avoid defining a class in open-ended terms, such as "those people interested in peaceful protest"[99] or by subjective intent, such as "those people who were eligible to apply for aid but who were dissuaded because of the relevant agency's treatment of others."[100] If the class prevails, or even if the class action is settled, the court will have to determine who will receive what

---

[97] Crown, Cork & Seal Co. v. Parker, 462 U.S. 345 (1983). This rule applies regardless of the basis on which class certification is rejected. For instance, suppose class certification is denied because the representative is inadequate. One might argue that such a representative should have no ability to toll the running of the statute for putative class members. The Court rejected such a notion, however, in favor of a clear, easily applied rule: Filing tolls the statute of limitations for all class members.

[98] This is because, in our hypothetical, Representative filed the putative class action on June 1, which was 14 days before the statute would have run (on June 15). Tolling means that the running of the statute was arrested on June 1. The statute starts to run again, however, as soon as the class certification is denied. The clock has 14 days left.

[99] See, e.g., Lopez Tijerina v. Henry, 48 F.R.D. 274, 277 (D.N.M. 1969) ("poor people within the state").

[100] See, e.g., Simer v. Rios, 661 F.2d 655, 669 (7th Cir. 1981) ("individuals certified for Crisis Intervention Program (CIP) but who were denied such or discouraged from applying for such").

remedy. The prudent lawyer will continually assure the judge that the case will be manageable. The first opportunity to do this is in the complaint, and counsel will do well to impose reasonable temporal and geographic limitations on the class, to convince the court from the start that the class will be determinable.

We see in §13.3.5 that there are different types of class actions. One type — under Rule 23(b)(3) — requires that the identifiable members of the class be given individual notice of the pendency of the case. That type of class action usually involves claims for monetary relief. In such cases, because the court will need to give individual notice and (if the class wins) to award money to the various class members, the court will expect especial specificity in the class definition. In contrast, another type of class action — under Rule 23(b)(2) — involves claims for injunctive or declaratory relief. Because there is no requirement of notice to individual members of such a class, or to find and distribute damages to individuals, courts require relatively less specificity in defining a class in such cases. Again, however, even though there is a greater need for specificity in the Rule 23(b)(3) class action, prudent lawyers take great care in defining the class in all cases.

Can a class include future members? That is, can a class action seek recovery on behalf of those who, while not yet injured, will be injured in the future? The answer is yes, but in limited circumstances. An illustrative example is *Robertson v. National Basketball Association*,[101] in which the Hall of Famer Oscar Robertson brought a class action to challenge the merger of two professional basketball leagues. The merger made it impossible for players to have the two leagues engage in bidding wars over them. Robertson alleged that the merger violated the antitrust laws by causing an anticompetitive result. He sought to represent a class consisting of (1) present players, (2) players who were active at the time of the merger, and (3) future players in the NBA. The defendants objected to inclusion of the future players and noted that of the thousands of people who play college basketball each year, only a handful will become professionals. The court upheld inclusion of the future members because the group was well defined, and relatively small and discrete. It emphasized that of the millions of high school and college basketball players, only a relative handful (a few hundred) will ever make it to the NBA. Accordingly, "[t]his court can determine at any time whether a particular individual is a member of the class."[102] Thus, inclusion of future members is possible but somewhat rare.

Assuming the existence of a "class," Rule 23(a) sets forth four prerequisites, usually referred to, respectively, as "numerosity," commonality, typicality, and adequacy of representation. Though all four should be

---

[101] 389 F. Supp. 867 (S.D.N.Y. 1975).
[102] *Id.* at 897.

addressed in any case, they are not hermetically sealed from one another. Indeed, there is a good argument that the four can be collapsed into two: numerosity and adequacy of representation.[103] Of course, the burden of persuading the court that all requirements are satisfied rests on the party seeking class certification.

Rule 23(a)(1): Numerosity. This "word" (if it is one) does not appear in Rule 23; courts made it up to cover the requirement in Rule 23(a)(1) that the class be "so numerous that joinder of all members is impracticable." This requirement ensures that the class action is necessary. If the number of class members involved is low enough that joinder would be practicable, a class action simply is not needed; the affected persons can join as co-plaintiffs under Rule 20(a)(1). Whether a proposed class satisfies Rule 23(a)(1) involves a case-by-case analysis of the facts.

One factor, of course, is the sheer number of putative class members. Some classes are so large that numerosity is obvious. For example, some classes have many hundreds or thousands (or even millions) of members. Even though courts should consider other factors besides sheer numbers, as we discuss in a moment, such large groups generally pose no numerosity problems. When is numerosity not obvious? Most courts agree that there are no automatic rules and there is no magic number. Some, however, have espoused this rule of thumb: Generally, fewer than 21 members is insufficient, more than 40 members is sufficient, and the range in between varies depending upon other factors.[104] Again, however, this is at best a general rule, and there are cases in which courts have certified classes with fewer than 21 members[105] and cases in which courts have denied certification of classes with scores of putative members.[106]

Such cases often demonstrate the importance of factors other than the raw numbers. For instance, geographic dispersion of class members is relevant. In one case, the court rejected class status for a putative class of 350 political subdivisions of a state because the members were not geographically dispersed and could join in a single case in which a state officer could represent them all.[107] On the other hand, a relatively small group might be seen as numerous if the members are geographically widespread,

---

[103] The Supreme Court has treated commonality and typicality as essentially collapsing into the requirement of adequate representation. General Tel. Co. of the Southwest v. Falcon, 457 U.S. 147, 157 n.13 (1982).

[104] *See, e.g.,* Cox v. Am. Cast Iron Pipe Co., 784 F.2d 1546, 1553 (11th Cir. 1986), *cert. denied,* 479 U.S. 883 (1986).

[105] *See, e.g.,* Allen v. Isaac, 99 F.R.D. 45, 53 (N.D. Ill. 1983) (17 members); Davy v. Sullivan, 354 F. Supp. 1320, 1325 (M.D. Ala. 1973) (10 members).

[106] *See, e.g.,* Liberty Lincoln Mercury, Inc. v. Ford Mktg. Corp., 149 F.R.D. 65, 73 (D.N.J. 1993) (123 purported members).

[107] Utah v. American Pipe & Constr. Co., 49 F.R.D. 17, 19 (C.D. Cal. 1969).

since joinder would be relatively more difficult.[108] We see in §13.3.6 that, for diversity of citizenship purposes, the court looks only to the citizenship of the class representative, not all the class members. If joinder of the individual members would make it impossible to satisfy the complete diversity rule, joinder is arguably impracticable.

Another relevant factor is the ability of members to pursue individual litigation. If individual claims are so small that members would not be expected to pursue them, joinder may be seen as impracticable. The Supreme Court recognized this possibility in *Phillips Petroleum Co. v. Shutts*, a case involving a class of claimants whose claim averaged $100; the Court explained "most of the plaintiffs would have no realistic day in court if a class action were not available."[109]

The court may consider other issues that affect an individual's incentive or ability to pursue individual litigation. In one case, for instance, the court concluded that a class of 19 was proper, in part because the individuals would be too intimidated to bring individual discrimination claims.[110] Similarly, factors such as limited financial resources, mental disability, or inability to speak English may render joinder impracticable.[111]

Rule 23(a)(2): Commonality. Rule 23(a)(2) requires that there be "questions of law or fact . . . common to the class." Though the rule uses the plural word "questions," courts routinely conclude that a single common question is sufficient.[112] As a practical matter, it is almost impossible for a class not to satisfy Rule 23(a)(2). Commonality is implicit in the existence of a class. It would simply not be a class if there were not some commonality among the members. In other words, without some commonality, the efficiency that is the hallmark of the class action would simply not be possible.

To the extent that commonality is hotly litigated, it is in the context of a class action under Rule 23(b)(3). In such cases, as we see below, the common question must *predominate over individual questions*. That requirement may be difficult to meet, depending upon how many individual issues will arise in the case. But nothing in Rule 23(a) requires that common questions predominate. All that is required is that some commonality

---

[108] *See, e.g.*, Alvarado Partners, L.P. v. Mehta, 130 F.R.D. 673, 675 (D. Colo. 1991) (joinder of 33 individuals impracticable in part because they resided in different areas of the United States).

[109] 472 U.S. 797, 809 (1985). *Shutts* is an important case concerning personal jurisdiction in the class action. See §13.3.8.

[110] Arkansas Educ. Assn. v. Board of Educ., 446 F.2d 763, 765-766 (8th Cir. 1971).

[111] *See, e.g.*, Jackson v. Foley, 156 F.R.D. 538, 542 (E.D.N.Y. 1994) (low-income claimants less likely to be able to bring individual suits); Rodriguez v. Berrymore Farms, Inc., 672 F. Supp. 1009, 1013 (W.D. Mich. 1987) (inability to speak English and lack of knowledge of legal system render individual suits unlikely).

[112] *See, e.g.*, Becher v. Long Island Lighting Co., 164 F.R.D. 144, 150 (E.D.N.Y. 1996).

exists among the class members. So Rule 23(a)(2) presents no significant problem.

Rule 23(a)(3): Typicality. Rule 23(a)(3) mandates that the representative's claims be typical of those of the class.[113] This factor is closely related to the next, which is that the representative fairly and adequately represent the class. Both requirements focus on the relationship between the class members and their representative. Remember that the function and goal of the class action is to bind the entire class to the judgment obtained by the representative. As discussed in §13.3.2, this cannot be accomplished, as a matter of due process, unless the representative adequately represents the interests of the class members. The requirement that the representative's claim be typical of the claims of class members helps to ensure adequate representation. If the representative has suffered a similar harm — if she can "feel the pain" of the class members — it is more likely that her representation will be adequate. Stated another way, without a typical claim, it is difficult to see what incentive the representative would have to assert the class claims vigorously.

Rule 23(a)(3) does not require that the representative's claims be *exactly* the same in all particulars as those of class members. Instead, courts focus on the "essential characteristics" of the claims and recognize that minor factual differences, even as to damages, will not make class treatment improper.[114] Obviously, though, if the class members' claims will require a high degree of individualized proof, class treatment is not appropriate, and the representative's claim will not be typical of those of the group.[115]

- ∘ Retail Store engages door-to-door salespeople to sell refrigerators. Fifty salespeople go to various neighborhoods and enter into discussions with residents, during which they offer to sell the refrigerator on discount if the person agrees on the spot. About 200 people agree to buy and make the required payment, and Retail Store never delivers the refrigerators. In a class action for common law fraud, one serious problem will be the substantive requirement of showing a misrepresentation of fact by the defendant. If each representation by a salesperson to a prospective purchaser was unique, a class action would seem impossible, because nobody's claim would be typical of anyone else's claim. But if Retail Store provided its sales force with a standard sales pitch to be memorized and

---

[113] Or, in a defendant class, that her defenses are typical of those of the class.

[114] *See* 5 Moore's Federal Practice §23.24[4].

[115] *See, e.g.,* In re Am. Med. Sys., Inc., 75 F.3d 1069, 1083 (6th Cir. 1996) (various members of putative class used different prosthetic model and experienced different harms).

delivered to each person, a class action might be possible. In such a situation, the misrepresentations would have been identical, even though each conversation was slightly different.[116]

Beyond this, it is important that the representative suffer the same general kind of harm suffered by the class.

○ The class consists of Mexican-American persons who applied for employment with Defendant. They claim that Defendant refused to hire them on the basis of their national origin. Representative is a Mexican-American who is employed by Defendant, but who claims that Defendant refused to promote him because of his national origin. Representative cannot represent the class, because he did not suffer the same harm. While both he and the class assert that they were hurt by Defendant's discriminatory behavior, they were hurt in different ways. The class members were never hired. Representative was hired (but not promoted), and thus his claim could not be typical of those of the class members.[117]

Moreover, the fact that a representative is subject to a defense that class members generally are not may preclude a finding of typicality (or adequacy of representation). The existence of such a defense will require litigation unrelated to class interest, and may distract the representative from prosecuting the class claim. For example, in one case, the fact that the named representative bought certificates of deposit from the defendant after the alleged fraud was uncovered subjected it to a unique defense and defeated typicality.[118] Similarly, the fact that the representative of a class of prostitutes was subject to deportation (and other class members were not) defeated typicality.[119]

It is also important that the representative suffered a typical harm at the hands of the same defendants as the class members.

---

[116]These facts are similar to those in *Vasquez v. Superior Court*, 484 P.2d 964, 966-967 (Cal. 1971). *See also* Rosario v. Livaditis, 963 F.2d 1013, 1018 (7th Cir. 1991) (claim typical because part of same overall fraudulent course of dealing). In securities fraud claims under Rule 10b-5, a federal court will presume reliance if the alleged misstatement was included in a public press release. In establishing this rule, the Supreme Court expressly noted that a contrary rule would make it impossible to prosecute such cases as class actions, because of the variations from class member to class member. Basic Inc. v. Levinson, 485 U.S. 224, 246-247 (1988).

[117]General Tel. Co. of the Southwest v. Falcon, 457 U.S. 147, 158. The Court recognized that the question might be seen as one of typicality or of adequacy of representation. *Id.* at 157 n.13. Note also the potential for conflict of interest between Representative and the class members. If the class succeeds, the members will be hired, which will create greater competition for the promotion Representative seeks.

[118]Gary Plastic Pkg. Corp. v. Merrill Lynch, 903 F.2d 176, 178-180 (2d Cir. 1990).

[119]Hagan v. City of Winnemucca, 108 F.R.D. 61, 65-66 (D. Nev. 1985). The court noted that the probable deportation proceedings against the representative would be an "outside entanglement" that would also rob her of her ability to be an adequate representative.

○ The class consists of persons in a city who did business with pawn shops that allegedly violated federal truth in lending laws. There are five defendant pawn shops, joined under Rule 20(a). The representative, however, dealt only with one of the defendants. The fact that she was not harmed by the other four pawn shop defendants means that her claim is not typical of the class members, who dealt with the other four. She did not suffer at the hands of those other four and cannot represent persons who did.[120]

There are some ways around this problem. First, the case may be structured with multiple representatives, one having dealt with each of the defendants. Then the representative who dealt with Defendant 1 has a claim typical of all class members who dealt with Defendant 1, the representative who dealt with Defendant 2 has a claim typical of all class members who dealt with Defendant 2, and so forth. This solution will not work, however, if there are too many defendants for practicable joinder. In such a situation, however, the case might be structured with a defendant class; if certified, the representative defendant will represent all defendants, who will then be bound by the judgment (just as plaintiff class members are bound by the judgment).

Second, if the defendants had engaged in a conspiracy to violate the truth in lending laws, the representative need not have had dealings with each defendant. The idea here is that each class member, including the representative, was harmed by the concerted efforts of the defendants; thus, one person so harmed can speak for others so harmed.[121]

Third, it is possible that members of a class have a *juridical relationship* that enables the court to conclude that one may speak for and bind the others. The term is not well defined, and seems limited to persons who occupy coordinate governmental positions. For example, in one case, plaintiffs sued a class of defendant jailers, who allegedly segregated prisoners unconstitutionally. Though the plaintiffs had not dealt with each jailer, all the defendant class members were officers of a single state. Their juridical relationship meant, in essence, that a plaintiff who had dealt with one could assert a claim against all.[122]

Rule 23(a)(4) (and Rule 23(g)): Protecting the Class Interests. Rule 23(a)(4) requires that the representative "fairly and adequately protect the interests of the class." It is the most important factor in Rule 23(a), because it is the linchpin for assuring that the class members can be bound

---

[120] These facts are similar to those in *LaMar v. H&B Novelty & Loan Co.*, 489 F.2d 461, 466 (9th Cir. 1973). The problem presented here is similar to the notion of standing. One who has not been harmed by a defendant has no standing to raise claims of others against that defendant.

[121] The *LaMar* case in the preceding footnote has a well-known discussion of this point. *See* 489 F.2d at 466. *See also* Thillens, Inc. v. Community Currency Exch. Assn., 97 F.R.D. 668, 676 (N.D. Ill. 1983).

[122] Washington v. Lee, 263 F. Supp. 327, 330 (M.D. Ala. 1966).

consistent with due process. As discussed immediately above, this factor overlaps greatly with the Rule 23(a)(3) requirement of typicality. Indeed, some courts treat the two as virtually interchangeable. While recognizing overlap between the two, it is important to see, however, that certain factors must be addressed under Rule 23(a)(4). Though that Rule refers only to adequacy of the *representative*, recall from §13.3.3 that the court must appoint class counsel (under Rule 23(g)) who will provide fair and adequate representation of class members' interests.

In contrast to class counsel (who, under Rule 23(g)(2), must be the applicant "best able to represent the interests of the class"), there is no requirement that the class representative be "the best" available. Rule 23(a)(4) requires "adequate" protection of the class interests. The representative owes a fiduciary duty of loyalty to the class. Thus, at a minimum, her interests cannot be antagonistic to those of the class. Mere differences of opinion concerning litigation strategy will not defeat class certification. Rather, a disqualifying conflict is one that relates to the core subject of the case and is immediate, not speculative. In structuring the case, counsel should be careful to proffer a putative representative whose interests are not antagonistic to those of the class.

As we noted above in discussing typicality, a representative may *not* be adequate if she is subject to a unique defense, one not available against class members generally. Such a defense may distract the representative from her job of litigating on behalf of the class members, and may, if successful, remove the representative from litigation. Similarly, if the representative's credibility is subject to legitimate attack, the court may find her inadequate.[123] In addition, some courts have found a representative inadequate if she has a close personal, business, or familial relationship with the class lawyer.[124] In such a case, the representative might be tempted to approve settlement on terms favorable to the lawyer and relatively less favorable to the class members.

The class representative must litigate with vigor. She must ensure that the motion to certify the class be heard with appropriate promptness. She must also provide at least some supervision over the actions of the class lawyer. To do so, she must have at least a general sense of the nature of the litigation and of the class action device. Defendants sometimes attempt to defeat class certification by arguing that the representative has no knowledge of the underlying claims or even of the underlying facts. Courts generally recognize that the representative is rarely a lawyer, and thus cannot be expected to have detailed knowledge of the law. At some level, however, the representative must have at least some rudimentary understanding of the nature of the dispute. Otherwise, she cannot serve as a brake on the actions of the class counsel. If the representative is wholly

---

[123] *See, e.g.*, Dubin v. Miller, 132 F.R.D. 269, 272 (D. Colo. 1990).
[124] *See, e.g.*, Kirby v. Cullinet Software, Inc., 116 F.R.D. 303, 309-310 (D. Mass. 1987).

clueless on such things, the class is essentially "headless," and is run entirely by the lawyer. Such a situation robs class members of a measure of representation and permits suit essentially by the lawyer, who lacks standing to bring the claim.[125]

Defendants also often challenge a class representative by pointing to her lack of financial ability to prosecute the litigation. Many lawyers take plaintiff class actions on a contingent fee basis, so the representative need not pay attorneys' fees as the litigation proceeds.[126] But the representative must pay various costs of the litigation as they are incurred. For example, there are filing fees, witness fees, and costs of discovery. In a class action under Rule 23(b)(3), as we see in §13.3.4, the representative must pay to give the required notice to class members. If the litigation is successful, the losing side generally will have to pay the prevailing party's costs. In the interim, however, the representative must bear the expenses as they are incurred. Thus, the court must be convinced that the representative can finance this aspect of the litigation.

Can the class counsel advance money to the representative to pay these expenses? Historically, the answer was yes, so long as the representative agreed to reimburse the lawyer if the class lost the litigation. Recently, Rule 1.8(e) of the American Bar Association Model Rule of Professional Responsibility permits the lawyer to advance litigation expenses on a contingent basis. That is, the lawyer advances the expenses, and the client repays them only if the client wins the underlying class litigation. Class action plaintiffs lawyers like this provision because it makes it easier for them to enlist representatives. On the other hand, there is a serious concern that absence of a requirement that the client reimburse the lawyer for these costs allows the lawyer to "buy" a class claim. In such a case, it

---

[125] Standing is one of several "justiciability" doctrines that you may study in detail in courses on Constitutional Law or Federal Courts. It requires, basically, that the person asserting a claim be one who was actually harmed by the defendant's behavior. This ensures that there is a true dispute — a "case or controversy" — as required by Article III of the Constitution for invocation of federal subject matter jurisdiction.

[126] With a contingent fee arrangement, the lawyer does not charge the plaintiff a fee by the hour or on any other basis. Rather, the lawyer and client agree that the lawyer's fee will be a percentage of the plaintiff's recovery, whether that recovery comes from a judgment or settlement. The lawyer is taking a calculated risk. If the plaintiff loses, the lawyer simply receives no fee. On the other hand, if the recovery is huge — as might be the case in a class action, where the claims of many are asserted in one proceeding — the lawyer's recovery is correspondingly huge. The fact that a lawyer on a contingent fee is, in essence, financing the litigation explains the concern that she might want to settle rather than go to trial. By settling, she is guaranteed some recovery; by going to trial, she invests a tremendous amount of time while potentially recovering no pay. This conflict of interest for the lawyer emphasizes the need for an active class representative — to ensure that the class members' desires, and not those of the lawyer, govern what action is taken. (Of course, defendants cannot get lawyers to work on a contingent fee. They pay their lawyers by the hour.)

seems to be the lawyer, and not the representative, who is the interested party in the litigation.

Recognizing potential abuses of the class action, Congress passed the Private Securities Litigation Reform Act in 1996.[127] With this Act, Congress intended to ensure that sophisticated institutional investors serve as representatives — or "lead plaintiffs" — in federal court class actions based upon alleged violations of federal securities law. Among other requirements, the Act provides that the court must appoint as lead plaintiff the person having the largest financial interest in the class claim. The provisions of the Act apply, however, only in litigation arising under the federal securities laws.

§13.3.5 Types of Class Actions Recognized Under Rule 23(b)

Assuming the party seeking certification convinces the court that the prerequisites of Rule 23(a) are satisfied, that party then must demonstrate that the case fits within one of the types of classes recognized by Rule 23(b). Thus, under Rule 23(b), there is a choice; the party seeking certification need only satisfy one of the types of classes recognized. On the other hand, nothing in Rule 23 precludes the representative from seeking certification under more than one type of class action, and some parties do seek certification under more than one type.

Rule 23(b)(1): The "Prejudice" Class Action. Reading Rule 23(b)(1) will remind you of Rule 19(a)(1)(B). The Rules Advisory Committee amended the two (along with Rule 24(a)(2)) together in 1966 expressly to emphasize their similarities. In §12.6.1, we saw that Rule 19(a)(1)(B) mandates the joinder of an absentee in either of two situations: (1) when nonjoinder of an absentee might subject the absentee's interest to practical impairment or (2) when nonjoinder of the absentee might subject the defendant to the risk of incurring multiple or inconsistent obligations.[128] Rule 23(b)(1) addresses the same potential harms, but in the class context, where there are so many absentees that their joinder is not feasible. Just as Rule 19(a)(1)(B) consists of two subparts, so does Rule 23(b)(1). Because the Rule is concerned with avoiding potential prejudice (either to the absentees or to a party), we can refer to the Rule 23(b)(1) classes as "prejudice" class actions.

Rule 23(b)(1)(A) permits a class action if individual suits "would create a risk of inconsistent or varying adjudications with respect to individual class members that would establish incompatible standards of conduct for the party opposing the class." This is the class analog to Rule 19(a)(1)(B)(ii); the focus is on the impact of non-class litigation on the

---

[127] 15 U.S.C. §§77z-1, 78u-4.

[128] In both instances, the absentee must claim an interest in the subject of the litigation.

party opposing the class. Assuming a plaintiff class, the focus thus is on the defendant. The court asks this question: If the putative class members sue individually (not in a class), might it subject the defendant to incompatible standards of conduct?

- ◦ Stockholders of a corporation claim that the corporation must convert their stock from one class to another. If the stockholders sue individually, some may win and some may lose, which would leave the corporation uncertain as to how to treat this class of stockholders. To avoid that potential uncertainty, a stockholder may sue on behalf of the other stockholders under Rule 23(b)(1)(A).[129]

As we saw with Rule 19, inconsistent outcomes in damages claims will not satisfy Rule 23(b)(1)(A), because such inconsistent claims do not constitute "incompatible standards of conduct."

- ◦ A train operated by TrainCo crashes and injures 120 people. If the 120 people sue individually, some may win and some may lose. This possibility does not satisfy Rule 23(b)(1)(A), however, because the individual cases against TrainCo will not subject it to incompatible standards of conduct. There is nothing incompatible in this sense between writing a check to one passenger and not to another.

The focus here — as in Rule 19(a)(1)(B)(ii) — is on the effect of individual litigation on the ways in which the defendant must do something in the real world. In the first hypothetical above, for example, individual litigation might leave the corporation subject to orders (1) that this class of stock be converted into another class of stock and (2) that this class of stock not be converted into another class of stock. The corporation could not satisfy one without violating the other. In the TrainCo hypothetical, in contrast, there is no comparable inconsistency in having to pay a judgment to one passenger but not to another.

Rule 23(b)(1)(B) provides for a class action if individual suits "would create a risk of adjudications with respect to individual class members that, as a practical matter, would be dispositive of the interests of the other members not parties to the individual adjudications or would substantially impair or impede their ability to protect their interests." This is the class analog to Rule 19(a)(1)(B)(i); the focus is on the would-be class members. The court asks this question: If the putative class members sue individually, might some be harmed as a practical matter? Such harm might be caused by the fact that there is a limited fund from which all class members can recover. Individual actions might deplete the fund, leaving some

---

[129] *See* Van Gemert v. Boeing Co., 259 F. Supp. 125 (S.D.N.Y. 1966) (similar facts, but concerning holders of debentures, which are securities, but differ from stock in ways not relevant here).

essentially without a remedy. Everyone seems to accept the theory behind these "limited fund" classes. Courts take different approaches, however, about the degree of proof required to invoke Rule 23(b)(1)(B).

> ∘ A fire raged through a crowded dinner theater and killed over 100 people. Based upon litigated claims for wrongful death in the area, the judge estimated that the total liability, though not precisely subject to calculation before trial, could exceed $16 million. In addition, defendants' lawyers estimated that the defendants had a net worth of approximately $3 million. Based upon these estimates, the court certified a Rule 23(b)(1)(B) class, because it found "good reason to believe" from these estimates "that total judgments might substantially exceed the ability of defendants to respond."[130]

Notice the reason for invoking Rule 23(b)(1)(B). If the claimants sued separately, according to the court, they would likely recover judgments totaling $16 million. But the pool of assets from which those judgments could be satisfied totaled only $3 million. If the litigations proceeded individually, the first few successful plaintiffs would exhaust the $3 million.[131] That scenario would prejudice those plaintiffs who were not first in the litigation line. Those whose cases went to trial later might win, but the victory would be hollow, because the defendants at that point would have no assets from which the judgment could be satisfied. To avoid that harm — to avoid the possibility that "individual actions would as a practical matter be dispositive of the interests of the other[s] not parties . . . or substantially impair their ability to protect their interests" — the group may proceed as a class action. In that way, each member will receive a proportional part of what money there is. Instead of some plaintiffs' recovering their full damages and many recovering nothing, this theory would allow all plaintiffs to recover a percentage of their damages.

The problem is that some courts have erected a dauntingly high burden of proof for invoking the limited fund class action under Rule 23(b)(1)(B). An example is the Ninth Circuit opinion in *In re Northern District of California Dalkon Shield IUD Products Litigation*,[132] which concerned claims related to an allegedly defective intrauterine birth control device. Injured women filed thousands of claims throughout the United States.

---

[130] Coburn v. 4-R Corp., 77 F.R.D. 43, 45 (E.D. Ky. 1977).

[131] Not only that, but the net worth of the defendants would be eroded further by the attorneys' fees and other litigation expenses from over 100 separate cases. By the way, notice how this fact pattern could raise issue preclusion concerns. If the first plaintiff won, and established at trial that the defendants' negligence caused the fire, could successive plaintiffs take advantage of that finding? The answer might be yes, if the applicable law adopted nonmutual offensive issue preclusion. See §11.3.5.

[132] 693 F.2d 847 (9th Cir.), *cert. denied*, 459 U.S. 1171 (1982).

The opinion involved the punitive damages claims[133] of a nationwide class of injured women. The district court added the punitive damages claims asserted by all class members; the total was $2.3 billion. The court then noted the net worth of the defendant, as asserted in discovery documents, which was $280 million. Finding an "unconscionable possibility that large numbers of plaintiffs who are not first in line at the courthouse door will be deprived of a practical means of redress," the district court certified a class under Rule 23(b)(1)(B).[134]

The Ninth Circuit reversed and criticized the district court for failing to undertake sufficient factual inquiry into the value of the claims and the net worth of the defendant. According to the Ninth Circuit, a limited fund class action is appropriate only when individual judgments "inescapably will alter the substance of the rights having similar claims." Nothing in Rule 23 even remotely requires such a degree of proof; the phrase "inescapably will alter" is not found in the Rule. Moreover, the Ninth Circuit opinion failed to indicate what kind of evidence would suffice to satisfy the standard it set for invoking Rule 23(b)(1)(B).

The Supreme Court addressed the limited fund class action in the important case of *Ortiz v. Fibreboard Corp.*,[135] which involved part of the massive litigation arising from exposure to asbestos.[136] The parties, including a large manufacturer of asbestos and its insurance companies, entered a very complicated "Global Settlement Agreement" settling millions of personal injury claims. The agreement set out a complex system for compensating the victims from a fund that was created mostly from insurance money; the manufacturer contributed some money to the fund, but ended up with nearly its entire net worth intact.

The Supreme Court rejected use of the Rule 23(b)(1)(B) limited fund class action on the facts of the case. In discussing three problems with such certification, the Court set out three requirements for a limited fund class action. First, the parties must *demonstrate* (not merely assert) that the available funds are insufficient to cover the numerous claims. In *Ortiz*, the parties simply stipulated about how much money was available; there

---

[133] Punitive damages are intended to punish the defendant. They are sometimes called *exemplary* damages, because they make an example to the defendant that its behavior was so outrageous that it should be hit with liability beyond that for merely compensating the plaintiff for the harm done to her.

[134] In re Northern Dist. of Cal. Dalkon Shield IUD Prods. Liab. Litig., 526 F. Supp. 887, 893 (N.D. Cal. 1981).

[135] 527 U.S. 815 (1999).

[136] We mentioned asbestos litigation in §11.3.4. Asbestos is a fire-resistant building material used routinely throughout much of the twentieth century. In the last third of the century it became clear that exposure to asbestos could cause deadly forms of cancer. Innumerable plaintiffs filed personal injury and wrongful death claims; in addition, there were thousands of claims concerning the financial responsibility for the federally mandated clean-up of asbestos from buildings. Asbestos has created more litigation than any other product in history.

was no proof, for example, of the value of the available insurance funds. Second, the proposed distribution must be equitable. The proposed settlement in *Ortiz* simply did not ensure that all claimants would be treated fairly. Third, the Court was quite concerned that the agreement permitted the manufacturer to retain nearly all its net worth; it contributed relatively little to the settlement fund. In the "historical use" of the limited fund class, the Court noted, the defendant is essentially wiped out by the litigation. In sum, the problem was that the defendants simply stipulated how much they would make available for potential plaintiffs. Individual suits might result in determinations that more insurance money was available and certainly could have recovered greater amounts from the manufacturer. Thus, there was no showing of a true limited fund that was insufficient to cover the prospective claims. While not ruling out the possibility of limited fund class actions under Rule 23(b)(1)(B), *Ortiz* certainly raises significant barriers to their use.[137]

The Court was also concerned that the actions under Rule 23(b)(1) are "mandatory" class actions. This means that the class members have no right to opt out; they are stuck in the class, and they are bound by the judgment in the class litigation. In contrast, as we see below, members of a Rule 23(b)(3) class have a right to opt out and pursue individual litigation. Traditionally, damages claims have been pursued under Rule 23(b)(3). Because the limited fund theory robs individuals of control over their own claim, the Court in *Ortiz* counseled caution.

Though it seems strange, sometimes the *defendant* will seek certification of a *plaintiff* class under Rule 23(b)(1)(B). In the classic limited fund class action, the defendant understands that it will be wiped out financially by the judgments to be rendered against it. The claims vastly exceed the defendant's net worth. (This is why some courts refer to limited fund classes as "constructive bankruptcy" classes.) Rather than litigate each claim individually, the defendant might prefer to have the entire liability decided in a class action under Rule 23(b)(1)(B). Functionally, such a case starts to look a bit like interpleader (discussed in §13.2), in which the net worth of the defendants is considered as the stake to which the numerous class members have claims. Ironically, *plaintiffs* might oppose such a class, because they (or their lawyers) might prefer to litigate alone and recover their individual judgments in full.[138] By doing so, they may be paid in full, while others run the risk of being left out in the cold.

---

[137] *See, e.g.*, Doe v. Karadzic, 192 F.R.D. 133, 139 (S.D.N.Y. 2000) (noting that though Rule 23(b)(1)(B) requires only "risk of impairment," courts have interpreted the phrase narrowly).

[138] In *Coburn* and *Northern District of California Dalkon Shield IUD Prod. Litig.*, defendants sought certification of a plaintiff class. In addition to avoiding serial litigation concerning the same events, a class action would probably reduce the amount paid by the defendant in attorneys' fees; this, in turn, would preserve more of defendant's assets for recovery by injured plaintiffs.

In addition to the limited fund, there is another theory, called *limited generosity*, on which Rule 23(b)(1)(B) classes might be certified. It concerns only claims for punitive damages, which, as we said in footnote 133, are intended to punish the defendant for outrageous conduct. Many observers have argued that it is unfair — perhaps even unconstitutional — to impose multiple punitive damages awards against a defendant for a single bad act.[139]

> ° *D* engages in a single example of outrageous conduct that injures hundreds of plaintiffs. Of course, each plaintiff has a claim against *D* for compensatory damages. Suppose the plaintiffs sue for punitive damages as well. Let's say the first several plaintiffs all win punitive damages against *D*. At some point, a court might say to the next plaintiff, in essence: "*D* has been punished enough for the outrageous conduct; nobody else may recover punitive damages against *D* for this act."

This conclusion means, of course, that no other plaintiffs may recover punitive damages. The argument is that these later plaintiffs have suffered the kind of harm that triggers Rule 23(b)(1)(B) — they lose out because they got to trial later than the ones who recovered punitive damages. That is, the possibility that some court may step in and say "enough is enough" on punitive damages might rob later plaintiffs of the chance to recover them. According to the argument, the court should certify a class action for punitive damages; that way, each plaintiff will recover a proportional share of punitive damages and none will be left out.[140] This theory has met with some success.

Finally, no matter what theory is used under Rule 23(b)(1)(B), it is important that all potential claimants be members of the class. Otherwise, the litigation risks precisely the harm the Rule was intended to avoid. In one case, a class of school districts sued to recover the expenses of having to comply with the federal mandate to remove asbestos from buildings. The court refused to certify a Rule 23(b)(1)(B) class, in part because the class did not include all such claimants. The class would have the incentive to recover first, precisely to leave other claimants out in the cold.[141]

Rule 23(b)(2): Equitable Relief. The Rule 23(b)(2) class action is appropriate when the party opposing the class (usually the defendant) "has acted or refused to act on grounds that apply generally to the class, so

---

[139] *See* Nancy J. King, *Portioning Punishment: Constitutional Limits on Successive and Excessive Penalties*, 144 U. Pa. L. Rev. 101 (1995); Richard W. Murphy, *Superbifurcation: Making Room for State Prosecution in the Punitive Damages Process*, 76 N.C. L. Rev. 463 (1998).

[140] *See, e.g.*, In re School Asbestos Litig., 789 F.2d 996, 1003-1004 (3d Cir. 1986), *cert. denied*, 479 U.S. 852 (1986).

[141] *Id.* at 1006 (because thousands of other claimants are not in the class, there is still "a race to the courthouse door").

that final injunctive relief or corresponding declaratory relief is appropriate respecting the class as a whole." Thus, there are two basic requirements: one relating to the action or inaction of the party opposing the class and one relating to the relief sought by the class. Typical class actions under Rule 23(b)(2) deal with employment discrimination or with claims to restructure public institutions. Each of the following examples would be appropriate under Rule 23(b)(2). In each, the defendant has treated class members "on grounds generally applicable to the class." And in each, the class seeks the type of equitable relief specified in the Rule.

- A group of workers claims that Employer has denied them promotion because of their national origin, in violation of federal law. They seek an injunction compelling Employer to promote them (or a declaratory judgment that they are entitled to such relief).[142]
- A group of pretrial detainees (persons charged with a crime and in custody while awaiting trial) claims that Sheriff is denying them "contact" visits from family members, in violation of the Constitution. They seek an injunction ordering Sheriff to permit such visits (or a similar declaratory judgment).

While we can see that these cases satisfy the Rule, we might ask why we should go to all the trouble of a class action. Why not just have one person from the affected group sue? If a single plaintiff proves that Employer is discriminating against a group of workers on the basis of national origin and wins an injunction against such discrimination, won't all the affected workers "win"? The answer may be no. Suppose one Plaintiff brings the suit and wins. The result is an injunction ordering Employer to promote Plaintiff, including, let's say, some broad language about not discriminating against the group on the basis of national origin. Now Employer promotes Plaintiff but continues to discriminate against the other members of that group. Can they sue to enforce the injunction against the Employer? Probably not, because they were not parties (or represented by a party) to that case and thus cannot enforce the judgment. The benefit to proceeding as a class action here is that any member of the class can later enforce the injunction against Employer. So if the class sues and wins, and Employer later continues to discriminate against a member of the class, the member can ask the court to hold Employer in contempt for violating an injunction entered in favor of all class members.

Though Rule 23(b)(2) speaks only of equitable relief, there is some authority for allowing class members to recover money in limited circumstances. Specifically, if damages (1) "flow automatically" from the grant

---

[142] As we noted in §4.6.3, a declaratory judgment is a judicial decree of the rights of the parties. It developed in equity.

of injunctive or declaratory relief and (2) can be readily calculated, they may be recovered in a Rule 23(b)(2) class.[143]

○ Suppose the class being discriminated against on the basis of national origin, noted above, wins an injunction requiring Employer to promote them. That order avoids future harm to the class members simply by ordering Employer to do what the law requires. But what about the past discrimination? After all, the class members were denied their rightful promotions for some time and thus were underpaid. Recovery of damages for the past discrimination will remedy that harm, and should be permitted in the Rule 23(b)(2) class. First, the damages for past harm flow automatically from the injunction; the injunction puts the class members at the proper pay level, but they were denied that pay level before the injunction. Second, the damages are easily calculated; the court can simply apply a formula based upon the difference between the two pay grades and the length of time each was discriminated against.

This result — permitting recovery of damages in the Rule 23(b)(2) class action — is to be encouraged in appropriate cases. It permits recovery of both forms of relief necessary to make the class whole in a single proceeding. It avoids any need for a second action for damages (which might, in turn, raise a concern of claim preclusion[144]). It also permits recovery of damages without having to satisfy the especially stringent (and perhaps expensive) requirements of a Rule 23(b)(3) class action. Specifically, for instance, as we see in §13.3.6, the representative of a Rule 23(b)(2) class need not pay to give individual notice to class members. On the other hand, such damages are proper in a Rule 23(b)(2) class action only if the two-part test discussed above is satisfied. Only in such circumstances are the economies of the class action not endangered by injection of individual issues. Like the Rule 23(b)(1) class, the Rule 23(b)(2) class is also mandatory. Class members have no right to opt out, and are bound by the judgment in the case.

Rule 23(b)(3): Common Questions Predominate. A class action under Rule 23(b)(3) is appropriate when (1) common questions *predominate* over individual questions, *and* (2) the class action is superior to other means of adjudicating the dispute. Though the Rule does not require that the class seek any particular form of relief, Rule 23(b)(3) class actions usually (but not always) involve claims for damages. (In fact, some people use the shorthand "damages class action" for a Rule 23(b)(3) class.)

The Rule 23(b)(3) class action is more controversial than the others. Classes certified under Rule 23(b)(1) and (b)(2) tend to involve fairly

---

[143] *See, e.g.*, Moody v. Albemarle Paper Co., 474 F.2d 134, 142 (4th Cir. 1973).

[144] Perhaps it could be argued that a class suing only for injunctive relief is barred by claim preclusion from asserting a damages claim. The claim for an injunction and that for damages might be a single "claim" for claim preclusion purposes. See §11.2.3.

cohesive groups, simply because of the nature of the actions. Under Rule 23(b)(1), the class members are so closely related that adjudication of their claims individually will subject someone — either the defendant or the other class members — to some sort of harm. Classes under Rule 23(b)(2), by definition, involve members who have been subjected to the same treatment by the defendant. But the Rule 23(b)(3) class is held together only by common facts. Frequently, the class members just happened to be in the same place at the same time — perhaps travelers on an ill-fated flight or investors in an ill-fated venture. If they sued individually, the fact that some would win and others would lose would create none of the problems that underlie the need for the class action under Rule 23(b)(1) or (b)(2).

Because the Rule 23(b)(3) class tends to be a disparate group, the drafters imposed special procedural protections, which we address in §13.3.6. First, the court must give notice to all class members of the pendency of the class action, including individual notice to those who can be identified with reasonable effort. Second, class members have the right to "opt out" — to leave the class action and proceed on their own (or, perhaps, decide not to sue). These protections are required *only* in the Rule 23(b)(3) class action. Before investigating them, however, we address the two requirements for certifying a Rule 23(b)(3) class.

The Need for Predominant Common Questions. We know from Rule 23(a)(2) that all class actions have common questions; the existence of common questions among all class members is part of the definition of the class itself. In the Rule 23(b)(3) class, it is not enough simply to have common questions; instead, the "questions of law or fact common to class members" must "predominate over any questions affecting only individual members." This requirement does not mean that the class members must share *every* issue in the case. Indeed, it is hard to imagine a case in which every issue — of causation, harm, and damages, for instance — will be identical to all class members.

The operative language defining the Rule 23(b)(3) class was part of the 1966 amendment to the Rule. Interestingly, the Rules Advisory Committee responsible for the language concluded in its Notes that a "mass accident resulting in injuries to numerous persons [would] ordinarily not [be] appropriate for class action"[145] under Rule 23(b)(3). Why? The Committee pointed out that individual questions, such as damages, and possibly defenses raised against individual class members, would require individual resolution. "In these circumstances," the Committee concluded, "an action conducted as a class action would degenerate in practice into multiple lawsuits separately tried."[146] Reflecting these concerns, courts initially were reluctant to use the Rule 23(b)(3) class in mass tort cases. In the 1980s,

---

[145] Fed. R. Civ. P. 23, advisory committee's notes (1966).
[146] *Id.*

however, as courts became increasingly crowded with mass tort litigation, many judges had a change in attitude, and some demonstrated creativity in adapting the Rule 23(b)(3) class action to mass tort situations. Doing so was relatively easier in cases involving a single cataclysmic event.

- ○ An explosion of a gas main in an office building injures scores of people. All were hurt at the same time in the same general locale by the same thing. Thus, litigation *en masse* of many issues — including causation and other questions related to liability — would be economical. The individual damages suffered by each class member — which might vary radically — can be left to individual proceedings.[147]

The requirement of predominant common questions seems more difficult to satisfy in toxic torts and other cases involving harm suffered at different places and at different times. For instance, consider hundreds of people harmed by an adulterated or defective product. Unlike injuries caused by a single cataclysm, here the harms are caused by hundreds of individual uses of the product. Still, class treatment is not out of the question. One example is *Jenkins v. Raymark Industries, Inc.*,[148] one of thousands of cases concerning personal injuries caused by exposure to asbestos. Class members suffered different levels of harm caused by different levels of exposure to asbestos over different periods in different places. Yet all their claims shared at least one thing: the assertion by the manufacturer-defendants that they could not be held liable under the "state of the art" defense; the argument was that they could not be responsible because the state of scientific knowledge at the time did not alert anyone to the risks of asbestos. Because each defendant had raised this defense in each individual injury case already litigated, the court upheld a Rule 23(b)(3) class simply to litigate *that issue* for all concerned.

Jenkins is good example of how it is easier to find predominance of common questions if one defines the class relatively narrowly. If one sees the class as all issues relating to the personal injury claims arising from asbestos exposure, there could be hundreds of individual issues. In this context, it is ridiculous to say that the common questions relating to the state of the art defense predominate over individual questions. But if one

---

[147] *See, e.g.,* Sterling v. Velsicol Chem. Corp., 855 F.2d 1188, 1197 (6th Cir. 1988), in which the court upheld the trial court's certifying a Rule 23(b)(3) class action on its own motion. The court explained: "In mass tort accidents, the factual and legal issues of a defendant's liability do not differ dramatically from one plaintiff to the next. No matter how individualized the issue of damages may be, these issues can be reversed for individual treatment with the question of liability tried as a class action. Consequently, the mere fact that questions peculiar to each individual member of the class remain after the common question of the defendant's liability have been resolved does not dictate the conclusion that a class action is impermissible."

[148] 782 F.2d 468 (5th Cir. 1986).

defines the class as raising only the viability of the state of the art defense, common questions obviously predominate; in fact, the common questions are the only questions. And class determination of the defense can bring great judicial economy. If the defense is upheld, all class members lose. If the defense is not upheld, the individual claims can proceed, and the defendants — having lost on this key defense — cannot raise the defense again.

The change in judicial attitude toward using the Rule 23(b)(3) class action in mass tort cases reflected the reality that the judicial system was under siege with mass tort litigation. The late Professor Charles Alan Wright was a member of the 1966 Advisory Committee and concluded then that mass torts could not be certified for class treatment. In the 1980s, however, he changed his mind: "I am profoundly convinced now that that is untrue. Unless we can use the class action and devices built on the class action, our judicial system is not going to be able to cope with the challenge of mass repetitive wrong."[149]

Predictably, perhaps, some trial courts went too far in forcing mass torts into the class action form. In the 1990s, several appellate opinions sent the message that trial judges had overreached in certifying mass tort class actions under Rule 23(b)(3). For example, in *In re Rhone-Poulenc Rorer, Inc.*,[150] the Seventh Circuit took the extraordinary step of issuing a writ of mandamus[151] to overturn the certification of a nationwide class action in a case concerning allegedly tainted blood products. In *Castano v. American Tobacco Co.*,[152] the Fifth Circuit reserved an absurd certification of a nationwide class of nicotine-dependent persons numbering in the millions. The trial judge had failed to analyze whether or how any common questions predominated. Not only did the complaint purport to rely on nine causes of action, but variations from state to state made the finding of predominant common questions nearly laughable. Such overzealous efforts, while perhaps borne of understandable frustration with the crowded dockets, created inappropriate pressure on defendants to settle.

Superiority of the Class Action. The second requirement for certification of a Rule 23(b)(3) class is that the class action be "superior to other available methods for fairly and effectively adjudicating the controversy." The Rule lists four nonexclusive factors to aid in the assessment. As a

---

[149] Charles Alan Wright, Transcript of Oral Argument July 30, 1984, at 106; In re School Asbestos Litigation, 594 F. Supp. 178 (E.D. Pa. 1984). Other leading commentators agreed. *See, e.g.*, Jack Weinstein & Eileen Hershenov, *The Effects of Equity on Mass Torts*, 1991 U. Ill. L. Rev. 269, 288 (1991): "In the earlier 1960's we did not fully understand the implications of mass tort demands on our legal system."

[150] 51 F.3d 1293 (7th Cir.), *cert. denied*, 516 U.S. 867 (1995).

[151] As discussed in §14.6, mandamus is appropriate only when the lower court has erred so profoundly that it has, in effect, overreached its jurisdiction. Today, interlocutory appellate review of class certification decisions is available through Rule 23(f).

[152] 84 F.3d 734 (5th Cir. 1996).

review of the factors reveals, the drafters clearly intended to force the judge to consider whether any other tools — joinder, multidistrict litigation under §1407,[153] consolidation, etc. — might be more readily managed than the class action. Obviously, the class action will not always be *easy* to manage and administer. It just has to be better than the other options. Just as obviously, the two requirements for a Rule 23(b)(3) class are closely related. If common questions do not predominate, manageability suffers. If the class can be defined with sufficient narrowness so that the common questions predominate, it might be relatively easy to manage.

§13.3.6 Notice to Class Members and "Opting Out"

Rule 23 has three separate provisions about notice. The first, found in Rule 23(c)(2)(B), is notice of the pendency of a class action, which applies *only* to Rule 23(b)(3) classes. The second, found in Rule 23(c)(2)(A), permits the court to give notice of the pendency of class actions under Rule 23(b)(1) and (b)(2). We discuss both of these (the first of which is far more important) in this subsection. The third, found in Rule 23(e)(1), concerns notice of a settlement or dismissal of a class action. It applies to all classes (not just Rule 23(b)(3) classes) and is discussed in §13.3.7.

We saw in the preceding subsection that the Rule 23(b)(3) class is more controversial than the other types because the group usually is bound together only by common questions and not by any legal relationship. The claims of class members generally are independent of one another. As a result, the Rule 23(b)(3) class presents great stress between the desire for efficient resolution of numerous claims and the requirements of due process. To address this stress, the drafters imposed a notice requirement in Rule 23(b)(3) class actions that simply does not exist in the other class actions. Under Rule 23(c)(2)(B), the court is required to direct notice to class members, "including individual notice to all members who can be identified through reasonable effort."

The purpose of this notice, which is sent out only after the class is certified under Rule 23(b)(3), is intended to protect the members' individual interests. Rule 23(c)(2)(B) requires the notice to inform class members of these things: (1) the nature of the action; (2) the definition of the class certified; (3) the class claims, issues, or defenses; (4) that a class member may enter an appearance through her own counsel if she desires; (5) that a class member may request exclusion (and when and how members may elect to be excluded); and (6) that the class judgment will bind class

---

[153] Section 1407 allows the Judicial Panel on Multidistrict Legislation (a panel of federal judges appointed by the Chief Justice) to transfer related cases to a district of its choosing for consolidated pretrial proceedings.

members who do not properly request exclusion. Requesting exclusion has traditionally been called *opting out* of the class action, though the Rule does not now use that phrase. This notice affirms to each class member that she does not have to depend on the class representative and class counsel to protect her interest. She can either request exclusion from the class and pursue her own remedy in a separate action (either alone or with others) or she can stay in the class, but have her own lawyer act to represent her interests. If she fails to request exclusion, and thus remains in the class, she will be bound by the class judgment.

Rule 23(c)(2)(B) requires that this notice be "the best notice that is practicable under the circumstances," including, as we said above, individual notice to those members who are identifiable with reasonable effort. This provision clearly seems more stringent than the Constitution would require. We saw in §3.2 that due process, interpreted in *Mullane v. Central Hanover Bank*,[154] requires notice "reasonably calculated, under all the circumstances, to apprise the parties of the pendency of the action. . . ." In addition, the Court spoke of giving "the best notice practicable."[155] In *Mullane* itself, however, the Court did not require individual notice to every person whose interest could be affected by the judgment, even if that person could be identified through reasonable effort. Nonetheless, in an appropriate abundance of caution, the drafters of Rule 23 require individual notice to those who can be identified reasonably. Such notice is usually given by mail, though nothing in the Rule specifies the manner in which it is to be given. It is not unusual to have some members who are reasonably identified and some who are not; in such a case, individual notice is given to those in the former group and publication notice — perhaps in newspapers or on television — is given to the latter.

Mailing individual notice to the reasonably identifiable class members can be an expensive proposition. Before the Supreme Court decision in *Eisen v. Carlisle & Jacquelin*,[156] courts occasionally would require the defendant to pay a percentage of the expense, based upon the court's assessment of the likelihood that the plaintiff class would prevail. *Eisen* rejected that practice, and the Court held that the expense of notice is a cost of litigation to be borne by the class representative. In other words, the court cannot impose any of that expense on the defendant at the outset. Of course, as a general rule, the loser is usually required to pay the winner's cost of litigation (as opposed to attorneys' fees) once the case is completed. So the representative will have to pay the expense of notice initially. Should the class prevail, however, that cost will ordinarily be

[154] 339 U.S. 306, 314-315 (1950).
[155] *Id.* at 318.
[156] 417 U.S. 156 (1974).

shifted to the defendant. Though Rule 23(c)(2)(B) was amended in December 2003, long after the *Eisen* decision, there is no reason to believe that the *Eisen* holding will not continue to apply.

Eisen undoubtedly made it more difficult to bring a class action. Many representatives are reluctant to advance the cost of notice, which often vastly outweighs the value of their claims. In *Eisen* itself, the class asserted a securities claim in which Mr. Eisen personally would stand to recover about $70. The cost of notice was over $225,000. Very few representatives will put up $225,000 for the course of litigation on the hope of recovering that sum as a cost of successful litigation, plus his own claim of $70.[157]

The Rule 23(c)(2)(B) notice emanates from the court. Judges rarely write such notices themselves, however. Ordinarily, the court asks the lawyers for the two sides to suggest notice. Not surprisingly, these efforts can be slanted. The plaintiff class lawyer usually wants the notice to say something like "you are a member of a class that has been ripped off by the greedy defendant, and you are lucky that we will do the litigating for you and will send you a check when it's all done; so don't opt out." The defendant's lawyer wants the notice to say something like "you are a putative member of a putative class that some lawyer is trying to gin up to sue the poor defendant, and none of the allegations has been proved and we did nothing wrong." From these extremes, the court usually requires the lawyers to work together to craft something both sides can live with. Unfortunately, the result is often unintelligible.

Professor Arthur Miller collected some telling responses to class notice from an actual case involving allegations that class members were overcharged for antibiotics.[158] The notice was the product of compromise, as described above, and attempted to tell the members the basics of the allegations. Class members were invited to respond with their opt-outs if they wanted to do so. In reading the responses below (which were actually received by the court), imagine how bad the notice must have been.

Dear Mr. Clerk: I have your notice that I owe you $300 for selling drugs. I have never sold any drugs, especially those you have listed; but I have sold a little whiskey once in a while.

Dear Sir: I received this paper from you. I guess I really don't understand it, but if I have been given one of those drugs, nobody told me why. If it means what I think it does, I have not been with a man in nine years.

Dear Sir: I received your pamphlet on drugs, which I think will be great value to me in the future. I am unable to attend your class, however.

---

[157] One interesting issue is whether the class lawyer can advance the cost of notice for the representative. After wrestling with the issue, the American Bar Association has concluded that the lawyer can do so on a contingent basis.

[158] Arthur Miller, *Problems of Giving Notice in Class Actions*, 58 F.R.D. 313 (1972). The article is very amusing.

In an effort to combat the sort of "legalese" that typifies notice sent to class members, Rule 23(c)(2)(B) requires that the notice "clearly and concisely state [the required contents] in plain, easily understood language."

It is important to remember that the notice we are discussing here — of the pendency of the class action and of one's membership in the class — is required only in the Rule 23(b)(3) class action. For Rule 23(b)(1) and 23(b)(2) classes, no notice is required. But Rule 23(c)(2)(A) does permit the court, in its discretion, to give notice in such cases. In addition, Rule 23(d)(1) arms the class action court with various tools with which to handle the complex litigation.

Can the lack of notice in these classes be constitutional? In §13.3.2, we noted that due process might be satisfied by providing notice or by ensuring adequate representation for the interests of class members. Rule 23 clearly envisions a combination of these protections in the Rule 23(b)(3) class. On the other hand, the drafters apparently concluded — given the close relationship of most class members in Rule 23(b)(1) and (b)(2) classes — that adequacy of representation (without notice) satisfies due process. No serious argument to the contrary has been mounted.

What about opt-outs? The Rule expressly permits them only in Rule 23(b)(3) classes. Some courts conclude, however, that they have discretion to allow opt-outs in other class actions. As amended in 2003, Rule 23 continues to allow requests for exclusions only in the Rule 23(b)(3) class and is silent on the issue in other cases.

§13.3.7 Judgment, Settlement, and Dismissal of a Class Action

A judgment in a class action binds all class members, except those who properly requested exclusion from a Rule 23(b)(3) class. Of course, it is this binding effect that makes the class action so efficient — the claims of numerous would-be plaintiffs are determined, and the determination is binding. This binding effect has always been understood and is now expressly stated in Rule 23(c)(3). Many class actions, however, do not go to judgment on the merits, either because they are settled or voluntarily dismissed. But the parties do not have autonomy in determining whether the case should be disposed of in such a way.

In most civil litigation, the parties are free to settle the dispute on whatever terms they consider appropriate. Likewise, any plaintiff is free to dismiss her case voluntarily if she meets the requirements of Rule 41(a). In neither situation — settlement or voluntary dismissal — does the court play any role in the usual case. In the class action, however, things are different. Because class actions are fraught with the potential for conflicts of interest, as we discussed in §13.3.1, Rule 23 does not permit the parties to settle or to enter voluntary dismissal of a class action. Instead, Rule 23(e) requires that the court approve either a settlement or a voluntary dismissal. To that end, it also requires notice to class members of the proposed settlement or voluntary dismissal. The class members are invited to share any feedback they may have concerning the fairness of the terms of the proposed action.

For years, courts were vexed by whether Rule 23(e) applied to cases filed as class actions but which had not yet been certified as class actions. Most courts concluded that the answer depended upon what was being settled or dismissed. If the parties had agreed to settle only the representative's claim, and not to compromise the class members' claims, courts generally concluded that Rule 23(e) did not apply, and the class members need not be given notice. On the other hand, if the settlement or dismissal related to class members' claims, courts concluded, quite rightly, that Rule 23(e) was implicated.

In December 2003, Rule 23(e) was amended to bring welcome clarity. It provides, in Rule 23(e)(1), that "[t]he claims, issues, or defenses in a certified class action may be settled, voluntarily dismissed, or compromised only with the court's approval." Thus, Rule 23(e) applies only if the court has actually certified the class, and only if the settlement, dismissal, or compromise affects class issues.

Most cases settle. Most class actions settle. Usually, counsel for the representative and for the defendants agree on terms of the settlement and present the terms to the court. The court then undertakes its first review of the terms, to determine whether they appear fair to the class members. Courts should be especially wary of settlements that give class members little of value while lining the pockets of the plaintiff's lawyer. If the court feels that the settlement is simply not fair, it will send the lawyers back to the bargaining table, without giving notice to class members. If, on the other hand, the court concludes that the settlement appears fair, it will direct notice under Rule 23(e)(1), which requires that the court "must direct notice in a reasonable manner to all class members who would be bound by the [proposed settlement, voluntary dismissal, or compromise]."[159]

Under Rule 23(e)(5), class members have the right to object to the proposed settlement, voluntary dismissal, or compromise of the class action. Rule 23(e)(2) says that "[t]he court may approve a settlement, voluntary dismissal, or compromise that would bind class members only after a hearing and on finding that [it] is fair, reasonable, and adequate." The court holds a "fairness hearing" to determine whether to approve the settlement. Obviously, the judge will consider the reaction of the class members. But

---

[159] Remember, the notice under Rule 23(e) applies in all class actions. The notice in Rule 23(c)(2) (which is notice not of settlement but of the pendency of the class action) is required only in Rule 23(b)(3) classes.

the question of whether to approve the settlement is not determined by vote of the class members. The court has the sole authority to decide whether the settlement terms are fair. If it so concludes, it will approve the settlement. If not, it will inform counsel, who may then reconsider the terms.

Some courts have been too willing to approve settlements. In one case, a district judge approved a proposed settlement of millions of consumer claims relating to alleged overcharging on loans based upon anticipated income tax refunds. A lawyer for a defendant essentially agreed to settlement terms over lunch with three lawyers who at the time did not even have clients who were members of the class! The district judge insisted on various changes to the formal settlement later hammered out, and of which a large law firm had a hand in forging; the Seventh Circuit held that the trial court abused its discretion in approving the settlement.

Under Rule 23(e)(4), the court may refuse to approve settlement of a certified Rule 23(b)(3) class unless the settlement "affords a new opportunity to request exclusion to individual class members who had an earlier opportunity to request exclusion but did not do so." In §13.3.6, we saw that members of a Rule 23(b)(3) class have a right to request exclusion from the class (and thus to avoid being bound by class judgment). The right is afforded by Rule 23(c)(2)(B), which gives notice of pendency of the class action only in Rule 23(b)(3) classes. Rule 23(e)(4) grants such members a second right to opt out, one that comes up when the case is being settled. Thus, members of a Rule 23(b)(3) class who do not like the terms of the settlement are not bound by it, may request exclusion, and proceed on their own.

In addition, Rule 23(e)(3) requires the parties seeking approval to identify "any agreement made in connection with the [proposed settlement, voluntary dismissal, or compromise.]" This provision is intended to help the court determine whether the representative is being "bought off" in a "side agreement," leaving the class members with less than appropriate relief.

We suggested above that in most class actions, the certification decision is the principal event in the litigation. If the class is certified, usually the case will settle. If the case is certified under Rule 23(b)(3), as we saw in the preceding subsection, class members are entitled to notice and the right to request exclusion. Sometimes the lawyers will agree to settlement terms before that notice is sent out. In such a case, the class may receive unified notice under Rule 23(c)(2)(B) and Rule 23(e). That is, they will be told that they are members of a Rule 23(b)(3) class and have the right to request exclusion, and that the case is provisionally settled on terms listed in the notice. Thus, each member can decide whether to request exclusion, to object to the terms of the settlement, or to accept the terms of the settlement.

If a class action is destined to be settled, must the court go through the entire certification inquiry under Rule 23(a) and 23(b)? After all, if the parties are going to agree to settlement terms, cannot the court simply proceed to assessment of the fairness of the settlement terms? The Supreme Court addressed these issues in *Amchem Products, Inc. v. Windsor*,[160] in which it held that the court must certify the class before approving the settlement. The fact that the case will settle and thus not require a trial is relevant to the manageability of the class, but does not justify wholesale ignorance of the requirements of Rule 23(a) and 23(b). The holding in *Amchem Products* is salutary. Without certification, the parties and the court are free to allow settlement of massive disputes that do not fit within any recognized form of litigation. By requiring certification, *Amchem* properly limits the ability of the court to act in properly constructed litigative units.

§13.3.8 Jurisdiction and Related Issues

Personal Jurisdiction

The Supreme Court has rarely addressed the question of personal jurisdiction in a class action. In most cases, as we saw in our detailed consideration of personal jurisdiction in Chapter 2, the relevant question is whether the court has personal jurisdiction over the defendant. Indeed, the due process protections of cases such as *International Shoe v. Washington*[161] were aimed at ensuring that the court not enter a binding judgment *against* one who does not have sufficient contacts with the forum. There is no issue of personal jurisdiction over the plaintiff, because the plaintiff initiates the litigation and thereby submits herself to the personal jurisdiction of the court.[162] Thus, the plaintiff is bound by the outcome, even if it is negative.

In the class action context, however, the issue regarding plaintiffs may not be so clear. In the plaintiff class, the representative is a party and can be seen as having invoked the jurisdiction of the court. But the class members are not parties and did not choose the forum (or the representative or the class lawyer). Must they be subject to personal jurisdiction in the forum? The issue might not seem important if the class wins and the class members receive some benefit. But what if the class loses? The defendant has a right to expect that the class members are bound by the judgment and cannot sue her separately.

---

[160] 521 U.S. 591 (1997).

[161] We discussed this case in detail in §2.4.3.

[162] This is true even if the plaintiff lacked any contacts with the forum. Remember that personal jurisdiction is a waivable defense, and one who lacks minimum contacts with a forum may nonetheless submit to its authority. See §6.2.1.

The Supreme Court addressed the topic, at least in one context, in *Phillips Petroleum Co. v. Shutts*,[163] a class action brought in a Kansas state court. The class consisted of 33,000 owners of royalty interests in gas wells. They claimed that the defendant had delayed paying their royalties, and that they were entitled to recover interest on the delayed payments. The average claim of each member of the class was about $100. The class was certified under Rule 23(b)(3) (the Kansas class action rule mirrors the Federal Rule), and the court gave notice to the class members. About 3,400 opted out, leaving a class of over 29,000 members. Of these, however, only 1,000 were Kansas citizens. The defendant was concerned that the 28,000 non-Kansas class members would not be bound by the judgment because they lacked minimum contacts with Kansas. If that were true, those 28,000 could sue the defendant separately if the defendant won the class action.

The Supreme Court held that all class members — even the 28,000 non-Kansas citizens — were bound by the judgment. Though it recognized that an adverse judgment would extinguish the claims of the class members, the Court emphasized the difference between defendants — who must have minimum contacts with the forum — and the plaintiff class members. A defendant faces significant burdens: She generally must hire an attorney in the forum, must participate in discovery, and faces liability for damages, possibly other relief and litigation costs (and maybe attorneys' fees[164]) if she loses. In sum, "[t]hese burdens are substantial, and the minimum contacts requirement of the Due Process Clause prevents the forum State from unfairly imposing them upon the defendant."[165] In contrast, the member of a plaintiff class is not haled into court to face imposition of liability. Indeed, "[a] class-action plaintiff is not required to do anything. He may sit back and allow the litigation to run its course, content in knowing that there are safeguards provided for his protection."[166]

In view of these differences, the Court concluded that the class members' due process rights were protected by the state rule requiring individual notice to known class members and a right to opt out of the class. *Shutts* thus stands for the proposition that plaintiff class members need not have minimum contacts with the forum state. Rather, their choice — after receiving notice — not to opt out constitutes their submission to the *in personam* jurisdiction of the forum. This holding raises an interesting question. A class member will be bound by a class judgment unless she

---

[163] 472 U.S. 797 (1985).

[164] The general rule is that the prevailing litigant recovers her litigation costs from the losing side. Absent an exception, however, each side bears her own attorneys' fees. Thus, the losing defendant would routinely be expected to pay the plaintiff's costs, but could be required to pay the plaintiff's attorneys' fees if some exception to the general rule applied.

[165] *Shutts*, 472 U.S. at 808.

[166] *Id.*

takes the affirmative step of opting out. But how does a court with which the class member lacks minimum contact have the authority to command the class member to do something or else be bound by its judgment? The fact that the class member does not have minimum contacts with the forum would seem to make it impermissible for that court to command an affirmative act. The Court did not explain how this could be so in *Shutts*.[167]

Beyond this, *Shutts* leaves several questions unanswered. First, does the holding apply in class actions under Rule 23(b)(1) and Rule 23(b)(2)? The Court was careful to limit its holding to a 23(b)(3) class.[168] And, as noted, it relied heavily upon the fact that the class members did not opt out of the class in concluding that they had consented to *in personam* jurisdiction. Rule 23(b)(1) or (b)(2) classes, however, are "mandatory" — there is no right to opt out. Perhaps this fact augurs toward the conclusion that a class member in a mandatory class should not be bound unless she has minimum contacts with the forum. But such a conclusion would seem contrary to the Court's discussion of the differences between plaintiff class members and defendants. As a practical matter, it is hard to believe that the Court would not uphold the binding effect of a judgment in a mandatory class action. After all, if the right to opt out is essential to render a class judgment binding, the Court likely would amend Rule 23 to permit opt-outs of Rule 23(b)(1) and (b)(2) classes.[169]

Second, must there be minimum contacts over members of a *defendant* class? In *Shutts*, the Court made it clear that its holding did not address defendant classes.[170] Though defendant class members are not parties and may be "along for the ride," just as plaintiff class members are, they may be held liable for a judgment in favor of the plaintiff. Thus, it seems likely that only those defendant class members over whom the forum has *in personam* jurisdiction may be bound. Some courts have permitted judgments involving defendant classes so long as there is *in personam* jurisdiction over the representative, even if the other class members were not

---

[167] The Court did, however, reject the assertion that due process requires that class members opt in to be bound by the judgment. The provision for notice and a right to opt out satisfies due process. *Id.* at 812.

[168] In a footnote, the Court said it would "intimate no view concerning other types of class actions, such as those seeking equitable relief." *Id.* at 811-812 n.3.

[169] *White v. National Football League*, 41 F.3d 402 (8th Cir. 1994), was a mandatory class action by professional football players. The court approved a settlement despite objections from many class members. The objectors contended that they were not bound by the settlement because the court lacked *in personam* jurisdiction over them. The Eight Circuit upheld jurisdiction, however, by holding that the objectors' appearance before the trial court to contest the settlement constituted submission to jurisdiction. The court was thus able to avoid the issue we are discussing here.

[170] *Shutts*, 472 U.S. at 811-812 n.3.

subject to jurisdiction.[171] These cases were decided before *Shutts*, however, and seem of doubtful validity today.

Finally, even with regard to a plaintiff class, did the Court in *Shutts* underestimate the possibility that the class might lose and class members might be asked to contribute to an award of defendant's costs (or, if justified, attorneys' fees)? Suppose, for example, that the case is litigated and the defendant wins. The defendant would have a right, in the ordinary course, to recover her costs from the plaintiff. Should those costs be borne solely by the named plaintiff, or can she "pass the hat" to the class? The defendant raised this issue in *Shutts*, but the Court noted that it could find no case in which such an award has been made. It did not decide the issue.[172]

Choice of Law

We just saw that *Phillips Petroleum Co. v. Shutts* held that members of a plaintiff 23(b)(3) class who did not opt out had, essentially, submitted to the *in personam* jurisdiction of forum and thus were bound by the judgment. In the same case, the Court also addressed the choice of law rules in the plaintiff class. The class in *Shutts* contended that the defendant had delayed making royalty payments on gas leases, and that the class members were entitled to recover interest on the late payments. The legal interest rate for such claims may differ from state to state. Though the class included citizens of several states, the Kansas court applied Kansas law to determine the interest to be recovered by all 28,000 class members. The Supreme Court reversed this decision, and held that the law of a state may only apply to parties who have some significant connection with that state. Accordingly, even though Kansas had personal jurisdiction over all class members, Kansas law could not be applied to claims of the non-Kansas members.

The exact holding on this point is of interest in an upper-division class on Conflict of Laws. For present purposes, though, the issue is important because it raises the possibility of subclasses. Indeed, in *Shutts*, the Court remanded with instructions to consider their use. For example, Texas citizens, as to whom Texas law would apply, could constitute one subclass, Oklahoma citizens another, and Kansas citizens another. The court would apply Kansas law only to the Kansas class members, Texas law to the Texas class members, Oklahoma law to the Oklahoma class members,

---

[171] *See, e.g.*, Dale Electronics, Inc. v. R.C.L. Electronics, Inc., 53 F.R.D. 531 (D.N.H. 1971); Canuel v. Oskoian, 23 F.R.D. 307 (D.R.I. 1959).

[172] *Shutts*, 472 U.S. at 810 n.2. Similarly, in cases in which the prevailing party may recover her attorneys' fees from the losing party, there is a question of whether class members in an unsuccessful case could be required to contribute to the defendant's attorneys' fees. The Court in *Shutts* did not address this question either.

and so forth. Though this procedure is undoubtedly complex, the use of subclasses would enable the Kansas court to achieve the kind of efficiency for which the class action was designed.

Subject Matter Jurisdiction

Like any claim in federal court, the claims asserted by a plaintiff class (or against a defendant class) must invoke federal subject matter jurisdiction. We discussed the principal bases of federal subject matter jurisdiction in Chapter 4. They included federal question jurisdiction, diversity of citizenship, and alienage jurisdiction. In addition, the Class Action Fairness Act of 2005 has opened the door to federal court based upon minimal diversity, in an express effort to channel class cases from state to federal court.

Federal Question Jurisdiction. A plaintiff class may invoke federal question jurisdiction by asserting a claim that arises under federal law. Recall that in federal question cases, the citizenship of the parties is irrelevant and there is no amount in controversy requirement. The jurisdictional rules discussed at §4.6 apply in the class context. So if the claim itself (not an anticipated defense) arises under federal law, the class action may be heard in federal court, regardless of the citizenship of the parties and regardless of the amount in controversy. Many federal class actions invoke federal question jurisdiction.

- ° A class of investors who bought stock in reliance on a misleading corporate press release sues the corporation and appropriate officers, alleging that the press release violated federal securities laws. The class claims invoke federal question jurisdiction.

Diversity of Citizenship Jurisdiction. A class action might invoke diversity of citizenship jurisdiction. Here we discuss "regular" diversity of citizenship jurisdiction under §1332(a)(2). Below we discuss the expanded subject matter jurisdiction provided by the Class Action Fairness Act of 2005. Recall from §4.5 that in a "regular" diversity case, each plaintiff must be of a different citizenship from each defendant and the amount in controversy must exceed $75,000. In the plaintiff class context, these requirements present a very straightforward question: In determining citizenship and the amount in controversy, to whom does the court look — to the representative or the class members? The answer to the question is in one way easy and in another way quite unsettled.[173]

---

[173] The same issues arise in a class action invoking alienage jurisdiction under §1332(a)(2). As we discussed in §4.6, alienage cases must be between a citizen of a state (of the United States) and a foreign citizen, and the amount in controversy must exceed $75,000.

The Class's Citizenship. The law is clear regarding whose citizenship is relevant. In *Supreme Tribe of Ben-Hur v. Cauble*,[174] the Supreme Court established that only the representative's citizenship must be diverse from that of the opposing party. In that case, representatives, who were not citizens of Indiana, sued an Indiana defendant. After judgment, the Indiana class members asserted that they were not bound, since they were not of diverse citizenship from the defendant. The Court rejected the argument. So long as the representative was of diverse citizenship from the defendant, diversity was established, and the judgment bound all class members, including those who were Indiana citizens.

The holding in *Ben-Hur* is enormously helpful from a practical standpoint because it makes the class action more readily available in federal court. A requirement that each class member must be of diverse citizenship from the opposing party would make it quite difficult to invoke diversity of citizenship jurisdiction in a class action. Though the Court in *Ben-Hur* did not discuss its holding in these terms, the case may well be seen as an example of supplemental jurisdiction. First, the representative's claim against the diverse opposing party invokes diversity of citizenship jurisdiction. Second, the claims of the class members seem sufficiently closely related to the representative's claim to invoke supplemental jurisdiction under *United Mine Workers v. Gibbs*.[175] Supplemental jurisdiction, of course, permits a federal court to entertain claims that do not satisfy diversity of citizenship, alienage, or federal question jurisdiction, and therefore would permit the assertion of claims by class members who are not of diverse citizenship from the defendant.

The Court has never explained *Ben-Hur* in this way, however. Perhaps it is better simply to see the case as holding that, for purposes of subject matter jurisdiction, the representative is the only party on the class side, and thus the only one who must be diverse from the opposing party. The Court has never questioned its holding in *Ben-Hur*, which remains vital to this day.

- Representative, a citizen of Georgia representing a class consisting of citizens of Georgia and Alabama, sues *D*, who is a citizen of Alabama. Assuming the amount in controversy requirement is satisfied, diversity of citizenship is proper. Representative is diverse from *D*. It is immaterial that members of the class are not of diverse citizenship from *D* because only Representative's citizenship is relevant on the class side.

---

[174] 255 U.S. 356 (1921).
[175] We discussed the case at §4.7. The supplemental jurisdiction statute, §1367(a), codifies the *Gibbs* standard in its grant of supplemental jurisdiction.

The Amount in Controversy. How should the court assess whether the amount in controversy requirement is satisfied in a diversity of citizenship class action? Again, here we discuss only a "regular" diversity case under §1332(a)(1), and not the quite different standards under the Class Action Fairness Act of 2005, which we discuss at the end of this chapter. For starters, the Supreme Court established in *Snyder v. Harris*[176] that the aggregation rules applicable in diversity of citizenship cases generally also apply in the class action context. Those rules, which we saw at §4.5, provide that multiple plaintiffs generally may not aggregate (add together) their claims to satisfy the amount in controversy requirement.[177]

- The class consists of 100 members. Each class member has a claim of $760. The aggregate value of the claims is $76,000. This cannot satisfy the amount-in-controversy requirement, however, because class claims, under *Snyder*, cannot be aggregated. This is still the rule under §1332(a)(1).

Suppose, in contrast, that the representative's claim exceeds $75,000, but the class members' individual claims do not. This fact pattern is different from *Snyder*, because here the claim of the representative alone *does* meet the amount in controversy requirement. It is the same situation as in *Ben-Hur*, in which the representative's citizenship satisfies the jurisdictional rule, but those of the class members do not. Consistency with *Ben-Hur* would counsel that the court look only to the representative in determining whether the amount in controversy is satisfied. Inexplicably, in addressing this issue, the Court ignored *Ben-Hur* altogether. In the unfortunate decision of *Zahn v. International Paper Co.*,[178] the Court held that the claim of *each* class member — individually — must meet the amount in controversy requirement.

The holding in *Zahn* simply cannot be reconciled with *Ben-Hur*: In determining citizenship, the court looks only to the citizenship of the representative, but in determining amount in controversy, the court looks to each class member. The inconsistency is ridiculous, since both the complete diversity rule and the amount in controversy requirements are simply statutory rules; neither is mandated by the Constitution, so there is no apparent reason for treating them differently. The dissenters in *Zahn* have a far better argument. They point out that the majority failed to reconcile

[176] 394 U.S. 332 (1969).

[177] Some courts say that there is an exception to this rule if the claim asserted is *joint* or *common*. As discussed in §4.5.3, however, these terms do not help much outside the property context.

[178] 414 U.S. 291 (1973).

its holding with *Ben-Hur* and failed to address the plausibility of supplemental jurisdiction.[179] The majority opinion is fixated upon the problem of aggregation. As discussed above, aggregation was simply not an issue in *Zahn*, because the representative's claim independently met the amount in controversy requirement. Not surprisingly, commentators criticized *Zahn* as an unprincipled decision, and most seemed to agree that the opinion was the result of an anti-diversity jurisdiction bias.[180] The result, and seemingly the intent, of *Zahn* was to make it more difficult to bring diversity of citizenship class actions in federal court.

But *Zahn* may have met its demise in 1990. In that year, Congress passed the supplemental jurisdiction statute, §1367. Shortly after the statute went into effect, commentators noticed, that by its terms, the statute overruled the result in *Zahn*, at least in some cases.[181] Recall that we discussed the structure of §1367 in §4.7. Section 1367(a) grants supplemental jurisdiction to the full extent permitted by the Constitution, which the Supreme Court determined in *United Mine Workers v. Gibbs* to include claims sharing a common nucleus of operative fact with a claim that invokes federal subject matter jurisdiction. So if the representative's claim invokes diversity of citizenship jurisdiction because the representative is of diverse citizenship from the defendant and her claim exceeds $75,000, §1367(a) grants supplemental jurisdiction over all appropriately related claims by class members, even if those claims do not exceed $75,000.

Section 1367(b) then cuts back on the grant of supplemental jurisdiction, removing it over certain listed claims, but only in diversity of citizenship cases. Nowhere in the catalogue in §1367(b), however, did Congress mention claims asserted pursuant to Rule 23. Thus, by its terms, §1367 overruled *Zahn* and permitted a class of members whose individual claims do not satisfy the amount in controversy requirement (just so long as the representative's claim does). Evidently, drafters of the statute belatedly saw the problem, and inserted into the legislative history a disclaimer of this result. Specifically, the one-sentence addition to the legislative history says that Congress "did not intend" to overrule the result in *Zahn*.[182] Thus, courts were presented with a bizarre proposition: a statute that by its terms overrules *Zahn*, but whose drafters say, in essence, "we didn't mean it." Commentators criticized the statute for creating what could only result in confusion. Three law professors who participated in drafting

---

[179] *Zahn*, 414 U.S. at 302-312 (Brennan, J., dissenting).

[180] *See, e.g.*, 16 Moore's Federal Practice at 106-61 to 106-64.1; 7A Wright & Miller at 74-76; Thomas D. Rowe, Jr., *Beyond the Class Action Rule: An Inventory of Statutory Possibilities to Improve the Federal Class Action*, 71 N.Y.U. L. Rev. 186, 193-194 (1996).

[181] The first critic of the statute to make this argument was Richard D. Freer, *Compounding Confusion and Hampering Diversity: Life After* Finley *and the Supplemental Jurisdiction Statute*, 40 Emory L.J. 445, 485-486 (1991).

[182] H.R. Rep. No. 734, H.R. Rep. No. 101-734, at 29 (1990).

the statute, however, saw no need for alarm, and concluded that the one-sentence legislative history fixed the problem and saved *Zahn*.[183]

Predictably, confusion reigned. Six Courts of Appeals — the Fourth, Fifth, Sixth, Seventh, Ninth, and Eleventh Circuits — concluded that §1367 overruled *Zahn* and permitted assertion of claims by class members that do not meet the amount in controversy requirement (again, as long as the representative's did).[184] These courts reached the conclusion by applying fundamental tenets of statutory construction. First, the court consults the language of the statute. Second, only if that language is ambiguous or would lead to absurd results does the court look to legislative history. Here, as noted above, the language of §1367 unambiguously grants supplemental jurisdiction. And the result of that language — that *Zahn* was overruled — is not absurd. Indeed, given the criticism of *Zahn*, overruling its holding made good sense. Accordingly, these six courts refused to address, let alone be bound by, the legislative history. As the first appellate case on the issue concluded, "the statute is the sole repository of congressional intent where the statute is clear and does not demand an absurd result."[185]

On the other hand, four other Courts of Appeals — the First, Third, Eighth, and Tenth Circuits — concluded that *Zahn* survived the supplemental jurisdiction statute, and thus that each class member's claim must exceed $75,000.[186] The Eighth Circuit opinion on this point was dicta, because in that case the named representative's claim did not exceed $75,000 and thus failed to invoke diversity of citizenship jurisdiction as a preliminary manner.[187] The Tenth Circuit reached its conclusion by adopting a theory that a court does not obtain "original jurisdiction" over a diversity of citizenship case unless it has subject matter jurisdiction over *each* claim in the case.[188] Because a court lacks independent subject matter

[183] Thomas Rowe, Stephen Burbank & Thomas Mengler, *Compounding or Creating Confusion About Supplemental Jurisdiction? A Reply to Professor Freer*, Emory L.J. 943, 960 n.1 (1991).

[184] *See* Olden v. Lafarge Corp., 383 F.3d 124 (6th Cir. 2004); Allapattah Servs., Inc. v. Exxon Corp., 333 F.3d 1248, 1253-1254 (11th Cir. 2003), *rehearing en banc denied*, 362 F.3d 739 (2004), *cert. granted*, 125 S. Ct. 314 (2005); Rosmer v. Pfizer, Inc., 263 F.3d 110, 114-119 (4th Cir. 2001); Gibson v. Chrysler Corp., 261 F.3d 927, 933-940 (9th Cir. 2001); In re Brand Name Prescription Drugs Antitrust Litigation, 123 F.3d 599, 607 (7th Cir. 1997); In re Abbott Laboratories, 51 F.3d 524, 527-529 (5th Cir. 1995), *aff'd by an equally divided court*, 529 U.S. 333 (2000).

[185] In re Abbott Laboratories, 51 F.3d at 529.

[186] *See* Ortega v. Star-Kist Foods, Inc., 370 F.3d 124 (1st Cir. 2004), *reversed*, Exxon Mobil Corp. v. Allapattah Servs., Inc., 545 U.S. 546 (2005); Trimble v. ASARCO, Inc., 232 F.3d 946, 961-962 (8th Cir. 2000); Meritcare, Inc. v. St. Paul Mercury Ins. Co., 166 F.3d 214, 218-222 (3d Cir. 1999); Leonhardt v. Western Sugar Co., 160 F.3d 631, 637-641 (10th Cir. 1998).

[187] *Trimble*, 232 F.3d at 964-965. Accordingly, the court had no occasion to discuss the supplemental jurisdiction issue.

[188] The theory was proposed in James E. Pfander, *Supplemental Jurisdiction and Section 1367: The Case for a Sympathetic Textualism*, 148 U. Pa. L. Rev. 109 (1999).

jurisdiction over the claims by class members that do not exceed $75,000, the theory goes, it would have no subject matter jurisdiction over any claim — not even the representative's claim. Thus, no claim is properly in federal court.[189] The Third Circuit justified its holding by resorting to the legislative history.[190]

In 2005, the Supreme Court resolved this lamentable split of authority with its decision in *Exxon Mobil Corp. v. Allapattah Servs., Inc.*[191] The Court concluded that §1367 effectively overruled *Zahn*. The Court adopted the reasoning of the majority of Courts of Appeals — that the result was clear from the face of the statute, and that legislative history is not available to alter that result unless the statutory language compels an absurd result. The Court criticized drafters of the statute for "a *post hoc* attempt"[192] to alter the result compelled by the statutory language. In stinging language, the Court said: "One need not subscribe to the wholesale condemnation of legislative history to refuse to give any effect to such a deliberate effort to amend a statute through a committee report."[193] The Court also rejected the theory that the district court does not obtain original jurisdiction over the case unless each and every claim asserted satisfies the amount in controversy.[194] Though the Court finally resolved the *Zahn* issue, it is worth reflecting on the uncertainty and expense occasioned by Congress's inability to draft a statute that comported with its legislative history. For 14 years, lawyers and courts labored in uncertainty and parties were put to great expense because of the poor effort put forth by Congress.

- ○ Representative sues on behalf of a class of purchasers of a product, alleging violation of state antitrust laws. By statute, each class member's claim is limited to $20,000. Representative, however, is entitled to seek recovery of attorneys' fees, so her claim exceeds $75,000. The representative's

---

[189] *Leonhardt*, 160 F.3d at 637-641. This reasoning has not been adopted in any other appellate holding, and is criticized by the opinions of the Fourth and Ninth Circuits and in Richard D. Freer, *The Cauldron Boils: Supplemental Jurisdiction, Amount in Controversy, and Diversity of Citizenship Class Actions*, 52 Emory L.J. 55, 79-85 (2004). It is defended in James Pfander, *The Simmering Debate over Supplemental Jurisdiction*, 2002 U. Ill. L. Rev. 1209.

[190] *Meritcare*, 166 F.3d at 21-22.

[191] 545 U.S. 546 (2005). In a companion case, the Court addressed the analogous issue in the non-class context, as we discussed at pages 629-630.

[192] 545 U.S. at 570.

[193] *Id.*

[194] 545 U.S. at 559-567. The Court was unwilling, however, to let supplemental jurisdiction overcome the complete diversity rule. See pages 631-632. Five years earlier, the Court had granted *certiorari* to resolve the same issue. Free v. Abbott Laboratories, Inc., 529 U.S. 333 (2000). Justice O'Connor recused herself from the case, and the remaining Justices split four-to-four. Thus, the Court affirmed the lower court opinion without opinion. Such a disposition by the Supreme Court has no precedential value.

citizenship is diverse from that of the defendant. Can this class action proceed in federal court?[195]

∘ The answer now is clear. First, Representative's claim invokes diversity of citizenship jurisdiction; she is of diverse citizenship from the defendant and her claim exceeds $75,000. Second, the claims by class members do not satisfy the requirements of diversity of citizenship jurisdiction because they do not exceed $75,000. Third, the claims by the class members invoke supplemental jurisdiction under §1367(a) because they arise from a common nucleus of operative fact with Representative's claim (if this point is fuzzy, see §4.7). Fourth, though §1367(b) applies in cases that invoke diversity of citizenship jurisdiction, as this one did, it does not remove supplemental jurisdiction over claims asserted under Rule 23.

Though the Supreme Court has resolved the split among the circuits on whether *Zahn* survived §1367, another problem lurks. Specifically (and oddly), §1367 may only overrule *Zahn* in cases involving a single defendant. Recall that §1367(b), which applies only in diversity of citizenship cases, removes supplemental jurisdiction over claims joined "by plaintiffs against persons made parties under Rule . . . 20." Rule 20 is the provision allowing joinder of multiple plaintiffs or defendants. If a plaintiff class action were asserted against multiple defendants (joined, obviously, under Rule 20), even if the court accepts the argument that §1367 has overruled *Zahn*, this provision of §1367(b) would deprive the court of supplemental jurisdiction over the claims by class members.[196] There is no definitive interpretation of this Rule 20 issue. So at the end of the day, the wasteful litigation spawned by this poorly drafted statute may not be ended.

Venue

There is no special venue provision for class actions. Thus, unless the case involves a claim for which there is a special venue provision, the general venue statute, 28 U.S.C. §1391, will apply. Recall from Chapter 5 that the general choices for venue are the same in diversity of citizenship cases (under §1391(a)) as they are in federal question cases (under §1391(b)). Specifically, as we discussed in §5.4.1, as a general matter, venue is proper in any district where all defendants reside or in which a substantial part of the claim arose.

---

[195] These are the facts from *Abbott Laboratories*, note 185 above.
[196] The Fifth Circuit did not address this point in *Abbott Laboratories*. It should have done so, since the case involved multiple defendants joined under Rule 20. The Supreme Court did not decide the issue in *Allapattah*, note 191 above.

The Class Action Fairness Act of 2005

At the end of §13.3.1, we discussed Congress's motivation in passing the Class Action Fairness Act of 2005 (CAFA). The clear purpose of the Act, which applies to cases filed on or after February 18, 2005, is to open the doors of federal court as widely as possible to accommodate large interstate class actions and "mass actions." Though plaintiffs can take advantage of the broad grant of federal subject matter jurisdiction in CAFA, the clear expectation is that defendants will more readily avail themselves of the right to remove such cases from state to federal court. As we discussed above, there is a widespread sense that defendants fare better in such cases in federal court than in state court.

CAFA is a very large and complicated piece of legislation, the full discussion of which is beyond our scope.[197] Our purpose here is to sketch the broad outline of the Act, to demonstrate how it facilitates access to federal court. Provisions of CAFA are spread throughout Title 28 of the United States Code. Section 1711 contains definitions for the Act. Section 1712 defines "coupon settlements," and requires that when a proposed settlement of a class action in federal court provides coupons for class members, the attorneys' fee attributable to the award of coupons must be based upon the actual value of the coupons to the class members. This provision, at §1712(a), is intended to avoid the award of large counsel fees to lawyers who procure for the class coupons that are essentially worthless. The remainder of §1712 deals with other attorneys' fee awards and judicial scrutiny of coupon settlements. Section 1713 addresses settlements in which a class member is required to pay class counsel, resulting in a net loss to the class member. Such settlements can be approved "only if the court makes a written finding that nonmonetary benefits to the class member substantially outweigh the monetary loss." Section 1714 prohibits approval of a settlement that discriminates in favor of class members geographically situated closer to the court than others. Section 1715, a very detailed provision, is aimed at requiring notification of a federal officer (usually the Attorney General) and a state officer of a proposed settlement of a case. The court cannot approve final settlement of a case under CAFA earlier than 90 days after such notice is given. The purpose of §1715 is to allow governmental input on the desirability of the settlement.

For our purposes, the most important parts of CAFA are found in amendments to §1332. The Act reorders some provisions of that statute; for instance, §1332(d) (providing that citizens of various federal enclaves such as the District of Columbia be deemed citizens of a state for diversity purposes (we saw this in §4.5.3)) is reenacted as §1332(e). Most significantly, CAFA inserts a new §1332(d), which, in §1332(d)(1) defines terms, including class action, which is a case "filed under rule 23 of the Federal Rules

---

[197] For an excellent comprehensive discussion of CAFA, *see* Vairo, note 75 above.

of Civil Procedure or similar State statute or rule. . . ." That subsection also defines "class certification order" as one "issued by a court approving the treatment of some or all aspects of a civil action as a class action."

The core of CAFA is found in the grant of subject matter jurisdiction in §1332(d)(2). The amount in controversy is one that "exceeds the sum or value of $5,000,000, exclusive of interest and costs." According to §1332(d)(6), this figure is determined by aggregating the claims of all class members. Thus, the statute represents a radical departure from the method of determining amount in controversy in a "regular" diversity of citizenship class action, which we discussed above. In addition, the CAFA grant of subject matter jurisdiction requires a class action in which any of three things is true:

1. Under §1332(d)(2)(A), "any member of a class of plaintiffs is a citizen of a State different from any defendant"; or
2. Under §1332(d)(2)(B), "any member of a class of plaintiffs is a foreign state or a citizen or subject of a foreign state and any defendant is a citizen of a State"; or
3. Under §1332(d)(2)(C), "any member of a class of plaintiffs is a citizen of a State and any defendant is a foreign state or a citizen or subject of a foreign state."

As with §1332(a), which we studied in Chapter 4, the capitalized use of "State" refers to a state of the United States; the uncapitalized use of the word refers to a foreign country. The most significant provision is §1332(d)(2)(A), which permits the exercise of minimal diversity. All CAFA requires is that a single member of the class be of diverse citizenship from any defendant. This provision is broader even than the practice permitted under the *Ben-Hur* case in "regular" diversity cases, which we discussed above. Under that case, the *representative* of the class must be diverse from *every* defendant. Under CAFA, however, a case invokes subject matter jurisdiction even if the representative and the defendant are co-citizens — so long as *some* member of the class is diverse from a defendant. And note, unlike in a "regular" diversity case, there need not be complete diversity. So long as a class member is diverse from *any* defendant, the statute is satisfied. Clearly, this statute reaches to the full extent of the constitutional grant of diversity of citizenship jurisdiction. As we discussed in §13.2.2, the Supreme Court upheld the constitutionality of such a grant in the Federal Interpleader Act. So there is no doubt of the constitutionality of CAFA.

The real importance of the Act is found in its creation of §1453, which permits removal of cases under §1332(d)(1). Here, too, Congress has reached further than it did in "regular" diversity cases. In §4.8, when we discussed removal of such a diversity case invoking §1332(a)(1), we saw that (1) removal was not permitted if any defendant was a citizen of the forum, and (2) no diversity case could be removed more than one year after the case was filed in state court. Neither of these restrictions applies, however, in removal of cases invoking CAFA.

- ◦ *P*, a citizen of Alabama, is named the representative of a class action filed in Alabama state court. Class members are citizens of Alabama, Mississippi, and Georgia. The complaint names five defendants, one of which is a citizen of Alabama. The defendants cannot remove this case under the regular provisions applicable to diversity of citizenship cases. First, there is no diversity because the representative is not of diverse citizenship from all defendants. Second, one of the defendants is a citizen of the forum, which defeats removal under §1446(b).
  - ◦ Under CAFA, however, diversity is satisfied because at least one class member is of diverse citizenship from at least one defendant. And the restriction of §1446(b) — precluding removal if a defendant is a citizen of the forum — does not apply under CAFA.

Clearly, then, CAFA is intended to make it nearly impossible for plaintiffs to structure a case in state court to make it "removal-proof." In this hypothetical, assuming the aggregate class claim exceeds $5 million, the case can be removed to federal court in Alabama.

Section 1332(d) is a startlingly complex provision. While the key to it is the grant of subject matter jurisdiction, we should note three other aspects of the statute. First, under §1332(d)(3), the federal court has discretion to decline subject matter jurisdiction "in the interests of justice and looking at the totality of the circumstances." This discretion is engaged if more than one-third but fewer than two-thirds of the members of the plaintiff class "and the primary defendants" are citizens of the state in which the case is filed. The section directs the court to consider various factors, including whether the claims involve matters of national or interstate interest. There are many problems with the provision, including the lack of a definition of "primary defendants" and the difficulty of determining how many class members are citizens of the forum. Nonetheless, the thrust of the provision seems clear: Even if the class satisfies the jurisdictional grant of §1332(d)(2), if a substantial number of those involved are citizens of the forum and the claims are mainly local in nature, the federal court might decline to exercise subject matter jurisdiction and allow the parties to litigate in state court.

Second, in §1332(d)(4), CAFA *requires* the federal court to decline subject matter jurisdiction if more than two-thirds of the members of the plaintiff class and at least one defendant from whom "significant relief is sought" and whose "alleged conduct forms a significant basis for the claims asserted" are citizens of the state in which the case is filed. There are other requirements, and, again there are definitional problems, but the idea is clear — a class action meeting these requirements is essentially local and should not proceed in federal court.

Third, CAFA recognizes something new called a *mass action*, which is addressed in §1332(d)(11) and which is a case "in which monetary relief claims of 100 or more persons are proposed to be tried jointly on the ground that the plaintiffs' claims involve common questions of law or fact." This provision is aimed at the practice in some state courts of permitting joinder of hundreds of plaintiffs in a single case, without certification as a class action.[198] Such cases can invoke subject matter jurisdiction on the same bases as class actions under CAFA. They also can be removed on the same bases. CAFA contains a staggering array of other provisions in §1332(d), including exceptions for certain securities claims and for cases involving internal affairs or governance of a corporation, and definitions and rules for determining citizenships of various litigants. It is controversial and seems aimed at permitting defendants to get virtually any large, truly interstate class action or mass action into federal court. There, the critics argue, the relatively high procedural hurdles for such cases will make it difficult and often impossible to proceed with litigation *en masse*. That being the case, they assert, CAFA fosters channeling complex cases into the federal court system, where they will fail. Without doubt, CAFA skews the historic allocation of class action litigation between the state and federal courts. Whether this is a good idea, and what effect it will have on litigation and, potentially, on the economy and the administration of justice, remain to be seen.

[198] *See* Vairo, note 75 above, at 32-38.

Chapter *14*

Appellate Review

§14.1 Defining the Issue

Almost everything we study in Civil Procedure relates to proceedings in a trial court. In this chapter, we study what happens at the appellate level of judicial systems, a topic we introduced in §1.2.2. A party who is dissatisfied with the outcome of litigation in a trial court might seek review by an appellate court. There is no federal *constitutional* right to appeal in a civil case.[1] Nonetheless, many state systems provide a right of appeal, either by statute or state constitution. The federal system has long granted a *statutory* right to appeal "final decisions" from the trial court (the United States District Court) to the United States Court of Appeals.[2] From those intermediate federal appellate courts, there is the possibility of discretionary review by the Supreme Court of the United States. So in the federal system, there are two appellate courts — the Court of Appeals and the Supreme Court. They play quite different roles, however, as we see in §14.2.

---

[1] *See, e.g.,* Estate of Kanter v. Commissioner of Internal Revenue, 337 F.3d 833, 884 (D.C. Cir. 2003).

[2] 28 U.S.C. §1291. In very rare circumstances (beyond our scope), there is direct review of district court rulings in the Supreme Court of the United States.

Many state court systems, including those in California and New York, also adopt this tripartite model, in which the three levels of courts — trial, intermediate appellate, and supreme court — function similarly to those in the federal system.[3] But states are not required to adopt this model, and some, including Maine, Nevada, and Wyoming, have opted for a two-level system, in which there are trial courts and a supreme court, but no intermediate court of appeals. In still other states, such as Virginia and Georgia, there is an intermediate court of appeals, but it hears appeals only in specialized types of cases and not in the relatively typical civil suit. In such states, there is simply no right to appeal a civil judgment. The state supreme court has discretion to review trial court results.[4]

§14.2   Purposes of Appellate Review

Appellate courts serve two functions. First, they review the trial court proceedings to determine whether the trial judge committed reversible error.[5] This function ensures that the trial court applied the law properly in resolving the case. In the federal system, this function is performed by the United States Court of Appeals. In many state court systems, it is performed by the intermediate court of appeals to which there is often some right to appeal. In these courts, the party taking the appeal is usually called the *appellant*, and the other party is the *appellee*.

Second, appellate courts interpret and exposit the law, thereby providing clarity and guidance for citizens and for the lower courts. This function is performed primarily by the ultimate court of the judicial system, where review is usually discretionary, rather than provided as a matter of right. As to matters of federal law, of course, this ultimate tribunal is the Supreme Court of the United States. In matters of state law, it will be the state supreme court. Such courts usually decide to hear cases only if they present an opportunity to clarify or elucidate the law, or to resolve splits

---

[3] States are free, of course, to call their courts whatever they wish. In New York, for example, the supreme court is the trial court, the intermediate court of appeals is called the appellate division, and the ultimate court is the New York Court of Appeals. In most states, the term *supreme court* applies to the ultimate court. In California, the intermediate appellate court is the court of appeal (singular). In most states in which an intermediate appellate court exists, it is the court of appeals (plural).

[4] In many states, the supreme court has mandatory review of capital criminal cases.

[5] Do not confuse this function with the renewed motion for judgment as a matter of law under Federal Rule 50(b), or the motion for new trial under Federal Rule 59(a), or the motion to set aside a judgment under Federal Rule 60(b) (all of which we discussed in Chapter 9). Those motions are addressed to the trial court, not an appellate court.

of authority among the lower courts.[6] The party seeking such review has a heavy burden — she must convince the highest court that the issue presented is of such importance as to require elucidation by the ultimate court. In most court systems, the party whose case the supreme court agrees to hear is called the *petitioner*, because she petitions the court to exercise its discretionary jurisdiction, and the other party is the *respondent*.

Historically, there was an important distinction between whether one sought review at the United States Supreme Court by appeal or by discretionary writ of *certiorari*. By statute, certain rulings could be reviewed by appeal; in theory, the Supreme Court had no discretion in such matters and was required to take the case. Other cases, in contrast, could be reviewed only if the Supreme Court granted the writ of *certiorari*, a decision over which it had complete discretion. Through the years, however, the Court came to treat review by appeal essentially as discretionary. Recognizing this, in 1988 Congress largely abolished Supreme Court review by appeal, meaning that today the Court has virtually unfettered discretion in deciding which cases to hear.

In deciding whether to grant the writ of *certiorari* and hear a case, the Court uses an informal "rule of four." This means the Court will take the case if four of the nine Justices agree that it is worthy of review. The Court grants *certiorari* in very few cases. In recent years, though *certiorari* is sought in several thousand cases, the Court grants the writ and hears oral argument in between 80 and 90 cases per year. In a handful of others, the Court may grant *certiorari* and enter an order without oral argument. For example, it might grant the writ and remand a case to the court of appeals for reconsideration in light of a new Supreme Court opinion.

Of course, there is no further judicial review after the Supreme Court has entered its final decision. As the late Justice Jackson put it, famously: "We are not final because we are infallible, but we are infallible only because we are final."[7] In the words of many others, if you lose at the Supreme Court, your only appeal is to God.

§14.3 Appellate Procedure in General

Sections 14.4 and 14.5 address the sorts of trial court orders that can be appealed. Here, we assume that the trial court has entered an order that is subject to appellate review, and the question is how an aggrieved

---

[6] Lower courts are sometimes referred to as *inferior* courts. This term is descriptive of the position of the court in the judicial system and is not pejorative.

[7] Justice Jackson's remark, Brown v. Allen, 344 U.S. 443, 540 (1953) (concurring opinion).

party gets the appropriate appellate court[8] to perform its review function. It is important to emphasize that practice varies from state to state, and counsel must be careful to research the applicable requirements in her jurisdiction. We can draw some general observations, however, based upon the practice in the federal courts. Throughout this book, we have referred to many provisions of the Federal Rules of Civil Procedure (Federal Rules). Those Rules, some of which are relevant to appeal, govern practice in federal trial courts. Here we must also become aware of the Federal Rules of Appellate Procedure (FRAP), which is a different body of provisions (also contained in your rules pamphlet), which govern practice in the United States Courts of Appeals.

Under FRAP 3(a)(1), the appellant must file a "notice of appeal." Surprisingly, perhaps, the notice of appeal is *not* filed in the court of appeals; it is filed in the district court.[9] Under FRAP 3(d)(1), the clerk of the district court then serves a copy of the notice on counsel for every other party to the case. The notice of appeal is a relatively simple document, which, under FRAP 3(c)(1), must specify the party or parties taking the appeal, the order from which appeal is taken, and the court to which the appeal is taken. Courts are fairly liberal, however, in accepting documents that fail to satisfy even these minimal requirements. As long as the notice identifies the parties and makes clear the desire of one of them to appeal a judgment of the trial court, it is likely to be found sufficient.[10]

This assumes, however, that the notice of appeal is filed in a timely fashion. The general rule, contained in FRAP 4(a)(1)(A), requires the appellant to file the notice of appeal within 30 days after entry of the appealable order.[11] We see some problems with applying the 30-day rule in §14.4.2. It is imperative to understand that this timing requirement is *jurisdictional*,

---

[8] In the federal system, each district court is located within a particular circuit. The courts of appeals are arranged geographically into these circuits. One appeals, obviously, from the district court to the circuit in which that district sits. So, for example, all appeals from district courts in New York go to the United States Court of Appeals for the Second Circuit; all appeals from district courts in Texas go to the Fifth Circuit. In some states, the practice is similarly arranged geographically. In others, however, the intermediate appellate court sits only in one city, and all appeals from trial courts throughout the state go there.

[9] The same seems to be universally true in state court systems: The notice of appeal is filed in the trial court.

[10] *See* Foman v. Davis, 371 U.S. 178 (1962). Courts have been very strict, however, with the requirement that the name of the appellant be stated. Torres v. Oakland Scavenger Co., 487 U.S. 312 (1988) (inadvertent omission of one of 17 appellants' names from notice of appeal fatal to the one omitted). In 1993, Fed. R. App. P. 3(c) was amended to allow general terms in naming appellants; an appeal will not be dismissed as to someone for whom the intent to appeal is clear from the notice as a whole. *See* 1993 Advisory Committee Note to Fed. R. App. P. 3(c).

[11] Under FRAP 4(a)(5), the district court may extend the time for filing a notice of appeal if a party makes such a motion no later than 30 days after the time prescribed for filing the notice has expired and shows excusable neglect or good cause.

so that failure to meet it means that the appellate court has no power over the case. The Supreme Court reiterated this fact in *Bowles v. Russell*, in which it noted that although the timing is set in a Federal Rule of Appellate Procedure, that rule is based upon a federal statute.[12] And because Congress has the power to set federal court jurisdiction (within the context of Article III), it can remove jurisdiction to hear an appeal not filed within set limits.

After filing the notice of appeal (timely), the appellant must take other steps to perfect the appeal. None of these steps is jurisdictional, though failure to satisfy these time requirements gives the appellate court the discretionary authority to dismiss the appeal. The appellant is required to pay certain filing fees and may be required to post a bond to cover costs on appeal. Interestingly, the pendency of an appeal does not stay the trial court's judgment. Indeed, a judgment against a defendant is still enforceable unless the defendant/appellant posts a bond. Such a bond — called *supersedeas* or a *suspending bond* — will "suspend" the operation of the judgment and preclude the plaintiff from executing on the judgment in the meantime. This requirement of a bond means that the defendant will have to deposit money with the court. How much money? It is usually the amount of the judgment plus interest set by law. This ensures that if the plaintiff ultimately wins, she will get not only her judgment, but post-judgment interest on the judgment, which compensates her for the time during which she did not have access to the money.

- ○ The trial court enters a final judgment in favor of Plaintiff, requiring Defendant to pay Plaintiff $250,000. Defendant files a notice of appeal. The appellate process will take months — maybe even years. Plaintiff wants her money now. The fact that Defendant has noticed an appeal does not stop Plaintiff from enforcing the judgment by having property belonging to Defendant seized and sold to raise the judgment amount. To stop Plaintiff from doing that, Defendant will have to post a suspending bond. The bond amount will be $250,000 plus some percentage thereof, to ensure that Plaintiff (if she wins on appeal) receives interest on the judgment.[13]

---

[12] 127 S. Ct. 2360, 2363-2366 (2007). Such jurisdictional timing rules are to be distinguished from claim-processing rules, which are not jurisdictional and therefore may be extended. Such claim-processing rules, according to the Court, include the time for objecting to a discharge in bankruptcy, Kontrick v. Ryan, 540 U.S. 443, 454-455 (2004), and the time in which to seek a new trial in a criminal case, Eberhart v. United States, 546 U.S. 12, 20 (2005). The Court's line-drawing in this regard has not always been convincing. For an excellent discussion of these matters, including competing policies, *see* E. King Poor, *Jurisdictional Deadlines in the Wake of* Kontrick *and* Eberhart: *Harmoninzing 160 Years of Precedent*, 40 Creighton L. Rev. 181 (2007). Mr. Poor is a distinguished lawyer who argued the *Kontrick* case at the Supreme Court.

[13] As a general rule, a winning claimant is entitled to recover interest on the judgment, commencing the day the judgment is entered. Stated another way, she is entitled to

In addition, the appellant is responsible for ensuring that the record of the trial court is transmitted to the appellate court. Under FRAP 10(a), this record consists of the original papers and exhibits filed in the district court, the transcript (if any) of proceedings at the trial court, and a certified copy of the docket entries prepared by the district court clerk.[14] Counsel must work with the office of the clerk at the district court to have the record prepared and transmitted to the appellate court.

Then counsel for each side will brief the issues raised on appeal. The appellant's brief is filed first, followed by the appellee's brief, sometimes followed by a "reply brief" by the appellant. The parties also prepare and file an appendix, which is a collection of the most important and useful documents from the record. This puts the relevant materials directly in the hands of the appellate judges who will be hearing the case. The appellant generally can seek reversal only on the basis of an objection she made in the trial court. It is critical, therefore, that counsel make objections on the record, so they can be the basis for an appeal. Objections at the trial court must be timely; for example, objections to jury instructions usually are waived if not made before the jury retires to deliberate.[15] The appellee can defend the judgment on any basis that is supported in the record. The appellee may also file a cross-appeal if she wishes to raise matters not addressed at trial or to gain relief not accorded her by the trial court.

Of course, appellate courts do not hold trials. They do not hear the presentation of evidence. Rather, the judges of the appellate court read the briefs and, in appropriate cases, hear oral argument by counsel for appellant and appellee. An appellate court's functions, then, are discharged "on the record."[16] The court is there to review what happened at the trial court, not to augment the record by taking evidence or considering issues not

---

"post-judgment" interest. She is not entitled to "pre-judgment" (or "aleatory") interest. So assume a plaintiff sues for $100,000. Generally, she is not entitled to recover interest on that sum for the time spent in litigation in trial court (even if that takes years to complete). Once the judgment is entered, however, she is entitled to recover that amount plus interest (set by law).

[14] Notice that FRAP 10(a)(2) refers to the transcript "if any." There is no requirement that trial proceedings be recorded stenographically, but they almost always are, at least in federal court. Having the stenographic record converted to transcript form is an expensive proposition and is a cost the appellant must bear. She pays the court reporter for this service. In some states, where there is no transcript, counsel may prepare a written summary of the trial, which is presented to the trial judge for correction before being transmitted to the appellate court.

[15] See, e.g., Larson v. Neimi, 9 F.3d 1397 (9th Cir. 1993) (requirement strictly enforced).

[16] In some state court systems, a party may "appeal" the judgment of a trial court to another trial court. Such a procedure usually involves what are essentially small claims courts. For example, in Virginia, the general district court can hold trials in civil cases involving damages of $15,000 or less. An aggrieved litigant may "appeal" to the circuit court, which is the trial court of general subject matter jurisdiction. This "appeal," however, consists of a trial de novo. In other words, the case is treated as if it had been filed originally in the

addressed to the trial court. Oral argument, when permitted, is strictly limited — often to 20 or 30 minutes per side — and is usually punctuated by active questioning from the judges. Most intermediate appellate courts, including the United States Courts of Appeals, hear cases in panels of three judges.[17] In contrast, all justices[18] of supreme courts, including the Supreme Court of the United States, usually sit at oral argument.

After oral argument, the judges retire to "conference," where they decide the case. This conference is attended only by the judges, and the discussions are confidential and closely guarded. The senior judge of the panel, if she is in the majority, assigns to herself or one of the other judges in the majority the task of writing the opinion. If she is in the minority, she may issue a dissenting opinion. Drafting the opinion — even in a case in which the judges are unanimous — may take several months. The judge then circulates her draft opinion to the other judges on the panel. There may be some give-and-take on language and reasoning. Eventually, however, the majority signs the opinion and it is released to the parties. The court will then decide whether the opinion should be published. Opinions of the United States Courts of Appeals are published in the Federal Reporter.

The court of appeals may dispose of the appeal in one of several ways. It might affirm what the trial court did. Or it may reverse and command the trial court to enter a particular order. It might reverse and remand for further proceedings. It may vacate the trial court order, which essentially expunges it from the record. No doubt you have seen examples of each of these in reading cases for your various courses. One bit of terminology should be emphasized (one we mentioned in §1.2.2). When an appellate court disagrees with the result reached by a lower court in the same case, it may "reverse" that order. When an appellate court decides that an earlier case should no longer be considered precedent for its jurisdiction, it "overrules" that opinion. Thus, for example, in the famous *Erie* case (which is the focus of Chapter 10), the Supreme Court overruled *Swift v. Tyson*.

---

circuit court. Because this is not a true appellate review on the record, the general district courts are known as courts "not of record."

[17] In extraordinary cases, as when panels of the same circuit have rendered inconsistent opinions, a United States Court of Appeals might hear a case "en banc," which means that all active judges of that circuit would participate in the oral argument and decision. *See* FRAP 35(a).

[18] In the federal system, the term *justice* refers only to a member of the Supreme Court. Members of the United States Courts of Appeals and the federal district court judges are referred to as "judge." It is rather surprising how often one hears lawyers who should know better refer to a judge of the court of appeals as a "justice." State practice varies. In New York, the term *justice* refers to the trial judge. (Remember, New York calls its trial court the supreme court, see note 3 above.) Judicial officers on the other courts in New York are called *judges*.

§14.4   The Final Judgment Rule

§14.4.1   Section 1291

In the federal system, 28 U.S.C. §1291 provides that the courts of appeals "shall have jurisdiction of appeals from all final decisions of the district courts of the United States. . . .[19] Thus, the statutory right to appeal is limited to "final decisions." For present purposes, it is helpful to consider that every order and decision by a trial court is either "final" or "interlocutory." The two are mutually exclusive. A final judgment is one that resolves the entire case. As the Supreme Court has said: A final judgment is one that "ends the litigation on the merits and leaves nothing for the [trial] court to do but execute the judgment."[20] Such rulings are appealable under §1291. All other trial court rulings are interlocutory, and are not appealable under §1291.[21]

Obviously, most decisions made during a case are interlocutory. Indeed, there may be hundreds of interlocutory decisions during a case. For example, orders permitting an amended pleading, allowing permissive intervention, compelling answers to discovery, setting a trial date, limiting cross-examination, overruling or granting objections to evidence at trial are all interlocutory. These issues may be important — even pivotal — to the outcome of the case, and they might be decided once and for all, but they do not resolve the *case* finally, and thus cannot be appealed as "final decisions" under §1291. In addition, *denials* of motions that would resolve the case — such as denials of motions to dismiss or for summary judgment or for judgment as a matter of law — are interlocutory. Again, they may be important, but such decisions do not resolve the case. They leave the case in status quo and thus cannot be appealed as "final decisions" under §1291.

Does the final judgment rule mean that the litigant who lost the ruling on an interlocutory order is without appellate remedy? No. Such a litigant has two possible routes to the appellate court: Either the issue qualifies for an exception to the final judgment rule (see §14.5 below) or she must await entry of the final judgment. Under the final judgment rule, review is

---

[19] The provision makes an exception for the United States Court of Appeals for the Federal Circuit, which has specialized subject matter jurisdiction, including appeals in patent cases. *See* 28 U.S.C. §§1292(c) and 1295(d) regarding the Federal Circuit.

[20] Catlin v. United States, 324 U.S. 229, 233 (1949).

[21] An order remanding a case from federal court to state court (after the case was removed — see §4.8) ends the jurisdiction of the federal court. Nonetheless, by statute, the order generally cannot be reviewed by appeal or otherwise. 28 U.S.C. §1447(d). There is an express exception in the statute for remand of certain civil rights cases from state court. And courts occasionally find ways to permit appellate review in the federal system of some remand orders, but only in limited and somewhat complicated circumstances. *See* 19 Moore's Federal Practice §205.08[1].

delayed until the entire case is resolved. So the final judgment rule does not *preclude* appellate review of interlocutory rulings — it simply *delays* such review.

The final judgment rule is based upon the policy of avoiding piecemeal review of issues as they arise in the trial court. If the system permitted a disgruntled party to appeal each issue as it came up, the trial court proceedings could be delayed markedly. It would interrupt the flow of the trial court proceedings and, at some point, the trial judge would come to resent the constant intrusion of the appellate court. In addition, the final judgment rule ultimately avoids appellate review of many issues altogether. That is, a litigant who feels that the trial judge made various errors, but who ultimately wins the case, will not appeal. If the issues had been appealable as they arose in the case, the appellate court would have made determinations that, in the long run, were unnecessary. Further, the final judgment rule permits the appellate court to have the entire case before it at once. This allows it to view the various alleged errors in context, which may inform its ultimate resolution.[22]

Despite these benefits, some jurisdictions reject the final judgment rule and permit piecemeal appeals throughout the course of litigation. New York seems to have the most broad-ranging practice in this regard.[23] On the positive side, such review does permit the appellate court to remedy an error before it can compound problems at the trial court. But this benefit can be realized in a jurisdiction adopting the final judgment rule by recognizing exceptions to permit interlocutory review when it would be ameliorative.

§14.4.2 The Single Litigative Unit Approach to "Final Decision"

Jurisdictions might adopt different definitions of what constitutes a final decision that can be appealed under the final judgment rule. For example, one might consider that once the trial court has definitively resolved a particular issue in the case, that decision is "final" and can be appealed. Such a reading might be especially appropriate in federal court under §1291 because that statute permits appeals from final "decisions," and does not mention final "judgments." But the federal courts have not adopted such an interpretation. Instead, federal courts embrace the notion that the *entire case* before the trial court constitutes a single litigative unit for

---

[22] Cohen v. Beneficial Industrial Loan Corp., 337 U.S. 294, 305 (1962) (final judgment rule "combine[s] in one review all stages of the proceeding that effectively may be reviewed and corrected if and when final judgment results").

[23] New York permits appeal of any order, including an interlocutory order, that "involves some part of the merits" of the case. N.Y. CPLR §5701(a)(2)(iv).

which there can be but a single final judgment and a single appeal.[24] This idea made sense under older joinder rules, when the entire case consisted only of closely related parties and claims. Then, awaiting the final judgment, while occasionally frustrating, worked no particular hardship on anyone. After all, because the claims and parties are related, everyone will probably be engaged in the litigation pending the final outcome.

Under modern joinder principles such as those applicable in federal court, however, the single litigative unit theory can make far less sense. As we saw in Chapter 12, a single civil case in federal court can involve many completely unrelated claims and parties. For example, under Federal Rule 18, which we discussed in §12.3, a plaintiff may assert any claims she has against a defendant, regardless of factual or legal relatedness. Similarly, a defendant may inject into the case claims wholly unrelated to the underlying dispute by filing a permissive counterclaim, which we saw at §12.5.1. As interpreted in federal court under the single litigative unit theory, however, an order completely resolving one claim — but leaving unrelated claims to be determined — is not a "final decision" under §1291. And because it does not resolve the *entire case*, it is not appealable.

- P sues D for injuries from a tort and asserts a completely unrelated claim for breach of contract in a business deal between the two. The court dismisses the tort claim as barred by the statute of limitations. Under the single litigative unit theory, P cannot appeal that dismissal now, because the contract claim is still pending.
- P sues D on a tort claim; D asserts a permissive counterclaim under Federal Rule 13(b) for a completely unrelated contract claim. The court grants summary judgment in favor of D on P's claim. Again, under the single litigative unit theory, P cannot appeal now, because the contract claim is still pending.
- Mother and Daughter, as co-plaintiffs, sue a pharmaceutical company. They allege that a drug it manufactured, and that Mother took while pregnant with Daughter, caused harm to both. The court dismisses Mother's claim as barred by the statute of limitations. Under the single litigative unit theory, Mother cannot appeal now, because the claim by Daughter remains pending.[25]

In such instances, application of the single litigative unit theory can be wasteful and even unfair. Suppose, for example, that in each of these three examples, the parties spend two years litigating the remaining claim before final judgment is entered. Then the appellate court reverses the dismissal of the first claim and remands that claim for trial. In the meantime, the parties have lost over two years in prosecuting a wholly unrelated claim at the trial court. During the delay, witnesses might have died or forgotten

---

[24] *See, e.g.,* Collins v. Miller, 252 U.S. 364, 370 (1920).

[25] *See* Robinson v. Parke-Davis & Co., 685 F.2d 912 (4th Cir. 1982).

key facts or evidence might have disappeared. Clearly, a more flexible approach would be appropriate in cases involving final disposition of separate and unrelated claims. (Federal Rule 54(b) provides such a flexible approach, as we see in §14.4.3.)

We saw in §14.3 that FRAP 4(a)(1)(A) requires the appellant to file her notice of appeal in the district court within 30 days after entry of the appealable order, and that this requirement is jurisdictional. In most cases, the date on which the 30 days starts to run will be clear.[26] As we saw in §9.3, Federal Rule 58 provides that a judgment of the district court is effective only after it is entered in a separate document in accordance with Federal Rule 54 and noted on the docket sheet in the district court. One reason for such mechanical requirements is to set a precise date from which to measure the time for filing a notice of appeal. The situation becomes more complicated, however, when a party makes a post-judgment motion in the district court.

Suppose the district court enters final judgment on June 1. As we saw in §§9.5 and 9.6, the losing party might, within ten days after entry of that judgment, move for a new trial or make a renewed motion for judgment as a matter of law (assuming she had met the requirements for doing so). Suppose a party makes such a motion on June 9, and the district court rules on the motion on June 20. When did the 30-day period under FRAP 4(a)(1)(A) start to run — on June 1 or on June 20? Fortunately, the answer is made clear by FRAP 4(a)(4)(A), which provides the 30-day period starts to run on the date on which the court rules on the motion (assuming, of course, the motion was timely). So the party taking an appeal would have 30 days from the court's ruling on the motion in which to file her notice of appeal.[27]

Of course, the court's ruling on a post-trial motion might render nonfinal a judgment that was final. How? Suppose the district court enters final judgment. Instead of taking an appeal from the final judgment, the losing party makes a timely motion for new trial. If the court *grants* the motion for new trial, the other party (the one who won the judgment) cannot appeal. Why? An order of new trial is not a final judgment — it does not wrap up the litigative unit. Indeed, as we discussed in §9.6, it constitutes the court's holding that the case go back to trial. On the other hand, grant or denial of a renewed motion for judgment as a matter of law would be final. Either ruling will end the litigation at the trial court. Why? Because

---

[26] We discussed timing in general in §7.3.3. The day on which the judgment is entered does not count toward the 30 days. The following day is Day 1 of the 30. The notice of appeal must be filed no later than Day 30. If that day falls on a Saturday, Sunday, or holiday, the notice of appeal may be filed on the next business day.

[27] The same would be true under FRAP 4(a)(4)(A) if a party had moved to alter or amend the judgment under Federal Rule 59, or to amend or make additional factual findings under Federal Rule 52(b), or to set aside the judgment under Federal Rule 60(b) (if such motion was filed within ten days after entry of judgment).

either the court leaves the judgment exactly where it is or it enters judgment for the other side; either way, the trial court case is over.

One post-trial motion that has gotten litigants into trouble is the motion for an award of attorneys' fees under Federal Rule 54. Under the general American Rule, discussed at §§1.1 and 9.3, each side bears her own attorneys' fees, but exceptions to that rule permit a prevailing party in some circumstances to recover her attorneys' fees from the losing side. In *Budinich v. Becton Dickinson & Co.*,[28] the trial court entered final judgment. The prevailing party then moved for an award of attorneys' fees under an exception to the American Rule. The court entered its order awarding fees. Only then did the losing party file a notice of appeal. It filed within 30 days after entry of the order awarding fees — but more than 30 days after entry of the final judgment. The Supreme Court held that the appeal was late; the appellate court had no jurisdiction. In other words, the motion for attorneys' fees (or for taxation of costs) does *not* extend the time for filing the notice of appeal.

This matter is expressly addressed in FRAP 4(a)(4)(A)(iii), which provides that the 30-day period will run from the district court's ruling on a motion for attorneys' fees *only* if the district court extended the time to appeal under Federal Rule 58. The latter Rule provides, *inter alia*, that the time for appeal is not extended "to tax costs or award fees, except that, when a timely motion for attorneys' fees is made under Rule 54(d)(2), the court, before a notice of appeal has been filed . . . may order that the motion have the same effect under [FRAP] 4(a)(4) as a motion [for new trial]." Thus, ordinarily, a motion for attorneys' fees does not extend the time for appeal. Only if the district court expressly orders that the motion has the effect of a new trial motion will the motion extend the time in which to appeal.

In any case, the prevailing party generally is permitted to recover her costs from the losing party. She will make a motion to recover such costs after entry of the judgment. A motion for the award of costs does not extend the time for filing the notice of appeal. As the Court in *Budinich* made clear, assessment of fees and costs is merely a "housekeeping" matter that has no bearing on the outcome of the case on the merits, and therefore should not delay the time for taking an appeal.

§14.4.3   Federal Rule 54(b) and Multiclaim or Multiparty Cases

Federal Rule 54(b) is not an exception to the final judgment rule. Rather, it shifts the focus away from the single litigative unit theory and allows appeal of final judgments of discrete parts of a case — parts that involve

---

[28] 486 U.S. 196 (1988).

final determination of one or more (but fewer than all) claims or one or more (but fewer than all)[29] parties. The Rule has three requirements. In discussing them, we refer back to the three hypotheticals that appeared shortly above (after the second paragraph of text in §14.4.2).

First, the case must involve "more than one claim for relief" or "multiple parties." In most instances, it will be obvious whether this requirement is met. The first two examples of the three hypotheticals in §14.4.2 clearly involve multiple claims for relief, since the assertions of liability involved unrelated factual circumstances.[30] Similarly, the third example falls within Rule 54(b) because it involves disposition of the entire claim involving one of multiple parties; after the ruling, Mother has no role in the litigation. Unfortunately, not all cases are this clear. The definition of "more than one claim for relief" has proved difficult in some contexts. For starters, the fact that a claimant seeks to recover under different legal theories does not necessarily mean that the case involves multiple claims. In one case, for example, the plaintiff alleged separate counts for negligence and strict liability, but the court concluded there was only one "claim" and thus that Rule 54(b) did not apply.[31]

In making the assessment of whether there are multiple claims, some courts have drawn an analogy to claim preclusion. They conclude that Rule 54(b) will not apply if the claims would be considered a single claim under principles of claim preclusion.[32] Though this proxy may be useful, it cannot always be determinative.[33] In §11.2.3 we saw that most courts define "claim" for claim preclusion purposes as all rights to relief arising from a transaction or occurrence. The Supreme Court has held, however, that the fact that claims arise from the same transaction or occurrence does not automatically mean that they are not separate for purposes of Rule 54(b).[34]

A more useful proxy may be to ask whether the different "claims" would support only a single recovery.[35] If so, they cannot be separate claims under Rule 54(b). As we have seen in other areas, however, the search for a single test is futile. Matters of this sort are best decided pragmatically,

---

[29] Obviously, if a judgment concluded all claims as to all parties, it would be appealable as a final judgment under §1291.

[30] See, e.g., Hudson River Sloop Clearwater, Inc. v. Department of the Navy, 891 F.2d 414 (2d Cir. 1989) (factually distinct claims are separate under Federal Rule 54(b)).

[31] See, e.g., Indiana Harbor Belt R.R. v. American Cyanamid Co., 860 F.3d 1441 (7th Cir. 1988).

[32] See, e.g., Automatic Liquid Packaging, Inc. v. Dominik, 852 F.2d 1036 (7th Cir. 1988).

[33] See Olympia Hotels Corp. v. Johnson Wax Dev. Corp., 908 F.2d 1363 (7th Cir. 1990) (suggesting limits of claim preclusion analogy).

[34] Cold Metal Process Co. v. United Engineering & Foundry Co., 351 U.S. 445 (1956) (fact that unadjudicated claim was a compulsory counterclaim, arising from the same transaction or occurrence as the adjudicated claim did not preclude appeal under Rule 54(b)).

[35] In re Southeast Banking Corp., 69 F.3d 1539, 1549-1550 (11th Cir. 1995).

with sensitivity to the underlying purpose of the Rule. The ultimate question is whether on the facts of each case assertions for relief are sufficiently different as to justify immediate appeal when they are resolved.[36]

Second, the trial court's order must be a final judgment as to at least one claim or as to at least one party. As noted above, Rule 54(b) does not obviate the final judgment rule. Rather, it changes the focus. Instead of requiring a final judgment as to the *overall case*, there must be a final judgment as to at least one claim or party.[37] One helpful way to assess this factor is to ask whether the order would be a final judgment if the claim adjudicated had been a separate, hypothetical case.[38] In each of the three examples at page 788, the answer would be yes. If *P*'s tort claim in the first and second examples were a separate case, the order dismissing it under the statute of limitations would be a final judgment under §1291. Likewise, if Mother's claim in the third example had been a separate suit, the dismissal would have been a final judgment as to it.

- Suppose in the case by Mother and Daughter that the trial court orders that Mother answer particular questions at her deposition, over her objection. Can Mother use Federal Rule 54(b) to gain appellate review of that issue now? No, because the order does not constitute a final judgment on the claim involving Mother. If Mother's case were seen as a separate suit, this order would not be appealable under §1291.

Third, Rule 54(b) requires that the trial court "may direct entry of a final judgment as to one or more" claims or parties, but only if it "expressly determines that there is no just reason for delay." So not only must the judge refer to the order as a final judgment as to the claim or party involved; she must also make the express determination on the record that there is no just reason to delay appeal on that claim or as to that party. These express requirements are salutary, because they ensure that there is no doubt about when the time for appeal starts to run.

- Assume the trial court enters an order disposing of one of multiple claims or of all matters regarding one of multiple parties. But the trial court does not make the express certification required by Rule 54(b). Can the

[36] Curtiss-Wright Corp. v. General Electric Co., 446 U.S. 1, 8 (1980) (court should "consider such factors as whether the claims under review were separable from the others remaining to be adjudicated and whether the nature of the claims already determined was such that no appellate court would have to decide the same issues more than once even if there were subsequent appeals").

[37] The Supreme Court has upheld the validity of the Rule under 28 U.S.C. §2072(c), which is part of the Rules Enabling Act (discussed in §10.6). Sears, Roebuck & Co. v. Mackey, 351 U.S. 427 (1956).

[38] See Horn v. Transcon Lines, 898 F.2d 589, 593 (7th Cir. 1990) ("ask whether [the order adjudicating the claim] would count as a final decision in a hypothetical independent case").

appropriate party take an appeal now? No. Rule 54(b) only applies if the court makes the express determination required on the record.[39] If it fails to do so, Rule 54(b) does not apply. In that case, the single litigative unit theory applies. Because this order did not resolve the overall litigation, it is not appealable under §1291.

The trial court's certification that the requirements of Rule 54(b) have been met is not binding on the appellate court. That court must determine whether the requirements are met and thus whether the appeal is properly before it.[40] Again, Rule 54(b) is not an exception to the final judgment rule — it just changes the focus on what constitutes a final decision. We turn now to actual exceptions to the basic rule requiring entry of a final judgment.

§14.5 Exceptions to the Final Judgment Rule

The final judgment rule imposes a significant restriction on appellate jurisdiction. Systems adopting the final judgment rule approach, including the federal system, recognize the need for exceptions to permit occasional appeal of interlocutory orders. In the federal system, authority for interlocutory review can be found in statutes and Federal Rules, as well as in judge-made doctrine. In each, it is important to note the policy interests that permit the appellate court to override the usually controlling principal of avoiding piecemeal appeals.

§14.5.1 Statutory and Rules-Based Exceptions

Section 1292(a)

The three subsections of 28 U.S.C. §1292(a) expressly permit appeal from specific types of interlocutory orders: (1) those "granting, continuing, modifying, refusing or dissolving injunctions, or refusing to dissolve or modify injunctions"; (2) those "appointing receivers, or refusing orders to wind up receiverships or to take steps to accomplish the purposes thereof"; and (3) those "determining the rights and liabilities of the parties to admiralty cases in which appeals from final decrees are allowed." Congress has determined that these orders are so important that appellate review should not await final judgment. In other words, as to such orders,

---

[39] Reiter v. Cooper, 507 U.S. 258 (1993) (no appeal of final determination of claim in multiclaim case absent Rule 54(b) determination and direction).

[40] Liberty Mutual Ins. Co. v. Wetzel, 424 U.S. 737 (1976) (trial court incorrectly concluded that it had finally adjudicated one of multiple claims).

the policy against piecemeal appeals — reflected in the final judgment rule — is overborne by the importance of immediate appellate review.

- ◦ *P* sues *D* for a permanent injunction to stop *D*'s operation of a business that allegedly violates zoning restrictions and damages *P*. The trial court enters a preliminary injunction shutting down *D*'s business pending final disposition of the case (or refuses so to order). That order (or the refusal so to order) is appealable immediately under §1292(a). Clearly, the order has such immediate and important consequences that permitting inter-locutory review outweighs the usual policy of avoiding piecemeal appeals.
- ◦ Would that order for (or refusing) a preliminary injunction be appealable under Rule 54(b) (which we saw in §14.4)? No. The trial court could not have certified the issue for immediate appeal under Rule 54(b) because it is not a final judgment. Remember that Rule 54(b) requires a final judg-ment (not an interlocutory order) as to one or more claims or parties in a case.

Because it permits appeal without final judgment, many courts have concluded that §1292(a) must be strictly construed.[41] On the other hand, courts have taken a pragmatic approach to whether an order falls within the statute. Thus, an order that has the *effect* of an injunction will trigger §1292(a) even if the court did not refer to it as an injunction.[42] Conversely, the fact that relief is referred to as injunctive does not ensure that §1292(a) applies. Again, it is the practical effect of the order that controls.[43]

In addition to considering the actual effect of the order — whether it is injunctive in nature — the courts impose requirements that do not appear on the face of the statute: (1) that the order create the risk of serious con-sequences for the appealing party, and (2) that the order effectively be unreviewable if the parties must await final judgment. In *Carson v. Ameri-can Brands, Inc.*,[44] the trial court refused to approve a class action settle-ment. The refusal created a serious possibility of harm to the erstwhile class members because it denied them the terms of the settlement (includ-ing injunctive relief). Thus, the Supreme Court characterized the order as having the practical effect of the denial of an injunction. For this reason, and because serious harm could result, which would not effectively be sub-ject to review if the parties awaited final judgment, the order was appeal-able under §1292(a). Similarly, in another case, grant of partial summary

---

[41] *See, e.g.,* In re Ingram Towing Co., 9 F.3d 513, 515 (5th Cir. 1995).

[42] *See, e.g.,* Aetna Cas. & Ins. Co. v. Markanian, 114 F.3d 346 (1st Cir. 1997) (order pre-venting party from leaving jurisdiction, although called writ of *ne exeat*, operates as an injunction and invokes §1392(a)).

[43] *See, e.g.,* Metex Corp. v. ACS Industries, Inc., 748 F.2d 150 (3d Cir. 1984) (although styled as a motion for injunction, in effect the order sought discovery; not appealable under §1392(a)).

[44] 450 U.S. 79 (1981).

judgment invoked §1292(a) because it had the injunctive effect of terminating employee contributions to a union's pension fund and thus threatened serious consequences for the fund's beneficiaries.[45]

One area of uncertainty is whether §1292(a) applies to orders concerning temporary restraining orders (TROs). The general rule is that TROs are not subject to interlocutory review as injunctive orders under §1292(a).[46] This rule makes good sense, since TROs are usually of very limited duration; the issue will almost always be moot by the time the appellate court could entertain the appeal.[47] As with other topics, however, the courts look to the substance of the matter, and not the terminology. So if what the trial court called a TRO has in effect become a preliminary injunction, §1292(a) will apply.[48] Similarly, although denial of a TRO is not generally appealable, a party may invoke §1292(a) if she can show that the denial effectively removes the possibility of receiving any injunctive relief and causes serious harm that could not be reviewed meaningfully on final judgment.[49]

Section 1292(b)

Section 1292(b) of the Judicial Code (28 U.S.C. §1292(b)) permits appeal of interlocutory orders if both the trial and appellate courts agree that three things are true. When they do so, the two levels of the judiciary are in accord that the situation warrants a departure from the final judgment rule. First, the order must "involve[] a controlling question of law." Second, that controlling question must be one "as to which there is substantial ground for difference of opinion." And third, "an immediate appeal from the order may materially advance the ultimate termination of the litigation." The district judge must first conclude that these requirements are established, after which the appellate court must agree that the interlocutory review should be permitted.[50] The procedure is usually referred to as "certification" of the issue by the district court to the court of appeals.

---

[45] Manchester Knitted Fashions, Inc. v. Amalgamated Cotton Garment & Allied Industries Fund, 967 F.2d 688 (1st Cir. 1992).

[46] *See* Board of Governors v. DLG Financial Corp., 29 F.3d 993 (5th Cir. 1994).

[47] A TRO cannot exceed ten days unless the trial court extends it up to an additional ten days on showing of good cause. It may be extended further on agreement of the parties. Fed. R. Civ. P. 65(b).

[48] *See, e.g.,* Baker Elec. Cooperative v. Chaske, 28 F.3d 1466 (8th Cir. 1994) (TRO in effect 30 months had become injunction).

[49] *See, e.g.,* Religious Tech. Center v. Scott, 869 F.2d 1306 (9th Cir. 1989) (denial of TRO effectively denial of preliminary injunction and thus appealable).

[50] The party taking the appeal must apply to the court of appeals within ten days of the district court's certification as to the first two requirements. 28 U.S.C. §1292(b). Note the contrast between §1292(b) and Federal Rule 54(b). In the former, both the trial and appellate courts must independently agree that the three requirements are satisfied. In the latter, the appellate court may only review whether the trial court properly assessed the

This statute strikes a salutary balance between the general policy of avoiding piecemeal appeals and the need to permit some interlocutory review. Unlike §1292(a), it is not subject-specific. The interlocutory order might involve any substantive issue, just so the three requirements are met. When they are, the final judgment rule is appropriately obviated to permit decision of an important and difficult question, the resolution of which may speed the ultimate disposition of the dispute. Whether the statute is satisfied is a fact-specific, ad hoc determination.

The issue subject to appeal might be wholly unrelated to the substance of the underlying controversy. Indeed, one use of this device has been to assess subject matter jurisdiction.

> ∘ *P* sued two defendants, *D-1* and *D-2*. As to *D-1*, *P*'s claim invoked diversity of citizenship jurisdiction. As to the claim against *D-2*, however, *P* sought to invoke supplemental jurisdiction. The case arose before the passage of the supplemental jurisdiction statute, and the supplemental jurisdiction issue was a difficult one, on which the courts of appeals had disagreed. The trial court concluded that it had supplemental jurisdiction, but certified the question under §1292(b). The court of appeals agreed to hear the issue, as did the Supreme Court, which ultimately held there was no supplemental jurisdiction.[51]

This case demonstrates the utility of the statute. Had the issue not been certified and reviewed on an interlocutory basis, the parties would have had to litigate the case on the merits fully before obtaining appellate review. In view of the ultimate holding that there was no subject matter jurisdiction over the claim by *P* against *D-2*, such litigation would have been a complete waste of time, effort, money, and judicial resources.

But judicial savings alone does not justify use of §1292(b). The matter must involve a question of law on which there is ground for disagreement and, thus, a reasonable chance of reversal. Accordingly, topics addressed to the discretion of the trial judge, on which there is little likelihood of reversal, may be less appropriate for treatment under §1292(b). Moreover, the issue may be so collateral to disposition of the case that its expeditious resolution will not advance the ultimate disposition of the case.[52]

---

requirements. Of course, the major difference between the two provisions is that the former applies to interlocutory rulings while the latter addresses final rulings disposing of fewer than all claims or parties in the case.

[51] These are the facts in *Finley v. United States*, 490 U.S. 595 (1989), which led to the passage of the supplemental jurisdiction statute. See §4.7.

[52] *See, e.g.*, People Who Care v. Rockford Bd. of Education, 921 F.2d 132 (7th Cir. 1991) (appellate review of attorneys' fee award will not advance ultimate disposition of dispute).

○   Suppose in the preceding case the district court had held there was no supplemental jurisdiction over the claim against *D-2* and had entered dismissal of *P*'s claim as to that defendant. Could *P* have sought appellate review under §1292(b)? No. Such an order would have been a final judgment in a multiparty case, and thus would have been eligible for treatment under Rule 54(b). Because it thus was not an interlocutory order, §1292(b) would not apply.

Federal Rule 23(f)

This provision gives the Court of Appeals discretion to review a trial court order either granting or denying certification as a class action. Federal Rule 23(f) became effective in 1998 and is an excellent addition to the Federal Rules. Before its promulgation, appellate review of class certification orders was problematic. Obviously, a decision either to certify a class or to deny such certification is not a final judgment, because it leaves the merits of the underlying dispute unresolved (indeed, unaddressed). On the other hand, the decision has enormous practical impact, as we saw in §13.3.3. The parties usually consider the class certification issue the watershed event in the litigation; its resolution often determines whether the case will proceed to trial or settle, and on what terms. Thus, some appellate courts decided to review denials of class certification, on the theory that such denial of class status sounded the "death knell" of the case.[53] But the Supreme Court rejected the death knell doctrine in 1978, in a case that also rejected use of the collateral order doctrine,[54] which we see at §14.5.2 below. After that, courts wrestled unsatisfactorily with whether orders about class certification could be reviewed by extraordinary writ, which we see in §14.6.[55] The addition of Rule 23(f) brings certainty by giving the appellate court discretion to review class certification orders.

Under Rule 23(f), the party seeking review — either of a grant or denial of class certification — must petition the court of appeals within ten days of the order. The decision whether to engage in appellate review is entirely in the appellate court; the trial court plays no role. The pendency of a petition for appellate review does not stay proceedings at the trial court. Indeed, even if the court of appeals decides to hear the appeal, proceedings at the trial court are not stayed, unless either the trial court or the court of appeals so orders.

---

[53] The leading case was *Eisen v. Carlisle & Jacqueline*, 370 F.2d 119, 120-121 (2d Cir. 1967) (accepting appellate jurisdiction when denial of class certification would end the litigation because the plaintiff would abandon his individual claim).

[54] Coopers & Lybrand v. Livesay, 437 U.S. 463, 468 (1978) (the fact that an interlocutory order denying class certification "may lead a party to dismiss his claim before final judgment is not a sufficient reason for considering it a 'final judgment' within . . . §1291").

[55] *See, e.g.,* In re Rhone-Poulenc Rorer, Inc., 51 F.3d 1293 (7th Cir. 1995) (issuing mandamus to decertify class).

Should the existence of Rule 23(f) affect the potential availability of other forms of interlocutory review? The answer should be yes. Rule 23(f) should be seen as the exclusive method for seeking appellate review of a class certification order. The Seventh Circuit has concluded that "district judges should not, and we shall not, authorize appeal under 28 U.S.C. §1292(b) when appeal might lie under Rule 23(f)."[56] Similarly, the existence of Rule 23(f) should obviate the availability of an extraordinary writ to review class certification orders. Such writs, which we discuss in §14.6 below, are not proper if an avenue for appeal exists. Rule 23(f) provides such an avenue, even when the appellate court refuses to take the appeal.

When Rule 23(f) was promulgated in 1998, many observers thought that it might be used to the advantage of defendants. That is, appellate courts might be more willing to grant review under Rule 23(f) to reverse orders certifying classes than to reverse denials of class certification. Preliminary empirical work on the issue supports this assumption. One study, based upon cases through 2007, found that 52 percent of the cases in which courts of appeals undertook review under Rule 23(f) resulted in reversals of class certification. Only 10 percent resulted in reversals of denials of certification.[57]

§14.5.2 Judicial "Exceptions"

The federal courts have occasionally interpreted some interlocutory orders as "final" for purposes of appeal under §1291. The Supreme Court insists that such interpretations do not eviscerate the final judgment rule. Rather, they give that rule a "practical rather than a technical construction."[58] Thus these case-law rules are not so much "exceptions" to the final judgment rule as they are doctrines manipulating the interpretation of the word "final" in §1291. The effect is the same, however: These doctrines permit immediate appeal of rulings that do not satisfy the general understanding of the final judgment rule.

[56] Richardson Electronics, Ltd. v. Panache Broadcasting of Pennsylvania, Inc., 202 F.3d 957, 959 (7th Cir. 2000). Federal Rule 23(f), unlike §1292(b), does not require that the appeal raise a controlling issue of law on which there is substantial ground for difference of opinion. The court recognized that some cases might present an issue satisfying §1292(b) and not involving the merits of class certification. *Id.*

[57] Richard D. Freer, *Interlocutory Review of Class Action Certification Decisions: A Preliminary Empirical Study of Federal and State Experience*, 35 W. St. U. L. Rev. 13, 19 (2007).

[58] Firestone Tire & Rubber Co. v. Risjord, 449 U.S. 368, 375 (1981) (*quoting* Cohen v. Beneficial Indus. Loan Corp., 337 U.S. 541, 546 (1949)).

Collateral Order Doctrine

The Supreme Court established the collateral order doctrine in *Cohen v. Beneficial Industrial Loan Corp.*[59] *Cohen* was a shareholder derivative suit[60] in federal court. The defendant argued that a state statute required the plaintiff to post a bond as security for costs and made a motion for an order requiring such a bond.[61] The trial court denied the motion. The defendant sought to appeal that decision to the Second Circuit. Although that court held the order nonappealable, the Supreme Court disagreed. It upheld appealability under §1291 and established the three requirements of what has become known as the collateral order doctrine.

First, the issue appealed must be both legally significant[62] and "not an ingredient of the cause of action and does not require consideration with it."[63] It is, as more commonly stated, an important issue "collateral" to the merits of the underlying dispute. Because of this, immediate appellate review will not violate the policy against piecemeal appeals; the issue presented here is unrelated to the merits, so review of this issue will not interfere with consideration of the merits by the trial court. Second, the issue appealed must have been decided finally by the trial court. It was "concluded and closed,"[64] and not subject to amendment during the pendency of the case. Third, waiting for final judgment would effectively deny appellate review of the issue.

On the facts of *Cohen*, all requirements were met. The question of whether the plaintiff had to post a bond was important and could affect other derivative litigation. It was also collateral to the merits of the underlying dispute, which had to do with alleged breaches of duties by corporate management. The issue had been resolved completely by the district court; there was little chance that the court would revisit it. And, finally, the issue could not be reviewed effectively if the parties awaited final judgment, because in the meantime the appellant would have to suffer

---

[59] 337 U.S. 541 (1949).

[60] This is a specialized kind of litigation you will study in an upper-division course on Corporations. We noted it briefly in §13.1; it is a claim against corporate managers for violating duties that they owe to the corporation. (An easy example is when corporate directors steal corporate assets; that breaches their duty of loyalty to the corporation.) If the corporation itself does not bring the suit, however, a shareholder is permitted to assert the claim.

[61] The Court determined that Federal Rule 23.1, and not state law, governed. We saw this case in discussing the *Erie* doctrine, §10.5.

[62] This goes without saying. It is hard to imagine that anyone would argue for an exception to a well-established rule to permit immediate appeal on a legally insignificant issue. The whole idea is to get something that matters before the court of appeals more quickly than would otherwise be the case.

[63] *Cohen*, 337 U.S. at 546-547.

[64] *Id.* at 546.

through litigation that would be obviated if the plaintiff had been required to post a bond.

The Supreme Court has interpreted *Cohen* sparingly. In *Firestone Tire & Rubber Co. v. Risjord*,[65] it held that an order denying a motion to disqualify attorneys from representing a party in the case was not appealable under the collateral order doctrine. Although the order was collateral to the merits and had been determined conclusively, there was no reason the ruling could not be effectively reviewed after final judgment. In *Cunningham v. Hamilton County*,[66] the Court refused to apply *Cohen* to an order imposing a monetary discovery sanction against an attorney, even though she no longer represented a party in the case. First, the order was not collateral to the merits of the case; whether the sanction was justified would require a review of the underlying facts.[67]

This is not to say that the *Cohen* doctrine is never successfully invoked. In *Puerto Rico Aqueduct & Sewer Authority v. Metcalf & Eddy, Inc.*,[68] the defendant, an agency of the Puerto Rican government, claimed immunity from being sued in federal court under the Eleventh Amendment.[69] The trial court's denial of the motion to dismiss satisfied the collateral order doctrine. It raised an important legal issue that was collateral to the merits of the underlying claim against the agency. The issue had been determined finally by the district court. And the issue could not effectively be reviewed on appeal from a final judgment. Without immediate appeal, the very protection claimed under the Eleventh Amendment (immunity from suit itself — not just from immunity from liability) would be lost.

The Court went a step farther in *Will v. Hallock*,[70] which involved rather complicated facts. In that case, federal officers seized plaintiff's computer as part of a criminal investigation; they damaged the computer, resulting in loss of data and ultimately causing plaintiff's business to fail. She sued the United States under the Federal Tort Claims Act, which waives the federal government's sovereign immunity in some circumstances. The government won that case, however, because the court found that the officers had acted in good faith, which was an exception to the government's

---

[65] 449 U.S. 368 (1981).

[66] 527 U.S. 198 (1999).

[67] In *Coopers & Lybrand v. Livesay*, 437 U.S. 463 (1978), the Court rejected use of the collateral order doctrine concerning an order certifying a class action. Such orders are continually subject to reconsideration by the trial court in light of factual development and thus intimately connected with the merits. *Coopers & Lybrand* is most notable for its rejection of the "death knell" doctrine, discussed in §14.5.1 above with regard to Federal Rule 23(f).

[68] 506 U.S. 139 (1993).

[69] The Eleventh Amendment shields states from being sued for damages in state court. It provides not just immunity from *liability*, but from being *sued in federal court at all*. Thus, making a defendant wait until final judgment to raise the issue on appeal robs it of this protection from being sued.

[70] 546 U.S. 345 (2006).

waiver of immunity. Plaintiff then sued the individual officers, alleging that they had violated her constitutional right to due process. The officers raised as a defense the ruling in the previous case in favor of the government. By statute, judgment in favor of the government constitutes a bar to suit against individual officers. The district court rejected the defense, however, because it held that the judgment in favor of the government was based upon a procedural ground and did not bar the suit against the officers.

The question was whether that order — denying the officers' motion to dismiss — was appealable under *Cohen*. The Court held that it was not. It emphasized that something more than merely avoiding trial had to be at stake — "some particular value of high order."[71] In *Puerto Rico Aqueduct*, for example, forcing the defendant to endure trial would have imposed the burden of litigation *and* have constituted a denigration of Puerto Rico's dignitary interest as a government entitled to protection by the Eleventh Amendment. On the facts in *Will*, the Court found no such important interest beyond the ordinary desire to avoid the rigors of trial. Avoidance of litigation "for its own sake" is not sufficient; if it were, "collateral order appeal would be a matter of right whenever the government lost a motion to dismiss under the Tort Claims Act...."[72] After *Will*, use of the collateral order doctrine would appear to be limited indeed — perhaps rarely to be invoked outside a state's right to be free from suit under the Eleventh Amendment.

Other Case-Law Relaxation of the Final Judgment Rule

From time to time, the Supreme Court has indicated some willingness to relax the final judgment rule. In the old case of *Forgay v. Conrad*,[73] the Court permitted an interlocutory appeal basically to avoid hardship on one of the parties. There, the trial court made a partial adjudication of the claim but directed the defendant to deliver property to the plaintiff. It seemed to treat the order as a final judgment. Although no final accounting had been made, and the order thus was interlocutory, the Court permitted the appeal. The holding was borne of necessity; the defendant simply needed immediate access to the appellate court, and the Supreme Court permitted it.[74] *Forgay* has not been invoked frequently.[75]

---

[71] 546 U.S. at 352.

[72] *Id.* at 353-354.

[73] 47 U.S. 201 (1848).

[74] In *Gillespie v. United States Steel Corp.*, 379 U.S. 148 (1964), the Court seemed to say that it would allow interlocutory review whenever it would be salutary. The broad language has not generated support. Indeed, the Court later criticized it. *Coopers & Lybrand*, above, 437 U.S. at 477 n.30.

[75] *See, e.g.*, Richard A. Matasar & Gregory S. Bruch, *Procedural Common Law, Federal Jurisdictional Policy, and Abandonment of the Adequate and Independent State Grounds*

Finally, the federal courts will allow immediate appeal of a criminal contempt citation. This is an especially important thing to remember in the discovery context. Discovery orders generally will not satisfy the collateral order doctrine. Consider a case in which the trial court rejects a claim of privilege and compels a party to respond to a discovery request. The appropriate course for the party opposing discovery is to disobey the order and be held in contempt, and then to appeal the contempt citation.

§14.6   Review by Extraordinary (or "Prerogative") Writ

What we have seen above are circumstances in which one party may appeal an order of a trial court to an appellate court. In addition, an aggrieved litigant may, in rare circumstances, ask an appellate court to issue a writ — an order — to the trial court. A party seeking such a writ actually commences a new proceeding by filing a petition for the appropriate writ *in the appellate court*. That party is the "petitioner" and the other parties in the case at the trial court are "respondents" in the writ proceeding.[76] Technically, in some judicial systems, the trial judge or court is actually named as a respondent in the petition for the writ,[77] although only the litigants brief and argue the issue. This was true in federal practice until 1996, when the applicable rule was amended to provide that only litigants are to be named as respondents. Accordingly, in the federal system, writ proceedings no longer bear the name of the district judge or the district court. Writ proceedings are entitled "In re [name of petitioner]."[78]

The main extraordinary writs are those of *mandamus* (or "mandate") and *prohibition*. Technically, mandamus lies to order the trial court to do something it has a mandatory duty to do. Prohibition lies to stop the trial

---

Doctrine, 86 Colum. L. Rev. 1291, 1354 n.314 (1986). *See also* In re Chateaugay Corp., 922 F.2d 86, 91 (2d Cir. 1990).

[76] FRAP 21(a)(1).

[77] Sometimes the trial judge is named personally. An example is *World-Wide Volkswagen v. Woodson*, which we studied in §2.4.4. Woodson was the state court trial judge who held that there was personal jurisdiction over the two New York defendants. When those two defendants sought an extraordinary writ from the state appellate court, Woodson was named as respondent. In some systems, the court (rather than the specific trial judge) is named in the application for a writ. An example is *Asahi v. Superior Court*, another personal jurisdiction case discussed in §2.4.4. There, the state trial court had upheld jurisdiction over Asahi, which then sought a writ from the state appellate court. In the federal system, before 1996 amendments to FRAP 22, the district court was named as a respondent. Now, however, only the other parties to the case are respondents. The appellate court may invite the trial judge to participate in the writ proceeding, although this is rarely done.

[78] FRAP 21(a)(2)(A).

court from doing something it has no jurisdiction to do. The distinctions between these two have eroded, however, and the label used is not terribly important in federal practice;[79] most litigants seem to use "mandamus" as the label of choice. The main point is that whatever label is used, issuance of such writs is extraordinary; it is limited to exceptional and rare circumstances.

In the federal judicial system, the All Writs Act[80] permits the courts of appeals to issue appropriate writs to district courts.[81] The writ must be "in aid of" the court of appeals' jurisdiction, which basically means it is necessary to confine a lower court to the lawful exercise of its jurisdiction or to compel that court to exercise its power when there is a duty to do so.[82] So it is important to understand that an extraordinary writ is *not* a vehicle simply for correcting legal error. Rather, it is a device to confine the lower court to its proper jurisdiction. Issuance of a writ is never automatic, but is vested in the discretion of the court of appeals. It is limited to cases in which the district court has done something it has no power to do or has so abused its discretion as to have usurped power.[83] The error must be clear and indisputable, and not just a matter on which the court of appeals has a difference of opinion with the district court. Clearly, then, writ practice is not a substitute for appeal.[84] As a general matter, a petition for a writ will be denied if the aggrieved party has any other remedy, including appeal.[85]

A trial court that has improperly exercised personal or subject matter jurisdiction may be reined in by an extraordinary writ from the appellate court.[86] In addition, a transfer of venue to a different circuit might be corrected by writ to protect the jurisdiction of the appellate court.[87] Mandamus has been invoked to review a judge's refusal to disqualify herself from

[79] Indeed, federal courts have long been forgiving about the technical misnaming of a writ. *See* In re Simons, 246 U.S. 231 (1918) (form or label of writ not important to ultimate disposition).

[80] 28 U.S.C. §1651(a) ("The Supreme Court and all courts established by Act of Congress may issue all writs necessary or appropriate in aid of their respective jurisdictions and agreeable to the usages and principles of law.").

[81] The Act applies to any court created by Congress, and thus applies to the Supreme Court of the United States and federal district courts as well. It permits a court to issue a writ to a lower court within its jurisdiction. The most common use — the one on which we focus — is by a court of appeals to make an order to a district court.

[82] *See* United States v. Victoria-21, 3 F.3d 571, 575 (2d Cir. 1993).

[83] *See* Mallard v. United States District Court, 490 U.S. 296, 309 (1989). *See also* 20 Moore's Federal Practice §321.15 (3d ed. 2005) (discussing different showings required for issuance of mandamus in different circuits).

[84] *See, e.g.,* In re Chesson, 897 F.2d 156, 159 (5th Cir. 1990).

[85] *See* In re Ivy, 197 F.2d 7, 10 (2d Cir. 1990).

[86] See note 77 above (personal jurisdiction cases involving appellate review by writ).

[87] *See, e.g.,* Roofing & Sheet Metal Servs., Inc. v. La Quinta Motor Inns, Inc., 689 F.2d 982, 988 (11th Cir. 1982) (intercircuit transfer more appropriately reviewed by writ than intracircuit transfer).

presiding over a case.[88] Likewise, mandamus is appropriate to correct the lower court's refusal to permit jury trial under the Seventh Amendment.[89] Mandamus will lie when a trial court abdicates its responsibility by referring all aspects of a case to a judicial surrogate.[90] These examples show the use of an extraordinary writ to compel the lower court to act within its power.

Moreover, however, such use of the "heavy artillery"[91] of mandamus serves a didactic function. It sends a message to the lower courts as a whole about proper exercise of their authority. This use of the writ has been called *supervisory mandamus*. Indeed, the Supreme Court has said that use of the writ to exercise "supervisory control of the district courts by the Courts of Appeals is necessary to proper judicial administration."[92] A judge's improper refusal to disqualify herself, for example, casts a cloud not only on the individual case, but on the judicial process itself.[93]

There was some thought in the 1990s that the courts of appeals were expanding the use of the extraordinary writ beyond the traditional use of confining a lower court to its proper jurisdiction. Most of the high-profile cases, however, involved issuance of mandamus to overturn district courts' certification of class actions.[94] The cases predate the promulgation of Rule 23(f), which, as we saw in §14.5.1, expressly permits the court of appeals to review orders granting or denying class certification. Today, then, the availability of Rule 23(f) should preclude requests for an extraordinary writ regarding class certification. Outside the class-certification context, there have been occasional broad invocations of mandamus. In one case, for instance, a trial court rejected a party's assertion of privilege and compelled it to disclose a document in discovery. Although interlocutory discovery orders have never been readily reviewed by appellate courts, the Second Circuit issued a writ to overturn the order compelling

---

[88] By statute, federal judges may be required to "recuse" (disqualify) themselves from sitting on a case. For example, a judge who owns stock in a corporate litigant must recuse. 28 U.S.C. §455(b)(4).

[89] Beacon Theatres, Inc. v. Westover, 359 U.S. 500 (1959), discussed in §9.2.2, was such a case.

[90] LaBuy v. Howes Leather Co., 352 U.S. 249 (1957) (involving wholesale abdication of case to a special master, who should be used as an adjunct, with ultimate authority resting in the district judge).

[91] In re Bituminous Coal Operators' Assn., 949 F.2d 1165, 1168 (D.C. Cir. 1991).

[92] *LaBuy*, note 90 above, 352 U.S. at 259-260.

[93] *See* Union Carbide Corp. v. U.S. Cutting Serv., Inc., 782 F.2d 710 (7th Cir. 1986).

[94] *See, e.g.*, Jackson v. Motel 6 Multipurpose, Inc., 130 F.3d 999 (11th Cir. 1997) (decertifying nationwide class allegedly suffering discrimination); In re American Medical Syst., Inc., 75 F.3d 1069 (6th Cir. 1996); In re Rhone-Poulenc Rorer, Inc., 51 F.3d 1293 (7th Cir. 1995) (decertifying nationwide class regarding allegedly tainted blood products). *See, e.g.*, Amy Schmidt Jones, *The Use of Mandamus to Vacate Mass Exposure Tort Class Certification Orders*, 72 N.Y.U. L. Rev. 232 (1997).

production.[95] The order was surprising given the fairly clear precedent that appellate review in such instances is available through appeal of a contempt citation, as we noted in §14.5.2. Still, despite the occasional arguably expansive use of mandamus in such cases, it seems unlikely that the extraordinary writ will become a free-wheeling substitute for appeal in the federal system.[96]

§14.7 Standards of Review

In this section, we assume that a case is properly before the appellate court. The issue here is the standard by which that court will review what the trial court did. Different issues are reviewed by different standards. It is useful to think of the varying standards employed by the appellate court as being relatively more or less deferential to the trial court. On some issues, the appellate court may give no deference at all, and may be free to substitute its own conclusion. On other issues, the court of appeals may give enormous deference, concluding that it will affirm the trial court unless its result is simply bizarre. On still other issues, there may be some intermediate position.

The determination of how much deference is due the trial court is based upon a variety of factors. First, of course, is the concern that the judicial system "get it right," that it apply the law correctly and reach the appropriate decision. Second, there is a concern with the relative expertise of the two judicial levels. For example, the appellate court should defer to the trial judge on matters such as credibility of witnesses, since only the trial judge saw the witnesses testify. Third, we are concerned with finality — that cases not be reversed for silly, insubstantial reasons.

Matters of Law

On issues of law, the appellate court gives no deference to the trial court ruling. There is no presumption that the trial court "got it right." The court of appeals is required to assess the issue de novo. This intrusive review is appropriate because the determination of what the law is, is not something on which the trial court would have especial expertise. It is not dependent upon anything that goes on in the trial. It is a dry question of research, which the appellate court may actually be better equipped than the trial court to perform. After all, part of its very function is to explicate the law

---

[95] In re Steinhardt Partners, L.P., 9 F.3d 230 (2d Cir. 1993).

[96] Some states, notably California, permit more liberal use of mandamus than the federal system.

for the benefit of the parties, the lower courts, and the community at large.[97]

There are many pure questions of law that may arise in any case, such as whether the trial judge properly instructed the jury on the elements of the claim or a defense, whether the trial judge properly allocated the burden of proof at trial, or whether she applied the correct standard for summary judgment or a motion to dismiss for failure to state a claim or a motion for judgment as a matter of law. On all such questions, the appellate court may substitute its judgment for that of the trial court.

Questions of Fact

By questions of fact, we mean what the Supreme Court has called *historical facts*;[98] that is, what happened in the real world. Was the traffic light red or green? Did the defendant drink alcohol before driving? If so, how much and when? Did the plaintiff sign the letter? What, if anything, did the defendant say to the plaintiff? Did the plaintiff pay for the goods? Is that witness lying? Such questions are important to the immediate parties, to be sure, but do not have the community-wide impact of a ruling on a question of law. Moreover, because only the fact-finder saw the witnesses and heard the testimony, an appellate court should defer at least in some measure to the determination of the fact-finder at trial. And indeed, that is the case.

The fact-finder at trial, of course, might be the judge or a jury. In §9.2, we discussed the right to a jury trial in civil cases in federal court. If there is no right to a jury trial, or if the parties waive the right to jury trial, the judge will act as the finder of fact in what is called a *bench trial*. Federal Rule 52(a)(6) provides that the trial judge's determination of the facts in a bench trial must be affirmed on appeal unless they are "clearly erroneous." Further, the Rule expressly requires that "due regard shall be given to the opportunity of the trial court to judge the credibility of the witnesses." Thus, such findings are presumptively correct; the appellate court defers to the trial judge's findings unless, "on the entire evidence [it] is left with the definite and firm conviction that a mistake has been committed."[99] The appellate court does not have to conclude that the trial judge necessarily got it "wrong." Instead, it must find that there is not enough

---

[97] In fact, the appellate court may decide that the law was properly applied but ought to be changed. Its holding on this point would create precedent and, under the doctrine of *stare decisis*, be binding on all lower courts in the jurisdiction. We discussed precedent at §1.2.2.

[98] Pullman-Standard v. Swint, 456 U.S. 273, 289 n.19 (1982).

[99] United States v. United States Gypsum Co., 333 U.S. 364, 395 (1948) (the leading definition of "clearly erroneous").

evidence in the record to support the finding. Deference reflects the institutional judgment that the trial judge was in a position to see and study the witnesses, and to put testimony and other evidence into an overall context before making her decision. The appellate court is able to do none of these things. Not surprisingly, because of this deferential standard, few cases are reversed because of erroneous fact-finding by the judge.

But what if the trial consisted mostly of deposition testimony in the record, without live witnesses? In such a case, some courts concluded that the trial court's findings of fact were entitled to less, or even no, deference.[100] They reasoned that an appellate court could review deposition testimony as readily as the trial judge.[101] The Supreme Court rejected this notion, however, in *Anderson v. City of Bessemer City*.[102] *Anderson* holds that all bench findings are entitled to review under the clearly erroneous standard, "even when the district court's findings do not rest on credibility determination, but are based instead on physical or documentary evidence or inferences from other facts."[103] The Court further noted that when the judge bases findings on her assessment of credibility of witnesses, "Rule 52(a) demands even greater deference to the trial court's findings. . . ."[104]

Rule 52(a)(1) does not apply to cases involving jury trial. Jury findings of fact are entitled to even greater deference than judge findings, because of the reexamination clause of the Seventh Amendment. That clause provides that "no fact tried by a jury, shall be otherwise re-examined in any Court of the United States, than according to the rules of common law." The appropriate standard of review on appeal of a jury verdict is similar to that used by a trial judge in determining whether to grant a motion of judgment as a matter of law under Federal Rule 50(a)(1).[105] Specifically, then, the appellate court views all evidence — including credibility determinations and inferences — in the light most favorable to the verdict, and

---

[100] *See, e.g.*, Orvis v. Higgins, 180 F.2d 537 (2d Cir. 1950).

[101] While this is true, the courts adopting this approach overlooked (1) that Rule 52(a) did not make such a distinction and (2) that even if the appellate court was in as good a position to judge the facts as the trial court, disregarding the trial court's findings "impairs confidence in the trial courts and multiplies appeals with attendant expense and delay." Wright & Kane, Federal Courts 691.

[102] 470 U.S. 564 (1985).

[103] *Id.* at 574. Federal Rule 52(a) was amended within months of the *Anderson* decision to apply the clearly erroneous standard to all bench findings of fact, "whether based on oral or documentary evidence." This requirement is now set forth at Rule 52(a)(6).

[104] *Id.* at 575.

[105] Most states refer to this motion as one for a directed verdict. We discussed this motion at §9.5.

must affirm so long as a reasonable fact-finder could have reached that conclusion.[106]

Mixed Questions of Law and Fact

The preceding discussion treated questions of law and questions of fact as clearly identifiable, separate things. In some cases, the exercise of drawing the line between law and fact proves difficult, and "varies according to the nature of the substantive law at issue."[107] Moreover, the two — law and fact — are not hermetically sealed from one another. Sometimes, trial courts will be called upon to decide "mixed questions of law and fact." There are two sources of great confusion concerning such mixed questions. First, what are they? Second, what is the standard of review of a mixed question? The issue is important because a great many cases state that mixed questions are reviewed de novo.[108] Under this view, mixed questions are treated as questions of law, with the appellate court free to substitute its own conclusion, based upon the entire record.

The Supreme Court has defined mixed questions as

> questions in which the historical facts are admitted or established, the rule of law is undisputed, and the issue is whether the facts satisfy the statutory standard, or to put it another way, whether the rule of law as applied to the established facts is or is not violated.[109]

This definition does not always yield a clear answer. Perhaps it is best to see what courts have done with this definition in different cases, to get a feel for what constitutes a mixed question. The words and actions of the defendant are pure facts, but whether they constitute intentional discrimination on the basis of race or national origin has been considered a mixed question of law and fact.[110] The representation the defendant made is a pure question of fact, but whether it is material for purposes of securities

---

[106] *See, e.g.*, Dresser-Rand Co. v. Virtual Automation Inc., 361 F.3d 831, 838 (5th Cir. 2004); Abvan v. Level 3 Communications, Inc., 353 F.3d 1158, 1164 (10th Cir. 2003).

[107] Bose Corp. v. Consumers Union of the United States, Inc., 466 U.S. 485, 501 n.17 (1984).

[108] *See, e.g.*, Cooper Tire & Rubber Co. v. St. Paul Fire & Marine, 48 F.3d 365, 369 (8th Cir. 1994); Banker v. Nightswander, Martin & Mitchell, 37 F.3d 866, 870 (2d Cir. 1994) (whether efforts to mitigate damages were reasonable). The Supreme Court has hinted that this is the appropriate general rule in Strickland v. Washington, 466 U.S. 668, 698 (1984), but has not ruled definitively. Pullman-Standard v. Swint, 456 U.S. 273, 289 n.19 (1982).

[109] Pullman-Standard v. Swint, 456 U.S. 273, 289 n.19 (1982).

[110] Woods v. Graphic Contractors, 92 F.2d 1195 (9th Cir. 1991). On the other hand, the Supreme Court has held that the question of discriminatory intent is one of fact. Pullman-Standard v. Swint, 456 U.S. 273, 274 (1982).

fraud has been seen as a mixed question of law and fact.[111] The *interpretation* of a contract is considered a mixed question of law and fact,[112] as is the question of whether use of copyrighted material constituted a permitted "fair use."[113] Whether a worker is a "seaman" covered by the Jones Act is also seen as a mixed question of law and fact.[114] Whether parties agreed to arbitrate a dispute apparently presents a mixed question of law and fact.[115]

The characterization of an issue as a mixed question affects the standard of appellate review. It is worth asking, however, why a mixed question of law or fact ought to be reviewed de novo. The most famous example of such a case is *Bose Corp. v. Consumers Union of United States, Inc.,*[116] in which Bose sued for product disparagement. It alleged that the defendant had made a false statement about Bose's product, and that the false statement was made with actual malice.[117] Bose won at trial, and the issue was whether the appellate court was limited to reviewing the actual malice question under the "clearly erroneous" standard of Federal Rule 52(a)(6). While the trial judge's assessment of witness credibility was subject to deference under Rule 52(a), the existence of actual malice presented a mixed question of law and fact. As such, the Court held, it was subject to de novo review on appeal. Why? To protect First Amendment rights. The appellate court had to be free to search the entire record to be sure the result in the case did not impinge on the defendant's constitutional right of free speech.[118] In other words, whether the defendant had actual malice — an issue that seems at first blush purely factual — will have a direct impact on an important constitutional right. Thus, the appellate court cannot be hampered in its review.

As the cases cited in the paragraph preceding the discussion of *Bose* make clear, courts have not limited the finding of "mixed questions of law and fact" to cases involving constitutional rights. Thus, the rationale of *Bose* — that searching appellate inquiry is necessary to protect a constitutional right — is not the only justification for characterizing an issue as a mixed question. It is impossible to rationalize or explain the variety of approaches on this issue seen in the case law. There is enough elasticity

---

[111] TSC Indus., Inc. v. Northway, Inc., 426 U.S. 438 (1976); ABC Arbitrage Plaintiffs Group v. Tchuruk, 291 F.3d 336 (5th Cir. 2002).

[112] Tyler v. Cuomo, 236 F.3d 1124 (9th Cir. 2000).

[113] Harper & Row, Publishers, Inc. v. The Nation Enterprises, 471 U.S. 539, 560 (1980).

[114] Endeavor Marine v. Crane Operators, Inc., 234 F.3d 287 (5th Cir. 2000).

[115] Bailey v. Fannie Mae, 209 F.3d 740 (D.C. Cir. 2000).

[116] 466 U.S. 485 (1984).

[117] In Constitutional Law, you will study *New York Times, Inc. v. Sullivan,* 376 U.S. 254 (1964), which requires plaintiffs to show actual malice in some (not all) defamation cases.

[118] The case of *New York Times v. Sullivan,* discussed in the preceding footnote, stands for the proposition that the First Amendment freedom of speech protects erroneous statements unless they are uttered with actual malice.

in these concepts to allow an appellate court to characterize close issues as mixed questions, thereby justifying de novo review.

Discretionary Matters

During the course of a case, the trial judge may be called upon to decide any number of matters vested in her "sound discretion." Issues such as whether to permit amendment of pleadings, permissive intervention, to compel discovery, to consolidate cases, to order separate trials, and a hundred similar issues relating to the management of the case are examples. The determination of whether there is no just reason for delaying appeal under Rule 54(b), which we saw at §14.4 above, is also an example.

Such issues present fact-specific circumstances, and appellate courts are very deferential to whatever the trial court orders. The court of appeals can reverse on such matters only if the trial judge "abused her discretion." This means the appellate court must affirm even if the appeals judges would have decided the matter differently. As long as the trial judge's decision was not plainly wrong or without basis, the appellate court will affirm. This high degree of deference is appropriate because the trial judge is in the best position to place the issue at hand in the context of the entire case and weigh all competing factors. Moreover, the decisions on many of these issues simply cannot be "right" or "wrong." Different reasonable people might disagree. About all the appellate court can do here is ensure that the trial judge exercised her discretion and made a decision that is "in the ballpark" — within the realm of reasonable decisions on the facts.

Table of Cases

Table of Cases

Table of Cases

Table of Cases

Table of Cases

Table of Authorities

Table of Authorities

Table of Authorities

Table of Authorities

Table of Authorities

Index